LIFE

Siobhán Scott-Sweeney BSc, HDE, FIBiolI
Kevin Maume MA, MSc, PDSLE, HDE, MIBiolI

First published in 2015 by Folens Publishers

Hibernian Industrial Estate, Greenhills Road, Tallaght, Dublin 24

© Siobhán Scott-Sweeney and Kevin Maume 2015

Illustrations: Oxford Design Studio, Luca Guerriero

Photographs: Science Photo Library, Fotolia

ISBN 978-1-78090-548-8

All rights reserved. No part of this publication may be reproduced, stored in a retrieval system or transmitted in any form or by any means, electronic, mechanical, photocopying, recording or otherwise, for whatever purpose, without the prior written permission of the publisher, or a licence permitting restricted copying in Ireland issued by the Irish Copyright Licensing Agency, 25 Denzille Lane, Dublin 2.

To the best of the publisher's knowledge, information in this book was correct at the time of going to press. No responsibility can be taken for any errors.

The FOLENS company name and associated logos are trademarks of Folens Publishers, registered in Ireland and other countries.

The publisher has made every effort to contact all copyright holders but if any have been overlooked, we will be pleased to make any necessary arrangements.

Any links or references to external websites should not be construed as an endorsement by Folens of the content or views of these websites.

Contents

- Biology Syllabus Synopsis iv
- Preface v
- Laboratory Safety vi
- Mandatory Student Activities vii
- How to Use this Book viii

01 The Study of Life

01	The Scientific Method 2
02	The Characteristics of Life 12
03	Food and Biomolecules 17
04	Introduction to Ecology 34
05	The Effects of Humans on the Environment 49
06	Ecological Relationships and Population Dynamics (HL only) 60
07	The Study of an Ecosystem 72

02 The Cell

08	Cell Structure 95
09	Cell Diversity 107
10	Movement Through Membranes 115
11	Cell Continuity 124
12	Enzymes 136
13	Photosynthesis 153
14	Respiration 165
15	DNA, RNA and Protein Synthesis 178
16	Genetic Inheritance 197
17	Variation, Evolution and Genetic Engineering 221

03 The Organism

18	Classification and Viruses 234
19	Monera (Prokaryotae) 242
20	Fungi and Protists 256
21	Flowering Plant Structure and Tissues 271
22	Transport, Nutrition and Food Storage in the Flowering Plant 289
23	Transport in Humans 301
24	The Blood 325
25	Human Nutrition 332
26	Homeostasis and Gaseous Exchange 348
27	Excretion and Osmoregulation 365
28	Plant Response to Stimuli 377
29	The Human Nervous System 388
30	The Sense Organs 401
31	The Endocrine System 412
32	The Musculoskeletal System 421
33	The Human Defence System 432
34	Sexual Reproduction in Flowering Plants 442
35	Asexual Reproduction in Flowering Plants 469
36	Human Reproduction 1: The Reproductive Systems and the Menstrual Cycle 476
37	Human Reproduction 2: From Fertilisation to Birth 491

38	The Examination 506
■	Glossary 513
■	Index 522

Biology Syllabus Synopsis

The Biology syllabus

The Leaving Certificate Biology syllabus is intended to be relevant to your everyday life. It aims to inspire and motivate you about Biology and science in general. It is hoped that through studying this course you will develop many skills, including becoming scientifically literate, and will be able to analyse and make judgements on information, material and issues that affect you in your daily lives and into the future.

Syllabus structure

The syllabus consists of approximately 70% pure science with the remaining 30% dealing with contemporary issues and technology. **Life** Leaving Certificate Biology is written specifically for this syllabus. It follows the syllabus in a logical order and it covers the Learning Outcomes of the syllabus completely. The Learning Outcomes are the material that you are expected to know and the skills that you will gain as a result of studying this course. Every chapter begins with a set of Learning Outcomes and these are highlighted throughout each chapter, focusing your learning.

There are 22 Mandatory Student Activities to be carried out, which include both laboratory and fieldwork (see page vii). Each of these activities is described in detail in the appropriate chapter and many are presented in a readily accessible visual format with the protocol steps laid out in diagrams. In addition, a video clip of each of the laboratory activities is available on folensonline.

The syllabus is divided into three units:

Unit 1 The Study of Life

Unit 1 introduces you, the learner, to the characteristics associated with all organisms, the biomolecules of which they are made and the place of living things in the environment.

Syllabus sub-unit	Chapters in *Life* Leaving Certificate Biology
1. The scientific method	Chapter 1
2. The characteristics of life	Chapter 2
3. Nutrition – food and biomolecules	Chapter 3
4. General principles of ecology	Chapters 4, 5, 6
5. A study of an ecosystem	Chapter 7

Unit 2 The Cell

Unit 2 deals specifically with the structure and workings of the cell, which is the basic unit of all living things. The role of the parts of a cell is explored as the chapters unfold. Starting with the detailed structure of a typical plant and animal cell, the chapters of this unit explore the need for and identification of different types of cells, give an explanation of how substances move in and out of cells, describe how cells divide and grow and explain how the chemical reactions within cells are controlled and function. The final section of this unit deals with DNA, genetic inheritance and evolution.

Syllabus sub-unit	Chapters in *Life* Leaving Certificate Biology
1. Cell structure	Chapter 8
2. Cell diversity	Chapter 9
3. Movement through membranes	Chapter 10
4. Cell continuity	Chapter 11
5. Cell metabolism	Chapters 12, 13, 14
6. Genetics	Chapters 15, 16, 17

Unit 3 The Organism

Unit 3 is the longest section of the syllabus. Entitled 'The Organism', it begins by looking at how organisms are classified into five main groups or kingdoms. It then takes the characteristic features of living things (Chapter 2) and applies them to a member of each of the kingdoms to illustrate the wide diversity of life with particular reference to the flowering plants and humans.

Syllabus sub-unit	Chapters in *Life* Leaving Certificate Biology
1. Diversity of organisms	Chapters 18, 19, 20
2. Organisation and vascular structures	Chapter 21
3. Transport and nutrition	Chapters 22, 23, 24, 25
4. Breathing system and excretion	Chapter 26, 27
5. Responses to stimuli	Chapters 28, 29, 30, 31, 32, 33
6. Reproduction and growth	Chapters 34, 35, 36, 37

Preface

Life Leaving Certificate Biology is a brand new, fully updated edition of the well-received New Senior Biology textbook. Written with ten years' experience of the 'new' syllabus, **Life** attempts to move the learning of Biology forward. Written to the syllabus and guidelines specifications, this book has all you need to know to succeed in the Leaving Certificate Biology examination.

The chapters in the textbook cover all of the syllabus material. Some sub-units are spread over more than one chapter, i.e genetics (2.5) is a sub-unit and are in chapters 15,16 and 17; general principles of ecology (1.4) are covered in chapters 4, 5 and 6.

Each chapter opens with a list of Learning Outcomes, which summarise the syllabus and inform and direct your learning. These should be used both before and after studying a topic.

A feature of modern Biology is the way in which new terms are emerging. A knowledge of these is very important to your understanding of the subject. To help with this, any new words are clearly identified by being highlighted in blue type. There are also key definitions reinforced by definition boxes and which can also be found in the Glossary at the back of the book. The precise learning of these definitions is recommended.

Within a chapter the Learning Outcomes are highlighted when and where they are covered. This provides an ordered pathway through the topic. A concise Summary is to be found at the conclusion of each chapter and includes all the key points. This is followed by three sets of questions:

1. Review questions – test knowledge of the chapter content.
2. Examination style questions – a series of questions which reflect the style and structure of the actual Leaving Certificate examination.
3. Leaving Certificate examination questions – include numerous examples of actual Leaving Certificate questions at both Ordinary and Higher Level.

Practising examination questions plays an essential part in improving your exam success potential. Finally there is a list showing the occurrence of questions asked from 2004 to 2014.

A HL pink wash clearly identifies material that is Higher Level only. This is found in the text, the Summary and the Review and Examination Style questions.

All 22 Mandatory Activities are included, a list of which can be found on page vii. Each activity is to be found in the appropriate chapter, with clear instructions, often accompanied by helpful, labelled, diagrams. In many cases, expected outcomes and observations are described. Developing practical skills is a key feature in studying the science of Biology and every opportunity should be taken to develop and improve these.

Biology is a constantly changing branch of science with many applications in our lives – these range from our study of the environment (Unit 1), genetics and heredity (Unit 2) to how we, as animals and other organisms carry out the characteristics of life (Unit 3). We hope you enjoy studying Biology and that **Life** helps you achieve success.

We would like to thank the many people who helped bring this project to fruition. Thanks go to the extraordinarily dedicated team in Folens: Michele Staunton, Adam Brophy, Emma O'Dwyer, Suzanne Gannon, Sara Hulse and the many teachers who read the manuscript, for their insightful suggestions and interest, to our families for their encouragement and tolerance and above all to the many students we have taught over the years, who through their interest in Biology have inspired us to write this book.

Siobhán Scott-Sweeney   Kevin Maume

Laboratory Safety

Carrying out investigations is an integral part of any science course. As a consequence, there are Mandatory Investigations for the Leaving Certificate Biology course. You will be expected to have carried out these investigations over the course of the two-year study of this subject. Experimental work, either in a laboratory or in the field, has risk associated with it. It is expected that you will appreciate this risk and take all the necessary precautions to ensure that your experimental work is done in as safe a way as possible.

All school laboratories will have a set of rules that everyone using the laboratory is required to follow to keep everyone as safe as possible. You are expected to know the rules associated with your laboratory and have an appreciation of the risks involved in the practical work you undertake. To this end, safety symbols are attached to each investigation in this book. These should be used as aids to inform your behaviour within the laboratory/the field and to determine how you will handle various chemicals or equipment that you will come in contact with during your study of Biology.

It is essential that you check, at all times, that you understand the risk associated with the chemicals or equipment you are using during your practical work. The most up to date symbols universally used to indicate risks are shown on page 5 (and below). You are expected to be able to identify these symbols and the precautions that you need to take for each symbol.

Safety Glasses	Harmful or Irritant	Flammable	Corrosive	Toxic	Oxidising	Explosive
Eye protection must be worn.	These substances are less of a health risk than toxic substances. However, they must still be handled with care.	These substances may easily catch fire in a laboratory under normal conditions.	These substances can cause chemical burns to skin and eyes.	These substances may cause serious health risks or death if inhaled, swallowed or if they penetrate the skin.	These substances may produce much heat when they react with other substances, particularly flammable substances.	These substances may explode if ignited in air or exposed to heat. A sudden shock or friction may also cause an explosion.

Mandatory Student Activities

The following is a list of the Mandatory Student Activities in the order in which they appear in the textbook. Experiments in bold are Higher Level only.

Activity number	Activity title	Page reference
1 (a)	To test for the presence of reducing sugars (simple carbohydrates).	Investigation 3.1 A, p. 25
1 (b)	To test for polysaccharides, e.g. starch.	Investigation 3.1 B, p. 25
1 (c)	To test for fat (lipid) in olive oil: brown paper test.	Investigation 3.2, p. 26
1 (d)	To test for protein in milk or in egg albumen: biuret test for soluble protein.	Investigation 3.3, p. 26
2 (a)	To identify three habitats within a selected ecosystem.	Page 76
2 (b)	To identify five flora and five fauna using simple keys.	Page 78
3	To identify and use various pieces of apparatus to collect plants and animals in an ecosystem.	Page 78
4 (a)	To conduct a quantitative survey of plants in an ecosystem.	Pages 82–83 [for plants]
4 (b)	To conduct a quantitative survey of animals in an ecosystem.	Page 85 [for animals]
5	To investigate any three abiotic factors in a selected ecosystem.	Investigation 7.1, p.80 Investigation 7.2, p.80 Investigation 7.3, p.80
6	To be familiar with and use a light microscope.	Investigation 8.1, p. 100
7 (a)	To prepare and examine animal cells – unstained and stained, under the light microscope.	Investigation 8.1, p.101
7 (b)	To prepare and examine plant cells – unstained and stained, under the light microscope.	Investigation 8.2, p.101
8	To conduct an activity to demonstrate osmosis.	Investigation 10.1, p.119
9	To investigate the effect of pH on the rate of enzyme activity.	Investigation 12.1, p.139
10	To investigate the effect of temperature on the rate of enzyme activity.	Investigation 12.2, p.141
11	**To investigate the effect of heat denaturation on the activity of an enzyme (HL only).**	**Investigation 12.3, p.143**
12	To prepare an enzyme immobilization and examine its application.	Investigation 12.4, p.144
13	To investigate the effect of light intensity OR carbon dioxide on the rate of photosynthesis.	Investigation 13.1, p.155, Investigation 13.2, p.156
14	To prepare and show the production of alcohol by yeast.	Investigation 14.1, p.169
15	To isolate DNA from a plant tissue.	Investigation 15.1, p.185
16	To investigate the growth of leaf yeasts using agar plates and controls.	Investigation 20.1, p.261
17	To prepare and examine microscopically the T.S. of a dicotylodonous stem (×100, ×400).	Investigation 21.1, p.280
18	To dissect, display and identify an ox's or a sheep's heart.	Investigation 23.1, p.309
19 (a)	To investigate the effect exercise on pulse rate.	Investigation 23.2, p.313
19 (b)	To investigate the effect of exercise on breathing rate.	Investigation 26.1, p.353
20	To investigate the effect of IAA growth regulator on plant tissue.	Investigation 28.1, p.380
21	To investigate the effect of water, oxygen and temperature on germination.	Investigation 34.1, p.455
22	To use starch or slimmed milk plates to show digestive activity during germination.	Investigation 34, p.456

How to Use this Book

This icon represents a Mandatory Activity. All Mandatory Activities are included in light blue-coloured panels, at the relevant part of the topic.

S — This icon represents the Summary which is to be found at the end of each chapter, before the questions. It is a good starting point to revise a topic.

Q — This icon represents a series of Review questions at the end of each chapter which cover the main points of that chapter.

Q — This icon represents a series of Examination Style questions, which reflect the style and difficulty of the Leaving Certificate examination. They contain Section A, Section B and Section C style questions.

Q — This icon represents actual past Leaving Certificate questions. Ordinary Level questions are listed first followed by Higher Level questions.

* — This icon is to be found at the very end of each chapter. It represents a listing of the year in which the topic appeared in the Leaving Certificate examinations from 2004-2014, including the SEC sample papers.

This icon represents the Learning Outcomes. These are listed at the start of each chapter and represent the syllabus requirements for each topic. They are repeated throughout the chapter at the place where the Learning Outcome is covered.

D — This is a definition box and contains the SEC accepted definition of the term. These should be learned off by heart. They are also to be found in the chapter Summary and in the Glossary, at the back of the book.

E — This icon identifies a balanced chemical equation that you are required to know.

SYLLABUS REQUIREMENT: This label indicates a specific syllabus requirement or alternative.

HL — This indicates that this chapter, section of a topic or Learning Outcome is Higher Level only.

UNIT 01

THE STUDY OF LIFE

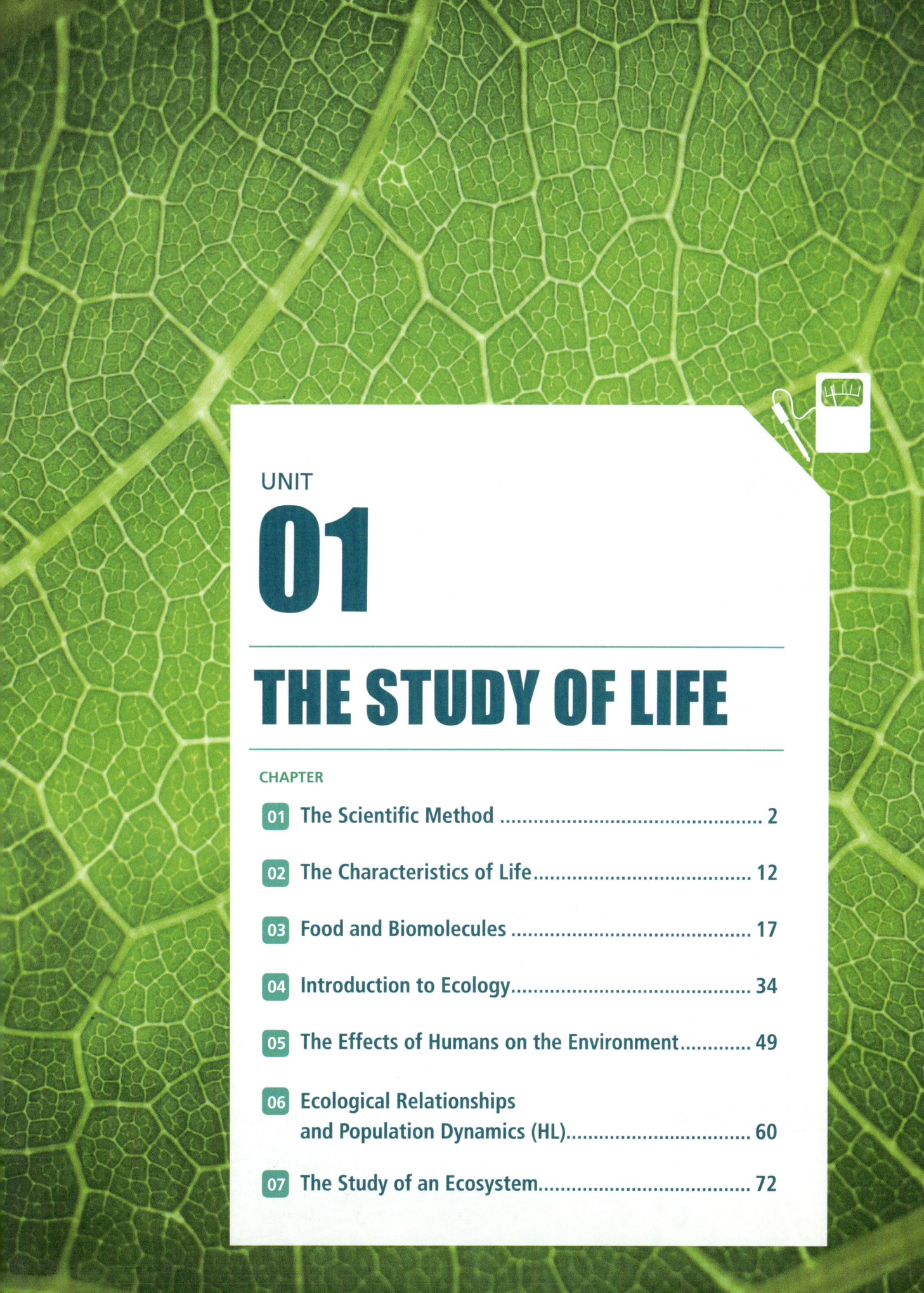

CHAPTER

01 The Scientific Method 2

02 The Characteristics of Life 12

03 Food and Biomolecules 17

04 Introduction to Ecology... 34

05 The Effects of Humans on the Environment............. 49

06 Ecological Relationships and Population Dynamics (HL)................................. 60

07 The Study of an Ecosystem.. 72

01 The Scientific Method

After studying this chapter you should be able to:

1. Define the term biology and give three examples of some of the areas studied within biology.
2. Outline the basic steps of the scientific method, including definitions of the terms data, experiment, hypothesis, replicates and theory.
3. Describe the principles of experimentation, including explanations of the terms control, conclusion, double-blind testing, freedom from bias, random selection.
4. Discuss the limitations of the value of the scientific method.

Living things

Biology is the study of life. In choosing to study the science of biology you have chosen to study the most complex of all things known – living things (Fig 1.1). Biologists learn about living things, or organisms, as they are more correctly known, by observing them and by experimentation. Biology is a very large subject area with many different branches of study.

Biology is the study of living things.

Botany	the study of plants.
Biochemistry	the study of the chemistry of organisms.
Bioinformatics	the collection and analysis of biological information using computers.
Biotechnology	the use of micro-organisms or enzymes to make useful products, e.g. the use of bacteria to make antibiotics (see Chapter 19).
Ecology	the study of organisms and their environment.
Genetics	the study of inheritance.
Microbiology	the study of tiny microscopic organisms such as bacteria.
Mycology	the study of fungi.
Zoology	the study of animals.

1.1 Living things

1.2 Biologists at work

The scientific method

A biologist, like any good scientist, learns about the natural world by observing, by asking questions and by carrying out experiments (Fig 1.2). Questions asked by biologists might include: where does it live?, how does this work?, what does it use that structure for?, why does it eat this food and not that?

In order to answer such questions and to find out more about the living world, biologists use a method for gathering information known as the **scientific method**.

> **D** The **scientific method** is a step-by-step process that leads to knowledge.

The scientific method begins with an **observation**. Suppose a farmer notices that her barley crop is not growing healthily and strong. Why is this?

First the farmer will think of a possible explanation for the observation – perhaps the plants are not getting enough nitrogen from the soil. A scientist calls this a **hypothesis**.

> **D** A **hypothesis** is an educated guess based on observation.

Then she would test her hypothesis to see whether it is true. This is done by carrying out a properly designed **experiment**, for example she might increase the amount of nitrogen fertiliser given to the crop.

On the basis of the information gathered (**data**) from the experiment the farmer would analyse the results and form a conclusion.

If the conclusion does not support (agree with) the hypothesis the farmer will have to suggest another hypothesis. If the conclusion does support the hypothesis, i.e. if the plants thrive with more nitrogen, then the original hypothesis would appear to be correct. She would then **replicate** the experiment to confirm her hypothesis.

> **D** An **experiment** is a series of steps carried out to test a hypothesis.

A tested hypothesis in turn can lead to new knowledge, **theories** and laws.

Experiments are usually written up and published so that the discoveries and research are made available to everyone and can be tried by others. Only when others can replicate them will they be accepted. Publication is needed to verify the results. Usually results are verified by other scientists – this is referred to as **peer review**.

> **D** **Data** are the measurements, observations or information gathered from an experiment.

Most biological work is published in the various biological and scientific journals, such as *Nature*: *The Journal of Plant Science* or *International Journal of Biological Sciences*, which are published regularly, in both paper and online formats (Fig 1.3). Posting results and theories on internet sites such as Wikipedia does not mean they have been verified. Only reputable sites and journals are acceptable.

> **D** A **replicate** is a repeat of an experiment or procedure.

1.3 Scientific journals

01 The Scientific Method

The scientific method involves the following steps:

1. Making an observation.
2. Forming a hypothesis.
3. Designing a controlled experiment to test the hypothesis.
4. Collecting and interpreting data.
5. Forming a conclusion.
6. Comparing the conclusion to existing knowledge.
7. Developing theories and principles.
8. Reporting and publishing the results.

Using the scientific method (Fig 1.4), scientists develop theories and principles to explain the natural world. A hypothesis becomes a **theory** when it is supported by a large number of observations and experiments and has, so far, not been proven wrong, e.g. the **cell theory**. The cell theory is based on many observations and experiments. It states that all living things are composed of cells. This theory was proposed by two German biologists, Schleiden and Schwann (Fig 1.5), in 1839 and it still holds true today. Proven theories can become laws or **principles** that aim to explain how the natural world works.

D A **theory** is a hypothesis that is supported by experiment.

D A **principle** is a proven theory.

Experimentation

A good experiment should:
- Be carefully **planned** and **designed**.
- Be carried out with **safety** in mind.
- Include a **control**.
- Be **free from bias (prejudice)**.

Planning and design

The planning and design of an experiment are very important. The following are some of the things that you need to think about.

- What is the purpose of your investigation?
- How can you be sure it is a **fair test**?
- What controls will you need?
- What is the most suitable equipment?
- How many times are you going to repeat the experiment?
- How are you going to record and present your results?

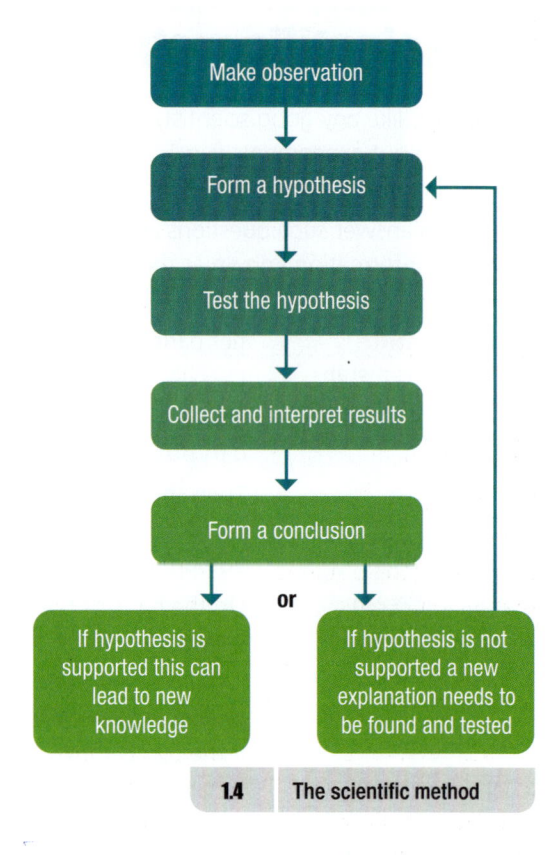

1.4 The scientific method

Flowchart: Make observation → Form a hypothesis → Test the hypothesis → Collect and interpret results → Form a conclusion → or → If hypothesis is supported this can lead to new knowledge / If hypothesis is not supported a new explanation needs to be found and tested (loops back to Form a hypothesis)

1.5 Schleiden and Schwann

Safety

In most cases, common sense will ensure no accidents occur when using equipment, apparatus, chemicals and other materials. Following a standard set of laboratory rules should ensure good safety practices. Throughout this book the safety symbols in Fig 1.6 are used.

Safety Glasses	Harmful or Irritant	Flammable	Corrosive	Toxic	Oxidising	Explosive
Eye protection must be worn.	These substances are less of a health risk than toxic substances. However, they must still be handled with care.	These substances may easily catch fire in a laboratory under normal conditions.	These substances can cause chemical burns to skin and eyes.	These substances may cause serious health risks or death if inhaled, swallowed or if they penetrate the skin.	These substances may produce much heat when they react with other substances, particularly flammable substances.	These substances may explode if ignited in air or exposed to heat. A sudden shock or friction may also cause an explosion.

1.6 Safety symbols

Controlled experiments

In carrying out an experiment, all conditions should be kept the same (constant) except the one being tested. In the test for starch (Fig 1.7), 3 drops of iodine solution are added to 5 cm³ of starch solution. In the presence of iodine, starch forms a blue-black colour. To show that it is the starch and not some other chemical that has this effect, the same amount of iodine solution is added to the same amount of water, which we know has no starch. The water acts as a comparison or control.

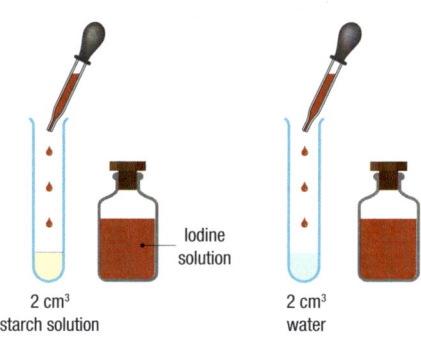

In Investigation 12.2 (page 141) you will be comparing the rate of enzyme action at different temperatures. In this case all the conditions of the investigation should be kept constant except the temperature. This is known as the **experimental (or independent) variable**. The variable that is being measured in the experiment is called the **dependent variable**. To be absolutely sure that the results are due to the experimental variable and not some unknown factor, a control group is set up. In Investigation 12.3 (page 143) you would run the experiment using everything the same but using boiled enzyme instead of active enzyme.

1.7 Testing for starch

> **D** A **control** is a standard against which the experiment is compared.

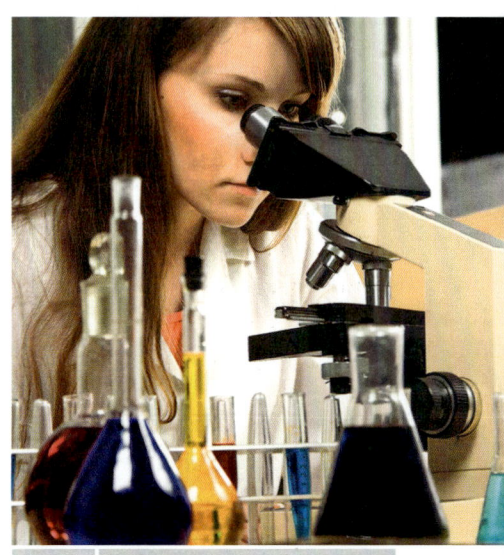

Freedom from bias

Freedom from bias means that the scientist does not come to the experiment thinking he already knows what the result will be. This can be achieved by a number of methods including:

- The use of a large number of samples.
- Random selection.
- Carrying out replicates.
- **Double-blind** testing.

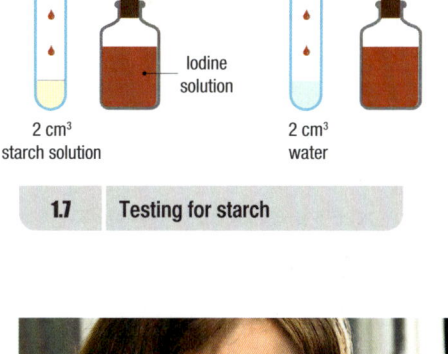

1.8 Working in a laboratory

Large sample size

Experimental samples must be large enough to ensure that the effects of individual differences do not matter. For example if you wanted to carry out a survey to find out who likes jazz music best, if you only asked 10 people, then the results would not be very representative. The larger the number of samples taken, the more likely we are to make valid assumptions (Fig 1.9).

Random selection

Again taking the example of the survey of people who like jazz music, even if you took a sample of 1000 people but they were all aged between 10 and 17 years, you do not have a representative sample. You need to choose people from across a wide range of age groups to make your assumption valid.

If you wanted to find out the number of buttercups in a meadow it is not practical to count every single buttercup plant. Instead you would carry out random sampling of the meadow. This means you would divide the meadow up into a grid of numbered squares and then select 20 squares at random and count the number of buttercups in each of them. By using several samples chosen at random you will even out the chances of selecting samples that are either full of buttercups or ones with none at all.

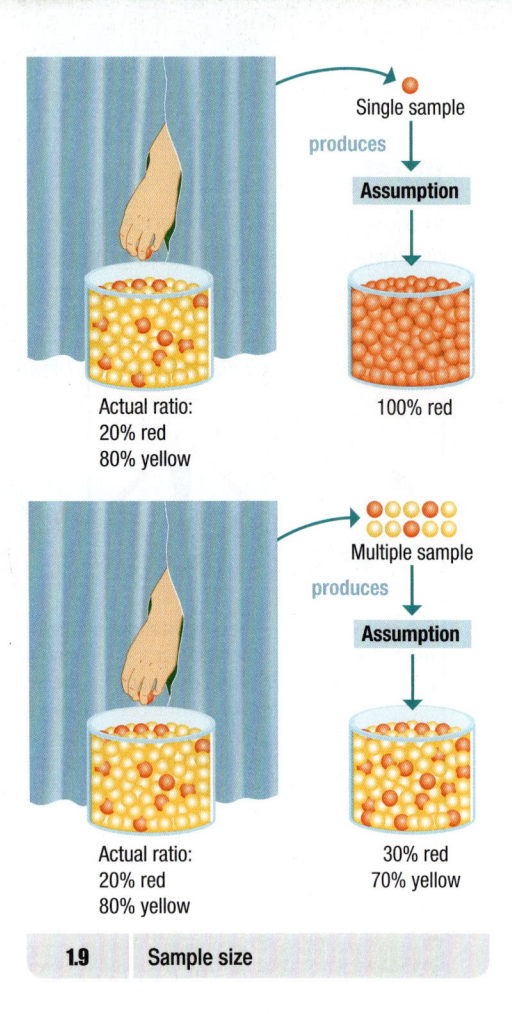

1.9 Sample size

Carry out replicates

Repeating an experiment many times helps to verify the results and prevents us jumping to a conclusion based on a single set of results. Generally speaking anyone using the same set of instructions (protocol) should get the same results. Often, in the classroom situation, many groups of students are performing the same experiment, each one therefore acting as a replicate for the others.

Double-blind testing

Double-blind testing is an important way of avoiding bias in an experiment and is best described by an example.

- A group of researchers wanted to test the hypothesis that students who received added fluorine in their diets developed fewer dental cavities (i.e. they had fewer fillings).
- To test their hypothesis, the researchers took a sample of 450 nine-year-olds who had no dental cavities.
- They gave each child a fluorine pill every day for six months and then checked to see whether any of them had developed dental cavities.
- According to their results, 88% of the children had not developed any dental cavities during the period of testing.
- But how do we know that it was the added fluorine that caused this and not some other factor? Maybe some of the children ate less sugary food or paid more attention to brushing their teeth properly.
- To prevent differences like this affecting the results the experiment had to have a control.

- A second group of 450 nine-year-olds were given a **placebo**, a harmless starch pill the same size, shape and taste as the fluorine pill being tested. The placebo acts as a control.
- But, when the researchers were handing out the placebo pills perhaps they somehow indicated to the children which pill they were given. Maybe they smiled at them and some of the children knew.
- To make sure the test is absolutely fair, neither the children nor the researcher should know who was getting the fluorine pill and who was getting the placebo.
- This method of avoiding bias in an experiment is known as double-blind testing. The pills are coded so that only after the experiment is over and the data gathered is it possible to distinguish between the control and the experimental group of children.

1.10 Drug testing trial

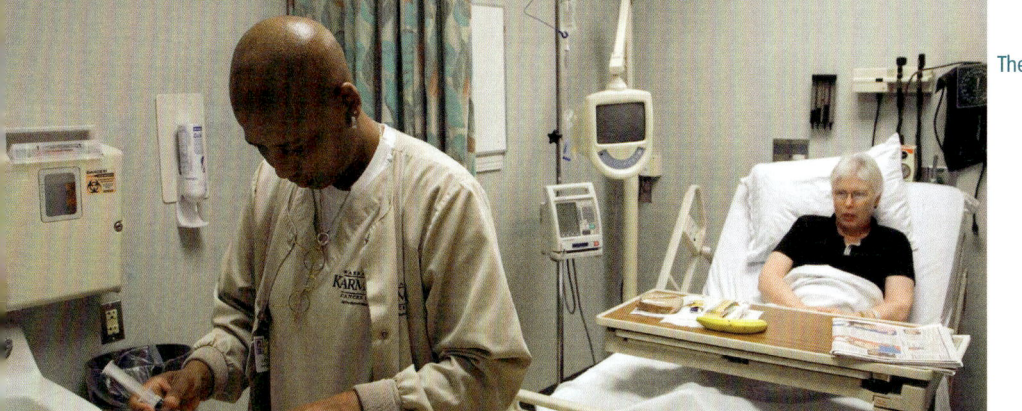

> **Double-blind** testing is a method of preventing bias where neither the tester nor the person being tested knows who is getting the placebo or who is getting the test chemical.

Limitations of the value of the scientific method

The value of the scientific method is limited by a number of factors:
- (i) The extent of our basic knowledge.
- (ii) The basis of investigation.
- (iii) Our ability to interpret results.
- (iv) The changing natural world.
- (v) Accidental discovery.

The extent of our basic knowledge

Until microscopes were invented we knew nothing about what living things are made of, i.e. **cells**. It was only when the electron microscope was invented that a true understanding of what cells are and how they work became known. You will learn more about the electron microscope in Chapter 8. Our understanding of the world around us is limited by what we already know and by what questions to ask. If we knew all the questions we would be a lot nearer to knowing all the answers!

The basis of investigation

We have already seen that hypotheses must be verifiable and repeatable. But there are some things that the scientific method cannot be used to prove, such as the existence of supernatural beings or whether there is life on other planets. This is because there is no experiment that can test these ideas. An investigation may also be limited by the accuracy of the instruments we are using. Until scales were invented that could weigh to a very small mass, being able to determine the effects of tiny amounts of a chemical or material was impossible.

Our ability to interpret results

Over the centuries it has often been the case that the results of an experiment or investigation suggest a particular conclusion. It is not always easy to interpret the results of experiments. In the early days of using microscopes to view cells scientists used many different staining techniques to make the structures more visible. Sometimes they identified what they thought were special new structures in a cell. This occurred after looking at the cells time and time again but on occasion the new 'structure' eventually turned out to be the result of how the cells were stained and not a structure at all.

The changing natural world

The constantly changing natural world means that assumptions we make may have to be changed or altered as nature changes. When antibiotics were first discovered they were referred to as 'magic bullets' because they were able to kill what were, up until then, often deadly diseases. Over time disease-causing bacteria have changed so that they have become immune to many of these life-saving **antibiotics** and they no longer work.

Accidental discovery

In 1848 an English doctor, John Snow, was trying to fight a dreadful disease called cholera. In those days the cause of cholera was not known. Some people said it was caused by 'bad air' or rats, but no one really knew. One day, almost by chance, Dr Snow realised that a lot of people in his area who suffered from cholera had one thing in common – they all got their water from the same pump in the street. This pump was found to be polluted by a leak from a nearby sewer. Dr Snow went on to prove that the polluted water contained germs that caused cholera (Fig 1.11).

1.11 Poor conditions in urban areas in the 1850s led to outbreaks of cholera

The discovery of the antibiotic penicillin by Sir Alexander Fleming in 1929 is another example of a chance discovery.

Ethics

Many advances in medicine have happened with the help of the scientific method. It is now possible to test your DNA to see if you carry the gene for serious illnesses such as cystic fibrosis or Huntington's disease. However this knowledge can have ethical issues. Should a person who has such a gene, e.g. for Huntington's disease, be told about it, even though there is no treatment for this serious condition?

These and many other issues – such as cloning animals and using stem cells from human embryos to make tissues and organs – need careful consideration.

D **Ethics** refers to whether something is right or wrong.

Summary

- Biology is the study of living things.
- There are many branches of biology including biochemistry, genetics, botany and zoology.
- Scientists use the scientific method to learn more about the natural world.
- The steps in the scientific method are:
  1. Making an observation.
  2. Forming a hypothesis.
  3. Designing a controlled experiment.
  4. Collecting and interpreting data.
  5. Forming a conclusion.
  6. Comparing the conclusion to existing knowledge.
  7. Reporting and publishing the results.
  8. Developing theories and principles.
- A hypothesis is an educated guess to explain an observation.
- A hypothesis can develop into a theory.
- An experiment is a series of steps used to test a hypothesis.
- A control is a comparison against which the experiment can be judged.
- A variable is something that changes in an experiment.
- Replicates are repeats of the procedure or experiment.
- Data refers to the observations and measurements gathered during an experiment.
- A conclusion is what the data lead us to understand.
- A theory is a supported hypothesis.
- A principle is a proven theory.
- The principles of experimentation state that an experiment should be well planned, well designed, safe and include a control.
- Avoiding bias in experimentation can be achieved by random sampling, using a large sample size, carrying out replicates and by double-blind testing.
- The interpretation of experiments and the value of the scientific method are limited by the extent of our existing knowledge, the basis of investigation, our ability to interpret results, the fact that the natural world is in a state of change and accidental discovery.

Review questions

01 (a) What is biology?
(b) Name two branches of biology that deal with animals.
(c) Name the branches of biology that people in the following jobs need to know about: a nurse, a park keeper, a surgeon, a lifeguard, a forest warden, a farmer, a beautician.

02 The term organism means 'living thing'. Which of the following are organisms: (a) a cat, (b) a mushroom, (c) a bacterium, (d) a jellyfish, (e) a fossil, (f) a human?

03 Find out what kind of work is carried out by each of the following professions: (a) a biochemist, (b) a marine biologist, (c) a taxonomist, (d) a geneticist.

04 (a) Explain the term 'scientific method'.
(b) Rearrange the following steps of the scientific method so that they are in the correct order:
(i) experimentation, (ii) conclusion, (iii) make observations, (iv) publication, (v) form a hypothesis.

05 Explain the terms: hypothesis, experiment, replicate, data, theory.

06 (a) Why is it important to report and publish the results of scientific work?
(b) Where would a scientist publish the results of their findings?

07 (a) List the principles of experimentation.
(b) Explain what is meant by a control in an experiment.
(c) What is the importance of a large sample size?
(d) In an experiment, what name is given to the factor that is changed?

08 Give examples to explain the importance of the following as they apply to the principles of experimentation:
(a) random sampling, (b) sample size, (c) double-blind testing.

09 List the limitations of the value of the scientific method and describe any one in more detail.

10 In an experiment to show that green plants need light to make food, two plants are used. Plant A is placed in the light and plant B is placed in the dark. Which plant, A or B, represents the control in this experiment? Give a reason for your answer.

11 An investigation into intelligence and vitamin intake in the diet of teenagers was carried out as follows: 1500 17-year-old students from six different schools were chosen for the survey; 750 students were given one tablet enriched with vitamins to be swallowed on each day of the survey. The other 750 students were given a tablet of the same size, shape and colour as that of the other group but containing no vitamins. Neither the investigators nor the students knew who was given which type of tablet. At the end of the survey, the levels of intelligence of all the students were tested using standard techniques.

(a) What hypothesis is being tested?
(b) Why were 1500 students chosen for the survey instead of 15 or 150?
(c) Which group of students represents the control?
(d) Identify the variable in this investigation.
(e) What name is given to the tablet without the vitamins?
(f) Summarise the importance of 'double-blind testing' in relation to experiments.

12 A group of students set up an experiment as follows. Three Petri dishes containing sterile nutrient agar were labelled A, B and C. Nutrient agar supplies food for bacteria. Samples of milk were spread across the surface of the nutrient agar in dishes A and B. The lids of the dishes were replaced and the dishes sealed. Dish C was left untouched. The dishes were then placed in an incubator (laboratory oven) at 25°C for 2–3 days. The results are shown below.

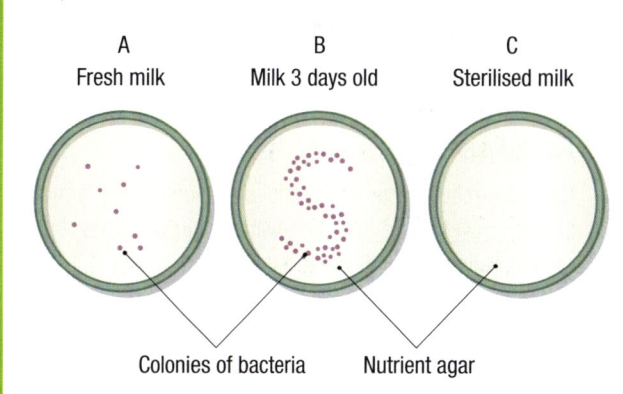

A — Fresh milk
B — Milk 3 days old
C — Sterilised milk

Colonies of bacteria   Nutrient agar

(a) What were the students trying to investigate?
(b) Which set-up, A, B or C, is the control?
(c) What conclusion can be drawn by comparing the result obtained for dish A and dish B?
(d) Suggest why you think the dishes were left at 25°C and not at 0°C or 100°C.
(e) Explain why the dishes were left in the incubator for 2–3 days and not 2–3 hours.
(f) Suggest what scientists might conclude from the results of this investigation.

01 The Scientific Method

Examination style questions

Section A

01 (a) Scientists must ensure that their experiments follow the 'scientific method'. The following steps in the scientific method are not in the correct order. Rewrite the steps in the correct order (use the numbers of the steps).
  (1) Collecting and interpreting data.
  (2) Working out a hypothesis.
  (3) Reporting and publishing results.
  (4) Making observations.
  (5) Reaching conclusions.
  (6) Designing a controlled experiment.

(b) State the purpose of each of the following methods used to avoid biased results.
  (i) Replicates (repeating the procedure many times).
  (ii) Random sampling.
  (iii) Double-blind testing.
  (iv) Large sample size.

02 Distinguish between the following pairs of terms:
(a) Hypothesis and theory.
(b) Data and conclusion

(c) Where experiments are reported and where they are published.
(d) Dependent and independent variables.
(e) Sample size and random sampling.

Section C

03 A number of years ago, a biological journal published a paper in which the paper's author made the claim that plants grew better when watered with a very dilute solution of the chemical **fluorescein.** The author thought there might be a connection between fluorescein and plants because both respond to light. Suggest how you could design an experiment to test the hypothesis that very dilute solutions of fluorescein make plants grow better. You should include a description of:
  (a) how you might prepare very dilute solutions;
  (b) what adequate controls you would set up;
  (c) how you would measure 'growth';
  (d) the expected results if the hypothesis is supported and what results would not support the hypothesis.

Leaving Certificate examination questions

Section A

01 Answer the following, which relate to the scientific method, by completing the blank spaces.

(a) As a result of her observations a scientist may formulate a _____. She will then progress her investigation by devising a series of _____ and then carefully analysing the resulting _____.

(b) Why is a control especially important in biological investigations?
(c) If a scientist wished to determine the effect of a certain herbicide on weed growth she would include a control in the investigation. Suggest a suitable control in this case.
(d) The use of replicates is an important aspect of scientific research. What, in this context, are replicates?
(e) Suggest where a scientist may publish the results of her investigations.

2008 HL Q. 3

02 Explain each of the following terms in relation to the scientific method:
(a) Hypothesis
(b) Control
(c) Data
(d) Replicate
(e) Theory

2005 HL Q. 2

03 Answer the following in relation to the scientific method:
(a) What is a hypothesis?
(b) What might a hypothesis develop into?
(c) Why is a control important in an experiment?
(d) Give an example of a control in a **named** experiment.
(e) State **two** ways in which the results of an experiment may be presented.

SEC Sample HL Q. 4

Leaving Certificate examination questions

Section B

04 (i) The scientific method involves making a hypothesis, carrying out experiments, recording results and forming conclusions. Why is it a good idea to repeat an experiment many times?
(ii) Why is a control used when carrying out experiments?

2011 OL Q. 8 (a)

05 (i) Give **one** example of a limitation of the scientific method.
(ii) Where do scientists usually publish the results and conclusions of their investigations?

2014 HL Q. 9 (a)

06 (a) In relation to the scientific method explain each of the following: (i) experiment, (ii) theory.
(b) Scientists investigated the effect of a certain mineral on the growth of wheat. Use your knowledge of biology and laboratory procedures to answer the following questions.

(i) Suggest a reason why the seeds used were all taken from one parent plant.
(ii) The compost in which the wheat plants were grown was sterilised at the start of the investigation.
  1. Suggest a way in which the scientists may have sterilised the compost.
  2. State **one** reason why it was important to sterilise the compost.
(iii) Why did the scientists divide the young wheat plants into two equal groups?
(iv) During the investigation the scientists kept the two groups of plants under identical conditions. Why was this?
(v) Name **two** conditions you think the scientists would have kept constant during the investigation.
(vi) Why did the scientists repeat the investigation several times before publishing their results in a scientific journal?

2011 HL Q. 7

Past examination questions

OL	2013 Q. 3 (e), (f)	2011 Q. 8 (a)					
HL	2014 Q. 9 (a)	2013 Q. 9 (a)	2011 Q. 7	2010 Q. 8 (a)	2008 Q. 3	2005 Q. 2	SEC Sample Q. 4

02 The Characteristics of Life

After studying this chapter you should be able to:

1. Appreciate that there is a wide variety of living organisms.
2. Identify the common features and behaviours that identify something as living.
3. Define the terms continuity of life and metabolism.
4. Define the following characteristics of living things: organisation, nutrition, response, excretion and reproduction.
5. Define life.

What is life?

We are surrounded by living things. The trees and flowers in the garden, other human beings, our pets and other animals are all **organisms**. Even the fungus on our mouldy bread is alive. **Biodiversity** is a term that describes the wide variety of **life** on the planet (Fig 2.1). But what do we mean when we say something is alive? How can we define life? There are no simple answers to these questions. However, if we examine how living things work and what they do, we find that organisms have many features or characteristics in common.

- All living things are composed of tiny units called **cells**.
- They are all highly organised.
- They react to changes in their surroundings.
- They use food to grow and to move.
- They reproduce and pass on information from one generation to the next.

Non-living things do none of these.

> **D** An **organism** is a living thing.

> **D** **Biodiversity** (or biological diversity) is a term used to describe the variety of living things on Earth.

> **D** **Life** may be defined as something that possesses metabolism and continuity.

Metabolism and continuity

The organisation of living things is made possible by their taking in substances and energy from their surroundings. Living things use these for growth and repair. **Metabolism** is the term used to describe all the chemical reactions that take place within living cells. These reactions allow an organism to grow, break down food, release energy, respond and reproduce.

So metabolism is essential for life. You will meet two different types of metabolism, **anabolism** and **catabolism**, in Chapter 12. Also essential is **continuity**. We all know that humans only give birth to human babies and not to baby cats or daisies

2.1 There is a wide variety of life on the planet

or fish. In other words, there is continuity of life. Continuity is the ability of each type of organism to exist from one generation to the next. If they cannot do this their type becomes extinct, like the dinosaurs and the Tasmanian tiger (Fig 2.2).

> **D** **Metabolism** is the sum of all the chemical reactions that occur in an organism.

> **D** **Continuity** is the ability of organisms to exist from one generation to the next.

2.2 The Tasmanian tiger, thought to have become extinct in 1936

The characteristics of life

It is true to say that we can only define life in terms of the features or characteristics that all living things show. These are known as the **characteristics of life**.

The five characteristics common to all organisms are: **organisation**, **nutrition**, **excretion**, **response** and **reproduction**.

1. Organisation

All organisms are highly organised, and are composed of tiny units called **cells**. Cells are made up of atoms and molecules, i.e. chemicals.

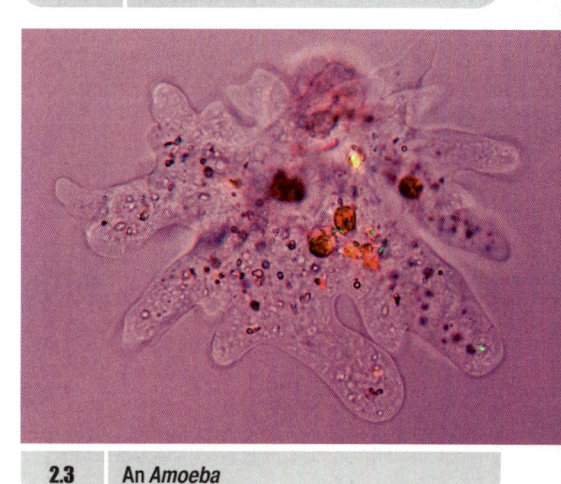

> **D** **Organisation** refers to organisms being made up of cells (which are themselves highly organised), tissues, organs and systems.

2.3 An *Amoeba*

These chemicals themselves are not alive but they combine together to form structures in the cell called **organelles**. The organelles, such as the nucleus, carry out particular functions in the cell. The role of the nucleus is to control the cell – if it is removed, the cell will die. It is the whole cell, working as a unit, which carries out the activities of life.

Some organisms consist of only one cell, e.g. the *Amoeba* (Fig 2.3). In these **unicellular** organisms all the processes of life are carried out in a single cell. Most organisms, however, are made up of many cells. These are called **multicellular** organisms, e.g. jellyfish, earthworms, insects, roses, grass, mushrooms and human beings. In multicellular organisms, not all the cells are identical, nor do they all have the same job to do. Groups of similar cells form **tissues**. Muscle is an example of a tissue. Different tissues make up **organs** like the heart in humans and the leaves and roots of a plant. Different organs working together then form **systems** of the body, e.g. the circulatory system in humans, and the different systems form **individuals** (Fig 2.4).

cells → tissues → organs → systems → individuals

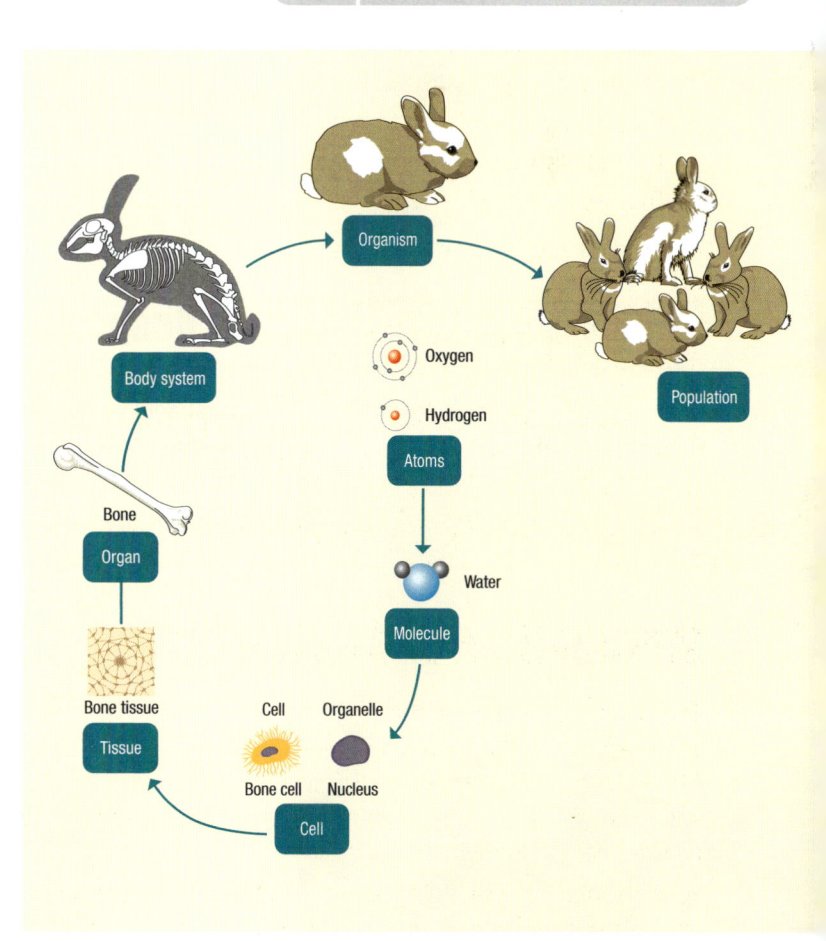

2.4 Levels of organisation

02 The Characteristics of Life

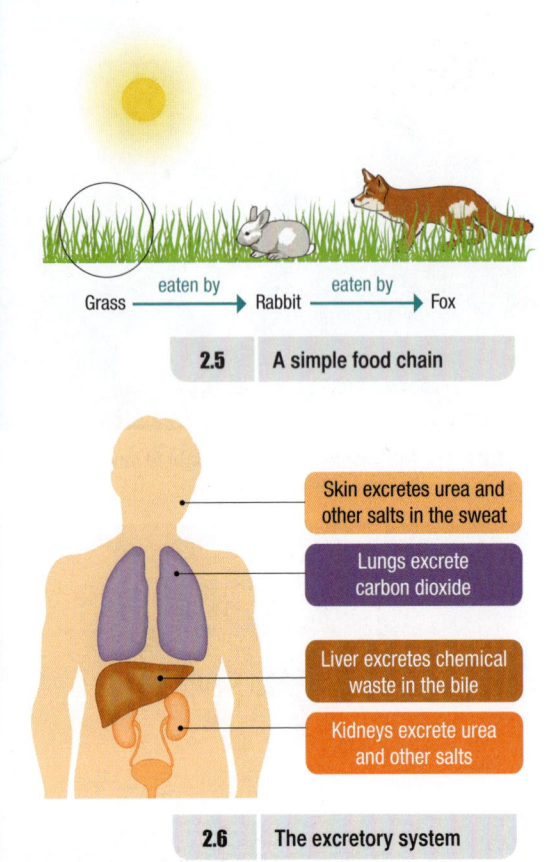

2.5 A simple food chain
Grass → eaten by → Rabbit → eaten by → Fox

2.6 The excretory system
- Skin excretes urea and other salts in the sweat
- Lungs excrete carbon dioxide
- Liver excretes chemical waste in the bile
- Kidneys excrete urea and other salts

2.7 Stomata on a leaf

2.8 Plant showing response

2. Nutrition

We usually think of nutrition as something to do with food. More correctly nutrition is the process by which living things obtain and use food from their surroundings. Food is needed to provide energy and to allow the organism to carry out the other characteristics of life.

There are two types of nutrition – **autotrophic** and **heterotrophic**.

Plants are autotrophic. This means they make their own food from simple raw materials in the environment. Plants combine water and carbon dioxide to make food using energy from the sun. This process is called **photosynthesis**.

Animals, on the other hand, cannot make their own food. Animals are heterotrophs. Heterotrophs obtain their nutrients by either eating plants or by eating other animals. As a result, energy from the sun is first passed into plants and from there it flows from one animal to the next. This flow of energy in nature is called a **food chain** (Fig 2.5).

3. Excretion

As a result of the chemical reactions that take place in living cells, wastes are produced, which may be harmful. Excretion is the removal of the waste products of metabolism. If there was a build-up of harmful wastes, the organism would be poisoned.

Animals, like humans, produce a nitrogen-containing waste called **urine**. Urine is made of urea, water and salts. The urea is made in the liver and passes from the liver to the kidneys in the bloodstream.

Excess carbon dioxide gas made in our cells is excreted through the lungs and excess water and salt is removed through the skin as sweat (Fig 2.6).

Plants do not produce a large amount of nitrogenous (nitrogen-containing) waste. Simple wastes such as excess oxygen from photosynthesis and carbon dioxide from respiration pass out of the leaves through tiny openings called **stomata** (Fig 2.7).

Other waste chemicals move into the leaves and are removed when the leaves fall in the autumn.

4. Response

All organisms react to changes in their environment and to things happening inside their bodies. Response is essential for an organism to survive and to allow it to carry out its daily activities. Animals respond to sound, touch and light using sense organs and the nervous system.

In plants there are no specific sense organs but certain cells respond to the force of gravity, and to light, touch, chemicals and water. The stem of a plant grows in the direction of light so the leaves can get light to make food, and the 'tentacles' of the sundew respond to touch (Fig 2.8).

> **Nutrition** is the getting/producing and use of food.

> **Excretion** is the removal of the wastes of metabolism (the wastes made in the cells of an organism).

> **Response** is the ability of organisms to react to both internal and external changes.

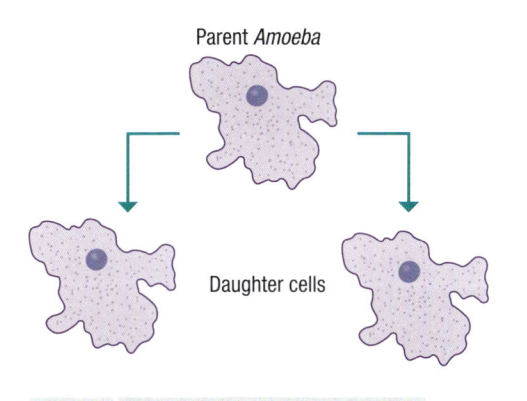

The Characteristics of Life | 02

2.9 Asexual reproduction in *Amoeba*

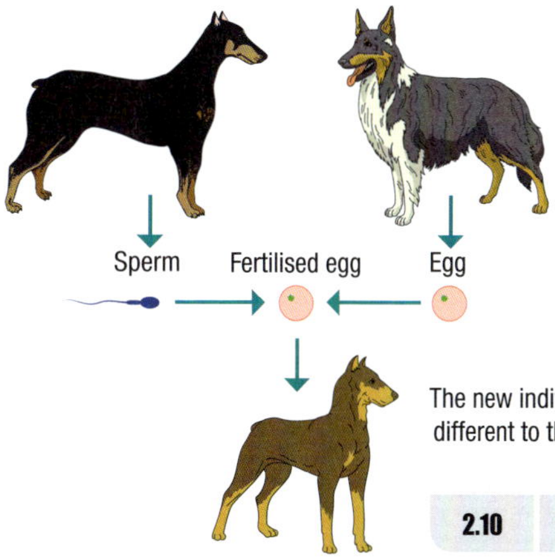

2.10 Sexual reproduction

Asexual reproduction	Sexual reproduction
No sex cells (gametes) produced.	Male and female sex cells produced.
Common in single-celled organisms such as *Amoeba* and in most plants.	Common in animals and flowering plants.
Offspring are identical to the parent (clone).	Offspring are similar to but not identical to the parents.

5. Reproduction

Reproduction is needed to make sure a particular type of organism survives. We have already seen how this continuity of life is important.

There are two types of reproduction – **asexual** and **sexual** (Figs 2.9 and 2.10).

> **Reproduction** is the ability of an organism to produce new individuals of its own kind.

Conclusion

Finding a definition of life is not easy. It involves the interaction of metabolism and continuity, both of which involve the characteristics we say all living things possess. Metabolism requires the interaction of organisation, nutrition, excretion and response. Continuity requires organisation, nutrition, response and reproduction.

To define something as 'alive' it must possess and carry out all of the characteristics of life. No one characteristic alone is sufficient. Crystals forming in the laboratory were once thought to be alive because they appear to grow. But they do not reproduce, nor do they respond to change. They cannot feed or excrete and so growth alone does not mean that crystals are alive. Growth in crystals is quite different to growth in living things. Crystals grow by gathering material around themselves from the solution they are in. Organisms grow from within their own bodies.

Summary

- Something is 'alive' if it shows *all* of the following five characteristics: organisation, nutrition, excretion, response and reproduction.
- Metabolism is the sum of the chemical reactions that take place in cells.
- Continuity of life is the ability of organisms to exist from one generation to the next.

Organisation	Living things are composed of cells, tissues, organs and organ systems.
Nutrition	The way living things obtain and use food.
Excretion	Getting rid of the wastes of metabolism.
Response	The ability to react to internal and external changes.
Reproduction	The ability to produce new individuals of the same type.

- Life means having the characteristics of both metabolism and continuity.

02 The Characteristics of Life

Review questions

01
(a) State another name for a 'living thing'.
(b) What do we mean when we say we are 'alive'?
(c) Give the name for all the chemical reactions that go on in living cells.

02
(a) What is a cell?
(b) What name is given to organisms that are made of only one cell?
(c) Name a 'one-celled' organism.
(d) What do 'one-celled' organisms have in common with human beings?

03
(a) What is the ultimate source of energy for life on earth?
(b) Explain the term nutrition.
(c) Distinguish between an autotroph and a heterotroph, including named examples of each.

04
(a) What is excretion?
(b) Name two substances excreted by humans.
(c) List two excretory organs in humans.
(d) Name two substances excreted by plants.
(e) What are stomata? Where are they found?

05
(a) Living things respond to stimuli. What does the term stimulus mean?
(b) Suggest one difference in the way an earthworm and a tree respond to light.

06
(a) Which characteristic of life may be defined as the ability to produce offspring?
(b) Explain the term offspring. Whose offspring are you?
(c) Distinguish between sexual and asexual reproduction.

07 Which characteristics of life are shown by the following activities?
(a) Rabbits running away from a fox.
(b) A tennis player hitting a ball.
(c) An oak tree growing from an acorn.
(d) A sweet pea plant climbing up some wire netting.
(e) A sprinter sweating after the race.

08 Some people do not consider plants to be living things. Explain the ways in which plants show all the characteristics of life.

09
(a) What is metabolism?
(b) Explain the term continuity of life and outline its importance.

Examination style questions

Section C

01 Biology is the study of living things. Living things can be distinguished from non-living things because they all share the following characteristics: organisation; nutrition; excretion; response and reproduction.

(a) Explain any *three* of the characteristics listed.
(b) Explain how each characteristic you have defined applies to animals.
(c) Explain the terms metabolism and continuity of life.

Leaving Certificate examination questions

Section A

01
(a) Metabolism is the sum of all the chemical reactions in the body: true or false?
(b) Nutrition is the way living things get rid of their waste: true or false?

2013 OL Q. 3

Past examination questions

OL 2013 Q. 3 (a), (c)   2012 Q. 12 (a)(i)

HL 2005 Q. 1 (f)

Food and Biomolecules

03

After studying this chapter you should be able to:

1. Appreciate that all living things are made of chemicals.
2. Explain the need for food.
3. Name the chemical components of food.
4. For each of carbohydrates, proteins and lipids describe the elements present, the structure, their source in the diet and their functions, both structural and metabolic.
5. Distinguish between fats and oils.
6. Explain the role of vitamins in general.
7. For one water-soluble and one fat-soluble vitamin describe its function, source in the diet and a disorder associated with a deficiency of it.
8. Describe the requirement and use of any two minerals in plants and two in animals.
9. Explain the importance of water to all organisms.
10. Define anabolic and catabolic reaction pathways.
11. Describe how to carry out a laboratory test to show the presence of each of the following in a sample of food: reducing sugar, starch, protein and lipid.

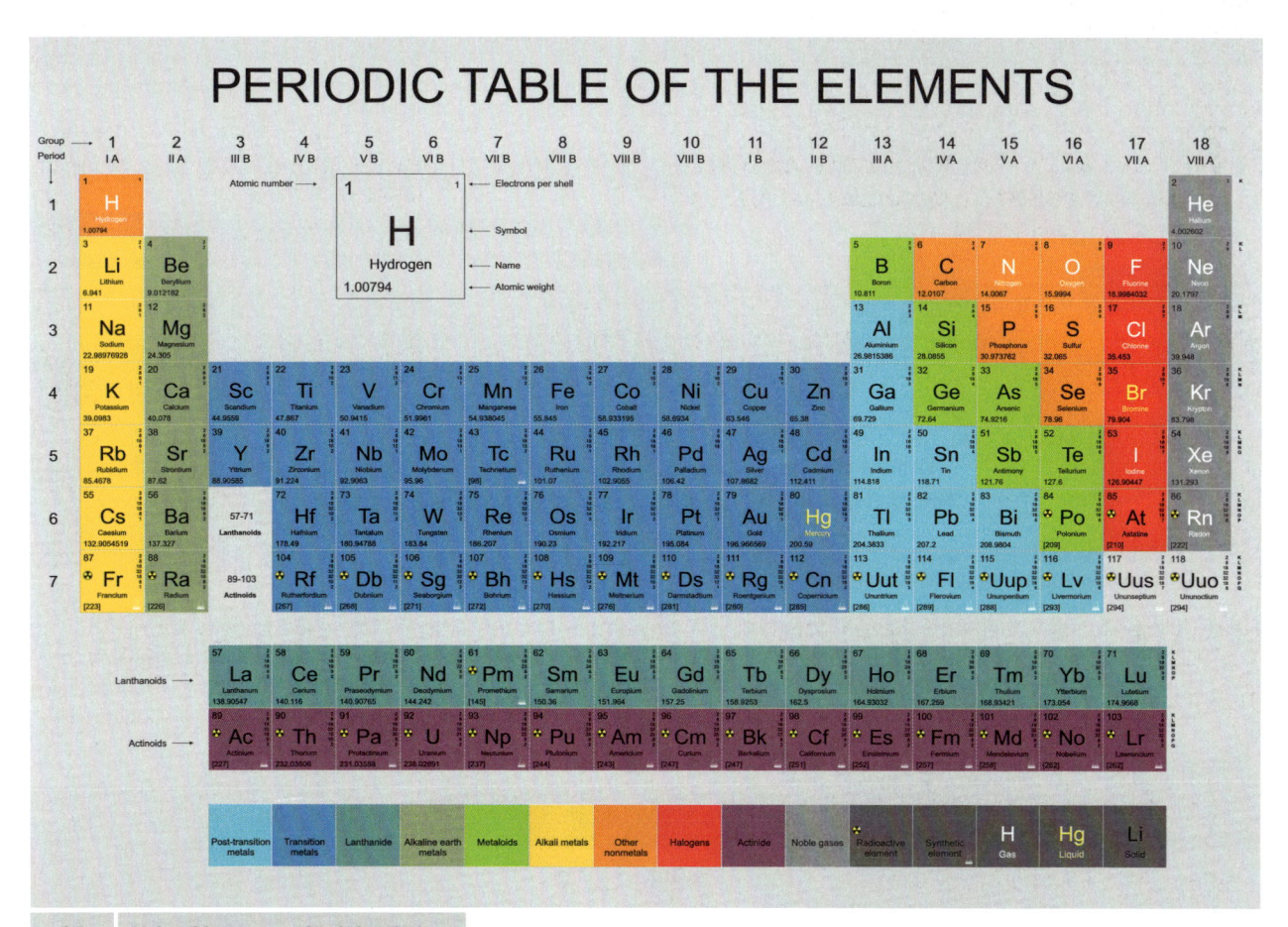

3.1 Living things are made of chemicals

03 Food and Biomolecules

Chemicals and living things

Until the 1800s, scientists believed that only non-living things were made of chemicals. They thought that living things were different and possessed what was called a 'vital force'. We now know that all things (matter) have a chemical make-up.

Sometimes it is difficult for us to realise that living things are also made up of chemicals. When we look at a cat or a flower we see a whole organism but, as we learned in the previous chapter, **organisms** are composed of **organ systems**. Organ systems are made of **organs** and organs are made of **tissues**. Tissues are groups of **cells** and cells are composed of molecules, and molecules are made up of chemical elements (Fig 3.1).

Chemical elements found in living things

Over 98% of all living things are made up of six **main chemical elements**. These elements join together (or bond) in different combinations (ratios) to form most of the molecules found in living organisms (Fig 3.2). The molecules in organisms are known as biochemicals or **biomolecules**.

Table 3.1 The six main elements found in organisms

Main element	Chemical symbol	Needed for
Carbon	C	Making all organic molecules such as carbohydrates, proteins, lipids and vitamins.
Hydrogen	H	
Oxygen	O	
Nitrogen	N	Making all proteins, DNA, RNA, ATP.
Phosphorus	P	Making ATP.
Sulfur	S	Making some proteins.

In addition to the six elements listed above, others are found as ions in **dissolved salts**.

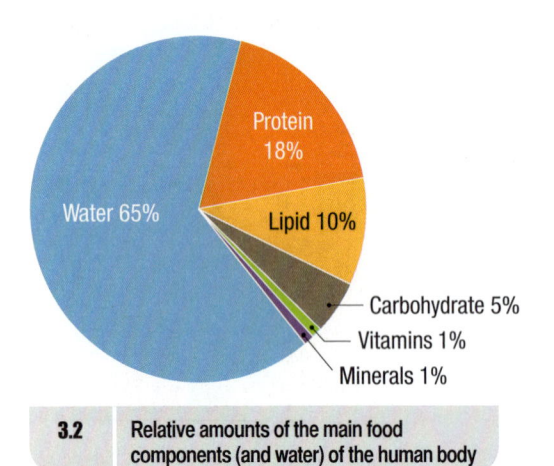

Table 3.2 Elements found in dissolved salts

Element found in dissolved salts	Symbol
Chlorine	Cl
Sodium	Na
Potassium	K
Magnesium	Mg
Calcium	Ca

3.2 Relative amounts of the main food components (and water) of the human body

- Water 65%
- Protein 18%
- Lipid 10%
- Carbohydrate 5%
- Vitamins 1%
- Minerals 1%

Finally, there are some elements that are found in only tiny amounts in organisms. These are known as **trace elements** and play a vital role in running chemical reactions in cells. Trace elements are usually found in combination with large organic molecules, like proteins.

Table 3.3 Trace elements

Trace element	Symbol
Copper	Cu
Zinc	Zn

Biomolecules are the chemicals found in living things.

03 Food and Biomolecules

Food for life

All living things need food. Food consists of carbohydrates, lipids, proteins, vitamins and minerals. It is made up of different molecules (Fig 3.3).

The functions of food

1. For **energy**.
2. To provide the **raw materials** that organisms use to build and repair their body parts.
3. To control the chemical reactions in cells, i.e. to control their **metabolism**.

3.3 Food is essential for life's activities

Chemical components of food

Traditionally, molecules that were found in living things and contained carbon were known as organic molecules. Now we call them biomolecules.

There are four major types of biomolecule found in food: **carbohydrates**, **lipids**, **proteins** and **vitamins**. These are known as organic molecules. Minerals (e.g. calcium), carbon dioxide (CO_2) and sodium chloride (NaCl) are examples of inorganic molecules.

1. Carbohydrates

① Monosaccharides Single sugar molecules e.g. glucose

② Disaccharides Double sugar molecules e.g. sucrose

③ Polysaccharides Many sugar units e.g. glycogen

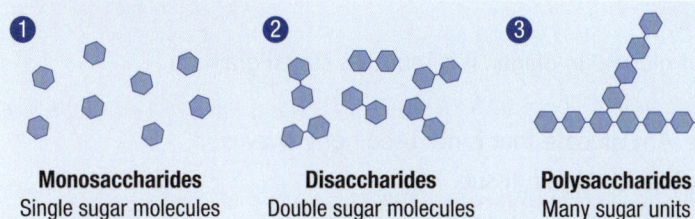

3.4 Three types of carbohydrate

Elements

Carbohydrates contain the elements carbon, hydrogen and oxygen (C, H and O). Carbohydrates contain twice as many hydrogen atoms as oxygen atoms. Many carbohydrates have the general formula $C_x(H_2O)_y$, where x is approximately equal to y. A simple carbohydrate is glucose, which has the chemical formula $C_6H_{12}O_6$.

Structure

1. Monosaccharides consist of a single 'sugar unit'. Examples include glucose, fructose and galactose. They are commonly referred to as simple sugars. Monosaccharides are soluble in water and are sweet to taste.
2. Disaccharides consist of two 'sugar units' joined together, e.g. sucrose and lactose. Sucrose is made of glucose and fructose combined together. Disaccharides are soluble in water and are sweet to taste.
3. Polysaccharides consist of many sugar units joined together, e.g. starch, glycogen, cellulose and chitin. Starch, glycogen and cellulose are made up of long chains of glucose molecules. Polysaccharides are not soluble in water and they do not taste sweet.

Sources of carbohydrates in the diet

Carbohydrate	Name	Source
Monosaccharide	Glucose Fructose	Fruit Fruit
Disaccharide	Sucrose Lactose	Table sugar/cane sugar Milk
Polysaccharide	Starch Cellulose	Bread, pasta, potatoes Vegetables, wholemeal bread

Table 3.4 Sources of carbohydrate in the diet

3.5 Good sources of carbohydrate

03 Food and Biomolecules

The role of carbohydrates

(a) Structural carbohydrates

The polysaccharide cellulose forms the wall of all plant cells (Fig 3.6). Human beings cannot digest cellulose, but cellulose is important in the diet as fibre (see Chapter 25). Chitin is a structural polysaccharide found in the cell walls of fungi (see Chapter 20). It also forms the skeleton of insects and crabs.

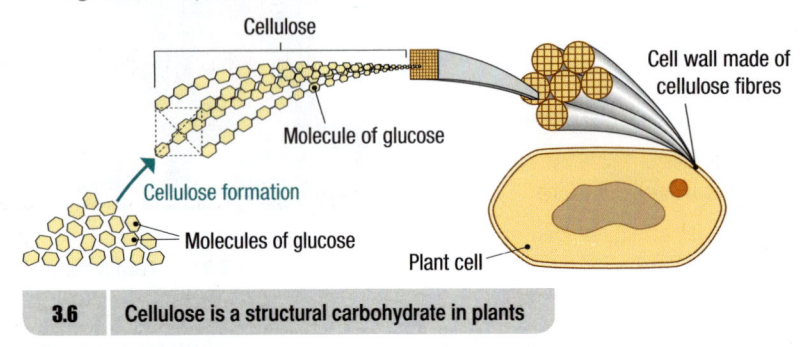

3.6 Cellulose is a structural carbohydrate in plants

(b) Metabolic carbohydrates

- Glucose provides **energy** when it breaks down during **respiration**:

$$C_6H_{12}O_6 + 6O_2 \rightarrow 6CO_2 + 6H_2O + \text{energy}$$

- Glucose is formed in **photosynthesis**:

$$6CO_2 + 6H_2O \rightarrow C_6H_{12}O_6 + 6O_2$$

- Starch is a storage carbohydrate. It is the store of glucose in plants. It is found as starch grains in the cytoplasm (Fig 3.7).
- Glycogen is the store of carbohydrate in animals. Any glucose that is not used right away is converted to glycogen and stored in the muscle, liver and brain tissue.

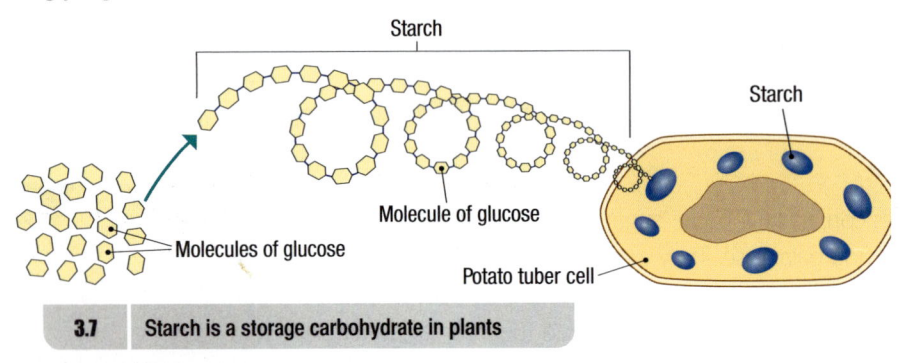

3.7 Starch is a storage carbohydrate in plants

2. Lipids (fats and oils)

Elements

Lipids contain the elements carbon, hydrogen and oxygen (C, H, O) but in a different ratio to that in the simple carbohydrates.

Structure

Lipids are composed of two main types of molecule: **fatty acids** and **glycerol**. The smallest lipid is called a **triglyceride** because it consists of three fatty acid molecules and one glycerol molecule (Fig 3.8). Lipids are commonly known as fats and oils. Fats and oils have the same basic chemical structure, but at room temperature (20°C) fats are solid whereas oils are liquid. All lipids are insoluble in water.

Phospholipids

If one of the fatty acids of a lipid molecule is replaced by a phosphate group, then a **phospholipid** molecule is formed (Fig 3.9). Phospholipids are important in the formation of cell membranes.

3.8 A triglyceride (lipid molecule)

3.9 A phospholipid molecule

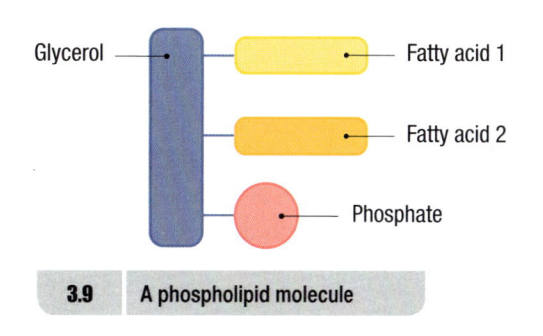

Sources of lipids in the diet

Fats are commonly found in butter, margarine, cream and cheese. Oils are mainly found in plants, e.g. sunflower oil, and also in fish oils such as mackerel and salmon.

The role of lipids

(a) Structural lipids

- Phospholipids and lipoproteins (lipid combined with protein) form a major component of cell membranes.
- Lipids are also important as storage molecules, forming the long-term energy store of organisms, whereas glucose is an immediate source of energy. Lipid is also important under the skin for insulation, for example, and as protection around body organs, e.g. the kidney.
- Lipids are found as myelin on some nerve cells. The myelin helps the nerve cell carry messages faster than nerve cells without myelin.
- Finally, oils secreted by the skin help to waterproof the body, and form on the epidermis of plants as the cuticle.

(b) Metabolic lipids

Lipids release energy when broken down in respiration. Lipids produce twice as much energy per gram as do carbohydrates.

3. Proteins

Elements

Proteins contain the elements carbon, hydrogen, oxygen and nitrogen (C, H, O, N). In addition, proteins may contain sulfur. Some proteins also combine with phosphorus and other elements such as iron. Examples of proteins found in cells include **enzymes**, **hormones**, pigments and myosin, the protein in muscles.

Structure

Protein molecules are made up of sub-units called **amino acids**, which link together in long, often twisted, chains. There are about 20 different kinds of amino acid commonly found in proteins. These amino acids can link up in any combination or sequence to form many different protein molecules. The bond between amino acids is called a **peptide bond** (Fig 3.10(a)).

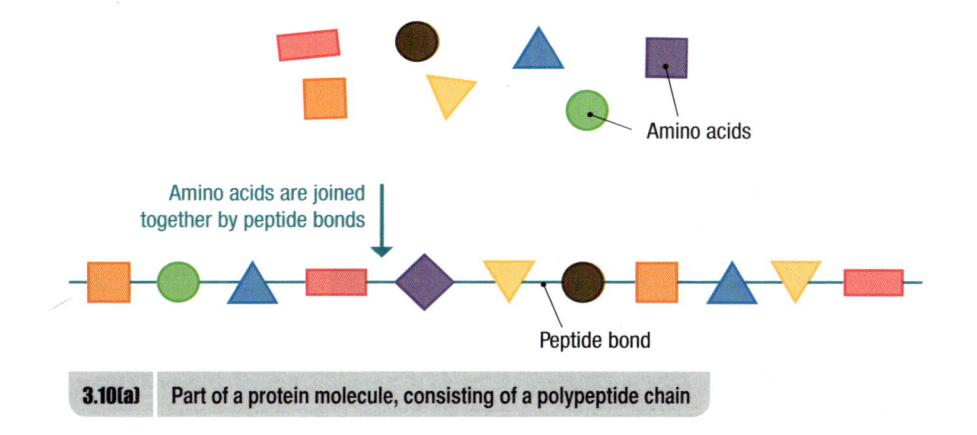

3.10(a) Part of a protein molecule, consisting of a polypeptide chain

A peptide consists of a chain of as many as 20 amino acids. A polypeptide consists of more than 20 amino acids and a typical protein has 200 amino acids.

Some polypeptide chains become:
- twisted, e.g. fibrous protein in hair and nails (Fig 3.10(b)(i))
- folded, e.g. globular proteins in enzymes and hormones (Fig 3.10(b)(ii)), or
- folded, and in addition have another chemical in the fold, e.g. haemoglobin in red blood cells and glycoproteins on cell membranes (Fig 3.10(b)(iii)).

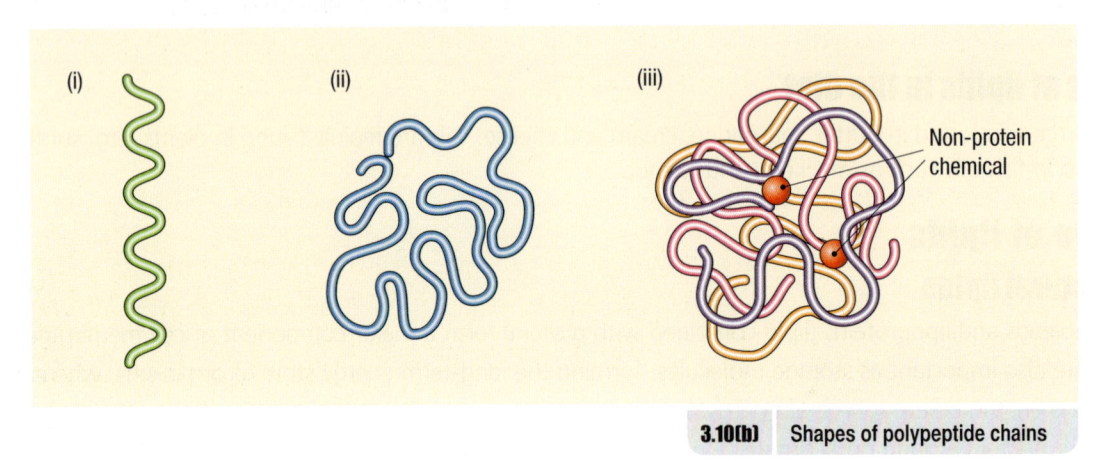

3.10(b) Shapes of polypeptide chains

Sources of proteins in the diet

Proteins are found in lean meat, egg white, fish, soya and pulses, e.g. beans, lentils and chick peas.

The role of proteins

(a) Structural proteins

Proteins are found as keratin in hair, skin and nails and as myosin in muscle.

(b) Metabolic proteins

- Molecules called enzymes which control the chemical reactions in cells are all made of protein. Chapter 12 deals specifically with enzymes and how proteins are made in cells is covered in Chapter 15.
- Hormones are proteins that regulate body functions, e.g. the hormone insulin (Fig 3.11) controls the amount of glucose in the bloodstream (Chapter 31).

Pigments such as chlorophyll and haemoglobin are proteins. Chlorophyll traps sunlight energy during the process of photosynthesis (Chapter 13).

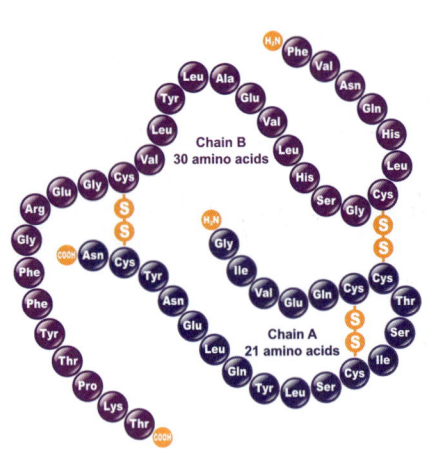

3.11 An insulin molecule

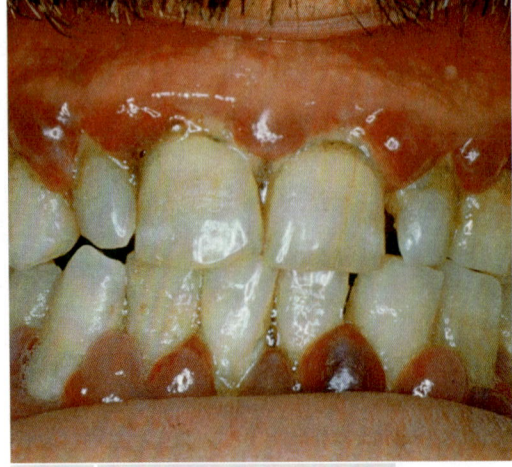

3.12 Scurvy – the result of vitamin C deficiency

3.13 Rickets – the result of vitamin D deficiency in a child

4. Vitamins

Vitamins are organic compounds. They all differ chemically from each other. Vitamins are needed in only tiny amounts but are essential for the normal functioning of living things. In the early 1900s, a biologist named Hopkins was investigating the nutrition of young rats. He used two groups of rats, a test group and a control group. He fed the test group a diet of pure protein, carbohydrate, lipid, minerals and water. After a few weeks these rats failed to grow properly. The second group of rats was fed exactly the same diet but with the addition of a small amount of milk. These rats thrived (grew vigorously). Hopkins concluded that something in the milk must be necessary for the rats to grow. This 'something' was found to be vitamins.

Vitamins are known by letters of the alphabet (A, B, C, D, E, K), or by names based on their chemical structure. Vitamin C is the chemical ascorbic acid and vitamin D is the chemical calciferol.

Vitamins can be classified by their solubility in either water or fat.
(i) Vitamins B and C are water-soluble vitamins.
(ii) Vitamins A, D, E and K are fat-soluble vitamins.

Vitamin	Solubility	Function	Source in diet	Deficiency disorder
Vitamin C	Water soluble	To form connective tissue, e.g. bone, cartilage, blood.	Oranges, kiwi fruit, broccoli.	Scurvy, a condition in which the gums bleed and wounds are slow to heal (Fig 3.12).
Vitamin D	Fat soluble	To help calcium absorption and form bone.	Dairy products such as milk, butter, yoghurt. Vitamin D can also be made in the skin on exposure to sunlight.	Rickets in children and osteo-malacia in adults. Both result in weakened bones (Fig 3.13).

Table 3.5 Vitamins

SYLLABUS REQUIREMENT:
You are required to know about one water-soluble and one fat-soluble vitamin.

5. Minerals

Minerals are inorganic chemicals that animals and plants need in very small amounts to function properly. Important minerals include sodium, calcium, magnesium, iron, iodine and fluorine. The main uses of minerals to plants and animals are:

1. Minerals form part of the rigid body structure, e.g. calcium is necessary to form bones and teeth. In plants calcium is needed to make the middle lamella that binds cells together.
2. Minerals form part of certain biomolecules such as pigments. Iron is needed to form haemoglobin, the red colour (pigment) of blood. Magnesium is essential for the formation of the plant pigment, chlorophyll.
3. Minerals regulate the cell and body fluids, e.g. sodium helps to balance the water content of cells, and manganese is an enzyme activator in cells.

	Mineral	Source	Function
Plants	Magnesium (Mg) Calcium (Ca)	As salts in the soil As salts in the soil	Forms part of chlorophyll. Helps form middle lamella between plant cells.
Animals	Iron (Fe) Calcium (Ca)	Red meat, liver, green vegetables Milk, cheese	Forms part of haemoglobin. Helps form healthy bones and teeth.

Table 3.6 Minerals

SYLLABUS REQUIREMENT:
You are required to know about two minerals in plants and two minerals in animals.

Water

Water is essential for life. Living things consist of 65–90% water, e.g. cabbage contains 95% water and fish comprise 80%. As much as 75% of a human cell consists of water. In the body, water forms a major part of the body fluids, e.g. in the blood.

03 Food and Biomolecules

The importance of water to living things

Water is a chemical molecule with the formula H_2O. Although it is a small molecule, water is very important to living things:

1. Water is a **universal solvent**. This means that water can dissolve many different kinds of substance, and it provides a **medium** in which chemical reactions can occur.
2. Water is a good **absorber of heat** energy. This means it holds its heat and is slow to cool down. This property of water is most important for organisms that live in water as it ensures they have a fairly constant external temperature.

    Because water is slow to heat up and cool down and the fact that it makes up such a large proportion of living things means that the internal temperature of organisms can also be kept fairly constant. This in turn protects the chemical reactions in cells, which can only take place within a narrow temperature range. Above certain temperatures, enzyme-controlled reactions cease. If the temperature is too low the chemical reactions slow down and in certain cases this can cause the death of an organism, e.g. hypothermia in human beings.
3. Water has a role to play in many chemical reactions:
    (a) It is the main source of the oxygen produced by plants during photosynthesis ($6CO_2 + 6H_2O \rightarrow C_6H_{12}O_6 + 6O_2$).
    (b) When two monosaccharides join to form a disaccharide, water is removed, e.g. glucose + fructose minus water forms sucrose (Fig 3.14).
4. Substances such as glucose move in and out of cells dissolved in water. The control of this movement is very important to cells, as we will see in Chapter 10. Water also controls the shape of cells. Take a houseplant that has not been watered for some time. The stem and leaves of the plant will droop (wilt). If the plant is watered, a short time later the stem becomes upright and the leaves will stand out from the stem once more. Water moving into the cells of the plant is responsible for the result you see.

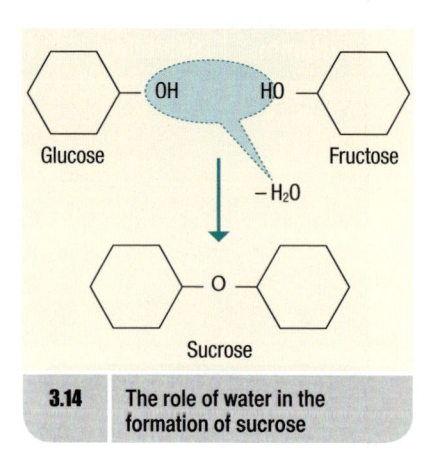

3.14 The role of water in the formation of sucrose

Metabolism

Metabolism is the sum of all the chemical reactions in an organism. There are two types of metabolic reactions.

Anabolic reactions, in which smaller molecules combine to form larger molecules. Anabolic reactions require **energy**. Photosynthesis is an example of an anabolic reaction:

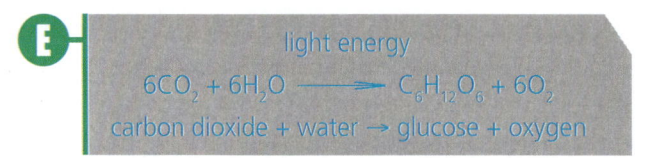

$$6CO_2 + 6H_2O \xrightarrow{\text{light energy}} C_6H_{12}O_6 + 6O_2$$
carbon dioxide + water → glucose + oxygen

Catabolic reactions, in which larger molecules are broken down to smaller molecules. Catabolic reactions release energy. Digestion, for example of starch, is an example of a catabolic reaction, as is respiration:

$$C_6H_{12}O_6 + 6O_2 \rightarrow 6CO_2 + 6H_2O + \text{energy is released}$$

Food test investigations

Qualitative tests for (i) a reducing sugar, (ii) starch, (iii) fat, (iv) a protein

For each test note:
1. The initial colour of the contents of the test tube.
2. Whether any precipitate* forms on heating.
3. The sequence of colour changes that occur.
4. The final colour of the contents of the test tube.

*A precipitate is small pieces of an insoluble solid that form in a liquid and sink to the bottom.

> **Anabolic** reactions are reactions in which smaller molecules are combined to form larger molecules.

> **Catabolic** reactions are reactions in which larger molecules are broken down to form smaller molecules.

Investigation 3.1

Tests for the presence of carbohydrates

A. To test for the presence of reducing sugars (simple carbohydrates)

Reducing and non-reducing sugars

Benedict's solution (blue) contains copper sulfate. If, on heating, a sugar changes the copper sulfate to form an orange/red precipitate, we call it a reducing sugar. All monosaccharides and some disaccharides are reducing sugars. Lactose is a disaccharide that is a reducing sugar; sucrose is a disaccharide that is not a reducing sugar. Fehling's solutions A and B may be used instead of Benedict's solution.

Note: The usual test for reducing sugars is heating with Benedict's reagent.

Procedure

1. Set up a boiling water bath.
2. If the substance being tested is not already in liquid form, crush some in a mortar with a pestle and add a little distilled water.
3. Place 2 cm^3 test solution into a test tube and add an equal volume of Benedict's solution (blue). Swirl gently to mix.
4. Place the test tube in the water bath and leave for 3 minutes.
5. Note any colour changes. If reducing sugars are present, a precipitate forms. The precipitate is usually green, orange or brick-red. In general, the greater the quantity of reducing sugar the more red in colour and heavier the precipitate.
6. Record your result.
7. To set up a control, replace the test solution with the same volume of water and repeat the procedure.
8. Write an account of this investigation in your practical notebook.

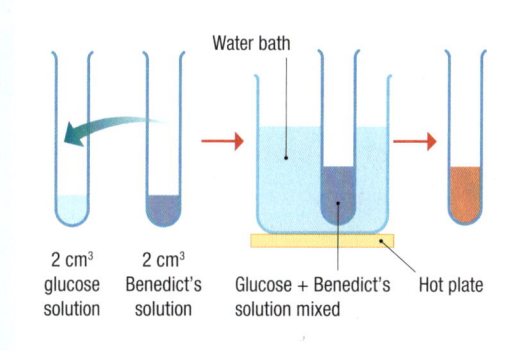

3.15   To test for reducing sugars

B. To test for polysaccharides, e.g. starch

1. Add 2–3 drops of dilute iodine solution (brown) to 2 cm^3 of the test solution in a test tube (or directly onto the substance if a solid, e.g. a piece of apple).
2. A blue/black colour develops if starch is present.
3. Record your result.
4. To set up a control, use water as the test solution and repeat the procedure.
5. Write an account of this investigation in your practical notebook.

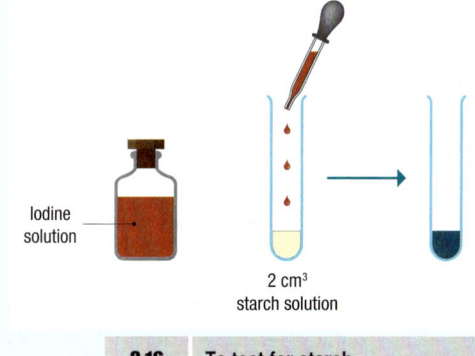

3.16   To test for starch

03 Food and Biomolecules

Investigation 3.2
Tests for the presence of fats

To test for fat (lipid) in olive oil: brown paper test

Procedure

1. Rub some of the food on a piece of brown paper. Allow to dry.
2. Hold the piece of paper up to the light.
3. A translucent mark develops if fat is present (translucent means light can pass through a substance).
4. Record your result.
5. To set up a control, use water as the test substance and repeat the procedure.
6. Write an account of this investigation in your practical notebook.

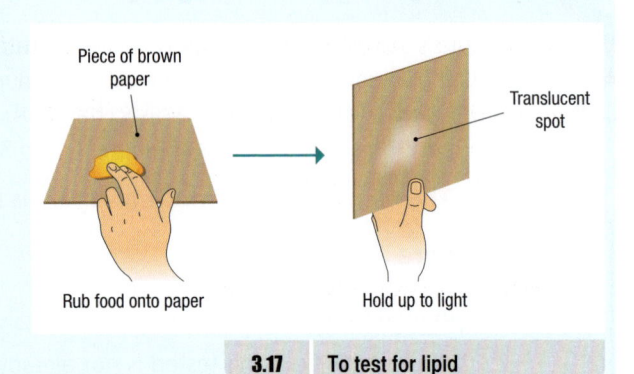

3.17 To test for lipid

Investigation 3.3
Test for the presence of protein

To test for protein in milk or in egg albumen: biuret test for soluble protein

Procedure

1. Add 2 cm³ of sodium hydroxide solution to the test solution.
2. Add 2–3 drops of copper sulfate solution (pale blue colour).

   (Or add 2 cm³ of Biuret solution to the test solution instead of steps 1 and 2.)

3. Swirl gently to mix.
4. A mauve/purple colour forms if protein is present.
5. Record your result.
6. To set up a control, use water instead of the test solution and repeat the procedure.
7. Write an account of this investigation in your practical notebook.

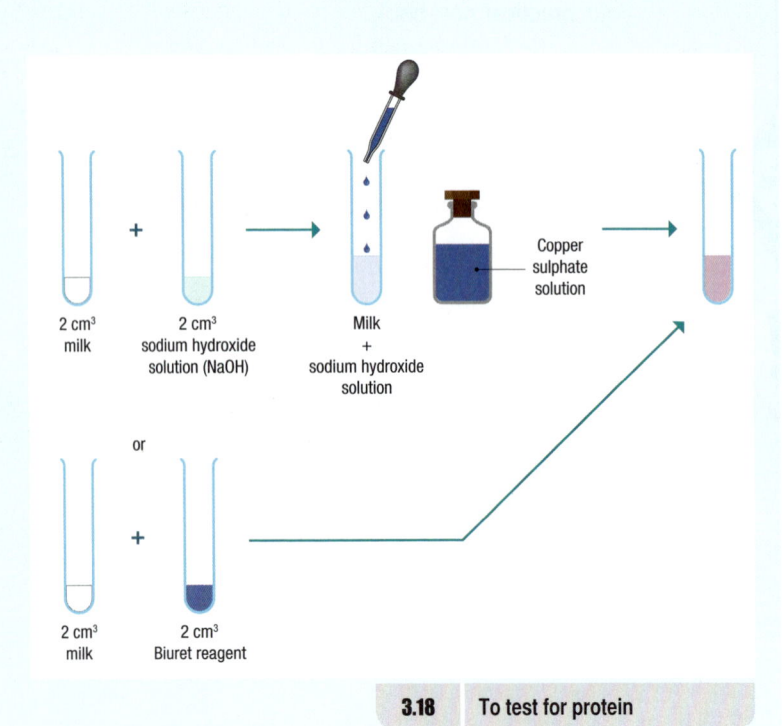

3.18 To test for protein

Summary

- All living things are composed of chemicals.

- The most common chemical elements in living things are: C, H, O, P, N, S, which make up most organic molecules; Na, Mg, Cl, K, Ca, which occur dissolved as salts; and Fe, Cu, Zn, which occur as trace elements.

- Living things need food for growth and repair and the energy necessary for the activities of life.

- Biomolecules are the chemicals that are formed in living things.

- The four types of biomolecule found in food are carbohydrates, lipids, proteins and vitamins.

Table 3.7 Summary of food molecules

Type of biomolecule	Elements	Example	Structure (basic units)	Source in diet	Functions/Role Structural	Role Metabolic	Test
Carbohydrate	C, H, O	Glucose, fructose	Monosaccharides – single sugar unit	Fruit	None	Immediate source of energy	Benedict's solution
		Sucrose, lactose	Disaccharides – two sugar units	Table sugar, cakes	None	Immediate source of energy	
		Starch	Polysaccharide – many sugar units	Bread (starch)	None	Store of energy in all plants	Iodine solution
		Glycogen	Polysaccharide – many sugar units	Meat (glycogen)	None	Store of energy in all animals	
		Cellulose	Polysaccharide – many branched sugar units	Plants cell walls (cellulose)	Cell walls of plants	Source of fibre in humans	
		Chitin	Polysaccharide – many sugar units	Mushrooms	Cell wall of fungi		
Lipids	C, H, O	Oils and fats	Triglyceride	Sunflower oil, butter, cheese	Form a component of cell membranes	Source of energy	Brown paper
Protein	C, H, O, N (maybe S and P)	Myosin, keratin	Chains of amino acids	Lean meat, soya beans	Form muscle and hair	None	Biuret solution
		Enzymes (e.g. amylase)	Chains of amino acids		None	Control cell reactions	
		Hormones (e.g. insulin)	Chains of amino acids		None	Regulate blood glucose	
Vitamins		Vitamin C – water-soluble	Ascorbic acid	Oranges, kiwi fruit	Form connective tissue		
		Vitamin D – fat-soluble	Calciferol	Dairy products, cheese, butter		Help calcium absorption	

03 Food and Biomolecules

Summary

- Minerals are inorganic chemicals required in small amounts by animals and plants.
- Animals: Calcium (Ca) for bones and teeth. Iron (Fe) for haemoglobin.
- Plants: Magnesium (Mg) for chlorophyll formation. Calcium to form the middle lamella between plant cells.
- Water comprises about 75% of living cells and is essential for life.
- Water is an important solvent: it is a medium for chemical reactions; it takes part in chemical reactions; it controls the shape of cells; it helps in the movement of substances into and out of cells; and it helps to maintain the internal environment of all living things.
- Food tests:

Table 3.8 Summary of food tests

Biomolecule	Food substance tested	Test reagent	Is heat needed?	Original colour	Final colour if positive
Carbohydrates (reducing sugars)	Glucose solution	Benedict's solution	Yes	Blue	Brick-red
Carbohydrates (polysaccharide)	Starch	Iodine solution	No	Brown	Blue-black
Lipids	Sunflower oil	Brown paper	No (but allow paper to dry)	Opaque	Translucent spot
Proteins	Milk	Biuret (copper sulphate and sodium hydroxide solutions	No	Pale blue	Purple/mauve/lilac

Food and Biomolecules 03

Review questions

01 Living things need food. Name three activities for which you need food.

02 (a) Give the name of six major elements common to living things.
(b) Give the chemical symbol for each of the elements you have named in (a).

03 (a) Name the elements whose symbols are given: Cl, Ca, Cu, Na, K.
(b) Which of the following elements are trace elements? Na, Cu, N, Ca, Zn, Cl.
(c) What does the term 'trace' mean in reference to the elements listed in part (b)?

04 (a) What are biomolecules?
(b) Name three biomolecules.
(c) What is meant by the term organic molecule?
(d) Give two examples of organic molecules.
(e) Name two examples of inorganic molecules or compounds.

05 (a) Name the chemical elements that make up a carbohydrate.
(b) Name a carbohydrate other than glucose.
(c) What is the function of glucose?
(d) Distinguish between a monosaccharide and a disaccharide.

06 (a) What elements make up starch?
(b) What molecule is starch formed from?
(c) Is starch a disaccharide or a polysaccharide?
(d) Which of the following solutions is used to test for starch: Benedict's, iodine, Biuret?
(e) What colour indicates a strong positive result in the test for starch?

07 Distinguish between:
(a) a monosaccharide and a disaccharide;
(b) a reducing and a non-reducing sugar;
(c) a metabolic and a structural carbohydrate.

08 (a) Name a good carbohydrate store in: (i) plants, (ii) animals.
(b) For each store mentioned in (a) give one location in the organism where the named carbohydrate would be stored.

09 (a) Name the types of molecule of which lipids are made.
(b) What is the difference between a fat and an oil?
(c) Are fats and oils lipids? Explain your answer.
(d) State three good sources of lipids in the human diet.

10 (a) What is a phospholipid?
(b) Draw an outline sketch to show the structure of a typical phospholipid.
(c) Where in a cell would you expect to find phospholipids?

11 (a) Proteins are composed of four main elements. Name these elements.
(b) Name the sub-units of which proteins are made.
(c) What is (i) a peptide bond, (ii) a peptide, (iii) a polypeptide?
(d) Name the test for proteins.
(e) Give the colour change you would expect for a positive result to the protein test.
(f) Identify two structural proteins from the following list: chlorophyll • keratin • amylase • insulin • myosin
(g) What is the shape of most metabolic proteins?

12 (a) What are vitamins? Are vitamins biomolecules?
(b) Distinguish between water-soluble and fat-soluble vitamins.
(c) Give two good sources of vitamin D.
(d) What is the function of vitamin D?
(e) Name a deficiency disorder caused by a lack of vitamin D.
(f) State the connection between vitamin D and calcium.

13 (a) Give two good sources in the diet of vitamin C.
(b) The main function of vitamin C is to form connective tissue. Give two examples of connective tissue.
(c) Name a deficiency disorder caused by a lack of vitamin C.

14 (a) What is meant by the term 'metabolism'?
(b) Explain the term 'anabolic'.
(c) Distinguish between anabolic and catabolic reactions in terms of energy loss or gain.
(d) Give an example of a catabolic reaction.

15 (a) What are minerals in the context of food? Are minerals biomolecules?
(b) List two main functions of minerals to organisms.
(c) Name and give the chemical symbol for each of two minerals needed in: (i) plants, (ii) animals.

16 Describe three ways in which water is essential for life.

Examination style questions

Section A

01 Answer **five** of the following:
(a) What term is used to represent all the chemical reactions in cells?
(b) Give one example of a monosaccharide.
(c) Name a mineral required by the body.
(d) Give a **good** source of lipids in the diet.
(e) State the colour that would be a negative result for the test for glucose.
(f) How many amino acids are there in a peptide?

03 Food and Biomolecules

Examination style questions

02 Answer the following by selecting the correct answer in each case.
  (a) Which of the following items in a human's diet is mainly protein?
     oranges; butter; lean meat; boiled potatoes
  (b) Which of the following is a storage carbohydrate?
     glucose; starch; sucrose; cellulose
  (c) Biomolecules are molecules found in: plants only; all dead things; bacteria only; all living things?
  (d) Which of the following vitamins is needed for healthy bones and teeth?
     vitamin D; vitamin C; vitamin B; vitamin A
  (e) An example of a monosaccharide is:
     glycogen; starch; sucrose; glucose

03 Match the terms in column A with the descriptions in column B. Write your matching pairs into your copybook.

A – term	B – description
Anabolism	Glucose
Element	Inorganic chemical
Component of fat	Reaction in which more complex molecules are built up
Molecule	Amino acid
Mineral substance	Consisting of only one type of atom
Monosaccharide	Glycerol
Catabolism	Smallest unit of a chemical substance
Sub-units of a protein	Reaction in which molecules are broken down

04 Distinguish between the following pairs of terms by writing a brief sentence on each.
  (a) Monosaccharide and polysaccharide.
  (b) Reducing and non-reducing sugar.
  (c) Fat and oil.
  (d) Vitamin C and vitamin D.
  (e) A peptide and a polypeptide.
  (f) A triglyceride and a disaccharide.

05 (a) Which food may be identified in the laboratory by use of the Biuret reagent?
  (b) Give a role for a named mineral in humans.
  (c) Give a role of lipids in cells.
  (d) Give one way in which one protein may differ from another in terms of its shape.
  (e) Give the general formula for a carbohydrate.
  (f) Name a storage polysaccharide.

Section B

06 (a) (i) Name a reducing sugar other than glucose.
       (ii) What is the function of sugars in organisms?
  (b) An experiment was set up to test for the presence of reducing sugars.
       (i) Name the chemical you used to show the presence of reducing sugars.
       (ii) Identify the pieces of apparatus labelled X, Y and Z in the diagram below.

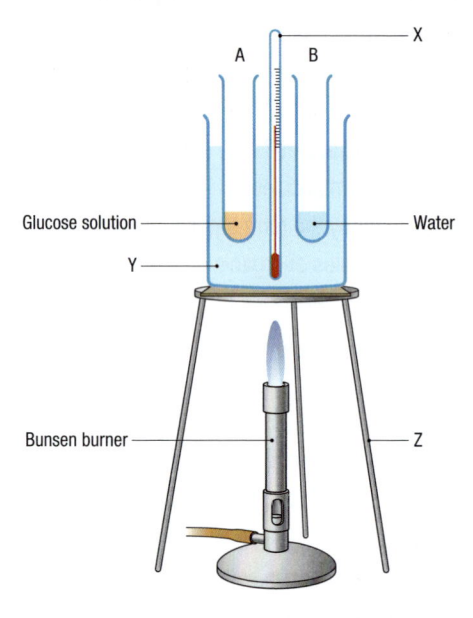

       (iii) Copy the table below and state the colour in each tube before and after the reducing sugar test was carried out.

Tube	Colour before test	Colour after test
A		
B		

       (iv) What was the purpose of having Tube B as part of the experiment?

07 (a) (i) Name the elements present in a lipid.
       (ii) Name the biomolecular sub-units of a lipid.
  (b) (i) Name the reagent (or reagents) used when testing for protein.
       (ii) What further treatment is required after the reagent or regents have been added?
       (iii) What colour change takes place if protein is present?
       (iv) Describe the control used in the protein test.
       (v) Why is a control necessary in an investigation?
       (vi) Give an example of a food that tests positive for protein.
       (vii) Outline how the food sample named in (vi) can be tested for lipid.

Food and Biomolecules

Examination style questions

Section C

08 A picnic hamper contained wholemeal brown bread, butter, tomatoes, lettuce, cucumber, hard-boiled eggs, tinned salmon, apples, oranges, tea, sugar and milk.
  (a) From the contents of the hamper indicate one good source of each of the following: soluble carbohydrate, insoluble carbohydrate, protein, lipid, vitamin D, fibre and two **named** minerals.
  (b) State a function of (i) vitamin D and (ii) one of the minerals you named.
  (c) Outline laboratory tests, one in each case, to show the presence of the following in food: protein; a reducing sugar.

09 (a) Carbohydrates and lipids are described as primary sources of energy for our metabolic activity. Explain the underlined term and suggest why protein is not included in the list of primary energy sources.
  (b) Enzymes regulate our metabolic activity. Name another group of substances that play an important role in our body's metabolic activity.
  (c) State the general function of vitamins in our diet.
  (d) Name a fat-soluble vitamin needed in our diet and state the effect of a diet deficient in the named vitamin.
  (e) Name two minerals needed by plants and give one function of each named mineral.

Leaving Certificate examination questions

Section A

01 Answer any **five** of parts (a) to (f).
A meal in a fast-food restaurant consists of fish and chips with a glass of water to drink.
  (a) Give a **good** source of protein from this meal.
  (b) Give **one** function of protein in the human body.
  (c) Chips contain starch. What chemical is used to test for the presence of starch?
  (d) State the **colour** of the chemical referred to in (c) if starch is present.
  (e) Water has many functions in the human body. State any **one** of these functions.
  (f) Suggest a reason why eating too much fast food could be bad for your health.

2014 OL Q. 1

02 Use your knowledge of nutrients to answer the following questions:
  (a) Proteins always contain the elements carbon, hydrogen, oxygen and _____.
  (b) Glucose is an example of which type of biomolecule?
  (c) An example of a fat-soluble vitamin is _____.
  (d) A solution used to test for the presence of glucose is _____.
  (e) Calcium and iron are examples of essential _____.

2013 OL Q. 1

03 A student brings a tuna and sweetcorn sandwich, an apple and a bag of crisps for her lunch.
  (a) Which food in the student's lunch is: (i) a **good** source of protein? (ii) a **good** source of fat?
  (b) Vitamins form part of a healthy diet and prevent many disorders.
    (i) Name **one** water-soluble vitamin.
    (ii) Suggest **one** food in the lunch that contains the water-soluble vitamin you have named.
  (c) Name **one** structural protein in humans.
  (d) Give **one** function of fat in the human body.
  (e) What term is used to describe all the chemical reactions in the human body?

2012 OL Q. 1

04 Indicate whether each of the following statements is true or false by rewriting each sentence and adding 'True' or 'False' in each case.

Example: Polysaccharide molecules contain many sugar units. True
  (a) Cellulose is a protein.
  (b) Iodine turns starch to a blue-black colour.
  (c) Lipids are made of amino acids.
  (d) All vitamins are fat soluble.
  (e) Eggs are a good source of fat in the diet.
  (f) Nitrogen is a trace element.
  (g) Glucose is a monosaccharide.

2010 OL Q. 1

05 Choose a term from the following list and place it in Column B to match the description in Column A.

The first one has been completed as an example:

amino acid, nitrogen, haemoglobin, keratin, enzyme

03 Food and Biomolecules

Leaving Certificate examination questions

Column A	Column B
A protein present in blood	haemoglobin
An element always present in proteins along with C, H, O	
A protein which changes reaction rates	
The end product of protein digestion	
A structural protein	

2008 OL Q. 1

06 (a) The following biochemical reactions took place in some living cells:
  (i) A → B + C + D
  Is this an example of anabolism or catabolism?
  (ii) Fat $\xrightarrow{X}$ fatty acids + Y
  Identify X and Y.
(b) (i) How does a phospholipid differ from a fat?
  (ii) Name a fat-soluble vitamin.
  (iii) State a disorder due to a dietary deficiency of the vitamin referred to in (b) (ii).
  (iv) Give any **two** functions of minerals in organisms.

2014 HL Q. 2

07 In the case of any **five** of the following pairs of terms, clearly distinguish between the first term and second term by writing a brief sentence about each.
(a) Starch and glucose.
(b) Amino acids and proteins.
(c) Cellulose and keratin.
(d) Enzymes and hormones.
(e) Biuret test and Benedict's (Fehling's) test.
(f) Fats and oils.

2013 HL Q. 1

08 Answer **five** of the following:
(a) Name a monosaccharide.
(b) Give the formula of the monosaccharide referred to in (a).
(c) Name a polysaccharide that can be formed from the monosaccharide referred to in (a).
(d) Give **one** way in which an amino acid differs from a monosaccharide, in terms of chemical composition.
(e) What do carbohydrates and fats have in common, in terms of chemical composition?
(f) How may one fat differ from another, in terms of chemical composition?

2012 HL Q. 1

09 (a) In carbohydrates, which two elements are in the ratio 2:1?
(b) Cellulose is a polysaccharide. Explain the term *polysaccharide*.
(c) Name a polysaccharide other than cellulose.
(d) Where precisely in a plant cell would you expect to find cellulose?
(e) Name a test or give the chemicals used to demonstrate the presence of a reducing sugar.
(f) In relation to the test referred to in (e) which of the following is correct?
  (i) No heat needed.
  (ii) Heat but do not boil.
  (iii) Boil.

2009 HL Q. 1

Section B

10 (a) Give **two** reasons why water is important for all living organisms.
(b) Answer the following questions in relation to food tests that you carried out as part of your practical work.
  (i) What chemical did you use to test the food for starch?
  (ii) Was heat necessary for this test?
  (iii) How did you know that starch was present?
  (iv) What control did you use in this test?
  (v) Another food was tested for the presence of protein. What solution was used to test for protein?
  (vi) What was the initial colour of the protein-testing solution before you put it on the food?
  (vii) Was heat necessary for this test?
  (viii) What colour indicated that protein was present in the food?

2012 OL Q. 9

11 (a) The main ingredient in a sports drink is water.
  (i) Give **one** reason why the body needs water.
  (ii) Give **one** way in which water is lost from the body.
(b) The composition of a **colourless** sports drink is to be investigated. Use your knowledge of food testing to answer the following:
  1. (i) Name the test **or** name the chemical used to test the sports drink for the presence of glucose (reducing sugar).
    (ii) If glucose is present in the drink, what colour change would you expect to see? In your answer give the initial **and** final colour of the test solution.
    (iii) Is heat necessary for this test?
  2. (i) Name the test **or** give the chemicals used to test the sports drink for the presence of protein.

Leaving Certificate examination questions

(ii) If protein is present in the drink, what colour change would you expect to see? In your answer give the initial **and** final colour of the test solution.

(iii) Is heat necessary for this test?

2009 OL Q. 7

12 (a) State a use for the Biuret test in the biology laboratory.

(b) (i) In the course of your practical studies you used a solution of iodine in different investigations. State **two** different uses of the iodine solution.

(ii) State **two** different uses of a water bath in biological investigations.

2011 HL Q. 8

Section C

13 (a) Water has many functions in the human body. State **three** of these functions.

(b) (i) Name the chemical elements present in carbohydrates.

(ii) Give an example of a carbohydrate that has a structural role. Where would you expect to find this carbohydrate in a living organism?

(iii) State a role of carbohydrates other than a structural one.

(iv) Name a test that you would carry out to show the presence of a reducing sugar (e.g. glucose).

(v) Describe how you would carry out the test that you have named in (iv).

(c) (i) Name a chemical element found in proteins that is **not** found in carbohydrates.

(ii) State **two** good sources of protein in the human diet.

(iii) Proteins are digested to simpler substances. What are these simpler substances called?

(iv) State **one** function of protein in the human body.
(v) Name a test for protein.
(vi) Describe how you would carry out the test that you have named in (v).

2004 OL Q. 4

14 (a) (i) The same elements are found in carbohydrates and fats. Name these elements.

(ii) State one way in which carbohydrates differ from fats.

(iii) How do phospholipids differ from other lipids?

(b) Carbohydrates are classified as monosaccharides, disaccharides and polysaccharides.

(i) Name a monosaccharide and state a role for it in living organisms.

(ii) What is a disaccharide?

(iii) Cellulose is a polysaccharide. What is it formed from? State a role for cellulose in living organisms.

(iv) Name a polysaccharide that has a different role to cellulose. What is the role of the polysaccharide that you have named?

(v) Describe a test for a named polysaccharide.

(c) Answer the following in relation to a test for
1. a reducing sugar
2. a protein
   (i) Name the reagent(s) used.
   (ii) State the initial colour of the reagent.
   (iii) State whether the test requires heat.
   (iv) What colour indicates a positive result?

SEC Sample HL Q. 10

Past examination questions

OL	2014–2009 Q. 1	2008 Q. 2	2007 Q. 1, Q. 8	2006 Q. 3	2005 Q. 5	2004 Q. 5, Q. 10
HL	2014 Q. 2	2013–2005 Q. 1	SEC SAMPLE Q. 10			

04 Introduction to Ecology

After studying this chapter you should be able to:

1. Define the following terms: biosphere, ecology, ecosystem, food chain, food web, habitat, niche, pyramid of numbers.
2. Distinguish between abiotic and biotic components of an ecosystem.
3. Define and give examples of abiotic, biotic and climatic factors that affect aquatic and terrestrial environments.
4. Define and give examples of edaphic factors that affect terrestrial environments.
5. Describe the flow of energy in the ecosystem. Define producer, consumer and decomposer.
6. Describe and give examples of a grazing food chain. Define herbivore, carnivore and omnivore.
7. Give an example of a food web and define trophic level.
8. Define and construct a pyramid of numbers.
9. **HL** Explain a pyramid of numbers in more detail.
10. **HL** Describe the limitations of the use of a pyramid of numbers.
11. Distinguish between the niche and the habitat of an organism. Define competition.
12. Define the term nutrient recycling.
13. Outline the carbon and nitrogen cycles.

Ecology

1. The environment of an **organism** consists of both living and non-living parts. The life of a frog living in a pond is affected by living things such as flies to eat, plants to shelter behind and rest upon, mates to breed with, and also by non-living things such as the temperature of the water and the amount of minerals and oxygen present.

D **Ecology** is the study of the interaction between groups of organisms and their environment.

D An **ecosystem** consists of organisms and their interactions with the environment.

Together the living and non-living parts of the environment make up what is known as an **ecosystem**. Major ecosystems include the tundra, savannah, desert and tropical regions of the world. On a smaller scale, the school grounds, the seashore, woodland and meadow are all different ecosystems (Fig 4.1). Each will have unique organisms that are suited to that environment.

4.1 A variety of ecosystems

Introduction to Ecology | 04

Ecology is the study of ecosystems. The whole Earth is itself a true ecosystem as no part is completely isolated from the rest. All ecosystems collectively result in the **biosphere**, i.e. the parts of the Earth and its atmosphere in which life can exist (Figs 4.2 and 4.3).

The place in an ecosystem where an organism lives is its **habitat**. For example the habitat of an earthworm is the soil and that of a trout is freshwater rivers and lakes.

> **D** The **biosphere** is the parts of the Earth and its atmosphere in which life can exist.

4.2 The biosphere

Environmental factors

The life of an organism is affected by a number of environmental factors. These include **biotic**, **abiotic**, **climatic**, **edaphic** and **aquatic** factors.

Biotic factors

Biotic factors are living factors that are caused by the organisms present and how they affect other organisms. They include **competition**, **predation**, disease, decomposition and the effects of humans. Some relationships that exist between organisms in ecosystems include the following:

> **D** Organisms can be divided into groups depending upon nutrition:
> - **producers**, which make their own food (the green plants);
> - **consumers**, which feed on the plants and animals, and
> - **decomposers**, such as bacteria and fungi which feed on dead and decaying plants and animals.

- All animals depend either directly or indirectly on plants to supply food and oxygen.
- Many plants depend on animals for pollination and for dispersal of their seeds and fruits.
- There is competition between plants for resources such as water, light and space.
- Animals compete for food, space and mates.
- Animals and plants can carry diseases which affect other organisms.
- Micro-organisms such as bacteria and fungi act as decomposers, recycling nutrients in the ecosystem.

The biosphere is made up of ecosystems.

Ecosystems are made up of communities of organisms and the environment.

Communities are made up of populations of different species of organisms.

4.3 Relationships in the biosphere

Abiotic factors

Abiotic factors (Fig 4.4) are the non-living factors that affect organisms. These include things such as:

- Exposure, for example to wind or salt spray near the sea.
- Altitude (height above sea level). The higher you are the lower the temperature.
- Aspect (the direction the ecosystem faces): south-facing sites are warmer than north-facing ones.

Climatic, edaphic (soil) and aquatic factors described on the next page are also examples of abiotic factors as they are all non-living factors.

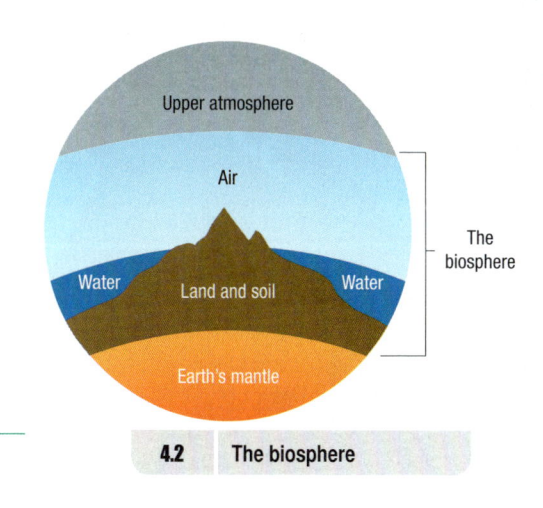

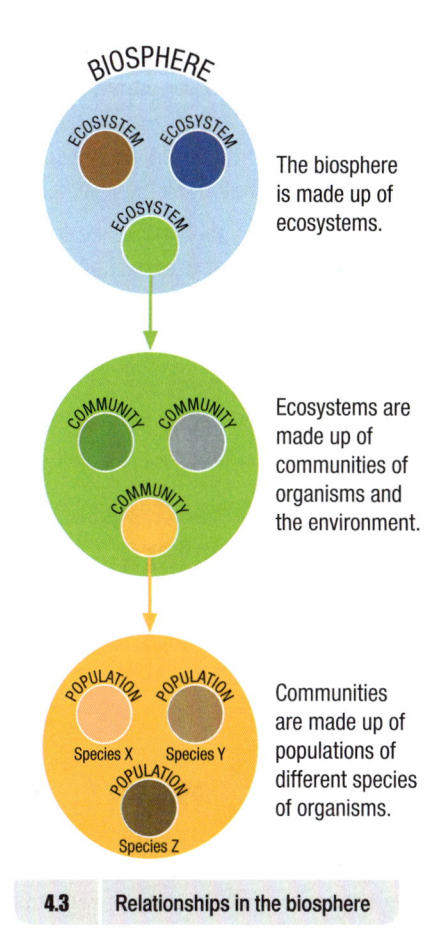

> **D** **Competition** is the struggle between organisms for resources that are in short supply, such as food or light.

> **D** **Biotic** – an organism's influence on another organism.

> **D** **Abiotic** – the influence of a non-living part of the environment on an organism.

LIFE LEAVING CERTIFICATE BIOLOGY | UNIT 1 THE STUDY OF LIFE | 35

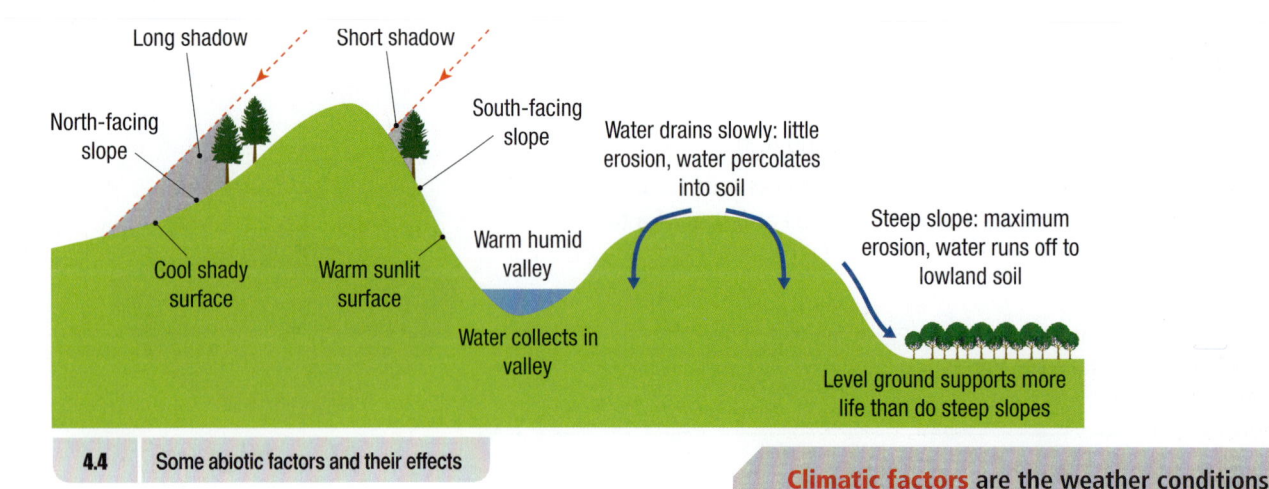

04 Introduction to Ecology

4.4 Some abiotic factors and their effects

> **Climatic factors** are the weather conditions that affect organisms in an ecosystem.

Climatic factors

Weather refers to conditions of the atmosphere over short periods of time, e.g. a day or a week. **Climate** refers to conditions of the atmosphere over long periods of time, such as years and decades. If it is snowing on a particular day then we are speaking of the weather, whereas if it snows from November to February every year somewhere, then we are speaking of the climate.

Climatic factors that influence the life of the organisms in an ecosystem include the rainfall, humidity, temperature, light intensity and day length.

Aquatic factors

In aquatic ecosystems like ponds, rivers and the sea, factors such as how far light can penetrate into the water and the effect of currents and waves and the salinity of sea water have an important role to play.

> **Aquatic factors** are those that affect organisms that live in water.

> **Edaphic factors** are soil factors that affect organisms.

Edaphic factors

Edaphic factors are factors related to the soil. The type of soil, its pH and its ability to hold water and minerals will affect the different types of plants and animals that will live there. For example, very few animals live in a heavy clay soil as this type of soil has few air spaces. As a result, oxygen and water cannot pass through it easily.

Energy flow in the ecosystem

All organisms need energy to live. The sun is the primary (main) source of energy for life on earth. Energy then flows from one organism to the next by means of the feeding relationships between organisms (Fig 4.5).

Producers (green plants) make their own food using energy from the sun (see Chapter 13). The producers are eaten by the primary consumers (**herbivores**). These in turn are eaten by the secondary consumers (**carnivores**) and these may be eaten by tertiary consumers (top carnivores).

- Producers: organisms that make their own food, e.g. green plants such as grass.
- Carnivores: organisms that feed on animals only, e.g. ladybirds.
- Herbivores: organisms that feed on plants only, e.g. greenfly.
- Omnivores: organisms that feed on both plants and animals, e.g. humans, robins.

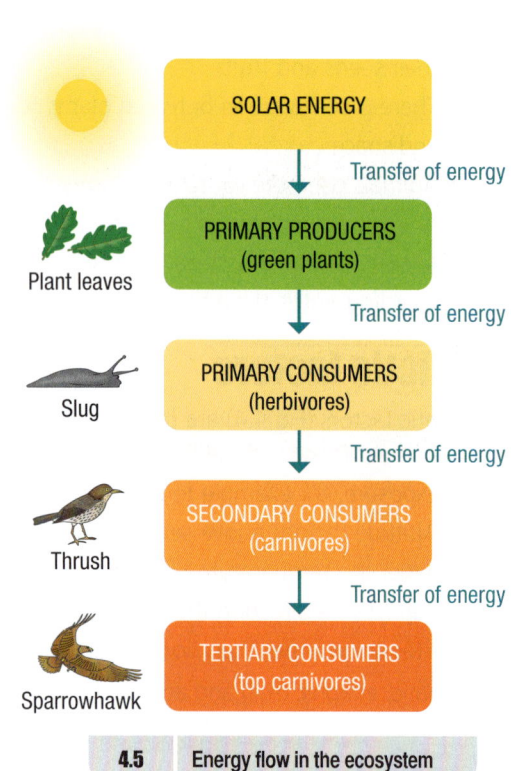

4.5 Energy flow in the ecosystem

Food chains and food webs

A **food chain** shows who eats whom in an ecosystem. In a food chain the energy absorbed by the plants is used to make food materials and new cells. However, a large proportion of the energy absorbed by the plant is lost as heat. This means that very little of the energy absorbed from the sun is passed on to the next organism in the chain.

Eventually, when organisms die and decompose, all the energy from the sun that was passed into the producers disperses as heat. Therefore energy does not cycle in nature.

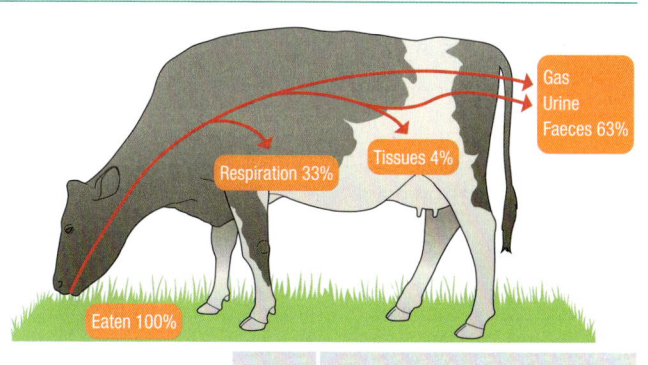

4.6 Energy transfer in the ecosystem

The simplest type of food chain is a **grazing food chain** in which the primary consumer feeds on a living green plant, e.g. buttercup leaf → caterpillar → thrush (Fig 4.7).

4.7 Grazing food chain

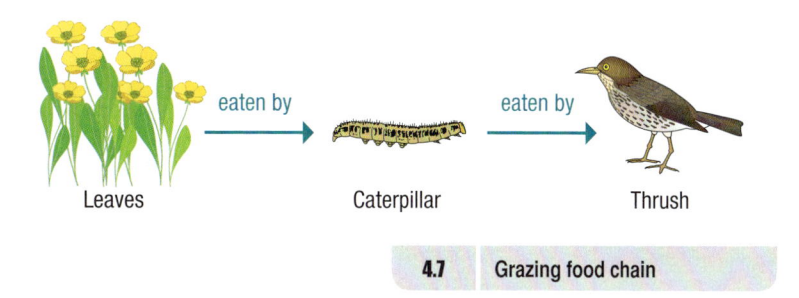

Another type of food chain exists in which the primary consumers feed on dead organisms (detritus), e.g. dead leaves → woodlouse → blackbird. This is known as a **detritus food chain** (Fig 4.8).

When drawing a food chain the arrow head (>) always points to the organism being eaten.

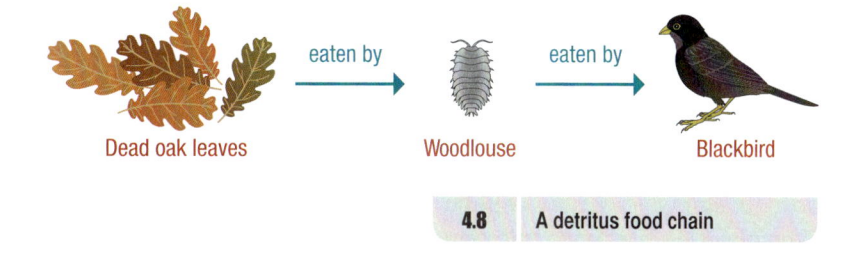

4.8 A detritus food chain

> **A food chain is the feeding relationship between organisms in which energy is transferred.**

Trophic level	1st	2nd	3rd	4th
Feeding relationship	Producer	Primary consumer	Secondary consumer	Tertiary consumer
Type of organism at each level	Plant (can make its own food)	Herbivore	Carnivore/omnivore (predator)	Carnivore (predator)
Grassland	Dandelion	Butterfly	Thrush	Sparrowhawk
Woodland	Oak leaves	Snail	Hedgehog	Fox
Seashore	Seaweed	Limpet	Edible crab	Herring gull

Table 4.1 Food chains from different ecosystems

04 Introduction to Ecology

Food webs

In nature, most food chains overlap with other food chains. This results in a **food web** (Fig 4.9).

Fig 4.9 shows a woodland food web in which plants are eaten by different herbivores. These, in turn, are eaten by a variety of carnivores, any one of which may be eaten by the sparrowhawk.

Trophic levels

In a food chain, the flow of energy is described in terms of **trophic** or feeding **levels**. The primary producers form the first trophic level; the primary consumers form the second trophic level; the secondary consumers form the third trophic level; and the tertiary consumers form the fourth trophic level (Fig 4.10).

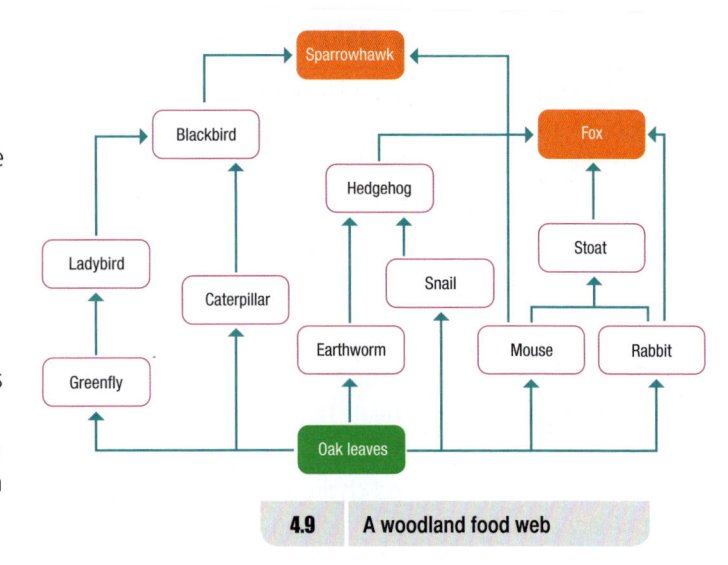

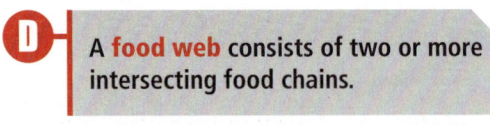

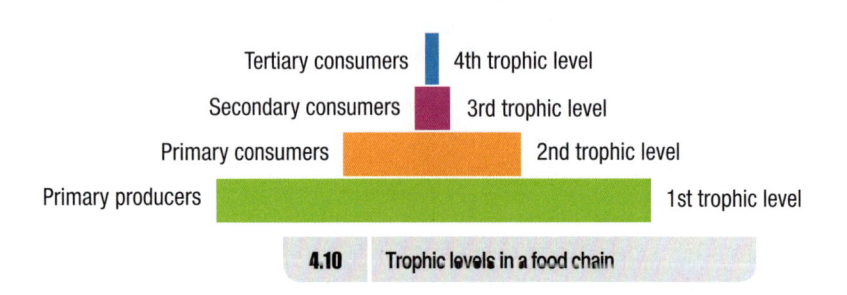

4.9 A woodland food web

> **D** A **food web** consists of two or more intersecting food chains.

> **D** A **trophic level** is a feeding level in a food chain.

> **D** A **pyramid of numbers** is used to show the numbers of individuals at each trophic level of a food chain.

4.10 Trophic levels in a food chain

Ecological pyramids

We can compare the trophic levels of different communities of organism in an ecosystem by means of models called **ecological pyramids**. There are a number of different types of ecological pyramid, one of which is a **pyramid of numbers**. A pyramid of numbers is a bar chart indicating the relative numbers of organisms at each trophic level. In a typical grazing food chain there are generally fewer herbivores than the plants they eat, and in turn fewer consumers than herbivores. The pyramid of numbers in Fig 4.11(a) illustrates this.

To construct a pyramid of numbers:
- Count all the primary producers and place this number at the base of the pyramid.
- Count the primary consumers and place this number on top of that for the primary producers.
- Count the secondary consumers and place this number on top of that for the primary consumers.
- Finally count the tertiary or top consumers and place this number on top of that for the secondary consumers.

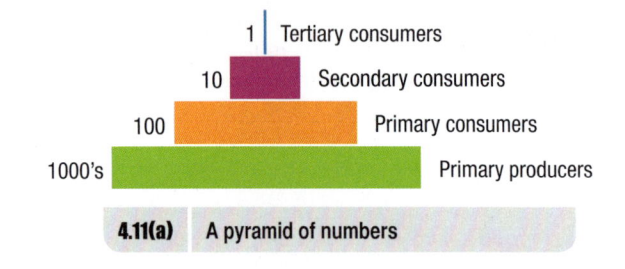

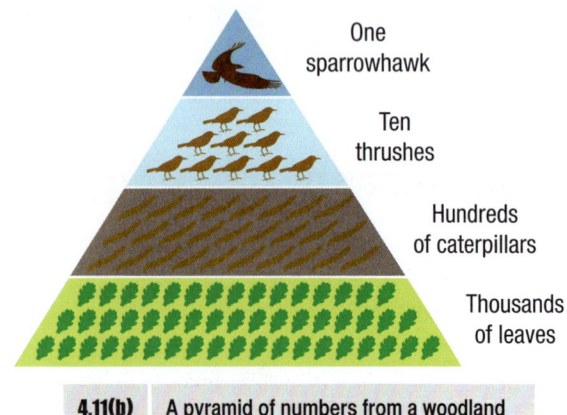

4.11(a) A pyramid of numbers

4.11(b) A pyramid of numbers from a woodland

Introduction to Ecology | 04

HL

Pyramid of numbers

In a food chain and food web, the flow of energy is described in terms of trophic levels. The transfer of energy from one trophic level to the next is very small. Of the energy absorbed by the green plants, only 10% is used for growth of the plant. Most of the energy is used up in **metabolism** or is lost as heat. When the plant is eaten, only 10% of the energy it absorbed is passed on to the consumer (i.e. 10% of 10%). In turn only 10% of this energy is transferred when the primary consumer is eaten by the secondary consumer.

As we can see, the organisms at each trophic level pass on less energy than they receive. This is because in nature:

(a) not all available food organisms are caught and eaten;
(b) some of the food that is eaten is indigestible and leaves the animal's body as undigested material (faeces); and
(c) of the food that is digested, only a small amount becomes part of the organism (which in turn could be eaten by the next consumer).

Because of this loss in energy from one trophic level to the next, food chains do not normally contain more than four or five levels (Fig 4.12).

In summary, each trophic level contains less energy than the previous level, most of the energy being lost as heat that cannot be recaptured. Therefore energy does not cycle through the ecosystem but has to be constantly added to the ecosystem from the sun.

Ecological pyramids are models that compare different communities within an ecosystem in order of different feeding (trophic) levels (Fig 4.13).

From looking at the pyramid you will note:

1. The number of organisms usually decreases as you move up the pyramid. This is because the energy available to the tertiary consumers is far less than that available to the producers. For this reason, the number of trophic levels in a pyramid is limited to four or five.
2. The size of the animal usually increases as you move up the pyramid.
   A fox is larger than the rabbit it captures and eats. Because of energy losses as you move up through the food chain, a fox will need to eat
   many rabbits, which in turn eat huge quantities of vegetation.

Limitations of the use of pyramids of numbers

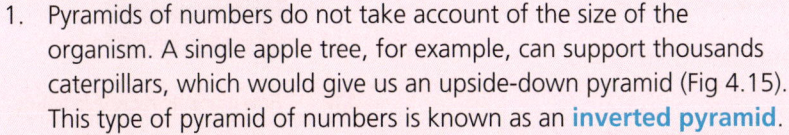

1. Pyramids of numbers do not take account of the size of the organism. A single apple tree, for example, can support thousands caterpillars, which would give us an upside-down pyramid (Fig 4.15). This type of pyramid of numbers is known as an **inverted pyramid**.
2. Pyramids involving parasites (Fig 4.14) also show an inverted shape. The huge numbers that are sometimes involved, such as hundreds of mites living on a sparrow, cannot be represented to scale.

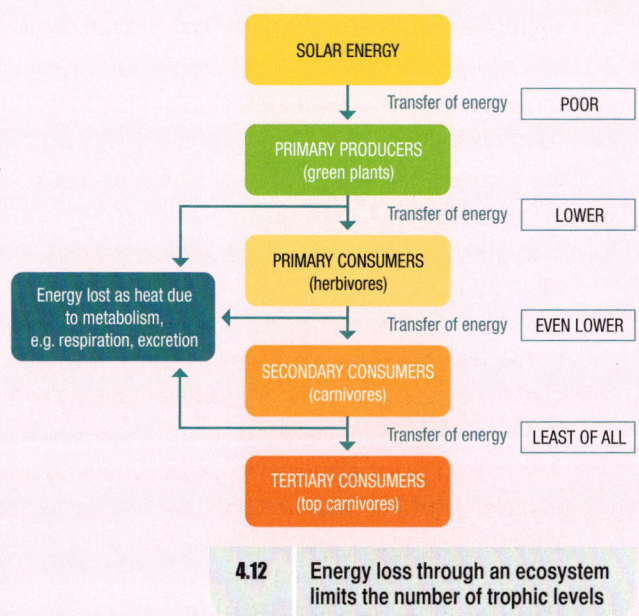

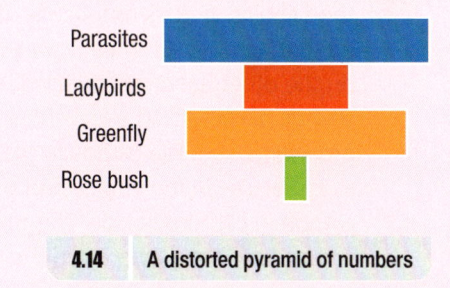

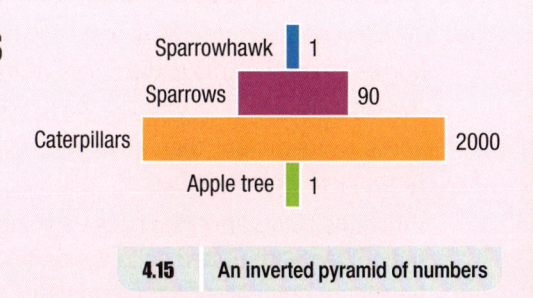

4.12 Energy loss through an ecosystem limits the number of trophic levels

4.13 A normal pyramid of numbers

4.14 A distorted pyramid of numbers

4.15 An inverted pyramid of numbers
- Sparrowhawk 1
- Sparrows 90
- Caterpillars 2000
- Apple tree 1

04   Introduction to Ecology

Habitat and niche

11 The **habitat** of an organism is the place where it lives, i.e. its 'address'. Examples of habitats include the soil, a pond, a rock pool, and a wood.

The **niche** of an organism refers to the role an organism plays in an ecosystem, i.e. how it lives, what it does in its community, i.e. its 'profession'.

For example, the habitat of a perch may be a lake: its niche is that of a large, fish-eating carnivore. Another example is a plant such as an oak tree. The habitat of the oak may be a woodland; its niche is that of a large primary producer.

In general no two species can occupy the same niche in the same habitat if they have the same requirements. Organisms living in the same habitat can do so because they occupy different niches within the habitat.

The bank vole and the field mouse share the same habitat, but the bank vole is diurnal (active during the day) and the field mouse is nocturnal (active at night) (Fig 4.16). Swallows and blackbirds can occupy the same habitat because they don't compete. They occupy different niches. The swallows feed on insects on the wing whereas the blackbirds eat worms and fruit.

However, if a second animal arrives to occupy the same niche, the first may die out. This has happened where the grey squirrels have taken over the niche of the red squirrels.

> **D**   A **habitat** is the place where an organism lives.

> **D**   The **niche** is the role of an organism in an ecosystem.

4.16 A bank vole (above) and a field mouse (below)

Recycling of nutrients

12 Energy from the sun flows through the ecosystem via food chains. It does not recycle. It is constantly being lost as heat, and needs to be replaced. Nutrients (C and N), on the other hand, are recycled. Each nutrient element spends part of its time locked up in molecules inside living organisms, e.g. the carbon in glucose and part of its time as molecules in the abiotic part of the ecosystem, e.g. the carbon in carbon dioxide. This means that nutrients can be used over and over again (Fig 4.17).

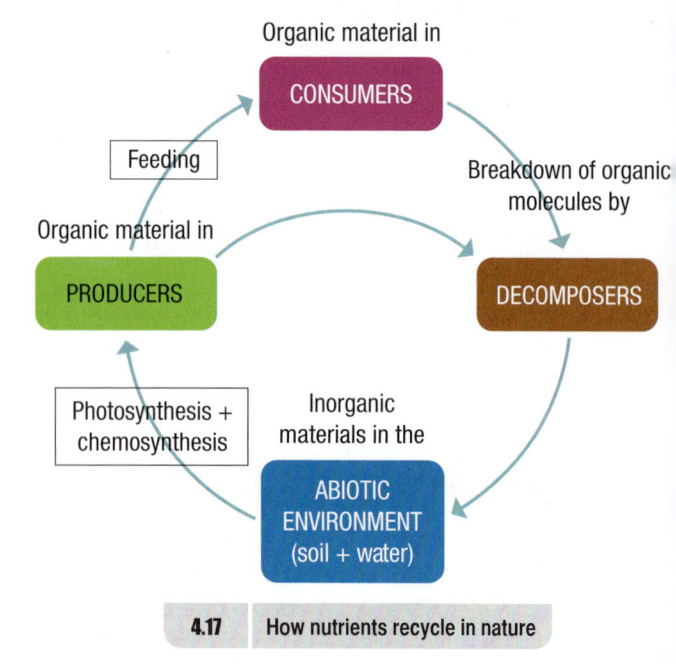

The role of living organisms in recycling these chemicals

The decomposers (**bacteria** and **fungi**) break down the bodies of dead plants and animals. In the process minerals are released that pass into the soil or water.

These nutrients are then absorbed by plants and used to form new plant tissues.

When the plants are eaten by the animals (primary consumers), the nutrients are passed on to the next link in the chain. This transfer of nutrients occurs on up to the tertiary consumers. Along the way, the consumers die and sooner or later the minerals once more find their way into the non-living environment.

4.17 How nutrients recycle in nature

> **D**   **Nutrient recycling** is the way nutrients are exchanged between the biotic and abiotic parts of the ecosystem.

Introduction to Ecology | 04

The carbon cycle

- Carbon is needed by organisms to make many molecules, such as glucose $C_6H_{12}O_6$, proteins and lipids.
- The carbon cycle is the way in which carbon is taken from and added to the environment by organisms (Fig 4.18).

The role of organisms in the carbon cycle

1. Green plants take in carbon in the form of carbon dioxide, CO_2, from the air. They use this CO_2 to make food in the process of **photosynthesis**.

   carbon dioxide + water → glucose + oxygen

   Plants also return CO_2 to the atmosphere during **respiration**:

   food + oxygen → carbon dioxide + water + energy

2. Animals eat plants as food. They also release CO_2 during respiration when they break down their food to produce energy.
3. The decomposers (fungi and bacteria) break down dead plants and animals, releasing CO_2 during respiration.

The burning of fossil fuels such as coal and oil releases more CO_2 into the atmosphere. The removal of tropical forests also increases the amount of CO_2 in the air, as there are fewer plants to take it in. These increasing amounts of CO_2 in the atmosphere are causing other problems, notably 'global warming'. This excess carbon dioxide forms a 'blanket' around the Earth, preventing the escape of heat radiating from the Earth. As a result the temperature of the Earth is increasing.

In summary:

- Photosynthesis removes CO_2 from the atmosphere.
- Respiration and combustion put CO_2 back.

4.18 The carbon cycle

The nitrogen cycle

- Organisms need nitrogen to make proteins, **DNA**, **RNA** and **ATP**.
- The main source of nitrogen in nature is N_2 gas in the atmosphere.

The main function of the nitrogen cycle is to enable organisms to get nitrogen in a form they can use.

Although 79% of the air is N_2 (also known as free nitrogen), most organisms cannot use nitrogen in this form. **Nitrate** is the form in which plants can absorb nitrogen. Once available, the plants absorb nitrate from the soil and use it to make proteins. Plants are eaten by animals who convert the plant protein into animal protein (assimilation).

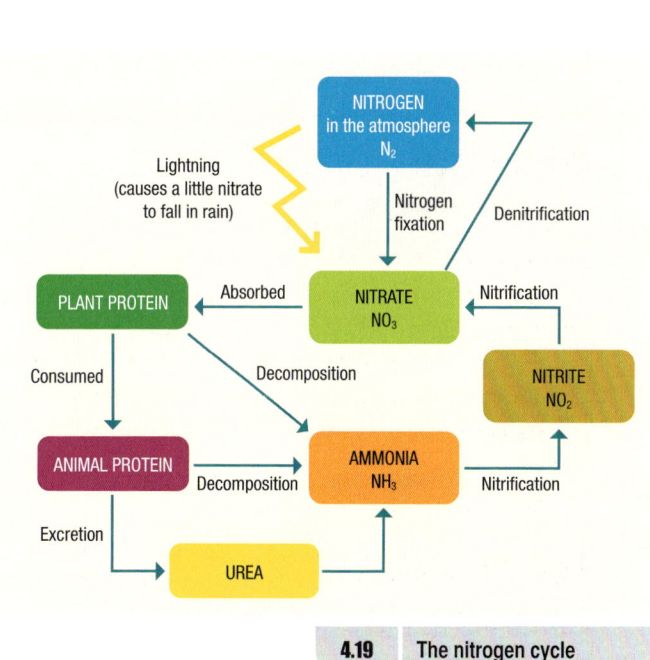

There are some plants, primarily those of the legume family (peas, beans, clover), which have tiny swellings or **nodules** on their roots (Fig 4.20). A group of bacteria known as the **nitrogen-fixing bacteria** live in these nodules and are able to convert free nitrogen from the soil air into nitrate ions, which are used by the plant to make protein. Other nitrogen-fixing bacteria are found living in the soil. Therefore, bacteria play a major role in making atmospheric nitrogen available to plants (see Table 4.3).

Nitrogen-fixing bacteria living in the root nodules are an example of a **symbiotic** relationship. This is where two organisms of different species live together and where at least one of them benefits. In this case both organisms are benefitting.

4.19 The nitrogen cycle

When plants and animals die, bacteria in the soil break them down. During this decomposition, protein is converted into **ammonia** (NH_3). Ammonia and other nitrogen-containing compounds such as urine are also released by animals during excretion. Plants cannot absorb this form of nitrogen. Certain other bacteria in the soil, known as the **nitrifying bacteria**, convert the ammonia into **nitrite** (NO_2) and the nitrite to **nitrate** (NO_3), which is then absorbed by the plants. These bacteria use the nitrogen as a source of energy to make their food (**chemosynthetic bacteria**, see Chapter 19).

> **D** — **Symbiosis** is a relationship between two organisms of different species in which at least one of them benefits.

There is also a group of bacteria that can undo the good work of the nitrifying bacteria. These are the **denitrifying bacteria** and they break down nitrates back into ammonia and nitrogen, making N_2 unavailable to living organisms once more (Fig 4.19).

Finally, humans have a role to play in the nitrogen cycle when fertilisers are being manufactured and used. In the industrial production of fertilisers, gaseous nitrogen (N_2) is converted into nitrates, which can be sold for use by farmers and gardeners. However, excessive use of inorganic (manufactured) nitrogen leads to a short-term increase in nitrate content in the soil. Much of this nitrate (or indeed organic fertiliser) is not used by plants and it may be washed off the land into neighbouring rivers and lakes. This results in the lakes becoming over-enriched with nutrients, a condition known as **eutrophication**, which in turn can lead to pollution (Chapter 5).

In summary, the nitrogen cycle (see Table 4.3) involves:
- three types of organism – plants, animals, micro-organisms (bacteria and fungi);
- four forms of nitrogen – N_2 gas, nitrate, nitrite and ammonia;
- four types of bacteria – nitrogen-fixing, bacteria of decay, nitrifying, denitrifying;
- five processes – nitrogen fixation, decomposition, nitrification, denitrification and assimilation.

4.20 (a) Legumes (peas and beans), (b) root nodules containing nitrogen-fixing bacteria

Summary

- Ecology is the study of the interactions between living organisms and their environment.
- Ecology is concerned with energy flow and nutrient cycles.
- An ecosystem is a community of organisms and their non-living environment interacting together, e.g. a pond, a woodland, a raised bog.
- The biosphere is the parts of the Earth where life can exist.
- The habitat of an organism is the place where it lives, e.g. the habitat of a crab is the seashore.
- The life of an organism is affected by abiotic, biotic, climatic, edaphic and aquatic factors.
- The biotic factors are an organism's influence on another organism, such as competition, predation and the effect of humans.
- The abiotic factors are the influence of the non-living part of the environment on an organism and include exposure, aspect and altitude.
- Climatic factors include the influence of weather, rainfall and seasonal changes.
- Climate refers to long-term atmospheric conditions, weather relates to day-to-day atmospheric conditions.
- Edaphic factors are soil factors that affect organisms, e.g. soil type, soil pH.
- In aquatic environments, factors such as light penetration, currents and wave action influence the life and distribution of organisms.

- Feeding relationships include (a) producers: organisms that make their own food, e.g. grass; (b) consumers: organisms that feed off other organisms, e.g. herbivores, carnivores, omnivores and detritovores (detritus feeders); (c) decomposers: organisms that cause the breakdown of dead plant and animal tissues, e.g. bacteria and fungi.
- Herbivores feed on plants only, e.g. snails, limpets.
- Carnivores feed on animals only, e.g. spiders, sparrowhawks.
- Omnivores feed on plants and animals, e.g. robins.
- The sun is the primary source of energy for the Earth.
- A food chain is the feeding relationship between organisms in which energy is transferred.
- A grazing food chain begins with a green plant, e.g. rose leaves → greenfly → ladybird.
- A detritus food chain begins with decaying plant or animal material, e.g. dead leaves → earthworm → blackbird → sparrowhawk.
- The number of steps in a food chain is usually limited to four or five due to the loss of energy through the chain. Most of the energy is lost as heat.
- A food web is a complex series of intersecting food chains in which there are various feeding (trophic) levels.
- A trophic level is a feeding level – primary producer, primary consumer, secondary consumer, etc.
- A pyramid of numbers shows the relationship between the numbers of organisms in a food chain.
- **HL** In general as you go up the pyramid the size of the organism increases and the number of organisms decreases.
- A pyramid of numbers may not represent the flow of energy in the ecosystem very accurately, because (a) it does not take into account the size of the organism; (b) it is not always possible to represent large numbers to scale.
- The niche of an organism describes the role of the organism in an ecosystem.
- Competition is the struggle between organisms for resources that are in short supply, such as food or light.
- Eventually, all members of a food chain die and decompose. In this way, minerals such as nitrogen and carbon are recycled, but the energy is lost as heat.
- Minerals cycle in nature, energy does not.
- The carbon cycle makes carbon available to organisms through the process of photosynthesis.

Table 4.2 The carbon cycle

Process	Organism	Action
Photosynthesis	Plants	Removes CO_2 from the atmosphere
Respiration	Plants, animals, decomposers	Adds CO_2 to the atmosphere
Combustion	None	Adds CO_2 to the atmosphere

The nitrogen cycle involves the following:

Table 4.3 The nitrogen cycle

Process	Organism	Location	Action
Nitrogen fixation	Nitrogen-fixing bacteria	Root nodules/soil	Convert N_2 to nitrate
Decomposition	Bacteria of decay	Soil	Breakdown of dead organisms, release of ammonia
Nitrification	Nitrifying bacteria	Soil	Convert ammonia to nitrite, nitrite to nitrate
Denitrification	Denitrifying bacteria	Soil	Convert nitrate back to N_2 in air
Farming	Humans	Soil	Addition of artificial fertiliser

04 Introduction to Ecology

Review questions

01 In your answers to the questions below, use examples from an Irish ecosystem.
   (a) Give the meaning of the following terms, with a clear example of each: ecosystem, biosphere, habitat.
   (b) Distinguish between abiotic and biotic factors that affect an ecosystem.
   (c) From the factors (a)–(g) select those that are (i) abiotic and (ii) biotic:
   (a) light   (d) currents   (g) hailstones
   (b) predators   (e) parasites   (h) competition
   (c) mineral salts (f) wind

02 Name a terrestrial ecosystem. State two abiotic factors and two climatic factors that influence the ecosystem you have named.

03 Name an aquatic ecosystem. List three factors that influence organisms in the ecosystem you have named.

04 What are edaphic factors? Give examples of edaphic factors that affect a terrestrial environment.

05 Explain the importance of the following factors in an ecosystem: (a) oxygen, (b) light intensity, (c) temperature.

06 (a) What is the primary source of energy for our planet?
   (b) Describe briefly how energy flows in an ecosystem.
   (c) What is: (i) a food chain? (ii) a grazing food chain?
   Give an example in each case, other than those given on page 37.

07 Match each of the terms A–E with the definitions (a)–(e) below.
   A biotic factor   (a) place where an organism lives
   B community   (b) influence of one organism on another
   C ecosystem   (c) a number of species interacting in a locality
   D food web   (d) feeding relationships of organisms
   E habitat   (e) interaction of organisms with each other and with the abiotic environment

08 The diagram shows a food web.
   (a) Give two food chains, each with four links, from the food web shown.
   (b) Name a primary producer, a secondary consumer and a tertiary consumer from the food web.
   (c) Blackbirds are omnivores. What does this mean? What similar term can be applied to the sparrowhawk?
   (d) Suggest what effect the killing of all the caterpillars might have on the numbers of (i) blackbirds, (ii) cabbages, (iii) spiders.

09 (a) Explain what is meant by a pyramid of numbers.
   (b) The diagram shows a pyramid of numbers from an ecosystem.
      (i) Which organism in this pyramid is a primary consumer?
      (ii) At which trophic level is the greatest amount of energy found?
      (iii) This pyramid of numbers is from which of the following ecosystems: rock pool; grassland; lake; hedgerow?
      (iv) Which organism in the pyramid is a producer?
      (v) Write out the food chain shown by this pyramid of numbers.

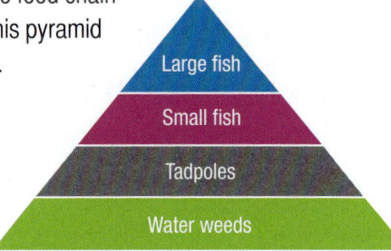

10 (a) Draw a pyramid of numbers to represent each of the following food chains:
      (i) sycamore tree → aphids → blue tits → kestrels
      (ii) seaweed → limpets → dog whelks → crabs → sea birds
   (b) Give a reason why a pyramid of numbers does not always have the same shape.
   (c) Outline two limitations of the use of pyramids of numbers.

11 Distinguish between the following pairs of terms giving examples in each case: (i) habitat and niche, (ii) biotic and abiotic, (iii) primary and secondary consumers.

12 The table below shows some animals and examples of the food they eat.

Animal	Ladybird	Fox	Owl	Rabbit	Greenfly	Small birds
Food the animal eats	Greenfly	Rabbits, mice, small birds	Mice, frogs	Grass	Leaves, small plants	Ladybird, caterpillars

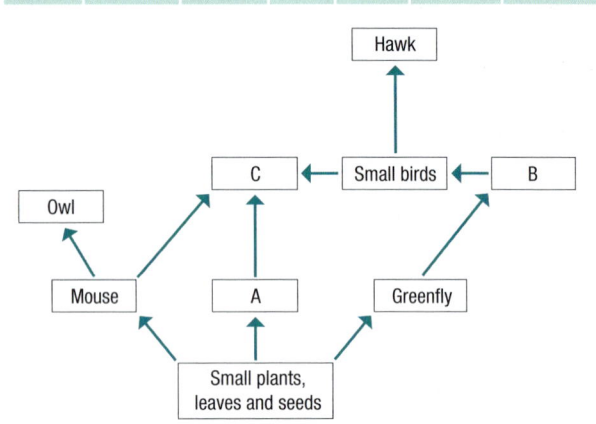

   (a) Copy and complete the boxes A, B and C in the food web with names of animals from the table.
   (b) Select, from the following list, the word that describes the greenfly in the food web: decomposer, producer, herbivore, carnivore.
   (c) Name the energy source on which all living things on Earth depend.
   (d) Suggest what might happen to the ladybirds if all the greenfly died?

Review questions

13 (a) Explain what you understand by nutrient recycling in nature.
(b) The diagram below shows an outline of the carbon cycle. Which letter(s) on the diagram correspond(s) to the following processes?
  (i) death
  (ii) combustion
  (iii) photosynthesis
  (iv) micro-organism
  (v) animal respiration
  (vi) plant respiration
  (vii) assimilation
  (viii) respiration

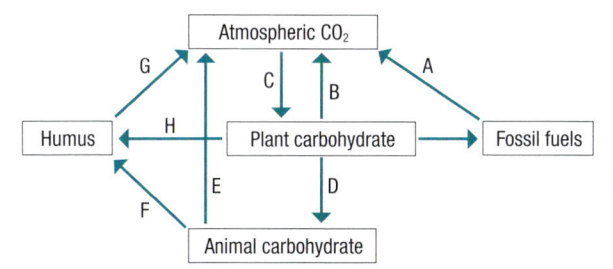

[Diagram: Atmospheric CO_2 connected by arrows labelled G, C, B, A, H to Humus, Plant carbohydrate, Fossil fuels; E, D, F connecting to Animal carbohydrate]

14 (a) Why do organisms need nitrogen?
(b) What is the function of the nitrogen cycle?
(c) What is meant by the term decay, in relation to the nitrogen cycle?
(d) Name a type of organism that causes decay.
(e) What is meant by the term nitrification?

15 Organic farmers do not put any artificial fertilisers on their crops.
(a) Suggest why organic farmers often grow more peas and beans than other farmers.
(b) Suggest why organic farmers often keep cows and pigs even if they mainly grow crops such as wheat.

16 (a) Global warming is thought, in part, to be due to a build-up of carbon dioxide in the Earth's atmosphere. Suggest how an imbalance in the carbon cycle may contribute to this build-up of carbon dioxide.
(b) Nitrogen, like carbon, is circulated in nature. State one difference between the carbon cycle and the nitrogen cycle.

17 (a) Name two activities of humans that cause an increase in the amount of CO_2 in the air.
(b) Name an activity of plants that causes a reduction of CO_2 in the air.
(c) Find out which of the following is the normal percentage of CO_2 in the air: A 0.3%, B 3.0%, C 0.003%, D 0.03%.
(d) State one useful function of nitrates in plants.
(e) Why are farmers encouraged to reduce the use of nitrate fertilisers?
(f) Describe how nitrogen in the air is converted into a form suitable for use by flowering plants.

Examination style questions

Section A

01 Explain the following terms by writing a brief description of each: (a) ecology, (b) abiotic, (c) producer, (d) niche, (e) food chain.

02 Rewrite and complete the following sentences:
(a) The study of the interactions between living organisms and their environment is called _____.
(b) The close relationship between two different species living together where at least one gains an advantage is called _____.
(c) The term used to refer to the non-living components or factors of the environment that affect living organisms is _____.
(d) The position or feeding level of an organism in a food chain is called its _____.
(e) The place where an organism lives and to which it is adapted is called its _____.
(f) A food web is a series of interconnected _____.

Section C

03 During the month of May, some students from a biology class studied the animals that can be found on a single sycamore tree. They collected a number of the animals, identified them and put together the following information.

Ladybirds feed on aphids.

Caterpillars eat the leaves of the sycamore tree.

Whitefly suck sycamore leaf juices.

Spiders feed on aphids, whitefly and ladybirds.

Beetles feed on leafhoppers who in turn feed on the leaves.

Birds, such as robins, feed on caterpillars and beetles.

Aphids suck the sycamore leaf juices.

(a) Construct a food web from this information.
(b) Name the primary producer(s) in the food web.
(c) Give two food chains from the web, each with four links.
(d) The aphids and leafhoppers found on the sycamore tree leaves were green in colour. What can you conclude from this observation?
(e) Construct a pyramid of numbers for a food chain in the web.

04 | Introduction to Ecology

Examination style questions

04 The diagram shows part of a seashore food web.

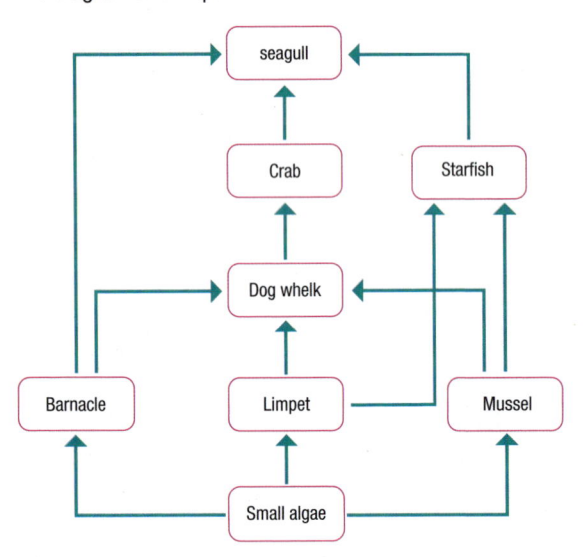

Examine the food web and answer the following questions:

(a) How many consumers are there?
(b) Name **two** herbivores from the food web.
(c) Name a producer from the food web.
(d) Draw a food chain with four links from this food web.
(e) Suppose all the starfish were killed off due to pollution. State what would happen to the number of mussels. Give a reason for your answer.
(f) Suggest what might cause pollution in this ecosystem.

05 The diagram shows three different examples of pyramids of numbers.

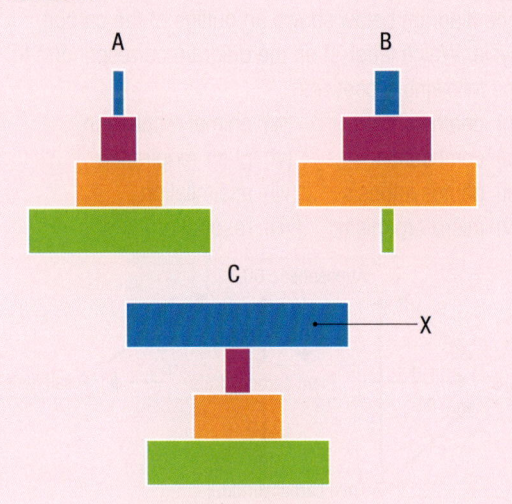

(a) In pyramid A, give a possible reason for the decrease in number of organisms up the pyramid.
(b) In pyramid B, explain the low number of organisms at the base of the pyramid.
(c) In pyramid C, explain the large number of organisms at level X.
(d) If a persistent insecticide, which accumulates in the tissues of organisms, had been used in an ecosystem containing pyramid A or B, which trophic level would eventually have the highest concentration? Explain your answer.
(e) From the habitat that you have studied or know, give an example of a pyramid of numbers.
(f) What is the trophic level of a secondary consumer?
(g) Other than food supply, state a factor that influences the population of organisms at the second trophic level.

Leaving Certificate examination questions

Section A

01 Use your knowledge of ecology to answer the following:

(a) What do we mean by the word *ecology*?
(b) The following food chain is from a grassland ecosystem:
grass → rabbit → fox
 (i) Name a secondary consumer from the above food chain.
 (ii) Name a producer from the above food chain.
 (iii) Name a herbivore from the above food chain.
 (iv) Show the above food chain as a pyramid of numbers.
 (v) If all the foxes were killed, what would happen to the *number* of rabbits?

2014 OL Q. 6

Leaving Certificate examination questions

02 Choose a term from the following list and place it in **Column B** to match a description in **Column A**. The first one has been done as an example:

trophic level   niche   habitat   ecosystem   biosphere

Column A	Column B
Where an organism lives	Habitat
All places where life is possible	
Organism's role in ecosystem	
Position in a pyramid of numbers	
Organisms and their environment	

2009 OL Q. 2

03 The following food chain is from a hedgerow.

hawthorn leaves → caterpillar → blue tit → sparrowhawk

Complete any **four** of the following by reference to **this** food chain.

(a) The primary consumer in this food chain is _____,

(b) If the number of sparrowhawks increases, the number of blue tits may _____.

(c) In this food chain the hawthorn leaves represent the _____.

(d) A carnivore from this food chain is _____.

(e) The number of trophic (feeding) levels in this food chain is limited by the small transfer of _____ from one level to the next.

2004 OL Q. 6

04 From your knowledge of ecology explain *any five* of the following terms: (a) biosphere, (b) niche, (c) biotic factor, (d) trophic level, (e) competition, (f) symbiosis.

2014 HL Q. 1

05 Answer the following questions in relation to food chains.

(a) Where in a food chain are primary producers found?
(b) What term is used to describe organisms that feed on primary producers?
(c) Why are most food chains short (i.e. consist of a few trophic levels)?
(d) What deduction may be made if the organisms at the start of the chain are less numerous than those that feed upon them?
(e) Can a parasite be the first member of a food chain? Explain your answer.
(f) Energy enters food chains in the form of light. In which form do you think most energy is lost from food chains?

2012 HL Q. 2

Section C

06 (a) In relation to ecology, explain the terms (i) abiotic; (ii) edaphic; (iii) habitat.

(b) Read the passage below and answer the questions that follow.

In the wild meerkats live in South America and Namibia, in dry, open plains and scrubland. They are mainly insectivores – but also eat lizards, snakes, spiders, eggs, small mammals, millipedes, centipedes, birds and plant roots. They are also very fond of a fungus called the desert truffle. They have no excess body fat stores and must forage for food every day. A colony of meerkats lives in a network of burrows with many entrance and exit holes. Meerkats memorise the locations of holes within their territory, so they can run to the nearest one at a moment's notice to avoid a predator. Each member of the group takes on a specific task – from baby-sitting and teaching youngsters how to survive, to sentry duty and foraging for food. When resting, they sunbathe or sleep in the shade. Meerkats have a high immunity to snake venom and scorpion stings. They usually bite off the scorpion's sting and then eat its body.

Meerkats at Dublin Zoo (series 4, 2013) adapted from RTÉ programme website notes and other sources.

(i) Name *one* country where meerkats live in the wild.
(ii) Where do colonies of meerkats make their home?
(iii) Explain the term *predator*.
(iv) What evidence is in the passage that meerkats are omnivores?
(v) Meerkats have a high immunity to the sting of which animal?
(vi) Name the three kingdoms of organisms represented in the passage above.
(vii) Give *two* reasons suggested by the photograph why meerkats make good sentries.

2014 OL Q. 11

07 (a) Explain the following terms as used in ecology: (i) producer, (ii) niche, (iii) habitat.

(b) There is now widespread evidence that the emission of greenhouse gases into the Earth's atmosphere is causing global climate change. Major changes are expected in terms of temperature and rainfall. One of the main greenhouse gases is carbon dioxide, released when fossil fuels are burned. Another is methane gas released by cattle. The gases cause pollution of the air. They are called greenhouse gases as they have an effect similar to that of a greenhouse – they prevent some of the sun's heat escaping back into space.

(i) Name **one** greenhouse gas.
(ii) Why are greenhouse gases so called?
(iii) What is meant by the term *pollution*?
(iv) Suggest **one** way to reduce the levels of greenhouse gases in the air.

04 Introduction to Ecology

Leaving Certificate examination questions

(v) The diagram below shows the carbon cycle. Match the terms from the list below to the letters A, B, C, D and E in the diagram.

photosynthesis   respiration   eaten by   combustion   decay

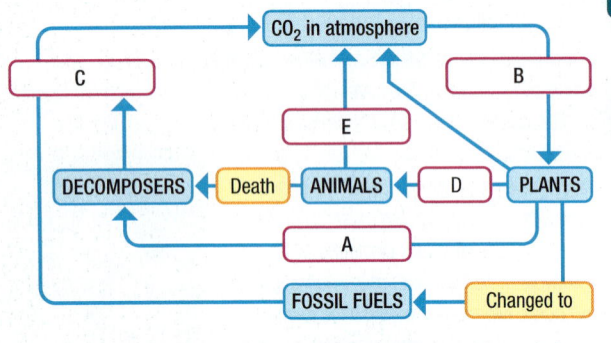

2013 OL Q. 11(a) and (b)

08 (a) In ecology we study ecosystems, habitats and communities, in which every organism has its own niche. Explain what is meant by: (i) an ecosystem, (ii) a habitat, (iii) a niche.

(b) (i) Name an ecosystem you have studied **and** construct a simple food chain from that ecosystem.
(ii) What is meant by a *trophic* level?
(iii) Name the trophic levels A, B and C in the pyramid of numbers shown below.

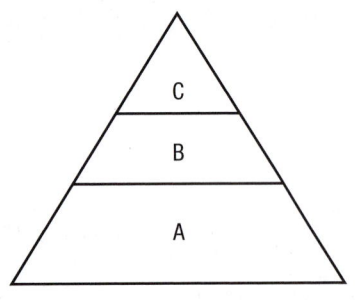

(iv) If all the organisms at C were removed (e.g. by disease) suggest what would happen to the organisms at B.

2010 OL Q. 10

09 Describe the role of 1. plants and 2. animals in the nitrogen cycle and the carbon cycle.

2014 HL Q. 15 (c) (vii)

10 (i) Draw a large labelled diagram to illustrate the main features of the nitrogen cycle.
(ii) Outline two biological similarities between the nitrogen cycle and the carbon cycle.
(iii) Suggest why continual monitoring of the environment is valuable.
(iv) In the case of the following pairs of terms, distinguish between the members of each pair by writing a sentence about each term.
1. Edaphic and aquatic.
2. Climate and weather.

2013 HL Q. 15 (b)

11 (a) Explain the following terms that are used in ecology: biosphere, habitat, niche.
(b) In ecological studies it is found that the distribution of organisms is influenced by abiotic and biotic factors.
 (i) Distinguish between the underlined terms.
 (ii) Name an ecosystem that you have investigated and give an example of an abiotic factor that influences the distribution of a named plant in the ecosystem.
 (iii) In the case of your named ecosystem give an example of a biotic factor that influences the distribution of a named animal.
 (iv) What is meant by a pyramid of numbers? Construct a pyramid of numbers from organisms in the ecosystem that you have studied.
 (v) What term is used by ecologists to describe the organisms that form the base of the pyramid?

2004 HL Q. 10

Past examination questions

OL	2014 Q. 6, Q. 11 (a), (b)	2013 Q. 3 (d), (g)	2013 Q. 11 (a), (b)	2012 Q. 10 (a), (b) (i)
	2011 Q. 11 (a), (b) (i)–(iv)	2010 Q. 1, Q. 10 (a), (b)	2009 Q. 2, Q. 10 (a)	2008 Q. 1, Q. 10 (a)
	2007 Q. 2, Q. 10 (a), (b)	2006 Q. 1, Q. 10 (a), (b)	2005 Q. 1, Q. 10 (a)	2004 Q. 6
HL	2014 Q. 1, Q. 15 (c) (vii)	2013 Q. 2, Q. 15 (b)	2012 Q. 11 (a), (b)	2011 Q. 3
	2010 Q. 5, Q. 12 (a), (c)	2009 Q. 11 (b)	2008 Q. 7 (a), (b) (i)	2007 Q. 2, Q. 12 (a), (b)
	2006 Q. 2	2004 Q. 10 (a), (b)		

The Effects of Humans on the Environment

05

After studying this chapter you should be able to:

1. Define the term pollution.
2. State the effects of one pollutant from any of the following areas: domestic, agricultural or industrial.
3. Outline one way in which the pollution can be controlled in the area mentioned in (2).
4. Refer to the ecological impact of one human activity that causes pollution.
5. Define the term conservation.
6. Outline one conservation practice from one of the following areas: agriculture, fisheries or forestry.
7. Explain the term waste management.
8. Describe the problems associated with waste disposal.
9. Give one example of waste management in agriculture, fisheries and forestry.
10. Outline methods of waste minimisation.
11. Explain the role of micro-organisms in waste management and pollution control.

Our environment and pollution

Almost everything in Ireland, apart from our few native oak woods, has been created by human activity. Ireland was once a land covered by deciduous woodland. Over time, humans have cut down the forests and cleared the land for agriculture. From the mid-1600s onwards, farmers started planting hedgerows around their fields and this provided *habitats* for many plants and animals. We have built towns and cities, roads and waterways, all of which have an effect on our surroundings (Fig 5.1). In just about everything we do, we influence the environment, for good and for bad. When harmful substances such as certain chemicals are put into the environment, it gives rise to concern, particularly where they affect our health.

5.1 A typical Irish landscape today

Types of pollution	Examples
Domestic	Household wastes such as food waste, paper, plastic, polystyrene, glass, aluminium cans.
Agricultural	Disposal of slurry, the use of sprays to kill insect pests and weeds, excess use of fertilisers.
Industrial	Waste from factories such as harmful acids, detergents, gases gases such as sulfur dioxide (SO_2) and oil which may leak into rivers and lakes.

Table 5.1 Types of pollution

05   The Effects of Humans on the Environment

5.2   Pollution

1. **Pollution** is the process by which harmful substances are added to the environment by humans. Common types of pollution include domestic, agricultural and industrial pollution (Fig 5.2). Pollutants are anything that causes pollution. Pollutants can affect:

- the air we breathe;
- freshwater rivers and lakes;
- the sea; and
- the land.

> **Pollution** is the addition of harmful substances to the environment.

SYLLABUS REQUIREMENT:
You are required to study the effects of any *one* pollutant, which must relate to the habitat studied, from any of the following areas: domestic, agricultural or industrial.

Agricultural pollution

Causes of agricultural pollution

(a) Overuse of fertilisers

2. **Fertilisers** are used to replace the minerals taken up by plants growing in the soil. If the plants are harvested and not allowed to die in the soil, then the nutrients do not return to the soil (see page 43). The soil becomes deplete of essential nutrients so fertilisers in the form of manure, compost or manufactured fertilisers are spread on the soil.

The problem

If excess artificial (or organic) fertilisers, **phosphates** and **nitrates** in particular, are washed into rivers and lakes then enrichment of the water with nutrients occurs, a process called **eutrophication**. As a result there is a rapid increase in the growth of microscopic algae – this is known as an **algal bloom**. When the algae die, they are broken down by bacteria that use up all the available oxygen in the water. This results in the death of aquatic organisms such as fish.

Control measures

3. Controlled use of fertilisers and a reduction in the run-off of chemicals from land into nearby water supplies would help reduce the problems of this type of water pollution. Legislation and a system of fines provide a deterrent and help reduce the problem.

(b) Use of pesticides

4. Farmers use chemicals called **pesticides** to kill pests that attack their crops. Chemicals which specifically kill insects are known as insecticides, while those that kill weeds are herbicides and fungicides kill fungal diseases of crops (Fig 5.3).

5.3   Spraying fertiliser

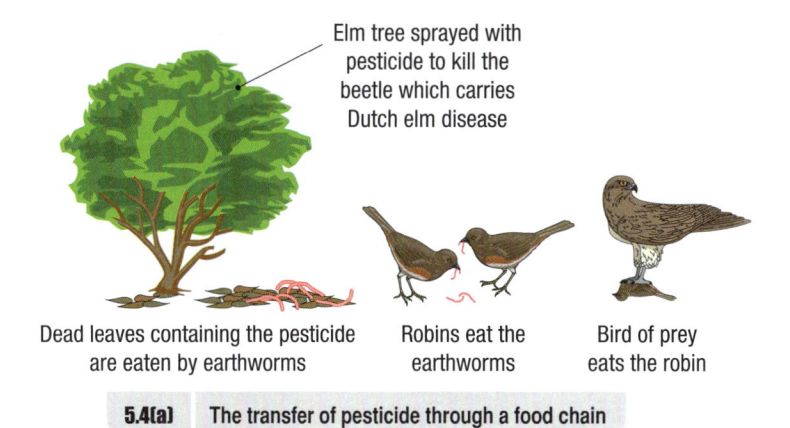

5.4(a) The transfer of pesticide through a food chain

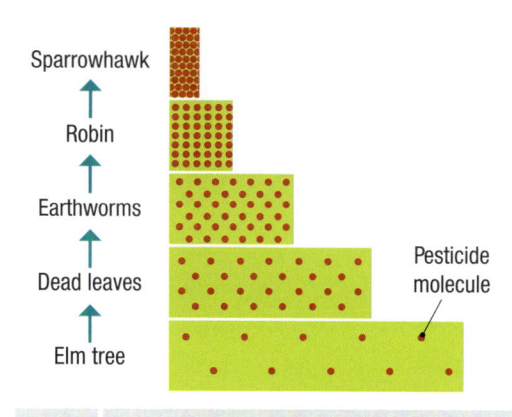

5.4(b) The build-up of pesticide through a food chain

The problem

Spraying crops with insecticides gets rid of harmful insects, but it may also kill off other useful insects such as bees and butterflies that are so necessary to the **pollination** of flowers.

If a pesticide gets into a food chain it may eventually become hazardous for humans. Excessive amounts of pesticides and fertilisers can also find their way into nearby streams and lakes. In turn they may become part of the food chain. Figs 5.4(a) and (b) show the effects of pesticides in a parkland habitat. As you move through the food chain, the pesticide becomes more concentrated in the **organisms**.

Control measures

1. In some cases, certain insects that feed on the harmful insects can be introduced to control the pest without the use of chemicals. For example in glasshouses, ladybirds can be introduced to kill the greenfly that may destroy the crops. This method of pest control is called **biological pest control**.
2. The use of pesticides (herbicides and fungicides as well) is strictly regulated (Fig 5.5). Chemicals that are left over or the residue in containers should be poured onto the land where the pesticide was being used. This allows time for the chemicals to break down in the soil. They should never be poured down a sink or drain or allowed to get into nearby streams and rivers. Even the smallest amount can, over time, build up in the food chain.
3. The over-use of both fertilisers and pesticides are examples of the ecological impact of the activities of humans. We have a responsibility to future generations to minimise the negative impact of our activities on the environment.

5.5 Use of pesticides is strictly controlled by legislation

Conservation

Conservation is the way in which we as humans manage the environment. Conservation aims to balance our use of resources with maintaining wildlife and their habitats. Nobody really knows how many **species** of organisms there are. Scientists have 'described' and named about 1.7 million. But damage to habitats by humans is causing many species to become extinct.

5.6 Some species are now endangered, such as the natterjack toad (top) and the red squirrel (bottom)

05 The Effects of Humans on the Environment

5.7 White-tailed eagle

Many animals are threatened with extinction, such as the giant panda in China and, closer to home, the corncrake, the barn owl, natterjack toad and red squirrel (Fig 5.6). Conservationists try, by protecting the habitats and breeding grounds of such animals, to ensure they will survive.

Here in Ireland we have a number of designated nature reserves – areas set aside by government where plants and animals are protected. Our national parks include those at Killarney, Co. Kerry, Letterfrack in Connemara, Glenveagh in Donegal and the Burren, Co. Clare, to name but a few. The role of the national parks is to maintain and promote habitats and biodiversity.

In 2007 white-tailed eagles from Norway were successfully reintroduced to Ireland. These magnificent birds had become extinct here over 100 years ago (Fig 5.7).

Reasons for conserving organisms

1. To prevent extinction.
2. To preserve habitats.
3. To maintain biodiversity (the wide range of organisms).
4. To provide aesthetic and recreational facilities for ourselves.
5. To provide food supplies.
6. As a possible source of new drugs or other materials.

Good conservation practices

Conservation practices can be found in agriculture, forestry and fishing.

> **Conservation** is the wise management of our environment.

SYLLABUS REQUIREMENT:
You are required to outline any one conservation practice, from agriculture, fisheries or forestry.

1. Agriculture
   - The use of crop rotation and mixed farming can help to prevent excessive mineral loss from the soil and overgrazing of land.
   - The controlled use of fertilisers (see page 50).
2. Forestry
   - Plant deciduous trees, which provide habitats for a variety of plant and animal life as well as being of recreational value and a good source of renewable raw material.
3. Fisheries
   - Net – mesh size and shape. Square mesh netting keeps its shape under tension, allowing young fish to escape and breed (Fig 5.8). Diamond mesh netting closes up under tension, preventing the escape of young fish.
   - Over-fishing leads to a reduction in the breeding stocks, which may last for decades. Specific quotas (maximum numbers allowed to be caught) are set for different species of fish. This helps ensure that sufficient numbers survive to breed and continue the species. But more needs to be done to ensure these quotas are being adhered to.

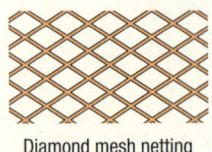

Diamond mesh netting relaxed

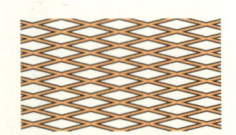

Diamond mesh netting closed under towing tension; prevents young fish escaping

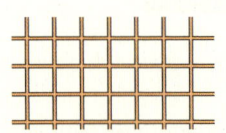

Square mesh netting under tension does not alter its shape; allows young fish to escape

5.8 Fish mesh sizes

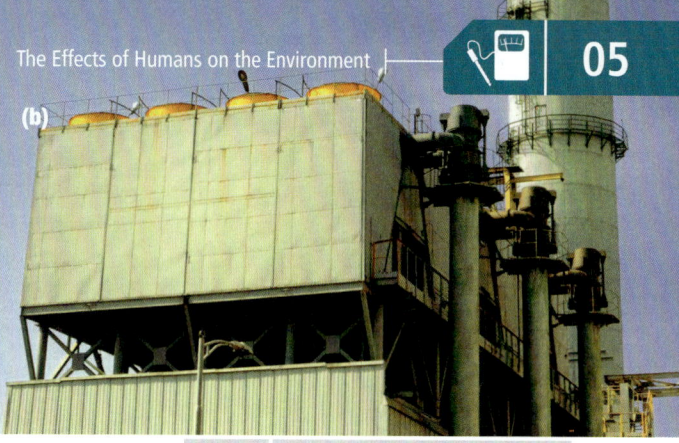

5.9 (a) Landfill and (b) incinerator

Waste management

Waste refers to any substance that a person wishes to dispose of. Waste may be in solid, liquid or gaseous form. The vast majority of waste produced in Ireland is in the solid form. It is made up of domestic, industrial, commercial, agricultural, building and demolition waste as well as sewage sludge and litter.

Waste management is the way we as a society deal with our waste. The amount of domestic waste being generated by households in Ireland has fallen significantly in recent years, mainly due to increased levels of recycling. In addition more and more household waste is being burned in incinerators than is being sent to landfill sites (Fig 5.9). However, few people seem happy to have large incinerators located near them as there may be problems with the release of toxic fumes.

Landfill involves burying the waste in large pits in the ground. Bacteria and fungi break down any organic material in the waste. Heat released by the micro-organisms is trapped and this speeds up the breakdown process. The anaerobic biodegradation produces a large amount of biogas. This can be collected from the landfill and used as fuel.

Problems with disposal of waste

> **Waste management** is the way we deal with our waste.

1. There may not be sufficient landfill sites available.
2. The waste may be toxic.
3. Too little is being recycled.
4. It may be non-biodegradable. It takes 500 years for a plastic bottle to break down.
5. It may be unsightly and have an odour.
6. Some liquid wastes can contaminate ground water supplies.

Examples of waste management

Agriculture

- More than 28 million tonnes of solid waste are produced each year in Ireland, and 22 million tonnes of this is agricultural waste! One of the main pollution problems in farming comes from the over-use and incorrect use of chemical fertilisers and animal manure (slurry).
- Slurry should be diluted and spread on dry land.

Fisheries

- Aquaculture is the cultivation of fish and shellfish such as salmon, trout, mussels and oysters. These fish are bred in fish farms at specialised sites around the coastline and in rivers and lakes (Fig 5.10).
- It is not in the interests of fish farmers to dispose of any wastes in a way that would be harmful to the stock. Certain chemicals are needed from time to time to treat parasites, like the sea lice that attach themselves to salmon. Other chemicals may be given to the fish to give the flesh a particular colour, e.g. pink for salmon. Strict regulations govern the use of such additives.

5.10 A marine fish farm

05 The Effects of Humans on the Environment

5.11 Bark mulch is good for suppressing weeds

5.12 Wood chips can be used to make fibreboard

- The fish waste can be neutralised, pulped and dried and used as a fertiliser (fish and bone meal).

Forestry

- Care must be taken when planting trees for forestry. The trees must not be planted too close to rivers and streams. If the leaves (needles) of conifers fall into nearby streams, they cause the waterways to become acidic.
- Wastes from tree processing in sawmills and timber yards can be recycled. The small branches can be made into mulch for use on flowerbeds, paths and playgrounds while the clippings from trees can be used to make fibreboard and other wood products. (Figs 5.11 and 5.12).

5.13 Tin cans

Methods of waste minimisation

In order to reduce the bulk of the material that is put into landfill sites, the following practices are recommended: reduce, re-use and recycle.

1. Reduce
- Waste can be reduced in the packaging of goods and in wrapping and transporting goods to shops.
- Customers can choose not to buy overly packaged goods.

2. Re-use
- Glass jars, plastic bottles and containers can be washed and re-used.
- Plastic and paper bags can be re-used when shopping.

3. Recycle
- Glass, aluminium cans, scrap metal, oil, paper and plastic containers can be recycled, thus reducing the amount of waste for disposal. It takes 11 months to make a tin can, from extraction of the ore to being on a shelf, but only 1 day to recycle and at only 5% of the energy costs.

Remember the three Rs of waste management are: reduce, re-use, recycle (Fig 5.14).

5.14(a) Recycle bins help reduce waste

5.14(b) Recycling glass bottles

5.15 Micro-organisms break down waste material in a compost bin

The role of micro-organisms in waste management and pollution control

1. We saw in Chapter 4 that soil micro-organisms, such as bacteria and fungi, break down dead and decaying plants and animals, recycling the nutrients in the nitrogen cycle. Microbes actively break down wastes in landfill sites and garden compost bins (Fig 5.15).
2. Bacteria play a major role in sewage treatment plants where they break down the sludge.
3. Some types of bacteria can absorb heavy metals such as cadmium and zinc, which may contaminate soils.
4. Bacteria that feed on oil can be used to treat pollution from oil leaks at sea.

Summary

- Pollution is any harmful addition to the environment by humans.
- Pollution affects the air, fresh water, land and sea.
- Domestic pollution is caused by wastes such as glass, paper, plastic, raw and cooked food and polystyrene and aluminium cans.
- Agricultural pollution is caused by over-use of pesticides and fertilisers, by the dumping of silage and other slurry into water and onto the land.
- Agricultural pollution can be controlled by means of legislation, disposing of chemicals safely and only spreading slurry in dry conditions.
- Industrial waste such as the emission of gases, e.g. SO_2 from industrial plants and power stations, causes air pollution.
- Conservation is the wise management of species and their environment.
- Conservation is an active process, not simply a case of preservation.
- Conservation is necessary to ensure biodiversity, maintain habitats and prevent extinction.
- In agriculture the practice of crop rotation ensures that the land does not become depleted of nutrients.
- In fisheries the use of nets that allow the young fish to escape and breed ensure the stock levels in the seas.
- In forestry, replanting deciduous trees is necessary to conserve our forests.
- Waste management is the way that we deal with our waste. It involves strategies for waste prevention and waste minimisation.
- Reduce, re-use and recycle are methods of waste minimisation and management.
- Composting biodegradable waste is one solution to the disposal problem – micro-organisms break down organic waste and the compost can then be used in the garden.
- Microbes that can absorb heavy metals help control soil pollution.

05 The Effects of Humans on the Environment

Review questions

01 (a) Define the terms: (i) pollution, (ii) pollutant.
(b) List two pollutants of each of the following: (i) air, (ii) water, (iii) land.
(c) Describe how any one of the pollutants you list in part (b) can be controlled.

02 Give two examples of either water pollution or air pollution and state one harmful effect of each example on the environment.

03 Lichens are a combined organism consisting of part fungus and part green alga. Each component depends on the other. The alga makes food for both itself and the fungus and the fungus absorbs water and minerals for itself and the alga. Some organisms are easily damaged by sulfur dioxide in the air and these can be used as pollution indicators. Lichens can act as 'indicator species'. If lichen is present in an area, then the air is clean. If lichen is absent from the area, then the air is polluted.

In a survey of the effects of air pollution around an industrial town, three different species of lichen, A, B and C, were examined. In the survey, an estimate was made of the density of each type of lichen growing on tree trunks at different distances along a line from the centre of the town.

The results of the survey are shown on the graph.

(a) What is a lichen?
(b) Which one of the three types of lichen is the most sensitive to air pollution? Give a reason for your choice.
(c) Find from the graphs the distance from the town centre at which lichen B shows half its maximum density.
(d) Suggest two substances that may cause air pollution in towns.
(e) Suggest two ways of reducing the air pollution in towns.

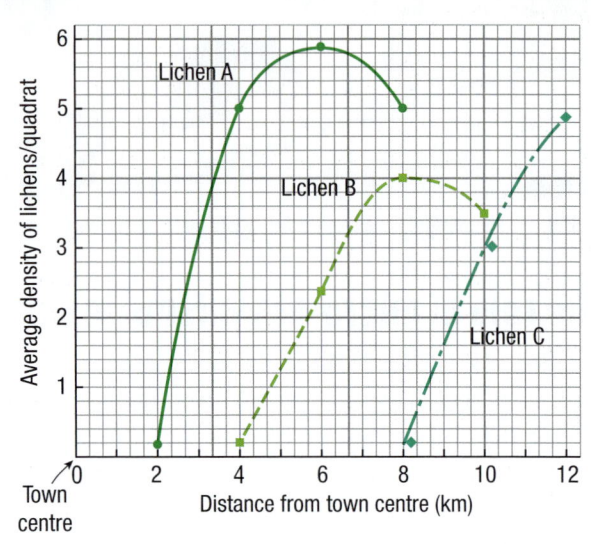

04 Write an essay on pollution describing the possible ecological impact that the activity of humans has had or could have on life on Earth. Include reference to the following: the source of pollution, the ecological effects and 'indicator species'. Use books and the internet as references. List your references.

05 (a) Explain what you understand by the term 'conservation'.
(b) State three reasons why it is considered a good idea to conserve species of organisms.
(c) Name any one species that is currently (i) under threat and (ii) being conserved, in Ireland.

06 Outline one conservation practice from two of the following: agriculture, fisheries, forestry.

07 (a) What is meant by waste management?
(b) Outline the problems associated with waste disposal.

08 (a) Describe one waste management practice in agriculture.
(b) Outline two methods of waste minimisation.

09 One of the major problems that we have to face in the 21st century is the disposal of domestic and industrial wastes. Nobody wants landfill sites or thermal/incinerator plants near them. So what can we do if we cannot bury or burn our waste? Outline the advantages and disadvantages of:
(a) landfill sites, (b) incinerators.

Examination style questions

01 (a) Define the term pollution.
(b) Give one example of a pollutant. State whether the pollutant is from an industrial, agricultural or domestic source. Describe the effects of the pollutant on the environment.
(c) Outline **one** way in which pollution may be controlled in an area.

02 A factory was found to be discharging toxic (poisonous) waste into a nearby river. The concentration of the waste was measured at regular distances downstream from the factory and the results are shown in the table below:

Distance from factory (m)	0	200	400	600	800	1000
Concentration of waste (mg/l)	50	31	20	13	8	4

(a) Using graph paper, plot a graph of these results. Put distance on the horizontal axis.
(b) From the graph, estimate the concentration of pollutant at 300 m from the factory.
(c) Suggest a reason for the decrease in the concentration of the pollutant from its point of discharge to 1000 m from the factory.
(d) Suggest a type of pollutant that might be discharged into this river.

03 Waste materials are produced in large amounts by human activity in Ireland today.
(a) Give **three** major sources of waste apart from domestic households.
(b) Outline the problems connected with the disposal of one form of waste.
(c) Discuss the role of micro-organisms in waste control.
(d) What are the three Rs of waste minimisation?

04 (a) What is meant by conservation in ecology?
(b) Give any two benefits of conservation to humans.

05 Read the following extract from an article in the magazine *Wild Ireland*, and then answer the questions that follow:

In 1998 almost 2 million tonnes of household and other domestic waste was generated in Ireland. Over 90% of this waste was placed in landfill sites around the country. Modern landfill sites have come a long way from the 'dumps' of the past. However there are a number of issues to consider when managing landfill sites.

Litter control: the spread of litter from landfills is mainly caused by wind and birds. Control measures include limiting the amount of waste left uncovered at any one time.

Run-off management: when organic waste breaks down it releases chemicals which can be harmful if they get into surrounding land and water supplies. A system of collecting this liquid waste and treating it is usually put in place.

Odours and noise: odours can be reduced by limiting the amount of uncovered waste. Noise pollution can be limited by positioning the site away from built-up areas.

Biogas: organic waste is decomposed by bacteria producing a biogas. This biogas consists mainly of methane, an extremely flammable gas. Of the 40 official landfill sites only five have the ability to recover the biogas and convert it to energy in the form of electricity.

Although disposal of waste in landfill is at the bottom of the list of preferred waste management, landfill gas collection provides one way to make the best of a bad situation.

(Adapted from *The Green Guide* by Cepa Giblin, Wild Ireland, July–August 2003)

(a) What percentage of our waste ends up in landfill sites?
(b) What causes the spread of litter from the landfill sites to nearby property?
(c) How can the spread of litter be controlled?
(d) When is 'run-off' from landfill sites harmful?
(e) What is biogas? How is it formed?
(f) How can the problem of the production of biogas be dealt with?
(g) If landfill is the last choice for waste management, what is the more preferred method of managing our waste?

06 Read the following extract and then answer the questions below.

The vast majority of micro-organisms live on dead plant and animal remains and thereby recycle the mineral elements tied up in this waste material. The recycling of dead waste material is known as biodegradation and forms the basis of well-known nutrient cycles such as the carbon cycle. Sometimes these micro-organisms will attack and break down materials that have been manufactured by humans and which play an important role in our everyday lives. Microbes are capable of breaking down metals in buildings, timber in joists and furniture, lubricating oils and even stone and concrete with acids they produce. Attack on materials of economic benefit is called biodeterioration. Humans try to encourage biodegradation, whilst discouraging biodeterioration.

(Adapted from Biological Science Review 4.4)

(a) Explain the term 'biodegradable'.
(b) State one way in which biodegradation and biodeterioration are similar and one way in which they are different.
(c) The carbon cycle is one example of a nutrient cycle. Name one other nutrient cycle in which bacteria are involved.
(d) Select one example of biodeterioration from the passage. Describe a possible result of this biodeterioration that may affect our everyday lives.

05 | The Effects of Humans on the Environment

Leaving Certificate examination questions

Section A

01
(i) Give *two* problems associated with waste disposal.
(ii) Mention *two* ways of minimising the amount of waste produced.
2014 OL Q. 11 (c)

02
(i) What is meant by *pollution*?
(ii) Name **one** human activity that causes pollution.
(iii) State **two** problems associated with waste disposal in Ireland.
(iv) List **two** ways of minimising waste.
(v) Give **one** example of the use of microorganisms in waste management.
2011 OL Q. 2

03 (a)
(i) What does an ecologist mean by the term *conservation*?
(ii) Suggest a reason why nature reserves are important for conservation.
(b)
(i) Explain the term *pollution*.
(ii) Pollution may result from domestic, agricultural or industrial sources. Select **one** of these areas **and** state an effect that may be produced by a **named** pollutant.
(iii) How may the pollution referred to in (ii) be controlled?
(c) In relation to the incineration of domestic waste, suggest: (i) an advantage of the process, (ii) a disadvantage of the process.
2012 HL Q. 4

04
(a) What is meant by pollution?
(b) Give an example of a human activity that results in the pollution of air or water.
(c) Suggest a means of counteracting this pollution.
(d) Explain conservation in relation to wild plants and animals.
(e) Suggest **two** reasons for conserving wild species.
(f) State **one** conservation practice from agriculture **or** fisheries **or** forestry.
2004 HL Q. 5

05 Place **each** term from the following list into **Column B** to match a description in **Column A**. The first one has been completed as an example.

Pollution   ~~Niche~~   Recycle
Burning fuel   Conservation   Smell

Column A	Column B
The role of the organism in the habitat.	Niche
(a) Any harmful addition to the ecosystem.	
(b) A problem associated with waste disposal.	
(c) A way to minimise waste.	
(d) Wise management of an ecosystem.	
(e) A possible cause of pollution.	

2012 OL Q. 5

Section C

06 Improper waste disposal may cause pollution.
(i) State any **two** types of pollution associated with waste disposal.
(ii) 1. Give **one** example of a waste associated with agriculture or forestry or fisheries.
2. State how the named waste is managed.
(iii) Give **three** ways to minimise waste.
(iv) Give **one** example of the use of micro-organisms in waste management.
2013 OL Q. 11 (c)

07
(i) Suggest what could happen to biological diversity as the human population continues to increase.
(ii) The vast amount of waste generated is one of the consequences of the huge increase in the human population. Mention **three** main ways in which waste can be minimised.
(iii) What is pollution?
(iv) What is the role of microorganisms in pollution control?
2014 HL Q. 15 (c)

05 The Effects of Humans on the Environment

Leaving Certificate examination questions

08 A paper factory pumps liquid effluent into a river. The effluent contains sugar. Oxygen demand is the amount of oxygen needed by organisms living in a river. Oxygen concentration is the amount of oxygen dissolved in the river water. The graph shows changes in water conditions for several kilometres downstream from the factory outflow.

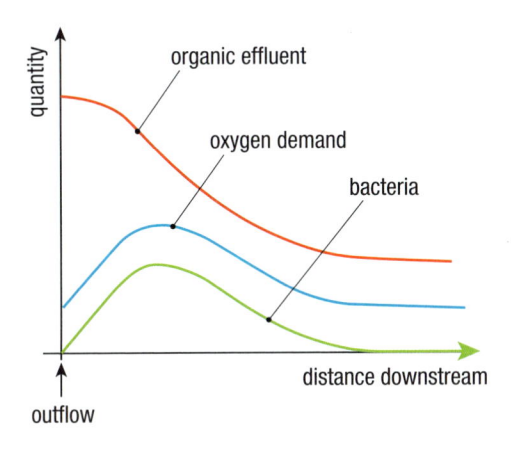

(i) To which kingdom do bacteria belong?
(ii) Give **one** reason why the number of bacteria increases immediately downstream from the outflow.
(iii) Give **one** reason why the number of bacteria then decreases further downstream from the outflow.
(iv) Describe how the oxygen demand changes as the number of bacteria in the water changes.
(v) Give a reason for your answer to part (iv).

The graph shows the changes in oxygen concentration and the number of fish in the same river.

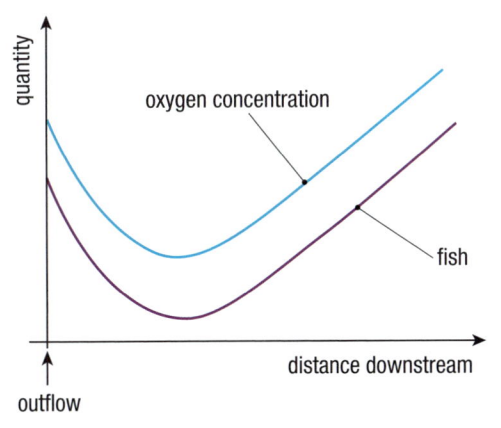

(vi) Explain why the curve for fish numbers is the same shape as that for oxygen concentration.
(vii) The oxygen concentration in the river water eventually increases with distance from the outflow. Suggest **two** ways by which this oxygen may enter the water.

(Adapted from *Biology for You* by Gareth Williams, 2nd edn, Stanley Thomas (Publishers) Ltd, 2002)

2010 HL Q. 12 (b)

09 Waste management is a matter of growing concern in Ireland as the population expands.
(i) Outline **three** problems associated with waste disposal.
(ii) Give an example of waste produced in agriculture or fisheries or forestry and describe how it is managed.
(iii) Suggest **two** methods of waste minimisation.
(iv) Give one example of the use of micro-organisms in waste management.

2008 HL Q.10 (c)

Past examination questions

OL	2014 Q. 11 (c)	2012 Q. 11 (c)	2012 Q. 5	2011 Q. 2	2010 Q. 10 (c)	2008 Q. 10 (c)
	2005 Q. 10 (c)	SEC Sample Q. 14				
HL	2014 Q. 15 (c)	2012 Q. 4	2011 Q. 4	2010 Q. 12 (b)	2008 Q. 10 (c)	2006 Q. 10 (c)	2004 Q. 5

06 Ecological Relationships and Population Dynamics

ALL OF THE MATERIAL IN THIS CHAPTER IS HL ONLY

After studying this chapter you should be able to:

1. Define and give an example of a population.
2. Define the following factors that control populations: competition, predation, symbiosis and parasitism, giving examples in each case.
3. Distinguish between contest and scramble competition and relate competition to population size.
4. Describe an adaptive technique of a named plant and animal to survive competition.
5. Describe three adaptive techniques of predators and prey.
6. Give an example of a predator/prey relationship.
7. Outline the contributory factors in predator/prey relationships.
8. Explain the effects of famine, disease, wars, and contraception on the human population.

Populations

A **population** is a group of individuals of the same **species** living in an **ecosystem** at any given time, for example the diving beetles in a particular pond or the oak trees in a woodland. **Organisms** live in populations for a number of reasons, including:

- The **habitat** provides food and shelter.
- It may be safer for individuals.
- For breeding purposes.

Biologists study populations to find out how their numbers change (Fig 6.1). Many insects destroy food crops and studying insect pest populations has led to a reduction in the damage these insects do to the crops (Fig 6.2).

Monitoring the populations of endangered species, such as the corncrake that lives in hay meadows, has helped in their **conservation** (Fig 6.3). Some species of organisms act as indicators of the state of the **environment**. For example, lichens vary in their tolerance to SO_2 (sulfur dioxide gas) in the atmosphere. Carrying out surveys of lichen populations provides useful information on air pollution.

6.1 A population (flock) of geese

6.2 A population of caterpillars on a cabbage crop

6.3 A corncrake

Population size

The size of a population is controlled by a number of factors, including **competition**, **predation**, **symbiosis** and **parasitism**.

D A **population** is the number of a particular species in a particular ecosystem.

Ecological Relationships and Population Dynamics | 06

D **Competition** is when two or more organisms fight for a resource that is in short supply.

D **Contest competition** is an active physical confrontation between two organisms in which only one wins the resource.

D **Scramble competition** is a struggle between organisms for a scarce resource in which each organism gets some of the resource.

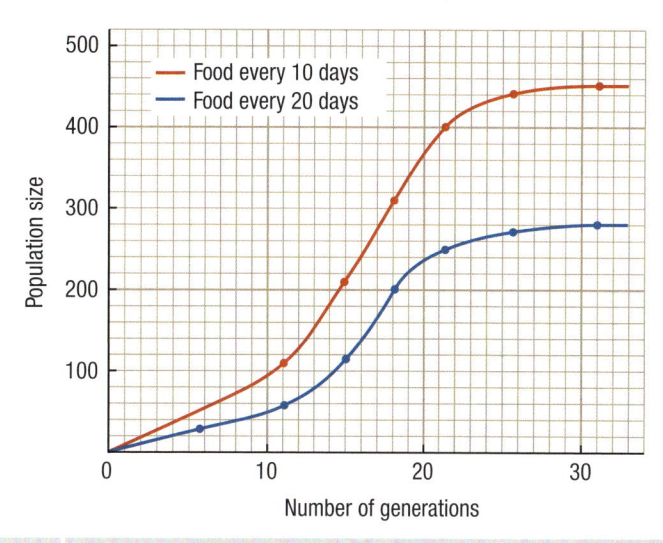

6.4 The changing size of two beetle populations given limited food supplies

Competition

Competition occurs when organisms seek a resource that is in short supply in a habitat:
- Plants growing close together will compete for light, water and minerals.
- Animals may compete for food, mates and territory. A good example of territorial competition is seen in robins, who compete strongly for territory that they defend all year round.
- In general competition between members of the same species is more intense than between different species as they are competing for the same resources.

A shortage of food amongst a population of animals will give rise to competition and some animals may starve to death. As a result, the size of the population will be affected. The availability of resources sets a limit on the population size in a habitat (Fig 6.4). Competition tends to reduce population size.

Types of competition

There are two types of competition – **contest competition** and **scramble competition**.
1. Contest competition: An active physical confrontation between two organisms in which only one wins the resource. This type of competition is seen amongst red deer during the breeding season when the stags (males) are seeking mates. Competing stags lock antlers and fight by pushing against each other until one of them withdraws (Fig 6.5).
2. Scramble competition occurs when each organism tries to get as much of the resource as possible. It results in all the organisms getting some of the resource. Young birds in the nest depend on food brought by their parents. If there are a large number of chicks and a relatively limited amount of food there will be jostling in the nest and the strongest chicks will get the food. The number of birds that reach adulthood will be reduced (Fig 6.6).

6.5 Two stags competing with each other for a mate

6.6 Young chicks all scrambling for some of the food

06 Ecological Relationships and Population Dynamics

ALL OF THE MATERIAL IN THIS CHAPTER IS HL ONLY

So how do organisms adapt to survive competition?

Take the example of weeds in the garden. A weed may be described as a plant growing in the wrong place at the wrong time. Weeds compete with other plants in the flower bed for water, minerals and light. Weeds are very good competitors. They are well adapted to survive competition because:

- many produce huge numbers of seeds;
- they are usually able to flourish in relatively poor soil conditions; and
- their seeds germinate (grow) quickly in poor soil.

Animals can adapt by moving away from areas of large populations, e.g. bees swarm and move on when the colony gets too crowded.

Table 6.1 Ways in which organisms adapt to reduce competition

Organism	Resource	Adaptation	Example
Plants	Water	Take water from different depths	Grass roots lie near the surface, dandelion roots take water from further down.
Animals	Food	Occupy different food niches	Swallows feed on insects on the wing, blackbirds feed on earthworms and fruit.

Predation is the act of hunting, killing and eating prey.

Predator: the organism that hunts, kills and eats its prey.

Prey is the organism that is eaten by the predator.

Predation

The second most important factor controlling population size is predation. Predation occurs when an organism (the **predator**) lives by hunting, killing and eating another organism (the **prey**). For example, spiders are predators of many insects (Fig 6.7); birds eating seeds are also predators as they kill the embryo (baby) plants; and humans are predators when they catch fish and hunt game birds as food.

Predator adaptations

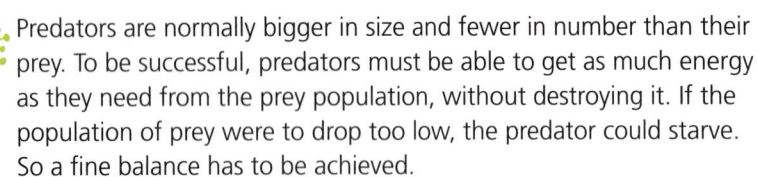

Predators are normally bigger in size and fewer in number than their prey. To be successful, predators must be able to get as much energy as they need from the prey population, without destroying it. If the population of prey were to drop too low, the predator could starve. So a fine balance has to be achieved.

- Keen eyesight, hearing and sense of smell and dentition (number and arrangement of teeth) suited to killing prey (Fig 6.8).
- Catching whatever is easiest – spending a long time chasing prey is a waste of energy. Often it is easier to catch old or sick prey or to scavenge.
- Being able to change diet as numbers of prey change reduces the risk of starvation. Foxes and spiders will do this.
- Living in groups (packs) can help locate food and also may make prey easier to catch.
- Being able to migrate to areas where the prey is more plentiful.
- Camouflage, which allows the predator to be concealed while hunting its prey.

6.7 A spider preying on a fly

6.8 Birds of prey have keen eyesight and sharp talons

Ecological Relationships and Population Dynamics | 06

ALL OF THE MATERIAL IN THIS CHAPTER IS HL ONLY

| 6.9 | Cactus spines deter predators |

| 6.10 | The peacock butterfly |

Prey adaptations

Just as predators have adaptations to help them survive, prey also have special features to prevent them being caught and eaten by predators. There are a number of these defence adaptations:
- Many plants, such as holly and cacti, have developed thorns, spines and stings to ward off predators (Fig 6.9).
- Some plants and animals have a nasty taste to deter predators, e.g. giant hogweed and the caterpillar of the large white butterfly.
- Staying in large groups – in flocks and herds, like deer – can help survival.
- Camouflage colouration enables prey to blend in with their surroundings, e.g. greenfly.
- Warning colouration as seen in many butterflies and moths (Fig 6.10) affords protection. When the peacock butterfly opens its wings, the spots on the wings appear as eyes. This frightens off predators.

Predator/prey relationships

A delicate balance exists between populations of predators and their prey in a habitat.
- If the number of prey increases, this leads to an increase in the number of predators.
- The prey population declines (it is being eaten), and this results in competition between the predators, which may eventually lead to a decrease in the number of predators. Some may be killed or starved and some will move away to find food elsewhere.
- This in turn allows the numbers of prey to increase again, which leads to an increase in the predator population, and so on.

Fig 6.11 shows the typical fluctuations in population numbers of predators and prey. The predator curve follows closely the pattern of the prey but it lags behind as time is needed for the changes to take effect.
Tip: the predator line will always appear lower and slightly to the right of the prey line.

Symbiosis

The term symbiosis literally means 'living together'. Symbiosis is a relationship between two organisms of different species in which at least one benefits. There are different types of symbiosis, two of which are mutualism and parasitism.

D **Symbiosis** can be defined as a close relationship between two organisms of different species in which at least one of them benefits.

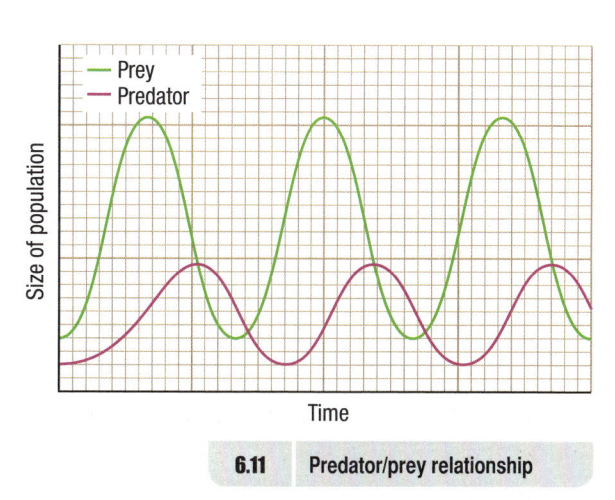

| 6.11 | Predator/prey relationship |

LIFE LEAVING CERTIFICATE BIOLOGY | UNIT 1 THE STUDY OF LIFE | 63

06 Ecological Relationships and Population Dynamics

ALL OF THE MATERIAL IN THIS CHAPTER IS HL ONLY

6.12 Lichen

6.13 A liver fluke

Mutualism

In mutualism, both organisms benefit from the relationship and neither suffers harm.

- Lichens are a good example of mutualism (Fig 6.12). Lichens consist of an algal part and a fungal part. The algal part has chlorophyll and makes food for both itself and the fungus, and the fungal part absorbs minerals and water for both itself and the alga.
- A mycorrhiza is a relationship between a fungus and the roots of a plant. The term mycorrhiza literally means fungus ('mykos') root ('riza'). The plant provides food for the fungus and the fungus supplies minerals for both itself and the plant. The thread-like hyphae of the fungus are better at absorbing minerals than the root hairs of the plants. Mycorrhizal relationships are found in many plants, e.g. in the silver birch tree and in the bee orchid.
- Nitrogen-fixing bacteria in the root nodules of legumes (see Chapter 4).

Parasitism

A **parasite** is an organism that lives on or in another organism (host), feeding on it and causing harm. This is a form of symbiosis. Examples of parasites include disease-causing bacteria, fleas, lice, tapeworms and the potato blight fungus *Phytophthora infestans*.

> **Parasitism** is a relationship between two organisms of different species living together where one benefits and does harm to the other.

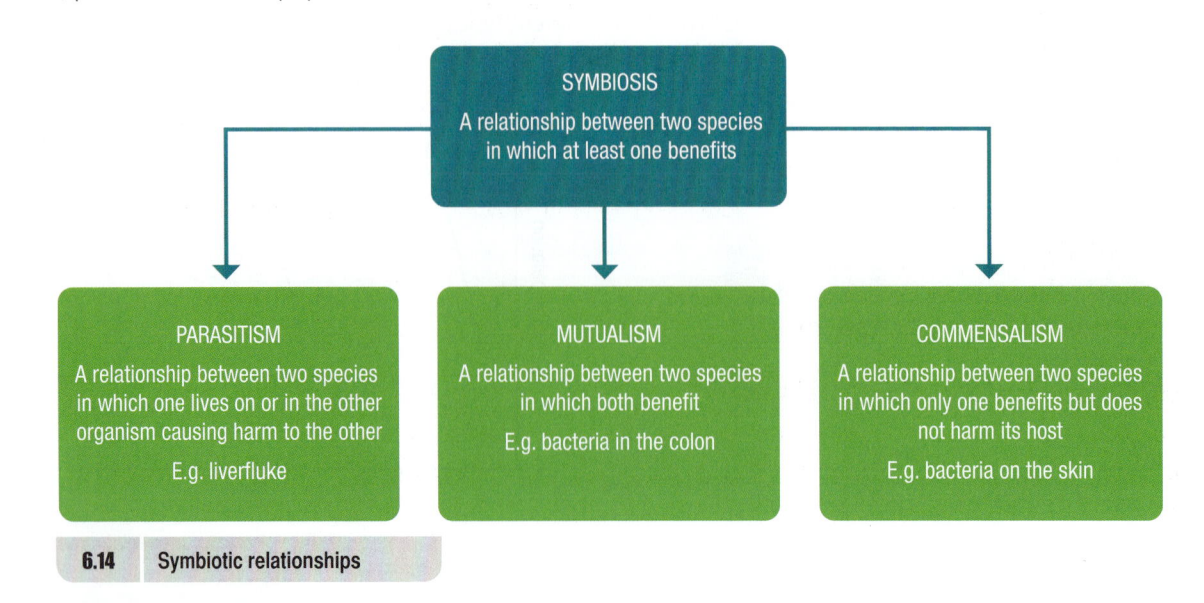

There are two types of parasite:

1. Endoparasites live inside their host, causing harm, e.g. tapeworm, liver fluke (Fig 6.13) and the organism that causes malaria.
2. Ectoparasites live on the outside/surface of the host, causing harm, e.g. fleas, the athlete's foot fungus, sea lice on salmon.

Parasites generally do not kill their host, at least not until their life cycle has been completed. Parasites are well adapted to allow them to survive inside their hosts. The reduction in the numbers of sea trout has been blamed on the parasitic sea louse. Depending on conditions, certain parasites can decimate populations of organisms, e.g. potato blight fungus can destroy whole crops of potatoes, the malaria parasite can kill thousands of humans in an area. In general, parasitism reduces populations.

SYMBIOSIS
A relationship between two species in which at least one benefits

- **PARASITISM**
A relationship between two species in which one lives on or in the other organism causing harm to the other
E.g. liverfluke

- **MUTUALISM**
A relationship between two species in which both benefit
E.g. bacteria in the colon

- **COMMENSALISM**
A relationship between two species in which only one benefits but does not harm its host
E.g. bacteria on the skin

6.14 Symbiotic relationships

ALL OF THE MATERIAL IN THIS CHAPTER IS HL ONLY

Ecological Relationships and Population Dynamics | 06

Population dynamics

Population dynamics is the study of changes that occur in a population and the factors that cause these changes.
- Population numbers change when new individuals are born and when individuals die.
- Populations also change as a result of individuals moving into an area (immigration) or leaving the area (emigration) (Fig 6.15).
- Population numbers change due to the effect of other species in the form of competition, predation and symbiosis.

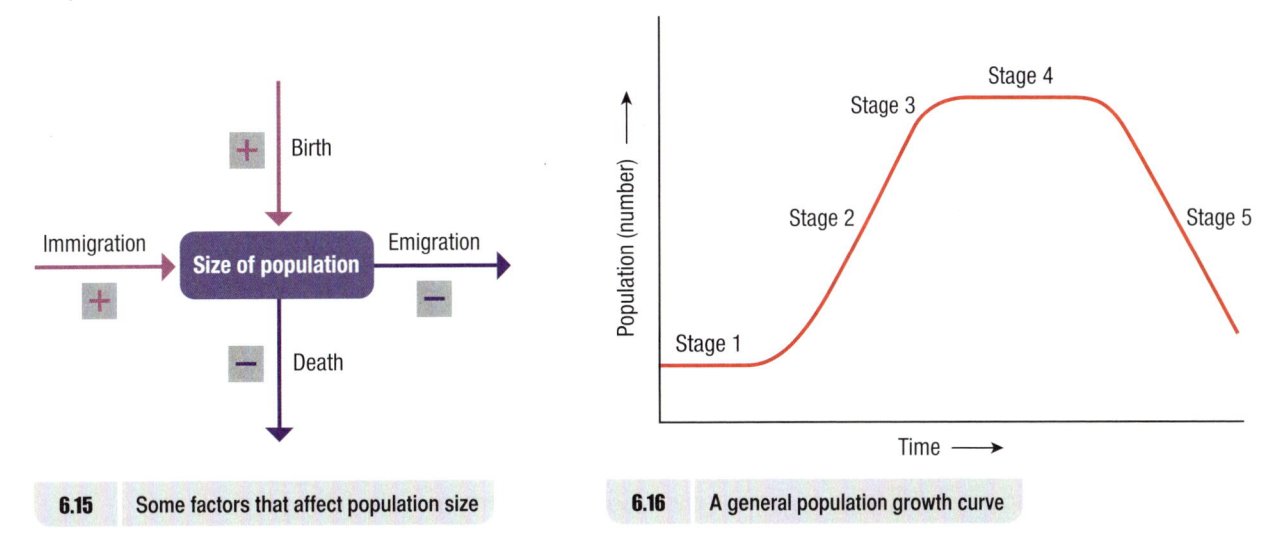

6.15 Some factors that affect population size

6.16 A general population growth curve

General population curves

The graph in Fig 6.16 shows a general population curve. Notice how the population grows quite slowly at first (stage 1) and then over a short period of time the numbers increase very rapidly (stage 2). In stage 3 the population growth slows down and stabilises (stage 4), and eventually the population growth declines (stage 5).

When a few individuals of a species enter a new habitat they have to adjust to the new environment. At this stage little increase in population happens (stage 1). If food is plentiful and conditions are right they start to breed. The numbers increase, slowly at first, but then more rapidly (stage 2), and finally the numbers level off (stage 3).

Why does the growth slow down? Possible causes include:
- The food begins to run out and some individuals starve or move to another area.
- There is not enough room for the pairs of animals to find breeding sites.
- Overcrowding can lead to the spread of disease and wastes begin to build up.
- Because numbers are higher, individuals are more easily killed off by predators.

In some cases, population sizes remain constant, e.g. trees in a well-established woodland. But in general, natural populations fluctuate.

In predator/prey relationships, some of the factors that contribute to the fluctuating numbers are:
- food availability;
- concealment;
- movement to an area of more abundant food.

Changes in the human population

Sometimes populations do not level off. Instead they keep on increasing, as for example with the human world population (Fig 6.17). However, some people (the optimists) believe that the human population growth rate will slow down eventually.

06 Ecological Relationships and Population Dynamics

ALL OF THE MATERIAL IN THIS CHAPTER IS HL ONLY

Fig 6.17 shows how world population has grown from earliest times to the present day. Until 1750, the population grew slowly. Then the rate of growth steadily increased until it literally 'exploded' in the 20th century. This sudden increase was a result of fewer infant deaths and people living longer as a result of improved sanitation and medicines, education and disease eradication programmes.

The size of the human population continues to rise, despite fluctuations in many countries, and reached 7 billion in 2013. Some of the reasons why human populations can go down include famine, disease, wars and **contraception**.

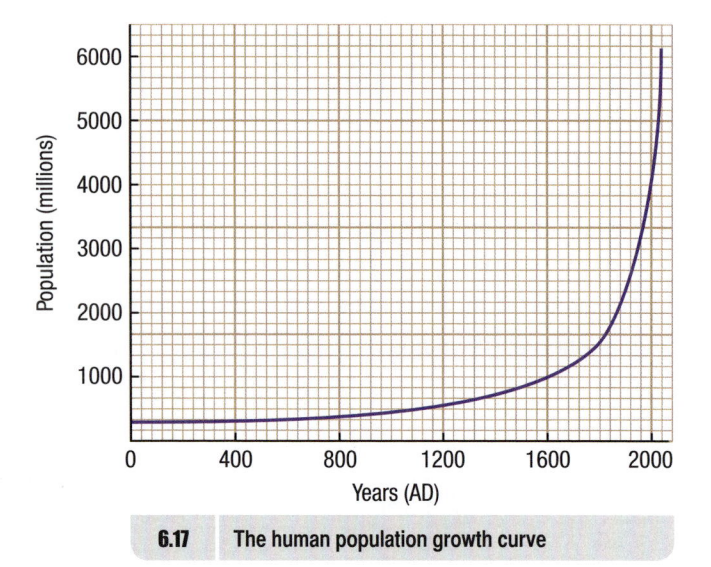

6.17 The human population growth curve

Famine

In 1841, the population of Ireland was 8,175,000; by 1851, it had fallen to 6,552,000. This huge drop in numbers was caused mainly by the failure of the potato crop, which was the staple food of most people. What followed was starvation, death and mass emigration. In 1961 the Irish population was only 2,818,341. The 2011 census shows the population to have reached 4.13 million.

In recent times, famine has devastated populations in many parts of the world, including Ethiopia, Sudan and India. It is estimated that 15 million people die each year from hunger.

Famine is defined as chronic, persistent hunger and it occurs when an acute shortage of food affects a population. Famine may be due to poor farming techniques, crop failure or badly managed food supplies, like the use of cash crops. Starving people cannot work and produce food as efficiently as well-nourished people can.

Disease

Disease is the most frequent cause of human deaths:
- In 1918–19, a world-wide outbreak of influenza claimed the lives of 15–20 million people.
- In 1999 more than 13 million people died from infectious diseases.
- Measles kills approximately 1 million people every year.
- Over 2 million people die each year of malaria.

Wars

Wars are also responsible for reducing the size of the human population (Fig 6.18). In wartime, there is an increased death rate of both soldiers and civilians. Families are separated and there is a decrease in birth rate. During the Second World War (1939–45), over 22 million people died. More recently, conflicts in Syria, in Afghanistan and in parts of Africa have resulted in thousands of deaths. Some 849 people are said to be killed each day due to armed conflict somewhere in the world – that's 35 people every hour.

Contraception

By the mid-19th century (1850), the average number of children born to mothers in Ireland was 8.2. Just over a hundred years later, this number was halved to 4.07 and by 1992 it was 2.1. Better education and more reliable methods and use of contraception have been mainly responsible for the decrease in birth rate, not only in Ireland but in most of the developed world. Contraception, or birth control, is the prevention of conception. More information on the methods of contraception can be found in Chapter 37.

Worldwide, the number of children born each year is greater than the number of people dying. Modern medical practices and disease-prevention programmes involving **vaccination** and **immunisation** have contributed to the reduction in the death rate.

6.18 Armed conflict

ALL OF THE MATERIAL IN THIS CHAPTER IS HL ONLY

Ecological Relationships and Population Dynamics

Summary

- A population is a group of individuals of the same species living in an ecosystem, e.g. the number of daisies in a lawn.

- The size of a population is governed by a number of factors. These include:
    (i) competition
    (ii) predation
    (iii) symbiosis
    (iv) parasitism

- Competition occurs when organisms seek the same resource in a habitat. Competition occurs between organisms for food, space, mates, shelter, light, water and minerals.

- Contest competition is an active physical confrontation between two organisms that allows one to win the resource.

- Scramble competition is a struggle between organisms for a scarce resource in which each organism gets *some* of the resource.

- Plants and animals develop adaptations to avoid competition (see Table 6.1, page 62).

- Predation is the hunting, killing and eating of one organism (the prey) by another (the predator), e.g. ladybirds are predators of greenfly.

Table 6.2 Predator and prey adaptive techniques

Predator adaptive techniques	Prey adaptive techniques
1. Catch large, rather than many small prey.	Animals: 1. Camouflage and warning colouration. 2. Travel in groups.
2. Catch whatever is easy, prevents wasting energy.	Plants: 1. Stings 2. Thorns and hairs
3. Ability to move to areas of more plentiful prey.	

- Symbiosis is a relationship between two organisms of different species in which at least one benefits, e.g. nitrogen-fixing bacteria living in the root nodules of pea plants.

- Parasitism is a relationship between two organisms of different species living together where one benefits and does harm to the other.

- A parasite is an organism that lives on or in another organism of a different species, feeding on it and causing harm. Examples include disease-causing bacteria like the cholera bacterium, viruses, tapeworms, mould on leaves, and fleas and ticks on animals.

- Most populations in an ecosystem show fluctuations in numbers over a period of time. These fluctuations occur because of:
    - births
    - deaths
    - immigration
    - emigration
    - the effect of other species in the form of competition, predation and symbiosis.

- The human population continues to rise despite war, famine, disease and contraception.

Review questions

01 (a) Explain the term population and give an example.
(b) List three factors that control populations.

02 (a) What is meant by competition in relation to population size?
(b) Outline an example of competition amongst (i) plants and (ii) animals.
(c) How can organisms reduce competition in a habitat?

03 (a) Distinguish between contest competition and scramble competition, giving examples in each case.
(b) State, giving a reason for your answer, whether competition is more intense or less intense between members of the same species.
(c) State one adaptive technique of (i) an animal and (ii) a plant to survive competition.

04 (a) What is a predator?
(b) List three features that enable predators to be successful.

05 (a) Look at the photograph of the peacock butterfly (Fig 6.10, page 63). Do you think the butterfly is a predator or prey? Explain your choice of answer.
(b) Suggest what you think the defence mechanisms of the following organisms are: (i) wasps, (ii) zebras, (iii) cactus, (iv) greenfly, (v) nettles.

06 The graph shows the changes in a population of microscopic algae in a lake over the period of one year.

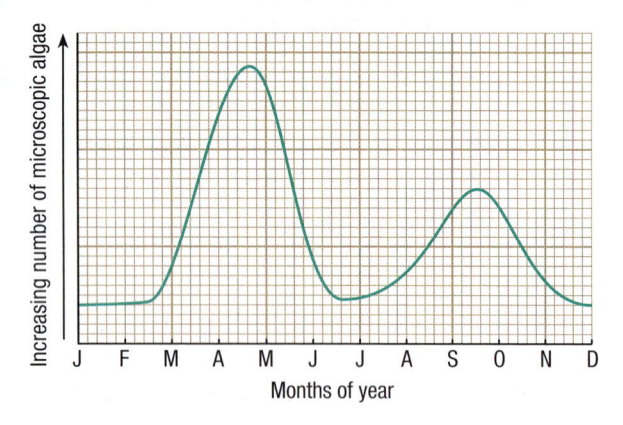

(a) Suggest a reason for the sudden rise in numbers of the algae in spring.
(b) These algae are eaten by water fleas. Copy the graph and then draw in the curve to show the fluctuations in the water flea population over the course of the year.

07 The diagram shows part of a woodland food web.

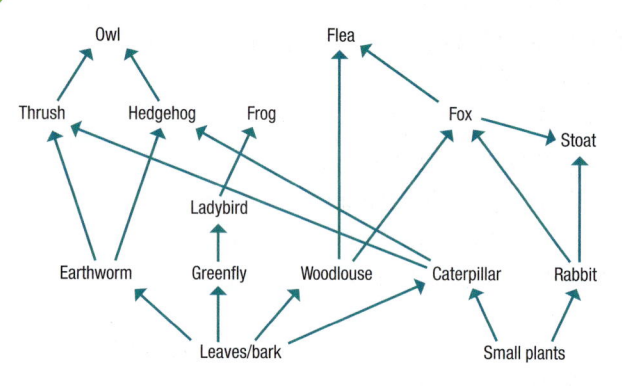

(a) Construct a food chain with four organisms from the food web.
(b) From the food web name (i) a producer, (ii) the prey of the ladybirds.
(c) How many trophic levels are there in this food web?
(d) Draw a pyramid of numbers to represent one of the food chains in the web.
(e) Use the words 'increase', 'decrease' or 'stay the same' to suggest what might happen to the populations of caterpillars and ladybirds if all the greenfly were removed. In each case give a reason for your answer.

08 A classic example of predation is the fluctuations in population numbers of the Canadian lynx (a member of the cat family) and the snowshoe hare, which provides up to 90% of the diet of the lynx. Changes in the population were recorded over 60 years, as the graph below shows.

(a) Explain the terms 'predator' and 'prey'.
(b) Use the graph to identify which line represents the predator and which is the prey. Give one reason for your choice.
(c) How does the predator respond to increased numbers of prey?
(d) What changes took place in the prey population between 1880 and 1900?
(e) What is the mean maximum population density of the lynx during the period shown?

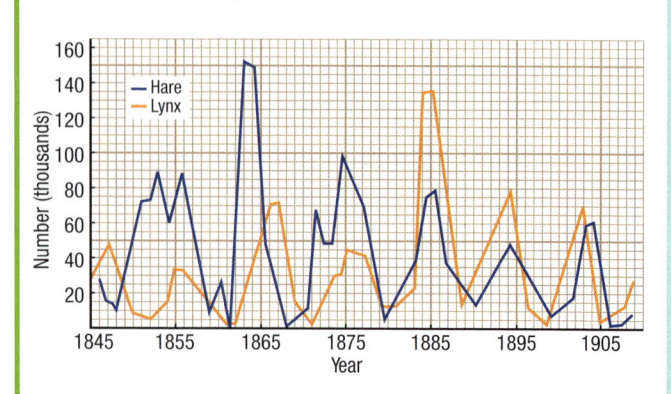

Examination style questions

Section A

01 Distinguish between the following pairs of terms as used in ecology.
(a) A population and a community.
(b) Scramble and contest competition.
(c) Immigration and emigration.
(d) Predator and prey.
(e) Parasitism and symbiosis.

02 Study the graph of human population and answer the following questions.

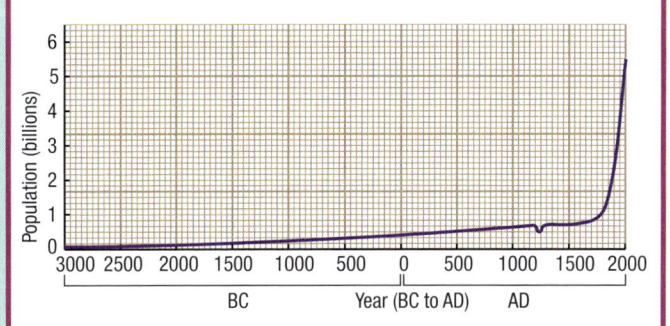

(a) Suggest two reasons why the population showed little increase between 3000 BC and AD 1000.
(b) The graph shows an interruption in the population growth between AD 1000 and AD 1500. Suggest a reason for this.
(c) Give two possible reasons for the eventual huge increase in the human population.
(d) A population cannot continue to increase indefinitely. Suggest one reason for this.
(e) A population of wild animals is very unlikely to show a pattern of population growth similar to the human one. Why do you think this is the case?

Section C

03 A population is a group of individuals of the same species which occupies a particular habitat. Over a period of time the size of wild animal populations tends to stay reasonably constant despite fluctuations within any one year and between years.

(a) Give three possible reasons that could account for fluctuations in the size of a population in a habitat.
(b) Give two examples of the possible consequences if a population should be wiped out.
(c) For a named animal outline how you would monitor its population.

04 The graph below shows the changes in the moose population on Isle Royale in Lake Superior, Canada. Moose colonised the island at the beginning of the 20th century. No predators were present until the arrival of timber wolves in 1949. Moose then became the main prey species of the timber wolves.

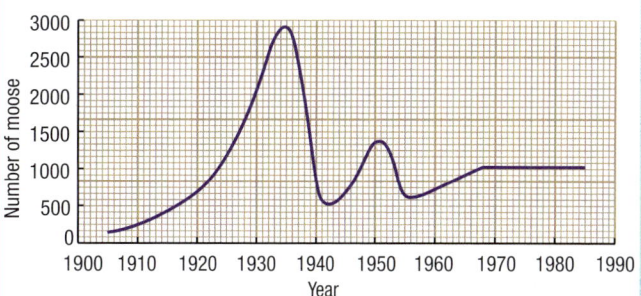

(a) Explain the terms predator, prey and parasite.
(b) Suggest a reason for the rapid expansion of the moose population between 1925 and 1935, other than the absence of predators.
(c) Suggest a reason for the decline in the moose population between 1935 and 1940.
(d) What changes took place in the moose population after the arrival of the timber wolves?
(e) Would you expect a similar population trend for moose if an ectoparasite rather than a predator arrived on the Isle Royale in 1949? Explain your answer.

05 (a) Name the habitat you have studied.
(b) What is a predator? Name a predator in the habitat you have studied.
(c) At which trophic level(s) would you find predators in a food web?
(d) In the case of the predator that you named in (b) above describe an external feature that is an adaptation to its life in the habitat.

06 Ecological Relationships and Population Dynamics

ALL OF THE MATERIAL IN THIS CHAPTER IS HL ONLY

Leaving Certificate examination questions

Section A

01
(i) Name **three** factors that can affect the human population.
(ii) Suggest **two** reasons why the human population increased so rapidly from the mid-1800s.
(iii) Suggest what could happen to biological diversity as the human population continues to increase.

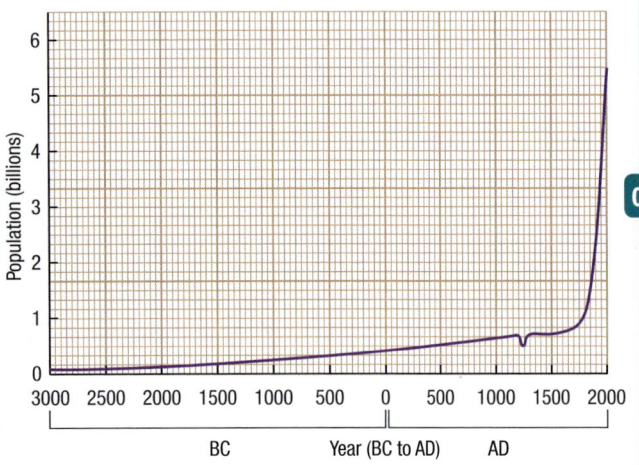

[Graph: Population (billions) vs Year (BC to AD), from 3000 BC to 2000 AD, showing population rising from near 0 to over 5 billion]

2014 HL Q. 15 (a)

02 The graph below shows the fluctuations in the population of a predatory species over many years.

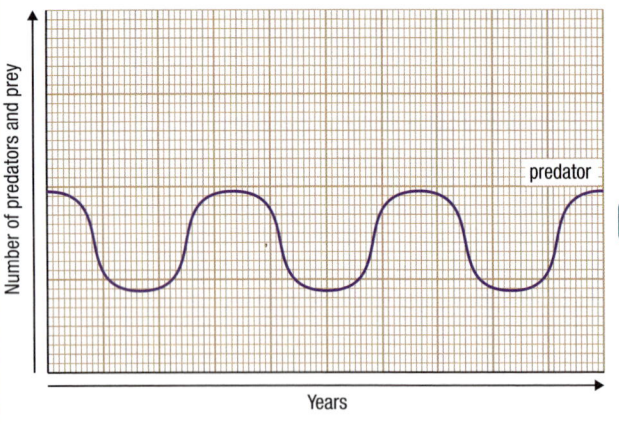

[Graph: Number of predators and prey vs Years, showing oscillating predator curve]

(a) Copy the graph into your answer book. Then on the same axes and using a dashed line (-----), show how you think the population of the predator's main prey might vary over the same time span.
(b) Give an explanation of the graph you have drawn for the **prey** species.
(c) Do you think that population graphs for a host species and its main parasite would show similar fluctuations? Explain your answer.
(d) Suggest a role for parasites in the overall scheme of nature.
   (i) Name **two** predators.
   (ii) Give **one** adaptive technique in the case of **each** predator.

2013 HL Q. 15

03 (a) (i) Distinguish between contest competition and scramble competition by writing a sentence about each.
(ii) Name a factor, other than competition, that controls wild populations.
(b) What deduction is it possible to make from each of the following observations?
   (i) In a particular area the population of a predator did not decline following a big reduction in the population of its main prey.
   (ii) Mortality levels resulting from infection by a particular virus tend to decline over the years.
   (iii) Where some members of a species remain in the same general area throughout life and some members are migratory, mortality levels tend to be higher in the migratory part of the population.

2011 HL Q. 10

04 (i) What term do ecologists use to describe an animal that kills and eats other animals?
(ii) What term is used to describe the animal that is killed and eaten?
(iii) If the population of the animals in (b) declines, suggest **two** possible consequences for the animals in (a).
(iv) Give **four** factors that influence the size of the human population.

2007 HL Q. 12 (c)

Ecological Relationships and Population Dynamics 06

ALL OF THE MATERIAL IN THIS CHAPTER IS HL ONLY

Leaving Certificate examination questions

05 The graph below shows the relative sizes of a lemming population (histogram or bars) and the percentage phosphorus in forage (curve) over a number of years.

(i) What relationship is indicated between the percentage of phosphorus in forage and the size of the lemming population?

(ii) Suggest an explanation for this relationship.

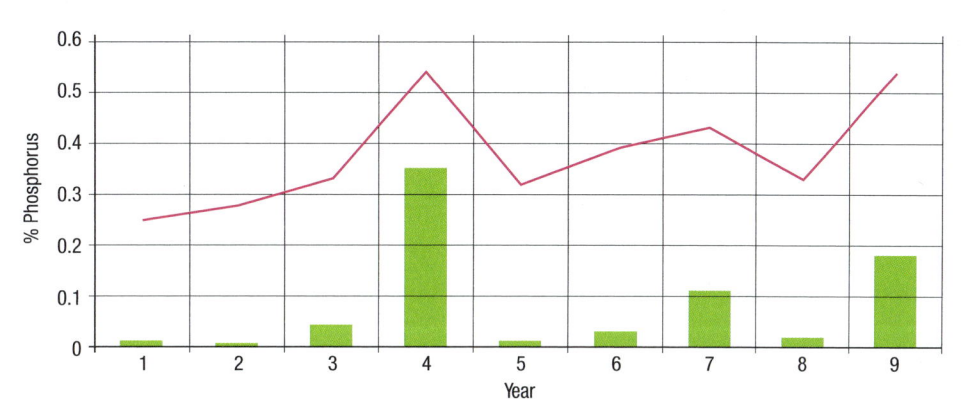

2006 HL Q. 10 (a)

06 Lemmings are small rodents that are widespread in northern latitudes. The graph shows the fluctuations in lemming numbers in northern Manitoba between 1929 and 1943.

[Adapted from J. P. Finerty (1980), *The Population Ecology of Cycles in Small Mammals*, Yale University Press, New Haven.]

(i) The graph indicates that population peaks occur at fairly regular intervals. What is the approximate average time between these peaks?

(ii) What is the mean maximum population density (numbers per hectare) for the period covered by the graph?

(iii) What is a predator? The Arctic fox is a predator of the lemming. Copy the graph into your answer book and draw on it a graph to show how you would expect the population of the Arctic fox to have varied in northern Manitoba during the period 1929–1943.

(iv) Suggest **two** factors other than predation that might account for the declines in lemmings shown in the graph.

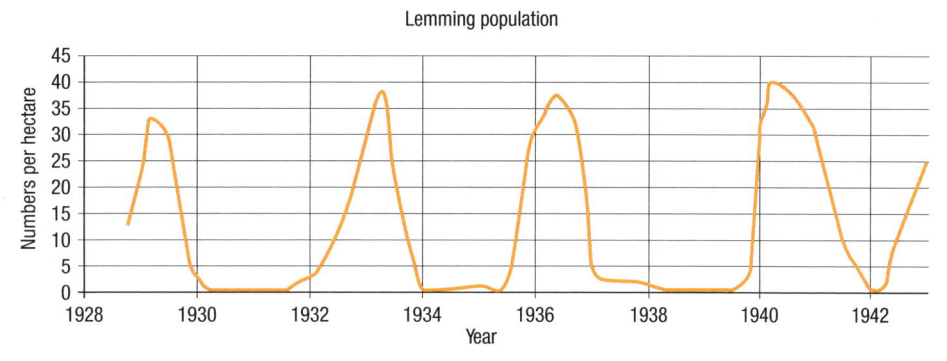

2004 HL Q. 10 (c)

Past examination questions

HL	2014 Q. 15 (a), (b) (ii)–(v), (c) (i)–(iii)	2013 Q. 15 (a), (c)	2011 Q. 10 (a), (b)	2008 Q. 10 (a), (b)
	2007 Q. 12 (c)	2006 Q. 10 (a)	2005 Q. 12 (a), Q. 13 (a)	2004 Q. 10 (c)

07 The Study of an Ecosystem

After studying this chapter you should be able to:

1. Appreciate the diversity of living organisms in your chosen ecosystem and study their interrelationships with each other and with the non-living environment.
2. Map the ecosystem and identify a number of habitats in it.
3. Identify and know how to use a number of different collection apparatus for use in the study of an ecosystem.
4. Identify using a simple key five plants (flora) and five animals (fauna) from a selected named ecosystem. Note any one adaptation for one of the flora and one of the fauna named.
5. Identify the abiotic factors in the ecosystem and investigate any three.
6. Distinguish between a qualitative and a quantitative survey of an ecosystem.
7. Describe both percentage frequency and percentage cover techniques and conduct one quantitative survey of plants in your named ecosystem.
8. Conduct one quantitative survey of animals in your named ecosystem.
9. Compile two food chains, a food web and a pyramid of numbers from the information obtained in your study of the ecosystem.
10. Prepare a report of the results obtained to include an analysis of the results, identification of sources of error and of any ecological issues related to the ecosystem.

Introduction to ecosystems

1. **Ecosystems** are ecological units consisting of a living (**biotic**) and a non-living (**abiotic**) component. A woodland, hedgerow, meadow, pond, seashore and the school grounds are all examples of ecosystems (Fig 7.1). (See Tables 7.1 to 7.5 for an overview of a number of ecosystems.)

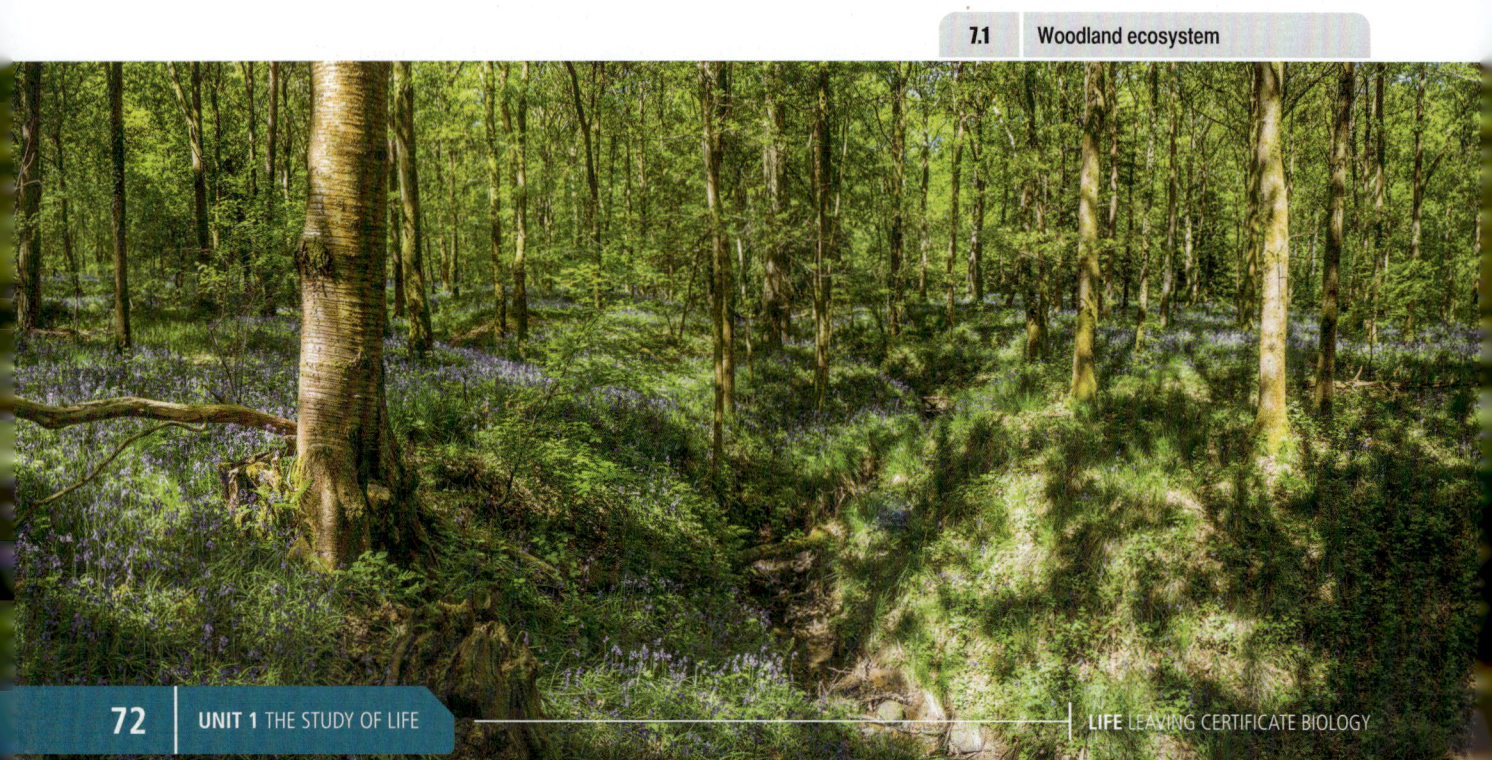

7.1 Woodland ecosystem

7.2 Different habitats in a pond ecosystem

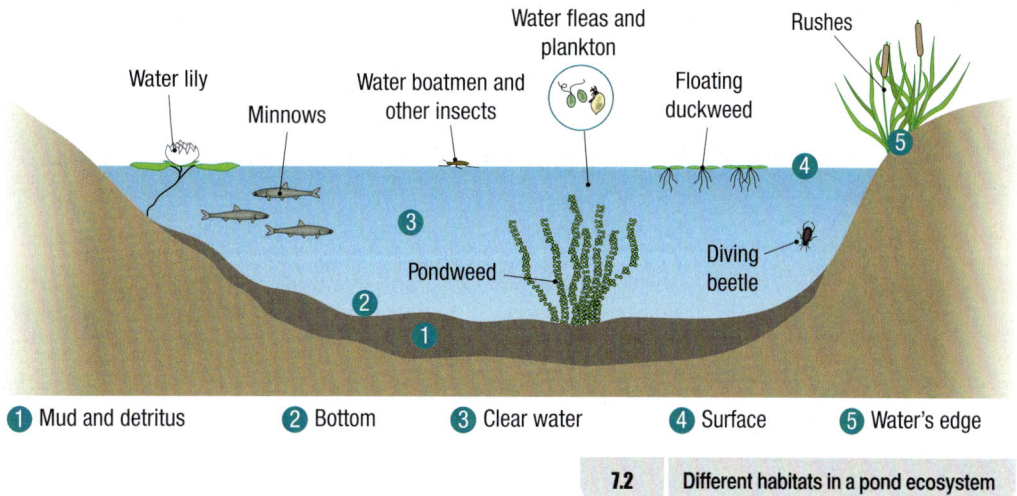

Ecosystems in turn consist of numerous **habitats** in which communities of **organisms** live and interact.

A map can be constructed of an ecosystem to illustrate the position of the different habitats within it (Fig 7.2).

We study ecosystems in terms of the organisms present and their non-living surroundings. In our study, we are trying to answer a number of questions, including:

1. What organisms are present?
2. Where in the ecosystem do they live?
3. Who do they eat and/or who eats them?
4. In what ways do they relate to each other, other than in terms of feeding?
5. What abiotic factors are important in the ecosystem?
6. How do we as humans impact on the ecosystem?

> A **community** is made up of groups of different species living together.

Selecting an ecosystem

The ecosystem you choose to study will depend upon a number of things, but most important is ease of access. You must be able to visit the area on a regular basis so that you can observe the organisms easily, and learn how they adapt to and survive in their environment.

The school grounds are an obvious choice of ecosystem and they often contain a number of habitats, e.g. the playing field(s), a hedge, pond, old wall, etc. Other ecosystems to study might be a woodland, a meadow, a stream or some wasteland. The rocky seashore and rock pools are examples of marine ecosystems that abound with life and may be suitable if your school is near the coast. Whatever ecosystem you choose, bear in mind the following before you set out:

- Obtain the owner's permission to carry out an investigation on private property.
- Dress properly for the area, time of year and weather. Suitable footwear is especially important.
- Leave the habitats undisturbed, as far as possible. If you turn over a stone or a rock, always remember to replace it, otherwise the animals that live there might die.
- Do not pick or collect any protected species. A number of species, such as the common frog, are protected under the Wildlife Act 1975 and Amendment 2000.
- Close gates behind you and take your litter home.
- Be aware of dangers such as the depth of water in streams and ponds.

Overview of a grassland, a woodland and a seashore ecosystem

Grassland

Most grassland ecosystems are created by humans, e.g. fields, meadows and lawns. They are generally used for grazing livestock, growing crops such as barley, and as an amenity in parks and gardens. Most are exposed to a lot of light and the plants that grow well are tolerant of the sun. Common plants and animals of grassland are listed below.

Plants: broad-leaf grass, plantain, buttercup, vetch, chickweed, dandelion, daisy, clover.

Animals: earthworm, snail, greenfly, bee, spider, blackbird, robin, field mouse.

Organisms show a variety of adaptations that allow them to survive in a given habitat. Some examples of adaptation shown by grassland flora and fauna can be found in Table 7.1.

Grassland plant or animal	Adaptations
Broad-leaf grasses	Shoot tips are below the ground to survive grazing.
Dandelions and daisies	Have broad leaves to capture the sunshine for photosynthesis. Their flowers attract pollinators.
Greenfly	Green colour gives good camouflage. Piercing mouthparts to suck sap.
Blackbird	Shape of beak suited to getting earthworms out of the soil.

Table 7.1 Some grassland plant and animal adaptations

Woodland

A woodland is made up of five layers above the ground and the soil beneath. The layers above ground are the canopy (tree), shrub, field, ground and leaf litter. The dominant plants are either deciduous or non-deciduous trees. The shading effect of the taller trees limits the available light to the layers below and this in turn determines what plants and animals will be found. In Ireland there are two main woodland types, based on the soil type. Typically oak woods are found on acid soil and ash/elm on more alkaline soil.

Plant layer	Oak wood pH < 5.5	Ash/elm wood pH > 6.0
Canopy	Oak	Ash, elm
Shrub	Holly, mountain ash	Hazel, hawthorn
Field	Wood sorrel, foxglove, ferns	Primrose, bluebell, ferns
Ground	Mosses	Mosses
Leaf litter	Dead/decomposing leaves	Dead/decomposing leaves

Table 7.2 Plant layers in a woodland

Animals of the woodland: earthworm, badger, greenfly, caterpillars, butterflies, moths, slugs, snails, mice, blackbirds, chaffinches.

Woodland plant or animal	Adaptations
Bluebell and primrose	Flower early in spring before the leaves of the canopy layer reduce the light.
Oak, ash, elm	Trees have thick bark to protect against cold, and attack by insects.
Badger	Sharp claws for digging.
Woodlice, earthworm	Dark body colour provides camouflage and protection from predators.

Table 7.3 Some woodland plant and animal adaptations

The rocky seashore

The rocky seashore is an interesting ecosystem to study, with nearly every major group of animal represented. The tides play a very important part in the life of seashore organisms. When the tide is out, the plants and animals are exposed to the air and fresh water, if it rains. When the tide is in, the organisms are submerged in sea water. Seashore plants and animals have special adaptations to help them cope with their ever changing environment (see Table 7.5).

The rocky shore can be divided into four zones – the splash zone, upper shore, middle shore and lower shore.

Zone	Location	Plants and animals
Splash	Nearest the road and is never covered by the tide.	Plants: sea pinks, green algae Animals: periwinkles
Upper shore	Only covered by water during very high tides. [Flat wrack marks the boundary with middle shore.]	Plants: channel weed. Animals: limpets, periwinkles, acorn barnacles, sandhoppers.
Middle shore	Covered by water twice a day. [Serrated wrack marks the boundary with the lower shore.]	Plants: sea lettuce, flat wrack, serrated wrack, bladderwrack (the wracks are all brown algae). Animals: periwinkles, limpets, top shells, dog whelks.
Lower shore	Always covered by water, except for very low tides.	Plants: red seaweeds, oar weed (kelp). Animals: sea urchins, shanny, blenny, starfish, sea anemones, sponges, mussels, shrimps, crabs.

Table 7.4   Some plants and animals of the rocky shore

Rocky shore plant or animal	Adaptations
Brown algae, such as bladderwrack	Have strong root-like structures (holdfast) to anchor them to the rocks to withstand wave action. They have air bladders to allow them to float.
Brown algae	Have a brown pigment in addition to chlorophyll, which allows light absorption under water.
Limpets, barnacles and whelks	Have a hard shell to prevent drying out when the tide is out.
Blenny and shanny	Streamlined body which makes it easier to swim.

Table 7.5   Rocky shore plant and animal adaptations

The steps involved in an ecosystem study

Once you have selected the ecosystem you are going to study you are ready to begin your fieldwork. The study of an ecosystem involves the following steps.

1. Make a simple **map** of the ecosystem.
2. **Identify** a number of **habitats** within the ecosystem.
3. Observe the variety of organisms in the ecosystem and make a **collection** of plants and animals using suitable methods and pieces of equipment.
4. **Identify** five plants and five animals present using a simple **key**.
5. Observe, **measure** and record three **abiotic factors**, together with the seasonal changes that affect the ecosystem.
6. Carry out a **quantitative survey** of the plants and animals to obtain information about the numbers and distribution of organisms.
7. **Analyse** and assess the **results** obtained.

1. Make a simple map

Use bamboo canes and string to mark out and measure the baseline of the ecosystem.

1. Choose a suitable scale (e.g. 0.5 m = 1 cm) and draw your baseline to scale on a piece of graph paper.
2. Use a tape measure to measure the perpendicular distance of any natural landmarks, such as trees, gates, paths and ponds, from the baseline.
3. Transfer the measurements to the graph paper and join the points to get the shape of the landmarks. Label the landmarks.

07 | The Study of an Ecosystem

4. Find the direction of North using the compass and mark this on your map, and also include the scale used (Fig 7.3).

If the ecosystem is on a slope, e.g. the rocky seashore, then a profile map needs to be drawn.

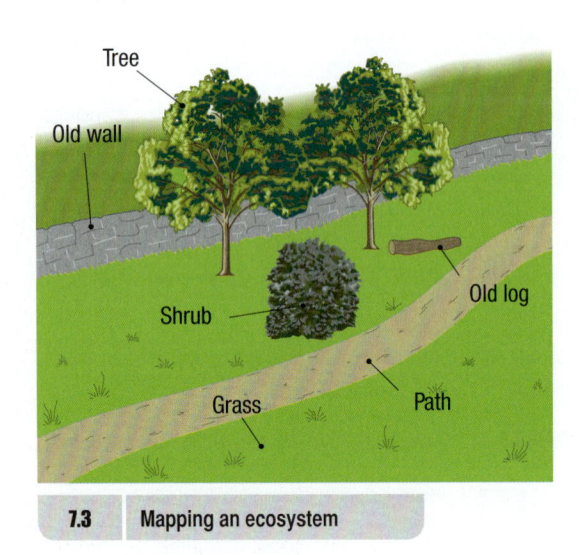

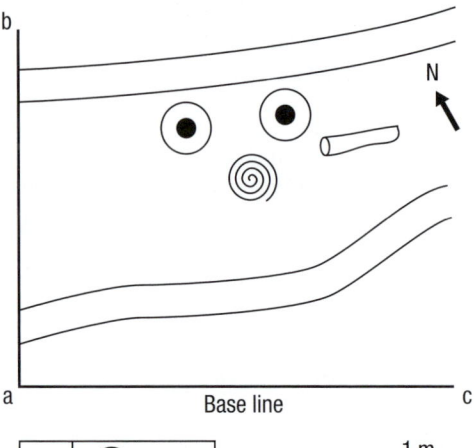

7.3 Mapping an ecosystem

2. Identify the habitats

Within any ecosystem there are a number of habitats. For example, in the school grounds there may be an old wall, a garden, playing fields, paths, a hedge and even a pond. Each of these habitats will have its own community of organisms that interact with each other and with the non-living environment.

Most organisms are found in a certain habitat because they can adapt to the environment in a particular way. The brown seaweed *Fucus* is adapted to living on the rocky shore by having strong root-like structures to anchor it to the rocks and by secreting mucilage to prevent it drying up when the tide goes out. Greenfly are green in colour and can blend in with the leaves of the plants on which they live (Fig 7.4 and 7.5).

A study of the different habitats in the ecosystem can be carried out by different groups within the class and the results pooled to reflect the ecology of the whole ecosystem.

7.4 Fucus

3. Collect plants and animals

The purpose of collecting plants and animals is to identify what is present in the ecosystem. If an organism can be identified in situ, i.e. where it is found, then it is not necessary to collect a specimen.

Plants

Small plants, such as microscopic algae found in ponds, can be collected using a plankton net (Table 7.6).

No special equipment is needed for collecting larger plants. Trees are easily identified by their leaves and bark. To identify an unknown plant, a piece of the stem/branch with leaves, and flowers if possible, can be photographed or collected and brought back to the laboratory. Each type of plant need be picked only once and placed in a plastic bag labelled with the place in which the plant was found.

Animals

Most animals move around from place to place and are not always easy to see. A variety of special collection methods is necessary to reveal and catch them. Simple methods include digging the soil with a trowel and looking under stones and rocks.

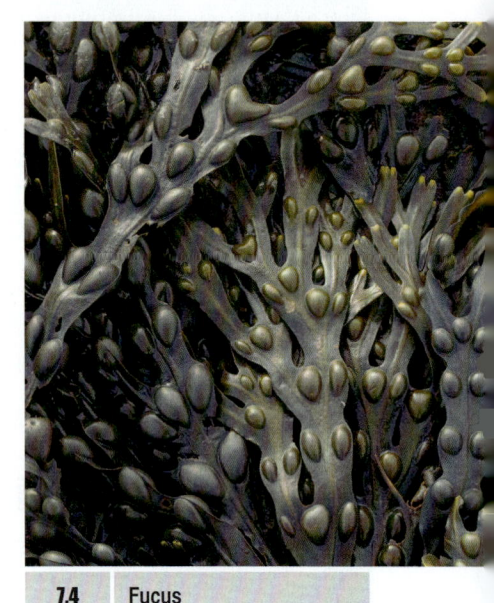

7.5 greenfly show good adaptations for survival

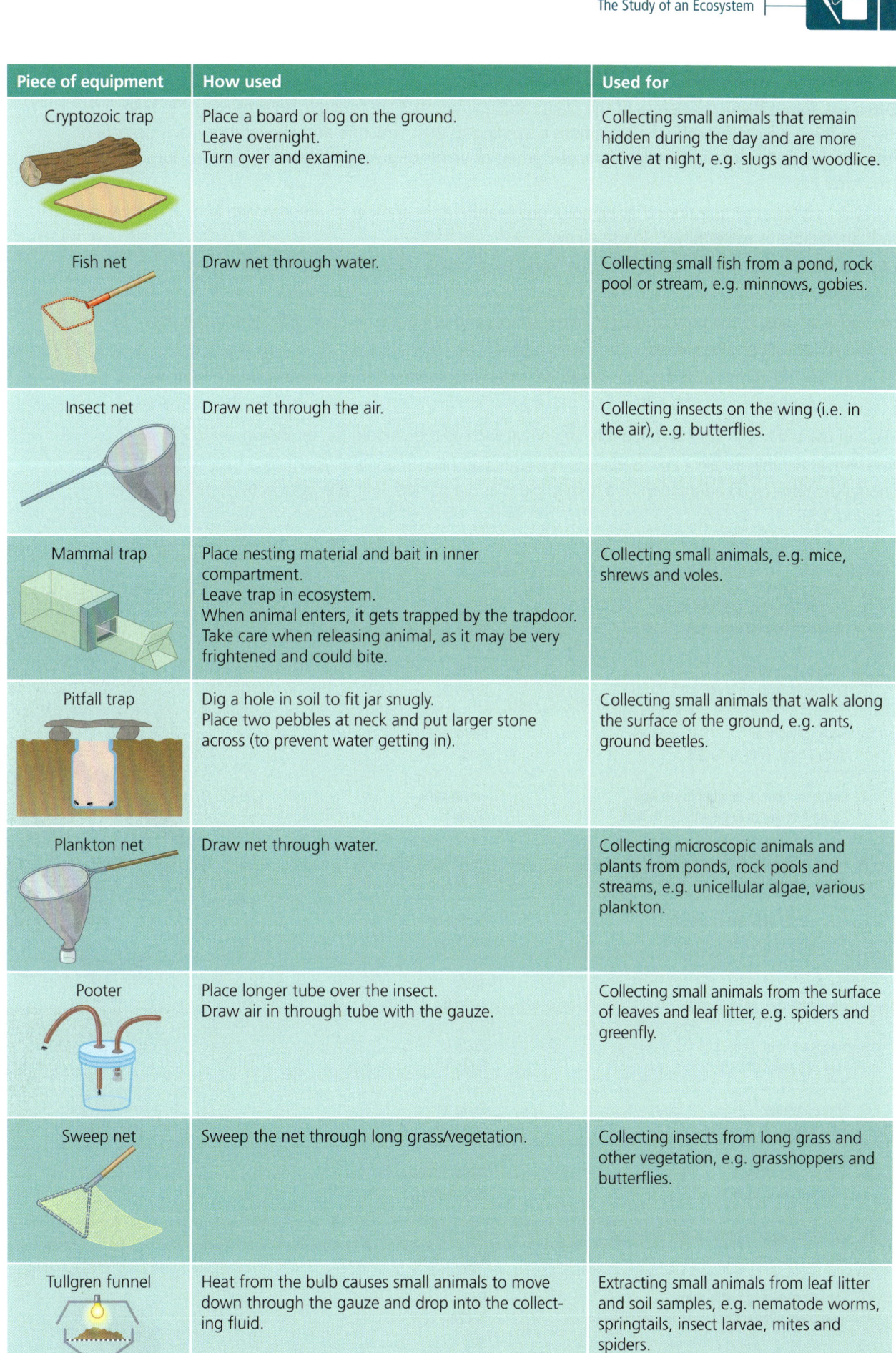

Piece of equipment	How used	Used for
Cryptozoic trap	Place a board or log on the ground. Leave overnight. Turn over and examine.	Collecting small animals that remain hidden during the day and are more active at night, e.g. slugs and woodlice.
Fish net	Draw net through water.	Collecting small fish from a pond, rock pool or stream, e.g. minnows, gobies.
Insect net	Draw net through the air.	Collecting insects on the wing (i.e. in the air), e.g. butterflies.
Mammal trap	Place nesting material and bait in inner compartment. Leave trap in ecosystem. When animal enters, it gets trapped by the trapdoor. Take care when releasing animal, as it may be very frightened and could bite.	Collecting small animals, e.g. mice, shrews and voles.
Pitfall trap	Dig a hole in soil to fit jar snugly. Place two pebbles at neck and put larger stone across (to prevent water getting in).	Collecting small animals that walk along the surface of the ground, e.g. ants, ground beetles.
Plankton net	Draw net through water.	Collecting microscopic animals and plants from ponds, rock pools and streams, e.g. unicellular algae, various plankton.
Pooter	Place longer tube over the insect. Draw air in through tube with the gauze.	Collecting small animals from the surface of leaves and leaf litter, e.g. spiders and greenfly.
Sweep net	Sweep the net through long grass/vegetation.	Collecting insects from long grass and other vegetation, e.g. grasshoppers and butterflies.
Tullgren funnel	Heat from the bulb causes small animals to move down through the gauze and drop into the collecting fluid.	Extracting small animals from leaf litter and soil samples, e.g. nematode worms, springtails, insect larvae, mites and spiders.

Table 7.6 Pieces of equipment used to collect animals in an ecosystem

4. Identify organisms using a simple key

Often we do not know the names of the plants and animals that are found in an ecosystem. To help identify them we can describe the specimens according to their structure and appearance. Each description forms a clue that helps us identify a particular group of plants or animals. We call this set of clues a biological key.

A key asks a series of questions that pinpoint one feature after another of an organism and, in a stepwise fashion, enable us to identify it. To use a key:

- Answer 'yes' or 'no' to each pair of questions, by deciding what set of features suits your specimen best.
- You then look to the right of the set of questions, and using the number indicated, move down to the correct set of alternatives.
- Continue doing this until a name is reached, often accompanied by a drawing, which matches your specimen.

We can use the key in Fig 7.6 to identify an animal such as the woodlouse, as shown in Fig 7.7.

You should be able to use a key to identify five plants and five animals in your chosen ecosystem. A note should be made of an adaptation of a named plant and a named animal in your ecosystem (see Tables 7.1, 7.3 and 7.5).

SIMPLE KEY TO IDENTIFY ANIMALS IN A SOIL SAMPLE

1.	Body not segmented* externally	Go to 2
	Body segmented externally	Go to 4
2.	Body soft, with shell	snail
	Body soft, with no shell	Go to 3
3.	Body cylindrical**	nematode
	Body plump with tentacles	slug
4.	Large number of segments, no legs	earthworm
	Large number of segments, with legs	Go to 5
5.	Many segments and > 14 pairs legs	Go to 6
	Many segments and < 14 pairs legs	Go to 7
6.	One pair of legs per segment	centipede
	Two pairs of legs per segment	milipede
7.	No legs	grub
	Has legs	Go to 8
8.	Has 3 pairs of legs	Go to 9
	Has > 3 pairs of legs	Go to 10
9.	Has no wings	Go to 11
	Has wings	Go to 12
10.	Has 4 pairs of legs	spider group
	Has > 4 pairs of legs	woodlouse
11.	Wingless insect, jumps when disturbed	springtail
	Larva	beetle larva
12.	One pair of wings with veins	fly
	Two pairs wings, front ones act as covers	beetle

* segmented means divided up into sections or rings
** cylindrical means shaped like a tube

7.6 A key to identify soil animals

1. Body not segmented externally   2
   Body segmented externally   4

   The animals has segments so go to Number 4.

4. Large number of segments, no legs   earthworm
   Large number of segments, with legs   5

   The animal has a large number of segments with legs, so go to number 5.

5. Many segments and > 14 pairs legs   6
   Many segments and < 14 pairs legs   7

   Your specimen hasn't got more than 14 pairs legs, so go to number 7.

7. No legs   fly larva (grub)
   Has legs   8

   The animals has legs, so go to 8.

8. Has 3 pairs of legs   9
   Has > 3 pairs of legs   10

   The creature has > 3 pairs of legs, so go to 10.

10. Has 4 pairs of legs   spider group
    Has > 4 pairs of legs   woodlouse

    The animal you have has > 4 pairs legs so according to this key it is a woodlouse.

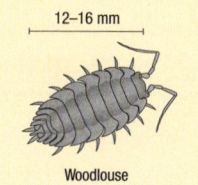

7.7   Using the key to identify a woodlouse

5. Measure three abiotic factors

The abiotic (non-living environment) component affects the number and distribution of organisms in an ecosystem. The abiotic factors you will be concerned with will depend upon the type of ecosystem you are studying, e.g. terrestrial or aquatic. You are required to measure three abiotic factors that affect your ecosystem.

Abiotic factor	Importance	Instrument/technique used
Temperature (soil/water/air)	Temperature on a given day is not of much value; it is longer-term seasonal temperatures that affect organisms.	Thermometer/digital thermometer.
Light intensity	Light is essential for photosynthesis.	Light meter/light probe.
pH (soil/water)	pH affects the growth of most plants. If the soil is too acidic, plants may die.	Universal indicator solution (paper) pH meter and a probe.
Air currents	For seed and fruit dispersal/affect pollinators such as bees.	Anemometer measures wind speed.
Salinity of water	Affects what organisms can survive.	Conductivity probe and meter.

Table 7.7   Measurement of some abiotic factors

SYLLABUS REQUIREMENT:

You need to know how to measure any three abiotic factors affecting your habitat.

07 | The Study of an Ecosystem

Investigation 7.1
To measure the temperature of soil in a habitat

1. Place a soil thermometer (Fig 7.8) into the soil.
2. Leave for 3 minutes to adjust.
3. Take the reading and record.
4. Repeat twice and get an average.
5. Take readings in a number of places in the habitat.

The temperature at a given moment is not of great value. Changes in temperature over 24 hours and over seasons is of more use to ecologists.

Note: Air temperature should be taken in the shade and not in full sunlight.

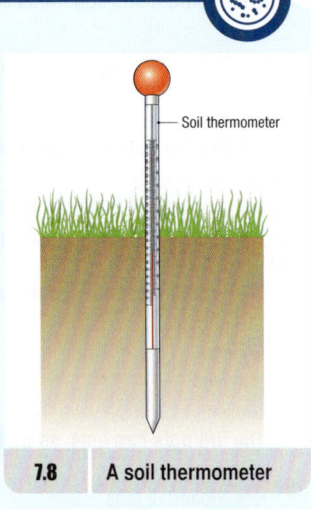

7.8 A soil thermometer

Investigation 7.2
To measure the light intensity in a habitat

A photographic light meter (Fig 7.9) may be used to measure light intensity. It is important to take a number of readings, because light intensity can change quickly, due to cloud cover for example. It is best to measure the light falling on the object rather than the light source itself.

A light probe connected to a data logger can give readings over a 24-hour period.

1. Place the light meter out of direct sunlight.
2. Remove the cap of the light meter.
3. Set the meter so it will read to the correct light level.
4. When the reading stops fluctuating press the 'hold' button.
5. Record the reading.
6. Repeat twice and get an average.
7. Take readings in a number of places in the habitat.

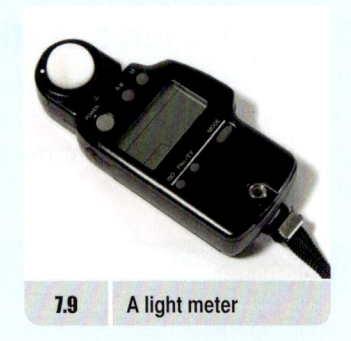

7.9 A light meter

Investigation 7.3
To measure the pH of soil in a habitat

1. Take a sample of soil from about 5 cm depth.
2. Place 1 cm^3 soil in a test tube.
3. Add 2 cm^3 distilled water, stopper, and shake.
4. Add three drops of universal indicator, stopper, and gently invert the tube to mix the sample.
5. Allow the soil to settle and then hold the tube against a white background (piece of paper) and note the colour formed (Fig 7.10).
6. Compare the colour against the colour chart to read the pH value.
7. Record the pH value.

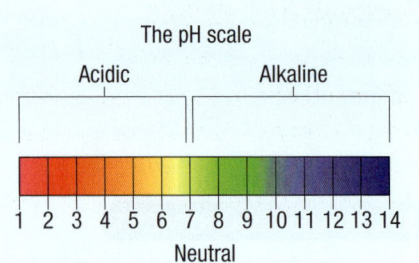

7.10 Testing the pH of a soil sample

Surveys

Two types of survey are commonly carried out in an ecosystem: a qualitative survey and a quantitative survey.

1. A **qualitative survey** is a record of the types of organisms present or absent in the ecosystem. It answers the question 'Who lives in the ecosystem?' A qualitative survey is carried out by collecting and identifying the species found (see pages 76–79).
2. A **quantitative survey** deals with the numbers of organisms present. It answers the question 'How many of a particular species are present?' A quantitative survey tells us more about the interrelationships in the ecosystem and is more useful.

> A **qualitative survey** records if a species is present or not.

> A **quantitative survey** records the numbers of a species present.

Surveys of plants

Subjective estimates

1. Abundance estimates

An estimate of the abundance of different plants in a habitat can be made by just looking at them and giving each species of plant present a subjective rating of abundance. However, using subjective estimates has a number of limitations:

1. No two people are likely to give the same score to the same set of plants.
2. Species that occur in clumps are more obvious than those that are more evenly scattered.
3. There is no guideline to say how common a plant has to be to be given a particular rating.

2. Random sampling

It is virtually impossible to count all the individuals in a given area. For example, imagine trying to count all the grass plants on a playing field! Instead, we take samples that enable the population of organisms in a habitat to be estimated. To be meaningful, the samples taken must be representative and without bias on the part of the investigator. This is done by taking random samples using a **quadrat**.

A quadrat is a square frame used to mark out an area of the habitat. Quadrats can be made from wood or plastic, by bending a piece of wire into a square shape or using four metal skewers and a piece of string (Fig 7.11).

- Quadrats vary in size depending on the size of the area being examined.
- A 0.5 m x 0.5 m quadrat is a useful size for most ground vegetation, whereas a 10 cm x 10 cm quadrat is a better size for estimating lichen and moss numbers on a wall or barnacles on a rock.
- Quadrats are placed at random in the habitat and the different species present are identified and the names transferred to a recording sheet.

Quantitative surveys of plants

Percentage cover

Percentage cover is a measure of the area of the ground covered by the aerial parts of a plant, expressed as a percentage of the total quadrat area. In other words, percentage cover is the percentage of the ground covered by a species in a quadrat.

7.11 A gridded quadrat

07 The Study of an Ecosystem

Investigation 7.4
To estimate percentage cover

Use a gridded quadrat, e.g. one with 25 squares.

Method

1. Select the sample area in the ecosystem and mark it off.
2. Place a quadrat at random. One way to do this is to throw a pencil over your shoulder and then place the quadrat over where the pencil has landed. Take care when throwing the pencil that no one is likely to be hit by it. Equally a quadrat itself should not be thrown, as it could hit someone or damage something.
3. Place a pin (knitting needle) at the top right-hand corner of each square. A plant scores a 'hit' if it is touched with the pin, or simply note any plant present at the top right-hand corner of each square.
4. Count and record the number of 'hits' for each plant.
5. Repeat the procedure (steps 2 to 4) 20 times. The more times you place the quadrat, the more representative your results.
6. Use the formula below to calculate the percentage cover for each plant species.
7. Record the results.
8. Transfer the data to a graph or a bar chart.

% cover = number of hits / total number of pins x 100/1

Sample Results

Quadrat number	1	2	3	....	20	Final no. of hits	Total no. of pins	% cover
Name of plant	No. of hits	No. of hits	No. of hits				250	
Buttercup	1	3	6					
Grass	24	18	19					
Daisy	0	3	0					
Self-heal								

Table 7.8 Percentage cover sample results table

Because you only record the plants that are touched by the pin, rare plants may not be touched at all and so will score no points. If the gridded quadrat is divided into a larger number of squares, say 100, then a more accurate estimate of cover is obtained (Fig 7.12).

7.12 A gridded quadrat with 100 squares

Percentage frequency

Percentage frequency is defined as the percentage probability of a plant occurring within a quadrat. For example, if a plant has a frequency of 20%, then you would expect it to occur on average once in every five quadrats examined.

To determine the percentage frequency, you have to record both the presence and absence of the species (the number is not important). Before you begin, you must decide what constitutes presence. It might be:

- any plant that is inside, touches or overhangs the quadrat;
- only plants rooted in the quadrat.

> **Percentage cover** is the area of the ground covered by a species of plant in a quadrat.

> **Percentage frequency** is the chance of finding a particular plant (or sedentary animal) in a quadrat.

Investigation 7.5
To measure percentage frequency

It is very simple to measure the frequency, but it is difficult to interpret, because frequency depends upon the quadrat size.

Method

1. Select the sample area in the ecosystem and mark it off.
2. The quadrat is placed at random. One way to do this is to throw a pencil over your shoulder and then place the quadrat over where the pencil has landed. Take care when throwing the pencil that no one is likely to be hit by it. Equally a quadrat itself should not be thrown, as it could hit someone or damage something.
3. Make a list of all the plants you are going to study.
4. Record the presence or absence of your chosen plants in a table, like in Table 7.9 below.
5. Repeat for 20 quadrat throws.
6. Use the formula below to calculate the percentage frequency of each plant species.
7. Transfer the data to a graph or a bar chart.

% frequency = number of quadrats containing plant/number of quadrats thrown x 100/1

Name of plant	Quadrat number									Total	% Frequency
	1	2	3	4	5	....	98	99	100		
Moss	*	*	*	*	*		X	X	*	86	86%
Heather	X	X	*	X	*		X	X	X	29	29%
Bent grass	*	*	*	*	*		*	*	*	96	96%
Blackberry	*	*	X	X	X		X	*	*	50	50%
Bracken	X	X	X	X	*		X	*	X	19	19%

Table 7.9 Percentage frequency table

Your results will let you see those species that are characteristic of the area and those that appear only now and then. In Table 7.9, heather is seen to be present in 29 out of 100 quadrats. This means that there is a 29% frequency for heather.

07 The Study of an Ecosystem

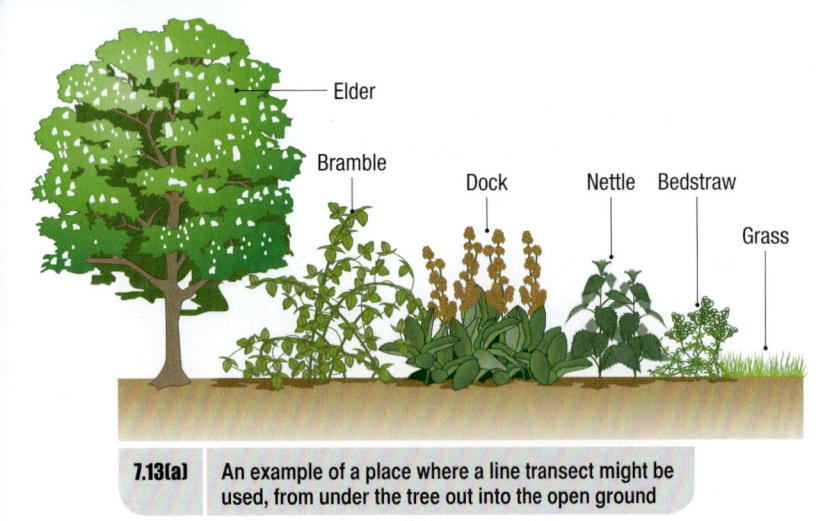

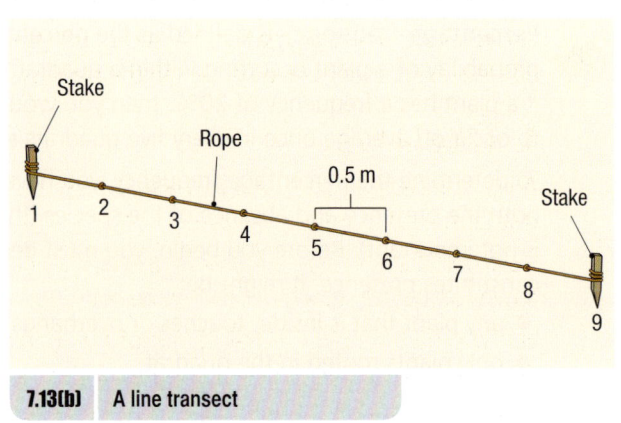

7.13(a) An example of a place where a line transect might be used, from under the tree out into the open ground

7.13(b) A line transect

Transects

A **transect** is a technique used to study changes in vegetation and animal life across a habitat, for example across the sea shore, from the water's edge to the road or from shade to full sunlight outside a wooded area. If a record of the abiotic conditions (light intensity, wet/dry soil, temperature) along the transect is made, it is possible to relate the distribution and abundance of organisms to the changing environment.

Transects are a non-random sampling technique because *you* decide where the transect will be positioned. One type of transect is a line transect.

Line transect

- A line transect consists of laying out a line of string or rope across the area to be studied.
- The two ends of the string should be staked into the ground and pieces of string tied at regular intervals along the line forming 'stations'.
- The interval chosen between stations, e.g. 10 cm, 0.5 m, depends upon the length of the transect line.
- The names and height of organisms (normally plants) that are touching the line at the stations are recorded (Fig 7.13(a) and (b)).

Table 7.10 Data from a line transect

Station	Name of plant	Height of plant (m)
1	Elder tree	4.0
2	Dock	0.3
3	Nettle	0.2
4	Grass	0.25
5	Grass	0.15

Belt transect

A belt transect is another type of transect. It consists of two line transects laid parallel, usually 1 m apart. The belt is then marked out in 1 m squares by tying string across between the lines forming a row of quadrats. The plants found in each quadrat are listed and their percentage cover and frequency measured, recorded and mapped. In addition the environmental conditions at each quadrat (light intensity, soil temperature, pH, etc.) should be recorded. In this way the belt transect provides information about the frequency and distribution of vegetation in relation to the abiotic environment. Results from a belt transect can be plotted on bar charts, histograms or belt transect maps.

Quantitative surveys of animals

Unlike plants, most animals move about and are not always easy to see. Sometimes we know certain animals are present because we see their tracks, footprints or pellets, or we hear them calling.

1. Transects

A line transect, as described on page 84, can be used to obtain information about the frequency and distribution of animals in an area.

However, there are certain problems when trying to obtain numbers for animals because many animals move too quickly to allow them to be counted, and very often they may not even be visible.

Earthworms can be encouraged out of the ground by marking out an area, removing the top layer of grass, if present, and spraying the area with a detergent solution such as washing-up liquid in water. If this is done for a number of quadrats, the population of earthworms can be estimated.

The population of more sedentary animals, such as limpets on the rocky shore, can also be determined using a quadrat.

2. Capture/recapture method

This is a quantitative method to estimate the size of a population of a given species of motile animal. The method involves capturing a number of the animals you wish to study. The number of animals caught will depend on the size of the area. Each animal is then marked and released. Later a further collection is made and a formula applied to calculate the population.

Investigation 7.6

To estimate the population of an animal species using the capture/recapture method

Method

1. Select the sample area in the ecosystem and mark it off.
2. Select an animal to study and make a collection of the selected animal.
3. Mark the animal using 'Tippex' or enamel paint in such a way that it does not harm them, it does not make them more visible to predators and the mark is not likely to rub off too soon.
4. Release the animals back into the same area of the ecosystem they were collected from.
5. A day (or a week) later, another sample is collected in the same area and the number of any marked/tagged individuals is noted.
6. The size of the population can be calculated using the following formula:

$$N = \frac{C1 \times C2}{M2}$$

where

N = the size of the population

$C1$ = number of animals caught on day 1

$C2$ = number of animals caught on day 2

$M2$ = number of animals caught on day 2 that have the mark or tag

For example, in an investigation 60 woodlice were collected on day 1, marked and released. On day 2, another 50 woodlice were captured, of which 10 were marked. Using the formula, the number of woodlice in the habitat is:

$$\frac{60 \times 50}{10} = \frac{3,000}{10} = 300.$$

The method works well for woodlice, snails and beetles.

7.14 A whale shark that has been tagged

Analysis and results

With the help of books and the internet compile two **food chains**, a **food web** and a **pyramid of numbers** from the information obtained in your study of the ecosystem. These give information on the feeding relationships in the ecosystem.

Presentation of results

Prepare a report of the results obtained to include an analysis of the results, identification of sources of error and of any ecological issues related to the ecosystem. Using the information gathered during your fieldwork, you can list examples of adaptations of organisms you have found to the environment.

This might include the following:

1. Drawings or photographs of five plants and five animals.
2. The methods of nutrition of the organisms.
3. Food chains, food webs and pyramids of numbers using organisms in the ecosystem.
4. A record of the abiotic factors that determine the numbers and distribution of organisms present.
5. Examples of adaptations of some of the organisms to the environment.
6. Results of the quantitative surveys can be presented in a number of ways, e.g. tables, diagrams, graphs, histograms (Fig 7.15).
7. Any ecological issues relating to your ecosystem and any sources of error that could have affected your survey.

Ecological issues related to the ecosystem

It is important to consider the effect of local ecological issues on the survival of your ecosystem. Is there to be a new shopping centre built on the local playing fields? Is a wooded area to be cut down to allow for a new road to pass through? Is the local farmer spraying pesticides nearby, which may affect the insect life in your habitat? Situations like these all have an impact on our ecosystems and careful planning and regulation is needed to ensure the safe survival of our habitats.

Possible errors

In conclusion, it is important to bear in mind that investigations in the field are always more complex than those in the laboratory.

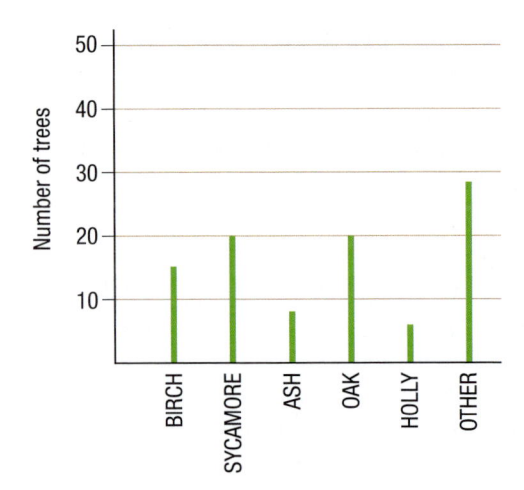

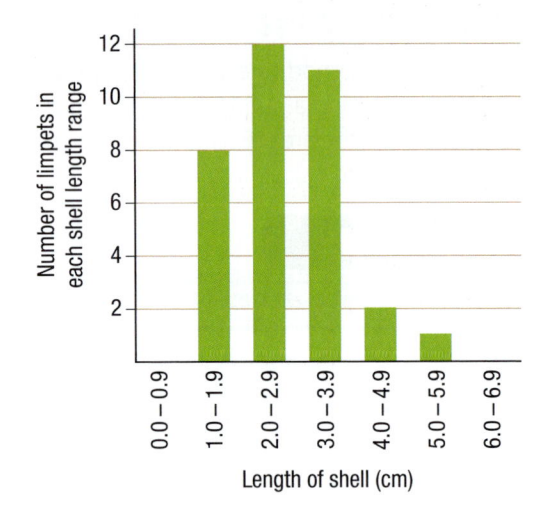

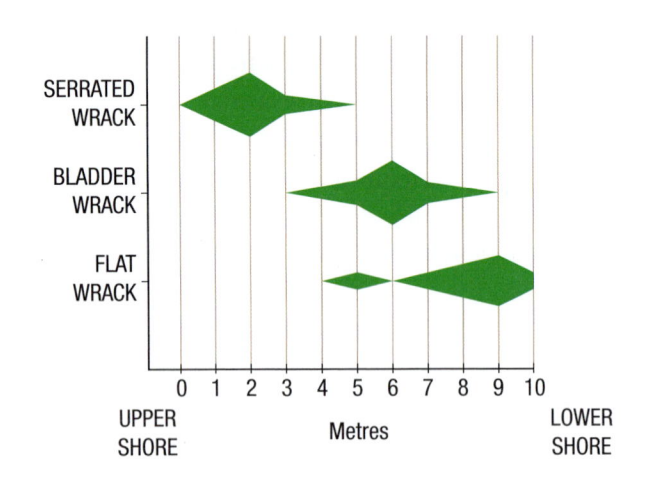

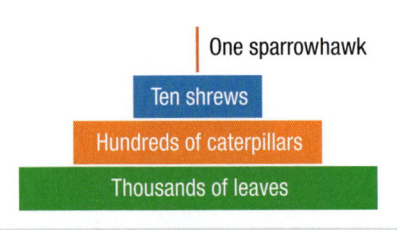

7.15 Various ways that results of surveys can be represented

- Organisms are always changing. No two individuals of a species are identical. What they do and where they live may depend on their age, their sex and the condition they are in.
- The weather conditions and time of day during which samples are taken may affect the organisms present, e.g. sampling on a warm sunny day may produce quite different results to samples taken when it is raining. Few insects can fly when it is very windy and equally on wet days, animals in particular will hide away. Nocturnal animals that feed and are active at night are rarely found during the day but they play an important role in the life of an ecosystem.
- Chance can also play a part. You might just happen to throw a quadrat onto an area with a very large number of a particular plant or animal. This may give a biased result.
- Although it can be time-consuming, the more samples you take the more reliable will be the overall picture of the whole area. A small number of samples may not show the presence of rare plants or animals.

Summary

- The study of an ecosystem involves the following:
  - Make a map of the ecosystem.
  - Note the habitats within the ecosystem.
  - Identify the plants and animals present.
  - Measure and record the abiotic factors.
  - Carry out surveys to estimate the numbers of plants and animals.
  - Analyse the results.
  - Present the information.
  - Be aware of errors and ecological issues that may affect the ecosystem.

- A simple map includes a sketch, a scale, labels/key, obvious plants named and the direction of North marked on it.

- Plants and animals can be identified using a key.

- Plants and animals can be collected using a variety of methods.

Table 7.11 Methods of collecting plants

Plant type	Collection method
Seaweeds	Knife
Plankton	Plankton net
Flowers, leaves, seeds and fruits	Hand pick

Summary

Table 7.12 Methods of collecting animals

Equipment	Type	Used to collect
Traps	Cryptozoic	Woodlice, slugs
	Pitfall	Ground beetles, ants, spiders
	Mammal	Field mice, shrews, voles
Nets	Fish	Small fish and pond insects
	Insect	Butterflies, moths, shield bugs
	Plankton	Plankton in streams, ponds, lakes
	Sweep	Insects such as grasshoppers and flies in long grass
Pooter		Greenfly, spiders, mites, ants
Tullgren funnel		Nematode worms, springtails, small spiders in soil

- The abiotic environment can affect the number and spread of plants and animals in the ecosystem (see Table 7.7 for methods of measuring abiotic factors).
- A qualitative survey is a record of the types of species present.
- A quantitative survey is a record of the number of each species. Quantitative surveys can be either subjective or objective.
- Subjective surveys tend to be less reliable because they depend upon personal opinions and no two people necessarily judge things exactly the same.
- One type of subjective survey is to use a visual estimate of the numbers of plants or animals in an area.
- A quadrat is a square wooden, plastic or metal frame used to mark out an area of a habitat.
- Quadrats are used to make random samples in a habitat.
- Objective surveys

  For plants:
  (a) Quadrats: used to find percentage cover and percentage frequency.
  (b) Transects: used to get information across an ecosystem, e.g. a line transect.

  For animals:
  (a) Transects, as above.
  (b) Capture/recapture technique using $N = C_1 \times C_2/M_2$
      where N = number of animals in the population, C_1 = number caught on first visit, C_2 = number caught on second visit and M_2 = number caught on second visit that were marked.

- Percentage cover is the percentage of the ground covered by a species in a quadrat.
- Percentage frequency is the percentage chance of finding a plant within a quadrat.
- Transects (line and belt) are a non-random method of sampling. They are used to examine and record the distribution of plants and animals in an area along an environmental gradient, e.g. across a hedgerow.
- Sources of error and issues of ecological importance should be noted.

Review questions

All questions should be answered with reference to the *ecosystem you studied* unless otherwise indicated.

01
(a) Name three ecosystems in Ireland.
(b) Name the ecosystem you have studied.
(c) List three habitats in the ecosystem.
(d) Name five plants and five animals found in the ecosystem.
(e) What did you use to identify the plants and animals you found?
(f) Give one adaptation for one named plant and one named animal in your ecosystem.

02
(a) Name three producers, three primary consumers and three secondary consumers in the ecosystem you have studied.
(b) Using the organisms named in (a), construct two simple food chains.

03
(a) Describe **two** named plants from your ecosystem by drawing a labelled diagram of each.
(b) For each plant named give one adaptation to life in the ecosystem.

04
(a) Use the following beetle key to identify the two species shown in the drawings below.

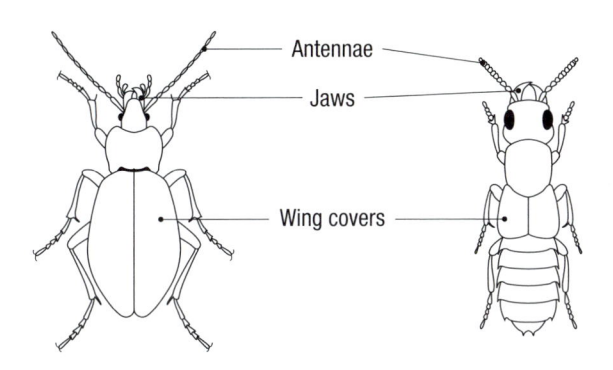

1. Wing covers short and six body segments uncovered	Go to 2
Wing covers long and a maximum of two body segments uncovered	Go to 3
2. Large jaws that stick out	Large jawed rove beetle
Without large jaws that stick out	Devil's coach horse beetle
3. Antennae end in a group of flat plates	Go to 4
Antennae do not end in a group of flat plates	Go to 5
4. Last body segment visible	Cockchafer beetle
Last body segment not visible	Dung beetle
5. Antennae club-shaped	Go to 6
Antennae not club-shaped	Ground beetle
6. Spots present on wing covers	Ladybird beetle
Spots not present on wing covers	Pill beetle

(b) Using information from the key, describe three features of (i) a ground beetle and (ii) a ladybird beetle.

05 The following key can be used to identify some trees.

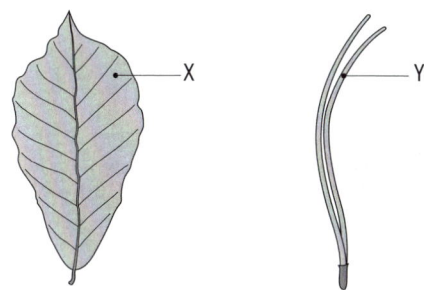

1. Leaves broad	Go to 2
Leaves narrow	Go to 5
2. Leaf divided into separate parts	Go to 3
Leaf not divided into parts	Go to 4
3. Leaf has five pointed parts	Sycamore
Leaf has many rounded parts	Oak
4. Leaf edge smooth	Beech
Leaf edge saw-toothed	Elm
5. Leaves grow singly	Yew
Leaves grow in groups	Go to 6
6. Leaves in pairs	Scots pine
Leaves in tufts	Larch

(a) Use the key to identify the leaves X and Y drawn above.
(b) The leaves of elm have a saw-toothed edge. Using information in the key give two other features of elm leaves.

06
(a) Name three biotic factors that affect an ecosystem.
(b) List three abiotic factors that affect a named ecosystem.
(c) Describe the effect of any one of the factors named in (b) on plants in the ecosystem.
(d) Outline how the factor named in (c) can be measured.

07 The Study of an Ecosystem

Review questions

07 (a) Identify the pieces of collection equipment labelled A, B and C.
For each piece state (i) a named animal it is used to collect; (ii) how it is used.
(b) Explain the role of X, Y and Z.

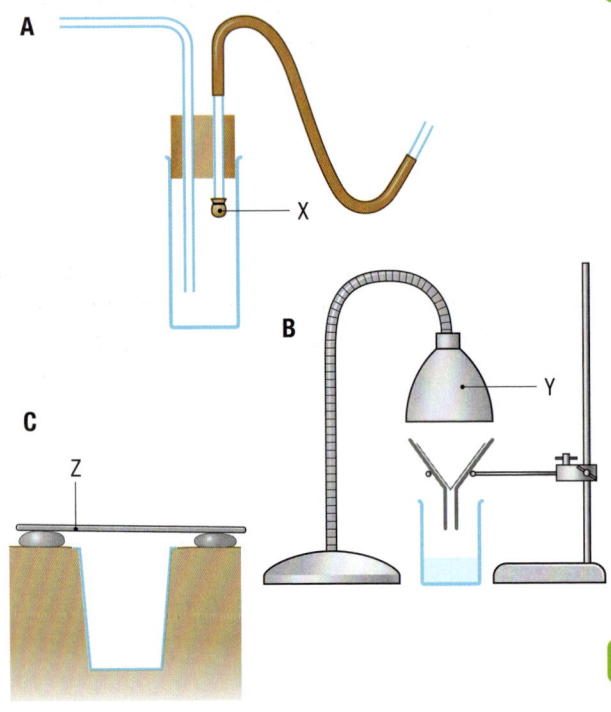

08 (a) Name a piece of equipment used for collecting microscopic organisms in a stream.
(b) Draw a labelled diagram of it.
(c) State how it is used.

09 Name one type of animal you might expect to collect in each of the following:
(a) a Tullgren funnel
(b) a pitfall trap
(c) a sweep net
(d) a cryptozoic trap

10 Distinguish between each of the following pairs of terms:
(a) Quantitative and qualitative surveys.
(b) % cover and % frequency.
(c) Random and non-random sampling.

11 A group of students carried out a survey of the frequency of dandelions in a field. A quadrat, 1 m², was thrown ten times at random and the presence or absence of dandelions recorded for each throw. The results obtained are shown in the table below.

Quadrat no.	1	2	3	4	5	6	7	8	9	10
No. of dandelions	X	O	O	O	X	O	O	O	O	O

O = presence, X = absence

(a) Draw a diagram to represent a quadrat.
(b) Why was it important to throw the quadrat at random?
(c) Describe how a quadrat can be thrown at random.
(d) Draw a bar chart of the results on graph paper. Mark in the axes.
(e) Calculate the % frequency of dandelions (show your working).

12 Describe how you would estimate the population of a named animal in the named ecosystem you have studied.

13 (a) Give a detailed account of how you would find the % cover of a named plant in the ecosystem you have studied.
(b) List two errors that might affect the results of your survey.

Examination style questions

Section A

01 (a) Draw a labelled diagram of a Pooter.
(b) Describe how a Pooter is used.
(c) Name three organisms that you might expect to find using a Pooter.

02 (a) What is meant by percentage cover in a survey of an ecosystem?
(b) Name the equipment you would use to estimate percentage cover.
(c) What is the frequency of a plant species if it is present in 12 out of 50 randomly thrown quadrats?

The Study of an Ecosystem 07

Examination style questions

Section B

03 (a) (i) Dandelions are producers. What is the meaning of the term producer?
  (ii) Dandelions produce many fruits that are light and have a parachute of fine hairs. Suggest one advantage of having this type of fruit.
 (b) (i) In the case of a named animal describe how you would carry out a quantitative survey in the ecosystem you have studied.
  (ii) Describe how you recorded the results of your survey.
  (iii) Suggest a possible source of error in your study.

04 (a) (i) Distinguish between abiotic and biotic factors in ecology.
  (ii) State the name of the piece of equipment you used to measure a *named* abiotic factor.
 (b) (i) What is meant by the term 'fauna'?
  (ii) Name *five* plants in the ecosystem you have studied.
  (iii) Describe how you carried out a quantitative survey of any one of the plants named in (ii).
  (iv) Why is it important to carry out a random survey?

05 (a) (i) What is meant in ecology by a *quantitative* survey?
  (ii) Name two animals you would expect to capture in a pitfall trap.
 (b) The diagrams below show leaves of four different trees. Use the key to identify each of the leaves. As you work through the key for each leaf, tick the boxes in the table to show how you got your answer. Leaf A has been completed for you.

Leaf	1(a)	1(b)	2(a)	2(b)	3(a)	3(b)	4(a)	4(b)	5(a)	5(b)	Name of tree
A	O		O								Horse chestnut
B											
C											
D											

	Name of tree
1. (a) Leaf divided into leaflets	Go to 2
(b) Leaf not divided into leaflets	Go to 3
2. (a) Leaflets form a fan on the leaf stalk	Horse chestnut
(b) Leaflets are in pairs along the leaf stalk	Ash
3. (a) Leaf edge has spikes	Holly
(b) Leaf edge has no spikes	Go to 4
4. (a) Leaf edge smooth	Beech
(b) Leaf outline lobed	Sycamore

Section C

06 (a) Name **three** habitats found in your ecosystem.
 (b) Name **three** animals found in the ecosystem and state **two** features that enabled you to identify any **one** of the named animals.
 (c) Explain how **one** of the animals named in (ii) is adapted to life in the ecosystem.

07 Cryptozoic traps, sweep nets, mammal traps and Tullgren funnels are all pieces of equipment that can be used to collect animals during ecology fieldwork.

For any **one** piece of equipment listed, draw a labelled diagram to show it and describe how it is used in an ecosystem.

(a) Give a brief description of the **named** ecosystem you have studied. The description may be given in the form of a labelled diagram or a map.
(b) Draw a diagram of a food web, from your named ecosystem, of at least eight species and four trophic levels.
(c) From the food web name: (i) a primary consumer, (ii) a secondary consumer.
(d) From the food web give: (i) a food chain of four trophic levels; (ii) a pyramid of numbers.

07 The Study of an Ecosystem

Leaving Certificate examination questions

Section A

01 A survey of field mice was carried out in a field of 2.5 hectares using the capture/recapture method. The field mice were caught using small mammal traps set at random points in the field. Forty field mice were captured, tagged and released at their capture points. One month later the traps were set again at the same locations and 40 field mice were caught. Five of these were found to be tagged. Estimate the population of the field mice in numbers per hectare.

(1 hectare = 10 000 m^2)

SEC Sample HL Q. 5 (b)

Section B

02 (a) Name an ecosystem that you have studied. Name **three** animals that are **normally** present in this ecosystem.

(b) Select **one** of the animals that you have named in (a) and answer the following questions in relation to it.
Which animal have you selected?
State **two** features that allowed you to identify the animal.
Name an organism on which this animal normally feeds.
Explain how you attempted to find out how many of these animals were present in the ecosystem.
Using the axes below draw a graph to show how you would expect the numbers of this animal to vary in the ecosystem in the course of a year.

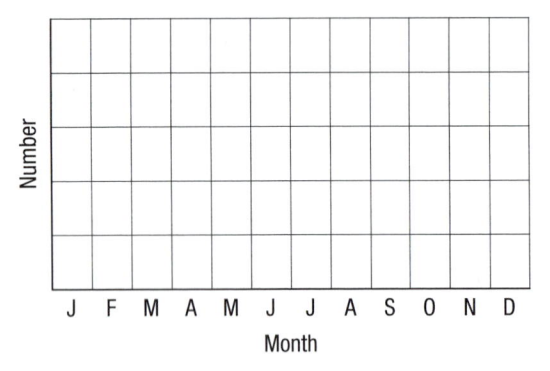

2004 OL Q. 8

03 Answer the following questions by reference to a named ecosystem that you have investigated.

(i) Name of ecosystem.
(ii) List **three** abiotic factors that you investigated.
(iii) For each of the three abiotic factors that you have listed describe how you carried out the investigation.
(iv) In the case of a named organism give an adaptation feature that you noted.
(v) Briefly explain how the adaptation feature that you have given in (iv) is of benefit to the organism.

2008 HL Q. 7 (b)

Section C

04 (i) A quantitative survey was carried out to show the effect of poor waste management on the plants in an ecosystem. What is meant by the term quantitative?

(ii) Describe how you carried out a quantitative survey on a species of plant in this habitat.

2014 OL Q. 11 (c)

05 (i) All organisms in an ecosystem are influenced by <u>biotic</u> and <u>abiotic</u> factors. Explain the underlined words.

(ii) Name any **two** abiotic factors from an ecosystem you have studied and describe how you measured **each** one.

(iii) Keys may be used to identify animals. Use the following key to identify animals A, B and C.
The animals are not drawn to scale.

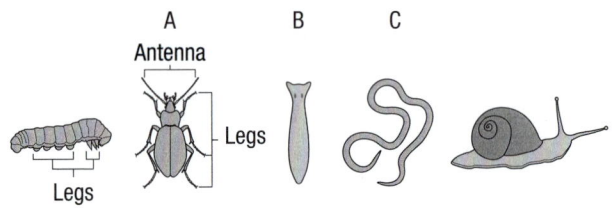

1. Animal has a shell	Helix
Animal does not have a shell	Go to 2
2. Animal has legs	Go to 3
Animal does not have legs	Go to 4
3. Animal has three pairs of legs	Tribolium
Animal has more than three pairs of legs	Pieris larva
4. Animal has long rounded body	Nematode
Animal has flat body with two eye spots	Planarian

(iv) All organisms are adapted to their own habitat.
1. Name **one** animal from the ecosystem you have studied.
2. Describe **one** way in which it is adapted to its habitat.

2012 OL Q. 10 (b)

06 (i) Distinguish between a quantitative and a qualitative survey by writing a sentence about each.

(ii) 1. Name one plant from the ecosystem you have studied.
2. Describe how you carried out a quantitative survey to determine its frequency.

(iii) As a result of pollution, a species of plant disappears from an ecosystem. Suggest **two** possible effects that the disappearance of this plant might have on the other plants and animals living in the area.

2012 OL Q. 10 (c)

Leaving Certificate examination questions

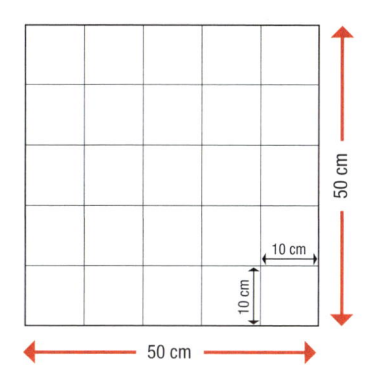

07 (i) Distinguish between quantitative and qualitative surveys in an ecosystem.
(ii) Name the piece of equipment shown above, which is used in a quantitative study of an ecosystem.
(iii) Why is the above piece of apparatus unsuitable for studying most animal populations?
(iv) Suggest a plant that would not be suitable to survey using the above apparatus.
(v) Outline how this piece of apparatus is used for studying plant populations.
(vi) How did you present your results?
(vii) State **one** possible source of error in a survey of an ecosystem.

2009 OL Q. 10 (b)

08 **Name the ecosystem** that you investigated during your study of ecology.
(i) Explain the terms: 1. *Flora*, 2. *Fauna*.
(ii) Name **one** animal from your named ecosystem **and** describe how you carried out a quantitative study of that animal.
(iii) Suggest **one** way in which marking an animal might endanger it.
(iv) Ecosystems are subject to changes, both natural and artificial.

Mention **one** of **each** type of change as it applies to your named ecosystem.

2012 HL Q. 11 (c)

09 (i) In relation to a study of an ecosystem distinguish clearly between *qualitative* and *quantitative* surveys by writing a sentence about each.
(ii) How were you able to identify the different plants in the ecosystem that you investigated?
(iii) Describe how you carried out a quantitative survey of the major plant species.
(iv) Give **two** possible sources of error that may have arisen in the course of your survey.

2011 HL Q. 10 (b)

Past examination questions

OL 2014 Q. 11 (c) (iii), (iv)   2013 Q. 9 (b)   2012 Q. 10 (b), (c)   2011 Q. 11 (b) (v), (vi)
2009 Q. 10 (b)   2007 Q. 9 (c), Q. 10 (c)   2006 Q. 8   2005 Q. 10
2004 Q. 8   SEC Sample Q. 8

HL 2014 Q. 15 (c) (iii)–(vi)   2013 Q. 7 (b)   2012 Q. 10 (c)   2011 Q. 10 (c)   2009 Q. 11 (c)
2008 Q. 7 (b)   2006 Q. 2 (b), Q. 9 (b), Q. 10 (b)   SEC Sample Q. 5

UNIT

02

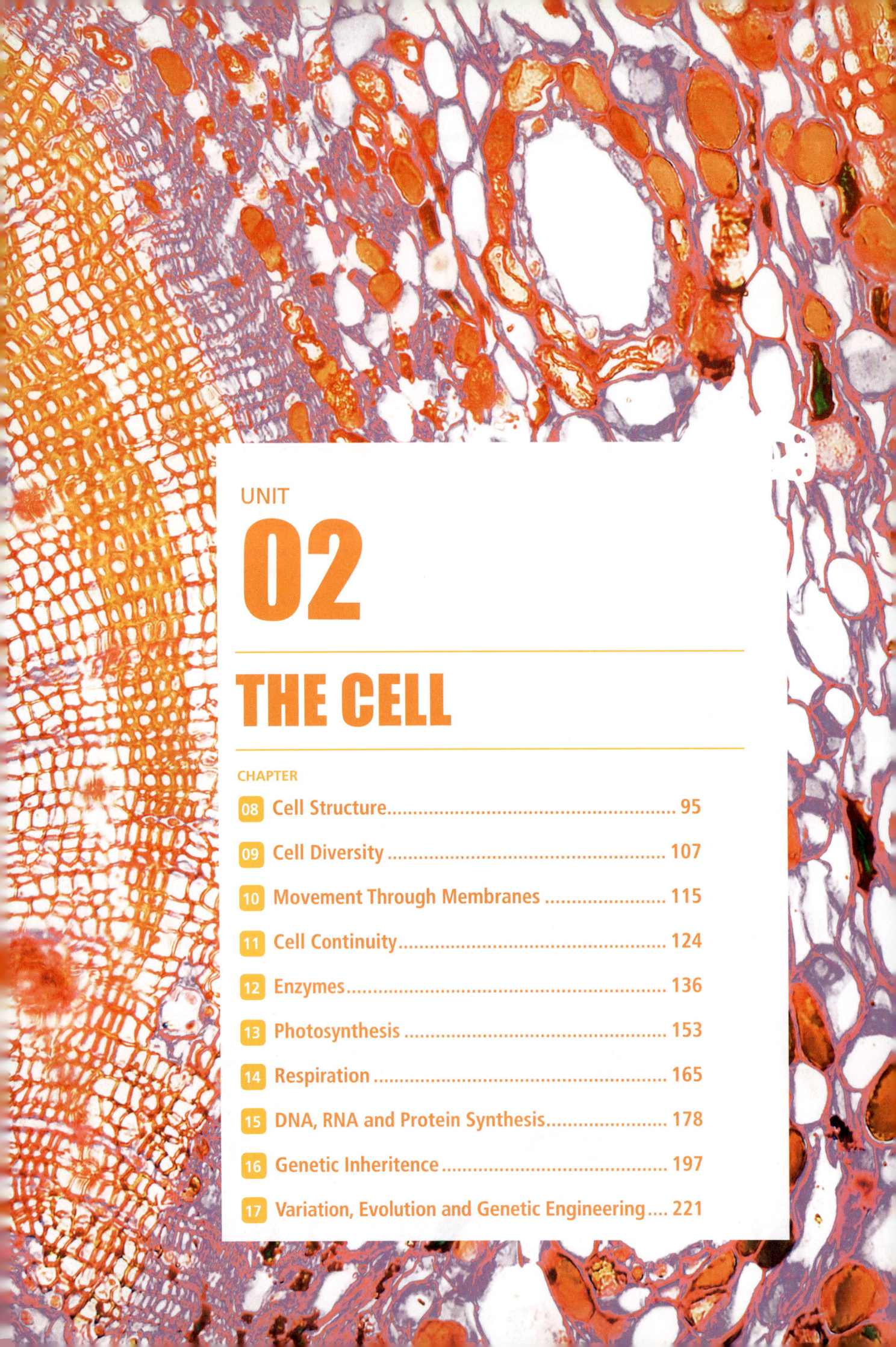

THE CELL

CHAPTER

08	Cell Structure	95
09	Cell Diversity	107
10	Movement Through Membranes	115
11	Cell Continuity	124
12	Enzymes	136
13	Photosynthesis	153
14	Respiration	165
15	DNA, RNA and Protein Synthesis	178
16	Genetic Inheritence	197
17	Variation, Evolution and Genetic Engineering	221

Cell Structure

08

After studying this chapter you should be able to:

1. Describe a bright-field light microscope.
2. Draw a diagram of a plant and an animal cell as seen under the light microscope and describe the functions of the visible structures.
3. Describe the function of, indicate the position and identify the cell membrane.
4. Draw a diagram of the ultrastructure of a typical animal cell and plant cell.
5. Describe the function of and identify the mitochondrion, the chloroplast, the nucleus, nuclear pores, ribosomes and DNA.
6. Prepare and examine an animal and a plant cell, stained and unstained, under a light microscope.
7. **HL** Define prokaryotic and eukaryotic cells.
8. **HL** State the differences between prokaryotic and eukaryotic cells.

Cells

All living organisms are made up of units called **cells**. A few large cells such as fish eggs are visible to the naked eye. Nearly all other cells are so small that we need to use microscopes to make them visible. In the middle of the 17th century, Anton van Leeuwenhoek, a Dutchman, studied a large number of microscopic organisms using his microscope. An Englishman, Robert Hooke, who described what he saw when he looked at a piece of cork, was the first to use the term 'cell'. The small structures that he saw reminded him of the rooms in a monastery and he therefore used the term 'cell' to describe them. By the middle of the 19th century the cell theory was formulated, which stated that all living things were made up of cells and all cells were made by pre-existing cells, as stated in Chapter 1.

Microscopes

Scientists use a wide variety of microscopes to study cells. They are divided into two main groups:
- those that use light (Fig 8.1);
- those that use electrons (Fig 8.2).

The microscope that you will use in your school is called a bright-field light microscope (often simply called a light microscope). This type of microscope shines a beam of light through the specimen, which can be stained to increase the detail that is visible. Microscopes we use now have more than one lens in combination and are called compound microscopes (Fig 8.3).

To see even more detail than the light microscope, the transmission electron microscope can be used. This microscope shines a beam of electrons through the specimen and the image is shown on a computer screen. A print can be produced from this image if a 'hard copy' of the image is required or the image can be stored. A scanning electron microscope can be used to give a lower magnification, frequently showing the surface of a specimen.

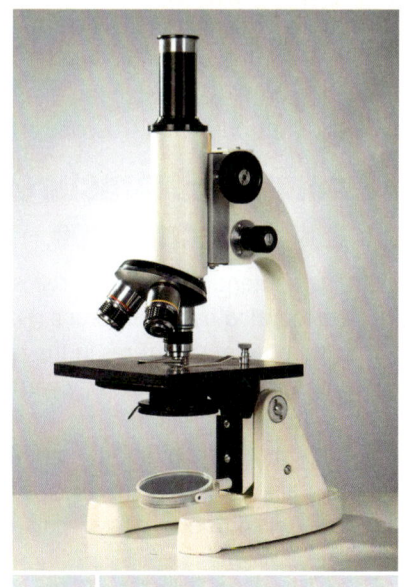

8.1 A light microscope

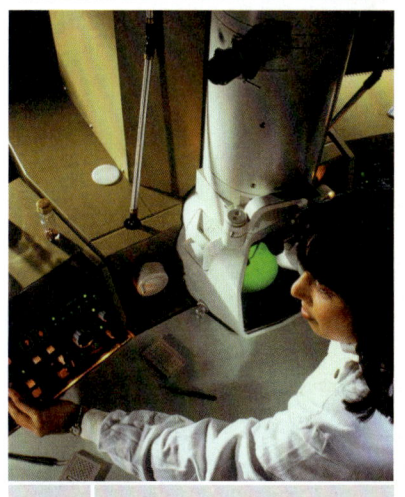

8.2 An electron microscope

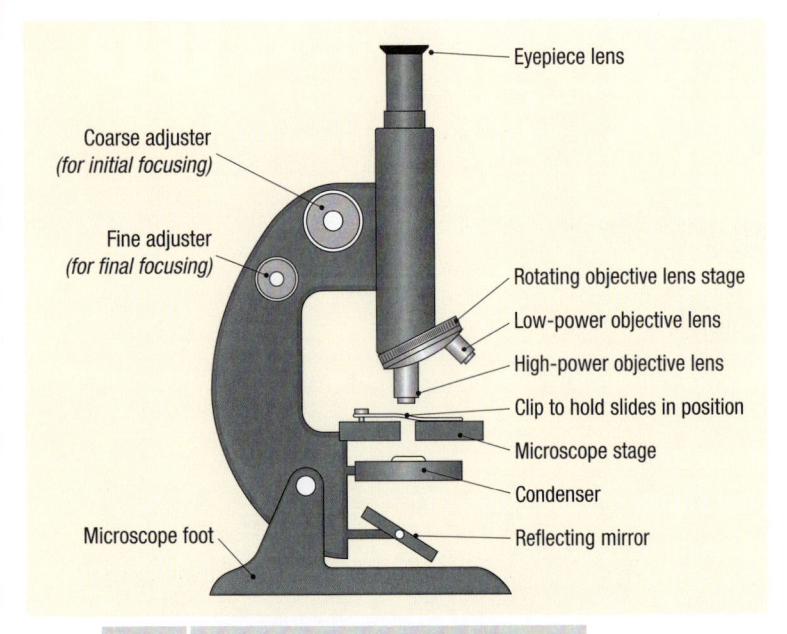

08 Cell Structure

8.3 The parts of a compound light microscope

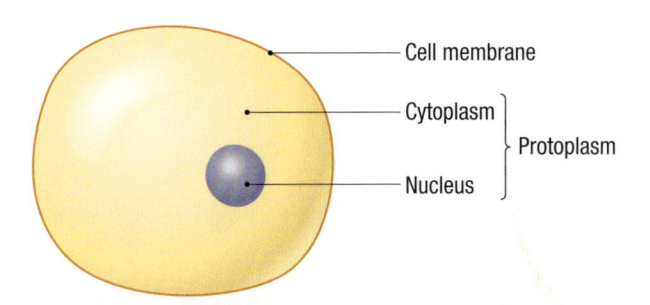

8.4 A typical animal cell as seen under a light microscope

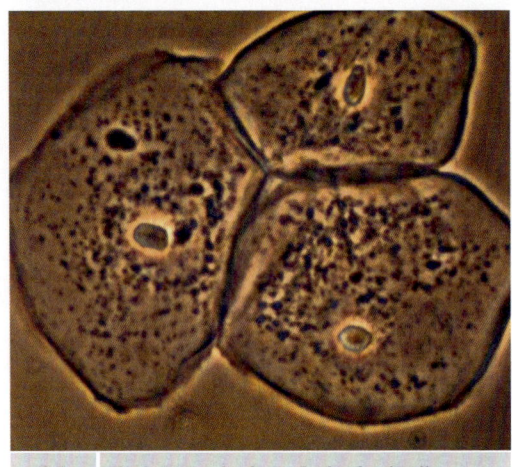

8.5 A photograph of a typical animal cell as seen under the light microscope

By looking at a large number of different animal and plant cells under the light microscope, scientists have noted what structures appear in most cells and these have been used to draw a 'typical' animal and a 'typical' plant cell. These structures are called cell **organelles** and are shown in Figs 8.4 to Fig 8.7. It was discovered that all cells have a cell membrane and contain a substance called cytoplasm. Photographs of a cell taken through a microscope are called photomicrographs.

Animal cell structures as seen under a light microscope

The content of an animal cell is called **protoplasm** and is surrounded by a membrane (Fig 8.4). Membranes surround a number of structures in the cell as well as the cell itself. All membranes are selectively permeable and are called **plasma membranes**. Membranes are composed of protein and phospholipids. Different membranes have different proteins contained in them and these proteins determine what chemicals can get through that particular membrane.

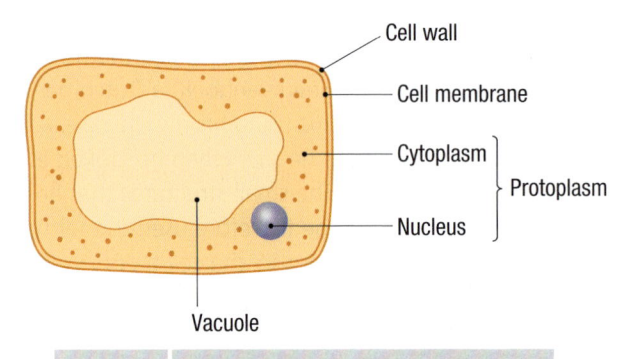

Cell membrane

The cell membrane is the boundary between the cell and the outside, thus giving shape to the cell. This cell membrane has no regular shape and has the important task of determining what gets into the cell and what gets out. It is selectively permeable (Fig 8.8).

- Cell membranes are composed of phospholipids and proteins.
- There is a double layer of phospholipids (called a lipid bilayer). This prevents the passage of most chemicals through the membrane.

The function of the proteins varies:

- Some create gaps in the membrane, called channels or pores, through which certain chemicals can pass.
- Some can pull chemicals through the membrane using energy (active transport).

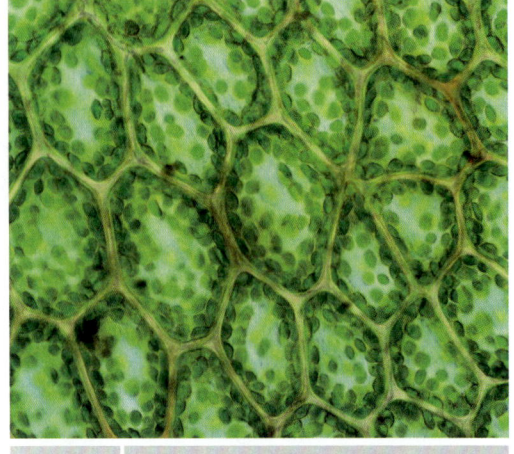

8.6 A typical plant cell as seen under a light microscope

8.7 A photograph of a typical plant cell as seen under a light microscope

8.8 The structure of the plasma membrane

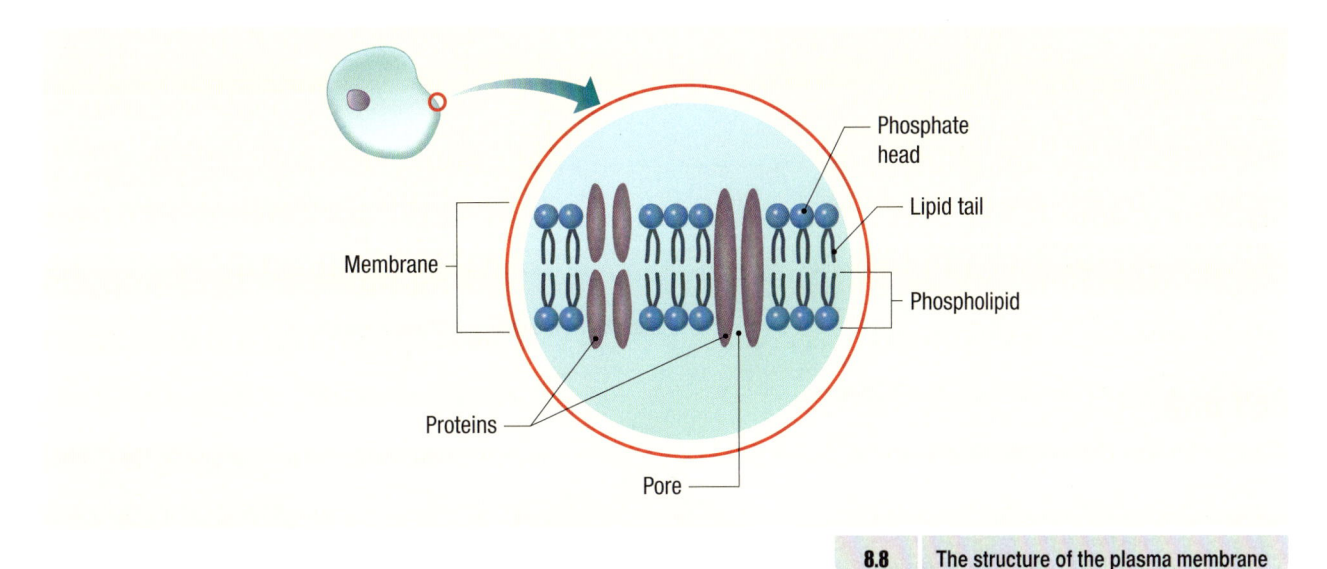

- Some take part in the immune system.
- Many cells can be identified by their surface proteins.

Within the protoplasm there are two structures visible under the light microscope – the **nucleus** and the **nucleolus**.

Nucleus
The most prominent structure in the animal cell is the nucleus.
- This is surrounded by a nuclear envelope made up of a double membrane.
- The nucleus is the control centre of the cell.
- It contains **DNA** (deoxyribonucleic acid), which is the hereditary material that makes up the **genes** and **chromosomes**.

Nucleolus
The nucleolus is an area in the nucleus that stains darker than the rest of the nucleus.
- Sometimes more than one nucleolus is present in a nucleus.
- It is here that the nucleus is most active, making another chemical called **RNA** (ribonucleic acid).

Cytoplasm
The rest of the contents of the cell, between the nucleus and the cell membrane, are called the **cytoplasm**.
- Cytoplasm is a colourless gel-like liquid containing mainly water with **enzymes**, salts, other molecules and **organelles**.
- Most of the metabolic activities of the cell take place in the cytoplasm.
- The cytoplasm contains a number of structures surrounded by membranes called organelles.
- The remainder is called the **cytosol**.

Plant cell structures as seen under a light microscope
Most of the structures found in animal cells are also present in plant cells. A typical plant cell also contains a number of additional structures visible under the light microscope (Fig 8.6).

Vacuole
The most obvious visible difference in a plant cell, as compared with an animal cell, is the large **vacuole** that normally fills the centre of the plant cell (animal cells may contain vacuoles but they are usually very small).
- The vacuole has a membrane surrounding it.
- It is filled with cell sap, a solution containing sugar and salt.
- The function of the vacuole is to fill the centre of the cell – this tends to push the rest of the cell contents to the edge of the cell. With the cell wall this gives shape to the cell and makes the cell ridged.

08 Cell Structure

Plant cells	Animal cells
Have a large central vacuole	Have small vacuoles generally
Have a cell wall	Do not have a cell wall
May have chloroplasts (chlorophyll)	Do not have chloroplasts (chlorophyll)

Table 8.1 Comparison of plant and animal cells

Cell wall

The contents of the cell are held in place by the **cell wall**.
- This is a tough and slightly elastic structure found just outside the cell membrane.
- The cell wall is made of the polysaccharide cellulose.
- It is fully permeable.
- The function of the cell wall and the vacuole is to give shape to a plant cell, as we shall see in a later chapter.

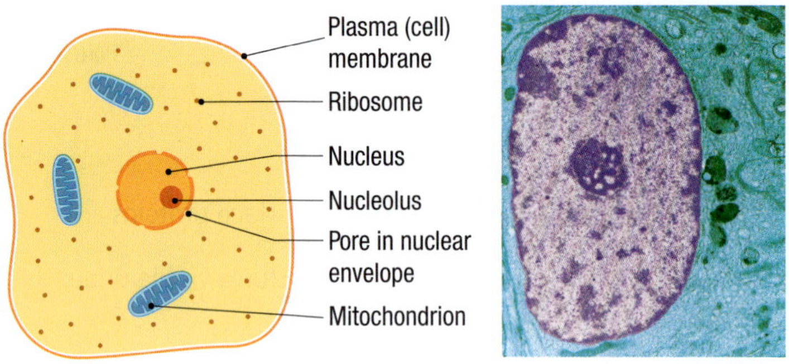

Chloroplasts

Most plant cells contain membrane-bound structures called **chloroplasts**.
- These contain the pigment **chlorophyll**.
- The function of the chloroplast is **photosynthesis**. In this process plants use light to make glucose.

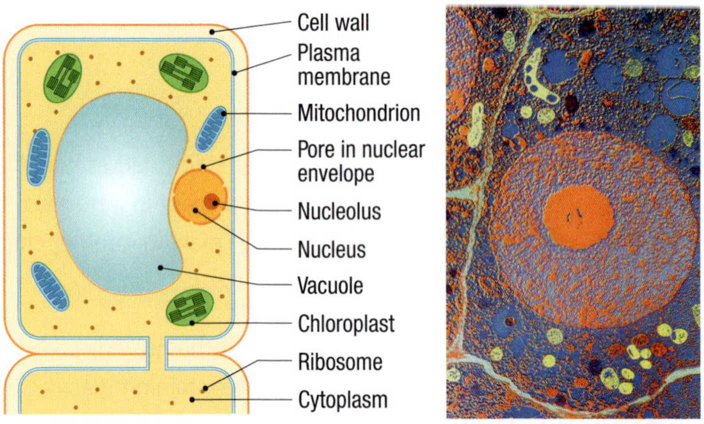

Cell ultrastructure

If animal and plant cells are studied using electron microscopes, more structures and more detail can be seen (Figs 8.9 to 8.12). Some of these are described below.

Mitochondrion

Both animal and plant cells contain **mitochondria** (Figs 8.13 and 8.14).

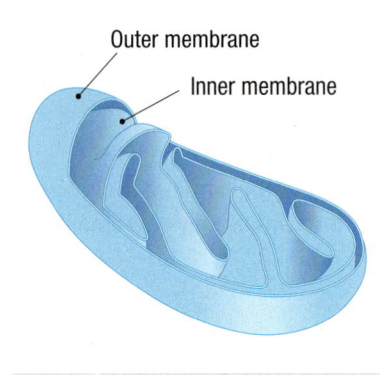

8.9 and 8.10 An animal cell as seen under an electron microscope

8.11 and 8.12 A plant cell as seen under an electron microscope

8.13 A diagram of a mitochondrion

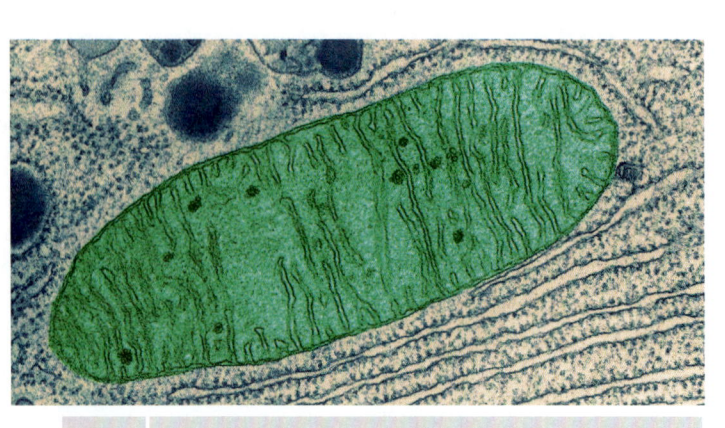

8.14 A mitochondrion as seen under an electron microscope

- These are tiny rod-like structures with double membranes, the inner of which is folded.
- The function of the mitochondrion is **aerobic respiration** (the part requiring oxygen). In this process the energy contained in food is given to a chemical called **ATP** that can be used in the cell as a source of energy for metabolic activity.
- Cells that are very active have many mitochondria.
- Mitochondrion contain DNA and can make copies of themselves.

Chloroplasts

Chloroplasts are only found in plant cells and have a complex structure (Figs 8.15 and 8.16).
- On the outside they have a double membrane, and inside there are a large number of membranes that are arranged in flattened discs piled up on top of one another.
- The chlorophyll they contain is attached to the membranes.
- The function of the chloroplast is photosynthesis.
- They contain DNA and can make copies of themselves.

Nucleus

Under the electron microscope more detail is visible in the nucleus (Figs 8.17 and 8.18).

The nucleus of the cell contains the genetic material in the form of DNA. This DNA is combined with protein to form **chromosomes**. Most of the time chromosomes are not visible as structures and are called **chromatin**. Any particular organism will have a specific number of chromosomes that will contain all the information needed to produce any protein required by that organism.
- The nuclear envelope that surrounds the nucleus has a double membrane.
- There are a large number of nuclear pores in this envelope. These pores are not simple holes but have a very complex structure containing proteins that carefully control all chemicals entering and leaving the nucleus.

Ribosomes

Ribosomes are visible as grainy structures under the electron microscope and can be found floating in the cytosol or attached to membranes. The function of the ribosomes is the production of proteins (protein synthesis).

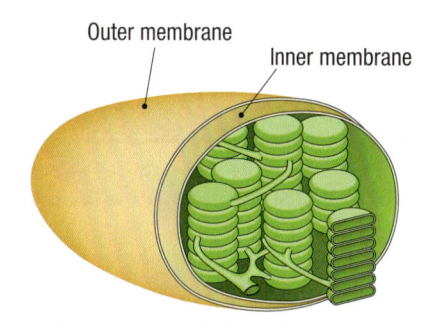

8.15 A diagram of a chloroplast

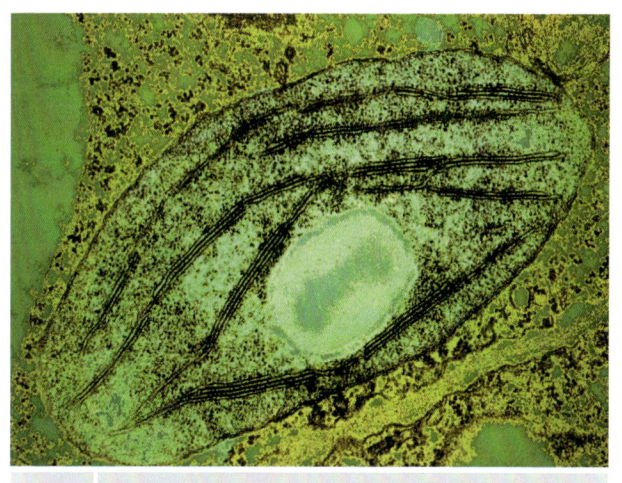

8.16 A chloroplast as seen under an electron microscope

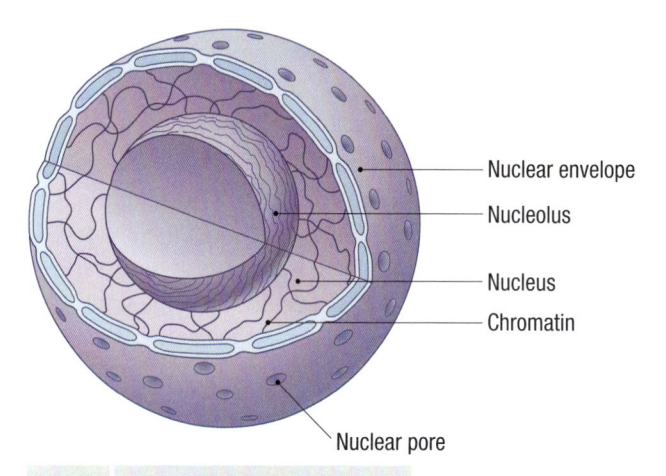

8.17 A diagram of a nucleus

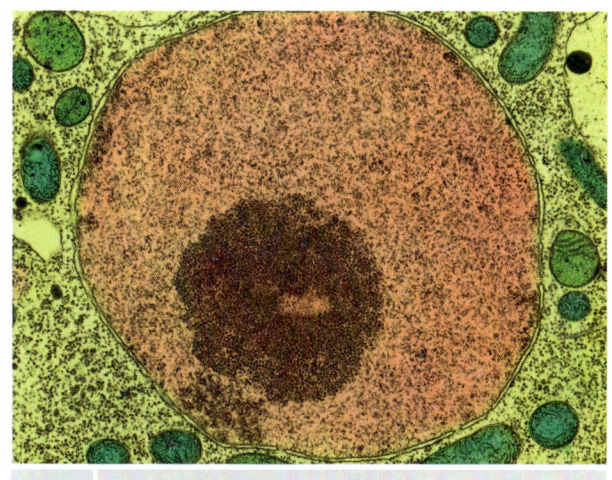

8.18 A nucleus as seen under an electron microscope

08 Cell Structure

Investigation 8.1

Observing animal cells under a light microscope

A. Preparing the slide of an unstained cell

1. Place a drop of water onto a clean glass slide (to prevent cells drying up).
2. Scrape the inside of your cheek with a clean spatula (to gather cells).
3. Add the cells onto the drop of water.
4. Hold a coverslip (to protect the lens) at an angle of 45° in the drop of water.
5. Gently lower the coverslip (to prevent air bubbles forming) (Fig 8.19(a)).

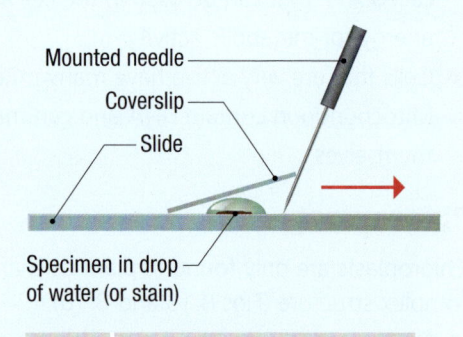

8.19(a) Preparing a slide

B. Using the microscope

1. Turn the low power objective lens into position on the microscope (Fig 8.19(b)).
2. Place the slide onto the stage and hold in place with the clips.
3. Move the stage to its highest position.
4. Looking down the eyepiece, turn on the light (or turn the mirror until the light is reflected up through the slide).
5. Move the objective lens using the coarse focus knob until the image on the slide is in focus. If necessary, move the slide on the stage until some cells are in the centre of the field of view.
6. Turn the nosepiece until the second objective lens has clicked into place.
7. Use the fine focus knob only to move the stage away from the lens (or the lens up from the slide) until the image is once more in focus.
8. Close the iris on the condenser and move the condenser focus knob until the image is as sharp as possible.
9. Move the highest power lens into position and repeat the focusing procedure.
10. Draw what you can see in your practical notebook.

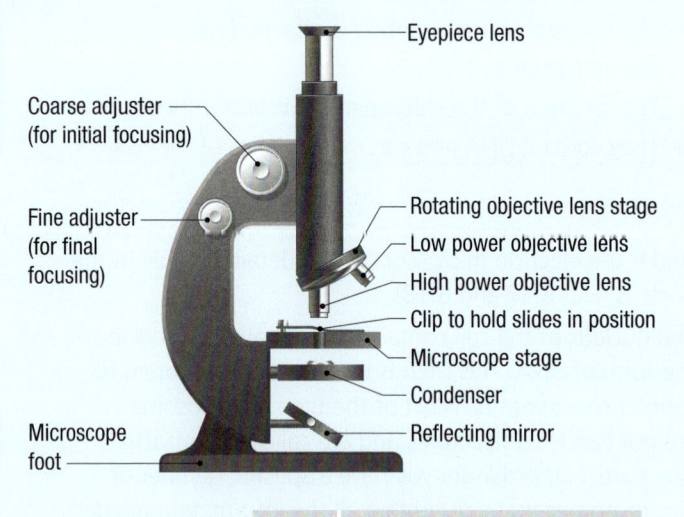

8.19(b) A light microscope

The eyepiece in many microscopes has a symbol 10× on it, which means it magnifies the image ten times. The objective lenses can vary but they commonly are 4×, 10× and 40×. This means they magnify what you are looking at four, ten or forty times.

Combined, this results in the image you see as being (4 × 10) 40, (10 × 10) 100 or (40 × 10) 400 times bigger than it is.

If the size of the image you see at the lowest magnification is 0.4 mm then the actual size is 0.4/40 = 0.01 mm.

Cell Structure | 08

Investigation 8.1
Observing animal cells under a light microscope

C. Staining the cells

1. Place a drop of methylene blue stain on one side of the slide just beside the coverslip (the stain makes the cells more visible) (Fig 8.19(c)).
2. Place a piece of filter/tissue paper in the water on the other side of the coverslip and draw the stain under the coverslip (to prevent over-staining of the specimen).
3. Place the spatula, coverslip and slide in a disinfectant solution at the end of this investigation (to kill any microbes).

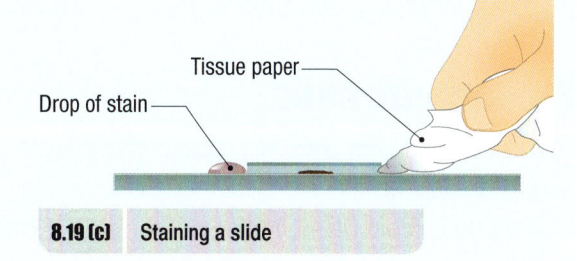

8.19 (c) Staining a slide

Investigation 8.2
Observing plant cells under a light microscope

A. Preparing the slide

1. Place a drop of water onto a glass slide.
2. Take a fleshy leaf from an onion bulb and remove the transparent epidermis (outer skin) from either side of the leaf (Fig 8.20).
3. Place the cells in a drop of water and place a coverslip over the onion as described in Investigation 8.1A.

B. Viewing the cells

1. View and draw the cells under a microscope as described in Investigation 8.1B.

C. Staining the cell

1. Place a drop of iodine solution onto the slide and draw the stain under the coverslip as described in Investigation 8.1C.
2. View and draw the stained cells.

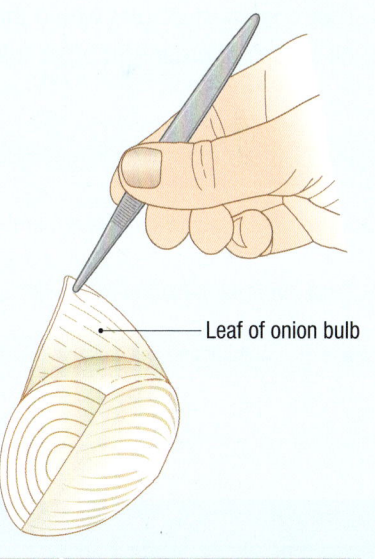

8.20 Removing the epidermis of an onion

08 Cell Structure

HL Prokaryotic and eukaryotic cells

All cells are divided into two main types – **prokaryotic** and **eukaryotic**. The distinction is due to the structures present in the cell.

> **D** A **prokaryotic cell** is one that does not possess a nucleus or other membrane-bound organelles.

> **D** A **eukaryotic cell** is one that has a nucleus and other membrane-bound organelles.

Prokaryotic cells

- These cells do not contain a nucleus (the term prokaryotic means 'before the nucleus').
- They do contain DNA but it does not have a membrane surrounding it.
- They do not contain membrane-bound organelles, e.g. mitochondria or chloroplasts.

Bacteria are the largest group of organisms that are prokaryotes.

8.21 A typical prokaryotic cell

Eukaryotic cells

- These cells contain a nucleus (the term eukaryotic means 'true nucleus').
- They contain structures within their cell that have membranes surrounding them.
- All groups of organisms other than bacteria are eukaryotic.

Prokaryotic cell	Eukaryotic cell
Does not have a nucleus with a membrane surrounding it	Has a nucleus with a membrane surrounding it
Has no membrane-bound organelles within the cell	Has membrane-bound organelles within the cell

Table 8.2 Comparison of a prokaryotic and a eukaryotic cell

8.22 Fungal cells are eukaryote cells

Summary

- All living things are made up of cells.
- Scientists use microscopes to view cells: light microscopes or electron microscopes.

Part	Composition	Function
Cell membrane	No definite shape Made of phospholipid and protein	Controls the passage of chemicals in and out of the cell (is selectively permeable) Acts as the boundary of the cell
Nucleus	Surrounded by a double membrane and contains chromosomes (DNA and protein)	Controls all activity of the cell
Nucleolus	DNA, RNA and proteins	Manufactures RNA
Nuclear membrane	Double layer of plasma membrane	Contains the nucleus
Nuclear pore	Gaps in the membrane with protein complexes	Controls the passage of material in and out of the nucleus, particularly RNA
Vacuole	Membrane-bound space in cytoplasm (large in plants)	Stores water, sugar and salt
Mitochondrion	Double-membraned organelle with own DNA	Aerobic respiration occurs here
Ribosome	RNA and protein	Manufactures protein
Cell wall*	Cellulose fibres	Give shape and rigidity (with vacuole); is fully permeable
Chloroplast*	Double-membraned organelle with chlorophyll and own DNA	Photosynthesis occurs here
*Plant cells only		

- Looking at cells:
  - Place cell on slide with water.
  - Cover with coverslip (to protect lens).
  - Lower the coverslip gently (to prevent air bubbles).
  - Stain (to make more visible):
    - Methylene blue for animal cells.
    - Iodine solution for plant cells.
  - Place on stage of microscope.
  - Focus with low then high power.
  - The total magnification is determined by multiplying the magnification of the eyepiece by the magnification of the objective lens.

HL
- There are two types of cells:
  1. Prokaryotic
     Has no membrane-bound structures within the cell
     Has no nucleus
     Example is bacteria.
  2. Eukaryotic
     Has membrane-bound structures within the cell
     Has a nucleus
     All organisms with the exception of bacteria are eukaryotes.

08 Cell Structure

Review questions

01
(a) What are the components all living organisms are made up of?
(b) What is the cell theory?
(c) Who formulated this theory (see Chapter 1)?

02
(a) What types of microscopes are there?
(b) Which type of microscope produces the most detailed images?
(c) Name the parts labelled 1 to 5 on the diagram of a microscope.
(d) Give the function of each part.

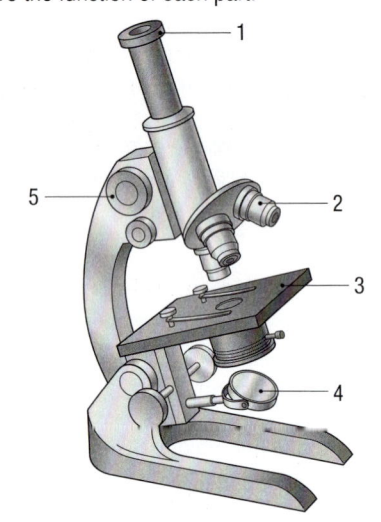

03
(a) What is the function of each of the following parts of a cell: the cell membrane, the cell wall, the nucleus, the vacuole, the cytoplasm?
(b) What structures are found in the nucleus?
(c) What is their function?

04 List three differences between animal and plant cells.

05
(a) What is the function of the mitochondrion?
(b) Kidney or muscle cells contain many mitochondria but a fat cell does not. Why do you think this is the case?

06 What is the function of the nucleolus? Is the nucleolus visible under the light microscope?

07
(a) Identify the cells shown in the diagram. 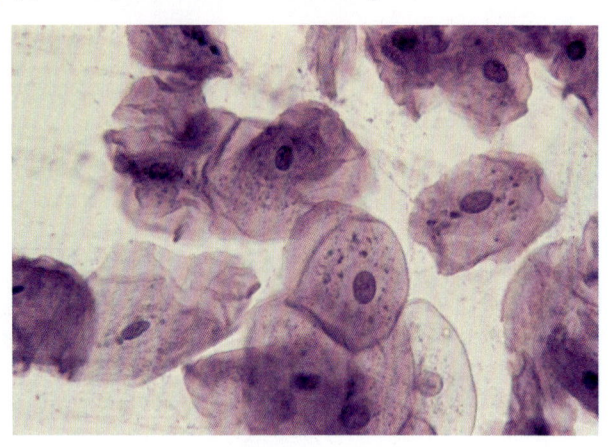
(b) Redraw one cell and label the nucleus, cytoplasm and cell membrane.
(c) State one way in which this cell differs from a typical plant cell.

08
(a) What is meant by the term eukaryote?
(b) What differences exist between eukaryotic and prokaryotic cells?
(c) What is the largest group of prokaryotic cells?

09
(a) Describe how you would prepare an animal cell for observation under a light microscope.
(b) What is the purpose of a stain?
(c) What is the function of a coverslip and why did you carefully lower it onto your cell?
(d) Describe how you use a microscope to view cells.

10 Draw a labelled diagram of:
(a) A plant cell as seen under a light microscope.
(b) An animal cell as seen under a light microscope.

Examination style questions

Section A

01 The diagram shows a plant cell as seen with an electron microscope.
(a) Name the parts labelled W, X and Y. 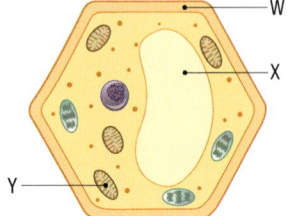
(b) What evidence is there in the diagram to show that the cell is being seen using an electron microscope?
　(i) Redraw the diagram into your copy and mark with the letter A on the diagram a part of the cell responsible for making enzymes.
　(ii) Mark with the letter B on the diagram a part of the cell responsible for making glucose.
(c) The nucleus of this cell has a darker stained area within it.
　(i) What is the name of this structure?
　(ii) Give one site in a plant where this cell would likely be found.

Cell Structure | 08

Examination style questions

Section B

02 All cells are small. A microscope is therefore needed to observe the detailed structure of cells.

(a) (i) What is the function of the nucleus?
 (ii) Name the type of cells that do not have a nucleus.
(b) (i) State the function of the parts of the microscope labelled A, B, C and D.

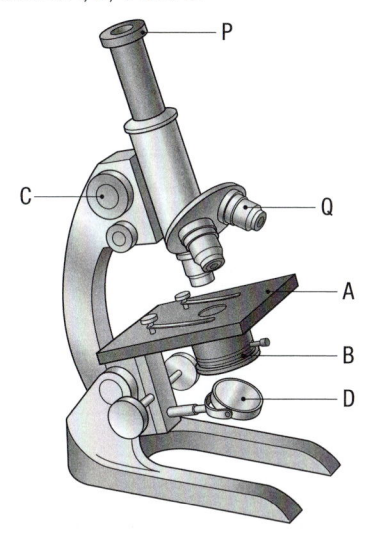

 (ii) Name the lenses labelled P and Q.
 (iii) If P is marked 10x and Q is marked 40x, what is the magnification achieved when both are used in combination?
 (iv) Describe how you prepared a slide of an animal cell for use in a light microscope.

Section C

03 (a) (i) Explain why a plant cell is described as eukaryotic.
 (ii) What is the term used to describe bacterial cells?
(b) Write brief notes on the following cell structures:
 (i) mitochondria, (ii) cell membrane, (iii) ribosomes, (iv) nuclear pores.
(c) (i) Draw a labelled diagram of a typical plant cell as observed with a light microscope.
 (ii) List **three** extra structures/details that can be observed in this cell that would be absent from an animal cell.
 (iii) Give the function of each of the items you named in (ii).

04 (a) (i) What is the term used to describe cells with no nucleus?
 (ii) Give two differences between these cells and plant cells.
(b) (i) Draw a well-labelled diagram of an animal cell as viewed under an electron microscope.
 (ii) Give the function of four of the structures labelled in (i).
 (iii) Where did you get an animal cell for viewing under a light microscope?
(c) (i) Name a stain used to observe plant cells more clearly.
 (ii) Describe how you applied this stain.
 (iii) Why did you apply it in the manner described in (ii)?

Leaving Certificate examination questions

Section A

01 Indicate whether each of the following statements is true or false.

Chloroplasts contain DNA.

The microscope lenses closest to the stage are the eyepiece lenses.

Animal cells do not have membranes.

2012 OL Q. 3

Section B

02 (a) Name the parts of the light microscope labelled A and B.
 If the magnification of A is 10x and the magnification of B is 40x, what magnification results when a slide is viewed using B?
(b) Answer the following in relation to preparing a slide of stained plant cells and viewing them under the microscope.
 (i) From what plants did you obtain the cells?
 (ii) Describe how you obtained a thin piece of a sample of the cells. 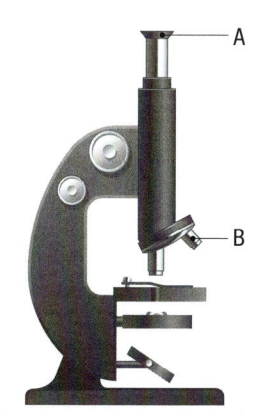
 (iii) What stain did you use for the cells on the slide?
 (iv) Describe how you applied this stain.
 (v) What did you do before placing the slide with the stained cells on the microscope platform?
 (vi) State two features of these cells that indicate they are typical plant cells.

2004 OL Q. 7

08 Cell Structure

Leaving Certificate examination questions

03 (a) Answer the following questions with reference to the microscope.
  (i) State the function of the part labelled A in the diagram.
  (ii) Lens E is marked 10x and lens O is marked 40x.

A cell is viewed through lenses E and O.

The image of the cell is 0.8 mm in diameter.

What is the actual diameter of the cell?

(b) Answer the following questions in relation to the procedures that you followed when preparing animal cells for examination with a light microscope.
  (i) Describe how you obtained a sample of cells.
  (ii) What stain did you use on the sample?
  (iii) Outline how you used the coverslip.
  (iv) Explain why a coverslip is used.
  (v) Describe how you examined the cells using the microscope.
  (vi) Draw a labelled diagram of the cells as seen at high magnification.

2014 HL Q. 8

04 (a) State the function of the following components of a cell: (i) ribosome, (ii) cell membrane.
(b) Answer the following questions in relation to the preparation, staining and microscopic observation of a slide of an animal cell.
  (i) What type of animal cell did you use? How did you obtain the cell? Name the stain that you used. Describe how you applied the stain.
  (ii) After staining a coverslip is placed on the slide. Give a reason for this.
  (iii) How did you apply the coverslip?
  (iv) Why did you apply it in this way?
  (v) Describe the difference in colour or depth of colour, if any, between the nucleus and cytoplasm when the stained cell was viewed under the microscope.

2006 HL Q. 8

Section C

05 (a) (i) Draw a labelled diagram of an animal cell as seen under a light microscope.
  (ii) Name another type of microscope that gives greater detail than a light microscope.
(b) The diagram below shows the ultrastructure of a section of a cell membrane.

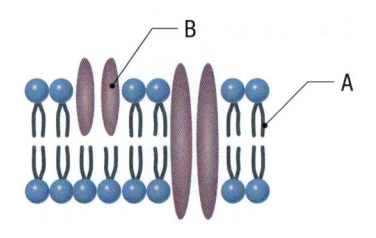

  (i) Give **two** functions of the cell membrane.
  (ii) Name the parts labelled A and B.
  (iii) Which organelle is known as 'the powerhouse of the cell'?
  (iv) Why does the nucleus of a cell have many pores?
  (v) List two differences between a plant cell and an animal cell.
  (vi) What is the primary source of energy for plant cells?

2013 OL Q. 13

06 (i) State the precise location of the cell membrane in plant cells.
(ii) With what type of cell do you associate membrane-bound organelles?
(iii) What is the corresponding term used to describe bacterial cells?

2011 HL Q. 14 (c)

Past examination questions

OL	2013 Q. 13 (a), (b)	2012 Q. 3 (c), (e), (f)	2011 Q. 8 (b) (iii), (v), Q. 9	2010 Q. 3	2007 Q. 3	2006 Q. 2
	2005 Q. 2	2004 Q. 2, Q. 7				

HL	2014 Q. 8	2012 Q. 12 (a)	2011 Q. 14 (c) (i)–(iii)	2010 Q. 8 (b) (ii), Q. 12 (b) (i)	2009 Q. 7	2006 Q. 8

Cell Diversity

09

After studying this chapter you should be able to:

1. Define the term tissue and give two examples of plant tissue and two examples of animal tissue.
2. Explain the term tissue culture and give two applications of a tissue culture.
3. Define the term organ and give one example from a plant and one from an animal.
4. Define an organ system and give two examples of an animal organ system.

Cell diversity

The vast majority of living **organisms** are multicellular. Although all the **cells** in such an organism carry the same **DNA** and are genetically identical, they are usually not physically identical. Different cells within the organism carry out different functions more efficiently and frequently look different, and in this way all the necessary activities occur to ensure the survival of the organism.

There are different ways of classifying **tissue** types, some depend more on function and others on structure. We classify here by function (Fig 9.1).

In animals, there are four major tissue types:

1. Epithelial tissue – groups of cells that line the body parts.
2. Connective tissue – groups of cells that support and hold the body structures together.
3. Muscular tissue – groups of cells that move the body parts.
4. Nervous tissue – groups of cells that respond to stimuli and transmit nerve messages.

> **D** **Tissues** are groups of similar cells that have the same structure and function.

PLANT TISSUE	ANIMAL TISSUE
Meristematic tissue (dividing)	Epithelial tissue (line the body)
Dermal tissue (protecting)	Connective tissue (hold body together)
Ground tissue (packing)	Muscular tissue (move the body)
Vascular tissue (transporting)	Nervous tissue (respond to stimuli and transmit nerve messages)

9.1 Plant and animal tissues

In plants, there are also four major tissue types:

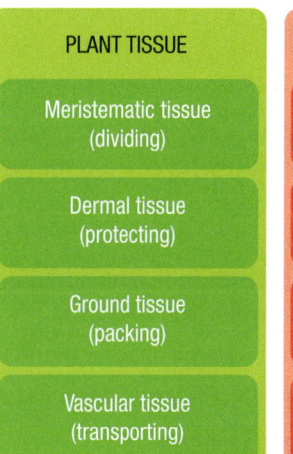

1. Meristematic tissue – groups of cells that are dividing and producing new cells for growth.
2. Dermal tissue – groups of cells protecting the outside of the plant.
3. Ground tissue – groups of cells filling the inside of the plant.
4. Vascular tissue – groups of cells that carry water and nutrients around the plant.

Animal tissues

Muscle tissue

Muscle tissue is unique because it has the ability to contract. This allows it to do two things: it can change its length or it can develop tension. There are three types of muscle tissue:

1. Cardiac muscle (found in your heart).
2. Skeletal muscle (attached to bones for movement).
3. Smooth muscle (in the walls of arteries).

09 Cell Diversity

Smooth muscle

Structure: Smooth muscle is made up of many long, slender cells called muscle fibres (Fig 9.2). These cells are pointed at either end and are about 0.2 mm long.

Role: Muscle can either cause movement or prevent movement due to an outside force.

Location: Smooth muscle (Fig 9.3) is found in the gut, blood vessels and other structures in the body cavity.

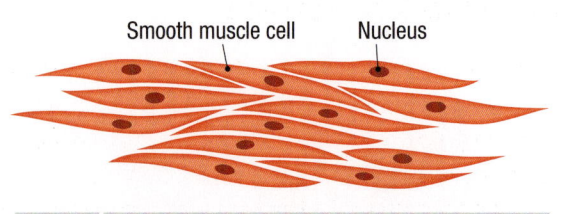

9.2 Animal tissue: smooth muscle

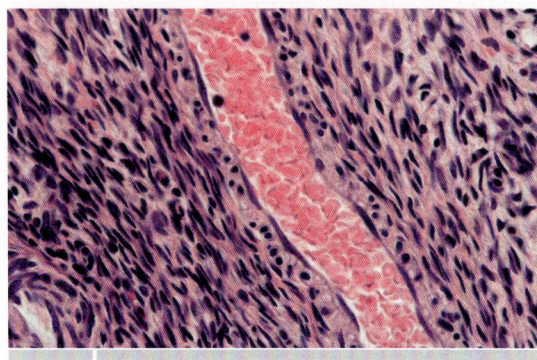

Connective tissue

There are many different types of connective tissue. Cartilage is one type of connective tissue, as is blood.

Structure: All connective tissue contains cells suspended in some form of matrix (non-cellular material). In cartilage a rubbery matrix that is flexible yet strong separates the cells.

Role: Connective tissues can hold body structures together, give support, protect and make blood.

Location: One type of cartilage is found in the tip of the nose and another type is found in our joints to stop wear and tear of bone (Fig 9.4).

9.3 Smooth muscle as seen under the electron microscope

Plant tissues

Dermal tissue

The outside of all plants is covered with dermal tissue (Fig 9.5).

Structure: These cells are tightly packed together and, in the aerial parts of the plant, are often covered with wax (cuticle). The epidermis (the outer dermal layer of cells on a leaf) may contain specialised cells, i.e. guard cells or root hairs.

Role: The epidermis protects the plant, controls gaseous exchange and absorbs water and minerals.

Location: The outside of a herbaceous (non-woody) plant is covered by a layer called the epidermis.

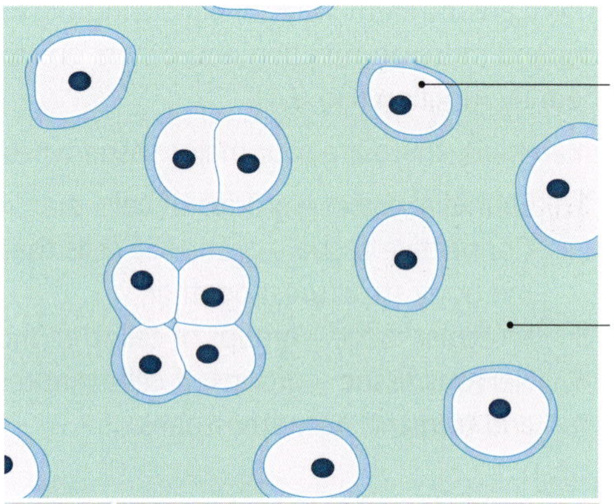

Meristematic tissue

The meristematic cells in a plant are the dividing cells from which all other cells are produced.

Structure: These cells are small with very thin walls, and have no chloroplasts or vacuoles.

Role: They divide and then differentiate into all the other plant cell types (Fig 9.6).

Location: They are found everywhere there is growth, e.g. root tip and shoot tip.

You will learn more about plant structure and plant tissues in Chapter 21.

9.4 Animal tissue: cartilage

9.5 Plant tissue (stained) as seen through a light microscope

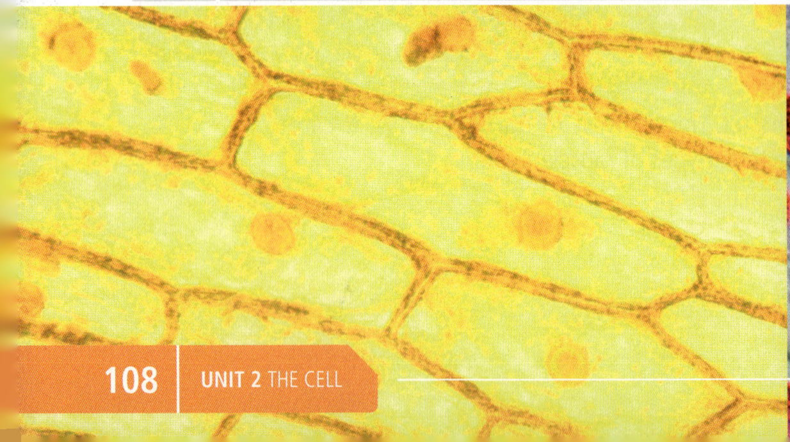

9.6 Meristematic cells as seen through the light microscope

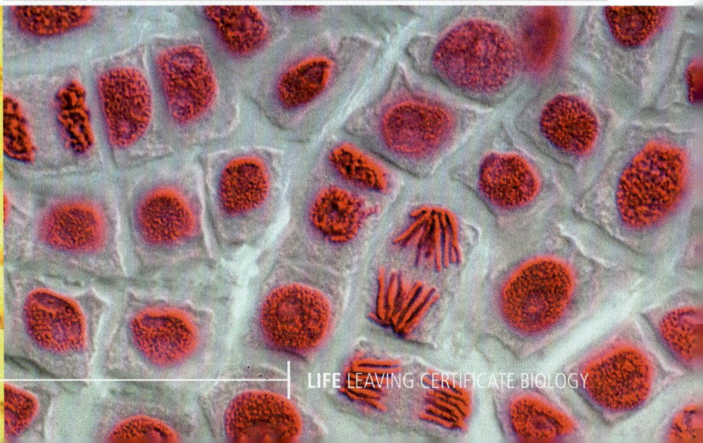

Tissue culture

It is now possible to grow both animal and plant tissue in the laboratory (Fig 9.7). These are called **tissue cultures**. The cells are grown in a sterile medium outside of the living organism. This is often called 'in vitro' growth of cells meaning growth 'in glass'. Frequently such cells are now grown in large **bioreactors**. For cells to grow in these bioreactors they need to be supplied with food, oxygen, the correct pH, the correct temperature and frequently specific chemicals called growth factors have to be supplied. The cells then grow and make the required product.

Plant tissue culture

- If pieces of carrot are put into a special culture medium they will produce a lump of cells called a callus.
- This callus (often after the addition of specific growth factors) will then produce new carrot plants that can then be transferred to soil. Each plant is genetically identical.
- This technique is particularly useful in **genetic engineering** experiments when **transgenic plants** (see Chapter 17) are being produced. It allows the experimenters to produce large numbers of identical plants (see Chapter 35).
- This process can be done with a number of plant species.

> **Tissue culture** is the growth of cells in a medium outside an organism.

> A **bioreactor** is a vessel (usually large) in which cells, organisms or enzymes are placed to manufacture specific products.

9.7 The micropropagation of plants

Animal tissue culture

- If human cells are taken and placed on a special medium, it is possible to grow sheets of human cells (Fig 9.8).
- The cells tend to grow in single layers.
- It is now possible to grow sheets of human skin in this manner to replace burnt skin.
- Bone tissue and cartilage are also grown for use in reconstructive surgery.
- There has been some success in growing large quantities of cells that manufacture a specific chemical, e.g. insulin-producing cells.

It is now possible, as the techniques develop, to grow layers of different tissues on a scaffolding to generate an **organ** (see below). This has been done for simple organs like the bladder and trachea. For some tissue culture, stem cells are used – these are cells that can grow into more than one type of cell.

In the case of the bladder a scaffolding of biodegradable plastic is used to grow the necessary tissues from the patient. In the case of the trachea a donated trachea (from a dead donor) is stripped of its cells and the patient's cells are grown on this cartilage framework. In both these cases the organs have the advantage that they are made from cells belonging to the person receiving them and tissue rejection is not a problem (see Chapter 33).

9.8 A piece of skin (epidermal strip) grown outside the body

09 | Cell Diversity

Organs

Organs contain at least two types of tissue, are distinct structures of the organism, and have particular functions.

In animals there are a frequently a large number of organs. For example, the human heart (Fig 9.9):

- contains cardiac muscle, valves and blood (connective tissue) and nerves;
- these tissues function together to act as a pump for the blood.

The human stomach:

- comprises smooth muscle, connective tissue, blood, nerve tissue and epithelial tissue;
- all of these various tissues work together in a coordinated manner to store the food, digest some of it and then pass it on to the next part of the digestive system.

In plants there are six organs: roots, leaves, stems, flowers, fruits and seeds.

Leaves are generally flat green structures primarily used for photosynthesis. The leaf (Fig 9.10) contains:

- dermal tissue on the outside for protection;
- ground tissue that has chloroplasts and can photosynthesise;
- vascular tissue for transporting food and water around the plant.

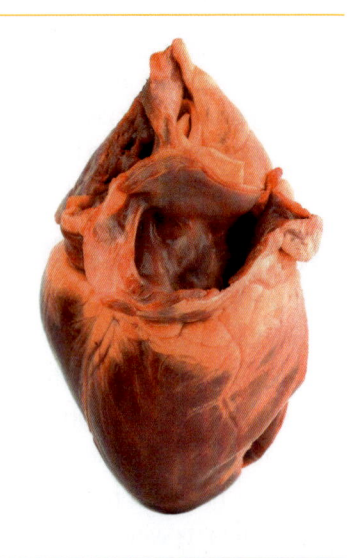

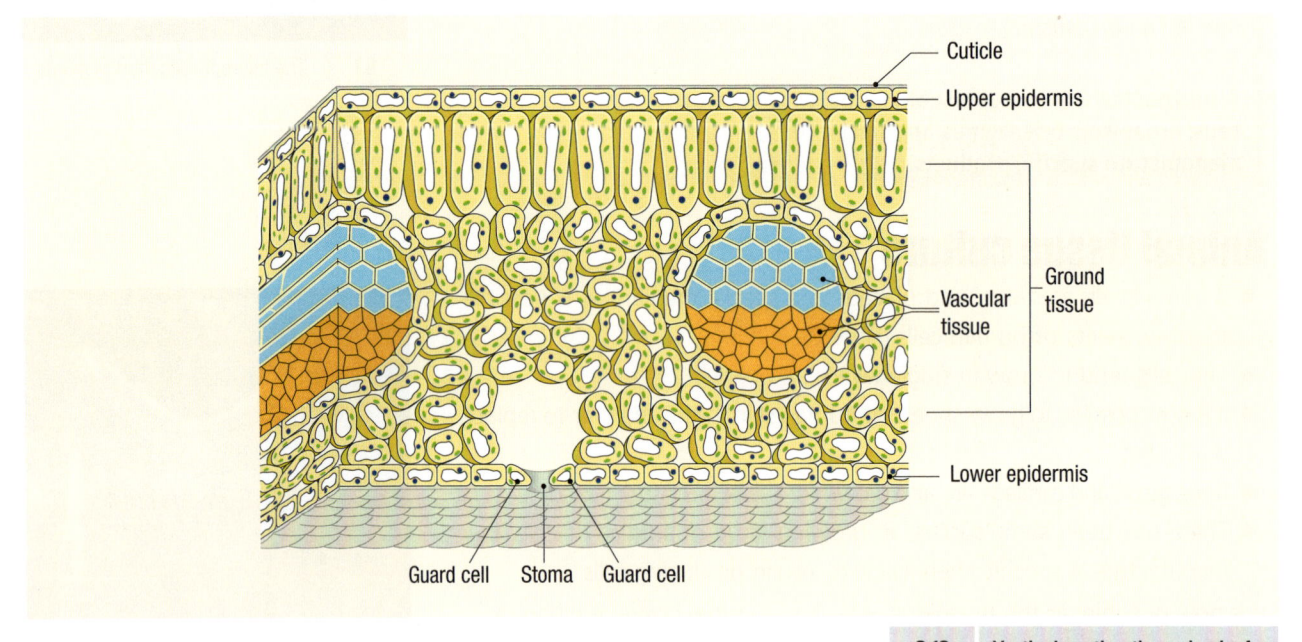

9.9 A human heart

9.10 Vertical section through a leaf

Roots in a plant are used for anchorage and for absorption of water and nutrients from the soil. The root contains:

- meristematic tissue for growth;
- dermal tissue for protection and absorption;
- vascular tissue for transport;
- ground tissue for bulk and food storage (see Fig 9.11).

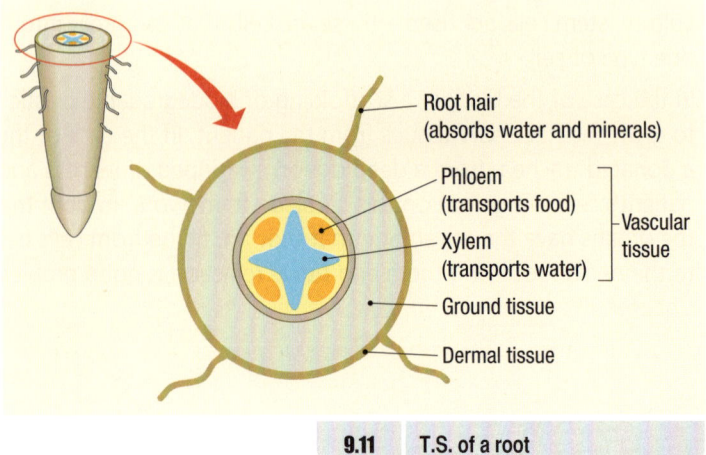

D An **organ** is a group of tissues that work together to carry out a function.

9.11 T.S. of a root

Organ systems

The next level of organisation found in animals is the **organ system**.

There are ten such systems in humans (Fig 9.12).

One of these is the urinary system (see Chapter 27).

- It comprises the **bladder**, **kidney**, **ureters** and the **urethra**.
- It has the function of removing waste material from the body and controlling the composition of many chemicals in the blood.

The skeletal system is also an organ system (see Chapter 32).

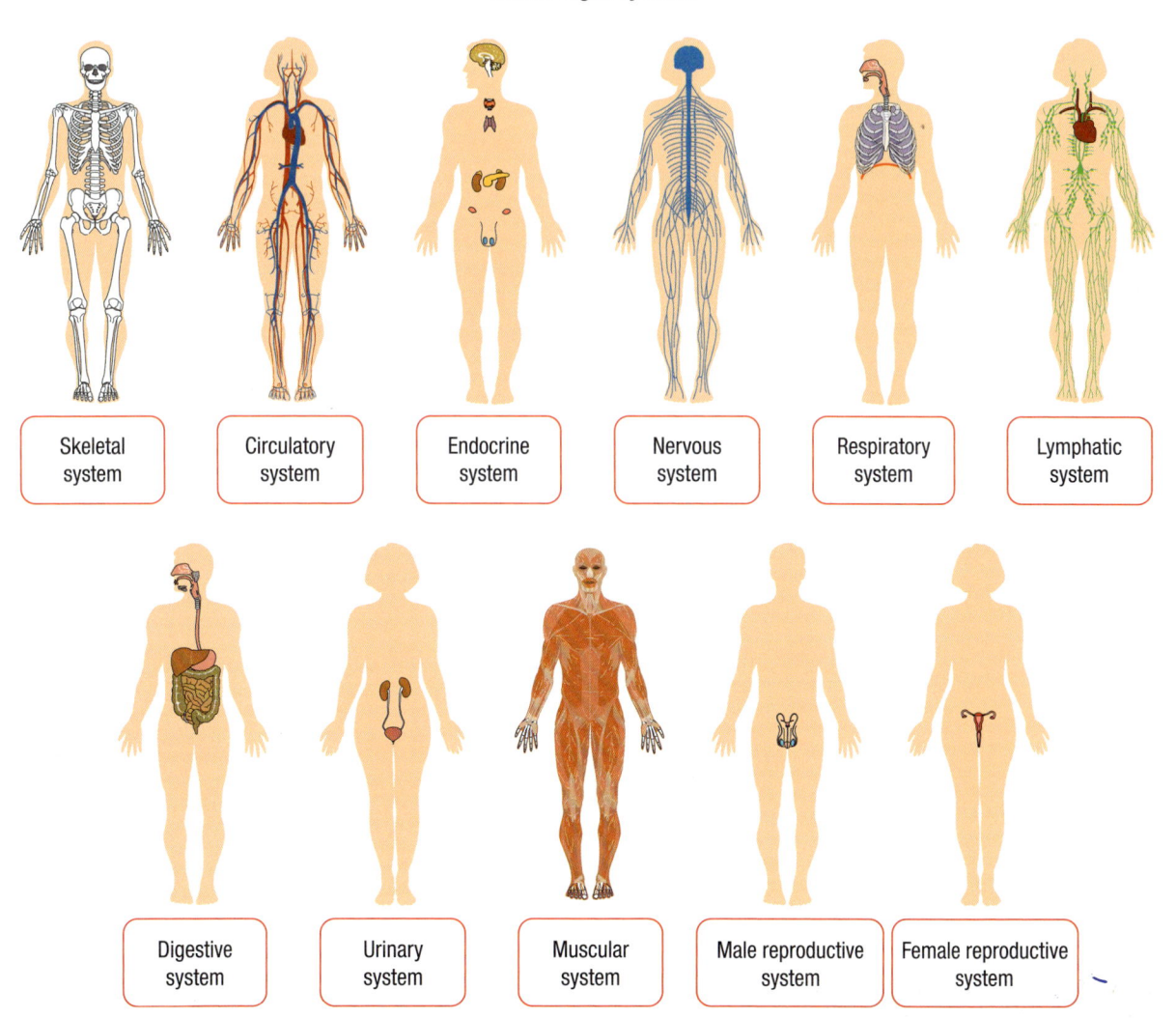

- It is made up of the **bones** and **cartilage**.
- This gives structure to the body, supports and protects the internal organs, allows movement and produces the blood cells.

> **Organ systems** are groups of organs working together to undertake specific functions.

Organism

Organs and organ systems combine to form an organism. A group of organisms that share a large number of physical features and can normally interbreed to produce fertile offspring is called a **species**. There are tens of millions of species on the planet. To study them, we need to have a way of classifying them to make such work manageable (see Chapter 18).

Human Organ Systems

Skeletal system | Circulatory system | Endocrine system | Nervous system | Respiratory system | Lymphatic system

Digestive system | Urinary system | Muscular system | Male reproductive system | Female reproductive system

9.12 Human organ systems

09 — Cell Diversity

Summary

- Tissues are groups of similar cells that carry out specific functions.
- Tissues allow a multicellular organism carry out its functions more effectively.
    - Animal tissues
        - Muscles:
          can contract and cause movement;
          are of three types: cardiac, smooth and skeletal.
            - Smooth muscle:
              comprises long narrow cells;
              is an involuntary muscle, i.e. it pushes the food through the gut;
              lines the gut.
        - Connective tissue:
          contain cells in a matrix.
            - Cartilage is a connective tissue:
              contains elastic fibres in a matrix;
              protects the bones from damage;
              found in the tip of the nose and at the end of bones in joints.
    - Plant tissues
        - Dermal tissue:
          consists of tightly packed cells;
          is used for protection, control of gaseous exchange and absorption of water;
          is found on the outside of plants.
        - Meristematic tissue:
          consists of dividing cells;
          is used to make new cells;
          is found in the root or shoot tip.
- Tissue culture is the growth of cells in a medium outside of the organism.
    - This is used to produce large numbers of identical plants.
    - The technology is particularly important in genetic engineering.
    - In humans it is used to grow simple tissues for surgery, e.g. skin, bone and cartilage.
    - Can be used to grow clones of chemical producing cells, e.g. insulin cells.
- An organ: Groups of tissues that work together to carry out a function:
    - contains at least two types of tissue;
    - carries out specific functions.
- The heart:
    - is found in animals;
    - contains cardiac muscle, valves and blood (connective tissue) and nerves;
    - pumps blood.
- The root:
    - is found in plants;
    - contains meristem, dermal tissue, vascular and ground tissues;
    - protects, stores food, and absorbs and transports water.
- Organ system: a group of organs that work together to carry out a function:
    - found in animals, e.g. the excretory system;
    - made of a number of organs;
    - carries out specific functions.
- Urinary (excretory) system:
    - comprises kidney, ureter, bladder and urethra;
    - removes waste.
- An organism is made of organs or organ systems.
- A group of interbreeding organisms that can produce fertile offspring is called a species.

Cell Diversity 09

Review questions

01 (a) What is a tissue?
(b) Name two types of animal tissue, then describe the structure and state the function of each tissue.

02 In the case of the dermis in plants:
(a) Describe the function of the tissue.
(b) Describe any specialised cells found in the dermis.

03 (a) What is the role of meristematic tissue in the plant?
(b) Where is this tissue found in the plant?

04 (a) What is a tissue culture?
(b) Describe how a plant tissue culture might be produced.
(c) What is the advantage of such a technique?
(d) Give three examples of the role of animal tissue culture in medicine.

05 (a) What is an organ?
(b) Name two plant organs.
(c) For each of these organs give its function and name the tissues found in the organ.

06 (a) Name two organs found in animals.
(b) For each organ give its function and name the tissues found in the organ.

07 (a) Define an organ system.
(b) Give the functions and structure of the urinary system.
(c) What are the functions of the skeletal system?
(d) Define a species.

Examination style questions

Section A

01 (a) What is a tissue?
(b) Name two types of human tissue.
(c) In the case of one of these tissues, state its function in the human body.
(d) Name two types of plant tissue.
(e) In the case of one of these tissues, state its function in the plant.

02 (a) Explain the term tissue culture.
(b) Give two examples of the use of tissue culture, one using plants and one using animal cells.
(c) What is an organ?
(d) Give one example of a plant organ and one example of an animal organ.
(e) What is an organ system?

Section C

03 (a) Explain the term tissue.
(b) Name one plant tissue, state its function and location of this tissue in a plant.
(c) Name one animal tissue, state its function and location of this tissue in an animal.
(d) In a laboratory process a small piece of carrot tissue is placed in a sterile growth medium. The tissue multiplies to form new carrot plants that are identical to the original carrot.

(i) Name the process.
(ii) Name three factors other than a sterile growth medium that are necessary for this process to occur and give the function of each.
(iii) Suggest the most suitable temperature for carrying out this process with human cells. Give a reason for your answer.
(iv) What type of cell division produces the new carrots?
(v) These new carrots are called clones. What does this mean?
(vi) Give two ways in which this process can be of benefit to humans.

04 (a) Explain the term organ.
(b) Give an example of one human organ, name the tissues that make up this organ and give the location of the organ in the human body.
(c) Give an example of one plant organ, name the tissues that make up the organ and give the location of the organ in a plant.
(d) What is an organ system?
(e) Give an example of a human organ system and give the function of this organ system.
(f) Explain the term species.

09 Cell Diversity

Leaving Certificate examination questions

Section A

01 Choose **each** term from the following list and place it in **Column B** to match a description in **Column A**.
The first one has been completed as an example.

skin graft   dermal   organ   leaf   tissue   *in vitro*   growth

Column A	Column B
A group of cells with the same function	Tissue
(a) A plant organ	
(b) Cells growing in a test tube	
(c) The heart	
(d) A use of tissue culture	
(e) A plant tissue	

2014 OL Q. 4

02 (a) (i) What is a tissue?
  (ii) Give an example of an animal tissue.
  (iii) State the role of the animal tissue referred to in (ii).
  (iv) Give one way in which tissue referred to in (ii) is adapted to carry out its function(s).

(b) (i) Explain the term *tissue culture*.
  (ii) Give **two** examples of the use of tissue culture.

2012 HL Q. 2

Section C

03 (a) (i) What is a tissue?
  (ii) Name **two** tissues found in animals.

(b) Tissue culture is used to make a skin graft for patients who have been severely burned.
  (i) What is meant by tissue culture?
  (ii) Name the gas needed to release energy to make a skin graft.
  (iii) Suggest the most suitable temperature to make skin cells grow.
  (iv) Suggest a reason why sterile conditions are needed in tissue culture.
  (v) What type of cell division, mitosis or meiosis, is involved in tissue culture?
  (vi) Give **one** other application of tissue culture apart from skin grafting.

2007 OL Q. 11

Past examination questions

| OL | 2014 Q. 4 | 2012 Q. 14 (c) (i), (ii) | 2009 Q. 9 (a) | 2007 Q. 11, Q. 14 (a) |

| HL | 2012 Q. 2 | 2010 Q. 4 | SEC Sample Q. 3 | |

Movement Through Membranes   10

After studying this chapter you should be able to:

1. Define the term diffusion and give examples.
2. Explain how cell membranes are selectively permeable.
3. Define the term osmosis and give examples.
4. Explain what is meant by the term turgid.
5. Describe how turgidity is used in plants for support.
6. Explain how a high salt or sugar concentration can be used to preserve food.
7. Describe an experiment to demonstrate osmosis.

Movement of molecules

If it were possible for you to look at the molecules surrounding a **cell**, you would see that they are in constant motion. This movement is completely random. As they move about, they hit off one another and collide but keep moving at all times. This movement is due to the kinetic energy that all molecules contain. Giving heat to the molecules can increase this energy. The temperature of something is simply a measure of the amount of kinetic energy it contains.

Diffusion

If a crystal of purple dye was placed in a test tube of water, the test tube of water would slowly turn purple (Fig 10.1). Why is it that the random movement of the dye caused a uniform mixture to be produced? When the dye was placed into the water, the molecules dissolved in the water and moved in a random manner. As there were a very large number of dye molecules concentrated in one area, more dye molecules on average moved away from this area to places in the liquid that had few dye molecules (Fig 10.2). This process of mixing is called **diffusion**.

> **D** **Diffusion** is the movement of molecules from areas of high concentration to areas of lower concentration.

10.1 The diffusion of a dye in water

10 Movement Through Membranes

(a) Crystal of dye is placed in water
(b) Diffusion of dye and water molecules
(c) Equal distribution of molecules results

10.2 The diffusion of a dye in water

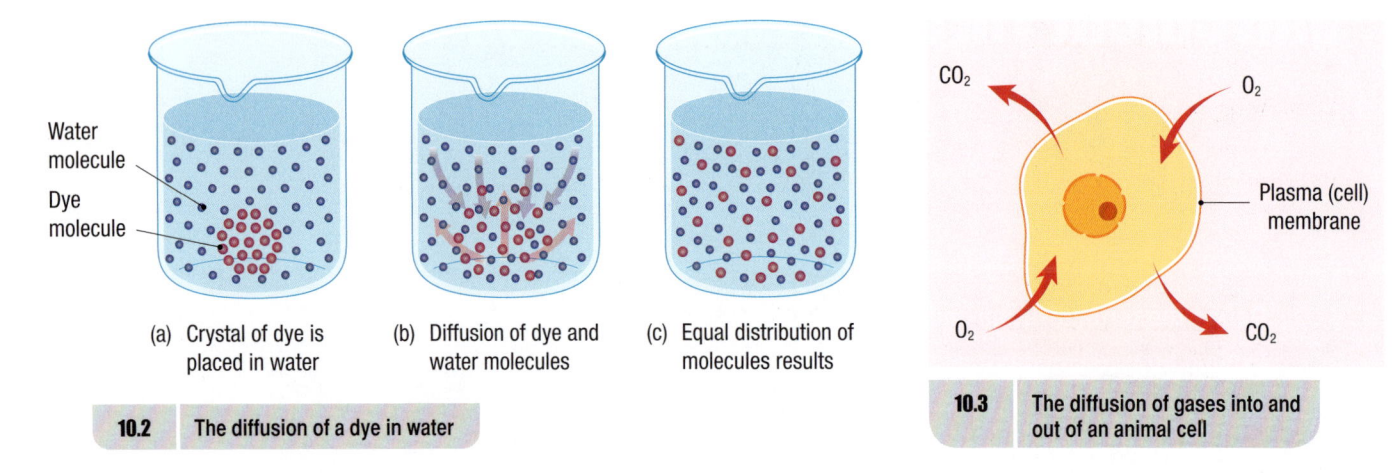

10.3 The diffusion of gases into and out of an animal cell

The gases oxygen and carbon dioxide diffuse freely into and out of cells. An active muscle cell in a human is surrounded by many tiny blood vessels filled with blood coming from the lungs that contains a high level of oxygen. The cell will have used all its oxygen in **respiration** and will have a high concentration of carbon dioxide in it. The difference in concentration of gases in these two areas is called the **concentration gradient**. Oxygen will diffuse into the cell and carbon dioxide will diffuse out of the cell (Fig 10.3). Diffusion will always take place when such a gradient occurs. Diffusion is a **passive** process that uses the natural heat energy concentration of a substance and does not require any other energy.

Osmosis

Membranes, around the cell or around cellular **organelles**, are barriers to the movement of molecules. Many molecules cannot pass across them. As we saw in Chapter 8 the membrane is made up of two types of chemicals, **phospholipids** and proteins.

- The phospholipids are a barrier to almost all chemicals but the proteins may allow certain chemicals through.
- Different proteins will let different chemicals pass through the membrane. Many of these chemicals will pass by diffusion although some may be pulled in by a process of **active transport** (see page 118).
- Depending on the different proteins present in the membranes found in the various cells in an **organism**, different chemicals can get into, or out of, the cells or cell **organelles**.
- Such membranes are called **selectively permeable** or **semi-permeable**.

Water is one of the few molecules that has the ability to cross most membranes freely. Many substances can dissolve in water.

- Water is, in this case, called a **solvent**.
- The chemical that is dissolved is called a **solute**.
- The mixture of these two is called a **solution**.

If a solution of sucrose (water and sugar) is separated from pure water by a semi-permeable membrane, only the water will move across the membrane. There is a higher concentration of water in the pure water as compared with the solution. Water will flow into the solution (Fig 10.4).

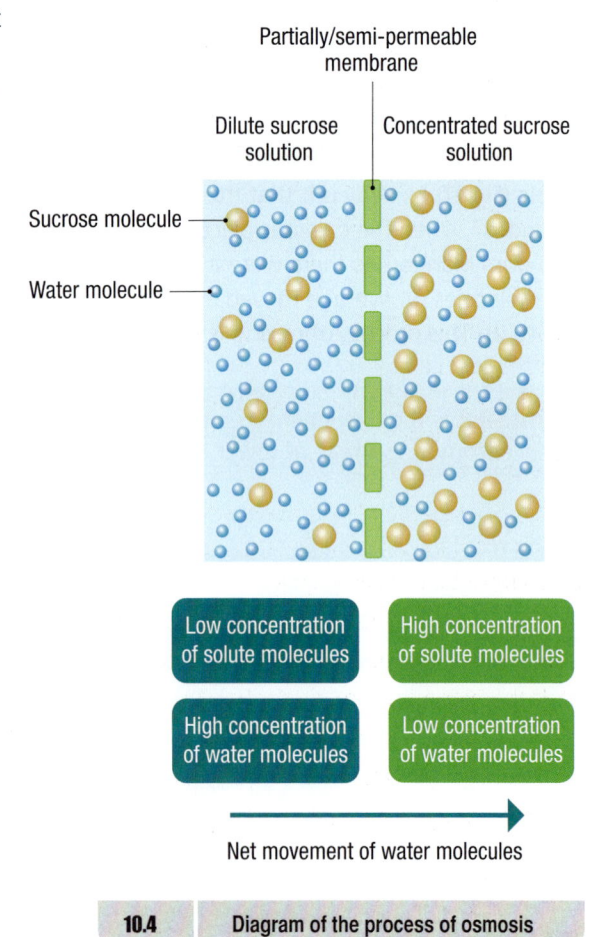

10.4 Diagram of the process of osmosis

10.5 A demonstration of osmosis

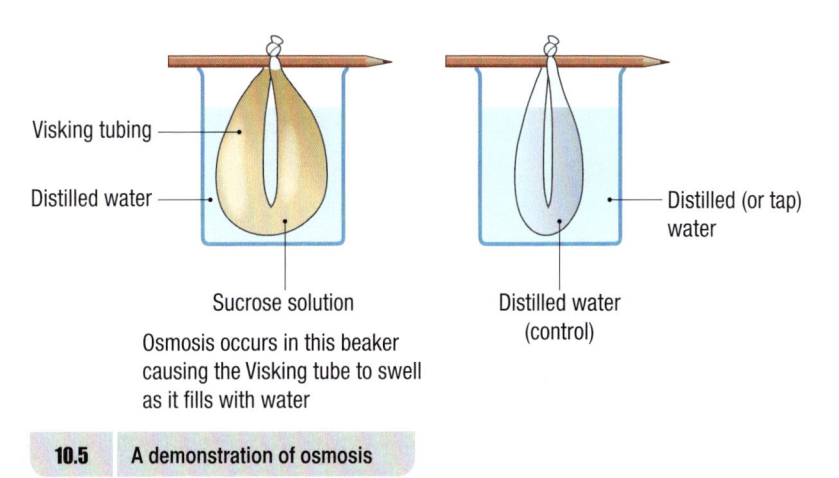

Osmosis (Fig 10.5) is the movement of water from an area of high concentration of water to an area of lower concentration across a semi-permeable membrane. Therefore, osmosis can be considered as a special form of diffusion.

> **Osmosis** is the movement of water from an area of high concentration of water to an area of lower concentration across a semi-permeable membrane.

Animal cells and osmosis

In animal cells, there is only a cell membrane separating the cell and the external environment. If such a cell was immersed in pure water the flow of water would be into the cell. Should this continue, then the cell membrane would be unable to withstand the pressure as the cell filled up with water and the cell would burst.

Such a problem exists for some single-celled organisms that live in fresh water. *Amoeba* is one such organism (see Chapter 20). It is not possible for the organism to stop the water coming in so it must get rid of the water before it causes a problem. To do this, *Amoeba* have a special structure called the **contractile vacuole** (Fig 10.6). As the water enters the cell, it is diverted into this vacuole. When the vacuole is full, the water is pushed out of the cell. This process requires **energy**.

If a red blood cell was put in a similar situation it would burst, as red blood cells do not contain contractile vacuoles. If the red blood cell was put into a solution containing a lot of salt, more water would leave the red blood cell than would enter and the cell would shrink (Fig 10.7).

Multicellular animals like ourselves have to carefully monitor the environment in which we keep our cells. The concentration of our blood must be kept exactly right or our cells will not work correctly.

- If the blood is more concentrated than the cells, water will leave the cells and flow into the blood.
- If the blood is more dilute than the cells, the cells will fill up with water from the blood.
- The **kidneys** carry out this process of **osmoregulation** in the body (see Chapter 27).

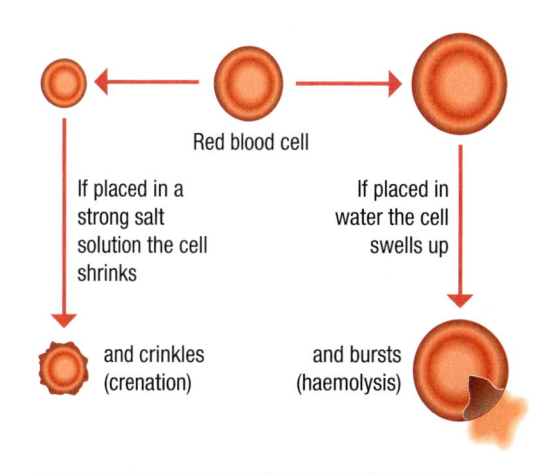

10.6 An *Amoeba* showing a contractile vacuole

10.7 The effect on red blood cells of solutions of different concentrations

> **Osmoregulation** is the control of the water and salt levels in the cell or the organism.

10 | Movement Through Membranes

> **Turgor pressure** is the force of the cell contents against the cell wall in plant cells.

> **Turgid cell**: a plant cell in which the contents of the cell are pushing against the cell wall due to turgor pressure.

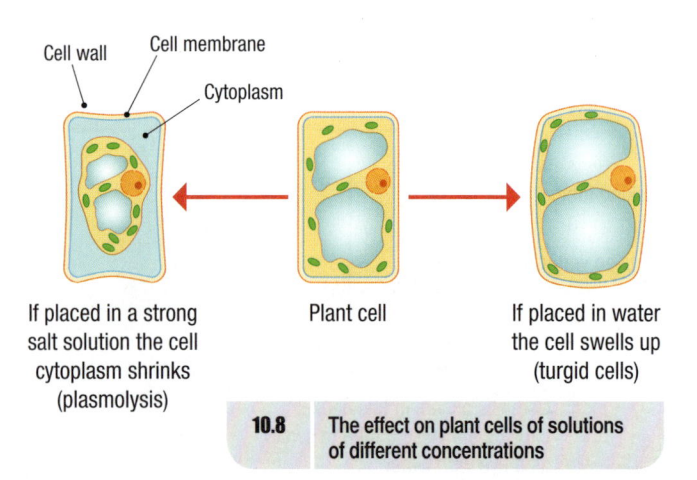

10.8 The effect on plant cells of solutions of different concentrations

If placed in a strong salt solution the cell cytoplasm shrinks (plasmolysis) — *Plant cell* — *If placed in water the cell swells up (turgid cells)*

Plant cells and osmosis

Plant cells have a cell wall around their membrane. The cell wall is fully permeable. If a plant cell is immersed in pure water, the water will enter the cell by osmosis and the cell will expand as the water flows into the vacuole. The cytoplasm and the membrane are pushed outwards against the cell wall. The cell does not burst because of the cell wall. This pushes back against the pressure on the cell membrane. The cell will expand but stops before it bursts. Such a cell is said to be **turgid**.

If a plant cell is placed in a solution that is highly concentrated, it will lose water to the surroundings. As the cell loses water, the cell membrane shrinks and pulls away from the cell wall, leaving a gap between the cell wall and the cytoplasm. This process is called **plasmolysis** (Fig 10.8).

The turgor pressure that develops in a plant is very important for the structural rigidity of **herbaceous** plants (see Chapter 21). The turgid cells packed tightly together hold the plant upright. When the plant loses too much water, it also loses turgor and the plant will **wilt** (see Fig 10.9).

10.9 The effect of water loss on a herbaceous plant

> **Plasmolysis** is the loss of turgor pressure in a plant cell due to loss of water from the cytoplasm.

Food preservation

The growth of micro-organisms on food may cause food to go bad. In order to help prevent this, food may be preserved. The death of cells of micro-organisms due to water loss because of osmosis is the mechanism by which some forms of food preservation work. In jam-making, a high level of sugar is added to the fruit. When micro-organisms land on the jam they lose water due to osmosis. The micro-organisms cannot survive without this water and thus die. This extends the shelf life of the jam. It also explains why modern low-sugar jams must be kept in the refrigerator to stop them from 'going off'. Adding salt to meat or fish has the same effect in preserving the food, e.g. bacon.

Active transport

Many cells need to take in chemicals that are already in high concentration within the cell. Diffusion would cause these chemicals to leave the cell. Active transport is the process where chemicals are taken into a cell against the diffusion gradient.

- This process requires energy.
- It is undertaken by proteins in the cell membrane, which drag the chemicals into the cell and keep them there.
- In certain circumstances, some minerals are taken into root hairs by this process, as is iodine into the **thyroid gland**.

> **Active transport** is the absorption of molecules into cells against the concentration gradient, using energy.

Movement Through Membranes | 10

10.10 Preserving food using sugar or salt

Investigation 10.1

Experiment to demonstrate osmosis

Procedure

1. Take one 50 cm strip of Visking tubing and cut into two equal lengths.
2. Place the two strips of Visking tubing into some tap water in a beaker for about 5 minutes (this will soften the tubing).
3. Tie a knot in one end of each softened strip.
4. Three-quarters fill one strip with distilled water (the control).
5. Three-quarters fill the second with 80% sucrose solution.
6. Tie the two ends of each tube together to form a circle, making sure to exclude as much air as possible.
7. Carefully wash and dry each piece of tubing.
8. Weigh each piece of tubing and note the turgidity (firmness) of each.
9. Suspend each piece of tubing in a beaker of distilled water using a pencil, remembering to identify each piece of tubing (see Fig 10.11).
10. After 20 minutes remove each piece of tubing from the beaker and re-dry.
11. Weigh and record the mass of each tube.
12. Note the turgidity of each tube.
13. Write up the investigation in your practical notebook and explain your observations.

10.11 The apparatus as set up for the experiment

You should expect the tubing with sucrose to be more turgid and heavier than it was at the start and the tubing containing distilled water not to have changed.

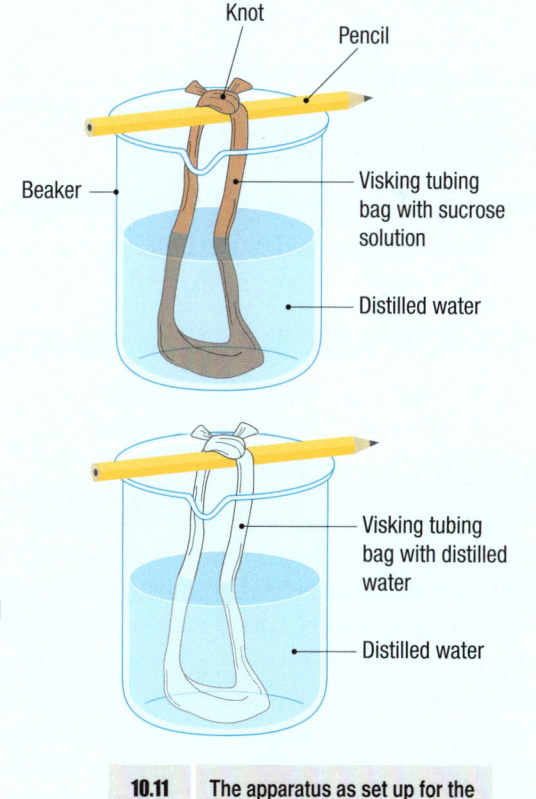

Movement Through Membranes

Summary

- All molecules are in constant motion, and the higher the temperature the faster the motion.
- Diffusion is the movement of molecules from areas of high concentration of water to areas of low concentration.
- Gases diffuse in and out of cells.
- Osmosis is the movement of water from an area of high concentration of water to an area of lower concentration across a semi-permeable membrane.
- The proteins in the membranes control which chemicals can get through the membrane.
- Different membranes let different chemicals through them as they contain different proteins.
- Single-celled organisms without a cell wall found in fresh water have to protect themselves from water flowing into them.
- *Amoeba* have a contractile vacuole that uses energy to expel water.
- If the cell has a cell wall and is in fresh water, e.g. a plant cell:
  - Water diffuses into the cell and the cell wall pushes against the expanding cell and the cells become rigid.
  - They are said to be turgid.
  - Green plants use this turgor pressure to keep upright.
- If the cell has a cell wall and is placed into a concentrated solution:
  - The water leaves the cell.
  - The cell membrane shrinks away from the cell wall.
  - The cell is said to be plasmolysed.
- Multicellular animals need to monitor the internal environment for water and salt balance.
  - Osmoregulation is the control of the water and salt balance in an organism.
  - Osmoregulation is carried out by the kidneys in humans.
- Micro-organisms can be killed if they are placed in high salt or high sugar solutions.
  - Preserving meat using salt: bacon.
  - Preserving fruit using sugar: jam.
- Active transport is the process by which chemicals are drawn into a cell against the diffusion gradient using energy, e.g. iodine into the thyroid gland.
- In an investigation Visking tubing containing sucrose solution, suspended in distilled water, gained weight but the one with distilled water remained the same. This demonstrated osmosis.

Movement Through Membranes | 10

Review questions

01 (a) What happens to molecules in a liquid when they are heated?
(b) Explain the term diffusion.

02 (a) If a crystal of purple potassium permanganate was placed into a dish of water, the water would eventually go purple. Why is this?
(b) How could you make this process occur faster?

03 Explain how diffusion is important to living organisms.

04 In what way does osmosis differ from diffusion?

05 (a) Where do you find semi-permeable membranes in nature?
(b) What part of the membrane determines what can get through it?

06 (a) What will happen to a plant cell if it is placed in pure water?
(b) How do plants use this process?

07 (a) On very sunny days, plants may wilt. Why does this happen?
(b) Draw what a plant cell would look like if it were placed in a solution with a high salt concentration.
(c) Why does this happen?

08 Explain why salt or sugar can be used to preserve food.

09 Describe an experiment to demonstrate osmosis.

10 Using a cork borer, ten potato 'chips' were cut from a raw potato. Each chip was 5 cm long and 0.5 cm in diameter. Five were placed in solution A and five in solution B. At the end of the day, the potatoes from solution A were 7 cm long and 1 cm wide. The potatoes from solution B were 3.5 cm long and 0.25 cm wide. Explain what happened and why it happened.

11 Suggest why boiling a membrane can stop osmosis.

Examination style questions

Section A

01 Diagram A shows a plant cell. Diagram B shows the same cell after it has been placed in a certain solution for a period of time.

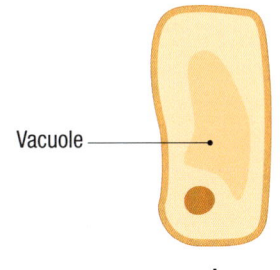

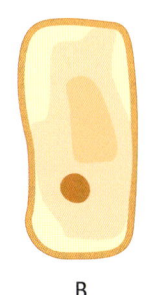

Vacuole

A   B

(a) Comment on the concentration of the solution in which the cell was placed.
(b) What term is used to describe the cell in diagram B?
(c) What is the effect on a plant to have cells in the state named in part (b)?
(d) Name two components of cell membranes.
(e) Name a substance, other than water, that you would expect to be present in the vacuole.

02 (a) What is meant by the term selectively permeable?
(b) What is the component of membranes that makes them selectively permeable?
(c) If the components in (b) are changed what will happen?
(d) What is osmoregulation?
(e) Why is it important for multicellular organisms?

Section B

03 (a) (i) What is meant by osmosis?
(ii) Give one example of osmosis in living organisms.
(b) In the course of your studies you carried out an investigation to demonstrate osmosis.
(i) Draw a fully labelled diagram of the apparatus you set up, including a control.
(ii) Explain the steps you took **after** the apparatus had been set up.
(iii) State the results you obtained.
(iv) Briefly explain the results described in (iii).

10 Movement Through Membranes

Examination style questions

Section C

04 (a) 'Osmosis is a special case of diffusion.' Comment on the validity of this statement.

(b) In an experiment, 10 cylinders of carrot tissue were obtained using a cork borer. The cylinders were divided into two sets of five. Each set was dried on the outside by a standard technique, the total length measured and the total mass recorded. One set was immersed in tap water and the other in a concentrated salt solution for 30 minutes and then the cylinders were re-measured.

The results are shown below.

(i) Suggest why each set of carrot cylinders was dried after being immersed in the water and the salt solution. Suggest a suitable method to dry them.

(ii) Give a precise biological explanation of the results of this experiment. Refer in your explanation to semi-permeable membrane, osmosis and turgor.

(iii) Describe **one** example of the application of high salt or high sugar concentration in food preservation.

(c) Describe using labelled diagrams what happens to animal cells when they are placed in solutions of differing concentrations.

	Group A (tap water)	Group B (salt solution)
Before immersion – mass	12.6 g	12.9 g
Length	31.4 cm	31.7 cm
After immersion – mass	13.2 g	11.3 g
Length	31.9 cm	31.1 cm

Leaving Certificate examination questions

Section A

01 (a) (i) In relation to structures such as the cell membrane, explain the term *selective permeability*.
(ii) Suggest an advantage to the cell of having a selectively permeable membrane.
(iii) Name **two** substances that enter a human muscle by diffusion.

(b) (i) Explain the term *turgor*.
(ii) Give a feature of a plant cell that allows it to remain turgid for long periods.
(iii) Suggest a way in which turgor is of value to plants.

2013 HL Q. 5

Section B

02 (a) (i) Which substance moves through cell membranes by osmosis?
(ii) Name **one** other term used in biology to describe the movement of substances through cell membranes.

(b) Answer the following in relation to an activity you carried out to demonstrate osmosis.

(i) Draw a labelled diagram of the apparatus you used in your demonstration.
(ii) Suggest a control that you might use in this activity.
(iii) State the result(s) of your investigation.
(iv) Briefly explain the result(s) referred to in part (iii).
(v) What is the purpose of a control in scientific experiments?

2013 OL Q. 8

03 (a) (i) Define the term *osmosis*.
(ii) Give an example of osmosis in plants.

(b) Answer the following questions in relation to practical work you carried out to investigate osmosis.

(i) Draw a labelled diagram of the apparatus you used in the investigation.
(ii) Describe how you used this apparatus to carry out the investigation.
(iii) State the result(s) of your investigation.
(iv) Briefly explain the result(s) you have given in part (iii).

2009 OL Q. 8

Leaving Certificate examination questions

Section C

04
(i) Water enters the roots of plants by osmosis. Explain what is meant by osmosis.
(ii) Describe how you demonstrated osmosis as part of your practical activities.

2008 OL Q. 15 (a)

05
(i) State the precise location of the cell membrane in plant cells.
(ii) With what type of cell do you associate membrane-bound organelles?
(iii) What corresponding term is used to describe bacterial cells?
(iv) The cell membrane is described as being *selectively permeable*. What does this mean?
(v) Why is diffusion alternatively known as *passive transport*?
(vi) Osmosis may be described as 'a special case of diffusion'. Explain why.
(vii) Describe, with the aid of a labelled diagram, how you demonstrated osmosis in the laboratory.
(viii) Name the structure by which *Amoeba* get rid of excess water that has entered by osmosis.

2011 HL Q. 14 (c)

06
(i) In relation to membranes in cells, explain what is meant by *selective permeability*.
(ii) Give **two** locations in a cell at which there is a selectively permeable membrane.
(iii) 1. What is diffusion?
2. In the case of a named molecule, give a precise location at which it diffuses in the human body.
(iv) Explain the biological basis for the use of high sugar or high salt concentrations in the preservation of food.

2010 HL Q. 14 (c)

Past examination questions

OL	2013 Q. 8	2009 Q. 8	2008 Q. 15 (a) (i), (ii)	2005 Q. 7	
HL	2013 Q. 5	2012 Q. 15 (c)	2011 Q. 14 (c)	2010 Q. 14 (c)	2008 Q. 14 (c)

11 Cell Continuity

After studying this chapter you should be able to:

1. Explain the term cell continuity.
2. Explain the term chromosome.
3. Explain the term diploid.
4. Explain the term haploid.
5. Describe the activities that occur in a cell when it is dividing and when it is not dividing.
6. Explain the term mitosis and give the primary function of mitosis in a single-celled and multicellular organism. With the aid of diagrams, show what is happening during mitosis.
7. **HL** Give a detailed description of the stages of mitosis with the aid of labelled diagrams.
8. Explain the term cancer.
9. Give any two causes of cancer.
10. Explain the term meiosis.
11. Give the functions of meiosis.

Cell division

All living **cells** are capable of division to produce new cells. The role of cell division can be for **reproduction**, growth or repair.

- In single-celled **organisms**, this cell division results in reproduction.
- All multicellular organisms start life as a single cell. To become a multicellular organism, that one cell needs to divide. This process of growth can go on for some considerable time in the life of the organism.
- Cell division in multicellular organisms may also be used to replace damaged cells during the life of the organism.

In all cases cells are produced by division of a pre-existing cell. Continuity of life is a characteristic of all living things as we saw in Chapter 1.

> **Cell continuity** means that all cells develop from pre-existing cells.

Chromosomes

The genetic material (**DNA**) is found in the nucleus of cells (providing, of course, that the cells have a nucleus). The DNA is not found in one piece in most cells but in a number of smaller packages called **chromosomes**. Chromosomes contain about 60% protein around which the DNA is wrapped. This material containing DNA and protein is called **chromatin**. Most of the time in the cell, the chromatin is a long thin molecule and is visible as a grainy material in the nucleus. Along the length of the DNA there are areas that code for proteins – these are called **genes**.

> A **chromosome** is a structure made of DNA and protein which can be inherited.

When cell reproduction is taking place, the chromosome coils around itself and becomes visible as a distinct structure in the nucleus (Fig 11.1). Every species has a characteristic number of chromosomes. In humans, this is 46. This number includes two of each type of chromosome, one from each parent (23 pairs). This is called the **diploid** number (2n).

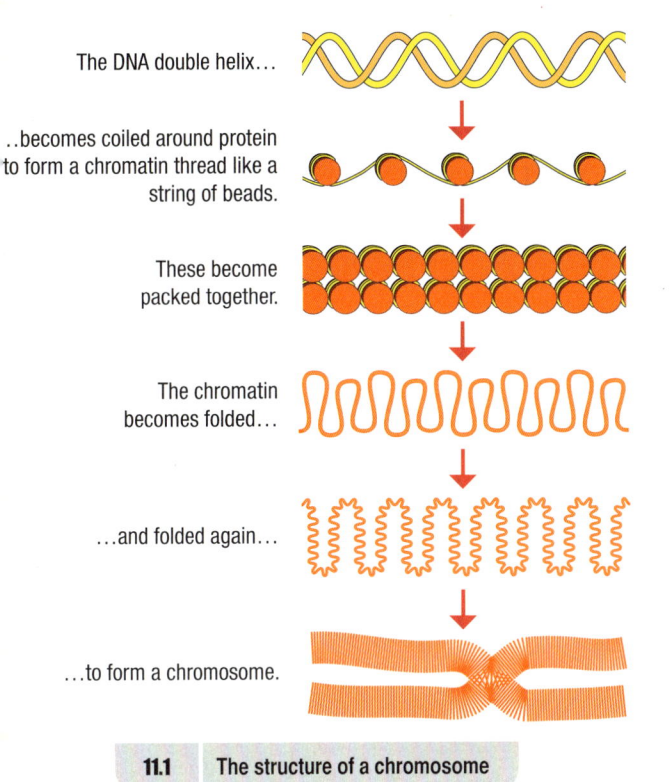

Cell Continuity

The DNA double helix…

..becomes coiled around protein to form a chromatin thread like a string of beads.

These become packed together.

The chromatin becomes folded…

…and folded again…

…to form a chromosome.

11.1 The structure of a chromosome

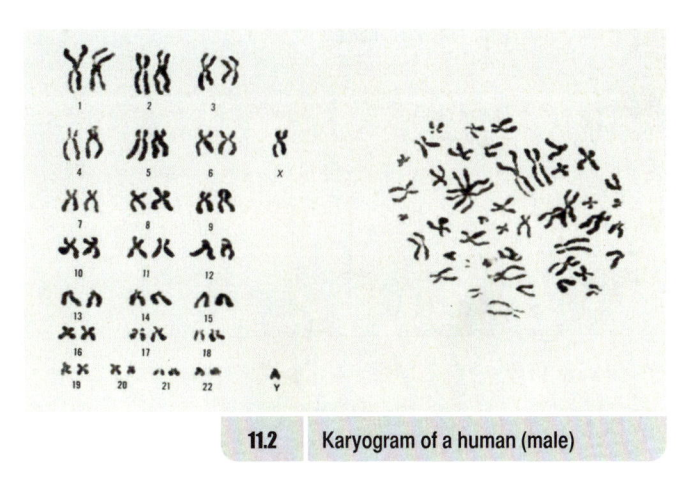

11.2 Karyogram of a human (male)

A **diploid** cell (2n) contains two copies of each chromosome.

A **haploid** cell (n) contains one copy of each chromosome.

When a cell is dividing, the chromosomes can be seen with a microscope and a photograph can be taken of them. A picture of chromosomes that have been arranged in matching pairs is referred to as a karyogram (Fig 11.2). Matching chromosomes are called **homologous** pairs (more about chromosomes in Chapter 15).

In **sexual reproduction**, two cells fuse to produce the new organism. Should two diploid cells fuse, the number of chromosomes would double in each generation and eventually the cell would be filled with a nucleus. To overcome this problem, special sex cells are produced which contain only half the diploid number of chromosomes. They are said to be **haploid**.

In many organisms, these sex cells or **gametes** are the only cells that are haploid. Some other organisms are haploid for most, if not all, of their life span and not diploid (see *Rhizopus* and yeast in Chapter 20).

The cell cycle

Cells, when looked at under the microscope, can be either physically dividing or not dividing. In cells that are dividing:
- The process of division is clearly visible under the microscope.
- Chromosomes thicken and become visible in the nucleus.
- Chromosomes are pulled apart.

When the cell is not dividing, it is said to be in **interphase**:
- Originally, scientists believed that cells in this state were resting. We now know that the cells are most active in this stage.

Towards the end of interphase:
- DNA is replicated and a copy of each chromosome is made.
- The cellular **organelles** are replicated.
- Energy (**ATP**) is produced and new proteins are made.

These changes that take place in the life of a cell give rise to the cell cycle.

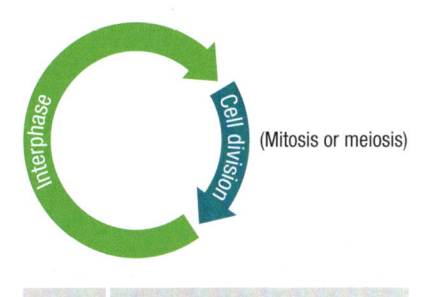

11.3 The cell cycle

(Mitosis or meiosis)

Mitosis and meiosis

There are two different types of nuclear division:
- **Mitosis**, which produces two cells that are genetically identical to the original parent cell.
- **Meiosis**, which produces four cells that are not genetically identical to the parent cell and have only half the genetic information (Fig 11.4).

11 Cell Continuity

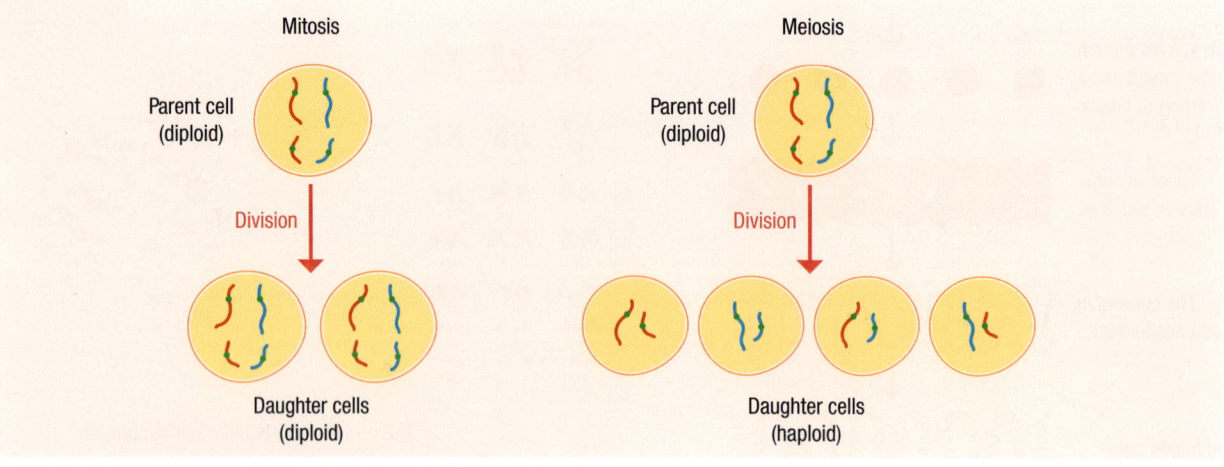

11.4 The different types of cells produced by meiosis and mitosis

The role of mitosis

In mitosis, a cell divides and produces two new cells that are genetically identical to the original cell. This type of cell division is used in growth and repair in multicellular organisms. Mitosis may also be used for **asexual reproduction** (see Chapter 35). This type of reproduction is particularly common in unicellular organisms, e.g. *Amoeba*.

The process of mitosis

There are a number of stages in mitosis (Figs 11.5 to 11.8).

Stage 1
- The chromosomes thicken.
- The chromosomes become visible as a pair of structures.
- The nuclear membrane starts to disappear.
- Thread-like fibres become visible in the cytoplasm.

Stage 2
- The nuclear membrane is gone.
- The fibres are at either end of the cell (poles) and are attached to the chromosomes.
- The chromosomes are pulled by the fibres into the middle of the cell.

Stage 3
- The fibres contract and pull the chromosomes apart.
- One copy of each chromosome is pulled into each half of the cell.
- This means that each half of the cells gets an identical copy of each chromosome.

Stage 4
- The chromosomes become less visible.
- The nuclear membrane reappears.
- The cell divides into two.
- Each cell is an exact copy of the original cell.

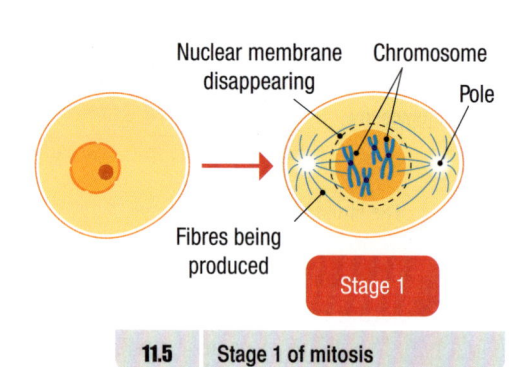

11.5 Stage 1 of mitosis

11.6 Stage 2 of mitosis

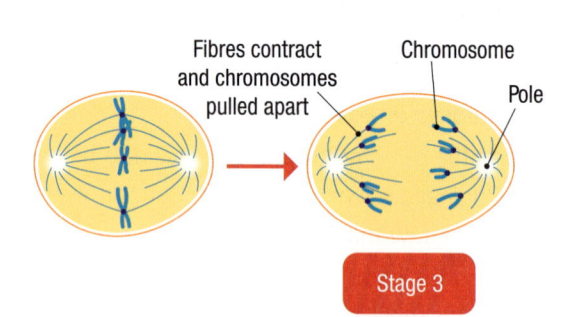

11.7 Stage 3 of mitosis

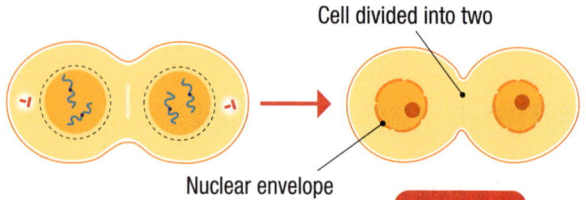

11.8 Stage 4 of mitosis

Cell Continuity | 11

HL Mitosis: extended study

Mitosis (and also meiosis) is a process of nuclear division followed by cell division. **Prokaryotic** cells such as bacteria cannot undertake either of these forms of division as they do not have a nucleus.

Mitosis occurs in four stages:

1. Prophase

As the cell starts to divide (Fig 11.9):
- The chromosomes are visible as **chromatid pairs** joined together at a region called the **centromere**. These pairs of chromatids are called sister chromatids.
- The nucleolus disappears.
- Tiny tubules are formed in the cell called microtubules. These form a structure known as the **spindle**.
- In some cells, this spindle has a **centriole** at either end of it. The locations of the centrioles are at either side of the old nucleus and are thus said to be at the poles.
- Finally the nuclear envelope breaks down.

Metaphase is said to have started when the envelope has disintegrated.

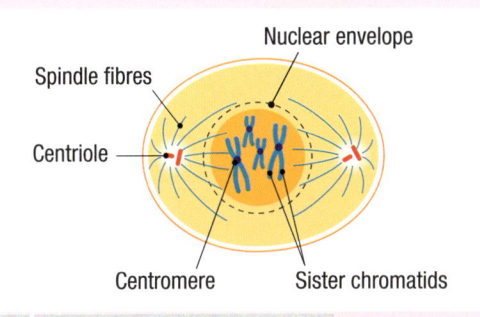

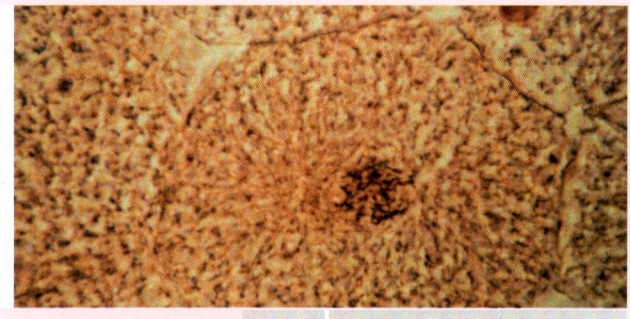

11.9(a) Prophase of mitosis

11.9(b) Prophase in an animal cell

2. Metaphase

In metaphase:
- The chromatid pairs migrate to the centre of the cell (the equator).
- Some of the spindle fibres attach themselves to the centromere of the chromatid pairs and align them so that the sister chromatids face opposite poles.
- Other spindle fibres run from pole to pole and do not attach to the chromatids (Fig 11.10 (a)(b)).

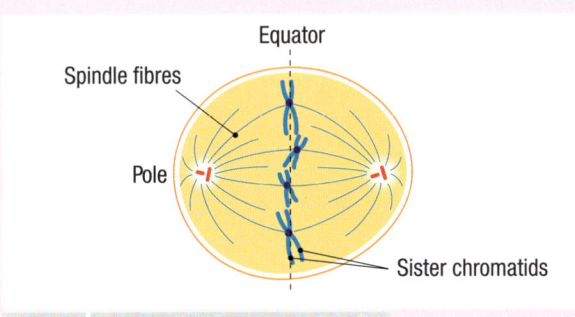

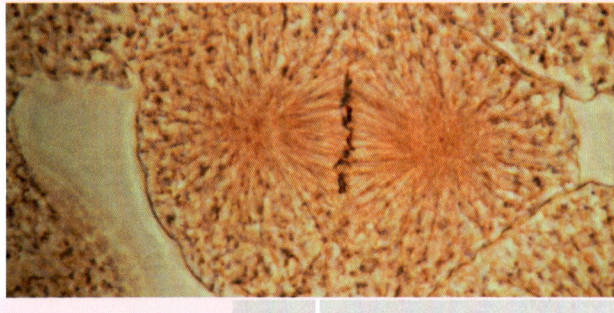

11.10(a) Metaphase of mitosis

11.10(b) Metaphase in an animal cell

3. Anaphase

At the beginning of anaphase:
- The centromeres of the chromatid pairs split.
- The sister chromatids separate and move to opposite poles.
- This is achieved by the spindle fibres attached to the centromeres contracting, splitting the centromeres and pulling the chromosomes to the poles.
- The poles also move further apart as the spindle fibres attached from pole to pole elongate, pushing the poles away from one another.

Anaphase has finished when the chromosomes arrive at the poles (Fig 11.11).

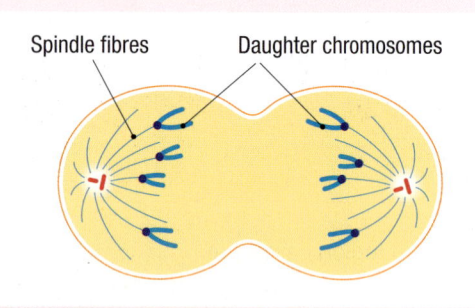

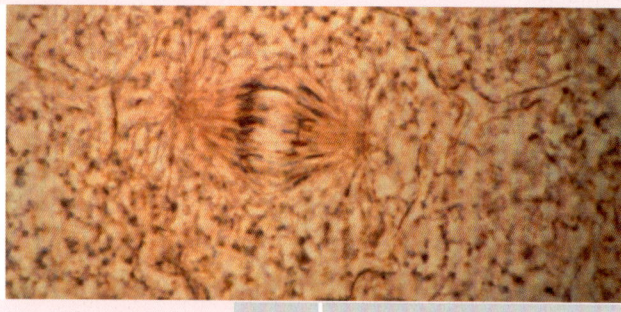

11.11(a) Anaphase of mitosis

11.11(b) Anaphase in an animal cell

4. Telophase

Telophase is the final stage in mitosis during which most of the processes that occurred in prophase are reversed.

- The spindle fibres disassemble.
- A nuclear envelope is formed around each new nucleus in which a nucleolus reappears.
- The chromosomes uncoil to become the more diffuse **chromatin threads**.
- The division of the original cell into two new cells is then completed. The cytoplasmic division of the two cells is called **cleavage**.
- In animal cells, the membrane around the middle of the cell is drawn inwards to form a cleavage furrow. The furrow gets deeper and deeper until the cells split into two new cells (Fig 11.12).

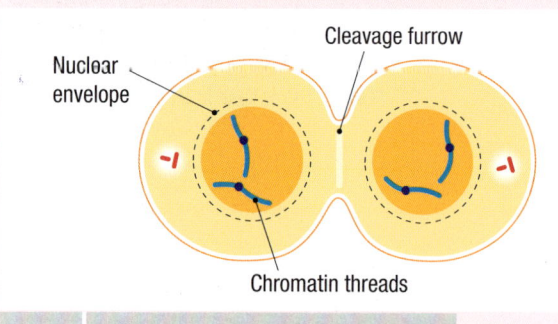

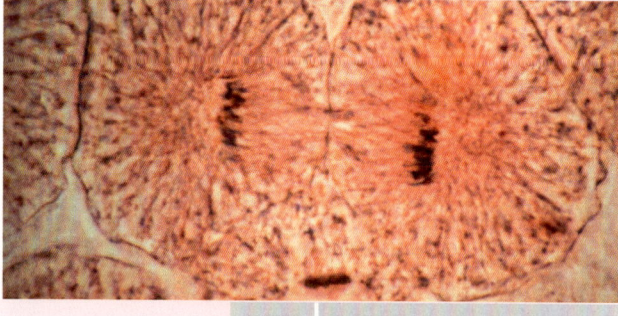

11.12(a) Telophase of mitosis in an animal cell

11.12(b) Telophase in an animal cell

A plant cell cannot cleave (divide) in this fashion as it has a rigid cell wall. Plant cells produce small membrane-bound sacs (**vesicles**), which migrate to the equator of the original cell. These vesicles contain all the cellulose and other chemicals that are required to make the cell wall and plasma membrane. The vesicles fuse to produce a **cell plate** along which the new cell wall and membrane are constructed (Fig 11.13).

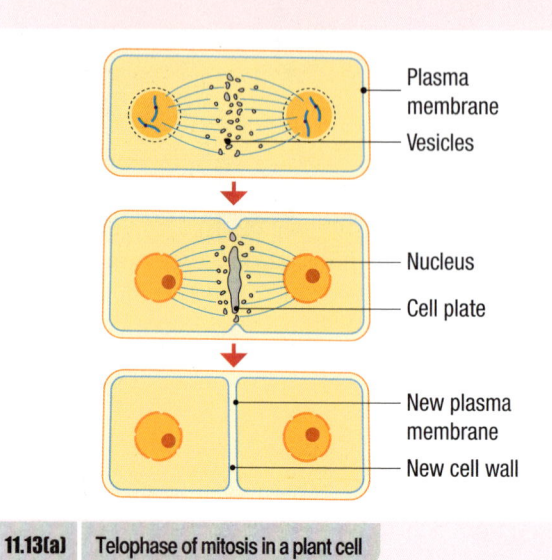

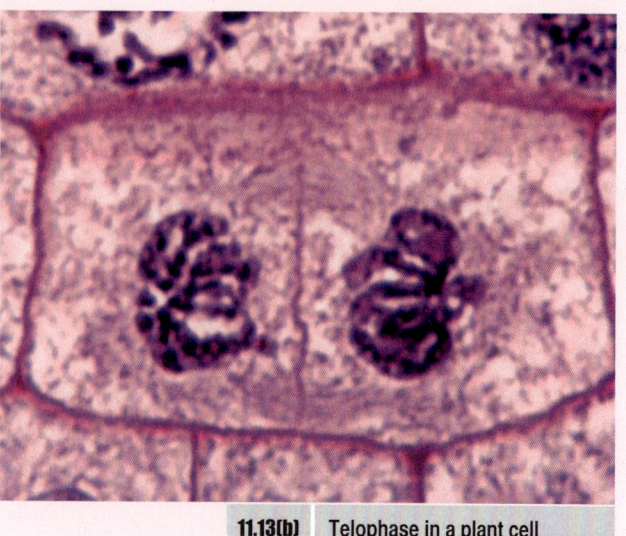

11.13(a) Telophase of mitosis in a plant cell

11.13(b) Telophase in a plant cell

Cancer

Occasionally the control mechanisms of mitosis will break down, resulting in uncontrolled growth of cells called **cancer**. Cancer is not a single disease but a whole series of diseases that affect different parts of the body. In all cases of cancer, the control of cell division is lost. A large mass of cells is produced, called a **tumour**. Some parts of this tumour may then spread to other parts of the body.

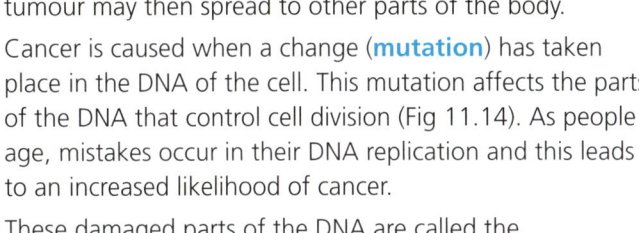

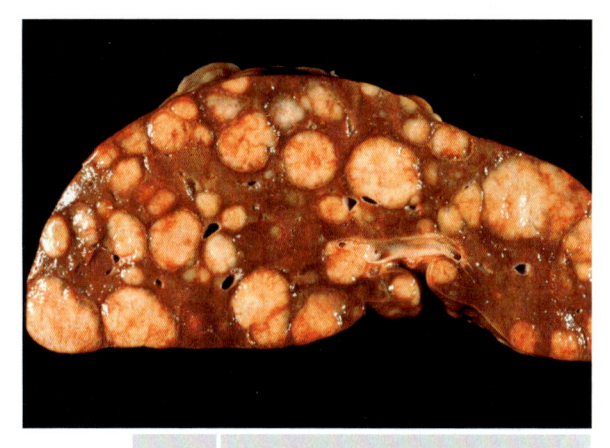

Cancer is caused when a change (**mutation**) has taken place in the DNA of the cell. This mutation affects the parts of the DNA that control cell division (Fig 11.14). As people age, mistakes occur in their DNA replication and this leads to an increased likelihood of cancer.

These damaged parts of the DNA are called the **oncogenes**. When enough oncogenes are present, control of cell division is lost resulting in cancer. Any factor in the environment that mutates DNA is called a **carcinogen**. It is possible to say that the risk of cancer increases with age (as the number of mutations builds up). There are three main environmental factors that increase the risk of cancer – chemicals, radiation and diet. It is also possible that some people may inherit an increased likelihood of getting a certain small number of cancers. It is also the case that some **viruses** increase the risk of cancer.

11.14 Cancerous liver cells forming tumours

> **Cancer** is the abnormal and uncontrolled growth of cells by mitosis.

SYLLABUS REQUIREMENT:
You only need to know about two causes of cancer.

Carcinogens

Certain chemicals are now known to be carcinogens.

- Cigarette smoke contains a number of chemical carcinogens. Smoking causes lung cancer and 90% of the deaths from lung cancer are due to smoking.
- Some types of radiation are also carcinogenic. Ultra-violet radiation from the sun, which causes tanning, is one such carcinogen. Exposure to sunlight, particularly if skin is sunburnt, may cause skin cancer in later life. X-rays may also damage cells, particularly dividing cells. As a result, X-rays of pregnant women are avoided to prevent damage to the developing foetus. Radiation released from radioactive chemicals is carcinogenic. This has resulted in a high level of certain types of cancer, i.e. leukaemia, from accidents that released radiation in nuclear power plants. There is also some evidence that exposure to low levels of radiation over a long period of time by workers in these plants may be dangerous.

Viruses

Viruses work by taking over the nucleus of the cell they are attacking. Some viruses appear to damage the genes of cells and hence may cause cancer. There is a body of evidence that suggests that some cervical cancers in women are due to the presence of the human papilloma virus (HPV). To reduce this risk girls are now offered **vaccinations** against this virus.

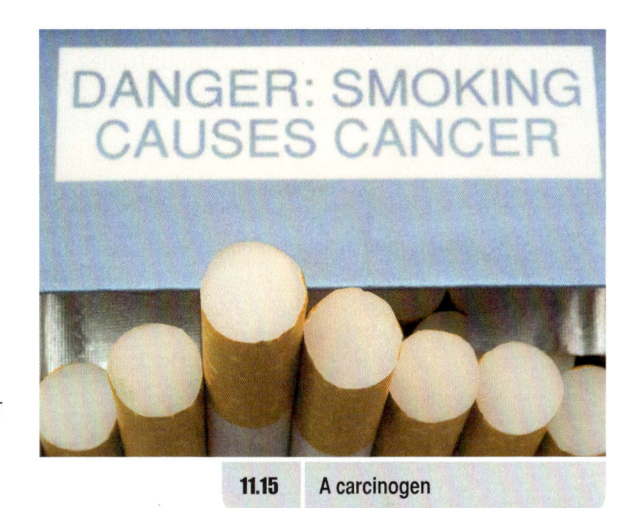

Diet

Diet appears to be important in cancer. There is a lot of debate as to what types of food are cancer causing or cancer preventing. It is safer to be moderate in intake of all types of foods. In particular, it is better to cut down on our fat, sugar and alcohol intake and increase our fibre, fresh fruit and vegetable intake (see Chapter 25 on a balanced diet).

11.15 A carcinogen

Genetics

In a certain number of cancers, researchers found that certain families tended to have a higher risk of getting the disease. These families were found to have mutations in certain genes that controlled cell division in some cells. If these people are exposed to carcinogens then they may get that particular type of cancer more quickly. Therefore we rarely say that cancer is inherited. There is, however, a tendency for a number of cancers to run in families.

Treatment

Many types of cancer are now very curable, particularly if they are discovered early. There are three main types of treatment for cancer:
1. Surgery, in which the tumour is removed.
2. Chemotherapy, in which chemicals are used to kill the cancer cells.
3. Radiotherapy, in which targeted radiation is used to kill the cancer cells.

The role of meiosis

Meiosis is a form of nuclear division in which a diploid cell divides to produce four new cells each of which is haploid (Fig 11.16).

- Meiosis will halve the number of chromosomes in a cell, i.e. produce haploid cells.
- These haploid cells are usually the sex cells, which will then fuse with other sex cells to produce a new diploid cell.
- Gametes are not always produced from meiosis (see sexual reproduction in *Rhizopus* in Chapter 20).
- Each of the haploid cells produced is given one chromosome from each chromosome pair in the original cell. Chromosomes from the chromosome pairs are passed on to the haploid cells independently of one another. As a result, a large number of genetically different haploid cells may be produced. If we take humans as an example of this:
  - There are 23 chromosomes in a human haploid cell. This means there are 2^{23} possible combinations of chromosomes (approximately 8.4 million) in each gamete (see a three chromosome example in Fig 11.17).
  - If these gametes are used in sexual reproduction then there are $(2^{23})^2$ (approximately 70.5 million million) different combinations of these cells possible.
  - Thus meiosis not only halves the number of chromosomes in a cell, but it also recombines the chromosomes. This in turn leads to variation from one generation to the next.

11.16 The products of meiosis

11.17 The possible combinations from three pairs of chromosomes

Mitosis	Meiosis
Produces two daughter cells	Produces four cells
The daughter cells have the same number of chromosomes as the parent	The daughter cells have half the number of chromosomes as the parent
The daughter cells are genetically identical	The daughter cells are genetically different

Table 11.1 Differences between mitosis and meiosis

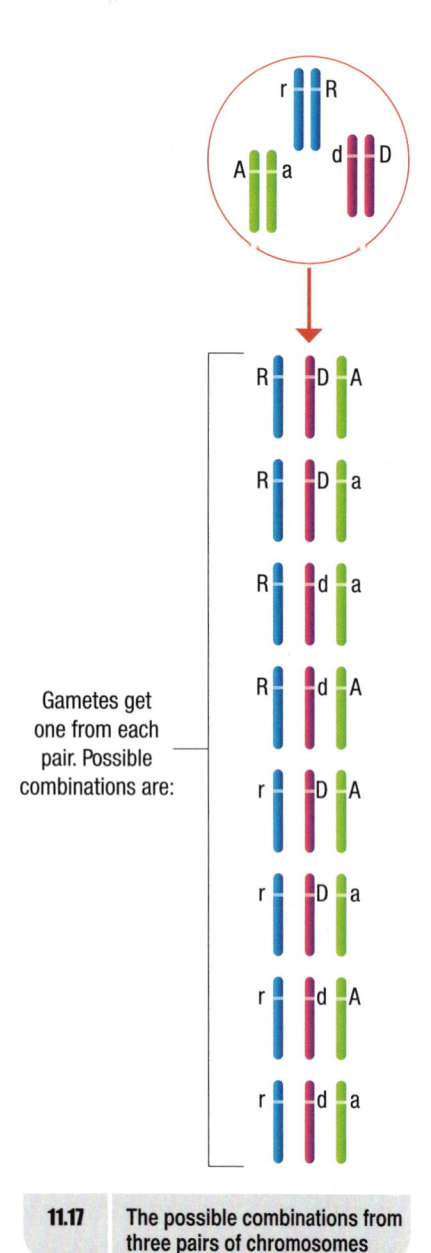

Cell Continuity | 11

Summary

- Cells divide for two purposes: (a) for reproduction and (b) repair and growth of multicellular organisms.
- Chromosomes are:
  - the genetic material of the cell;
  - found in the nucleus;
  - composed of protein and DNA coiled together.
- Each organism has a characteristic number of chromosomes in each cell (humans = 46). Most organisms contain two of each type of chromosome and are called diploid (2n).
- The diploid (2n) number is when a cell has two copies of each chromosome.
- In sexual reproduction, the cells fuse. To keep the number of chromosomes constant, special sex cells (gametes) are produced containing one set of chromosomes. These are called haploid cells (in humans they have 23 chromosomes).
- The haploid (n) number is when a cell contains one copy of each chromosome.
- Mitosis:
  - is a form of nuclear division;
  - produces two identical cells;
  - is used for growth and repair in multicellular organisms;
  - is used for asexual reproduction in unicellular organisms;
  - is divided into four stages.
- Mitosis is divided into four stages (the terms highlighted in pink are HL only):
- Stage 1 Prophase:
  - Chromosomes visible as chromatid pairs joined at centromeres.
  - Nuclear envelope disappears.
  - Spindle fibres are produced by the centrioles at the poles.
- Stage 2 Metaphase:
  - The chromatid pairs are pulled to the equator by the spindle fibres.
- Stage 3 Anaphase:
  - The chromatid pairs, pulled by the spindle fibres, split at the centromeres and move to the poles.
- Stage 4 Telophase:
  - The chromosomes unwind and become non-distinct.
  - The nuclear membrane re-forms.
  - The cell divides in two: in animals, the cell pinches in to form a cleavage furrow at either side which eventually joins. In plants, a cell plate forms where a new cell wall is made.
- Cancer:
  - is the abnormal uncontrolled growth of cells by mitosis;
  - produces a tumour;
  - is due to damaged DNA (mutation);
  - is caused by carcinogens;
  - is more likely as you age.
- Types of carcinogens are: smoke produced by tobacco, which causes 90% of lung cancer; radiation, e.g. X-rays, UV light, radioactive chemicals, and viruses.
- Meiosis:
  - is a form of nuclear division;
  - produces four haploid cells, all of which are different from each other and the parent;
  - results in enormous variety;
  - is essential in the production of gametes.

11 Cell Continuity

Review questions

01 (a) Why do cells divide?
(b) In what circumstances is cell division used for reproduction?

02 (a) What is a chromosome?
(b) Where are these normally found?
(c) What are they made up of?
(d) What is their function?
(e) In what circumstances is a chromosome visible?
(f) How many chromosomes are present in a human skin cell?

03 (a) Explain what is meant by the terms diploid and haploid.
(b) Why do gametes need to be haploid cells?

04 (a) What are the stages of the cell cycle?
(b) What happens in each stage?
(c) Why do you think scientists originally believed the cell was resting in one of these stages?
(d) In which stage does a cell spend most of its time?

05 (a) What is the name of the type of cell division that produces identical cells?
(b) With the aid of diagrams, describe in simple terms the process named in (a).
(c) Why does this process produce identical cells?

06 (a) What are the names of the stages of mitosis?
(b) Describe using labelled diagrams the process of mitosis.

07 Explain the following terms: centromere, sister chromatid, centriole, spindle, cleavage furrow, cell plate.

08 (a) What has happened to a cell that is cancerous?
(b) In what way are cancerous cells different from a normal cell?
(c) What does the term carcinogen mean?
(d) Why do carcinogens cause cancer?
(e) Give two examples of carcinogens.

09 (a) (i) What is meiosis?
(ii) Why does meiosis lead to variation in cells?
(b) (i) Compare the end products of mitosis and meiosis.
(ii) Why is meiosis necessary for sexual reproduction?
(iii) What happens in mitosis to ensure the daughter cells are identical?

10 (a) Draw a labelled diagram of a cell at anaphase of mitosis when the chromosome number is 8.
(b) Name the stage which precedes anaphase.
(c) In what stage in the cell cycle does the DNA duplicate?
(d) In a human cell how many chromosomes will be present in (a) a sperm cell, (b) a zygote, (c) an egg cell, (d) a skin cell.

Examination style questions

Section A

01 (a) When a cell divides, the genetic material can divide by mitosis, meiosis or neither of these. Complete the table below by placing a tick (✓) in the box to indicate the process by which you would expect the genetic material to divide in each case.

	Mitosis	Meiosis	Neither
The stage in the formation of female gametes in the ovule of a flowering plant in which haploid daughter cells are formed from a haploid parent cell.			
The division of the genetic material in bacterial reproduction.			
The stage in the life cycle of fungi such as *Rhizopus* at which the zygospore germinates.			
Cell division which takes place in the growth of a human testis during pregnancy.			

(b) The diagram represents the cell cycle.

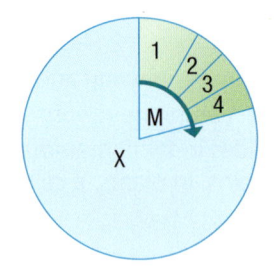

(i) Draw the diagram in your copy and mark on the diagram the stage where the chromosomes line up on the equator of the cell.
(ii) Identify Stage X and state two processes that occur during X which are necessary for cell division to take place.

02 (a) What name is given to a haploid sex cell?
(b) In what stage of the life cycle of humans does meiosis take place?
(c) What is the name given to the loss of control of mitosis?
(d) Name two factors that increase this loss of control.

Cell Continuity 11

Examination style questions

03 (a) What stage of mitosis is represented by the following diagram?

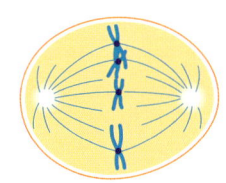

(b) What is the name of the thread-like structures seen in the diagram?
(c) How many of the structures mentioned in (b) would be found in a haploid cell from this organism?
(d) What type of cell division would produce such a cell?
(e) Give a possible function of the cell mentioned in (c).

Section C

04 (a) 'The products of meiosis are always gametes.' Discuss.
(b) Distinguish between the following pairs of terms:
  (i) Chromatin and chromosome.
  (ii) Haploid and diploid.
  (iii) Mitosis and cell division.
  (iv) Mutation and mutagen.

(c) (i) Explain how meiosis is essential in the life cycle of organisms that reproduce sexually.
  (ii) Compare the results of mitosis and meiosis under the following headings:
    1. Number of daughter nuclei.
    2. Chromosome number of the daughter nuclei.
    3. Genetic likeness between the daughter nuclei.
    4. Genetic likeness between daughter nuclei and parent nucleus.
  (iii) Name one site in the flowering plant where (1) meiosis and (2) mitosis takes place.

05 (a) Meiosis is sometimes termed 'reduction division'.
  (i) Suggest why meiosis is often given this alternative title.
  (ii) At what stage in the life cycle of the fungus known as *Rhizopus* does meiosis occur?
(b) Meiosis is involved in the production of very specialised cell types in flowering plants and humans.
  (i) Name these four specialised cells.
  (ii) Outline the role of mitosis in humans.
  (iii) State one unfortunate consequence of uncontrolled cell division by mitosis in humans.
  (iv) What are carcinogens? List three of these.
  (v) How do carcinogens damage cells?
(c) Describe the process of mitosis with the help of labelled diagrams.

Leaving Certificate examination questions

Section A

01 The diagram shows the cell cycle.

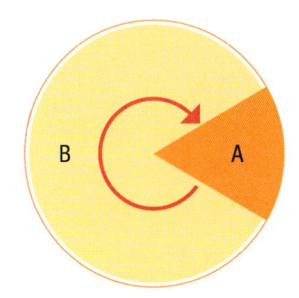

(a) There are two parts to the cell cycle – cell division and interphase. Match these two parts to the letters in the diagram.
(b) Name the **two** types of cell division.
(c) Cancer is the uncontrolled multiplication of abnormal cells. Give **two** causes of cancer.
(d) Suggest a possible treatment for cancer.

2013 OL Q. 4

02 Indicate whether the following statements are true (T) or false (F).

Example: The cells produced by meiosis are haploid.   T

(a) The cells produced by mitosis are identical.
(b) Meiosis gives rise to variation.
(c) Mitosis always produces four new cells.
(d) Meiosis is never involved in gamete formation.
(e) Single-celled organisms use mitosis for reproduction.

2009 OL Q. 4

11 Cell Continuity

Leaving Certificate examination questions

03 The diagram shows a stage of mitosis.

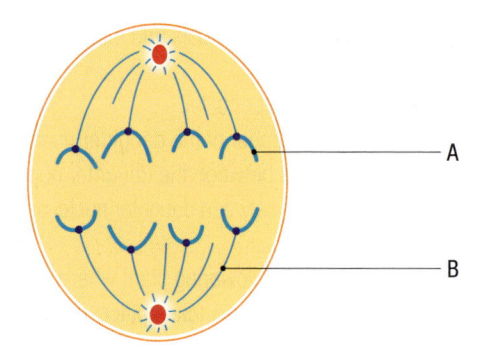

(a) Name A and B.
(b) What is happening during this stage of mitosis?
(c) How many cells are formed when a cell divides by mitosis?
(d) For what purpose do single-celled organisms use mitosis?

2005 OL Q. 4

04 Indicate whether the following statements are true (T) or false (F).
(a) Single-celled organisms use meiosis for asexual reproduction.
(b) In telophase of mitosis, a cleavage furrow forms in plant cells.
(c) When a cell is not dividing it is said to be in prophase.
(d) The nuclear membrane disappears in the early part of mitosis.
(e) Centromeres give rise to the nuclear spindle.
(f) Mitosis is a source of variation.
(g) In multicellular organisms mitosis is primarily used for growth.

2014 HL Q. 5

05 The diagram shows a stage of mitosis.

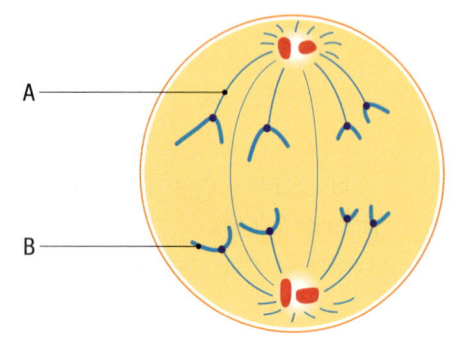

(a) Name this stage of mitosis.
(b) Give a feature from the diagram that allowed you to identify this stage.
(c) Name the parts of the diagram labelled A and B.

(d) What is the function of mitosis in single-celled organisms?
(e) Give **one** function of mitosis in multicellular organisms.
(f) Give **one** location where mitosis occurs in flowering plants.

2009 HL Q. 5

06 The diagram represents the cell cycle.

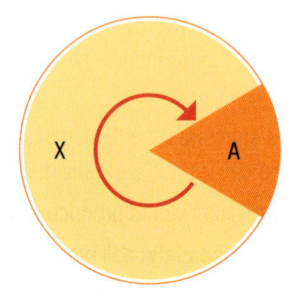

(a) What stage of the cycle is represented by X?
(b) Give the names of the two processes involving DNA which take place during stage X.
(c) For convenience of study, mitosis is divided into four stages. List these in order starting at A.
(d) In which of the stages of mitosis that you have listed in (c) would you expect to see the spindle fibres contracting?
(e) Explain the term diploid number.
(f) What term is used to describe a group of disorders of the body in which cells lose the normal regulation of mitosis?

2008 HL Q. 2

07 Study the diagram of a stage of mitosis in a diploid cell and then answer the questions below.

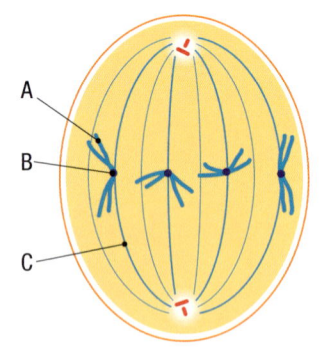

(a) Name A, B and C.
(b) What stage of mitosis is shown? Give a reason for your answer.
(c) What is the diploid number of this nucleus which is undergoing mitosis?
(d) Give a role of structure A.
(e) Some cells in the human body undergo meiosis. Give one function of meiosis.

2007 HL Q. 3

Leaving Certificate examination questions

Section C

08 The diagram shows a cell undergoing division.

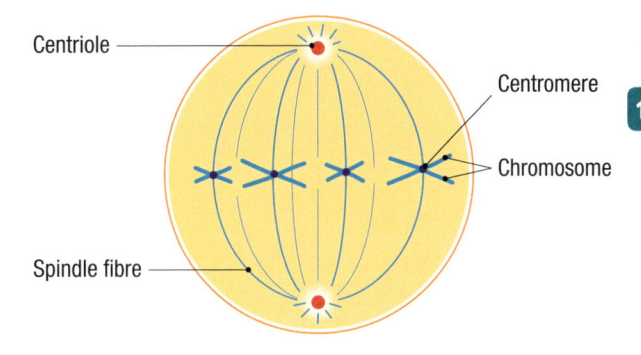

[Diagram of cell in mitosis with labels: Centriole, Centromere, Chromosome, Spindle fibre]

(i) On which structure in the diagram are the genes located?
(ii) This type of cell division is called mitosis.
   1. How many cells are formed when a cell divides by mitosis?
   2. Name the other type of cell division.
(iii) 1. What is the purpose of mitosis in single-celled organisms?
   2. Name a single-celled organism.
(iv) Which genetic structure changes when a mutation occurs?

2014 OL Q. 10 (c)

09 (i) What medical term is used to describe the disease caused by uncontrolled mitosis in human cells?
(ii) Give **two** causes of this uncontrolled cell division.
(iii) Draw a labelled diagram to show the normal cell cycle.
(iv) What is the function of meiosis?

2012 OL Q. 14 (c)

10 The <u>haploid number</u> of chromosomes is found in the human egg and sperm.
Explain the underlined term.

2008 OL Q. 11 (a)

11 Answer the following questions, which relate to events in the cell cycle.
(i) What name is applied to the period of the cell cycle in which division is **not** taking place?
(ii) Give a cellular process that occurs during this period in which the nucleus is not dividing.
(iii) Draw a labelled diagram to show the position of the chromosomes during metaphase of mitosis in a nucleus in which 2n = 6.
   1. State a function of one of the structures, other than chromosomes, that you have labelled in your diagram of metaphase.
   2. How does the structure carry out this function?
(iv) What term is used for the group of disorders in which control has been lost over the rate of mitosis?

2013 HL Q. 11 (c)

12 Distinguish between the terms in the following pair by writing one sentence about each member.
(i) Haploid and diploid.

2010 HL Q. 10 (c)

Past examination questions

OL	2014 Q. 10 (c)	2013 Q. 4	2012 Q. 11 (a)–(i), (ii), Q. 14 (c) (v)–(viii)	2011 Q. 3 (a)N, (c), Q. 10 (c) (i)–(ii)	
	2009 Q. 4	2008 Q. 11 (a)	2007 Q. 4 (c)	2005 Q. 4	2004 Q. 3	SEC Sample Q. 6

HL	2014 Q. 5	2013 Q. 11 (c)	2011 Q. 2	2010 Q. 10 (c) (i)	2009 Q. 5	2008 Q. 2
	2007 Q. 3	2005 Q. 5				

12 Enzymes

After studying this chapter you should be able to:

1. Define what is meant by the term metabolism.
2. Define the term enzyme.
3. Describe the protein nature and folded structure of enzymes.
4. Describe the role of enzymes in plants and animals, particularly in metabolism.
5. **HL** Describe using the active site theory how an enzyme functions.
6. **HL** Explain the specificity of an enzyme.
7. Explain the effect of pH on enzyme action.
8. **HL** Explain what is meant by the 'optimum' pH of an enzyme.
9. Carry out an investigation to demonstrate the effect of pH on an enzyme.
10. Explain the effect of temperature on enzyme action.
11. Carry out an investigation to demonstrate the effect of temperature on an enzyme.
12. **HL** Explain how high temperatures denature enzymes.
13. **HL** Carry out an investigation to demonstrate heat denaturation of an enzyme.
14. Describe the process of immobilising enzymes.
15. Give the advantages and the use of immobilised enzymes in bioreactors.
16. Immobilise one enzyme and demonstrate its effect.
17. **HL** Describe the nature and role of ATP in cells.
18. **HL** Describe the production on ATP from ADP, phosphate and energy.
19. **HL** Describe the role of NAD and NADP in the transfer of electrons and hydrogen ions.

Cell metabolism

All **cells** carry out many different chemical reactions – building up molecules or breaking them down. These reactions are called cell **metabolism**.

> **Metabolism** is the sum of all the chemical reactions that occur in an organism.

In all chemical reactions, the chemicals that react with one another are called the **reactants**, and the chemicals produced as the result of the chemical reaction are called the **products**. There are two types of chemical reactions:

> **Solar energy** is the energy that comes from the sun.

1. **Anabolic** or synthetic reactions involve the building up of molecules to form more complex molecules. These reactions normally require energy to take place, e.g. **photosynthesis**.

   A + B ⟶ AB + energy

2. **Catabolic** reactions involve the breakdown of complex chemicals into simpler chemicals. These reactions normally release energy, e.g. **respiration**.

   AB + energy ⟶ A + B

Within the **biosphere**, there is a continuous flow of energy. The primary source of this energy is the sun.

12 Enzymes

12.1 The flow of energy through the biosphere

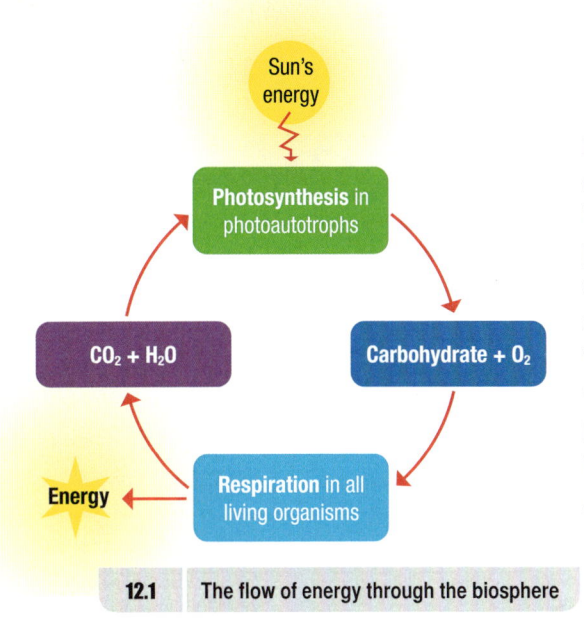

Plants have the ability to use this light energy to make a complex chemical (sugar) from simple chemicals (carbon dioxide and water). This reaction requires a green pigment, **chlorophyll**, and is called photosynthesis. The sugar produced is used by the plants as an energy source to build up all the other chemicals that the plant needs to function, and for the energy needed for the cells to function. The reaction in which the cells get energy from sugar is called respiration.

In the end, the energy is lost from the system in the form of heat. Thus the Earth requires a constant input of energy from the sun. All life ultimately depends on this solar energy to survive (Fig 12.1).

> **Cellular energy** is the energy stored in the chemicals found in cells.

Enzymes

All metabolic activity in a cell is controlled. Chemicals called **catalysts** control many chemical reactions.

In cells there are special types of catalysts called **enzymes**. These are made of protein and they are used to control cell metabolism.

> **Catalysts** have the ability to speed up (or indeed slow down) chemical reactions without being used up in the reaction.

> **Enzymes** are protein catalysts found in living organisms.

Enzyme structure

Proteins are made up of long chains of amino acids. These long chains do not remain as long straight chains but fold over and take up a very specific shape. Enzymes are made at the **ribosomes** in the cell. Enzymes will only work if they have the correct shape to allow them to function properly. This is because the shape lets the enzyme attach to the molecule they are changing (Fig 12.2).

Enzyme action

The chemical (or chemicals) that an enzyme reacts with is called the **substrate** and the chemical (or chemicals) produced at the end of the reaction is called the **product**.

> A **substrate** is the chemical or chemicals with which the enzyme reacts.

> The **product** is the chemical or chemicals made in the reaction.

E substrate + enzyme ⟶ product

Enzyme	Substrate	Product
Amylase	Starch	Maltose
Catalase	Hydrogen peroxide	Oxygen and water

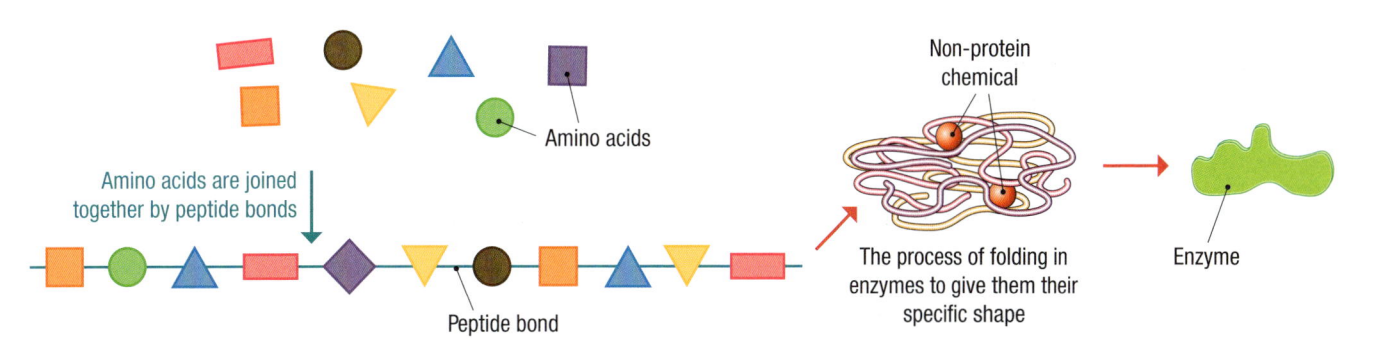

12.2 The process of folding in enzymes to give them their specific shape

12 Enzymes

Even chemical reactions that give out a lot of energy do not normally happen spontaneously. The coal in your grate will not light automatically. It will require a flame to 'light' it and then it will give out much more energy than was contained in the match.

The energy of the match is called the **activation energy**. Some reactions need a large activation energy to get started. If a chemist was starting up such a reaction, then they would simply heat the reaction. Living cells would not survive such heating. They use enzymes to lower the energy required to get the reaction started and thus, reactions occur in the cell at a temperature that the cell can tolerate (Fig 12.3).

This is similar to you attempting to roll a boulder down a hill from a little hollow at the top. The boulder gives out plenty of energy as it speeds down the hill but first you have to give it a push so it can get on its way (Fig 12.4). Using an enzyme is like using a spade to lower the edge of the hollow so the boulder could be more easily pushed on its way down the hill.

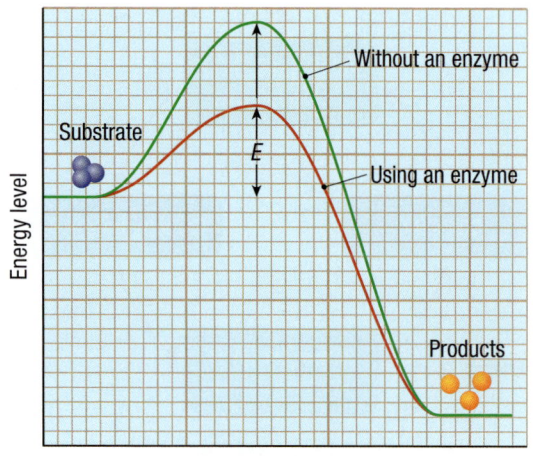

12.3 Progress of a reaction with and without an enzyme

12.4 The boulder analogy for an enzyme reaction

HL How enzymes work

Enzymes work by joining to the substrate molecules. The position on the enzyme where this happens is called the **active site**. An enzyme is specific for a particular substrate because it acts like a mould that fits the substrate very closely. Any other chemicals that do not fit exactly onto the active site cannot react with the enzyme.

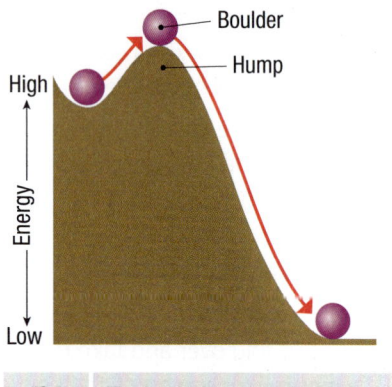

> **D** An **active site** is the place on the enzyme where the substrate attaches and the reaction takes place.

The enzyme will usually work in one of two ways:
1. It will either strain a bond in the substrate so much that the bond breaks and the products will be released (catabolic reaction).

Or

2. It will bring two molecules close together at the active site and will encourage the formation of a bond making a new chemical (anabolic reaction).

Occasionally a combination of the two will occur.

It is now believed that the active site is not a fixed shape on the enzyme. When the substrate joins the enzyme, it will change the shape of its active site slightly to make a better fit for the substrate. This is called the **induced fit theory** (Fig 12.5).

This is similar to you sitting on a beanbag. As you sit into the bag, it changes its shape to fit you more perfectly until it is tightly wrapped around you.

In an enzyme-controlled reaction, the enzyme and the substrate(s) combine to form the **enzyme–substrate complex**. The substrate molecules react, the products are released and the unchanged enzyme is then available to catalyse again. Enzymes are said to be **specific** as the active site will only fit a single substrate and thus will only catalyse a single reaction, e.g. amylase will only break down starch. Anything that changes the shape of the enzyme will tend to prevent the enzyme from working as expected.

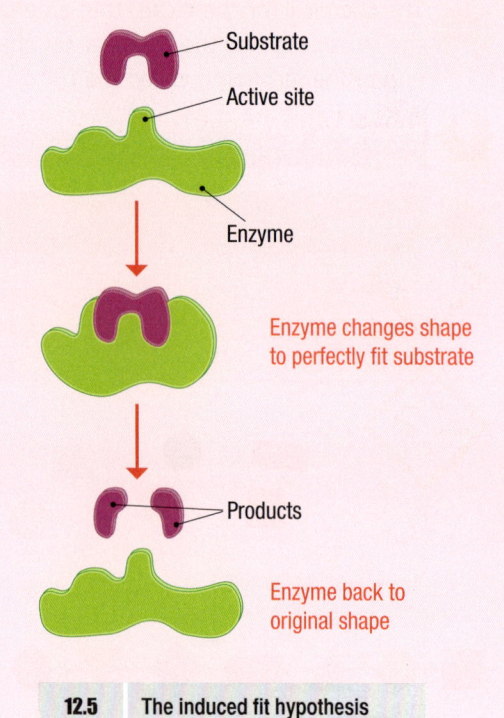

> **D** **Enzyme specificity** means that the enzyme will only catalyse one reaction.

12.5 The induced fit hypothesis

Factors affecting enzyme action
pH

pH is a scale that measures how acidic or how basic (alkaline) a solution is: 0 to 7 is acidic, 7 is neutral, and 7 to 14 is basic.

Any factor that affects the shape of an enzyme will affect how well it works because the shape will determine how well it can catalyse the reaction. pH will tend to change the shape of the enzyme, and it will affect the rate at which the enzyme will carry out its function. As a consequence, an enzyme will only have its correct shape at a specific pH. The enzyme becomes less efficient on either side of this pH. Often the effect is very dramatic, as seen in Fig 12.6. The best pH for one enzyme will not necessarily be the best pH for another enzyme. If we look at two human digestive enzymes, we see that trypsin, found in the small intestine, works best at a pH of about 8 whereas pepsin, found in the stomach, works at a pH of about 2.

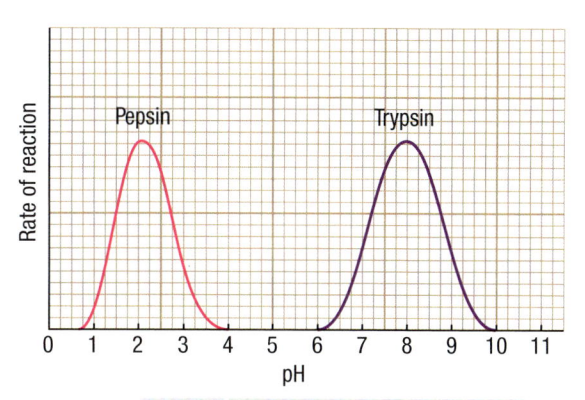

12.6 The effect of pH on the enzymes pepsin and trypsin

HL The shape of the enzyme, as we have seen, is the most important feature of the enzyme in relation to its function. Anything that alters its shape will tend to make the enzyme less effective. One of the important factors in the shape of an enzyme is **hydrogen bonding** between various amino acids in the protein. If the pH in the **environment** surrounding the enzyme changes, this affects these bonds.

Each enzyme has a specific pH at which it has the shape that lets it work best. This pH is known as the **optimum pH**. If an experiment is carried out in which the concentration of the enzyme, the concentration of the substrate and the temperature are kept constant, but the pH is varied, it is found that the rate of reaction varies as in Fig 12.7. Under these constant conditions, the pH at which the enzyme works best is said to be the optimum pH for this enzyme. As the pH varies from the optimum the enzyme may permanently lose its shape and function and is said to be **denatured** (see page 143).

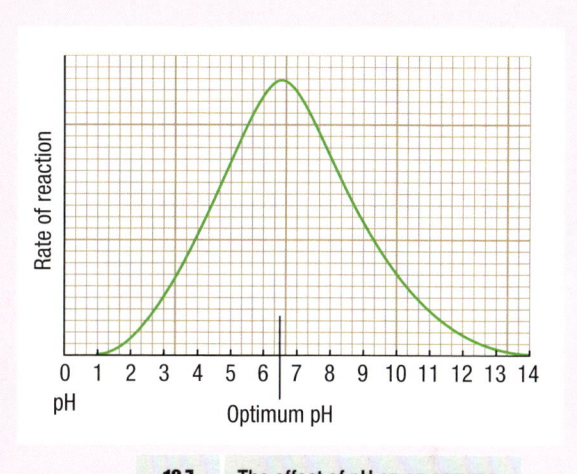

12.7 The effect of pH on an enzyme

Investigation 12.1

To investigate the effect of pH range on the rate of catalase activity

Enzyme	Substrate	Product
Catalase	Hydrogen peroxide	Water + oxygen

Procedure

1. Finely cut up a few celery stalks.
2. Add 20 cm³ of a buffer solution to each of four measuring cylinders. Use a different buffer solution for each cylinder, i.e. pH 9, pH 7, pH 5, etc. (The buffer solution will stabilise the pH.)
3. Weigh 5 g of the chopped celery and add to each measuring cylinder.
4. With a pipette add one drop of washing-up liquid to each measuring cylinder (to generate foam).

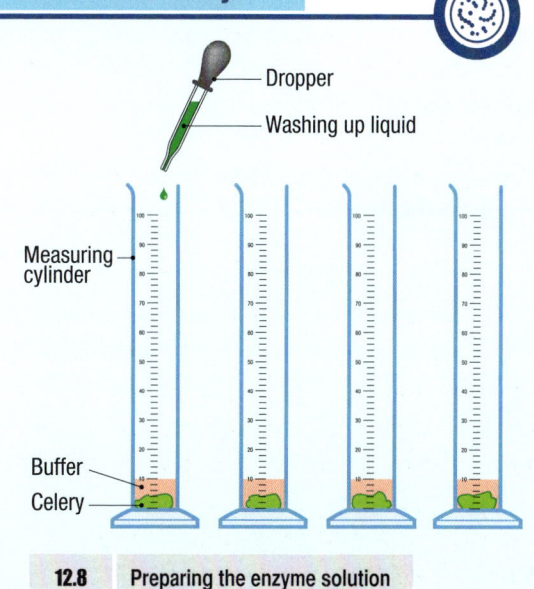

12.8 Preparing the enzyme solution

12 Enzymes

5. Put 2 cm³ of '12 vol' hydrogen peroxide solution into four test tubes.
6. Place the four measuring cylinders and the four test tubes into a water bath at 25°C and leave for 10 minutes (to bring all test tubes to this temperature).
7. Add one test tube of hydrogen peroxide solution to each measuring cylinder, note the volume and immediately start a stopwatch.
8. Measure the volume of each measuring cylinder after 2 minutes.
9. Add two drops of universal indicator to each cylinder to check the pH.

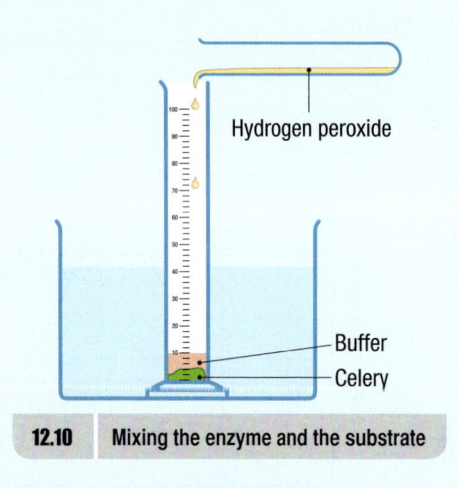

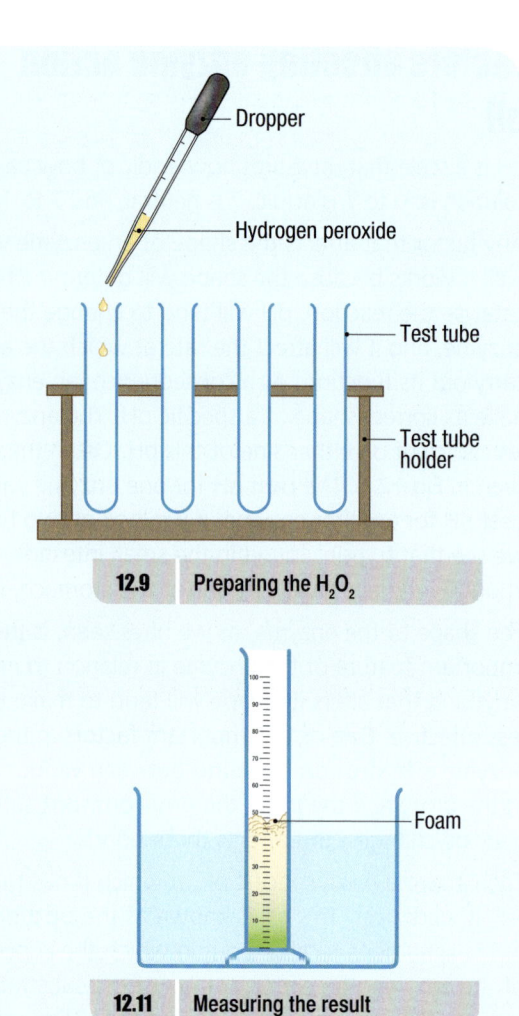

12.9 Preparing the H_2O_2

12.10 Mixing the enzyme and the substrate

12.11 Measuring the result

10. Repeat the investigation using 5 g of boiled celery at each pH (to act as a control).

Results:

Unboiled celery:

pH of buffer	Initial volume (cm³)	Final volume (cm³)	Volume of foam produced (cm³)

Boiled celery:

pH of buffer	Initial volume (cm³)	Final volume (cm³)	Volume of foam produced (cm³)

1. Write an account of this investigation in your practical notebook and include a graph of pH against enzyme activity (volume of foam). Place pH on the x-axis (horizontal axis).
2. Explain your results.

You should expect the greatest volume of foam to be generated at pH 9 and the volume to drop off noticeably on either side of this.

Temperature

Temperature will also affect the rate of enzyme activity. As with all chemical reactions, as the temperature rises so will the rate of reaction as the enzymes and substrate get more energy. In enzyme-controlled reactions, the rate of reaction will increase with an increase of temperatures seen in the graph (Fig 12.12). In general plant enzymes will work better at lower temperatures than enzymes found in humans, which generally work best at body temperature (37°C). If the temperature becomes too high then it may damage the enzyme and the reaction will stop (see HL material).

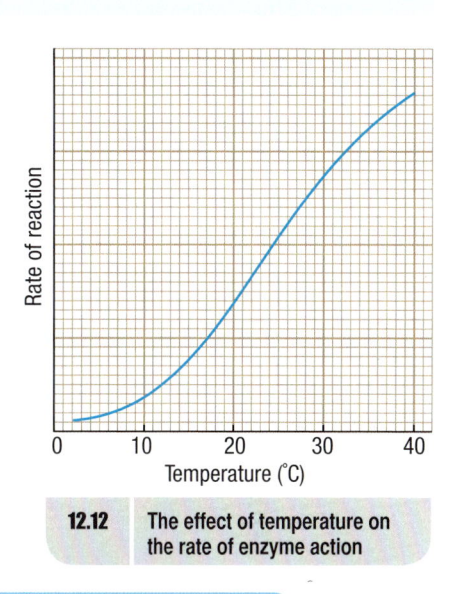

12.12 The effect of temperature on the rate of enzyme action

Investigation 12.2

To investigate the effect of temperature range on the rate of catalase activity

Enzyme	Substrate	Product
Catalase	Hydrogen peroxide	Water + oxygen

Procedure

1. Set up four water baths, each one between 4°C (ice cold) and 60°C.
2. Finely chop up a couple of stalks of celery.
3. Put 20 cm³ of buffer at pH 9 into four measuring cylinders (this is the optimum pH for catalase).
4. Put 5 g of the celery into the measuring cylinders (as a source of catalase).
5. Add 1 drop of washing-up liquid to each measuring cylinder (to produce foam).
6. Put 2 cm³ of a '20 vol' hydrogen peroxide solution into four test tubes.
7. Place one test tube of hydrogen peroxide solution and one measuring cylinder into each water bath.
8. Leave the solutions in the various water baths for 10 minutes (to reach correct temperature).

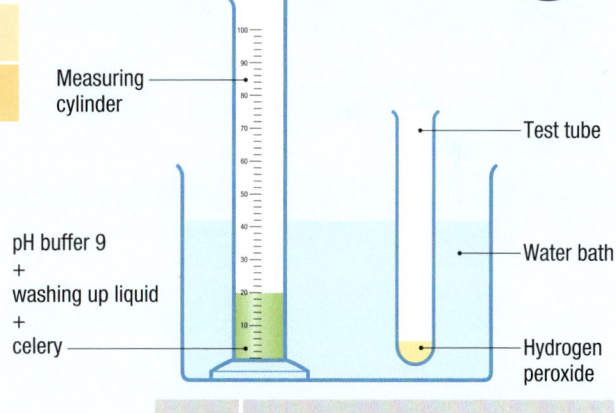

12.13 Preparing the enzyme and the substrate

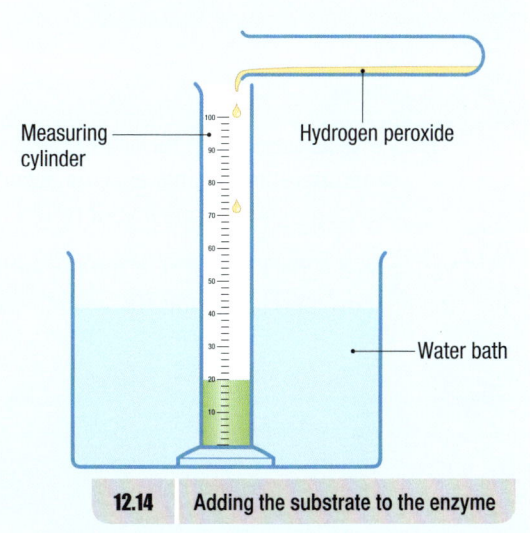

12.14 Adding the substrate to the enzyme

12 | Enzymes

9. Add the hydrogen peroxide solution to the measuring cylinder in each water bath.
10. Immediately note the volume and start a stopwatch.
11. After 2 minutes note the volume.
12. Repeat the investigation at each temperature with boiled celery (to act as a control).

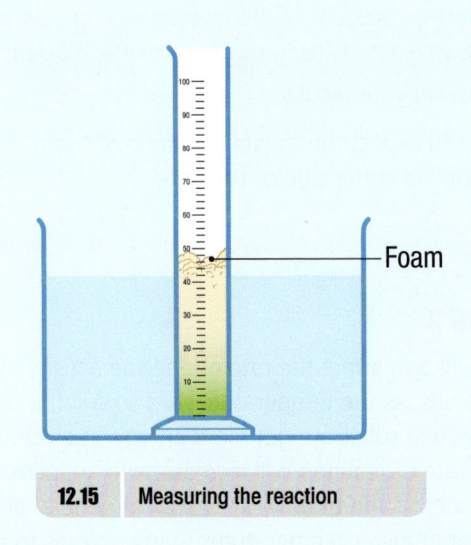

12.15 Measuring the reaction

Results

Unboiled celery:

Temperature (°C)	Initial volume (cm³)	Final volume (cm³)	Volume of foam produced (cm³)

Boiled celery:

Temperature (°C)	Initial volume (cm³)	Final volume (cm³)	Volume of foam produced (cm³)

1. Write an account of this investigation in your practical notebook and include a graph of temperature against enzyme activity (volume of foam). Put temperature on the x-axis (horizontal axis). Explain your results.

You should expect to find that the higher the temperature up to 20°C the greater the volume of foam; above and below this the volume should be lower.

HL Heat denaturation

With all chemical reactions, it can generally be said that an increase of 10°C will double the rate of reaction. This is due to the fact that heat is energy, and as more heat is added to a reaction, the molecules move around more rapidly, collide more often and more molecules have the **activation energy** when they collide, thus they react more quickly.

The same can be said for enzyme-controlled reactions except that, as the temperature rises, another feature comes into play. The shape of the enzyme changes, often permanently, when the temperature becomes too high. Such an enzyme is said to be **denatured** and rapidly loses its enzyme action. As a result, it will be found that, as the temperature increases in an enzyme-controlled reaction, there is initially an increase in activity but this increase halts and a rapid decrease in activity occurs at whatever temperature that particular enzyme is denatured (Fig 12.16).

Extremes of pH or high salt concentration may also denature enzymes.

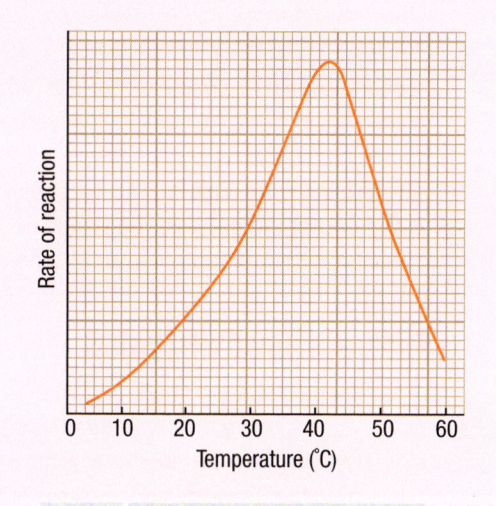

12.16 The effects of temperature on enzyme action showing denaturation

> **D** An enzyme is said to be **denatured** when it has permanently lost its function due to loss of shape.

Investigation 12.3

To investigate the effect of heat denaturation on the activity of catalase

Procedure

1. Finely chop some stalks of celery.
2. Place 5 g of the celery into two measuring cylinders.
3. Place one of the measuring cylinders into a boiling water bath for 10 minutes (this denatures the enzyme catalase in the celery).
4. Remove the measuring cylinder from the water bath and cool to room temperature.
5. Add 20 cm^3 of buffer at pH 9 (as this is the optimum pH for catalase) and one drop of washing-up liquid (to produce foam) to each measuring cylinder.
6. Place 5 cm^3 of hydrogen peroxide solution into two test tubes.
7. Place the two test tubes and the two measuring cylinders in a 25°C water bath for 10 minutes (to bring everything to the same temperature).
8. Pour the hydrogen peroxide into the measuring cylinders and estimate the height of foam generated after 2 minutes.
9. Record the results.

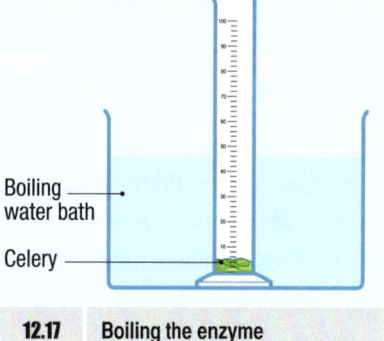

You will expect to find the boiled celery produces no foam.

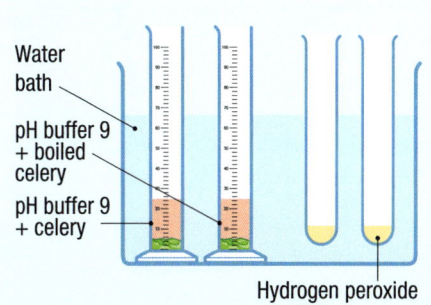

12.17 Boiling the enzyme

12.18 Preparing the enzyme and substrate

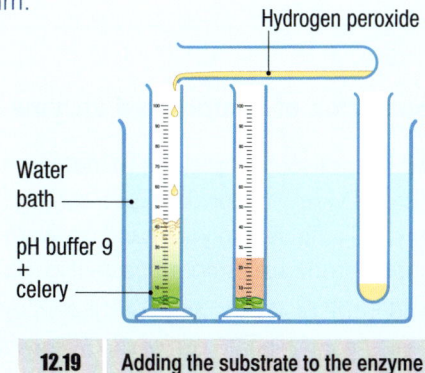

12.19 Adding the substrate to the enzyme

12 Enzymes

Industrial use of enzymes

Enzymes are used widely in industry. They can be used as an effective way of carrying out a specific reaction. Using enzymes, **organisms** or cells in industrial processes is called **bioprocessing**.

A cheap source of sweetener for the food industry is corn syrup, which is made by converting corn starch into sugar. A very effective way of doing this is to use enzymes. One practical problem is that, at the end of the process, you would be left with a mixture of syrup and enzyme. To separate the enzyme from the syrup is difficult and expensive.

> **Bioprocessing** is the use of organisms, cells or enzymes to make specific products.

> **Immobilised enzymes** are biological catalysts attached to an inert material chemically or physically.

Immobilised enzymes

A technique has been developed where the enzymes are not added directly to the corn starch solution. Rather the enzyme is put into a gel (sodium alginate) which will not let the enzyme diffuse out. The sodium alginate containing the **immobilised enzyme** is made into small beads. Dripping the gel into a solution of calcium chloride makes these beads. Enzymes may also be immobilised in a number of other ways including; attaching them onto the surface of glass or plastic beads, or placing them in membranes.

The beads are placed into a large vessel, usually a stainless steel column called a **bioreactor** (Fig 12.20). The corn starch solution is added to the top of the column and the corn syrup will emerge at the bottom.

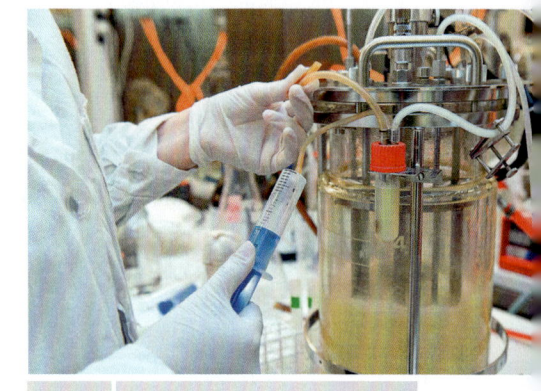

> A **bioreactor** is a vessel (usually large) in which cells, organisms or enzymes are placed to manufacture specific products.

12.20 A bioreactor

Advantages of immobilisation

- It is a very effective way of getting the product (syrup) without the enzyme being mixed through it. This removes the cost/difficulty of separating these.
- It is also a very efficient way of using the enzymes as the gel beads can be used over and over again.
- The gel beads are easily used in large-scale industrial processes using big tanks filled with the beads (bioreactors).
- This process is generally slower than using the enzyme without the gel.

Investigation 12.4

To prepare an enzyme immobilisation and examine its application

Enzyme	Substrate	Product
Amylase	Starch	Maltose

Procedure

1. Preparation of immobilised enzyme

1. Add 3 g of sodium alginate to 100 cm^3 distilled water in a beaker use a stirring rod to mix while holding in your hand (to warm it) until it produces a smooth paste (Fig 12.21).
2. Add 5 cm^3 of a 0.1% amylase solution to the beaker containing 30 cm^3 of the 3% warm sodium alginate solution (to immobilise the enzyme).

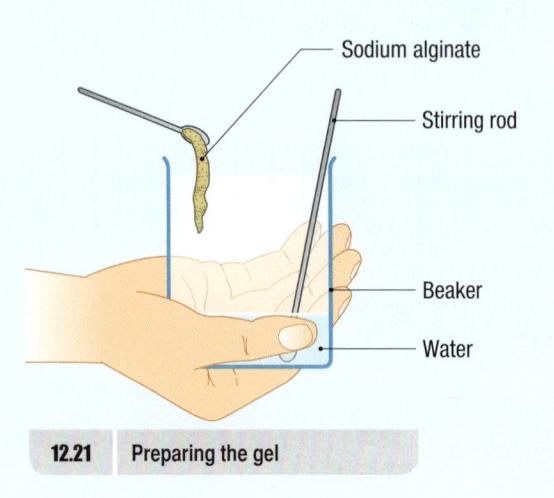

12.21 Preparing the gel

3. Mix this solution well. Put the mixture into a 10 cm³ syringe.

4. Hold the syringe over a beaker containing 50 cm³ of a 2% calcium chloride solution and gently squeeze the sodium alginate mixture into the calcium chloride solution drop by drop (Fig 12.22). (This will produce the beads containing the enzyme.)

5. Leave the gel beads in the calcium chloride solution for 15 minutes to harden.

6. Wash the sodium alginate beads with distilled water through a sieve (to remove any unbound enzymes).

2. Application

7. Place into a funnel with one end sealed with a tap (as shown in Fig 12.23).

8. In a second funnel add 50cm³ of 0.1% amylase solution (to act as control).

9. Add 50 cm³ of 1% starch solution to the top of each funnel.

10. Open the tap at intervals of 10 minutes, withdrawing about 5 cm³ of the liquid.

11. Place this liquid in a test tube and test for reducing sugar using Benedict's solution (see Investigation 7.1).

12. Write an account of this investigation in your practical notebook and explain your results.

You would expect that the non-bound enzyme will work faster but you will run out of the enzyme and the enzyme is mixed with the product.

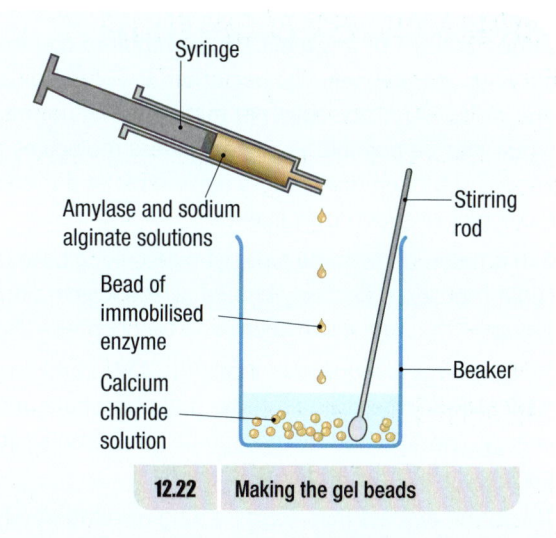

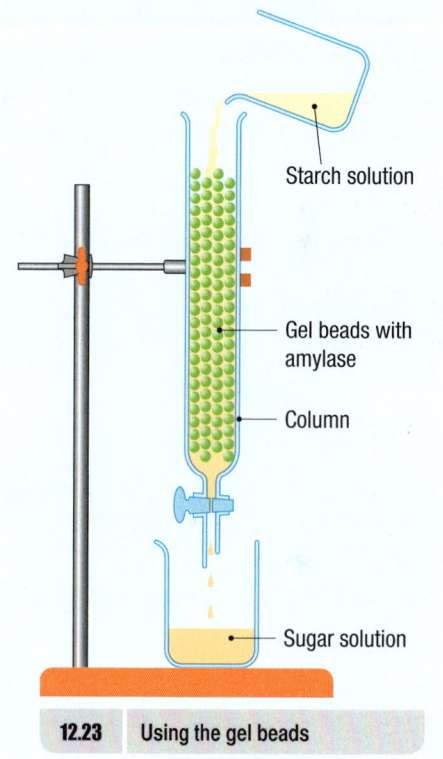

12.22 Making the gel beads

12.23 Using the gel beads

HL ATP, NADP and NAD

ATP

Metabolic reactions in cells take place in many small steps. For these steps to work well, small amounts of energy must be available to cells. Breaking down a sugar molecule every time energy is required would be very wasteful, as sugar contains a large amount of energy.

Cells have overcome this problem by producing a large number of molecules that contain just the right amount of energy to power the steps in **cell metabolism**. The molecule that acts as a broker of energy is called **ATP (adenosine triphosphate)**.

D | **ATP** traps and transfers energy for cell reactions.

Large numbers of this molecule are required continuously in a cell if it is to operate well. The bacterium *E. coli* needs approximately one million ATP molecules per minute for its normal cell activity. It would not be possible to make all these molecules as quickly as they are being broken down. Cells reassemble and then reuse the same molecules over and over again.

ATP is made up of three types of molecule: a base (adenine) and a sugar (ribose), collectively known as adenosine; and three phosphate groups – thus the name adenosine triphosphate (Fig 12.24).

When energy is required in a cell, the ATP is broken down into **ADP** (**adenosine diphosphate**) and phosphate and this releases energy. The ADP and the phosphate group can be re-formed back to ATP by the addition of energy.

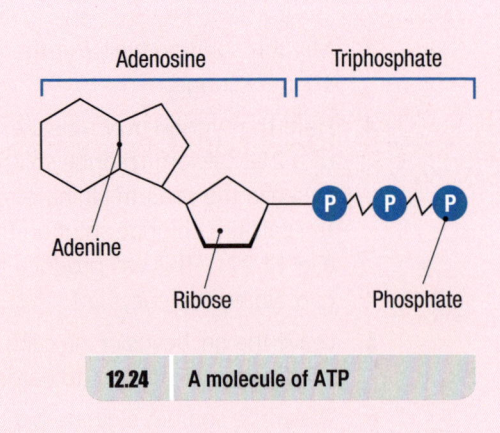

This is the process that occurs during respiration where the energy from the breakdown of sugar is used to re-form ATP (Fig 12.25). ATP is also made during photosynthesis as a source of energy that can then be used to make sugar.

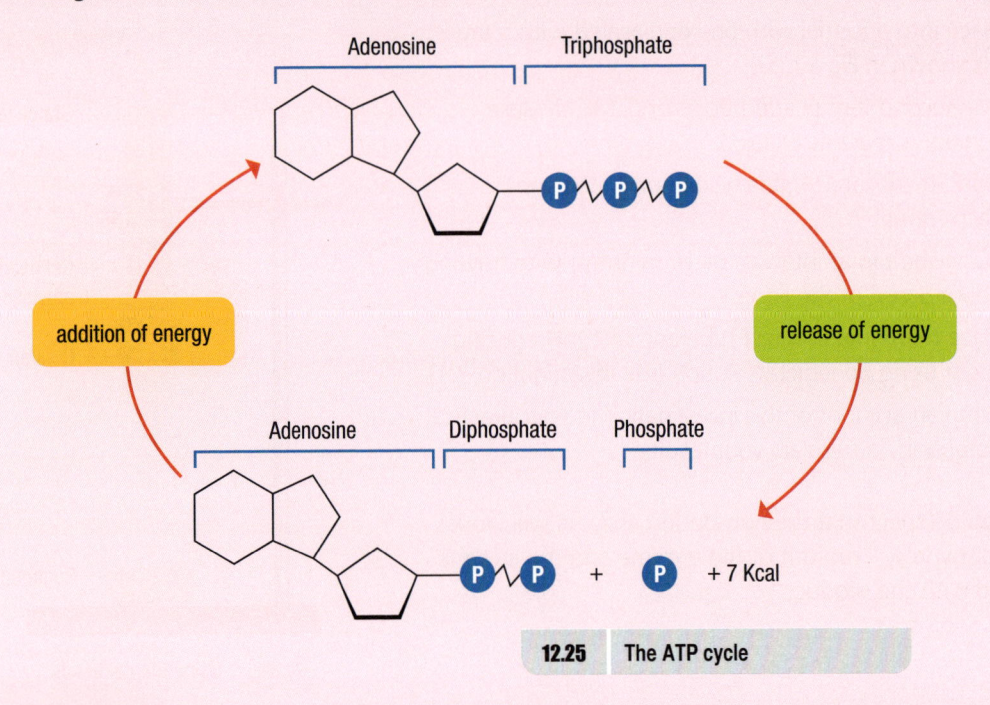

12.24 A molecule of ATP

12.25 The ATP cycle

NAD⁺ and NADH

In catabolic (breakdown) reactions, energy and hydrogen ions, or energy and electrons, are released. These hydrogen ions or electrons need to be attached to something. A chemical, **NAD⁺ (nicotinamide adenine dinucleotide)**, is used to carry these hydrogen ions and electrons.

- When NAD accepts these hydrogen ions, it is reduced (accepts hydrogen and electrons) and becomes NADH (Fig 12.26).
- NADH can then be oxidised (releases hydrogen) by other hydrogen acceptors.
- This oxidation will release energy in small quantities so it can be used to make ATP.

HL NAD is a **coenzyme**, i.e. a non-protein chemical that assists some enzymes in their function. NAD is produced from a B vitamin called niacin.

D | **NAD traps and transfers hydrogen ions and electrons in cell reactions.**

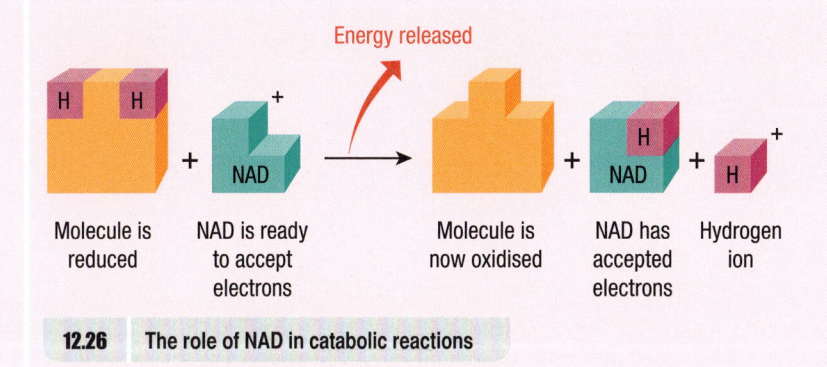

12.26 The role of NAD in catabolic reactions

NADP⁺ and NADPH

In anabolic (synthetic) reactions, hydrogen ions are often needed to make more complex chemicals, i.e. glucose from carbon dioxide in photosynthesis. In these reactions, a similar molecule called **NADPH** is used to reduce (add hydrogen to) the substrate (Fig 12.27).

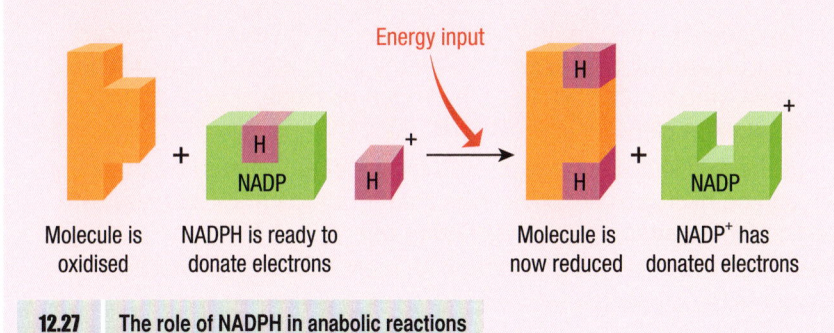

12.27 The role of NADPH in anabolic reactions

In photosynthesis a similar molecule **NADP⁺ (nicotinamide adenine dinucleotide phosphate)** is present in the chloroplast
- During photosynthesis, the light energy is used to make NADPH.
- NADPH is made from NADP⁺, electrons and hydrogen ions (Fig 12.28).
- NADPH can then be used to manufacture sugar by reducing carbon dioxide.

D | **NADP traps and transfers hydrogen ions and electrons in cell reactions.**

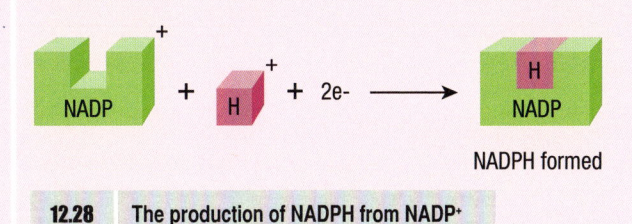

12.28 The production of NADPH from NADP⁺

Summary

- All the energy on the planet ultimately comes from the sun.
- The energy from the sun is called solar energy.
- The energy contained in the chemicals in a cell is called cellular energy.
- Cell metabolism is the sum of all the chemical reactions in an organism.
- Anabolic reactions are chemical reactions that build molecules.
- Catabolic reactions are chemical reactions that break down molecules.
- Enzymes:
    - are biological catalysts made of protein;
    - are made at the ribosomes in cells;
    - control cell activities by lowering the activation energy of a reaction;
    - are made of folded amino acid chains called proteins;
    - their shape controls their function;
    - **HL** change the shape of the active site to fit the correct substrate exactly (induced fit theory);
    - have an active site – the place on the enzyme where the substrate attaches and the reaction takes place;
    - produce an enzyme–substrate complex temporarily;
    - produce product(s) and an unchanged enzyme finally;
    - will have their shape affected by pH and work best at one specific pH;
    - **HL** have an optimum pH at which the shape of the active site best fits the substrate and the rate of activity is highest;
    - can be shown to vary their action dependent on pH, i.e. if you add catalase from celery to hydrogen peroxide at different pHs the amount of foam will vary depending on the pH; the most foam will be produced (O_2 released) at the pH the enzyme has its 'best fit' to hydrogen peroxide;
    - will stop working if the temperature gets too high;
    - will increase their rate of reaction as the temperature increases; this can be demonstrated by changing the temperature of catalase when adding hydrogen peroxide – the amount of foam will increase with increased temperature up to a certain temperature (approx. 60°C with celery);
    - **HL** increase their movement at increased temperatures thus reacting with more substrate molecules; will stop working when the temperature denatures the enzyme; denaturation: when the enzyme has permanently lost its function due to loss of shape – this can be demonstrated by boiling catalase and adding to hydrogen peroxide [no foam (O_2) produced];
    - are used widely in industry;
    - can be combined with gel, immobilised, and put in bioreactors for industrial processes; this can be demonstrated by:
        - adding amylase to sodium alginate
        - dropping into calcium chloride to make beads
        - placing beads into a funnel and adding starch
        - sugar without starch present will be produced
        - the enzymes can be used repeatedly.
- **HL** ATP (adenosine triphosphate):
    - traps and transfers energy for cell reactions;
    - carries energy in small manageable quantities around the cell;
    - is made up of adenosine and three phosphate molecules;
    - releases energy when it is broken down to produce ADP and phosphate;
        - can be reformed during respiration or photosynthesis from ADP and phosphate.
- NAD (nicotinamide adenine dinucleotide)
  traps and transfers hydrogen ions and electrons in cell reactions;
  when hydrogen is released during catabolic reactions, it is added to NAD to form NADH.
- NADP (nicotinamide adenine dinucleotide phosphate)
  traps and transfers hydrogen ions and electrons in cell reactions;
  in photosynthesis, NADPH is manufactured and is used as a reducing agent to make carbohydrate.

Review questions

01 (a) What is the name given to the chemical reactions in cells?
    (b) Explain the difference between a catabolic reaction and an anabolic reaction.

02 Explain the following terms:
    (a) reactants
    (b) products
    (c) solar energy
    (d) cellular energy

03 (a) What are catalysts?
    (b) How can enzymes be considered catalysts?
    (c) In what way do enzymes differ from other catalysts?

04 (a) On what important feature of proteins does an enzyme's function depend?
    (b) What is the activation energy of a reaction?
    (c) What factors will affect the enzyme action?

05 Describe with the aid of diagrams how an enzyme functions.

06 (a) Explain the following terms:
        (i) active site
        (ii) induced fit theory
        (iii) enzyme–substrate complex.
    (b) Comment on the statement 'shape is all-important for an enzyme'.

07 What effect does the pH have on the action of an enzyme?

08 Explain how the pH affects the rate of an enzyme-controlled reaction.

09 How does increased temperature affect the rate of an enzyme reaction?

10 (a) What does the term denaturation mean?
    (b) What conditions will denature enzymes?
    (c) What happens to an enzyme when it is denatured?

11 (a) Explain the meaning of the following terms:
        (i) bioprocessing, (ii) bioreactor, (iii) immobilised enzymes.
    (b) What are the advantages to immobilising enzymes?
    (c) How might enzymes be immobilised?

12 (a) For what do the letters ATP stand?
    (b) What chemicals make up ATP?
    (c) What important role does ATP have in the transfer of energy in a cell?

13 (a) What is the function of NAD^+ and NADH in the metabolism of a cell?
    (b) What is the role of NADPH in photosynthesis?

Examination style questions

Section A

01 (a) Enzymes are made from what type of biomolecule?
    (b) What is an enzyme?
    (c) Name an enzyme and its substrate that you have used in an experiment.
    (d) What was the product of this enzyme?
    (e) How did you test for this product?

02 (a) What is an immobilised enzyme?
    (b) What is a bioreactor?
    (c) What chemical was used to immobilise an enzyme in your experiment?
    (d) How did you make your beads of immobilised enzyme?
    (e) What are the advantages of immobilising enzymes?

Section B

03 (a) Enzymes are biological catalysts made of protein. (i) What is a catalyst? (ii) Name the biomolecular subunits of protein.
    (b) Answer the following questions based on the investigation of the effect of temperature on the rate of enzyme activity.
        (i) Name the enzyme you used in this investigation.
        (ii) Name the specific substrate the enzyme acted on.
        (iii) Name the product(s) of the reaction between the named enzyme and substrate.
        (iv) Outline how one particular temperature was achieved and kept constant.
        (v) Why is a control necessary at each temperature?
        (vi) Describe the control.
        (vii) Describe the result of the control.
        (viii) Draw an outline graph of the expected results.

04 Answer the following questions based on an experiment to investigate the effect of pH on the rate of enzyme action.
    (a) (i) Where precisely in the cell are enzymes made?
        (ii) Outline what is meant by pH.
    (b) (i) Name the enzyme and the substrate used in the experiment.
        (ii) State the optimum temperature for the named enzyme.
        (iii) Explain how the experiment is run at the optimum temperature.
        (iv) Why must the temperature be kept constant at the optimum level?
        (v) Describe how different pH values are obtained.
        (vi) How is the pH of the solution measured?
        (vii) Describe the control for this investigation.
        (viii) How is the rate of enzyme action measured?

05 (a) Enzymes are proteins which, by virtue of their shapes, catalyse specific chemical reactions.
        (i) Which four chemical elements must be present in enzymes?

12 Enzymes

Examination style questions

(ii) Name the part of the enzyme which has a complementary shape to the substrate that binds to it and where the catalysis takes place.

(b) Excessive heat can raise the temperature high enough to cause enzymes to denature. Answer the following, referring to the investigation you carried out to show the effect of heat denaturation on enzyme activity.
  (i) Name the enzyme you investigated.
  (ii) Name the substrate specific to the named enzyme.
  (iii) How precisely did you denature the enzyme?
  (iv) Describe a suitable control for this investigation.
  (v) At what pH was the procedure conducted?
  (vi) At what temperature was the procedure conducted?
  (vii) How was the temperature kept constant during the experiment?
  (viii) Describe the difference between the experiment and control.

Section C

06 (a) (i) Enzymes play an essential role in metabolism. Explain the underlined term.
  (ii) Of which biomolecule are enzymes composed?
  (iii) Where in a cell are enzymes produced?

(b) (i) Describe, with the aid of diagrams, the induced fit theory of enzyme action.
  (ii) How may the flexibility of the enzyme assist the catalytic ability of the enzyme?
  (iii) Explain why an enzyme is specific in the reaction it catalyses, e.g. amylase converts starch to maltose but has no effect on protein.
  (iv) What is a denatured enzyme?

(c) Immobilised enzymes are often used in the large-scale production of useful substances in industry.
  (i) Explain the term immobilised enzymes.
  (ii) Give two advantages of using immobilised enzymes over using enzymes in solution in the reaction medium.
  (iii) Give one example of the use of enzymes in industry.
  (iv) What is a bioreactor?
  (v) In a bioreactor the pH is maintained at a particular value. Why is it important that the pH should not change during the reaction?

07 (a) (i) What role do enzymes play in a cell?
  (ii) From what type of chemical are proteins made?
  (iii) How would you test for this chemical?

(b) (i) What is an enzyme?
  (ii) Catalase is an enzyme that speeds up the breakdown of hydrogen peroxide resulting in the release of oxygen gas. The table shows the results of an experiment in which catalase was added to hydrogen peroxide solution at different pH values and the time taken to collect 10 cm^3 of the oxygen gas produced was recorded.

pH of solution	4	5	6	7	8
Time (minutes)	18	10	8	13	16

  1. Draw a graph to show these results, placing pH on the horizontal axis (x-axis).
  2. From the graph, state the optimum pH for catalase activity.
  3. How is the pH maintained constant at each pH?
  4. State the other factors which must be kept constant at each pH.
  5. What control should be used to show catalase is responsible for the breakdown of hydrogen peroxide?

(c) (i) Describe with the aid of a labelled diagram how you carried out an experiment to demonstrate the effect of temperature on the activity of an enzyme.
  (ii) What results did you obtain?
  (iii) Explain these results.

Leaving Certificate examination questions

Section A

01 Draw this table in your copy. Choose each term from the following list and place it in Column B to match a description in Column A. The first one has been completed as an example.

amylase   temperature   substrate
immobilised   reusable   protein

Column A	Column B
An example of an enzyme	Amylase
(a) The group of biomolecules to which enzymes belong	
(b) Enzyme activity is affected by this	
(c) Enzymes trapped in an inert substance	
(d) The substance with which enzymes react	
(e) Advantage of using immobilised enzymes	

2013 OL Q. 5

Section B

02 (a) (i) What is an enzyme?
  (ii) Explain what is meant by the term *pH*.

(b) Answer the following questions in relation to your investigation into the effect of pH on the rate of enzyme activity.

Leaving Certificate examination questions

(i) Name the enzyme you used in this investigation.
(ii) Name
  1. The substrate of this enzyme.
  2. The product of this enzyme.
(iii) Draw a labelled diagram of the apparatus you used in your investigation.
(iv) How did you vary the pH?
(v) Name **one** factor you kept constant.
(vi) How did you keep the named factor constant?

2010 OL Q. 8

03 (a) (i) What term is used for the substance(s) that result(s) from the action of an enzyme on its substrate?
(ii) In relation to an enzyme, explain the term *optimum activity*.
(b) Answer the following in relation to an activity that you carried out to investigate the effect of heat denaturation on the activity of an enzyme.
  (i) Name the enzyme **and** the substrate that you used.
  (ii) Describe how you carried out the investigation, and in your description outline how you measured the activity of the enzyme.
  (iii) Using suitably labelled axes, draw a graph of the results you obtained.

2013 HL Q. 8

04 (a) Answer the following in relation to enzymes.
  (i) What is their chemical nature?
  (ii) Comment upon their molecular shape.
(b) Answer the following in relation to an investigation that you carried out into the effect of temperature on the rate of enzyme action.
  (i) Name the enzyme that you used.
  (ii) Name the substrate of this enzyme.
  (iii) Why was it necessary to keep the pH constant in the course of the investigation?
  (iv) How did you keep the pH constant?
  (v) How did you vary the temperature in the course of the investigation?
  (vi) How did you know that the enzyme was working?
  (vii) Use the axes below to summarise the results of your investigation. Do this by
    1. Labelling the axes.
    2. Drawing a graph to show how the rate of enzyme action varied with temperature.

2012 HL Q. 9

05 (a) (i) To which group of biomolecules do enzymes belong?
(ii) Name a factor that influences the activity of an enzyme.
(b) In the course of your practical investigations you prepared an enzyme immobilisation. Answer the following questions in relation to that investigation.

(i) Describe how you carried out the immobilisation.
(ii) Draw a labelled diagram of the apparatus that you used to investigate **the activity** of the immobilised enzyme.
(iii) Briefly outline how you used the apparatus referred to in (b) (ii) above.

2009 HL Q. 9

Section C

06 Enzymes are used in many processes in both plants and animals.
(i) What is an enzyme?
(ii) Name any **one** enzyme, **and** its substrate, **and** its product.
(iii) The rate of activity of enzymes can be affected by various factors. Name any **two** factors that can affect enzyme activity.
(iv) Enzymes are sometimes immobilised in industrial processes. What is meant by the term *immobilised* in relation to enzymes?
(v) Give **one** advantage of using immobilised enzymes.

2011 OL Q. 12 (c)

07 (i) To what group of biomolecules do enzymes belong?
(ii) Name the small molecules that are the building blocks for these biomolecules.
(iii) The action of the enzyme amylase on its <u>substrate</u> starch is an example of a <u>catabolic</u> reaction. Explain **each** of the underlined terms.
(iv) What is meant by immobilisation of an enzyme?
(v) Describe how you immobilised an enzyme in the course of your practical work.
(vi) Give **one** advantage of bioprocessing using an immobilised enzyme.
(vii) Suggest **one** reason why enzymes are not found in body soap or shampoo.

2009 OL Q. 15 (c)

08 (a) Study the graphs of enzyme activity below and answer the questions that follow.

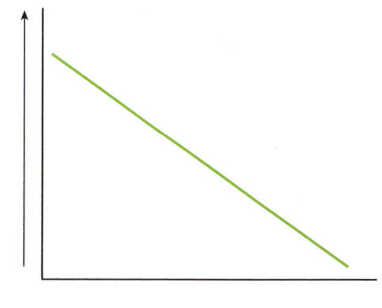

Graph A

12 Enzymes

Leaving Certificate examination questions

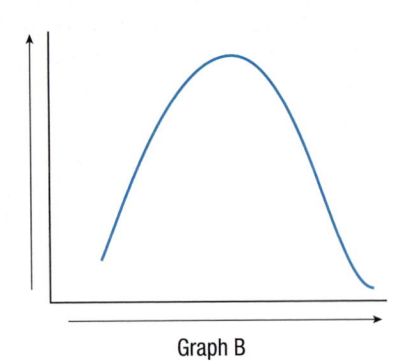

09
(a) [Graph B — bell-shaped curve]

Graph B

(i) In the case of **each** graph state the relationship between the rate of reaction (*y*-axis) and another factor (*x*-axis).
(ii) In the case of graph B, what factor could be responsible for the changes in activity of the enzyme?

(b) (i) Give a detailed account of how enzymes work, referring in your answer to their specificity.
(ii) Name **two** processes that occur in plant or animal cells that require the use of enzymes.
(iii) Some biological washing powders contain enzymes similar to the ones found in our digestive system. Many of these enzymes are extracted from bacteria.
 1. Suggest why such enzymes are included in washing powder.
 2. Why is 40°C the recommended temperature for these washing powders?
 3. Suggest what would happen to these enzymes in an 80°C wash.

(c) In the course of your practical studies you immobilised an enzyme and then investigated its activity. You also prepared alcohol using yeast.
Give **two** advantages of using immobilised yeast cells in the production of alcohol.

2014 HL Q. 13

09
(i) What is meant by the term *metabolism*?
(ii) 'Enzymes are essential for metabolism'. Explain why this statement is true.
(iii) In **each** of the following cases state whether the process is anabolic or catabolic.
 1. Protein synthesis.
 2. Conversion of ADP to ATP.
 3. Reactions in which product molecules are larger than substrate molecules.
(iv) State **one** way by which an enzyme may be denatured.
(v) Give **two** features of a denatured enzyme.
(vi) Apart from carbon, hydrogen and oxygen, there is one other element always present in the building blocks of enzymes. Name that element.

2011 HL Q. 14 (b)

10
(i) What is an enzyme?
(ii) What is meant by the specificity of an enzyme?
(iii) Explain how the active site theory may be used to explain the specificity of enzymes.
(iv) Bioprocessing often involves the use of immobilised enzymes in a bioreactor.
 1. What does the term *immobilisation* refer to when used about enzymes?
 2. Explain the term *bioreactor*.
(v) Give **one** example of the use of immobilised enzymes in bioreactors. In your answer name the enzyme, the substrate and the product.

2010 HL Q. 14 (b)

Past examination questions

OL	2013 Q. 5	2012 Q. 3 (d)	2011 Q. 8 (b) (vi), Q. 12 (c)	2010 Q. 8	2009 Q. 15 (c)
	2007 Q. 7	2005 Q. 8			

HL	2014 Q. 13 (a), (b), (c) (ii)		2013 Q. 8, Q. 14 (c)	2012 Q. 9	2011 Q. 14 (b)	2010 Q. 14 (b)
	2009 Q. 9	2008 Q. 9	2007 Q. 7, Q. 11 (c)	2006 Q. 3	2005 Q. 7	SEC Sample Q. 7

Photosynthesis

13

After studying this chapter you should be able to:

1. Define photosynthesis.
2. State the role of photosynthesis.
3. Give a balanced equation for the overall reaction of photosynthesis.
4. Identify the location of chlorophyll.
5. Describe how light energy causes electrons to be released by chlorophyll, which combine with protons and carbon dioxide to form carbohydrate. The protons come from the splitting of water, which also releases oxygen.
6. Identify the source of light, water and carbon dioxide for photosynthesis.
7. Carry out an experiment to show the effect of light intensity or carbon dioxide concentration on photosynthesis.
8. Refer to the methods by which humans can artificially modify the rates of photosynthesis in horticulture.
9. **HL** Describe the two stages of photosynthesis: the light-dependent stage producing ATP, NADPH and oxygen; the light-independent stage which uses CO_2, ATP and NADPH and produces carbohydrate.

Energy for cells

Energy is required by all living **organisms** to survive. All **cells**, including plants, get this energy when they break down complex chemicals (carbohydrates) to more simple chemicals, releasing energy for cell **metabolism**. These carbohydrates, therefore, must be produced continuously. Green plants have the unique ability to produce carbohydrates from simple chemicals using the sun's energy. This reaction, called **photosynthesis**, is the process of making food (synthesis) with light (photo).

Almost all living things depend, directly or indirectly, on green plants and therefore the sun for their energy. In the breakdown process, most living things also use the oxygen produced in photosynthesis to release the energy. Oxygen and carbohydrate produced in photosynthesis (from carbon dioxide and water) are converted back into carbon dioxide and water during **respiration**. In respiration, energy that originally came from the sun is made available to living organisms (Fig 13.1).

> **D** **Photosynthesis** is the process in which plants make carbohydrate and oxygen using (sun)light energy, water, carbon dioxide and chlorophyll.

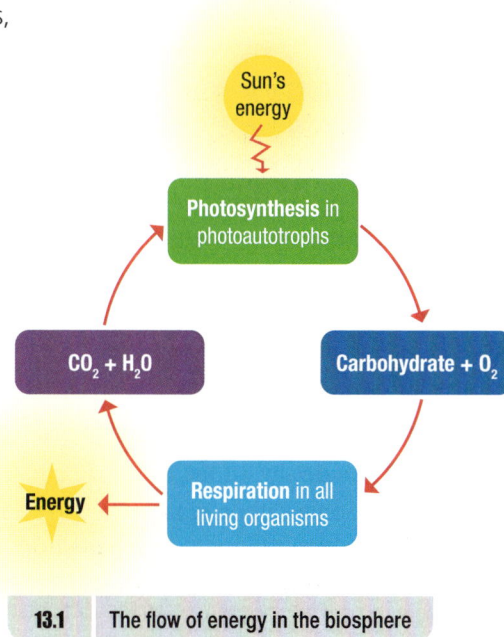

13.1 The flow of energy in the biosphere

Photosynthesis

Glucose is one of the two products of photosynthesis. This is rapidly converted into starch by most plants. The second product is oxygen, which usually escapes through the **stomata** (pores on the underside of a leaf). The production of either of these can be used to demonstrate that photosynthesis has occurred (Fig 13.2).

13 Photosynthesis

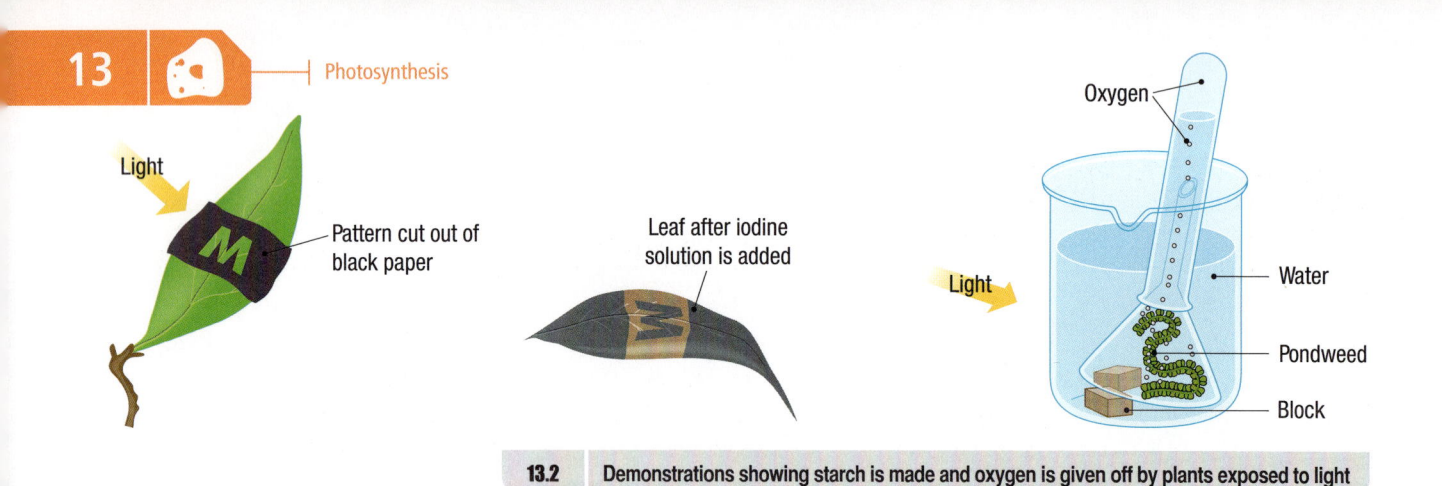

13.2 Demonstrations showing starch is made and oxygen is given off by plants exposed to light

By measuring the amount of oxygen given off by a plant in a given time, the rate of photosynthesis can be measured. An equation to summarise photosynthesis is:

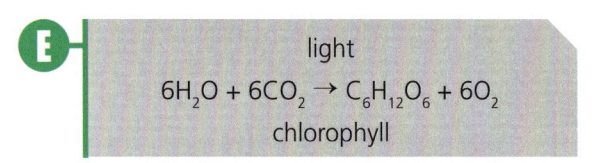

$$6H_2O + 6CO_2 \xrightarrow[\text{chlorophyll}]{\text{light}} C_6H_{12}O_6 + 6O_2$$

Photosynthesis:
- Requires the presence of a green pigment, **chlorophyll**, in the plant cell.
- This pigment is found in a special cellular **organelle** called a **chloroplast**.
- The process of photosynthesis is therefore restricted to those structures.
- The highest concentration of cells containing chloroplasts is found in the leaves of most plants. The cells containing the largest number of chloroplasts are usually found in the upper half of the leaf (Fig 13.3).

13.3 A cross-section through a leaf

In the chloroplast, the energy from the light is **absorbed**.
1. Some light energy is used to release high-energy electrons from chlorophyll.
2. Some light energy is used to split water into H^+ ions (protons), electrons and oxygen.
   - The H^+ ions go into a common pool of protons in the chloroplast.
   - The electrons from water go to the chlorophyll to replace those lost.
   - Most of the oxygen gas is released as a waste product out of the leaf through the stomata.
   - Some of the oxygen produced will be used in the cells of the leaf for respiration.

Carbon dioxide is then combined with the protons and the high-energy electrons and produces glucose (Fig 13.4).
1. The carbon dioxide
   - Enter the leaf through the **stomata**, found mainly on the underside of the leaf.
   - Some carbon dioxide used in photosynthesis comes from respiration within the plant itself.
2. The light for photosynthesis comes from the sun in the natural environment.
3. The water for photosynthesis comes up to the leaf from the roots via the **xylem** vessels in the veins (see Chapter 21).

SYLLABUS REQUIREMENT:

Students are expected to do either Investigation 13.1 or Investigation 13.2 (not both).

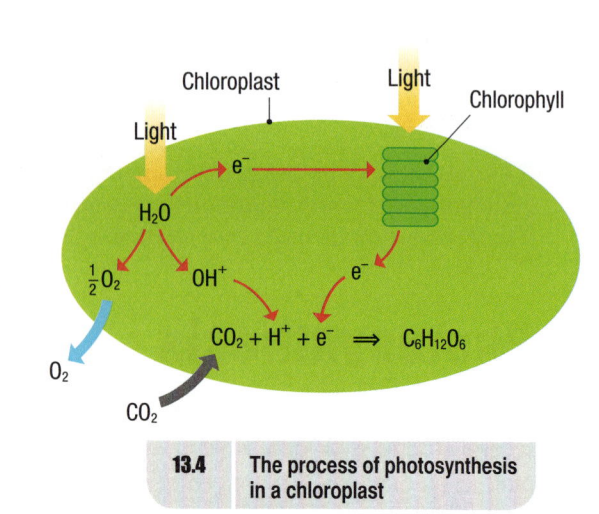

13.4 The process of photosynthesis in a chloroplast

Investigation 13.1

To investigate the influence of light intensity on the rate of photosynthesis

Procedure

1. Place *Elodea* (use a water plant so you can see bubbles of oxygen) in a large test tube of saturated sodium hydrogen carbonate (this ensures CO_2 is in excess). Place this in a larger beaker containing water at 25°C to act as a water bath (see diagram). If you are using data logging, place a pressure or oxygen sensor attached to a one-hole cork on top of the test tube and connect to your logging equipment.

2. Place a lamp of fixed wattage close to the water bath.

3. Measure the distance of the lamp away from the water bath.

4. Leave the apparatus for 5 minutes to let the plant adjust.

5. Count the number of bubbles given off by the plant per minute (to measure the rate of photosynthesis).

6. Repeat the count at least three times and get the average.

7. Move the lamp further away from the water bath, measure the distance in centimetres (d), leave to adjust and count bubbles as before.

8. Repeat with the lamp at other distances from the water bath.

9. Hold a light meter the same distances from the light as the water bath and measure the light intensity at each distance.

10. Write up the investigation in your practical notebook, drawing a graph of rate (number of bubbles per minute) against light intensity. $10{,}000/\text{distance}^2$ (cm^{-2}) is a good way of estimating light intensity (or you can use a light meter as used in ecology).

11. Explain your results.

12. What would you use as a control in this experiment?

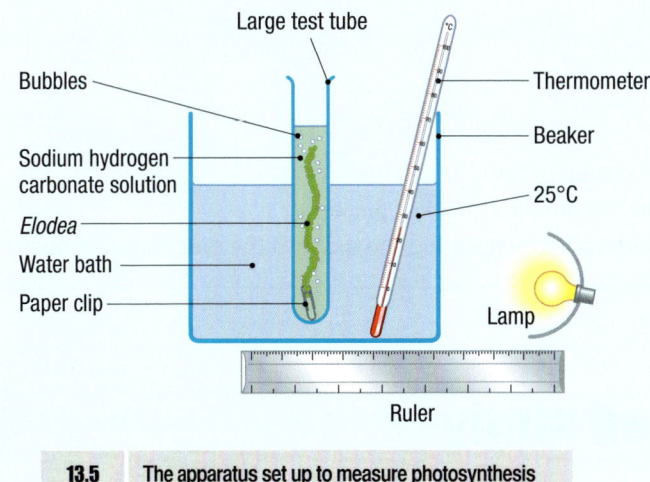

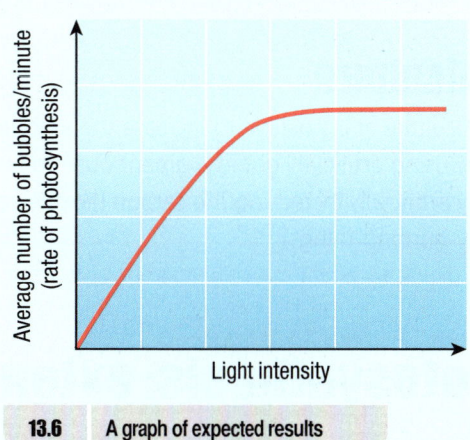

13.5 The apparatus set up to measure photosynthesis

13.6 A graph of expected results

13 | Photosynthesis

Investigation 13.2

To investigate the influence of carbon dioxide concentration on the rate of photosynthesis

1. Place *Elodea* (use a water plant so you can see bubbles of oxygen) in a large test tube containing a 2% solution of sodium hydrogen carbonate. Place this in a beaker containing water at 25°C to act as a water bath (see diagram). If you are using data logging, place a pressure or oxygen sensor attached to a one-hole cork on top of the test tube and connect to your logging equipment.
2. Place a lamp at a set distance from the water bath.
3. Leave the experiment for 5 minutes to adjust.
4. Count the number of bubbles given off per minute (to measure the rate of photosynthesis).
5. Repeat the count at least twice more and get the average result.
6. Repeat the entire experiment with 4%, 6% and 8% solutions of sodium hydrogen carbonate ($NaHCO_3$).
7. Write up the investigation in your practical notebook, drawing a graph of rate (number of bubbles per minute) against percentage solution of $NaHCO_3$.
8. Explain your results and describe a control you could use.

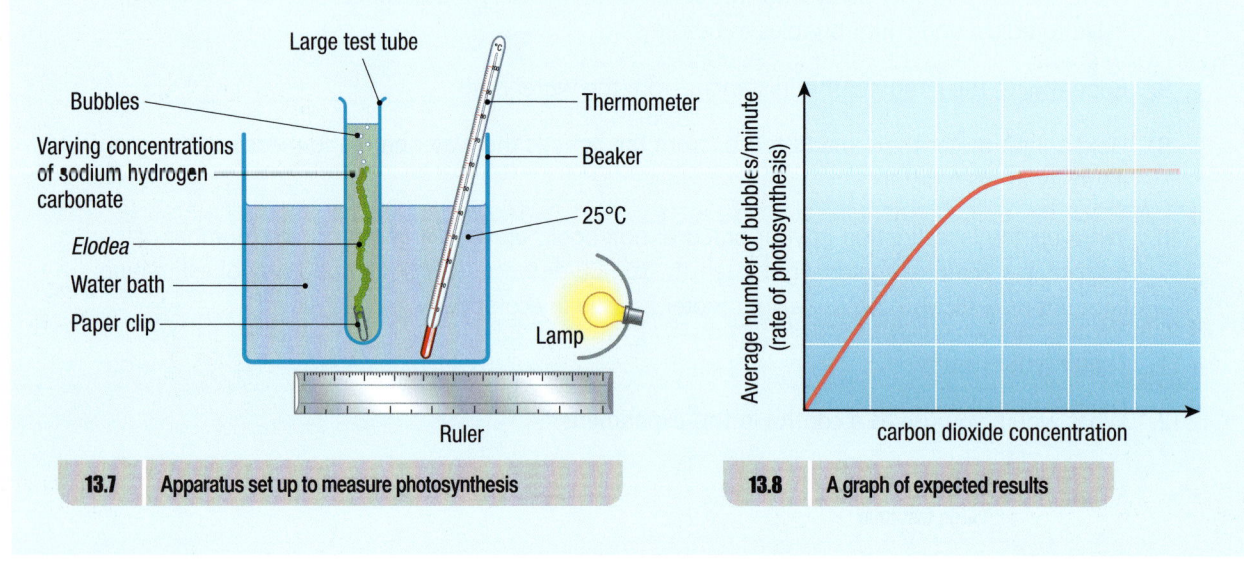

13.7 Apparatus set up to measure photosynthesis

13.8 A graph of expected results

Horticulture

In horticulture, it is possible to increase the amount of photosynthesis in two main ways:
1. By using artificial light in a greenhouse to extend the time that it takes place.
2. By artificially increasing the carbon dioxide concentrations by releasing the gas into the greenhouse (usually by burning things).

HL Photosynthesis: extended study

Photosynthesis is a very complex reaction that uses the energy of the sun to manufacture sugar from carbon dioxide and water.

The reaction has two main stages. The first stage is called the **light-dependent stage**, as it only takes place in the presence of light. In these reactions, **NADPH** and **ATP** are made and water is split, releasing oxygen. This process uses the chlorophyll pigment molecules (see Fig 13.9).

HL The second stage is dependent on the products of the light phase, i.e. NADPH and ATP. Carbon dioxide is reduced to sugar using these products. As light is not directly required in these reactions, it is called the **light-independent stage** (Fig 13.10).

The light-dependent stage

The light-dependent stage (Fig 13.10) takes place using the pigments that make up chlorophyll:
- Having more than one pigment means more wavelengths (colours) of light can be absorbed.
- These molecules are grouped together in a funnel-shaped structure. The broad base of the funnel is pointed to the sun.
- A photon of light energy is absorbed by one pigment molecule and the energy is passed at random from one pigment molecule to the next.
- At the end of the funnel is the reaction centre, a **chlorophyll a** molecule.
- The chlorophyll a molecule absorbs the energy, and electrons in the chlorophyll are excited.
- These energised electrons leave the chlorophyll and go to an **acceptor molecule** (Fig 13.11).

There are two possible pathways that these electrons can take.
1. In the first pathway:
   - They will return to a chlorophyll molecule via a series of carrier molecules.
   - This process releases energy in steps that can be used to generate ATP from ADP and P (photophosphorylation).
2. In the second possible pathway:
   - The electrons are passed from the acceptor to NADP$^+$.
   - This results in chlorophyll being deficient in electrons.
   - The electrons needed to replenish the chlorophyll come from the splitting of water.

E $H_2O \rightarrow 2H^+ + 2e^- + \frac{1}{2}O_2$ (is released as a gas)

- The NADP$^+$ receives two electrons from the chlorophyll to become NADP$^-$.
- H$^+$ ions (from a pool of such protons in the chloroplast) are attracted to the NADP$^-$ forming NADPH.

E $NADP^+ + 2e^- + H^+ \rightarrow NADPH$

- The H$^+$ ions released by the splitting of water replenish the proton pool in the chloroplast.
- The remaining oxygen is released as a gas.

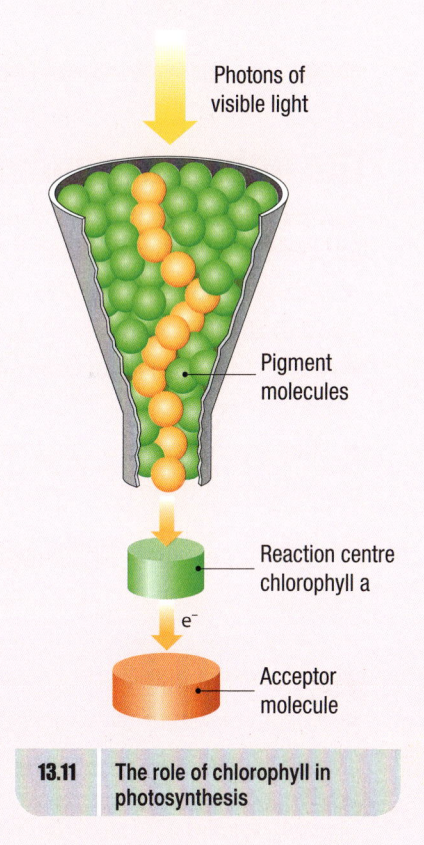

Products of the light-dependent stage

There are three products of the light-dependent stage (Fig 13.12): NADPH, ATP and oxygen gas.
- The NADPH is used to reduce (convert) carbon dioxide to glucose.
- The ATP provides energy for this production of glucose.
- The oxygen is released as a waste gas or used in respiration.

Increasing or decreasing the light intensity is the main factor that controls the rate of these reactions.

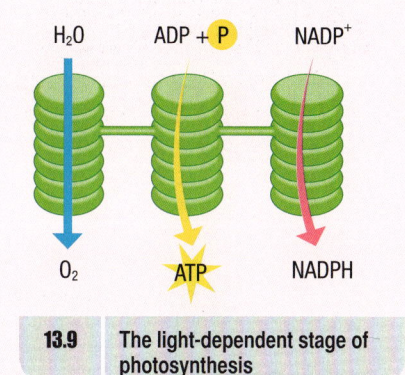

13.9 The light-dependent stage of photosynthesis

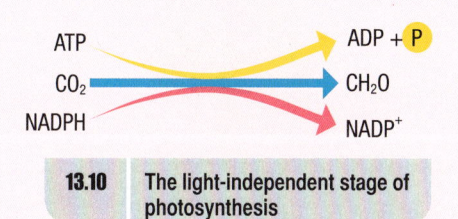

13.10 The light-independent stage of photosynthesis

13.11 The role of chlorophyll in photosynthesis

13 Photosynthesis

HL

Possible pathway 1

13.12(a) The light-dependent stage first pathway

Possible pathway 2

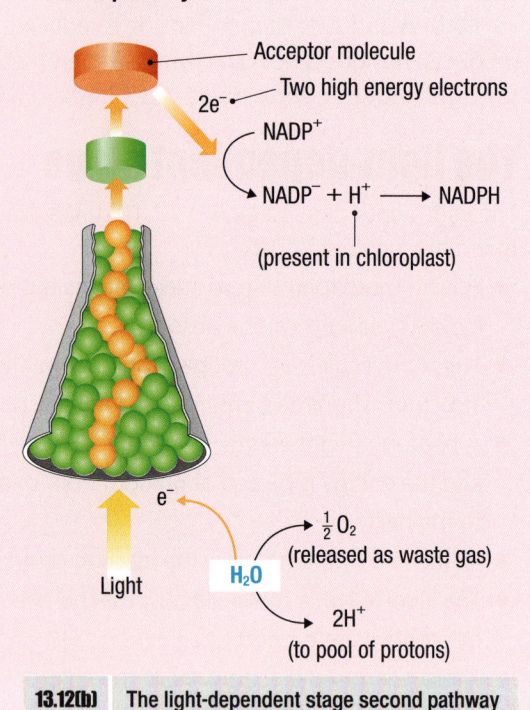

13.12(b) The light-dependent stage second pathway

The light-independent stage

The light-independent stage needs NADPH and ATP if it is to work. In this reaction:
- A carbon dioxide molecule is reduced (hydrogen is added) using NADPH.
- The energy needed to allow the reaction to take place comes from ATP.
- The carbon dioxide is converted into a carbohydrate $C_x(H_2O)_y$.

The simplest of these carbohydrates would be **glucose** ($C_6H_{12}O_6$) (Fig 13.13).

13.13 The light-independent stage

Products of the light-independent stage

There are four products of the light-independent stage: glucose, $NADP^+$, ADP and P.
- The glucose can be used in respiration or stored as starch.
- The $NADP^+$ returns to the light-dependent stage where it can be used to regenerate NADPH.
- ADP and P return to the light-dependent stage and regenerate ATP again.

The reactions in the light-independent stage are controlled by **enzymes**. The levels of CO_2 and the temperature will affect the rate of these reactions as well as the amount of NADPH and ATP available. The levels of these last two (NADPH and ATP) are determined by the rate of the light-dependent stage.

Conclusion

Photosynthesis occurs in two stages:
1. The light-dependent stage, which converts H_2O, $NADP^+$, ADP and P into NADPH, ATP and O_2 using chlorophyll and sunlight.
2. The light-independent stage, which converts CO_2 into glucose using NADPH and ATP. This process generates $NADP^+$, ADP and P, which can be reused in the light-dependent stage.

Thus photosynthesis converts carbon dioxide and water into sugar and oxygen (which is given off as a waste gas), using chlorophyll and sunlight.

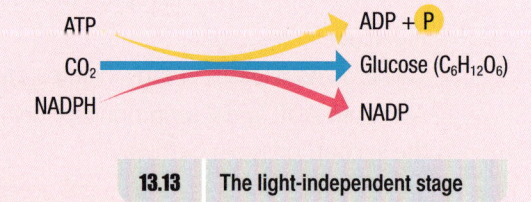

13 Photosynthesis

Summary

- Green plants produce carbohydrates from sunlight by the process of photosynthesis.
- Photosynthesis is the process in which plants make carbohydrate and oxygen using (sun)light energy, water, carbon dioxide and chlorophyll.
- Photosynthesis:
    - requires carbon dioxide, water, chlorophyll and light (usually from the sun);
    - produces oxygen, and sugar or starch (showing the production of any of these can be used to demonstrate that photosynthesis has occurred): $6H_2O + 6CO_2 \rightarrow C_6H_{12}O_6 + 6O_2$.
- Chloroplasts:
    - contain chlorophyll and are required for photosynthesis;
    - are at their highest concentration in cells at the top of the leaf;
    - combine H^+ from water with CO_2 from the air to produce sugar.
- CO_2:
    - comes from the air into the leaf via stomata;
    - some is produced in the plant by respiration.
- H_2O:
    - comes into the plant from the ground;
    - travels to the leaf in the xylem vessels;
    - is split to produce O_2 and H^+ ions and electrons.
- Photosynthesis can be increased in greenhouses by using electric light and by increasing CO_2 concentrations.
- In an experiment the rate of photosynthesis can be measured by counting the bubbles given off per minute by *Elodea* placed in a test tube of $NaHCO_3$ (sodium hydrogen carbonate) standing in a transparent water bath:
    - By moving a light source towards and away from the plant the effect of light intensity on the rate can be measured.
    - By changing the amount of $NaHCO_3$ (sodium hydrogen carbonate) in the test tube the effect of changing CO_2 concentration on the rate can be measured.

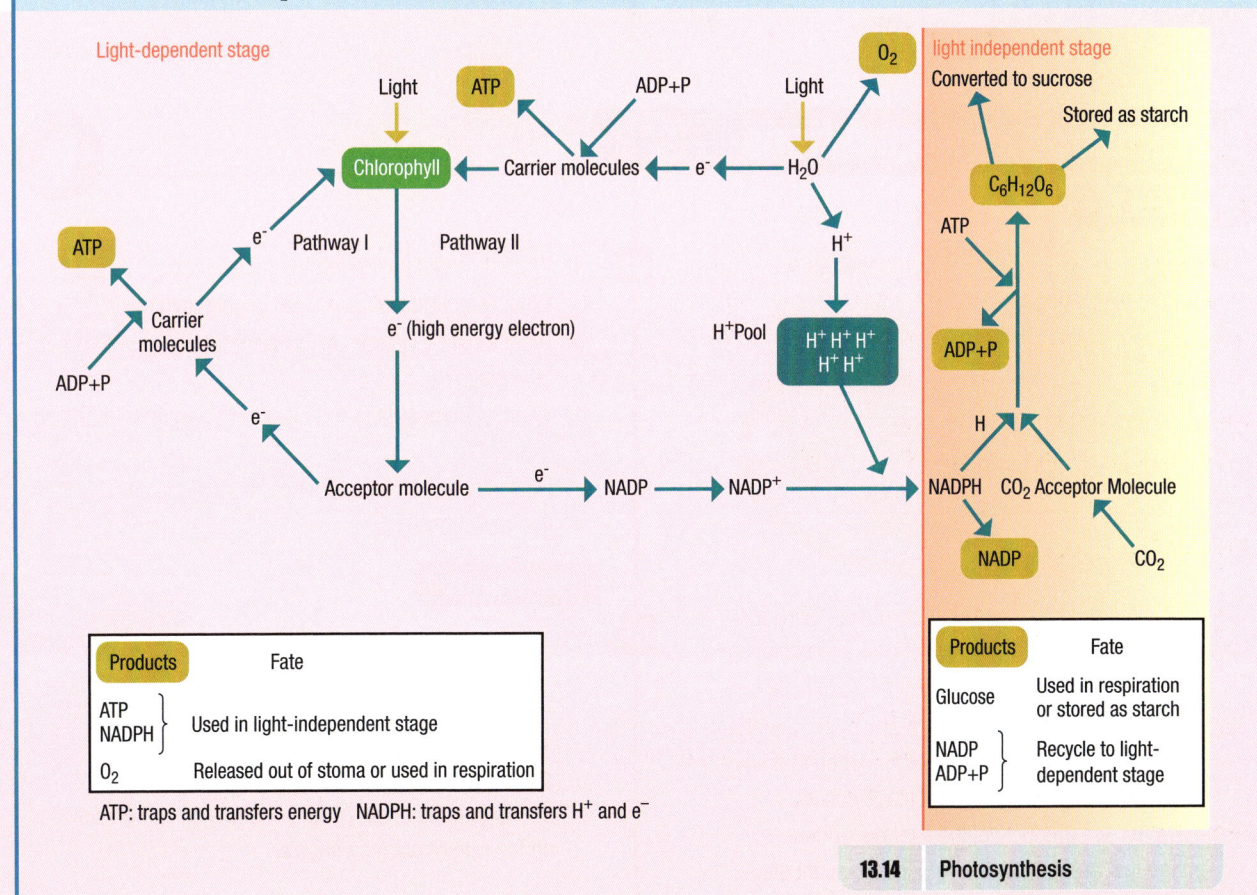

HL

Light-dependent stage

Products	Fate
ATP, NADPH	Used in light-independent stage
O_2	Released out of stoma or used in respiration

ATP: traps and transfers energy   NADPH: traps and transfers H^+ and e^-

light independent stage

Products	Fate
Glucose	Used in respiration or stored as starch
NADP, ADP+P	Recycle to light-dependent stage

13.14 Photosynthesis

13 Photosynthesis

Review questions

01 (a) What is photosynthesis?
(b) In what type of organism does it take place?
(c) Where in the cell does it occur?
(d) What pigment is required for it to happen?

02 (a) Write a simple balanced equation for photosynthesis.
(b) Give two benefits of photosynthesis for plants.
(c) From where do plants get the two chemicals necessary for photosynthesis?

03 It is sometimes said that 'animals depend on photosynthesis'. Comment on this statement.

04 (a) What is the function of chlorophyll and where is it found?
(b) From where does chlorophyll get energy?

05 When light is absorbed by chlorophyll water is split.
(a) What three things are produced when water is split?
(b) What happens to each of the things mentioned in (a)?
(c) Which of these products would be considered waste?
(d) What else does chlorophyll release?

06 (a) What happens to carbon dioxide in photosynthesis?
(b) Where might the carbon dioxide come from for use in photosynthesis?
(c) How do plants get water for use in photosynthesis?

07 How does the structure of the leaf help it carry out its function?

08 In horticulture growers may wish to increase the yield from their crops.
(a) Describe two ways in which they could do this.
(b) Explain how each of these methods could increase the yield.

09 Describe an experiment, with the aid of a labelled diagram, to show the effect of changing light intensity or carbon dioxide concentration on photosynthesis and explain the results you found.

10 (a) Name the two stages in photosynthesis.
(b) Compare these two stages.

11 (a) In what organelle is chlorophyll found?
(b) What does light cause to happen in chlorophyll?
(c) What are the two possible pathways used by the products named in (b)?

12 Does changing the temperature affect the (a) light-dependent, (b) the light-independent stages of photosynthesis? In each case explain your answer.

13 The light-independent stage of photosynthesis will not happen in the absence of light. Why is this the case?

14 (a) Describe how ATP and NADPH are produced in the first stage of photosynthesis.
(b) What are the roles of ATP and NADPH in the second stage of photosynthesis?

15 Why can it be said that 'recycling is an important part of photosynthesis'?

Examination style questions

Section A

01 The diagram shows a sub-cellular organelle as seen through an electron microscope.

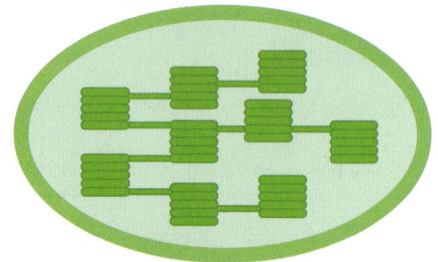

(a) Name the organelle and state its overall function.
(b) In what region of a leaf would you expect to find cells with the highest concentration of this organelle?
(c) Draw a diagram of the structure and mark X on the diagram to indicate where the light-dependent stage and Y where the light-independent stage occurs.
(d) Give the two products of the light-dependent stage that are used in the light-independent stage.

02 (a) What is meant by the term photosynthesis?
(b) What two chemicals are used in photosynthesis?
(c) What must be present in the plant for photosynthesis to take place?
(d) What is the benefit to the plant in having more than one pigment?
(e) How might a market gardener improve the crop yield in the greenhouse?

Section B

03 (a) (i) How does carbon dioxide enrichment in greenhouses promote crop growth?
(ii) State one suitable method by which the carbon level in greenhouses can be raised.
(b) The diagram shows a set-up that can be used to investigate the effect of light intensity or carbon dioxide on the rate of photosynthesis.

Examination style questions

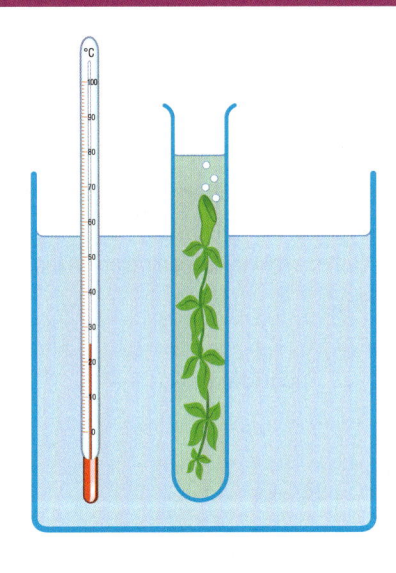

Name the factor you changed in the investigation you carried out. Refer to this when answering questions (a)–(h) below.

(a) Name a plant suitable for this experiment.
(b) At what temperature was the experiment conducted?
(c) How was the temperature kept constant?
(d) Name one other factor you kept constant.
(e) Name the gas given off by photosynthesis.
(f) How is the rate of photosynthesis measured?
(g) Why is it necessary to take several measurements at each value of the factor under investigation?
(h) How did you vary the factor under investigation?

Section C

04 (a) Photosynthesis occurs mainly in the leaves of plants.
   (i) Give one way in which leaves are adapted to their role in photosynthesis.
   (ii) One of the raw materials for photosynthesis is water. State a source of this water and state the precise role of water in the process.
(b) An experiment was carried out to measure how quickly the pond weed *Elodea* photosynthesises.

The *Elodea* was exposed to different light intensities. The rate of photosynthesis was estimated by counting the number of bubbles produced per minute. The results are given below.

Relative light intensity	0	1	2	3	4	5	6
Number of bubbles per minute	0	11	22	35	45	45	45

(i) Plot the results on graph paper. Put light intensity on the horizontal (*x*) axis.
(ii) What is the effect of increasing light intensity on the rate of photosynthesis?
(iii) At what light intensity did the *Elodea* produce 35 bubbles per minute?
(iv) Name the gas that makes the bubbles.
(v) What would be the effect of doing this experiment at 4°C?

(c) (i) Draw a labelled diagram to show the normal external structure of a leaf from a typical dicotyledonous plant, e.g. oak or ash.
(ii) Draw a diagram to show the internal structure of a leaf. Label the following: guard cell, dermal tissue, stoma.

05 (a) ATP is produced in the light-dependent stage of photosynthesis. Describe the structure of ATP and state its general function in living cells.
(b) (i) Distinguish between the light-dependent and the light-independent stages of photosynthesis.
(ii) Outline how ATP is generated in the light-dependent stage of photosynthesis.
(iii) NADPH is the other product of the light-independent stage. Describe the production of NADPH.
(iv) Why is oxygen considered to be a 'waste' of the light-independent stage?
(v) What use can the photosynthetic cell make of the oxygen produced in the light-independent stage?
(c) The rate of photosynthesis at different light intensities was determined by experiment in the laboratory. The results are given below.

Light intensity						
(% of noon light intensity in summer)	0	20	40	60	80	100
Rate of photosynthesis (arbitrary units)	0	4.2	5.1	5.6	5.7	5.7

(i) Plot the results on graph paper placing light intensity on the *x*-axis.
(ii) Describe the relationship between light intensity and the rate of photosynthesis.
(iii) Why were external factors, such as temperature and carbon dioxide concentration, kept constant at the different light intensities?
(iv) Describe how one of the factors you name in (iii) was kept constant.

13 Photosynthesis

Leaving Certificate examination questions

Section A

01 The diagram shows part of a section through a leaf.

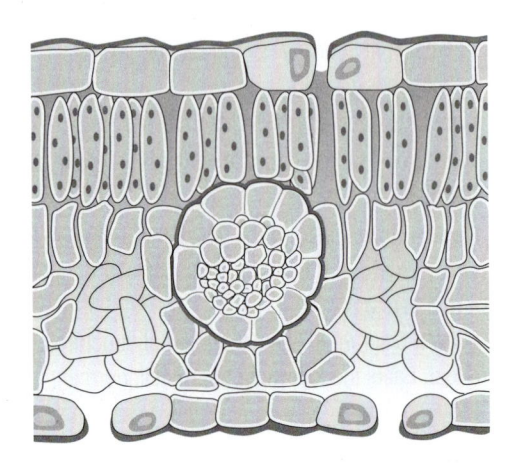

(a) Use the letter **A** to show a point of entry of carbon dioxide. Name this point.
(b) Name a gas that **leaves** the leaf at this point.
(c) Use the letter **B** to show the part of the leaf in which most photosynthesis occurs.
(d) Name the structures in plant cells in which photosynthesis occurs.
(e) In addition to carbon dioxide another small molecule is needed for photosynthesis. Name this other molecule.

2006 OL Q. 4

02 The following graph shows how the rate of photosynthesis varied when a plant was subjected to varying levels of light intensity **or** carbon dioxide concentration.

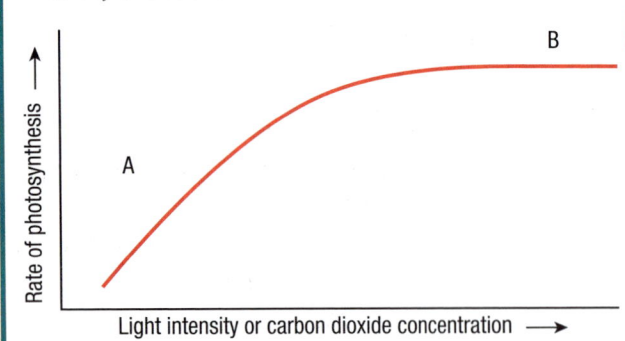

(a) What is happening at A?
(b) What is happening at B?
(c) Suggest a reason for your answer in (b).
(d) Where in a cell does photosynthesis take place?
(e) Give **two** sources of the carbon dioxide that is found in the atmosphere.
(f) Suggest **one** way in which the rate of photosynthesis of plants in a greenhouse could be increased.

2005 HL Q. 4

Section B

03 (a) (i) Where in a plant does photosynthesis take place?
  (ii) Name the gas released during photosynthesis.
(b) Answer the following questions in relation to an investigation that you carried out to study the effect of light intensity or carbon dioxide concentration on the rate of photosynthesis.

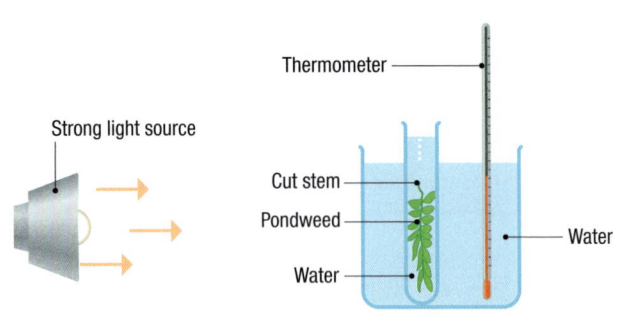

Name the factor you will refer to.
  (i) Name the plant that you used.
  (ii) How did you vary the light intensity **or** the carbon dioxide concentration?
  (iii) Name **one** factor you kept constant during the investigation.
  (iv) How did you keep that factor constant?
  (v) How did you measure the rate of photosynthesis?
  (vi) What was the result of your investigation?

2013 OL Q. 7

04 (a) State a precise role for each of the following in photosynthesis: (i) carbon dioxide, (ii) water.
(b) Answer the following questions in relation to an activity that you carried out to investigate the influence of light intensity OR carbon dioxide concentration on the rate of photosynthesis.
  (i) Name the plant that you used.
  (ii) How did you vary light intensity OR carbon dioxide concentration?
  (iii) State a factor that you kept constant during the investigation.
  (iv) How did you ensure that the factor that you mentioned in (iii) remained constant?
  (v) How did you measure the rate of photosynthesis?
  (vi) Using labelled axes, sketch a graph to show how the rate of photosynthesis varied with the factor mentioned in (ii) above.

2007 HL Q. 9

Leaving Certificate examination questions

Section C

05 (a) What is the main source of energy for photosynthesis?

(b) The diagram shows a section through a leaf.

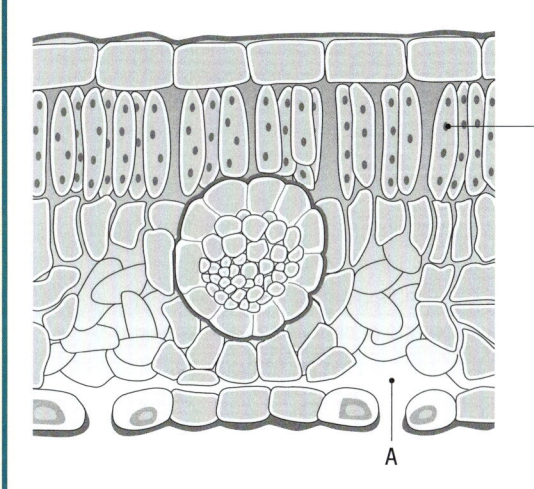

(i) Name the green pigment present in leaves that is essential for photosynthesis.
(ii) Name the cell structures, present in large numbers in part B, that are needed for photosynthesis.
(iii) Name the opening labelled A that is used for gas exchange.
(iv) Name the gas in the air needed for photosynthesis.
(v) In photosynthesis, water is split into three products. Name these **three** products.
(vi) From your knowledge of photosynthesis, suggest **two** ways of improving the rate of photosynthesis of plants in a greenhouse.

2014 OL Q. 13

06 (a) (i) What is meant by the term *photosynthesis*?
(ii) A gas from the air is needed for photosynthesis. Name this gas.
(iii) Name the part of a plant cell in which photosynthesis takes place.

(b) (i) Write a balanced equation for photosynthesis.
(ii) Plants contain the green pigment chlorophyll. What is the role of chlorophyll in photosynthesis?
(iii) The apparatus shown below may be used to investigate the effect of an environmental factor on the rate of photosynthesis.
  1. Name any **two** environmental factors affecting photosynthesis that could be investigated using the apparatus shown.
  2. How would you measure the rate of photosynthesis using the apparatus below?

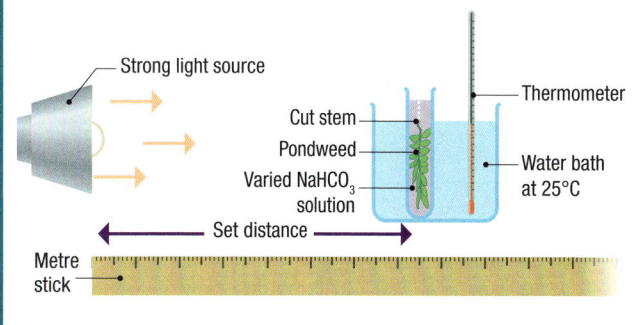

2011 OL Q. 12

07 (a) (i) In what main part of a plant does most photosynthesis take place?
(ii) In what cell structure does photosynthesis take place?

(b) (i) What is the main source of energy for photosynthesis?
(ii) Suggest **two** reasons why life on Earth might not continue without photosynthesis.
(iii) In photosynthesis water (H_2O) is split into three products.
  1. Name these **three** products.
  2. State what happens to each of these products.

(c) Describe an activity that you carried out to investigate the influence of light intensity **or** carbon dioxide concentration on the rate of photosynthesis. Include a diagram of the apparatus that you used in your answer.

2008 OL Q. 12

08 The scheme below summarises the process of photosynthesis.

Photosynthesis: First Stage { Pathway I / Pathway II } → Second Stage

(i) Give the name of the first stage.
(ii) In the first stage pathways I and II relate to the passage of energised electrons.
  1. Explain what happens to these electrons in pathway I.
  2. Describe the events of pathway II.
(iii) Give the name of the second stage.
(iv) Explain why the second stage is given the name referred to in part (iii).
(v) Give **one** reason why the second stage cannot happen without the first stage.
(vi) Outline the major events of the second stage.

2013 HL Q. 14 (a)

09 (a) (i) From the following list, **write into your answer book** any term that describes the nutrition of a typical plant:
parasitic   heterotrophic   saprophytic   autotrophic

13 Photosynthesis

Leaving Certificate examination questions

(ii) Identify, **in your answer book**, the cell organelles A and B.

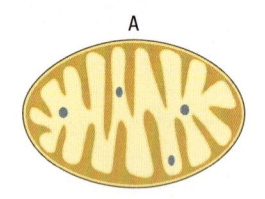

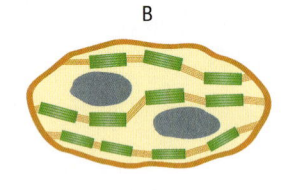

A   B

(b) Chlorophyll is composed of various pigments. Two of these pigments are **chlorophyll a** and **chlorophyll b**.

The graph below shows the amount of light of different colours absorbed by chlorophyll a and chlorophyll b.

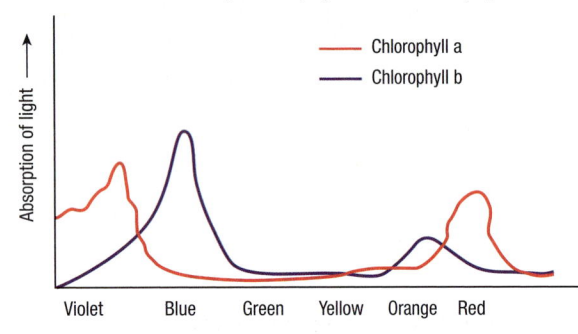

(i) 1. What **colours** of light are absorbed most by chlorophyll a?
2. What **colour** of light is absorbed most by chlorophyll b?
(ii) What happens to yellow light when it strikes a leaf?
(iii) Suggest **one** possible benefit to plants of having more than one chlorophyll pigment.
(iv) From the information provided by the graph suggest how a commercial grower might try to increase crop yield in his glasshouses or tunnels.
(v) 1. What is the main source of carbon dioxide used by plants in the dark stage of photosynthesis?
2. State **one** role of NADP and **one** role of ATP in the dark stage of photosynthesis.

2012 HL Q. 12

10 The graph shows the results of a classroom investigation into the factors affecting the rate of photosynthesis. The variable investigated was **either** light intensity **or** CO_2 concentration.

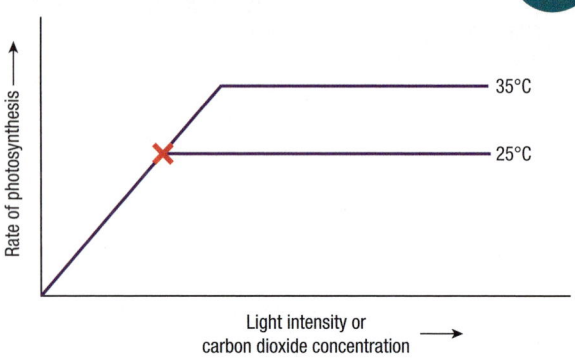

In your answer book, indicate clearly which factor you chose to address and answer the following questions:
(i) Suggest a suitable plant for such an investigation.
(ii) How was the rate of photosynthesis measured?
(iii) Name a factor that must be kept constant during this investigation.
(iv) Explain how you would keep constant the factor referred to in (iii).
(v) Why is it necessary to keep that factor constant?
(vi) 1. What happens to the rate of photosynthesis at X when the investigation is: (a) carried out at 25°C, (b) carried out at 35°C?
2. Give a reason for each answer.

2011 HL Q. 14 (a)

11 (i) Where in a plant cell does photosynthesis take place?
(ii) Give the alternative name of the first stage of photosynthesis.
(iii) During the first stage of photosynthesis energised electrons enter two pathways.
1. Where do the energised electrons come from?
2. Briefly describe the main events of **each** of these pathways.
(iv) 1. In the second stage of photosynthesis compounds of the general formula $C_x(H_2O)_y$ are formed. What name is given to this group of compounds?
2. From which simple compound does the plant obtain the H used to make compounds of general formula $C_x(H_2O)_y$?
(v) Name the simple compound that supplies the necessary energy for the second stage reactions.

2010 HL Q. 14 (a)

Past examination questions

OL	2014 Q. 13 (a) (ii), (b)	2013 Q. 7	2012 Q. 14 (b)	2011 Q. 12 (a), (b)	2010 Q. 12 (c)	2009 Q. 15 (a)
	2008 Q. 12	2006 Q. 4	2005 Q. 11 (a), (b)	2004 Q. 13		

HL	2013 Q. 9 (b) (i), Q. 14 (a)	2012 Q. 12 (a), (b)	2011 Q. 14 (a)	2010 Q. 8 (b) (ii), Q. 14 (a)	2009 Q. 12 (c)
	2008 Q. 14 (a)	2007 Q. 9	2006 Q. 11	2005 Q. 4, Q. 5 2004 Q. 11 (b), (c)	SEC Sample Q. 12

Respiration   14

After studying this chapter you should be able to:

1. Define aerobic respiration and give a balanced equation for the reaction.
2. Describe the two-stage reaction in aerobic respiration: the first which releases energy and the second, requiring oxygen, which produces a lot of energy.
3. Define anaerobic respiration and give a word equation for the reaction.
4. (HL) Describe the stages in respiration: glycolysis followed by the Krebs cycle and the electron carrier system or glycolysis followed by fermentation (in the absence of oxygen).
5. Describe the process of fermentation and the use of micro-organisms in industrial fermentation.
6. Describe the use of immobilised cells in industry.
7. Carry out an experiment to demonstrate the production of alcohol by yeast.

Respiration

Respiration is the process by which glucose molecules are broken down to release energy for cell metabolism. This process normally requires oxygen and releases energy, carbon dioxide and water. In respiration, glucose is oxidised. The breakdown of sugar with oxygen is called aerobic respiration. When organisms find themselves short of oxygen, many can break down glucose temporarily. The breakdown of sugar without oxygen is called anaerobic respiration. The end products of this reaction are usually damaging to the cells so the reaction will eventually stop. For a few micro-organisms, oxygen is a poison and these organisms can only respire in the absence of oxygen.

D Respiration is the breakdown of food (carbohydrate) to release energy.

Aerobic respiration

Aerobic respiration is the breakdown of sugar in the presence of oxygen. A simple balanced equation for aerobic respiration is:

E $C_6H_{12}O_6 + 6O_2 \rightarrow 6CO_2 + 6H_2O + 2820 \text{ kJ}$

Respiration is not a very efficient reaction and a lot of the energy is lost from the reaction in the form of heat. This is the heat you feel when you do hard physical work. Most organisms use oxygen in the breakdown of sugar in an attempt to be as efficient as possible.

The breakdown is a two-stage process.
1. In the first stage of the process:
   - Glucose is broken down into two three-carbon compounds.
   - Oxygen is not required.
   - Very little energy is released.
   - Takes place in the cytosol of the cell.
2. In the second stage of the process:
   - The three-carbon compounds are broken down into carbon dioxide and water.

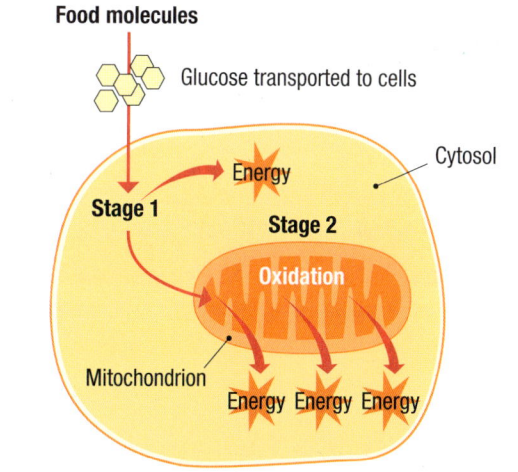

14.1 The process of respiration in a cell

14 Respiration

- Oxygen is required.
- A large amount of energy is released.
- Takes place in the **mitochondria** of the cell.

As with all metabolic reactions in a cell, **enzymes** regulate both stages of respiration (Fig 14.1).

> **Aerobic respiration** is the breakdown of food (carbohydrate) with oxygen to release energy.

> **Anaerobic respiration** is the breakdown of food (carbohydrate) in the absence of oxygen releasing energy.

Anaerobic respiration

Anaerobic respiration is the breakdown of sugar in the absence of oxygen. Anaerobic respiration is based on the first stage of respiration:

- Glucose is broken down to two three-carbon compounds releasing a little energy.
- In humans, the three-carbon compound is broken down to lactic acid. This eventually damages the cells in the muscles and causes cramp.
- In yeast the three-carbon compound is further broken down into ethanol and carbon dioxide (see Investigation 14.1). This process is known as **fermentation**.

A simple word equation for anaerobic respiration is:

> In muscle: glucose → lactic acid + very little energy
> In yeast: glucose → ethanol + carbon dioxide + very little energy

HL Respiration: extended study

Energy from the sun has been stored in carbohydrate molecules in the process of **photosynthesis**. For cell activity, this energy needs to be released gradually and converted into **ATP** (ATP traps and transfers energy for cell reactions, see Chapter 12). This is done in respiration. Respiration is a two-stage reaction, as we have already seen.

First stage

The first stage is called **glycolysis**.

- A six-carbon (6C) sugar (glucose) is converted into two three-carbon (3C) compounds called pyruvic acid (pyruvate).
- This process occurs in the cytosol of the cell.
- It produces two ATP molecules (Fig 14.2).

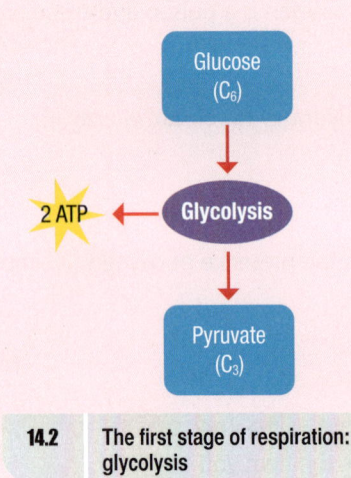

Glucose (C_6) → Glycolysis → Pyruvate (C_3) (2 ATP)

14.2 The first stage of respiration: glycolysis

- If oxygen is not present, the pyruvic acid (pyruvate) is converted into either lactic acid or ethanol and carbon dioxide (Fig 14.3).

A simple equation for anaerobic respiration is:

> Glucose → lactic acid + 150 kJ
> Glucose → ethanol + carbon dioxide + 210 kJ

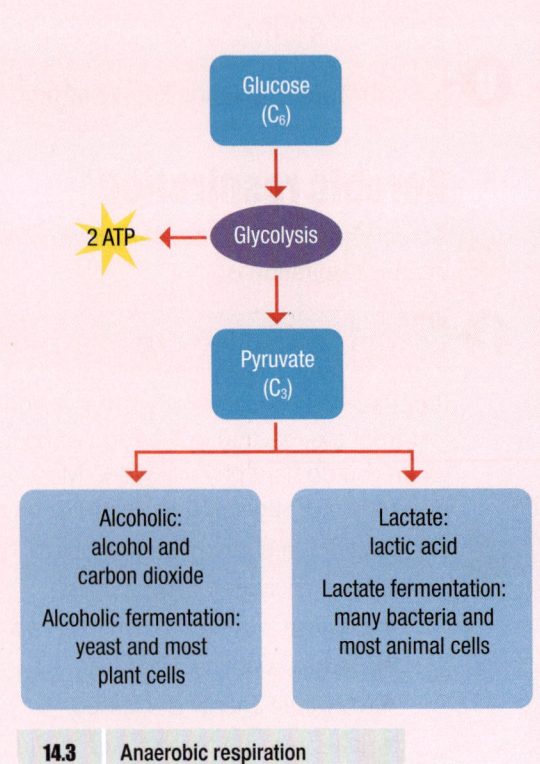

Glucose (C_6) → Glycolysis (2 ATP) → Pyruvate (C_3) →
- Alcoholic: alcohol and carbon dioxide. Alcoholic fermentation: yeast and most plant cells
- Lactate: lactic acid. Lactate fermentation: many bacteria and most animal cells

14.3 Anaerobic respiration

Respiration | 14

HL Second stage

If oxygen is present, the pyruvic acid enters the mitochondrion. The second stage of respiration occurs here.

- One carbon atom is removed from pyruvic acid in the form of carbon dioxide.
- The remaining acetyl (two-carbon group) produces a compound called acetyl coenzyme A and is passed into a series of reactions called the **Krebs cycle** (Fig 14.4).
- This cycle converts the acetyl group into carbon dioxide and hydrogen.
- The CO_2 is released as a waste gas.
- NADH is generated from **NAD** and the hydrogen.

The electrons from the hydrogen atoms are transferred down an **electron carrier chain** (the electron transport system).

- The energy released by the transport of the electrons is used to manufacture ATP from ADP and P.
- Finally the H^+, electrons and oxygen are combined to form water (Fig 14.5 and Summary diagram, page 171).

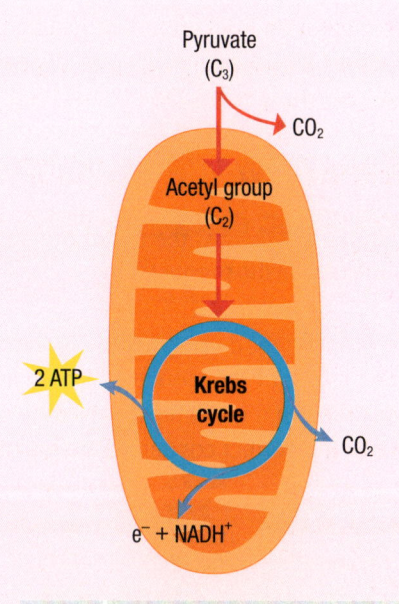

14.4 The Krebs cycle in the mitochondrion

Electron Transport system

Site: Mitochondria

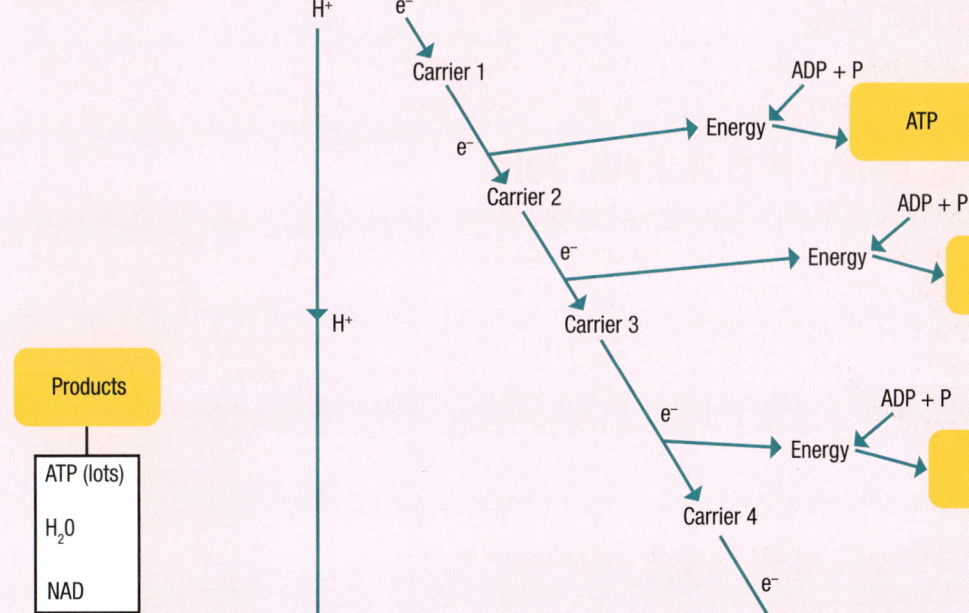

Products
- ATP (lots)
- H_2O
- NAD

14.5 The electron transport chain in the mitochondrion

LIFE LEAVING CERTIFICATE BIOLOGY | UNIT 2 THE CELL | 167

14 | Respiration

Industrial fermentation (bioprocessing)

Fermentation is an important reaction in the food and drink industry. Activities such as brewing, baking, yoghurt and cheese-making all depend on anaerobic respiration. In these processes, micro-organisms are used to ferment the original food to produce the desired result. In brewing, yeast is added to a sugar solution and, in the absence of oxygen, ethanol is produced. This is probably the oldest form of **biotechnology**. In 6000 BC beer was produced in the Middle East.

> **Biotechnology** is the use of organisms, cells or enzymes to make specific products.

To produce food using micro-organisms (a process often called **bioprocessing**), the correct conditions for the growth of the required microbe are needed and you also need to prevent the growth of the wrong microbes. In most cases the microbe is added to a **substrate** in a **bioreactor** and the product is made when the correct conditions are maintained in the reactor (see Chapter 12).

Name of product	Type of micro-organism
Ethanol (beer, wine, etc.)	Fungi (yeast) and bacteria
Yogurt	Bacteria
Methane (biogas)	Bacteria
Antibiotics	Fungi and bacteria
Vitamins	Bacteria

Yoghurt manufacture

Yoghurt is produced from milk: The milk is **pasteurised** and a bacterial culture is grown then added to the milk. This converts the milk in to yogurt and then various flavours, fruit etc. can be added.

Bioprocessing using immobilised cells

In some industrial alcohol production, yeast cells are not free in the solution. The cells are **immobilised** on sodium alginate beads (see Chapter 12). In these processes, the sugar solution is passed down through a bioreactor of yeast containing beads. The alcohol is produced by the fungi and runs out of the bottom of the column. In this process, the bioreactor can be continuously used without the need to stop the reaction and separate the cells from the alcohol (see Chapter 19 HL).

> **Immobilised cells** are cells attached to an inert material by chemical or physical means.

> A **bioreactor** is a vessel (usually large) in which cells, organisms or enzymes are placed to manufacture specific products.

14.6 A yoghurt culture

Respiration | 14

Investigation 14.1

To prepare and show the production of ethanol by yeast

Procedure

1. Boil 400 cm^3 (approx.) glucose solution in a conical flask for 5 minutes (to remove all the oxygen).

2. Divide the solution into two conical flasks and cool.

3. Add 2 g of powdered yeast in 10 cm^3 of water (this is your yeast suspension).

4. Boil half of this yeast suspension for 5 minutes.

5. Into one of the conical flasks, put 1 cm^3 of the unboiled yeast suspension.

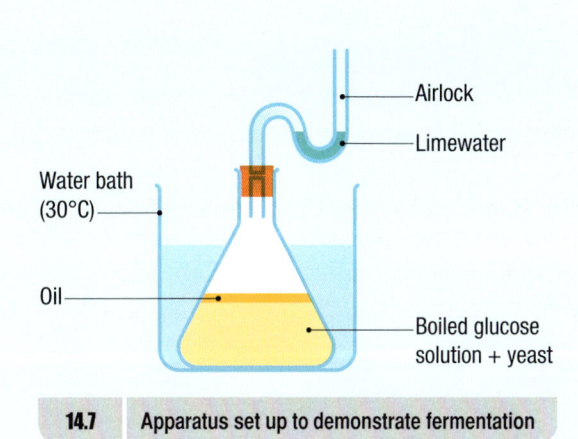

6. Into the second flask, add 1 cm^3 of the boiled yeast suspension (this is your control).

7. Cover the liquid in both flasks with oil (to exclude oxygen).

8. Put a one-hole rubber bung with fermentation lock attached containing limewater in each flask (see diagram).

9. Place the flasks into a water bath at 30°C.

10. Leave for 24 hours and record any changes in the limewater.

11. Filter the solutions in the flasks and add 5cm^3 of the solutions into test tubes.

12. Add 3 cm^3 of potassium iodide solution and 5 cm^3 of sodium hypochlorite solution to each test tube (the brown colour should disappear).

13. Place the test tube in a hot water bath (the appearance of pale yellow crystals is a positive test for ethanol).

14. Write up the investigation in your practical notebook and explain your results.

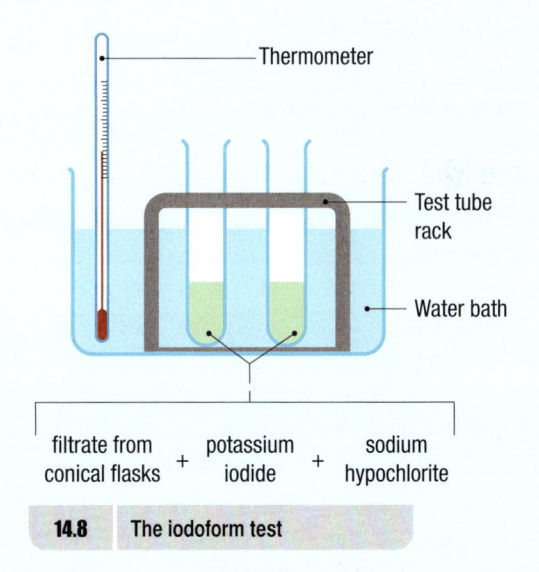

14.7 Apparatus set up to demonstrate fermentation

14.8 The iodoform test

You would expect to get a positive alcohol test only when you add unboiled yeast.

14 Respiration

Summary

- Respiration is:
    - the controlled release of energy in cells;
    - enzyme regulated;
    - carried out in two stages.

- Stage 1 in the cytoplasm does not require oxygen, produces little energy.

- Stage 2 in the mitochondrion requires O_2 and produces a lot of energy.

Aerobic	Anaerobic
The production of energy using oxygen	The production of energy in the absence of oxygen
Produces a lot of energy	Produces a little energy
Occurs in the cytosol and the mitochondrion	Occurs in the cytosol only
Has two stages	Has one stage
Produces: energy, carbon dioxide and water	Produces energy, ethanol and carbon dioxide (yeast) or Produces energy and lactic acid (animals)
Requires O_2	Does not require O_2
$C_6H_{12}O_6 + 6O_2 \longrightarrow 6 CO_2 + 6H_2O + energy$	Glucose → lactic acid in animals Glucose → ethanol and carbon dioxide in fungi

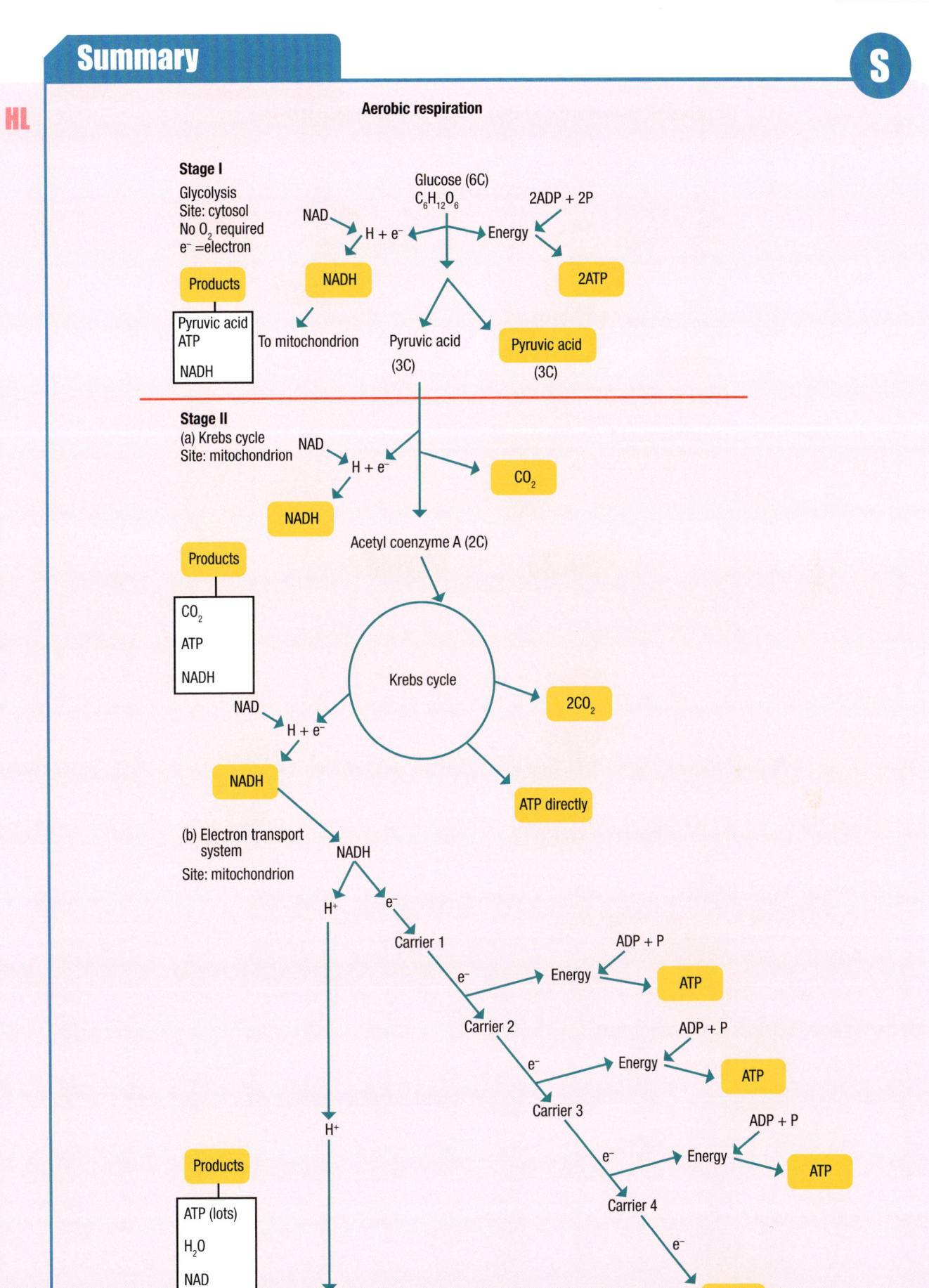

Summary

HL

Aerobic respiration

Stage I
Glycolysis
Site: cytosol
No O_2 required
e^- = electron

Products
- Pyruvic acid
- ATP
- NADH

Glucose (6C) $C_6H_{12}O_6$

NAD → H + e^- → NADH → To mitochondrion
Glucose → Energy ← 2ADP + 2P → 2ATP
Glucose → Pyruvic acid (3C)
Glucose → Pyruvic acid (3C)

Stage II
(a) Krebs cycle
Site: mitochondrion

NAD → H + e^- → NADH
Pyruvic acid → CO_2
Pyruvic acid → Acetyl coenzyme A (2C) → Krebs cycle

Products
- CO_2
- ATP
- NADH

Krebs cycle → $2CO_2$
Krebs cycle → ATP directly
NAD → H + e^- → NADH

(b) Electron transport system
Site: mitochondrion

NADH → H^+ and e^-
e^- → Carrier 1 → e^- → Energy (+ ADP + P) → ATP
→ Carrier 2 → e^- → Energy (+ ADP + P) → ATP
→ Carrier 3 → e^- → Energy (+ ADP + P) → ATP
→ Carrier 4 → e^- → H_2O

H^+ → H_2O
O_2 → H_2O

Products
- ATP (lots)
- H_2O
- NAD

14 Respiration

Summary

Anaerobic respiration (fermentation) – incomplete breakdown of glucose

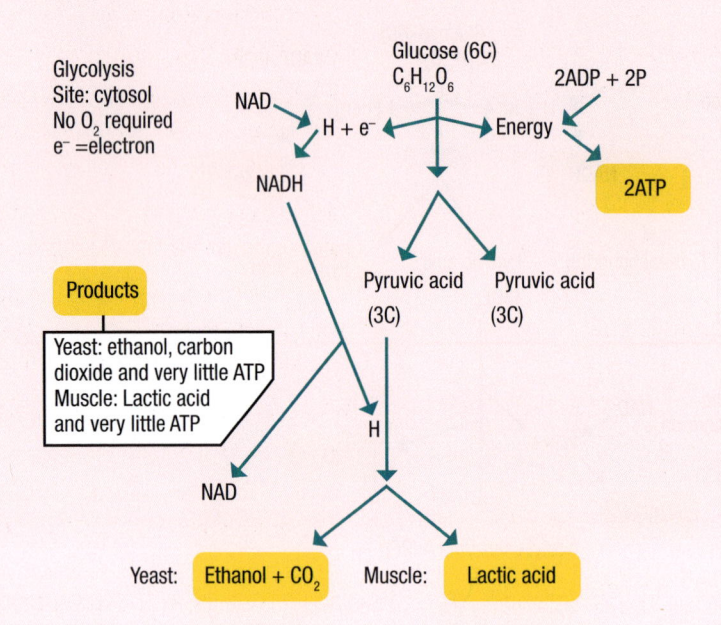

Glycolysis
Site: cytosol
No O_2 required
e^- = electron

Glucose (6C) $C_6H_{12}O_6$

NAD → H + e^-
Energy → 2ADP + 2P → 2ATP
NADH
Pyruvic acid (3C)   Pyruvic acid (3C)

Products
Yeast: ethanol, carbon dioxide and very little ATP
Muscle: Lactic acid and very little ATP

NAD
H

Yeast: Ethanol + CO_2 Muscle: Lactic acid

- Yoghurt manufacture:
  - pasteurise milk, cool and add yoghurt culture.

- Immobilising the cells:
  - If you add the yeast to gel and immobilise it, a sugar solution can be added to one end of a gel column and alcohol will emerge from the other end.

- The production of alcohol:
  - Add yeast cells to a solution of glucose.
  - Exclude oxygen and keep at 40°C.
  - CO_2 is given off (limewater test).
  - Ethanol is produced (iodoform test).
  - The control contains boiled yeast.

Respiration | 14

Review questions

01
(a) What is respiration?
(b) Give three differences between anaerobic and aerobic respiration.
(c) Write balanced chemical equations for aerobic respiration.
(d) Write word equations for anaerobic respiration in (i) a muscle, (ii) yeast.

02
(a) Explain the term aerobic respiration.
(b) Compare the two stages that occur in aerobic respiration.
(c) What type of chemicals control the process of respiration in cells?

03
(a) Explain the term anaerobic respiration.
(b) What end products can be produced by this process in (i) animal cells, (ii) fungal cells, i.e. yeast.
(c) Why do you think that human muscles stop working shortly after they start anaerobic respiration?

04 Answer the following questions in relation to glycolysis.
(a) What is glycolysis?
(b) Where in the cell does it take place?
(c) State the main products.
(d) How much energy is produced?

05
(a) Where in the cell does the second stage of respiration take place?
(b) Describe the process.
(c) What is the role of acetyl coenzyme A?
(d) What are the products of the Krebs cycle?
(e) What happens to each of the products named in (d)?
(f) What is the role of oxygen in this process?

06 'Both photosynthesis and respiration use high energy electrons.' Comment on this statement.

07 In one industrial accident at a brewery, a worker collapsed and died when he climbed into a recently emptied vat of beer. What do you think was in the empty vat that could kill him?

08 What is the advantage of immobilising the fungi in a gel in some industrial processes?

09
(a) With the aid of a labelled diagram describe an investigation you carried out to demonstrate anaerobic respiration.
(b) How did you exclude oxygen?
(c) Describe the tests you carried out to show your investigation was successful.
(d) What control did you use in this investigation?

Examination style questions

Section A

01
(a) Explain the term respiration.
(b) What is necessary for aerobic respiration but not anaerobic respiration to occur?
(c) Where in the cell do these types of respiration occur?
(d) What are the differences in the energy produced by these two processes?
(e) What are the end products of these two processes?

02
(a) What is fermentation?
(b) What use is made of this in industry?
(c) Write a simple word equation for fermentation.
(d) Where in the cell does fermentation take place?

Section B

03
(a) (i) Give another name for the process of fermentation.
(ii) What is a bioreactor?
(b) In your course of study you carried out an investigation to look at fermentation. Answer the following questions in relation to this investigation.
(i) Name the organism you used.
(ii) What substrate did you add?
(iii) How did you exclude oxygen from the apparatus?
(iv) What were the end products you produced?
(v) How did you test for ethanol?
(vi) Draw a labelled diagram of the apparatus you used.
(vii) What was your control?

Section C

04
(a) Compare aerobic and anaerobic respiration (in yeast) under the following headings:
(i) the need for oxygen
(ii) the place in the cell where it takes place
(iii) the products formed
(iv) the amount of energy produced.

14 Respiration

Examination style questions

(b) To investigate anaerobic respiration in yeast, the apparatus shown in the diagram below was set up.

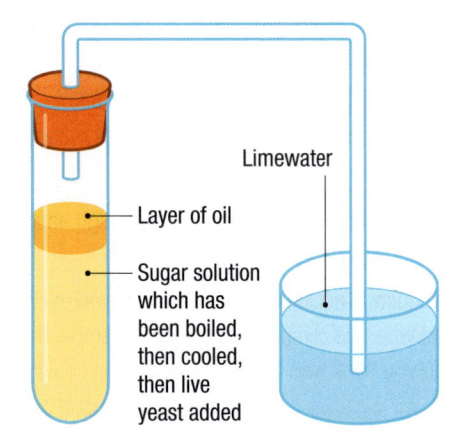

- Limewater
- Layer of oil
- Sugar solution which has been boiled, then cooled, then live yeast added

(i) Name the gas that would be given off by the yeast.
(ii) What is the purpose of the layer of oil?
(iii) Name a substance, other than the gas mentioned in (i), that you would expect to find in tube A after a few hours.
(iv) Describe a test to show the presence of this substance. Suggest a control for this investigation.

05 (a) (i) Give a balanced chemical equation for aerobic respiration.
  (ii) Is the process of respiration affected by temperature? Explain your answer.
(b) The first stage of respiration is called glycolysis.
  (i) Name the products of glycolysis.
  (ii) Where does glycolysis take place in a cell?
  (iii) Is oxygen necessary for glycolysis?
  (iv) The second stage of respiration involves Krebs cycle and an electron transport chain.
    1. Where does the Krebs cycle take place?
    2. What is the function of Krebs cycle?
    3. What happens to the products of Krebs cycle?
(c) Answer the following in relation to an experiment you carried out to show the production of ethanol by yeast.
  (i) Draw a labelled diagram of the apparatus you set up.
  (ii) State two experimental procedures which ensured anaerobic conditions.
  (iii) What control did you use in this experiment?
  (iv) Why is a control necessary in an experiment?
  (v) Outline the test that you carried out to show the presence of ethanol in the product formed.

06 (a) (i) What is the fundamental role of respiration in living cells?
  (ii) Distinguish between aerobic and anaerobic respiration.

(b) The diagram shows an outline of some of the events in the breakdown of glucose in a cell.

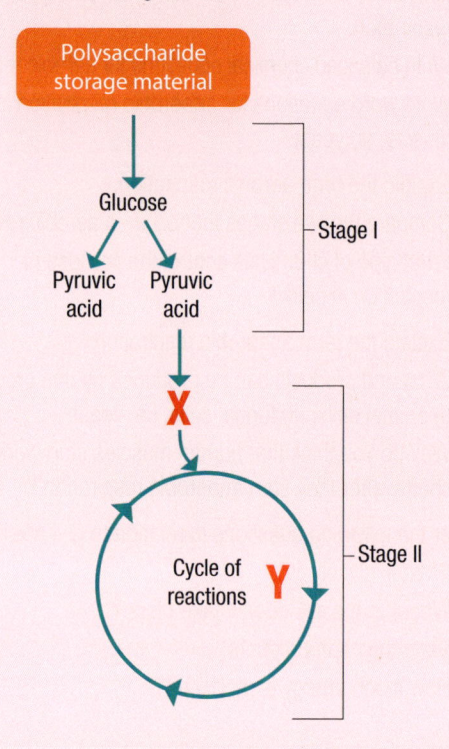

- Polysaccharide storage material
- Glucose
- Pyruvic acid / Pyruvic acid — Stage I
- X
- Cycle of reactions Y — Stage II

(i) Give a balanced chemical equation to summarise the process of aerobic respiration.
(ii) Name the polysaccharide storage material in humans from which the glucose is produced for respiration.
(iii) Name stage 1 and state where in the cell this stage takes place.
(iv) Identify the intermediate compound X.
(iv) If oxygen is present in the cell the stage 2 process occurs involving a series of reactions Y and an electron transport system.
  1. List the products of the series of reactions Y.
  2. Describe how the electron transport system produces ATP.

07 A form of respiration is frequently used in industrial processes to manufacture food.
(a) Name this form of respiration.
(b) Name two foods that can be produced using this reaction.
(c) Briefly describe the industrial production of a named food.

Leaving Certificate examination questions

Section A

01 Choose each term from the following list and place it in **Column B** to match a description in **Column A**. The first one has been completed as an example.

alcohol   oxygen   water
mitochondria   lactic acid   ~~large~~

Column A	Column B
The amount of energy released in aerobic respiration.	large
(a) A substance required for aerobic respiration.	
(b) A product of anaerobic respiration in muscles.	
(c) A product of aerobic respiration.	
(d) A product of anaerobic respiration in yeast.	
(e) The cell structures in which stage 2 of aerobic respiration takes place.	

2011 OL Q. 5

02 Indicate whether the following are true (T) or false (F) by placing the letter T or F beside the letter of the statement.

Example: Carbon dioxide is produced during respiration.   F

(a) Stage 1 of respiration requires oxygen
(b) Stage 1 of respiration takes place in the cytoplasm
(c) Stage 2 of respiration also takes place in the cytoplasm
(d) Some of the energy released in respiration is lost as heat
(e) Lactic acid is a product of anaerobic respiration

2008 OL Q. 3

03 (a) Suggest an advantage of using ATP as an energy store in cells.
(b) Name **two** processes requiring ATP that occur in cells.
(c) Name **two** substances, other than carbon dioxide, into which pyruvate may be broken down under aerobic conditions in cells.
(d) What is the name of the two-carbon compound into which pyruvate is broken down under **aerobic** conditions?
(e) Briefly describe the fate, under **aerobic** conditions, of the two-carbon compound referred to in part (d).

2014 HL Q. 6

04 Cellular respiration may occur in one stage or two stages.

(a) Give **two** differences, other than location, between Stage 1 and Stage 2.
(b) Where in a cell does Stage 1 occur?
(c) What term is used to describe respiration in which only Stage 1 occurs?
(d) Name a chemical end product of the type of respiration referred to in (c).
(e) In Stage 2 of respiration electrons pass along an electron transport chain, releasing energy. In what molecule is this energy stored in the cell?

2011 HL Q. 6

05 (a) Write a balanced equation to represent aerobic respiration.
(b) The first stage of respiration takes place in the cytosol. What is the cytosol?
(c) Does the first stage of respiration release a small or large amount of energy?
(d) What is fermentation?
(e) Where in the cell does the second stage of aerobic respiration take place?
(f) Is oxygen required for the second stage of aerobic respiration?
(g) Suggest a situation in which some cells in the human body may not be able to engage in the second stage of aerobic respiration.

2008 HL Q. 5

06 (a) What is the first stage process of respiration called?
(b) In this first stage there is a release of ATP as glucose is converted to another substance. Name this other substance.
(c) To what is the substance you have named in (b) converted under anaerobic conditions in (i) yeast, (ii) a human muscle cell?
(d) Under aerobic conditions the substance that you have named in (b) is converted to an acetyl group and in the process a small molecule is released. Name this small molecule.
(e) The acetyl group now enters a cycle of reactions. What name is given to this cycle?
(f) Where in the cell does this cycle take place?

2006 HL Q. 4

Section B

07 (a) Yeast cells produce ethanol (alcohol) in a process called fermentation. Is this process affected by temperature? Explain your answer.
(b) Answer the following in relation to an experiment to prepare and show the presence of ethanol using yeast.
  (i) Draw a labelled diagram of the apparatus that you used.
  (ii) Name a substance that yeast can use to make ethanol.
  (iii) What substance, other than ethanol, is produced during fermentation?
  (iv) Describe the control that you used in this experiment.
  (v) Explain the purpose of a control in a scientific experiment.

Respiration

Leaving Certificate examination questions

(vi) How did you know when the fermentation was finished?
(vii) Why were solutions of potassium iodide and sodium hypochlorite added to the reaction vessels after a certain period of time?
(viii) Name a substance produced during aerobic respiration that is not produced during fermentation.

2004 HL Q. 7

Section C

08 (i) What is meant by the term *respiration*?
(ii) Name the **two** types of respiration.
(iii) Which type of respiration results in the production of acid in our muscles?
(iv) In the type of respiration referred to in (iii), is a little or a lot of energy produced?
(v) What is the name of the acid produced in the muscles?
(vi) Suggest what might happen to this acid in the muscles afterwards.

2014 OL Q. 13 (c)

09 Answer the following questions in relation to an investigation you carried out into fermentation by yeast cells.
(i) Explain what is meant by *anaerobic respiration*.
(ii) Where in the cell does anaerobic respiration occur?
(iii) Describe, with the aid of a diagram, how you kept the yeast under anaerobic conditions during the investigation.
(iv) Name the **two** substances produced by the yeast in the process of fermentation.
(v) How do you know that fermentation had ceased?

2013 OL Q. 13 (c)

10 (i) What is meant by *aerobic respiration*?
(ii) Aerobic respiration takes place in two stages.
 1. Where **in a cell** does stage 1 occur?
 2. Where **in a cell** does stage 2 occur?
(iii) Which type of respiration, aerobic or anaerobic, produces more energy?
(iv) In yeast cells, alcohol is produced by fermentation. Draw a labelled diagram showing how alcohol may be produced in the laboratory.
Answer the following questions in relation to the activity:
1. Name another substance that is produced during the fermentation process.
2. How would you detect this other substance?
3. How would you know when fermentation had finished?

2012 OL Q. 14 (a)

11 (a) (i) Explain briefly what is meant by respiration.
(ii) Distinguish between aerobic and anaerobic respiration.

(b) (i) Copy the table below into your answer book and complete the final column.

Type of respiration	Energy source	End products
Aerobic respiration	Glucose	
Anaerobic respiration in muscle	Glucose	
Anaerobic respiration in yeast	Glucose	

(ii) In stage 1 of respiration, glucose is partly broken down. Where in the cell does this happen?
(iii) Name the cell component shown in the diagram in which stage 2 of respiration takes place.

(iv) Which stage of respiration releases more energy?
(c) (i) Draw a labelled diagram of the apparatus in which you used yeast to produce alcohol.
(ii) The water that you used in the apparatus was previously boiled and cooled. Why was this?
(iii) In your investigation it was necessary to exclude air. How was this done?
(iv) Describe briefly a test to show that alcohol had been produced.

2007 OL Q. 12

12 In the course of your practical studies you immobilised an enzyme and then investigated its activity. You also prepared alcohol using yeast.
(i) Draw a labelled diagram of the apparatus you used to prepare alcohol.
(ii) Give **two** advantages of using immobilised yeast cells in the production of alcohol.
(iii) How did you test for the presence of alcohol?

2014 HL Q. 13 (c)

13 (a) Write short notes on each of the following topics. You are required to make a minimum of **three** points concerning **each** topic. Marks will **not** be given for word diagrams alone.
(i) Metabolism
(ii) Krebs cycle
(iii) ADP

Leaving Certificate examination questions

(b) (i) Explain the term *fermentation*.
   (ii) Name the organism that is used in industrial fermentation.
   (iii) To which kingdom does this organism belong?
   (iv) Name the compound which is used as a carbon source in the fermentation referred to in part (ii).
   (v) In industrial fermentations bioprocessing with immobilised cells is sometimes used.
      1. Explain the terms *bioprocessing* and *immobilised*.
      2. Give the advantage of using immobilised cells.
      3. Name the compound from which the immobilised beads are formed in the laboratory.
      4. Give the general name for the vessel used in such reactions.

2013 HL Q. 14

14
(i) What name is given to the first stage of respiration?
(ii) The first stage ends with the formation of pyruvate (pyruvic acid). In **anaerobic** conditions, what is produced from this pyruvate:
   1. In muscle cells?
   2. In yeast cells?
(iii) If conditions are **aerobic**, pyruvate next passes to an organelle in which the second stage of respiration takes place. Name this organelle.
(iv) In this organelle pyruvate is broken down to CO_2 and a two-carbon compound. Name this two-carbon compound.
(v) This two-carbon compound passes directly into a series of reactions in the second stage of respiration. Name this series of reactions **and** give **one** product, other than electrons, of these reactions.
(vi) The electrons released from the above reactions pass along a transport chain and in the process energy is released.
   1. To what use is this energy put?
   2. At the end of the transport chain what happens to the electrons?

2009 HL Q. 12 (b)

15 (a) (i) Distinguish between aerobic and anaerobic respiration.
   (ii) Write a balanced equation to summarise aerobic respiration.
(b) Answer the following questions in relation to the first stage of respiration.
   (i) Where in the cell does this stage occur?
   (ii) During this stage a small amount of energy is released. Explain the role of ADP in relation to this released energy.
   (iii) What is the final product of this stage under aerobic conditions?
   (iv) If conditions in the cell remain aerobic the product you have named in (iii) is used for the second stage of respiration. Where does this second stage take place?
   (v) If conditions in a human cell (e.g. muscle) become anaerobic the product named in (iii) is converted to another substance. Name this other substance.
   (vi) When the substance named in (v) builds up in the blood, a person is said to be in oxygen debt. This debt must eventually be paid. Suggest how the debt is paid.
(c) If yeast cells are kept in anaerobic conditions alcohol (ethanol) and another substance are produced.
   (i) Describe, with the aid of a diagram, how you would keep yeast under anaerobic conditions in the laboratory.
   (ii) Name a carbohydrate that you would supply to the yeast as an energy source.
   (iii) Give an account of a chemical test to demonstrate that alcohol (ethanol) has been produced. Include the initial colour and final colour of the test.
   (iv) What is the other substance produced under anaerobic conditions?
   (v) Alcohol (ethanol) production is an example of fermentation. How would you know when fermentation has ceased?
   (vi) Why does fermentation eventually cease?

2005 HL Q. 11

Past examination questions

OL	2014 Q. 13 (c)	2013 Q. 13 (c)	2012 Q. 14 (a)	2011 Q. 5	2010 Q. 12 (b)	2009 Q. 15 (b)
	2008 Q. 3	2007 Q. 12	2006 Q. 13	2005 Q. 11 (c)		

HL	2014 Q. 6 (c)–(e), Q. 13 (c)	2013 Q. 14 (b)	2012 Q. 7 (b) (ii), Q. 12 (c)	2011 Q. 6
	2009 Q. 12 (a), (b)	2008 Q. 5	2007 Q. 11 (b)	2006 Q. 4	2005 Q. 11	2004 Q. 7

15 DNA, RNA and Protein Synthesis

After studying this chapter you should be able to:

1. Define gene and gene expression and explain the role of the gene.
2. Describe the structure of a chromosome.
3. Describe the simple structure of DNA.
4. **HL** Describe the structure of DNA in more detail.
5. Describe the simple replication of DNA.
6. Define DNA profiling, and describe the main processes used in profiling.
7. Give two examples of the uses of DNA profiling.
8. Explain the meaning of the term genetic screening.
9. Describe an experiment used to extract DNA from plant tissue.
10. Describe the structure of RNA, and give the function of mRNA.
11. Describe the process of protein synthesis in the cell using RNA and ribosomes.
12. **HL** Describe the process of protein synthesis in more detail.

The gene

It is now known that the genetic information is carried on the **DNA** (deoxyribonucleic acid) molecule. The structure of DNA was discovered in 1953 by James Watson and Francis Crick. This discovery was aided by the work of Rosalind Franklin and Maurice Wilkins. This structure will be described below. Sections of DNA are able to code for specific proteins, which normally give rise to a trait (characteristic) in the **organism**. Such a section of DNA is called a **gene**.

> A **gene** is a section of DNA that codes for a particular protein.

> An **allele** is an alternative form of a gene.

In humans, an example of such a gene is the gene for tongue rolling. There are two possible genes that you may have, one of which will give you the ability to roll your tongue, the other will not give you this ability (Fig 15.1). These alternative forms of the same gene are called **alleles**.

Just because an organism has a gene in their **cells** it does not mean it will be used, e.g. in humans, the gene for growth **hormone** is expressed at different times of your life. Certain factors come into play (described later) that will determine which genes the organism will use. When the gene is switched on by the organism this will lead to **expression** of the gene. You might inherit the genes to make you grow to be 6 feet tall but if you don't get the correct nutrition you will not grow properly.

> **Gene expression** is the process of converting the information in a gene into a protein.

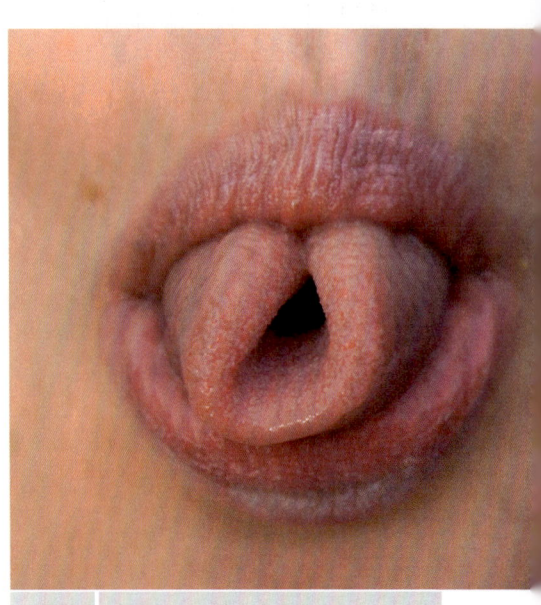

15.1 A person rolling their tongue

DNA, RNA and Protein Synthesis | 15

Chromosomes

The DNA in an organism is found in strands. These strands are tightly wound around a protein scaffold. These structures are called **chromosomes** (Fig 15.2):

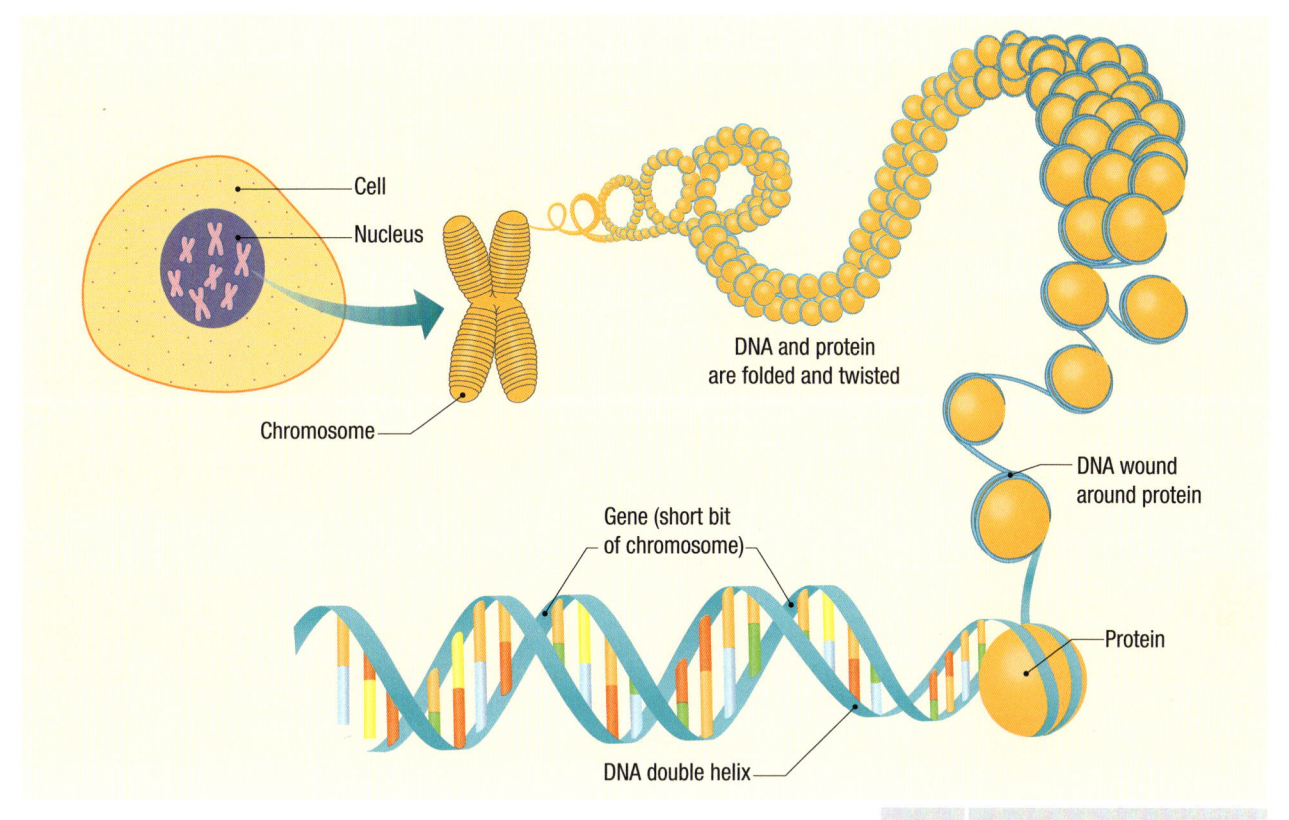

15.2 The structure of a chromosome

- Each chromosome comprises a large number of genes.
- Chromosomes are made of DNA and protein, i.e. in human chromosome no. 1 there are 2968 genes.
- Cells normally contain two sets of chromosomes and are said to be **diploid (2n)**.
- As a result, each cell has two copies of each gene.
- These interact to produce the traits visible in the organism.

In **sexual reproduction**, an offspring gets information from each parent. To prevent a doubling of the amount of DNA at each generation, special cells or **gametes** are produced that contain only one copy of each chromosome and thus each gene. Such cells are **haploid (n)**.

Fertilisation occurs when two gametes fuse and the resultant cell (**zygote**) has two copies of each gene.

> **D** A cell is **diploid** when it has two copies of each chromosome.

> **D** A cell is **haploid** when it has only one copy of each chromosome or gene.

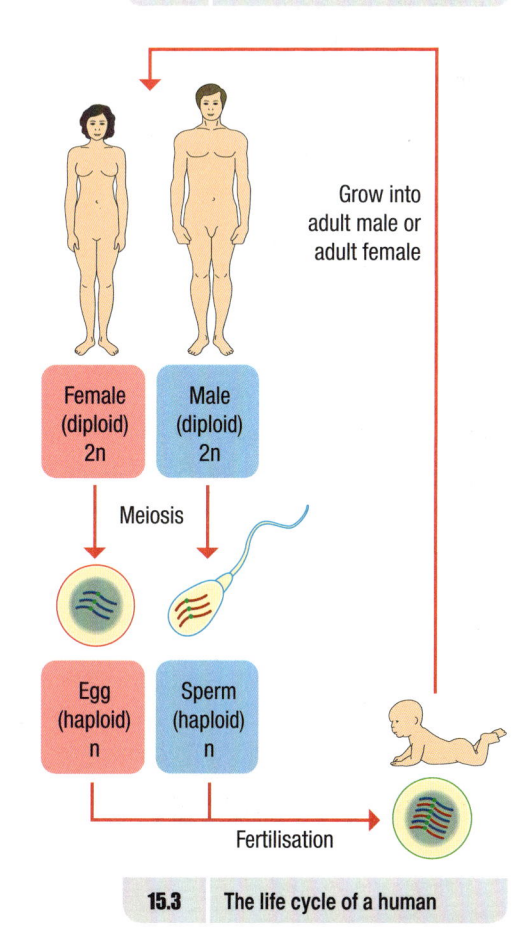

15.3 The life cycle of a human

LIFE LEAVING CERTIFICATE BIOLOGY | UNIT 2 THE CELL | 179

15 | DNA, RNA and Protein Synthesis

Coding and non-coding DNA

Not all of the DNA carries messages; in fact the majority of the DNA does not code for proteins at all. The coding parts of the DNA are called exons and the **non-coding** pieces of DNA are called introns (junk genes) and are highly variable (Fig 15.4). Non-coding parts of the DNA can be found within a particular gene or between two genes. It is these highly variable parts of the DNA that are used when taking a **DNA profile** (fingerprint). It was originally thought that these non-coding regions had no function but now it is realised that some of them have a major role in determining what genes are switched on or off at any one time in the cell cycle. Thus these areas are rarely called junk genes now.

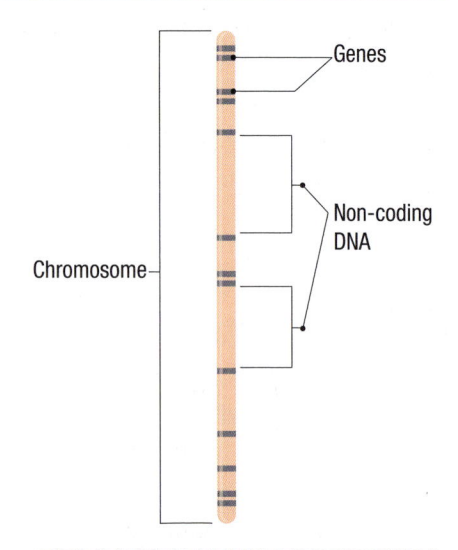

> **Non-coding DNA (introns)** is an area of a chromosome that does not produce a protein.

15.4 Coding (genes) and non-coding areas of a chromosome

DNA

DNA is a very long coiled molecule called a **double helix**. It consists of two strands made up of **sugars** and **phosphate**, one strand running up the helix and one strand running down. These two strands are linked together by **bases** (Fig 15.5). The bases are paired one on each strand. They form a ladder-like structure which is then twisted into the characteristic double helix of DNA. There are four different bases possible.

- adenine (A)
- thymine (T)
- guanine (G)
- cytosine (C)

These are known by their initials A, G, C or T.
- A is always paired with T.
- C is always paired with G.

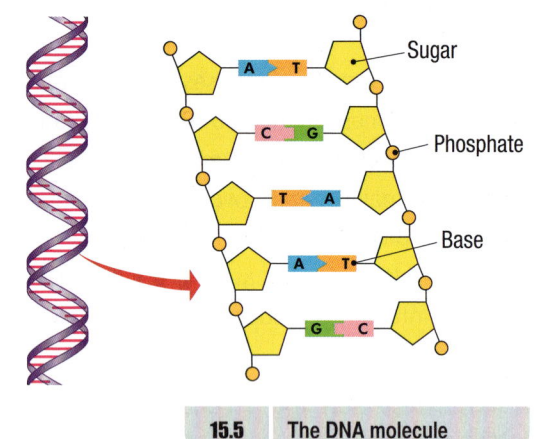

15.5 The DNA molecule

These pairs of bases are called **complementary base pairs**. These four bases can be found in any order along the strand of DNA. Each DNA molecule has its own unique order of bases along its strand. It is the order of the bases along the DNA that codes for the **proteins** made by the cell. Each message for a particular protein is called a gene.

DNA: extended study

As has already been seen DNA has a complex structure. The basic unit that makes up the DNA is much simpler and is called a **nucleotide**. The nucleotide is composed of three basic chemicals – a five-carbon sugar called deoxyribose, a phosphate group and a nitrogenous base (Fig 15.6).

There are four possible bases in DNA: adenine, guanine, cytosine and thymine, abbreviated to A, G, C and T.

- Adenine and guanine are double-ringed **purine** bases.
- Cytosine and thymine are single-ringed **pyrimidine** bases.

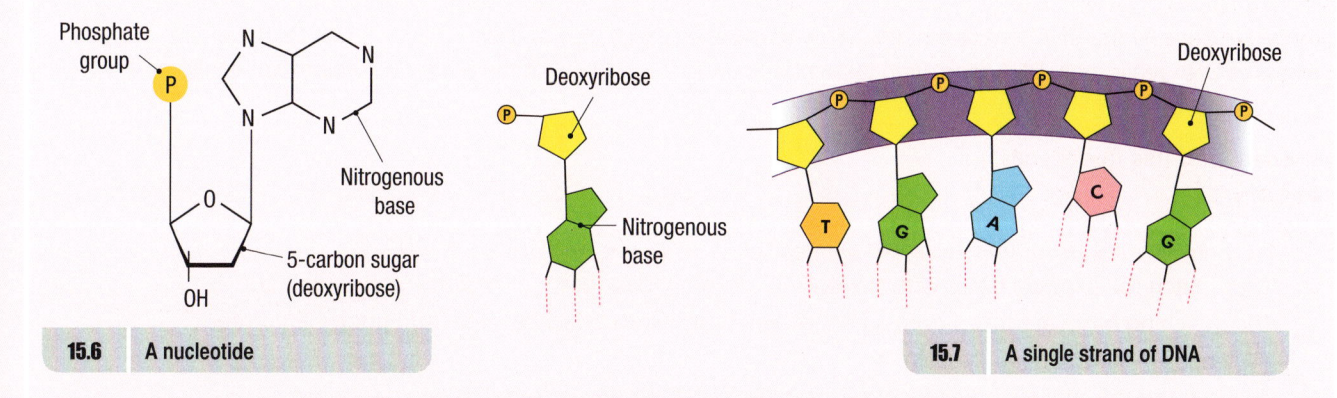

15.6 A nucleotide

15.7 A single strand of DNA

Long chains of nucleotides can be produced by attaching one nucleotide to the next. This is done by bonding the phosphate group of one nucleotide to the sugar of the next. An average DNA molecule has 130×10^6 nucleotides. This forms the 'backbone' of the molecule (Fig 15.7).

The resulting chain has almost no limit to its length. Protruding from this chain are the bases attached to the sugar. Due to their structure, these bases are able to form bonds, called **hydrogen bonds**. In DNA, the bases form these hydrogen bonds with other bases. Because of the structure of each base, each base can only form hydrogen bonds with one specific base, i.e. A will only bond with T and C with G. These pairs of bases are thus known as **complementary base pairs**. Complementary means that each base has a matching (corresponding) base. This results in a DNA molecule that looks like a ladder.

- The sides of the ladder are made of alternating sugar and phosphate groups.
- The rungs of the ladder are made up of complementary base pairs.
- The two sides of the ladder are held together by the enormous number of hydrogen bonds formed down the length of the molecule (Figs 15.8 and 15.9).

These two chains coil around each other to form a **double helix** (Fig 15.10).

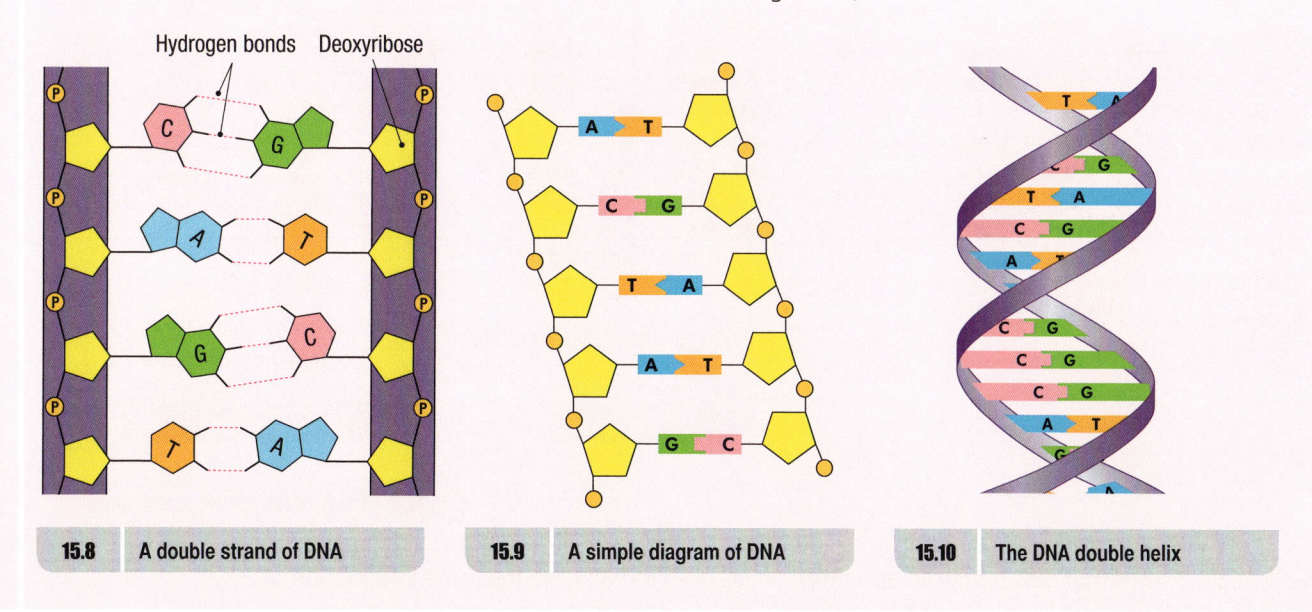

15.8 A double strand of DNA

15.9 A simple diagram of DNA

15.10 The DNA double helix

DNA replication

The messages that the DNA carries are vital for the survival of the cell. When a cell **replicates** it produces an identical copy of itself.

> **Replication** is the production of an identical copy of the DNA in a cell.

To accomplish this it is essential that an **exact copy** of the DNA be made for the new cell. This is the only way the cell is sure a correct set of information is given to each new cell, e.g. when you cut yourself you need to repair your damaged skin by making new cells identical to the old ones.

It is the structure of the DNA that gives it the ability to make an exact copy of itself. **Enzymes** control the entire process of DNA replication. DNA replication takes place during **interphase** of the cell cycle. Replication requires:

- enzymes;
- a supply of free nucleotides;
- energy.

1. Enzymes unwind the double helix and pull apart or 'unzip' the two strands of DNA.
2. They match the exposed bases with their complementary base pair, i.e. A with T and C with G. The matching bases are taken from a pool of free bases, with attached sugar and phosphate (free nucleotides), surrounding the DNA.
3. The result of this process is two identical strands of DNA produced from the original strand.
4. Each now twists to form two identical helices.
5. One side of each new DNA molecule comes from the original and one is new.
6. The order of bases on the two new DNA molecules is identical. As a consequence, the genes on each chromosome are the same (Fig 15.11).

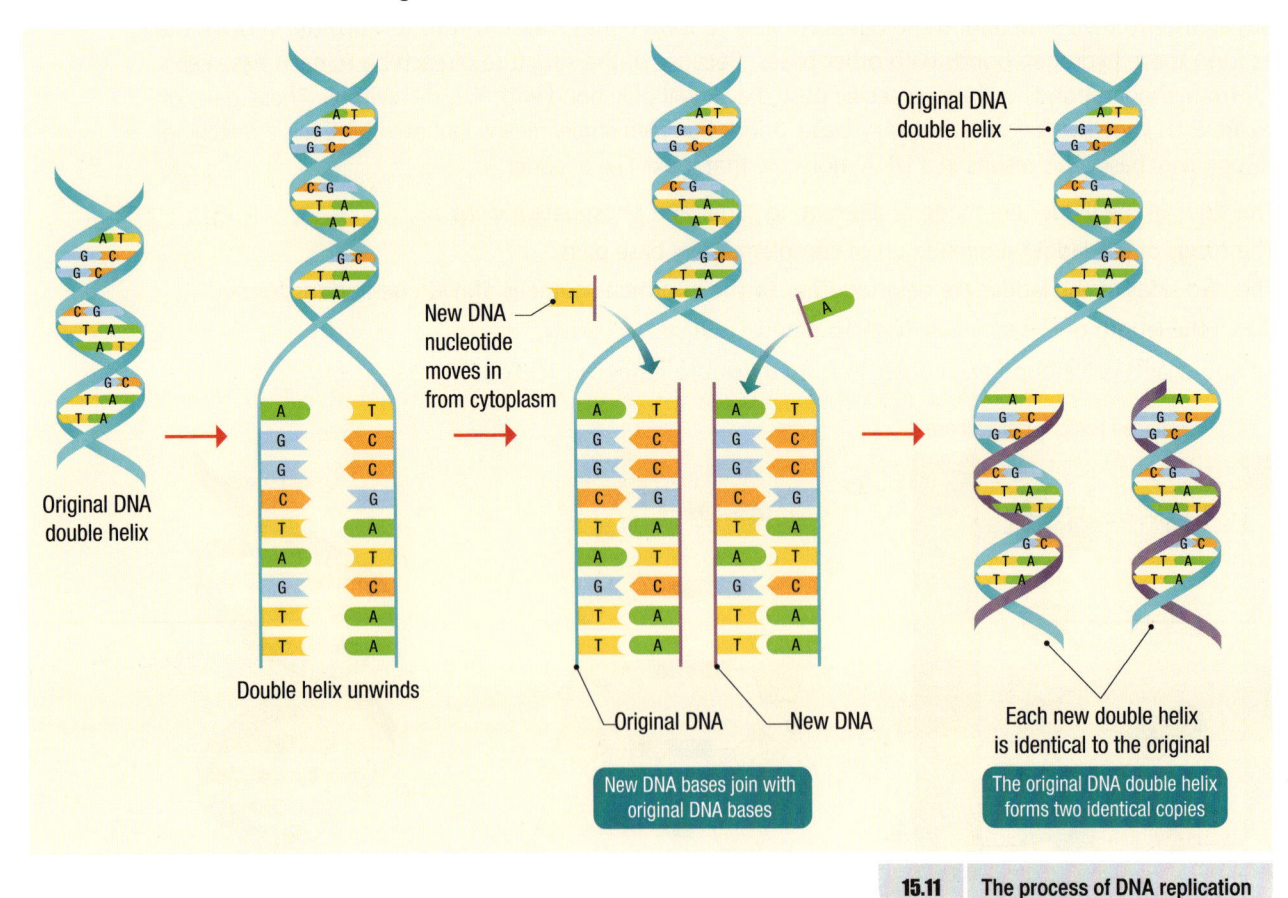

15.11 The process of DNA replication

Replication ensures that cells produced as a result of cell division will have the same information as each other and they will be identical to the cell that produced them. As a consequence all the cells in a multicellular organism have **identical genetic information**.

DNA profiles

A **DNA profile** is the unique pattern a person's DNA can make when it is cut into lengths using enzymes. In 1984 the English scientist Alex Jeffreys noted that certain pieces of a person's non-coding DNA varied enormously between individuals. He used this information to produce what we now call a DNA fingerprint or DNA profile (Fig 15.12).

The procedure for DNA profiling (fingerprinting) is:

1. Take a sample of cell-containing material, e.g. cheek cell or semen.
2. Extract the DNA from the cells by breaking up the cell membrane.
3. Treat the extracted DNA with special **enzymes**. These enzymes recognise specific sequences of DNA and cut the DNA at those sites. Most of the sites cut will be in the **non-coding DNA** (introns) that are highly variable from one person to the next.
4. These enzymes produce a large number of **DNA fragments**, which will vary in length. Due to the differences between each member of a species, it is almost impossible that two members of a **species** will produce exactly the same DNA fragments (unless they are identical twins).
5. The DNA fragments are placed at one end of a gel.
6. When an electric charge is passed through the gel the fragments will move down the gel. This is because DNA is negatively charged so it will move towards the positive electrode. This will separate the fragments. The smaller pieces will move faster.
7. The distance travelled by the pieces of DNA can be seen by putting a stain onto the gel to visualise the DNA.
8. The result is a series of bands similar to the bar codes used on groceries. A permanent copy of this pattern can be made for various uses as described below (Fig 15.13).

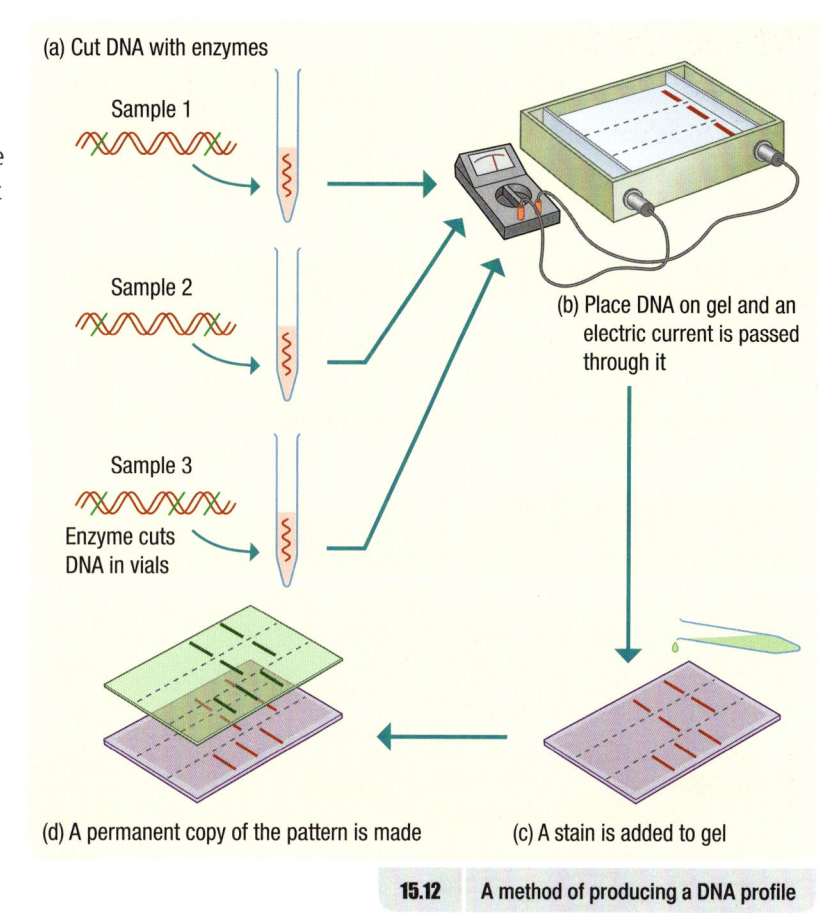

15.12 A method of producing a DNA profile

(a) Cut DNA with enzymes
(b) Place DNA on gel and an electric current is passed through it
(c) A stain is added to gel
(d) A permanent copy of the pattern is made

> **D** **DNA profiling** is the process of making a pattern of bands from a person's DNA to compare with other DNA patterns.

15.13 A number of DNA profiles

15 | DNA, RNA and Protein Synthesis

Uses of DNA profiling

These DNA profiles can then be used for a number of different purposes:

- They can be used to identify criminals from blood (only the white blood cells will have DNA), semen or other tissue left at the scene of a crime. The DNA profiles will be identical (Fig 15.14).
- To identify species, particularly plants.
- To see whether twins are identical.
- To look for genetic matches in organ transplants.
- To identify specific strains of pathogens.
- To identify family relationships in refugee cases.
- They can be used to identify fathers in paternity cases. In this case any band in the child's profile which does not have a match in the mother's profile must have a match in the father's (Fig 15.15).

SYLLABUS REQUIREMENT:
You only need to know about two applications.

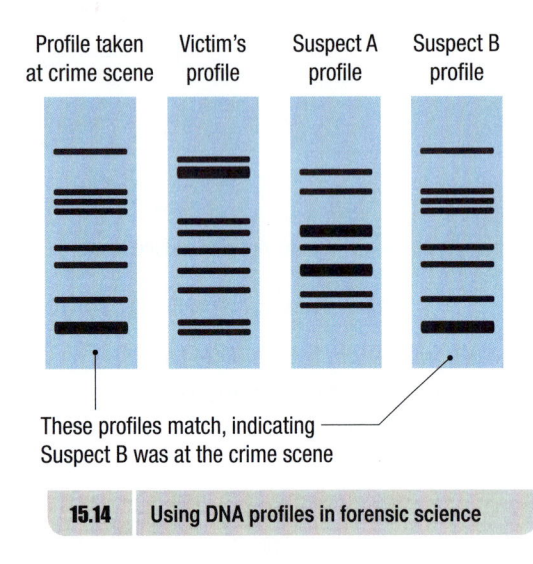

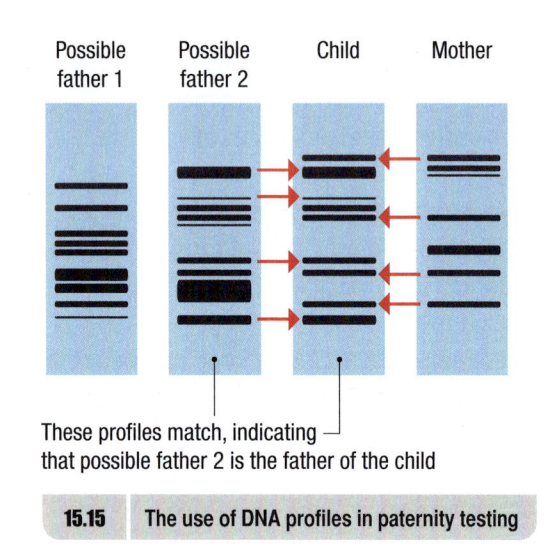

These profiles match, indicating Suspect B was at the crime scene

15.14 Using DNA profiles in forensic science

These profiles match, indicating that possible father 2 is the father of the child

15.15 The use of DNA profiles in paternity testing

Genetic screening

There is a related procedure called **genetic screening**. In genetic screening, a single gene is looked for to see whether a person is carrying a particular gene(s) for a **genetic disorder**.

1. This could result in them getting a particular genetic disorder. For genetic disorders for which there is a cure, it could be important to find out if a person has a gene or genes which will give them that disorder. In some cases it is important to know as soon as possible if the person carries the gene, to effect a cure or to prevent damage, e.g. haemochromatosis is a disorder caused by a defective gene in which a person accumulates a dangerous level of iron in the body. The damage due to this can be prevented by removing blood on a regular basis from the sufferer.
2. Some people may have one copy of the incorrect gene. They will not have the disorder themselves if the **allele** is recessive, but they could pass on the gene to their children, e.g. a gene to cause cystic fibrosis. If a couple know that each of them carries a gene for a genetic disorder, they could use this information to decide whether or not to have a family.

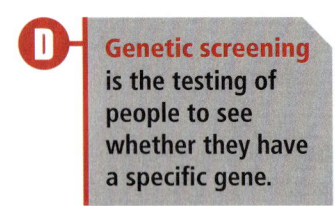

> **D** **Genetic screening** is the testing of people to see whether they have a specific gene.

There is a serious ethical problem as to whether people should be tested for a genetic disorder (or told the results if tested), if there is nothing the medical profession can do for that individual. Genetic screening may also have major consequences for insurance businesses. If the insurance company knows you carry certain genetic defects, will they refuse to insure you? Will people refuse to employ you? These are some of the ethical issues that are raised by these DNA manipulation techniques.

DNA, RNA and Protein Synthesis | 15

Investigation 15.1

The isolation of DNA from onion cells

Procedure

1. Add 10 cm³ of washing-up liquid and 3 g of salt to 100 cm³ of water in a beaker and stir well to dissolve the salt. (The washing-up liquid will break down the cell membranes and the salt will protect the DNA.)

2. Chop up a medium-sized onion with a knife (to increase surface area for reaction) and add to the mixture and stir.

3. Place the beaker into a 60°C water bath for 15 minutes (the purpose of this step is to inactivate the enzymes that break down DNA).

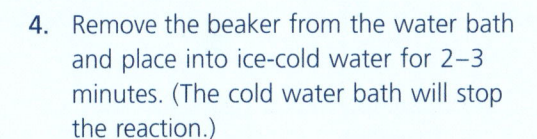

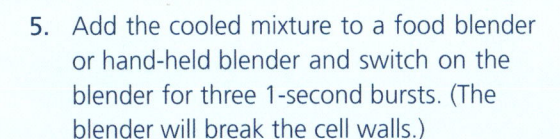

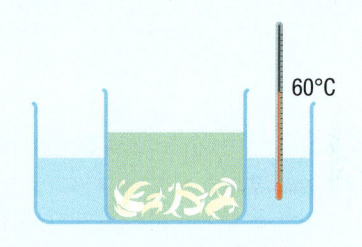

4. Remove the beaker from the water bath and place into ice-cold water for 2–3 minutes. (The cold water bath will stop the reaction.)

5. Add the cooled mixture to a food blender or hand-held blender and switch on the blender for three 1-second bursts. (The blender will break the cell walls.)

10 cm³ Washing up liquid, 3 g salt and 100 cm³ water

60°C

Ice

Blender

DNA, RNA and Protein Synthesis

6. Put the blended mixture into a large funnel containing coarse filter paper such as a coffee filter (the pores in this paper will let DNA through).

Coarse (coffee) filter paper

7. To about 10 cm³ of the filtrate, add three drops of a protease enzyme and mix. (The protease will break down the protein scaffold around the chromosome leaving just the DNA.)

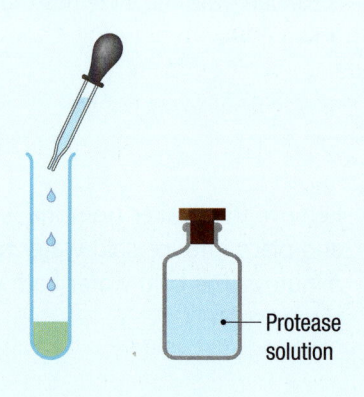

Protease solution

8. Very carefully, add 10 cm³ of freezer-cold ethanol from the freezer down the side of the test tube containing the filtrate. The white threads that become visible in the ethanol layer are the DNA molecules. (DNA is insoluble in freezer-cold ethanol.)

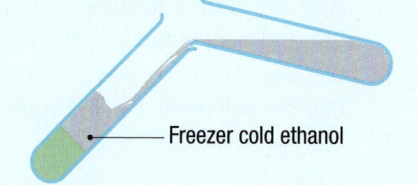

Freezer cold ethanol

9. Gently twist a glass rod or inoculating rod to attach the DNA. This can then be removed.

10. Write up the investigation in your practical notebook.

RNA

There is a second nucleic acid present in cells called **RNA** (ribonucleic acid). RNA is similar to DNA but it differs in the following ways:

1. RNA does not contain the base thymine, but instead has the base uracil (U).
2. RNA contains the sugar ribose instead of deoxyribose.
3. RNA is found as a single strand not a double strand.
4. RNA can move out of the nucleus unlike DNA.

One type of RNA can be made using the DNA as a template – this is called **messenger RNA (mRNA)**. The mRNA is complementary to the DNA, e.g. if the order of bases in the DNA is GGCCAATT then the order of bases in the RNA will be CCGGUUAA (Fig 15.16).

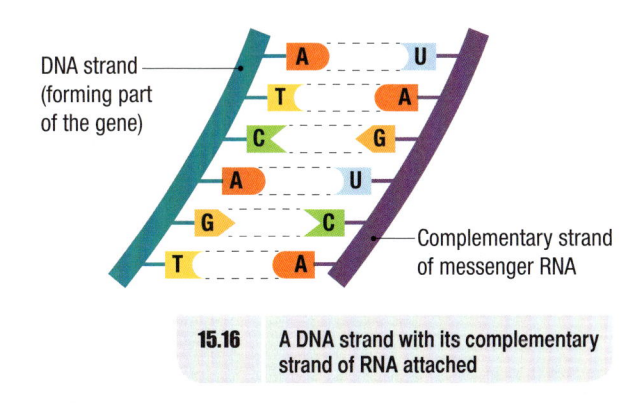

15.16 A DNA strand with its complementary strand of RNA attached

Protein synthesis

The ability to replicate is only half of the function of DNA. DNA must be able not only to pass on its message from one generation to the next, but also to convert its message into **proteins**. This is called the genetic code. These proteins will then 'run' the cell. There are about 20 amino acids used to make up the majority of the proteins found in cells.

- The number and order of amino acids determines the type of protein that is made.
- The DNA molecule controls both of these.
- The DNA has a code on one side of the double strand that determines the order of the amino acids in the protein.
- This code is made up of groups of three bases in sequence. Each group of three bases will code for a specific amino acid that will be placed in the protein at that position – this is called the **codon**.

Transcription is the copying of a section of DNA, a gene, into mRNA.

When a cell needs to make a protein a number of processes need to occur:

1. The first thing that happens is that the piece of DNA which codes for that protein is rewritten (**transcribed**) into mRNA (Fig 15.17). The enzyme RNA polymerase facilitates this transcription of the DNA into mRNA.

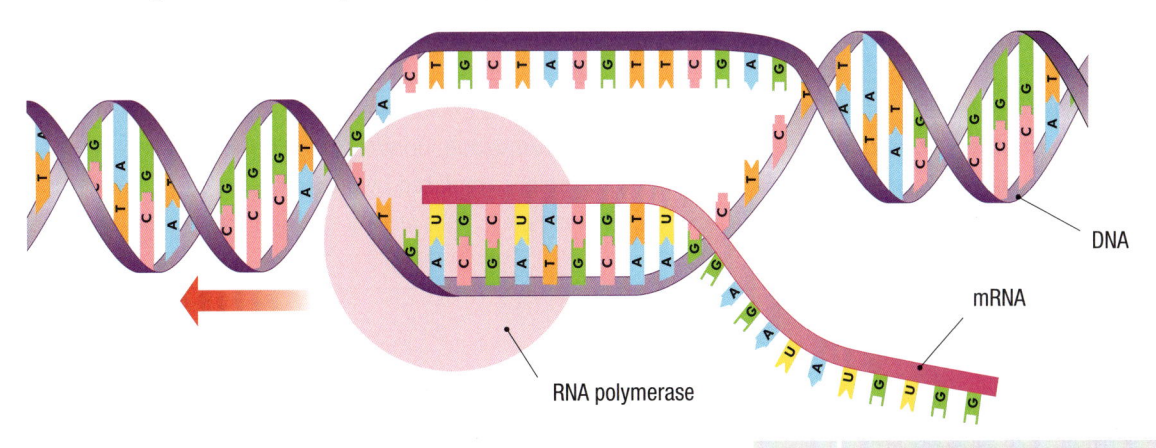

15.17 The transcription of DNA into mRNA

2. The new mRNA molecule will leave the **nucleus** and travel to the **ribosome**.
3. Here the message is **translated** using a number of chemicals. These will assemble the protein with the correct sequence of amino acids, which was determined by the order of the bases on the DNA. The number of coding bases in the gene determines the length of the protein.

Translation is the manufacture of protein based on the sequence of bases on the mRNA.

4. When the amino acids have been bonded together, the long chain will fold to give the three-dimensional shape to the protein (Fig 15.18). The folded protein will then be able to carry out its function.

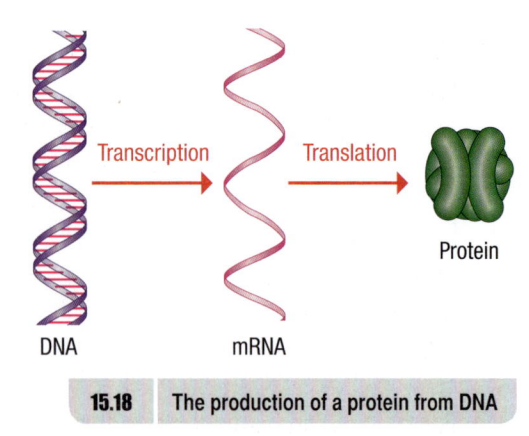

15.18 The production of a protein from DNA

HL Protein synthesis: advanced study

As has been explained in the previous section (do study this first), the DNA is a long molecule made up of nucleotides. As the sugar and phosphate groups do not change, the parts of the DNA molecule that carry the messages are the bases. The bases can be found in any order along the length of the DNA chain. It is the **order of the bases** that determines the **order of the amino acids** in the protein. DNA is therefore a code for the synthesis of proteins.

This code has four letters in it: A, T, C and G.

- These letters are read in groups of three called a codon.
- Each group of three bases in sequence (triplet) codes for one specific amino acid in the final protein structure.
- As there are more codes than there are amino acids, some codes double up and code for the same amino acid, e.g. GGA and GGG code for the same amino acid.
- The non-coding side of the DNA double strand will have the complementary set of bases to the code, i.e. if the codon is GGA the complimentary codon is CCT. This is called the anti-codon.
- As the bases can occur in any order along the DNA strand, any amino acid can be placed beside any other in the protein structure. This gives the DNA the freedom to code for any protein required by the cell.
- There is also a code to tell the enzymes where to start transcribing the mRNA and one to stop the transcription.

DNA remains in the nucleus. Proteins are not manufactured there. Some method has to be used to get the message from the DNA in the nucleus to the site of protein synthesis. A second type of nucleic acid is used for this function. This nucleic acid is called messenger RNA (mRNA).

1. mRNA is made when the DNA is 'unzipped' and one side of the DNA is used as a **template** to make a **complementary copy** of mRNA. An enzyme, **RNA polymerase**, does this copying of DNA into mRNA.
2. The mRNA has bases similar to the DNA except that thymine is replaced by uracil and the order of bases in the mRNA is determined by the order of bases in the DNA molecule. This process is called **transcription**.

> **D** **Transcription** is the copying of a section of DNA, a gene, into mRNA.

3. The mRNA has the ability to leave the nucleus, via the **nuclear pores**, and to go to a ribosome where the proteins are synthesised.
4. The ribosome is made up of another nucleic acid called **ribosomal RNA (rRNA)**. This rRNA is able to bond weakly to the mRNA. The ribosome is the site where a third type of RNA, **transfer RNA (tRNA)** is used.

5. tRNA uses the coded message to connect the amino acids together in the correct sequence (Fig 15.19). tRNA is found in the cytoplasm of the cell. tRNA has a structure where it has an amino acid attached at one end with a corresponding group of three exposed bases at the other end called the anti-codon. This group of three bases determines the amino acid that can bind to the tRNA. The three exposed bases can bind with the bases on the mRNA. This three-base unit is called the '**binding site**'.
6. Thus the mRNA carries its code in each group of three bases. The mRNA also carries a 'start' and a 'stop' code to indicate where the protein begins and ends.
7. Two tRNA molecules bind to the mRNA at a time. The amino acids attached at the other end of the tRNA molecule are then bonded together to form the protein. This process of manufacture of the proteins is called translation.

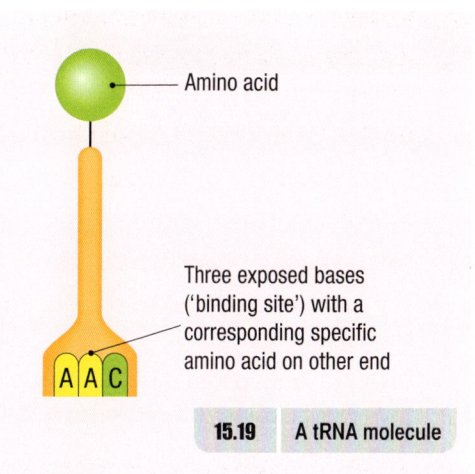

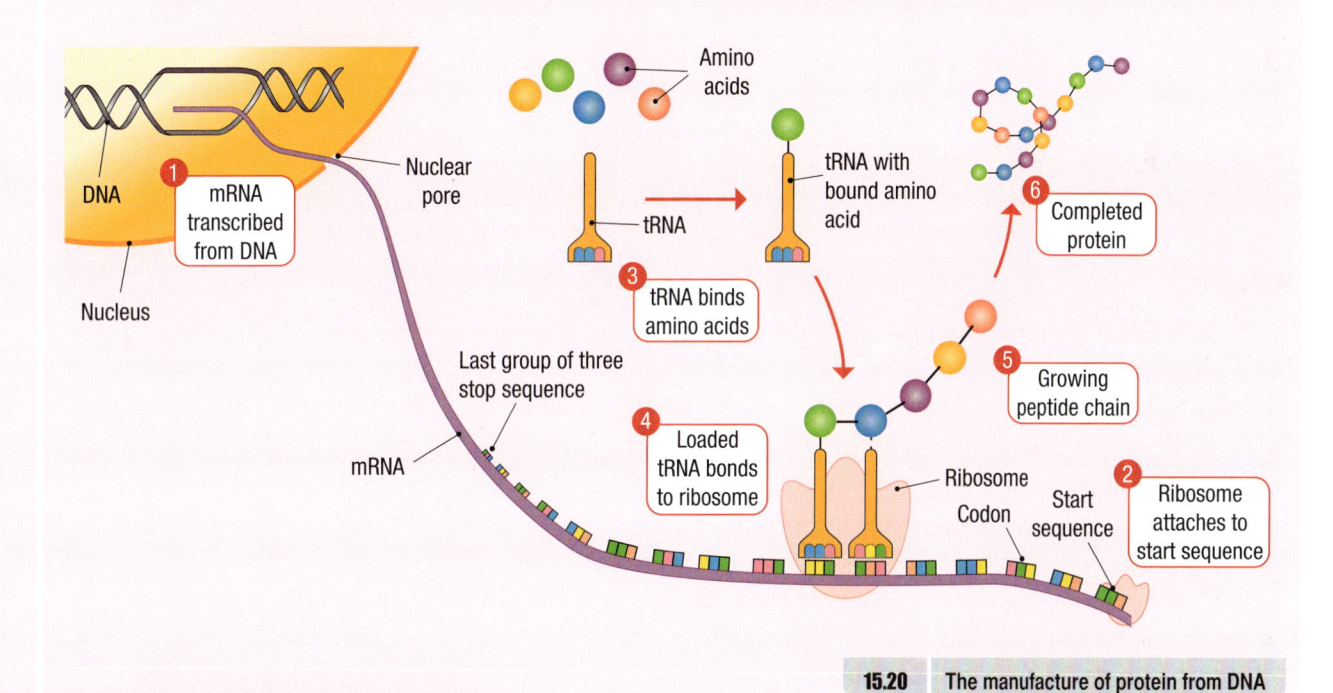

15.19 A tRNA molecule

15.20 The manufacture of protein from DNA

> **D** **Translation** is the manufacture of protein based on the sequence of bases on the mRNA.

The entire process of transcription followed by translation is controlled by enzymes. It is in this way that the nucleus (made up of DNA) controls the cell by determining the proteins present in the cell (Fig 15.20).

15 DNA, RNA and Protein Synthesis

Summary

- Genetic information is carried on the DNA molecule.
- Each section of a DNA molecule that carries the information for a particular trait is called a gene.
- A DNA strand and its attached protein scaffold are called a chromosome.
- Most organisms have two copies of each chromosome and are described as being diploid (2n).
- The gametes produced by diploid organisms have half the information (one set of chromosomes) and are haploid (n).
- DNA is a long, coiled molecule made up of sugars, phosphates and four bases. The bases are adenine, thymine, guanine and cytosine (A, T, G and C).
  - The DNA strand is held together by the bases.
  - A bonds with T and G with C.
  - The order of bases along the DNA molecule codes for proteins.
  - The stretches of DNA that code for proteins are called coding DNA.
  - Most of the DNA is made up of non-coding pieces of DNA (junk genes).

HL
- DNA is made up of nucleotides containing a sugar (deoxyribose), a phosphate and one of four bases.
  - The bases are adenine (A), thymine (T), cytosine (C) and guanine (G). A and G are purine bases, C and T are pyrimidine bases.
  - DNA is a ladder-like molecule, the sides of which are made up of sugars and phosphates. The steps are made up of the bases attached to their complementary base by hydrogen bonds holding the two sides together – A to T and G to C.
  - The completed DNA is coiled around itself as a double helix.
  - The bases can be in any order along the DNA strand, but only their complementary base will be opposite them.

- DNA replication:
  - Using enzymes, the DNA unwinds to form two halves and each half of the strand makes a complementary copy of itself by binding the appropriate base, i.e. A to T and G to C.
  - This produces two identical strands of DNA.
  - This occurs in interphase (shortly before mitosis/meiosis).
  - It ensures that the new cells produced by cell division have identical information, i.e they are clones.

- DNA profiles (fingerprinting):
  - DNA profiling is the process of making a pattern of bands from a person's DNA to compare with other DNA patterns.
  - This process identifies the DNA contained in a tissue sample, which is unique to each organism.
  - The DNA is cut using enzymes and the segments are separated according to size, using an electric current, along a piece of gel. The fragments of DNA are made visible by staining. The fragments form a pattern that can be analysed. A permanent record can be made of the pattern.
  - DNA profiles can be used to identify people from crime sites, for paternity cases, identifying pathogens or tissue matching.

- Genetic screening is the process of looking to see whether a person has a particular gene, e.g testing to see whether a person has the gene for cystic fibrosis or haemochromatosis.

- The genetic code is the ability of three bases (or codon) in sequence to code for one amino acid; these amino acids in sequence produce a protein.

- Protein synthesis:
  - Each group of three bases (codon) along the DNA molecule will code for one of the amino acids that make up a protein.
  - The order of bases along the DNA strand will therefore determine the protein that is made.
  - The DNA is transcribed into mRNA. This mRNA will leave the nucleus and travel to the ribosomes where it is translated into a protein structure.

Summary

HL
- Protein synthesis:
  - Proteins are made at the ribosomes from messages sent from the DNA. The piece of DNA to be translated into a protein structure (the gene) is transcribed into a complementary piece of mRNA (RNA has a different sugar and uracil (U) instead of thymine).
  - The mRNA goes to the ribosome (made of rRNA). The ribosome binds to the mRNA.
  - The ribosome binds tRNA to the mRNA using three bases along the mRNA for each tRNA. tRNA contains three exposed bases at one end corresponding to a specific amino acid at the other end. In this way, the correct order of amino acids is assembled to produce the necessary proteins.

Type of RNA	Where it functions	Functions
mRNA	Produced in nucleus Used at ribosome to make protein	Copy of the genetic message Used as a template to make protein
rRNA	A component of the ribosome	'Reads' the message on the mRNA Used to attach tRNA to the mRNA
tRNA	It attaches to mRNA at the ribosome	Places amino acids in the correct sequence to make a protein

- The order of the amino acids is ultimately determined by the order of bases on the DNA. There are three types of triplet codon: (i) a codon for a specific amino acid; (ii) a 'start' codon, (iii) a 'stop' codon.

Differences between DNA and RNA	
DNA	**RNA**
Double strand	Single strand
Has deoxyribose sugar	Has ribose sugar
Contain the bases A, T, G, C	Contains the bases A, U, G, C
Remains in the nucleus	Can leave the nucleus

15 DNA, RNA and Protein Synthesis

Review questions

01
(a) What is the name of the molecule that carries genetic messages?
(b) What is a gene?
(c) What is an allele?
(d) What is gene expression?

02
(a) What two chemicals make up a chromosome?
(b) What is non-coding DNA?
(c) What modern forensic process is based on introns (non-coding DNA)?

03
(a) What is meant by the term haploid?
(b) Why are gametes always haploid?

04 Describe in simple terms the structure of DNA.

05
(a) What are the components of a nucleotide?
(b) What are the purine bases?
(c) What are the pyrimidine bases?
(d) What holds the two sides of a DNA molecule together?
(e) What is a complementary base pair?

06 Using a labelled diagram, describe the detailed structure of DNA.

07
(a) Describe in simple terms the process of DNA replication.
(b) What controls the process of DNA replication?
(c) Why are the two new chromosomes identical?

08
(a) Describe the process of making a DNA profile.
(b) What must be present in a sample to make a DNA profile?
(c) What uses are there for DNA profiles?

09
(a) What is genetic screening?
(b) What are the uses for genetic screening?

10
(a) Where are proteins made?
(b) In what form does the message in the DNA get out of the nucleus?
(c) Name the smaller chemicals that are assembled to produce proteins.

11 How does DNA code for proteins?

12 Describe the process of protein manufacture from DNA, describing the role of mRNA, rRNA and tRNA.

13
(a) What are the differences between DNA and RNA?
(b) In protein synthesis what is meant by the terms (i) transcription and (ii) translation?

14
(a) Describe an experiment to extract DNA from cells.
(b) Explain why the following were used:
　(i) salt
　(ii) washing-up liquid
　(iii) a water bath at 60°C
　(iv) coarse filter paper
　(v) freezer-cold ethanol

Examination style questions

Section A

01
(a) Name the **four** bases of DNA.
(b) Copy the table below and complete to give two structural differences between DNA and RNA.

DNA	RNA

(c) What is *genetic screening*? Give one advantage of genetic screening.

02 A sequence of a section of one of the two strands of DNA is TTACCG.
(a) What is the sequence of the corresponding region on the complementary strand of DNA?
(b) What is the sequence on the corresponding region of mRNA synthesised from the TTACCG sequence?
(c) What term is used for the copying of a DNA sequence into a RNA sequence?
(d) What is the sequence of the corresponding region of the two tRNAs used in translating the mRNA base sequence?
(e) What is the product formed by the translation of mRNA by tRNA?
(f) In what part of the cell is the DNA copied into RNA?
(g) In what part of the cell is mRNA translated?

03 The diagram represents part of a DNA molecule.

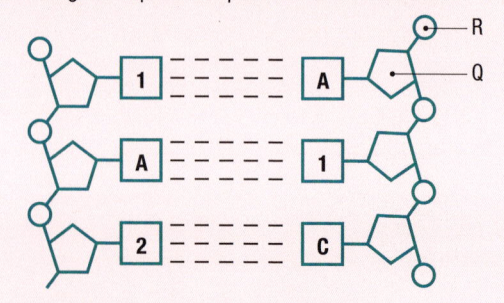

(a) What do the letters DNA stand for?
(b) Label the parts of the diagram R and Q.
(c) Circle one nucleotide on the diagram.
(d) Identify the missing bases in the shapes numbered 1 and 2.
(e) Which of the bases is not present in RNA?
(f) Distinguish between purine and pyrimidine bases.

Examination style questions

Section B

04 (a) DNA is the hereditary material in all living organisms. The DNA in eukaryotic cells is present in chromatin.
  (i) Chromatin is a mixture of DNA and _____.
  (ii) Condensed chromatin observed during nuclear division is called _____.

(b) The following questions relate to the extraction of DNA from live plant tissue.
  (i) What technique did you use to break the plant cell walls?
  (ii) What liquid is used to break down the membranes of the cell?
  (iii) Why is it necessary to break down the membranes?
  (iv) How is the protein separated from the DNA?
  (v) Name the freezer-cold organic solvent that is gently added to the DNA solution.
  (vi) How is the organic solvent added to the DNA solution?
  (vii) What is observed at the junction between the DNA solution and the organic solvent?
  (viii) What is seen to happen after the organic solvent is added?

Section C

05 (a) (i) What is a gene?
  (ii) What is meant by the term gene expression?

(b) (i) What is the name used to describe the general shape of the DNA molecule?
  (ii) Draw a labelled diagram of sufficient of a DNA molecule to show three base pairs (minimum of eight labels).
  (iii) Circle and label **one** nucleotide on your diagram.

(c) As soon as Watson and Crick proposed their model of DNA in 1953, scientists realised that the linear sequence of bases in DNA could form a series of code words, or codons, that would specify the corresponding linear sequence of amino acids in protein. [Adapted from B. Guttman, A. Griffiths, D. Susuki, T. Cullis, *A Beginner's Guide to Genetics.* One World, Oxford (2004).]

The diagram summarises the process of protein synthesis.

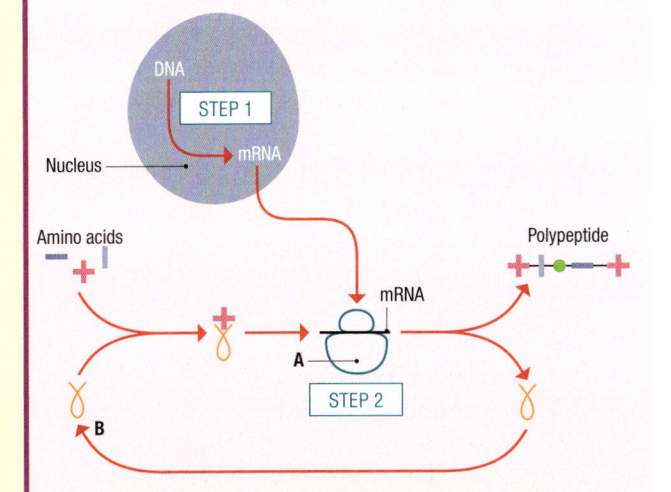

  (i) Identify Step 1.
  (ii) Name an enzyme involved in the formation of mRNA.
  (iii) The site of Step 2 is A. Identify A and Step 2.
  (iv) Identify B and outline its role in the formation of protein.
  (v) Copy the following chart into your answer book and complete it by matching the letters in column X with the appropriate term from the following list and write it in column Y.

  codon   triplet   anti-codon

Column X	Column Y
DNA	
mRNA	
tRNA	

06 (a) (i) What is genetic screening?
  (ii) Give two possible ethical problems associated with genetic screening.

(b) 'DNA, the secret of life. One simple shape; endlessly, effortlessly fertile, dividing, reforming itself from the beginning to the end of the world.' [BBC drama documentary, *Life Story*, on the discovery of the structure of DNA.]

The diagram is of a small section of DNA showing the base sequences of the two complementary strands of DNA. Use this diagram as a starting point to answer
(b) (i) of this question.

  (i) Describe, with the aid of labelled diagrams, the replication of DNA.
  (ii) Outline the significance of DNA replication.
  (iii) At what stage in the cell cycle does DNA replication take place?

(c) Each individual has a unique sequence of bases along their DNA. Modern genetic engineering techniques can treat a sample of a person's DNA to produce a pattern of DNA fragments unique and constant to that person.
  (i) What is the term used for this genetic procedure?
  (ii) Outline, in the correct sequence, the stages involved in producing the unique pattern of DNA fragments. (It is important to give a brief explanation for each step in the process.)
  (iii) Give two possible applications of this procedure.

15 DNA, RNA and Protein Synthesis

Leaving Certificate examination questions

Section A

01 Indicate whether the following are true (T) or false (F) by placing the letter T or F beside the statement.

Example: Alleles are different forms of the same gene.   T

(a) Chromosomes are made up of DNA and protein.
(b) A human sperm cell contains 23 chromosomes.
(c) Phenotype is the genetic make-up of an organism.
(d) Replication is the copying of DNA.
(e) RNA contains the base thymine.
(f) Genetic engineering is the manipulation and alteration of genes.
(g) The copying of the DNA code into mRNA is called transcription.

2014 OL Q. 2

02 The diagram represents a part of a DNA molecule. A and C represent nitrogenous bases.

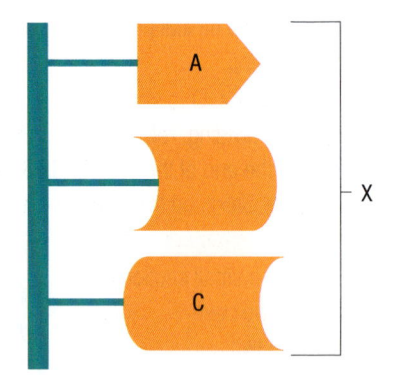

Complete the following in relation to DNA.

(a) Name the nitrogenous bases whose first letters are A and C.
(b) The structure labelled **X** is called a _____.
(c) Where in the cell would you expect to find most DNA?
(d) DNA contains the instructions needed to make protein. These instructions are called the _____ code.

2008 OL Q. 5

03 (a) (i) In DNA, nitrogenous bases occur in complementary pairs. Explain the term complementary as used here.
  (ii) In each case, name the complementary base in RNA for
     1. Adenine
     2. Cytosine
  (iii) Name a carbohydrate that is a component of nucleotides.
  (iv) Name a component of a nucleotide that is neither a carbohydrate nor a nitrogenous base.
(b) (i) What does the 'm' stand for in mRNA?
  (ii) Give one difference between RNA and DNA, other than the nitrogenous bases.
  (iii) Give the role of the enzyme RNA polymerase.

2013 HL Q. 6

Section B

04 In one of your laboratory activities you isolated DNA from a plant tissue.

(a) (i) Where in plant cells is DNA found?
  (ii) What is meant by DNA profiling?
(b) (i) Give one reason why you first chopped the plant material into very small pieces.
  (ii) Detergent and salt were added to the chopped plant material, which was then heated. Explain why the detergent was used.
  (iii) How was this mixture heated?
  (iv) Why was this mixture heated?
  (v) Later in the activity the mixture was blended for a maximum of 3 seconds. What would happen to the DNA if the mixture was blended for longer than 3 seconds?
  (vi) Protease was then added to the mixture. Why was protease added?
  (vii) The mixture was then filtered. After filtration, where was the DNA of your plant tissue to be found?
  (viii) What should you do next to make the DNA visible?

2010 OL Q. 10

05 (a) (i) How are the two strands of a DNA molecule joined together?
  (ii) What is 'junk' DNA?
(b) Answer the following questions by referring to the procedures that you used to isolate DNA from a plant tissue.
  (i) Having obtained a plant tissue e.g. onion:
     1. What was the first procedure that you followed?
     2. What was the reason for that procedure?
  (ii) Washing-up liquid is then used in the isolation. Give a reason for its use.
  (iii) Salt (sodium chloride) is also used in the isolation. Give a reason for its use.
  (iv) 1. What is a protease?
     2. Why is a protease necessary when isolating DNA?
  (v) The final stage of the isolation involves the use of freezer-cold ethanol.
     1. Describe how it is used.
     2. For what purpose is it used?

2011 HL Q. 9

Leaving Certificate examination questions

Section C

06 The diagram shows a short section of a DNA molecule.

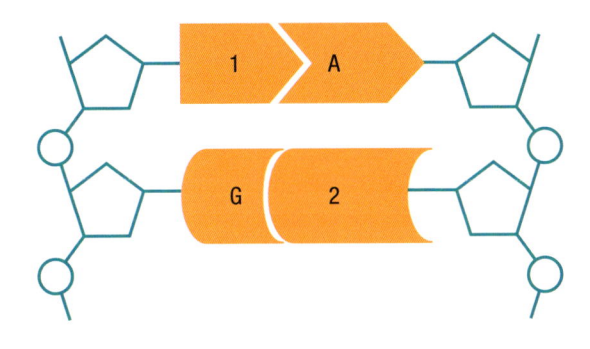

(i) Name the bases numbered 1 and 2 in the diagram above.
(ii) Protein synthesis involves both transcription and translation.
Where in a cell does **transcription** occur?
(iii) What type of RNA is involved in transcription?
(iv) In what organelle does **translation** occur?
(v) Name the small biomolecules that are joined together to make a protein.
(vi) What must happen to the newly formed protein before it can begin to work?
(vii) Give **one** function of proteins in living organisms.

2010 OL Q. 11 (c)

07 (i) What is meant by DNA profiling?
(ii) In DNA profiling, what are used to cut DNA strands into fragments?
(iii) On what basis are these fragments then separated?
(iv) Give two applications (uses) of DNA profiling.
(v) Name the plant from which you isolated DNA in your practical studies.
(vi) For what precise purpose did you use freezer-cold ethanol (alcohol) in your isolation of DNA?

2009 OL Q. 11 (c)

08 (a) (i) Explain the term *species*.
(ii) What is meant by the term *gene expression*?
(b) Last year it was discovered, by DNA analysis, that meat products labelled as beef contained meat from other animals, particularly horses and pigs.
(i) Name the biomolecule that is the major component of meat.
(ii) Where in a cell are these biomolecules manufactured?
(iii) Name the molecule, formed from DNA, which carries the instruction to manufacture these biomolecules.
(iv) Name **and** outline the procedure used for analysing the DNA samples that revealed the presence of horse meat in products labelled as beef.
(v) Would the result obtained from the procedure referred to in (iv) be the same if the beef were contaminated with pig meat? Explain your answer.

2014 HL Q. 10

09 Part (a) deals with DNA structure and replication.
(a) (i) Name the base in DNA that pairs with cytosine.
(ii) What are the two main events in the replication of DNA?

Part (b) deals with protein synthesis.
(b) (i) Explain the terms *transcription* and *translation*.
(ii) In which structures in the cell does translation occur?
(iii) How many bases in sequence make up a codon in mRNA?
(iv) Each mRNA codon specifies one of three possible outcomes during protein synthesis. Name these **three** possible outcomes.
(v) What does the letter 't' stand for in tRNA?
(vi) During translation one end of a tRNA molecule attaches to an mRNA codon. What is usually attached to the other end of the tRNA molecule?

(c) Distinguish between the terms in the following pair by writing **one** sentence about **each** member of **the** pair.
(i) Haploid and diploid.

2010 HL Q. 10

10 (i) DNA is made of units called nucleotides. Draw a labelled diagram of a nucleotide to show its three constituent parts.
(ii) Which of the labelled parts in your diagram in (i) may vary from nucleotide to nucleotide?
(iii) The genetic code is contained within the DNA of chromosomes. Briefly describe the nature of this code.
(iv) What is meant by non-coding DNA?
(v) Give **one** structural difference between DNA and RNA.
(vi) Name a cell organelle, apart from the nucleus, in which DNA is found.

2008 HL Q. 14 (b)

15 DNA, RNA and Protein Synthesis

Leaving Certificate examination questions

11 (a) (i) The DNA molecule is composed of two strands held together by paired bases.
1. Which base can link only to thymine?
2. Which base can link only to cytosine?
(ii) Name the type of bonding which occurs between members of a base pair.
(b) (i) Explain what is meant by the term DNA profiling.
(ii) Give a brief account of the stages involved in DNA profiling.
(iii) Give **two** applications of DNA profiling.
(iv) What is genetic screening?
(c) "The same amount of DNA is present in nuclei of cells taken from the liver, heart, pancreas and muscle of a rat."
(i) Use your knowledge of DNA and mitosis to explain this statement.
(ii) Name a cell produced by the rat which will contain a different amount of DNA in its nucleus to those mentioned above.
(iii) Briefly outline how you isolated DNA from a plant tissue.

2007 HL Q. 10

Past examination questions

OL	2014 Q. 2	2013 Q. 10 (b)	2012 Q. 3 (a)	2011 Q. 8 (b) (viii), Q. 10 (c) (iii)–(v)	
	2010 Q. 7	2009 Q. 11 (c)	2004 Q. 12 (c)		
HL	2014 Q. 10 (a), (b)	2013 Q. 6	2012 Q. 10 (a)	2011 Q. 9	2010 Q. 8 (b) (iii), Q. 10 (a), (b), (c) (i)
	2008 Q. 14 (b)	2007 Q. 10	2006 Q. 7 (b) (iii)	2005 Q. 8	

Genetic Inheritance   16

After studying this chapter you should be able to:

1. Define the following terms: species, heredity, allele, homozygous, heterozygous, genotype, phenotype, dominant, recessive and incomplete dominance (codominance).
2. Define gamete and fertilisation and give the function of gametes in sexual reproduction.
3. Explain a genetic cross for a homozygous cross.
4. Explain a genetic cross for a heterozygous cross.
5. Understand the use of a Punnett square.
6. Explain a genetic cross for a sex determination cross.
7. **HL** State the two laws of Gregor Mendel and describe the experiments used to formulate these laws.
8. **HL** Work out a dihybrid cross using the Punnett square technique.
9. **HL** Define the term linkage and explain the change in the probability of the results as compared to a dihybrid cross.
10. **HL** Explain sex-linked traits, and describe a sex-linked cross.
11. **HL** Describe the inheritance of non-nuclear DNA.

Heredity

There are a huge number of different living **organisms** on Earth. To make it easier to study them we classify all living things into groups of similar organisms. There is no one accepted way to classify all living things, but one widely accepted method divides all living things into five kingdoms (see Chapter 18). Living organisms are further divided into smaller and smaller groups until we reach the smallest division called the **species**.

> **D** A **species** is a group of organisms that can interbreed and produce <u>fertile</u> offspring.

> **D** **Heredity** is the passing of traits, using genes, from one generation to the next.

Humans, for example, are considered one species, *Homo sapiens*, as all humans are capable of interbreeding and producing fertile offspring. When members of a species interbreed, they pass on information from one next generation to the next. This makes the new generation similar to the previous one. This process is called **heredity**.

Gene function

> **D** A **gene** is a section of DNA that codes for a protein.

> **D** An **allele** is an alternative form of a gene.

As we know from the previous chapter a **gene** is a length of **DNA** that codes for a particular protein. This protein usually leads to a specific trait in the organism. An **allele** is an alternative form of a gene. A human either has the ability to roll their tongue or they don't. There is no intermediate stage where you can half roll your tongue.

16 Genetic Inheritance

A gene is always found at a specific position on a **chromosome**, which is called the **locus** of the gene (Fig 16.1). As a consequence **diploid** cells, which have two copies of each chromosome, have only two alleles for any one gene. They could be the same or they could be different.

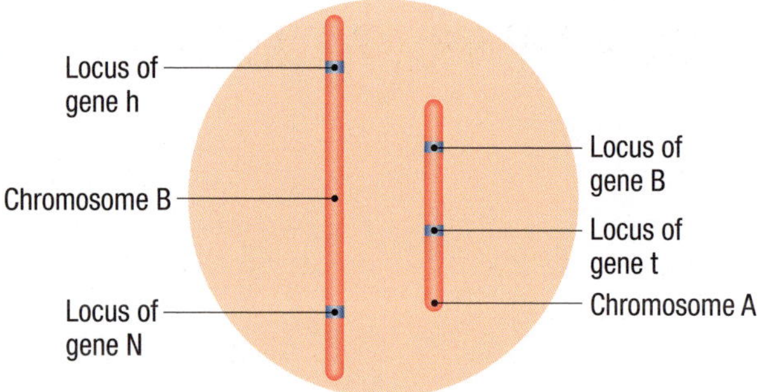

> **D** — The **locus** is the position of the gene on a chromosome.

If you are **homozygous** for the trait, you have only one type of allele to express and you show this trait, e.g. if you have two copies of the allele for tongue rolling, then you can roll your tongue.

> **D** — **Homozygous** means an individual has identical alleles.

But what happens if you have the **heterozygous** condition, e.g. one allele for tongue rolling and one for non-tongue rolling?

In this case, only one of the two traits is expressed. It is found that the same trait is always expressed in this circumstance. If you are heterozygous for tongue rolling, you will be able to roll your tongue. The allele for tongue rolling is said to be the **dominant allele** and it is expressed in the heterozygous condition.

A capital letter is used to show the dominant allele when writing down the allele contained in an individual, e.g. **R** = the gene for tongue rolling. If you cannot roll your tongue then you must have two copies of the non-rolling allele. Such a gene is said to be the **recessive allele** and it is written using the lower case letter, e.g. **r**. Such an allele is only expressed in the homozygous condition.

16.1 The loci (locus singular) of a number of genes on different chromosomes

> **Heterozygous** means an individual has different alleles. — **D**

> **Dominant allele** is the allele that is expressed in the heterozygous condition. — **D**

> A **recessive allele** is the allele that is only expressed in the homozygous condition. — **D**

From this we see that a person can roll his or her tongue whether they have one or two copies of the allele for tongue rolling **RR** or **Rr** but to express the trait for non-tongue rolling, he or she has to possess two copies of the non-tongue rolling gene **rr**.

Genotype and phenotype

The genes that an individual inherits are called the **genotype**. The physical appearance that an individual displays due to the genotype is called the **phenotype**. The genotype and the phenotype are not always the same as there are two possible phenotypes for tongue rolling and three possible genotypes for the trait (Fig 16.2).

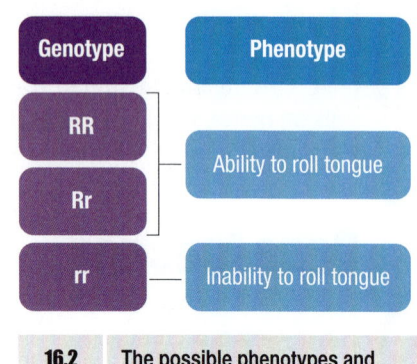

> **D** — **Genotype** is the genetic make-up of an organism.

> **D** — The **phenotype** is the physical appearance of the organism and is produced from the interaction of the genotype and the environment.

16.2 The possible phenotypes and genotypes for the tongue rolling gene

An individual whose phenotype is non-rolling has the genotype **rr**. An individual whose phenotype is rolling has two possible genotypes, **RR** or **Rr**. It is not possible to distinguish between these two genotypes from their external appearance. It may be possible to distinguish these two different genotypes by looking at the children that these people produce. The environment can also play a part in the phenotype, regardless of the genotype. You may inherit the genotype to make you 2 metres tall, but if you do not get enough food then you cannot grow to this size.

Genetic Inheritance | 16

Sexual reproduction

Most of the study of genetics involves the process of **sexual reproduction**. In this process the parents are almost always **diploid** and as a consequence have two alleles for each trait. If two of these normal (**somatic**) cells were to fuse then the next generation would have twice as much information in the nucleus and this process would eventually lead to a nucleus the size of the cell! To overcome this problem organisms have developed a process of sexual reproduction in which specialised sex cells (**gametes**) are produced that have half the amount of information of a somatic cell. These cells are **haploid** (see Chapter 11).

D — A **gamete** is a haploid sex cell capable of fusion.

When two of these gametes fuse in **fertilisation** then the resultant **zygote** is again a diploid cell.

D — **Fertilisation** is the fusion of two haploid gametes to produce a diploid zygote.

Solving genetic problems

If a man homozygous for tongue rolling reproduces with a non-tongue rolling woman, what type of tongue rolling ability will their children have?

1. To get an answer to this question you first need to see what the genotype of the parents is:
   a. The father is a tongue roller therefore he must have at least one dominant gene. But we are told he is homozygous so we know he is **RR**.
   b. The mother is a non-roller. This is the recessive phenotype so she has to be **rr**.
2. Next we need to find the gametes the parents can produce.
   a. Gametes have only one copy of each gene.
   b. Although each parent has two copies of the gene for tongue rolling they are both identical.
   c. Hence each parent can only produce one type of gamete. All of the father's gametes will contain the dominant allele (**R**). All of the mother's gametes will contain the recessive allele (**r**).
3. At fertilisation, the zygote will contain two alleles for tongue rolling, one from each parent **R** and **r**. This results in the heterozygous condition **Rr**, and each child will have the ability to roll their tongue as this is the dominant trait (Fig 16.3).

16.3 A cross between a homozygous tongue rolling man and a non-tongue rolling woman

16.4 A cross between two heterozygous parents

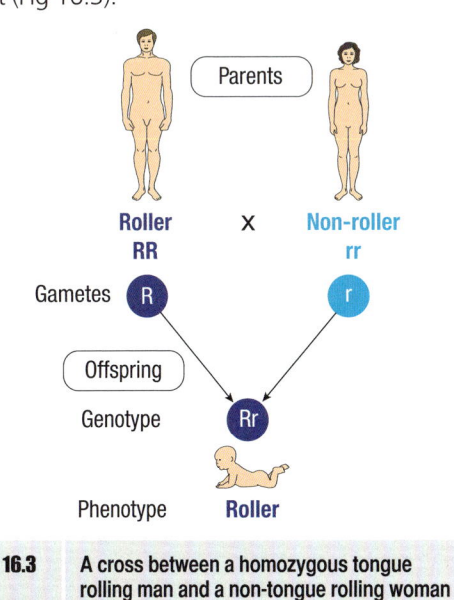

If a woman and a man who are both heterozygous for tongue rolling (**Rr**) have children, what would happen then?
1. Again, you need to see what gametes the parents could produce:
   a. Each parent can produce two different types of gamete, one containing the recessive allele (**r**) and one containing the dominant allele (**R**).
   b. These gametes are produced in equal numbers.

2. If you look at the father's gamete containing **R**:
   a. You can see that it is equally possible it would fertilise an egg containing **R** or **r**.
   b. The same can be said for the father's gamete containing the **r** gene.
   c. This will produce four possible results, each of which have an equal chance of occurring: **RR**, **Rr**, **Rr** and **rr** (note you always write the dominant gene first). This is shown in Fig 16.4.

As you can see from the diagram, there are four possible results (with two of the genotypes the same **Rr**) but there are only two possible phenotypes. The children either can or cannot roll their tongues. Children who are heterozygous for the trait (**Rr**) are said to be **carriers** of the trait (Fig 16.4). A carrier of a trait has one copy of the recessive allele and therefore shows the dominant allele but they can pass on the recessive allele to their offspring.

Punnett square

A **Punnett square** (Fig 16.5) is a device that is used to predict the possible genotypes of the offspring of a cross. Once the possible gametes of the parents are known, they are placed along the sides of the grid. Then the possible combinations (at fertilisation) are worked out and placed in the remaining squares. We can demonstrate the use of the Punnett square using the tongue-rolling example above, i.e. **Rr × Rr** (Fig 16.5).

Parents: Rr × Rr
Gametes: R, r × R, r

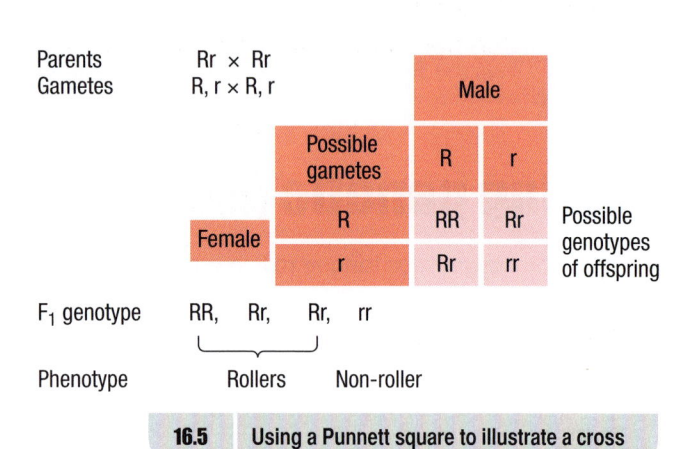

	Male	
Possible gametes	R	r
Female R	RR	Rr
r	Rr	rr

Possible genotypes of offspring

F_1 genotype: RR, Rr, Rr, rr

Phenotype: Rollers   Non-roller

16.5 Using a Punnett square to illustrate a cross

Worked example 1 (using Punnett square)

In peas, round seed shape (**R**) is dominant to wrinkled shape (**r**). A plant producing wrinkled seeds is crossed with a plant heterozygous for seed shape. (a) What is the genotype of each parent and what gametes can they produce? (b) Using a Punnett square work out the possible genotypes and phenotypes of their offspring.

Solution

(a) The plant producing wrinkled seeds can only have the genotype **rr**. Thus it can only produce gametes with the genotype **r**.

(b) The plant producing round seeds is heterozygous (stated in question) so its genotype is **Rr**. Therefore its gametes are **R** and **r** in equal numbers.

If we put this into a Punnett square the following results are obtained:

Parent   Rr × rr
Gametes   R × r × r

Possible Gametes	r
R	Rr
r	rr

16.6 Using a Punnett square to illustrate a cross

Possible genotypes   rr   Rr
Possible phenotypes   Wrinkled   Round
Ratio   1 :   1

Worked example 2

In a species of plant, yellow flower colour is dominant to white. Two yellow flowers were crossed and their seeds produced 294 yellow flowers and 89 white flowers. Explain.

Solution

1. From the information given, the letters **Y** for yellow and **y** for white are used (**Y** for the dominant allele).
2. Both parents are yellow so each must have at least one **Y** allele. The second allele could be either **Y** or **y**. How can you determine this?
3. Look at the offspring. Some of them are white. They must be **yy**. Therefore they must get a **y** allele from each parent.
4. We can therefore say the parents are both **Yy** (Fig 16.7).

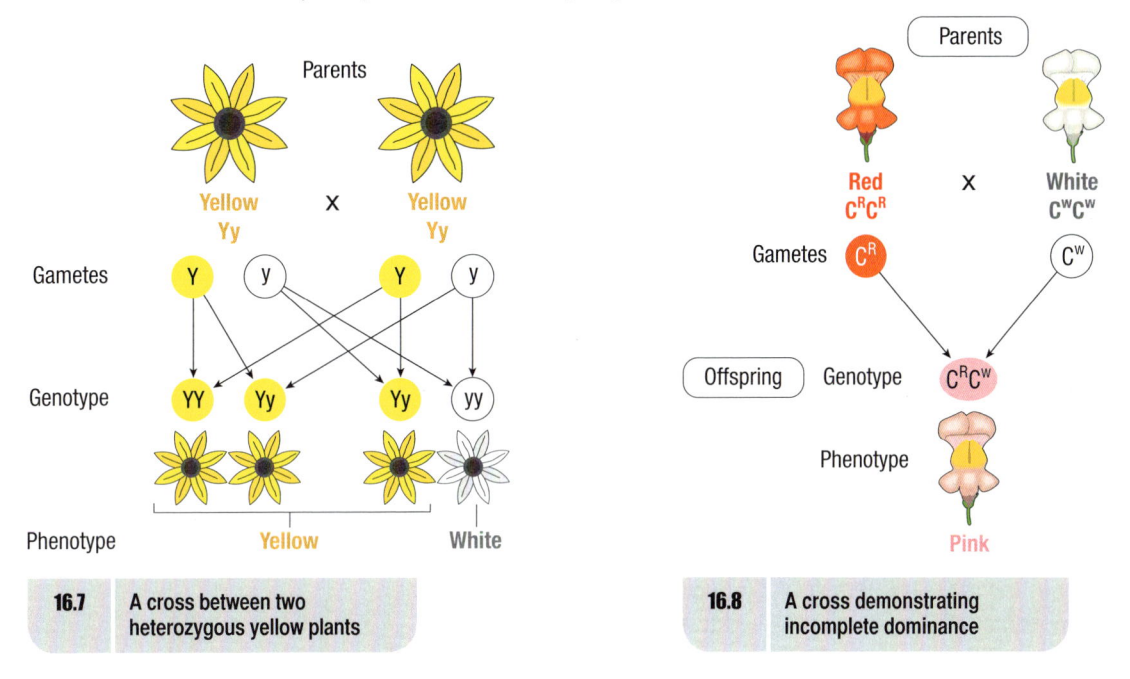

16.7 A cross between two heterozygous yellow plants

16.8 A cross demonstrating incomplete dominance

Incomplete dominance

In reality, things are rarely as simple as we have shown. Genetic inheritance can be very much more complex. Most of the possible variations on the inheritance of genes are beyond the scope of this syllabus.

One complication that is often seen is when neither of the two alleles is dominant. In snapdragon flowers, this is demonstrated when we look at flower colour. A cross between a red-flowered snapdragon and a white- flowered snapdragon will only give plants with pink flowers. This is a mix of the original two alleles and these alleles demonstrate **incomplete dominance** (**codominance**) (Fig 16.8).

> **D** In **incomplete dominance**, neither allele masks the expression of the other.

In this case incomplete dominance causes this third possible phenotype, not red or white but pink in the heterozygous condition.

Worked example 3

In short-horn cattle, red and white are incomplete dominant coat colours. The colour roan is produced in the heterozygous condition.

Because neither gene is dominant it is not correct to use a capital letter for one allele and a lower case for the other as neither is dominant. This exception is written using a letter **C** to stand for coat colour and using a capital letter with each to indicate the specific colour e.g. C^W for white coat colour and C^R for red coat colour. This unusual way of writing the two alleles will remind you it is not a normal cross.

16 Genetic Inheritance

Solution

If a red bull mates with a white cow, what results will be produced?

1. From the information given we would use the letters C^W and C^R for the alleles for coat colour.
2. The white cow must be $C^W C^W$.
3. The bull must be $C^R C^R$.
4. The cross would be as shown in Fig 16.9.

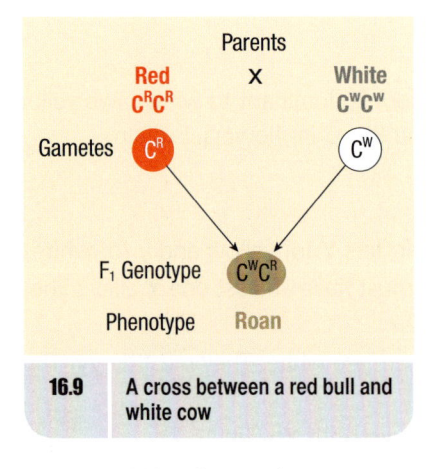

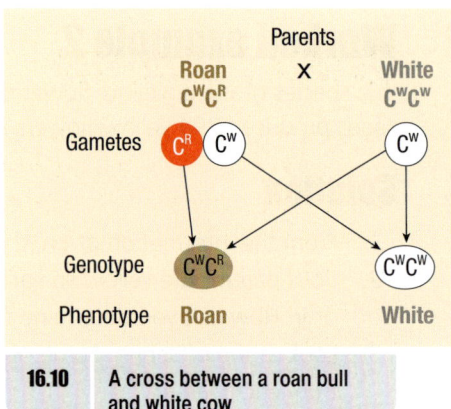

16.9 A cross between a red bull and white cow

If the white cow mates with a roan bull, what would be the results?

1. The cow must be $C^W C^W$.
2. The bull must be $C^R C^W$.
3. The cross would be as shown in Fig 16.10.

16.10 A cross between a roan bull and white cow

Sex determination

Every cell in a human, with the exception of the gametes, contains 46 chromosomes or 23 pairs. Twenty-two of these pairs have no function in determining the sex of an individual and are called **autosomes**. The sex of a human is determined by the last pair of chromosomes, the **sex chromosomes** (Fig 16.11), also called the **heterosomes**. These sex chromosomes contain the genes that determine the sex of the individual. The sex chromosomes differ in the male and female. All females have two sex chromosomes of the same size called the X-chromosomes and are depicted as XX. Males have one X chromosome and one much smaller chromosome called the Y chromosome, depicted as XY. The opposite is the case in birds and butterflies, where males are XX and females are XY.

- From this, it can be seen that females produce only one type of gamete as far as the sex chromosomes are concerned: all her eggs contain the X chromosome.
- Males, however, produce two types of sperm as far as the sex chromosomes are concerned: half contain the X chromosome and half contain the Y chromosome.
- Everyone receives an X chromosome from his or her mother but it is their father that determines his or her sex.
- If an egg is fertilised by an X-containing sperm, the resultant offspring will be female.
- If your mother's egg is fertilised by a Y-containing sperm then you will be a male.
- Thus the father determines the sex of a child.
- There is a 50:50 chance that any child will be female and a 50:50 chance that any child will be male (Fig 16.12).

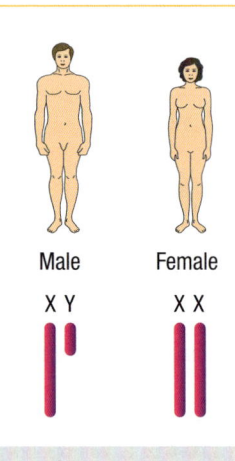

16.11 The sex chromosomes present in humans

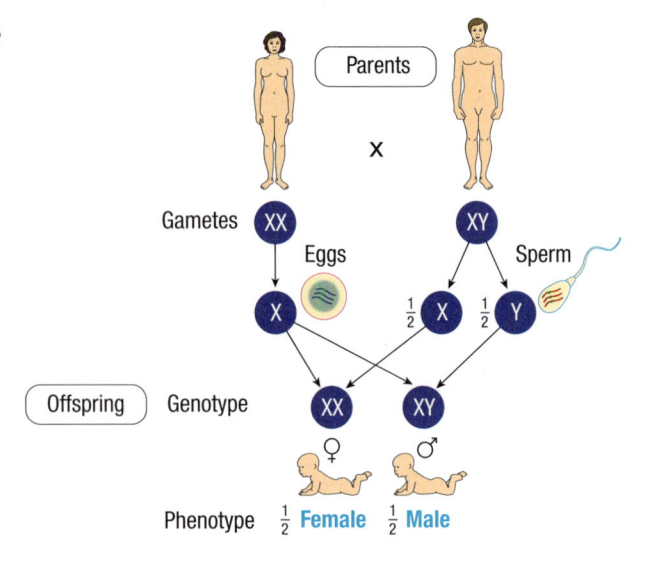

16.12 Sex determination in humans

Gregor Mendel

The basic rules governing genetics were discovered long before genes, chromosomes, mutations or the roles of the nucleus or meiosis were understood. These rules were discovered by a monk, Gregor Mendel (Fig 16.13), in 1860. Working in the garden attached to his monastery in the city now called Brno in the Czech Republic, Mendel did a series of breeding experiments. He was not the first person to study this area, but he was the first to approach genetics in a truly scientific manner.

Mendel's experiments

Mendel chose to study the pea plant.

1. He looked at contrasting traits that were easy to distinguish, i.e. tall versus short plants. Mendel studied large numbers of plants and statistically analysed his results.
2. To begin with, Mendel used **pure-breeding** plants. Pure-breeding plants, when crossed with one another, always produce offspring identical to the parents. Mendel called these plants the P generation (P for parental).
3. He also looked at only one contrasting trait at a time. Such an experiment is called a **monohybrid cross**.
4. In one of these experiments, Mendel crossed pure-breeding tall plants with pure-breeding short plants. To ensure that this was the only cross possible, he removed the anthers from tall plants and dusted the stigma of these tall plants with pollen from short plants. Pea plants normally self-pollinate so there was no danger of pollen from other plants arriving at the tall plants.
5. Mendel then planted the pea seeds and looked at the plants that were produced. He found that all the plants produced were tall. These plants were called the F_1 generation (for 'first filial' from the Latin for son or daughter).
6. It made no difference whether the male or female plant was tall or short, the results were always the same (Fig 16.14). This was not the result expected. The accepted theory at the time was that traits 'blended', so that medium-sized plants should have been produced.
7. Mendel then looked to see whether the information for short plants had disappeared. He let these F_1 plants self-fertilise. He then collected the pea seeds produced, planted them and looked at the new plants that were produced.
8. This second set of plants he called the **F_2 generation**. Both tall and short plants were present: 705 tall plants and 224 short plants. When Mendel analysed these results and the results from the other seven traits he studied, he found that there was approximately a **3 to 1 ratio** present (Figs 16.15 and 16.16).

16.13 Gregor Mendel

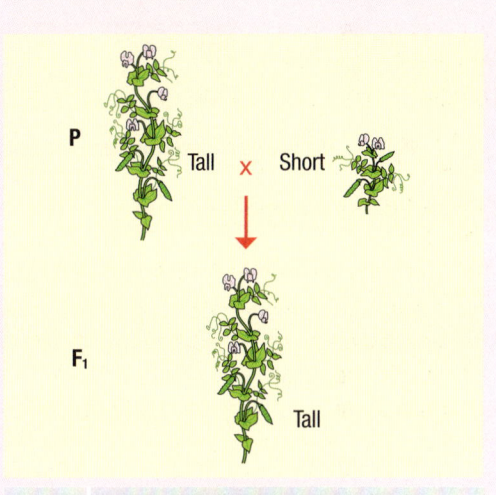

16.14 The result in one of Mendel's investigations looking at the F_1 generation

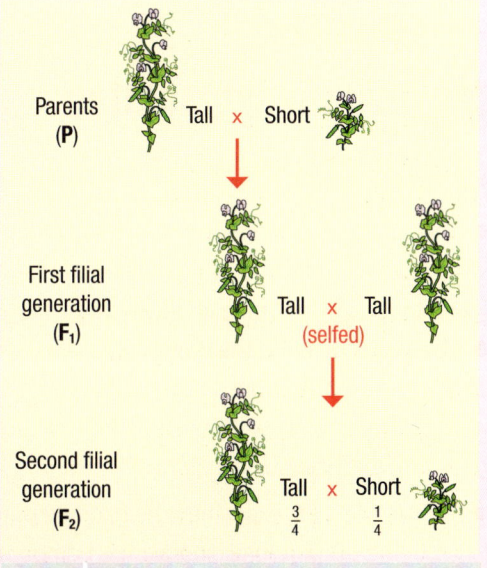

16.15 The results of one of Mendel's investigations looking at the F_2 generation

16 Genetic Inheritance

Trait	Dominant v Recessive	F₂ generation results		Ratio
		Dominant form	Recessive form	
Flower colour	Purple × White	705	224	3.15 : 1
Seed colour	Yellow × Green	6,022	2,001	3.01 : 1
Seed shape	Round × Wrinkled	5,474	1,850	2.96 : 1
Pod colour	Green × Yellow	428	152	2.82 : 1
Pod shape	Round × Constricted	882	299	2.95 : 1
Flower position	Axial × Top (Terminal)	651	207	3.14 : 1
Plant height	Tall × Small	787	277	2.84 : 1

16.16 The results achieved by Mendel looking at contrasting traits

The Law of Segregation states that organisms contain two factors for every trait. These factors separate in gamete formation, producing gametes with only one copy of each factor.

Mendel's conclusions

From these results, Mendel drew the following conclusions.

1. Each plant contains two 'factors' that control each trait.
2. There are two alternative forms of each factor, one of which is dominant (tall) and the other is recessive (small).
3. The dominant factor is always expressed, when present, whether there is one or two copies of it in the organism.
4. The recessive factor is only expressed when there are two copies present in the organism.

Mendel suggested that factors were transmitted from parent to offspring via the gametes. He proposed that the F₁ plants had one copy of each factor (tall and short), one factor coming from each parent. This led Mendel to draw up his first law, the **Law of Segregation**.

The modern explanation

We now know that genes exist, and we explain Mendel's results in terms of genes.

- There are two different forms of the gene for height. One produces tall plants and the other produces small plants. These alternative forms of the gene are called alleles.
- The allele for tall is the dominant allele as it is expressed when it is homozygous or when it is heterozygous. The allele for small is recessive because it will only produce small plants in the homozygous condition.
  1. In Mendel's experiment he had two pure-breeding plants. The tall pure-breeding plant is homozygous dominant. The small pure-breeding plant is homozygous recessive.

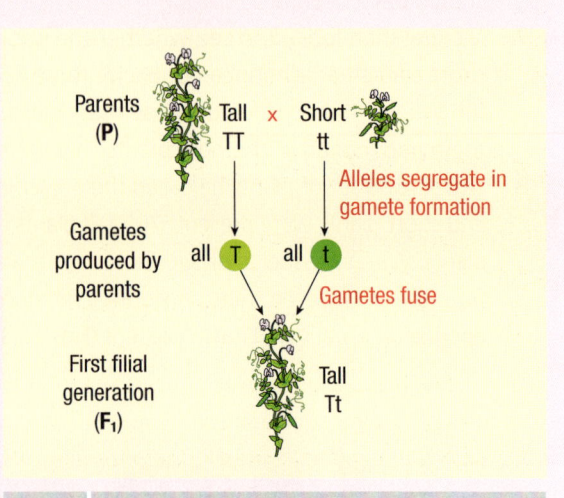

16.17 The modern explanation for Mendel's F₁ results

HL
    (a) These plants can only produce one type of gamete each because they have two copies of the same allele (see Fig 16.17).
    (b) When these gametes fuse, they produce the F_1 generation, all of which are heterozygous for the trait. In this situation, the dominant allele is expressed and all these plants are tall.
2. If these F_1 plants self-fertilise, then each plant can produce two types of gametes.
    (a) Half of the gametes will contain the **T** allele and half the gametes will contain the **t** allele.
    (b) These two gametes will fuse at random to produce all three possible genotypes (Fig 16.18): **TT**, **Tt** or **tt**. This cross can be demonstrated using a Punnett square, the use of which is described on page 200.

In our example, there are four possible results, two of which are the same:
- a quarter will be **TT**;
- half will be **Tt** (one quarter plus one quarter);
- and another quarter will be **tt**.

As **T** is the dominant gene, tall plants will be produced when plants receive one or two **T** genes. Thus three out of four of the plants will be tall and one out of four of the plants will be small. This three to one ratio of the phenotypes is the ratio that Mendel observed.

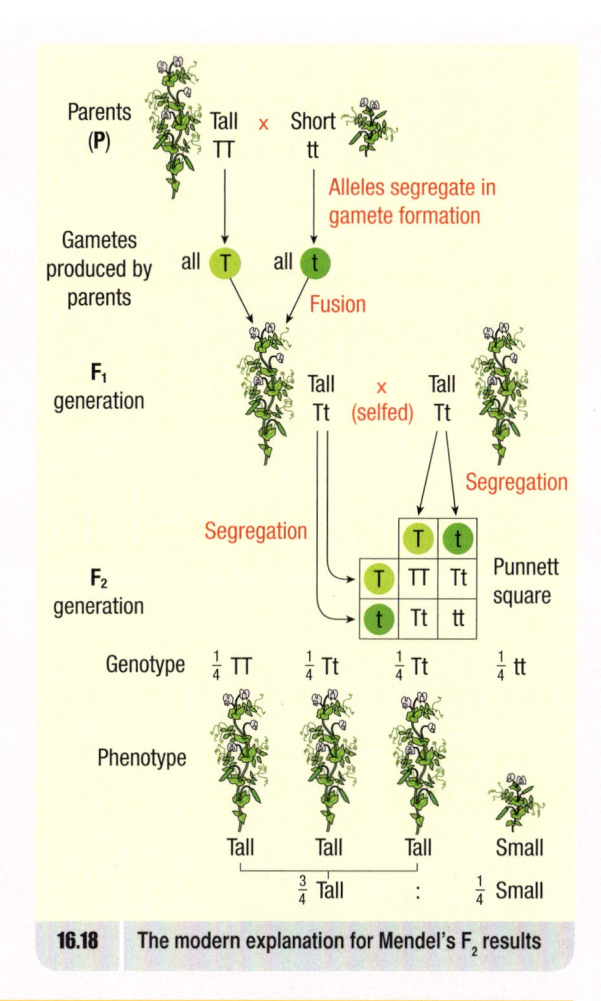

16.18 The modern explanation for Mendel's F_2 results

Probability

Three out of the four possible results in the above cross will give a tall plant. Therefore there is a 25%, or a one in four, chance that any plant will be small. There is a 75%, or three in four, chance that any plant will be tall. You must remember, however, that these are only **probabilities** and not certainties.

If you toss a coin into the air, you know there is a 50% chance it will come down heads. You also know that if it came down tails the last time, it does not mean it will come down heads this time. There is a 50% chance each time you throw it and it can easily come down tails three, four or even 20 times in a row, even if such a result is highly improbable.

The same can be said here. If two heterozygous plants cross and produce four seeds, it is highly likely that one of the seeds will produce a small plant. It is possible that none, two or three or four of the seeds will produce small plants. If you take a large number of plants in this position and look at all their offspring you will find that you will get a result of almost exactly three tall plants to each small plant. This is described as a 3:1 ratio.

Dihybrid crosses

All the crosses shown above were looking at one pair of contrasting traits at a time, e.g. height or petal colour in pea plants.
1. The next set of experiments that Mendel did was to study the inheritance of two pairs of **contrasting traits**. These are known as **dihybrid crosses**.
2. One of these experiments crossed a pure-breeding tall plant with purple flowers and a pure-breeding short plant with white flowers.
3. All of the F_1 plants were found to be tall with purple flowers.

HL

4. When these plants were allowed to self-fertilise, four different types of F₂ plants were produced – tall purple, tall white, small purple and small white.
5. Mendel again counted the offspring, and he got 96 tall purple, 31 tall white, 34 short purple and 11 short white. This gives a ratio of 9:3:3:1 (Fig 16.19).

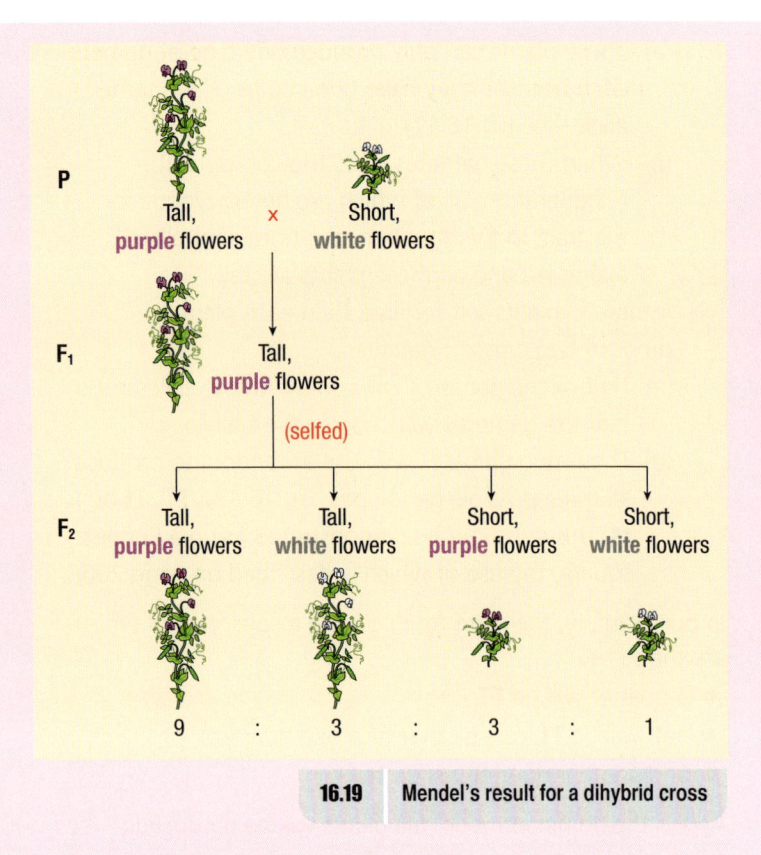

16.19 | Mendel's result for a dihybrid cross

The explanation

Using the information gained in the previous monohybrid cross, the results can be explained in the following way.

1. As Mendel started the experiment with pure-breeding plants, they both had to be homozygous for size and colour. The tall purple plant had the genotype **TTPP** and the small white plant had the genotype **ttpp**.
2. All the gametes from the tall purple plant contain the alleles **TP** and all the gametes from the short white plant contain the alleles **tp**.
3. When these gametes fuse they will produce plants all of which have the genotype **TtPp**. These plants are tall and purple.

To get the results in the F₂ generation, where all four possible combinations are seen, Mendel concluded that the F₁ plants must produce four types of gametes: **TP, Tp, tP** and **tp**.

A simple way of demonstrating this cross is to use a device called the Punnett square (after R. C. Punnett). This is shown in Fig 16.20.

In a Punnett square:

- all the possible types of gametes from one parent are written along the top of a series of squares;
- the types of gametes from the second parent are written down the side of the squares;
- all the possible products of fusion are then written into the squares;
- as there are four possible gametes meeting any one of four possible gametes, there are 16 possible results.

Genetic Inheritance | 16

HL As long as a plant receives one **T** gene, it will be tall. If it receives one **P** gene, it will be purple. It can be seen from the Punnett square (Fig 16.20) that nine are tall purple, three are tall white, three are small purple and one is small white. This was the result that Mendel produced. From this, Mendel formulated his second law, the **Law of Independent Assortment**.

> **D** **Mendel's Law of Independent Assortment** states that either member of a pair of alleles can pass into a gamete with either member of another pair of alleles.

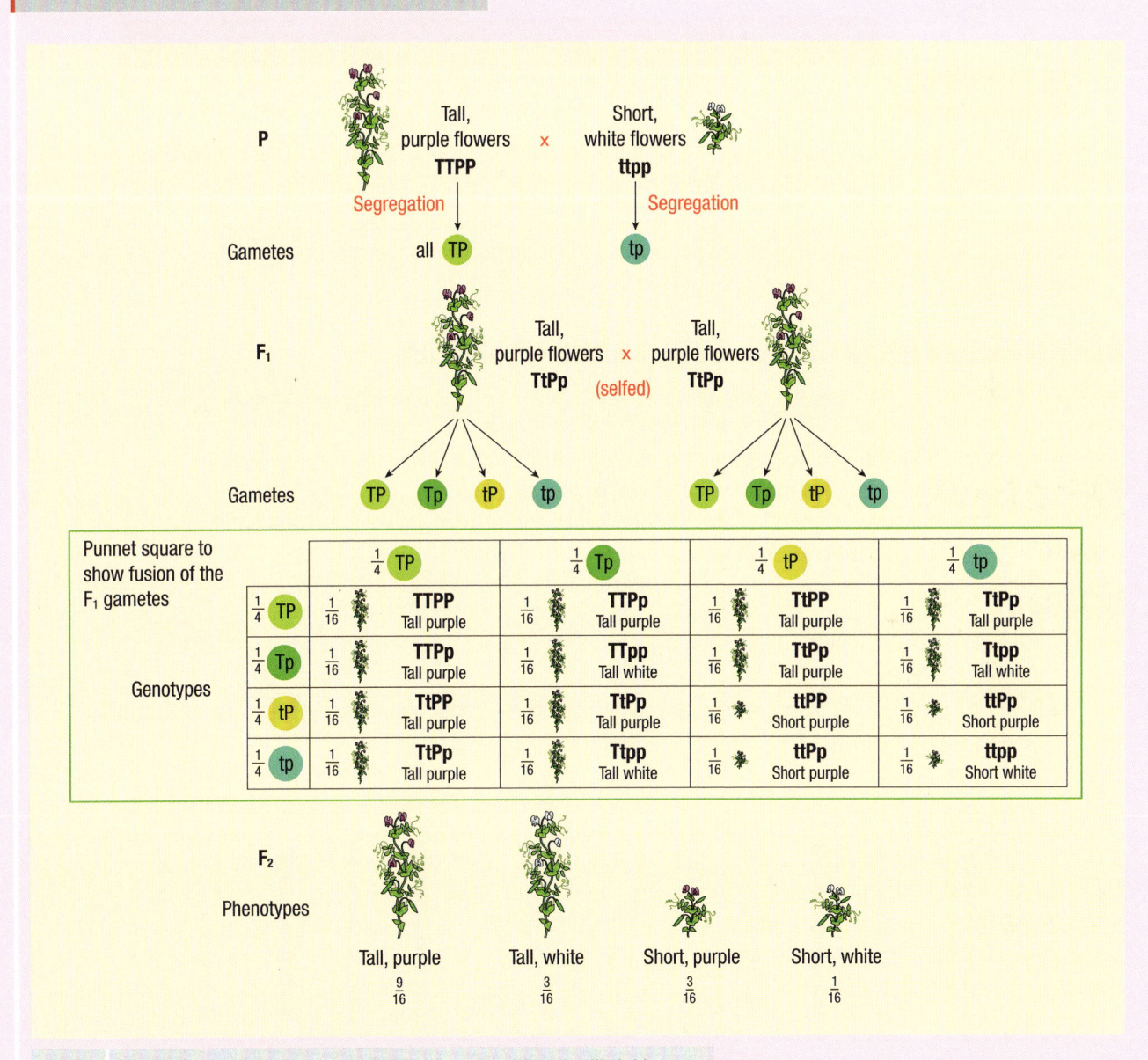

P Tall, purple flowers **TTPP** × Short, white flowers **ttpp**

Segregation / Segregation

Gametes all TP / tp

F₁ Tall, purple flowers **TtPp** × (selfed) Tall, purple flowers **TtPp**

Gametes TP, Tp, tP, tp / TP, Tp, tP, tp

Punnett square to show fusion of the F₁ gametes — Genotypes

	¼ TP	¼ Tp	¼ tP	¼ tp
¼ TP	1/16 TTPP Tall purple	1/16 TTPp Tall purple	1/16 TtPP Tall purple	1/16 TtPp Tall purple
¼ Tp	1/16 TTPp Tall purple	1/16 TTpp Tall white	1/16 TtPp Tall purple	1/16 Ttpp Tall white
¼ tP	1/16 TtPP Tall purple	1/16 TtPp Tall purple	1/16 ttPP Short purple	1/16 ttPp Short purple
¼ tp	1/16 TtPp Tall purple	1/16 Ttpp Tall white	1/16 ttPp Short purple	1/16 ttpp Short white

F₂ Phenotypes: Tall, purple 9/16 — Tall, white 3/16 — Short, purple 3/16 — Short, white 1/16

16.20 Using a Punnett square to show the modern explanation of a dihybrid cross

Dihybrid example 1

From Fig 16.16 we see that in pea plants, yellow seed colour (**Y**) and round seed shape (**R**) are the dominant traits, and green seed colour (**g**) with wrinkled seed shape (**r**) are recessive.

What results would be expected in a cross between a pea plant heterozygous for seed colour and seed shape and a plant recessive for both traits?

Genetic Inheritance

Solution

1. We know the plant recessive for both traits must be homozygous recessive for both or else it would show a dominant trait: thus its genotype is **yyrr**. The gametes it can produce are all **yr**.
2. We are told the second parent is heterozygous for both traits, thus its genotype is **YyRr**. There are four possible gametes it can produce: **YR, Yr, yR** and **yr**.
3. The cross will look as follows:

   Parents (p)   yyrr   x   YyRr
   Gametes   yr   x   YR, Yr, yR, yr

	YR	Yr	yR	yr
yr	YyRy	Yyrr	yyRr	yyrr

   Possible phenotypes: yellow round,   yellow wrinkled,   green round,   green wrinkled.
   The results give a ratio of 1:1:1:1, i.e. there is an equal chance that any one of the four phenotypes will be produced.
4. This is because Mendel's Law of Independent Assortment applies, and four possible gametes can be produced from the heterozygous parent (**YyRr**).

Dihybrid and incomplete dominance example

In snapdragon plants tall is dominant to dwarf but red and white petal colours show incomplete dominance, the heterozygous condition producing pink petal colour.

(a) Give the genotype of (i) a heterozygous tall red snapdragon, (ii) a dwarf pink snapdragon.
(b) Draw chromosome diagrams to show the genotypes in (a).
(c) Show, with the aid of a Punnett square, the genotypes and phenotypes of a cross between the plants whose genotypes you have given in (a).

Solution

(a) (i) Tall is dominant so a heterozygous tall plant has a genotype **Tt** and a red snapdragon is **C^{R}C^R**.
    Genotype = **TtC^{R}C^R**
   (ii) Dwarf is recessive so a dwarf plant is **tt** and because petal colour shows incomplete dominance, pink flowers have a genotype **C^{R}C^r**. Genotype = **ttC^{R}C^r**

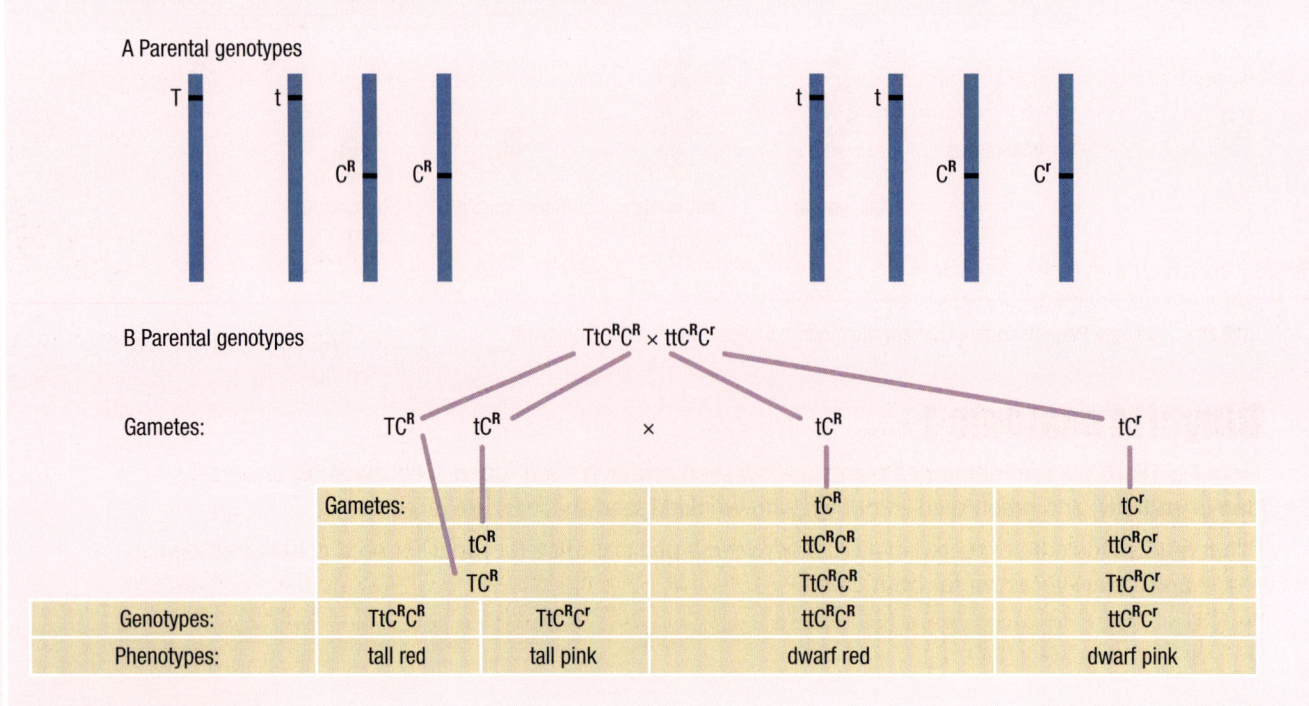

A Parental genotypes

B Parental genotypes   TtC^{R}C^R × ttC^{R}C^r

Gametes: TC^R tC^R ×   tC^R tC^r

Gametes:			tC^R	tC^r
	tC^R		ttC^{R}C^R	ttC^{R}C^r
	TC^R		TtC^{R}C^R	TtC^{R}C^r
Genotypes:	TtC^{R}C^R	TtC^{R}C^r	ttC^{R}C^R	ttC^{R}C^r
Phenotypes:	tall red	tall pink	dwarf red	dwarf pink

Linked genes

HL

This second law of Mendel was found not to be the case in all circumstances:

- When a dihybrid cross between a homozygous recessive parent and a heterozygous parent was carried out, in some cases the expected 1:1:1:1 ratio did not occur.
- The offspring were identical to one or other of the two parents.
- This was due to the fact that genes are carried on chromosomes and it is chromosomes, not genes, that separate out into gametes.
- If two genes are carried on the same chromosome they will tend to be inherited together (Fig 16.21).

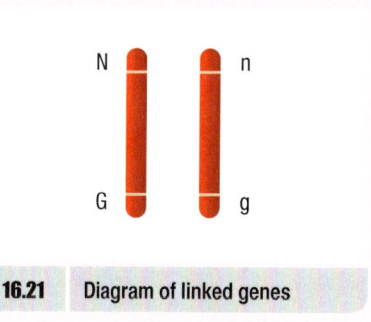

16.21 Diagram of linked genes

This is demonstrated in fruit flies. When we are illustrating these crosses the simplest way to show the linkage is to draw simple chromosome diagrams. This is demonstrated in Fig 16.21 using the letters **N** and **n** for one gene and **G** and **g** for the other pair. Note the following:

1. The alleles are always found at the **same loci** or position on the chromosome so it is impossible to have more than two alleles for a trait.
2. Genes for the different traits are found at **different loci** on the chromosomes.

Fruit flies can have long **L** or vestigial **l** (short) wings and broad **B** or narrow **b** abdomens. It was found that if a heterozygous long-winged, broad-abdomen fly produced offspring with another fly heterozygous for both traits, all the offspring would be:

- long-winged and broad abdomen or
- vestigial-winged with a narrow abdomen.

The other two alternatives do not occur. This is because the genes for wing length and abdomen shape are carried on the same chromosome and tend to be inherited together, i.e. the genes are linked (Fig 16.22).

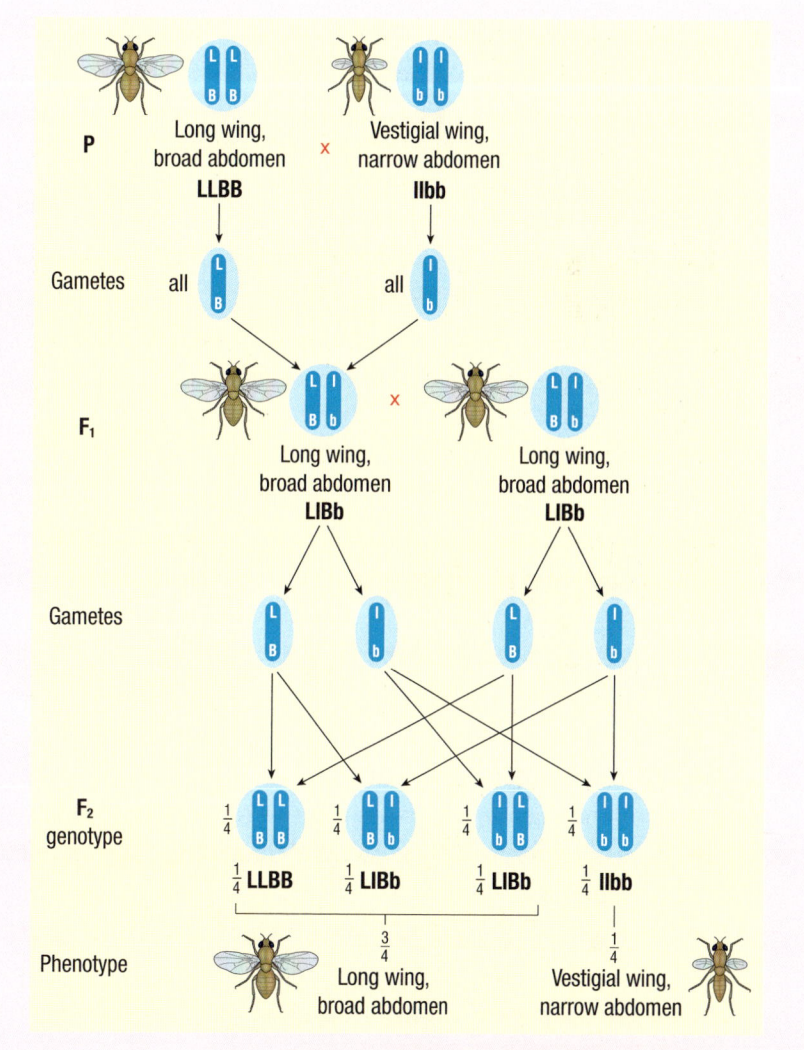

D **Linked genes** – where genes for different traits are contained on the same chromosome and tend to be inherited together.

16.22 A cross demonstrating linked genes

Linked genes example

In the fruit fly, fat body and hairy legs are linked genes. The recessive alleles for both of these are also linked and produce thin bodied and smooth legged flies.

When a fat bodied hairy legged fly was crossed with a thin bodied fly with smooth legs, all the resultant flies were fat with hairy legs. When these F_1 flies were crossed with thin bodied smooth legged flies an equal number of fat bodied hairy legged flies and thin bodied smooth legged flies were produced. Can you explain how these results came about?

Solution

As the genes were linked, the parental genotypes were:

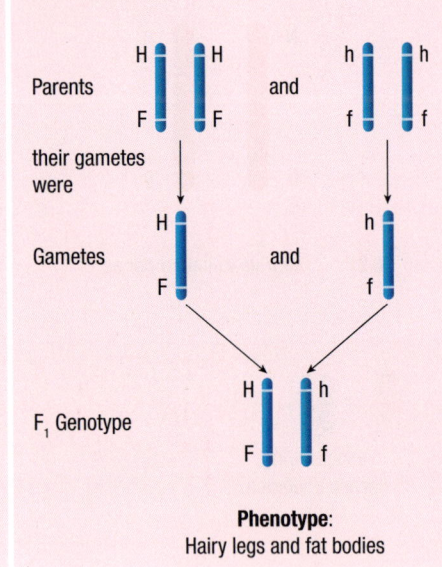

Parents: HHFF and hhff
their gametes were
Gametes: HF and hf
F₁ Genotype: HhFf

Phenotype:
Hairy legs and fat bodies

This fits in with Mendel's expected results.

However, when we cross these with the fat, hairy legged flies, Mendel would expect four possible results. This does not happen as the genes do not assort themselves independently of each other into the gametes. F is always found with H and f with h.

There are only two types of gamete from the F₁ flies: HF and hf

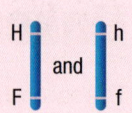

As a result, there are only two types of flies possible in the F₂ generation, *not* four as would be predicted by Mendel.

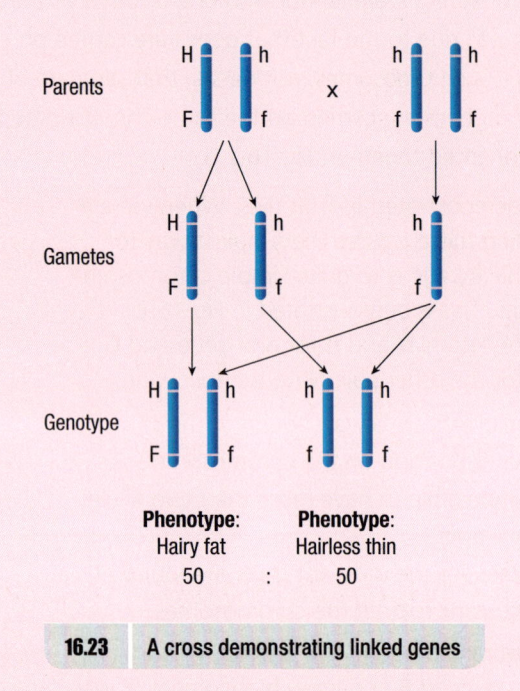

Parents: HhFf × hhff
Gametes: HF, hf and hf, hf
Genotype: HhFf, hhff, hhff, hhff

Phenotype: Hairy fat 50 : **Phenotype:** Hairless thin 50

16.23 A cross demonstrating linked genes

Sex-linked genes

As has been described earlier, the sex of an individual is determined by the sex chromosome. Females have two copies of the X chromosomes and males have one copy of the X chromosome and one copy of the Y chromosome.

- The X chromosome contains many more genes other than those that determine sex.
- The Y chromosome does not.
- As a consequence, a male has only one copy of many genes which are present only on his single X chromosome.
- There is no matching gene on the Y chromosome. In fact the Y chromosome is much smaller than the X chromosome.
- Some genes are found only on the Y chromosome, mainly those involved in producing male characteristics.

Sex-linked genes are genes found on the X chromosome or on the Y chromosome. The gene that gives the ability to distinguish between red and green light (the mutation causes red–green colour blindness) and the genes to allow correct blood clotting (the mutation causes haemophilia) are both sex-linked genes in humans.

In humans, the gene used to distinguish between red and green light is located on the X chromosome. Males have only one copy of this gene, which always comes from their mother (their father has to give them a Y chromosome if they are male). If they inherit the recessive gene from their mother, they have no corresponding gene from their father and they are red–green colour blind. Females can be red–green colour blind too but they need to inherit the recessive gene from both their mother and their father as they have two copies of the gene. Males are therefore far more likely to be red–green colour blind than females (Fig 16.22).

D **Sex-linked genes** are genes found on the X chromosome or on the Y chromosome.

HL Sex-linked example

Red–green colour-blindness is a sex-linked trait. If a normal man marries a woman who is a carrier of the trait, what is the likelihood that their first son would be colour blind?

1. If the trait is sex-linked, then it is on the X chromosome and the male has only one copy of it.
2. The parents have the following genotype: female X^CX^c, male X^CY
3. The female will produce two types of gametes: X^C and X^c
4. The male will produce two types of gametes: X^C and Y
5. For a male to be produced, the father has to provide a sperm with a Y chromosome.
6. The result would be X^CY or X^cY in equal numbers.
7. Thus the answer is a 50:50 chance (Fig 16.23).

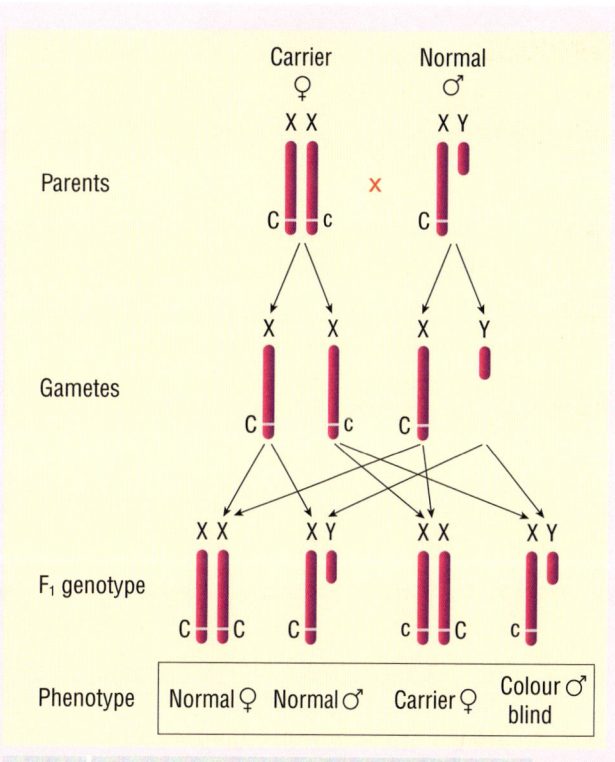

16.24 The inheritance of a sex-linked gene in humans

Non-nuclear inheritance

When two gametes fuse, they are not just two nuclei coming together. The male gamete is not much more than a motile nucleus but the female gamete contains a cell as well as a nucleus. The new individual also inherits this cell.

Mitochondria contain their own DNA (mtDNA), and these structures are inherited from the female only. When a cell replicates, it makes copies of mitochondria, including the DNA contained inside them. This results in some parts of the offspring's cells getting all of their genetic information from the maternal parent only. This is described as **non-nuclear inheritance**. In plant cells, **chloroplasts** also have their own pieces of DNA contained in them.

> **Non-nuclear DNA** is DNA not contained in the nucleus that is passed from one generation to the next.

Summary

- All living things are classified into five kingdoms.
- Each group of organisms capable of reproducing with each other and producing fertile offspring is called a species.
- Heredity is passing on of characteristics from one generation to the next using genes.
- Genes are units of DNA that code for the manufacture of a specific protein.
- There are two alleles for each trait:
  - The recessive allele is expressed only when you have two copies of that allele (homozygous condition). This allele is denoted using a lower case letter, e.g. r.
  - The dominant allele is expressed whether you have one or two copies of that allele (homozygous or heterozygous condition). This allele is denoted using an upper case letter, e.g. R.

16 Genetic Inheritance

Summary

- The genotype is the genetic make-up of the organism.
- The phenotype is the physical appearance of the organism, i.e. which genes are expressed.
- Sex determination:
  - Sex is determined in humans by the sex chromosomes, X and Y. Females are XX and males are XY.
  - It is the father's gamete that determines the sex of the children. In birds and butterflies XX is male and XY is female.
- Incomplete dominance (codominance):
  - This is where both alleles are expressed in the heterozygous condition, e.g. a red-flowered snapdragon crossed with a white-flowered snapdragon produces pink offspring.

HL
- Gregor Mendel discovered the basic rules of genetics in the 1860s. He studied pea plants in large numbers starting with pure-breeding plants, and he statistically analysed his results. From his results he formulated his two laws.
- Monohybrid cross:
  - Mendel crossed a pure-breeding tall plant with a pure-breeding small plant.
  - All the offspring (F_1) were tall.
  - If the F_1 generation were self-fertilised, then three tall plants were produced for every one small plant (F_2).
  - This led to the Law of Segregation: Organisms have two alleles for each trait and these segregate out in gamete formation.
- Dihybrid cross:
  - Mendel crossed pure-breeding, tall, purple-flowered plants with pure-breeding, small, white-flowered plants.
  - All the F_1 plants were tall and purple-flowered.
  - If the F_1 generation were self-fertilised, then there were four possible plants produced: tall purple, tall white, small purple and small white in the ratio 9:3:3:1.
  - This led to the Law of Independent Assortment, which states that either member of a pair of alleles can pass into a gamete with either member of another pair of alleles.
- One exception to Mendel's laws occurs when genes are linked:
  - These genes are contained on the same chromosomes and tend to be inherited together.
  - In fruit flies, if heterozygous, long-winged, broad-abdomen flies are crossed with vestigial-winged, narrow-abdomen flies, then four types of offspring would be expected in a 1:1:1:1 ratio.
  - But only two types of offspring are produced, similar to the parental types. Neither vestigial-winged, broad-abdomen nor long-winged, short abdomen flies are produced because these two pairs of alleles are contained on the same chromosome.
- Another exception to Mendel's laws occurs when genes are sex linked:
  - These are genes that are found on the X chromosome or on the Y chromosome.
  - Human females get two copies of the genes on the X chromosome and need to get two recessive alleles to show the recessive trait.
  - Human males have only one copy of this gene (from their mother) and if this is a recessive allele it will be expressed, thus they will show the recessive trail more often.
  - Red–green colour blindness and haemophilia are sex-linked traits in humans.
  - Co-dominance is also an exception to Mendel's laws (see above).
- Non-nuclear inheritance:
  - The inheritance of DNA not contained in the nucleus.
  - Mitochondria and chloroplasts contain their own DNA.
  - Each offspring gets a nucleus from the male parent and a nucleus plus a cell from the female parent.
  - The mitochondria or chloroplast produced in the new organism come from the mother and contain DNA from the mother only.
  - As the cell replicates, it is this maternal DNA that will be copied in each mitochondria or chloroplast.

Review questions

01 (a) What is a species?
(b) What is meant by heredity?
(c) Explain the terms (i) gene, (ii) allele, (iii) locus, (iv) gamete, (v) fertilisation.

02 (a) What is a dominant allele?
(b) What is a recessive allele?
(c) What allele is expressed in the heterozygous condition?

03 In humans the following applies:
(a) Having freckles is dominant to not having freckles.
(b) Being blue eyed is recessive to brown.
(c) Curly hair is dominant to straight hair.
(d) Detached earlobes is dominant to attached earlobes.

Use the information above to assign genotypes to each of the following:
  (i) A person with straight hair.
  (ii) A person heterozygous for eye colour.
  (iii) The egg of a woman who has freckles.
  (iv) Someone with detached earlobes whose mother has attached earlobes.
  (v) A brown-eyed heterozygote.
  (vi) A person heterozygous for freckles and curly hair.
  (vii) The gametes of individual (vi).
  (viii) A blue-eyed person with attached earlobes.

04 (a) What is the difference between a genotype and a phenotype?
(b) How might the environment affect the phenotype?

05 In rabbits, black fur (B) is dominant over white fur (b).
(a) What is the genotype of a white rabbit?
(b) If this rabbit should mate with: (i) a homozygous black rabbit or (ii) a heterozygous black rabbit, what offspring would result from each cross?

06 In pea plants height is controlled by a single pair of allelic genes. The allele for tallness (**T**) is dominant over the allele for shortness (**t**).
(a) Give the genotype of a plant that is (i) heterozygous for height, (ii) homozygous recessive for height.
(b) A homozygous tall plant was crossed with a homozygous short plant (cross 1). The offspring that resulted were then crossed with each other to produce the next generation (cross 2). Copy the following and give your answers in the spaces provided. (Genotype in brackets, phenotype on line.)

Cross 1
(i) The genotypes of the original parents ( ) ( )
(ii) The gametes produced by each parent ( ) ( )
(iii) The genotype of the offspring ( )
(iv) The phenotype of the offspring _____

Cross 2
The genotypes of the parents (i.e. the offspring of cross 1) ( ) ( )
The gametes produced by each parent ( ) ( )
(i) Use the Punnett square to find the genotypes of the second cross.
(ii) List the phenotype of the offspring.

07 In humans, freckles (F) is dominant over no freckles (f). A couple, both of whom have freckles, have one child with no freckles. Explain how this could happen.

08 When a homozygous black mouse was crossed with a homozygous white mouse all the offspring were black.
(a) Which of the colours is the recessive colour?
(b) What is the genotype of the offspring?
(c) If two of the black mice from this cross are mated what will be the possible genotypes and phenotypes of their offspring?
(d) A black mouse was crossed with a white mouse and half of the offspring were white. Explain how this could happen.

09 The flower colour of a snapdragon exhibits incomplete dominance between red and white. What would be the genotype and phenotype of the plants produced by crossing: (a) two pink plants or (b) a pink and a white plant?

10 (a) What is an autosome?
(b) Explain the term sex chromosome.
(c) 'The sex of the child is determined by the father.' Explain this statement.

11 (a) Who was Gregor Mendel?
(b) Why were Mendel's experiments successful?

12 (a) What is Mendel's first law?
(b) What experiments did Mendel carry out to demonstrate his first law?

13 What is meant by a dihybrid cross?

16 Genetic Inheritance

Review questions

14 In humans, brown eyes (B) is dominant to blue eyes (b) and normal pigment (N) is dominant to lack of pigment (albinism) (n). A brown-eyed normal pigmented man (heterozygous for both traits) marries a woman of the same genotype. What proportion of their children would be (a) blue-eyed with normal pigmentation, (b) have the allele for brown eyes but have no pigmentation? Show your answers in the form of a cross.

15 In cattle, uniform colouring (U) is dominant to spotted (u) and black coat colour (B) is dominant to white (b). Show the cross between two parents of genotype UuBb × uubb, including the possible gametes and the genotypes and phenotypes of the offspring.

16 In guinea pigs black coat colour is dominant to brown and short hair is dominant to long. A short-haired black guinea pig, heterozygous for both genes, was crossed with a long-haired brown guinea pig.
  (a) Give the possible genotypes and phenotypes of the progeny (offspring) of the above cross.
  (b) Could progeny with the same phenotypes be produced in the cross if the two pairs of alleles were linked? Explain your answer.

17 How did Mendel demonstrate his second law?

18 (a) What are linked genes?
  (b) How do linked genes affect the expected ratios of offspring?

19 (a) What is a sex-linked trait?
  (b) In humans, normal colour vision is a sex-linked trait and its allele is dominant to the gene for red–green colour blindness. If a woman who is colour blind has children by a man with normal vision what would be the expected distribution of colour vision in their children?

20 (a) What is non-nuclear inheritance?
  (b) In which organelles does this occur?

Examination style questions

Section A

01 (a) What is meant by the term allele?
  (b) In pea plants the allele for purple flower (P) is dominant to white flower (p). If a heterozygous purple plant is crossed with a white plant what would be:
   (i) The genotype of the parents?
   (ii) The possible gametes they could produce?
   (iii) The genotype of the offspring?
   (iv) The phenotype of the offspring?

02 (a) What meant by the term *heredity*?
  (b) What is a recessive allele?
  (c) What is a sex chromosome?
  (d) What are the sex chromosome(s) found in a man?
  (e) What is incomplete dominance or codominance?
  (f) In what way is a gene sex linked?

Section C

03 (a) (i) What is a gene?
   (ii) Where are genes found?
   (iii) What name is given to the alternative form of a gene?

  (b) Albinism is a genetically inherited condition where the skin pigment melanin is not produced. As a result sufferers have white hair, pale skin and no pigment in the iris of their eyes. The diagram shows the inheritance of albinism in a family. Normal melanin production is controlled by a dominant gene (N). Albinism is caused by the recessive gene (n).

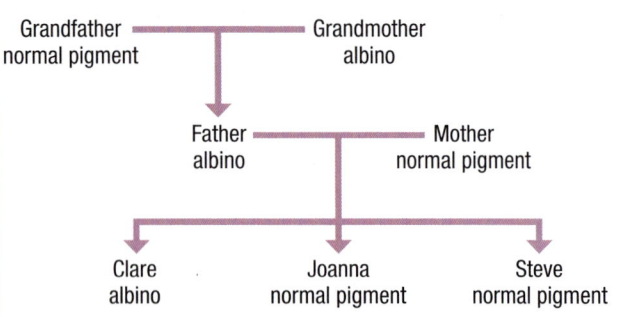

```
Grandfather ─────────── Grandmother
normal pigment           albino
        │
        ▼
      Father ─────────── Mother
      albino             normal pigment
        │
   ┌────┼────────┐
   ▼    ▼        ▼
 Clare  Joanna   Steve
 albino normal   normal
        pigment  pigment
```

Answer the following questions.
  (i) What is the genotype of:
   1) Clare?
   2) Her mother?

Genetic Inheritance 16

Examination style questions

(ii) Joanna marries a man homozygous for normal skin pigment. Copy and complete the table below to work out the possible genotypes and phenotypes of their children. (put the genotypes in the brackets, phenotypes on the lines).

Genotypes of parents	Joanna ( ) x Husband ( )
Genotypes of gametes	( )( ) x ( )
Genotypes of offspring	( )( )
Phenotypes of offspring	_____ _____

04 Hairy stemmed tomato plants were crossed with smooth stemmed tomato plants. All the next generation (F₁) of plants had hairy stems.

(a) Copy the following into your answer book and complete the spaces to show the cross (genotype in brackets, phenotype on the lines).

The genotypes of the parents   ( ) x ( )( ) ( )
The gametes produced by each parent   ( ) x ( )
The genotype of the offspring   ( )
The phenotype of the offspring   _____

(b) What advantage do you think having a hairy stem is to the plant?

05 (a) Give the meaning of the following terms as used in genetics: (i) allele, (ii) phenotype, (iii) dominant.

(b) In pea plants, the allele for tall plants (T) is dominant to the allele for dwarf plants (t).

(i) What advantage is it to pea plants to grow tall?
(ii) Copy the following into your answer book and complete the spaces to show the following crosses. (Put phenotypes on the lines and genotypes in the brackets.)

Cross 1. A homozygous tall pea plant was crossed with a dwarf pea plant and all the offspring were tall.

Genotypes of parents   ( ) x ( )
Genotypes of gametes   ( ) x ( )
Genotype of offspring   ( )
Phenotype of offspring   _____

Cross 2. The offspring of Cross 1 were then crossed with themselves.

Genotypes of parents   ( ) x ( )
Genotypes of gametes   ( )( ) x ( )( )
(To solve this use a Punnet square.)

Genotypes of the offspring   ( ) ( ) ( ) ( )
Phenotypes of the offspring
_____ _____ _____ _____

(c) In some plants the allele for red petals (C^R) is incompletely dominant (co-dominant) to that for white petals (C^W), the heterozygous condition being pink. Copy the following into your answer book and complete the spaces to show the cross between two pink plants.

The genotypes of the parents   ( ) x ( )
The genotypes of the gametes ( ) ( ) x ( ) ( )
The genotypes of the progeny   ( ) ( ) ( )
The phenotypes of the progeny
_____ _____ _____
(these must match the genotypes above)

06 (a) Define the following terms as used in genetics: (i) allele, (ii) genotype, (iii) recessive.

(b) In sweet pea, tall is dominant to small and white flower is dominant to purple.

A cross between a plant heterozygous tall white flower and a plant homozygous small purple flower yielded the following results:

36   Tall plants with white flowers
34   Tall plants with purple flowers
35   Small plants with white flowers
31   Small plants with purple flowers

Show (i) the genotypes of the parents, (ii) the genotypes of the gametes, (iii) the genotypes of the offspring.

(c) (i) What is meant by stating that certain genes in humans are 'sex-linked'?
(ii) Give an example of a human trait governed by a sex-linked gene.
(iii) Draw chromosome diagrams to illustrate the following genotypes for a sex-linked trait in humans: a heterozygous female, a male showing the recessive phenotype.
(iv) Name an animal cell organelle that contains its own DNA. What is the genetic consequence of this in human cells?

07 (a) (i) What is meant by linkage in genetics?
(ii) Explain why linked genes do not give a phenotype ratio of 1:1:1:1 for a dihybrid heterozygote crossed with a dihybrid recessive, i.e. AaBb x aabb.

(b) In pea plants studied by Mendel, yellow seed (Y) is dominant over green seed (y) and round seed (R) is dominant over wrinkled seed (r). The genes governing seed colour and seed shape are not linked.

16 Genetic Inheritance

Examination style questions

A yellow, round, homozygous parent crossed with a green, wrinkled parent produced only yellow, round, heterozygous offspring. When allowed to self-pollinate and self-fertilise, the second generation contained four different phenotypes in a ratio approximating 9:3:3:1. Show, by means of a cross diagram, how the genotype and phenotype results of the F_2 generation came about.

(c) Given that the allele A is dominant over a, and the allele B is dominant over b, draw simple chromosome diagrams to illustrate the following cases.

(i) The genes are not linked and the organism is heterozygous for both genes.
(ii) The genes are linked, A to B and a to b, and the organism is heterozygous for both genes.
(iii) The genes are not linked and the organism is heterozygous for A and homozygous for B.
(iv) Give the genotypes of both the gametes and offspring of a cross between the organism in (iii) and that in (i).

08 (a) (i) Explain what is meant by the term heredity.
(ii) What is a gene and what is meant by the term gene expression?

(b) The table below summarises some of the results obtained by Gregor Mendel in his investigation of the inheritance of seven traits of pea plants.

Trait	Original cross	F_1 progeny	F_2 progeny
Seed colour	Yellow × green	Yellow	6022 yellow, 2001 green
Seed form	Round × wrinkled	Round	474 round, 1850 wrinkled
Flower position	Axial × terminal	Axial	651 axial, 207 terminal
Flower colour	Red × white	Red	705 red, 224 white
Pod form	Inflated × constricted	Inflated	882 inflated, 299 constricted
Pod colour	Green × yellow	Green	428 green, 152 yellow
Stem length	Tall × small	Tall	787 tall, 277 small

Use suitable symbols to illustrate the genotypes of the following pea plants.
(i) Heterozygous in respect of seed form.
(ii) Homozygous recessive in respect of flower colour.
(iii) Homozygous in respect of tall stem.
(iv) Heterozygous in respect of pod colour.
(v) Terminal flower position.

State the phenotypes that would result from the genotypes given in (i), (ii) and (iv).
Give the genotypes of the gametes produced by the plant in (i).

(c) In a species of plant, the height of the plant is determined by one pair of allelic genes and leaf type by another pair.
(i) Using suitable symbols, give the genotypes of the following parents: heterozygous dominant for tall plant and rough leaf, homozygous recessive for small plant and smooth leaf.
(ii) State the phenotype ratio that would be expected from this cross if the genes were not linked.
(iii) What would be the effect on the phenotype ratio if the genes were closely linked?
(iv) Which of Mendel's laws do linked genes tend not to obey? You must state the name of the law.
(v) What is meant by a dihybrid cross in genetics?
(vi) Give the genotypes of the parents that produce offspring in the ratio 9:3:3:1.
(vii) Name the hereditary material that genes are made of.

16 Genetic Inheritance

Leaving Certificate examination questions

Section A

01 In pea plants the allele for tall (T) is dominant over the allele for dwarf (t).

A heterozygous tall plant is crossed with a dwarf plant. Complete the blank spaces below.

Genotypes of parents   (Tt)   ×   (tt)
(a) Possible gametes   ( )( )   ×   ( )
(b) Genotypes of offspring   ( )   ( )
(c) Phenotypes of offspring   _____   _____

2012 OL Q. 6

02 Choose each term from the following list and place it in **Column A** to match a description from **Column B**. The first one has been completed as an example.

dominant   gamete   gene   mutation   genetics   genotype

Column A	Column B
genetics	The study of biological inheritance
(i)	The genetic make-up of an individual
(ii)	A sex cell
(iii)	A change in the structure of DNA
(iv)	A part of DNA with information to make one protein
(v)	The allele expressed in the heterozygous condition

2010 OL Q. 4

03 In each of the following cases read the information provided and then, **from the list below**, choose the correct percentage chance of obtaining the indicated offspring in each case.

0%   10%   25%   50%   75%   100%

(a) In the fruit fly *Drosophila* the allele for full wing is dominant to the allele for vestigial wing. One parent was homozygous in respect of full wing and the other parent was heterozygous.

What is the % chance of obtaining offspring with **full** wing?

(b) In roses there is incomplete dominance between the allele governing red petals and the allele governing white petals. Heterozygous individuals have pink petals. A plant with pink petals was crossed with a plant with white petals.

What is the % chance of obtaining offspring with **white** petals?

(c) In Dalmatian dogs the allele for brown spots is recessive to the allele for black spots. The two parents were heterozygous in respect of spot colour.

What is the % chance of obtaining offspring with **black** spots?

(d) Red hair in humans is recessive to all other hair colours. A red-haired woman and a black-haired man, whose own father was red-haired, started a family.

What is the % chance of obtaining offspring with **red** hair?

2010 HL Q. 2

04 In tomato plants the allele responsible for purple stem (**P**) is dominant to that for green stem (**p**) and the allele for cut leaf (**C**) is dominant to the allele for potato type leaf (**c**). A plant with a purple stem and cut leaves was crossed with a plant with a green stem and potato type leaves. A total of 448 seeds was obtained. When the seeds were germinated four types of progeny resulted and they had the following phenotypes:

110 purple stem and cut leaves

115 green stem and potato type leaves

114 purple stem and potato type leaves

109 green stem and cut leaves

(a) What were the genotypes of the tomato plants that gave rise to these progeny?

(b) Do the progeny of this cross illustrate the Law of Independent Assortment?

(c) Explain your answer.

2004 HL Q. 3

Section C

05 (a) Explain the following terms as used in genetics:
(i) heterozygous, (ii) sex chromosome, (iii) diploid.

(b) In cats, black coat colour (B) is dominant to white coat colour (b).

If a white cat is crossed with a cat heterozygous for coat colour, state:

(i) The genotype of each parent cat.

(ii) The genotype(s) of the gametes produced by each parent.

(iii) The genotypes and the matching phenotypes of the kittens produced by the cross.

2014 OL Q. 10

16 Genetic Inheritance

Leaving Certificate examination questions

06 (a) Explain the following terms used in genetics: (i) gene, (ii) allele, (iii) genotype.

(b) In humans, sex is determined by genes located on pairs of chromosomes called sex chromosomes.
Using a Punnett square or otherwise, show that there is an equal chance of a child being male or female. In your answer give:
  (i) The genotypes and matching phenotypes of the parents.
  (ii) The possible genotypes of the gametes that can be produced by **each** parent.
  (iii) The genotypes of the offspring.

2013 OL Q. 10

07 (a) Explain the following terms that are used in genetics: (i) allele, (ii) heterozygous, (iii) phenotype.

(b) In humans, brown eye (B) is dominant to blue eye (b). Two parents, one heterozygous for eye colour and the other with blue eyes, start a family.
  (i) What is the genotype of the blue-eyed parent?
  (ii) What are the possible gametes that **each** parent can produce?
  (iii) Using a Punnett square or another method work out the possible genotypes **and** phenotypes of their children.

2011 OL Q. 10

08 (a) Many characteristics are passed on to children by their parents.
  (i) Give **one** example of an **inherited** human characteristic.
  (ii) Give **one** example of a **non-inherited** human characteristic.
  (iii) Which structures in sperm and egg nuclei are responsible for biological inheritance?

(b) When a pure-breeding black cat was mated with a pure-breeding white cat, all the kittens were black.
  (i) Which fur colour, black or white, is **recessive** in these cats?
  (ii) Using capital letters for dominant and lower case letters for recessive, give:
    1. The genotypes of the parent cats.
    2. The genotype of the kittens.
  (iii) Is the genotype of the kittens referred to as homozygous or heterozygous?
  (iv) Give a reason for your answer to part (iii).
  (v) In relation to fur colour, what will be the genotypes of the gametes that these kittens will produce?
  (vi) What are *alleles*?

2010 OL Q. 11

09 (a) Explain the following terms as used in genetics: (i) heterozygous, (ii) incomplete dominance, (iii) phenotype.

(b) In snapdragon plants the allele for red flower (**R**) is incompletely dominant to the allele for white flower (**r**). Heterozygous plants have pink flowers.
  (i) Using a Punnett square, or otherwise, give the genotypes of the parents and find the genotypes and phenotypes of the offspring of the following cross:
    Pink-flowered x Pink-flowered
     snapdragon   snapdragon
  (ii) If 120 new plants were produced in this cross, how many of them would you expect to have pink flowers? Explain how you got this answer.

2009 OL Q. 11

10 (a) Explain the following terms, which are used in genetics: allele, homozygous, genotype.

(b) (i) Name or draw the sex chromosomes that are present in a human body cell in the case of: 1. A male. 2. A female.
  (ii) Use a Punnett square to show that there is a 50% chance that fertilisation will lead to a male and 50% chance that it will lead to a female.

2006 OL Q. 11

11 The diagram shows part of the genotype of an individual of the Aberdeen Angus cattle breed. This breed is unusual in that the allele for the polled (hornless) condition is dominant to the one for the horned condition.

(i) What term is used to describe the allele pair Pp?
(ii) Is this a sex-linked condition? Explain your answer.
(iii) What is the phenotype *and* sex of the animal whose partial genotype is shown above?
(iv) Draw a diagram, similar to the one shown, to describe an Aberdeen Angus which, when crossed with the one above, would **ensure** the production of a polled calf.
(v) Name a group of organisms in which the XY chromosome pair gives rise to a different sex than in cattle.

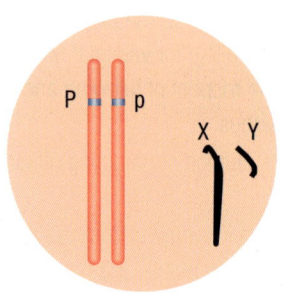

2014 HL Q. 10 (c)

Leaving Certificate examination questions

12 (i) Human males and females differ in one of their 23 pairs of chromosomes. What name is given to this pair of chromosomes?
  (ii) Draw this pair of chromosomes for a human male **and** for a human female and label them appropriately.
  (iii) Using the chromosomes referred to in part (b) (ii), show, using a Punnett square or otherwise, that a child strands an equal chance of being male or female.
  (iv) 1. What is meant in genetics by the term *sex linkage*?
       2. Name **two** common sex-linked traits.
  2013 HL Q. 11 (b)

13 In the sweet pea plant the texture and colour of the testa (seed coat) are governed by two pairs of alleles, which are not linked. The allele for smooth (S) is dominant to the allele for wrinkled (s) and the allele for yellow (Y) is dominant to the allele for green (y).
  (i) State the Law of Segregation **and** the Law of Independent Assortment.
  (ii) Using the above symbols, and taking particular care to differentiate between upper case and lower case letters:
       1. Give the genotype of a pea plant that is homozygous in respect of seed texture and heterozygous in respect of seed colour.
       2. State the phenotype that will result from the genotype referred to in 1.
  (iii) What phenotype will be produced by the genotype SsYy? Give another genotype that will produce the same phenotype. Do not use a genotype that you have already given in response to part (ii) 1.
  (iv) If the allele for smooth were linked to the allele for green and the allele for wrinkled were linked to the allele for yellow, give the genotypes of the **two** gametes that parent SsYy would produce **in the greatest numbers**.
  2012 HL Q. 10 (b)

14 (a) In the antirrhinum (snapdragon) there is no dominance between the allele for red flower and the allele for white flower. Heterozygous individuals have pink flowers. The allele for tall stem is dominant to the allele for short stem. These pairs of alleles are located on different chromosome pairs.
  (i) What is the significance of the fact that the two allele pairs are located on different chromosome pairs?
  (ii) A plant which had pink flowers and was heterozygous in respect of stem height was crossed with one which had white flowers and a short stem.
       1. Using suitable symbols determine the genotypes of all the possible offspring of this cross.
       2. For each of your answers, state the phenotype that would result.

(b) Distinguish between the members of each of the following pairs of terms, by writing a sentence about **each** member of each pair.
  (i) Gene and allele.
  (ii) Homozygous and heterozygous.
  (iii) Genotype and phenotype.
  (iv) Linkage and sex linkage.
  2011 HL Q. 13

15 (a) (i) State Mendel's Law of Segregation.
  (ii) Name two cell organelles, other than the nucleus, that contain DNA.

(b) In guinea pigs the allele for black hair (B) is dominant to the allele for brown hair (b) and the allele for short hair (S) is dominant to the allele for long hair (s). The alleles governing hair colour are located on a different chromosome pair to those governing hair length.
  (i) Explain the terms *alleles* and *dominant*.
  (ii) What term is used to describe alleles that lie on the same chromosome?
  (iii) Why is it significant that the two pairs of alleles, mentioned above in relation to guinea pigs, are located on different chromosome pairs?
  (iv) Determine all the possible genotypes and phenotypes of the offspring of a cross between the following guinea pigs:
       Brown hair, heterozygous short hair x heterozygous black hair, long hair
  2009 HL Q. 10

16 (a) Explain the following terms which are used in genetics: homozygous, recessive, phenotype.

(b) In the fruit fly, *Drosophila*, the allele for grey body (**G**) is dominant to the allele for ebony body (**g**) and the allele for long wings (**L**) is dominant to the allele for vestigial wings (**l**). These two pairs of alleles are located on different chromosome pairs.
  (i) Determine all the possible genotypes and phenotypes of the progeny of the following cross: grey body, long wings (heterozygous for both) x ebony body, vestigial wings.
  (ii) What is the significance of the fact that the two allele pairs are located on different chromosome pairs?

(c) Haemophilia in humans is governed by a sex-linked allele. The allele for normal blood clotting (**N**) is dominant to the allele for haemophilia (**n**).
  (i) What is meant by sex-linked?
  (ii) Determine the possible genotypes and phenotypes of the progeny of the following cross: haemophiliac male x heterozygous normal female.
  2008 HL Q. 11

16 Genetic Inheritance

Past examination questions

OL			
2014 Q. 10 (a), (b)	2013 Q. 10 (a), (c)	2012 Q. 6, Q. 11 (a)	2011 Q. 10 (a), (b)
2010 Q. 11 (a), (b)	2009 Q. 11 (a), (b)	2008 Q. 11 (a), (b)	2007 Q. 4 (b), (c), Q. 11 (c)
2006 Q. 11 (a), (b)	2005 Q. 13 (a)	2004 Q. 12 (a), (b)	

HL			
2014 Q. 10 (c)	2013 Q. 11 (b)	2012 Q. 10 (b)	2011 Q. 13 (b), (c)
2010 Q. 2, Q. 10 (c)	2009 Q. 10 (a), (b)	2008 Q. 11	2007 Q. 5
2006 Q. 12 (a), (b)	2005 Q. 10 (b), (c)	2004 Q. 3	SEC Sample Q. 11 (a), (b)

Variation, Evolution and Genetic Engineering

17

After studying this chapter you should be able to:

1. Define variation and describe how variation occurs from sexual reproduction and mutations and give two sources of mutations.
2. Define evolution.
3. Give the theory of natural selection including one source of evidence for the theory.
4. Define the term genetic engineering.
5. Describe the process of genetic engineering.
6. Give three applications of genetic engineering.

Variation

As we saw in the last chapter a **species** is a group of individuals who can interbreed and produce fertile offspring. Individuals belonging to a species are not all identical but show some **variation**.

This variation can be due to environmental or genetic causes. From an evolutionary viewpoint, the only important variation is genetic or **inherited variation** within a species. The second type of variation is **acquired variation**. An example of this would be your accent. We shall look at some causes of inherited (genetic) variation.

> **Variation** is the difference between individuals of the same species.

> **Inherited variations** are differences within a species that are controlled by genes.

> **Acquired variations** are differences within a species that develop over the life of the organism.

Causes of genetic variation

Sexual reproduction

Sexual reproduction itself causes variation. As one set of information comes from each parent, the offspring will have a different combination of genes than either of the original parents. As a result the offspring will be different from both of them.

Meiosis

Meiosis allows genes to be reshuffled. This can be demonstrated if we take an example of a cell with a **diploid** number of six. The cell has three pairs of **homologous chromosomes**, i.e. pairs of chromosomes with matching **genes**. Each set of homologous chromosomes (homologues) is given a different colour in the diagram. Homologous chromosomes are not usually identical, e.g. a pair of homologues could control flower colour but one might have the gene for red flowers and the other the gene for white flowers.

When you look at only one trait, homologous chromosomes could easily be identical, but chromosomes contain genes for hundreds of traits so the likelihood that they are identical is remote. Each **gamete** produced contains one copy of each chromosome. There are eight ways you can combine these three pairs of homologous chromosomes as shown in Fig 17.1. This is 2^3, i.e. 8.

Gametes get one from each pair. Possible combinations are:

17.1 The number of possible ways three pairs of chromosomes can be combined

17 Variation, Evolution and Genetic Engineering

In a human cell where there are 23 chromosome pairs, the resultant number of different gametes is 2^{23} or 8.4 million. Any one of these gametes may meet up with any one of the 8.4 million gametes produced by the second parent, so the total possible different fertilised eggs produced is $(8,400,000)^2$ which is approximately 70.5 million, million different possible combinations all leading to slightly different new individuals.

Gene mutation

Genes code for proteins in our cells, and for our cells to work correctly the proteins have to work in a very precise manner. Sometimes genes are damaged or are copied incorrectly. The new protein that is produced as a result of this change may not work in the same fashion or produce the same result as the normal protein. These changes are called **gene mutations**. **Mutations** may also lead to variation and some of the changes might be beneficial. Mutations are permanent changes in genes or chromosomes. Should these mutations occur in cells that develop into gametes then they can be passed from one generation to the next. In general, mutations are rare, they occur randomly and tend to be harmful.

> **D** A **mutation** is a change in the structure or amount of DNA in an organism.

An example of gene mutation in humans is the genetic disorder called **cystic fibrosis**. This is one of the most common serious genetic disorders in Caucasians and most common in Irish people. About one in every 25 Caucasians has the gene and about one in every 1,800 children has the disease. The gene codes for a protein found in the cell membrane that controls the flow of chloride ions into and out of the cell. The mutated protein does not allow the correct flow of chloride ions. This results in thick mucus that clogs the lungs and stops the correct functioning of the pancreas and liver.

The mutation is recessive and to get the disorder you need to inherit the gene from both of your parents. A person who carries one copy of such a gene has no symptoms of the disorder and is called a **carrier**. If both parents are carriers there is a one in four chance that any child they produce will get the disorder (Fig 17.2).

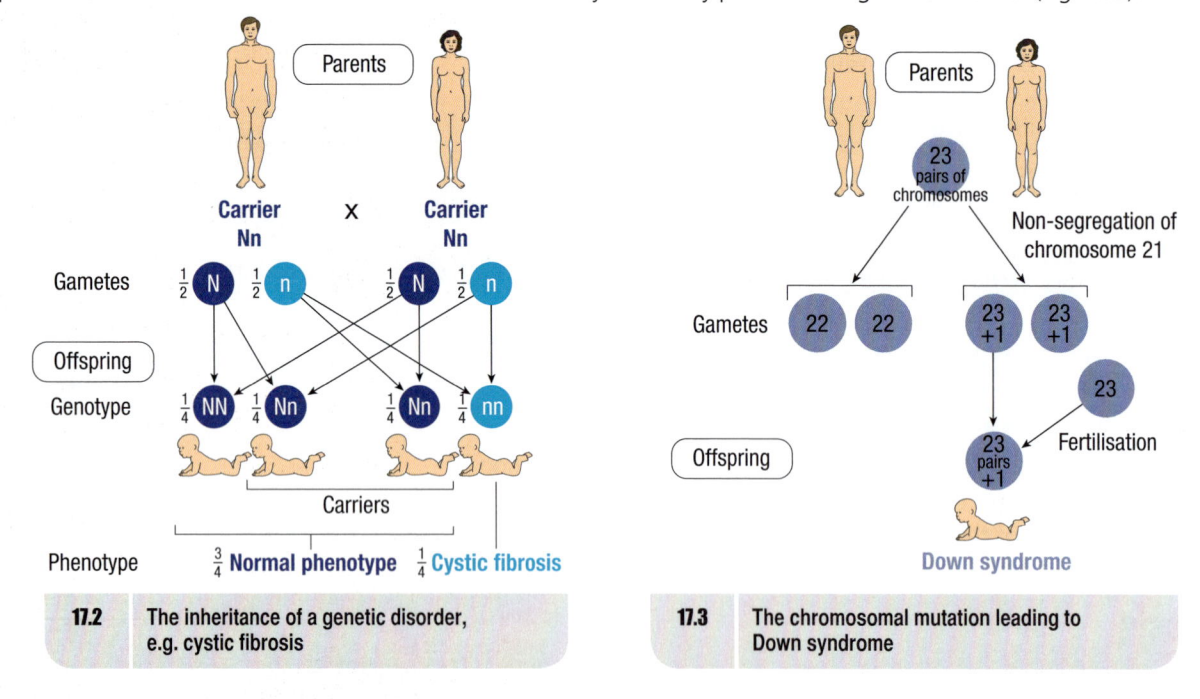

17.2 The inheritance of a genetic disorder, e.g. cystic fibrosis

17.3 The chromosomal mutation leading to Down syndrome

Chromosome mutation

Chromosome mutations occur in one of two ways:
- an individual chromosome is changed in some way;
- the number of chromosomes is changed.

The commonest human chromosome mutation is called **Down syndrome**. About one in 1,000 children worldwide have this condition. Such children have a characteristic appearance, with almond-shaped eyes and a round face. They have an intellectual disability and often have congenital heart defects. These children have an extra copy of **chromosome number 21 (trisomy 21)**.

This happens because one of the gametes has an extra copy of this chromosome. When the cell producing the gametes divided by meiosis, it failed to segregate (separate) the homologous chromosomes. Two of the four gametes had no copy of chromosome number 21 and two gametes contained two copies of the chromosome (Fig 17.3). When a gamete with one extra chromosome number 21 is fertilised by a second normal gamete, the result is Down syndrome. The incidence of Down syndrome increases markedly with increasing age of the parents, at about 35 for women and 55 for men.

Causes of mutation

Spontaneous changes will occasionally occur in the genetic material if a mistake is made in the normal copying mechanism of **DNA** in a cell. These changes are relatively rare but they do happen at a low but measurable rate.

Certain agents will increase this rate of change such as X-rays, gamma radiation and many chemicals, e.g. cigarette smoke. These agents, or **mutagens**, change the structure or the amount of DNA in the cell. Most mutagenic agents are **carcinogens** and vice versa (see Chapter 11).

> **Mutagens** are agents that change the DNA in a cell.

In a Japanese fishing village, a large number of children were born with severe birth defects. It was found that their parents were eating large amounts of shellfish that was contaminated with mercury from a nearby factory. This mercury was a mutagen and caused the genetic defects.

Evolution

The vast majority of biologists accept the theory of **evolution**, although there is much discussion as to how this process came about. The person most commonly thought of in relation to the theory of evolution is Charles Darwin. In 1831, Darwin went on a round-the-world trip on a survey ship The Beagle. On this trip Darwin saw an enormous variety of animals and plants as well as a large number of fossils. Darwin came to the conclusion that species must have evolved from one another. Others had proposed this **theory**, but Darwin was the first to suggest a mechanism for it to happen, and to have a large body of evidence to back his theory. However, Darwin did not publish his theory at that time.

Sixteen years later another biologist, Alfred Wallace, wrote to Darwin. Wallace was on a scientific expedition to the Malay archipelago and had independently come up with the same theory. A combined presentation of the two theories was given at a scientific meeting in London. Darwin followed this up by publishing his famous book *On the Origin of Species* in 1852. This book is without question one of the most important biology books ever written.

17.4 Charles Darwin (1809–1882)

> **Evolution** is the changes between members of a species and the emergence of new species from older species over time, in response to change in the environment, due to natural selection.

17.5 Alfred Wallace (1823–1913)

17 Variation, Evolution and Genetic Engineering

Natural selection

The Darwin–Wallace theory proposed a mechanism by which evolution occurred. This mechanism is called **natural selection**. From their studies, they observed four preconditions which led to two conclusions:

1. Individual members of a species are different from one another. There is variation within populations of a species.
2. Offspring in general resemble their parents (variation is inheritable).
3. Many more offspring are produced than can possibly survive and reproduce.
4. There is a struggle for existence and some individuals have variations that make them better suited to survive than other individuals.

From these four preconditions two observable conclusions occur:

1. The individual members of a species who survive to reproduce will tend to pass on to the succeeding generations the variation that allowed them to survive and this variation will become the norm.
2. As a result of this natural selection, populations change until they become so different from each other they will no longer interbreed and thus form a new species.

> **D** **Natural selection** is the mechanism by which members of a species, with genetic traits that allow them to survive in their environment, reproduce and pass these traits to the next generation.

Natural selection can be seen in action today. One form of rat poison is a chemical called **warfarin**. This is a substance that interferes with the correct clotting of the blood. Rats that ingest warfarin die from haemorrhaging (excessive bleeding). There is a **dominant allele** that confers resistance to warfarin, which was present in very low levels in the rat population. As the use of warfarin spread then the possession of the gene for warfarin resistance was a major advantage. Very quickly, the population of rats in the areas where warfarin was used became resistant to the poison. However, rats that carry the allele for warfarin resistance have a disadvantage in that they require large amounts of **vitamin K**. In areas where the poison is not used, it is a disadvantage to have the allele. In the long term, this type of natural selection could lead to two new species being produced. This process of generating new species is called **speciation**. It is also seen in the development of resistance to **antibiotics** by bacteria (see Chapter 19).

Evidence for evolution

There are many strands of evidence to suggest that evolution occurred. Some of this evidence was available to Darwin and Wallace but much has been discovered since they first published their theory. This evidence shows that there was common descent between different groups of organisms. Areas where evidence has been produced are varied and include some of the following:

1. The study of fossils
2. Comparative embryology
3. Comparative biochemistry
4. Comparative anatomy, which we will look at here in more detail.

Comparative anatomy

If we compare the structures found in different groups of organisms (comparative anatomy) we can obtain evidence of common descent. All the terrestrial groups of vertebrates, i.e. amphibians, reptiles, birds and mammals have a basic structure to their limbs that is common to them all.
This **pentadactyl (five-fingered) limb** is called a **homologous structure**. The limb is constructed from the same bones in each animal but in each case it is modified to do a different job (Fig 17.6).

- The human hand is the least specialised, as it is a general-purpose structure.
- The forelimb in the horse is modified for speed. The animal stands on one toe with the other toes miniscule or missing.
- Whales have broad paddle-like limbs for swimming.
- Bats have long extended fingers to hold the skin used for wings.

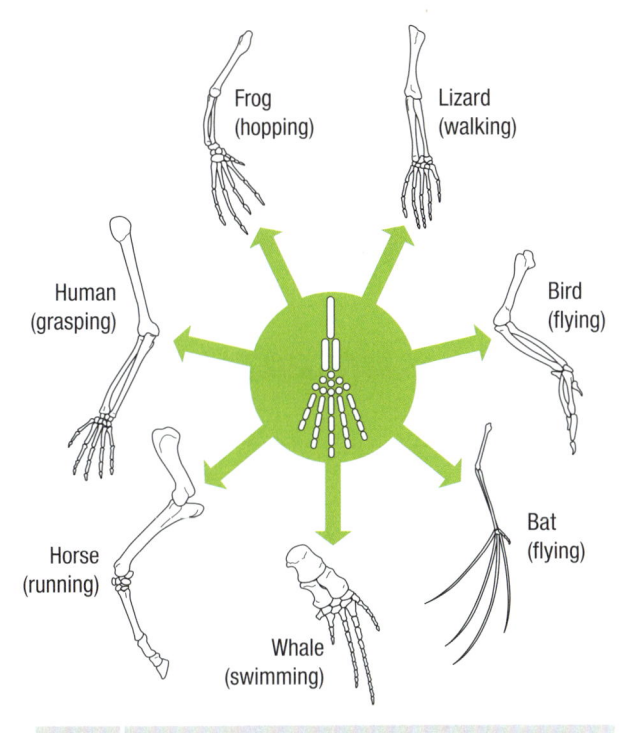

17.6 The pentadactyl forelimb in a number of vertebrates

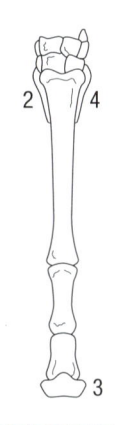

17.7 The forelimbs of a horse showing the remaining three toes

In some cases, structures have been lost, as they no longer serve a function. For example, the horse stands on its third toe. Toes number two and four are still present in a vestigial form (Fig 17.7), and toes one and five are no longer present.

Humans also have **vestigial structures** that point to evolution, e.g. ear lobe muscles. These structures had a function in the ancestors of the modern species. Their function is no longer required, but the structure has not been completely shed.

By using comparative anatomy, it is possible to show relationships between different organisms and get evidence for evolution.

Genetic engineering

Generations of farmers and plant breeders selectively bred animals or plants to suit their needs and as a result altered the species very considerably. Darwin was very interested, when researching evolution, in how pigeon fanciers had, in a few generations, changed the shape of a wild bird into hundreds of 'fancy' varieties. The same process is seen in the breeding of a huge number of 'thoroughbred' dogs from the original wolf (Fig 17.8).

Now it is possible to change the genetic make-up of organisms more radically. It is possible to alter the genes in one species or to take genes from one species and insert them into other species. This artificial process is called **genetic engineering**. The mechanism behind this is straightforward, even if it can be very difficult to get it to work successfully.

> **Genetic engineering** is the alteration and manipulation of genes.

There are six basic steps in genetic engineering:
1. Isolating the DNA.
2. Cutting the DNA.
3. Attaching the cut DNA to a vector (carrying) piece of DNA (ligation).
4. Transforming (changing) the target organism.
5. Cloning the transformed organism.
6. Getting the introduced gene expressed.

17.8 An example of one of many different types of dogs by selective breeding

17 Variation, Evolution and Genetic Engineering

The method of genetic engineering is illustrated by looking at how the **human growth hormone** gene was introduced into a bacterium.

1. Isolating the DNA:
   - The gene for growth hormone was identified (the source of the DNA). A copy of this gene was isolated from human cells.
2. Cutting the DNA:
   - The gene was cut out of the chromosome using an enzyme called a restriction enzyme that will cut DNA at specific places depending on the order of the bases.
   - A bacterial plasmid is used as a vector in this instance (it carries the human gene).
   - The plasmid is also cut using the same restriction enzyme.
3. Ligation of the DNA:
   - The plasmid and the gene that had been cut from the human cells were placed together with DNA ligase. This enzyme will stick cut pieces of DNA together.
4. Transforming the organism:
   - The plasmid was then inserted into a bacterial cell which is transformed.
5. Cloning the organism:
   - The bacterial cells were cloned and large numbers of the cells were produced.
6. Expressing the gene:
   - These bacterial cells then express the human gene and make the human growth hormone (Fig 17.9).

Organisms that have been altered using modern genetic engineering techniques are called **transgenic organisms**. There are many examples of these now.

Applications of genetic engineering
Bacteria

As we have seen above, bacteria have had the gene for human growth hormone inserted and have been engineered to produce human growth hormone.

- This is a cheaper method of producing human growth hormone than other available methods.
- In the past people were injected with HGH (human growth hormone) extracted from cadavers, which led to some people getting CJD, a human form of 'mad cow disease'.

Plants

Tomato plants have been genetically altered so that one of their genes, which produces an enzyme that leads to softening when ripe, no longer functions.

- The tomato plants produce tomatoes that ripen but remain hard.
- This fruit is much easier to harvest and results in a greater yield per acre (Fig 17.11).
- This tomato variety is used to produce tomato ketchup.

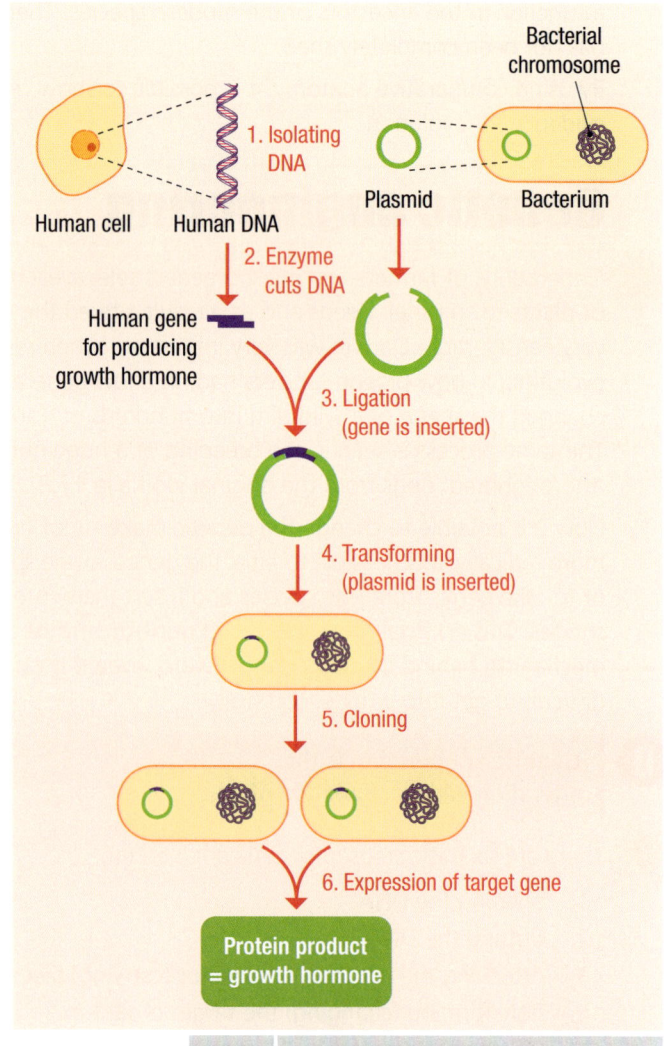

17.9 The production of transgenic bacteria that produce human growth hormone

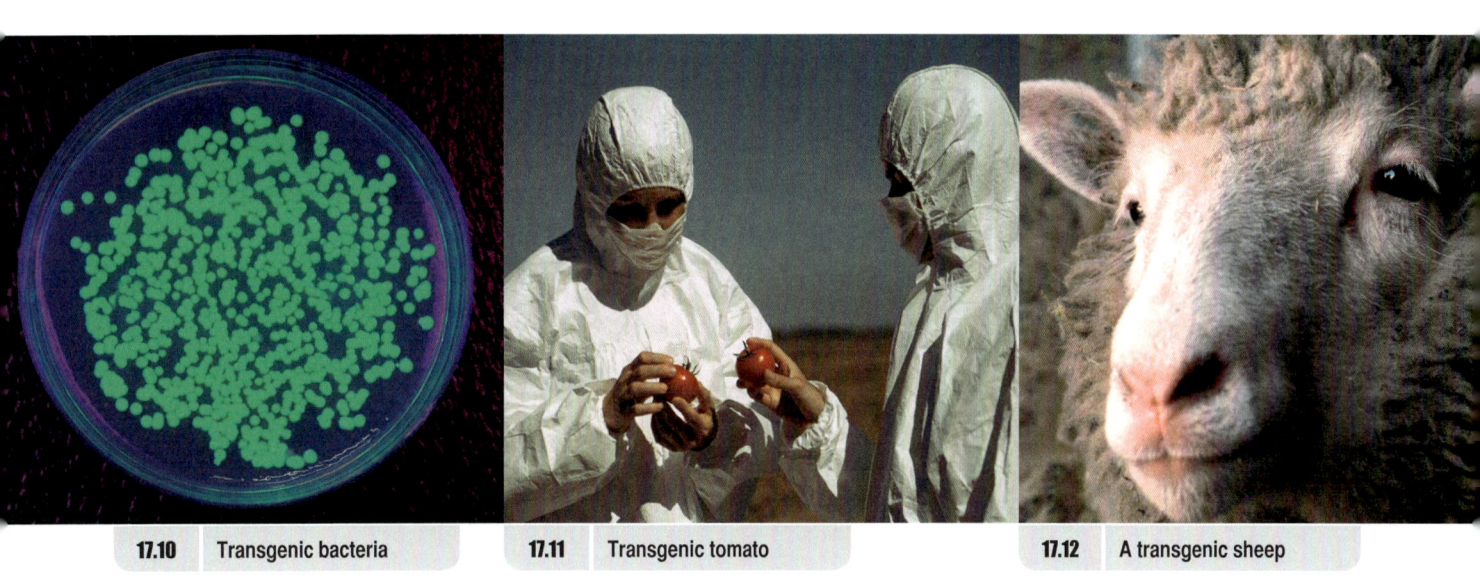

Variation, Evolution and Genetic Engineering | 17

17.10 Transgenic bacteria **17.11** Transgenic tomato **17.12** A transgenic sheep

Animals

Sheep have been produced into which the human gene for blood factor VIII has been introduced. The protein produced by this gene is needed for correct blood clotting in humans (Fig 17.12).

- Some haemophiliacs are missing this gene product and their blood does not clot. It is hoped that these sheep will provide a cheap and safe way to get factor VIII in the future by extracting it from their milk.

SYLLABUS REQUIREMENT:
Three applications of genetic engineering are required: one micro-organism, one plant and one animal.

Summary

- Variation is the difference between individuals of the same species. There are two types:
  - Acquired, which you pick up in your lifetime, e.g. playing a musical instrument.
  - Inherited, e.g. your eye colour.

- Inherited variation gives rise to evolution. Causes of this type of variation include:
  - Sexual reproduction, where the combination of chromosomes is shuffled in gamete formation and the fertilisation of these different chromosome combinations.
  - Mutation, either gene or chromosomal.

- Mutations are a change in the structure or amount of DNA. Types of mutation:
  - Gene mutation: Where a change is made in the DNA and thus a different protein is produced. This changed protein might be useful or might not.
  - Chromosome mutation can give rise to variation. In this case a piece of a chromosome or a whole chromosome is added or removed, e.g. Down syndrome.

- Mutations tend to be rare, random and harmful.

- X-rays, gamma rays and certain chemicals like mercury can cause mutations.

- These agents that cause mutations are called mutagens.

- Evolution is the changes between members of a species and the emergence of new species from older species over time, in response to changes in the environment, due to natural selection.

17 Variation, Evolution and Genetic Engineering

Summary

- Wallace and Darwin proposed the theory based on evidence that there was a common descent between different groups of organisms.
  - Darwin and Wallace noticed four things:
    1. Variation exists within a species.
    2. This variation is inheritable.
    3. Far more young are produced than can possibly survive.
    4. Some individuals within a species have a variation that gives them an advantage for survival.

    This is called the survival of the fittest.

    From this they concluded:
    1. That organisms that survive to breed will pass on the traits that gave them the advantage which allowed them to survive.
    2. Over time this will lead to the production of new species.

    This is known as the theory of natural selection.

- Evidence for evolution comes from:
  (i) fossils
  (ii) comparative embryology
  (iii) comparative biochemistry
  (iv) comparative anatomy. The pentadactyl limb, or its remnants, is found in all vertebrates modified to its specific function. This demonstrates descent from a common ancestor.

- Genetic engineering is the alteration and manipulation of genes. For this to occur six steps need to be taken:
  1. Isolating the DNA
  2. Cutting the DNA
  3. The cut DNA is attached to a vector piece of DNA (ligation)
  4. Transforming (changing) the target organism
  5. Cloning the transformed organism
  6. Getting the introduced gene expressed

- Applications of genetic engineering include:
  - The gene for softening is changed on the tomato plant.
  - A gene for a blood clotting factor is inserted into a sheep.
  - The gene for human growth hormone is inserted into bacteria.

Review questions

01
(a) What is a species?
(b) What are the two forms of variation?
(c) Which one is important in evolution?

02
(a) How does sexual reproduction lead to variation?
(b) What is the importance of meiosis in this process?

03
(a) What is meant by the term mutation?
(b) What are the two main types of mutation?
(c) Give an example of each type of mutation.

04
(a) What is wrong at the cellular level when someone has cystic fibrosis?
(b) How can two healthy parents produce a child with cystic fibrosis?

05
(a) What is a chromosome mutation?
(b) What causes Down syndrome to occur?

06
(a) Give two causes of mutations.
(b) What are agents of mutation called?
(c) Why are many of these carcinogenic?

07
(a) What is meant by the term evolution?
(b) Who were the scientists who first produced a credible theory of evolution?
(c) What was the process they suggested could cause evolution?

08 Different lines of evidence are currently used to support the theory of evolution.
(a) Give one example of these.
(b) Explain how it can be used to support the theory of evolution.

09
(a) What are the four observations on which the theory of natural selection was based?
(b) What conclusions can be drawn from these observations?

10
(a) What is genetic engineering?
(b) Genetic engineering could be said to be 'a modern development of an ancient process'. Comment on this statement.

11
(a) Describe the process undertaken to genetically modify an organism.
(b) What are transgenic organisms?
(c) Give one example of a transgenic plant, animal and bacterium.

Examination style questions

Section A

01
(a) Name the two types of variation.
(b) Which type of variation has an effect on evolution?
(c) Explain why this is the case.
(d) Name two causes of variation.
(e) Why is variation essential for evolution?

02
(a) What is meant by the term evolution?
(b) Name the two people associated with the scientifically accepted theory of evolution.
(c) Describe the process which they suggested caused evolution.
(d) Name one type of evidence that can be used to confirm the theory.
(e) How does this evidence confirm evolution?

17 Variation, Evolution and Genetic Engineering

Examination style questions

03 Diabetes mellitus is the most common worldwide endocrine disorder and its incidence is increasing at a dramatic rate. Many diabetics need daily injections of insulin hormone to treat this condition. Before DNA recombinant technology, insulin was only available from animal sources. Unfortunately, many people undergoing this treatment became allergic to this insulin. Since 1982 human insulin, produced by transgenic *E. coli* bacteria, has been available for the treatment of diabetes.

The flow chart below shows the main features involved in the production of human insulin by genetic engineering.

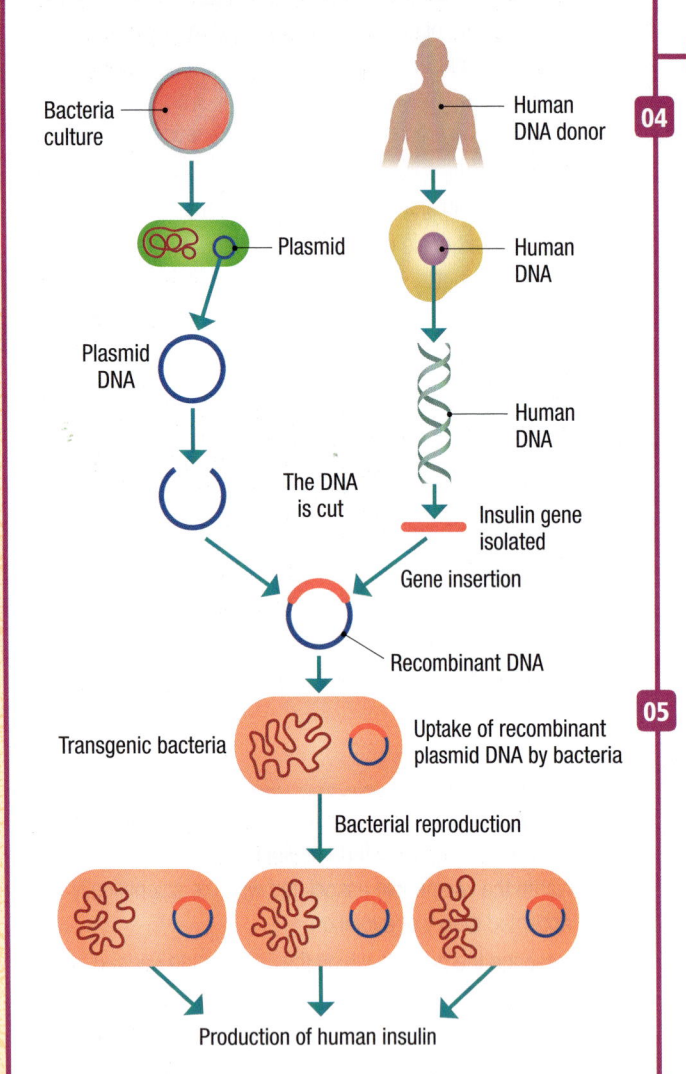

[Flow chart showing: Bacteria culture → Plasmid → Plasmid DNA → The DNA is cut; Human DNA donor → Human DNA → Insulin gene isolated; Gene insertion → Recombinant DNA → Uptake of recombinant plasmid DNA by bacteria → Transgenic bacteria → Bacterial reproduction → Production of human insulin]

(a) How is the insulin gene cut from the rest of the human DNA?
(b) What is a plasmid?
(c) The insertion of the insulin gene into the plasmid produced <u>recombinant DNA</u>. Explain the underlined term.
(d) The plasmid is used as a <u>vector</u> for the insulin gene. Explain the underlined term.
(e) Explain the term gene expression.
(f) Give one example in each case of the application of genetic engineering in the following: (i) plants, (ii) animals.

Section C

04 (a) (i) Explain the term *species*.
   (ii) A mule is a cross between a horse and a donkey. The diploid number of chromosomes is 64 in a horse and 62 in a donkey. How many chromosomes would there be in a somatic (body) cell of a mule? Explain your answer.

(b) (i) Define the term *evolution*. Give one source of evidence for evolution.
   (ii) Outline the main points of the Darwin–Wallace theory of evolution by natural selection.

(c) (i) What is meant by the term *genetic engineering*?
   (ii) Describe the process followed in the production of a genetically modified organism.
   (iii) Give an advantage of such an organism.

05 (a) (i) Explain the term *variation*.
   (ii) How is variation important in evolution?
   (iii) What are the possible types of variation?
   (iv) What are the causes of genetic variation?
   (v) Give an example of each type.

(b) (i) What is natural selection?
   (ii) What effect does this have on a population?
   (iii) How does this lead to evolution?
   (iv) Describe one source of evidence for evolution.

Leaving Certificate examination questions

Section A

01
(a) In genetics, what is meant by the term **variation**?
(b) Variation can result from mutation. Name **one** other cause of variation.
(c) Name **two** types of mutation.
(d) Name **two** agents responsible for increased rates of mutation.
(e) Briefly explain the significance of mutation in relation to natural selection.

2012 HL Q. 6

02
(a) What is *genetic engineering*?
(b) Name **three** processes involved in genetic engineering.
(c) Give an example of an application of genetic engineering in each of the following cases:
(i) a micro-organism, (ii) an animal, (iii) a plant.

2009 HL Q. 6

03 The diagram shows the distribution of heights in a group of men between the ages of 18 and 23.

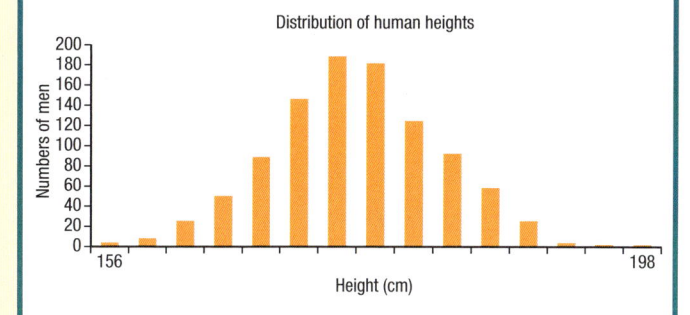

Distribution of human heights (bar chart: Numbers of men vs Height (cm), from 156 to 198)

What term is used by biologists to describe differences within a population with respect to features such as height?

State **two** factors that could be responsible for the differences shown.

Would you expect a similar distribution if the students were weighed instead of being measured for height?

Explain your answer.

What is a mutation?

State one cause of mutation.

Give an example of a condition, found in the human population, that results from a mutation.

2004 HL Q. 2

Section C

04
(a) The rabbit in the photograph has no pigment in its skin, fur or eyes. This is due to an inherited condition known as albinism. Such animals are unable to produce melanin, a protein pigment that gives colour to the skin, eyes, fur or hair. This condition makes an animal more likely to be preyed upon. Albinism is caused by genetic mutation. The gene that causes albinism (lack of pigment) is a recessive gene. If an animal has one gene for albinism and one gene for pigmentation, it will have enough genetic information to make pigment and the animal will not have this disorder. However, if both genes are recessive the result is albinism. At least 300 species of animal have albino individuals, e.g. rabbits, turtles, squirrels, deer and frogs.

(i) What are the main characteristics of albinism?
(ii) What is meant by the term *recessive* gene?
(iii) What is a mutation?
(iv) Mutations can lead to variation in organisms. Variations that make an organism better adapted to its environment can lead to evolution.
   1. What is meant by *evolution*?
   2. Name **one** of the scientists who first explained how evolution occurs by natural selection.
   3. Give **one** source of evidence for evolution.
(v) People with albinism should always apply a high-factor sunscreen when going outdoors and must avoid strong sunshine. Suggest a reason for these precautions.

(b) (i) Genetic engineering is regularly used in animals, plants and micro-organisms. What is meant by genetic engineering?
(ii) List **three** of the main procedures used in genetic engineering.
(iii) Give **two** examples of how genetic engineering is used.

2012 OL Q. 11

17 Variation, Evolution and Genetic Engineering

Leaving Certificate examination questions

05 (i) What is evolution?
(ii) What is natural selection?
(iii) Name **one** of the scientists who developed the theory of natural selection.
(iv) Give a brief account of the evidence for evolution from **one** named source.

2005 OL Q. 13 (c)

06 (i) Give a source of evidence for evolution.
(ii) Briefly outline the evidence from the source referred to in (i).

2013 HL Q. 11 (a)

07 (i) What is meant by the term *genetic engineering*?
(ii) In genetic engineering all or some of the following procedures may be involved:
Isolation
Cutting (restriction)
Transformation (ligation)
Introduction of base sequence changes
Expression

Briefly explain **each** of the above terms in the context of genetic engineering.
(iii) Give **one** application of genetic engineering in **any two** of the following:
1. An animal.
2. A plant.
3. A micro-organism.

2012 HL Q. 10 (c)

08 (i) Explain the term *species*.
(ii) Within a species a considerable degree of variation is usually seen. What is meant by *variation*? State **two** causes of variation.
(iii) What is the significance of inherited variation in the evolution of species?
(iv) State **two** types of evidence used to support the theory of evolution.

2009 HL Q. 10 (c)

Past examination questions

OL	2012 Q. 11 (b), (c)	2009 Q. 3	2008 Q. 11 (c)	2007 Q. 4 (e)
	2006 Q. 11 (c)	2005 Q. 13 (c)		
HL	2013 Q. 11 (a)	2012 Q. 6, Q. 10 (c)	2011 Q. 13 (a)	2009 Q. 6, Q. 10 (c)
	2006 Q. 12 (a), (c)	2005 Q. 10 (a)	2004 Q. 2, Q. 13 (c)	

UNIT 03

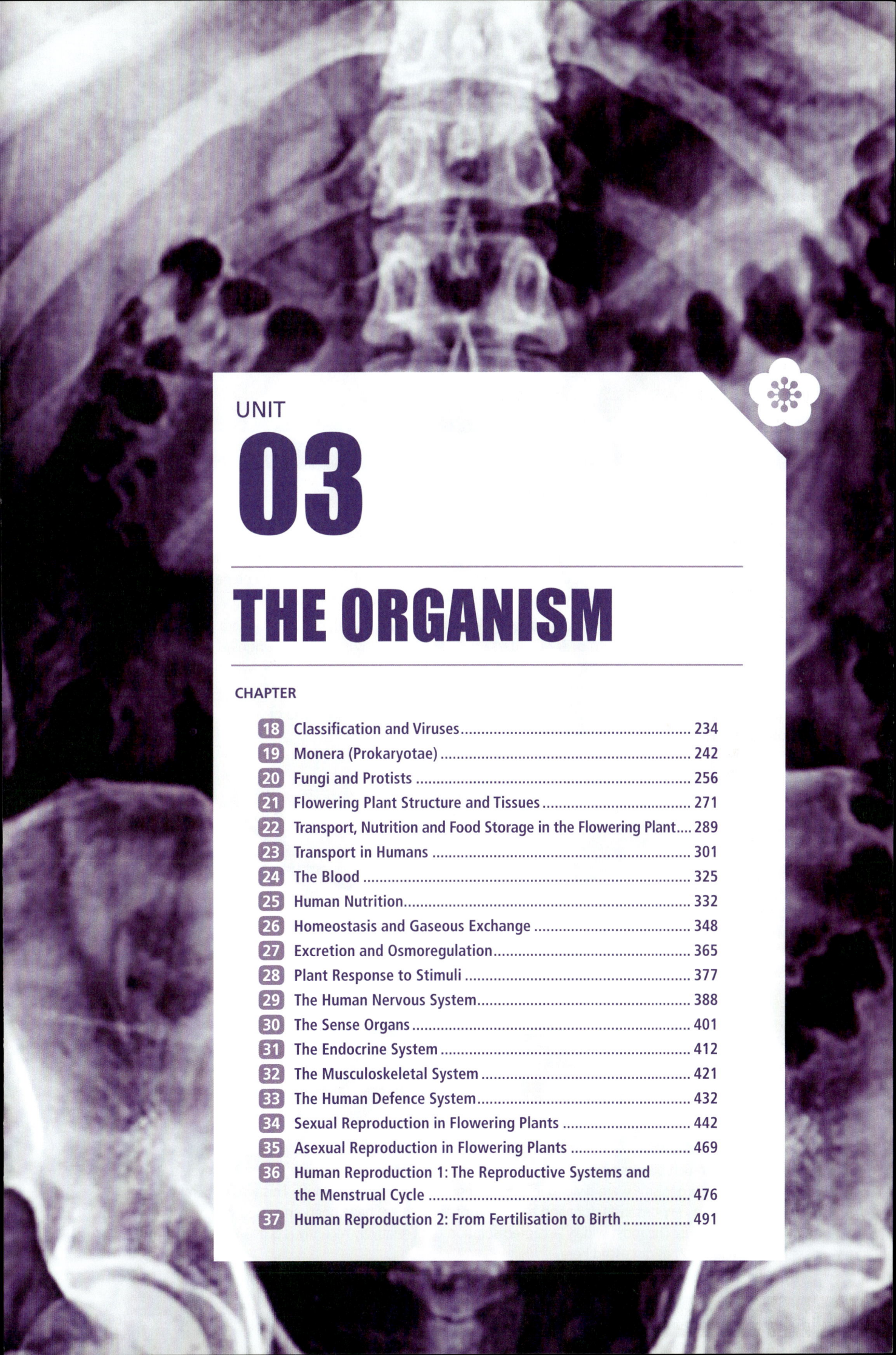

THE ORGANISM

CHAPTER

- 18 Classification and Viruses 234
- 19 Monera (Prokaryotae) 242
- 20 Fungi and Protists 256
- 21 Flowering Plant Structure and Tissues 271
- 22 Transport, Nutrition and Food Storage in the Flowering Plant 289
- 23 Transport in Humans 301
- 24 The Blood 325
- 25 Human Nutrition 332
- 26 Homeostasis and Gaseous Exchange 348
- 27 Excretion and Osmoregulation 365
- 28 Plant Response to Stimuli 377
- 29 The Human Nervous System 388
- 30 The Sense Organs 401
- 31 The Endocrine System 412
- 32 The Musculoskeletal System 421
- 33 The Human Defence System 432
- 34 Sexual Reproduction in Flowering Plants 442
- 35 Asexual Reproduction in Flowering Plants 469
- 36 Human Reproduction 1: The Reproductive Systems and the Menstrual Cycle 476
- 37 Human Reproduction 2: From Fertilisation to Birth 491

18 Classification and Viruses

After studying this chapter you should be able to:

1. Describe a five-kingdom system of classification.
2. Explain why viruses are not classified as living things.
3. Describe the structure and reproduction of viruses.
4. Give examples of medically and economically important viruses: one beneficial and two harmful from each.

Classification

A group of **organisms** that share a large number of physical features and can normally interbreed to produce fertile offspring is called a **species**. There are tens of millions of species on the planet. To study them, we need to have a way of classifying them to make such a study manageable.

Groups of closely related species are grouped together into a **genus** (plural, genera). Genera are grouped together into **families**, families into **orders**, orders into **classes**, classes into **phyla** (singular, phylum) and phyla into **kingdoms**. To name a specific organism, we use a **binomial system** in which we use the species and genus name, e.g. a human is called *Homo sapiens*.

There is little dispute between scientists about the species, genus and family name of most organisms (see Fig 18.1).

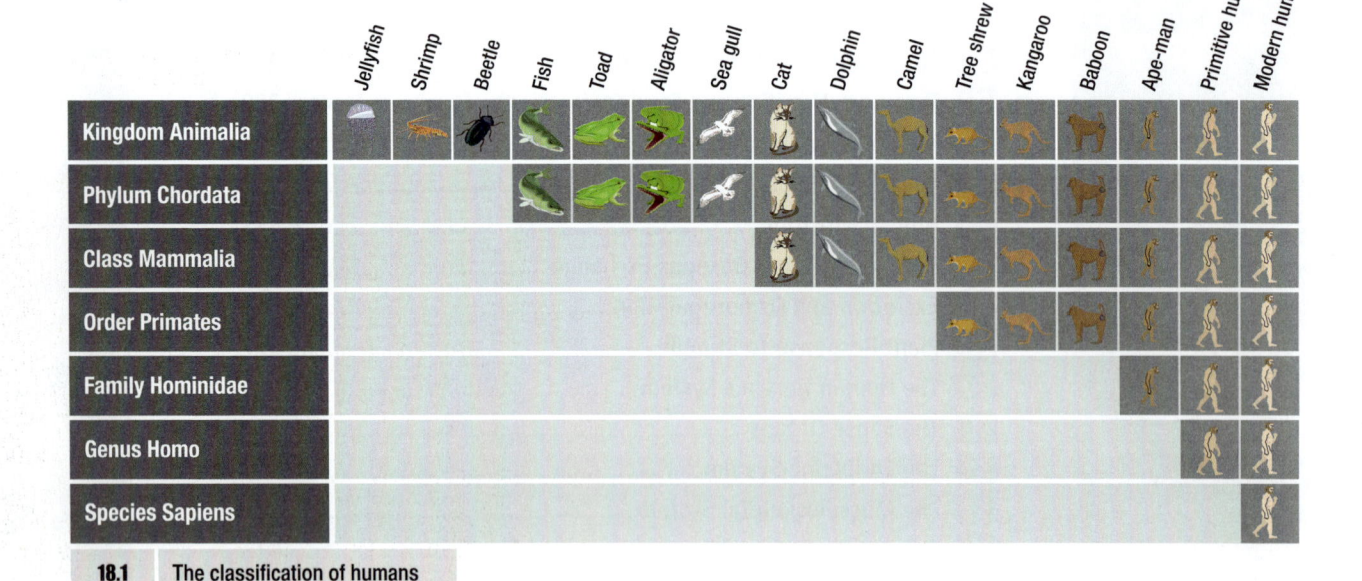

	Jellyfish	Shrimp	Beetle	Fish	Toad	Aligator	Sea gull	Cat	Dolphin	Camel	Tree shrew	Kangaroo	Baboon	Ape-man	Primitive human	Modern human
Kingdom Animalia	✓	✓	✓	✓	✓	✓	✓	✓	✓	✓	✓	✓	✓	✓	✓	✓
Phylum Chordata				✓	✓	✓	✓	✓	✓	✓	✓	✓	✓	✓	✓	✓
Class Mammalia								✓	✓	✓	✓	✓	✓	✓	✓	✓
Order Primates											✓	✓	✓	✓	✓	✓
Family Hominidae														✓	✓	✓
Genus Homo															✓	✓
Species Sapiens																✓

18.1 The classification of humans

However, there is much discussion and argument about much of the classification above this level. Originally all living organisms were divided into two kingdoms (animal and plant). This was generally recognised as being very unsatisfactory and a number of alternatives have been proposed with varying numbers of kingdoms. The most widely accepted solution until relatively recently is a five-kingdom classification (Fig 18.2) as discussed here.

Classification and Viruses | 18

The five kingdoms

1. Prokaryote
2. Protista
3. Fungus
4. Plant
5. Animal

PLANT KINGDOM (photosynthesis): Angiosperms, Gymnosperms, Ferns, Bryophytes, Horsetails

FUNGUS KINGDOM (absorb food): Fungi, Saccharomyces, Moulds

ANIMAL KINGDOM (ingest food): Vertebrates, Arthropods, Annelids, Molluscs, Cnidarians, Echinoderms, Nematodes, Flatworms

PROTIST KINGDOM: Red algae, Green algae, Brown algae, Water moulds, Ciliates, Amoeba, Protista

PROKARYOTE KINGDOM: Bacteria

18.2 The five-kingdom classification system

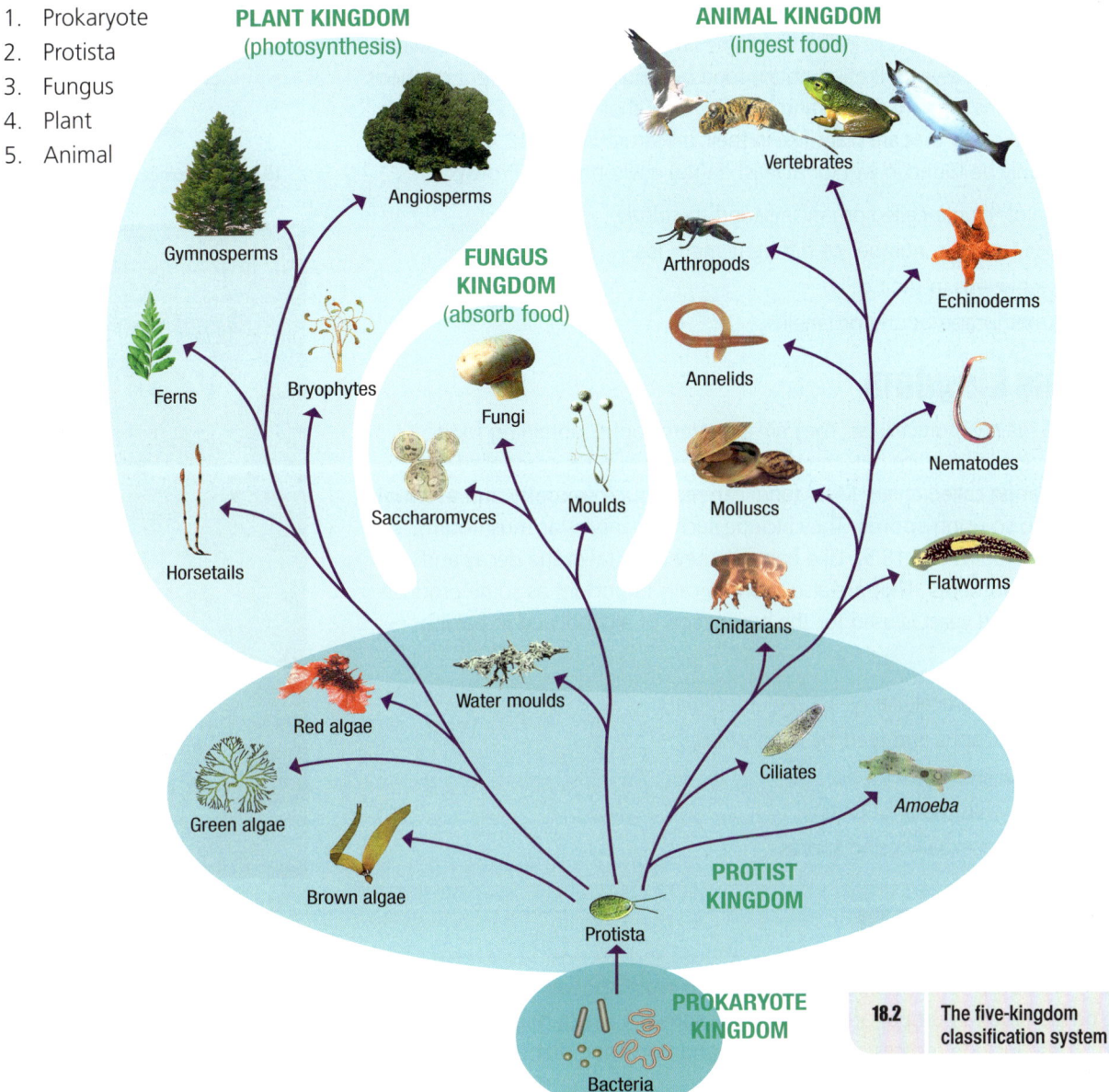

Monera (prokaryotae) kingdom

These are simple single-celled organisms that obtain food by a number of different methods – they are both **autotrophs** and **heterotrophs**. This group of organisms include the bacteria. They are found everywhere in the **biosphere**. They have been found in some of the most extreme environments on the planet. They are unquestionably the most numerous organisms on Earth. When most people think of bacteria they think of diseases they cause but in fact bacteria are essential for many activities that occur on the Earth without which we could not survive, e.g. the recycling of nutrients (see Chapter 4). They have a unique cellular structure as they have no **organelles** within the **cell** surrounded by membranes (Fig 18.3). These are called **prokaryote** cells.

Monera:

- are single-celled organisms;
- are heterotrophs or autotrophs;
- have no cell nucleus;
- have no membrane-bound organelles in their cells.

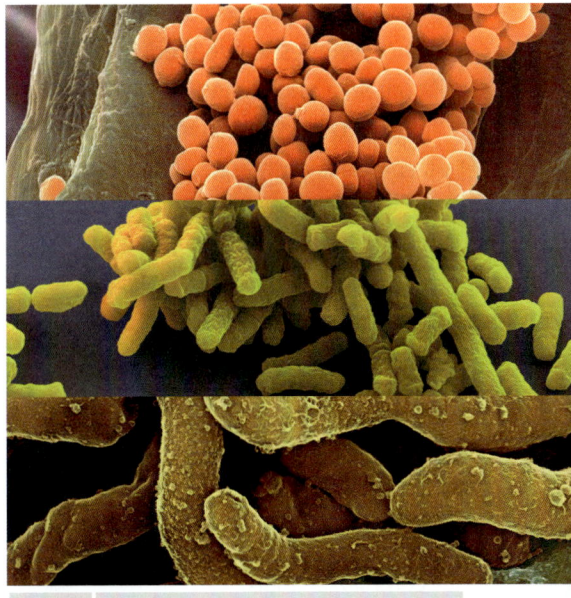

18.3 Monera as seen under an electron microscope

LIFE LEAVING CERTIFICATE BIOLOGY — UNIT 3 THE ORGANISM — 235

18 Classification and Viruses

Protista (protoctist) kingdom

This kingdom is made up of complex single-celled organisms and all of the algae. Many of the algae are single-celled but some are colonial or simple multicellular organisms, e.g. seaweed. Protists obtain food by a number of different methods. These organisms are very diverse and include many that are animal-like such as *Amoeba* and many that are plant-like in their cell structure (Fig 18.4). They will generally only be found in wet (or at least damp) environments. Protists:

- are mainly single-celled organisms (and the algae);
- obtain food by a number of different methods;
- have a nucleus in their cells;
- have membrane-bound organelles.

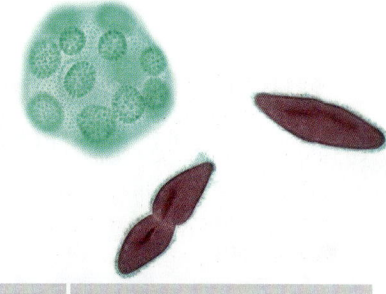

18.4 A number of protists

Fungus kingdom

Fungi are mainly multicellular. They are all heterotrophs, obtaining food by absorption. Like plant cells they have a cell wall but it is composed of a polysaccharide called chitin. Most fungi can reproduce **sexually** and **asexually** but they do so using **spores**. They include such organisms as mushrooms, yeasts and moulds (Fig 18.5). Like bacteria they are vital in the decay and recycling of nutrients. They are also economically important as some produce **antibiotics** and yeast is used for the production of alcohol and in baking.

Fungi:

- are mainly multicellular (yeast are unicellular);
- are heterotrophs and feed by absorption;
- have a nucleus in their cells;
- have cell walls made of chitin;
- reproduce asexually using spores.

Plant kingdom

These are autotrophic, multicellular organisms that **photosynthesise**. They are divided into a number of major groups, some of which might be familiar to you. These include mosses, ferns, conifers and flowering plants (shown in Fig 18.2). In general plants (Fig 18.6):

- are complex multicellular organisms;
- photosynthesise (are producers);
- contain a nucleus in their cells;
- have a cellulose cell wall;
- reproduce both asexually and sexually.

18.5 A fungus

18.6 A number of different plants in a woodland

Animal kingdom

Animals are multicellular heterotropic organisms that feed by ingestion. Even more so than plants, animals contain a large variety of different organisms from jellyfish and flatworms to insects and mammals. In general animals:

- are complex multicellular organisms;
- are heterotrophs and feed by ingestion;
- have a nucleus in their cells;
- have nervous and muscular systems (may not be present in less complex animals);
- reproduce sexually.

18.7 A number of different animals on the African plains

This five-kingdom method of classification is not perfect and not all organisms fit neatly into the group to which they are assigned. In more recent years a different form of classification has been proposed where all life is divided into three domains (or super-kingdoms): domain Bacteria, domain Archaea, which are the more advanced bacteria (this breaks up the Monera kingdom), and domain Eukarya. This final domain is divided into multiple kingdoms including the plants, fungi and animals. The Protist kingdom is split up into a number of groups in this classification.

SYLLABUS REQUIREMENT:

You only need to know about the five-kingdom classification.

Viruses

Viruses do not appear in the classification of living things (Fig 18.2). There is much discussion between biologists as to whether they are living or non-living. They have a structure that is simpler than cells, and they can **replicate** and pass on information from one generation to the next. However, they can only reproduce within the cell of another living organism and have no organelles or **metabolism** outside their host.

Viruses are too small to be seen by light microscopes and were discovered by a biologist looking at a tobacco plant with tobacco mosaic disease in 1892. The diseased plant was crushed and the resultant liquid was passed through a filter fine enough to prevent the passage of bacteria. This extract still caused the disease when rubbed on an uninfected plant. The filterable agent that caused the disease was called a virus, although it was some time before it was seen under an electron microscope. Examples of viruses include the influenza virus ('flu'), human immunodeficient virus (causes AIDS), tobacco mosaic virus (attacks tobacco plants) and chickenpox. Recently some very large viruses have been discovered but in general they are very small (Fig 18.8).

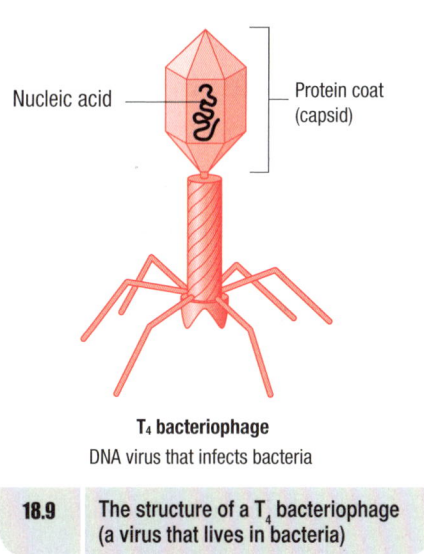

18.8 Some examples of viruses (the round structures) attached to cells

18.9 The structure of a T_4 bacteriophage (a virus that lives in bacteria)

T_4 bacteriophage
DNA virus that infects bacteria

Viral structure

All viruses have a simple structure consisting of:

- A core of nucleic acid (either **DNA** or **RNA**, never both).
- A coat of proteins (capsid) on its surface (Fig 18.9).

Obligate parasites can only replicate within another living cell.

Some animal viruses have a membrane coat outside this made from the membrane of the cell that was infected; this membrane usually has virus proteins inserted into it, e.g. influenza.

Viruses are not composed of cells and do not have any of the structures associated with either prokaryote or eukaryote cells except nucleic acid. They do not fulfil the cellular definition of living things. This has led some scientists to suggest that viruses are simply pieces of genetic material that have escaped from cells, as they are DNA or RNA surrounded by a protein coat.

When viruses come to make copies of themselves, they are incapable of doing this without using the metabolism of other living cells. They are not capable of reproducing, rather they replicate. As all viruses can only replicate within other living cells, they are described as **obligate parasites**. To infect a cell, the surface proteins of the virus must be able to bind with proteins on the surface of the cell. This is what causes the specificity of viruses.

Virus replication

When viruses arrive at their host cell:

1. First of all they attach to their target proteins on the surface.
2. They insert their nucleic acid into the cell thus infecting the cell.
3. The virus uses its DNA (or RNA) to inactivate the host DNA and the workings of the host cell.
4. The virus makes the host produce copies of the viral proteins and viral DNA or RNA.
5. These are then assembled into new viruses.
6. They are released by the lysis (bursting) of the host cell.

Alternatively, the viral DNA may be inserted into the host DNA where it is integrated, lies dormant and passed on from one cell to the next when replication takes place.

1. These cells are called **lysogenic cells**.
2. This viral DNA may have no apparent effect, but many generations later environmental factors, e.g. radiation or chemicals, may cause the virus to become active again, making more copies of itself and lysing the host cell (Fig 18.10).

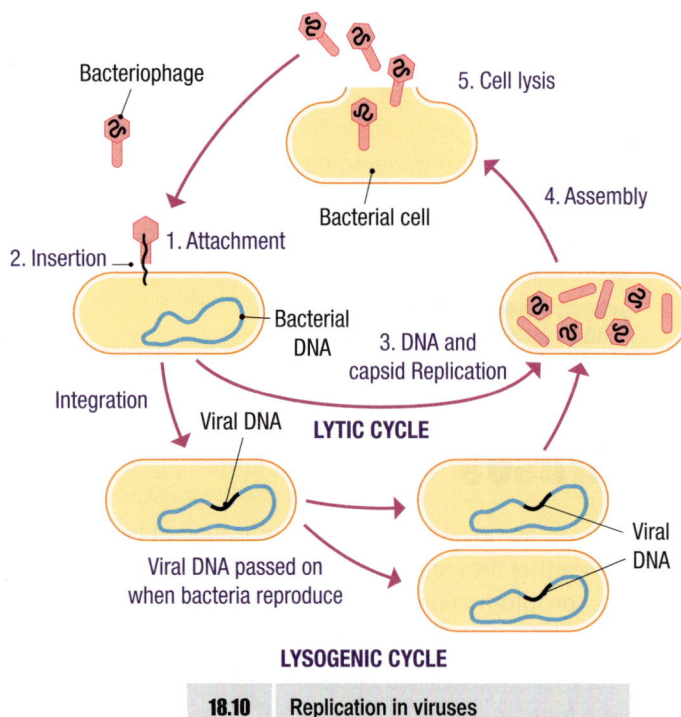

18.10 Replication in viruses

Economic effects of viruses

Harmful medical effects

Viruses are of major importance in medicine as they cause so many diseases:

- AIDS (HIV)
- Influenza ('flu')
- Hepatitis
- Measles
- Ebola
- Rubella

This is compounded by the fact that **antibiotics** cannot cure viral diseases. (Antibiotics are chemicals produced by micro-organisms which are only toxic to bacteria.) Some viral diseases can be protected against by using **vaccination**, e.g. chickenpox or measles. Other diseases cannot be protected against in this way, e.g. HIV. Some progress has being made in producing medicines that interfere with viral replication, called anti-viral medication.

Beneficial medical effects

Beneficial viruses are more difficult to find.

1. Lambda (D) bacteriophages attack *E. coli* and could be said to be useful, as they destroy this harmful bacterium.
2. Viruses can be used in the production of vaccines, i.e. MMR vaccine.

Harmful economic effects

1. Ill people also have an effect on the economy as they cannot work and need to be cared for. It is estimated that 35 million people are infected with HIV, causing devastation to their societies. In sub-Saharan Africa thousands of children have been orphaned due to the early death of their parents from AIDS.
2. Not only do viruses damage people's health, they are also of economic significance as they damage crops, e.g. tomato mosaic virus.

Beneficial economic effects

1. In genetic engineering many viruses are used as vectors to carry genes from the source to the host cell.
2. Viruses can be used as biological controls for pests, i.e. myxomatosis used to kill rabbits.

SYLLABUS REQUIREMENT:

You need to know one beneficial and two harmful effects from the medical and economic effects of viruses.

Summary

- Living things can be classified into five kingdoms.
- Monera (Prokaryotae) kingdom:
  - are single-celled organisms;
  - obtain food by a number of different methods (autotrophs and heterotrophs);
  - have no cell nucleus;
  - have no membrane-bound organelles in their cells;
  - are prokaryotes.
- Protist (Protoctist) kingdom:
  - are mainly single-celled organisms (and the algae);
  - obtain their food by a number of different methods;
  - have a nucleus in their cells.
- Fungus kingdom:
  - are mainly multicellular (yeast are unicellular);
  - are heterotrophs and obtain their food by absorption;
  - have a nucleus in their cells;
  - have cell walls made of chitin;
  - reproduce using spores.
- Plant kingdom:
  - are complex multicellular organisms;
  - photosynthesise;
  - contain a nucleus in their cells;
  - have a cellulose cell wall;
  - reproduce both asexually and sexually.
- Animal kingdom:
  - have a nucleus in their cells;
  - are complex multicellular organisms;
  - are heterotrophs and obtain their food by ingestion;
  - have nervous and muscular systems (may not be present in simple animals);
  - reproduce sexually mainly.
- Viruses:
  - are non-living;
  - are non-cellular and have no organelles;
  - contain DNA (or RNA), and a protein coat (capsid);
  - only replicate within another organism, i.e. they are obligate parasites;
  - do not have independent metabolism;
  - take over the host cell and make it produce more copies of the virus;
  - may sometimes remain dormant in the host.
- Harmful effects:
  - Viruses have a major effect on the medical and social life of a society by causing disease/death to humans or damaging food crops or animals, e.g. Ebola, Rubella, HIV, measles, tomato mosaic disease, AIDS orphans large numbers of children.
- Beneficial effects:
  - They can be useful by killing disease-causing bacteria/fungi.
  - They are used as vectors in genetic engineering.

18 Classification and Viruses

Review questions

01
(a) What is a species?
(b) What is binomial classification?
(c) Why do biologists classify organisms?

02
(a) Into what were all living things originally classified?
(b) Why was this unsatisfactory?

03
(a) What are the five kingdoms used to classify organisms now?
(b) Give two characteristics used to classify each kingdom.
(c) Why do you think scientists are changing their method of classification?

04
(a) Why are viruses not classified as living things?
(b) Do you think they should be?
(c) Justify your answer in (b).

05
(a) What are the two components of a virus?
(b) Where are these found?
(c) How does a virus target its host cell?
(d) What is meant by the term replicate in relation to a virus?

06
(a) Describe what happens when a virus meets its target cell.
(b) A virus is called an 'obligate parasite'. What does this mean?
(c) What are the two possible results when a virus enters a cell?

07
(a) Give two harmful and one beneficial effect of a virus.
(b) Why would it be wrong to give a person with a viral infection an antibiotic?
(c) How should this person be treated?

Examination style questions

Section A

01
(a) Into what kingdom would you put a mushroom?
(b) Give two reasons why you would place it here.
(c) What characteristic makes bacteria different from all other living things?
(d) Into what kingdom would you place bacteria?
(e) What type of nutrition is found in all plants?
(f) How is this type of nutrition different for animals?

02
(a) What are the components of all viruses?
(b) How does a virus target its host cell?
(c) What part of the virus structure affects the host cell?
(d) How does it do this?
(e) What is replication?

Section C

03
(a) (i) Draw a labelled diagram to show the structure of a typical virus.
(ii) Which part targets the host cell?
(iii) Which part affects the host DNA?
(b) (i) What are the difficulties in classifying viruses as living?
(ii) Viruses are described as 'obligate parasites'. What does this term mean?
(iii) Describe what can happen if a virus meets its host cell.
(iv) Give two harmful effects of viruses.
(v) Give one beneficial effect of viruses.
(c) Once a virus has entered its host it will replicate.
(i) What does this term mean?
(ii) Describe briefly how a virus will replicate.

04
(a) Why are viruses sometimes classified as non-living?
(b) The method of entry and use of a living cell by viruses is so ingenious that the virus may be mankind's deadliest enemy. Viruses have resisted the most advanced efforts of modern science to eliminate them. Describe how a virus enters and uses the living cell for viral reproduction.
(c) Give two examples of diseases caused by viruses.
(d) Draw a labelled diagram to show the structure of a typical virus.

Classification and Viruses 18

Leaving Certificate examination questions

Section A

01 (a) The living world may be divided into five kingdoms: Monera, Protista, Fungi, Plantae, Animalia.

In the case of each of the following pairs of kingdoms give any structural feature of members of the first-named kingdom not found in members of the second kingdom.
  (i) Fungi and Animalia.
  (ii) Plantae and Fungi.
  (iii) Animalia and Monera.
  (iv) Protista and Animalia.

(b) In **each** of the following cases, name an organism that fits the description.
  (i) A multicellular fungus.
  (ii) A member of the Protista that catches and consumes smaller organisms.
  (iii) A harmful member of the Monera.

2014 HL Q. 4

02 The diagram shows a virus attached to a host cell.

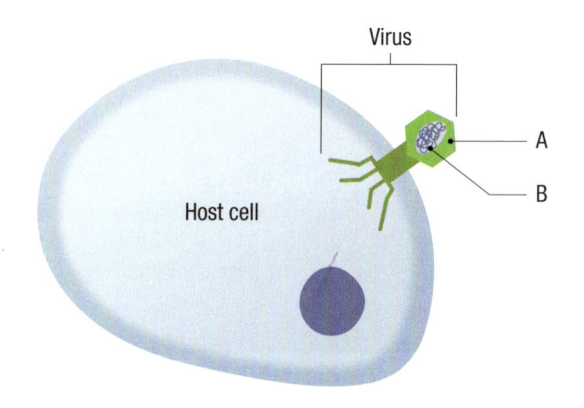

(a) (i) What is part A made of?
    (ii) What is part B made of?
(b) Briefly describe how viruses reproduce.
(c) During 2009 swine flu spread through the population of many countries. Younger people were more at risk of becoming ill with swine flu than older people. Using your knowledge of the immune system, suggest a reason for this.

2010 HL Q. 6

Section C

03 (i) Explain why it is difficult to classify viruses as living organisms.
(ii) Give the **two** main chemical components of a virus.
(iii) Briefly describe how viruses reproduce.
(iv) Give **one** way in which viruses are beneficial and **one** way in which they are harmful.

2009 OL Q. 12 (c)

04 (i) A virus has been described as a piece of genetic material that has escaped from a cell. Give one piece of evidence that supports this description.
(ii) Viruses are examples of obligate parasites. Explain why this is the case.
(iii) Give an example of how a virus might be beneficial to mankind.

2013 HL Q. 12 (a)

05 Just over fifty years ago the myxoma virus was brought to Ireland. The disease for which it is responsible in rabbits, myxomatosis, quickly decimated the wild population. Now, however, the disease is much less common and is responsible for far fewer deaths.
(i) Why do you think that the rabbit population was decimated when the myxoma virus was first brought to Ireland?
(ii) Suggest a reason why myxomatosis is no longer a major threat to the Irish rabbit population.
(iii) The use of one species to control the population of another species is called biological control. Suggest **one** advantage and **one** disadvantage of biological control.
(iv) The human immunodeficiency virus (HIV) is responsible for AIDS in the human population. Would you expect a similar trend to that shown by myxomatosis as time passes? Explain your answer.
(v) Outline briefly how a virus replicates (reproduces).

2008 HL Q. 15 (b)

Past examination questions

OL	2011 Q. 15 (c) (i) (ii)	2009 Q. 12 (c)		
HL	2014 Q. 4	2013 Q. 12 (a)	2010 Q. 6	2009 Q. 15 (c) (v)
	2008 Q. 15 (b)	2007 Q. 14 (b)	2005 Q. 15 (a)	SEC Sample Q. 15 (c)

19 Monera (Prokaryotae)

After studying this chapter you should be able to:

1. Explain how bacteria are divided into groups by shape.
2. Describe the structure of bacterial cells.
3. Describe the reproduction of bacteria.
4. Describe the nutrition of bacteria.
5. Describe the factors affecting the growth of bacteria.
6. Give examples of economically important bacteria: two beneficial and two harmful.
7. Explain the term pathogen.
8. Define antibiotics and give their role in medicine.
9. Describe the possible problems of misuse of antibiotics.
10. Distinguish between sterility and asepsis.
11. Describe the necessary safety precautions to be taken when working with micro-organisms, including procedures for the safe containment and disposal of contaminated material.
12. **HL** Distinguish between the prokaryotic nature of bacteria and the eukaryotic nature of other kingdoms.
13. **HL** Describe the growth patterns of micro-organisms.
14. **HL** Describe how industrialists can keep micro-organisms in the growth phase that best suits the production of the required product.

Monera (prokaryotae) kingdom

We will study one group of **organisms** from this kingdom. These are the bacteria, the study of which is called bacteriology. Bacteria are one of a few groups of organisms commonly called microbes.

As we discovered in the last chapter Monera have the following characteristics:

- They are single-celled organisms.
- They can be **heterotrophs** or **autotrophs**.
- They have no cell nucleus.
- They have no membrane-bound **organelles** in their cells.

1. Bacteria can be divided into groups using many different criteria. We shall simply divide them into three groups using shape (Fig 19.1):

   - Spherical (**cocci**): These can be found singly, in clusters, in pairs or in chains (Fig 19.2).
   - Rods: These can occur singly or in chains and may have flagella for movement (Fig 19.3).
   - Spiral: Often contain flagella for movement (Fig 19.4).

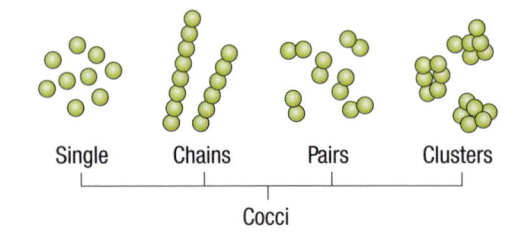

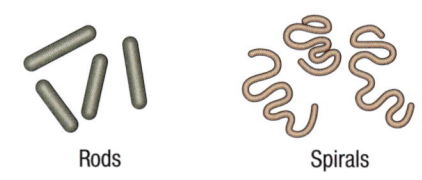

19.1 The three types of bacterial shapes

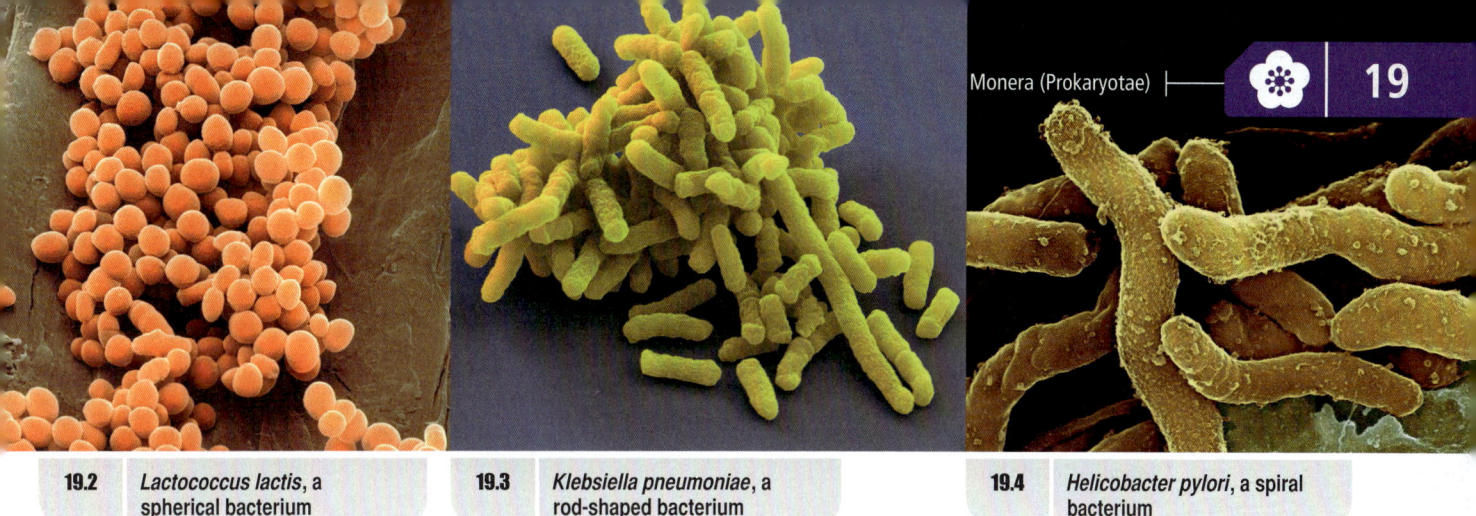

| 19.2 | *Lactococcus lactis*, a spherical bacterium | 19.3 | *Klebsiella pneumoniae*, a rod-shaped bacterium | 19.4 | *Helicobacter pylori*, a spiral bacterium |

Structure

All bacteria have a simple cellular structure (Fig 19.5):

- On the outside of all bacteria, there is a cell wall.
- Some bacteria have a gelatinous sheath around this cell wall, particularly if they are **pathogenic** (disease-causing); others may have a dry capsule.
- Motile bacteria have flagella.
- There is a cell (plasma) membrane between the cell wall and the cytoplasm of all bacteria.

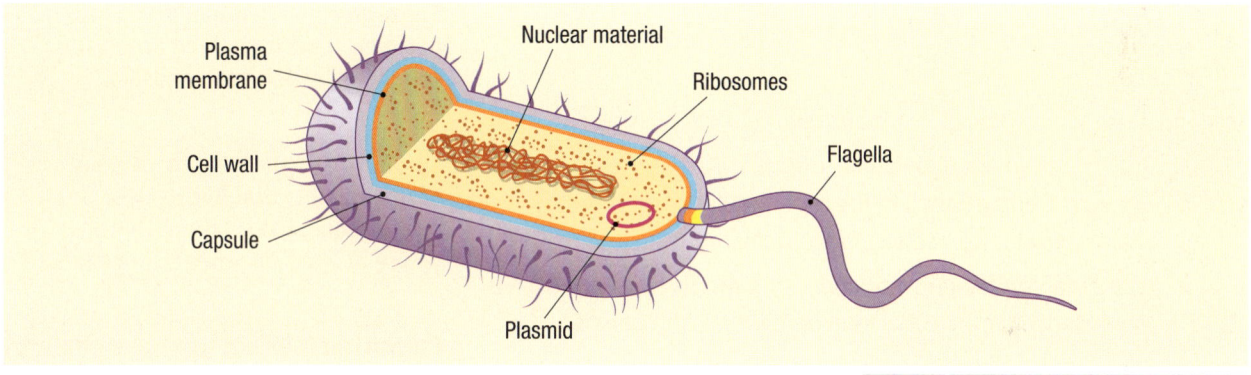

19.5 A diagram of a bacterial cell

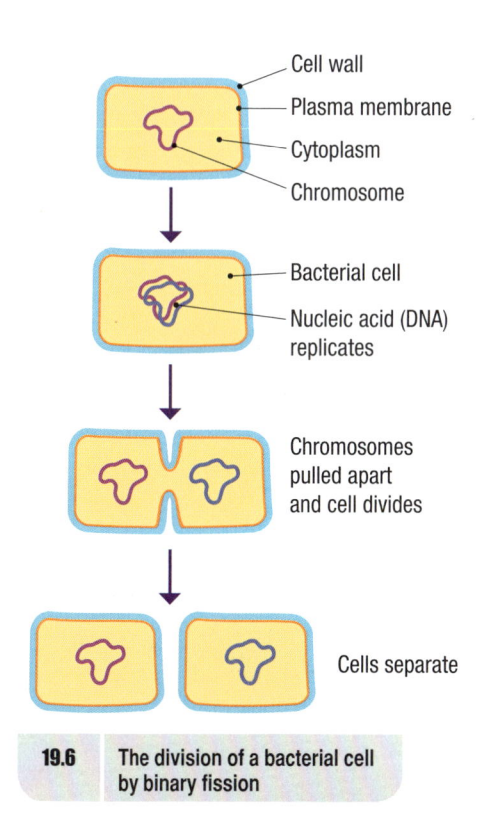

Internally, the bacterial cell is very simple:

- There are no membrane-bound **organelles** found within the cell but **cytoplasm** and **ribosomes** are present.
- The nucleic material is a single **chromosome** of **DNA** that is not contained within a membrane.
- Many bacteria also contain other circular pieces of DNA. These small pieces of DNA usually contain only a few **genes** and are called **plasmids**. In many disease-causing (pathogenic) bacteria, the genes for drug resistance are carried on these plasmids. Bacteria can **replicate** plasmids and can pass them on from one bacterium to the next. This is how drug resistance is spreading among pathogenic bacteria.
- Many bacteria produce **spores**, often endospores, in unfavourable conditions. Spores are thick-walled structures which allow the bacteria survive the unfavourable conditions (Fig 19.8).

Reproduction

Bacteria reproduce by a simple process of **binary fission**. This is a form of **asexual reproduction**.

In the process, the chromosome is replicated. Each chromosome is fastened onto the cell membrane. As the cell grows, the two chromosomes are pulled apart. When doubled in size, it divides down the middle and forms two equal sized cells each with one chromosome (Fig 19.6).

19.6 The division of a bacterial cell by binary fission

19 Monera (Prokaryotae)

Nutrition

Bacteria can be autotrophic or heterotrophic.

1. Autotrophic bacteria make their own food by one of two methods.
   (a) **Photosynthetic** bacteria make their own food by using light energy to make carbohydrate. This is done slightly differently to photosynthesis in plants. Cyanobacteria (blue-green bacteria) are one such group.
   (b) **Chemosynthetic** bacteria use the energy released by a chemical reaction to fuel for carbohydrate production. Nitrifying bacteria found in the soil belong to this group (see nitrogen cycle, Chapter 4).
2. Heterotrophic bacteria have to take in food produced by other organisms. These are the most common type of bacteria.

They are either free-living **saprophytes** or they live in a close relationship with other bacteria (**symbiotes**).

(a) Saprophytes live off dead material, e.g. bacteria involved in decay.
(b) There are three types of symbiotic relationships possible:
   1. Both organisms may benefit (**mutualism**), e.g. nitrogen-fixing bacteria in the root nodules of legumes, vitamin-producing bacteria in the human gut.
   2. One organism benefits but does not harm its host (**commensalism**), i.e. bacteria on the skin of a person.
   3. One organism benefits and harms its host (**parasitism**), e.g. disease-causing bacteria (*Streptococci*).

> **Autotrophic bacteria** are bacteria capable of making their own food using energy.

> **Photosynthetic bacteria** are bacteria that use sunlight to make their own food.

> **Chemosynthetic bacteria** are bacteria that are capable of making their own food using energy from a chemical reaction.

> **Heterotrophs** are organisms which are not capable of making their own food.

> **Saprophytes** are organisms which get their food from dead organisms commonly called decomposers.

> **Symbiotic organisms** are organisms of one species that live in close relationship with a second species where at least one organism benefits.

> **Parasitism** is where two organisms of different species live together, where one benefits and causes harm to the other.

19.7 Bacterial nutrition

Bacteria
- Autotroph
  - Photosynthetic
  - Chemosynthetic
- Heterotrophs (aerobic and anaerobic)
  - Saprophytes
  - Symbiotes
    - Mutualism
    - Commensalism
    - Parasitism

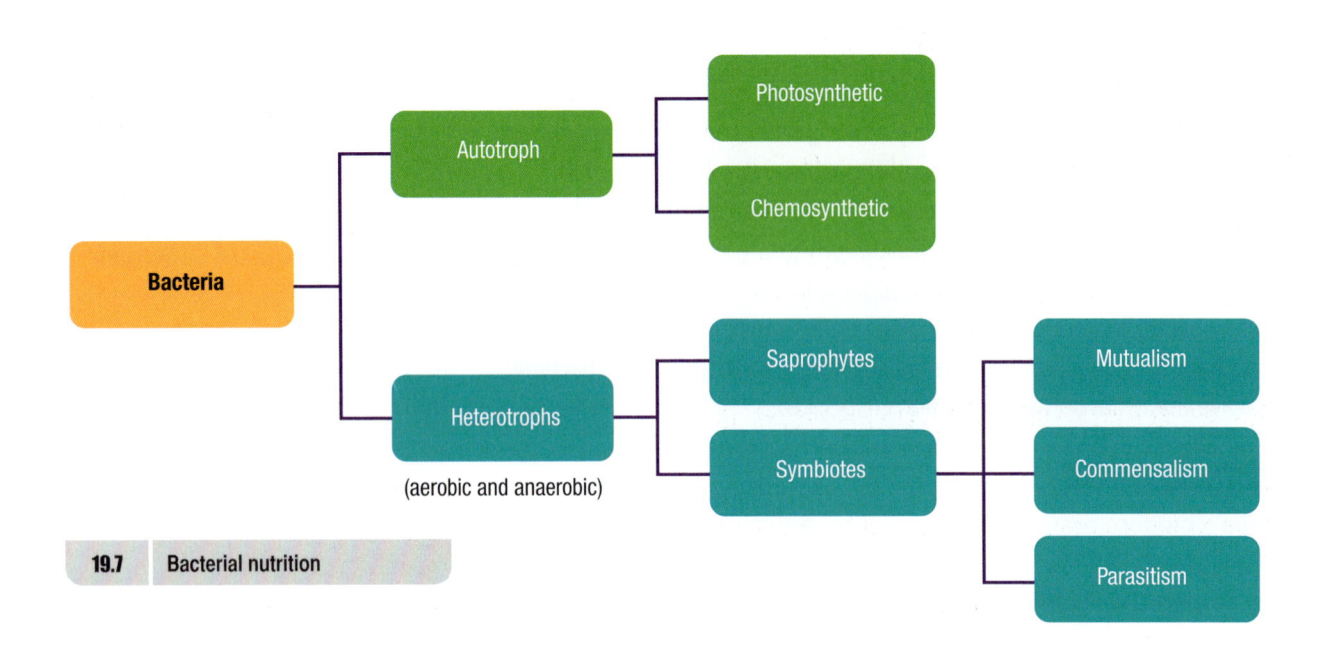

Factors affecting growth

There are many factors that affect the growth of bacteria.

Oxygen

Most organisms need oxygen to produce energy in respiration.

1. Many heterotrophic bacteria can live in the presence or absence of oxygen, undertaking **aerobic respiration** or **anaerobic respiration** as the conditions demand; such bacteria are called **facultative anaerobes**, e.g. *E. coli*.
2. Some bacteria cannot live in the presence of oxygen and are **obligate anaerobes**, e.g. *Clostridium botulinum* which causes botulism, a form of food poisoning.
3. Others are **obligate aerobes** that can only live in the presence of oxygen, e.g. *Streptococcus aureus* which can cause skin infections.

Temperature

Temperature will affect the growth of bacteria. This is because each type of bacteria will have its own specific **enzymes**, each of which will function best at a particular temperature:

1. Most grow in the temperature range 10–30°C.
2. Some grow better at high temperatures (e.g. bacteria found in hot springs).
3. Others grow better at lower temperatures (bacteria found in snow). But in general bacteria will have very slow growth rates or will stop growing at low temperatures.

pH

Different bacteria will grow better at different pHs. The enzymes found in each type of bacteria will function best at a specific pH. Most, but not all, live in the pH range 6–8. Those causing stomach ulcers, for example, live at a very low pH.

Environmental concentration

The concentration of the solutions that surround bacteria can also affect how they grow, e.g. certain bacteria found only in the Dead Sea, can survive high salt concentrations. For most bacteria solutions of a high salt/sugar concentration will cause them to lose water due to osmosis, and will kill them. This is the basis of preserving food using jam or sugar (see Chapter 10).

Other factors can affect the growth of bacteria, e.g. pressure (some bacteria are found exclusively in areas of high pressure, for example deep in the sea).

Survival in adverse conditions

When environmental conditions are unfavourable to the bacteria many of them have the ability to produce spores. The DNA of the bacteria replicates, the contents of the cell shrink and a tough outer coat is formed within the original cell, producing an **endospore** (Fig 19.8). These spores will resist desiccation and high temperatures and are the reason why very high temperatures are needed to ensure that all bacteria are killed. When favourable conditions return, the spores take in water and expand, breaking their tough outer wall. The new bacterium will divide by binary fission.

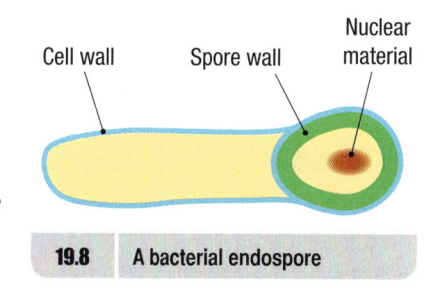

19.8 A bacterial endospore

The economic importance of bacteria

There are many bacteria that are harmful to humans and more that are beneficial (see Table 19.1):
- Harmful bacteria can lead to decay where we don't want decay, i.e. food spoilage.
- Bacteria can cause disease in humans and other animals and plants, i.e. typhoid-causing bacteria.
- Beneficial bacteria are important as decomposers in the treatment of sewage and in the production of compost.
- Bacteria can produce **antibiotics** (see page 246).
- Beneficial bacteria can produce cheese and yoghurt.

Beneficial bacteria	
Streptomyces spp.*	Produce antibiotics
Lactobacillus spp.*	Produce yoghurt and cheese
Escherichia coli	Produce vitamin K in the colon
Harmful bacteria	
Salmonella typhi	Cause typhoid
Vibrio cholera	Cause cholera
Mycobacterium tuberculosis	Cause TB

Table 19.1 Beneficial and harmful bacteria

spp*= there is more than one species of this organism.

SYLLABUS REQUIREMENT:
The Latin names are not required.

Bacteria, disease and antibiotics

7 Parasitic bacteria, called **pathogens**, cause diseases in their hosts and are the main reason we tend only to think of the negative aspects of bacteria. Although bacteria do cause many diseases, they are vital to us. There are many more beneficial bacteria than harmful ones.

8 One beneficial effect of some bacteria is their ability to secrete antibiotics.

Antibiotics are chemicals produced by micro-organisms that are toxic to bacteria. They have no effect against viruses or fungi. This is because they target chemical reactions unique to bacteria. Antibiotics were originally isolated from fungi, e.g. penicillin from *Penicillium*. Many are now isolated from bacteria, e.g. streptomycin. Antibiotics are very useful in medicine as they kill or prevent the growth of bacteria without affecting the human (unless there is an allergic reaction).

> **Pathogens** are disease-causing organisms.

> **Antibiotics** are chemicals produced by micro-organisms that are toxic to bacteria.

Most antibiotics are naturally occurring chemicals that give the micro-organism that produces them the ability to prevent the growth of competing microbes. Consequently, there are naturally occurring microbes which have the ability to grow in the presence of these antibiotics. The gene conferring this **antibiotic resistance** is usually carried on the **plasmids** in the bacteria. Bacteria have the ability to pass on these plasmids from one bacterium to the next and from one species of bacteria to another.

Misuse of antibiotics

9 When a patient is given an antibiotic, all the bacteria in that person are killed, including the beneficial microbes in the gut. Should antibiotic-resistant bacteria be present, then that bacterium has no competition, will not be killed and will quickly colonise the patient. When a disease-causing bacterium arrives, it can pick up the antibiotic resistance from the colonising bacteria and the antibiotic will not affect it. In this way, drug resistance is spreading in disease-causing bacteria and many antibiotics are of very limited use today (Figs 19.9 and 19.10).

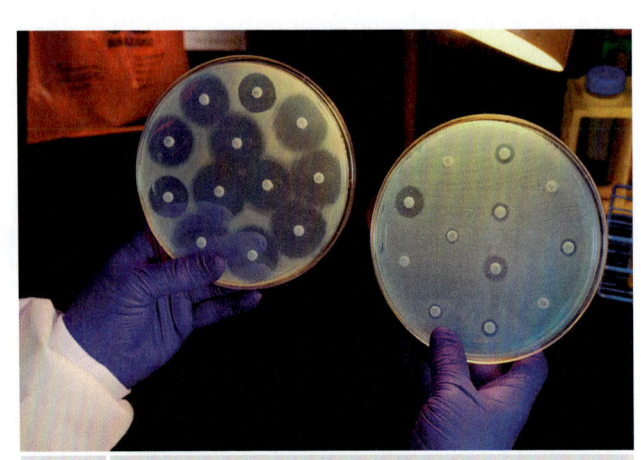

19.9 A test for drug resistance in bacteria: where the bacteria grows up to the paper disc containing the antibiotic the bacteria is resistant to that antibiotic

Care must be taken to ensure the correct use of antibiotics and to prevent their unnecessary use. It is also important that patients finish a course of antibiotics rather than stopping when they feel better, as this can also increase the risk of drug resistance. Some multiple drug-resistant, disease-causing bacteria are posing a serious health problem, e.g. multiple drug-resistant tuberculosis, MRSA and *C. difficile*. This is an example of the theory of **natural selection** in action. The small number of bacteria which have a resistance to the antibiotic survive to reproduce and their offspring carry this mutation and are more likely to survive. The fact that the gene for resistance is often on plasmids means that the resistance can be spread very rapidly from microbe to microbe.

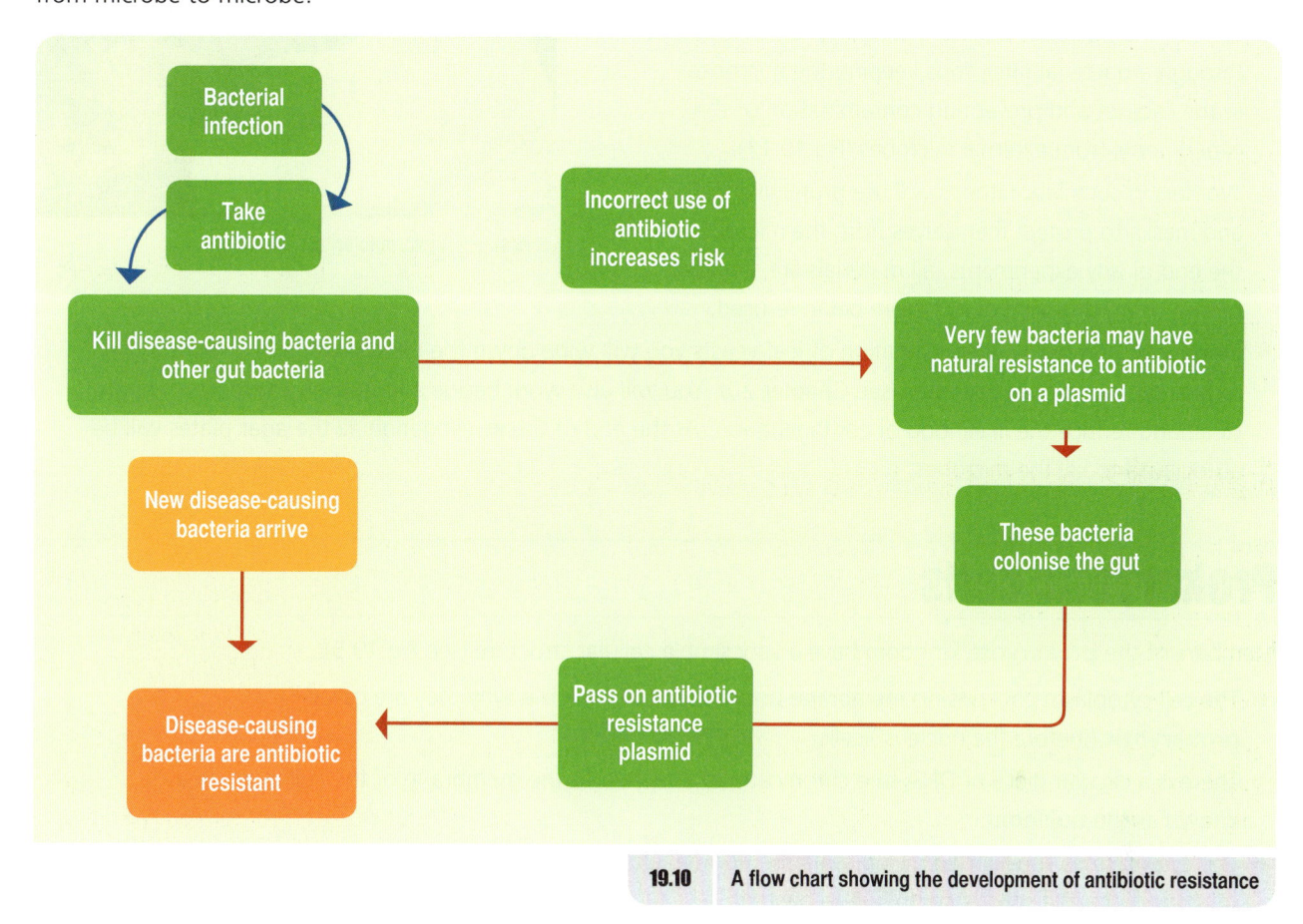

19.10 A flow chart showing the development of antibiotic resistance

Sterility and asepsis

Microbes are found everywhere. When you are working with them or if you are trying to reduce their numbers to prevent decay, you need to be able to destroy or remove all or some of the microbes.

1. A **sterile** substance is one that has been treated to kill all of the microbes and their spores. There are a number of ways in which this can be done. If the material is kept in damp heat (steam) at 120°C for 20 minutes, this will kill all microbes and spores. Sterilisation by this method is achieved by heating the water under pressure in an **autoclave** (pressure cooker).

> **D** A substance is **sterile** if it is free from all microbes.

In operating theatres, where it is not possible to sterilise all the people in the room, the principle of **asepsis** is used.

2. In asepsis, microbes are excluded from as much of the environment as possible. The clothes and skin of the people present are covered with sterile material and the air is filtered to prevent the entry of microbes.

> **D** **Asepsis** means excluding microbes from as much of the environment as possible.

19 — Monera (Prokaryotae)

11. In working with potentially dangerous microbes, most scientists:

- Will now only work in laboratories that have a negative pressure to the outside. This means that any escaping microbes will tend to be drawn back into the laboratory and will not be released to the outside.
- They also work in laminar air flow cabinets, which contain the microbes behind a curtain of air that passes through a bacterial filter, thus keeping the microbes in the cabinet and preventing contamination of the experiments from external microbes (Fig 19.11).
- Workers in such laboratories will use protective clothing and masks to protect themselves from the microbes. At the end of any experiments, all materials are sterilised before being disposed of or before being re-used.
- Before carrying out your investigation of leaf yeasts you will wipe down the bench with a disinfectant to reduce the number of microbes (see Chapter 20). You will also work beside a lit Bunsen to create an updraft of air and reduce the likelihood of contamination. At the end of the investigation all the agar plates will be autoclaved to kill the microbes.

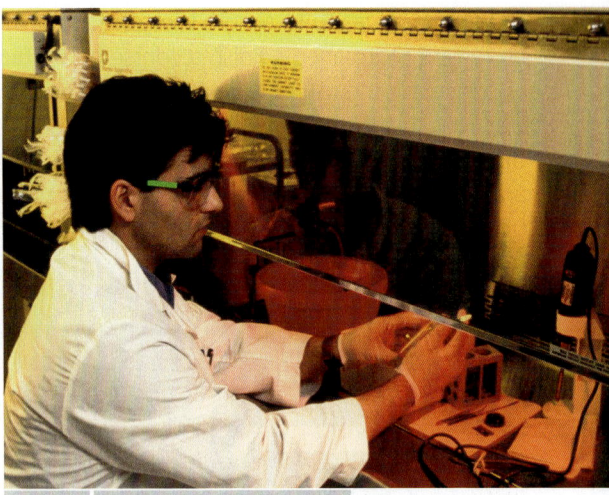

19.11 A microbiologist at work

HL Prokaryotic cells

12. Members of the **prokaryote** kingdom have a very simple cellular structure (see Fig 19.5).

- The cell cytoplasm contains no membrane-bound nucleus, which is why they are called **prokaryotic** ('before the nucleus') cells.
- There is a circular piece of DNA (the chromosome) attached to the membrane of the cell in an area known as the **nucleoid**.
- The cytoplasm is surrounded by a plasma membrane. Outside the membrane is a cell wall made of **peptidoglycan**, a substance unique to bacteria.

In addition:

- The chromosome does not contain the associated proteins as seen in the eukaryotic chromosome.
- In the rest of the cytoplasm, there are ribosomes, enzymes and food storage granules but none of the other structures as described in Chapter 8 are present.
- Some bacteria have a slimy or dry capsule outside the cell wall.
- Some may have flagella.

Eukaryotic cells

Members of all other kingdoms have a more advanced cellular structure as described in Chapter 8. These cells are called **eukaryotic** ('true nucleus') cells.

- These cells have a nucleus.
- These cells have many membrane-bound cellular organelles.

There is some evidence for a theory that eukaryotic cells developed from a number of prokaryotic cells coming together as one cell. The membrane-bound structures such as **chloroplasts** or **mitochondria** may have originated from individual prokaryote cells. This is due to the fact that both of these cellular organelles contain their own DNA.

Growth curves

HL

13 In a laboratory, when scientists are looking at bacteria they will most commonly grow them on agar. This is a gel to which different food can be added to feed the bacteria. As the bacteria grow on the surface of the agar they are easy to see and it is simple to isolate colonies. Alternatively bacteria may be grown in a liquid (broth) where individual colonies will not form but the medium will go cloudy as the microbes grow. It is in these conditions that growth rates are examined. When micro-organisms are introduced to a fresh medium, there is a common pattern of growth. This is shown in Fig 19.12 and is similar to the general population growth curve described in Chapter 6.

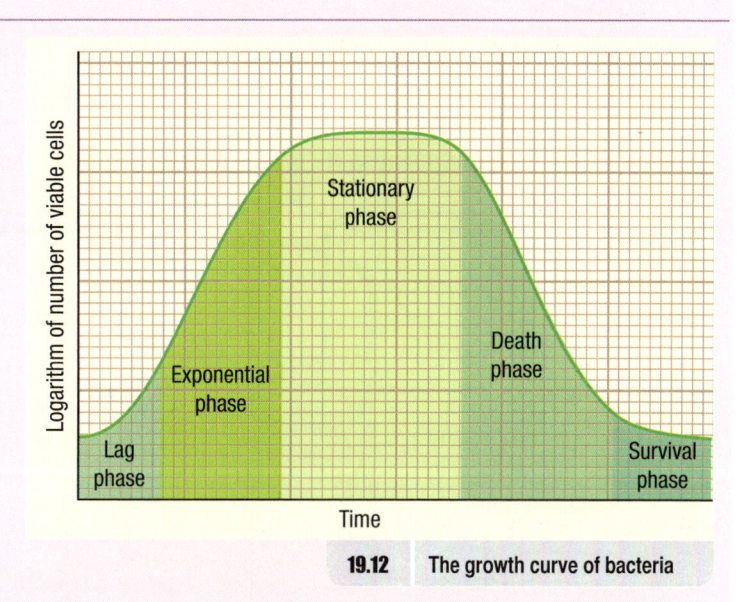

19.12 The growth curve of bacteria

At the start of the graph, the new medium has been inoculated with some microbes. The microbes are observed going through five specific stages of growth shown in Table 19.2.

Phase	Numbers of bacteria	Reason
1. Lag phase	Numbers of bacteria do not increase.	Bacteria adjusting to the environment and learning to produce the correct enzymes for the food source.
2. Log (exponential) phase	Numbers of bacteria increase rapidly over a short period of time.	Bacteria are reproducing as they have all the conditions they need – correct food, oxygen, etc.
3. Stationary phase	Numbers of bacteria level out because the numbers being produced equal the numbers dying.	The bacteria begin to run out of food, oxygen and space. Wastes build up.
4. Death or decline phase	Numbers decline rapidly.	Toxic wastes kill off the bacteria.
5. Survival phase	A small number of bacteria remain.	Some bacteria can form spores and become dormant until conditions improve.

Table 19.2 The growth stages of a typical microbe

Industrial microbiology

14 In industrial microbiology the microbes are grown in large vats called **bioreactors**. Some of the products that the industrial microbiologist is looking for may be produced in the log phase of growth. Other products may be produced during the stationary phase.

> A **bioreactor** is a vessel (usually large) in which cells, organisms or enzymes are placed to manufacture specific products.

Continuous flow method

Some microbes are eaten as a protein substitute. These are called **single-cell proteins (SCP)**.
- The most efficient way of producing a large amount of SCP is to keep the microbe in the log phase, reproducing at the fastest rate possible.

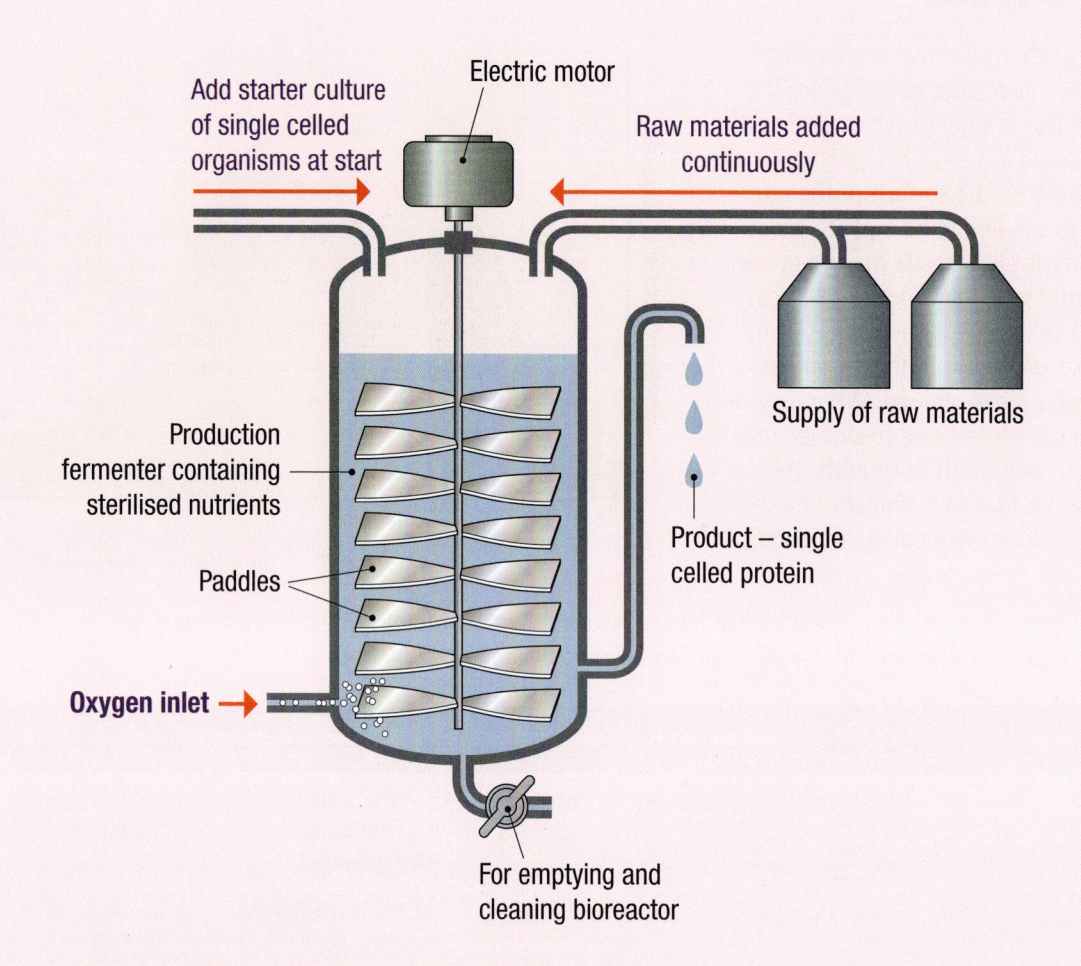

19 | Monera (Prokaryotae)

19.13 A diagram showing the continuous flow method of SCP production

- This is achieved by setting up a large bioreactor full of medium which is inoculated with the microbe.
- Oxygen is bubbled into the bioreactor.
- The temperature is carefully monitored and the medium is stirred using large paddles.
- When the microbe is in the log phase, fresh sterile medium is introduced at the top.
- A continuous flow of old medium with SCP is removed from the bottom.

In theory, this continuous flow method of production could go on indefinitely, but in practice the bioreactor has to be emptied after about 6 months due to contamination or the build-up of toxic by-products, etc.

> **D** The **continuous flow method** of production involves maintaining the microbes in the log phase of growth by the addition of fresh medium.

Monera (Prokaryotae) | 19

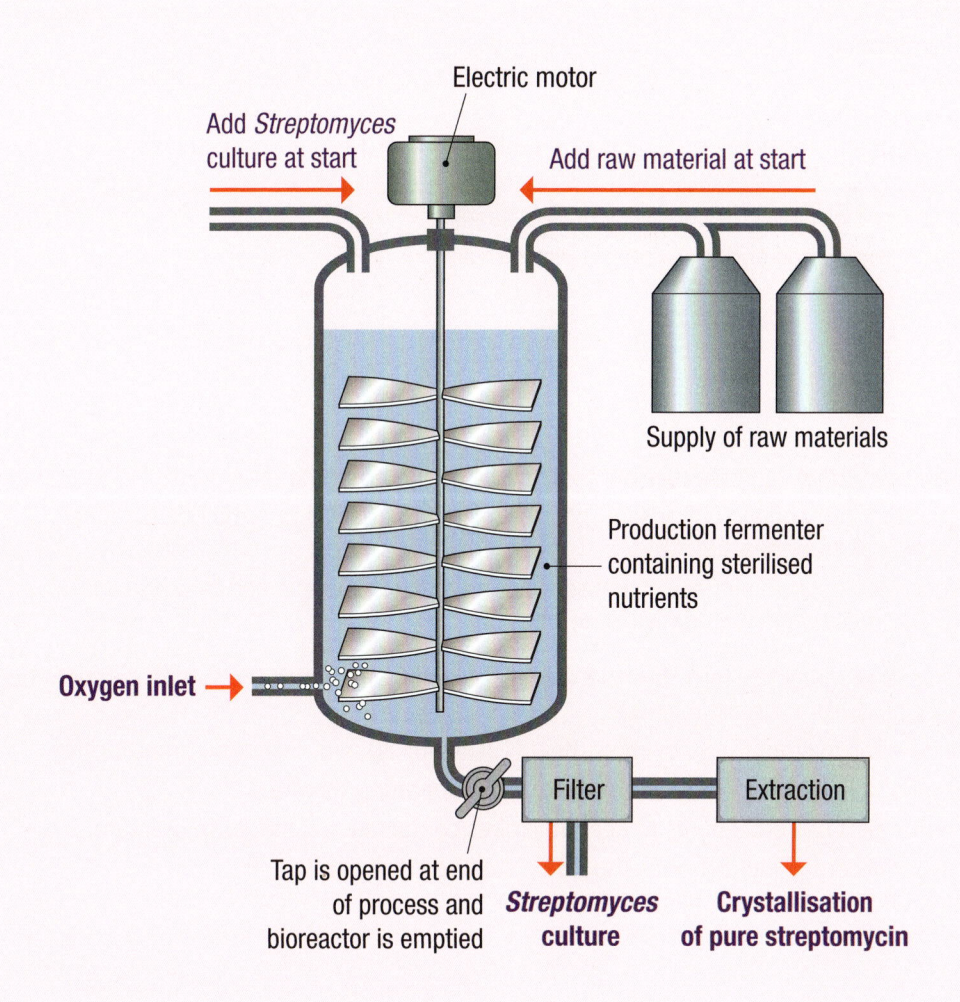

19.14 Diagram showing batch production of streptomycin

Batch flow method
An antibiotic such as streptomycin is produced by the batch method, in which:
- A bioreactor is filled with a fixed amount of nutrients and the *Streptomyces* culture.
- The bioreactor is kept at the correct temperature and is carefully stirred.
- The bacteria go through the lag, log, stationary and perhaps the decline phase.
- At the end of the process, the liquid is removed and filtered, extracting the *Streptomyces* culture, and the streptomycin is separated out of the remaining fluid (Fig 19.14).

> The **batch flow method** of production is when a fixed amount of nutrients are added to a bioreactor which is emptied of its contents at the end of production.

19 Monera (Prokaryotae)

Summary

- Monera (Prokaryotae) kingdom:
  - Structure
    - Simple single-celled organisms with no nucleus or membrane-bound structures within the cell, e.g. bacteria.
    - Have a cell wall and sometimes a capsule. May have a flagella.
    - Contain a circular chromosome and may contain plasmids.
    - Some produce spores.
    - Reproduction
    - Divide by binary fission.
  - Nutrition
    - Autotrophs (make own food) can be either photosynthetic or chemosynthetic.
    - Heterotrophs (take in food) and are either saprophytes (bacteria of decay) or symbiotic bacteria (mutualism, commensalism or parasitism).
    - Some need oxygen (aerobes), some need the absence of oxygen (obligate anaerobes) and some function with or without oxygen (facultative anaerobes).
  - Antibiotics are chemicals produced by microbes to kill other bacteria with which they are in competition. Overuse of antibiotics produces resistant microbes.
  - Sterilising is the killing of all microbes, e.g. by moist heat (120°C for 20 minutes) using an autoclave.
  - Asepsis is the removal of all possible contamination, e.g. in an operating theatre.
  - Laboratories with pathogens use procedures to keep microbes contained, e.g. negative pressure.
  - All contaminated material containing microbes should be sterilised before disposal.

HL
- Prokaryotic cells:
  - Are found in members of the Prokaryote kingdom.
  - Have no structures surrounded by membranes in the cell.
  - Have a circular piece of DNA attached to the cell membrane found at the nucleoid.
  - Have cell walls made of peptidoglycan.
- Eukaryotic cells:
  - Found in all other kingdoms.
  - Have a nucleus.
  - Have membrane-bound cellular organelles.
- Microbes can be grown for commercial use in a bioreactor.
  - If large numbers are needed, they can be kept in the exponential phase to produce the maximum quantity, e.g. SCP production.
  - If they are producing a product then they are grown by the batch method, e.g. streptomycin production.

Review questions

01. (a) What method is used to classify bacteria?
    (b) Name two types of bacteria.
02. (a) Draw a well-labelled diagram of a bacteria.
    (b) Give a function for each labelled part.
    (c) What is the function of a bacterial spore?
03. (a) What is the name given to reproduction in bacteria?
    (b) With the aid of a labelled diagram describe reproduction in bacteria.
04. (a) What are the different types of nutrition found in bacteria?
    (b) What is symbiosis?
    (c) What is the difference between mutualism, commensalism and parasitism?
05. (a) Explain the term pathogen.
    (b) Give two benefits to humans from bacteria.
06. (a) What is an antibiotic?
    (b) What is the problem with the overuse of antibiotics?
    (c) Why should you not treat (i) influenza, (ii) a fungal infection with antibiotics?
07. (a) What is meant by the term sterile?
    (b) Distinguish between an aseptic technique and a sterile technique.
    (c) Why is all microbial waste autoclaved before disposal?
08. (a) What is the difference between a prokaryotic cell and a eukaryotic cell?
    (b) What type of cell is a bacterium?
09. (a) Draw a graph describing the normal growth curve of bacteria.
    (b) Explain what is happening at each stage.
    (c) Give the advantage to the microbe of the last stage.
10. (a) Name the two ways in which microbes can be grown to produce chemicals.
    (b) Describe each of these methods.
    (c) What would determine which method of production would be used?
    (d) Give examples of both forms of production.

Examination style questions

Section A

01. (a) To what kingdom do bacteria belong?
    (b) What are autotrophs?
    (c) There are two types of autotrophic bacteria. Name them.
    (d) What is a saprophyte?
    (e) Give two examples of beneficial bacteria.
02. (a) What is an antibiotic?
    (b) What produces an antibiotic?
    (c) Why are these used in medicine?
    (d) Why is the incorrect use of antibiotics a problem?
    (e) Why is an antibiotic not used against the common cold?

Section C

03. (a) (i) Some bacteria are rod shaped and are classified as bacilli. Name the other two shapes of bacteria.
        (ii) Give a reason why bacteria are found everywhere in the biosphere.
    (b) The graph shows the number of bacteria growing in a culture in nutrient medium over a period of time at a temperature of 20°C.

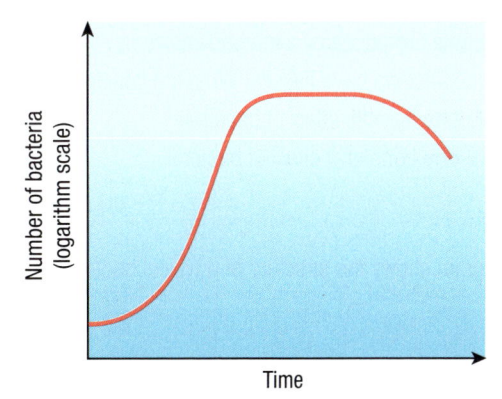

        (i) Explain how, after an initial period, the number of bacteria increase rapidly.
        (ii) Give two factors that limit the size of the bacterial population.
        (iii) What may the eventual fate of the bacteria be if the culture is left undisturbed?
        (iv) There are more bacteria living in our gut than the number of living cells making up our body.

19 Monera (Prokaryotae)

Examination style questions

This is an example of symbiosis.
1. Explain the underlined term.
2. How do we benefit from these bacteria?
3. How do the bacteria benefit from this relationship?

(c) The diagram shows the structure of a generalised bacterial cell.

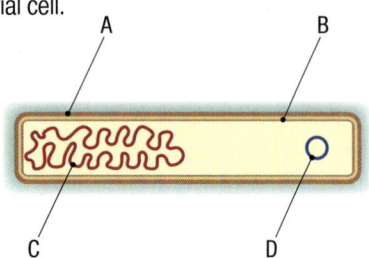

(i) Name the structures labelled A, B and C.
(ii) Name the small circle of symbiotic DNA labelled D. Outline the role of these structures in bacteria.
(iii) Name and describe the method by which bacteria reproduce.
(iv) Only a relatively small proportion of bacteria are pathogenic. Explain the term pathogenic.

Leaving Certificate examination questions

Section A

01 (a) The diagram shows three bacterial shapes. Match the correct letter with the name of **each** shape below:

rod   cocci   spiral

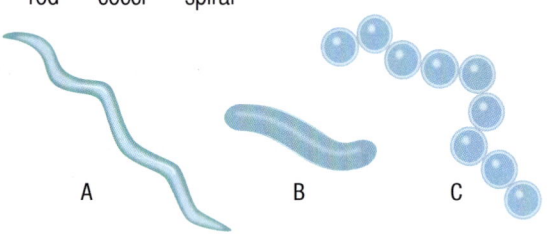

(b) Bacteria reproduce by a method known as _____.
(c) Some bacteria have flagella. What are flagella used for?
(d) Give **one** harmful effect of bacteria.
(e) Give **one** beneficial effect of bacteria.

2014 OL Q. 5

02 The diagram shows the structure of a typical bacterium.

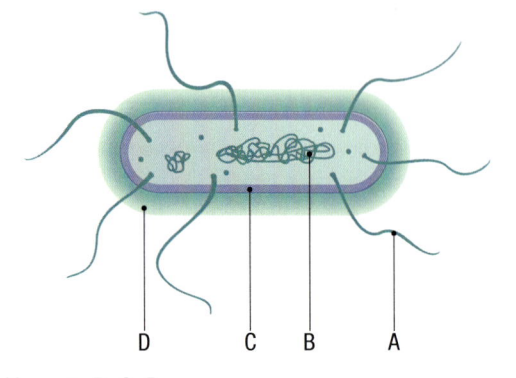

(i) Name A, B, C, D.
(ii) To which kingdom do bacteria belong?

2005 OL Q. 6 (b)

Section C

03 (a) All organisms may be classified (grouped) into five kingdoms.
   (i) Suggest **one** advantage of classifying organisms.
   (ii) Name the kingdom to which bacteria belong.
   (iii) Give **one** example of the economic importance of bacteria.
(b) (i) Draw a large labelled diagram of a typical bacterial cell.
   (ii) Bacteria may be classified by their shape. Name any **two** bacterial shapes.
   (iii) Name the method by which bacteria reproduce.
   (iv) What are *pathogenic* bacteria?
   (v) State **two** factors affecting the growth of bacteria.

2012 OL Q. 13

04 (a) The diagram shows a typical bacterial cell.

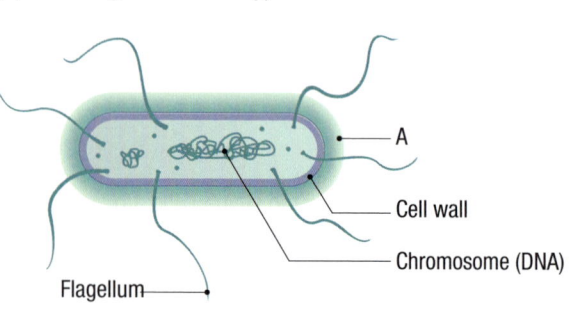

(i) Some bacteria have a layer outside the cell wall (labelled A in the diagram above). Name this layer and state its function.
(ii) Name a structure, other than A, which is not found in all bacteria.

254 UNIT 3 THE ORGANISM   LIFE LEAVING CERTIFICATE BIOLOGY

Leaving Certificate examination questions

(b) The table below shows ways in which bacteria obtain their food. Study the table and then answer the questions that follow.

Autotrophic	Heterotrophic
Photosynthetic	Parasitic
Chemosynthetic	Saprophytic

(i) Distinguish between autotrophic and heterotrophic nutrition.
(ii) What is saprophytic nutrition?
(iii) Why are saprophytic bacteria important in nature?
(iv) Briefly explain chemosynthesis.
(v) What term is used for the organism from which a parasite obtains its food?

2007 OL Q. 13

05 (i) Name the kingdom to which bacteria belong.
(ii) Draw a large labelled diagram of a bacterial cell to show:
  1. The relative positions of a cell wall, cell membrane, and capsule.
  2. A plasmid
(iii) 1. Under what circumstances does a bacterial cell form an endospore?
  2. Describe briefly how an endospore forms.
(iv) Name two types of heterotrophic nutrition used by bacteria.
(iv) Give **two** examples of harmful bacteria.

2013 HL Q. 12 (b)

06 The diagram shows a bacterial growth curve.

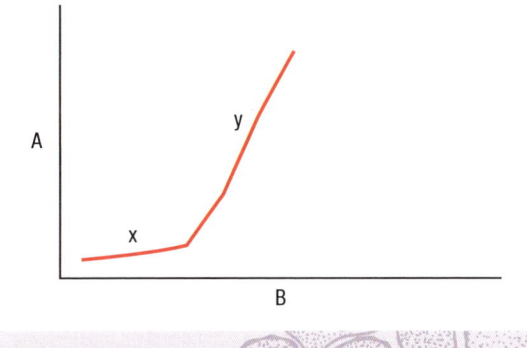

(i) **A** and **B** represent the labels on the axes. What does each of them stand for?
(ii) What term is applied to the part of the curve labelled **x**? What is happening during **x**?
(iii) What term is applied to the part of the curve labelled **y**? What is happening during **y**?
(iv) Copy the diagram into your answer book and continue the curve to show the next phase. Explain why you have continued the curve in this way.
(v) Distinguish between batch and continuous flow food processing using micro-organisms in the food industry.

2008 HL Q. 15 (b)

07 Answer the following in relation to bacteria.
(i) Distinguish between photosynthetic and chemo-synthetic bacteria. Give an example of each type.
(ii) Name **two** forms of heterotrophic nutrition found in bacteria.
(iii) What are antibiotics? For what purpose are they used?
(iv) Explain what is meant by antibiotic resistance and suggest how it may develop.

2006 HL Q. 15 (b)

08 (i) Draw and label a diagram to show the basic structure of a typical bacterial cell.
(ii) Other than being prokaryotic, state **two** ways in which a typical bacterial cell differs from a typical human cell (e.g. cell from cheek lining).
(iii) Describe how some bacteria respond in order to survive when environmental conditions become unfavourable.
(iv) What is meant when a bacterium is described as being pathogenic?
(v) What are antibiotics? Use your knowledge of the Theory of Natural Selection to explain the possible danger involved in the misuse of antibiotics.

2005 HL Q. 15 (b)

Past examination questions

OL	2014 Q. 5	2012 Q. 13 (a) (b)	2009 Q. 12 (a) (b)	2007 Q. 13 (a) (b)	2005 Q. 6 (b)
HL	2013 Q. 12 (b)	2010 Q. 15 (c) (ii)	2008 Q. 15 (c)	2007 Q. 14 (b) (v), (vi)	2006 Q. 15 (b)	2005 Q. 15 (b)

20 Fungi and Protists

After studying this chapter you should be able to:

1. Classify an organism as a fungus.
2. Describe nutrition in fungi and outline the role of saprophytes and parasites in nature.
3. Distinguish between edible and poisonous fungi and know a named example of each.
4. State the economic importance of fungi and give examples of two beneficial and two harmful fungi.
5. Describe the structure and nutrition of *Rhizopus*.
6. Describe the life cycle of *Rhizopus*.
7. Describe the structure and asexual reproduction of yeast.
8. Describe the economic importance of yeast.
9. Distinguish between asepsis and sterility.
10. Describe the necessary safety precautions when working with micro-organisms, including procedures for the safe containment and disposal of unwanted material.
11. Describe an investigation to show the presence of leaf yeasts using agar plates and controls.
12. Classify an organism as a Protist.
13. Describe the structure of *Amoeba*, to include the nucleus and sub-cellular structures.

Kingdom fungi

Classification of fungi

- Fungi are multicellular organisms (with the exception of yeast).
- The cells of fungi have a nucleus.
- They are made up of thread-like structures composed of many cells called **hyphae**.
- A single organism containing many hyphae is called a **mycelium**.
- The cell walls of fungi are composed of chitin. Chitin is an example of a structural polysaccharide (see Chapter 3).
- Fungi are **heterotrophic**.
- They reproduce by **spores**.

20.1 Common edible fungi – oyster mushrooms, chanterelles and common field mushrooms

20.2 Some poisonous fungi – deadly webcap, fly agaric and destroying angel

Nutrition in fungi

Fungi are heterotrophs, they do not have chlorophyll. They cannot make their own food. A large number of fungi are **saprophytes**, living and feeding on dead material. The role of saprophytes in nature is in decomposition – they recycle nutrients. The fruiting bodies of many saprophytes are edible, e.g. common field mushrooms, although care must be taken when picking fungi as a number of them are highly poisonous.

Some fungi are **parasites**, e.g. the fungus that causes athlete's foot. Parasitic fungi that attack food crops are particularly damaging economically. The role of parasites in nature is to reduce populations.

> A **saprophyte** is an organism that lives and feeds on dead things.

> A **parasite** is an organism that lives on or in another organism, feeding on it and causing harm.

Edible vs poisonous fungi

Some fungi, when eaten, produce toxins that can be lethal. It is extremely difficult to distinguish poisonous fungi from edible types. Features that can be used to identify fungi include the cap, spore type, colour, size and smell. Examples of edible fungi (Fig 20.1) are common field mushrooms, truffles, morels. Examples of poisonous fungi (Fig 20.2) include death cap, destroying angel and fly agaric.

The economic importance of fungi

Beneficial fungi (Fig 20.3):
- Yeasts can be used to make bread and alcohols such as beer and wine.
- Some fungi are a source of nutrition, e.g. button mushrooms.

Harmful fungi (Figs 20.4, 20.5 and 20.6):
- Fungi can attack crops and cause major financial losses. Examples include the smuts and rusts on corn and wheat and the potato blight fungus.
- Fungi such as those causing athlete's foot and ringworm of the scalp can infect animals.
- Fungi can spoil food, e.g. *Rhizopus* grows on bread, tomatoes and fruit.
- Fungi cause dry rot.

20.3 Beneficial fungi

20 Fungi and Protists

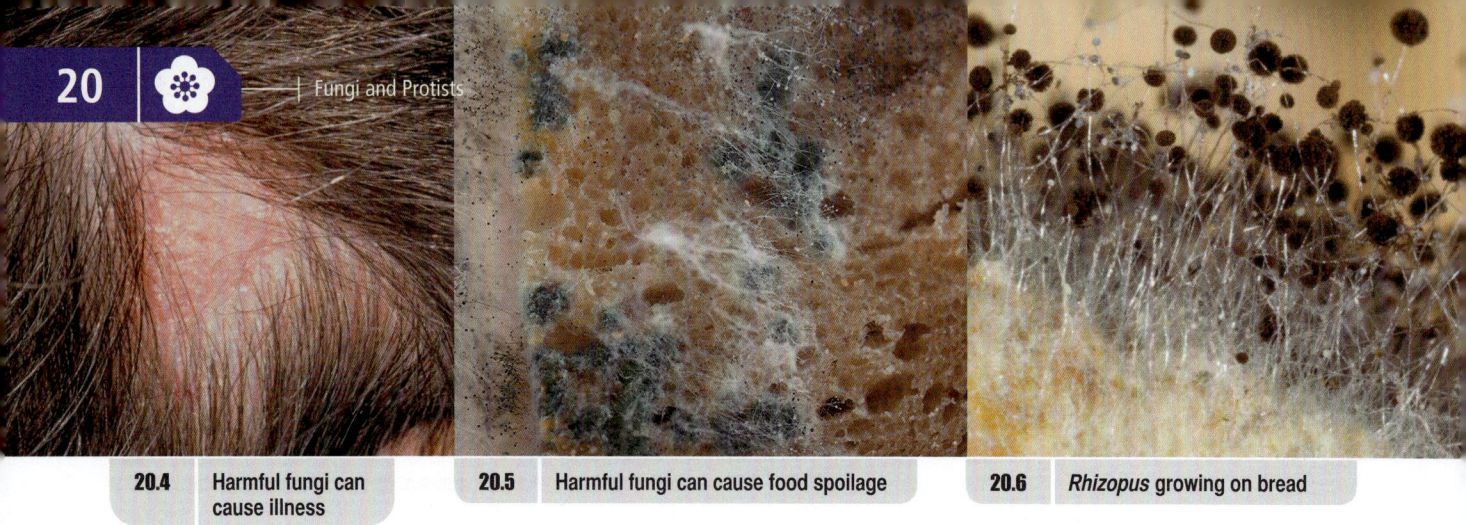

20.4	Harmful fungi can cause illness
20.5	Harmful fungi can cause food spoilage
20.6	*Rhizopus* growing on bread

Rhizopus

Structure

Rhizopus is an example of a type of fungus commonly called the black bread moulds (Fig 20.7). It consists of long thin threads called **hyphae**. The hyphae have no cross-walls and are multi-nucleate. The nuclei are all **haploid (n)** (Fig 20.7).

There are three types of hyphae in *Rhizopus*:

1. **Stolons** – hyphae that grow across the surface of the substrate, allowing the fungus to spread.
2. **Rhizoids** – hyphae that grow down into the substrate. Rhizoids provide anchorage and absorb digested food.
3. **Sporangiophores** – hyphae that grow vertically up above the substrate and produce the sporangium for reproduction.

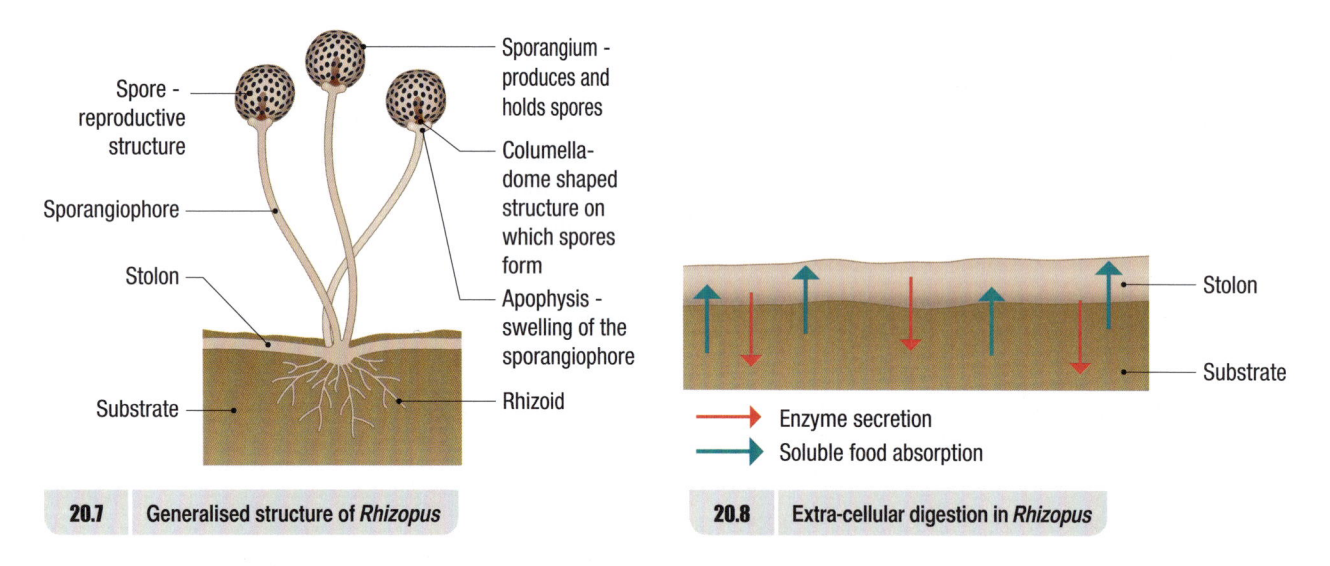

20.7 Generalised structure of *Rhizopus*

20.8 Extra-cellular digestion in *Rhizopus*

Mode of nutrition

Rhizopus is a saprophytic heterotroph, living on starchy or sugary foods. The mould gets its nutrition by releasing **enzymes** from the hyphae into the substrate (bread). Enzymes such as amylase break down the starch in the bread into soluble maltose. The digested food is absorbed back into the hyphae by diffusion and can be used for **respiration**. Digestion in *Rhizopus* is referred to as external or extra-cellular digestion (Fig 20.8).

Reproduction and life cycle

Rhizopus can reproduce both **asexually** and **sexually**. The normal method is asexual. Sexual reproduction takes place when *Rhizopus* is under harsh or adverse environmental conditions such as a lack of water or food.

Asexual reproduction – sporulation (the process of making spores)

Method

Some hyphae grow vertically up from the substrate and form a **sporangium**. **Mitosis** occurs within the sporangium producing a mass of haploid spores (Fig 20.9). Each cell develops a resistant wall and is now called a **spore**. In dry conditions the sporangium dries out and bursts, releasing spores into the air. If spores land on a suitable substrate they will germinate and a new mycelium will form.

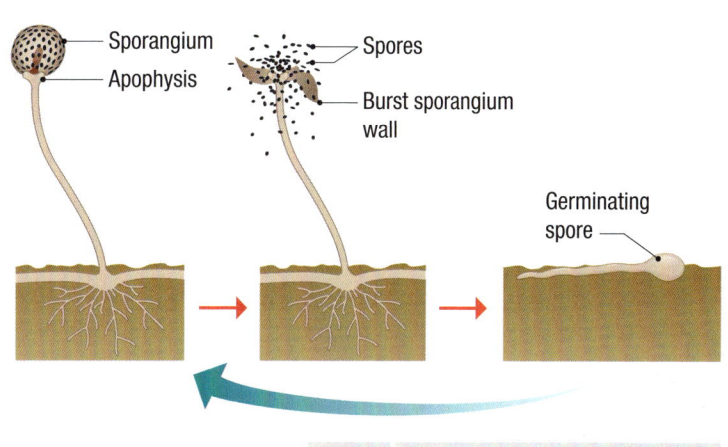

20.9 Asexual reproduction in *Rhizopus*

Sexual reproduction

Sexual reproduction is also possible. It occurs when *Rhizopus* is under harsh conditions and it is a means of survival. It involves the formation of tough, resistant **zygospores**.

There are no male and female mycelia. However, there are two different strains that are structurally identical but chemically different. These two strands are called the positive (+) strain and the negative (−) strain.

Method

1. + and − strains grow close together.
2. Swellings form along the length of the hyphae and touch.
3. Nuclei move into each swelling – now known as progametangia.
4. Cross-walls form to produce **gametangia**, which are held in place by suspensors.
5. The wall between the gametangia breaks down.
6. **Fertilisation** occurs when two nuclei fuse. Many **diploid** nuclei form.
7. A tough, resistant outer wall forms around the old gametangia, forming a zygospore (2n).

> **D** A **gametangium** is a structure that produces gametes in *Rhizopus*.

8. The parent hyphae die away and the zygospores are released.
   The zygospores can remain dormant for a number of months.
   When conditions are suitable the zygospore germinates by **meiosis**.
9. This produces a haploid hypha which grows and produces a sporangium.
10. Nuclei in the sporangium form spores by mitosis, which on release produce new hyphae and mycelia.

Role of meiosis in sexual reproduction in *Rhizopus*

In sexual reproduction in most organisms meiosis is associated with the formation of haploid gametes, prior to fertilisation. However in *Rhizopus* the parent organisms are already haploid so meiosis is not used in the production of the gametangia. Instead, in order to restore the chromosome number of the offspring, meiosis occurs at the germination of the zygospore (2n) (Fig 20.10).

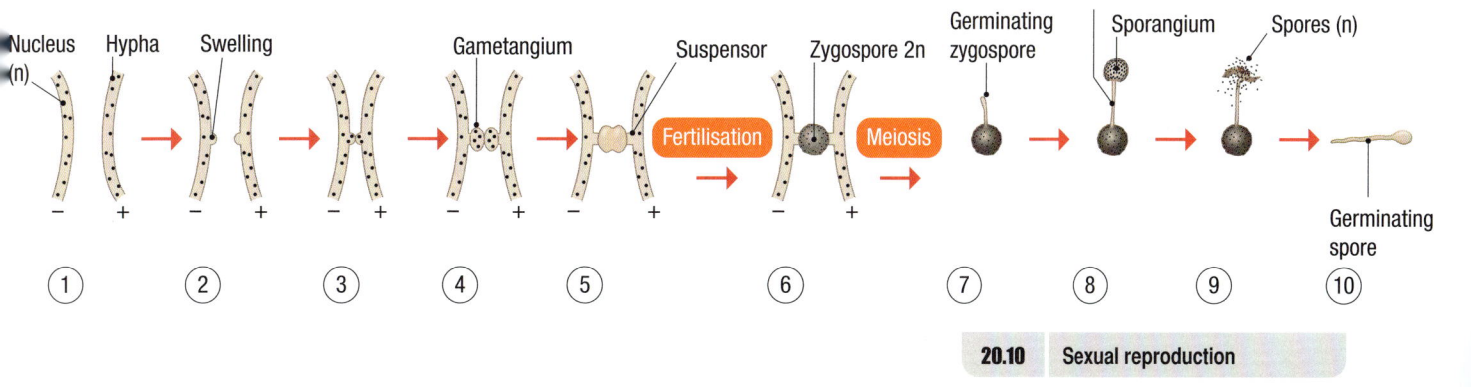

20.10 Sexual reproduction

Yeast

Structure

Yeast is unusual for a fungus in that it has a **unicellular** structure (Figs 20.11 and 20.12). Each cell is roughly oval or spherical in shape. It contains a single **haploid** nucleus, a large **central vacuole** and a thin cell wall.

Reproduction

The main method of reproduction in yeast is **asexual**. In this case, the process is called **budding**. In favourable conditions, a small extension (bud) forms on the cell. The bud enlarges and fills with cytoplasm. The parent cell nucleus divides by mitosis and the second nucleus moves into the bud. The bud will then grow and may separate from the parent cell (Fig 20.13). The new cell may remain attached and divide again, forming a colony.

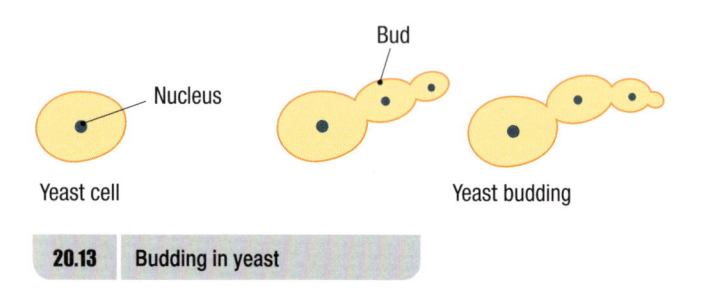

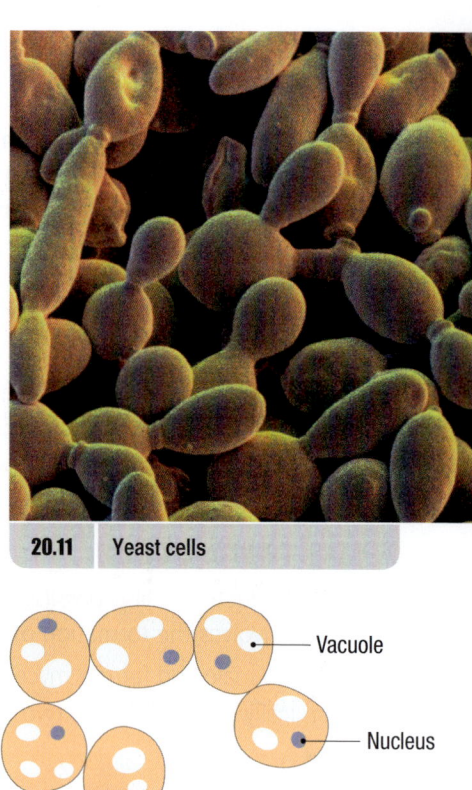

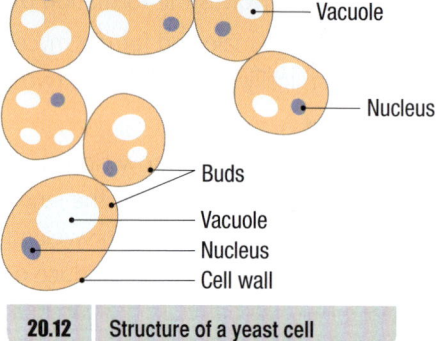

20.11 Yeast cells

20.13 Budding in yeast

20.12 Structure of a yeast cell

Economic importance of yeast

Yeasts are of great economic importance to humans. The **fermentation** of grain or fruit to produce alcohol was probably the first incidence of **biotechnology**. Under anaerobic conditions, *Saccharomyces cerevisiae* (baker's yeast) will respire and produce ethanol and carbon dioxide (see Chapter 14). *Saccharomyces cerevisiae* is also important in the baking industry. The carbon dioxide released during anaerobic respiration is what causes bread containing yeast to rise during baking.

Sterility and asepsis

Microbes are found everywhere. When you are working with them or if you are trying to reduce their numbers to prevent decay, you need to be able to destroy or remove all or some of the microbes.

There are a number of ways in which a substance can be made sterile. If the material is kept in damp heat (steam) at 120°C for 20 minutes, this will kill all microbes and spores. Sterilisation by this method is achieved by heating the water under pressure in an **autoclave**.

In operating theatres, where it is not possible to sterilise all the people in the room, the principle of asepsis is used. Each person must wash their hands with anti-microbial hand wash.

> **Sterile** means to be free of life.

> **Asepsis** means excluding microbes from as much of the environment as possible.

The clothes and skin of the people present are covered with sterile material and the air is filtered to prevent the entry of microbes.

In working with potentially dangerous microbes, most scientists will now only work in laboratories that have a negative pressure to the outside. This means that any escaping microbes will tend to be drawn back into the laboratory and will not be released to the outside. Workers in such laboratories will use protective clothing and masks to protect themselves from the microbes (Fig 20.14). At the end of any experiments, all materials are sterilised before being safely disposed of or before being re-used.

Precautions when using microbes

1. Swab the benches and wash hands with anti-microbial soap, before and after.
2. Use only sterile equipment and growth media.
3. All cultures of micro-organisms should be treated as potentially dangerous.
4. When inoculating an agar plate only open the lid a small amount, to prevent contamination.
5. Dispose of all materials safely, by autoclaving.

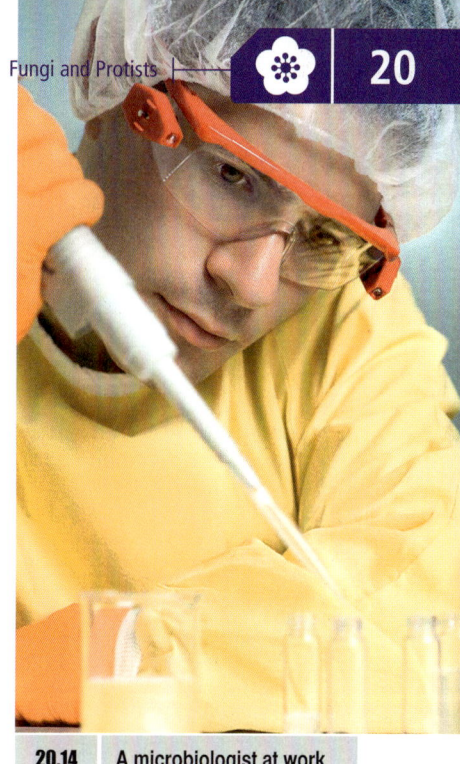

20.14 A microbiologist at work

Investigation 20.1
To investigate the growth of leaf yeasts

Microbes can be grown in the laboratory on Petri dishes of nutrient agar. The nutrient agar provides food for the microbes. In this investigation the nutrient is malt agar. Leaf yeasts can be found growing on the leaves of ash, sycamore and privet.

1. Wash your hands and wipe the surface of the bench and a cutting board with a disinfectant solution (to prevent contamination).
2. Take an ash leaf consisting of eight or nine leaflets. When picking the leaves, place them in a plastic bag (to prevent contamination).
3. Flame a cork borer (or scissors) by passing it through a Bunsen flame (to sterilise it). Take care not to burn your hand.
4. Take two sterile malt agar plates and label them A – experiment and B – control (the malt agar acts as a substrate or nutrient for the yeasts to grow).
5. Use the cork borer to remove a disc from the centre of each leaflet, making sure you get the midrib (Fig 20.15(a)).
6. Use cold, sterile tweezers to place small blobs of Vaseline® (about eight or nine) onto the underside of the lid of a malt agar plate. Place the agar plate upside down on the bench to prevent contamination as shown in Fig 20.15(b).
7. Flame a tweezers. Allow to cool.
8. Using the tweezers put the upper surface of the leaf discs onto the Vaseline®.
9. Place the agar dish back onto the lid.
10. Keep one agar plate unopened as a control.
11. Put a small piece of tape/parafilm on either side of the dishes to make sure they remain closed.

12. Turn the agar plates over so that the leaf discs are suspended over the agar (Fig 20.15(c)). (This allows the yeast spores to fall on to the agar.)
13. Leave the dishes in the laboratory out of direct sunlight or away from any heat source for 24 hours.
14. After 24 hours, turn each agar plate upside down (to prevent condensation forming).
15. Place the plates in an incubator at 20°C for 2–3 days, looking at them periodically.
16. Examine the plates. Leaf yeasts appear as shiny pink colonies. Draw a labelled diagram of each plate to record your results.
17. When you have looked at the microbes, place all the materials into an autoclave bag and sterilise everything in an autoclave.
18. Write up the investigation in your practical notebook and form a conclusion.

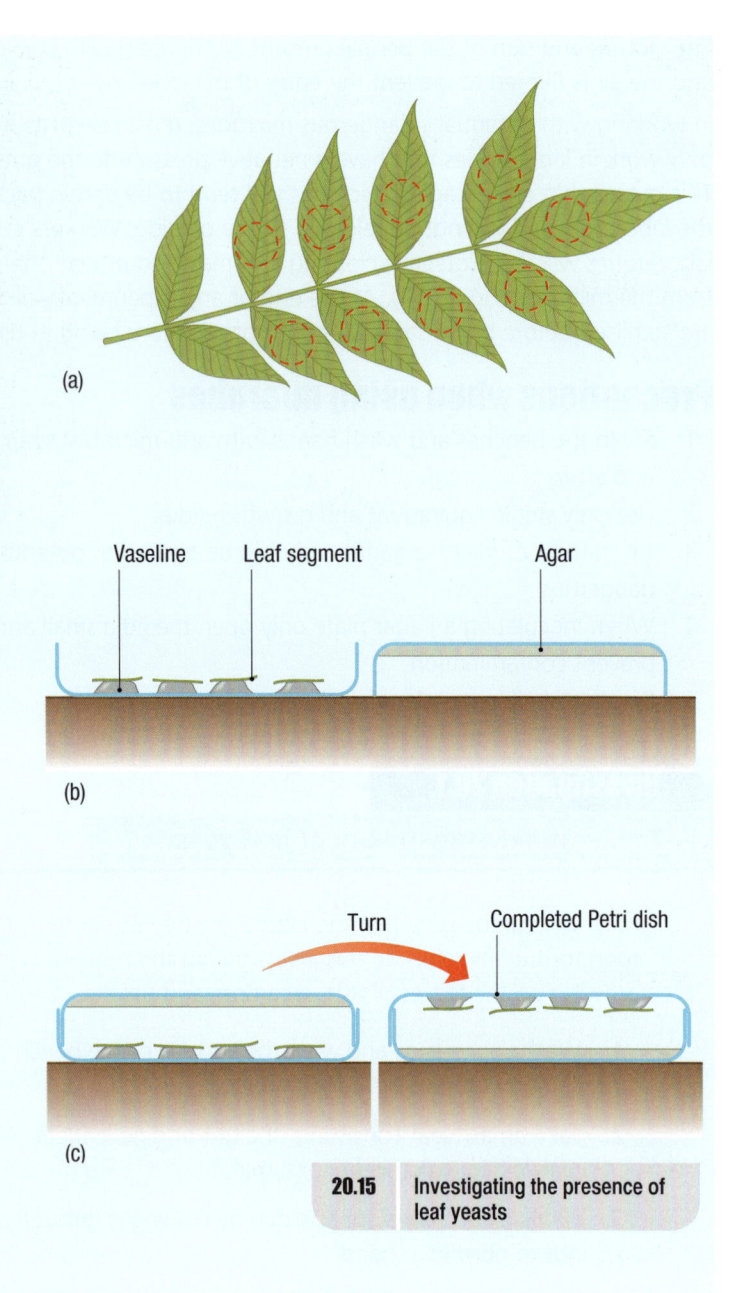

20.15 Investigating the presence of leaf yeasts

Kingdom Protista (Protoctista)

12. The Protist kingdom consists of organisms that all have a true nucleus, may be uni- or multi-cellular, heterotrophic or autotrophic. The group includes tiny cells such as *Amoeba* and the multi-cellular seaweeds (Fig 20.16).

20.16 Seaweeds are Protists

Amoeba

- *Amoeba proteus* is a single-celled organism. It is therefore microscopic (Fig 20.17).
- It is heterotrophic.
- It lives in fresh water, e.g. a pond.

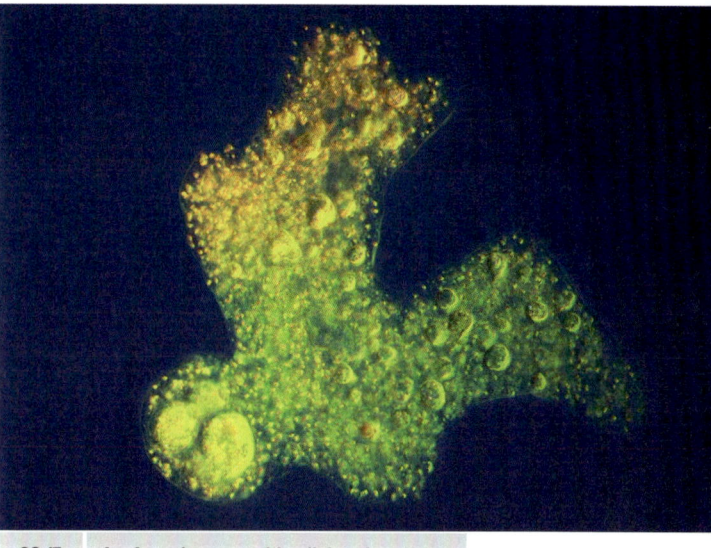

Structure

Amoeba consist of a small amount of cytoplasm surrounded by a cell membrane and has no fixed shape. This is because the cytoplasm can push outwards at any point on the surface to form **pseudopodia** (false feet). Inside the cytoplasm are a number of structures, including a nucleus and a number of specialised vacuoles. The names and functions of these structures are shown in Table 20.1 and Fig 20.18.

20.17 An *Amoeba* seen with a light microscope

Structure	Function
nucleus	controls the activities of the cell
food vacuole	digests ingested food particles
pseudopodia	engulfing prey and movement
contractile vacuole	osmoregulation
cell membrane	allows diffusion of gases/water

Table 20.1 Structures in *Amoeba* and their function

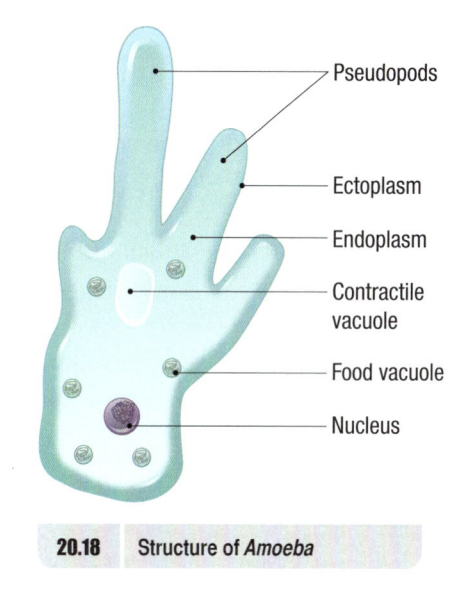

20.18 Structure of *Amoeba*

Contractile vacuole

The role of the **contractile vacuole** is to regulate the amount of water in the *Amoeba*. *Amoeba* that live in fresh water are constantly taking in water from the surroundings by **osmosis**. This constant inflow of water could cause the *Amoeba* to swell up and burst. To prevent this, a temporary vacuole, called a contractile vacuole, forms in the cytoplasm. The vacuole collects the excess water and then moves to the surface of the cell where it 'contracts' or bursts, releasing the excess water out of the cell. This action requires energy produced by the cell.

The function of the contractile vacuole is **osmoregulation**.

In marine *Amoeba* contractile vacuoles are less active. Can you think why this might be the case?

Fungi and Protists

Summary

- Fungus kingdom:
  - Are multicellular (except yeast) and the cells have a nucleus (eukaryotic).
  - Have thread-like structures called hyphae forming a mycelium.
  - A mycelium is a mass of hyphae.
  - Mode of nutrition is heterotrophic – saprophytes live and feed on dead matter; parasites live on or in another organism, feeding on it and causing harm.
  - Reproduce asexually by spores.
  - Fungi may be edible or poisonous. Colour, smell, cap and spore type can be used to identify poisonous fungi, e.g. death cap.
  - Beneficial fungi include yeast, which is used in baking and brewing.
  - Harmful fungi can cause illness (e.g. ringworm), destroy crops and spoil food.

- *Rhizopus*:
  - Mode of nutrition – heterotrophic (saprophtye).
  - Rhizoids release enzymes onto the substrate and absorb the digested food.
  - Asexual reproduction is the norm. Aerial sporangia produce tough spores by mitosis. On release, these spores produce hyphae.
  - Sexual reproduction occurs when *Rhizopus* is under adverse conditions. Gameteangia nuclei from two mycelia (+ strain and – strain) fuse to form a diploid zygote which develops into a resistant zygospore.
  - When conditions are favourable the zygospore germinates by meiosis to produce a sporangium and spores.

- Yeast:
  - Unicellular, with asexual reproduction by budding. Will produce alcohol and carbon dioxide under anaerobic conditions, so is used in brewing and baking.

- Sterilising is the killing of all microbes, e.g. by moist heat (120°C for 20 minutes) using an autoclave.

- Asepsis is the exclusion of microbes from as much of the environment as possible.

- All contaminated material containing microbes should be sterilised before disposal.

- Malt agar nutrient plates can be used to grow leaf yeasts from ash/sycamore leaves. The leaf yeasts grow as shiny pink colonies on the surface of the agar.

- Protist (Protoctist) kingdom:
  - Unicellular, e.g. *Amoeba* or multi-cellular, e.g. the algae.
  - *Amoeba* have no definite shape.
  - The cell membrane allows diffusion of gases.
  - The food vacuoles digest food.
  - The nucleus controls the cell's activities.
  - The pseudopods are used to engulf prey and for movement.
  - The contractile vacuole controls water and salt balance in the cell (osmoregulation).

20 Fungi and Protists

Review questions

01 (a) List three features that can be used to classify an organism as a fungus.
(b) Name two fungi.
(c) State the mode of nutrition of fungi.

02 (a) Name a poisonous fungus.
(b) Outline three features that would enable you to distinguish edible from poisonous fungi.
(c) Give an example of a beneficial fungus.

03 (a) Describe by means of a well-labelled diagram the structure of the fungus *Rhizopus*.
(b) One type of hypha is a sporangiophore. What is the function of a sporangiophore?
(c) Name another type of hypha.
(d) What is a mycelium?
(e) Is *Rhizopus* parasitic or saprophytic? Give a reason for your answer.

04 (a) State the normal method of reproduction in *Rhizopus*.
(b) Describe how *Rhizopus* reproduces by this method.
(c) Suggest a benefit to *Rhizopus* of this type of reproduction.

05 Give a function of each of the following in *Rhizopus*:
(a) stolon; (b) rhizoid, (c) gametangium, (d) sporangium, (e) meiosis, (f) zygospore.

06 (a) Use the following description to draw a labelled diagram of a yeast cell.
The cell is oval in shape, it has a thin cell wall, a haploid nucleus and a large central vacuole.
(b) Name two industries in which yeast plays a major part.
(c) State and describe the method of asexual reproduction in yeast.

07 (a) Distinguish between asepsis and sterility.
(b) Suggest why it is not possible to completely sterilise an operating theatre.
(c) Name one aseptic technique that you carried out in the laboratory and give a reason for doing so.
(d) How would you sterilise some Petri dishes in the laboratory?

08 (a) Describe how you could show the presence of leaf yeasts on leaves.
(b) Why is one plate left without any leaf discs (leaves) during the experiment?
(c) Why are the agar plates left in the incubator for 2–3 days?
(d) Describe the leaf yeasts that form.

09 (a) Give one characteristic of fungi that separates them from any other kingdom.
(b) Why would you classify *Amoeba* as a Protist?
(c) List three structural differences between (i) *Rhizopus* and *Amoeba*, (ii) *Amoeba* and yeast.

10 (a) Draw a labelled diagram of an *Amoeba*.
(b) Describe the function of each of the parts you label in (a).

Examination style questions

Section A

01 (a) Name the kingdom to which the organism shown belongs.
(b) Give two reasons for your answer.
(c) Name another member of the kingdom you have named in (a) that you have studied in your course.

02 (a) Name the organism shown in the diagram.
(b) Name the parts labelled A, B, C, D, E.
(c) State the function of parts A and D.
(d) Are the haploid structures produced in E formed as a result of mitosis or meiosis?

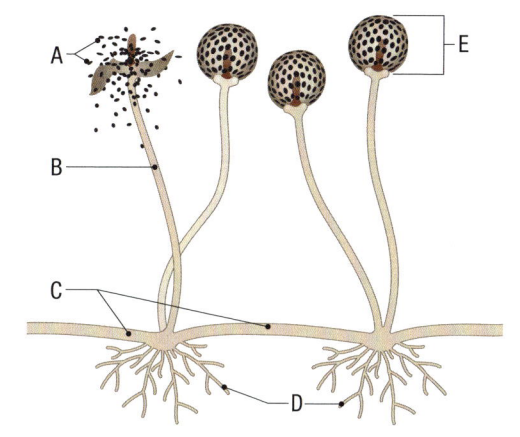

20 Fungi and Protists

Examination style questions

(e) What term is used to describe the type of nutrition used by this organism?

03 The figure shows asexual reproduction taking place in yeast.
(a) Name this type of reproduction.
(b) Are the products of this type of reproduction clones? Briefly explain your answer.
(c) Yeast can respire aerobically and anaerobically. Name the substances produced by anaerobic respiration.
(d) How does the oxygen, necessary for aerobic respiration, enter a yeast cell?
(e) State two ways in which a yeast cell differs from a typical plant cell.

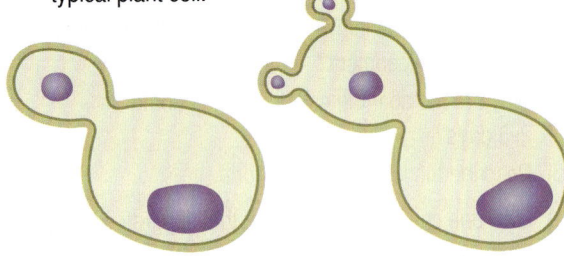

04 (a) Name the organism shown in the figure below.
(b) To which kingdom does this organism belong?
(c) Give two reasons for your answer.
(d) How is the structure of this organism similar to that of a bacterium?
(e) Name the parts labelled A to E.
(f) Give the main function of each of parts A to E.

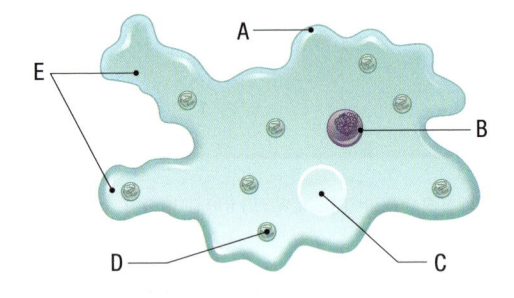

Section B

05 (a) (i) Distinguish between asepsis and sterile.
(ii) Describe one aseptic technique you have carried out in the laboratory.
(b) Leaf yeasts can be cultured in the laboratory.

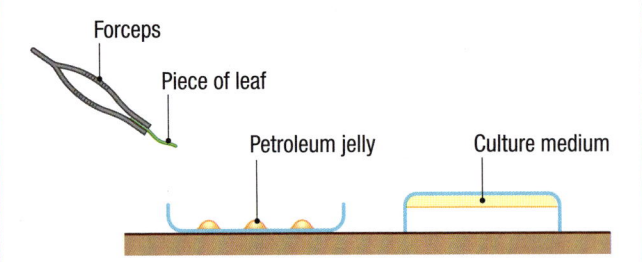

(i) How was the forceps sterilised before transferring the piece of leaf?
(ii) Name a suitable growth medium for leaf yeast.
(iii) Why was the base of the plate containing the growth medium placed upside down while the pieces of leaf were being transferred?
(iv) Describe a suitable control for this investigation.
(v) How is the yeast colony identified?
(vi) Name the asexual reproductive method by which the yeast colony grew.
(vii) What would the result of the control be if your technique did not cause contamination?
(viii) At the end of the investigation how should you dispose of the plates?

Section C

06 The diagram shows the structure of *Rhizopus* (the bread mould). Use the following list of terms to name the parts labelled A, B, C, D, E:
apophysis, columella, rhizoids, sporangium, stolon
(a) What is the function of the stolon and of the sporangium?
(b) To which kingdom of organisms does *Rhizopus* belong?
(c) Name another member of the same kingdom that you have studied in your course.
(d) Describe how *Rhizopus* reproduces asexually.
(e) Suggest two conditions that might cause *Rhizopus* to reproduce sexually. Of what benefit is this type of reproduction to *Rhizopus*?

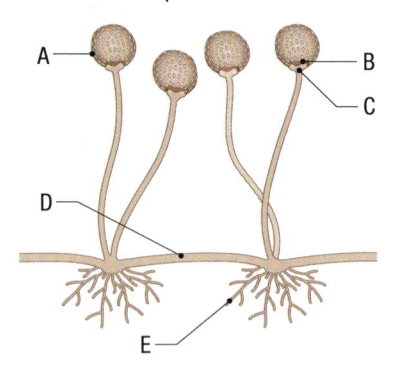

07 (a) (i) Give two reasons why fungi are not classified as plants.
(ii) Name one poisonous fungus.
(b) (i) Draw labelled diagrams of *Rhizopus* and yeast. Identify from your drawings two major differences in structure between these two fungi.
(ii) Outline how *Rhizopus* obtains its nutrients.
(iii) What is the role of fungi such as *Rhizopus* in the biosphere?
(iv) Write notes on each of the following in *Rhizopus*: gametangia, the role of meiosis in the life cycle, rhizoids.

Examination style questions

(c) Read the passage below and answer the following questions.

Yeasts such as the leaf yeast *Sporbolomyces rosacea* grow on the upper and lower surface of leaves of plants such as ash and privet. Its growth depends on such factors as sugars that ooze out of the leaves, on which it feeds, temperature and light intensity. The age of the leaf and its position on the tree also play a part in determining the presence and abundance of the yeast. In addition the type and amount of wax, the number and position of stomata on the leaf surface and the presence of hairs on the leaves will also play a part. This species grows as pink colonies and its abundance has been used to measure air quality. It is known as a 'mirror' yeast because it can forcibly discharge its spores which then grow on the agar forming a mirror image.

Adapted from Biology, Leaving Certificate, Support Materials. NCCA, DES, NBSS 2003

(i) Suggest on which side of the leaf the most leaf yeasts will grow. Give a reason for your answer.
(ii) Explain how the age and position of the leaf on the tree will affect the abundance of leaf yeasts.
(iii) State a use that the presence of these leaf yeasts has for humans.
(iv) Suggest a general role for the waxy layer and hairs on the leaves of plants.
(v) Outline an investigation you could carry out in the laboratory to show on which side of the leaf the most leaf yeasts grow.

Leaving Certificate examination questions

Section A

01 *Amoeba* is a tiny, one-celled organism. This diagram shows the structure of a freshwater *Amoeba* as seen through a microscope.

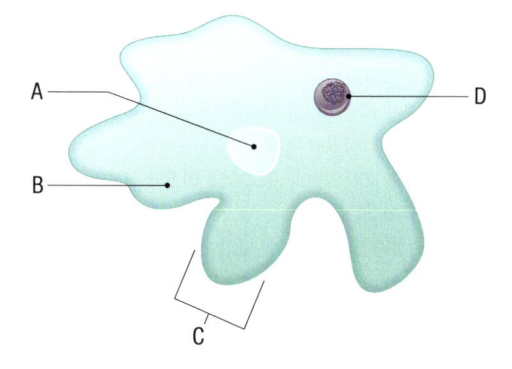

(a) Name the parts labelled A, B, C and D.
(b) State **one** function of part A and **one** function of part C.
(c) Give **one** difference between a plant cell and an *Amoeba*.

2012 OL Q. 2

02 The diagram shows a yeast cell, which is undergoing asexual reproduction.

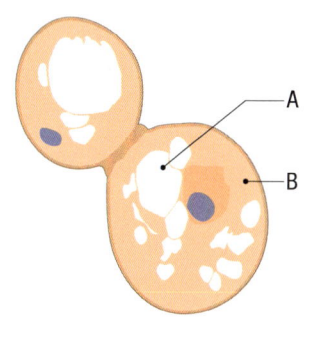

(a) Name A and B.
(b) What type of asexual reproduction is shown in the diagram?
(c) Which type of division, mitosis or meiosis, is involved in this form of reproduction?
(d) If yeast cells are kept under anaerobic conditions, alcohol (ethanol) and another substance are produced.
  (i) What are anaerobic conditions?
  (ii) Name the other substance produced.

2006 OL Q. 6

20 Fungi and Protists

Leaving Certificate examination questions

03 (a) The living world may be divided into five kingdoms: Monera, Protista, Fungi, Plantae, Animalia.
In the case of **each** of the following pairs of kingdoms give any structural feature of members of the first-named kingdom **not found** in members of the second kingdom.
  (i) Fungi and Animalia.
  (ii) Plantae and Fungi.
  (iii) Animalia and Monera.
  (iv) Protista and Animalia.

(b) In **each** of the following cases, name an organism that fits the description.
  (i) A multicellular fungus.
  (ii) A member of the Protista that catches and consumes smaller organisms.
  (iii) A harmful member of the Monera.

2014 HL Q. 4

04 The diagram shows the structure of *Amoeba*.

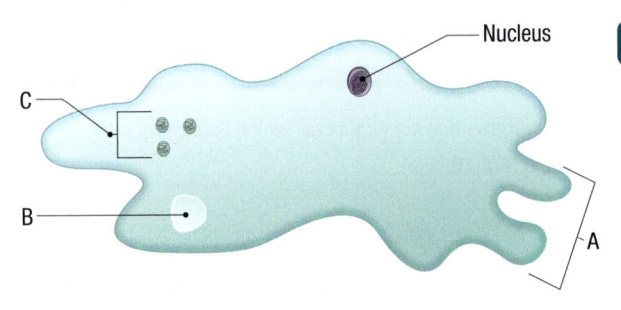

(a) Name the parts labelled A, B and C.
(b) To which kingdom does *Amoeba* belong?
(c) Is the cell of an *Amoeba* prokaryotic or eukaryotic?
(d) Give a reason for your answer to part (c).
(e) Give one function of A in an *Amoeba*.
(f) 1. Give one function of B in *Amoeba*.
    2. Suggest **one** reason why B is more active in freshwater *Amoeba* than in marine *Amoeba*.

2010 HL Q. 3

Section B

05 (a) Draw a labelled diagram of a single reproducing yeast cell.
(b) Answer the following questions in relation to your investigation into the growth of leaf yeast.
  (i) From what plant did you obtain the yeast?
  (ii) Name the nutrient medium on which you grew the yeast.
  (iii) Outline the steps you followed to get the yeast cells onto the nutrient medium.
  (iv) How long did it take for the yeast to become visible on the nutrient medium?
  (v) How did you recognise the yeast?
  (vi) Describe **one** aseptic technique you carried out during this investigation.

2011 OL Q. 7

06 It is important to use sterile apparatus when working with micro-organisms.
(a) (i) What is meant by sterile?
    (ii) How may apparatus be sterilised?
(b) Answer the following questions about an investigation that you carried out to show the growth of leaf yeast.
  (i) Name the container in which you grew the leaf yeast.
  (ii) What was present in this container to provide food for the yeast?
  (iii) Describe how you put leaf yeast into the container.
  (iv) How long did it take for the leaf yeast to appear?
  (v) Describe the appearance of the leaf yeast in the container.

2008 OL Q. 7

07 (a) (i) Are fungi prokaryotic or eukaryotic?
    (ii) Name **one** structure in plant cells not found in fungi.
(b) (i) What is the purpose of using agar when growing fungi or bacteria in the laboratory?
  (ii) Suggest **one** reason why leaf yeasts are more plentiful in July than in March.
  (iii) Describe how you introduced the leaf yeasts into agar plates.
  (iv) What was the precise purpose of a control in this investigation?
  (v) How did you recognise the leaf yeasts when they appeared on the agar?
  (vi) How did you safely dispose of the plates at the end of the investigation?
  (vii) Using the axes below, draw a graph to show how the number of leaf yeasts varied following their introduction into the plate.

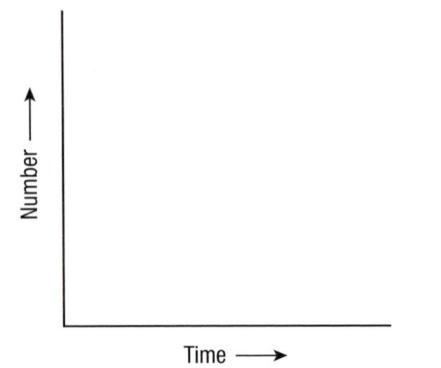

2012 HL Q. 8

Leaving Certificate examination questions

08 (a) (i) Name a fungus, other than yeast, that you studied during your course.
  (ii) Give **one** way in which the fungus that you have named in (i) differs from yeast.
(b) Answer the following questions in relation to your investigation of the growth of leaf yeast.
  (i) It was necessary to use a nutrient medium. What is a nutrient medium?
  (ii) Name the nutrient medium that you used.
  (iii) The nutrient medium should be sterile. Explain the underlined term.
  (iv) Describe, in words and/or labelled diagram(s), how you conducted the investigation.
  (v) What was the result of your investigation?

2007 HL Q. 8

Section C

09 The diagram shows part of the fungus *Rhizopus*.

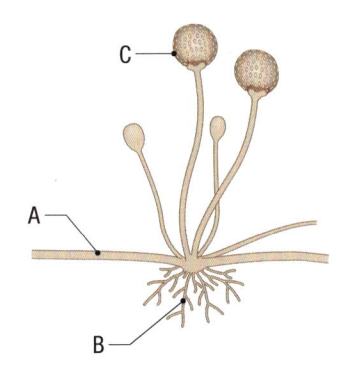

(i) Name the parts labelled A and B.
(ii) Give **two** functions of structure B.
(iii) Describe the role of part C in the reproduction of *Rhizopus*.
(iv) What is meant by *saprophytic* nutrition?
(v) Give **one** beneficial use of fungi.

2012 OL Q. 13 (c)

10 (i) Draw a labelled diagram to show the structure of *Rhizopus*.
(ii) *Rhizopus* uses both sexual and asexual reproduction. Give a brief account of its asexual reproduction, using diagrams.
(iii) The diagrams show stages of sexual reproduction of *Rhizopus*. Name the parts labelled A and B.

(iv) What is the function of B?

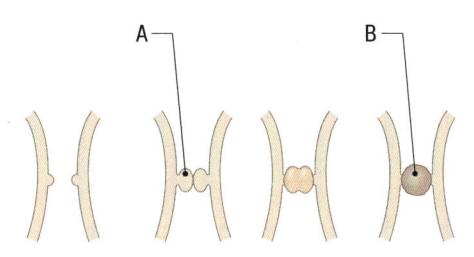

2007 OL Q. 13 (c)

11 (i) Answer the following questions in relation to sexual reproduction in the mould *Rhizopus*.
  1. Sexual reproduction in *Rhizopus* is normally triggered by an adverse environmental stimulus. Suggest **one** such stimulus.
  2. Draw diagrams to show the main events of sexual reproduction in *Rhizopus*. In your diagrams label **three** structures other than the zygospore.
  3. (i) Give **two** advantages to *Rhizopus* of zygospore formation.
    (ii) Answer the following questions in relation to asexual reproduction in yeast.
      1. What term is used to describe the process of asexual reproduction in yeast?
      2. What happens to the new cells formed in the process?
      3. How does asexual reproduction in *Rhizopus* differ from that in yeast?

2012 HL Q. 14 (c)

12 (i) Identify the organism shown in the diagram.
(ii) To which kingdom does this organism belong?
(iii) Name the parts labelled A, B and C.
(iv) 1. Give a role, other than anchorage, for structure X.
   2. Describe how X carries out this role.

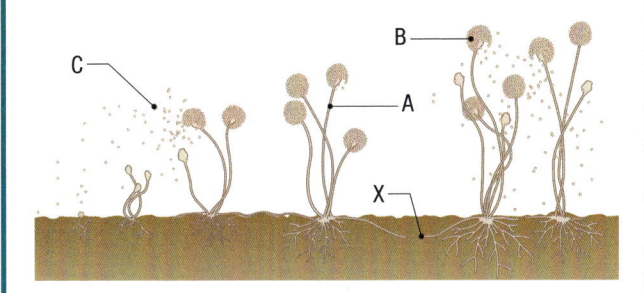

(v) Which term describes the mode of nutrition of this organism?

20 Fungi and Protists

Leaving Certificate examination questions

(vi) The cells of this organism are described as eukaryotic. Give **two** characteristic features of eukaryotic cells.

(vii) What corresponding term is used to describe bacterial cells?

2009 HL Q. 14 (c)

13 (i) Draw a labelled diagram to show the structure of *Rhizopus*. State **one** feature in your diagram that indicates that *Rhizopus* belongs to the kingdom Fungi.

(ii) Sexual reproduction in *Rhizopus* leads to the formation of a zygospore. Show, by means of labelled diagrams, the stages involved in the production of the zygospore.

(iii) Explain what happens when the zygospore reaches a location at which conditions for its germination are suitable.

2004 HL Q. 15 (c)

Past examination questions

OL	Fungi	2012 Q. 13 (c)	2011 Q. 7	2010 Q. 15 (c)	2008 Q. 7, Q. 15 (c)	
		2007 Q. 13 (c)	2006 Q. 6	2005 Q. 15 (c)		
	Protist	2012 Q. 2	2005 Q. 6 (a)			
HL	Fungi	2014 Q. 4 (a) (i), (ii), (b) (i)	2012 Q. 8, Q. 14 (c)	2011 Q. 15 (c)	2009 Q. 14 (c)	2007 Q. 8
		2006 Q. 6 (c)	2005 Q. 9, Q. 15 (c)	2004 Q. 15 (c)	SEC Sample Q. 8	
	Protist	2014 Q. 4 (a) (iv), (b) (ii)	2010 Q. 3			

Flowering Plant Structure and Tissues

21

After studying this chapter you should be able to:

1. Classify a flowering plant as belonging to the plant kingdom. Name some flowering plants.
2. Describe the organisation of a flowering plant into a root system and a shoot system.
3. Describe and give the functions of the root system.
4. Describe and give the functions of the shoot system.
5. Explain the term meristem and know the locations of meristems in the shoot and root. Give an overview of the function of dermal, ground and vascular tissue.
6. Draw and identify the position of dermal, ground and vascular tissue in a T.S. of a stem, root and leaf and an L.S. of a stem and root.
7. Describe the structure and function of xylem and phloem and be able to draw and identify them.
8. State the differences between (a) xylem and phloem, (b) xylem tracheids and xylem vessels, and (c) phloem sieve tubes and companion cells.
9. State the difference between herbaceous and woody plants, with examples.
10. Explain the term cotyledon and distinguish between named monocotyledons and dicotyledons.
11. Describe how to prepare and examine microscopically a T.S. of a herbaceous dicotyledonous stem.

The plant kingdom

1. - Flowering plants (Fig 21.1) such as roses, sycamore trees and dandelions belong to the plant kingdom because they are complex multicellular **organisms**. They:
   - are **autotrophic**, i.e they **photosynthesise** (are producers);
   - contain a nucleus in their cells (**eukaryotic**);
   - have a cellulose cell wall;
   - reproduce both **asexually** and **sexually**.

21.1 Flowering plants

21 Flowering Plant Structure and Tissues

External structure of a typical flowering plant

A typical flowering plant is made up of two parts: the root system below the ground and the shoot system above the ground (Fig 21.2).

The root system

Some plants have a main tap root which may produce side (lateral) roots, e.g. in the dandelion and wallflower. Others have fibrous roots which grow from the base of the stem, e.g. in grasses. These roots are very shallow (Fig 21.3).

The tip of a root, i.e. the part pushing down into the ground, is protected by a root cap and further back is an area covered with fine hairs called **root hairs**. The root hairs are used by the plant to absorb water and minerals. The greater the number of root hairs, the larger the surface area available for absorption.

The main functions of the root are:

- to anchor the plant in the ground

- to absorb water and minerals from the soil

- to store food (in certain plants, e.g. carrot)

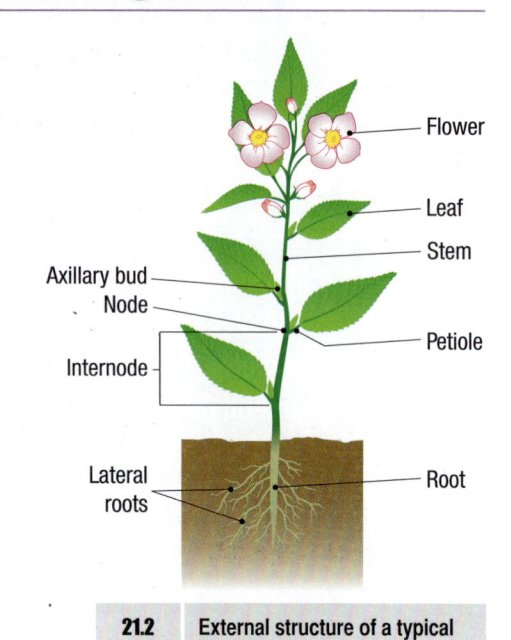

21.2 External structure of a typical flowering plant

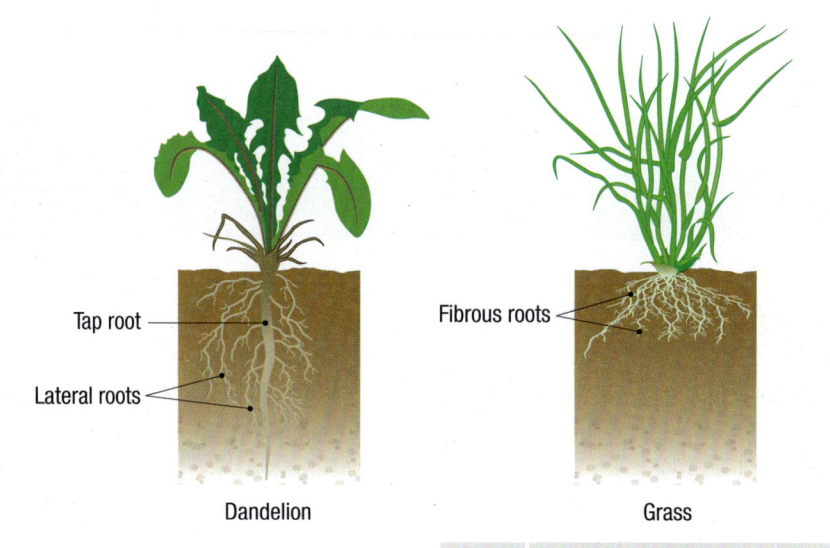

21.3 Root systems

The shoot system

The shoot system consists of an upright **stem** bearing buds, leaves and flowers.

The main functions of the stem are:

- to transport water and minerals from the roots to the leaves and flowers

- to transport food made in the leaves all around the plant

- to support the aerial parts of the plant, leaves, flowers, fruits

- to make food (photosynthesise) in the leaves

Buds

A bud is an undeveloped shoot. At the tip of the stem lies the **apical bud**, which is the place where upward growth takes place. Buds are also found on the side of the stem, usually in the **axil** of a leaf. Such side or **lateral buds** give rise to side shoots and branches. The axil of a leaf is the angle formed between the leaf and the stem. The place where leaves are attached to the stem is called a **node** and the space between nodes is an **internode** (Fig 21.8).

Leaves

Typically leaves are attached to the stem by a leaf stalk or **petiole**, but sometimes leaves are attached directly to the stem, in which case they are said to be **sessile**. The flattened leaf blade or **lamina** has many veins, which give the leaf support and allow transport of food, water and minerals. The veins may be arranged in a netted pattern as in the rose, wallflower and horse chestnut, or they may be parallel as in grasses, daffodils and spider plants (see Fig 21.4).

The main functions of the leaf are:

- to make food, in the process of photosynthesis

- to allow gaseous exchange, i.e. CO_2 in and surplus O_2 out – the gases pass in and out through tiny pores on the surface of the leaf called **stomata**

- to allow water to evaporate from the leaf in a process called **transpiration** (see Chapter 22), which helps draw water up the plant

- to store food, in some plants, e.g. cabbage and lettuce

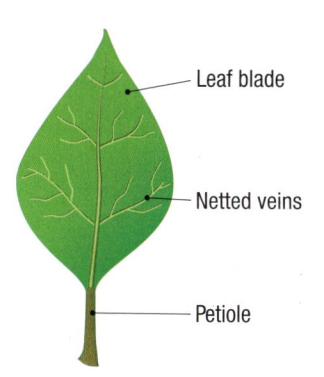

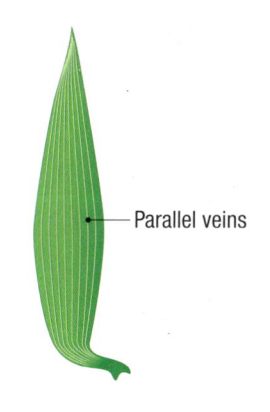

21.4 Veination in leaves

21.5 Different flower types

Flowers

Flowers are formed from flower buds, which once the flower is formed do not grow any more. Flowers may occur singly, as in the tulip, or in groups known as an **inflorescence** as in bluebells, wallflowers and foxgloves (Fig 21.5).

The function of the flower is for **sexual reproduction**. A typical flower consists of groups of modified (altered) leaves arranged in rings or whorls. There are four main whorls; the sepals, the petals, the stamens and the carpels (Fig 21.6). More detail of flower structure and function can be found in Chapter 34.

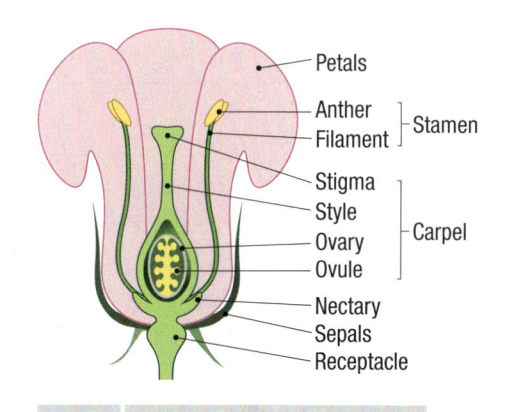

21.6 The structure of a typical flower

21 Flowering Plant Structure and Tissues

L.S. and T.S.

When examining plant tissues, the way you cut the **tissue** gives you a different view (Fig 21.7):

- A transverse section (T.S.) or cross-section (C.S.) is a cut made across the specimen.
- A longitudinal section or L.S. is a lengthwise cut through a specimen.

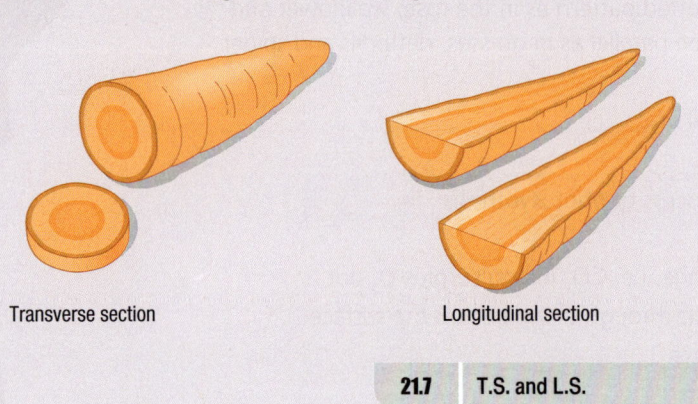

Transverse section

Longitudinal section

21.7 T.S. and L.S.

Growth and tissues in plants

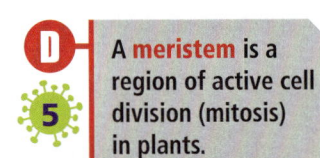

> **D 5** A **meristem** is a region of active cell division (mitosis) in plants.

Growth in a flowering plant happens as a result of cells dividing, i.e. they undergo **mitosis** (see Chapter 11). The region of active cell division in a plant is known as a **meristem**. Apical meristems are found at the tip of the shoot and the tip of the root, in buds and inside the vascular bundles of some stems (see Figs 21.8 and 21.9).

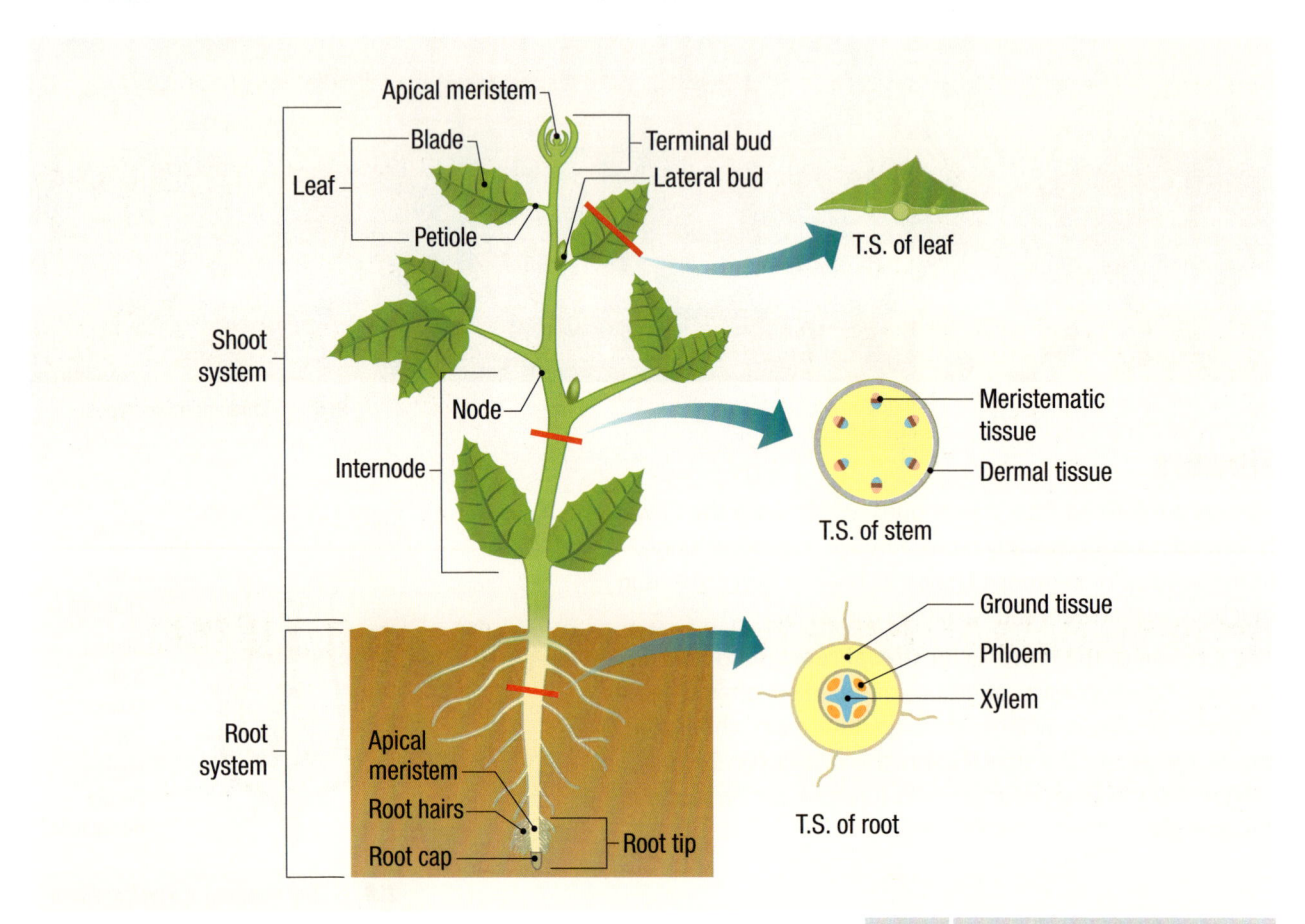

21.8 Organisation of plant tissues

Flowering Plant Structure and Tissues | 21

21.9 Plant tissue types

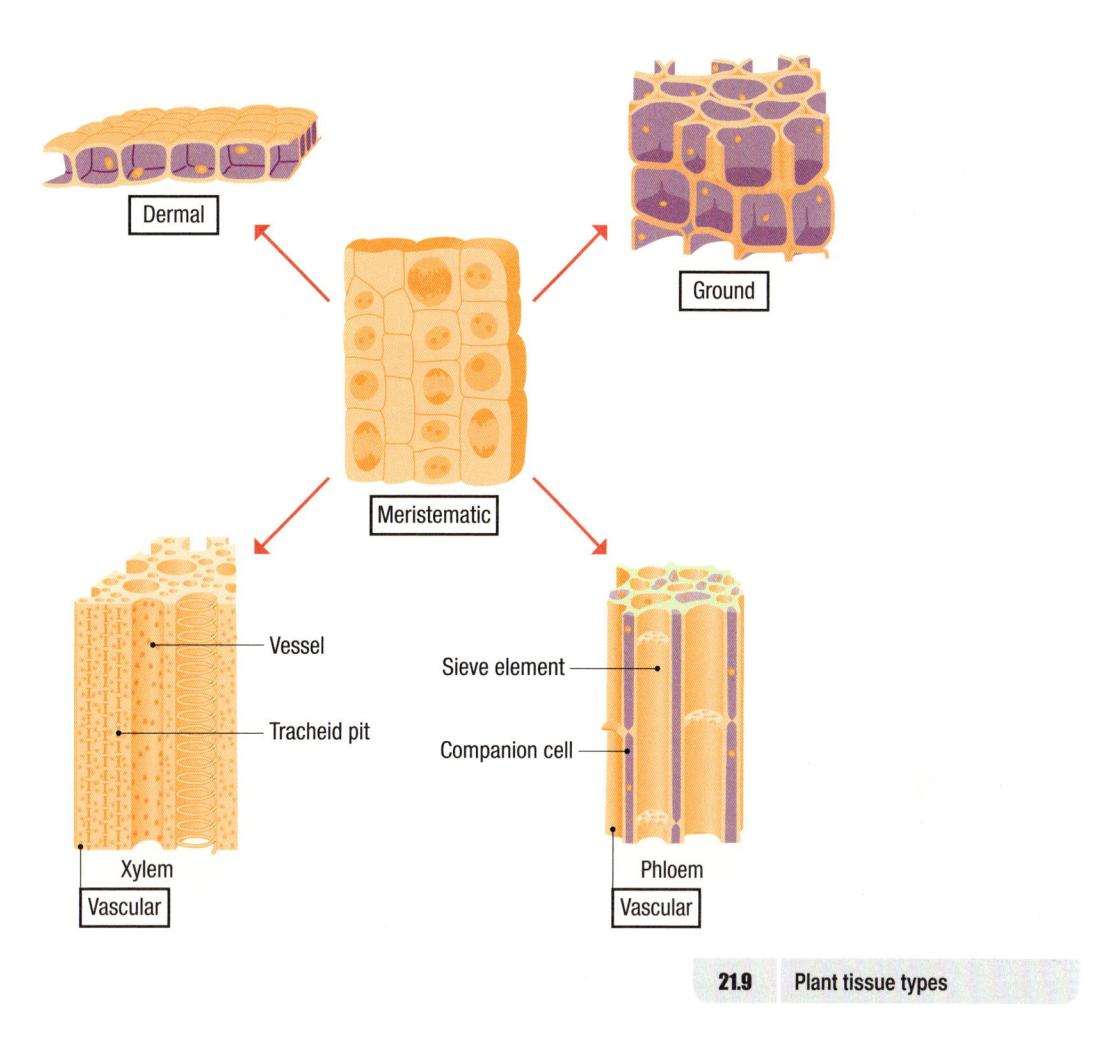

6. When cells in the apical meristems divide, they give rise to three main types of tissue: dermal, ground and vascular.

Tissue type	Location in plant	Function
Dermal	On the surface of the plant	Protection
Ground	Lies between the dermal and the vascular tissues	To make or store food and for strength
Vascular (xylem and phloem)	Veins of leaves Vascular bundles of stem Core of the root	Transport materials around the plant

Table 21.1 Plant tissues

Arrangement of tissue types in the root, stem and leaf

7. There is a specific and different arrangement of the plant tissue types in the root, stem and leaf.

In the root, the vascular tissue is found at the core (centre). There is more xylem than phloem as xylem is needed to transport the water and minerals that enter the plant at the root hairs. The ground tissue lies between the vascular and the dermal tissue.

21 | Flowering Plant Structure and Tissues

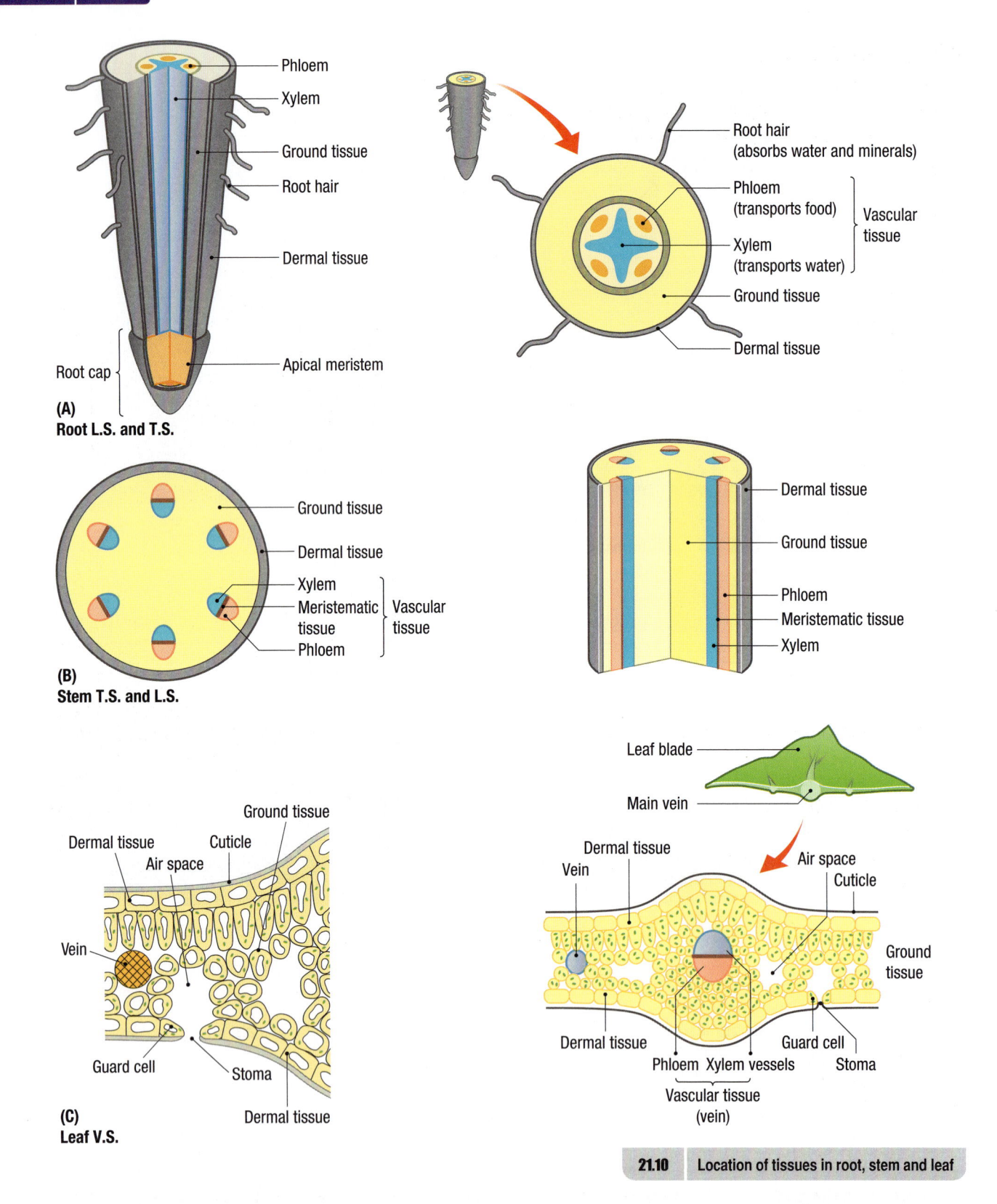

(A) Root L.S. and T.S.

(B) Stem T.S. and L.S.

(C) Leaf V.S.

| 21.10 | Location of tissues in root, stem and leaf |

In the stem the vascular tissue is parcelled off into discrete areas, surrounded by ground tissue. These areas are known as **vascular bundles**. The dermal layer lies on the outside. Sometimes dermal cells have extensions, forming hairs or thorns.

In the leaf, dermal tissue is found on both surfaces, forming the upper and lower epidermis. Sometimes the dermal cells are modified and have extensions, which form hairs. In addition some leaves have a non-cellular clear layer on the outside called a **cuticle**. The ground tissue lies between the two dermal layers, through which the vascular tissue runs as a mid-rib and veins.

Fig 21.10 shows the location of the main tissue types in a T.S and L.S. of a root, stem and leaf.

Flowering Plant Structure and Tissues | 21

Vascular tissue

8 As mentioned above the vascular tissue of flowering plants is located in the veins of the leaves, areas in the stem called vascular bundles and in the core of the root. There are two main types of vascular tissue, **xylem** and **phloem**.

Xylem

Functions
- Transport of water and minerals up the plant.
- Provides support.

Structure:
Xylem tissue consists of two kinds of conducting cells, **xylem tracheids** and **xylem vessels**.

1. Xylem tracheids are long, narrow cells, tapered at both ends, with pits in the walls. The pits allow water and minerals to move sideways from cell to cell. This feature can be important if a xylem cell becomes blocked by an air bubble. The cells are dead and hollow at maturity, i.e. they contain no cytoplasm or nucleus. The cells have end walls with gaps to allow passage of water. The walls of tracheids are thickened with a chemical called **lignin** which gives support (Fig 21.11).
2. Xylem vessels are hollow, dead, elongated cells with side walls thickened in spiral bands of lignin. They lack end walls, and when mature form a continuous conducting pipe. Vessel cells tend to be wider than tracheids and when stacked together are known as xylem vessels (Fig 21.12). You will learn more about how the xylem transports water in Chapter 22.

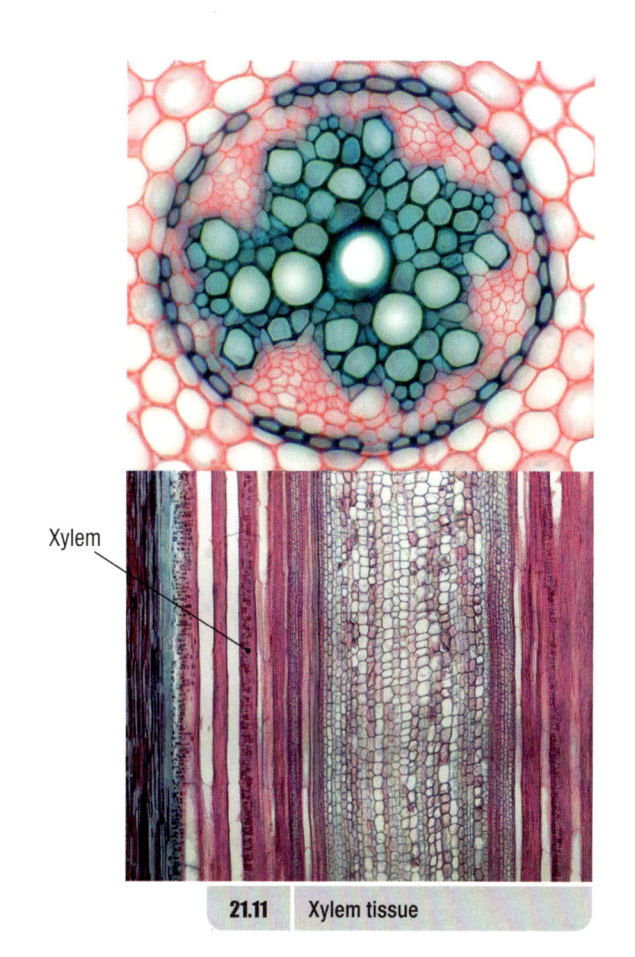

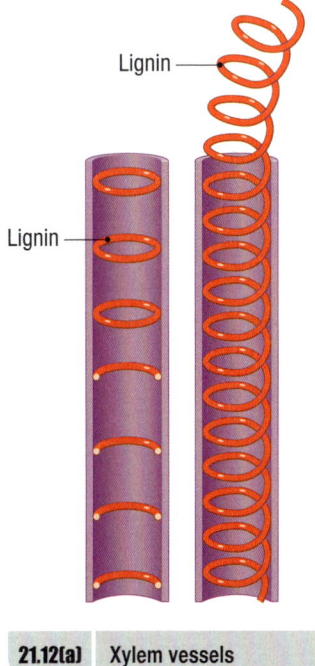

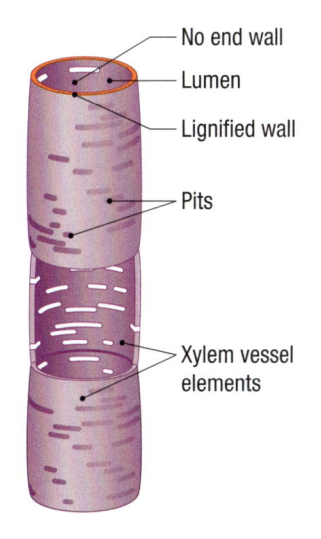

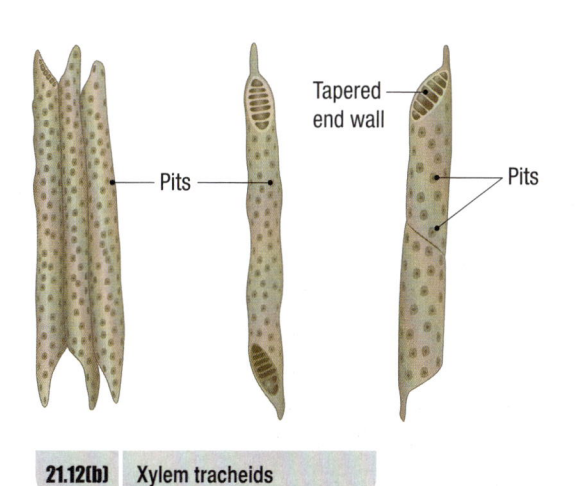

21.11 Xylem tissue

21.12(a) Xylem vessels

21.12(b) Xylem tracheids

Phloem

Function

- Transport of sugars, mainly sucrose, up and down the plant. Food made in the leaves may be needed in the root or above in the flowers.
- Transport of some plant growth regulators, e.g. **auxins** (see Chapter 28).
- Movement of food in the phloem is known as translocation.

Phloem tissue consists of two types of cells – phloem **sieve tube cells** (elements) and **companion cells** (Fig 21.14). Sieve tube cells are elongated cylindrical cells stacked end on end. The end walls have holes and are known as **sieve plates**. The sieve plates allow cytoplasm to move from one sieve tube cell to another. When mature, the nucleus of each tube cell disintegrates.

Each sieve tube cell has a companion cell beside it, which has a nucleus and is connected to the sieve tube cell by cytoplasmic connections. The nucleus of the companion cell controls the activities of both itself and the sieve tube cell. Phloem, unlike xylem, is considered a living tissue.

Xylem	Phloem
Dead, at maturity	Living
Lignified	Not lignified
Transports water and minerals, involved in support	Transports sucrose and auxins

Table 21.2 The differences between xylem and phloem

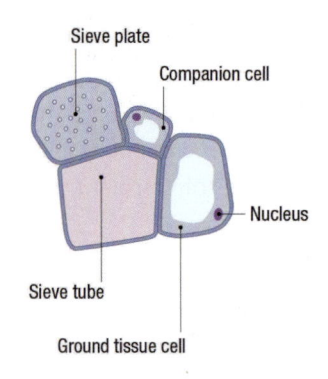

21.13 Phloem sieve tube and companion cells

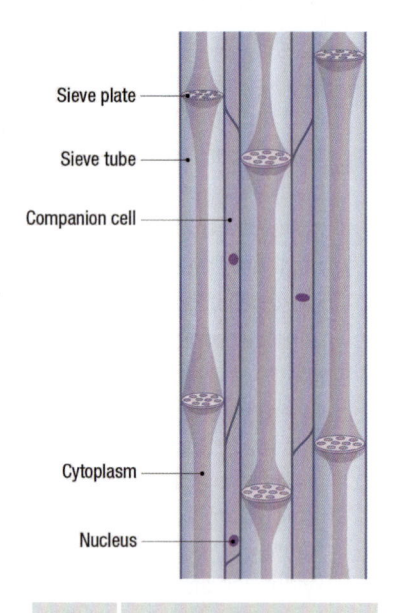

21.14 Phloem tissue

Classification of flowering plants

Flowering plants may be classed as:
- **woody**, e.g. trees and shrubs, or **herbaceous** (non-woody), e.g. grass, buttercup, lettuce;
- **monocotyledons** or **dicotyledons**, depending upon the number of **cotyledons** ('seed leaves') their seeds possess. The cotyledon provides nutrients for the developing **embryo** plant before it produces its own leaves, which can then photosynthesise.

> A **cotyledon** is an embryonic seed leaf.

> **Monocotyledons** have one seed leaf.

> **Dicotyledons** have two seed leaves.

Monocotyledons have only one cotyledon in the seed whereas dicotyledons have two cotyledons. Examples of monocotyledons are grass, bluebells, onions, and of dicotyledons are buttercups, horse chestnut, broad bean and sunflower.

Table 21.3 summarises the differences between monocotyledons and dicotyledons (also see Figs 21.15 and 21.16).

Flowering Plant Structure and Tissues — 21

	Monocots	Dicots
Number of seed 'leaves' (cotyledons)	One	Two
Arrangement of vascular bundles in the stem	Scattered	In a definite ring pattern
Leaf shape	Strap (elongated)	Broad
Leaf veination	Parallel	Netted (reticulate)
Number of flower parts, i.e. petals, sepals, stamens and carpels	In multiples of 3	In multiples of 4 and 5
Woody or herbaceous	Herbaceous	May be woody or herbaceous
Named examples	Grasses, daffodils, onions	Sycamore, roses, dandelions

Table 21.3 The differences between monocots and dicots

MONOCOT
- One cotyledon
- Vascular bundles scattered in stem
- Leaf veins parallel
- Flower parts in multiples of 3

DICOT
- Two cotyledons
- Vascular bundles in a distinct ring
- Leaf veins form a netted pattern
- Flower parts in multiples of 4 or 5

21.15 The differences between monocots and dicots

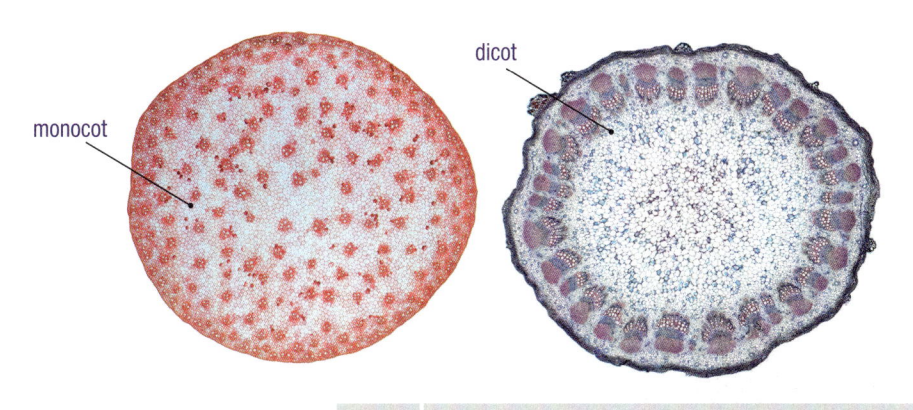

monocot   dicot

21.16 Photomicrographs of T.S. of monocot and dicot stems

21 Flowering Plant Structure and Tissues

Investigation 21.1

To prepare and examine a T.S. of a dicotyledenous stem

Method

A. To prepare the stem sections

1. Use part of a young (non-woody) plant stem (it is easier to cut), e.g. a piece of celery or buttercup stem.

2. Hold the stem as shown in Fig 21.17(a) or hold it with your hand against the cutting board.

3. With a sharp safety razor blade, cut very thin sections of the stem. Cut the stem between the nodes (to ensure only stem tissue is present). Always cut away from your body. (Hint: dipping the blade into water can help make a better cut.)

4. Transfer the sections to a dish of water (to prevent the tissue drying out Fig 21.17(b)).

5. If the sections are difficult to remove from the blade, use a fine paint brush to transfer them to the dish of water.

6. Place a drop of water onto a clean glass slide.

7. Using the paint brush, transfer two to three of the stem sections from the dish of water to the drop of water on the slide. Incomplete sections can also be used.

8. Cover the sections with a coverslip (to protect the lens of the microscope).

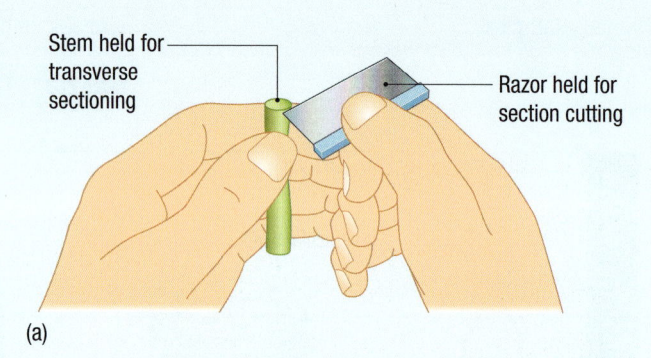

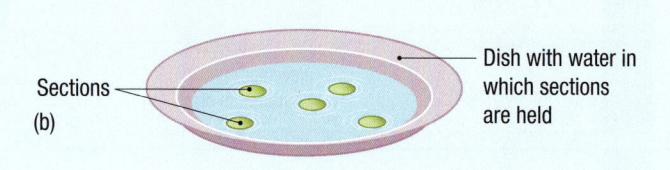

Take special care when using razor blades when making a stem section

21.17 (a) Cutting and (b) storing sections

B. To examine the stem sections:

1. Place the slide onto the microscope stage. Move the low power objective lens into position and bring the sections into focus.

2. Identify the dermal, ground and vascular tissues using Figs 21.16 and 21.18 as a guide. Draw an outline diagram to show the arrangement of the tissues.

3. Now increase the magnification to the medium power. Bring the sections into focus and examine the arrangement of tissues. Draw an outline diagram to show the arrangement of the tissues under medium power.

Flowering Plant Structure and Tissues | 21

4. Finally, increase the magnification to the highest power and once again identify the dermal, ground and vascular tissue.

5. The expected arrangement of tissues for celery is as shown in Fig 21.18.

6. Write up the investigation in your practical notebook.

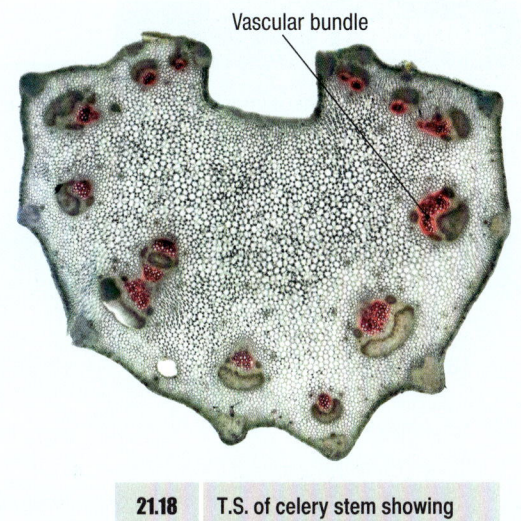

21.18 T.S. of celery stem showing arrangement of tissues

Summary

- A typical flowering plant consists of a root system below the ground and a shoot system (stem, leaves, buds and flowers) above ground.

Part	Main function(s)
Root	Absorbs water and minerals, anchorage, may store food
Stem	Supports aerial parts, allows conduction of materials
Bud	New growth (mitosis)
Leaf	Photosynthesis, gas exchange, transpiration
Flower	Sexual reproduction

- A meristem is an area of active cell division (mitosis) in a plant.
- Meristems are found at the shoot tip, the root tip and in the buds. Meristematic tissue divides to produce three types of plant tissue: (a) dermal tissue, (b) ground tissue, (c) vascular tissue.

Tissue	Function	Location
Meristem	Mitosis (growth)	Root tip, shoot tip, buds
Dermal	Protection	On the surface of the plant
Ground	Between the dermal and vascular tissues	Make food (in photosynthesis) and store food
Vascular	Transport materials	Veins of leaves, vascular bundles in stem, core of root

Summary

- Xylem transports water and minerals up the plant and gives support. There are two types of xylem cell: xylem tracheids and xylem vessels.

Xylem tracheids	Xylem vessels
Tapered with end walls	Not tapered, no end walls
Dead, hollow tubes	Dead, hollow tubes
Lignified	Lignified
Have pits	Have pits

Table 21.4 Xylem cells (Fig 21.12)

- Phloem transports sugars, e.g. sucrose, up and down the plant.
- There are two types of phloem cell: sieve tube cells and companion cells.

Phloem sieve tube elements	Companion cell
Living tubes with cytoplasm	Living cell
No nucleus at maturity	Has nucleus
Elongated cells with sieve plate	Small elongated cells, no sieve plate

Table 21.5 Phloem cells (Fig 21.13)

- Herbaceous plants produce little or no wood, e.g. buttercup.
- Woody plants have woody stems, e.g. rose bush, horse chestnut tree.
- Flowering plants may be classified as monocotyledons or dicotyledons based on the organisation of their tissues.
- A cotyledon (seed leaf) is a leaf formed in the embryo plant which acts as a food store.
- Cotyledons usually lack chlorophyll.
- Monocotyledons have one embryonic seed leaf, scattered vascular bundles in the stem, parallel veins in the leaves, and flower parts in threes and are mainly herbaceous, e.g. bluebells, grasses.
- Dicotyledons have two embryonic seed leaves, vascular bundles in a distinct ring pattern, netted veins in the leaves, and flower parts in fours or fives. Both woody and herbaceous types are common, e.g. roses, buttercups.
- Investigation 21.1 describes how to prepare and examine a T.S. of a dicotyledon stem.

Flowering Plant Structure and Tissues

Review questions

01 (a) Name two flowering plants.
(b) Identify the parts labelled A to F in the diagram below.
(c) State the main function of A, B and C.

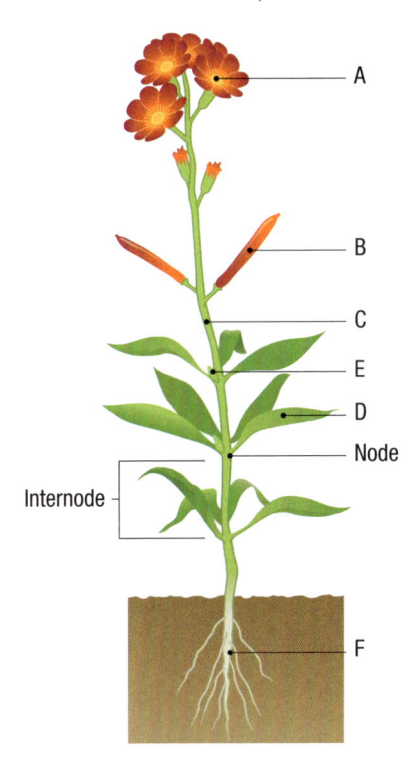

02 (a) Name the two types of root.
(b) List three functions of the root of a plant.
(c) Name a plant whose root you eat for food.
(d) State one way in which the structure of a root is adapted to its function.
(e) Suggest why roots are generally not green in colour.

03 (a) List the parts of the shoot system of a plant.
(b) State the function of each of the parts listed.
(c) Name a plant whose leaves can be eaten by humans.

04 (a) State the two types of leaf veination and for each, name a plant that has that type of leaf.
(b) Draw labelled diagrams to show the two types of veination in plant leaves.
(c) The leaf is an organ of the plant. Explain the term organ and name two other plant organs.

05 (a) What is a tissue?
(b) Meristematic tissue is an example of a plant tissue.
 (i) What is the function of meristematic tissue?
 (ii) List two places in a plant where meristematic tissue can be found.
 (iii) Name the three main tissue types which arise from the meristematic tissue.

06 Distinguish between the following:
(a) Root and shoot system.
(b) Dermal and ground tissue.
(c) Longitudinal and transverse sections.
(d) Xylem and phloem.
(e) Xylem vessels and xylem tracheids.

07 Draw a labelled diagram to show the position of the dermal, ground and vascular tissues in a transverse section of a stem.

08 (a) What is a cotyledon?
(b) Make a two-column table placing monocotyledons at the top of one column and dicotyledons at the top of the other column. Complete the table to compare and contrast the two types of plant under the following headings:
 (i) Number of cotyledons.
 (ii) Leaf veination.
 (iii) Nnumber of flower parts.
 (iv) Arrangement of vascular bundles in the stem.
 (v) A named example.

09 (a) Examine the diagram below and state which diagram, A or B, represents a T.S. of a dicotyledenous stem. Give a reason for your answer.
(b) Label the parts P, Q, R, S, T in the diagrams.
(c) Name an instrument suitable for making a T.S. of the stem.

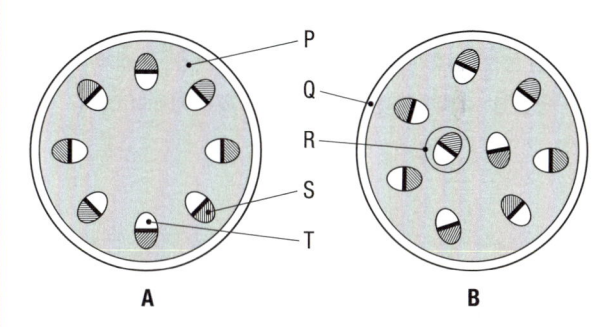

10 Answer the following in relation to an investigation you carried out to prepare and examine a T.S. of a dicotyledenous stem.
(a) Name the plant stem you used.
(b) Why did you use a young rather than an old stem?
(c) Describe how and where on the stem you cut the T.S.
(d) How did you transfer the cut sections to the dish of water?
(e) Why was it important to cut a very thin section?
(f) With what did you examine the T.S.?

21 Flowering Plant Structure and Tissues

Examination style questions

Section A

01 The diagram below shows a section of a green leaf.

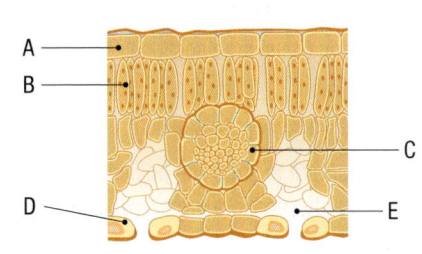

(a) Match the cell types A, B and C on the diagram, to one of the tissue types listed:
vascular tissue   dermal tissue   ground tissue
(b) What is the part labelled E?
(c) What is the function of cell D?
(d) On the diagram shade the area responsible for water transport.
(e) Carbon dioxide and oxygen pass through the stomata. Name one other substance that is lost to the atmosphere through the stomata.

02 The diagram shows a flowering plant tissue in transverse section.
(a) Name the tissue shown.
(b) Name the cell types labelled A and B.
(c) Where would you expect to find this tissue in the stem of a young dicot plant?
(d) What is the function of (i) cell type A and (ii) cell type B?
(e) In which zone of a young root is this tissue formed?

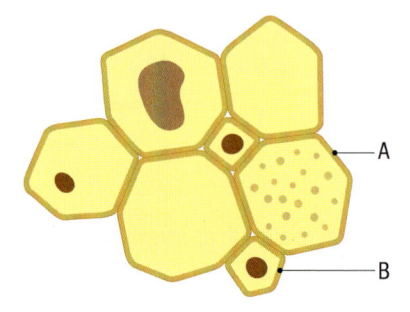

Section B

03 (a) (i) Give an example of a dicotyledonous plant.
(ii) Other than number of cotyledons, state one difference between a monocotyledon and a dicotyledon.
(b) (i) When preparing a transverse section (T.S.) of a dicotyledonous stem, what is the ideal age or condition of the stem?
(ii) With what did you cut the stem?
(iii) Why are the stem sections placed in water after they are cut?
(iv) Name the small thin sheet of glass that is placed over the cut section before viewing the stem section with a microscope.
(v) Draw a diagram to show some or all of your section of stem as seen under the microscope. Label the following parts: dermal tissue, ground tissue, vascular bundle.
(vi) Give one function in the stem for dermal and ground tissue.

Section C

04 (a) The diagram shows a 3D view of a root.

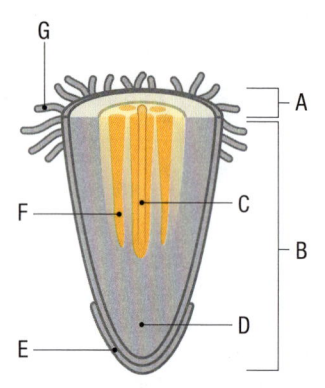

Which letter on the diagram:
(i) Shows the region that absorbs water from the soil?
(ii) Represents a T.S.?
(iii) Shows a region that carries food.
(b) (i) Name the type of tissue that transports food in plants.
(ii) Draw a labelled diagram of this tissue in L.S.
(iii) In what form is food transported?
(iv) How is this tissue similar to and different from the tissue type that transports water in plants?
(c) (i) What is a meristem?
(ii) Draw an outline diagram of a small flowering plant and on it mark the locations of meristems.
(iii) Name the three main tissue types that are formed from the cells produced by meristems.

05 (a) (i) Explain the term cotyledon.
(ii) Where in a plant are cotyledons to be found?
(iii) Name a dicotyledonous plant.
(b) (i) Distinguish between a transverse and a longitudinal section.
(ii) Draw a labelled diagram of a transverse section of a young, non-woody dicot stem to show the general arrangement of tissues.
(iii) In what way(s) does the T.S. you have drawn in (ii) differ from that of a monocot stem?
(iv) Indicate by means of the letter P the tissue in the stem you have drawn that has a role in the making and storing of food.

Examination style questions

(c) Write notes on any **three** of the following. You are required to make a minimum of **three** points concerning each.
   (i) Xylem tracheids.
   (ii) Roots.
   (iii) The functions of leaves.
   (iv) Phloem sieve tubes.

06 (a) (i) List the parts of the shoot system of a plant.
   (ii) Give **one** function for **two** of the parts listed.
(b) (i) Distinguish between the root and shoot system of a plant.
   (ii) List the functions of the root.
   (iii) What are root hairs? What is their function?
   (iv) State one way in which the structure of a root is adapted to its function.
   (v) Why are roots generally not green in colour?
(c) (i) Draw a labelled diagram to show the structure of a typical dicot root in L.S.
   (ii) What is a tissue?
   (iii) What is dermal tissue? State where it is located in the plant.
   (iv) Mark one location of dermal tissue on the diagram you have drawn.
   (v) When transplanting seedlings (young plants) suggest why gardeners are advised to ease the seedlings out of the ground rather than pulling them out.

Leaving Certificate examination questions

Section A

01 The diagram shows the structure of a flowering plant.
(a) Name the parts labelled A, B and C.
(b) Give **one** main function of each of the parts labelled A, B and C.
(c) Flowers are the organs of which type of reproduction in the plant?

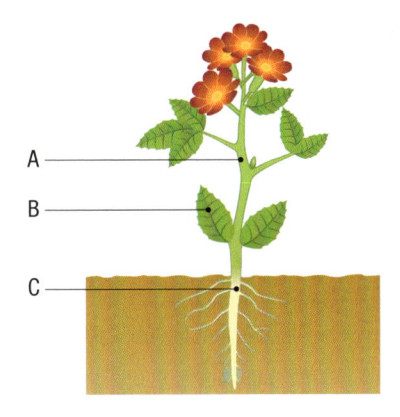

2013 OL Q. 2

02 The diagram below represents a transverse section through part of a plant.

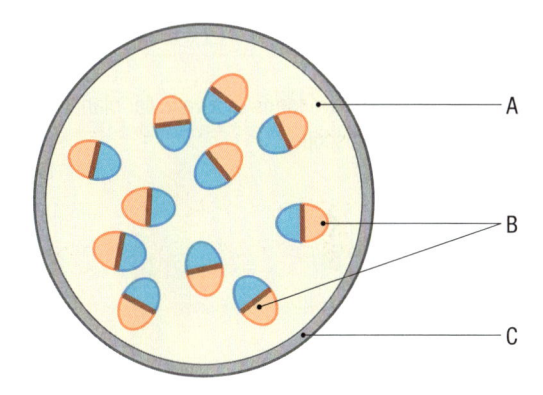

(a) Does the diagram represent a root or a stem?
(b) The letters A, B, C in the diagram represent three different tissue types. Match each letter with its correct tissue type in the following list:
   ground tissue   dermal tissue   vascular tissue
(c) State a function of vascular tissue.
(d) Name the **two** types of vascular tissue in plants.

2012 OL Q. 4

21 Flowering Plant Structure and Tissues

Leaving Certificate examination questions

03 The diagram shows a transverse section through the stem of a monocotyledonous (monocot) plant.
(a) What is meant by the term *monocotyledonous*?
(b) Give an example of a monocotyledonous plant.
(c) Name the structures labelled A.
(d) How do you know from the diagram that the section is taken from: (i) a stem? (ii) a monocot?
(e) How are the veins arranged in the leaves of monocots?
(f) How does the vein arrangement in the leaves of dicot plants differ from that in monocots?

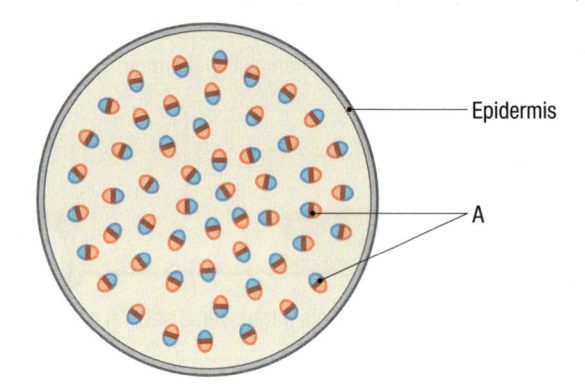

2012 HL Q. 5

04 The diagrams represent two forms of a vascular plant tissue, as seen under the microscope.

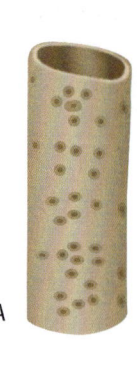

(a) Name this vascular tissue.
(b) Identify the two forms of this tissue, A and B.
(c) The walls of A and B are reinforced with a hard material. Name this material.
(d) Where precisely is this vascular tissue found in the stem of a young dicotyledonous plant?
(e) Name another vascular tissue.

2007 HL Q. 6

Section B

05 (a) (i) Why is a dicotyledonous (dicot) plant so called?
(ii) Give **one** function of vascular tissue in plants.
(b) Answer the following questions in relation to how you prepared and examined with a microscope a transverse section (T.S.) of a dicotyledonous stem.
(i) Name the plant that you used.
(ii) Why did you use a herbaceous (non-woody) stem rather than a woody one?
(iii) Outline how you made the section of the stem **and** prepared it for examination.
(iv) Describe how you examined your section of stem with the microscope.
(v) Draw a labelled diagram to best represent what was seen on your slide. Label the following on your diagram:
    ground tissue   xylem   phloem

2014 OL Q. 7

06 (a) (i) In biology, what is meant by the term *organ*?
(ii) In school, a light microscope is normally used to examine cells and tissues. Name a more powerful type of microscope that is used to show what cells are made of in much greater detail (cell ultrastructure).
(b) Answer the following questions in relation to how you prepared and examined with a microscope a transverse section (T.S.) of a dicotyledonous stem.
(i) Name the plant that you used.
(ii) How did you make a section of the stem **and** prepare it for examination?
(iii) Describe how you examined your section of stem once you had placed the slide on the stage of the microscope.

2010 OL Q. 9

07 (a) Observation of a transverse section of a dicotyledonous stem reveals vascular and other tissues. Name **two** of the tissues that are not vascular tissues.
(b) Answer the following questions in relation to the preparation of a microscope slide of a transverse section of a dicotyledonous stem.
(i) State **one** reason why you used a herbaceous stem rather than a woody one.
(ii) Explain how you cut the section.
(iii) Why is it desirable to cut the section as thinly as possible?
(iv) Draw a diagram of the section as seen under the microscope. Label the vascular tissues that can be seen.

2004 HL Q. 8

Leaving Certificate examination questions

Section C

08 The diagrams show two types of vascular tissue in plants.

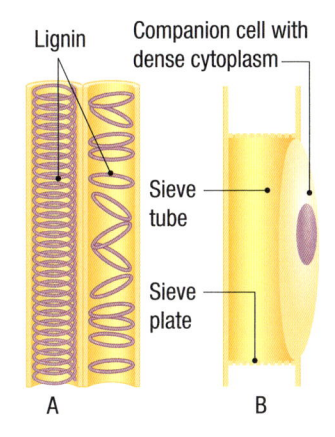

(i) Name the tissues A and B.
(ii) Which of the above tissues transports water from the roots?
(iii) Which of the above tissues transports food from the leaves?
(iv) Is tissue A living or dead?
(v) Suggest a role of the lignin in tissue A.
(vi) Name **one** process that causes water to move upwards through a plant.
(vii) Name the structures in the leaves through which water exits the plant.
(viii) Vascular tissue is one type of plant tissue. Name **two** other plant tissues.

2013 OL Q. 15 (c)

09 The diagram shows a transverse section through a dicotyledonous (dicot) root.

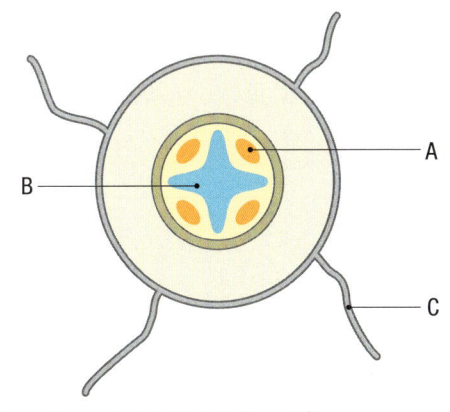

(i) Name the parts labelled A, B and C.
(ii) State two functions of a root.
(iii) From what part of a seed does the root develop?
(iv) Give one example of a root modified for food storage.
(v) Plants can be monocotyledonous or dicotyledonous. Give any **one** difference between a monocotyledonous plant and a dicotyledonous plant.
(vi) Give **one** example of a monocotyledonous plant **and** one example of a dicotyledonous plant.

2011 OL Q. 15 (b)

10 The photograph below shows the tissues in a **transverse** section of a dicotyledonous (dicot) stem.

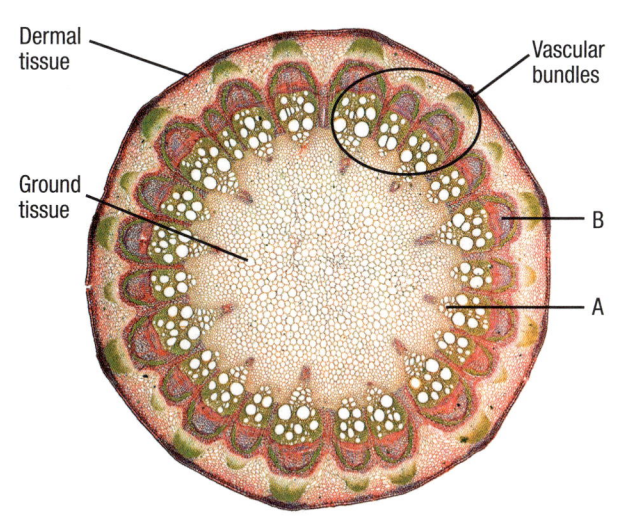

(i) Give **one** feature shown in the photograph that allows you to identify the section as a stem and not a root.
(ii) Name the **two** vascular tissues, A and B, found in a vascular bundle.
(iii) Draw a labelled diagram to show a **longitudinal** section of tissue B. Include the following labels in your diagram: sieve tube   sieve plate   companion cell
(iv) Give **one** function of **each** of the following:
   1. Dermal tissue.
   2. Ground tissue.
(v) 1. In which of the vascular tissues does water transport occur?
   2. State **one** way in which this tissue is adapted for water transport.
   3. In which direction does this transport take place?

2009 Q. 14 (a)

11 (i) Draw a diagram of a transverse section through a young dicotyledonous stem as seen under the low power lens of a microscope. Indicate on your diagram a location for each of the following: dermal tissue, ground tissue, vascular tissue.

21 Flowering Plant Structure and Tissues

Leaving Certificate examination questions

(ii) 1. Which of the above tissue types has a different location in a young root?
2. Where precisely is the tissue type referred to in 1. found in the root?
3. Give **one** function of ground tissue.
(iii) Draw labelled diagrams to show the detailed structure of the **two** vascular tissues of plants.
(iv) Which of the tissues referred to in (iii) is composed of living cells?
(v) What is the function of meristematic tissue?

2014 HL Q. 14 (b)

12 The diagram shows part of a transverse section through a dicotyledonous stem.

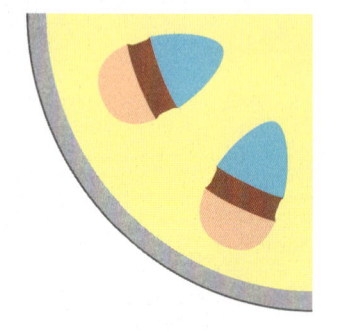

(i) Copy the diagram into your answer book and identify each of the following by placing the appropriate letter on your diagram:
phloem P   ground tissue G   xylem X   dermal tissue D
(ii) In which of the tissues that you have identified are sugars mainly transported?
(iii) State a function of D.
(iv) In the course of your practical work you cut and observed a transverse section of a stem. Answer the following in relation to that procedure:
1. What did you use to cut the section?
2. How did you support the stem while you were cutting the section?
3. How did you transfer the section to a microscope slide?
(v) State one way in which a transverse section through a monocotyledonous stem differs from the one that you cut.

2006 HL Q. 14 (c)

Past examination questions

OL	2014 Q. 4 (a), (e), Q. 7, Q. 13 (b) (i)–(iii)	2013 Q. 2, Q. 15 (c)	2012 Q. 4	2011 Q. 15 (b)	
	2010 Q. 9	2009 Q. 14 (a)	2008 Q. 15 (a)	2007 Q. 5, Q. 14 (a)	2006 Q. 4, Q. 14 (b)
	2005 Q. 15 (a)	2004 Q. 15 (c)			
HL	2014 Q. 14 (b)	2012 Q. 5	2009 Q. 7	2008 Q. 14 (c) (i)	2007 Q. 6
	2006 Q. 14 (c)	2004 Q. 4 (a), Q. 8			

Transport, Nutrition and Food Storage in the Flowering Plant

22

After studying this chapter you should be able to:

1. Outline the need for a transport system and appreciate that plants are autotrophic.
2. Describe how plants take up water and how water is transported through the plant.
3. Explain the term root pressure and understand its role in water movement.
4. Explain the term transpiration and understand its role in water movement.
5. **HL** Describe how the cohesion-tension model of water transport operates. Refer to the work of Dixon and Joly.
6. Describe how plants take up minerals and how minerals are transported through the plant.
7. Describe how plants take up carbon dioxide and how carbon dioxide is transported through the plant.
8. Describe how the products of photosynthesis (glucose and oxygen) are distributed through the plant.
9. Explain how leaves, stems and roots may be modified to store food in plants. Be able to give one example of each.

The need for a transport system

1 Flowering plants are **autotrophic**, i.e. they can make their own food in the process known as **photosynthesis**:

$$6CO_2 + 6H_2O \rightarrow C_6H_{12}O_6 + 6O_2$$

Plants are large, complex, multicellular **organisms** and they need a transport system: (i) to carry the raw materials for photosynthesis to where the food is made, (ii) to carry the products of photosynthesis to where they are needed around the plant.

In addition to water and food, plants transport minerals, gases and **plant growth regulators**.

Mineral, such as nitrates and phosphates are needed for various chemical reactions in the cells of plants. Gases such as carbon dioxide and oxygen are needed for photosynthesis and **respiration** respectively.
In addition, plant growth regulators are needed to control the rate of growth and the development of plants (see Chapter 28).

We learnt in Chapter 21 that plants have two types of transport tissue, the xylem and the phloem. We can now see how these tissues are used by plants.

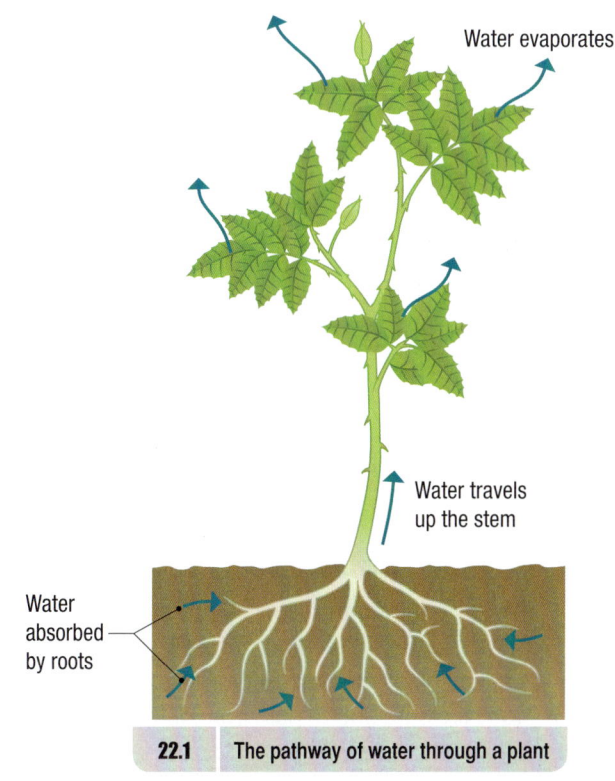

22.1 The pathway of water through a plant

Transport, Nutrition and Food Storage in the Flowering Plant

Uptake and transport of water in plants

1. The uptake of water into the plant

Water is needed for photosynthesis and to form part of the cytoplasm of cells. Here it has a role in keeping plant cells **turgid** and provides a medium for chemical reactions.

The source of water for a plant is the soil. Water enters the plant, through the root hairs, by **osmosis** (see Chapter 10). This occurs due to a difference in concentration between the high water concentration in soil and the lower water concentration in the **cytoplasm** of the root cells.

Adaptations of the root for water uptake
- The root hairs are very numerous and this greatly increases the surface area across which absorption can occur.
- Root hairs are thin walled.
- Root hairs do not possess a **cuticle** because they must be permeable to water.

2. Transport of water up the plant

The water **diffuses** across the ground tissue (cortex) and into the xylem (Fig 22.1). Water travels up the **xylem vessels** in the stem and out into the leaves. The xylem vessels form a continuous hollow pipeline through which water can pass.

Adaptations of xylem for water transport:

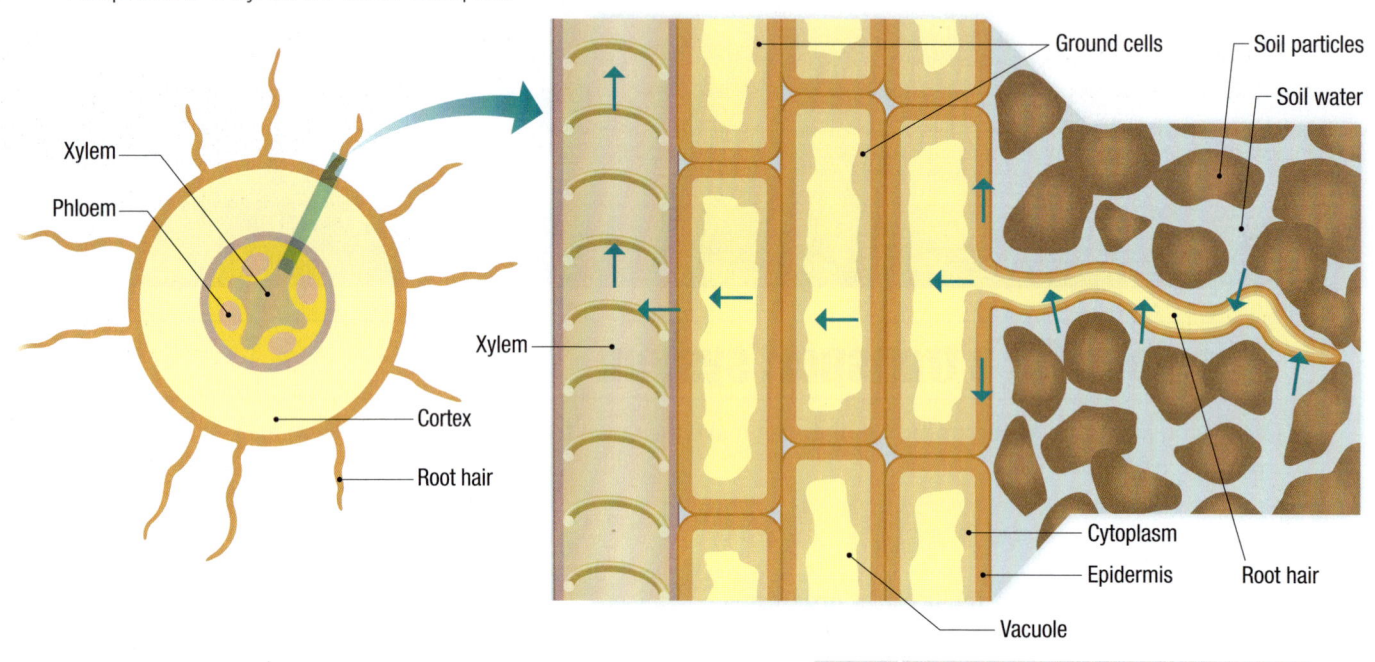

22.2 Movement of water into and across the root

- Thin, hollow, continuous tubes with narrow bore.
- Strengthened with lignin.
- Pits to allow sideways movement of water.

But how is it possible for water to rise against gravity up to the top of the highest trees?

Two processes combine to cause upwards movement of water in the plant – **root pressure** and **transpiration**.

> **Root pressure** is the force that pushes water up the stem from the root.

1. Root pressure

Water, entering the roots by osmosis, generates a pressure called root pressure. Root pressure helps to 'push' water up the xylem vessels. However, root pressure alone does not account for the ability of water to reach the top of the tallest plants. Water rises through the plant as a result of a 'push' from below – root pressure and a 'pull' from above – transpiration.

Transport, Nutrition and Food Storage in the Flowering Plant | 22

2. Transpiration

Only a tiny percentage of the water that moves up to the leaves is used in photosynthesis and other activities. Over 99% of the water evaporates from the cells inside the leaves and exits through the **stomata** as water vapour. This loss of water vapour from the surface of the plant is called transpiration. When water evaporates from the leaf cells these cells become less turgid. This causes water to move into them by osmosis from the xylem vessels. In this way, water is 'pulled' up the stem from the roots.

> **Transpiration** is the loss of water vapour from the surface of a plant.

Control of transpiration

1. Transpiration is controlled by the presence of a cuticle

The leaves of plants are covered with a transparent, non-cellular, outer layer called the cuticle. The cuticle prevents the loss of too much water from the plant. Some plants have a thin cuticle and in others it is much thicker, e.g. holly leaves. The presence of a cuticle is one of the ways in which flowering plants have adapted to living on land, surrounded by air and not in water.

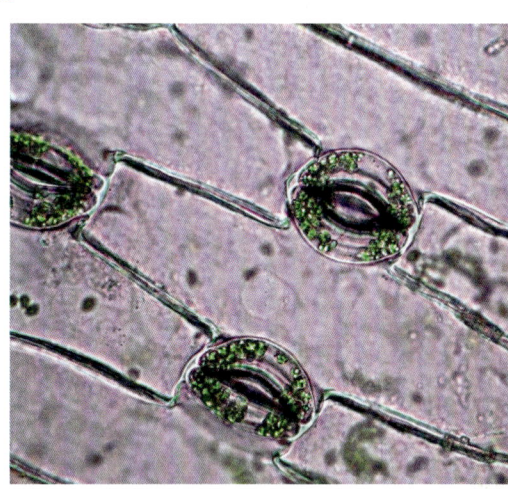

2. Transpiration is also controlled by the opening and closing of stomata

Stomata are tiny openings on the surface of the leaves and stems through which water vapour escapes (Fig 22.3). Most **dicotyledons** have a greater number of stomata on the lower surface of their leaves, whereas **monocotyledons** have a more or less equal number on both leaf surfaces.

22.3 Stomata on the under surface of a leaf

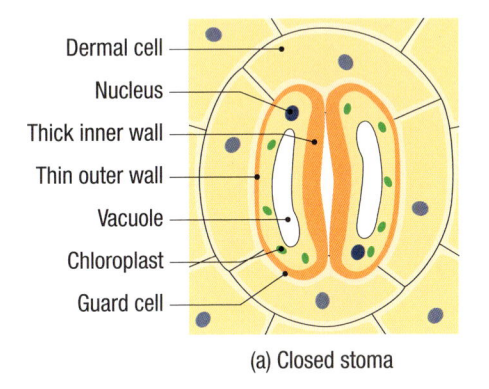

22.4 Guard cells control the opening and closing of the stomata

(a) Closed stoma
(b) Open stoma

Labels: Dermal cell, Nucleus, Thick inner wall, Thin outer wall, Vacuole, Chloroplast, Guard cell

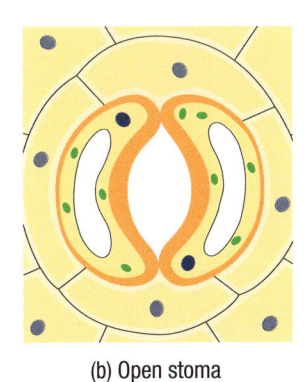

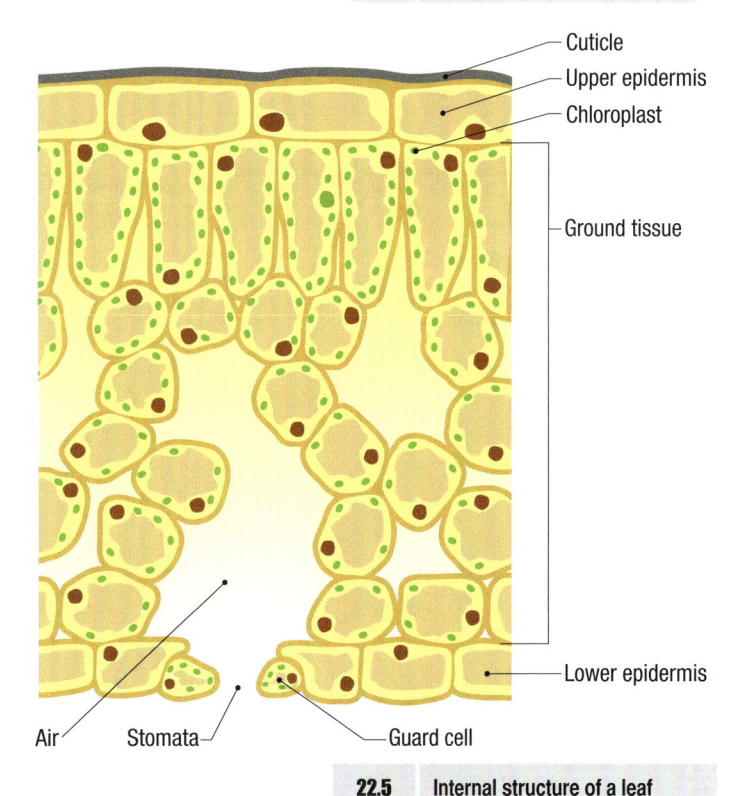

22.5 Internal structure of a leaf

Labels: Cuticle, Upper epidermis, Chloroplast, Ground tissue, Lower epidermis, Air, Stomata, Guard cell

Each stomata is bounded by a pair of sausage-shaped **guard cells** which control the opening and closing of the stomata. The stomata usually open during the day to allow for gas exchange and close at night. When the stomata are open, water loss increases and when the stomata close, water loss (transpiration) decreases. In general, plants transpire most during the day.

The opening and closing of the stomata is itself controlled by changes in the levels of carbon dioxide in the leaf air spaces, see page 350.

Environmental factors such as light intensity, humidity and air movements also affect the rate of transpiration.

HL The cohesion-tension model of water transport

So, how does water rise to great heights in plants, against the force of gravity? The answer lies in the properties of water and the structure of the xylem. In 1895 the cohesion-tension model of water movement in plants was put forward by two Irish scientists, Henry Dixon and John Joly.

1. Due to their polar nature, water molecules cling to each other, i.e. they are cohesive. In addition water molecules are adhesive in that they stick to the walls of the xylem vessels. The cohesive and adhesive properties of water ensure a continuous column of water can move upwards through the plant.
2. Water evaporates from the leaves through transpiration. More water is then pulled out of the xylem into the air spaces in the leaf, to replace it. This creates a tension (suction) which 'pulls' more water from the xylem into the leaf. The tension makes the xylem vessels narrower and the narrower the vessel, the greater the pulling force.
3. Because water molecules are cohesive, when some are pulled from the xylem into the leaf air spaces, others follow.
4. This means an unbroken column of water in the xylem can move upwards from the roots to the top of the plant.

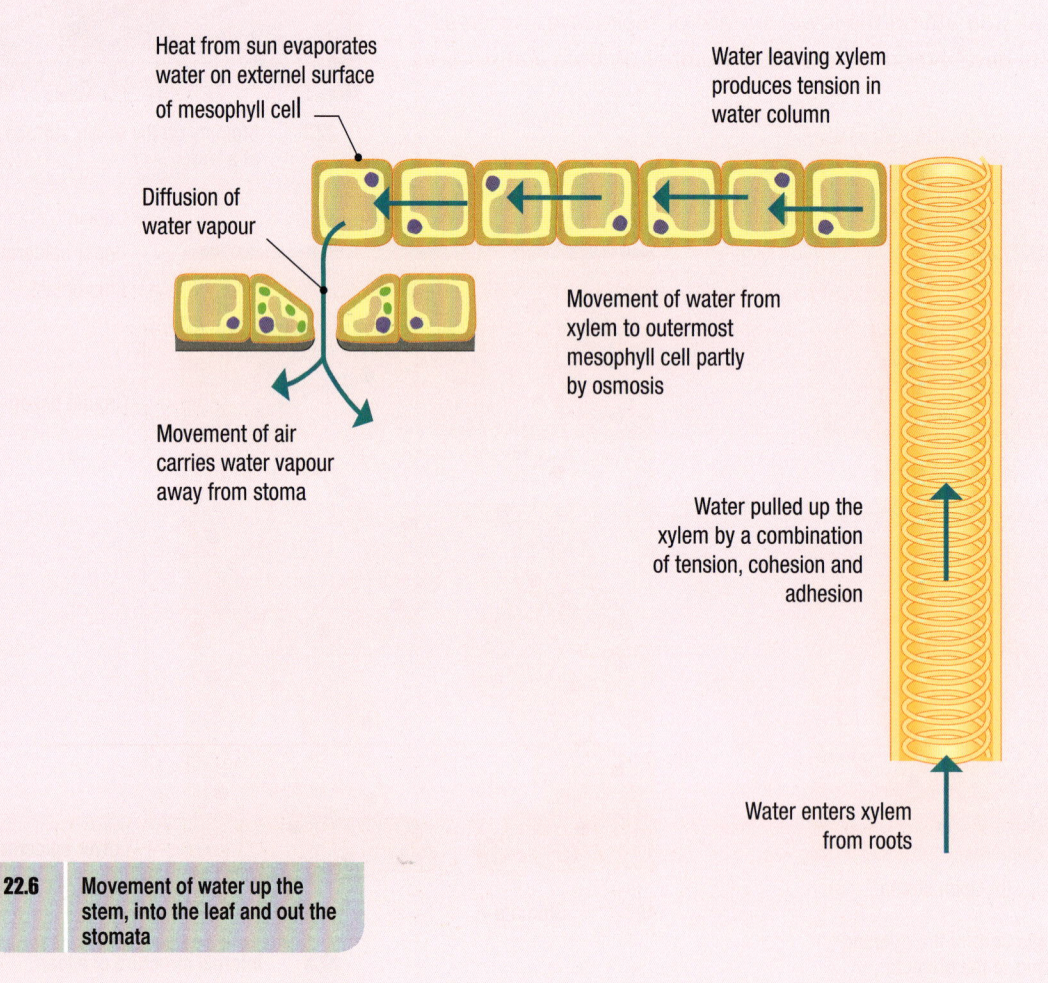

22.6 Movement of water up the stem, into the leaf and out the stomata

In summary, transpiration causes a tension in the leaf which pulls water up the xylem to the top of the plant. The cohesive and adhesive properties of water molecules make an unbroken column of water possible.

Uptake and transport of minerals
1. Uptake of minerals into the plant

Minerals are absorbed by plants from the soil, in the form of ions, e.g. magnesium is absorbed as Mg^{++}, calcium as Ca^{++}, sulphur as SO_4^{--}. The role of minerals in the plant is also discussed in Chapter 3.

Minerals enter the root through the root hairs by diffusion, due to a difference in concentration between the soil and the cytoplasm.

2. Transport of minerals through the plant

Once in the root, minerals pass across the ground tissue (cortex) to the xylem in the centre of the root. A layer of cells called the endodermis surrounds the vascular tissue of the root and certain minerals are unable to pass through this layer without the use of energy. Such minerals are taken through the endodermis by **active transport**. When they have reached the xylem, the minerals travel up the plant along with the water. The ions are then absorbed into cells where they are used or stored.

Uptake and transport of carbon dioxide
1. Uptake of carbon dioxide by the plant

Carbon dioxide is one of the raw materials needed for photosynthesis (see the equation for photosynthesis page 289).

The sources of carbon dioxide for the plant are either from respiration within its cells or by diffusion from the air through the stomata.

2. Transport of carbon dioxide through the plant

Carbon dioxide diffuses through the air spaces in the leaf and from cell to cell. It is used in cells to make food and is produced during respiration.

Transport of the products of photosynthesis

The products of photosynthesis are glucose and oxygen.

Photosynthesis produces food in the form of glucose. This glucose may be stored in the form of starch in the leaf or it may be transported in the form of sucrose (sugar), from the leaves, all around the plant. Sucrose travels around the plant in the phloem sieve tube cells.

The oxygen produced during photosynthesis may be used by the plant in respiration or released through the stomata during the day, by diffusion.

How plants store food

Plants use the food they make to get energy and to grow and develop. Any surplus food is stored, mainly as starch. Some plants store their surplus food as oil, e.g. in sunflower seeds.

Many plants store food to allow them to survive when they cannot make their food, for example, during the winter. Such plants have special modified storage organs which swell with food.

Fig (a) Food made in the leaves passes to parts underground.

Fig (b) Underground parts become swollen with food stores.

Fig (c) Parts above ground die away but the storage organ lies dormant in the soil.

Fig (d) The storage organ produces a new shoot using the stored food.

22.7 How plants store food to survive the winter

22 Transport, Nutrition and Food Storage in the Flowering Plant

A turnip is a modified root swollen with stored starch and so is a carrot. A potato is a modified swollen stem and an onion is a group of swollen leaves.

The storage organ can survive the winter underground and provide the next year's plant with food until it produces leaves and photosynthesises for itself (Fig 22.7).

Modified roots

In some plants, the first root of the plant grows straight down and forms the main root or tap root. The tap roots of many dicotyledonous plants may become swollen with starch, e.g. parsnip, carrot and radish. We eat a lot of swollen tap roots as 'root' vegetables (Fig 22.8(a)). The sugar beet plant stores food in the form of sucrose in large swollen roots. Sugar beet grows in temperate climates and is a very important commercial source of sugar for humans.

Modified stems

Horizontal, underground stems called **rhizomes** can become enlarged with food stores, for example in the iris, and nettle. Sometimes only the tip of the rhizome becomes swollen with food. Such tips are called tubers. A potato is an example of a stem tuber swollen with stored food for the new shoot (Fig 22.8(b)).

Modified leaves

An onion **bulb** is a group of leaves that swell and store food (Fig 22.8(c)). You may remember discovering this as stored starch grains in the cytoplasm of the onion cells turn a blue/black colour when stained with iodine solution. Heads of cabbage and lettuce are other examples of leaves modified for food storage, as are the leaf stalks (petioles) of rhubarb and celery.

As well as acting as stores of food, many of these modified roots, stems and leaves are used by the plant as a method of **asexual reproduction** (see Chapter 35).

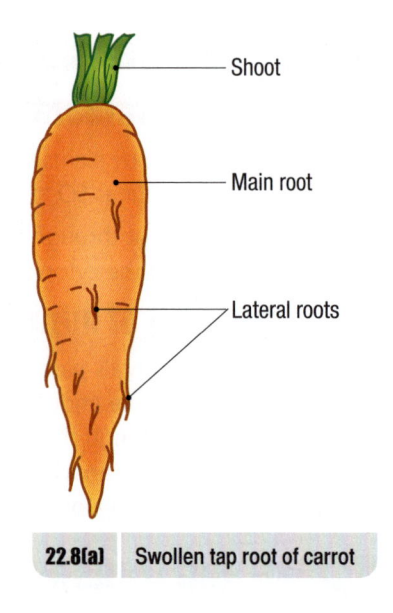

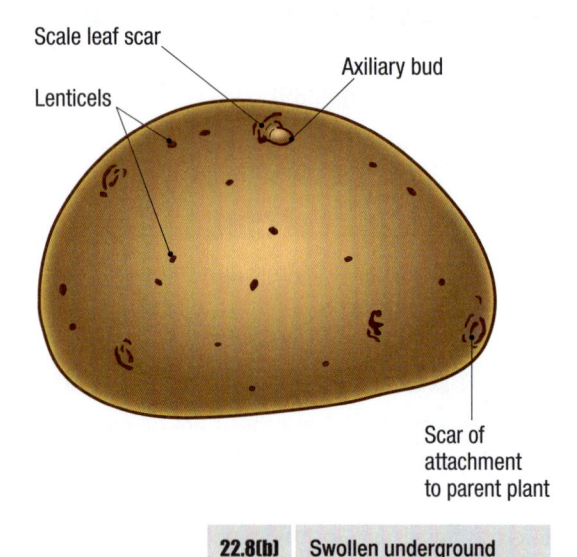

22.8(a) Swollen tap root of carrot

22.8(b) Swollen underground stem tuber of potato

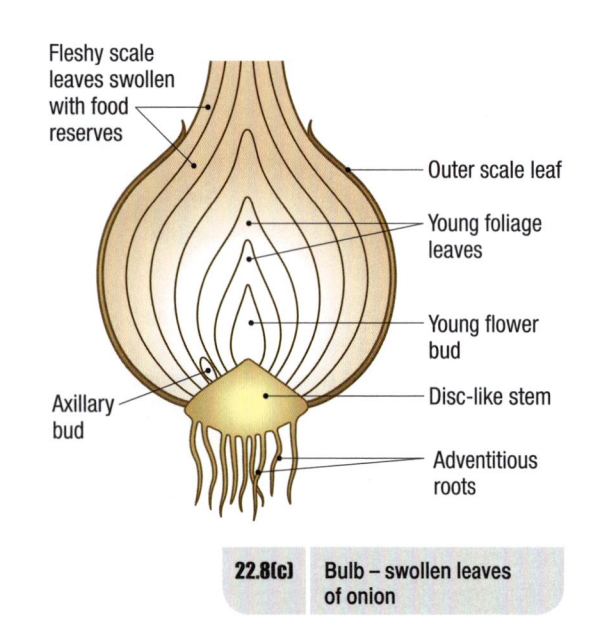

22.8(c) Bulb – swollen leaves of onion

22 Transport, Nutrition and Food Storage in the Flowering Plant

Summary

- Green plants are autotrophic, i.e. they can make their own food in photosynthesis.
- Photosynthesis requires the raw materials water and carbon dioxide. The basic equation for photosynthesis is $6CO_2 + 6H_2O \rightarrow C_6H_{12}O_6 + 6O_2$
- Transport of materials in plants involves the vascular tissues, transpiration and root pressure.
- Water and minerals enter the plant through the root hairs.
- Water is absorbed by osmosis, due to a difference in concentration.
- Plant roots have no cuticle. This assists absorption.
- Root hairs are very numerous and provide a greater surface area for absorption.
- Water moves up the stem in the xylem, as a result of root pressure and transpiration.
- Root pressure is a force which can push water up the stem.
- Transpiration is the loss of water vapour from the surface of the plant.
- Transpiration causes water and minerals to be moved up the plant from roots to leaves.
- Transpiration is controlled by:
  - The presence of a cuticle.
  - The opening and closing of the stomata.
  - Environmental factors e.g. light intensity, temperature.

HL
- The cohesion-tension model of water movement in plants explains how water rises up stems. Proposed by Dixon and Joly in 1895:
  - Transpiration causes a tension at the top of the plant.
  - This tension pulls a continuous chain of water molecules up the xylem into the leaf.
  - The tension causes the xylem vessels to narrow which increases the pulling force.
  - The unbroken column of water is made possible due to the cohesion and adhesion of water molecules.

- Xylem is adapted for water transport by being hollow, lignified and narrow.
- Minerals:
  are absorbed as ions, e.g. sulphur is absorbed as the sulphate ion, or SO_4^{--};
  diffuse into the root from the soil, due to difference in concentration;
  are transported up the plant along with water in the xylem vessels.
- Carbon dioxide:
  - diffuses into the plant, through the stomata, from the air;
  - is also a product of respiration in cells;
  - is transported around the plant from cell to cell by diffusion.
- Glucose:
  - is produced in photosynthesis;
  - is transported as sucrose, in the phloem sieve tube cells up and down the plant;
  - can be used in respiration or stored as starch.
- Oxygen:
  - is produced during photosynthesis;
  - may diffuse out of the plant through the stomata;
  - moves around the plant by diffusion;
  - is used in the plant for respiration.
- Plants store food for survival, in specially modified roots, stems and leaves.
- Modified roots for food storage include the tap roots of carrots and sugar beet.
- Modified underground stems, known as rhizomes store food, e.g. the potato tuber.
- Modified leaves for food storage include the onion bulb and the petiole of rhubarb.

22 Transport, Nutrition and Food Storage in the Flowering Plant

Review questions

01
(a) What term is given to organisms that can make their own food?
(b) Name two such organisms.
(c) Give the balanced chemical equation for photosynthesis.

02
(a) Why is a vascular system need in pants?
(b) Name the vascular tissues in plants.
(c) Name the vascular tissue in humans.

03
(a) Where does water enter the plant?
(b) What causes water to enter the plant?
(c) Name the process by which water moves into a plant.
(d) In what tissue is water transported in the plant?

04
(a) Explain the terms root pressure and transpiration.
(b) What is the importance of transpiration to plants?
(c) The graph shown below shows the relative rates of water uptake and transpiration by a plant in early summer.
  (i) How is the root of a plant adapted for water uptake?
  (ii) Why do you think the rate of transpiration is higher at 2 p.m. than the rate of water uptake?
  (iii) Why do you think the rate of water uptake drops rapidly after 6pm?

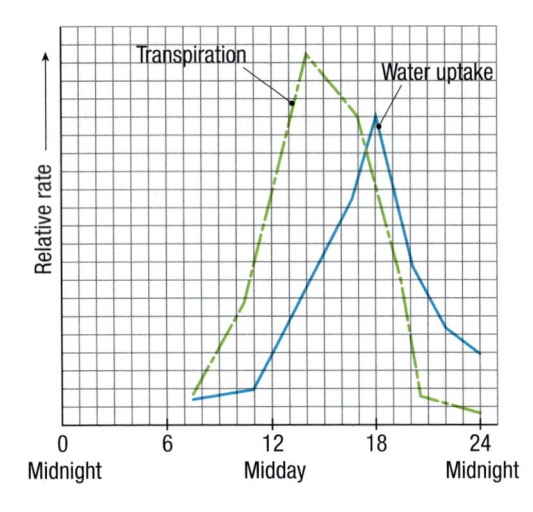

05
(a) Give two internal factors that control transpiration.
(b) Suggest two environmental factors that affect transpiration.
(c) Suggest which of the following sets of conditions will result in the greatest rate of transpiration:
  (i) a dry, dull day with a cool breeze.
  (ii) a damp, cool, windy day.
  (iii) a dry, bright day with a warm breeze.
  Give a reason for your choice.

06
(a) What are stomata?
(b) Suggest why, in general, more stomata are found on the under surface of leaves.
(c) Outline the role of stomata in transpiration.
(d) Draw a labelled diagram to show guard sells and a stomata as you would expect it to appear during the daytime.

07
(a) Name the Irish scientists who put forward the cohesion–tension model of water movement in plants.
(b) What did their model attempt to explain?
(c) Describe the cohesion-tension model of transport in detail.

08
(a) List three minerals required by plants.
(b) For any two named minerals state their role in the plant.
(c) State the source of minerals for plants.
(d) How are minerals absorbed by plants?
(e) How are minerals transported through the plant.

09
(a) Draw a labelled diagram of a T.S. of a root and use arrows to show the passage of minerals into the xylem.
(b) List two ways in which root hairs are adapted for water absorption.

10
(a) Name four substances transported by plants.
(b) For each named substance state its (i) source, (ii) how it is transported and (iii) its fate.

11
(a) List the products of photosynthesis and state their use to the plant.
(b) Where and in what form are sugars (i) transported, (ii) stored in plants?
(c) In which tissue is food transported in the plant?

12
(a) Identify each of the plant structures 1 and 2 below.
(b) Name a plant with which each structure can be associated.
(c) Give the name of the parts labelled A, B, C.

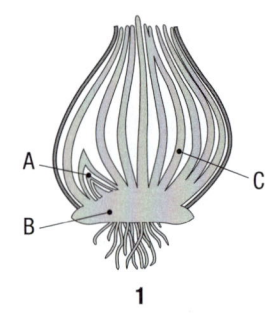

Transport, Nutrition and Food Storage in the Flowering Plant — 22

Examination style questions

Section A

01 The diagram shows a section of a green leaf.

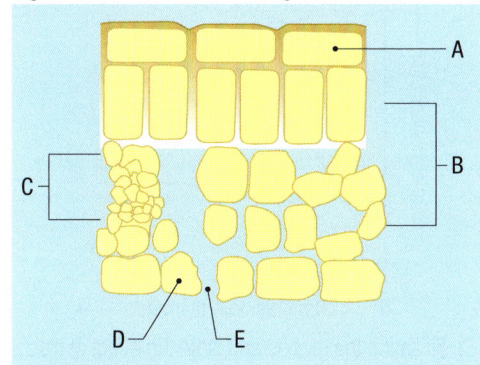

(a) Match the cell types A, B, C, D, E on the diagram to one of the following:
guard cell, vein, ground tissue, dermal tissue, stoma
(b) Name three substances that pass through E that are involved in the leaf's metabolism.
(c) What is the function of the tissue layers B?
(d) Identify a structure on the diagram that is non-cellular.
(e) Name the process by which water is lost from the leaf surface.

02 State whether each of the following statements is true or false. If false, rewrite the sentence correctly.

(a) The tissue in which water is transported is the xylem. T F
(b) Sugars are transported in the form of starch. T F
(c) Root hairs have a thick cuticle. T F
(d) The xylem does not carry water up and down the plant. T F
(e) Transpiration and Root pressure are involved in water transport. T F
(f) Minerals need energy to be absorbed. T F
(g) High humidity increases transpiration T F

Section C

03 (a) Xylem and phloem are the transport tissues in flowering plants.
 (i) Name one substance, other than water, transported by each of these tissues.
 (ii) State the direction of movement of substances in the xylem and phloem.
(b) (i) Draw a T.S. and an L.S of either xylem or phloem tissue.
 (ii) Describe three adaptations of xylem to its role in transporting water.
 (iii) Describe the pathway of water molecules from the soil to the leaf of a plant.

(c) (i) Explain the terms root pressure and transpiration.
 (ii) Explain why root pressure may be of great value for small plants but not for tall plants.
 (iii) An experiment to measure the water loss and water uptake by a flowering plant was set up as shown below. The apparatus was weighed at the start of the experiment and again after 24 hours. The results obtained are shown in the table below.

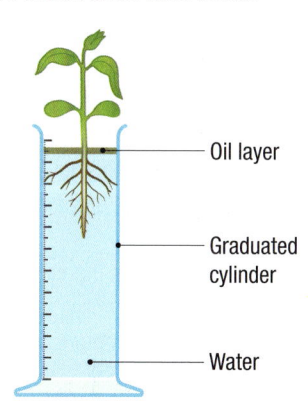

	Mass of apparatus with plant (g)	Volume of water in the cylinder (cm³)
At the start	210	100
24 hours later	200	86

1. Calculate the volume of water that has been absorbed by the roots of the plant in the 24-hour period.
2. What was the purpose of the oil layer?
3. Why is the volume of water lost by the plant not the same as the volume of water absorbed by the plant?
4. Under certain conditions, a plant growing in a natural environment, might lose a lot more water than it absorbs. Suggest one such condition and describe the effect it might have on the plant.
5. What control would you set up in this experiment?

04 (a) Food storage organs in plants include bulbs, stem tubers and tap roots.
 (i) Suggest one reason why plants might need to form food storage organs.
 (ii) State in what form the following plants store food:
  A carrot plant.
  A sunflower plant.
  A potato plant.
 (iii) Outline a laboratory test for a named food storage substance in plants.

Examination style questions

(iv) Name a plant, one in each case, that has (i) a stem modified for food storage, (ii) leaves modified for food storage.
(v) Draw a labelled diagram to show the structure of a bulb and indicate clearly where the food is stored.

(b) The tissue in which water travels through the plant is the xylem.
 (i) Name the two types of specialised water-conducting cells in xylem.
 (ii) Describe with the help of a labelled diagram how water enters the root and makes its way to the xylem, naming the tissue types through which it passes.
 (iii) Name one of the Irish scientists who proposed a theory to explain the upward movement of water in plant.
 (iv) By what name is this theory more correctly known?
 (v) Explain the role of transpiration, adhesion and cohesion in the movement of water up through the plant.

05 (a) (i) List three ways in which water is important to plants.
 (ii) Name the plant tissue in which water is transported in a plant.
(b) The graphs show the variations in the rate of transpiration in a pot plant plotted against stomatal pore diameter in windy conditions and in still air.

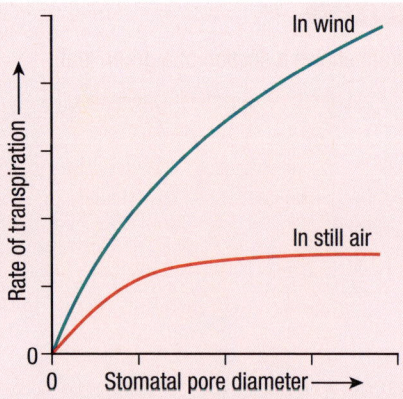

(i) Examine the graphs and state the effect of closure of the stomata on transpiration in (i) wind and (ii) in still air.
(ii) In still air conditions a thin layer of air exists on each surface of the leaf in which there is little or no movement of the air and the concentration of water vapour builds up to a level higher than in the general surroundings.
 Relate this high concentration of water vapour to the difference between transpiration in wind and in still air.
(iii) Draw a simple labelled diagram of a stoma in (a) the open position and (b) the closed position, as seen looking down on the surface of the leaf.
(iv) It is usually found that transpiration from the lower surfaces of leaves is greater than from the upper surfaces.
 Suggest two reasons for this based on leaf structure.
(c) (i) Name two minerals that are needed for plant health and outline the role of each.
 (ii) What is the source of minerals for the plant?
 (iii) Describe the uptake of minerals into the plant.
 (iv) State how minerals are transported in the plant.

Leaving Certificate examination questions

Section A

01 The diagram right shows the internal structure of a leaf.
 (i) Name the **one** tissue type that is found at **both** V and Y.
 (ii) The cells at W contain many organelles that carry out photosynthesis.
  Suggest why the cells at W contain more of these organelles than the cells at X.
 (iii) In layer X, gases can diffuse throughout the leaf. Name **one** such gas.
 (iv) State **one** function of the opening at Z.
 (v) Name the cells which are responsible for controlling the size of the opening at Z.

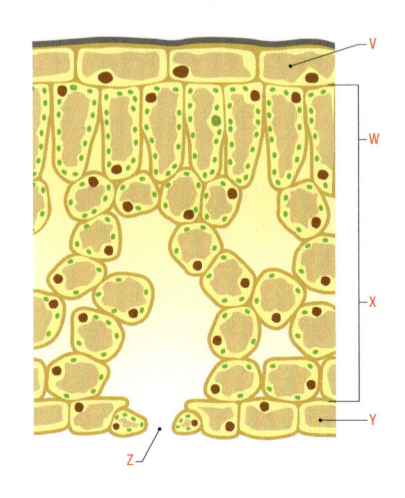

2010 OL Q. 6

Leaving Certificate examination questions

02 The diagram shows part of a section through a leaf.

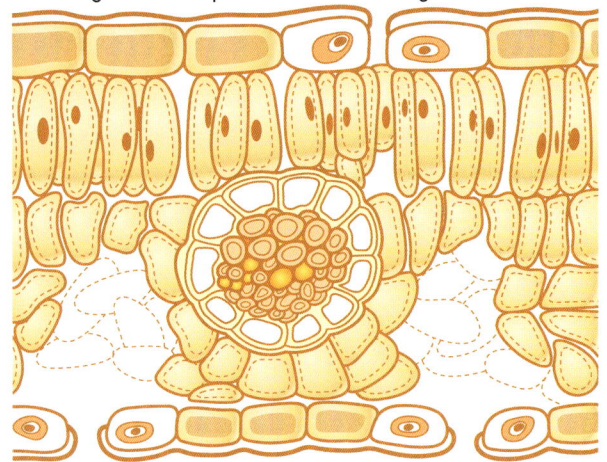

(a) Use the letter **A** to show a point of entry of carbon dioxide
(b) Name this point.
(c) Name a gas that **leaves** the leaf at this point
(d) Use the letter **B** to show the part of the leaf in which most photosynthesis occurs.
(e) Name the structures in plant cells in which photosynthesis occurs.
(f) In addition to carbon dioxide another small molecule is needed for photosynthesis.

2006 OL Q. 4

03 (a) The diagram shows part of the under surface of a leaf as seen through the microscope.
A is an aperture. B and C are cells. (note : an aperture is an opening)

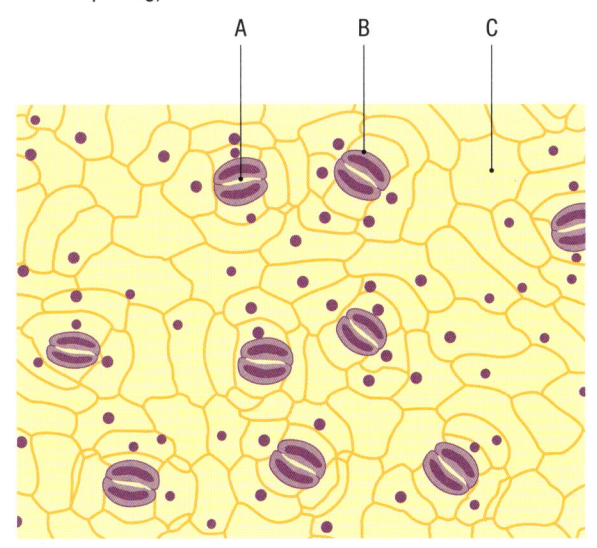

(i) Name A, B, C.
(ii) What is the function of A?
(iii) Name a factor that influences the diameter of A.
(iv) Name the apertures in stems that are equivalent to A.

(b) In some species of flowering plants the leaves are modified for the storage of food.
(i) Name a plant in which the leaves are modified for food storage.
(ii) Name a carbohydrate that you would expect to find in the modified leaves of the plant that you named above.
(iii) Name a type of modified stem that functions in food storage.

2004 HL Q. 4

Section C

04 Water is vital for the survival of living things. Plants absorb water from the soil.
(i) Through which microscopic **structures** does water enter a plant from the soil?
(ii) By what **process** does water enter a plant?
(iii) Name the **tissue** that water travels through in a plant.
(iv) Draw a labelled diagram of one cell of the tissue referred to in (iii) above.
(v) Name **one** process that causes water to move upwards in a plant.
(vi) Consider that night has fallen and the plant is in darkness. Suggest what will happen to the **amount** of water moving through the plant **and** give a reason for your answer.

2010 OL Q. 15 (a)

05 (i) Water enters the roots of plants by osmosis. Explain what is meant by osmosis.
(ii) Name the tissue that transports water from the root to the leaves.
(iii) Mention **one** way in which the tissue you have named in (ii) is adapted for the transport of water.
(iv) The diagram below shows another tissue that is involved in transport in plants.
(v) Name this tissue and name a substance that is transported in it.

2008 OL Q. 15 (a)

Leaving Certificate examination questions

06
(i) Explain how water enters root hairs and then passes to the vascular tissue.
(ii) In which of the vascular tissues will water now rise through the plant?
(iii) Give two features of the tissue referred to in (ii) that facilitate this upward movement of water.
(iv) Name and briefly explain any two processes involved in the upward movement of water in plants.

2014 HL Q. 14 (c)

07
(i) Name the tissue in plant stems through which water rises to the leaves.
(ii) Give **one** way in which this tissue is adapted for the transport of water.
(iii) Give a precise location of this tissue in the stem.
(iv) State another function of the tissue referred to in (i).
(v) The cohesion-tension model of transport attempts to explain water movement in plants against a particular force. Name this force.
(vi) Describe the principal features of the cohesion-tension model.
(vii) Name the two scientists mainly associated with the cohesion-tension model of transport.

2011 HL Q. 15 (b)

08 The passage of water through a plant is known as the transpiration stream. Answer the following questions in relation to the transpiration stream.
(i) Explain how water enters the plant at the root hairs.
(ii) Do minerals enter the plant by the process that you have indicated in (i)? Explain your answer.
(iii) How is xylem adapted for its role in water transport?
(iv) Strong forces of attraction exist between water molecules. Give an account of the importance of these forces in raising water to great height in trees.

2005 HL Q. 14 (a)

Past examination questions

OL	2013 Q. 15 (c) (ii), (vi)	2010 Q. 6, Q. 15 (a)	2008 Q. 15 (a)	2007 Q. 15 (b) (iii)–(v)	2006 Q. 4
HL	2014 Q. 14 (c)	2011 Q. 15 (b)	2008 Q. 14 (a) (i), (c) (v)	2006 Q. 11 (c)	
	2005 Q. 14 (a)	2004 Q. 4, Q. 14 (a)			

Transport in Humans

23

After studying this chapter you should be able to:

1. Appreciate the need (a) for organisms to be able to exchange materials between themselves and the environment and (b) for a transport system in animals.
2. Explain the term circulatory system and appreciate the efficiency of a closed circulatory system in humans.
3. Describe the two-circuit circulation system in humans.
4. Draw, label and give the functions of an artery, vein and capillary.
5. Compare the structure and functions of the three types of blood vessels.
6. Identify the external structure of the heart and know the role of the cardiac (coronary) blood vessels.
7. Draw and label the structure of the human heart.
8. Trace the pathway of blood through the heart and the body, including the hepatic portal system.
9. Describe how to dissect and display a bovine or a sheep heart.
10. Describe how the heart beats and how heartbeat is controlled.
11. Explain the heart cycle in terms of the systolic and diastolic periods.
12. Describe the control of heartbeat in more detail, with reference to cardiac muscle and the existence and location of the pacemaker nodes (S-A and A-V).
13. Explain the pulse and blood pressure.
14. Describe the effect of smoking, diet and exercise on the circulatory system.
15. Describe an investigation to determine the effect of exercise on the human pulse (or breathing rate).
16. Describe the structure and give three functions of the lymphatic system.

Exchange of materials

1. Most **cells** need a constant supply of oxygen and nutrients and a means of getting rid of waste materials. In single-celled **organisms**, e.g. *Amoeba*, exchange of materials is brought about by simple **diffusion** across the cell membrane (Fig 23.1).

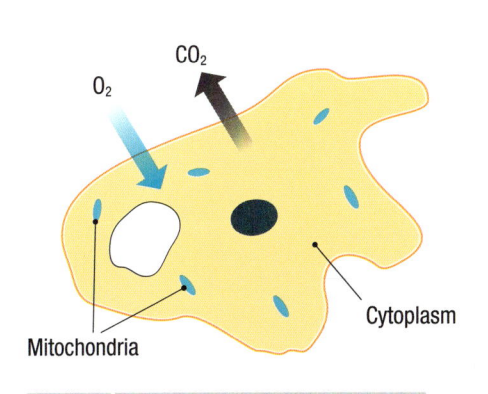

23.1 Exchange of materials in *Amoeba*

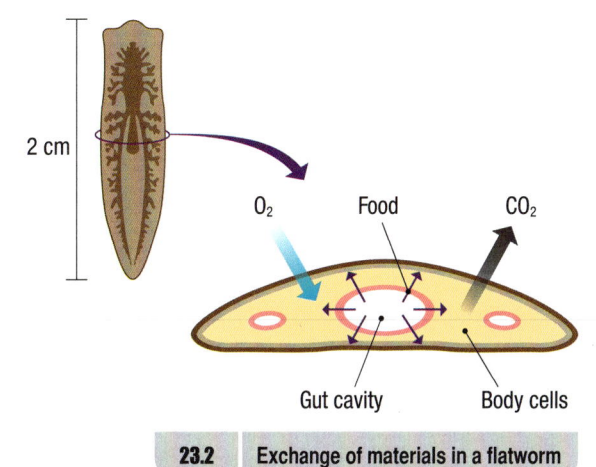

23.2 Exchange of materials in a flatworm

23 | Transport in Humans

In some multicellular animals, such as flatworms, materials can also be exchanged between the organism and its environment by diffusion. This is because the body of the animal is only a few cells thick (Fig 23.2). In either case, an internal transport or circulatory system is not needed. In more complex animals, including humans, a specialised circulatory system is required. This is because of the distance between the inner **tissues** and the external environment, which makes it impossible for materials to exchange large numbers of cells.

Circulatory systems

A typical circulatory system consists of:
- a fluid, e.g. blood;
- a pump called a heart;
- vessels or tubes to carry the blood to the cells of the body.

In this chapter, we will deal with the heart and the blood vessels. A study of the blood itself is in the next chapter.

There are two types of circulatory system: (a) open and (b) closed.

(a) An **open circulatory system** is one in which the blood is not always found in blood vessels. The blood is pumped into open-ended blood vessels. The blood then pours into the body cavity of the animal. Here it bathes the cells of the body and exchange of materials takes place. Later the blood passes back into blood vessels. An open blood circulatory system is found in insects.

(b) In a closed circulatory system, the blood remains in the blood vessels. Exchange of materials is possible because the walls of the smallest blood vessels are very thin. This enables diffusion of gas and nutrients from the blood into the fluid surrounding the body cells and from there into the cells themselves. This fluid, called **tissue fluid**, bathes the organs of the body and acts as a medium through which substances may be exchanged between the blood and the cells of the body. Closed blood systems are found in the earthworm and vertebrates, including humans. The closed blood system is a more efficient system than the open blood system seen in insects (Fig 23.3(a) and (b)).

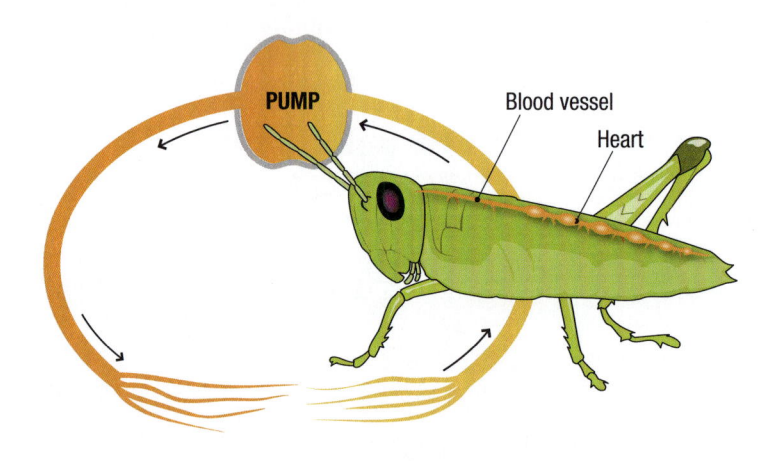

23.3(a) An open circulatory system

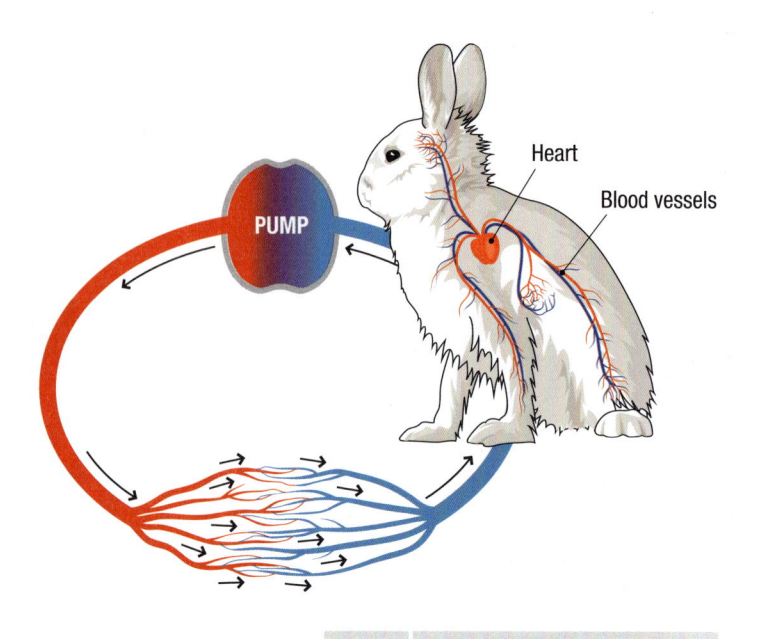

23.3(b) A closed circulatory system

The human circulatory system

Double circulation

Humans have a two-circuit or double circulatory system. This means that blood is pumped by the heart to the lungs and then back to the heart (**pulmonary circulation**) and from the heart to the rest of the body systems and back to the heart (**systemic circulation**) (Fig 23.4).

The pulmonary and systemic systems are separate because the heart is divided by a wall of muscle into left- and right-hand sides. The right side of the heart pumps deoxygenated blood to the lungs and the left side pumps oxygenated blood to the rest of the body. The advantage of this double circulatory system (Fig 23.4) is that it ensures adequate blood pressure for both systems and for oxygen and nutrients to be pumped around the body faster.

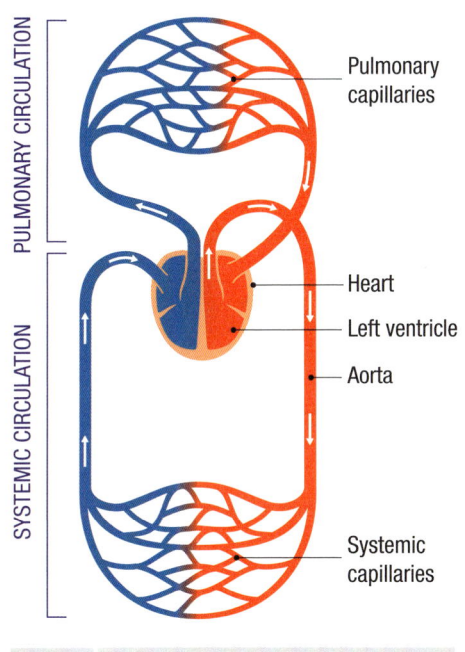

23.4 Double circulatory system in humans

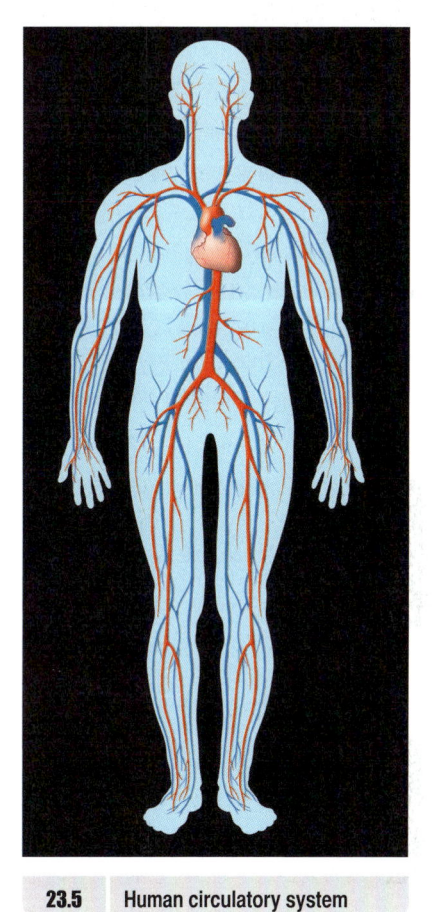

23.5 Human circulatory system

Blood vessels

The vessels that carry blood around the body are the **arteries**, **veins** and **capillaries**.

Arteries

Arteries (Fig 23.6) are thick-walled tubes with a small lumen (cavity) through which the blood passes. Arteries carry blood away from the heart to the organs of the body. The blood in the arteries is under pressure from the heart.

Veins

Veins (Fig 23.7) have a much thinner wall than arteries but have a larger lumen. In addition, veins have **valves**, which prevent a back-flow of blood. Veins carry blood from the body organs to the heart. Pressure in the veins is low. When the body muscles contract they squeeze the veins and help to push the blood back to the heart.

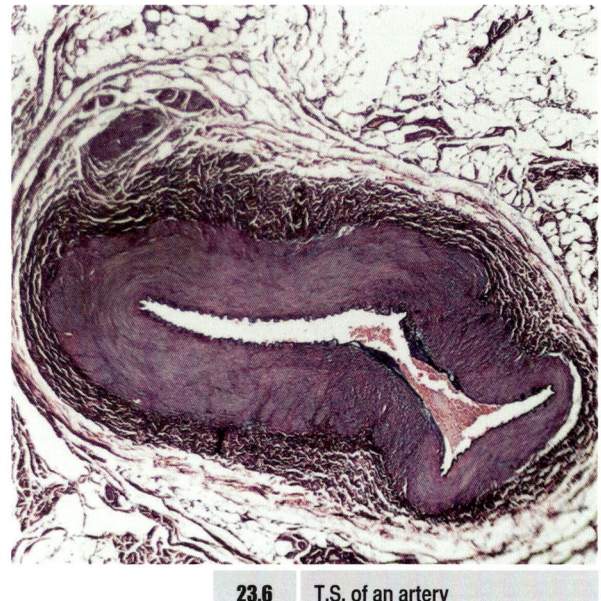

23.6 T.S. of an artery

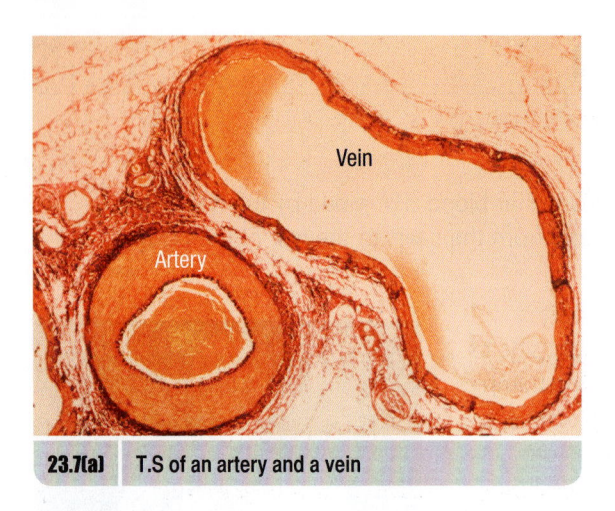

23.7(a) T.S of an artery and a vein

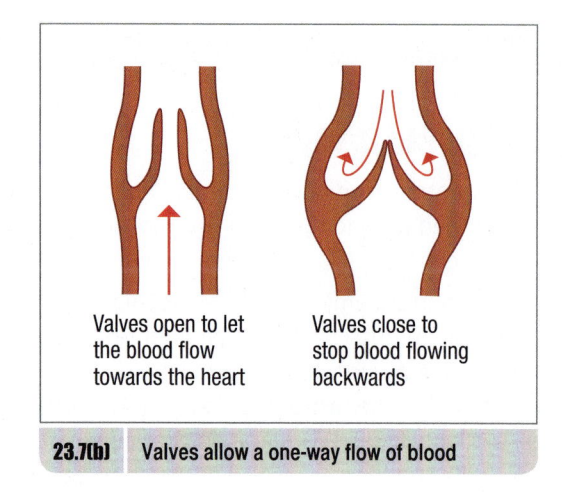

23.7(b) Valves allow a one-way flow of blood

Capillaries

When a main artery reaches a particular organ of the body, it branches into smaller vessels called **arterioles**. Arterioles in turn sub-divide into extremely tiny thin-walled vessels called **capillaries**. It is only through the thin capillary walls that necessary substances such as oxygen and glucose and wastes such as CO_2 can be exchanged between the blood and the body cells (Fig 23.8).

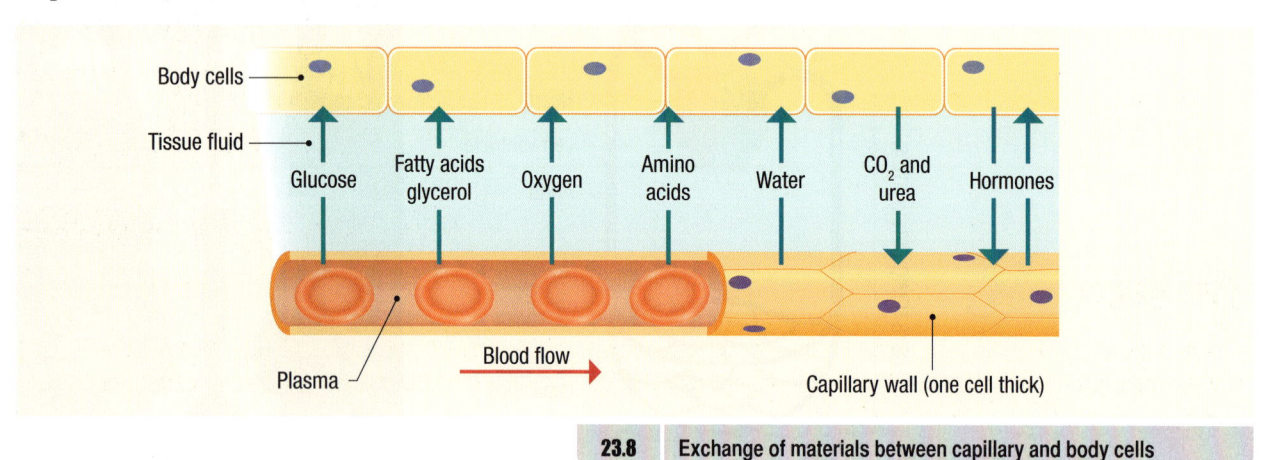

23.8 Exchange of materials between capillary and body cells

Blood leaves the body organs in capillaries and travels via small blood vessels known as **venules** to the veins, which in turn bring the blood back to the heart.

Capillaries lie close to nearly every cell in the body, thus ensuring efficient exchange of materials. Capillaries are the smallest blood vessels. Their walls are only one cell thick (Fig 23.9).

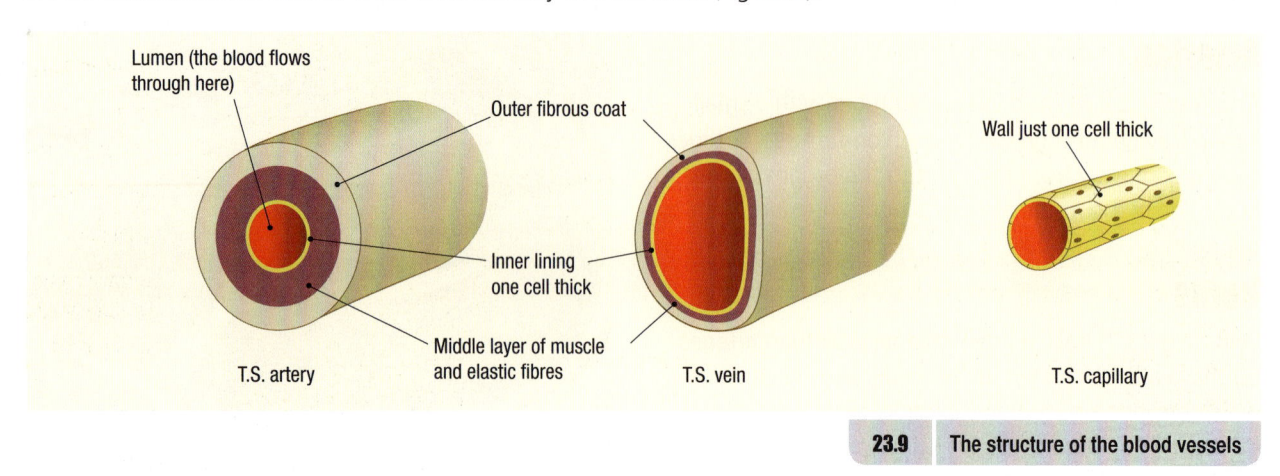

23.9 The structure of the blood vessels

5. The main differences in structure and function of these three types of blood vessel can be seen in Table 23.1 and Fig 23.9.

	Artery	Vein	Capillary
Structure	Thick, three-layered wall of muscle and elastin	Thin, three-layered wall of muscle and elastin	Wall only one cell thick
	Narrow lumen	Large lumen	Extremely narrow lumen
	No valves	Valves present	No valves
Function	Carry blood away from heart	Carry blood to heart	Allows exchange of materials between blood and body tissues
Blood flow	Rapid under pressure from heart	Sluggish under low pressure	Pressure reducing
	Blood flows in pulses	Blood flows steadily	Blood flows slowly

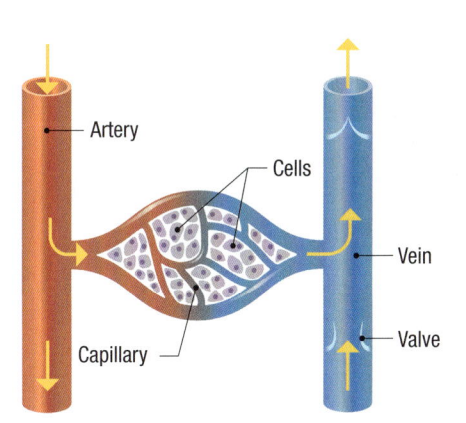

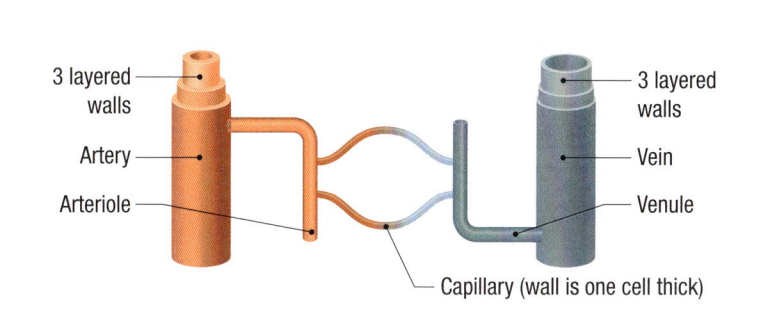

Table 23.1 The differences between arteries, veins and capillaries

23.10 Relationship between the blood vessels

The heart

The heart is a hollow muscular organ. It lies in the thorax behind the breastbone, slightly to the left-hand side of the chest, above the diaphragm. The average adult human heart is about the size of a clenched fist and has a mass of approximately 300 g.

Surrounding the heart is a tough, protective sac called the **pericardium**. Between the pericardium and the heart wall lies a fluid-filled chamber which allows friction-free movement of the heart when it is beating. The wall of the heart is made of a very special type of muscle called **cardiac muscle**. This type of muscle is not found in any other part of the body. It never tires. If given sufficient oxygen and nutrients, cardiac muscle will contract rhythmically without any nervous stimulation.

Cardiac blood supply

Cardiac muscle has its own blood supply consisting of the **coronary** (cardiac) **blood vessels**. The coronary arteries arise at the base of the aorta. They branch across the surface of the heart bringing oxygen and nutrients to the muscle cells from the aorta. Coronary veins carry blood rich in carbon dioxide and wastes back to the right atrium.

Emerging from the heart are the main blood vessels, the **aorta**, the **vena cavae** and the pulmonary arteries and veins (Figs 23.11).

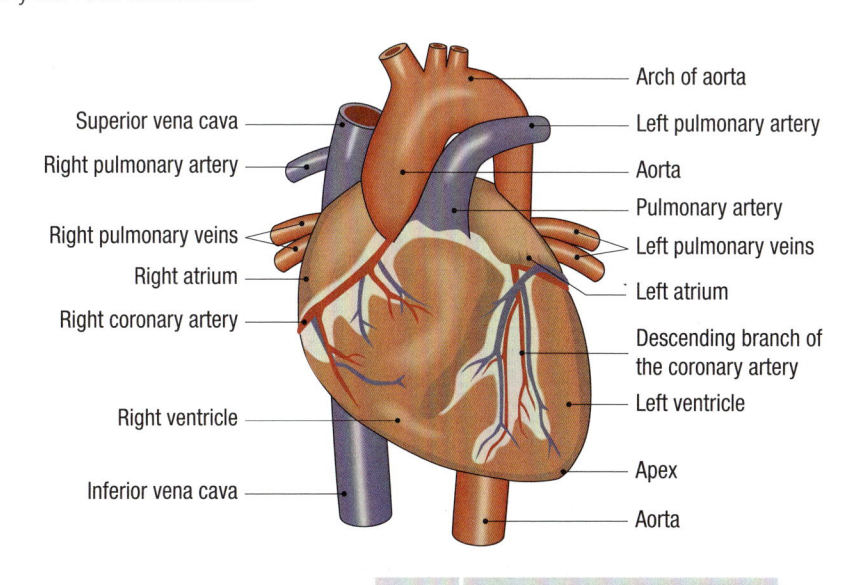

23.11 External view of the human heart

23 Transport in Humans

Internal structure of the heart

The heart consists of four separate chambers (Fig 23.12):

- The two upper chambers, left and right, are thin-walled and are called **atria** (singular atrium).
- The two lower chambers, left and right, the **ventricles**, are larger than the atria and are thick-walled.
- A thick muscle wall called the septum divides the heart into left and right halves. Blood cannot flow through the septum.

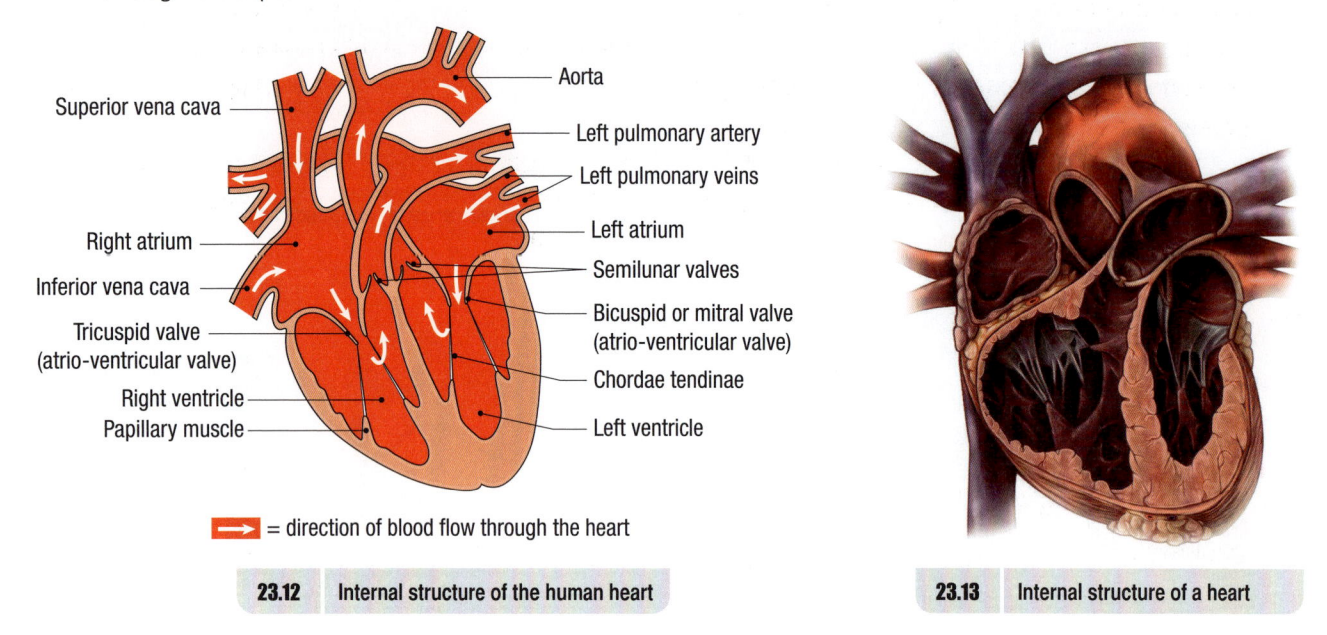

→ = direction of blood flow through the heart

23.12 Internal structure of the human heart

23.13 Internal structure of a heart

The two sides of the heart have distinct but interrelated functions:

- The right atrium receives blood from all around the body through the main vein, the vena cava.
- The right ventricle receives blood from the right atrium and pumps it to the lungs through the pulmonary arteries.
- The left atrium receives oxygenated blood from the lungs via the pulmonary veins.
- The left ventricle receives blood from the left atrium and pumps it to the body through the aorta.
  Because the left ventricle has to pump blood to all parts of the body, its wall is much thicker than that of the right ventricle, which has only to pump blood the relatively short distance to the lungs. The walls of the atria are thinner than those of the ventricles because they only have to pump blood down into the ventricles (Figs 23.12 and 23.13).

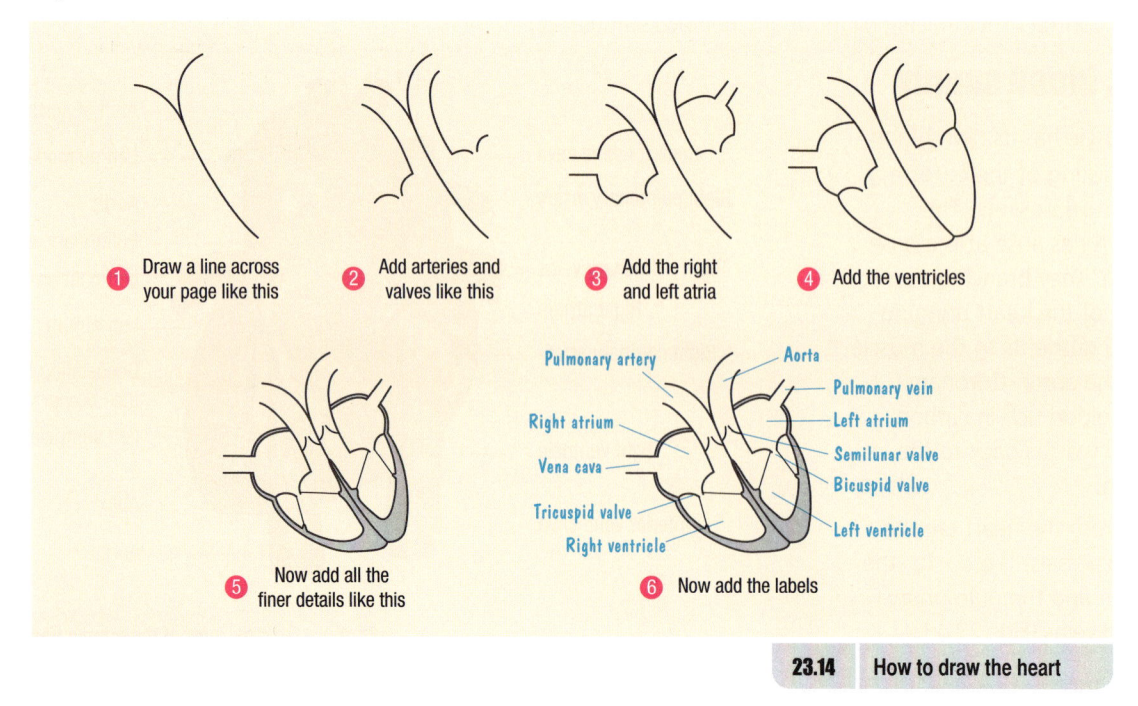

① Draw a line across your page like this
② Add arteries and valves like this
③ Add the right and left atria
④ Add the ventricles
⑤ Now add all the finer details like this
⑥ Now add the labels

23.14 How to draw the heart

Valves in the heart

To ensure that blood flows through the heart in one direction only, the heart has valves at the exits of each heart chamber.

A-V valves

- The valve between the right atrium and the right ventricle is called the **tricuspid valve**, that between the left atrium and left ventricle is called the **bicuspid or mitral valve**. Collectively, these valves are known as the **atrio-ventricular or A-V valves**. These valves are attached to papillary muscles on the ventricle walls by the chordae tendinae or 'heart strings'. The function of the A-V valves is to prevent a back-flow of blood from the ventricles to the atria.
- **Semi-lunar (half-moon) valves** are found between the right ventricle and the pulmonary artery and between the left ventricle and the aorta. The function of the semi-lunar valves is to prevent the blood flowing backwards into the heart (see the arrows in Fig 23.15).

You can examine the structure of a bovine or sheep heart in Investigation 23.1 (Fig 23.18).

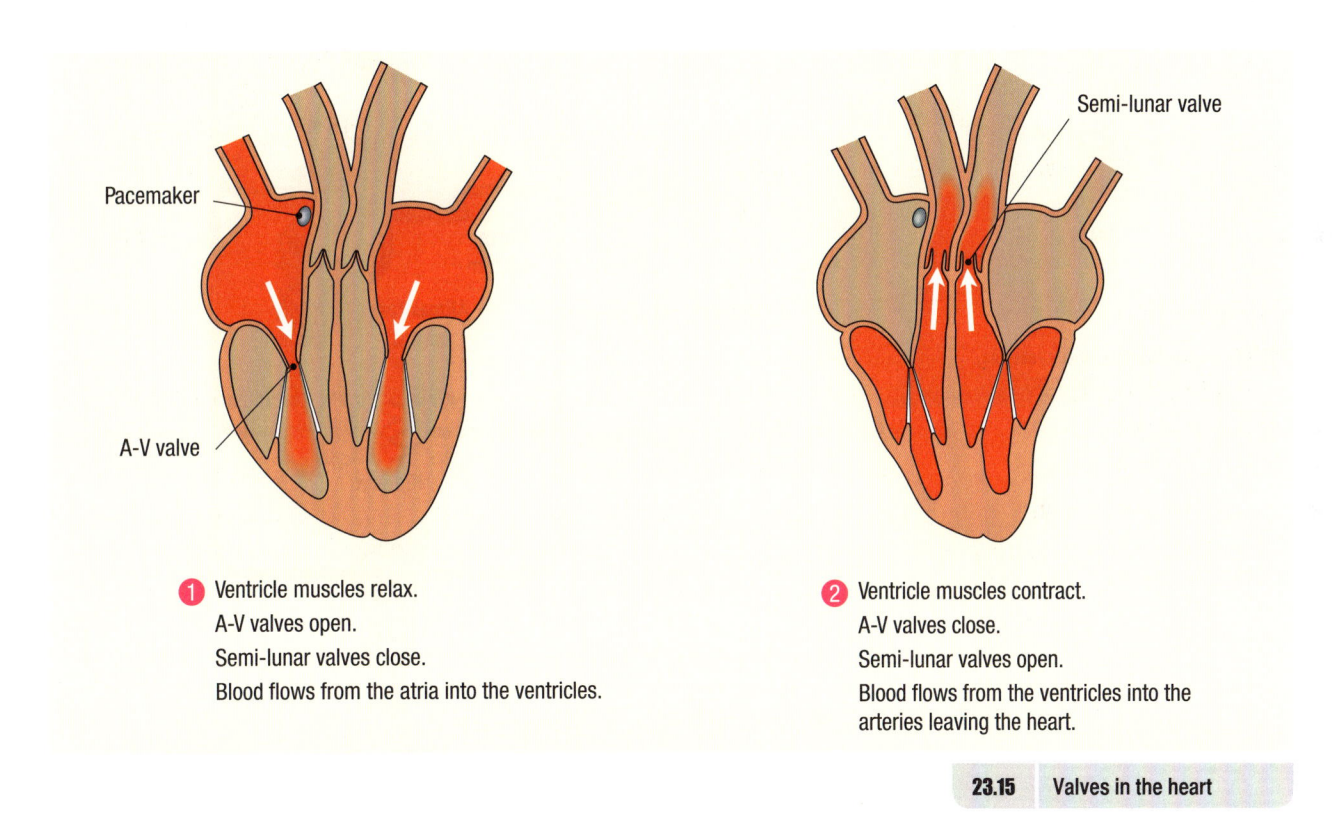

1 Ventricle muscles relax.
A-V valves open.
Semi-lunar valves close.
Blood flows from the atria into the ventricles.

2 Ventricle muscles contract.
A-V valves close.
Semi-lunar valves open.
Blood flows from the ventricles into the arteries leaving the heart.

23.15 Valves in the heart

23 | Transport in Humans

Blood flow through the heart and the portal blood system

As already mentioned, the human circulatory system consists of the pulmonary circulatory system and the systemic circulatory system (Fig 23.16).

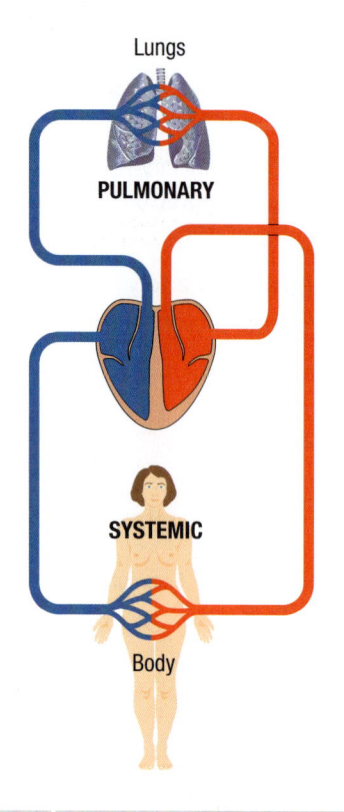

23.16 Pulmonary and systemic circulatory systems

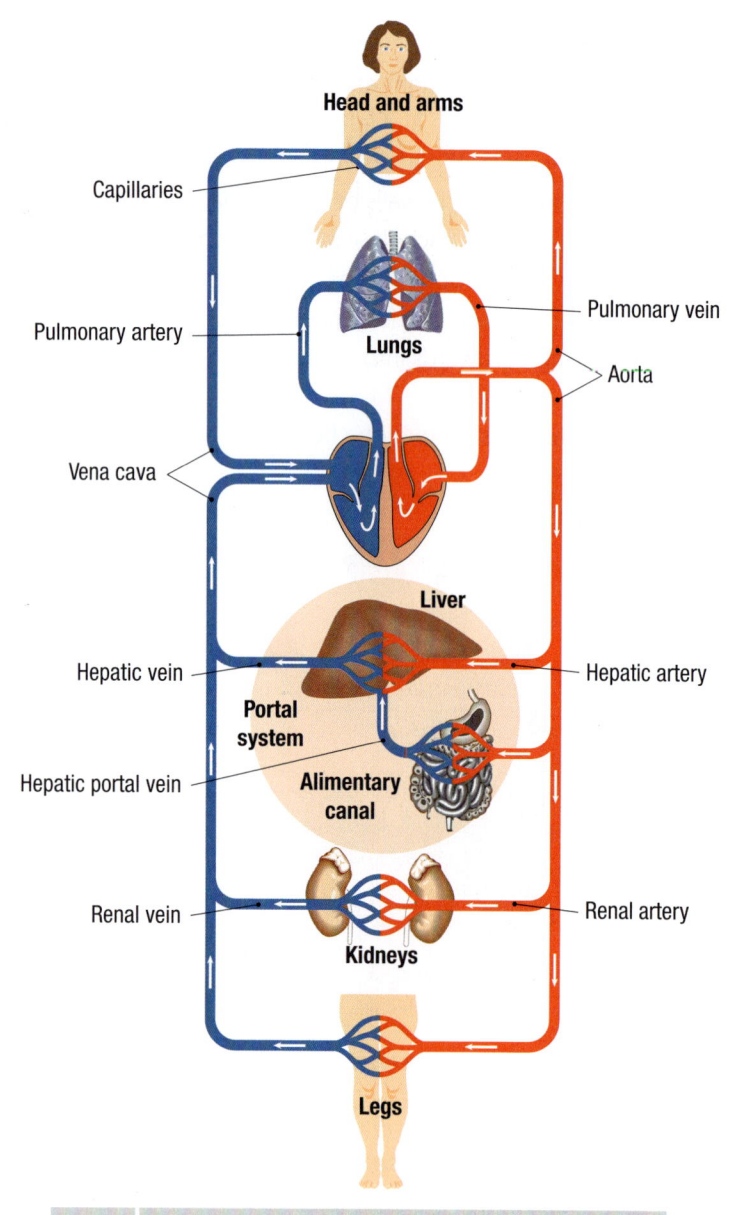

23.17 The human circulatory system showing the portal system

Pulmonary system

Heart → pulmonary artery → arterioles → capillaries (in lungs) → venules → pulmonary vein → heart

Systemic system

Heart → aorta → arterioles → capillaries in body organs → venules → veins → vena cava → heart

In addition there is the **portal system**, which begins and ends in capillaries that do not connect directly to the heart.

In humans, the hepatic portal system which connects the digestive system to the liver is an example of a portal system (Fig 23.17). In general blood flows from artery to capillary to vein. The portal system is an exception to this.

Portal system

Capillaries, e.g. in stomach and intestines → venules → hepatic portal vein → venules → capillaries in the liver

Transport in Humans | 23

Investigation 23.1
To dissect and display a sheep's heart

Procedure

1. Position the heart so that the front (ventral) surface is facing you. The front of the heart is recognised by the large coronary blood vessel running across the surface from top right to bottom left as you look at the heart. Also if you feel the heart walls, the wall on *your* right should feel firmer than the one on the left (Fig 23.18(a)).

2. Identify the major blood vessels that enter and leave the heart. Sometimes these vessels have been removed by the butcher.

3. Identify the following chambers: left and right atria (upper chambers); left and right ventricles (lower chambers).

4. Draw a labelled diagram of the external structure of the heart.

5. Using a scalpel make a shallow incision (cut) in the outside walls of the left atrium and left ventricle (Fig 23.18(b)).

6. Push open the heart and examine the internal structures (Fig 23.18(c)).

7. Locate the bicuspid valve with its two flaps and the attached chordae tendinae.

8. Feel the thickness of the wall of the atria and the ventricles, which are thin.

9. Make a second incision down the outside wall of the right atrium and right ventricle (Fig 23.18(b)).

10. Push open the heart and examine the internal structures.

11. Locate the tricuspid valve with its three flaps and the attached chordae tendinae. Note that in the sheep's heart there is an additional moderator muscle across the right ventricle. This structure is not present in the human heart.

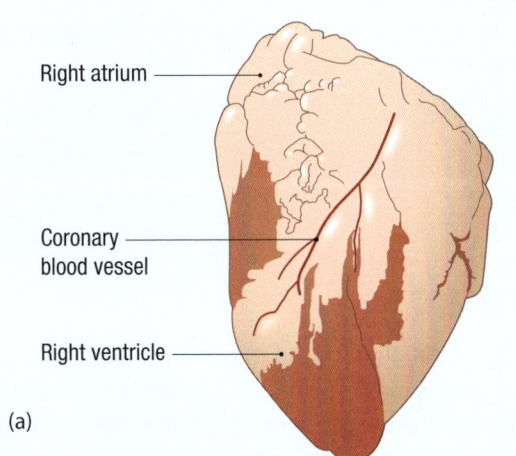

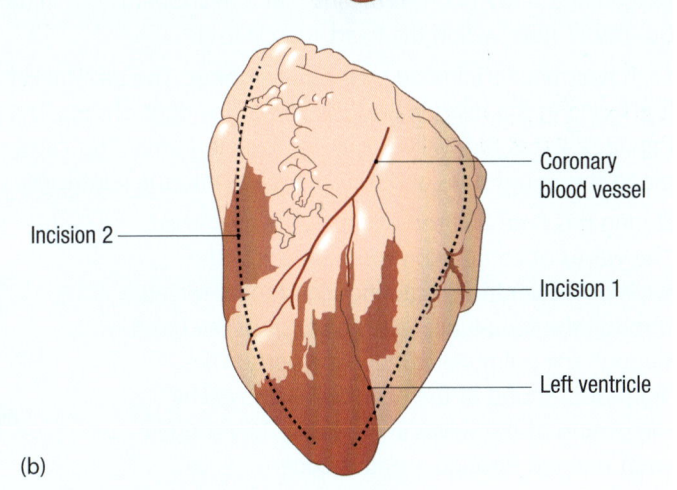

Take special care when using a scalpel

(a) Right atrium, Coronary blood vessel, Right ventricle

(b) Incision 2, Coronary blood vessel, Incision 1, Left ventricle

(c) Bicuspid valve, Chorda tendinae, Left ventricle wall

23.18 Steps in heart dissection

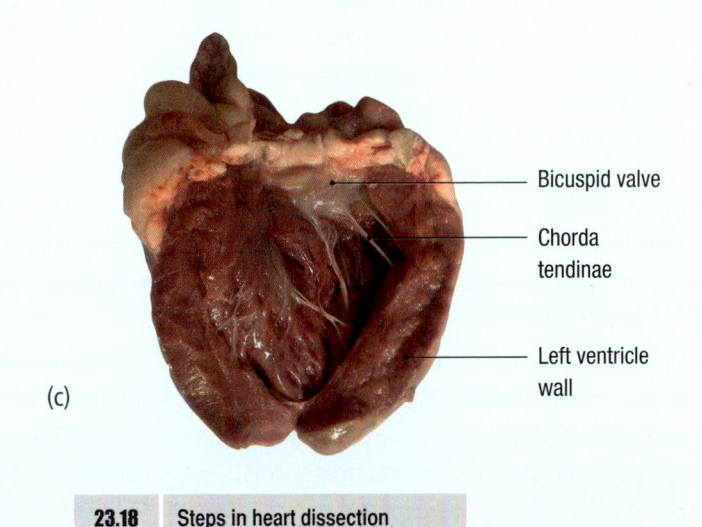

UNIT 3 THE ORGANISM | 309

23 — Transport in Humans

12. Feel the thickness of the right ventricle wall and compare it to that of the left.
13. Cut a square window in the pulmonary artery and aorta close to where they leave the heart to expose the semi-lunar valves, which have three flaps.
14. Locate two small openings at the base of the aorta (just above the semi-lunar valves). These are the entrance to the coronary artery. Insert a dropper to pump air into these openings. This will trace the pathway of the coronary artery.
15. Make flag labels of the major parts of the heart and insert them into your dissection for display.
16. Draw a labelled diagram of your dissected heart.
17. Dispose of the heart by wrapping in newspaper and placing in a plastic bag before sealing and placing in the waste bin.
18. Wash and sterilise the dissecting board and instruments after use. Wash your hands.

The heartbeat

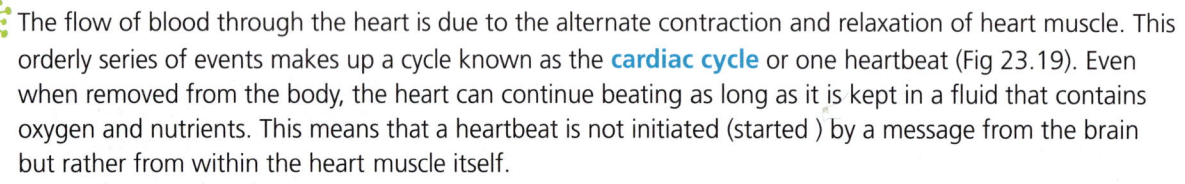

10 The flow of blood through the heart is due to the alternate contraction and relaxation of heart muscle. This orderly series of events makes up a cycle known as the **cardiac cycle** or one heartbeat (Fig 23.19). Even when removed from the body, the heart can continue beating as long as it is kept in a fluid that contains oxygen and nutrients. This means that a heartbeat is not initiated (started) by a message from the brain but rather from within the heart muscle itself.

Each heartbeat is initiated by the **pacemaker**. The pacemaker is a special group of cardiac muscle cells. It is found in the heart wall at the top of the right atrium. The pacemaker sends out a wave of electrical impulses across the walls of the right and left atria. This causes the atrial muscle to contract forcing the blood through the tri- and bicuspid valves into the ventricles.

During this time, the semi-lunar valves are closed. The waves of contraction continue across the walls of the ventricles, causing blood to be forced through the semi-lunar valves and out of the heart through the pulmonary artery and aorta. The 'lupp-dup' sound of the heartbeat is caused by the closing of the valves in the heart. This sound is what is heard through a stethoscope.

In summary, the pacemaker controls the heartbeat. The heart normally beats about 72 times every minute. One complete heartbeat takes 0.8 seconds and is known as the cardiac cycle.

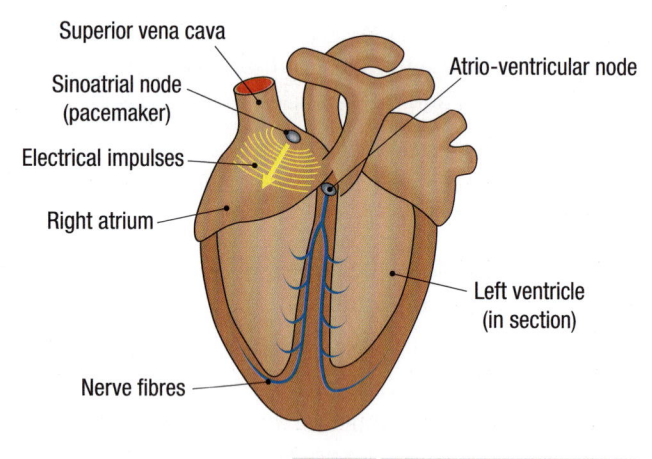

23.19 Heartbeat

HL

11 The alternate contraction and relaxation of the heart muscle ensures the constant movement of blood through the heart. The contraction of cardiac muscle is known as **systole** and the relaxation of cardiac muscle is referred to as **diastole**.

12 Heartbeat is initiated by a special group of muscles called the **sinoatrial node** (S-A node) or pacemaker. The S-A node is found embedded in the wall of the right atrium near where the superior vena cava enters the heart.

The S-A node sends out a wave of electrical impulses across the muscle tissue in both atria. This causes the muscles of the atria to contract (atrial systole). As the impulses pass down over the atrial muscle, they reach a second group of specialised muscle cells called the **atrio-ventricular node** (A-V node).

HL The A-V node lies at the bottom of the right atrium near the septum. Long muscle fibres run from the A-V node down either side of the septum and spread out across the ventricle walls (Fig 23.20). The impulses from the A-V node pass down the nerve fibres (Purkinje fibres) to all parts of the ventricles where they cause both ventricles to contract (ventricular systole). As the ventricles contract the atria relax (atrial diastole).

1 Diastole   **2** Atrial systole   **3** Ventricular systole

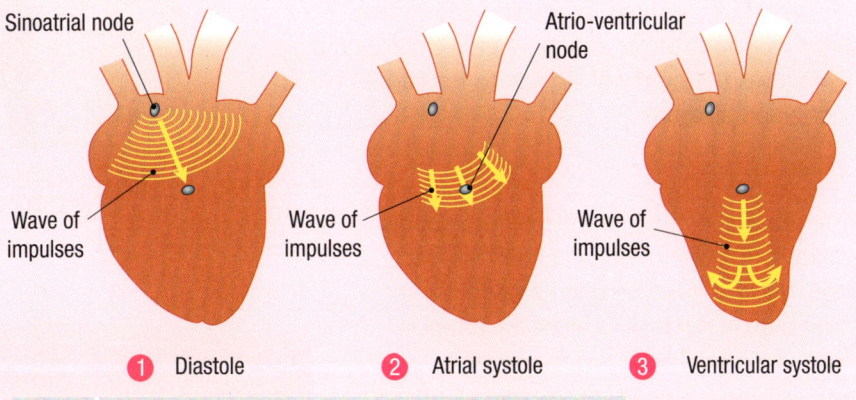

23.20 Waves of contraction of cardiac muscle during heartbeat

The pulse

When a nurse or a doctor takes your **pulse**, they are checking to see whether your heart is beating properly. When the ventricles of the heart contract, blood is forced through the aorta into the arteries. The rhythmic expansion and contraction of the walls of the arteries as blood is forced through them is called the pulse. A pulse can be easily detected where an artery is close to the surface of the skin and passing over a bone, e.g. at the wrist, temple and neck.

> **The pulse** is the expansion and contraction of the arteries due to the pumping action of the heart.

Blood pressure

Blood pressure is the flow of blood through the main arteries due to the pumping action of the heart. A person's blood pressure needs to be reasonably high to keep the blood moving in the blood vessels. The region of highest blood pressure is where blood is forced into the aorta by contraction of the left ventricle (systolic pressure). The lowest pressure occurs when the ventricles relax (diastolic pressure).

> **Blood pressure** is the force of blood as it passes through an artery.

Normally a person's blood pressure is taken from the artery of the upper arm using a blood pressure monitor (a sphygmomanometer). This machine measures the amount of pressure required to stop the flow of blood through this artery. The blood pressure reading from the machine is a reading of both the contraction and relaxation pressures recorded as a fraction.

A healthy young adult has a blood pressure reading of 120/80 where 120 represents the pressure when the ventricle contracts and 80 the pressure when it relaxes (Fig 23.21). Abnormally high blood pressure is known as **hypertension** and abnormally low blood pressure is **hypotension**.

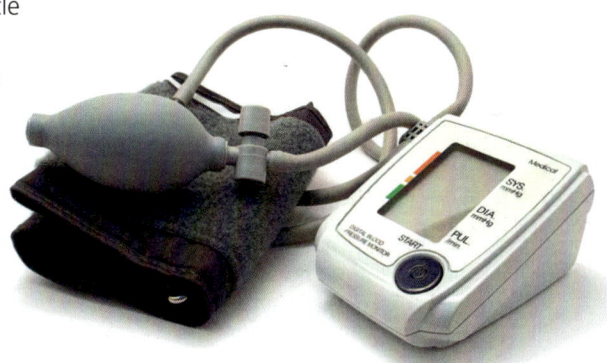

23.21 A blood pressure monitor

23 Transport in Humans

Maintaining a healthy circulatory system

1. Exercise

When we take exercise the heart beats faster. This pumps more blood around the body which brings nutrients and oxygen to the muscles that need them. Regular exercise such as running, swimming and cycling (Fig 23.22) makes the heart muscle stronger and more efficient at pumping blood. Regular exercise improves the supply of oxygen to the cardiac blood vessels and it also reduces blood pressure.

23.22 Regular exercise increases the strength of your heart

2. Diet

Cholesterol is an important fatty substance produced in the body. Certain forms of cholesterol, i.e. those found in animal fats, can cause heart disease. If too much of this type of cholesterol is included in our diet, it builds up in the inner wall of the arteries, blocking the flow of blood. If a blockage occurs in a cardiac artery, it will stop oxygen reaching the heart muscle and cause a heart attack (Fig 23.23). Improving the diet by eating less fat and sugar can reduce the risk of heart and circulatory disease.

Increased salt intake increases blood pressure and should be reduced in the diet.

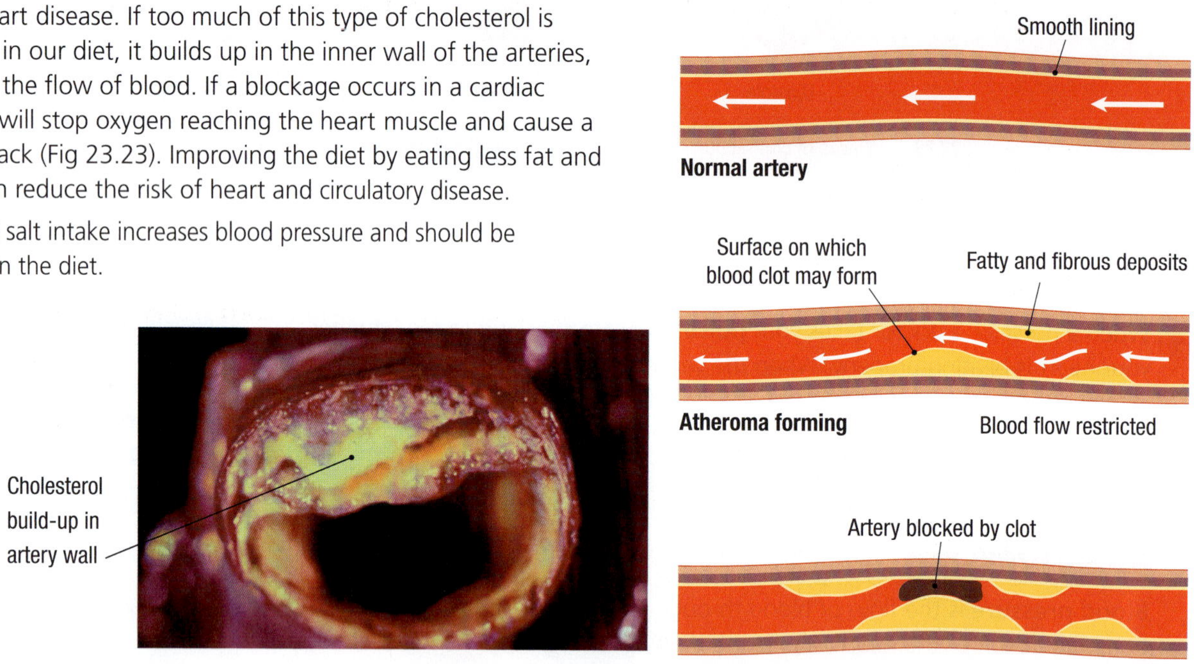

23.23 Hardening of an artery (atherosclerosis) reduces blood flow

3. Smoking

Smoking is now considered one of the major causes of coronary heart disease. Tobacco smoke contains many harmful substances, amongst them nicotine and carbon monoxide (Fig 23.24). Over time, nicotine can increase the blood pressure of a smoker. Carbon monoxide (CO) interferes with the transfer of oxygen to the body cells and damages blood vessels which can lead to poor circulation. High levels of CO in the blood of heavy smokers can cause hardening of the arteries and increase the risk of blood clots. Remember: the easiest way to give up smoking is never to start.

So to keep a healthy heart and circulatory system:
- Take regular exercise – to strengthen the heart.
- Reduce the fat, sugar and salt content of the diet – to reduce the risk of heart attack and obesity.
- Do not smoke – to reduce the risk of heart attacks and stroke.

23.24 Smoking is bad for your health

Investigation 23.2

To investigate the effect of exercise on the pulse rate of a human

SYLLABUS REQUIREMENT:

You have the choice to investigate the effect of exercise on pulse rate or on breathing rate (see Chapter 26).

Procedure

1. First of all, find your pulse rate at rest, i.e. when sitting down. To find your pulse place the fingers of one hand against the inside of the other wrist as shown in Fig 23.25. You should feel your pulse as a repeated throbbing.

2. Count the number of beats in one minute. Write down this number in Table 23.2.

3. Repeat step 2 three times. Work out your average pulse rate. This is your pulse rate at rest.

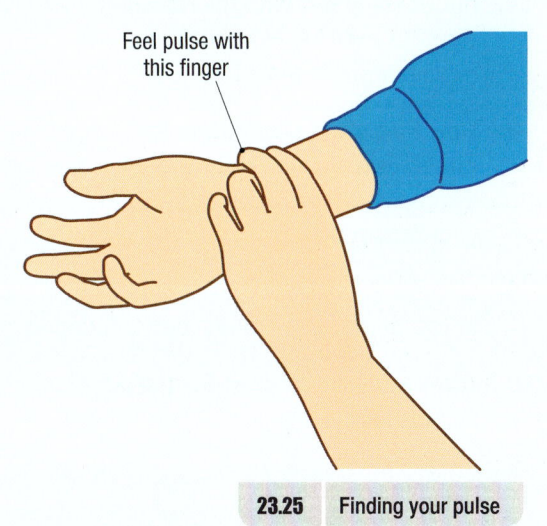

4. Take some easy exercise such as walking on the spot for 3 minutes. Immediately after walking take your pulse for 1 minute and record the figure in Table 23.2. When your pulse has returned to normal, repeat twice and get an average. Record the figures in the table.

5. Compare your resting pulse rate with the rate after gentle exercise. Try and explain any difference you find.

6. Now do some vigorous exercise such as running on the spot for 3 minutes or stepping up onto a stool and down again for 3 minutes.

23.25 Finding your pulse

	Pulse rate at rest	Pulse rate after gentle exercise	Pulse rate immediately after vigorous exercise
Trial 1			
Trial 2			
Trial 3			
Total			
Average			
Class average			

Table 23.2

23 | Transport in Humans

7. Immediately after the exercise take your pulse rate and do this every minute until your pulse rate returns to your resting rate. Record your pulse rate for each minute after exercise in Table 23.3. Compare your pulse rate at rest with the rate after vigorous exercise. How could you explain any difference?

8. How long did it take your pulse rate to return to the resting rate? Compare your results with those of your classmates.

Minutes after exercise	Pulse rate

Table 23.3

9. Suggest a relationship between the time taken to reach the pulse rate at rest after exercise and a person's degree of physical fitness.

10. Draw a graph to show how the pulse rate changes over time after a period of 3 minutes vigorous exercise.

Alternatively the effect of increasing exercise on heart rate can be investigated using datalogging equipment. Datalogging allows real-time data such as heart rate, pH and temperature changes to be collected using electronic sensors. This data is then transferred to a computer or other hardware for processing. Special software applications are required to allow the data to be displayed and manipulated on this hardware.

The system used to investigate pulse rate can use a chest transmitter belt and a sensor to measure the pulse (heart) rate. Because systems used can vary and are constantly being upgraded it is advisable to follow the instructions with the system in use in your school.

The lymphatic system

The **lymphatic (lymph) system** is part of both the immune system and the transport system of the body. The lymph system (Fig 23.26) consists of a fluid called **lymph**, **lymph vessels** and **lymph nodes**.

Lymph is a pale yellow-coloured fluid containing water, white blood cells, proteins and lipids (but no red blood cells or platelets).

Lymph vessels are blind-ending tubes that carry lymph. Many lymph vessels have valves.

Lymph nodes are small swellings along the length of many lymph vessels. Lymph nodes filter bacteria and produce and store white blood cells.

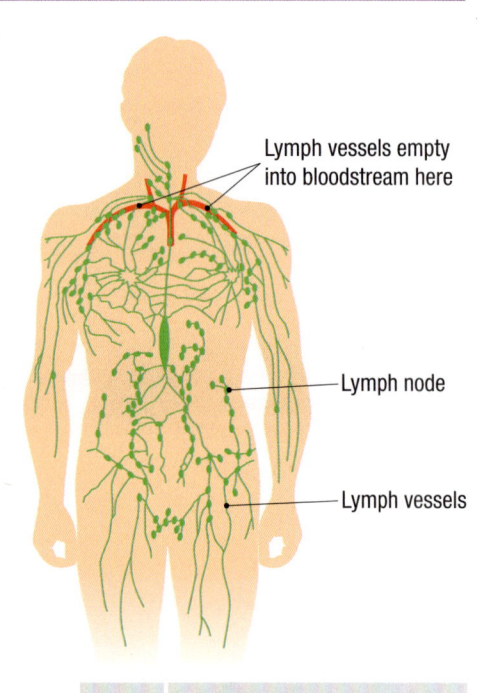

23.26 The lymph system

Transport in Humans | 23

Tissue fluid

All the cells of the body are bathed in a fluid called extra-cellular or **tissue fluid**. This fluid provides a medium through which materials exchange between the cells and the bloodstream. The composition of tissue fluid is similar to blood plasma but without the large plasma proteins. Some of the plasma which is forced, under pressure, from the arteries to the capillaries, leaks out to form tissue fluid.

Most of this fluid returns to the blood at the venous end of the capillaries. However, not all of it does and the rest enters the lymph vessels which lie between the cells (Fig 23.27). Tissue fluid which enters the lymph vessels becomes known as lymph.

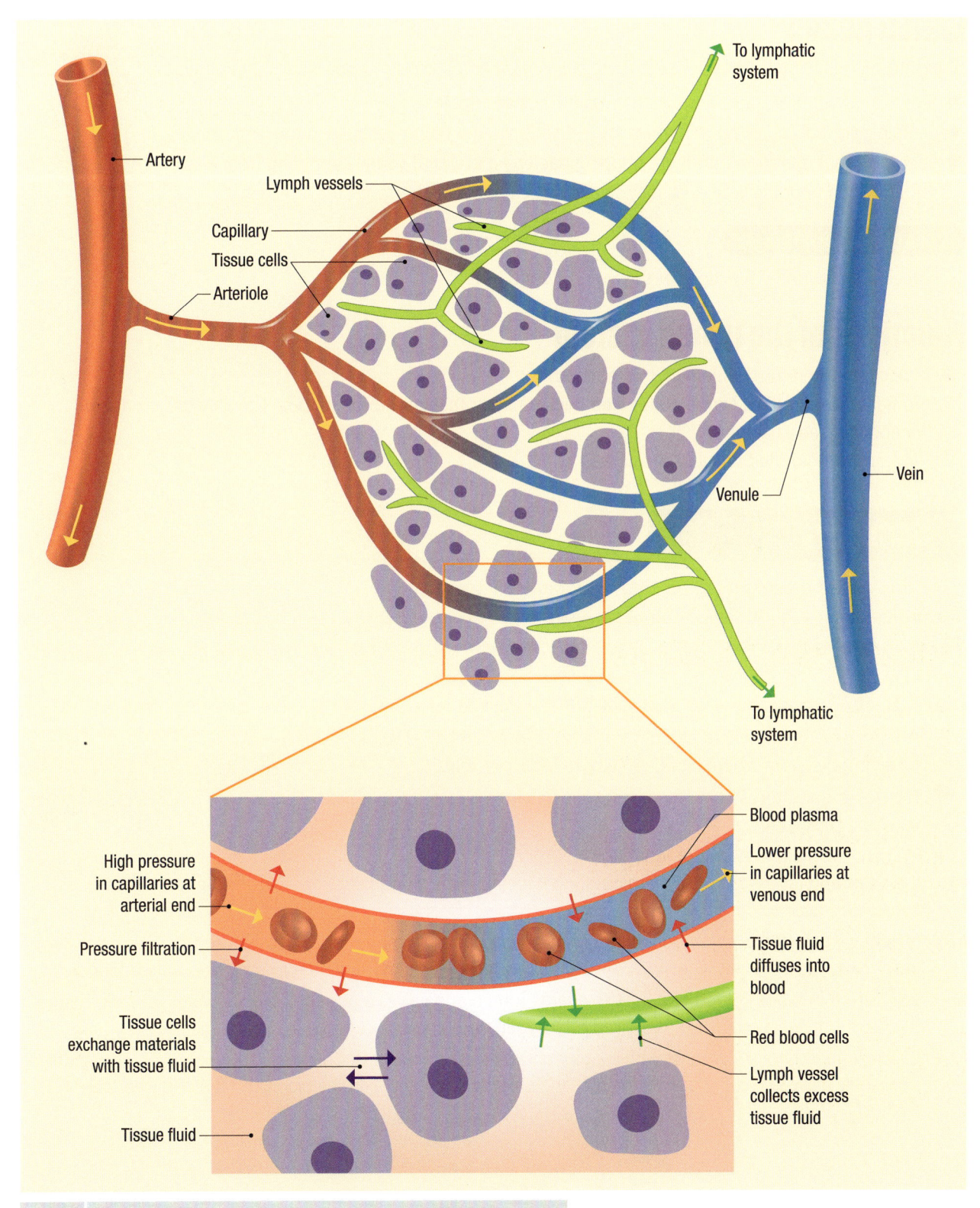

23.27 The relationship between the blood capillaries and the lymph vessels

LIFE LEAVING CERTIFICATE BIOLOGY | UNIT 3 THE ORGANISM

Lymph vessels

The lymph system is a one-way system of lymph vessels (lymphatics). Lymph vessels are similar to veins in that they have numerous valves along their length to prevent a back-flow of lymph. There is no heart to pump the lymph around and the lymph vessels rely on the contraction of the skeletal muscles to shunt the lymph along. The lymph vessels eventually lead to veins where they empty the lymph back into the bloodstream at the subclavian veins.

These veins lie just below the collar bones or clavicles. In this way the volume of fluid in the body remains more or less constant.

Lymph nodes

Along the length of many lymph vessels there are small swellings called lymph nodes. Lymph nodes:

- produce **antibodies** and transport them to the site of infection;
- contain cells that manufacture **lymphocytes** (specialised white blood cells in the lymph);
- filter the lymph as it flows through, trapping bacteria and dirt (if you are suffering from a sore throat, lymph nodes in your neck may swell and be painful as they fight the infection).

SYLLABUS REQUIREMENT:
You need to know three functions of the lymph system.

Functions of the lymph system

1. To collect and return tissue fluid to the blood.
2. To fight infection. The lymph nodes filter bacteria and other **pathogens**. Some lymphocytes produce antibodies (see Chapter 33).
3. To transport digested fats and hormones.

Summary

- Single-celled organisms rely on diffusion for internal transport.
- In some multicellular animals, internal transport by diffusion is also possible.
- As animals became more complex, a circulatory system developed to enable efficient internal transport of materials.
- There are two types of circulatory system:
  - An open system where blood is not always found in blood vessels (tubes).
  - a closed system where blood remains in blood vessels.
- The closed circulatory system in humans consists of the blood, the muscular heart and the blood vessels (arteries, veins and capillaries).
- Humans have a two-circuit or 'double' circulation – the pulmonary system which pumps blood to and from the heart and lungs and the systemic system which pumps blood from the heart to the rest of the body tissues and back to the heart.
- Arteries are thick-walled blood vessels. They have a narrow lumen and no valves. They carry blood away from the heart under high pressure. All arteries, except the pulmonary artery, carry oxygenated blood.
- Veins are thin-walled blood vessels with a large lumen and valves along their length. Veins return blood to the heart under low pressure. Veins carry deoxygenated blood, except for the pulmonary veins.
- Capillaries are very narrow tubes with walls of only one cell in thickness. Capillaries have no valves. They branch extensively between cells and allow the exchanges of materials between the blood and the cells (see Table 23.1).
- The heart is a muscular pump. It consists of the following parts:

Summary

Part of the heart	Function
Pericardium	Protects the heart
Two atria – upper chambers	Receive blood
Two ventricles – lower chambers	Pump blood out of the heart
Septum	Separates the left- and right-hand sides of the heart
Valves	Prevent a back-flow of blood
Tricuspid valve (A-V valve) (has an 'r' in its name as it is the valve on the 'right')	Separates right atrium from right ventricle
Bicuspid valve (A-V valve)	Separates left atrium from left ventricle
Semi-lunar valves	Prevent a back-flow of blood from the arteries into the ventricles
Cardiac (coronary) arteries (arise at base of aorta, where it leaves the heart)	Supply the heart muscle with oxygen and nutrients
Cardiac veins	Remove carbon dioxide and wastes from the heart muscle

Table 23.4 Summary of heart structure

- The systemic and pulmonary circulatory systems begin and end at the heart, e.g. the systemic blood flow follows the following pathway: heart → aorta → arterioles → capillaries → venules → veins → heart.
- A portal circulatory system does not directly involve the heart. It begins and ends at capillaries, e.g. the hepatic portal system which transports digested nutrients from the stomach and intestines to the liver.
- Heartbeat is controlled by the pacemaker. It regulates the contraction and relaxation of heart muscle.
  - The pacemaker is a special group of muscles found in the wall at the top of the right atrium.
  - Heartbeat sounds are caused by the closing of the valves in the heart.
- When the ventricles contract, they force blood into the arteries. This causes the arteries to expand.
- The pulse is the expansion and contraction of the wall of an artery.
- The heartbeat mechanism is as follows: pacemaker (S-A node) generates an impulse → atrial muscle → A-V node → muscle fibres → ventricle muscle

  Systole is the contraction of heart muscle. Diastole is the relaxation of heart muscle.
- The S-A node is located in the wall of the right atrium (at the upper end of the atrium). The A-V node is located in the septum near the tricuspid valve.
- Blood pressure is the force exerted by the blood on the walls of the blood vessels.
- Blood pressure is greatest as it leaves the heart in the aorta. As the blood passes through the arteries, arterioles, capillaries, venules and veins the pressure drops.
- To have a healthy heart and circulatory system we should eat a balanced low-fat, low-salt diet, take exercise and never smoke.
- The lymphatic system is a second circulatory system in the body.
- The lymphatic system consists of a fluid called lymph, a one-way system of lymph vessels (lymphatics) and lymph nodes.
- Lymph is a fluid containing white blood cells (lymphocytes), proteins and fats (no red blood cells or platelets). It is formed from tissue fluid that enters the lymph vessels.
- Tissue fluid is the excess fluid that leaks from the blood capillaries.
- Lymph vessels have thin, non-elastic walls, valves and a wide lumen.
- Lymph nodes lie along the length of the lymph vessels. They filter bacteria from the lymph and make white blood cells which help fight infection.
- Functions of the lymph system: (i) to keep the volume of the blood constant, (ii) to transport digested fats and hormones, (iii) to fight infection.

23 Transport in Humans

Review questions

01 (a) How do single-celled organisms transport substances into and out of the cell?
(b) Why do large multicellular animals need a transport system?

02 (a) What is a circulatory system?
(b) Explain the term closed circulatory system.
(c) Name an animal with an open circulatory system.

03 (a) What is meant by a double circulatory system?
(b) Outline the advantages to humans of having such a system.
(c) List the components of the human circulatory system.

04 (a) Draw a large well-labelled diagram to show the external structure of the heart.
(b) Give the precise location of the heart in the body.
(c) Name two structures that protect the heart.

05 (a) Identify the parts of the heart labelled A to I in the diagram below.

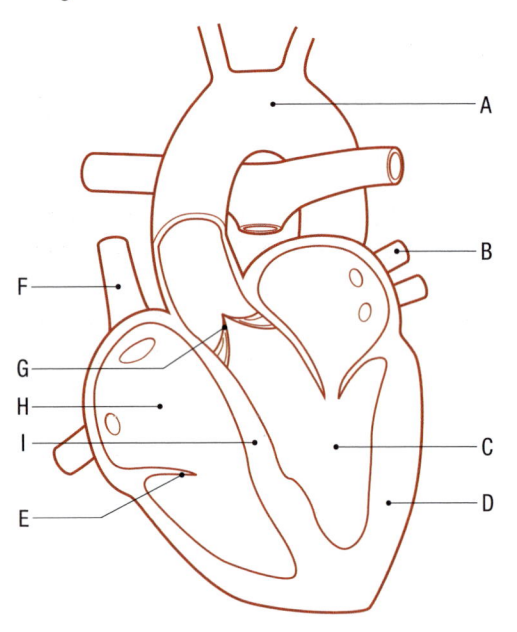

(b) State the function of parts A, C, E, G, I.
(c) Name the part of the heart from which the coronary artery derives.

06 (a) State the location of the pacemaker.
(b) Outline the role of the pacemaker in controlling heartbeat.

07 (a) Label the parts A to F on the diagram of the human circulatory system below.

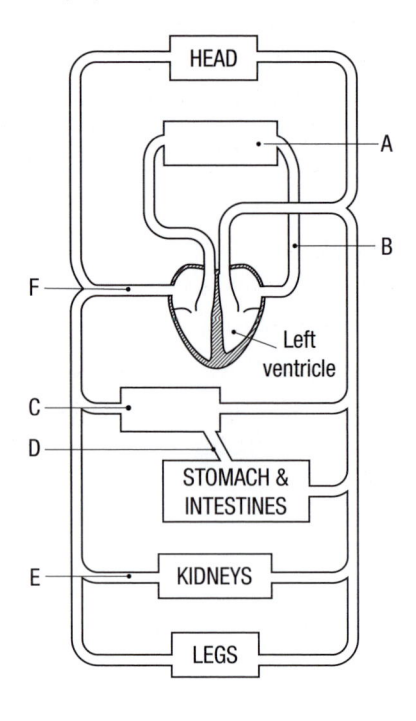

(b) List three parts of the diagram that represent (i) the pulmonary system, (ii) a portal system.

08 (a) What do T.S. and L.S. stand for in biology?
(b) Draw a labelled diagram of a T.S. and an L.S. of a vein.
(c) Draw labelled diagrams to show the difference in structure between an artery and a capillary in transverse section.

09 (a) Name the main gas carried by the pulmonary vein and the vena cava.
(b) List the structural differences between an artery and a capillary.
(c) List the functional differences between an artery, vein and capillary.

10 (a) Distinguish between the following pairs by writing a brief sentence about each.
(i) Heart beat and pulse.
(ii) A-V and semi-lunar valves.
(iii) Systole and diastole.
(iv) Cardiac arteries and cardiac veins.

Review questions

11 (a) Explain fully the role of the pacemaker in controlling heartbeat.
(b) Outline the stages in the human heart beat.
(c) The average speed of blood travelling through the arteries is far, far greater than that through the capillaries. Suggest a reason why this is so and also why exchange of materials can only occur from the capillaries.

12 (a) What is the pulse?
(b) How might you find a person's pulse?
(c) What is the normal pulse rate for an adult human?
(d) Suggest how increased exercise affects pulse rate.
(e) Do you think the heart rate of a fit person would be lower or higher than the average? Give a reason for your answer.

13 Explain the term blood pressure and outline the significance of raised blood pressure for an individual.

14 Why is it necessary to have a 'Healthy Heart Awareness Week' in Ireland each year? Design a poster to encourage teenagers to look after their hearts.

15 (a) Name the second circulatory system in humans.
(b) What is tissue fluid? From what is it formed?
(c) What is lymph? List three components of lymph.
(d) Distinguish between lymph and blood.

16 Describe the structure and functions of the lymphatic system.

17 Distinguish between the following pairs of terms by giving two points of information about each term:
(a) Open and closed circulatory systems.
(b) Arteries and veins.
(c) Atria and ventricles.
(d) Pulmonary artery and pulmonary vein.
(e) Lymph vessels and arteries.

Examination style questions

Section A

01 The diagram below shows the external structure of the mammalian heart together with the major blood vessels.
(a) Name parts X, Y, Z.
(b) Does blood flow into or out of the heart through Z?
(c) What is the function of the cardiac artery?
(d) Which of the labelled parts carries deoxygenated blood?
(e) If a clot were to form in the cardiac artery, what effect is this likely to have on the working of the heart?
(f) Suggest three ways to keep your heart healthy.

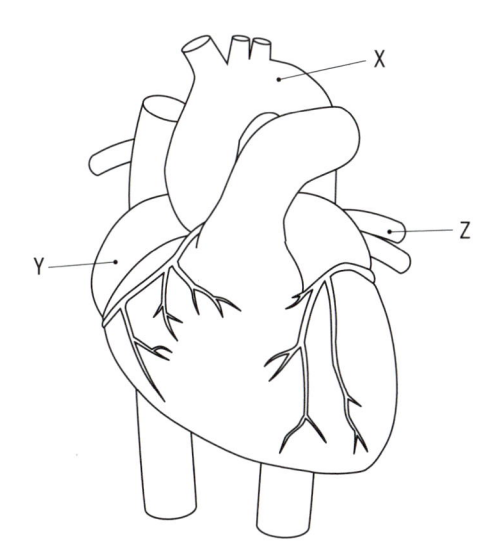

Section B

02 (a) (i) Name an artery that carries deoxygenated blood.
(ii) From which chamber of the heart does this blood vessel arise?
(b) (i) The diagram shows the external and ventral view of a heart. Name the parts labelled A, B, C, D.

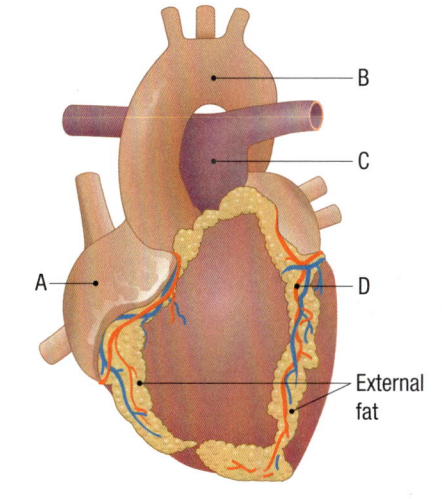

(ii) On the diagram, indicate the line of cuts you made in the heart in order to expose the interior of its four chambers.
(iii) Why are the walls of both atria equally thick?
(iv) Where would you expect to find a papillary muscle?
(v) Is the pacemaker visible in your dissected heart?
(vi) Describe one safety precaution you took while carrying out this activity.

23 Transport in Humans

Examination style questions

03 (a) (i) Name the arteries that supply the muscle of the heart with oxygenated blood.
  (ii) Name the artery that carries deoxygenated blood to the lungs.
(b) Answer the following question in relation to an investigation into the effect of exercise level on the breathing rate **or** pulse rate of a human.
  (i) How is the rate measured?
  (ii) Why is the rate at rest measured?
  (iii) Why are different intensity levels of exercise carried out?
  (iv) Why are at least three readings taken at each level of activity?
  (v) Why is there a period of rest after each exercise session?
  (vi) Explain the adaptive advantage to the change in rate during exercise.

Section C

04 (a) The human circulatory system is described as 'closed'.
  (i) What is meant by a closed circulatory system?
  (ii) There are three major loops or circuits in the human circulatory system. Name any **two**.
(b) (i) Draw a diagram of a vertical section of the mammalian heart to display its internal structure.
  (ii) Label the following parts on your diagram: left atrium, bicuspid valve, septum, papillary muscle, pulmonary artery and a semi-lunar valve.
  (iii) Indicate (pacemaker) on the diagram the location of the sino-atrial node.
  (iv) What is the function of the sino-atrial node?
  (v) What is the precise function of the bicuspid valve?
(c) The following diagram shows the relationship between blood and the lymphatic system and tissue cells.

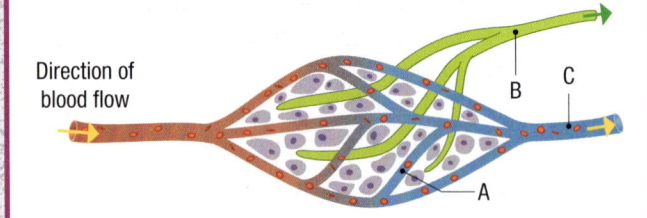

  (i) Name A, B and C.
  (ii) Describe how exchange takes place between the blood in C and the tissue cells.
  (iii) Outline the major difference in composition between blood and lymph.
  (iv) Outline how the lymphatic system forms an important part of the circulatory system.

05 (a) The diagram of the human heart shows the four chambers and the major blood vessels and valves.

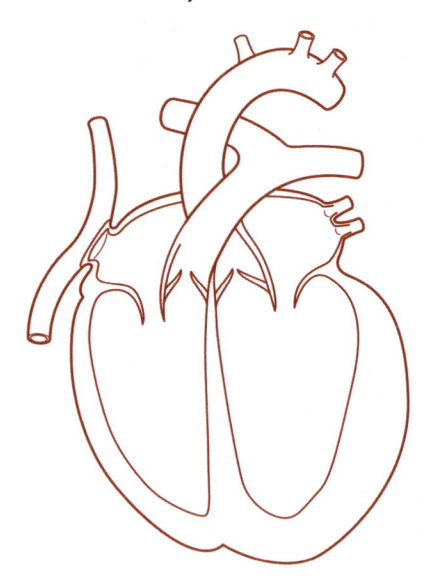

  (i) Copy the diagram into your answer book and indicate on it the positions of the SA node and the AV node.
  (ii) Describe in detail the role of the SA and AV nodes in the heart cycle.
(b) The real work of the blood circulatory system occurs at the capillaries where exchange between blood and tissue cells takes place. The heart, arteries and veins receive a much greater level of interest even though they are really just the supporting cast for the capillaries. William Harvey, who proposed the circulation of blood in the 17th century, could not directly prove his theory because the microscope had not been invented and capillaries are too small to be seen with the unaided eye.
  (i) Draw labelled diagrams to show the structure of a vein and a capillary.
  (ii) What are the adaptive features of a capillary for its role in exchange?
  (iii) Name the process by which materials pass out of the capillaries.
  (iv) Compare arteries and veins under the headings structure and functions.
(c) (i) What is lymph and what is it formed from?
  (ii) State **two** structural differences between blood and lymph.
  (iii) How is lymph circulated around the body?
  (iv) Describe **one** way in which the lymph system defends the body against harmful micro-organisms.
  (v) What is a lacteal? Where would you expect to find a lacteal? State the function of lacteals.

Examination style questions

06 The heart is a very active organ requiring an efficient supply of oxygen and nutrients along with the removal of its metabolic wastes. In regards to the coronary circuit:
(a) State from what major artery do the coronary arteries emerge?
(b) What is the function of the coronary arteries?
(c) Give the precise location of the point of origin of the coronary arteries.
(d) Describe in detail how you dissected a sheep/bovine heart to show the main chambers, valves and origin of the coronary arteries.
(e) Give **two** harmful effects of smoking on the circulatory system.
(f) Outline the benefit to the circulatory system of regular physical exercise.

Leaving Certificate examination questions

Section A

01 The diagram shows a section through a human heart.

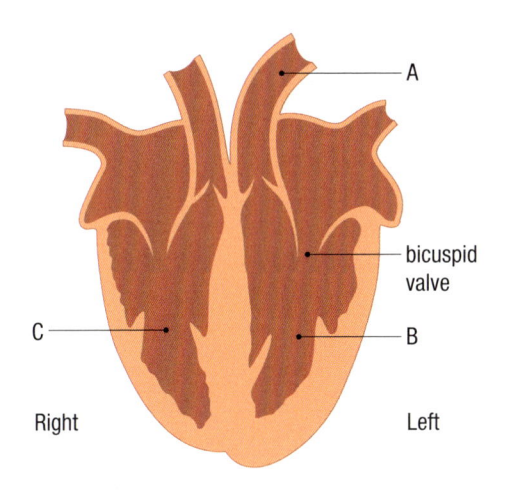

(a) Name blood vessel A.
(b) Is the blood in A oxygenated or deoxygenated?
(c) Name the chamber of the heart labelled B.
(d) Give one reason why the wall of chamber B is thicker than the wall of chamber C.
(e) What is the role of the bicuspid valve?

2008 OL Q. 4

02 The diagram shows a region of tissue that includes body cells and parts of the circulatory and lymphatic systems.

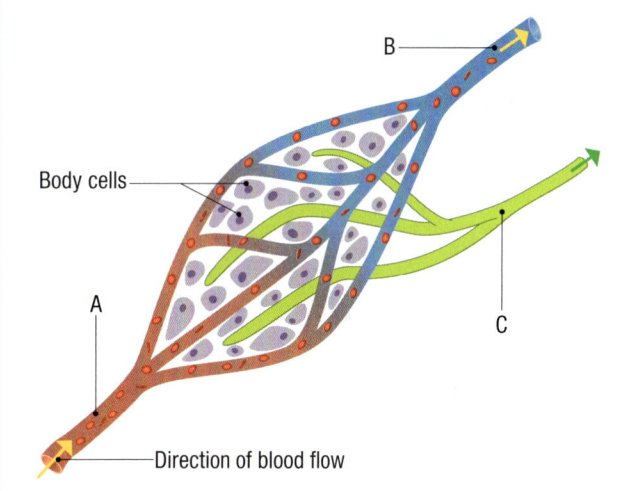

(a) Name part C.
(b) What type of blood vessel is A?
(c) If a transverse section of A were viewed under the microscope state **one** way in which it would differ from a transverse section through B.
(d) Give **two** functions of the lymphatic system.
(e) Give **one** way in which lymph differs from blood.
(f) Name a major blood vessel that returns the blood in B to the heart.

2014 HL Q. 3

Leaving Certificate examination questions

03 The diagram shows a section of human tissue containing an artery and a vein.

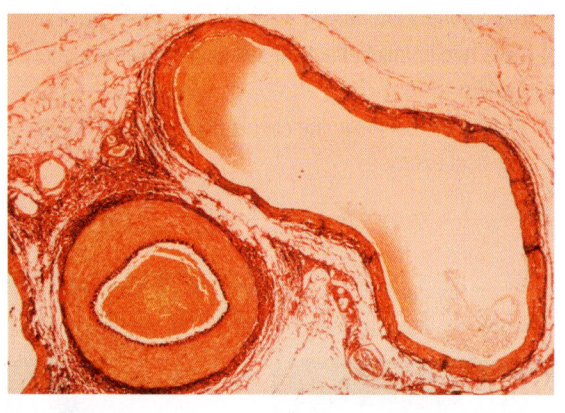

(a) Identify the artery by writing A on it and the vein by writing B on it.
(b) State two features of the artery that can be seen in the diagram which allowed you to identify it.
(c) Name two tissues that are present in the walls of arteries and veins and give a function of each of these tissues.
(d) Veins contain valves whereas arteries do not. What is the function of the valves?

SEC Sample HL Q. 4

Section B

04 (a) (i) What is the purpose of the valves in the heart?
(ii) What structure separates the right side of the heart from the left side?
(b) Answer the following questions in relation to the dissection of a heart.
(i) How did you distinguish between the left side and the right side of the heart?
(ii) What was the main instrument that you used for the actual dissection?
(iii) Describe how you carried out the dissection.
(iv) Name the valves found at the base of both the aorta and the pulmonary artery.
(v) Based on your dissection draw and label the following parts: bicuspid valve, left atrium, left ventricle.

2014 OL Q. 9

05 Answer the following questions about an activity that you carried out to investigate the effect of exercise on your breathing rate **or** your pulse rate.

Tick the rate you will refer to.		
	Breathing rate	
	Pulse rate	

(i) The investigation starts by measuring the resting rate. How did you measure the resting rate?
(ii) After measuring your resting rate, what other steps did you carry out to complete the investigation?
(iii) What was the result of your investigation?
(iv) Does this investigation give the same result for both fit and non-fit people?
(v) Give a reason for your answer.

2012 OL Q. 7 (b)

06 (a) Answer the following in relation to human breathing rate OR pulse rate. State which of these you will refer to.
(i) What is the average rate at rest?
(ii) State a possible effect of smoking on the resting rate.
(b) How did you measure the resting rate? Describe how you investigated the effect of exercise on this rate. Using the axes below draw a graph to show how rate is likely to vary as the exercise level increases.

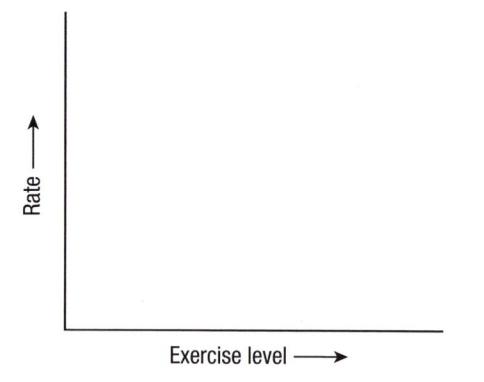

2004 OL Q. 9

07 (a) (i) Name the cavity of the body in which the heart and lungs are located.
(ii) State **one** way in which heart muscle differs from other muscles in the body.
(b) Answer the following questions in relation to a dissection that you carried out to investigate the structure of an ox's or a sheep's heart.
(i) Describe the steps that you followed in order to identify and display the inner structures of the heart. Use suitably labelled diagrams if necessary.
(ii) What did you do in order to expose a semi-lunar valve?
(iii) Draw and label sufficient of your dissection to show the tricuspid valve, the right atrium and the right ventricle.

2010 HL Q. 7

Leaving Certificate examination questions

Section C

08 (i) The heart pumps blood around the body.
  1. Name the structure in the heart that controls the heartbeat.
  2. Where is this structure located in the heart?
 (ii) What causes the sound of a heartbeat?
 (iii) Name the blood vessels that supply the heart cells with blood.
 (iv) Mention two ways to maintain a healthy heart.

2013 OL Q. 14 (b)

09 The diagram shows a section through the human heart.

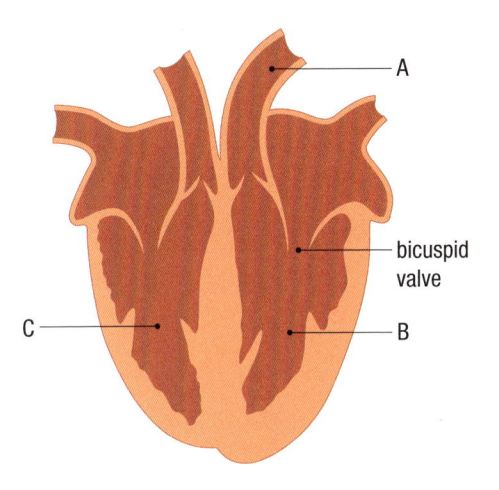

 (i) Name the blood vessel labelled A.
 (ii) Does A carry blood towards or away from the heart?
 (iii) Name the chamber of the heart labelled C.
 (iv) Why is the wall of chamber B thicker than the wall of chamber C?
 (v) Name the arteries that supply the heart wall with blood.
 (vi) What is the role of valves in the heart?
 (vii) The lymphatic system is another series of vessels carrying fluid in the body. Give any **two** functions of the lymphatic system.

2011 OL Q. 13 (b)

10 (a) Name the blood vessel referred to in each of the following cases:
  (i) The vein connected to the lungs.
  (ii) The artery connected to the kidneys.
  (iii) The vein that joins the intestine to the liver.
 (b) The following questions relate to the human heart.
  (i) Give the precise location of the heart in the human body.
  (ii) What structure(s) protects the heart?
  (iii) Name the upper chambers of the heart.
  (iv) Name the valve between the upper and lower chambers on the left-hand side.
  (v) What is the average resting human heart rate?
  (vi) Give **two** factors which cause an increase in heart rate.
  (vii) Name the blood vessels that bring oxygen to the heart muscle.
  (viii) Explain why the walls of the lower chambers of the heart are thicker than the walls of the upper chambers.
 (c) **Copy the table below into your copy** and use your knowledge of blood vessels and the information in diagrams A, B and C to complete the table. Some boxes have been filled as examples.

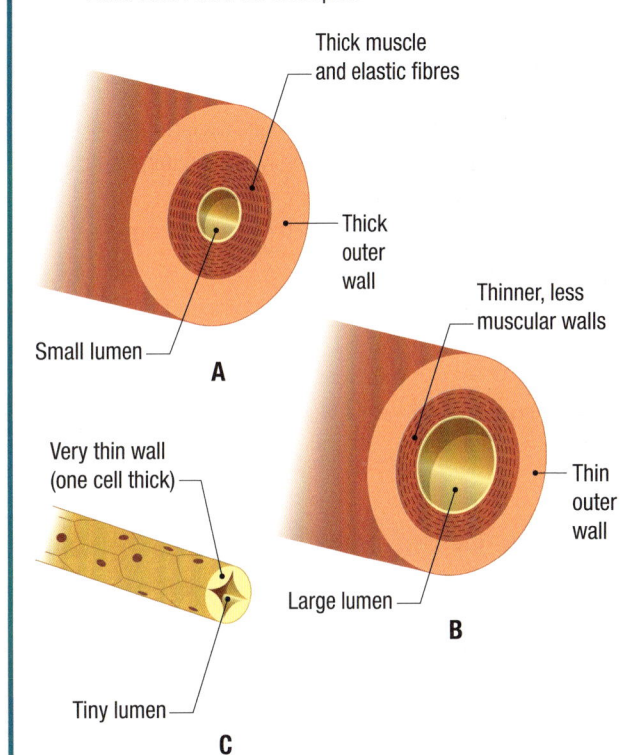

Vessel	A	B	C
Name		Vein	
Lumen	Small		
Wall			
Direction of blood flow			
Valves present			

2009 OL Q. 13

23 Transport in Humans

Leaving Certificate examination questions

11 Answer the following questions in relation to blood vessels in the human body.
   (i) Valves are present in veins. What is their function?
   (ii) Why are valves not needed in arteries?
   (iii) Which has the bigger lumen (cavity), an artery or a vein?
   (iv) The wall of capillaries is only one cell thick. How is this related to their function?
   (v) How does a portal vein differ from other veins?
   (vi) Name the following blood vessels:
      1. The vessels that carry blood from the aorta to the kidneys.
      2. The vessels that supply the heart's muscle with blood.

2005 OL Q. 14 (c)

12 (a) The human circulatory system has two circuits.
   (i) Give the name of each of these circuits.
   (ii) Which of these circuits involves the pumping of blood by the left ventricle?
   (b) (i) Write a short note on **each** of the following:
      1. Pulse.
      2. Blood pressure.

   (ii) Comment on the effect of **each** of the following on the circulatory system:
      1. Diet.
      2. Exercise.
   (iii) Give **two** ways, other than colour, in which a red blood cell differs in structure or composition from a typical body cell such as one in the cheek lining.
   (iv) What is the role of the SA (sino-atrial) and AV (atrio-ventricular) nodes in the heart? Give the **precise** locations of **both** the SA and the AV nodes in the heart.

2009 HL Q. 13

13 (i) Describe the structure of the lymphatic system.
   (ii) Give an account of **three** functions of the lymphatic system.

2006 HL Q. 13 (c)

Past examination questions

OL	2014 Q. 9	2013 Q. 14 (b) (v)–(viii)	2012 Q. 7	2011 Q. 13 (b)	2009 Q. 13
	2008 Q. 4, Q. 8		2006 Q. 7	2005 Q. 12 (a), 14 (c)	2004 Q. 9
HL	2014 Q. 3, Q. 9 (b), Q. 12 (c)	2010 Q. 7	2009 Q. 13 (a), (b)	2007 Q. 13 (a) (i)	
	2006 Q. 5 (a), (b), Q. 13 (c)	2004 Q. 9			

The Blood

24

After studying this chapter you should be able to:

1. List the components of blood.
2. Describe the structure and role of red blood cells, white blood cells and platelets.
3. **HL** Give a more detailed description of red blood cells.
4. **HL** Classify white blood cells as lymphocytes and monocytes.
5. Outline the functions of blood.
6. Name the four main blood groups and the Rhesus factors.

Composition of the blood

1. Blood (Fig 24.1) is the **vascular tissue** in humans. It is made up of:
   - a liquid called **plasma** (55% by volume);
   - three types of **blood cell** suspended in the plasma (45% by volume).

   The blood has a pH of 7.4, which is slightly alkaline.

Plasma

Plasma is a straw-coloured liquid consisting of 90% water and 10% dissolved substances. The water acts as a transport medium for blood cells and dissolved substances. The dissolved substances include:
- Nutrients: glucose, amino acids, fatty acids, glycerol.
- Wastes: carbon dioxide, urea, uric acid.
- **Hormones:** insulin, testosterone.
- Gases: carbon dioxide, oxygen.
- Salts: sodium bicarbonate.
- Large proteins: albumen, which makes the blood thicker, and fibrinogen, which helps in blood clotting.

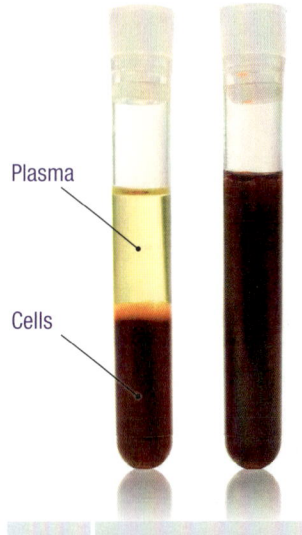

24.1 Composition of blood

Blood cells

2. There are three types of blood cell – **red blood cells**, **white blood cells** and cell fragments called **platelets** (Fig 24.2).

24.2 Blood cells

24 | The Blood

Red blood cells

Structure

Red blood cells are tiny, biconcave discs (Fig 24.3). Their shape gives them a large surface area which enables them to carry more oxygen. They have a flexible membrane that allows them to squeeze through the tiniest blood **capillaries**.

Red blood cells are filled with the pigment **haemoglobin**, which gives the blood its red colour. Haemoglobin is a complex protein molecule containing iron (Fe). The function of haemoglobin is to bind with the oxygen we breathe in to form **oxyhaemoglobin**. In this form, oxygen is transported to all the **cells** of the body.

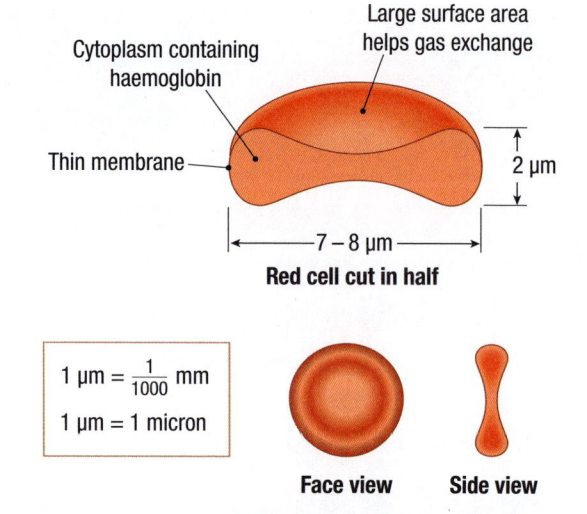

Site of production

Red blood cells are formed in the **red bone marrow** of bones such as the ribs and breastbone.

Function

The function of the red blood cells is to transport oxygen (and carbon dioxide).

> **HL 3**
>
> When fully formed, red blood cells do not have a nucleus or **mitochondria**. The lack of mitochondria enables red blood cells to transport and release oxygen which would otherwise be used in the mitochondria during **respiration**. Because they have no nuclei, red blood cells are very flexible, which allows them to squeeze through the capillaries. They are broken down in the liver and spleen (Fig 25.6), and most of the iron from their haemoglobin is re-used to make new red blood cells.

A lack of iron in the diet is the most common cause of the condition known as **anaemia**. So eating enough iron-rich foods is important for our health. Foods containing iron include red meats, liver, kidneys, chicken and turkey, eggs, sardines, many nuts, prunes, apricots, bananas and green vegetables.

White blood cells

Structure

White blood cells have a nucleus and are usually larger than red blood cells. They do not contain haemoglobin (Fig 24.4). There are a number of different types of white blood cell.

Site of production

White blood cells are formed in the red bone marrow and they mature in the lymph system (see Chapter 23).

Function

The main function of white blood cells is to protect against disease. White blood cells recognise dangerous things in the body and destroy them. White blood cells are far less numerous than red blood cells.

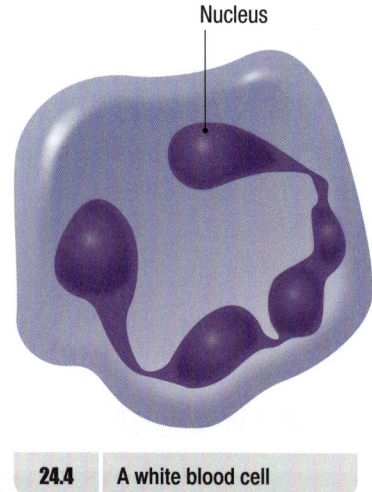

> **HL 4**
>
> There are two types of white blood cell – the **lymphocytes** and the **monocytes** (Fig 24.5).
>
> ### Lymphocytes
>
> Many lymphocytes originate in the red bone marrow and mature in the lymph system. Lymphocytes have a fairly large nucleus. They produce proteins called **antibodies** in response to 'foreign' **viruses** and bacteria which may invade the body. The antibodies destroy the foreign cells (Chapter 33).

HL ### Monocytes (phagocytes)

Monocytes are made in the red bone marrow and are the largest type of white blood cell. They function in protection by engulfing bacteria and dead cells.

You can learn more about how the white blood cells protect us against infection in Chapter 33.

24.5 Lymphocytes and monocytes

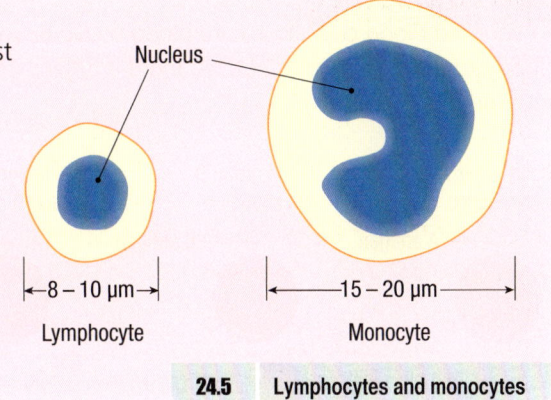

Platelets

Structure

Platelets are tiny fragments of larger cells made in the red bone marrow. They have no nucleus.

Site of production

Platelets are formed in the red bone marrow.

Function

The function of platelets (Fig 24.6) is in helping the blood to clot when the skin is cut at the surface and internally when blood vessels are damaged.

24.6 Platelets

Functions of blood

1. Transport

The blood transports a number of different groups of substances including:
- **Gases**: Oxygen is carried from the lungs to all the cells in the red blood cells. Carbon dioxide is carried from the cells to the lungs in the red blood cells and as bicarbonate ions in the plasma.
- **Nutrients**: Digested foods such as glucose are carried from the digestive system to all the cells.
- **Wastes**: are carried from the cells to the kidneys, skin and lungs.
- **Hormones**: are carried from one place to another, e.g. insulin, testosterone.

2. Protection

The white blood cells produce **antibodies** which fight against infection and disease.

The platelets play an important role in **blood clotting**.

3. Regulation

Blood helps to keep the amount of water and salts in the cells at the correct level. It helps maintain the body temperature.

Many of these functions of the blood are dealt with in more detail in other chapters.

Blood groups

Human blood is classified into four different blood groups. The blood group you belong to depends upon the presence or absence of different glycoprotein molecules on the surface of your red blood cells. Glycoproteins consist of a carbohydrate and a protein and they act as **antigens** (see Chapter 33).

24 The Blood

The blood groups are known as A, B, AB and O. If you are blood group A, it means you have A antigens on your red blood cells. If you are blood group B, you have B antigens on your red blood cells. If you are blood group AB, you have both A and B antigens. If you are blood group O, you have neither antigen on your red blood cells (Fig 24.7).

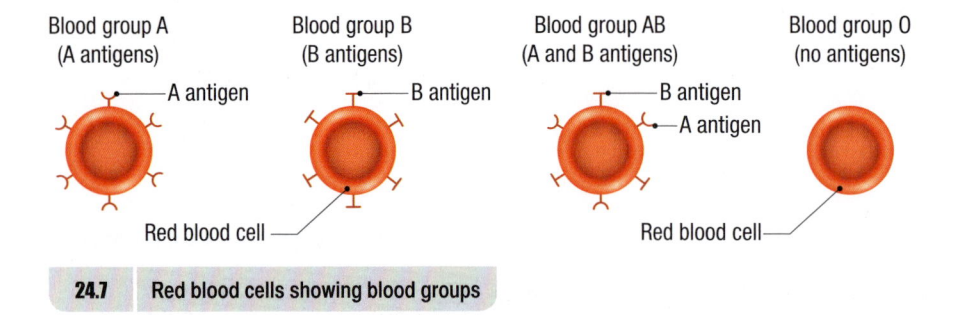

24.7 Red blood cells showing blood groups

The exact frequency of each blood group varies with different races of people. In Ireland the most common blood group is blood group O (55%) (see Table 24.1).

Blood group	Antigen on red blood cells	Ireland	USA (negroid)	US (Caucasian)
A	A	31%	25%	41%
B	B	11%	20%	7%
AB	A and B	3%	4%	2%
O	none	55%	51%	50%

Table 24.1 Blood group frequency

Knowing what blood group a person belongs to is essential for safe blood transfusions (Fig 24.8). If the bloods do not match correctly, then the blood may clump.

Rhesus factors

The Rhesus system is another blood grouping system. It was first discovered during experiments with Rhesus monkeys in 1940. This system involves a number of antigens, the most important of which is one called **factor D**. People who possess factor D are referred to as being **Rhesus positive** or Rh$^+$; those who do not possess the factor are **Rhesus negative** or Rh$^-$. Approximately 85% of people are Rh$^+$.

When a person's blood is classified, both the Rhesus system and the ABO blood grouping system are used. For example the majority of Irish people are O$^+$ (O positive). This means they have neither A nor B antigens but they do have factor D. The Rhesus factor is significant during pregnancy.

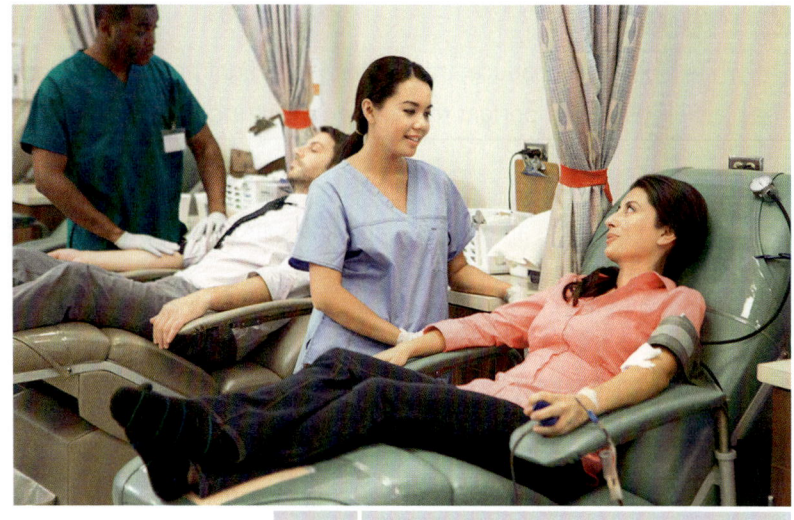

24.8 Being a blood donor could save someone's life

Summary

- Blood is the vascular (transport) tissue in animals.
- Blood is composed of plasma and blood cells.
- Blood plasma consists of 90% water and 10% dissolved substances such as digested nutrients, salts, gases and wastes.
- The functions of blood are: transport, protection and regulation.
- There are three types of blood cell:

	Red blood cells	White blood cells	Platelets
Appearance	Biconcave disc containing haemoglobin, with flexible membrane No nucleus	Varied shapes. Nucleus present	Fragments of larger cells No nucleus
	No mitochondria	Two types: lymphocytes (produce antibodies) and monocytes (phagocytic)	
Site of production	Red bone marrow	Red bone marrow	Red bone marrow
Function	Transport oxygen (as oxyhaemoglobin)	Defence against disease	Blood clotting

- There are four different human blood groups: A, B, AB and O.
- The blood group of an individual depends upon the presence or absence of a particular antigen on their red blood cells.
- The Rhesus factor is one of a number of antigens on the surface of red blood cells. It is known as anti-D.
- If a person is Rhesus positive, it means they have the D antigen. If they are Rhesus negative, it means they do not have the D antigen on their red blood cells.
- Knowing a person's blood group is important for blood transfusions and during pregnancy.

24 The Blood

Review questions

01
(a) What is vascular tissue?
(b) Name the vascular tissue in (i) flowering plants, (ii) humans.
(c) Suggest why a vascular system is necessary.

02
(a) List the components of (i) blood, (ii) blood plasma.
(b) List three ways in which red and white blood cells differ.
(c) State the main function of red and white blood cells.
(d) Where are blood cells made?

03
(a) What are platelets?
(b) Where are they made?
(c) Why are they important in the body?

04
(a) Red blood cells have no nucleus. What advantage does this have?
(b) What are mitochondria?
(c) What is their function?
(d) Why do red blood cells not possess mitochondria?

05 Give two points in each case to clearly distinguish between: (a) plasma and water, (b) red blood cells and platelets, (c) monocytes and lymphocytes.

06 The photograph shows a sample of blood cells.
(a) Do you think this photograph is a view of blood cells taken with a light microscope or an electron microscope? Explain your choice.
(b) How many white cells can you see? What is the function of the white cells?
(c) State two features of the red cells that allow them to be identified.

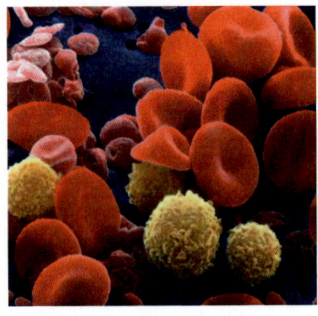

07
(a) What does it mean when we say a person is blood group B?
(b) Name the other human blood groups.
(c) What are Rhesus factors?
(d) Why is knowing a person's blood group and Rhesus factor important?

08 Compare and contrast red and white blood cells under the following headings: (a) size, (b) site(s) of formation, (c) main function, (d) shape.

09
(a) Distinguish between the cellular and non-cellular components of blood.
(b) Name the oxygen-carrying molecule present in red blood cells.
(c) Name the trace element that is the major component of this molecule.
(d) Name the cellular organelle that is absent from red blood cells that allows them to transport oxygen efficiently.
(e) What does it mean if your blood is classed as A negative (A$^-$)?

10 The table shows the blood composition of four people.

	Red blood cells/mm^3	White blood cells/mm^3	Platelets/mm^3
Mark	5,750,000	550	250,000
Sarah	2,220,000	5,000	600
Donal	8,200,000	6,000	260,000
Matt	5,000,000	8,000	250,000

(a) One person is suffering from anaemia (lack of iron in the diet). Who do you think it is? Give a reason for your choice.
(b) Suggest one symptom of anaemia.
(c) Say, giving a reason, which person has blood that will take a long time to clot?
(d) At high altitude, e.g. in the Andes, there is less oxygen in the air than at sea level, and more red blood cells are needed to carry oxygen efficiently. One of the people in the table lives at a high altitude. Who do you think it is? Explain your choice.

Examination style questions

Section A

01 Answer each of the following:
(a) State one function of white blood cells.
(b) Name the red pigment in the blood.
(c) Which type(s) of blood cell has no nucleus?
(d) Where in the body are blood cells made?
(e) Name the non-cellular component of the blood.
(f) What is the function of the platelets?
(g) Name the gas that is mainly transported as bicarbonate ions.

Examination style questions

Section C

02 (a) (i) What is the name given to the pale yellow liquid that forms about 55% of the blood?
  (ii) What is the major component of this liquid?
(b) In relation to mature red blood cells, state:
  (i) A precise location where they are formed in the body.
  (ii) One way, other than colour and function, that they differ from white blood cells.
  (iii) Two ways in which they differ from a typical plant cell.
  (iv) One way in which they are adapted to pass through narrow capillaries.
(c) (i) List three groups of materials transported by the blood.
  (ii) For each group listed give (1) a location where it enters the blood and (2) a location where it leaves the blood.
  (iii) When a person has lost blood in an accident they may be given a blood transfusion. Whenever possible the transfused blood should be the same blood group as the patient's blood. Name the four blood groups and say why it is important that the bloods be the same.

03 Give a biological reason for each of the following:
(a) When you are suffering from certain illnesses, the number of white blood cells in your bloodstream is greater than at other times.
(b) The importance of knowing a person's blood group before giving them a blood transfusion.
(c) During pregnancy, a woman is often given iron tablets.
(d) When viewed under a light microscope, the middle part of a red blood cell appears paler in colour than the outer part.

Leaving Certificate examination questions

Section A

01 (a) Name the liquid part of blood.
(b) Give **two** components of this liquid.
(c) Copy and complete the following table in relation to blood cells:

Cell type	One function
Red blood cell	
White blood cell	
Platelet	

2009 OL Q. 5

Section C

02 (i) Blood is made up of plasma and blood cells. What is plasma?
(ii) What is the function of white blood cells?
(iii) Where in the body are white blood cells produced?
(iv) Some people may have the blood group B positive (B+). What factor is present in their blood that makes it positive?

2013 OL Q. 14 (b)

03 Answer the following questions in relation to blood.
(i) What is blood plasma? Give a role for blood plasma.
(ii) Name two types of cell found in the blood and give a function for each type.
(iii) The ABO blood group system has four blood groups. What are these four groups?
(iv) Suggest a reason why it is important to know a person's blood group.

2008 OL Q. 15 (b)

04 (i) State two ways, other than colour, in which red blood cells differ from white blood cells.
(ii) Name a group of white blood cells, other than lymphocytes.

2012 HL Q. 15 (b)

05 (i) State a precise location in the human body at which red blood cells are made.
(ii) State two ways in which red blood cells differ from typical body cells, e.g. from the cheek lining.

2006 HL Q. 13 (a)

Past examination questions

| **OL** | 2013 Q. 14 (b) | 2009 Q. 5 | 2008 Q. 15 (b) |

| **HL** | 2012 Q. 15 (b) | 2006 Q. 13 (a) |

25 Human Nutrition

After studying this chapter you should be able to:

1. Define the terms heterotroph and autotroph and distinguish between the different types of heterotroph.
2. Define the term digestion and outline the need for digestion and a digestive system.
3. Draw a labelled diagram of the human digestive system and its associated glands, i.e. salivary glands, liver and pancreas.
4. State and explain the stages of human nutrition.
5. Distinguish between mechanical and chemical breakdown of food.
6. Describe digestion in the mouth including the role of the different teeth and state the dental formula of the human.
7. Define the term peristalsis and describe its effects.
8. Describe digestion in the stomach, duodenum and ileum.
9. Outline the role of the glands associated with the digestive system – the pancreas and the liver.
10. Outline the role, production site, pH at a named location of action and products of an amylase, a protease and a lipase enzyme.
11. Explain how the small intestine is adapted for its role in digestion and absorption.
12. Describe the structure of the large intestine in relation to its function.
13. Outline the role of symbiotic bacteria in the digestive system and the benefits of dietary fibre.

Heterotrophs and autotrophs

All animals, including humans, are **heterotrophs**. Heterotrophs cannot make their own food. Instead they feed on food that has been made by some other organism, e.g. cows eat grass, owls eat mice and humans eat meat and vegetables. Organisms that can make their own food are called **autotrophs**. Green plants are autotrophs.

> **Heterotrophs** are organisms that cannot make their own food.

There are three main types of heterotrophs (Fig 25.1):

1. **Herbivores** – which eat plant material only, e.g. sheep.
2. **Carnivores** – which eat other animals only, e.g. seals.
3. **Omnivores** – which eat both plant and animal material, e.g. humans.

25.1 Herbivores, carnivores and omnivores

Digestion

2 The food we eat consists of large, complex chemicals such as carbohydrates and proteins. These **biomolecules** are too large to pass directly into the body's cells. They must be broken down (digested) into a smaller, soluble form that can be absorbed into the bloodstream. Much of our food is digested by **enzymes**. If every cell of our body had to produce a full set of digestive enzymes it would be very inefficient and time-consuming. Instead **digestion** takes place in a specialised digestive system (Fig 25.2). The digestive

3 system or gut is a long, hollow, muscular tube which runs through the body from mouth to anus.

> **D** **Digestion** is the breakdown of large food molecules into smaller soluble ones.

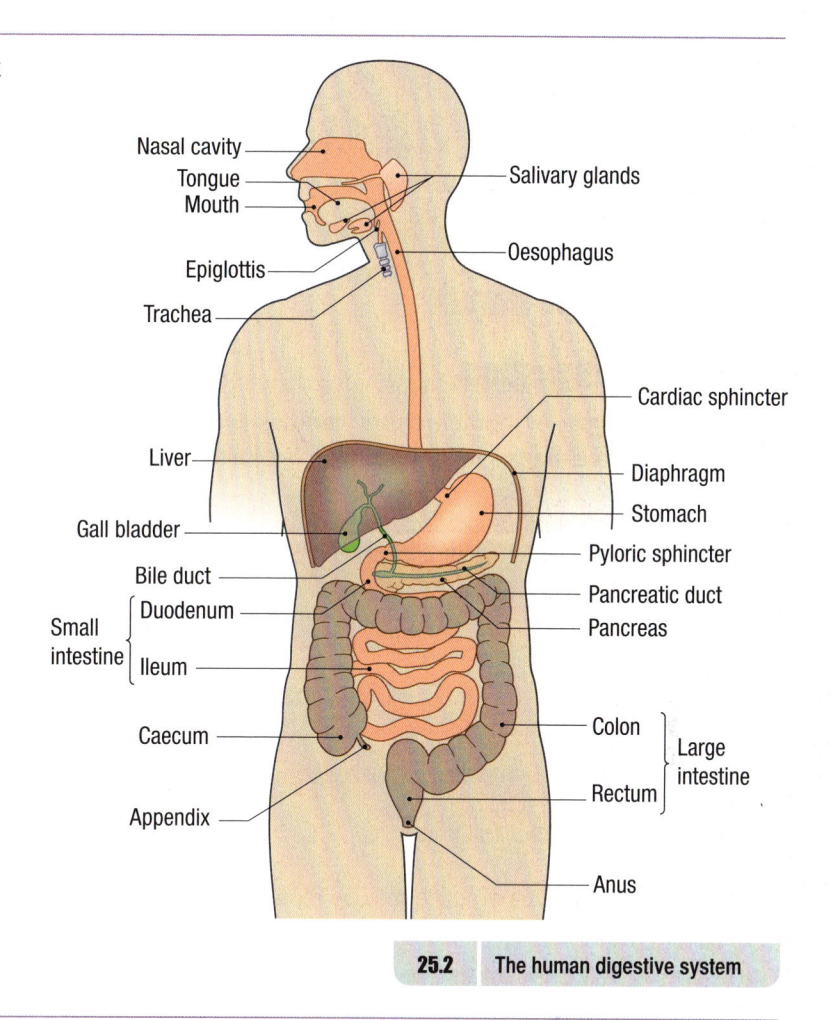

25.2 The human digestive system

Human nutrition

4 Human nutrition occurs in stages. These are:
1. **Ingestion**: the taking of food into the body, i.e. at the mouth.
2. **Digestion**: the physical and chemical breakdown of food into smaller soluble pieces. It takes place in the mouth, stomach and small intestine.
3. **Absorption**: the taking into the bloodstream of the digested food. It takes place through the walls of the stomach and intestines.
4. **Egestion**: the removal of the undigested material from the body, i.e. through the anus.

Types of digestion
Mechanical digestion

5 **Mechanical digestion** is the physical breakdown of food into smaller pieces (Fig 25.3). It begins in the mouth when food is cut and chewed by the teeth and continues throughout the gut by the muscles of the gut wall (**peristalsis**, see below).

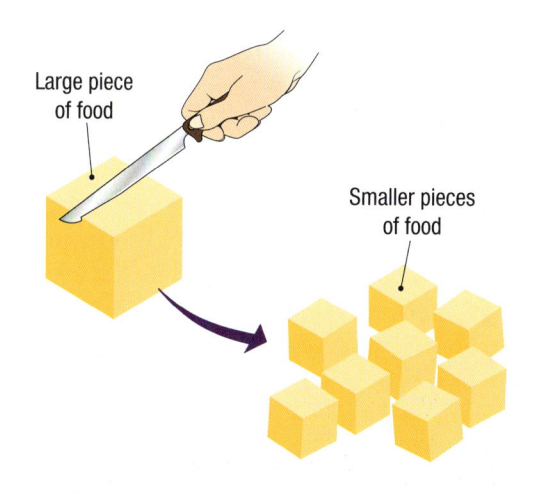

25.3 Cutting food into smaller pieces increases the surface area

25 Human Nutrition

D **Mechanical digestion** is the breakdown of food into smaller pieces by physical means such as teeth, chewing, churning.

D **Chemical digestion** is the breakdown of food into smaller molecules by enzymes, stomach acid or bile.

Chemical digestion

Chemical digestion is the action of enzymes, stomach acid and bile on the food. This type of digestion breaks down the large molecules into ones that are small enough to pass across the gut wall into the bloodstream.

Digestion in the mouth

Mechanical digestion

6 There are three types of tooth: **incisors**, **canines** and **cheek teeth** – the premolars and molars (Fig 25.4). The role of each tooth is described in Table 25.1.

Tooth type	Function
Incisor	Biting
Canine	Tearing
Cheek teeth: premolar and molar	Chewing

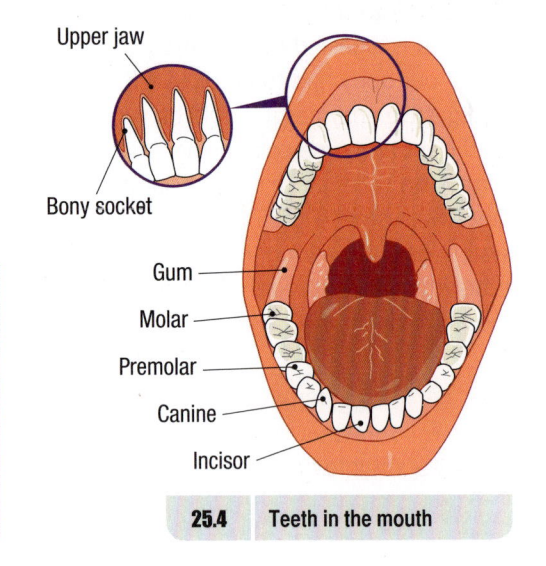

Table 25.1 The role of the different teeth

25.4 Teeth in the mouth

The number of each type of tooth may be represented as the **dental formula**. In adult humans the dental formula is: $i\frac{2}{2}$, $c\frac{1}{1}$, $pm\frac{2}{2}$, $m\frac{3}{3}$.

The letters represent the tooth type. The numbers represent the number of these teeth found on the upper and lower jaw of one side of the mouth. From the formula, we see that humans have two incisors on the top left-hand side of the mouth and two incisors on the bottom left-hand side, and the same number of incisors on the top and bottom right-hand sides, making eight incisors in all.

During our lifetime we possess two sets of teeth: the **milk** or **deciduous set** when we are young (20 teeth in all) and the **permanent set** (32 teeth), which replace the milk set from about the age of 6 or 7 onwards. The milk set has no molars.

Use the formula to find the number of premolars an adult human has.

Teeth break down food particles into smaller pieces. As a result of chewing, our food is easier to swallow and the small pieces provide a large surface area for enzymes to work on.

Chemical digestion

At the same time as the teeth are physically breaking down the food, saliva is pouring into the mouth from the salivary glands. Saliva consists of water, mucus and the enzyme **salivary amylase**.

- The water and mucus moisten and lubricate the food, making it easier to swallow.
- Salivary amylase acts on any starch in the food and breaks it down to the sugar maltose.
- Salivary amylase works best in a slightly alkaline environment, pH 7.5, which is the normal environment of the mouth.

The food now moves to the back of the throat where it is swallowed into a narrow muscular tube called the **oesophagus**.

The oesophagus and peristalsis

7 The wall of the oesophagus is lined with muscles that contract and relax in a rhythmic manner, pushing the food down to the stomach. All throughout the gut, the muscles in the walls of the gut help to shunt the food onwards. The alternate contraction and relaxation of the muscles of the gut wall is called peristalsis.

Peristalsis in the stomach churns the food and helps it to mix with the gastric enzymes. The churning action also helps the mechanical digestion of food.

> **Peristalsis** is the waves of muscular contraction of the gut wall that moves the food along.

In the small intestine, peristalsis produces a slower backward and forward shunting action. This allows for longer contact of the food with the digestive enzymes and with the wall of the intestine for absorption. Finally, in the large intestine, peristalsis causes much slower movement of the material.

The stomach

As food passes from the oesophagus into the stomach, it passes through a special ring of muscle called the **cardiac sphincter muscle**. When the sphincter muscle relaxes, it allows food to move into the stomach and when it contracts the opening closes. In this way, sphincter muscles regulate the opening and closing of various parts of the gut tube.

The stomach is a muscular J-shaped organ that lies to the left of the liver just under the diaphragm. Some of the food will remain in the stomach for between 3 and 4 hours, being churned by the muscle walls in the abdomen while enzymes act on it. If the food was not stored in the stomach, we would have to eat every 20–30 minutes.

The wall of the stomach has glands (gastric glands) which produce **hydrochloric acid**, **enzymes** and **mucus**.

- Hydrochloric acid (HCl) makes the environment of the stomach acidic (pH 1–2). This allows the enzyme gastric protease to work. HCl also kills bacteria and other micro-organisms that may be ingested with the food.
- The enzymes gastric protease (pepsin) and sometimes rennin act on long proteins, breaking them into shorter polypeptides. The enzyme rennin, if present, acts on protein in milk.
- Mucus protects the stomach wall from the acid and enzymes.

Muscles in the stomach wall churn the food and gastric juice, causing the food to convert into a creamy liquid called **chyme**. The chyme passes via the **pyloric sphincter muscle** into the small intestine.

The small intestine

The small intestine is so called because it is narrow. It is a tube some 6 m long that lies coiled in the abdomen. The main functions of the small intestine are:

- the further digestion of food;
- the absorption of the products of digestion into the bloodstream and **lymph** system.

The inner lining of the small intestine is not smooth, it is thrown into folds (Fig 25.5). The surface of these folds is covered by thousands of tiny finger-like projections called **villi** (singular villus). Villi increase the surface area for the release of enzymes and the absorption of digested food. It is estimated that if the small intestine had a smooth lining it would need to be more than 500 m long to provide a similar surface area.

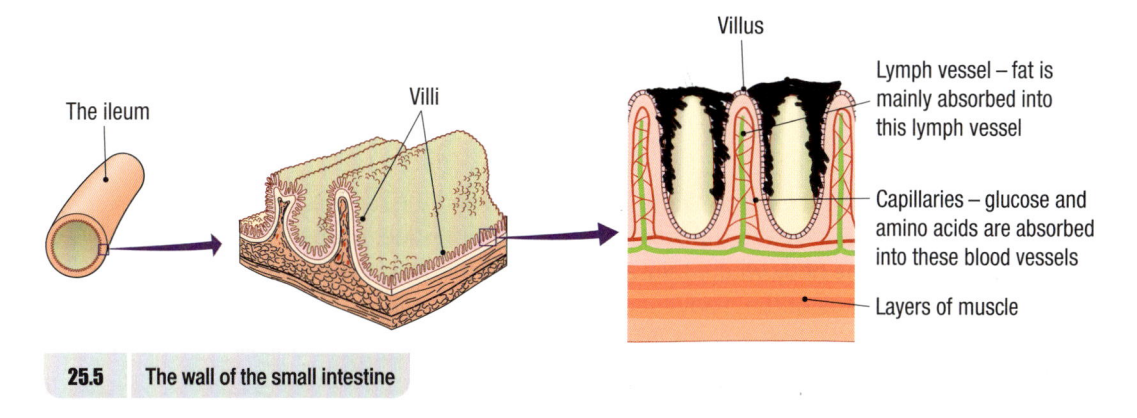

25.5 The wall of the small intestine

The small intestine consists of two main parts – the duodenum and the ileum.

The duodenum

The duodenum forms the first part of the small intestine. The wall of the duodenum secretes **intestinal juice**, which contains enzymes and these continue the process of digestion. The enzymes in the duodenum and the ileum act best in a slightly alkaline environment. Peristalsis shunts the food along the tube. The main role of the duodenum is chemical digestion.

In addition to its own wall, the duodenum receives juices from the pancreas and the liver (Fig 25.6).

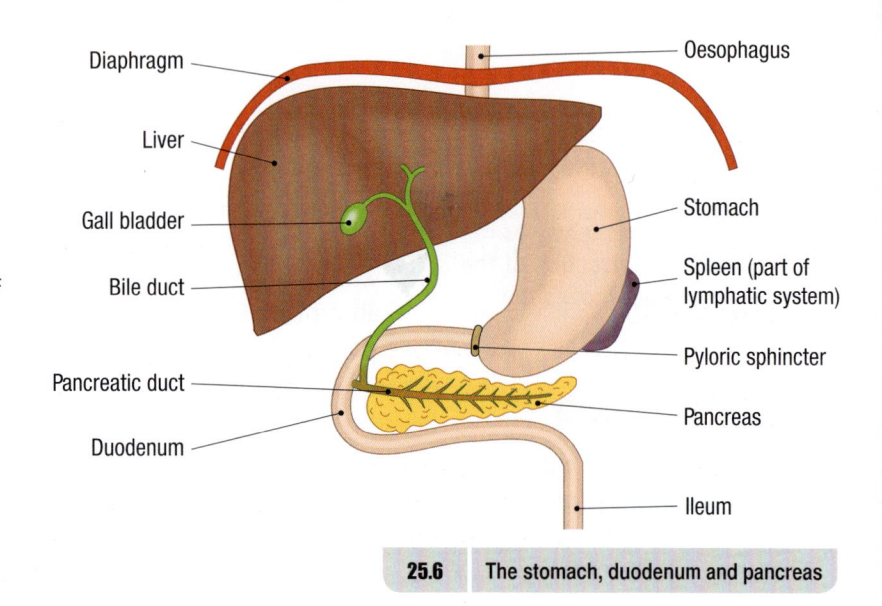

25.6 The stomach, duodenum and pancreas

The pancreas

The pancreas is an organ lying under the stomach. It secretes **pancreatic juice** into the duodenum through a duct called the pancreatic duct.

Pancreatic juice contains water, sodium bicarbonate to neutralise the acid chyme and enzymes to continue the digestion of the food. The main pancreatic enzymes are shown in Table 25.2.

Enzyme	Action in the duodenum
Pancreatic amylase	Breaks down starch to maltose
Pancreatic lipase	Breaks down lipids to fatty acids and glycerol
Pancreatic protease	Breaks down protein to peptides

Table 25.2 Enzymes of the pancreas

The role of the liver in digestion

The liver is the largest gland in the body, other than the skin. It lies to the right-hand side of the stomach, underneath the diaphragm. The role of the liver in the digestive process is to produce **bile**.

- Bile is a greenish/yellow coloured liquid which contains bile salts.
- Bile is produced from dead red blood cells.
- Bile is stored in the gall bladder.
- Bile passes into the duodenum through the bile duct.

Functions of bile in digestion:

1. Bile is alkaline and it helps **neutralise** the acid chyme from the stomach.
2. Bile salts **emulsify fats**, i.e. they break up the fats into fat droplets, which makes it easier for lipase to work.

Bile does not contain any enzymes.

More about the liver

The liver has a huge blood supply including the hepatic artery, hepatic vein and the hepatic portal vein. The hepatic portal vein carries digested nutrients to the liver from the small intestine. Nutrients travel from the liver via the bloodstream to cells in the body where they are needed. In this way, the food we eat reaches the various parts of our body. Some of the many functions of the liver include:

- Breakdown of dead red blood cells.
- Production of bile.
- Detoxification of the blood – poisonous substances and drugs can be made harmless in the liver.

- Storage – excess glucose is stored in the liver as glycogen. The fat-soluble vitamins such as vitamin A are stored in the liver, as are minerals, e.g. iron.
- Deamination of excess protein excess amino acids cannot be stored in the body. They are broken down in the liver to form urea. The urea is then transferred to the kidney by the blood for excretion.

The ileum

As with the duodenum, the wall of the ileum secretes enzymes which complete the process of **digestion**. It is also from the ileum that most of the digested food is absorbed into the blood and lymph (see next section).

Food may remain in the small intestine for up to 6 hours, during which time digestion is completed and the food is constantly being churned and moved along by peristalsis. Some of the food we eat contains cellulose, found in vegetables and fruits. Cellulose cannot be broken down by our digestive system because we do not produce cellulose-digesting enzymes. This undigested material is swept along into the large intestine (colon).

Name of secretion	pH	Site of production	Site of action	Substrate	Product(s) formed
Amylase (enzyme)	7–8	Salivary glands	Mouth	Starch	Maltose
Pepsin (enzyme)	1–2	Stomach wall	Stomach	Protein	Peptides
Amylase (enzyme)	8	Pancreas	Duodenum	Starch	Maltose
Lipase (enzyme)	8	Pancreas	Duodenum	Lipid	Fatty acids and glycerol
Protease (enzyme)	8	Pancreas	Duodenum	Protein/polypeptides	Peptides
Bile salts	8	Liver	Duodenum	Lipids	Lipid droplets
Maltase (enzyme)	8	Small intestine/duodenum	Duodenum and ileum	Maltose	Glucose
Peptidase (enzyme)	8	Small intestine/duodenum	Duodenum and ileum	Peptides	Amino acids
Lipase (enzyme)	8	Small intestine/duodenum	Duodenum and ileum	Lipid	Fatty acids and glycerol

Table 25.3 Summary of digestion

SYLLABUS REQUIREMENT:

You are required to know about any **one** carbohydrate-digesting enzyme, **one** lipid-digesting enzyme and **one** protein-digesting enzyme.

Absorption in the ileum

The main function of the ileum is **absorption** of the digested food.

The products of carbohydrate and protein digestion are glucose and amino acids. These molecules, together with other nutrients such as vitamins and minerals, are absorbed through the villi into the blood capillaries of the wall of the small intestine by **diffusion** (Fig 25.7). From here, they travel in the hepatic portal vein to the liver (see Fig 25.8 and section on the portal system in Chapter 23).

Digested lipids, i.e. fatty acids and glycerol, as well as fat-soluble vitamins, do not pass directly by diffusion into the bloodstream, instead they pass into the lymph vessels in the villi. These lymph vessels are called lacteals. From the villi, the fatty acids and glycerol and fat-soluble vitamins travel in the lymph system and eventually return to the bloodstream, and are finally transported to the liver.

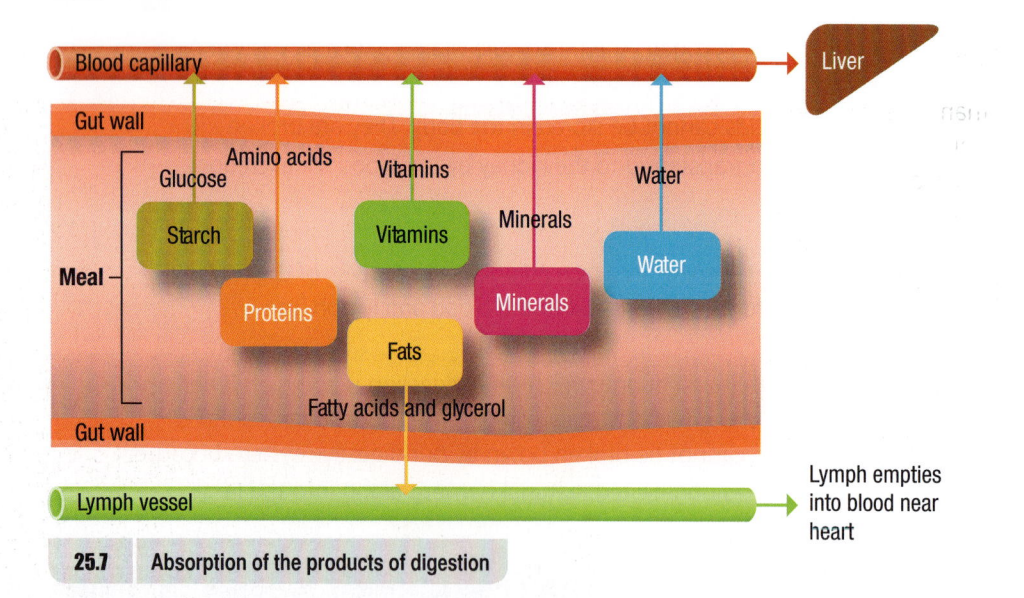

25 Human Nutrition

25.7 Absorption of the products of digestion

Product of digestion	Use in the body
Glucose	For energy in respiration, excess stored as glycogen
Fatty acids and glycerol	Form cell membranes, insulation under the skin
Amino acids	Form proteins, i.e. enzymes, hormones, pigments, nails and hair

Table 25.4 Uses of the products of digestion

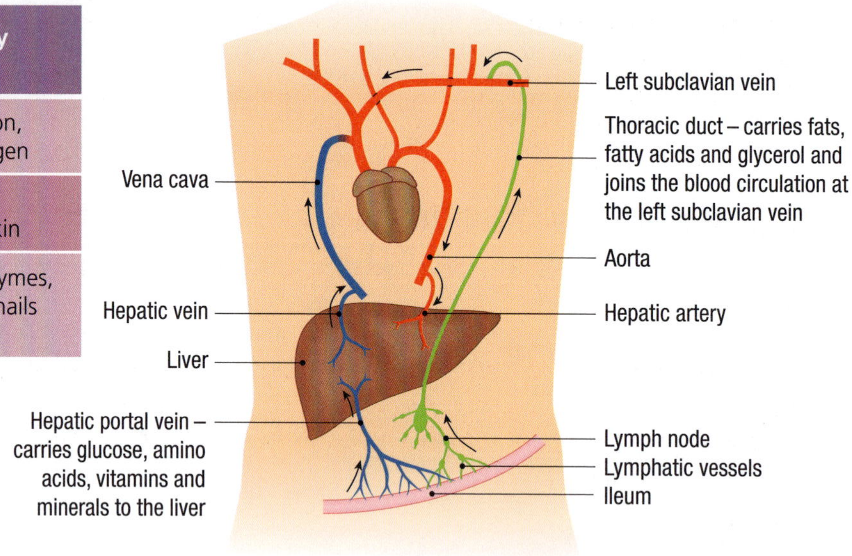

25.8 Pathways of absorbed foodstuffs

Adaptations of the ileum for absorption

The ileum is well adapted to its function in absorption because of the following features:

1. The ileum is very long. This allows digested food to come into contact with the ileum wall for longer.
2. The much folded wall and the presence of villi (Fig 25.9) greatly increase the surface area for absorption.
3. The cells lining the ileum are thin walled. This allows for the rapid movement of substances through them.
4. The wall is well supplied with blood vessels and lacteals to carry the digested food away.

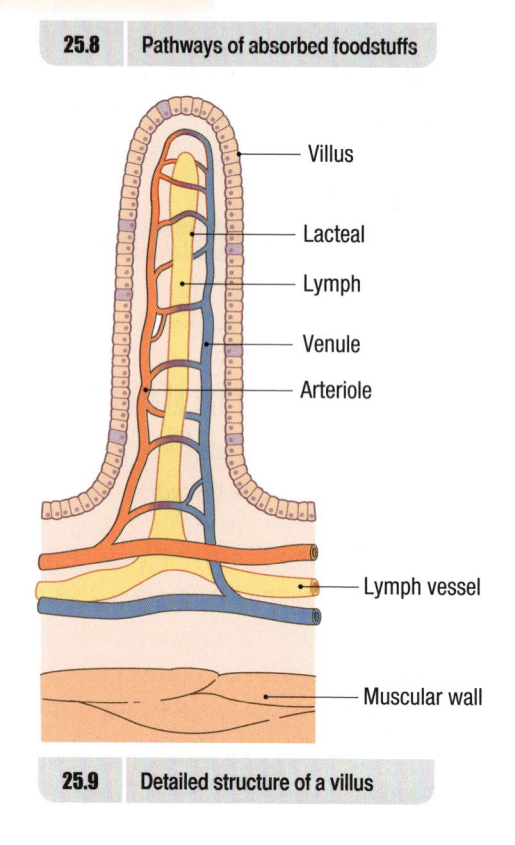

25.9 Detailed structure of a villus

338 UNIT 3 THE ORGANISM

Human Nutrition | 25

The large intestine

12 Although it is much shorter than the small intestine, the large intestine is so called because it has a larger diameter. The large intestine consists of the caecum, appendix, colon and rectum (Fig 25.2). The undigested remains of our food (cellulose, water and bacteria) pass from the ileum into the caecum. The caecum and appendix have no role to play in human digestion and the waste now enters the colon.

The colon is a muscular tube with a smooth inner, mucus-secreting lining (Fig 25.10). There are no villi in the colon. Material moves through the colon by peristalsis. The mucus secreted by the lining lubricates the material and helps it to move along the tube.

The main function of the colon is the **absorption of water** and mineral salts back into the blood. This prevents the body becoming dehydrated. As water is removed, the waste becomes more solid. This semi-solid waste, the faeces, now passes into the rectum where it is stored. Finally the faeces are released from the body through the anus. The release of faeces from the body is known as **egestion** and it is under the control of the anal sphincter muscle (N.B. this is not excretion).

25.10 T.S. of the colon

Symbiotic bacteria in the colon

13 Certain types of bacteria live in the colon and produce vitamin B and vitamin K, which are then absorbed by the body. These bacteria also digest some cellulose. This activity is an example of **symbiosis**, which is a relationship in which two different species of organism are living together where at least one benefits. In the case of bacteria living in the human gut, both organisms are benefiting from the relationship. This type of symbiosis is known as **mutualism** (see Chapters 6 and 19).

> **Symbiotic bacteria** are bacteria that live on or in another organism where at least one organism benefits.

Fibre in the diet

Dietary fibre or roughage is only found in plant food. Fibre is another name for the cellulose walls of plant cells which cannot be digested by humans and it passes through the gut unchanged.

There are a number of benefits of eating fibre in the diet:

- Fibre absorbs water, which keeps the faeces soft and easier to pass. This helps prevent constipation.
- Fibre provides bulk, which gives the muscles of the gut wall something to push against. In this way fibre helps to keep the contents of the gut moving.
- There is good evidence to suggest that fibre helps to prevent bowel (colon) cancer. Bowel cancer can be caused by cancer-causing chemicals (carcinogens) being produced by bacteria in the colon. These carcinogens are then present in the faeces. Fibre increases the bulk of the faeces, which dilutes the carcinogens.
- Eating fibre-rich foods often makes you feel full and it can therefore help prevent over-eating. Fibre-rich foods include wholegrain bread and cereals (Fig 25.11).

However, as with all foodstuffs, fibre needs to be eaten in moderation, together with other foods to ensure a balanced diet.

25.11 Fibre-rich foods

25 Human Nutrition

A balanced diet

A balanced diet is one that contains all the essential nutrients in the correct amounts. Remember, the essential nutrients are carbohydrates, lipids, proteins, vitamins and minerals. We also need water and dietary fibre. The best way to achieve a balanced diet is to eat a varied diet containing a little of everything. The food pyramid (Fig 25.12) indicates the recommended servings of each food group for teenagers.

A balanced diet depends on a number of factors including a person's age, gender, level of physical activity and general health.

Growing children and teenagers need a diet high in protein, calcium and iron. A person doing heavy work needs much more carbohydrate than a person sitting at a desk all day. Elderly people who may not be physically very active need less carbohydrate in their diet but still require a good supply of protein, minerals, vitamins and fibre to keep healthy.

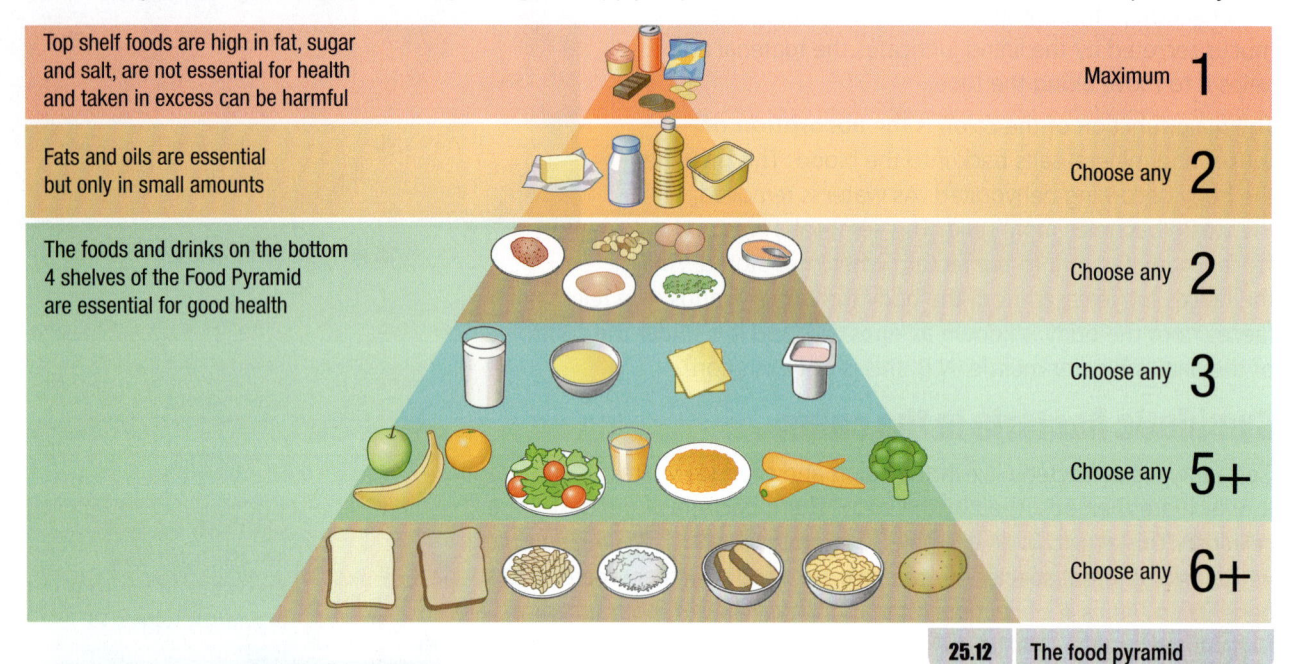

Top shelf foods are high in fat, sugar and salt, are not essential for health and taken in excess can be harmful — Maximum 1

Fats and oils are essential but only in small amounts — Choose any 2

The foods and drinks on the bottom 4 shelves of the Food Pyramid are essential for good health — Choose any 2

Choose any 3

Choose any 5+

Choose any 6+

25.12 The food pyramid

Summary

- Heterotrophs cannot make their own food. All animals are heterotrophs.
- Herbivores eat plant material only, e.g. horses.
- Carnivores eat other animals, e.g. pike.
- Omnivores eat both plants and animals, e.g. humans.
- The stages of human nutrition are:
  - Ingestion – the taking in of food, which occurs in the mouth.
  - Digestion – the mechanical and chemical breakdown of food into soluble form.
  - Absorption – is the passage of digested foods into the blood and lymph by diffusion.
  - Egestion – the removal of undigested material from the body.
  - Mechanical digestion is the breakdown of food into smaller pieces by physical means such as teeth, chewing, churning.
  - Chemical digestion is the breakdown of food into smaller molecules by enzymes, stomach acid or bile.
- There are three main types of tooth: incisors, canines, cheek teeth (premolars and molars).
- The dental formula is the number of these teeth found on the upper and lower jaw of **one** side of the mouth. The dental formula for an adult human is: i $\frac{2}{2}$, c $\frac{1}{1}$, pm $\frac{2}{2}$, m $\frac{3}{3}$.
- There are 32 teeth in the full adult set.
- The function of teeth is to cut the food and break it down into smaller pieces, which will allow the more effective action of enzymes.
- Peristalsis is the alternate contraction and relaxation of the muscles of the gut wall.
- Peristalsis occurs in every part of the gut and it is responsible for the movement of food through the gut.
- The main parts of the digestive system are: the mouth, oesophagus, stomach, duodenum, ileum, colon.

Summary

- The associated glands are the salivary glands, the liver and the pancreas.
- The liver:
  - is the largest gland in the body;
  - is located to the right of the stomach, under the diaphragm;
  - has a large blood supply;
  - produces bile;
  - breaks down dead red blood cells;
  - removes poisons from the blood;
  - stores fat-soluble vitamins, e.g. vitamin A;
  - produces urea from excess amino acids (deamination).
- Summary of chemical digestion (see Table 25.3, page 337).

Part of digestive system	Main function
Mouth	Ingestion Digestion: mechanical by the teeth Chemical: amylase breaks down starch to maltose
Oesophagus	Moves food to stomach by peristalsis
Stomach	Digestion: mechanical – churning Chemical: pepsin breakdown of protein to peptides
Liver (associated gland)	Produces bile which emulsifies lipids
Pancreas (associated gland)	Produces amylase, lipase and protease enzymes
Duodenum	Digestion Peristalsis
Ileum	Absorption Peristalsis
Colon	Absorption of water Peristalsis Production of B and K vitamins (by symbiotic bacteria)

- Absorption of digested foodstuffs takes place mainly from the villi in the ileum.
- Glucose, amino acids and minerals diffuse into the bloodstream and travel to the liver in the hepatic portal vein.
- Fatty acids and glycerol and fat-soluble vitamins diffuse into the lacteals of the villi and from there into the lymph system.
- The structure of the small intestine is adapted for its role in digestion and absorption of food:
  - It is very long (provides longer contact time of food with intestine wall).
  - It has a huge blood supply (to allow rapid diffusion of digested food).
  - It has thousands of villi, and micro-villi (increase surface area for digestion and absorption).
  - The walls of the villi are thin (allows rapid movement of substances through).
- The functions of the colon are to:
  - reabsorb water;
  - contain bacteria that produce B and K vitamins;
  - digest some cellulose.
- Symbiotic bacteria are bacteria that live on or in another organism where at least one benefits.
- A balanced diet contains the correct amounts of carbohydrate for energy, protein for growth and repair, lipid for energy, vitamins for general good health, minerals for metabolism, water and dietary fibre.
- Dietary fibre is the indigestible plant material in the diet, i.e. cereal grains, vegetable material and fruit.
- Dietary fibre helps prevent over-eating, constipation and bowel cancer.
- A balanced diet is essential for good health. We should eat a variety of foods from the different food groups: (i) breads and cereals, (ii) fruits and vegetables, (iii) milk and milk products, (iv) meat, fish and poultry.

25 Human Nutrition

Review questions

01 Distinguish between each of the following, giving examples in each case: (a) autotroph and heterotroph, (b) herbivore and carnivore, (c) omnivore and carnivore.

02 Distinguish between the following by briefly explaining each term: (a) ingestion and egestion, (b) digestion and absorption, (c) egestion and excretion.

03 List the stages in human nutrition.

04 Draw a large diagram to show the parts of the human digestive system to include the following structures and labels: mouth, salivary glands, oesophagus, stomach, pancreas, pancreatic duct, liver, bile duct, gall bladder, duodenum, ileum, small intestine, appendix, colon, rectum, anus, large intestine.

05 (a) What is digestion?
(b) Why is digestion necessary?
(c) Distinguish clearly between mechanical digestion and chemical digestion.

06 (a) List the main tooth types.
(b) State the function of each tooth type.
(c) Are the teeth an example of mechanical or chemical digestion?
(d) What benefit are teeth to the digestive process?
(e) Give the dental formula for an adult human.

07 The dental formula of an animal is given as i $\frac{0}{3}$, c $\frac{0}{1}$, pm $\frac{3}{3}$, m $\frac{3}{3}$. Use this information to:
(a) Give the total number of teeth in the adult animal.
(b) Suggest whether the animal is more likely to be a herbivore or a carnivore, giving a reason for your choice.

08 (a) Explain the term peristalsis and describe its effects.
(b) What is a sphincter muscle?
(c) Give one place in the body where you would find a sphincter muscle and outline its role.

09 (a) Give the precise location of the stomach.
(b) Outline the mechanical and chemical digestion of food in the stomach.
(c) Why does the stomach have the following:
(i) a pH of 1–2?
(ii) a lining layer of mucus?
(iii) the enzyme pepsin?
(iv) a thick muscle wall?

10 (a) What is bile?
(b) Where is bile made?
(c) From what is bile made?
(d) Where is bile stored?
(e) Where does bile mix with food?
(f) What are the functions of bile?

11 (a) State the location of the pancreas.
(b) Name an enzyme made in the pancreas that is used in the breakdown of each of the following: (i) starch, (ii) protein, (iii) fat.
(c) Where do the enzymes you named in (b) act?

12 (a) Name the two main parts of the small intestine.
(b) State the main function of each part.
(c) Why is the small intestine called 'small' when in fact it is some 6 m long?
(d) Explain two ways in which the wall of the small intestine is adapted for its function.

13 (a) Name the process by which digested food is absorbed into the bloodstream.
(b) State the final end products of the digestion of (i) carbohydrate, (ii) protein, (iii) fat.

14 Make a table to distinguish between a named carbohydrate-digesting enzyme, a named protein-digesting enzyme and a named fat-digesting enzyme under the following headings: site of production, site of action, substrate (food acted on), product(s), site of absorption.

15 The table shows the results of an experiment to show the time it took for an enzyme to break down a substrate at different pH values.

pH	5	5.5	6	6.5	7	7.5	8
Time taken (minutes)	6.5	4.5	3	2	1.25	1.25	3

(a) What is meant by pH?
(b) Draw a graph to show these results. Put pH on the horizontal (x) axis.
(c) Use your graph to find at which pH the fastest breakdown of the substrate took place.
(d) In this experiment, how and why would you keep the temperature constant?

16 Give an account of the digestion and absorption of protein from the time it enters the mouth until it reaches the liver.

17 (a) What are villi?
(b) Where in the body are villi found?
(c) Draw a labelled sketch to show the structure of a villus.
(d) In what form is digested protein absorbed?
(e) Name the process by which the digested protein is absorbed.
(f) In what way does the absorption of digested fats differ from the absorption of digested carbohydrate?

18 (a) Give the precise location of the liver in the body.
(b) Name the blood vessel which brings material from the intestine to the liver.

Review questions

(c) Bile is secreted by the liver. Where is it stored?
(d) State and explain three functions of the liver other than the secretion of bile.

19 Outline the structure and functions of the large intestine.

20 (a) What are symbiotic bacteria?
(b) Outline two functions of symbiotic bacteria in the human digestive system.

21 (a) What is fibre?
(b) Why is it important in the diet?
(c) What types of food are good sources of fibre?

22 Explain with examples what is meant by a balanced diet.

23 Give a biological reason for each of the following:
(a) The importance of chewing our food.
(b) Taking an antacid to relieve stomach upsets.
(c) The inner lining of the ileum is covered with villi.
(d) There is a sphincter muscle at the junction of the ileum and the caecum.
(e) There are bacteria living in the colon.

24 Describe the role of each of the following in the digestive system: bile, amylase, the rectum, the appendix, the pancreas, peristalsis.

Examination style questions

Section A

01 (a) Identify the parts A, B, C, D, E, F of the digestive system in the figure below.
(b) In which labelled part is the enzyme amylase active?
(c) From which labelled part are digested fats absorbed?
(d) Name the process by which the products of digestion are absorbed.

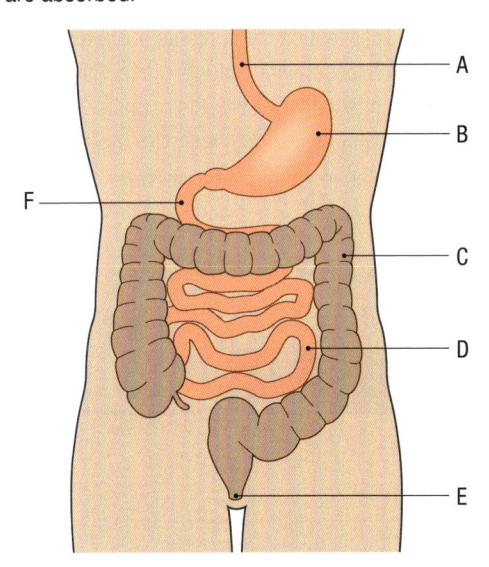

02 (a) Where is saliva produced?
(b) What does an enzyme in saliva break down starch into?
(c) Pepsin is an enzyme found in the stomach. What does pepsin digest?
(d) Name the enzyme that breaks down fats.
(e) Name a test to detect protein.

03 (a) What is meant by a balanced diet?
(b) What is dietary fibre?
(c) Name a good source of fibre in the diet.
(d) State its function in the body.
(e) Suggest a possible health problem due to a lack of fibre in the diet.

04 (a) State the location of the liver in the body.
(b) Name the blood vessel which connects the liver and the intestine.
(c) Where is bile made?
(d) Name the component of bile that neutralises stomach chyme.
(e) Into which region of the digestive system is bile released?
(f) The secretion of another gland is released into the same region of the digestive system as bile. Name this other gland.

Section C

05 The diagram shows part of the digestive system in humans.
(a) (i) State the meaning of the term digestion.
(ii) Why is digestion of food necessary?
(iii) Name the parts of the digestive system in which protein is digested.
(b) (i) Name the parts labelled P, Q, R, S and T of the diagram shown.
(ii) Outline the role the stomach plays in the transport and mechanical digestion of food.
(iii) Other than digestion suggest a role of the HCl secreted by the stomach wall.
(iv) Name a secretion of the part labelled T and outline its role in the process of digestion.
(v) Why is egestion not a type of excretion?

25 Human Nutrition

Examination style questions

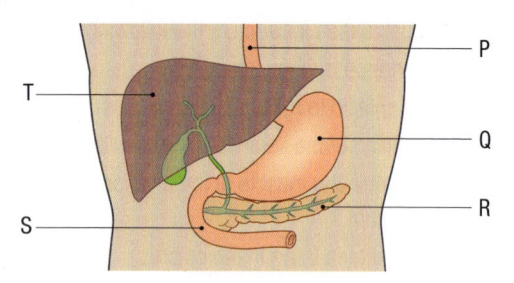

(b) A person eats a fish curry, some rice and chips and drinks a can of fizzy lemon drink.
   (i) What are the main nutrient biomolecules (i.e. protein, carbohydrate, etc.) in the rice, the fish, cooking oil, the fizzy drink?
   (ii) In what form are each of these nutrients when they are finally absorbed into the bloodstream?
   (iii) Name an enzyme involved in the digestion of protein and state where it is produced.
   (iv) Do you consider the meal described as a healthy meal? Give reasons for your answer.
   (v) What name is given to material such as the skins of fruit and the stalks of vegetables, which is not fully broken down in the digestive system? Why is it important to include such material in our diet?

06 (a) (i) Name three different foods that are rich in protein.
   (ii) In what form are proteins absorbed by the body?
(b) (i) Distinguish between mechanical and chemical digestion.
   (ii) Describe the role of each of the following in human nutrition: stomach, liver, ileum and pancreas.
   (iii) What is a villus? Describe the functions of the villi in the digestive system.

(c) An investigation was set up to create an artificial gut. A length of Visking tubing was tied tightly at one end. The tube was then three-quarters filled with a 1% starch solution.

A solution of amylase and maltase was then added to the starch solution and the tubing twisted at the top and secured using a paper clip. The contents of the tubing were mixed by shaking the tubing and then placed in a test tube of distilled water as shown in the diagram.

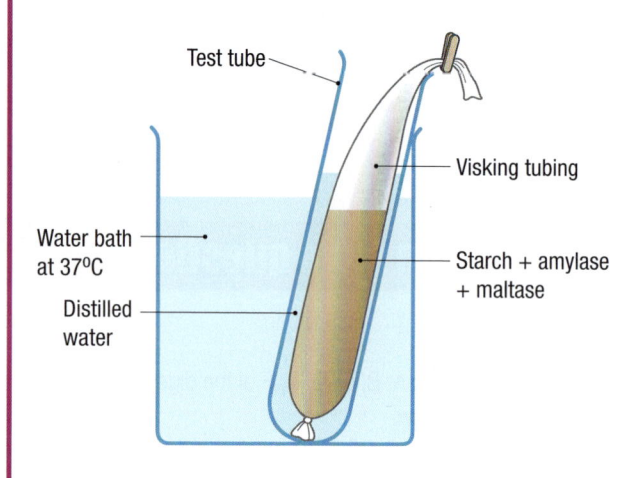

After a period of time tests were carried out on the samples as follows:
   (i) Benedict's test on the contents of the Visking tubing.
   (ii) Benedict's test on the contents of the test tube.
   (iii) A starch test on the contents of the Visking tubing.
   (iv) A starch test on the contents of the test tube.

For each of the tests (i)–(iv) state the result you would expect and the reason for your answer.

Leaving Certificate examination questions

Section A

01 (a) (i) What is meant by the term *digestion*?
   (ii) Why is digestion necessary?
   (iii) Distinguish between mechanical and chemical digestion by writing a sentence about each.
(b) The diagram shows part of the human alimentary canal and associated structures.
   (i) What part of the alimentary canal is labelled W?
   (ii) The bile duct is connected to X. Name X.
   (iii) From which part of the alimentary canal does food arrive into W?
   (iv) State **one** digestive function of the pancreas.

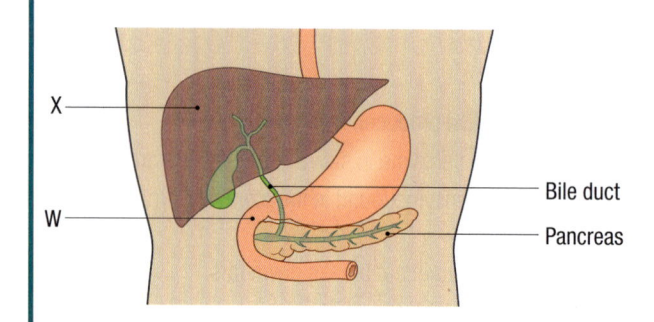

2011 HL Q. 5

Leaving Certificate examination questions

02 The diagram shows part of a section of the human small intestine.

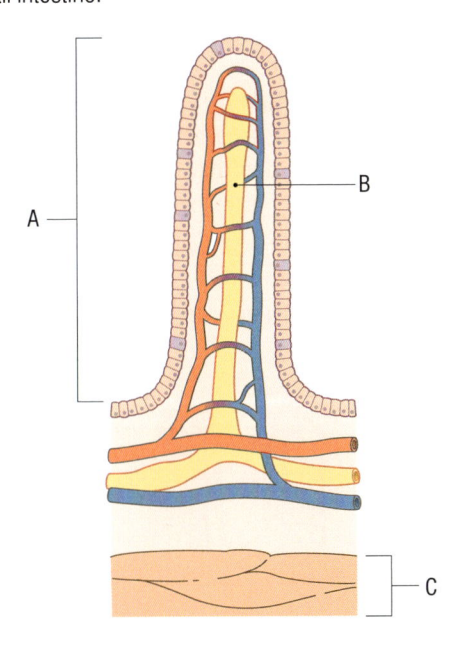

(a) Name A, B, C.
(b) State **two** ways in which A is adapted for the absorption of soluble foods.
(c) Name a process by which soluble foods are absorbed into the blood from the small intestine.
(d) What type of food is mainly absorbed into B?

_____ 2005 HL Q. 6

03 Answer the following questions in relation to the human alimentary canal.
(a) What is peristalsis?
(b) State **one** reason why a low pH is important in the stomach.
(c) Why is fibre important?
(d) Name an enzyme that is involved in the digestion of fat.
(e) What are the products of fat digestion?
(f) What is the role of bile in fat digestion?
(g) State a role of beneficial bacteria in the alimentary canal.

_____ 2004 HL Q. 6

Section C

04 The diagram shows the human digestive system.
(i) Name the parts labelled A, B and C.
(ii) Explain the term **digestion**.
(iii) Name **one** human tooth type **and** give its function.
(iv) Part C secretes hydrochloric acid onto the ingested food. Give **one** function of this acid.
(v) Give **one** digestive function of part D.
(vi) Give **one** digestive function and **one** non-digestive function of the pancreas.

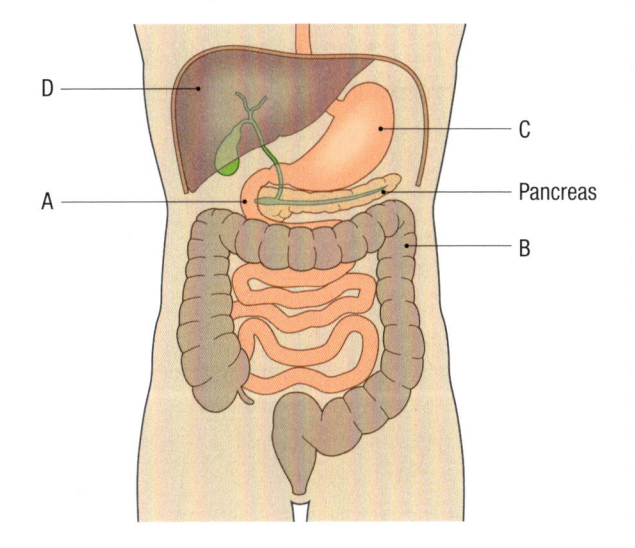

_____ 2012 OL Q. 15 (c)

05 (a) (i) What is meant by a 'balanced' diet?
   (ii) Distinguish between autotrophic nutrition and heterotrophic nutrition.
(b) (i) Explain the word *digestion*.
   (ii) Give **one** role for **each** of the following types of teeth:
      1. Incisors
      2. Molars
   (iii) Peristalsis begins when food enters the oesophagus. What is meant by *peristalsis*?
   (iv) Describe the following changes that happen to food in the stomach:
      1. Mechanical changes
      2. Chemical changes
   (v) What is the pH of the stomach contents?
   (vi) Where does the partially digested food go when it leaves the stomach?
(c) The liver, the gall bladder and the pancreas all play a part in digestion. Digested food is carried to the liver where it is processed. Undigested food enters the large intestine.
   (i) State
      1. **One** role of the pancreas in digestion.
      2. **One** role of the gall bladder in digestion.
   (ii) From what part of the digestive system does the digested food enter the blood?
   (iii) Name the blood vessel that carries the digested food to the liver.
   (iv) State **two** functions of the liver – other than the processing of digested food.
   (v) The colon contains many symbiotic bacteria – mostly 'good' bacteria. State **two** benefits we get from these bacteria.

_____ 2010 OL Q. 13

25 Human Nutrition

Leaving Certificate examination questions

06 (a) Bile is involved in digestion in the human body.
 (i) 1. Where is bile produced?
  2. Where is bile stored?
 (ii) Where does bile act in the alimentary canal?
(b) The diagram shows the digestive system of the human.

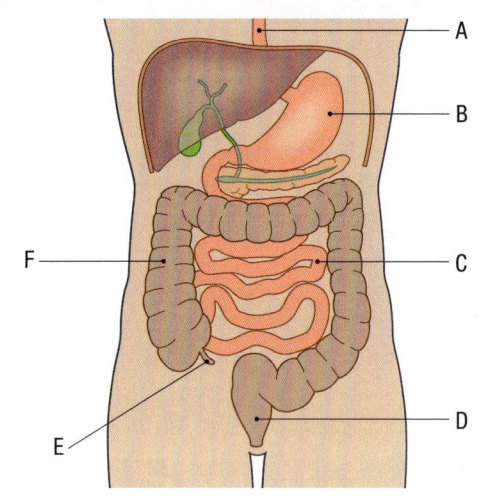

(i) Name the parts labelled A, B, C, D, E and F.
(ii) What is the role of peristalsis in the digestive system?
(iii) Where do the products of digestion enter the blood?
(iv) How do these products of digestion pass into the blood?

(c) (i) For each of the parts labelled B and C in the diagram above, state whether the contents are acidic, neutral or alkaline.
(ii) Amylase is an enzyme that is found in saliva. State the substrate and the product of this enzyme.
(iii) State **two** functions of symbiotic bacteria in the alimentary canal.
(iv) What is meant by egestion? From which labelled part of the diagram does egestion occur?

2008 OL Q. 13

07 (i) Copy the following table into your copy. Complete the table by inserting the correct terms from the following list: molar teeth, symbiotic bacteria, peristalsis, bile salts, lipase, stomach

	an organ for churning of food to chyme
	waves of contractions passing along the gut
	grind food into smaller pieces
	an enzyme that turns fats to fatty acids and glycerol
	emulsify fats
	produce vitamins

(ii) Copy the following passage into your copy and fill in the blank spaces.
"The passage of the products of digestion from the intestine to the blood is called _____ Folds in the lining of the intestine, called _____, increase the surface area for this passage. Amino acids from the digestion of _____ and monosaccharides from the digestion of _____ enter the blood in this process."

2007 OL Q.15 (c)

08 The diagram shows part of a transverse section through the small intestine.

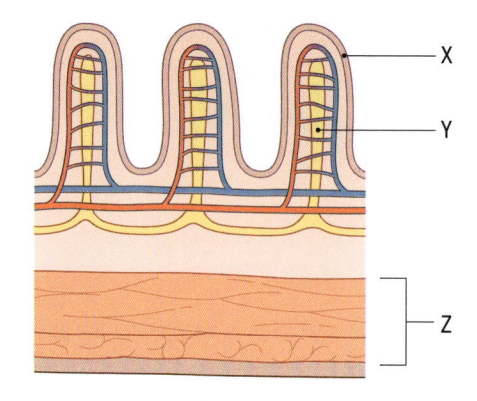

(i) Name structures X and Y.
(ii) What process results from the contraction of the two parts of tissue Z?
(iii) **In your answer book**, indicate which of the following most accurately represents the pH of the contents of the small intestine.
 acidic   neutral   alkaline
(iv) Name **two** glands that pass their secretions into the small intestine.
(v) 1. What are *symbiotic* bacteria?
 2. Give **two** functions of symbiotic bacteria in the human alimentary canal.
(vi) Where in the human alimentary canal is most water absorbed?

2012 HL Q. 15 (a)

09 (i) Draw a labelled diagram to show the relationship between the liver, the small intestine and the hepatic portal vein.
(ii) Name a substance transported to the liver by the blood in the hepatic portal vein.
(iii) Name the blood vessel that brings oxygenated blood to the liver.
(iv) Where in the human body is the liver located in relation to the stomach?
(v) Where is bile stored after it has been made in the liver?

Leaving Certificate examination questions

(vi) Give **one** role that the bile salts play in the digestive process.
(vii) Give **two** further functions of the liver, other than the manufacture of bile.

2010 HL Q. 15 (b)

10. (a) (i) Distinguish between mechanical and chemical digestion.
    (ii) Name a structure in the human digestive system, other than teeth, which is involved in mechanical digestion.

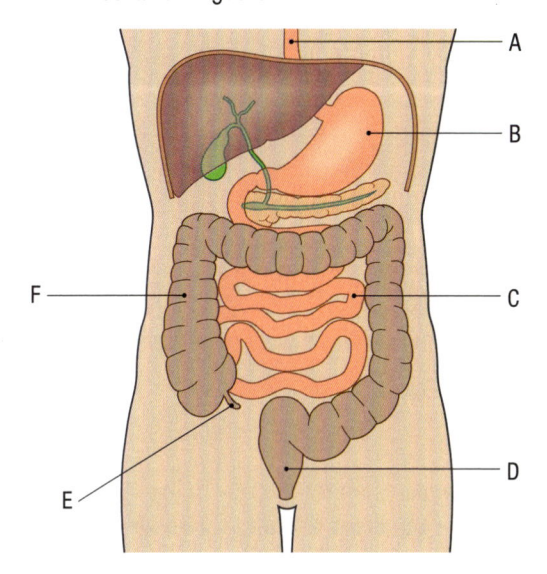

(b) The diagram shows the human digestive system.
  (i) Name the parts A, B, C, D, E and F.
  (ii) Describe **two** functions of bile in relation to digestion.
  (iii) Answer the following in relation to a lipase:
    1. Where is it secreted?
    2. Where does it act?
    3. What is the approximate pH at its site of action?
(c) (i) What are symbiotic bacteria?
  (ii) Give **two** activities of symbiotic bacteria in the human digestive system.
  (iii) Name the part(s) of the digestive system in which the following are absorbed into the blood.
    1. The products of digestion
    2. Water.
  (iv) Name a process involved in the passage of the products of digestion into the blood.
  (v) Explain how the structure that you have named in (iii) 1. is adapted for the absorption of the products of digestion.

2008 HL Q. 12

Past examination questions

OL	2012 Q. 15 (c)	2010 Q. 13	2008 Q. 13	2007 Q. 15 (c)	2006 Q. 12		
HL	2012 Q. 15 (a)	2011 Q. 5	2010 Q. 15 (b)	2008 Q. 12	2006 Q. 5	2005 Q. 6	2004 Q. 6

26 Homeostasis and Gaseous Exchange

After studying this chapter you should be able to:

1. Define homeostasis.
2. Understand why the exchange of gases, nutrients and waste is necessary.
3. Know the role of the leaf, stoma and lenticels in gas exchange in flowering plants.
4. Be able to draw and label a T.S. of a leaf and describe its role in gaseous exchange.
5. **HL** Explain the role of carbon dioxide in the control of gaseous exchange in plants.
6. Be able to draw and identify the main parts of the breathing system of humans.
7. Know the features of an efficient respiratory surface.
8. Be able to describe the mechanism of inhaling and exhaling.
9. Describe an experiment to investigate the effect of exercise on your breathing rate.
10. Understand the role of the blood in the transport of oxygen and carbon dioxide.
11. **HL** Explain the role of carbon dioxide in the control of gaseous exchange in animals.
12. Be able to discuss one breathing disorder, under the headings cause, prevention and treatment.
13. Explain the terms ectotherm and endotherm.
14. Be able to describe the role of skin in temperature regulation.

Homeostasis

Multicellular **organisms** may live in an external environment that can vary considerably but their individual **cells** could not live in such a variable environment. Single-celled organisms also need to keep the internal environment of their cell consistent. **Homeostasis** is the term used to describe the processes used by organisms to maintain such a steady environment.

Homeostasis is particularly necessary for animals. Multicellular animal cells are bathed in a liquid called tissue fluid (see page 315). This fluid produces an internal environment. Many variables need to be kept constant if the cells are to flourish. Some of the more important are:

- The temperature.
- The pH.
- The osmotic potential (this is achieved by controlling the concentrations of various salts in the blood).
- The concentration of glucose.
- The concentration of carbon dioxide (CO_2).

> **D** — **Homeostasis** is the maintenance of a constant internal environment.

Also important in the maintenance of a constant internal environment is the removal of the waste products from cell **metabolism**.

Gaseous exchange

Gases move into and out of cells by **diffusion**. In small organisms such as bacteria, the distance that gases have to travel is short and exchange is quick and efficient. In larger organisms such as flowering plants and vertebrate animals, diffusion alone is not sufficient to ensure efficient gaseous exchange. To overcome this problem, a number of strategies have developed in organisms to ensure that oxygen and carbon dioxide are readily exchanged. These strategies include:

- The body of the organism may be flattened. This reduces the distance the gases have to travel. We see this in the flattened bodies of flatworms and in the flattened leaves of plants (Fig 26.1).
- The surface area across which the gases are exchanged is increased, e.g. in the gills of fish and the alveoli of human lungs.
- The body may develop systems where gases are brought to the body surface, e.g. the breathing tubes of insects and mammals

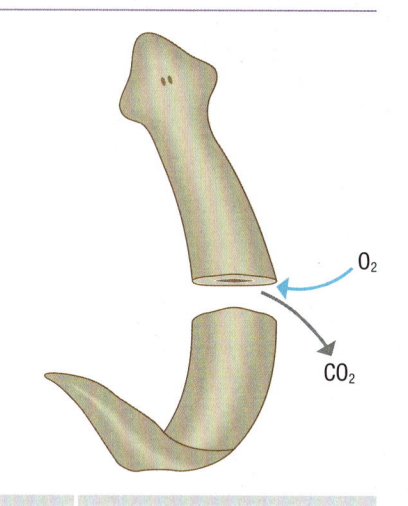

26.1 Gas exchange in a flatworm

Gaseous exchange in the flowering plant

In flowering plants, most of the oxygen and carbon dioxide are exchanged through the **stomata** (singular stoma). Stomata are tiny pores on the surface of leaves and green stems. During the day, carbon dioxide diffuses into the leaf through the stomata. The carbon dioxide moves to the **chloroplasts** where it is used by the plant to make glucose in the process of **photosynthesis**. Oxygen that is produced during photosynthesis diffuses out of the leaf through the stomata (Fig 26.2). Surrounding each stomata there are two **guard cells**. These cells can change their shape, which then opens or closes the stoma.

Leaves are well adapted to allow for rapid diffusion of gases:

- They are flattened.
- They have stomata.
- They have air spaces between the cells.
- The ground tissue is loosely arranged and their surfaces are moist.

In woody stems, gas exchange takes place through **lenticels**. Lenticels are small raised pores in the bark, formed by loosely arranged cells with air spaces between them (Fig 26.3).

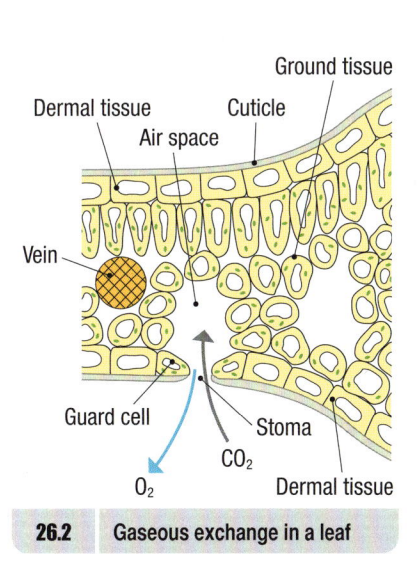

26.2 Gaseous exchange in a leaf

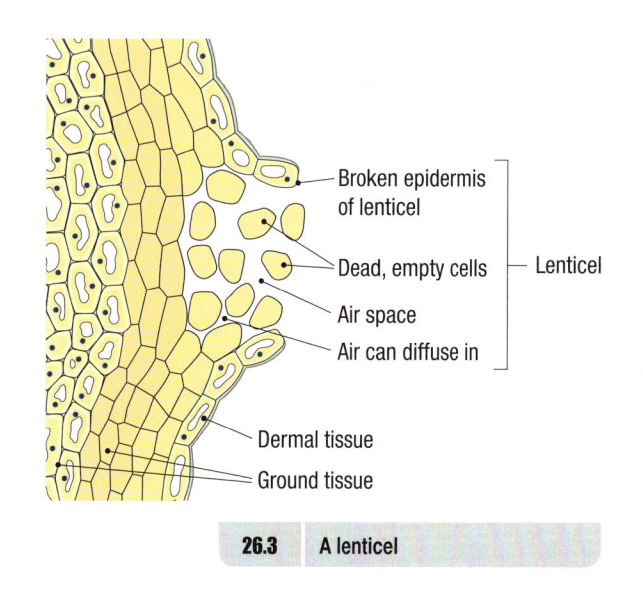

26.3 A lenticel

26 Homeostasis and Gaseous Exchange

HL Control of gaseous exchange in plants

5 In plants, the bulk of gaseous exchange takes place through the stomata. These pores are usually found in greater quantity on the underside of a plant leaf. On either side of the stomata, there is a special type of epidermal cell called a guard cell (Fig 26.4). The cell walls of the guard cells are not of uniform thickness. The cell walls where the two guard cells touch are much thicker than the outer cell walls.

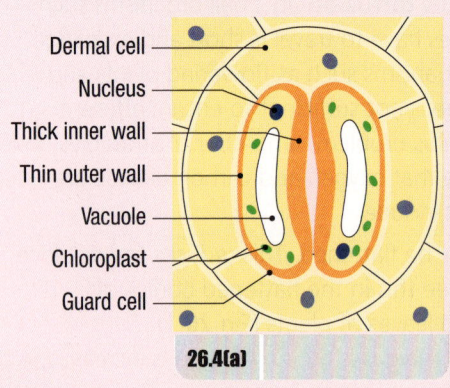

As water enters these cells, they expand unevenly and the tougher inner wall makes the cells bend away from one another, creating a gap between the two cells called the stoma (Fig 26.5).

It is the level of CO_2 in the air spaces of the leaf that determines the amount of water in the guard cells:

- If there is a low level of CO_2 in the air spaces (this will occur when the plant is photosynthesising), then water will enter the guard cell and the stoma will open (Fig 26.6(a)).
- If there is a high level of CO_2 in the air spaces (this will occur when there is no photosynthesis), then water will leave the guard cells and the stoma will close (Fig 26.6(b)).

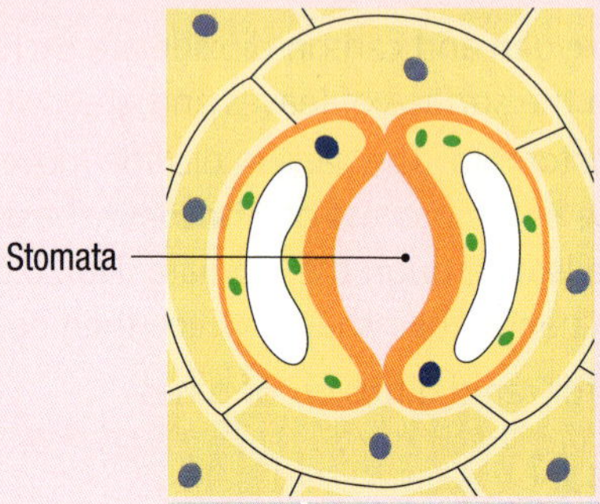

If the water loss becomes too great during the day, due to excess **transpiration**, the water will leave the guard cells and the stomata will close (see also Chapter 22).

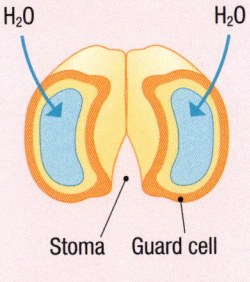

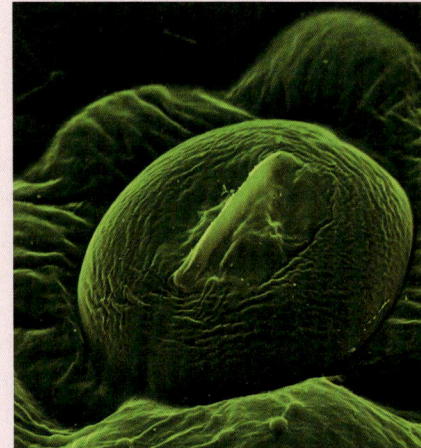

26.4(a)

26.4(b) A closed stoma

26.5(a)

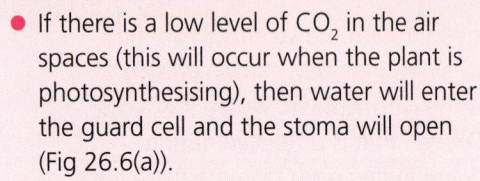

26.5(b) An open stoma

(a) Low CO_2 concentration
(b) High CO_2 concentration

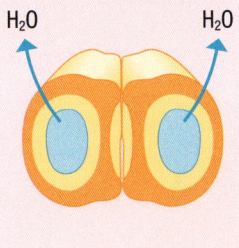

26.6 The effect of the concentration of CO_2 on the guard cells

Gaseous exchange in humans

6 Gas exchange in humans occurs at a special area called a **respiratory surface**. Another name for the human respiratory surface is the lungs. The lungs are part of the breathing system (Fig 26.7).

The lungs lie in the **thoracic (chest) cavity** above the diaphragm muscle. The lungs are enclosed and protected by the rib cage and the pleural membrane. A fluid called pleural fluid lies within these membranes. This allows friction-free movement of the lungs. The lungs have a role in homeostasis as these

Homeostasis and Gaseous Exchange | 26

remove waste **carbon dioxide**, produced during respiration, from the blood. This removal of CO_2 helps to maintain the correct pH in the blood. Water and heat are also normally lost from the lungs to the air.

The structure of the breathing system

The structure of the breathing system in shown in Fig 26.7 and the functions of the various parts are described in Table 26.1.

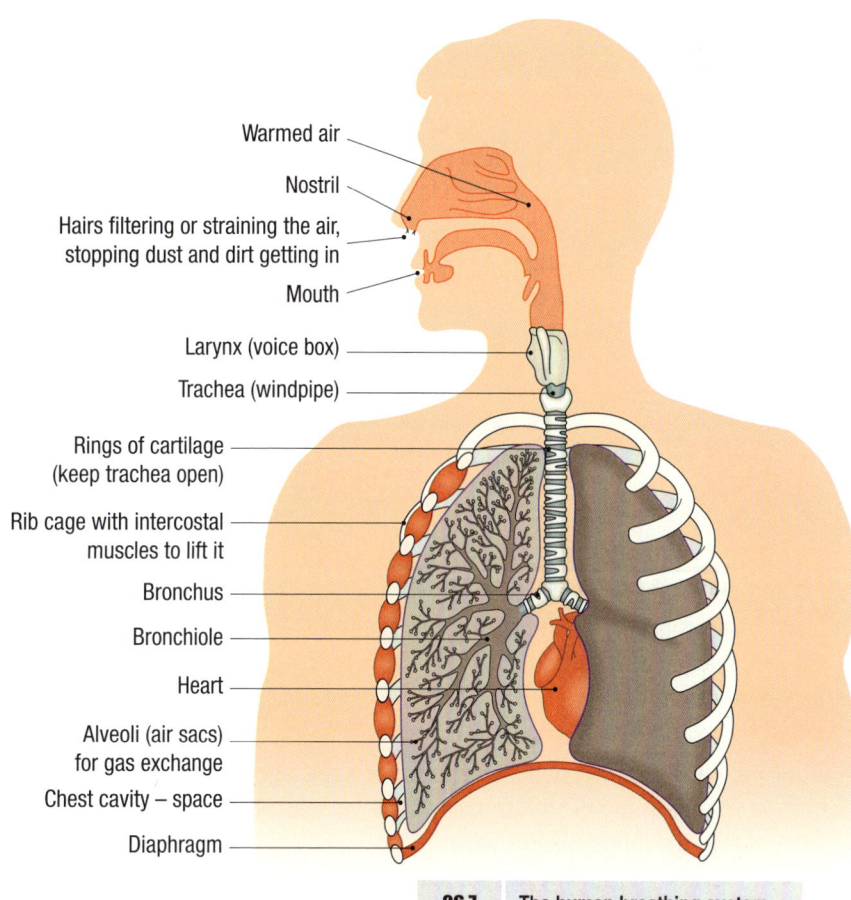

26.7 The human breathing system

Part	Function
Nostrils (openings to the nose)	Allow air to enter the nose
Nose	Warms, filters and moistens air
Pharynx (throat)	Connects nose and mouth to larynx
Glottis	Opening of the larynx
Epiglottis	Prevents food passing into the windpipe when you swallow
Larynx (voice box)	Makes sounds
Trachea (windpipe)	Allows air to pass to lungs
Cilia	Draws mucus and trapped dust/microbes out of lungs
Cartilage	Keeps trachea and bronchi open
Bronchus	Transports air into lung
Bronchiole	Transports air into alveoli
Alveoli (air sacs)	Site of gas exchange
Pleural membranes	Allow friction-free movement of lungs

Table 26.1 The function of the parts of the breathing system

26 Homeostasis and Gaseous Exchange

Pathway of air

Air enters the nostrils and passes via the nose, pharynx and larynx into the trachea. The nasal passages help to warm, moisten and filter dust particles from the air we breathe. The base of the trachea branches into two bronchi, down which air passes into the bronchioles. All these tubes in the lungs are covered in mucus and microscopic hairs called **cilia** (Fig 26.8).

- The mucus traps the dust and microorganisms in the air.
- The cilia beat upwards, dragging the mucus and the trapped particles up to the throat where they are swallowed into the stomach to be destroyed by the acid there.

Finally the air reaches the **alveoli**. It is at the alveoli that the gases are exchanged.

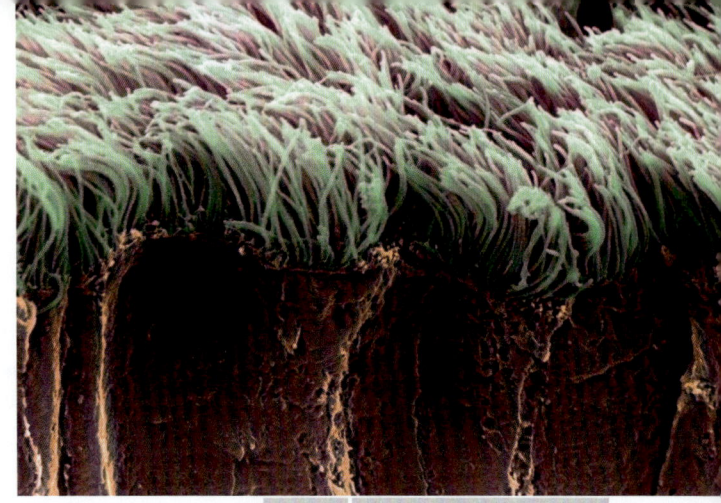

26.8 The cilia in the lungs

Features of a good respiratory surface

For gaseous exchange to be efficient, the surface across which oxygen and carbon dioxide diffuse must have the following features:

- It must have a large surface area. This is to ensure maximum contact between the surface and the air. The human respiratory surface consists of millions of tiny air sacs in the lungs called alveoli.
- It must be moist. Oxygen and carbon dioxide can only diffuse in solution across a respiratory surface.
- It must be very thin to allow rapid diffusion of gases.
- It must be in contact with a large blood capillary network to allow exchange of gases between the air and the bloodstream. The capillary walls are only one cell thick, which increases the rate of diffusion.
- It must receive a constant supply of air, i.e. it must have good ventilation. The breathing movements provide the ventilation mechanism in humans.

The alveoli are the respiratory surface of the lungs. The alveoli are specifically designed to maximise gaseous exchange.

Gaseous exchange in the alveoli

The exchange of gases between the air and the blood occurs at the alveoli by diffusion. The air in the alveoli is rich in oxygen, but the blood in the pulmonary capillaries coming from the heart is oxygen-poor. Therefore, oxygen diffuses from the alveoli into the blood capillaries. Carbon dioxide, on the other hand, is plentiful in the blood capillaries and low in the alveoli. Carbon dioxide diffuses out of the capillaries into the alveoli (Figs 26.9 and 26.10).

Rapid diffusion of the gases is possible because:

- Each human lung contains 350 million alveoli and the total surface area of the lung is about 90 m^2!
- The wall of each alveolus is one cell thick and it is surrounded by a thin layer of fluid.
- There is a huge blood capillary network surrounding each alveolus.
- The capillaries are very narrow and also one cell thick.

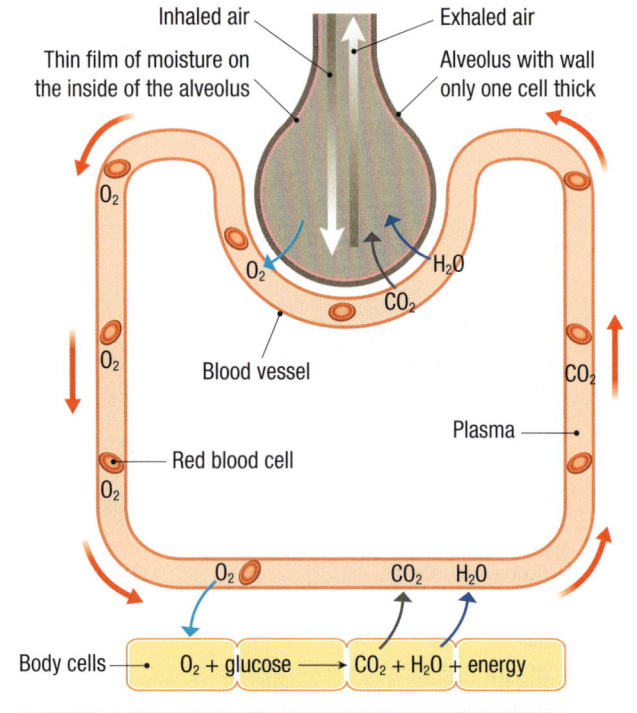

26.9 Gaseous exchange at the alveoli and at body cells

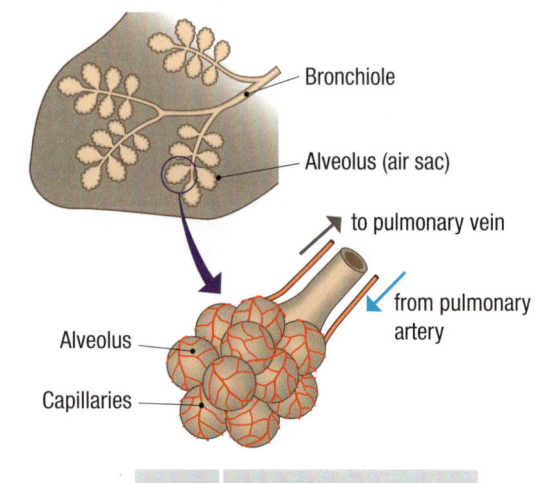

Body cells → O_2 + glucose → CO_2 + H_2O + energy

26.10 A cluster of alveoli

The process of breathing

Getting air into and out of the lungs occurs in two stages, called **inhaling** and **exhaling**. At rest, the average breathing rate is 17 breaths per minute (one inhalation + one exhalation = one breath). The process of breathing is an unconscious activity, i.e. breathing just happens. You don't have to think about it. Breathing is under the control of a part of the brain called the **medulla oblongata** (brainstem) (see Fig 29.9).

The intercostal muscles between the ribs and the diaphragm muscle at the bottom of the thorax play a major role in the process of breathing. You can see the effect of exercise on your rate of breathing in Investigation 26.1.

The breathing mechanism

Inhaling	Exhaling
The intercostal muscles contract and cause the rib cage to move up and out.	The intercostal muscles relax and the rib cage moves down and in.
The diaphragm muscle contracts and the diaphragm moves down.	The diaphragm relaxes and moves back up.
This enlarges the thorax from top to bottom. As a result, the volume of the lungs increases, i.e. the lungs can spread out into the larger space.	These actions reduce the volume of the thorax.
The air pressure in the lungs now decreases (because there is more room for the air molecules to move around). As a result, the pressure of the atmosphere (outside the body) is now greater than that inside the lungs.	This increases the pressure on the lungs as the ribs and diaphragm push on the lungs.
As a result, air flows into the lungs.	Air is pushed out of the lungs.
Inhaling requires energy. It is an active process.	Exhaling does not require energy. It is a passive process.

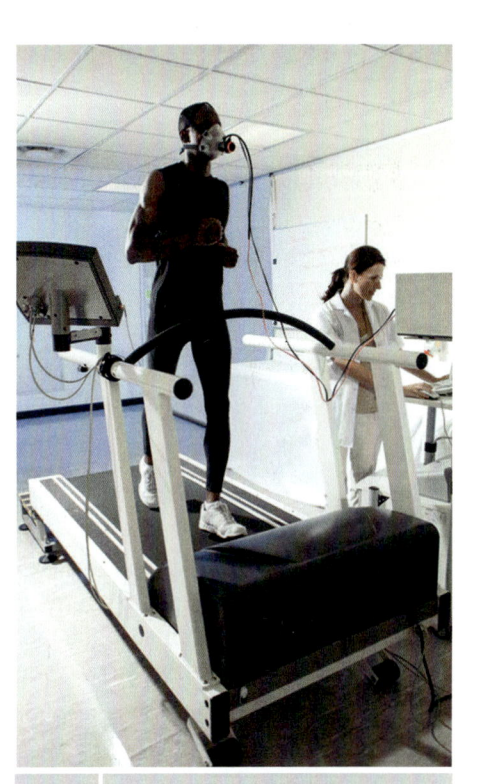

Table 26.2 The breathing process

26.11 The breathing rate of an athlete being measured

Investigation 26.1

To investigate the effect of exercise on the breathing rate of a human

SYLLABUS REQUIREMENT:

You are required to do either this investigation or Investigation 23.2.

Your breathing rate tells you the number of breaths you take per minute. One breath in and out is a single breath.

Procedure

1. First of all, find your breathing rate at rest, i.e. when sitting down. Do this by counting the number of breaths in 1 minute. Write down the number of breaths per minute in Table 26.3.
2. Repeat step 1 twice. Work out your average breathing rate. This is your breathing rate at rest.

Homeostasis and Gaseous Exchange

3. Take some easy exercise such as walking on the spot for 3 minutes.
4. Immediately after walking take your breathing rate for 1 minute and write down the figure. When your breathing rate has returned to normal, repeat twice and get an average. Record the figures in the table.
5. Compare your resting breathing rate with the rate after gentle exercise. Try and explain any difference you find.
6. Now do some vigorous exercise such as running on the spot for 3 minutes or stepping up onto a stool and down again for 3 minutes.

	Breathing rate at rest	Breathing rate after gentle exercise	Breathing rate immediately after vigorous exercise
Trial 1			
Trial 2			
Trial 3			
Total			
Average			
Class average			

Table 26.3

7. Immediately after the exercise take your breathing rate and do this every minute until your breathing rate returns to your resting breathing rate. Record your breathing rate for each minute after exercise in the table below. Compare your breathing rate at rest with the rate after vigorous exercise. How could you explain any difference?

Minutes after exercise	Breathing rate

Table 26.4

8. How long did it take your breathing rate to return to the resting rate? Did your breathing rate fall below the resting rate? Why do you think this might happen? Compare your results with those of your classmates.
9. Suggest a relationship between the time taken to reach the breathing rate at rest after exercise and a person's degree of physical fitness.
10. Write up the investigation in your practical notebook.

You would expect that your rate of breathing will increase as you do more exercise.

The transport of oxygen, carbon dioxide and water

10 The inhaled oxygen dissolves in the moist lining of the alveolus. It then diffuses through the wall of the alveolus and the wall of the capillary and into the red blood cells. Here it combines with the red pigment **haemoglobin** to form **oxyhaemoglobin**. In this way, the oxygen is carried to every cell in the body. When it reaches an area where oxygen is needed, the oxygen is released and passes from the capillary into the cells, again by diffusion.

Carbon dioxide is produced in the body cells during **respiration**. It diffuses from the cells into the blood. Some of the carbon dioxide will be carried in the red blood cells and some in the plasma. The carbon dioxide will reduce the pH of the blood, making it more acidic. The removal of carbon dioxide from the lungs ensures the pH of the blood is kept at the correct level.

As Table 26.5 shows, we usually exhale more water vapour than we inhale.

Gas	Inhaled air	Exhaled air
Nitrogen (N_2)	79%	79%
Oxygen (O_2)	20.0%	16.4%
Carbon dioxide	0.03%	4.1%
Water vapour	Variable	Saturated

Table 26.5 Composition of inhaled and exhaled air

Thus in the breathing system:

- Oxygen is carried in the red blood cell as oxyhaemoglobin.
- Carbon dioxide and water are mainly carried in the blood plasma.

HL The control of breathing

11 Breathing movements are under the control of the respiratory centre in a part of the brain called the **medulla oblongata**. Nerve cells in the medulla are connected to the diaphragm and intercostal muscles. There are **chemoreceptors** found in the walls of the aorta and the arteries leading to the head which are sensitive to the level of carbon dioxide in the blood and the pH of the blood. The medulla oblongata is also sensitive to these two factors. When the level of carbon dioxide rises in the blood (this will lower the pH), the chemoreceptors pick up this change and the medulla will increase the rate of breathing.

The level of oxygen in the blood has a very small effect on the rate of breathing. Normally, breathing is not under our conscious control.

26 | Homeostasis and Gaseous Exchange

Breathing disorders

SYLLABUS REQUIREMENT:
You are only required to know about one breathing disorder.

Asthma

Asthma results in the narrowing of the bronchioles which prevents air reaching the alveoli.

Symptoms: Breathlessness and wheezing.

Causes: Asthma can be triggered by a number of different things including pollen, house dust, vigorous exercise, cat and dog dander (scaly pieces of skin), infection, tobacco smoke and other air pollutants.

Prevention: If a specific cause is known to trigger the asthma then steps can be taken to avoid it. For example, if pet dander is responsible, then the person should not keep a pet or hold/play with one if possible.

Treatment: Inhaling a bronchodilator which widens the bronchioles is common. The technique for inhalation is very important and inhalers (Fig 26.12) should only be used on medical advice.

26.12 An inhaler used for asthma

Chronic bronchitis

Chronic bronchitis occurs when the bronchi become inflamed and narrowed.

Symptoms: A persistent cough, breathlessness and the production of a lot of phlegm (mucus).

Causes: The main cause of chronic bronchitis is smoking and other air pollutants.

Prevention: The single most effective measure is never to smoke. When a person smokes, tiny particles get trapped on the mucus lining of the bronchi (Figs 26.13 and 26.14). As a result more mucus is produced. This mucus collects in the bronchi and causes the familiar 'smoker's cough'.

Treatment: A bronchodilator (to open the bronchi) may be prescribed to relieve the breathlessness. In severe cases the patient may need to inhale oxygen from an oxygen cylinder.

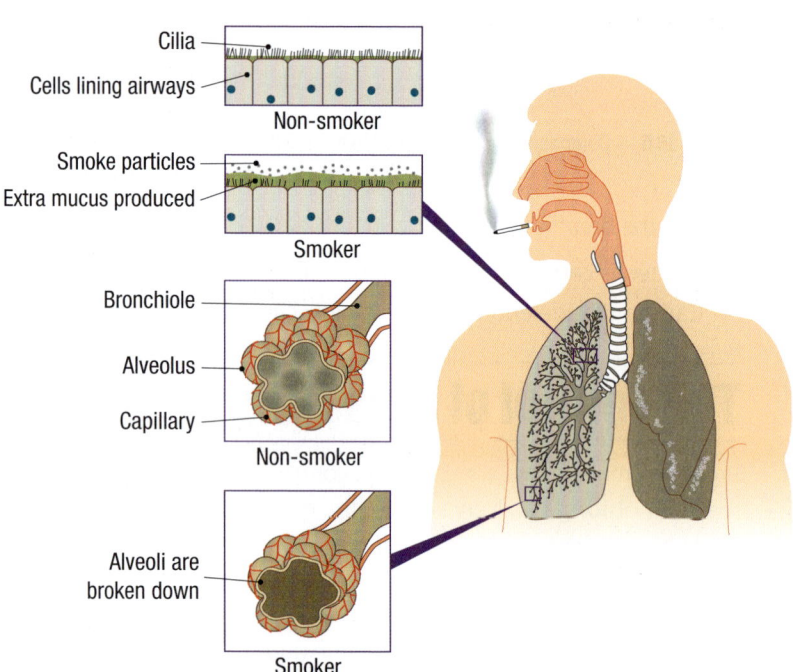

26.13 The effects of smoke on the lungs

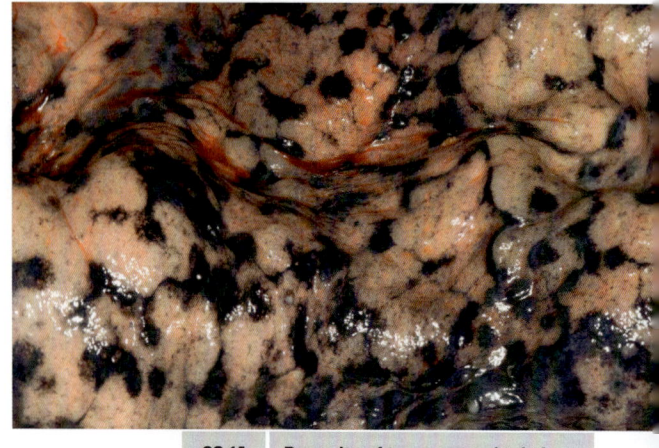

26.14 Deposits of tar on a smoker's lung

The skin and homeostasis

13 The skin is the largest organ in the body and it carries out many functions:

- excretion;
- protection;
- homeostasis;
- as a sense organ.

It acts as an excretory organ in the body in that it gets rid of water, salt and urea when sweating. However, sweating is more important in maintaining a constant body temperature as part of homeostasis, rather than a method of excretion. All organisms have certain temperature limits within which their cells can operate. Should the temperature go higher or lower than this, permanent damage may be done to the organism. Keeping a constant temperature is important to some animals, as a higher temperature, within limits, will allow the cell metabolism to occur faster and can provide the animal with more energy (Fig 26.15).

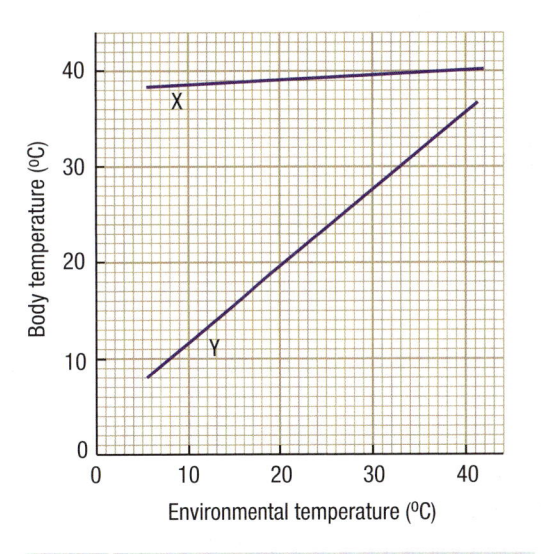

26.15 Relationship between external temperature and internal temperature for a cat X and a snake Y

> **D** An **ectotherm** is an animal whose body temperature varies with the external temperature.

> **D** An **endotherm** is an animal who maintains its body temperature independent of the external environment.

Some animals cannot regulate their internal temperature, e.g. reptiles. These animals are called **ectotherms**. If a snake is too cold, it will move into the sun to warm up, and if it is too hot, it will retreat into the shade.

Birds and mammals, i.e. a cat, can regulate their own internal temperature using the waste heat from cell activity to warm their bodies when they are cold. They also have methods of reducing their temperature if it gets too high. These animals are called **endotherms**.

The role of skin in maintaining body temperature

14 When body temperature rises, humans use their skin to get rid of any excess heat. As the body temperature rises:

- the blood vessels near the skin surface dilate (vasoconstriction), allowing more of the warm blood to the surface;
- the hairs covering the skin remain flat against the surface so there is no layer of air trapped close to the skin to act as insulation;
- the sweat glands release water onto the skin;
- the evaporation of the sweat removes some of the excess heat from the body.

Sweating may cause a lack of water in the blood if the body overheats. This is the reason why athletes drink large quantities of water during and after exercise, to replace the lost water. Various salts will also be lost in this way, e.g. potassium. The producers of 'sports' drinks will add salts to them to help replace those lost salts.

When body temperature falls the skin may also be used to try to retain heat.

- The erector muscles at the end of the hairs (Fig 26.16) can contract and pull the hairs upright (piloerection).
- The hairs will then trap a layer of air around the skin. This layer will get warm and then act as an insulation from the cold. This is what happens when we get 'goose pimples'.
- The blood vessels leading to the surface of the skin constrict and the flow of blood to the surface is greatly reduced. This retains the heat inside the body.
- The body fat held under the skin is a good insulator but this structural adaptation cannot be changed at will.

26 Homeostasis and Gaseous Exchange

- The brain will also increase the metabolic rate of the body to create more waste heat which will then warm up the blood. The brain can also cause shivering for the same reason.

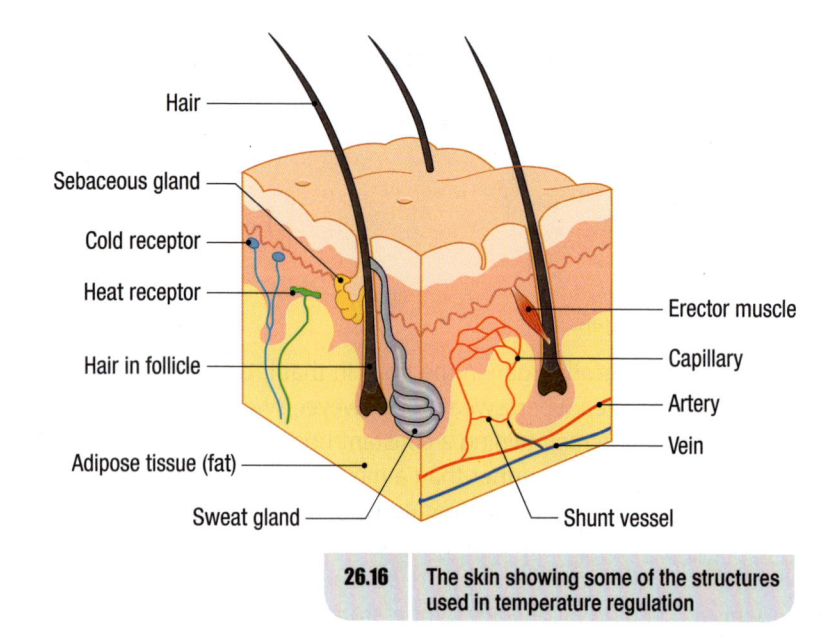

26.16 The skin showing some of the structures used in temperature regulation

Summary

- Homeostasis is the maintenance of a constant internal environment around the cells of a multicellular organism.
  - Among the characteristics that are controlled are: the temperature, the pH, the salt concentration, the oxygen concentration and the glucose concentration.
- In all organisms, gases are exchanged by diffusion.
- In flowering plants, gases diffuse in and out through stomata.
  - Stomata are pores in the leaves.
- Leaves are flat, thin and have air spaces, which allows for rapid diffusion of gases.
- Lenticels are raised pores in the bark.
  - Lenticels allow gaseous exchange in woody stems when the plant has lost its leaves, i.e. in the winter.
- **HL** The CO_2 level controls the gaseous exchange in plants. In plants:
  - Guard cells are found on either side of the stomata; they have thick inner cell walls.
  - When the cells fill with water they bend away from each other creating the stomata.
  - The amount of water taken in depends on the level of CO_2 in the air spaces of the leaf (perhaps because the CO_2 level is controlled by the amount of photosynthesis that occurs).
- In humans, gas exchange occurs at the respiratory surface, the lungs.
- The lung also acts in homeostasis as it controls the pH of the blood (it excretes CO_2). It also loses water and heat.
- A good respiratory surface:
  - has a good surface area and good ventilation;
  - is moist;
  - is thin;
  - is surrounded by a large blood capillary network.
- The breathing system consists of the nostrils, nose, pharynx, larynx, glottis, epiglottis, trachea, bronchi, bronchioles and alveoli.
- The functions of the parts of the breathing system can be found in Table 26.1.
- Inhaling means breathing in and it needs energy, as the muscles in the diaphragm and between the ribs have to contract.

Summary

- During inhalation the brain sends a message to the diaphragm and intercostal muscles causing them to contract. The diaphragm moves down and the rib cage moves up and out.
- The volume of the thorax increases which reduces the air pressure.
- Air moves into the lungs.
- Exhaling means breathing out, and it does not require energy.
  - The diaphragm and intercostal muscles relax. The diaphragm moves up and the rib cage moves down and in.
  - The volume of the thorax decreases, which increase the pressure on the lungs.
  - Air is forced out of the lungs.
- As you exercise your rate of breathing increases as you require more oxygen and have to remove more CO_2.
- Gas exchange takes place at the alveoli.
- O_2 is carried in the red blood cells as oxyhaemoglobin. CO_2 is carried in the red blood cells and the blood plasma, lowering the pH.

HL
- The CO_2 level controls the gaseous exchange in humans:
  - The rate of breathing is controlled by the medulla oblongata.
  - The level of CO_2 affects the pH of the blood as it produces bicarbonate ions.
  - An increase of CO_2 lowers the pH and the medulla increases the breathing rate.

- Note that CO_2 levels affect both the breathing rate and the rate of gaseous exchange in plants.
- Breathing disorders:

	Asthma	Chronic bronchitis
Symptoms	Breathlessness, wheezing	Persistent cough, breathlessness
Cause	Allergens (pollen, etc.)	Smoking
Prevention	Remove allergens	Stop/don't smoke
Treatment	Bronchodilator (inhaler)	Bronchodilator (inhaler)

- Ectotherms are animals which have a body temperature that varies with the environmental temperature, e.g. frogs and reptiles.
- Endotherms are animals which keep their body temperature constant independent of the environment, e.g. birds and mammals.
- Skin:
  - It loses water and urea as waste products when sweating.
  - Sweating normally takes place as a temperature control mechanism when the body is hot.
  - The blood capillaries near the surface dilate and the warm blood flows to the surface. The sweat evaporates removing the heat.
  - In cold conditions the hairs stand on end, pulled by the erector muscles, and trap a layer of air on the surface that insulates the skin.
  - The capillaries contract and the blood does not flow near the surface thus retaining heat.

Homeostasis and Gaseous Exchange

Review questions

01 (a) What is meant by the term homeostasis?
(b) Why is homeostasis necessary to organisms?

02 (a) Name three factors that would be controlled in homeostasis.
(b) For each of these explain why they would need to be controlled.

03 (a) What does the term gaseous exchange mean?
(b) Name the method of gas exchange in organisms.
(c) Name two gases that need to be exchanged in humans.

04 Match each of the following organisms to the method of gaseous exchange that they use:

humans	the entire body surface
fish	gills
buttercups	breathing tubes
flatworms	skin
bacteria	alveoli
	stomata

05 (a) List three ways in which leaves are adapted for rapid diffusion of gases.
(b) Explain how each of the ways listed in (a) help the process.

06 (a) What is the gas that controls rate of gaseous exchange in plants?
(b) What structures does this gas affect?
(c) Using labelled diagrams explain how gaseous exchange is controlled in plants.

07 (a) State the features of a good respiratory surface.
(b) Explain how each of the features in (a) help in gaseous exchange.
(c) Gaseous exchange in humans occurs at the alveoli. List four features of alveoli that make them suited to gaseous exchange.
(d) Draw a large labelled diagram of the human breathing system. Include the following labels: larynx, pharynx, trachea, rings of cartilage, lung, bronchi, bronchioles, alveoli, rib cage, pleural membranes, diaphragm, intercostal muscles.
  (i) Mark on your diagram X – the place where gas exchange occurs.
  (ii) Y – the muscles involved in breathing.
  (iii) Z – the part that produces sounds.

08 (a) Outline the processes that occur to allow for inhalation and exhalation in humans.
(b) The level of which gas regulates this process?

09 (a) Describe the role the lungs play in homeostasis.
(b) Explain which of these roles could be considered accidental to its main function.

10 Use Table 26.3 to answer the following questions:
(a) Which air sample, inhaled or exhaled, contains more oxygen?
(b) Explain why this is so.
(c) What happens to the nitrogen we breathe in?
(d) What do the figures for carbon dioxide tell us?
(e) Why does the amount of water vapour we inhale vary?

11 (a) Copy the diagram of the alveolus shown and explain what is happening at each of labels A to F.

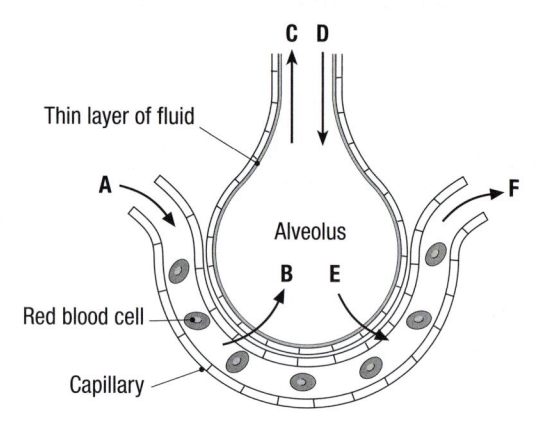

(b) What transports the oxygen in the blood?
(c) Where in the blood is the carbon dioxide carried?

12 Select one of the breathing disorders, asthma or bronchitis, and for each describe its causes, prevention and treatment.

13 (a) What is the role of carbon dioxide in the control of breathing?
(b) Outline the role of the brain in the control of breathing.
(c) Comment on the following statement: "Gaseous exchange is dependent on the level of carbon dioxide".

14 The graph shows changes in the nicotine content of a person's blood during and after smoking a cigarette. (Adapted from *Biology Principles and Processes*, Roberts et al. (1993).)

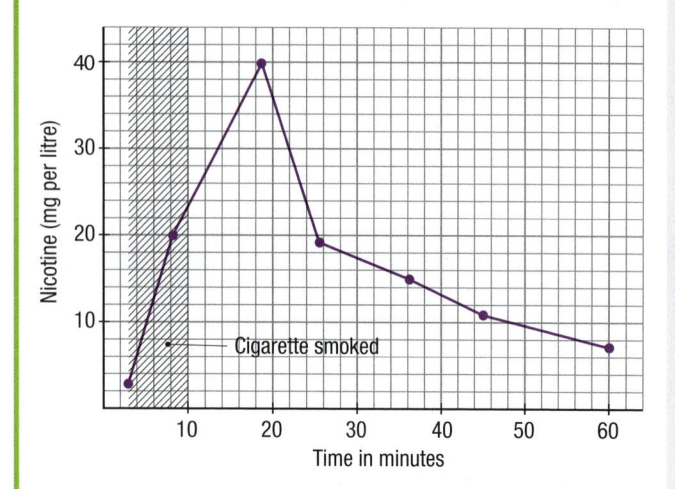

(a) Name the process by which nicotine enters the blood.

Review questions

(b) Into which artery does nicotine first pass?
(c) From the graph, find how long it takes for the nicotine to reach its highest concentration in the blood once the cigarette has been finished.
(d) Which organ of the body do you associate with the removal of harmful substances such as nicotine from the blood?
(e) Smoking is known to promote the formation of clots in blood vessels. Suggest one way death could result from the formation of a clot within a blood vessel.

15 (a) What role is played by the skin in homeostasis in a human?
(b) What are the other functions of the skin?
(c) Describe what happens in the skin when (i) the body temperature rises, (ii) the body temperature falls.

16 (a) Describe the investigation you carried out to examine the effect of exercise on breathing rate.
(b) What results did you get?
(c) Explain the results.

Examination style questions

Section A

01 Give the functions of each of the following:
(a) The pleural membranes.
(b) The rings of cartilage on the trachea and bronchi.
(c) The cilia in the trachea.
(d) The diaphragm.
(e) The alveoli.

02 (a) What is meant by the term gaseous exchange?
(b) By what process does this exchange occur?
(c) List the features of a surface that will help in this process of gaseous exchange.
(d) Where does this take place in (i) plants, (ii) humans?
(e) What gases are exchanged in humans?

03 (a) What is homeostasis?
(b) Give the function of the following organs in homeostasis: the lungs, the skin.
(c) What is an ectotherm?
(d) What is an endotherm?

04 (a) What is a stoma?
(b) What specialised cells are found surrounding a stoma?
(c) In what way are the cells mentioned in (b) different from a normal epidermal cell?
(d) What is the role of these cells?
(e) What structure on a woody stem has the same function as a stoma?

Section B

05 (a) (i) Name the structure in the lungs used for gaseous exchange.
(ii) Name the artery that carries deoxygenated blood to the lungs.

(b) Answer the following questions in relation to an investigation into the effect of exercise level on the breathing rate.
(i) How is the rate measured?
(ii) Why is the rate at rest measured?
(iii) Why are different intensity levels of exercise carried out?
(iv) Why are at least three readings taken at each level of activity?
(v) Why is there a period of rest after each exercise session?
(vi) What is the effect of exercise and the level of exercise on the rate?
(vii) Explain the adaptive advantage to the change in rate during exercise.

Section C

06 The leaf is the food factory for the plant. Many of the cells of the leaf have an abundance of chloroplasts, 'little green machines', that carry out photosynthesis. The atmosphere is the major source of carbon dioxide, a raw material needed for photosynthesis. The leaf is beautifully structured for photosynthesis.

(a) Draw a labelled diagram to show the normal external structure of a leaf from a typical dicotyledonous plant, e.g. oak or ash.
(b) (i) Draw a diagram to show the internal structure of a leaf. Label the following: guard cell, dermal tissue, stoma.
(ii) Outline how the leaf is adapted for gas exchange.
(iii) Name the factor that controls the opening of the stomata.
(iv) Name another plant structure that functions in gas exchange where the surface is covered in woody tissue.

26 Homeostasis and Gaseous Exchange

Examination style questions

(c) The diagram shows the structure of the respiratory system in humans.

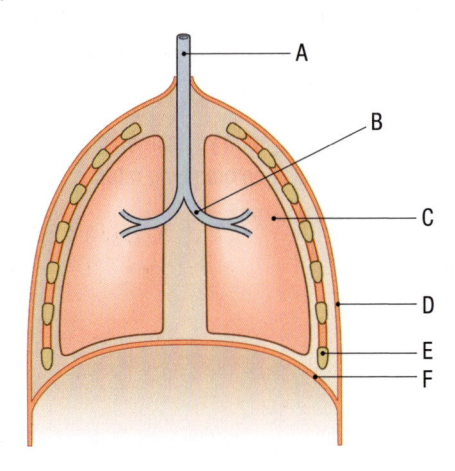

(i) Name A, B, C, D, E, F.
(ii) Give a detailed explanation of how air is expelled from the lungs, i.e. exhalation.
(iii) Why is exhalation considered to be a passive process?

07 (a) Outline a symptom, a cause and one preventive measure of one of the following breathing disorders: asthma or bronchitis.

(b) (i) Draw a labelled diagram of the breathing system in the human body. Insert the letters X where gas exchange takes place, Y where mucus is secreted by mucous membranes and Z where cartilage is found.
(ii) Outline how air is drawn into the lungs during normal breathing (inhalation).

(c) (i) With reference to the human breathing system, state three features of an efficient gas exchange structure.
(ii) Inspired air is changed before reaching the respiratory surface. State the advantages of any three changes that happen to the air as it passes to the lungs.
(iii) Compare the percentage of oxygen and carbon dioxide in ordinary air and breathed out air.

Leaving Certificate examination questions

Section A

01 The diagram shows a section through human skin.

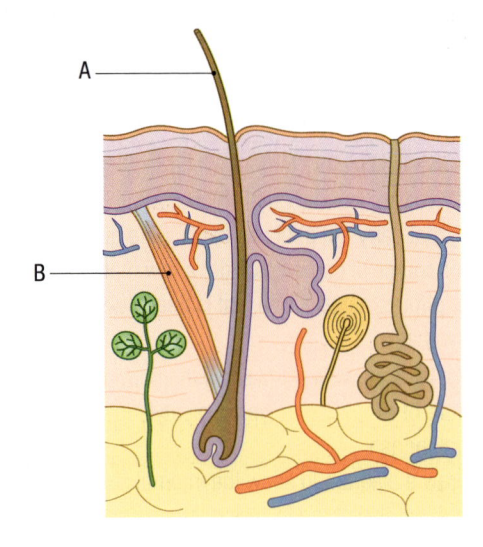

(a) Name parts **A** and **B**.
(b) Place **X** on the diagram to show where sweat reaches the skin surface.
(c) Apart from water, name **one** other substance which is found in sweat

(d) Describe briefly **one** way by which the skin helps to retain heat in cold conditions.

2008 OL Q. 6

02 The relationship between body temperature and environmental temperature for two animals is plotted below. One of these animals is a dog and the other is a lizard.

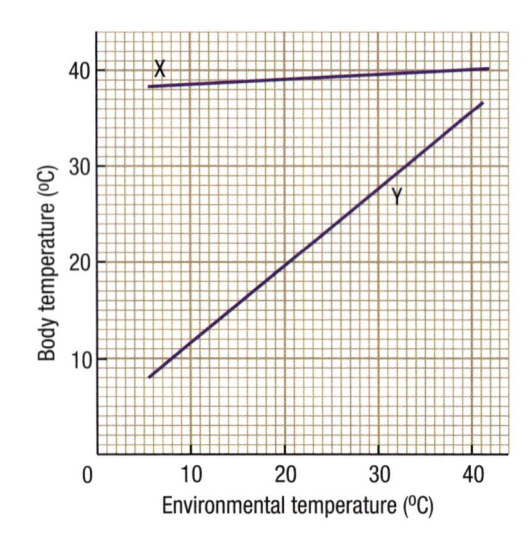

Leaving Certificate examination questions

(a) Which of the plots, X or Y, relates to the dog? Explain your answer.
(b) In relation to body temperature, what term is used to describe animals such as the dog?
(c) What is the main source of the dog's body heat?
(d) Suggest a value to dogs of the relationship between their body temperature and environmental temperature.
(e) In relation to body temperature, what term is used to describe animals such as the lizard?
(f) What is the main source of the lizard's body heat?

2013 HL Q. 3

03 (a) (i) What is an *endotherm*?
 (ii) What word is used to describe animals which are not endotherms?
 (iii) Suggest an advantage of being an endotherm.
(b) The graph shows daily variations of human body temperature over three days.

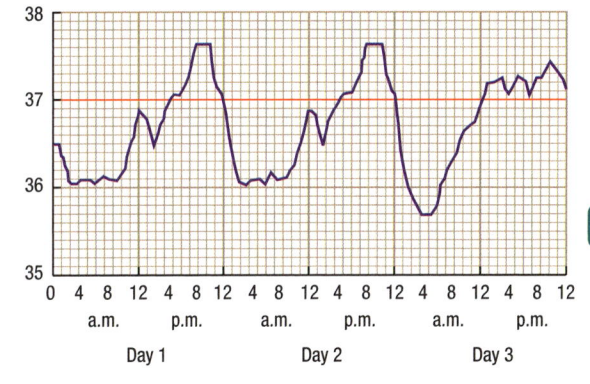

(i) What is the maximum range of body temperature under normal conditions as shown in the graph?
(ii) At what time each day does body temperature drop to its lowest level?
(iii) Suggest a reason for the drop in temperature at the time referred to in (ii).
(iv) Children typically have higher body temperatures than adults. Suggest a reason for this.

2011 HL Q. 4

Section B

04 (a) (i) Name **one** disorder of the human breathing system.
 (ii) Give **one** possible treatment for the disorder referred to above.
(b) Answer the following questions about an activity that you carried out to investigate the effect of exercise on your breathing rate.
 (i) The investigation starts by measuring the resting rate. How did you measure the resting rate?

(ii) After measuring your resting rate, what other steps did you carry out to complete the investigation?
(iii) What was the result of your investigation?
(iv) Does this investigation give the same result for both fit and non-fit people?
(v) Give a reason for your answer.

2012 OL Q. 7

05 (a) State the location in the human body of the following muscles which are used for breathing: (i) diaphragm, (ii) intercostals.
(b) Answer the following questions about an activity that you carried out to investigate the effect of exercise on the breathing rate of a human.
 (i) At the start of the investigation you asked the person who was about to do the exercise to sit down for a few minutes. Explain the purpose of this.
 (ii) How did you measure the breathing rate?
 (iii) Describe how you conducted the investigation after the period of rest.
 (iv) State the results of your investigation.

2008 OL Q. 8

Section C

06 Answer the following questions in relation to the human breathing system.
 (i) When we breathe we inhale air. What gas in the air is essential for respiration?
 (ii) One large muscle and one set of muscles are involved in inhalation. Name **both**.
 (iii) Describe in detail how we inhale air.
 (iv) 1. Name **one** disorder of the human breathing system.
   2. Suggest a possible cause of the disorder.
   3. Suggest a treatment for the disorder.

2014 OL Q. 15 (b)

07 (i) Draw a diagram of a section through a leaf. Label a stoma and a guard cell.
 (ii) Give a function of the guard cell.
 (iii) Name two gases that enter or leave the leaf.
 (iv) Name the process by which the gases move in or out of the leaf.

2007 OL Q. 15 (b)

08 (a) (i) Name the structures found in stems, equivalent to stomata in leaves, which are involved in gaseous exchange in plants.
 (ii) Name **two** compounds that leave the plant through the structures referred to in part (i).

26 Homeostasis and Gaseous Exchange

Leaving Certificate examination questions

(b) (i) Draw a large labelled diagram of the human breathing tract.
   (ii) Outline the details of the process of inhalation.
(c) Answer the following questions in relation to carbon dioxide.
   (ii) Give a feature of a capillary which allows the rapid uptake of carbon dioxide.
   (v) Briefly outline the role of carbon dioxide in the control of the human breathing rate.

2014 HL Q. 12

09 (a) (i) Name the blood vessel that returns blood to the heart from the lungs.
   (ii) Name the main gas transported in the blood vessel that you have named in (i). How is this gas transported?
(b) (i) Draw a large diagram of the human breathing system. Label the trachea, bronchus and lung.
   (ii) State the function of the following: epiglottis, larynx.
   (iii) Describe briefly the role of the diaphragm and intercostal muscles in inhalation. In your answer refer to volume and thoracic air pressure.

(c) (i) Give three ways in which an alveolus is adapted for efficient gas exchange.
   (ii) Name the process involved in the passage of gas between the alveolus and the blood.
   (iii) Name a breathing disorder.
   (iv) In the case of the breathing disorder that you have named in (iii) state:
      1. A cause.
      2. A means of prevention.
      3. A treatment.

2007 HL Q. 13

10 (i) What is homeostasis? Note one reason why it is important in the human body.
(ii) Draw a diagram of a section through human skin to show two structures involved in temperature regulation. Label each of these structures.
(iii) For one of the structures that you have labelled in your diagram briefly describe its role in temperature regulation.
(iv) What is meant by an ectotherm?

2007 HL Q. 15 (c)

Past examination questions

OL	2014 Q. 15 (b)	2012 Q. 7, Q. 15 (c)	2011 Q. 13 (c)
	2008 Q. 6, Q. 8, Q. 14 (c)	2007 Q. 15 (b)	2006 Q. 5 (a)
	2005 Q. 12 (b) (c)	2004 Q. 9	

HL	2014 Q. 9 (b) (ii), Q. 12 (a), (b), (c) (ii) and (v)	2013 Q. 3	2012 Q. 15 (c)
	2011 Q. 4 + Q. 8 (b) (iii)	2010 Q.5 (c) (v)	2009 Q. 13 (c), Q. 15 (c) (iii)
	2007 Q. 13, Q. 15 (c)	2004 Q. 12 (a), (c)	SEC Sample Q. 6, Q. 13

Excretion and Osmoregulation

27

After studying this chapter you should be able to:

1. Define excretion.
2. Explain the role of leaves and lenticels as organs of excretion in plants and explain how the process works.
3. Explain the role of the human excretory system in homeostasis and give the function, location and the waste products of the lungs, skin and urinary systems.
4. Describe the macrostructure and basic role of the urinary system.
5. Describe the role of the kidney in osmoregulation.
6. Identify the sites of filtration and reabsorption in the kidneys.
7. Describe the path of the urine to the urethra.
8. **HL** Describe the structure of the nephron in the kidney.
9. **HL** Describe the role of the nephron in the formation of urine.
10. **HL** Describe the function of the kidney and the hormone ADH in osmoregulation.

Excretion

1. **Excretion** is the removal of waste chemicals that have been produced by **cell** activity. This process takes place in all **organisms**. An organism must get rid of these waste chemicals because a build-up would be harmful. Some of the waste products are poisonous in themselves, e.g. urea or carbon dioxide. Others are not poisonous, but if they are allowed to build up they will affect the environment of the cells in the organism, which can damage the cells, e.g. the effects of excess water. Excretion is part of the process of **homeostasis**. By removing these waste products the internal environment of the organism is kept constant, as we have seen in the previous chapter.

> **D** **Excretion** is the removal of waste chemicals that have been produced by cell activity.

Excretion in plants

2. In plants, the major waste products are gases. **Photosynthesis** produces oxygen as a waste gas and **respiration** produces carbon dioxide and water as waste products. Photosynthesis produces the greatest amount of waste product and therefore the leaf is the major organ of excretion in plants.

Excretion of oxygen

The oxygen produced in photosynthesis leaves the photosynthetic cells and diffuses into the air spaces in the ground tissue (Fig 27.1). This gas then diffuses out of the **stomata** of the leaves. In this way, the plant removes the waste oxygen. This excretion of plants is demonstrated using pond weed, as shown in the investigations on photosynthesis (Investigation 13.1 or 13.2).

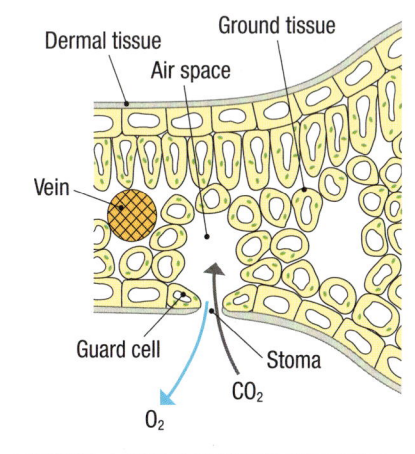

27.1 Gaseous exchange in a leaf

27 Excretion and Osmoregulation

In the stem of woody plants there are special spaces in the airtight cork layer which allow gaseous exchange. These are formed by loosely arranged cells that have air spaces between them to allow for the **diffusion** of gases used and produced in respiration. These specialised pores are called **lenticels** (Fig 27.2).

Excretion of carbon dioxide

Some of the oxygen produced in photosynthesis is used in the plant for respiration and this respiration will produce waste carbon dioxide. In the dark, the release of carbon dioxide can be shown as photosynthesis ceases. If a potted plant is placed in the apparatus as shown in Fig 27.3, the release of carbon dioxide can be demonstrated. The limewater in the second flask will remain clear but the limewater in the last flask will turn milky, showing the release of carbon dioxide by the plant.

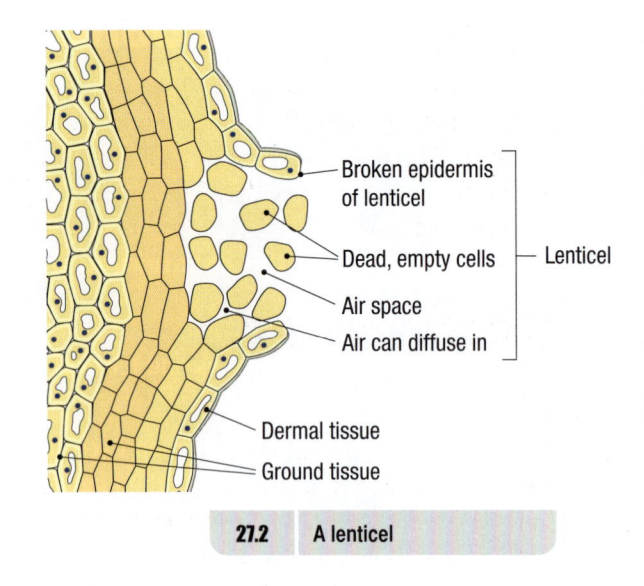

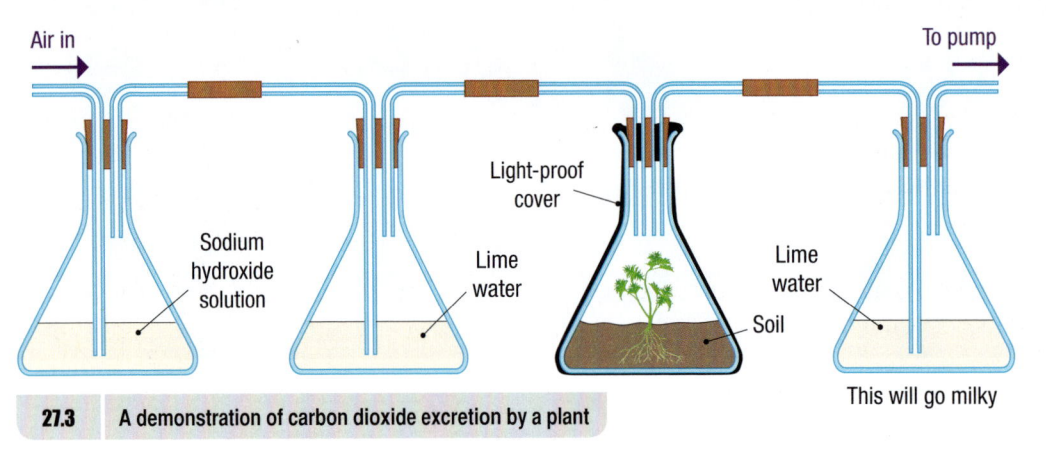

27.2 A lenticel

27.3 A demonstration of carbon dioxide excretion by a plant

The shedding of leaves by deciduous plants will also remove some waste products from the plant.

Excretion in humans

Lungs

The lungs, as seen in the last chapter, are located in the chest (thoracic) cavity (Fig 27.4). These remove waste carbon dioxide, produced during respiration, from the blood. Water and heat are also normally lost from the lungs to the air but the primary role of the lungs in excretion is the loss of carbon dioxide. In addition to excretion the lungs also have a role in homeostasis as they help control the water and carbon dioxide (pH) levels in the blood.

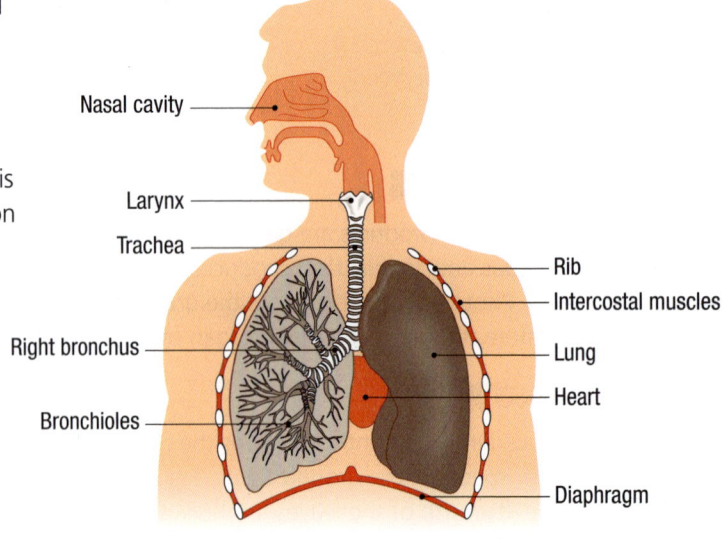

27.4 The lungs

The skin

The skin (Fig 27.5) acts as an excretory organ in the body in that it gets rid of **water** and **urea** when sweating. Sweating is more important in maintaining a constant body temperature than as a method of excretion. As we have seen in the last chapter the loss of water is primarily for homeostasis.

The urinary system

Role

Nitrogen-containing molecules such as protein or genetic material (**DNA** or **RNA**) will produce nitrogen-containing waste products. These waste products, mainly urea, are removed from the body by the kidneys, the main excretory organ of the body. The human has a pair of kidneys situated in the lower abdominal cavity (if you place your hands on your waist your thumb will be situated over your kidneys). The kidneys are brown, bean-shaped organs the size of a small fist.

Structure

Each kidney has a large artery (the renal artery) carrying blood to it from the aorta and a large vein (the renal vein) carrying the deoxygenated blood away. A third tube attached to each kidney is the **ureter**, which carries the urine away from the kidney to the bladder. The **bladder** is a muscular bag that stores the urine until it is got rid of from the body via the **urethra** by a process called **urination**. The urine is held in the bladder by a **sphincter muscle** at the base of the bladder that prevents the urine travelling along the urethra. In males, the urethra passes through the penis and in females it opens above the opening of the vagina (Fig 27.6).

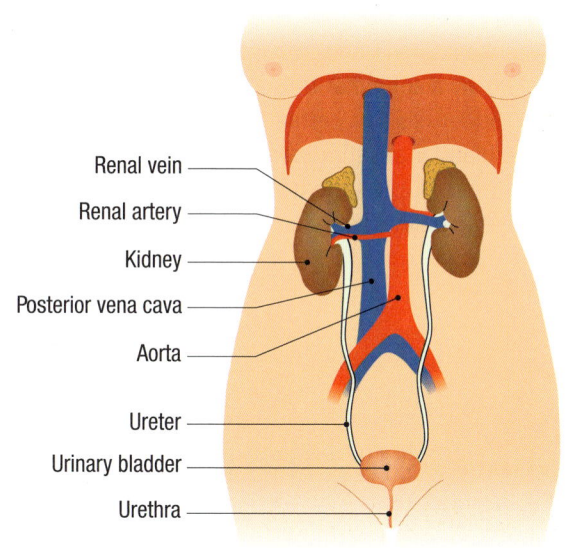

27.5 The skin as seen under the scanning electron microscope

27.6 The human urinary system

The kidneys

Structure

A longitudinal section through a kidney shows three main areas (Fig 27.7). The outer edge or **cortex** is a darker colour with a grainy appearance. Inside this is the **medulla**, made up of a number of **pyramids**, so called because of their shape. These pyramids have a striped appearance. The centre of the kidney contains a hollow area, the **pelvis**, which is connected to the ureter.

Functions

The kidneys are important in the removal of waste products from the blood and they have another important role in the control of the amount of salt and water present in the blood. This process is called **osmoregulation**. These two processes are carried out simultaneously in the kidney.

In the **cortex** of the kidney, the renal artery divides into small blood vessels (Figs 27.7 and 27.8).

- The high-pressure blood from the heart trying to force its way through these small vessels causes a leakage of the liquid component of the blood (the **plasma**) into the kidneys. The blood cells and plasma proteins do not pass out of the vessels. This process is called **filtration**.

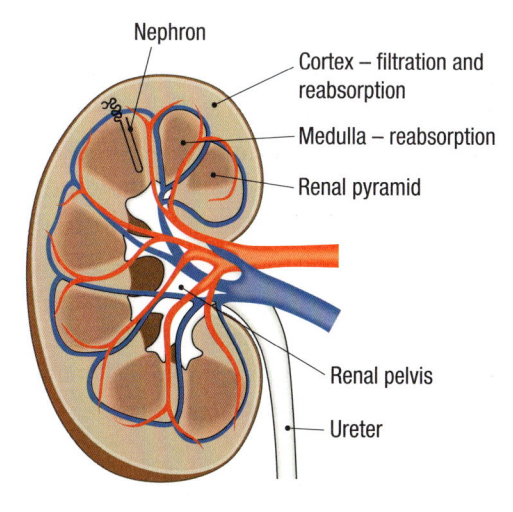

27.7 The structure of the human kidney

27 Excretion and Osmoregulation

- The filtration results in many beneficial chemicals (such as glucose) being forced into the kidney as well as the waste materials. These are reabsorbed into the blood along with much water in the cortex.
- Some materials such as penicillin or potassium ions are actively secreted into the kidney from the blood in the cortex.

The **medulla** is primarily involved in the control of the amount of water in the blood:

- Should the level of salts be too high in the blood, the medulla will be used to reabsorb the water from the kidney so the blood will become more dilute and the urine more concentrated.
- Should the blood be too dilute, the cortex is used to reabsorb more sodium ions to concentrate the blood and the medulla does not reabsorb water.

In this way, the kidneys can remove the waste products from the blood and control the levels of salt and water in the blood. The kidney is an organ of excretion and an organ of osmoregulation and homeostasis.

The waste material released by the kidneys is called urine and it contains mainly water, some urea, which is made in the **liver**, and various salts. The urine is released into the pelvis of the kidney, which acts as a funnel carrying the urine to the ureter. The urine trickles down the ureter to the bladder. The urine is held in the bladder by a sphincter muscle. Urination occurs when the bladder fills to a certain point and stretch receptors in the bladder are stimulated. This sets off a reflex action that empties the bladder. Older children and adults can delay this reflex.

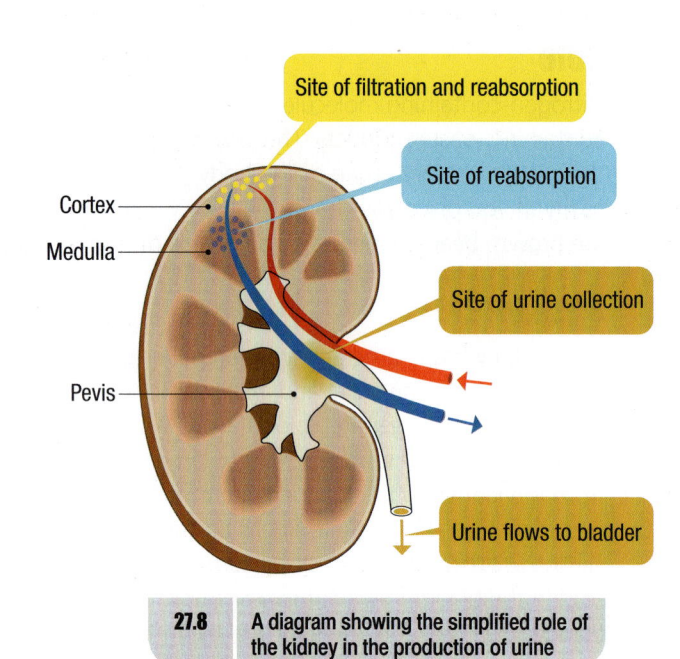

27.8 A diagram showing the simplified role of the kidney in the production of urine

More about the kidney

The kidney, as has been seen, is the main organ of excretion. It removes nitrogenous waste products from the body and controls the water/salt balance in the blood. Each kidney is made up of between 1 and 2 million microscopic structures called **nephrons** (Fig 27.9). These are the basic working units of the kidney.

Nephron structure

There are five parts found in the nephron:

1. The first part is a cup-shaped structure called the **Bowman's capsule**, which is like a soft football that has been pushed in on one side (Fig 27.10). A large group of small capillaries, the **glomerulus**, are found in this cup. There is an arteriole bringing the blood to the glomerulus, the **afferent arteriole** and a slightly narrower arteriole bringing the blood away, the **efferent arteriole**.

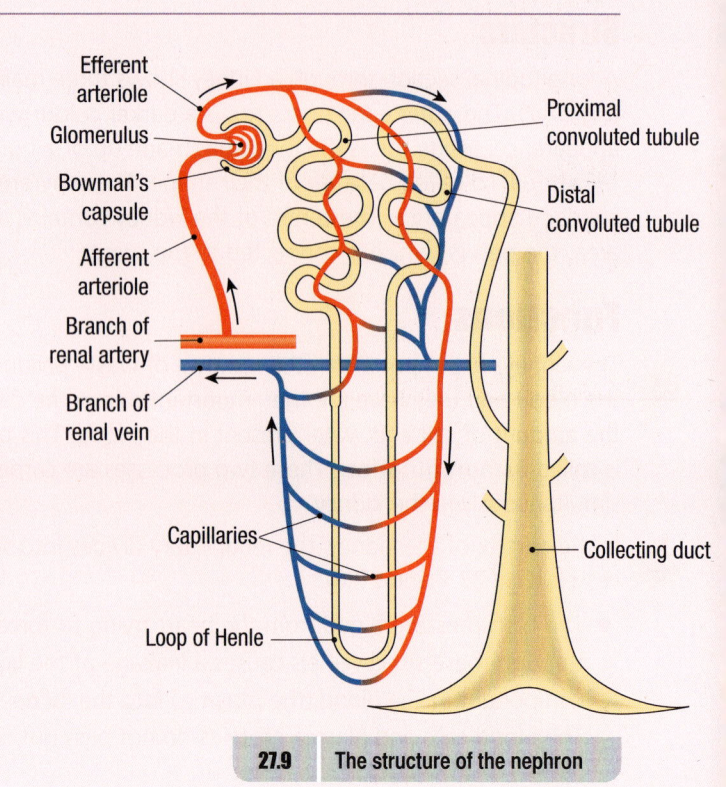

27.9 The structure of the nephron

HL

2. The Bowman's capsule leads to a highly coiled structure called the **proximal (near) convoluted (twisted) tubule**.
3. This leads to a U-shaped tubule, the **loop of Henlé**.
4. This is followed by the **distal (distant) convoluted tubule**.
5. This tubule opens into the **collecting duct**.

The Bowman's capsule and both convoluted tubules are found in the cortex of the kidney and the loop of Henlé is found in the medulla. A network of capillaries surrounds the entire structure (Fig 27.9).

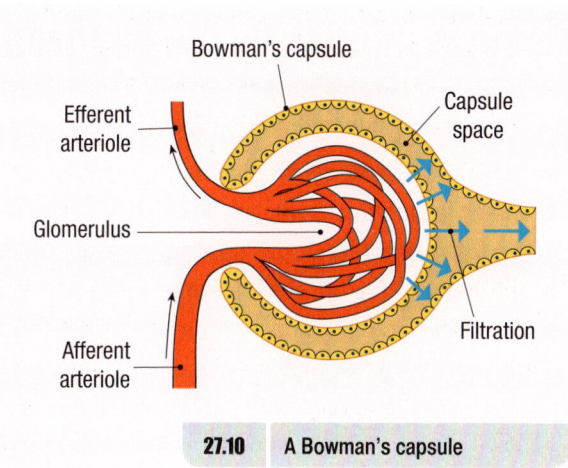

27.10   A Bowman's capsule

How the nephron makes urine

Bowman's capsule

- The blood that enters the glomerulus is under pressure and the narrowing of the arteriole leaving the glomerulus increases this pressure.
- This results in the **pressure filtration** of the plasma from the blood along with many dissolved chemicals into the Bowman's capsule.
- The blood cells and plasma proteins are too big to pass through the wall of the capillaries and do not pass into the Bowman's capsule but remain in the blood.
- The liquid (plasma) now present in the Bowman's capsule is called the **glomerular filtrate** and contains most of the waste products but also many chemicals the body requires, i.e. water and glucose, as these are small enough to pass through the wall of the Bowman's capsule.

Proximal convoluted tubule

- In the proximal convoluted tubule the glucose, nutrients and some of the salt and water are reabsorbed back into the blood supply by a combination of **diffusion**, **osmosis** and **active transport**.
- Active transport requires energy and ensures that all the glucose, for example, is reabsorbed from the nephron.

Loop of Henlé

Some water and salts are reabsorbed in the loop of Henlé but the main function of this loop is to generate a temporary **high salt concentration** at the bottom of the loop. This creates an area that will attract water out of the **collecting duct**, thus concentrating the urine.

Distal convoluted tubule

Some water and salts are reabsorbed in the distal convoluted tubule. The secretion of certain waste products out of the blood into the distal convoluted tubule occurs also by active transport.

Collecting duct

The remaining urine passes down the collecting duct into the pelvis and then the ureter.

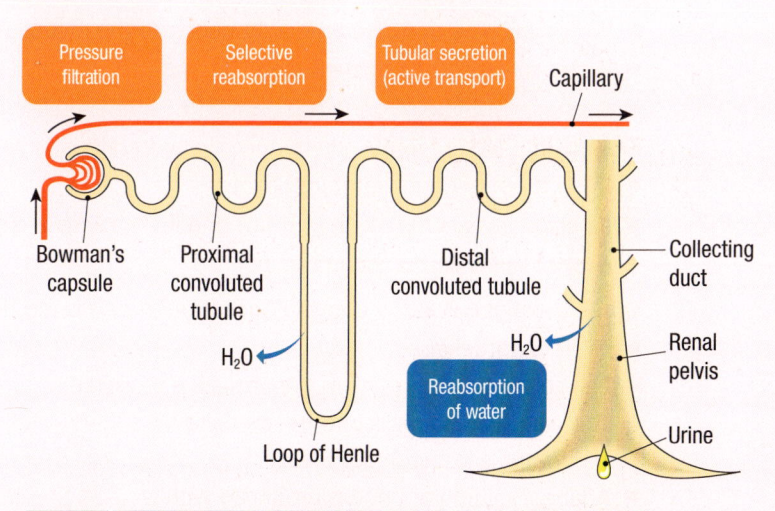

27.11   The functions of each part of the nephron in urine formation

27 Excretion and Osmoregulation

HL Osmoregulation by the nephron

It is in the collecting duct that the kidney plays a major role in the control of water loss from the body. It is the structure of the nephron that allows it to produce urine that is more concentrated than the blood.

- The loop of Henlé passes down into the medulla and then arrives back into the cortex.
- The collecting duct starts at the cortex and passes down through the medulla to the pelvis.
- Thus the collecting duct is passing the high salt concentration in the medulla (Fig 27.12).
- The water in the urine will attempt to move into the medulla due to osmosis.
- The collecting duct is normally impermeable to water so that any water that arrives here will be lost down to the pelvis and into the bladder and will not pass into the medulla.

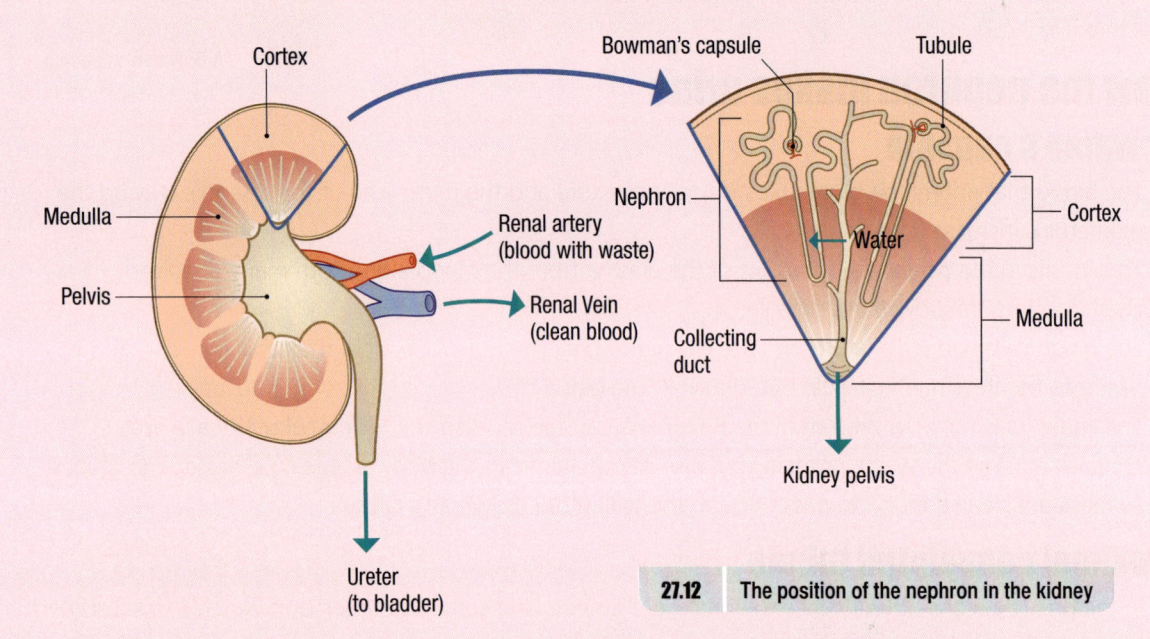

27.12 The position of the nephron in the kidney

The concentration and the volume of the urine produced by the body are largely determined by the collecting duct. This will change depending on the concentration of the blood plasma (Fig 27.13).

1. When the blood plasma is short of water (it is too concentrated) the following happens:
   - The **pituitary gland** releases a hormone **ADH (anti-diuretic hormone)**.
   - This hormone travels in the blood to the kidney, which causes the wall of the collecting duct to become permeable to water.
   - Water will pass from the collecting duct into the medulla due to osmosis.
   - Water is reabsorbed by the blood.
   - A smaller volume of urine is produced with more salt present.

   Reasons the blood plasma can be too concentrated include:
   - there is not enough water in the diet;
   - a person sweats too much (it is hot or a lot of exercise is taken);
   - a lot of salt is consumed in the diet.

2. When the blood is at the correct concentration or it is too dilute, the following happens:
   - ADH is not released.
   - The collecting duct remains impermeable to water.
   - The water cannot pass into the medulla.
   - The water is lost with the urea.
   - A larger volume of urine is produced with less salt present.

   This happens if:
   - there is too much water in the diet;
   - there is too little salt in the diet.

27 Excretion and Osmoregulation

HL A close contact between the nephron and the blood capillaries is necessary to allow for the water to pass back into the blood and the correct functioning of the kidney.

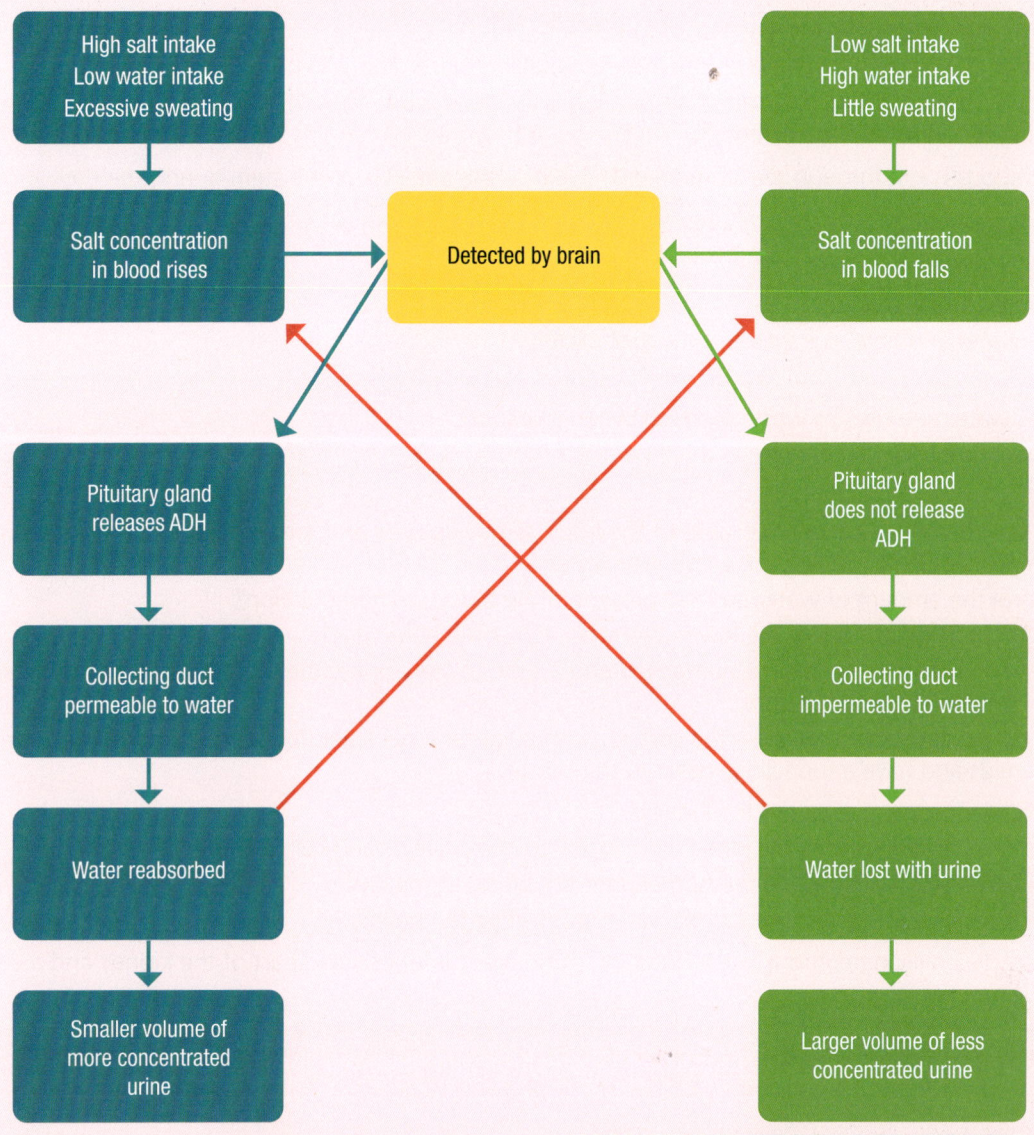

```
High salt intake                                    Low salt intake
Low water intake                                    High water intake
Excessive sweating                                  Little sweating
        ↓                                                   ↓
Salt concentration  →  Detected by brain  ←  Salt concentration
in blood rises                                      in blood falls
        ↓                                                   ↓
Pituitary gland                                     Pituitary gland
releases ADH                                        does not release ADH
        ↓                                                   ↓
Collecting duct                                     Collecting duct
permeable to water                                  impermeable to water
        ↓                                                   ↓
Water reabsorbed                                    Water lost with urine
        ↓                                                   ↓
Smaller volume of                                   Larger volume of less
more concentrated urine                             concentrated urine
```

27.13 The control of water loss in the kidneys

	Blood too dilute	Blood at the correct concentration	Blood too concentrated	Too much urea in blood
What can cause this	Take in too much water. Take in too little salt	Correct intake of water and salt	Take in too little water. Excessive sweating due to hot day or exercise	High protein diet
Effect on ADH level in blood	None present	None present	Released by pituitary into blood	No effect
Volume of urine produced	Large volume	Normal volume	Small volume	No effect
Level of salt in urine	Low level	Normal level	High level	No effect
Amount of urea in urine	No effect	No effect	No effect	High level

Table 27.1 How different types of blood condition affect the type of urine produced

27 Excretion and Osmoregulation

Summary

- Excretion is the removal of waste products of cellular metabolism from a cell or organism.
- Plants mainly excrete gases and water vapour:
  - Oxygen during the day when photosynthesis is taking place. This is lost via the stomata.
  - Carbon dioxide during darkness as respiration only is occurring. Most of this carbon dioxide is used during daylight for photosynthesis.
- Water vapour is lost through the stomata of the leaf or the lenticels of the stem during the day.
- Many organs in humans have a double function in homeostasis and excretion.
- Lungs:
  - excrete carbon dioxide;
  - lose water and heat as a waste product of excretion.
- Skin:
  - loses water and urea as waste products when sweating;
  - sweating normally takes place as a temperature control mechanism (homeostasis) when the body is hot.
- Kidneys:
  - are the specialised excretory organs of the body, removing urea and forming urine and are involved in homeostasis in controlling the amount of water;
  - control the amount of water and salt present in the blood (osmoregulation);
  - are situated to the rear of the lower abdomen above the pelvic girdle;
  - each has a large artery and vein attached and a tube to carry urine (the ureter) leading to the bladder, which empties via the urethra;
  - in L.S. are dark on the outside (the cortex), have a lighter inner layer (the medulla) containing the pyramids and have a funnel-like pelvis in the centre.
- The following activities occur in the kidneys:
  - Pressure filtration causes the blood plasma, minus the proteins and cells, to enter the cortex.
  - The beneficial chemicals are reabsorbed into the blood at the cortex.
  - The medulla controls the amount of water reabsorbed by the kidney.

HL
- There are 1–2 million nephrons in each kidney. These are the functioning part of the kidney and are made up of five parts:

The parts of the nephron and their function	
The Bowman's capsule	A thin-walled, cup-like structure containing a bunch of capillaries. Pressure filtration of the liquid component of the plasma occurs here. Large molecules and cells do not leave the blood.
The proximal convoluted tubule	Where diffusion and active transport remove all the required chemicals back into the blood, e.g. glucose, hormones, vitamins, salts.
The loop of Henlé	Some water and salt are reabsorbed. An area of high salt concentration is generated here.
The distal convoluted tubule	Some waste chemicals are put into the urine by active transport.
The collecting duct	This is impermeable to water. It passes by the medulla where the area of high salt concentration has been created. The water will try to leave the collecting duct by osmosis and travel to the medulla, but it can't. If the blood is too concentrated water is reabsorbed because the pituitary gland releases ADH to make the wall of the duct permeable to water. A small volume of concentrated urine is produced. If the blood is too dilute no ADH is released and the water is lost along with the urine. A large volume of dilute urine is produced.

Review questions

01 (a) What is excretion?
(b) What are the excretory products of a plant?
(c) Why are the excretory products of a plant not always released at the same time?
(d) How would you demonstrate the loss of carbon dioxide by a plant?

02 (a) Name the structures used by green plants for excretion.
(b) List the excretory products lost by these structures.
(c) What is the other function(s) of these structures?

03 (a) What are the main excretory products in an animal?
(b) List the excretory organs.

04 (a) What function(s) do the lungs have in excretion?
(b) What is the excretory function of the skin?
(c) What are the other functions of the skin?

05 (a) What are the functions of the kidney?
(b) Draw a simple labelled diagram of an L.S. of the internal structure of a kidney.
(c) Give a function for each part you have labelled.
(d) Indicate on your diagram where: (i) filtration takes place, (ii) reabsorption takes place, (iii) secretion takes place.

06 (a) Describe in simple terms the action of the kidney.
(b) What are the functions of the bladder, the ureter and the urethra?

07 (a) Draw a labelled diagram of the nephron including the blood supply.
(b) Describe the function(s) of each part.

08 (a) Where does pressure filtration happen?
(b) How does pressure filtration occur?
(c) What effect will pressure filtration have on: (i) urea, (ii) salt, (iii) blood cells, (iv) glucose?
(d) Give a reason for each of your answers in (iii).

09 (a) Why must active transport occur in the kidney?
(b) Name a substance that is affected by active transport in the kidney.
(c) Where in the kidney does active transport occur?

10 (a) What is osmoregulation?
(b) Describe the role of the kidneys in osmoregulation.
(c) What is the effect of ADH on the nephron?
(d) Describe the role of ADH in osmoregulation.

11 What will be the effect of each of the following on the composition of the urine:
(a) A hot day.
(b) A diet high in protein.
(c) A high level of exercise.
(d) A diet high in salt.
Give a reason for each of your answers.

Examination style questions

Section A

01 The diagram shows a human kidney in vertical section.

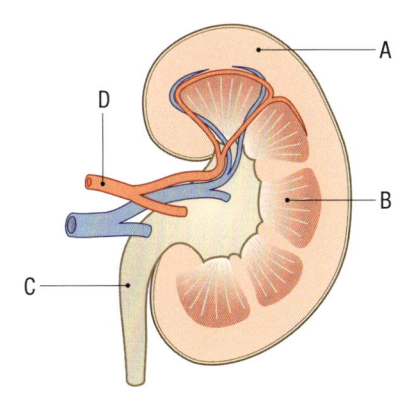

(a) Name the parts labelled A, B and C.
(b) Place an X on the diagram where you would expect to find a Bowman's capsule.
(c) To which major blood vessel does D connect?
(d) Part C joins the kidney to the _____.
(e) State a function of the kidney other than excretion.
(f) State the precise location of the kidneys in the human body.

02 (a) What are the functions of the kidney?
(b) What is pressure filtration?
(c) What is the role of the ureter in the kidney?
(d) What is the role of ADH in the kidney?
(e) What gland produces ADH?
(f) What would happen to the urine of a person who exercises a lot?

Section C

03 (a) When samples of urine from a patient were tested in the laboratory, the following results were obtained: blue litmus turned red and, on heating with blue Benedict's reagent (or with Fehling's solutions), the colour remained blue. What do these results indicate about the urine?
(b) (i) Draw a diagram of the kidney in vertical section. On the diagram show the location of the nephron.
(ii) Name the artery that supplies the kidney with oxygenated blood.

27 Excretion and Osmoregulation

Examination style questions

(iii) What effect would a very hot day (with no extra fluid intake) have on the concentration and volume of urine?

(c) The following questions relate to concentrations of some body fluids. State the difference in concentration of each substance(s) in each pair of fluids and explain the difference.
   (i) The concentration of urea in the blood of an artery supplying the kidney and a vein leading from the kidney.
   (ii) The concentration of dissolved substances in the urine on a cold day and in urine on a hot day.
   (iii) The concentration of salt in a blood vessel supplying the skin on a hot day and a blood vessel draining from the skin.

04 (a) The kidney plays a role in excretion.
   (i) Explain the term excretion and state one other function of the kidneys.
   (ii) Name two other organs that function in excretion.
(b) (i) Draw a diagram of the human nephron and its blood supply. Label the following parts: glomerulus, Bowman's capsule, loop of Henlé, proximal convoluted tubule, collecting duct, distal convoluted tubule.
   (ii) Draw a labelled outline sketch of an L.S. of a kidney to show the location of Bowman's capsule.
(c) The production of urine by the nephron involves filtration and reabsorption.
   (i) Name the site of filtration.
   (ii) Why are red blood corpuscles or proteins absent from the filtrate?
   (iii) In normal circumstances, where is glucose reabsorbed in the nephron?
   (iv) Name the process involved in the reabsorption of glucose.
   (v) Name one other substance reabsorbed by the same process.
   (vi) Where is the hormone ADH (anti-diuretic hormone) produced?
   (vii) Name one part of the nephron that is the target site for this hormone.
   (viii) Name the process by which the nephron reabsorbs water.
   (ix) Why is the term reabsorption used to describe the movement of water and glucose from the cavity (lumen) of the nephron into the blood?

Leaving Certificate examination questions

Section A

01 The diagram shows a vertical section through a human kidney.

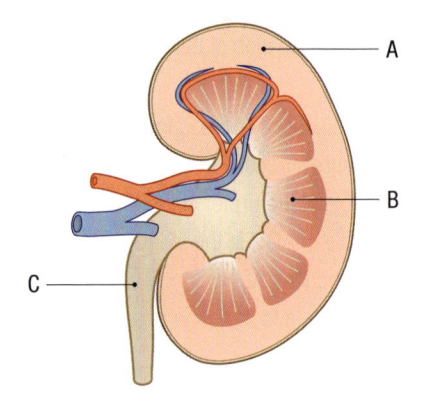

(a) Name the parts labelled A, B and C.
(b) Name the organ that is attached to the kidney by part C.
(c) Name one substance excreted by the kidneys.
(d) Name the site in the kidney where filtration takes place.
(e) Suggest one possible treatment for kidney failure.

2013 OL Q. 6

Section C

02 (i) Explain the term *excretion*.
(ii) Name **two** substances excreted by the kidneys.
(iii) The diagram shows the human urinary system.

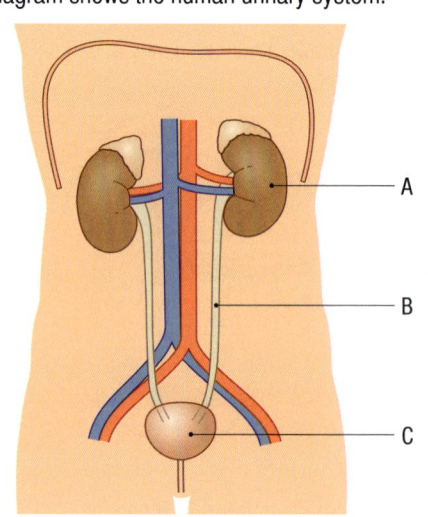

Name the parts labelled A, B and C.
(iv) Name the parts of the kidney in which each of the following takes place: filtration, reabsorption.
(v) Name **one** other excretory organ in the body.

2011 OL Q. 14 (c)

Leaving Certificate examination questions

03 The diagram shows a vertical section through a human kidney.

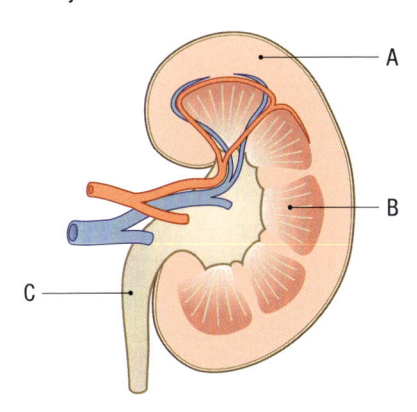

(i) Name the parts labelled A, B and C.
(ii) Which organ is attached to the kidney by part C?
(iii) In which of the three labelled parts does filtration of the blood occur?
(iv) Explain the term *excretion*.
(v) Name **two** substances excreted by the kidneys.
(vi) Give **two** other excretory organs in the human body.

2009 OL Q. 14 (b)

04 (i) What is meant by excretion?
(ii) Name **two** products excreted by the human.
(iii) Name **one** organ of excretion, other than the kidney, in the human body.
(iv) What is meant by osmoregulation?
(v) Study the diagram of a section through the kidney and answer the following questions.

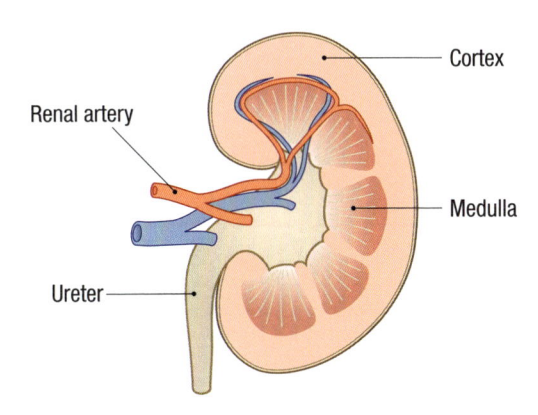

1. Where does filtration of blood take place?
2. Where does reabsorption of salt take place?
3. To what organ does the ureter link the kidney?
4. To which main blood vessel does the renal artery link the kidney?

(vi) Name the fluid present in the ureter.

2007 OL Q. 14 (b)

05 (a) (i) What is meant by the term *excretion*?
(ii) Mention **one** method of excretion in flowering plants.

(b) (i) Draw a large labelled diagram of a vertical section through a human kidney. Label the following parts of your diagram: cortex, medulla, pelvis.
(ii) Indicate clearly on your diagram where reabsorption takes place.
(iii) 1. Name the blood vessel that supplies blood to a kidney.
2. From which blood vessel does the blood vessel referred to in (iii) 1. arise?
(iv) In which cavity of the body are the kidneys located?
(v) Name **one** substance, other than water, excreted in the urine.
(vi) Give a feature of the kidney which indicates that it is an exocrine gland.

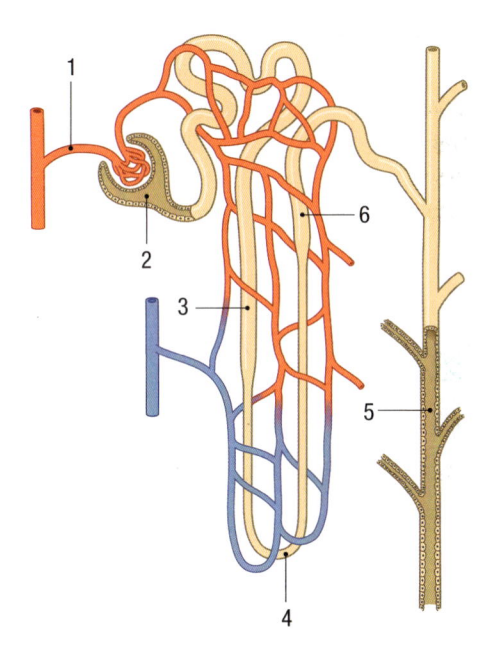

(c) (i) The diagram above shows the structure of a nephron and its associated blood supply.
1. Name the parts numbered 1 to 6.
2. Indicate clearly by number where filtration takes place.
3. Name the hormone associated with changing the permeability of the structure at 7.

(ii) A sample of urine was found to contain protein.
1. Would you consider this to be normal?
2. Explain your answer.

(iii) A sample of urine was found to contain glucose.
1. Would you consider this to be normal?
2. Explain your answer.

2011 HL Q. 12

Leaving Certificate examination questions

06 (a) (i) What is meant by excretion?
  (ii) Urea and carbon dioxide are excretory products of the human body. In the case of each product name a substance from which it is derived.
(b) The diagram shows the structure of a nephron and its associated blood supply.

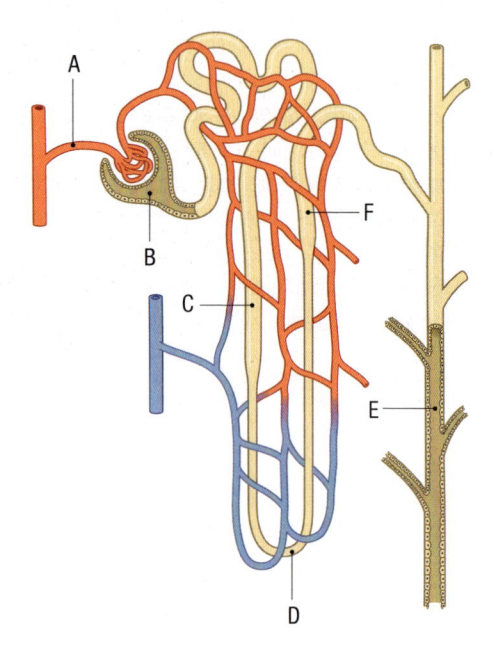

  (i) Name the parts A, B, C, D, E and F.
  (ii) From which blood vessel is A derived?
  (iii) Where in the kidney is B located?
  (iv) Give the part of the nephron in which each of the following takes place:
    1. filtration,   2. reabsorption of amino acids.
  (v) Give **two** features of the nephron that aid filtration.
  (vi) Name a group of biomolecules in the blood which are too large to pass through the filtration system of the nephron.
(c) (i) Suggest **two** situations which may result in a drop in the water content of the blood.
  (ii) When the water content of the blood drops a hormone is released. Name this hormone and the endocrine gland from which it is secreted.
  (iii) Give a precise target area for this hormone. How does the hormone reach the target area?
  (iv) Explain the role of the hormone at its target area, when the water content of the blood is low.

2008 HL Q. 13

07 Use your knowledge of the human vascular and excretory systems to answer the following.
  (i) Explain the terms, plasma, glomerular filtrate.
  (ii) Explain why red blood cells are normally absent from glomerular filtrate.
  (iii) The concentration of glucose is the same in plasma and glomerular filtrate. Why is this?
  (iv) Why is glucose normally absent from urine?
  (v) Following a period of heavy exercise an athlete may produce only a small volume of concentrated urine. Explain this observation and give an account of the process that concentrates the urine.

2006 HL Q. 13 (b)

Past examination questions

OL	2013 Q. 6	2011 Q. 14 (c)	2009 Q. 14 (b)	2007 Q. 14 (b)	2005 Q. 14 (a)
HL	2011 Q. 12	2010 Q. 15 (c) (iv), (v)	2009 Q 15. (c) (iii)	2008 Q. 13	2006 Q. 6 (b), Q. 13 (b)
	2005 Q. 3 (a)	2004 Q. 12 (b)			

Plant Response to Stimuli

28

After studying this chapter you should be able to:

1. Describe and name the various growth responses in plants, giving examples of phototropism and geotropism.
2. Describe the effect and the role of a growth regulator in plants.
3. Give any two uses of these growth regulators in horticulture.
4. Describe an experiment to investigate the effect of IAA on dicotyledonous plants.
5. Describe the production, function and effect of an auxin in a plant. *(HL)*
6. Explain the mechanism of a plant response to an external stimulus. *(HL)*
7. Give four mechanical or chemical ways in which plants protect themselves.

Responses to stimuli

One of the characteristics of all living things is that they respond to a stimulus. For this to happen, an **organism** has to be able to register a stimulus. This stimulus will cause a controlling mechanism to function that will produce some type of response in the organism.

In humans, for example, the eye could pick up light from a moving car. The image is sent via the nerves to the brain where a further message is sent to the muscles that use the skeleton to move the body out of the way. A second message is sent to the **adrenal gland**, which releases a chemical message to get the heart beating faster so the body has more oxygen available for fast action. Here a series of interconnected systems in the body is used to respond to a stimulus – the moving car.

A response may be on a much smaller scale. Should micro-organisms enter the body, the immune system responds by defending the body in a number of ways to prevent the micro-organisms doing any harm.

Plants also respond to stimuli. Light falling unevenly on a shoot will cause the release of a chemical that causes a growth response in the plant so that it grows in the direction of the sun. From these examples it can be seen that there are a number of different ways in which organisms respond to stimuli.

Plant tropisms

In flowering plants, the commonest response to an external stimulus is a change in the growth pattern of that plant. There are many different external factors that affect the growth of plants including length of day (or night), temperature, the force of gravity or type (wavelength) of light.

When the direction of that growth response is determined by the direction of the stimulus, the responses are called **tropisms**. A naturally occurring chemical called a **growth regulator** (or growth substance), which is produced in the **meristematic tissue** of the plant, controls the tropism. The main growth regulators involved in tropic responses are called **auxins**.

> **D** A **tropism** is a growth response of a plant to a directional stimulus.

There are a number of different tropisms. Each one is caused by a different stimulus. If the plant grows towards the stimulus it is said to be a positive tropism, i.e. a root growing towards the force of gravity. If the plant grows away from the stimulus it is said to be a negative tropism, i.e. a shoot growing away from the force of gravity.

28 Plant Response to Stimuli

28.1 Phototropism in cress seeds

Phototropism is the growth response of plants in response to unidirectional light. If a plant is illuminated from one side the plant will bend towards the light. Phototropism ensures that plants grow towards light and their leaves are facing the sun so maximum **photosynthesis** can take place. This can be easily demonstrated. If a group of cress seeds is left beside a window they will bend towards the light coming in the window (Fig 28.1). The stem is positively phototropic. Most roots will bend away from light – they are negatively phototropic.

Geotropism is the growth response of plants to the force of gravity. Geotropism ensures that the roots of a plant grow down into the soil and successfully anchor the plant. It will also ensure that the stem grows up out of the soil when a seed germinates, and will get the necessary light for photosynthesis. If seeds are planted in any position in the soil they will all produce stems that grow upwards and roots that grow downwards (Figs 28.2 and 28.3). Shoots grow away from the force of gravity and are said to be negatively geotropic. Roots grow towards the force of gravity and are said to be positively geotropic.

Thigmotropism is the growth response of plants to touch, i.e. the sweet pea produces tendrils which bend around a stake placed beside it. Climbing plants use this response to hold onto the structure that supports them (Fig 28.4). These plants are positively thigmotropic.

Hydrotropism is the growth response of plants to water, i.e. roots appear to grow towards water. This ensures the plants have the necessary water for photosynthesis and turgidity. Roots are positively hydrotropic.

Chemotropism is the growth response of plants towards certain chemicals, i.e. roots appear to grow towards certain chemicals in the soil, i.e. fertilisers. They will also tend to grow away from certain damaging chemicals. Roots can be negatively and positively chemotropic. Another example of chemotropism can be found in the growth of the pollen tube during plant **reproduction** (see Chapter 34).

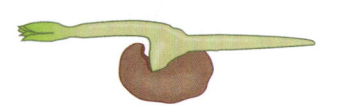

Seedling placed on side

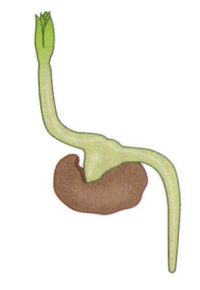

Response to force of gravity

28.2 Geotropism in a seed

28.3 Negative geotropism in a shoot

28.4 Thigmotropism in a climbing plant

Tropism	Response to	Part of plant affected	Benefit
Phototropism	Light	Shoot (+ve) Root (–ve)	Increase photosynthesis Anchor plant, get more water and minerals
Geotropism	Gravity	Shoot (–ve) Root (+ve)	Increase photosynthesis Anchor plant, get more water and minerals
Thigmotropism	Touch	Stem or tendrils (+ve)	Hold plant up, increase photosynthesis
Hydrotropism	Water	Root (+ve)	Absorb more water
Chemotropism	Chemicals	Root (+ve) and (–ve)	Take in minerals or avoid harmful chemicals

Table 28.1 Tropic responses in plants

Plant growth regulators

Plant growth regulators (PGRs) are chemicals produced in plants that affect the rate of growth or the development of plants when they are in very low concentrations.

- Some of these growth regulators are carried in the vascular system of plants.
- Others diffuse from cell to cell.
- PGRs are made in one site, e.g. the meristems.
- They do not function where they are made, they function at another place in the plant.

These features of PGRs are similar to the action of animal hormones.

> **D** A **plant growth regulator** is a chemical that at very low concentrations affects the development of plants.

There are a number of different types of growth regulator, each of which has a different effect on the plant. Some are growth promoters: **auxins**, **gibberellins** or **cytokinins**, and others are growth inhibitors: **abscisic acid** or **ethene** (ethylene). **Indoleacetic acid (IAA)** is a naturally occurring auxin, which affects the elongation of cells. It is commonly produced in the top of growing shoots.

1. The same growth regulator can have opposite effects on the root and the shoot, e.g. the same concentration of an auxin such as IAA will cause growth inhibition in a root but stimulate growth in a stem.
2. The same growth regulator can have the opposite effect at different concentrations, e.g. IAA at very low concentration stimulates root growth but at high concentrations inhibits it.
3. Sometimes, two of these growth regulators work together or against each other. This effect is seen in leaf fall (abscission). Ethene is responsible for leaf fall but auxin prevents leaf fall. Young leaves produce auxin that prevents leaf fall. As the leaf ages, auxin production stops and ethene production is increased due to longer nights. Thus, in most broad-leaved trees in Ireland, leaf fall occurs as autumn arrives.

These responses by plants due to the production of PGRs are sometimes compared to the hormonal response found in animals. This is because the response is due to chemicals which are produced in one place on the plant but they have their effect on a different place. The chemicals are also carried in the veins of plants, which is similar to the blood system transporting hormones.

Table 28.2 lists some naturally occurring PGRs.

	Type	Example	Function
Growth promoters	Auxins	Indoleacetic acid (IAA)	Cell elongation
	Gibberellins	Gibberellic acid (GA)	Stem elongation
	Cytokinins	Zeatin	Cell division
Growth inhibitors	Abscisic acid	Abscisic acid	Dormancy
	Ethene (ethylene)	Ethene (ethylene)	Abscission

Table 28.2 Plant growth regulators

28 Plant Response to Stimuli

SYLLABUS REQUIREMENT:
You need to know about the use of any two of these PGRs.

Commercial use of PGRs

Scientists have discovered many effects of growth regulators and have discovered some other chemicals that mimic the effect of growth regulators. These chemicals can be used to affect plant growth.

1. One such chemical is 2,4-D, the main component of many selective lawn weedkillers (Fig 28.5). 2,4-D will kill any broad-leaved plants (**dicots**), such as dandelions and daisies, in a lawn, but it will not kill the grasses (**monocots**).

2. Ethene will cause the ripening of fruit. Bananas are picked when green and ethene is released into the warehouse to ripen them when they are required for sale. This is also the reason why one 'bad' apple will make the barrel bad. The over-ripe apple will release ethene, which causes the other apples to ripen (see Chapter 34).

3. Seedless fruits can be produced by spraying the crop with gibberellins, which cause fruit formation without fertilisation and hence without seeds.

28.5 Spraying a selective weedkiller

Investigation 28.1
To investigate the effect of growth regulator on plant tissue

In this investigation we are trying to show the effect of different strengths of IAA on the growth of radish or cress seedlings.

Because auxins (IAA) work in very low concentrations it would be impossible to weigh out very small amounts. Instead a serial dilution is made of a stock solution of IAA.

A stock solution is a solution of known concentration, e.g. 100 ppm (100 parts IAA to 1 million parts distilled water).

A serial dilution is a series of solutions of different concentrations made from the stock solution. Usually each concentration is one-tenth that of the previous one.

Making the serial dilution

1. Label eight clean containers and eight pipettes A to H.
2. With a pipette (syringe) take 10 cm^3 of the stock solution (10^2 ppm) of IAA provided and place it in the container labelled A.
3. In the remaining containers place 9 cm^3 of distilled water.
4. Using a fresh pipette take 1 cm^3 of the solution from container A, add it to test tube B and mix well.

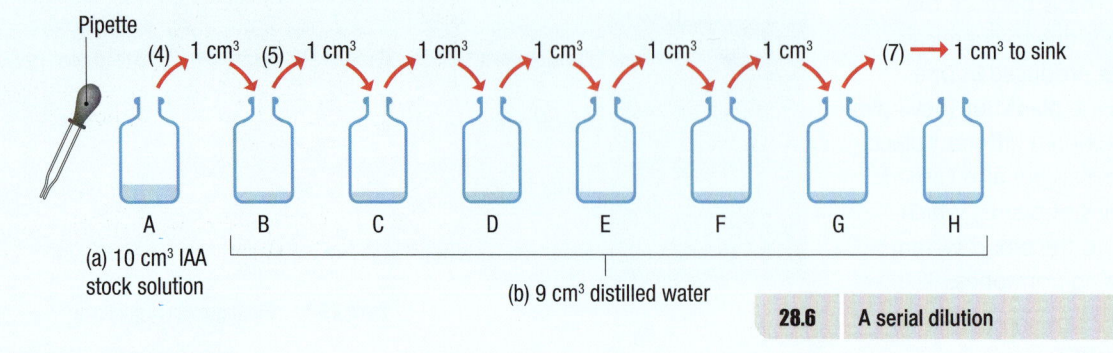

(a) 10 cm^3 IAA stock solution
(b) 9 cm^3 distilled water

28.6 A serial dilution

5. Using a clean pipette take 1 cm³ from container B, add to C and mix.
6. Using a clean pipette each time repeat for each container C to G.
7. Take 1 cm³ out of container G and discard in the sink.

This is called a serial dilution (Fig 28.6) – each solution is one-tenth as dilute as the previous one: 10^2, 10, 1, 10^{-1}, 10^{-2}, 10^{-3}, 10^{-4}. The final test tube (H) has no IAA and is the control.

N.B. container H will have 9 cm³ of distilled water only.

To set up the experiment

1. Cut eight circular pieces from a sheet of acetate, which has a photocopy of a grid on it, so it will just fit inside a Petri dish lid.
2. Label eight Petri dishes A to H and place the acetate in the lid of each while it is flat on the desk. (The grid allows you to line up the seeds in a row and to measure the shoot/root growth.)
3. Place five radish or cress seeds along a grid line of each acetate sheet in the eight Petri dishes. (Using a number of seeds increases the chance that at least some will germinate.)
4. Cover each set of seeds with a piece of filter paper.
5. Gently add the IAA solutions to each Petri dish.
6. Carefully place cotton wool on the filter paper to soak up the excess liquid. Make sure the cotton wool is thick enough to fill the depth of the Petri dish. Alternatively a cotton wool 'make-up' removable pad is suitable as it ensures all the dishes have the same volume of cotton wool.
7. Carefully tape the sides of the Petri dish in place, making sure the seeds do not move and the cotton wool holds the seeds firmly in place.
8. Stand the eight Petri dishes on their edges and leave in the incubator at 25°C for two or three days. (This allows the roots and shoots to grow so they can be measured Fig 28.8)
9. At the end of this time measure the length of each root and shoot using the acetate grid. Record your results in a table.

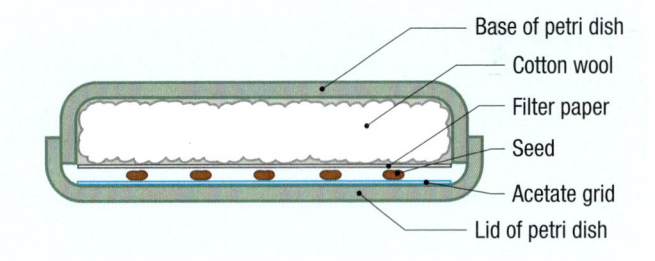

28.7 Seeds on the Petri dish lid

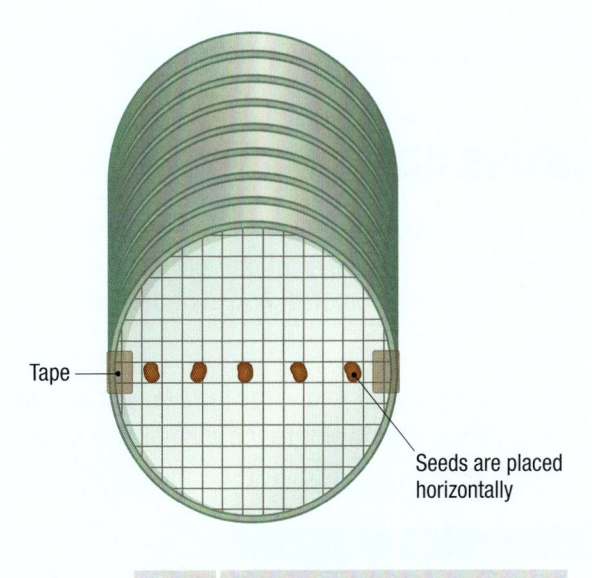

28.8 The Petri dishes set up for the investigation

Results

Concentration of IAA (ppm)	Length of roots/shoots (mm)					Total length (mm)	Average length (mm)	Percentage stimulation or inhibition
	Seed 1	Seed 2	Seed 3	Seed 4	Seed 5			
0 (control)								
10^{-4}								
10^{-3}								
10^{-2}								
10^{-1}								
1								
10^{1}								
10^{2}								

1. The percentage stimulation or inhibition of growth for each root or shoot is found by using the following formula:

$$\frac{\text{Average length} - \text{average length of controls}}{\text{Average length of controls}} \times \frac{100}{1}$$

2. Using your results draw a graph of percentage stimulation or inhibition against IAA concentration. IAA concentration is on the x (horizontal) axis.

It would be expected that the root would show stimulation of growth at very low concentrations and inhibition at medium and high concentrations. Shoots should show no effect at low concentrations, stimulation at medium concentrations and inhibition at high concentrations.

HL Auxins and the shoot

A sheath called a **coleoptile** covers the tips of oat seedlings and other similar plants. It was discovered by experimentation that the tip of the coleoptile was producing a chemical called an auxin that diffused down into the shoot and promoted growth of the shoot.

Auxins:

- Are chemicals produced in the meristematic cells in the shoot tip.
- They diffuse downwards to the zone of elongation.
- Higher levels in the shoot increase the size of the cells (cell elongation).

Other roles of auxins

1. Auxin also affects the growth of roots. In very weak concentrations, it stimulates root growth very slightly, but at concentrations that cause maximum shoot growth, it inhibits root growth strongly. As auxins are produced in the shoot tip and are destroyed by time, it is doubtful whether any auxin reaches the roots at all. So the effect of auxins on roots may not be of any consequence in nature.

Plant Response to Stimuli | 28

HL

2. It was believed that auxin was involved in the response of roots to the force of gravity but now it is suggested that a different growth factor, abscisic acid, is involved.
3. Auxins have effects other than on shoot and root growth. **Apical dominance** is the effect that is seen in many plants where the bud at the top of the shoot grows and inhibits the growth of side shoots. The apical shoot is producing auxin that is inhibiting the growth of lateral shoots. This is the principle by which pruning works. By pruning a shrub, apical dominance is removed and the shrub produces lots of side shoots.
4. The application of auxin to a plant cutting encourages the production of roots at the cut edge. Rooting powder works on this principle.

28.9 Phototropism in oat seedling

Phototropism

Light affects the growth of stems. Charles Darwin (1809–1882) and his son first investigated this. They found that when the tip of a coleoptile was lit from one side the shoot grew in the direction of the light (Fig 28.9).

Further experiments showed that there was more auxin on the shady side of the shoot than the lit side. It is now suggested that the auxin moves away from light and thus there is more auxin on the shady side. The cells on the dark side have weaker cell walls as a result and they elongate more, causing the shoot to bend in the direction of the light (Fig 28.10).

Plant protection

Plants have a number of ways in which they use anatomical (structural) or chemical means of protecting themselves (Figs 28.11 and 28.12).

28.10 The effect of an auxin on a shoot

SYLLABUS REQUIREMENT:

You need to be able to name four methods of chemical or anatomical adaptations.

Anatomical (structural)
- The thorns on blackberries and the spines on cacti.
- Fine hairs on many leaves prevent the plants from being eaten.

Chemical
- Ethene is released from wounds on some plants. This causes the production of many new cells, which form a callus that closes the wound (in this case ethene is acting as a growth promoter).
- Some plants produce poisons, which kill the insects that eat them. These poisons are released at the edge of the leaf when insects chew it. (Some insects are not killed by these poisons but put them in their own skin to poison their predators.)

28.11 Protective thorns

28.12 Protective spines on a cactus

- Some plants have 'heat shock' proteins. These are produced in high levels when the plant is exposed to stress. This stress may be caused by a sudden temperature jump, altered pH or lack of oxygen. These stressors make it difficult for proteins to fold in the correct way or may cause correctly folded proteins to unfold. Heat shock proteins stabilise proteins and are involved in the correct folding of incorrectly folded proteins. If these mis-folded proteins accumulate in the cells they may eventually kill the cell.

Summary

- All living things respond to stimuli. Plants respond most commonly by changing their growth patterns.
- A tropism is a growth response of a plant to a directional stimulus.
- The main chemical used to cause these effects is an auxin.
- Phototropism – growth response to light. The stem of a plant in a window bends towards the light.
- Geotropism – growth response to the force of gravity. The root grows downwards – positively geotropic, the shoot upwards – negatively geotropic.
- Thigmotropism – growth response to touch, e.g. sweet pea plant.
- Hydrotropism – growth response to water.
- Chemotropism – growth response to chemicals.
- A plant growth regulator is a chemical, which at very low concentrations, affects the growth of plants.
- Some regulators promote growth, e.g. auxins.
- Some regulators inhibit growth, e.g. ethene.
- Commercial use of growth regulators:
  - 2,4-D is an artificial growth regulator that kills broad-leaved plants. It is used as a selective weedkiller on lawns.
  - Ethene is released into banana stores to ripen the green fruit.
- The effect of IAA on the growth of plant tissue can be seen by:
  - soaking seeds with different concentration of IAA;
  - measuring the length of their roots and shoots.

HL
- The tip of an oat seedling (coleoptile) produces the auxin that affects plant growth. This was shown by experiments. It was since shown that the greater the concentration of the auxin, the greater the growth.
- Auxins:
  - have the opposite effect on roots than on shoots but they are probably not produced in roots in nature so the effect is seen in the laboratory only;
  - cause apical dominance: this stops the growth of side shoots and lets the stem elongate;
  - increase the production of roots (rooting powder contains auxins).
- Phototropism:
  - was investigated by Darwin and his son;
  - was demonstrated when light on one side of a plant caused the plant to bend to the light;
  - auxin is produced in the tip;
  - it diffused downwards;
  - more passes to the shady side of the shoot;
  - here it causes increased elongation;
  - resulting in the shoot bending towards the light.
- Ethene is released into banana stores to ripen the green fruit.

- Some plants protect themselves with structures, i.e. spines (cacti), stinging hairs (nettles).
- Some plants use chemicals, i.e. produce poisons that kill insects.
- Some plants release ethene at the site of injury. This causes cell growth covering the wound.

Plant Response to Stimuli | 28

Review questions

01 (a) What is a stimulus?
(b) Give an example of a stimulus and a response that affects (i) a plant, (ii) an animal.

02 (a) What is a tropism?
(b) What is a positive tropism?
(c) What is a negative tropism?
(d) What is a growth regulator?

03 (a) What is an auxin?
(b) Where is it produced?
(c) How does it travel?
(d) Give one function of auxins.

04 (a) List four tropisms.
(b) Give a benefit of each of the tropisms mentioned in (a).

05 (a) What effect do growth regulators have in plants?
(b) What are the two different effects that growth regulators can have?

06 Describe two commercial uses humans have made of growth regulators.

07 Describe an investigation you would carry out to demonstrate the effectiveness of a selective weedkiller.

08 (a) Where are the auxins produced that affect shoot growth?
(b) In what way do auxins affect shoot growth?
(c) How do auxins affect roots?

09 Describe with the aid of a labelled diagram how light from one side affects a plant shoot.

10 (a) Explain how pruning affects plant growth.
(b) Using this principle suggest how a gardener could produce a hedge of beech trees.

11 (a) Describe the two basic methods by which plants can protect themselves.
(b) Give two examples of each of the methods mentioned in (a).

12 (a) What is a serial dilution?
(b) Describe how you might use a serial dilution as described in (b) to demonstrate the effect of IAA on plant tissue.
(c) Describe the results you would expect in this investigation.

Examination style questions

Section A

01 (a) What is a tropism?
(b) Name three tropisms.
(c) Give the benefit of each of these to a plant.
(d) What is a growth regulator?
(e) Name two plant growth regulators.

02 (a) Give a role of ethene (ethylene) in plants.
(b) What is the name given to such chemicals in a plant?
(c) Name an artifical example of this.
(d) Give a role of this chemical in horticulture.
(e) Give an example of an auxin.
(f) Give a function of the auxin you have named in (e).
(g) Name a tropism where this auxin has a role.

Section B

03 (a) (i) What is the general role of IAA in plants?
(ii) By what name is IAA more commonly known?
(b) Answer the following in relation to an experiment you carried out to investigate the effect of IAA on plant tissue using serial dilutions.
(i) What is a serial dilution?
(ii) State the control you set up in this experiment.
(iii) Name the plant that you used in your investigation.
(iv) Draw a labelled diagram of one of the dishes you set up in this investigation.
(v) How did you determine the effect of IAA on the plant tissue?
(vi) Describe the results of your investigation.

Section C

04 (a) (i) What is a tropism?
(ii) List four tropisms and give their function in a plant.
(iii) What are plant growth regulators?
(iv) Describe the role of a plant growth regulator in fruit ripening.
(v) How might such a growth regulator be used in horticulture?
(b) One of the laboratory activities you carried out demonstrated the effect of different concentrations of IAA on plant tissue.
(i) What is IAA? State **two** functions of IAA in plants.
(ii) Name the plant/plant tissue that you used.
(iii) How long did you leave the experiment before you got your results?
(iv) Draw a labelled diagram to show the final apparatus you set up.

28 Plant Response to Stimuli

Examination style questions

(v) Describe how you measured the effect of the different concentrations of IAA on the plant tissue.

(vi) Copy the graph axes below in to your answer book and draw onto it the expected results for root growth.

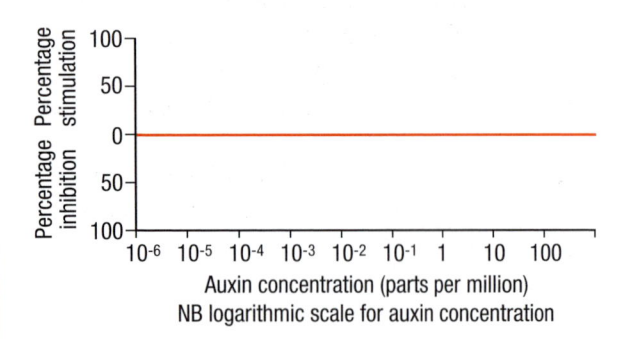

containing cress seedlings. Describe how you might use these to demonstrate phototropism in a plant.

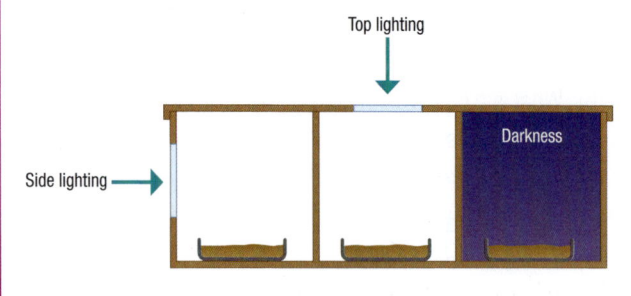

(ii) 2,4-D is a selective weedkiller. What is meant by the term selective weedkiller?

(iii) What might be the benefit of such a weedkiller?

05 (a) (i) Give three examples of protective structures found in plants.

(ii) Give a role for each of the structures you have named in (i).

(b) (i) You are given two boxes each with one window in it: (a) on top, (b) on the side and a third box with no window (see diagram). You are also given three Petri dishes

(c) Auxin is a plant growth regulator.
(i) Plant growth regulators are sometimes referred to as 'plant hormones'. Suggest **one** way in which they are similar to and one way in which they differ from animal hormones.
(ii) Explain the adaptive advantage of the positive phototropic response of stems.
(iii) Explain in detail the mechanism of one plant response to any one external stimulus, phototropism or geotropism.

Leaving Certificate examination questions

Section A

01

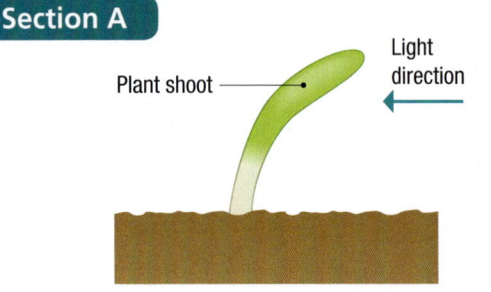

(a) Give the term used for the growth response shown by the plant shoot in the diagram above.
(b) Why is this growth response of benefit to plants?
(c) Name the group of substances that controls such responses.
(d) Name the tissue through which the substances named in (c) are transported in the plant.
(e) Name another growth response found in plants.

2009 OL Q. 6

02 The diagram shows a young plant growing in a tilted seed box.
(a) Name the growth response shown by A.
(b) Name the growth response shown by B.

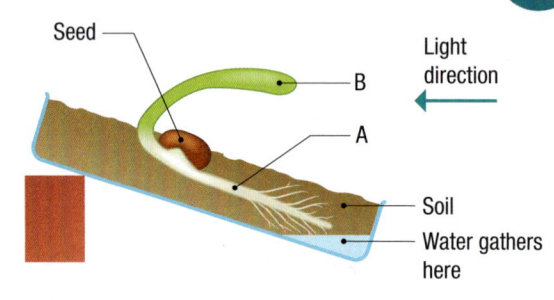

(c) Suggest a benefit to the plant of the growth response shown by B.
(d) Give an example of a regulator in plants that inhibits growth.
(e) Give **two** uses of plant growth regulators in horticulture.

2009 HL Q. 2

Section B

03 (a) (i) What is a tropism?
(ii) What is a plant growth regulator?
(b) Answer the following in relation to an investigation that you carried out into the effect of the growth regulator IAA on plant tissue.
(i) What plant tissue did you use?

Leaving Certificate examination questions

(ii) Describe how you carried out the investigation.
(iii) Describe the control that you used.
(iv) Compare the results that you obtained in the experiment and in the control.
2010 HL Q. 9

04 Growth regulators in plants can promote growth or inhibit it.
(a) Give an example of each of the following:
   (i) A growth regulator that promotes growth.
   (ii) A growth regulator that inhibits growth.
(b) In the course of your studies you investigated the effect of a growth regulator on plant tissue. Answer the following questions in relation to that investigation.
   (i) Name the plant that you used.
   (ii) Describe how you carried out the investigation.
   (iii) Give a safety precaution that you took while carrying out the investigation.
   (iv) State the results that you obtained.
2008 HL Q. 8

Section C

05 In relation to plant responses:
1. What name is given to a plant's response to light?
2. Name **one** growth regulator produced in plants.
3. Where in a plant are growth regulators produced?
4. Give one way by which plants can protect themselves from attack.
2012 OL Q. 15 (b) (i)

06 (i) State two ways in which growth regulators in plants are similar to hormones in animals.
(ii) Name a plant growth regulator that promotes growth and give a precise location for a site of its action.
Through which part of a stem are growth promoters transported?
Outline two uses of growth promoters in horticulture.
Give an example of a growth regulator that inhibits growth.
2013 HL Q. 10 (c)

07 (a) (i) What do you understand by the term *adverse external environment*?
(ii) Give two ways in which plants protect themselves from adverse external environments.
(b) (i) Name the group of substances in plants which control responses to external stimuli.
   (ii) 1. What name is given to the regions in plants in which these substances are produced?
   2. Give locations for two of these regions.
   (iii) Most plant shoots are positively phototropic. Explain the underlined term.
   (iv) How does the plant benefit from this response?
   (v) Explain the mechanism of response by a plant to a named external stimulus.
2011 HL Q. 11 (a), (b)

08 The graph shows the effect of varying auxin concentration on the root and shoot of a plant.

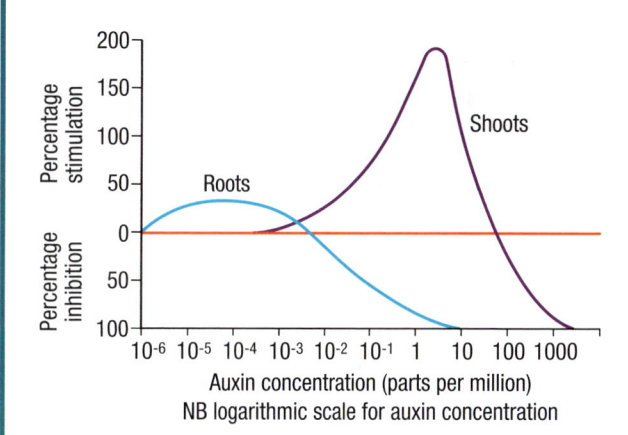

(i) What is an auxin?
(ii) At what approximate auxin concentration does the root receive maximum stimulation?
(iii) At what approximate auxin concentration does the shoot receive maximum stimulation?
(iv) What is the effect on the root of an auxin concentration of 10^{-2} parts per million?
(v) Give two examples of uses of synthetic (man-made) auxins.
(vi) Describe three methods used by plants to protect themselves from adverse external environments.
2005 HL Q. 14 (b)

Past examination questions

OL	2012 Q. 15 (b) (i)	2011 Q. 8 (b) (viii)	2009 Q. 6	2004 Q. 1 (c)		
HL	2013 Q. 14 (c)	2011 Q. 11 (a), (b)	2010 Q. 9	2009 Q. 2	2008 Q. 8	2006 Q. 6 (d), Q. 7 (b) (i)
	2005 Q. 14 (b)	2004 Q. 15 (b)	SEC Sample Q. 9			

29 The Human Nervous System

After studying this chapter you should be able to:

1. Describe the structure and function of the human nervous system.
2. Describe the structure of the neuron.
3. Name and give the role of the different types of neuron.
4. Describe how nerve impulses travel along and between nerves.
5. Describe the parts of the central nervous system.
6. Locate the cerebrum, the cerebellum, the hypothalamus and the medulla oblongata on a diagram of the brain and give their functions.
7. Draw a labelled diagram of a cross-section of the spinal cord.
8. Describe the peripheral nervous system.
9. Describe the mechanism and function of reflex actions.
10. Give a cause, prevention and treatment for paralysis or Parkinson's disease.

Animal response to stimuli

In complex animals like humans, responses to change in the environment have to be coordinated if the organism is going to respond in an organised way. The two coordinating systems in the human are the nervous system (see Chapter 29) and the endocrine system (see Chapter 31). These two systems work with the sensory system and the musculoskeletal system. For coordination to work, a receptor is required to pick up a stimulus, e.g. the eye is a receptor that picks up information about the external environment. This receptor needs to send a message to an effector to get a response. The message that is sent may be either a nervous message or a chemical message, depending on which system is being used. Generally, where fast, short responses are required, the nervous system is used and where slower, more long-term responses are needed, the endocrine system is used. The structures that produce the response are called effectors. The muscles (often working with the skeletal system) or glands are the most commonly used effectors.

Nervous system	Endocrine system
Electrochemical message	Chemical message
Carried in nerve cells	Carried in the blood
Fast-acting	Slow-acting
Short-term effect	Long-term effect

Table 29.1 A comparison of the nervous and endocrine systems

29 | The Human Nervous System

The nervous system

1 The human nervous system is made up of two parts (Fig 29.1): the **central nervous system (CNS)** and the **peripheral nervous system (PNS)**.

The central nervous system includes the **brain** and the spinal cord. The CNS acts as the central controlling region of the nervous system. It processes information (often from the senses), makes decisions and issues instructions to the effectors.

The peripheral nervous system includes the nerves fibres carrying messages to and from the CNS. These nerves are made up of bundles of tiny nerve cells called **neurons**. A cross-section of one such nerve will look like a section through a large telephone cable, where hundreds of fine insulated wires are held in a bundle (Fig 29.2).

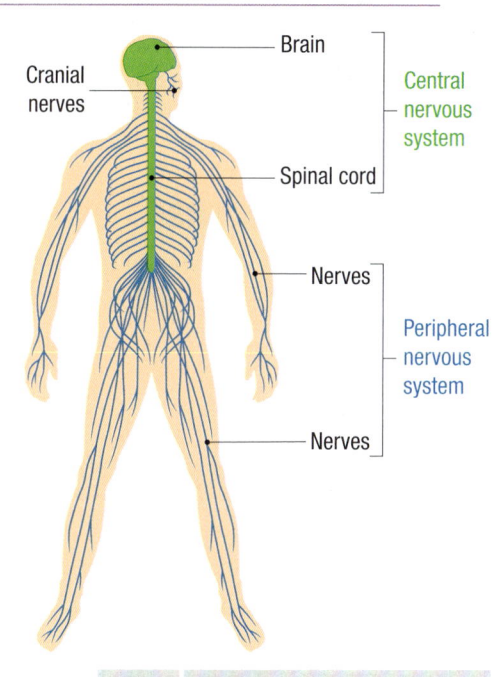

Neurons

2 Neurons are the basic unit of the nervous system. They are very specialised cells, designed to carry information as an electrochemical message.

> A **neuron** is a nerve cell.

Structure

- Neurons have a **nucleus** like most other **cells**. This nucleus is contained in a structure called a **cell body** (Fig 29.3). The cell body contains all the usual organelles found in every other cell and produces the chemicals (one such chemical is a neurotransmitter) and energy required by the neuron.
- Short branch-like structures, called **dendrites**, are connected to one end of the cell body. Dendrites carry messages towards the cell body.
- Extending out of the cell body is a single long tube called the **axon**, which carries messages away from the cell body.

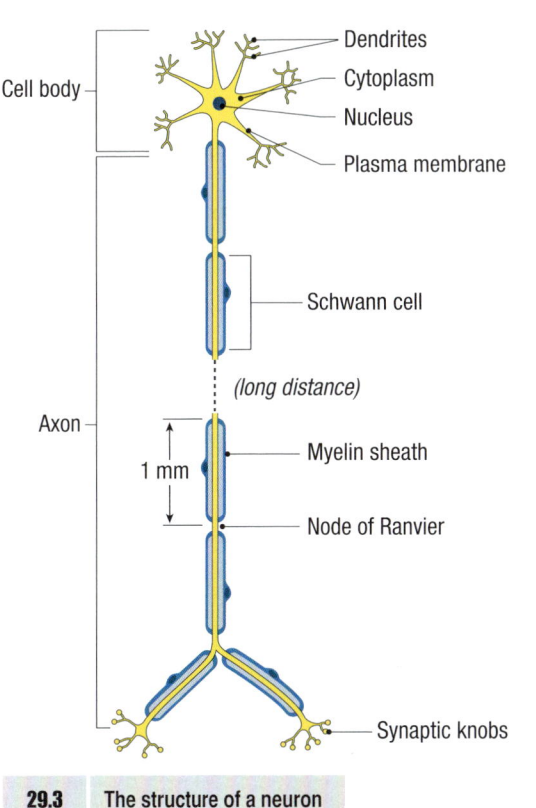

29.1 The human nervous system

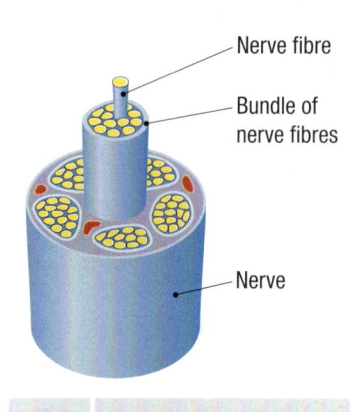

29.2 The structure of a nerve

29.3 The structure of a neuron

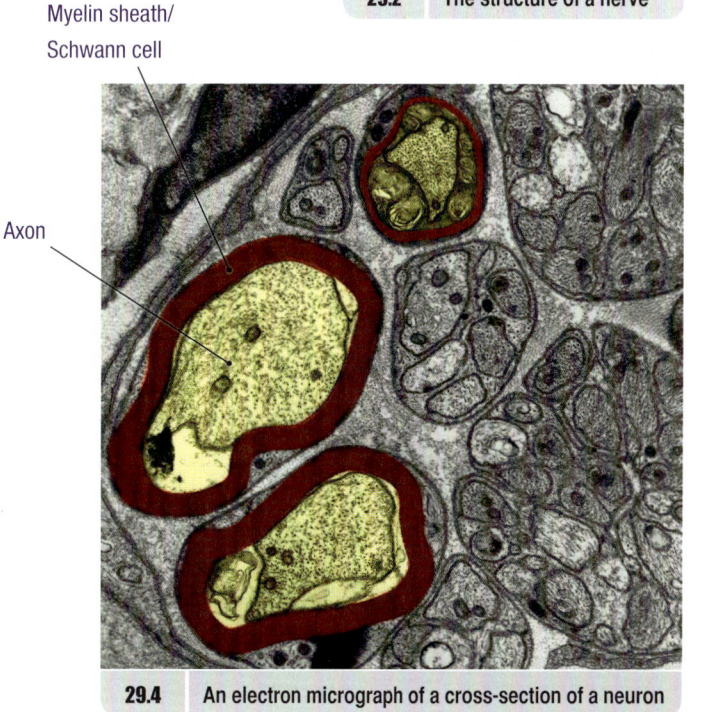

29.4 An electron micrograph of a cross-section of a neuron

LIFE LEAVING CERTIFICATE BIOLOGY | UNIT 3 THE ORGANISM | 389

29 | The Human Nervous System

- In many neurons, there is a fatty **myelin sheath** around the axon that acts as an insulating layer and speeds up the transport of messages along the neuron. The myelin sheath is produced by specialised **Schwann cells**, which wrap around the neuron but do not completely cover it, leaving small gaps called nodes of Ranvier between each Schwann cell. These gaps help to speed up the message transfer along the neurons.
- The axon eventually divides into a number of fine branches that end in little bulbs called **synaptic knobs** (Fig 29.3).

Types of neurons

There are three main types of neuron (neurone) found in the nervous system. Each type of neuron has a different function and a slightly different structure (Fig 29.5).

1. The **motor neurons** carry messages from the central nervous system to effectors, i.e. the muscles. These neurons have short dendrites and a long axon.

> A **motor neuron** is a nerve cell that carries messages from the CNS to an effector.

2. The **sensory neurons** carry messages from the receptors, i.e. the eye, into the central nervous system. These neurons have a cell body at the end of a short branch to one side of the axon.

> A **sensory neuron** is a nerve cell that carries messages to the CNS from a sense organ.

3. The **interneuron** carries messages from one nerve cell to another and is found only within the central nervous system. These have axons of differing lengths.

> An **interneuron** carries messages between nerve cells.

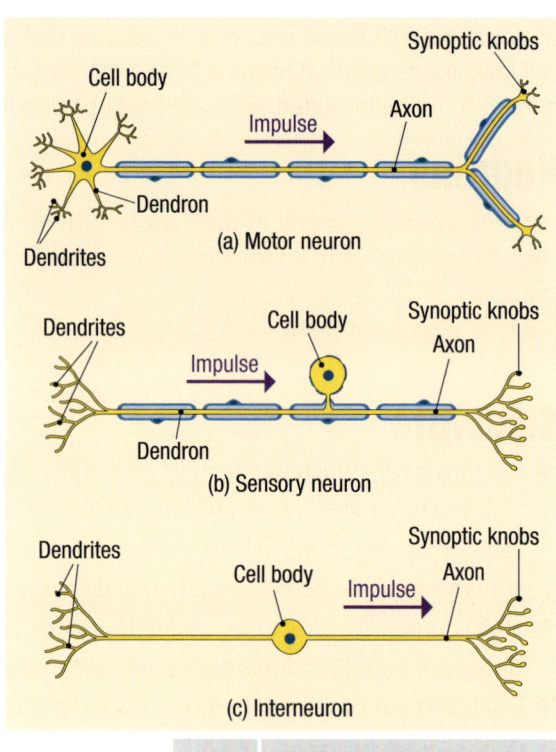

29.5 The three types of neurons

Message transfer

- The neuron will carry messages down its length once there is a stimulus of sufficient strength at the dendrites.
- If the stimulus is not sufficiently strong, no message is transmitted.
- Once this **threshold** level is reached, a message is transmitted. It does not matter if the stimulus is above the required strength, as the same message is sent even if the stimulus is twice that required. The message sent in all neurons is the same.

> The **threshold** is the minimum stimulation required to send a message along a neuron.

- The neuron acts like a simple switch. It is either switched on (it sends a message) or it is switched off (it does not send a message). This is known as the 'all or nothing rule'. This simple procedure ensures the message is not interfered with as it travels up the neuron.
- The message is an **electrical impulse** moving along the neuron.
- When the impulse reaches the end of the neuron it arrives at a **synaptic knob**.
- The electrical impulse is generated by ions moving from one side to the other of the cell membrane.

> A **synapse** is the region where two neurons meet.

> A **synaptic cleft** is the gap between two neurons.

- The electrical impulse cannot be transmitted to the next neuron, as there is a tiny gap called the **synaptic cleft** between each neuron (Fig 29.6).
- In the synaptic knob, there are tiny vesicles containing chemicals called **neurotransmitters**. One common neurotransmitter is **acetylcholine**.
- These chemicals are released by the pre-synaptic neuron when the impulse arrives at the synapse.
- They travel across the synaptic cleft and cause an impulse to start in the post-synaptic neuron.
- **Enzymes** are then released into, or are present in, the synaptic cleft, which break down the neurotransmitters.
- As a result, only one impulse is sent each time a neurotransmitter is released across a synaptic cleft.
- The broken down products of the neurotransmitters are then reabsorbed by the pre-synaptic neuron and used to manufacture more neurotransmitters in the cell body (Fig 29.7).
- Before a second message can pass the synapse the system has to be 'reset' – this is called the **refractory period**. So there is a slight delay between one message and the next.

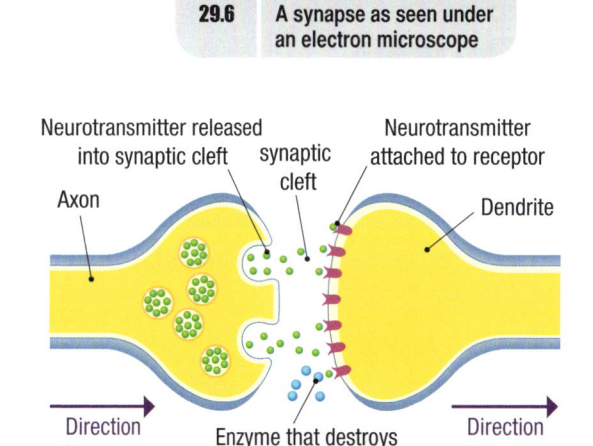

29.6 A synapse as seen under an electron microscope

> A **neurotransmitter** is a chemical that carries a nerve message across a synapse.

29.7 Message transfer at a synapse

Drugs and the nervous system

Many drugs that influence the central nervous system affect the synapse by increasing or decreasing the production of the neurotransmitter or by affecting the rate of breakdown of the neurotransmitter. Cocaine, for example, interferes with the normal breakdown of a neurotransmitter, **dopamine**. Dopamine is involved in pleasurable feelings. When dopamine is not broken down, the synapse keeps on transmitting messages and euphoria follows. The body reduces its production of dopamine, which results in addiction as the user has to take cocaine to produce enough dopamine to feel 'normal'. Also, more and more cocaine needs to be taken to give the effect originally felt as the body becomes tolerant of cocaine.

The central nervous system

The entire central nervous system, which is made up of the brain and spinal cord, is surrounded by bone for protection. Also surrounding the CNS is a triple-layered membrane, the **meninges**. The innermost layer of the meninges is very fine. The middle layer is fibrous, filled with **cerebrospinal fluid** and the arteries for the brain or spinal cord. The outermost layer is very tough (Fig 29.8).

As the central nervous system has developed from a tube, the centre of it is hollow. This hollow centre of the brain and the spinal cord is filled with cerebrospinal fluid.

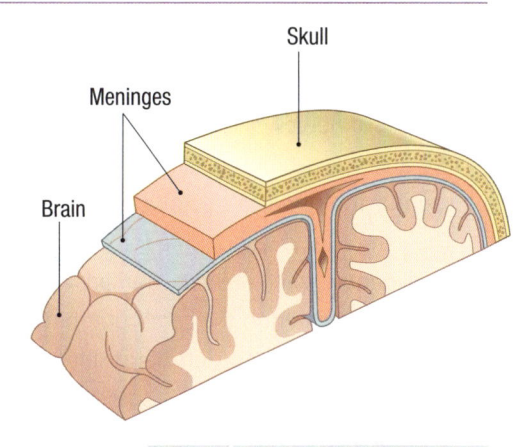

29.8 Protection for the brain

Grey matter is the part of the CNS that contains cell bodies and has a darker colour.

White matter is the part of the CNS that contains the axons and has a lighter colour.

The central nervous system is made up of neurons and other specialised cells. Groups of cell bodies from the neurons have a dark or grey appearance. The myelin sheath surrounding the axons and dendrites give them a white appearance. This is the origin of the **grey matter** and **white matter** of the central nervous system. The parts of the CNS that have a lot of cell bodies present have a grey appearance (this is where decisions are made) and the parts of the CNS that are primarily made up of axons have a white appearance (these carry messages).

The brain

When the brain develops in the embryo, it starts out as three swellings on the nerve cord. These three sections develop into the main sections of the brain:

1. The **cerebrum** (cerebral cortex) for higher thought and interpretation of sensory information.
2. The **thalamus** and **hypothalamus**, which process incoming information.
3. The **cerebellum** and **medulla oblongata** for motor coordination and involuntary muscle control (Fig 29.9).

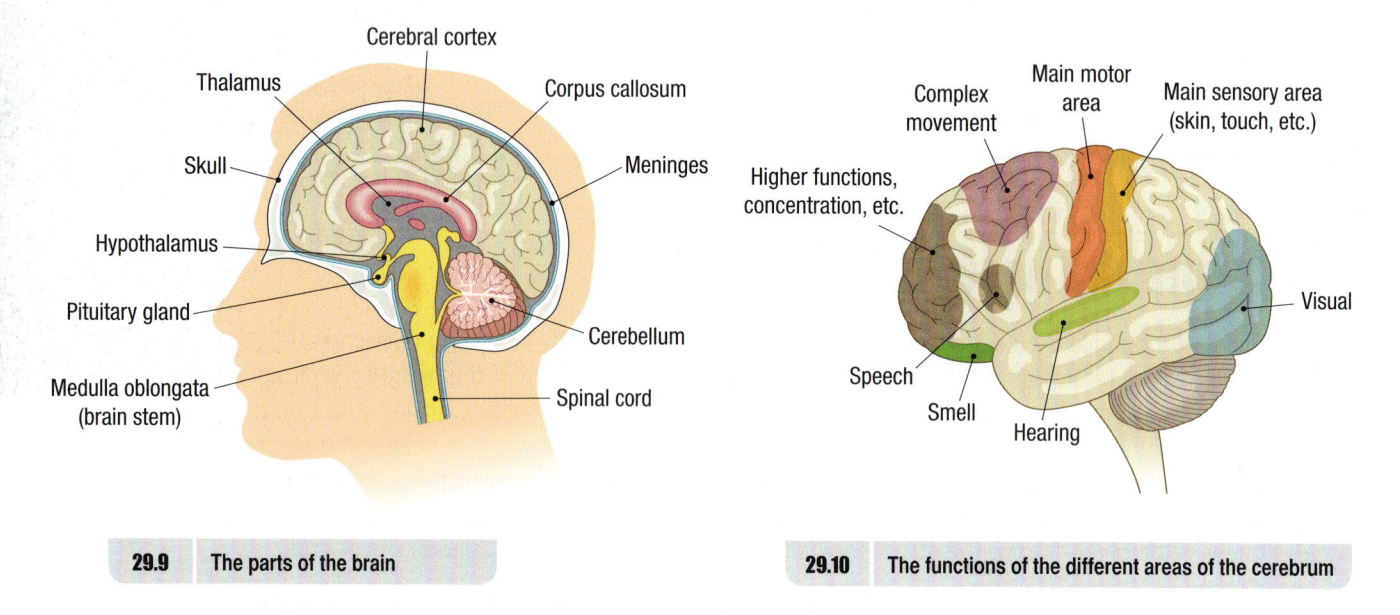

| 29.9 | The parts of the brain |

| 29.10 | The functions of the different areas of the cerebrum |

The cerebrum

The largest part of the human brain is the cerebrum.

- This is divided into two halves called **cerebral hemispheres**. These two hemispheres are connected by a bundle of nerves called the **corpus callosum**. The surface or cortex of the cerebrum is grey, and to increase the area for decision making is very heavily folded. It is estimated that the surface area of the cerebrum is roughly the same as a pillowcase.
- The cerebrum is responsible for consciousness and it is the section of the brain that governs reason and intelligence. Of all animals, humans have the most developed cerebrum.
- The nerves entering the cerebrum through the corpus callosum cross over so the right-hand side of the cerebrum controls the left-hand side of the body and vice versa.
- Each half of the cerebrum also organises different skills. The left-hand side is generally responsible for language and mathematical ability whereas the right-hand side is responsible for musical and spatial sense.
- Some areas on the surface of the cerebrum have been shown to be the controlling areas for specific functions. These are shown in Fig 29.10. These areas of the **cortex** control various parts of the body or receive sensory information from the same parts of the body.

Thalamus and hypothalamus

Directly beneath the cerebrum are the thalamus and hypothalamus.

- The thalamus receives all the messages from the senses and directs them to the correct place in the cerebrum.
- The hypothalamus is concerned with the maintenance of a steady state in the body or **homeostasis** (see Chapters 26 and 27). Some of the actions it controls are: hunger, sleep, thirst, **osmoregulation** and sexual activity.
- Attached to the underside of the hypothalamus is the **pituitary gland**. This **endocrine gland** is controlled by the hypothalamus and this is the link between the nervous and hormonal systems (see Chapter 31).

The cerebellum

The second biggest part of the brain, the cerebellum (little brain) is found beneath and to the back of the cerebrum.

- It is a very dense tissue with a lot of nerve cells.
- Its function is to coordinate the voluntary muscles so they function in a smooth manner.
- The cerebellum is also involved in the maintenance of balance.

The medulla oblongata

Connecting the brain to the spinal cord is the medulla oblongata or brain stem.

- This controls the involuntary muscles such as the heart and the muscles involved in breathing and swallowing.

The spinal cord

The remainder of the CNS is called the spinal cord. This runs down the middle of the vertebral column. A cross-section of the spinal cord is shown in Figs 29.11 and 29.12.

- The spinal cord acts as a coordinating centre, sending messages from the body to the brain.
- The spinal cord also controls most of the **reflex actions** that occur in the body.
- The hollow central canal of the spinal cord is filled with cerebrospinal fluid. The grey matter, in a butterfly shape (cell bodies), surrounds the hollow centre. Outside this is the white matter (fibres). Like the brain, the spinal cord is protected by the meninges.
- Leading into the spinal cord are the spinal nerves of the peripheral nervous system (PNS). There are 31 pairs of spinal nerves. Each spinal nerve branches into two as it enters the spinal cord.
- The dorsal root leads into the back of the cord and contains a swelling or ganglion containing the cell bodies of the sensory neurons.
- The ventral root comes out the front of the cord. Because the ventral root contains the motor neurons, it therefore has no ganglion as the cell bodies of motor neurons are found in the grey matter.

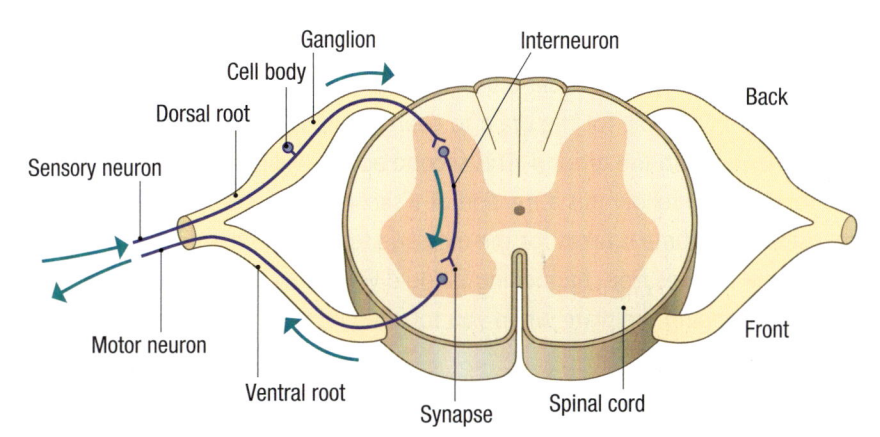

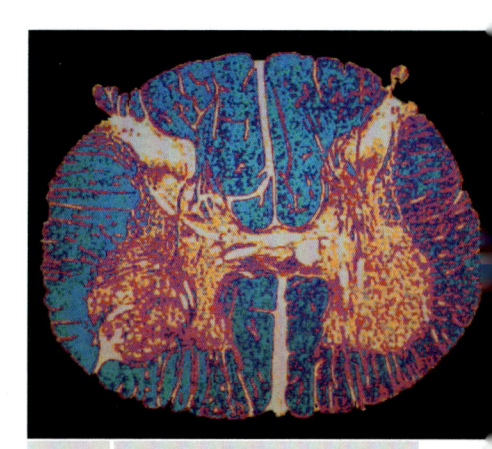

29.11 A section through a spinal cord

29.12 T.S. of the spinal cord

The peripheral nervous system

The peripheral nervous system is that part of the nervous system which is outside of the CNS. This mostly comprises the motor and sensory neurons which take the messages to and from the CNS (Fig 29.1).

- Motor neurons take messages away from the CNS in a long axon and their cell bodies are found with the grey matter of the CNS.
- Sensory neurons take massages from the senses into the CNS in a long dendron and their cell bodies are found in a swelling (ganglion) on the dorsal root of the spinal cord.

Reflex actions

The control of reflex actions is an important function of the spinal cord. A reflex is an automatic, involuntary response to an internal or external stimulus. Some reflexes in the head, i.e. blinking, use the brain. Other responses, such as the 'knee jerk', use the spinal cord and by-pass the brain. The pathway, as shown in Fig 29.13, is called the **reflex arc**.

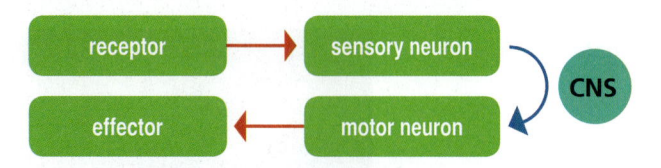

> **D** A **reflex action** is the unthinking response to a nerve stimulus.

> **D** A **reflex arc** is the nerve pathway of a reflex action.

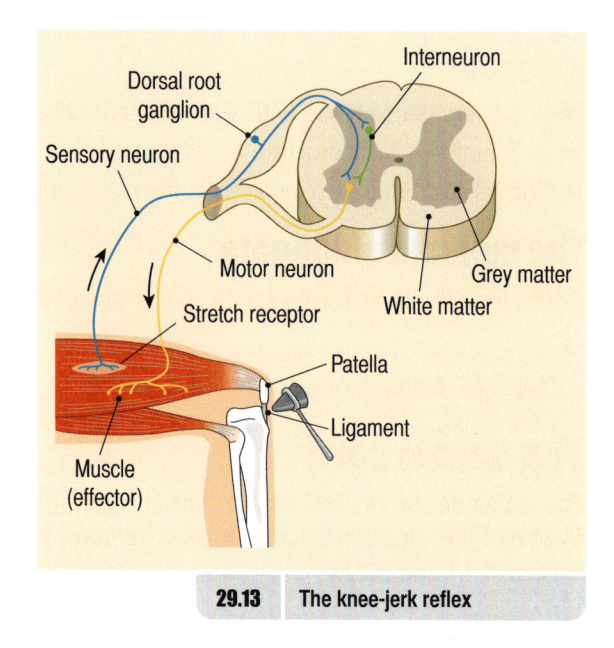

29.13 The knee-jerk reflex

- The knee-jerk reflex is the simplest type of reflex action. When a sharp knock is given below the kneecap, the kneecap pulls on the muscle stimulating a stretch receptor in the muscle. The nerve impulse is sent up to the nerve cord and stimulates a motor neuron attached to the same muscle. This causes the muscle to contract, pulling the lower leg outward. This reflex is used to keep you upright. If you are standing and begin to fall backwards, the stretch receptor is stimulated as you pull on your kneecap and this reflex brings you upright again (Fig 29.13).
- The blinking reflex uses the brain as the eye is connected to the brain directly and not through the spinal cord. There is still no conscious thought involved in the action.
- Reflexes allow you to respond quickly to danger without any delay in the transfer of messages to the brain for decision making.
- Some reflexes are more complex than these simple responses. If you pick up a hot plate, the heat receptors in the skin will register this fact and you will send nerve messages to cause a number of muscles in your hand and arm to withdraw your hand from the hot object. You may also send a message to the larynx, causing a shout. To achieve this, the spinal cord needs to send the message along its length to different motor neurons.
- The brain is not involved, but it is possible for the brain to override the reflex. If your dinner is on the plate you may try to save it from landing on the ground. This second action will occur after the first. Your hand first pulls away from the plate, then you follow this a fraction of a second later with a grab for your dinner! The second response demonstrates the time it takes for the message to travel to the brain and back.
- It is also possible to stop some reflexes from happening. Should you know in advance that the plate was hot, you could stop yourself dropping the plate when you touched it by consciously preventing the reflex from occurring.

Nervous system disorders

SYLLABUS REQUIREMENT:
The syllabus requires you to know about one disorder.

Parkinson's disease

There are some disorders of the nervous system that are caused by problems with neurotransmitters. **Parkinson's disease** is one such disorder.

Cause

Patients suffering from Parkinson's disease are missing **dopamine**, due to the loss or damage of tissue in the brain that makes dopamine. Dopamine is used to regulate the nerves controlling muscle activity.

Prevention

There is no known preventative treatment available.

Treatment

There is currently no cure for this disease. Many symptoms can be reduced by the drug levodopa, which the body converts into dopamine, helping to replace the missing neurotransmitter. Some experiments have been done in transplanting dopamine-producing tissue into the patient's brain. The results have been variable to date. For some patients an electrical stimulation system implanted into the brain has had some success in reducing the symptoms of the disease.

29.14 The effect of paralysis

Paralysis

Cause

Paralysis can occur due to physical damage to the spinal cord. A protein that prevents growth surrounds neurons, which run up and down the white matter of the spinal cord. Damage to these neurons cannot therefore be repaired in the normal way.

Prevention

Much can be done to reduce the damage to the spine of accident victims if they are handled in such a way that damage is not increased when they are being moved. In most cases, this involves immobilising the neck and head. However, once the nerves are severed the damage is irreversible.

Treatment

At the moment, there is no cure for such damage (Fig 29.14). Some experimental work has been done in bridging such gaps with other neurons or by splicing the broken neurons through the grey matter, which will allow growth. This work has only been carried out using experimental animals.

Summary

- Humans use two systems to respond to stimuli: the nervous system for fast action and the endocrine system for slower responses.
- The nervous system is made up of:
  - The central nervous system (CNS) that processes messages and controls our responses.
  - The peripheral nervous (PNS) that carries messages to and from the CNS.
- Individual nerve cells are called neurons. They contain:
  - The cell body – containing the nucleus.
  - The dendrites – short branches carrying messages to the cell body.
  - The axon – a long tube carrying messages from the cell body.

29 The Human Nervous System

Summary

- Synaptic knobs – swollen ends of the axon used to connect with the neighbouring cell.
- Myelin sheath – a fatty layer to insulate the neuron: produced by Schwann cells.

Neuron type	Location of cell body	Direction of impulse	Structure
Motor	In the CNS	Away from the CNS to effectors	Long axon, short dendrites
Sensory	Outside the CNS	Towards CNS from receptor	Short axon, cell body to one side
Inter	In the CNS	Carry messages around the CNS	Axons of varying length

- Neurons are either switched on or off. The strength of their message does not differ. The message is an electrical impulse sent down the neuron using ions. Once a message is sent, the neuron has to rest for a short while.
- The region where two neurons meet is called the synapse, where messages are carried as chemicals (neurotransmitters) such as dopamine. Once used, these are broken down by enzymes.
- The CNS:
  - comprises the brain and spinal cord;
  - is hollow and filled with cerebrospinal fluid;
  - is surrounded by the meninges (three layers);
  - contains the grey matter (cell bodies) to make decisions and the white matter (axons) to transport messages.

Parts of the brain	Function(s)
Cerebrum	Controls sight, hearing, intelligence, memory
Thalamus	Relays messages to the cerebrum
Hypothalamus	Homeostasis
Pituitary gland	Produces hormones
Cerebellum	Controls coordination of voluntary muscles and balance
Medulla oblongata	Controls involuntary muscles, e.g. the diaphragm and muscles in the gut wall

- The spinal cord has the grey matter on the inside and white matter on the outside (opposite to the brain), with 31 pairs of spinal nerves containing motor and sensory neurons leaving it.
- Grey matter is the part of the CNS that contains cell bodies and has a darker colour.
- White matter is the part of the CNS that contains the axons and has a lighter colour.
- Reflex actions occur when you have an involuntary response to a stimulus, e.g. the knee jerk.
- A reflex arc is the nerve pathway of a reflex action.
- Reflex actions help to protect the body.

Disorders of the nervous system	Parkinson's disease	Paralysis
Cause	The absence of a neurotransmitter (dopamine).	Damage to spinal cord
Prevention	It cannot be prevented	No prevention or cure
Treatment	Some symptoms can be relieved by levodopa	No treatment to reverse paralysis

Review questions

01. (a) What are the two methods or response that a human has to a stimulus?
    (b) Compare these two systems.
02. (a) What are the two parts of the nervous system?
    (b) What are the components of each of the parts mentioned in (a)?
03. (a) Draw a labelled diagram of a nerve cell.
    (b) Give the function of each part.
    (c) What is the name of this cell?
04. (a) What are the differences between a motor and a sensory neuron?
    (b) What is the purpose of the interneuron?
05. (a) Messages sent in the nervous system are sent by the 'all or nothing rule'. How does this work?
    (b) What is the threshold in relation to nerve action?
    (c) What is a synapse?
    (d) Describe what happens when a nervous message reaches a synapse.
06. (a) What is a neurotransmitter?
    (b) Name a neurotransmitter.
    (c) Why are enzymes required at the synapse?
07. (a) What are the component parts of the CNS?
    (b) List the main areas of the brain.
    (c) Give a function for each part.
    (d) Where are the meninges found?
    (e) What makes up the meninges?
    (f) What is the function of the meninges?
    (g) Where do the nervous system and the hormonal system interconnect?
08. (a) Draw a labelled diagram of a T.S. of the spinal cord.
    (b) Give a function for each part.
    (c) What is present in the grey matter?
    (d) What is present in the white matter?
    (e) Distinguish between the CNS and PNS.
09. (a) With the aid of a labelled diagram describe a reflex action.
    (b) What is the advantage of not having the brain involved in a reflex action?
    (c) What is the purpose of reflex actions?
    (d) How might you demonstrate a reflex action?
10. (a) In the case of a person suffering from Parkinson's disease give: a cause, a treatment and a preventative measure (if any).
    (b) Give a cause, a treatment (if any) for paralysis.

Examination style questions

Section A

01. The diagram represents a transverse section through the spinal cord of a mammal to show a reflex arc.

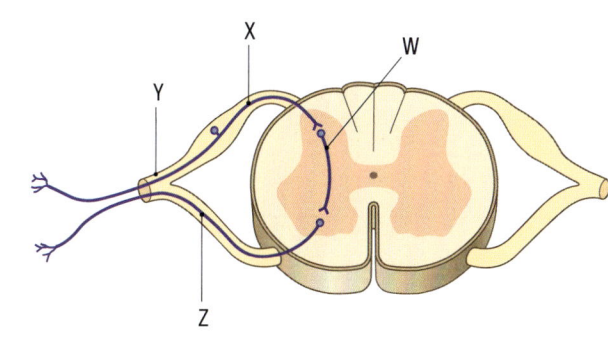

    (a) Name the parts labelled W, X, Y and Z.
    (b) Draw the diagram into your copy and mark E on the diagram to show the position of the effector.
    (c) Place arrows on the diagram to illustrate the direction of the reflex arc nerve pathway.
    (d) Suggest a function of a reflex action for humans.

02. (a) What is the CNS?
    (b) What are the components of the CNS?
    (c) Name the three types of neuron found in a human.
    (d) What is a neurotransmitter?
    (e) Name a neurotransmitter.

Section C

03. (a) (i) Draw a diagram to show the structure of a motor neuron.
        (ii) Label the following parts: cell body, dendrites, axon, Schwann cell, synaptic knobs.
        (iii) Mark on the diagram the direction of travel of nerve impulses along the neuron.
        (iv) Give the function of any three of the listed parts.
        (v) What is a nerve impulse?
    (b) Write notes on three of the following:
        (i) Neurotransmitters.
        (ii) The central nervous system.
        (iii) Synapses.
        (iv) A named nervous system disorder.

29 The Human Nervous System

Examination style questions

04 (a) (i) What is the PNS?
   (ii) Name two components of the PNS.
(b) (i) What is a synapse?
   (ii) Describe the sequence of events that occurs when a nerve message arrives at a synapse.
   (iii) Cocaine has the effect of blocking the normal breakdown of a neurotransmitter. It is a stimulant.
      a. Why is it necessary to break down the neurotransmitter?
      b. Explain why you think cocaine is a stimulant.
(c) (i) What are the main areas of the brain?
   (ii) Give a function for each of the areas mentioned in (i).
   (iii) What is the name of the nerve action that occurs when the brain is not involved.
   (iv) With the aid of a labelled diagram describe how this reaction occurs.

05 (a) (i) Distinguish between white matter and grey matter.
   (ii) What is the function of the meninges?
(b) (i) Explain the term synapse.
   (ii) Describe the events that occur between the arrival of a nerve impulse at one side of a synapse and the generation of a nerve impulse on the other side of the synapse.

(c) Certain drugs work by copying the action of acetylcholine, a transmitter substance that is released from swellings at the ends of neurons. Other drugs work by blocking the action of acetylcholine.
The table below shows some of the effects of some substances on the human nervous system.

Substance	Site of action	Most common effect
Botulinum toxin	Pre-synaptic membrane	Prevents release of acetylcholine
Nicotine	Post-synaptic membrane	Copies the action of acetylcholine
Curare	Junction between nerve and muscle	Blocks the action of acetylcholine

(i) By means of a large labelled diagram of a synapse, indicate the precise site of action of the following substances, using the appropriate letters.
W = botulinum toxin.   X = nicotine
(ii) Suggest the effect you would expect each substance named in the table to have on the post-synaptic generation of a nerve impulse.

Leaving Certificate examination questions

Section A

01 The diagram shows a motor neuron.

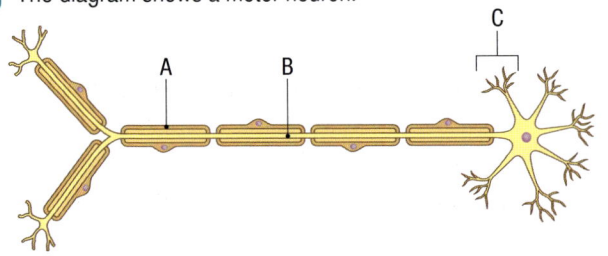

(a) Identify parts A, B and C.
(b) Give a function of A.
(c) Place an arrow on the diagram to show the direction of the impulse.
(d) Give a function of C.
(e) Place an X on the diagram at a point at which a neurotransmitter substance is secreted.
(f) What is the role of the motor neuron?

2008 HL Q. 4

Section C

02 The diagram shows the human nervous system.

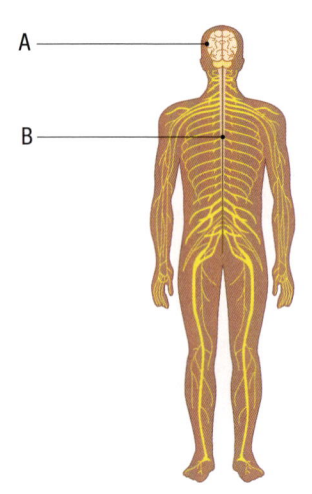

(i) Name the parts labelled A and B.
(ii) Nerve impulses are carried around the body by neurons. Name any two types of **neuron**.

Leaving Certificate examination questions

(iii) Tiny gaps are found where one neuron ends and the next one begins.
  1. What are these gaps called?
  2. What substances carry nerve impulses across the gaps?

(iv) 1. Name **one** disorder of the human nervous system.
  2. Give **one** cause of the disorder.
  3. Suggest a means of treating the disorder.

2014 OL Q. 12 (b)

03 The diagram shows part of a reflex arc.

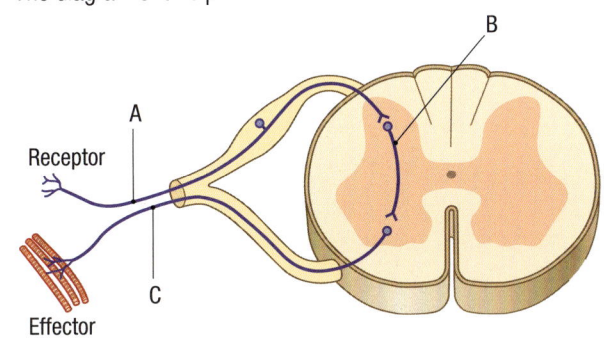

(i) Name neurons A, B and C.
(ii) In which direction is the impulse transmitted A → B → C or C → B → A?
(iii) Name the small gaps between neurons.
(iv) Neurons produce neurotransmitter substances. What is their function?
(v) Give an example of a reflex action in humans.
(vi) Why are reflex actions important in humans?

2007 OL Q. 15 (a)

04 (a) Answer the following questions in relation to the human nervous system.
  (i) Name the **type** of particle whose movement in and out of neurons is an essential feature of nerve impulse transmission.
  (ii) One of the roles of particles referred to in (i) is the activation of neurotransmitters.
  Give an account of how neurotransmitters work.
  (iii) 1. Distinguish between the position of the cerebellum and the position of the cerebrum in the human brain.
  2. State **three** functions of the cerebrum.

(b) Read the following extract and then answer the questions below.

Alzheimer's diseases (a degenerative brain condition), like many other degenerative illnesses, is driven by genes and recently scientists have identified a group of genes that are thought to be associated with this disease. The disease is thought to be caused by a build-up of protein-based plaques in the brain, and investigators now believe they have an understanding of ways to interrupt that process. Technology is helping too, as researchers exploit new ways to scan the brain and detect the first signs of trouble, peering deeper into human and animal neural tissue to pinpoint the very molecules that give rise to the disease.

(Adapted from Alzheimer's Unlocked, TIME, Vol. 176, No. 17, 2010.)

  (i) What do you think is meant by the term 'degenerative illnesses'?
  (ii) Is Alzheimer's disease driven by a single gene or by many genes?
  (iii) What is thought to cause the disease?
  (iv) Suggest a possible symptom of Alzheimer's disease.
  (v) How is the advance of technology helping in the fight against the disease?
  (vi) There are probably more people suffering from the disease now than ever before. Suggest a reason for this.
  (vii) Name another disorder of the nervous system **and** give a possible treatment for it.

2014 HL Q. 11

05 (a) (i) Distinguish between the central nervous system and the peripheral nervous system. Include a clear reference to each in your answer.
  (ii) Give one way in which a nervous response differs from a hormonal response.

(b) (i) Draw a large labelled diagram of a motor neuron.
  (ii) Give one function each of any two parts found only in neurons.
  (iii) Place an arrow on or near your diagram to indicate the direction of impulse transmission.
  (iv) Name and state the role of any two types of neuron, other than the motor neuron.

(c) (i) State one function for each of the following parts of the human brain: cerebrum; hypothalamus; cerebellum; medulla oblongata.

29 | The Human Nervous System

Leaving Certificate examination questions

(ii) In relation to the nervous system, distinguish between grey matter and white matter. Include a clear reference to each in your answer.
(iii) In the case of either paralysis or Parkinson's disease state:
  1. A possible cause, other than accident.
  2. A method of treatment.
  2012 HL Q. 13

06 (a) (i) Name a disorder of the human nervous system.
  (ii) In the case of the disorder referred to in part (i) state:
    1. A possible cause.
    2. A means of prevention or a treatment.
  (b) (i) What is a reflex action?
  (ii) Give one example of a reflex action.
  (iii) Suggest an advantage of reflex actions.

(iv) The parts of the nervous system involved in a reflex action make up a reflex arc. Draw a large labelled diagram to show the structures involved in a reflex arc. Place arrows on your diagram to show the direction of impulse transmission in the reflex arc.
2010 HL Q. 11

07 (a) (i) Draw and label sufficient of two neurons to show a synaptic cleft.
  (ii) Describe the sequence of events that allows an impulse to be transmitted across a synapse from one neuron to the next.
  (iii) Suggest a possible role for a drug in relation to the events that you have outlined in (ii).
  2004 HL Q. 15 (a)

Past examination questions

OL	2014 Q. 12 (b)	2012 Q. 15 (b) (ii)	2007 Q. 15 (a)			
HL	2014 Q. 11 (b), (c)	2012 Q. 13	2010 Q. 11 (a), (b)	2009 Q. 15 (c) (ii)	2008 Q. 4	2006 Q. 14 (b)
	2005 Q. 14 (c) (iii)	2004 Q. 15 (a)				

The Sense Organs

30

After studying this chapter you should be able to:

1. Describe the role of the brain in interpreting sensory messages from different sense receptors.
2. Describe the five senses.
3. Describe the structure and function of the ear.
4. Describe the corrective measures necessary for long-sightedness and short-sightedness or for hearing loss.
5. Describe the structure and function of the eye.

Receiving messages in the brain

1 The **brain** interprets messages sent to it by the **sensory neurones**. These messages are a response to various stimuli. Before they can be sent along the neuron, the stimuli are converted into nervous messages by sensory receptors, which the brain then interprets. All nervous messages are the same. The messages coming from the eye and the ear are identical nerve impulses, but messages arriving at the auditory centre of the brain are interpreted as sound, and those arriving in the visual centre are interpreted as light. Sense cells are classified by the type of stimulus to which they respond.

- Some receptors respond to changes inside the body, i.e. blood pressure receptors in the arteries.
- Other receptors respond to changes in the external environment, i.e. light receptors in the eye.

The receptors are further divided into:

- **Chemoreceptors** that respond to chemicals, e.g. taste in the tongue, smell in the nose and receptors to blood pH.
- **Photoreceptors** that respond to light, e.g. rods and cones in the eye.
- **Mechanoreceptors** that respond to physical change, e.g. pressure receptors in the skin, sound receptors in the ear and receptors used in balance.
- **Thermoreceptors** that respond to temperature change, e.g. heat and cold receptors in the skin.
- **Proprioceptors** that give information about the position and movement of the body, e.g. stretch receptors in the muscles

Some specialised sense cells are grouped together to form sense **organs**. These produce the five senses – taste, smell, touch, hearing and sight.

Taste and smell

2 Smell and taste are two closely related senses. The sense of smell is located in the nose. Chemicals enter the nose along with the air and stimulate receptors in a moist membrane in the back of the nose (Fig 30.1).

Different chemicals stimulate different receptors and these responses are translated into 'smells' by the brain in the area of the **cerebrum** dealing with smell (see Chapter 29).

Taste is also a response to chemicals dissolved in the mouth. There are a very limited number of chemicals to which the tongue responds. The taste buds register four basic tastes: sweet, sour, bitter and salt. These responses are located on different parts of the tongue (Fig 30.2). Recently a new 'taste' has been described called umami. This is believed to make other tastes more intense.

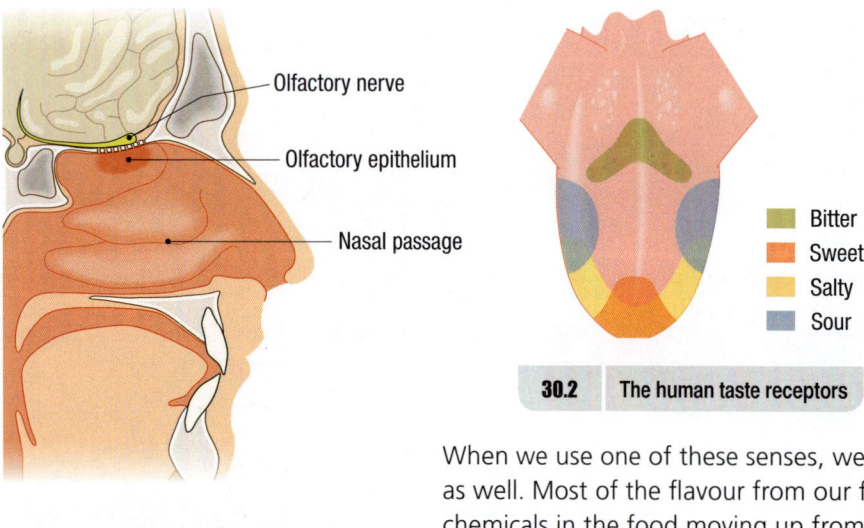

30.1 The smell receptors in the nose

30.2 The human taste receptors

- Bitter
- Sweet
- Salty
- Sour

When we use one of these senses, we usually use the other as well. Most of the flavour from our food comes from the chemicals in the food moving up from the back of our mouth to the nose, thus when we have a heavy cold, food is 'tasteless'. When we smell something, some of the chemicals can pass into the mouth and be 'tasted'.

Touch

Touch is a very generalised sense that is located in the skin (Fig 30.3). It involves the ability to sense a number of stimuli:

- **Touch receptors** have the ability to respond to a gentle force on the skin and are found mainly in hairless skin, i.e. palm of the hand.
- **Pressure receptors** respond to a greater force, and are found over the whole skin.
- **Pain receptors** are found over the whole skin.
- **Heat receptors** are found over the whole skin and respond to increases in heat.
- **Cold receptors** are found over the whole skin and respond to decreases in heat.

The final two senses are hearing and sight, which we will cover in detail below.

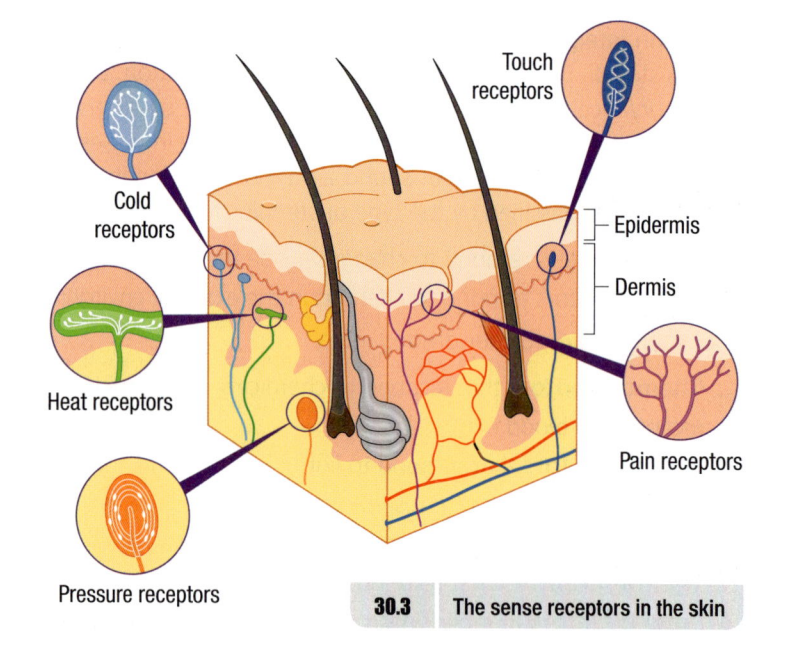

30.3 The sense receptors in the skin

Hearing

The ear is the sense organ that responds to sound. The ear is made up of three parts – the outer, middle and inner ear. These are protected by the bones of the skull. The outer and inner ear are air filled and the inner ear is fluid filled.

Hearing is the sensing of waves of pressure in the air (sound) as they hit your eardrum.

1. The sound is picked up by the **pinna** of the ear and funnelled into the **ear (auditory) canal**.
2. This ends in the **eardrum**, a membrane that is stretched across the canal (Fig 30.4). The tiny differences in air pressure cause the eardrum to vibrate. To ensure that this vibration is a true response to the pressure differential, there must be the same air pressure on both sides of the eardrum.
3. This is achieved by connecting the middle ear to the outside via the **Eustachian canal** (tube) that runs down into the back of the throat. This is why your ears 'pop' when exposed to sudden changes in pressure, e.g. when in a plane taking off.

The Sense Organs | 30

4. The vibration of the eardrum is transferred across the middle ear by the **ear ossicles** (Fig 30.5). These are the three smallest bones in the body and are called the **hammer**, the **anvil** and the **stirrup**. The hammer, anvil and stirrup are so called because of their shapes.
5. The last of these bones, the stirrup, is connected to a second membrane, the **oval window**. The hammer picks up the vibrations from the eardrum and the three bones act as levers, passing the vibrations to the oval window. Due to this leverage effect, and the fact that the oval window is smaller than the eardrum, the sound vibrations are amplified 20-fold.
6. The oval window leads into a coiled, fluid-filled structure called the **cochlea** (Fig 30.6). Tiny receptors in the shape of hairs pick up the vibrations and convert them into nerve messages.
7. These messages are carried along the auditory nerve to the brain for interpretation.
8. The vibrations pass along the cochlea, and are lost back into the middle ear at the **round window**.
9. The receptors nearest to the oval window respond to high-frequency sounds (whistle blowing) and the receptors at the apex of the cochlea farthest from the oval window respond to low-frequency sounds (drum beats).

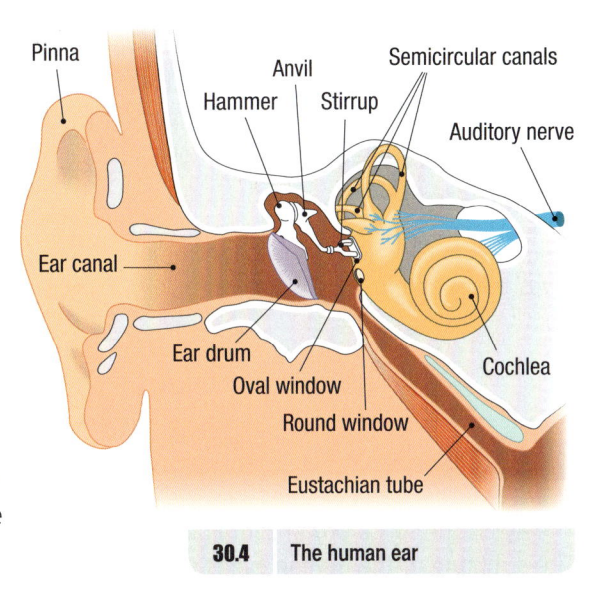

30.4 The human ear

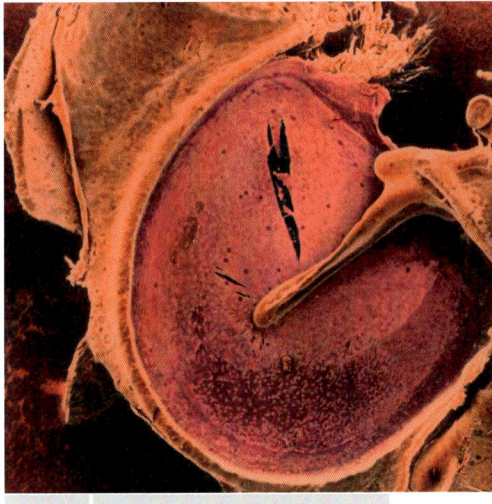

Balance

The inner ear has a function in balance. As well as the cochlea, the inner ear contains the **semi-circular canals**. These are fluid-filled structures containing receptors that respond to movement or to the position of the head. These are used to keep your posture and balance.

> **SYLLABUS REQUIREMENT:**
> You need to know about either the corrective measures for hearing loss or sight problems.

Hearing defects

1. Exposure to continuous loud noise, or sudden very loud noise (gunshot), causes so much vibration that the hairs in the **cochlea** are damaged and do not function. These receptors are irreplaceable. The hairs nearest the oval window are more likely to be damaged, so our response to high-frequency sounds is lost first. Some loss of receptors occurs with age, but hearing loss happens in younger people who are over-exposed to loud noises at work, e.g. using pneumatic drills or during leisure activities, e.g. rock concerts, or listening to loud music with ear phones.

30.5 The ear drum with attached hammer

Correction

Some help may be given to victims of such deafness with hearing aids (Fig 30.7).

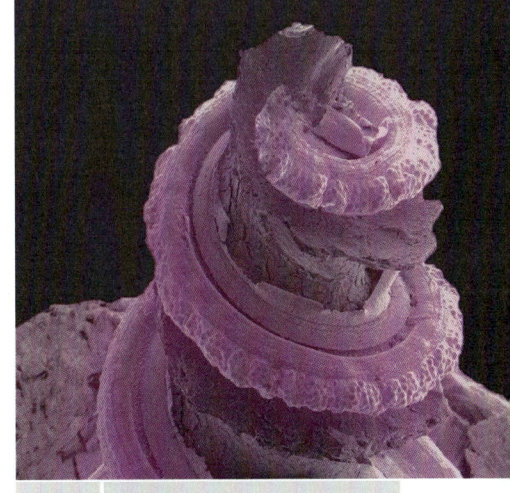

30.6 A cochlea as seen under a scanning electron microscope

LIFE LEAVING CERTIFICATE BIOLOGY | UNIT 3 THE ORGANISM | 403

30 The Sense Organs

2. In some cases, a problem develops with the outer or middle ear. Glue ear is a frequent cause of deafness in young children. This is due to a collection of sticky fluid in the middle ear and is more common in the children of smokers.

Correction

Inserting small drainage tubes (grommets) into the ear commonly cures this problem.

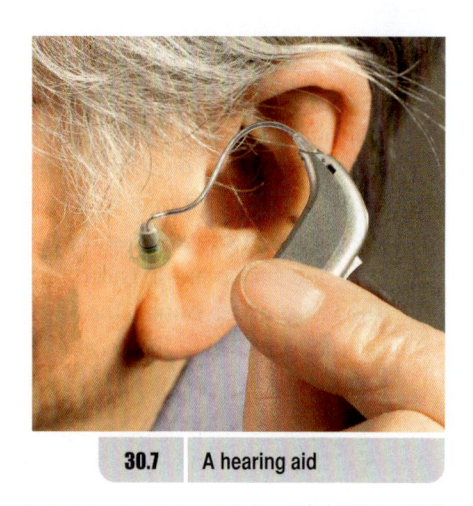

30.7 A hearing aid

5 Vision

The eye is the sense organ containing the photoreceptors. The structure of the human eye is shown in Fig 30.8.

1. The outermost layer of the eye is the **sclera**, a tough, fibrous, white layer which is used for muscle attachment, and for keeping the eye in its correct shape. The sclera is opaque.
2. The front of the sclera, the **cornea**, is transparent and allows the light to pass through it into the eye. It also bends (refracts) the light and helps to focus it onto the **retina**.
3. Covering the cornea and the front of the eye is the **conjunctiva**, which is a thin layer of cells for protection.
4. The second layer that makes up the eye is the **choroid**, a brown/black layer containing a large blood supply. The dark layer absorbs the light to prevent reflection within the eye while the large blood supply gives nourishment to the eye.
5. The front of the choroid enlarges to become the **ciliary body**, which contains a circular muscle, the **ciliary muscle**. This muscle along with the ligaments control the shape of the lens.

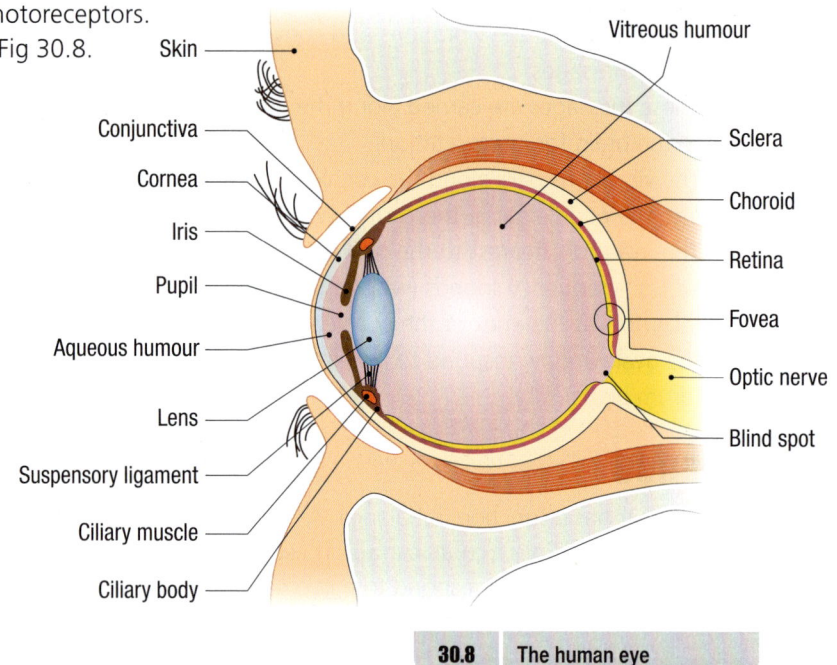

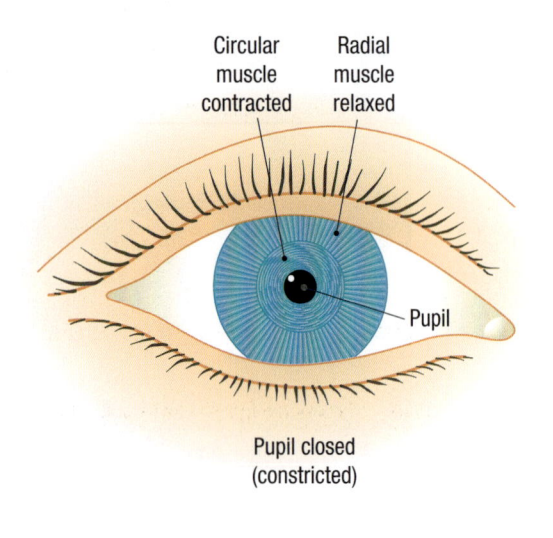

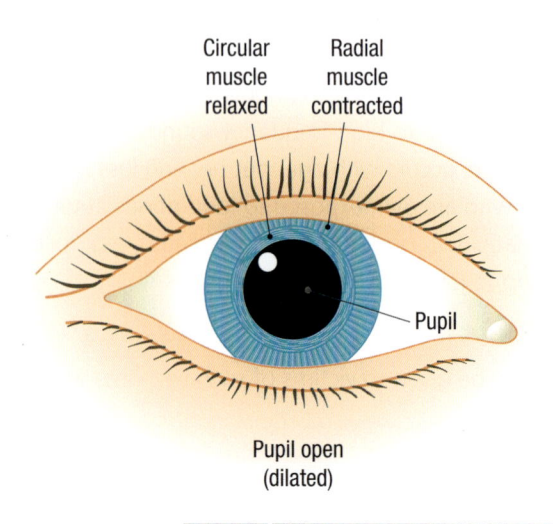

30.8 The human eye

Pupil closed (constricted) — Circular muscle contracted, Radial muscle relaxed

Pupil open (dilated) — Circular muscle relaxed, Radial muscle contracted

30.9 The opening and closing reflex in the iris

6. Suspensory ligaments attach the ciliary muscle to the transparent **lens**. The lens is involved in the focusing of light onto the retina.
7. An extension of the ciliary body becomes the **iris** to the front of the lens. The function of the iris is to control the amount of light entering the eye. The iris is the coloured part of the eye, and has a circular opening in the middle of it (the **pupil**), surrounded by circular and radial muscles. In bright light, the circular muscle contracts, and the radial muscle relaxes to produce a small pupil and reduce the amount of light entering the eye. In dim light, the reverse happens and the pupil is made larger, thus increasing the amount of light entering the eye (Fig 30.9).
8. To keep the shape of the eye, the centre spaces are filled with solutions. The chamber to the front of the lens is filled with a watery fluid called **aqueous humour**, and the chamber behind the lens is filled with a jelly-like solution called **vitreous humour**. Both of these liquids exert an outward pressure on the eye, keeping its shape. Food and oxygen diffuse across these liquids to keep the transparent lens and cornea alive, as they do not have a blood supply of their own.
9. The innermost layer of the eye is the retina, which is the light-sensitive section of the eye. There are two types of photosensitive receptors in the retina: **rods** and **cones**.
   (a) The rods are sensitive to low light intensities. They are not sensitive to different colours so they only see in black, white and various shades of grey. Neither do they see things very clearly so the edges are indistinct. Rods are used in dim light and are responsible for night vision.
   (b) Cones only function in good light intensity. There are three types of cones, each of which is sensitive to a different primary colour. From these three types of cones, all colours can be detected. Cones give sharp images.
   (c) In the centre of the retina straight behind the lens is a small yellowish pit called the **fovea** or yellow spot. This has the highest concentration of cones in the eye, and is where the light is focused for the most accurate vision.
   (d) The optic nerve carries the nerve impulses to the brain.
   (e) Where the optic nerve leaves the retina, there are no light receptors and this is called the **blind spot**. This is in a slightly different place in each eye so it is not normally noticed.

SYLLABUS REQUIREMENT:

You need to know about either the corrective measures for hearing loss or sight problems.

Eye defects

Two very common defects of the eye are long-sightedness (**hypermetropia**) and short-sightedness (**myopia**).

1. A long-sighted person cannot focus on objects close to the eye, but can focus on distant objects. This is due to the eyeball being too short and the image is focused behind the retina. This can be corrected by using a convex lens that bends the light inward (Fig 30.10).

A long-sighted person…

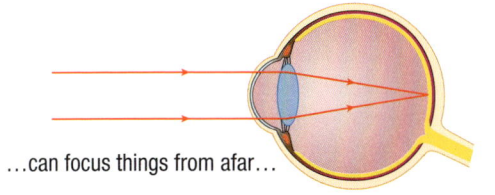

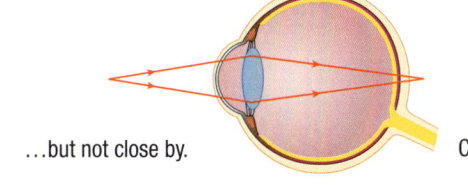

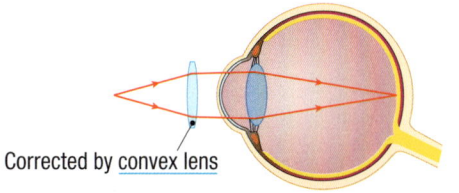

…can focus things from afar… …but not close by. Corrected by convex lens

30.10 Long-sightedness and its correction

2. A short-sighted person cannot focus on objects at a distance but can focus on near objects. This is due to the eyeball being too long. Objects at a distance are focused in front of the retina. This condition is corrected by using a concave lens that bends the light outward (Fig 30.11).

A short-sighted person…

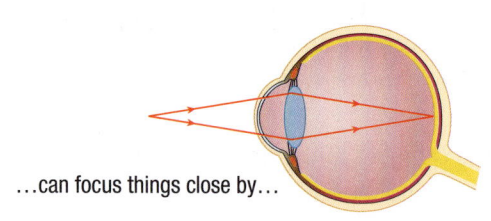

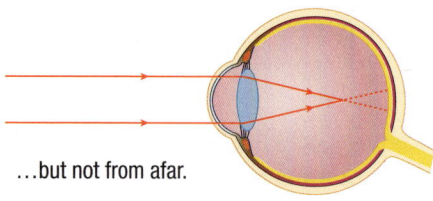

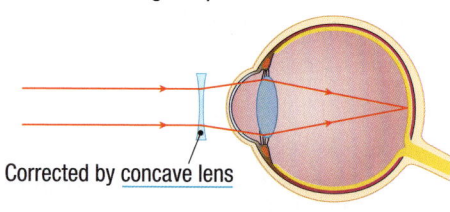

…can focus things close by…   …but not from afar.   Corrected by concave lens

30.11 Short-sightedness and its correction

Summary

- All messages arriving at the brain are identical. We interpret them differently depending on which area of the brain they are sent to, i.e. the area for vision 'sees' the messages as pictures.
- Receptors in the body respond to different stimuli, both internal and external:
  - If they respond to chemicals, they are called chemoreceptors.
  - If they respond to light, they are called photoreceptors.
  - If they respond to physical change, they are called mechanoreceptors.
  - If they respond to heat, they are called thermoreceptors.
- Receptors in some cases are grouped into sense organs.
- Smell and taste are very similar senses. They respond to chemicals dissolving in the liquid around the receptor. Smell responds to thousands of chemicals but taste only responds to bitter, salt, sweet and sour and a newly discovered taste, umami.
- Touch, pressure, pain, hot and cold receptors are found in the skin.
- The ear is the organ of hearing.
- Hearing responds to very small changes in air pressure. It contains the following parts:

Part	Function
Outer ear: air-filled	
Pinna	Directs sound waves into the auditory canal.
Auditory canal	Protective (lined with hairs and wax to trap dirt and bacteria).
Eardrum	Transfers sound waves into middle ear.
Middle ear: air-filled	
Ear ossicles (hammer, anvil and stirrup)	Magnify and intensify the sound waves.
Eustachian tube	Equalises air pressure either side of the ear drum.
Inner ear: fluid-filled	
Cochlea	Has hair receptor cells which respond to sound waves. Responsible for hearing.
Auditory nerve	Carries nerve impulses to the brain for interpretation.
Semi-circular canals	Have receptors which respond to the position of the head and body. Responsible for posture and balance.

Summary

- A build-up of a sticky fluid in the middle ear can cause deafness in children. It can be relieved by inserting drainage tubes (grommets) in the ear drum.
- Deafness can be caused by damage to the hairs in the cochlea. There is no cure but hearing aids can help.
- The eye is used for sight and responds to light. It contains the following parts:

Part	Function
Sclera	Tough outer coat for protection.
Cornea	Transparent front to eye for focusing.
Conjunctiva	Protect the front of the eye.
Choroid	Black layer for absorbing light.
Ciliary body	Contains the ciliary muscle to focus lens.
Suspensory ligaments	Attached to the lens, control the shape of the lens with the ciliary muscle.
Lens	To focus light onto the retina.
Iris	Controls the amount of light entering eye.
Aqueous humour	Maintains the shape of the cornea and supplies it with food.
Vitreous humour	Maintains the shape of the eyeball and supplies it with food.
Retina	Houses the light receptors.
Rods	Light-sensitive cells respond to low light intensity and to black and white.
Cones	Light-sensitive cells respond to high light intensity and to colour.
Yellow spot (fovea)	Area of most accurate vision on retina.
Optic nerve	Carries the nerve impulses to the brain.
Blind spot	The place on the retina where the optic nerve exits. No vision here.

- Eye defects:
    - If you are long-sighted, you can see distant objects but not near ones. Long-sightedness is corrected using a convex lens.
    - If you are short-sighted, you can see near objects but not distant ones. Short-sightedness is corrected using a concave lens.

30 The Sense Organs

Review questions

01
(a) Name the five senses.
(b) Name a sense organ associated with each of the senses you have named.
(c) Give a precise location in the body for each of the sense organs you have named or draw a simple diagram of the human body and position each of the organs you have named in (b).
(d) Suggest the main benefit of having sense organs to humans.

02
(a) What role does the brain play in the sensory system?
(b) If all nerve messages are the same, how do we distinguish between senses?

03
(a) Give an example of a receptor that responds to stimulus from the outside of the body.
(b) In what way are these receptors divided?
(c) When these receptors are grouped together what is produced?

04
(a) What do the senses of taste and smell have in common?
(b) What are the four basic tastes?

05 To what stimuli does your skin respond?

06
(a) Describe the role of the various parts of the ear in the process of hearing.
(b) What does a loud noise do to cause deafness?
(c) What is a treatment for deafness?

07
(a) Name the parts labelled A to D on the diagram of the ear.
(b) What is the function of the parts labelled B and C?
(c) What would be the effect if A were damaged?

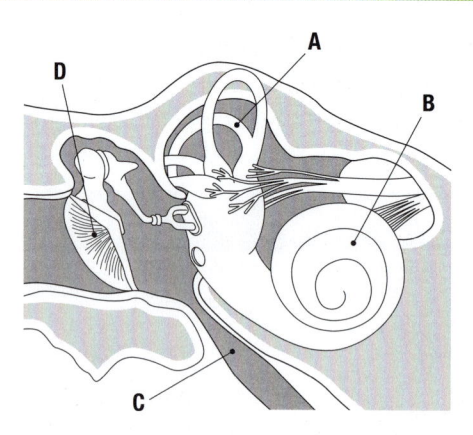

08 The diagram shows a section through the eye.

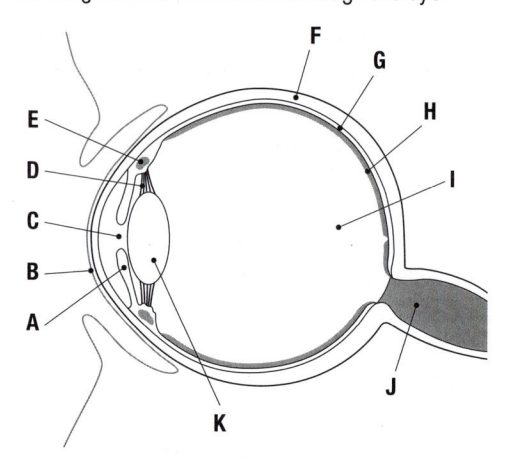

(a) Name the parts labelled A to K.
(b) Give one function for each part.

09
(a) Why is the choroid layer of the eye brown/black?
(b) Why is it important that the inside of the eye is filled with liquid?

10
(a) What is the problem if you are short-sighted and how do you correct it?
(b) What is the problem if you are long-sighted and how might you correct this (include diagrams in your answer)?

Examination style questions

Section A

01
(a) Name the parts labelled in the eye and give a function for each labelled part.
(b) What is the function of the fovea?
(c) What is missing from the blind spot?
(d) Why is the blind spot so named?
(e) How would you correct short-sightedness or a named hearing defect?

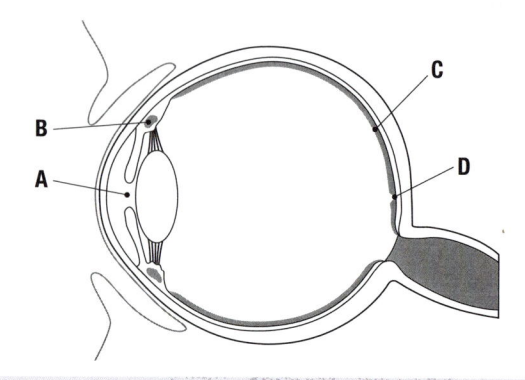

Examination style questions

02
(a) What is the function of the ear drum?
(b) What is found on the inside of the ear drum?
(c) What is the function of these structure/s?
(d) What does the Eustachian tube (canal) connect to the middle ear?
(e) What happens when the hairs in the cochlea are damaged?

Section C

03
(a) (i) Draw a diagram of a vertical section through the eye and label the following parts: cornea, retina, iris, vitreous humour, optic nerve, fovea.
 (ii) Which part of the eye:
  1. Is responsible for controlling the amount of light entering the eye?
  2. Has no light receptors?
  3. Is a type of light receptor that is used in bright light?
  4. Controls the shape of the lens?
(b) (i) Long- and short-sightedness are examples of common eye defects. Explain how these defects may be corrected.
   OR
   Name a hearing defect. State its cause. Outline how this defect may be corrected.
 (ii) Name three sense organs of the body other than the eye and the ear.
 (iii) For two of the named organs, state the type of environmental factor they are sensitive to.

04
(a) The diagram shows the general structure of the ear.

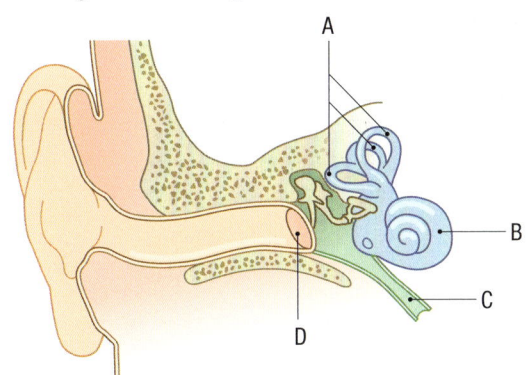

 (i) Name the parts labelled A, B, C and D.
 (ii) Give two functions of the three small bones of the middle ear.
 (iii) Give the general function of the part labelled A.
 (iv) Give the general function of the part labelled B.
 (v) The part labelled C is usually closed. Give one method of opening part C and state the purpose of opening it.
 (vi) Suggest why part F is much smaller in humans than in most other wild mammals.
(b) (i) Give the function of the following in the eye: iris, retina, conjunctiva, ciliary muscle, lens.
 (ii) Give the name of the two types of sensory receptor in the eye.
 (iii) What is the difference in their function?
 (iv) Are they both evenly distributed in the eye?
 (v) Explain your answer in (iv).

Leaving Certificate examination questions

Section A

01 The diagram shows a vertical section through the human eye.
(a) Name the parts labelled A, B, C.
(b) Name the coloured part of the eye.
(c) What is the function of the pupil in the eye?
(d) In which labelled part would you find the rods and cones?
(e) What is the function of the cones?

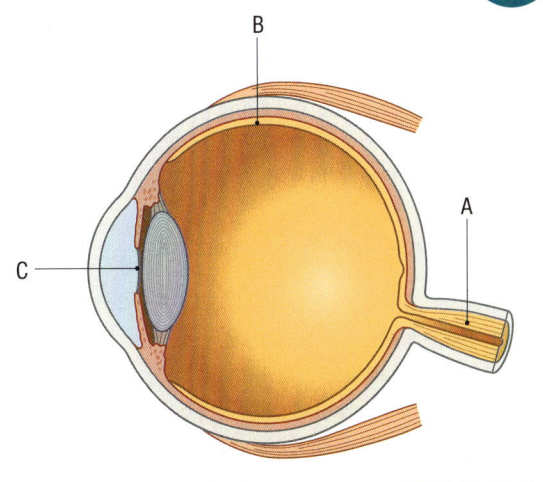

2011 OL Q. 6

30 The Sense Organs

Leaving Certificate examination questions

02 The diagram shows the external and internal structure of the human ear.

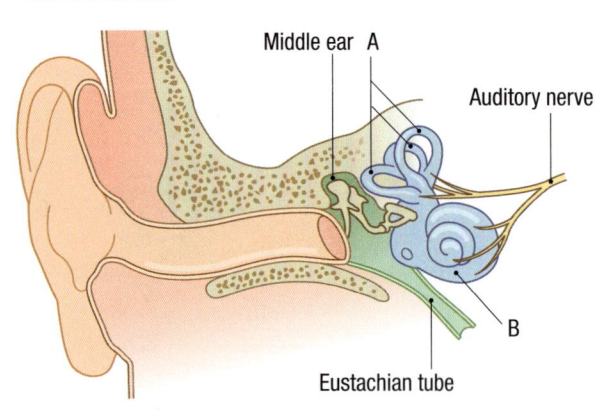

(i) Name the parts labelled A and B.
(ii) What is the function of B?
(iii) What is connected to the middle ear by the Eustachian tube?
(iv) What is the function of the Eustachian tube?
(v) Name one disorder of the ear or of the eye and give a corrective measure for the disorder you have named.

2010 OL Q. 5

Section C

03 The diagram shows a section through the human eye.

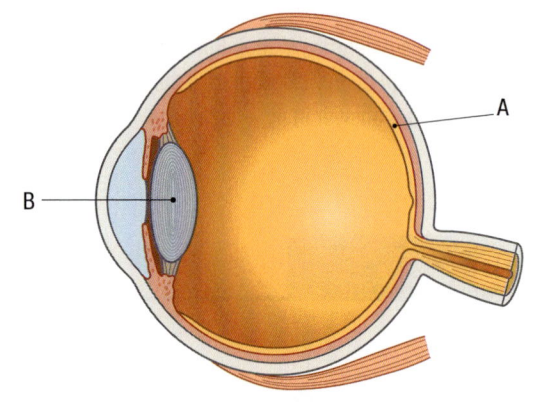

(i) Name the parts labelled A and B.
(ii) Name and give a function of the coloured part of the eye.
(iii) The eye is filled with fluid. What is the function of this fluid?
(iv) Explain in detail how the eye works.

2014 OL Q.15 (a)

04 The diagram shows the human ear.
(i) Name the parts labelled A and B.
(ii) What is the function of part A?
(iii) What is the function of part B?
(iv) What is connected to the middle ear by the Eustachian tube?
(v) What surrounds the bones in the middle ear?

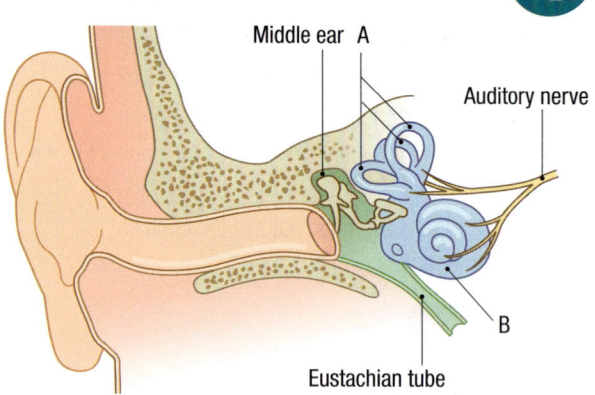

(vi) The ear is an example of a sense organ. Name two sense organs, other than the ear and the eye, in the human body.
(vii) Name one disorder of the ear or the eye and give corrective measures for the disorder referred to.

2013 OL Q. 14 (c)

05 (i) Copy the diagram of the front of the eye into your answer book and label the iris and the pupil.

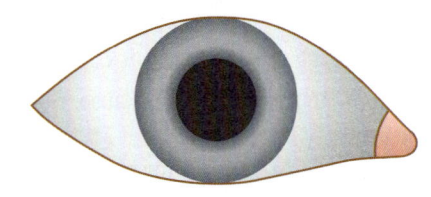

(ii) Is the eye shown in the diagram above adapted for dim light or bright light? Explain your answer.
(iii) Where in the eye is the retina located?
(iv) Two types of cells that receive light are found in the retina. Name each of these.
(v) Give one difference between the two types of cell that receive light.
(vi) The optic nerve is attached to the eye. What is the function of the optic nerve?

2008 OL Q. 14 (b)

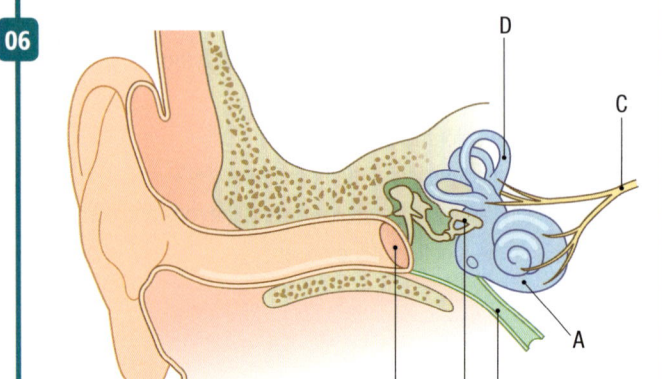

06

(i) The diagram above shows the internal structure of the human ear.
 1. Name the structures labelled A, B, C.

Leaving Certificate examination questions

2. Give the functions of parts D and E.
3. Which letters denote the parts of the ear in which nerve impulses are generated?
  (ii) In what part of the eye are nerve impulses generated?
  (iii) Suggest one way by which the ear may be protected.
  (iv) Explain how a corrective measure for a named defect of hearing or vision works.

2011 HL Q. 15 (a)

07 The diagram shows the human eye.
  (i) Name the parts labelled V, W and X.
  (ii) Give the functions of parts Y and Z.
  (iii) 1. Suspensory ligaments. 2. Cones. 3. Optic nerve. 4. Brain. Outline the roles in vision of any three of the above structures.
  (iv) Explain how the iris works.
  (v) Suggest a reason why two eyes are better than one.

2009 HL Q. 15 (b)

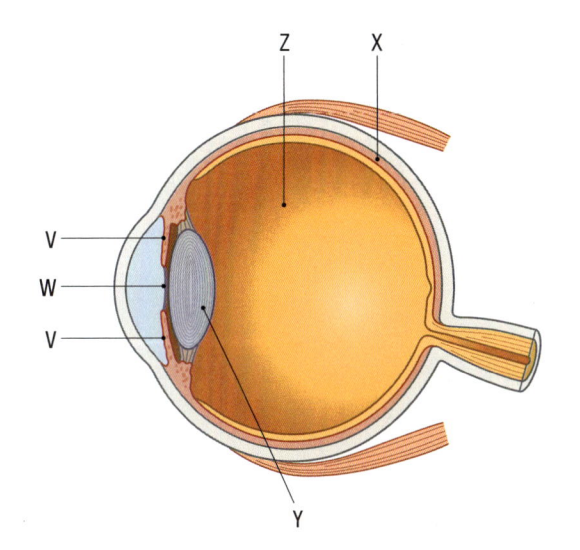

Past examination questions

OL	2013 Q. 14 (c)	2011 Q. 6	2010 Q. 5	2008 Q. 14 (b)	2006 Q. 15 (b)	2004 Q. 15 (a)
HL	2014 Q. 15 (a)	2011 Q. 15 (a)	2009 Q. 15 (b)			

31 The Endocrine System

After studying this chapter you should be able to:

1. Define a hormone.
2. Distinguish between endocrine and exocrine glands, giving examples.
3. Compare the action of the endocrine system with the nervous system.
4. Give the location of each endocrine gland, a hormone produced there and its function.
5. Give a description of the symptoms of an excess or shortage of one hormone and possible corrective measures.
6. Give two examples of the use of hormone supplements.
7. **HL** Describe the feedback control mechanism of a hormone.

The endocrine system

1. The **endocrine system** produces **hormones**:
   - Hormones are chemical messengers produced in one part of the body that cause a response in another part of the body.
   - Hormones are usually carried in the bloodstream.
   - Hormones are carried to all parts of the body and can affect many different target **organs**.
2. - The glands that produce hormones are called **endocrine** or **ductless glands** because they have no tubes leading from them to carry these chemicals, which are secreted directly into the blood.

Exocrine glands in contrast release their chemicals into ducts that carry them to their destination, e.g. the salivary gland.

> **D** **Endocrine glands** are ductless glands that produce hormones.

> **D** **Hormones** are chemical messengers produced in ductless glands, carried in the blood, for use in another part of the body.

> **D** **Exocrine glands** have ducts (tubes) leaving them which carry their products.

Function of hormones

The function of the hormones is to regulate the activities of the various systems in the body. Hormones are used to regulate cell **metabolism** on a continuing basis, e.g. the control of the sugar level in the blood by insulin. Hormones are particularly useful in controlling processes in which there is a wide range of changes required in many different cells, e.g. the effect of the sex hormones on sexual development.

3.

Nervous system	Endocrine system
Electrochemical message	Chemical message
Carried in nerve cells	Carried in the blood
Fast-acting (travel in the nerves as electrical messages)	Slow-acting (chemicals travelling in the blood)
Short-term effect	Long-term effect

Table 31.1 A comparison of the nervous and endocrine systems

The endocrine glands

SYLLABUS REQUIREMENT:
You need to know the name of only one hormone produced from each endocrine gland.

The seven major endocrine glands and their locations are shown in Fig 31.1.

The hypothalamus

The hypothalamus is located in the brain and produces some hormones such as anti-diuretic Hormone **ADH**, which it sends to the **pituitary gland** immediately below it. The pituitary gland then releases these hormones, i.e. ADH which controls osmoregulation (see Chapter 27).

Other hormones released by the hypothalamus travel the short distance to the pituitary gland causing it to release hormones the pituitary manufactures itself, i.e. **thyroid releasing hormone (TRH)** is a hormone produced by the hypothalamus when cell activity is too low. This hormone causes the pituitary to release **thyroid stimulating hormone (TSH)**.

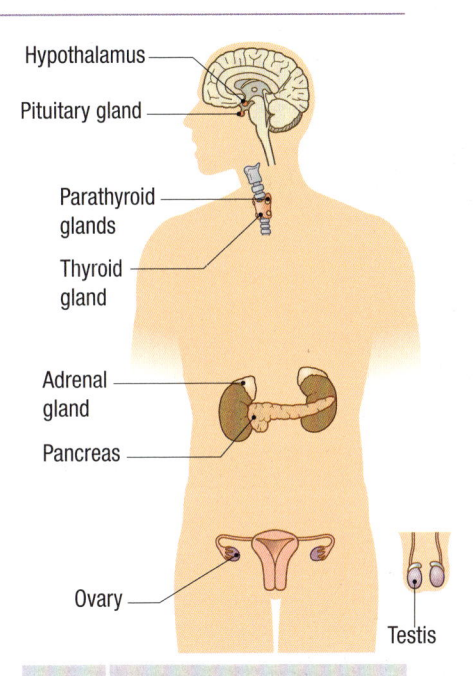

31.1 The principal endocrine glands in a human

Pituitary gland

The pituitary gland is located on the underside of the brain. It is sometimes called the master gland as it produces a number of hormones that control the functioning of the other glands. The pituitary releases thyroid stimulating hormone (TSH) to control the thyroid gland.

The pituitary also produces some hormones that affect organs other than glands, e.g. **growth hormone**, **follicle stimulating hormone (FSH)**, **luteinising hormone (LH)**, prolactin and **oxytocin**.

The thyroid gland

The **thyroid gland** is situated in the neck. It produces **thyroxine**, which requires **iodine** in its manufacture. Thyroxine controls the rate of cell metabolism. The higher the level of thyroxine present in the blood the more rapidly you will respire. In children, thyroxine will help control the rate of growth.

The parathyroid glands

The **parathyroids** are situated behind the thyroid gland. They release **parathyroid hormone** which increases the release of calcium into the blood from the bones.

The adrenal glands

The **adrenal glands** (Fig 31.2) are situated on top of the **kidneys**. They produce **adrenaline**, which is called the **'flight or fight'** hormone, as it prepares the body for a dangerous situation, giving it the potential for great physical activity. It does this by increasing the heart rate and speeding up metabolism.

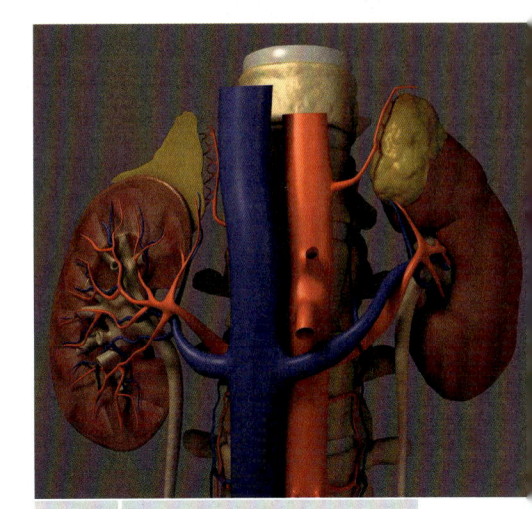

31.2 An adrenal gland on top of each kidney

The pancreas

The **pancreas** is situated under the stomach. It is both an exocrine and an endocrine gland and can be called a dual function gland. Areas of the gland called the **islets of Langerhans** carry out its endocrine function. The islets of Langerhans produce **insulin**, which lowers the level of sugar in the blood and increases the storage of glycogen in the liver and the uptake of glucose by cells. The exocrine function of the pancreas is to produce digestive enzymes.

31 The Endocrine System

The ovaries
The **ovaries** (in women) are situated in the lower abdomen. They produce the sex hormones **oestrogen** and **progesterone**. These are involved in the control of the **menstrual cycle**, **pregnancy** and the production of the **secondary sexual characteristics** (see Chapter 36).

The testes
The **testes** (in men) are situated in the scrotum. They produce **testosterone**, the male sex hormone. This causes the development of the male secondary sexual characteristics (see Chapter 36). Muscle development is one of these characteristics, and this has led to the development of the 'anabolic steroids'. These are very useful in medicine, but athletes can abuse them. Many of these 'anabolic steroids' are based on testosterone and can have a number of harmful and unwelcome side effects (Fig 31.3).

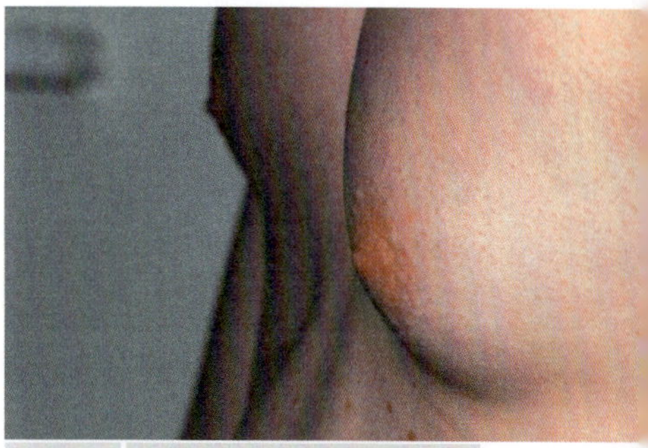

31.3 Male breast enlargement due to anabolic steroids

Gland	Location	Hormone	Function
Hypothalamus	In the brain above pituitary gland	ADH Thyroid-releasing hormone (TRH)	Osmoregulation Controls the level of TSH
Pituitary	Just under the brain	Thyroid-stimulating hormone (TSH) Growth hormone	Controls the level of thyroxine Stimulate growth
Parathyroids	Behind the thyroid	Parathyroid hormone	Controls the release of calcium from bone
Thyroid	Neck	Thyroxine	Controls metabolic rate
Thymus	Under the breastbone	Thymosine	Development of lymphocytes
Adrenal	Above the kidney	Adrenaline	'Flight or fight' response increase the heart rate and cell metabolism
Pancreas (islets of Langerhans)	Under the stomach	Insulin	Controls sugar level in blood
Ovaries (female)	Lower abdomen	Oestrogen + progesterone	Control sexual development
Testes (male)	Scrotum	Testosterone	Control sexual development

Table 31.2 The endocrine glands, their hormones and the function of the hormones

Underproduction or overproduction of hormones

Should the body produce too much or too little of any one hormone, there can be many effects which sometimes require medical intervention.

1. If the pituitary gland fails to produce growth hormone in a child, the person fails to grow and remains a pituitary dwarf (Fig 31.4).

A pituitary giant (Fig 31.5) is caused by the production of excessive amounts of growth hormone (often due to a pituitary tumour).

31.4 A pituitary dwarf

Corrective measures
A low level of growth hormone can be cured if growth hormone is given by injection to the child. This is an example of a **hormone supplement**. The growth hormone has to be given before normal growth would stop in the child to be effective.

An overactive pituitary may be corrected by surgically removing the tumour. It will of course not reduce any growth that has already taken place.

2. If a person has **sugar diabetes type I** (*diabetes mellitus*), their pancreas may not be producing insulin.

Corrective measures

In this case, they can regulate their sugar levels by monitoring their blood sugar level and injecting insulin (Fig 31.6) as a hormone supplement when their sugar levels are rising.

Type II diabetes is caused when your cells stop responding to the insulin you produce. The risk of this is increased by fat in the body. Being overweight or obese will greatly increase your risk of this type of diabetes.

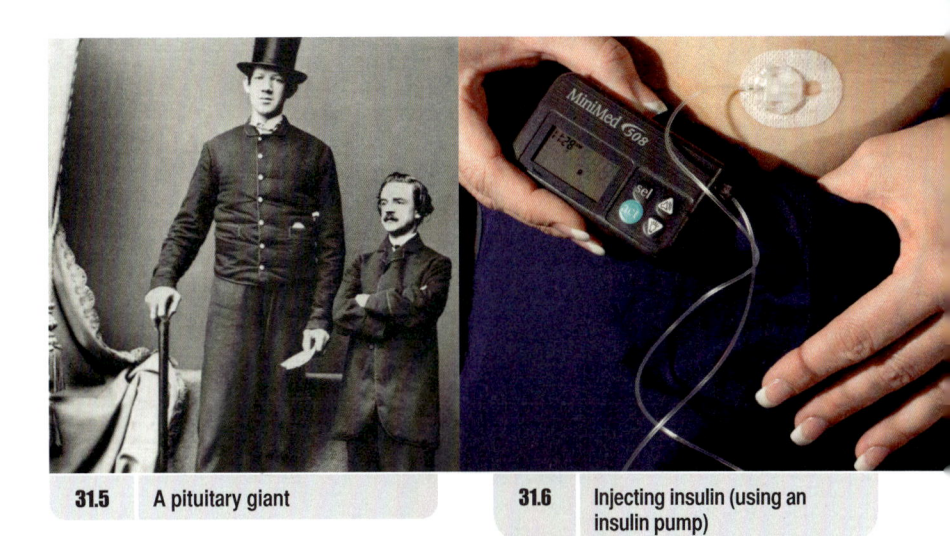

31.5 A pituitary giant

31.6 Injecting insulin (using an insulin pump)

Hormone supplements	Function
Insulin	Used to replace missing natural insulin to regulate sugar levels
Human growth hormones	Used to replace growth hormones missing in pituitary dwarfs

Table 31.3 Examples of hormone supplements in medicine

HL Feedback mechanism of hormone control

The level of the hormones is regulated in the body and this in turn will regulate the function that the hormone in question is carrying out in the person. **Feedback** occurs when the level of a hormone controls the production of itself or another hormone. There are a number of ways this can be done and we will examine how this control occurs with the hormones insulin and glucagon. Insulin is the hormone released by the pancreas to regulate the sugar level in the blood but the pancreas also releases a second hormone, glucagon, that helps in this process. In the body the normal level of glucose is about 90 mg/100 mL of blood.

1. If the level of glucose should rise (for example when you eat a lot of carbohydrates) then your islets of Langerhans in the pancreas release insulin.
2. The rising level of insulin in the blood causes the liver to take in glucose and store it as glycogen and your body cells to take up more glucose.
3. The glucose level in your blood falls and at a set concentration, slightly lower than the norm (90 mg/100 mL), less insulin is released.
4. If the blood glucose level falls below 90 mg/100 mL (for example when you miss a meal) then the islets of Langerhans release glucagon.
5. The rise in glucagon causes your liver to break down glycogen and release glucose.
6. The glucose level in your blood now rises and at a set glucose concentration, slightly higher than the norm (90 mg/100 mL) the production and release of glucagon falls.

By using both of these hormones you are able to keep your glucose level in your blood close to the preferred optimum of 90 mg/100 mL.

Both of these hormones work by a process called **negative feedback**:

Chemical A (the hormone) causes an effect B (change in glucose levels). B then switches off the production of the chemical A.

The release of insulin causes a reduction of glucose that eventually switches off the production of insulin.

The release of glucagon causes an increase in blood glucose that eventually switches off the production of glucagon (Fig 31.7).

Feedback occurs when the level of hormone in the blood controls the production of another hormone or the production of itself.

Negative feedback occurs when the increasing level of a hormone in the blood stops the production of itself.

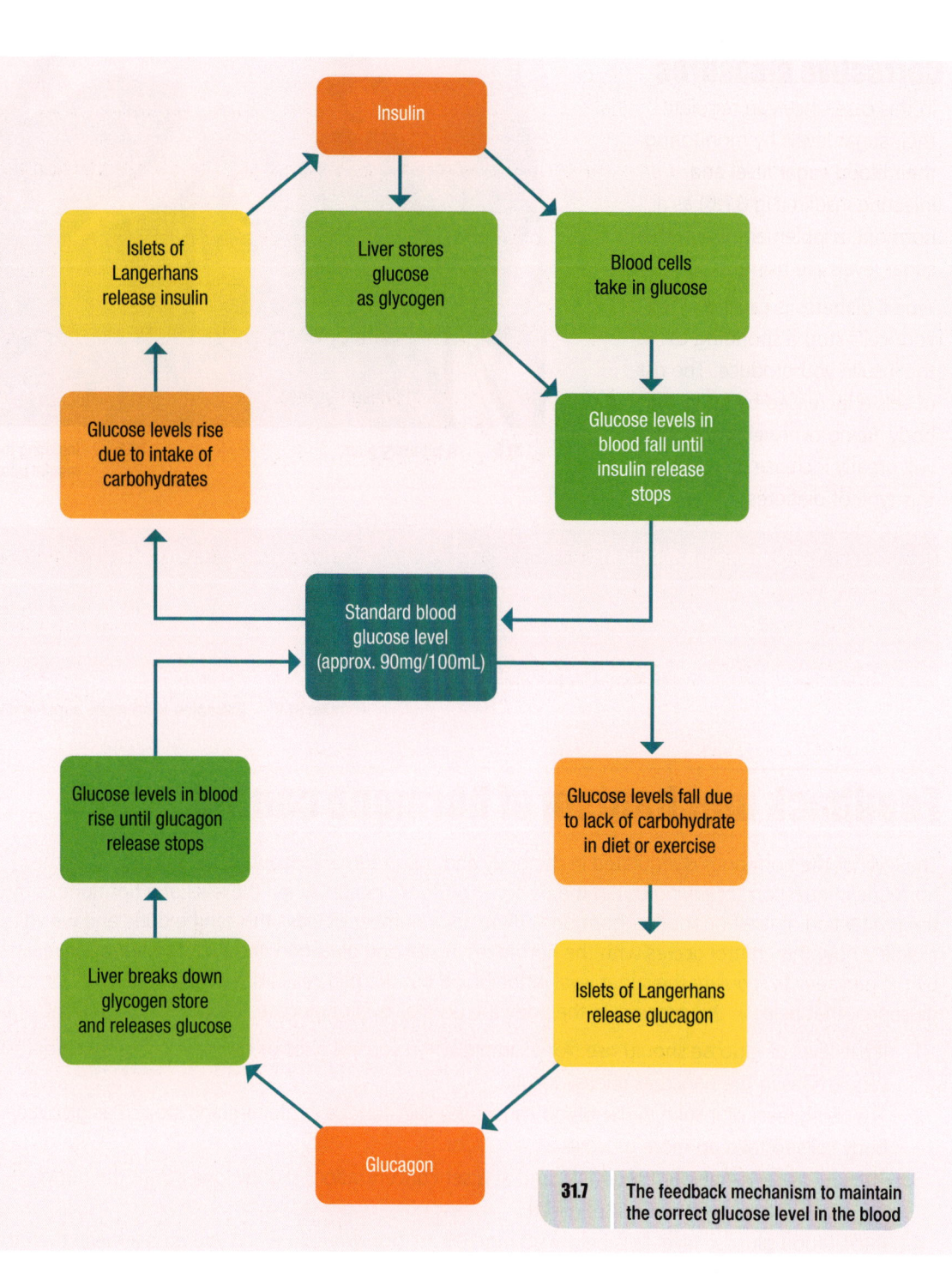

31 The Endocrine System

Figure 31.7 The feedback mechanism to maintain the correct glucose level in the blood

Flow diagram:
- Insulin → Islets of Langerhans release insulin, Liver stores glucose as glycogen, Blood cells take in glucose
- Glucose levels in blood fall until insulin release stops → Standard blood glucose level (approx. 90mg/100mL)
- Glucose levels rise due to intake of carbohydrates → Islets of Langerhans release insulin → Insulin
- Standard blood glucose level → Glucose levels fall due to lack of carbohydrate in diet or exercise → Islets of Langerhans release glucagon → Glucagon
- Glucagon → Liver breaks down glycogen store and releases glucose → Glucose levels in blood rise until glucagon release stops → Standard blood glucose level

Summary

- The endocrine system produces hormones.
- Endocrine glands are ductless and produce hormones; exocrine glands are ducted and release their chemicals using ducts (see Table 31.2).
- Hormones are chemical messengers produced in ductless glands for use elsewhere.
  - Hormones are carried in the blood.
  - The chemical nature of most hormones is protein (or protein-like), e.g. adrenalin.
  - Hormones can be steroids, e.g. oestrogen.
- Overproduction of the growth hormone produces a pituitary giant. This is treated by surgically removing part or all of the gland.

Summary

- Underproduction produces a pituitary dwarf – this can be treated by giving the growth hormone as a hormone supplement.
- Another use of a hormone supplement is the injecting of insulin by diabetics.
- **HL** Many hormones are controlled by negative feedback. The level of glucose in the blood is monitored:
  - if the level of glucose rises above 90 mg/100 mL;
  - it causes the release of insulin which removes glucose from the blood as the liver turns glucose into glycogen;
  - the glucose levels falls and the pancreas stops making insulin.
- If the level of glucose falls below 90 mg/100 mL:
  - it causes the release of glucagon which releases glucose into the blood as the liver turns glycogen into glucose;
  - the glucose level rises and the pancreas stops making glucagon.
- Feedback occurs when the level of hormone in the blood controls the production of another hormone or the production of itself.
- Negative feedback occurs when the increasing level of a hormone in the blood stops the production of itself.

Nervous system	Endocrine system
Electrochemical message	Chemical message
Carried in nerve cells	Carried in the blood
Fast-acting	Slow-acting
Short-term effect	Long-term effect

- Hormones and plant growth regulators share a number of characteristics (see Chapter 28).

Endocrine system	Plant growth regulators
Chemical messages	Chemical messages
Made in one site and function in a second	Made in one site and function in a second
Carried in the vascular system	Can be carried in vascular system

31 The Endocrine System

Review questions

01 (a) What is a hormone?
(b) How are hormones carried around the body?
(c) Where are hormones produced?

02 (a) What is an exocrine gland?
(b) How does it differ from an endocrine gland?

03 (a) What is the chemical difference between the two main types of hormones?
(b) List the seven main endocrine glands.
(c) Give the precise location of each of these.
(d) Name a hormone produced by each.

04 (a) Why is the pituitary gland called the master gland?
(b) Why is adrenaline called the 'flight or fight' hormone?
(c) What does insulin do in the body?

05 (a) Give an example of a malfunctioning gland.
(b) Describe how the problem can be solved.
(c) Give two examples of the use of hormone supplements.

06 Compare the endocrine system with the nervous system.

07 (a) Describe the control mechanism for production of a hormone.
(b) Why is it important that such control mechanisms exist?

Examination style questions

Section A

01 Complete the following table.

Hormone	Site of production	Function
		Stimulates growth
Thyroxine	Thyroid	
	Islets of Langerhans	
Adrenalin		

02 (a) Where is growth hormone produced?
(b) What effect does this hormone have on your body?
(c) Does it always have this effect?
(d) Explain your answer in (c).
(e) Why might athletes abuse this hormone?

Section C

03 (a) (i) Distinguish between exocrine and endocrine glands.
(ii) Give the precise location of one named exocrine gland.
(b) (i) What is a hormone?
(ii) Indicate the precise positions of the following endocrine glands: pituitary, thyroid, pancreas. You may indicate their positions by drawing an outline diagram of the human body and marking their positions on the diagram.
(iii) Name any one hormone produced by one of these glands and state a precise function of the named hormone.
(iv) Give one example of the use of hormone supplements.
(v) Give two differences between hormonal and nervous action.
(c) Regulation of the secretion of hormones and the formation of lymphocytes (specific defensive white cells) are very important aspects of maintaining a suitable metabolic environment within the body.
(i) What is meant by a feedback mechanism in regard to the secretion of hormones in humans?
(ii) Describe how the secretion of one named hormone is regulated by such a feedback mechanism.

04 (a) What is a hormone?
(b) Name the gland that produces insulin.
(c) Give the precise location of the gland named in (b).

31 The Endocrine System

Examination style questions

The graph below shows how an injection of insulin affects the level of blood glucose in a person.

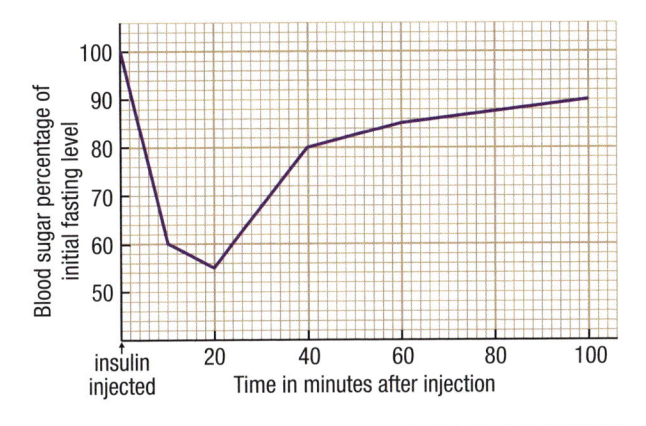

(d) Using the graph describe the effect of injecting insulin.
(e) Following the injection for how long did the insulin affect the level of glucose in the blood?
(f) What could happen to the glucose other than its breakdown in respiration?
(g) What would be the difference between this hormonal response and a nervous response?
(h) What are the similarities between the hormonal and nervous responses?

Leaving Certificate examination questions

Section C

01 Obesity is an excessive level of body fat. It is generally caused by over-eating and lack of exercise. Obesity may contribute to the development of type II diabetes. Type II diabetes is caused by the resistance of certain body cells to the hormone insulin. Diabetes may also be caused by a lack of insulin in the body. Insulin is produced by the pancreas, which is an endocrine gland. Symptoms of diabetes include thirst and fatigue.

(i) What is meant by the term *obesity*?
(ii) What is meant by the term *endocrine*?
(iii) Where in the human body is the pancreas located?
(iv) How are hormones carried around the body?
(v) 1. Give one cause of diabetes.
    2. Give two symptoms of diabetes.
    3. Suggest one treatment for a person who suffers from diabetes

2014 OL Q. 12 (c)

02 (i) The diagram shows some parts of the human endocrine system. Name the glands labelled A and B.

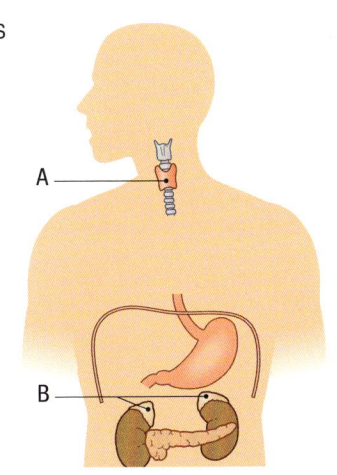

(ii) Name any **one** hormone produced by the body.
(iii) Give a deficiency symptom of the hormone named in (ii) above.
(iv) Give **one** example of the use of hormone supplements.
(v) The central nervous system is made up of **two** main parts. Name **each** part.
(vi) Name a disorder of the nervous system. Give **one** cause of the disorder **and** suggest a means of treating the disorder.

2011 OL Q. 14 (b)

03 (i) What is a hormone?
(ii) Draw an outline diagram of the human body and indicate on it the location of the following hormone-producing glands by using the following letters:
W Pituitary
X Thyroid
Y Pancreas (islets of Langerhans)
Z Adrenals
(iii) In the case of one of the hormone-producing glands that you have located in your diagram, state:
  1. The gland and a hormone that it produces.
  2. A function of this hormone.
  3. A deficiency symptom of this hormone.
(iv) State one way in which hormone action differs from nerve action.

2004 OL Q. 15 (b)

04 (a) (i) What term is used for glands that secrete hormones?
(ii) How do these glands differ from those that do not secrete hormones?

31 The Endocrine System

Leaving Certificate examination questions

(iii) Explain why the pancreas may be described as a dual-function gland.

(b) Answer the following by reference to hormones, other than the sex hormones, which you have encountered in the course of your studies.
  (i) What is the chemical nature of many hormones?
  (ii) In the case of each of two named hormones secreted in the human body state:
    1. The precise location of the gland that secretes it.
    2. A function of the hormone.
  (iii) In the case of one hormone referred to in part (b) (ii):
    1. Give a deficiency symptom.
    2. Give a symptom of excess secretion.
    3. Give a corrective measure for either its deficiency or its excess, stating clearly which you have chosen.
    4. Explain why hormonal responses are slower than nervous responses.

2013 HL Q. 10

05 (i) What is a hormone?
(ii) State **two** ways in which hormones are similar to the group of substances called plant growth promoters.
(iii) 1. What is meant by **feedback** in relation to hormone action?
    2. Give a brief account of the feedback mechanism for a **named** hormone.
(iv) Describe **one** deficiency symptom of a **named** hormone.

2011 HL Q. 11 (c)

06 (i) What term is used to describe the glands that secrete hormones in the human body?
(ii) 1. Name a hormone-producing gland in the human body.
  2. Where in the body is the gland located?
  3. Name a hormone that this gland secretes.
  4. State a role of this hormone.
  5. Describe what happens if the body experiences a deficiency of this hormone.
(iii) Give **two** examples of the use of hormone supplements.

2010 HL Q. 11 (c)

07 (i) Other than the secretion of hormones, how does an endocrine gland differ from an exocrine gland?
(ii) State two ways in which hormone action differs from nerve action.
(iii) Copy the following table into your answer book and fill each of the empty boxes.

Endocrine gland	Location	Hormone	Role of hormone
	Pancreas	Insulin	
Thyroid gland			
			'fight or flight'

(iv) In the case of a named hormone give:
  1. A deficiency symptom.
  2. A corrective measure.

2007 HL Q. 15 (b)

Past examination questions

OL 2011 Q. 14 (b)   2004 Q. 15 (b)

HL 2013 Q. 10 (a), (b)   2011 Q. 11 (c)   2010 Q. 11 (c)   2008 Q. 13 (c) (ii)   2007 Q. 4, Q. 15 (b)
2005 Q. 3 (c), Q. 14 (c) (i) (ii)

The Musculoskeletal System

32

After studying this chapter you should be able to:

1. Describe the structure and function of the axial and the appendicular skeleton.
2. Describe the structure of a long bone.
3. Give the function of compact bone, spongy bone, red marrow and yellow marrow.
4. Classify and give the location and function of the joints.
5. Give the role of cartilage, ligaments and tendons.
6. Describe how the muscles work in antagonistic pairs to move the skeleton, giving one example.
7. Give one possible cause, prevention and treatment for arthritis or osteoporosis.
8. **HL** Describe the role of the osteoblasts and calcium in bone formation and renewal.
9. **HL** Explain why increase in height does not occur in adults.

Reacting to stimuli

Producing **hormones** is one way we react to stimuli. The second way in which the body can react to a stimulus is to move. This is achieved by using the muscles in conjunction with the **skeleton**. These two sets of structures are so closely interconnected that they are referred to as one system: the **musculoskeletal system**.

The human skeleton

The skeleton in the human is composed of rigid structures called **bones**. There are 206 bones in the skeleton. Where one bone meets another, **joints** are formed. Bone tissue and **cartilage** are the two types of tissue that comprise the bulk of the skeleton. Bone is harder than cartilage. Cartilage is found mainly as a shock absorber at the joints. **Ligaments** attach bones to bones. Bones move due to the forces produced by muscles which are attached to the bones by **tendons**.

Functions of the skeleton

There are four functions of the skeleton:

1. It **supports** the body and gives it **shape** with the help of the muscles.
2. The muscles pull on the skeleton causing the bones to move. Thus the skeleton is required for **movement**.
3. It **protects** the organs of the body; in particular those it completely surrounds, i.e. the brain.
4. It **manufactures blood cells** in the inside (**red bone marrow**) of certain bones.

The skeleton is subdivided into two parts: the **axial skeleton** and the **appendicular skeleton**. The human skeleton is shown in Fig 32.1.

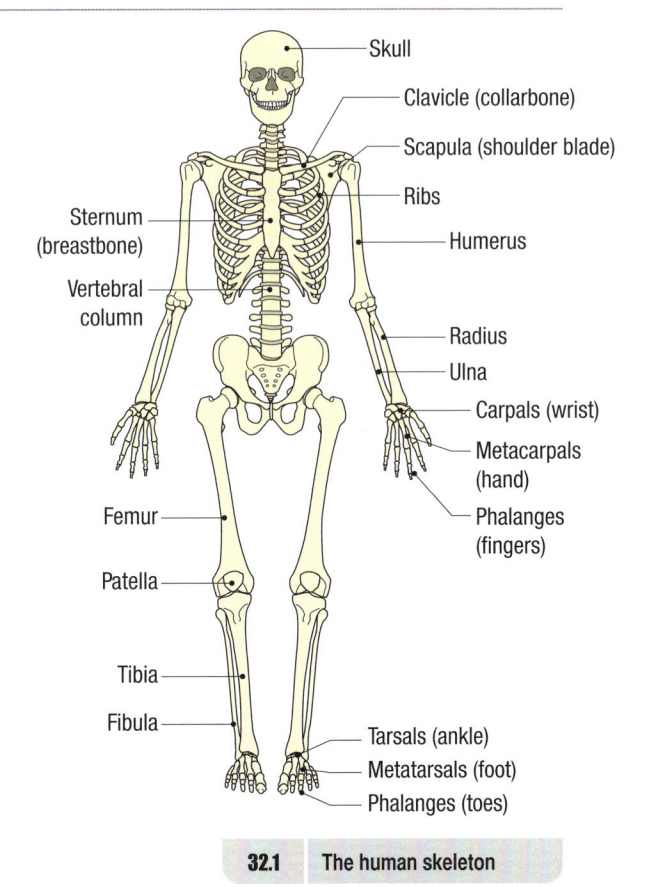

32.1 The human skeleton

32 The Musculoskeletal System

The axial skeleton

The axial skeleton is made up of the **skull**, **vertebrae** and the **rib cage**.

- The skull is made up of a number of bones, some of which are fused together to form the **cranium**, which encases the brain. The skull is attached to the top of the **vertebral column** (backbone or spine).
- The vertebral column comprises 26 vertebrae (Fig 32.2). These are grouped together into regions:
  - The region nearest the neck contains seven **cervical** vertebrae.
  - The next region contains twelve **thoracic** vertebrae, each of which have a pair of ribs attached to them.
  - Below these vertebrae are the five **lumbar** vertebrae, followed by the **sacrum** and the **coccyx**. These last two regions are fused together.
- Each vertebra fits into the one above and below it. Vertebrae are held together by muscles and ligaments. Between each vertebra, there is a **disc** of cartilage, giving a total of 24 discs. Each disc gives a little bit of flexibility and all 24 allow a reasonable amount of bending in the column. These discs also prevent the bones from grinding against one another and act as shock absorbers up the spine.
- The twelve pairs of ribs are attached to the vertebrae. The first seven curve around to the front of the chest and fasten to the **sternum** (breastbone). The next three pairs are attached to cartilage that is attached to the sternum and the remaining two pairs do not attach to the sternum (floating ribs). The ribs protect the lungs and heart, and are used in breathing (Fig 32.3).

D The **axial skeleton** comprises the skull, vertebral column, ribs and sternum.

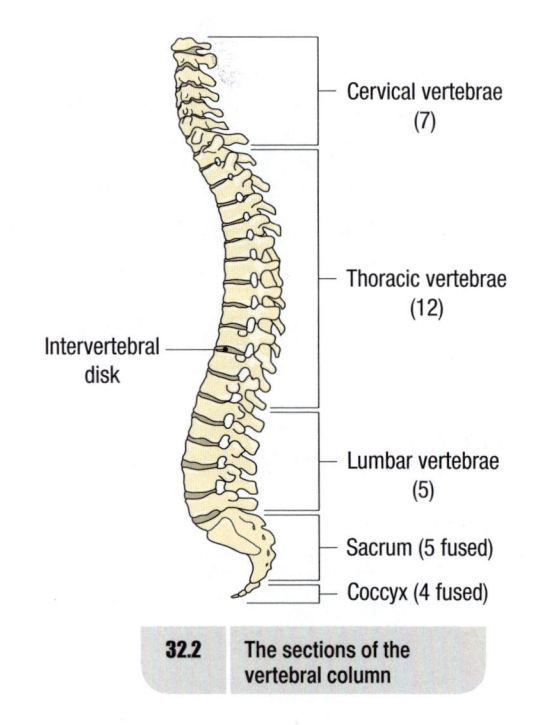

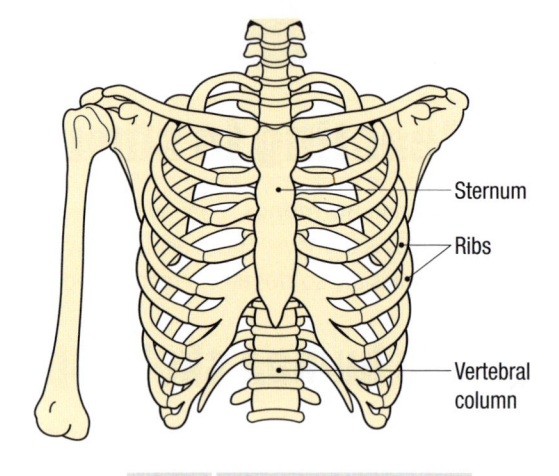

32.2 The sections of the vertebral column

32.3 A rib cage

The appendicular skeleton

The appendicular skeleton comprises the limb bones and the **girdles** that attach them to the axial skeleton.

- The **pectoral girdle** or shoulder comprises the two large flat bones called the shoulder blades (scapula), each of which is attached to a collarbone (clavicle). Attached to the pectoral girdle are the arms and hands.
- The arm in the human is comprised of the humerus, radius and ulna, followed by the carpals, metacarpals and the phalanges in the hand.
- The **pelvic girdle** or pelvis comprises the two hip bones. Attached to the pelvis is the leg, as shown in Fig 32.5.

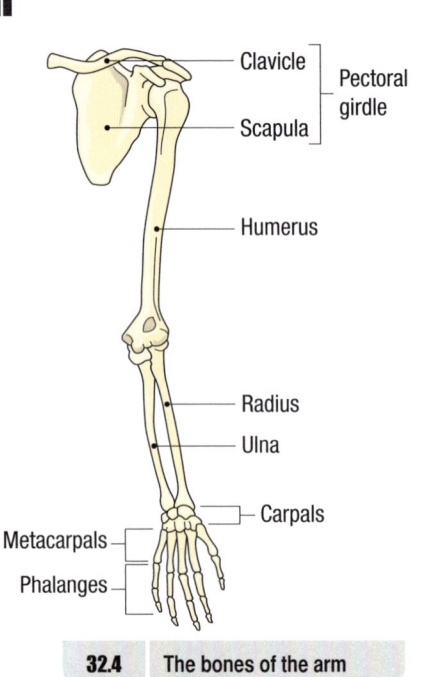

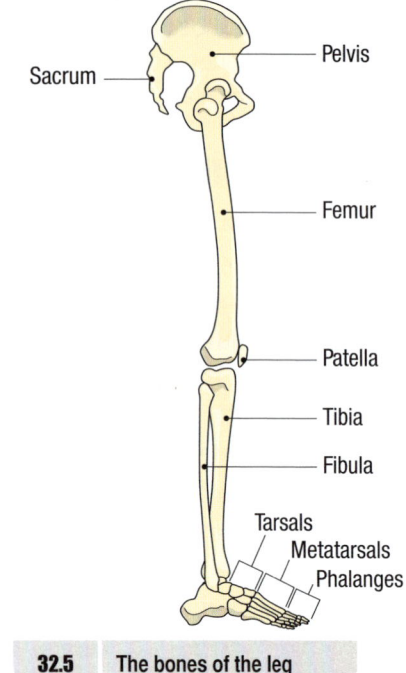

32.4 The bones of the arm

32.5 The bones of the leg

- The leg in the human is comprised of the femur, the fibula and tibia, followed by the tarsals, metatarsals and phalanges in the foot.
- Arms and legs are examples of the **pentadactyl (five-digit) limbs** found in **vertebrates** (Figs 32.4 and 32.5). These comprise a large, long bone followed by a pair of smaller long bones. Next is a group of small bones making up the wrist or ankle, and then the bones of the fingers or toes (digits). This order of bones is found in the limbs of most vertebrates (see Chapter 14).

> The **appendicular skeleton** comprises the girdles and the limbs.

Bone structure

Bones provide support so they need to be strong, but they cannot be too heavy or the muscles would not be able to move them. Bone has a shape similar to that in Fig 32.6, giving maximum strength with minimum weight.

- The tops of the bone are called the epiphysis or head.
- The long section is called the diaphysis or shaft.
- On the outside of the bone is a fibrous coat.
- Beneath this is compact bone for strength. The compact bone contains living cells and it therefore has to have a good blood supply to nourish those cells. There is also a good nerve supply in bone.
- The next layer is spongy bone, so called because it has an irregular lattice-like arrangement of bone tissue to minimise weight. **Red bone marrow** is found in the spaces of the spongy bone. Red bone marrow produces blood cells (see Chapter 24).
- The centre of the long bones is hollow (the medullary cavity) and contains **yellow bone marrow**, which is used for the storage of fat.
- Cartilage is found at the end of the bones, at the joint. This comprises cells in a rubbery matrix which may contain elastic fibres made of protein (see Chapter 9). Cartilage is flexible and prevents the hard bones from rubbing against each other, which would cause damage.

Joints

Joints are found where bones meet other bones. There are three types of joints found in the body:

1. The **immovable joints (fused joints)** are found where bones are held tightly together without cartilage. These are found in the skull where the bones of the cranium grow into one another (Fig 32.7).
2. The **slightly movable** joints are found where flexibility with little movement is required. Discs of cartilage separate the bones in the vertebral column, which allow a limited amount of movement and act as shock absorbers (Fig 32.8).
3. In **freely moveable joints**, there is cartilage and a space at the junction of the bones. These joints are also called **synovial joints**.

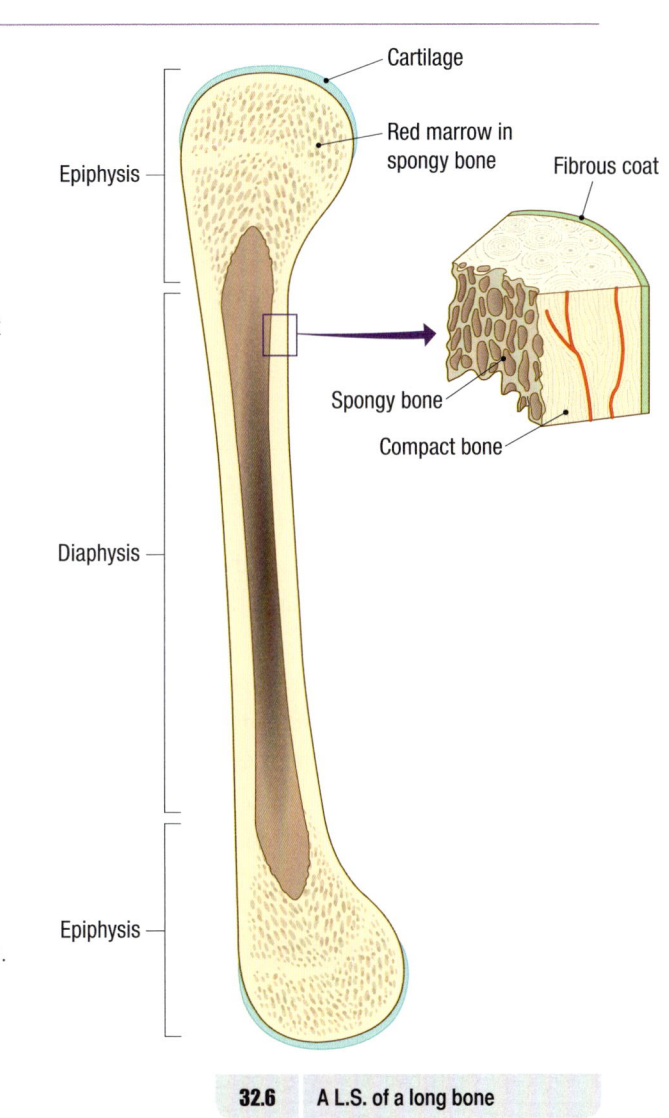

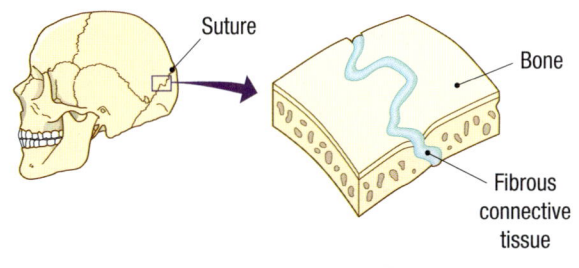

32.6 A L.S. of a long bone

32.7 An immovable joint

32 | The Musculoskeletal System

All synovial joints have a common structure as shown in Fig 32.9.

A membrane called the **synovial membrane** surrounds the joint. The synovial membrane secretes **synovial fluid**. This fluid acts as a lubricant for the joint. The bones are covered at the joint by pads of **cartilage** to prevent the bones from rubbing against one another. The bones are held together by flexible **ligaments** which allow them to move without coming apart. Muscles are attached to bones by inelastic **tendons** which transfer the 'pull' of the muscle to the bone.

There are four types of synovial joints in the human:

1. **Ball and socket joints** give the most freedom of movement and are found in the hip and shoulder.
2. **Hinge joints** allow for movement in one plane only (just like a door hinge) and are found at the elbow, knee and fingers.
3. **Gliding joints** are found where bones slip over one another, and are found at the wrist and ankle.
4. **Pivot joints** occur where one bone pivots on another and one is found in the neck between the top two vertebrae.

> **D** — A **synovial joint** is a freely movable joint comprised of synovial membrane and fluid and cartilage.

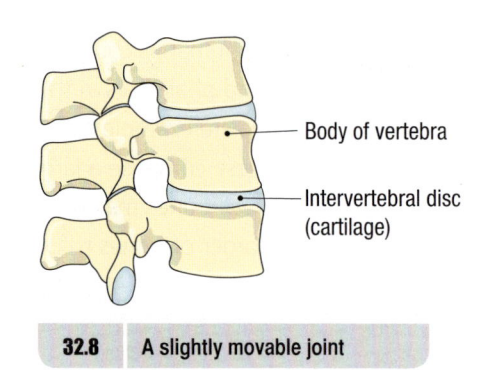

32.8 A slightly movable joint

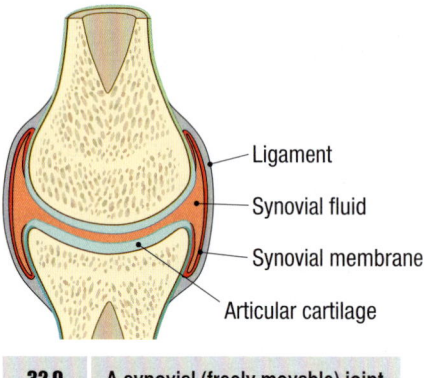

32.9 A synovial (freely movable) joint

Movement

There are three types of muscle in the body, as discussed in Chapter 9: **cardiac**, **smooth** and **skeletal** muscle.

- Cardiac muscles are found in the heart, they can contract strongly but they do not tire and they are not under conscious control.
- Smooth muscles are found in the digestive system, they contract and tire slowly and are not under conscious control.
- Skeletal muscles are found around the skeleton, they contract and tire quickly. Skeletal muscle is used in the body to move the bones. An example of this is shown in Fig 32.10, showing the two muscles in the upper arm, the **biceps** and the **triceps**.

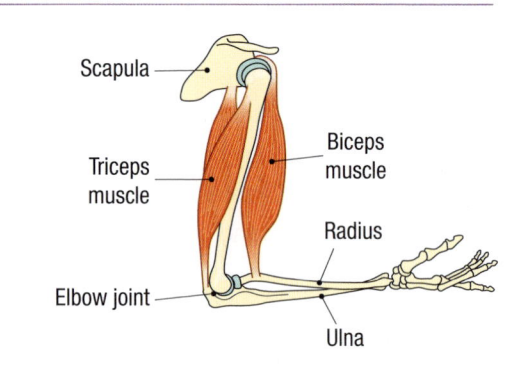

Antagonistic muscles

The biceps causes the arm to bend at the elbow while the triceps straightens it out (Fig 32.10).

The triceps pulls two bones further away from each other.

It can be seen that the two muscles cause opposite effects. Any two muscles that oppose each other in this way are called **antagonistic muscles** (pairs).

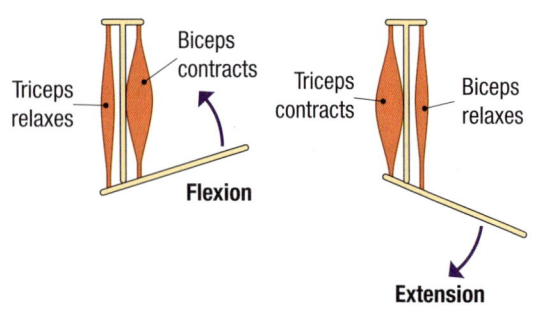

Muscles can only contract and relax (they cannot 'push'), and therefore need to be pulled back to their original length once contraction is finished. Having muscles in antagonistic pairs achieves this in the body.

32.10 The biceps and triceps, an antagonistic pair of muscles, showing their action

> **D** — **Antagonistic muscles** are pairs of muscles that pull against each other.

Muscles are attached to the bones by tough, inelastic tendons. These tendons transfer the pulling force from the muscles to the bone. The bones at a joint are held together by ligaments. Ligaments are elastic to allow bones to move at joints, and they are tough to hold the bones together.

Table 32.1 The role of the structures involved in movement

Structure	Properties	Located	Function
Muscle	Can contract	Attached to tendons as antagonistic pairs	Move bones
Tendon	Tough and inelastic	Connect muscles to bone	Transfer muscle 'pull' to bone
Ligament	Tough but elastic	Connect bone to bone	Allow bones to move at a joint
Cartilage	Tough and flexible	At the end of bones, also in the trachea and at nose and ear tip	Prevent bones rubbing

Skeletal disorders

SYLLABUS REQUIREMENT:

You need to know about arthritis or osteoporosis.

Medical problems can arise with the musculoskeletal system.

Arthritis
Cause

If the surfaces of the joints wear faster than the body can repair them, they will tend to wear out. This damage is described as **osteoarthritis**. Similar damage is sometimes due to an auto-immune disease such as **rheumatoid arthritis** where the immune system of the person causes inflammation and pain by attacking the joints (Fig 32.11).

Prevention

Osteoarthritis is due to wear and tear of the joints. This can be reduced by reducing the weight on the joints when exercising, i.e. swimming or cycling rather than running on a hard surface, and also by wearing the correct footwear when exercising.

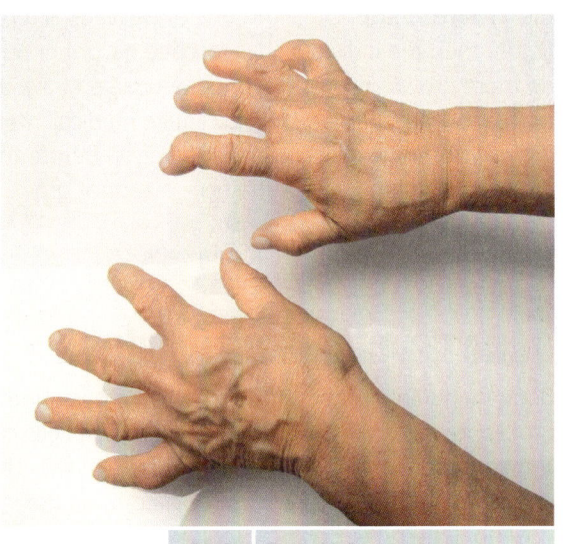

32.11 Damage due to arthritis

Treatment

If the damage to the joints in either type of arthritis gets very severe, then the joints can be replaced by artificial replacements. This is commonly done in the hip joint. In the operation, the top of the femur is replaced by a metal implant and a plastic socket is attached to the pelvis. This removes the pain and returns mobility to the patient.

Osteoporosis
Cause

Osteoporosis (brittle bone disease) is another disease that may affect the skeletal system. In this disease, the **bone density** gradually reduces with age, and eventually the patient will get bone fractures, particularly disintegration of the vertebral column. This disease is more common in women than in men, and it becomes very noticeable in women after the **menopause** (when their normal monthly hormonal cycle stops). This is because at this time **oestrogen** levels fall, and oestrogen is responsible for maintaining bone calcium.

Prevention and treatment

The disease can be recognised before it causes damage by taking X-rays of bone density. Damage can then be limited by increasing vitamin D and calcium intake as well as weight-bearing exercise, e.g. walking.

32 The Musculoskeletal System

HL

Growth and development of bone

Original bone development

In the human **embryo**, the skeleton is originally made of cartilage and is later replaced with bone. This process (**ossification**) continues until the person stops growing. Ossification is brought about by specialised cells called **osteoblasts**. These osteoblasts (Fig 31.12) produce collagen, which is then hardened with a compound of calcium and phosphate. Once this hardening occurs then the osteoblasts are trapped in the bone and remain dormant and are called **osteocytes**.

This hardening process starts in the middle of the long bones but eventually a second site of ossification occurs at the ends of the bones. Between these two sites, a disc of cartilage remains called the **growth plate**. Once this disc of cartilage is replaced by bone tissue, then the individual has reached his or her adult height, as no more growth is possible. Should a person have a lack of growth hormone (see Chapter 31) and require medical intervention, growth hormone injections must be given before the cartilage discs have disappeared or the person cannot grow.

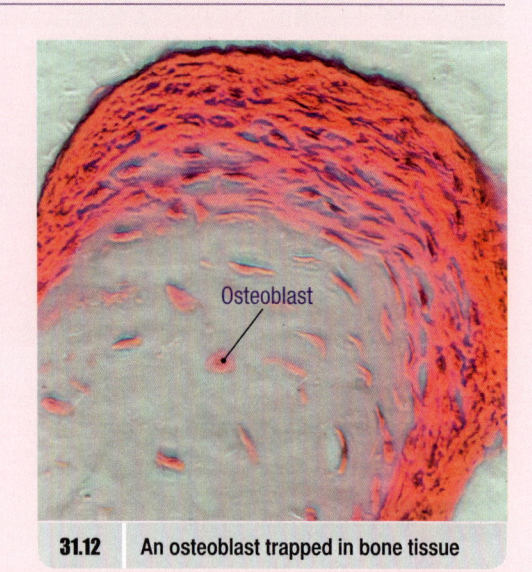

31.12 An osteoblast trapped in bone tissue

D **Osteoblasts** are bone-producing cells.

Bone development in adults

Bone manufacture does not stop when a person reaches adulthood, as the bones are continually being broken down and built up again. Specialised cells called **osteoclasts** from the bone marrow break down the bone and release the calcium into the blood. This is controlled by the **parathyroid hormone**. The osteoblasts now released from the hard bone tissue make new bone. This new bone is made along load-bearing lines in the bone caused by everyday activity. This means that the bone is made where it is needed and removed from places where it is not required. The result is a strong structure with minimum weight. Although surrounded by this rigid material, the cells in bones are living and have to be supplied with oxygen and food. Consequently, there is always a good blood supply to bones. The continued renewal of bone is dependent upon physical activity, hormone levels and diet.

D **Osteoclasts** are bone-digesting cells.

Summary

- The skeleton is made up of bones (hard) and cartilage (flexible).
- Bones are held together by elastic ligaments and moved by muscles attached to them by inelastic tendons.
- The functions of the skeleton are:
  - to give support;
  - movement;
  - protection;
  - blood cell production.
- The skeleton comprises the axial skeleton and the appendicular skeleton.

32 The Musculoskeletal System

Summary

- The axial skeleton comprises:
  - the skull containing fused bones;
  - the vertebral column made up of vertebrae: seven cervical, twelve thoracic with ribs, five lumbar, the sacrum and coccyx; between each vertebra is a disc of cartilage.
- The appendicular skeleton comprises:
  - the pentadactyl (five-digit) limbs made up of one long bone followed by two long bones, followed by a set of little bones and then the palm and digit bones;
  - the girdles, which attach the limbs to the axial skeleton.
- Bones have a fibrous coat, a layer of solid bone, and a spongy (honeycomb) layer of bone with red marrow and a hollow centre with yellow marrow. Cartilage is found at the end of bones.

Structure	Properties	Located	Function
Muscle	Can contract	Attached to tendons as antagonistic pairs	Move bones
Tendon	Tough and inelastic	Connect muscles to bone	Transfer muscle 'pull' to bone
Ligament	Tough but elastic	Connect bones to bone	Allow bones to move at a joint
Cartilage	Tough and flexible	At the end of bones	Prevent bones rubbing
Synovial fluid	Liquid	Inside synovial joints	Lubrication
Synovial membrane	Tough	Around synovial joint	Make and hold synovial fluid

- There are three types of joint.
  1. Immovable joints (fused):
     no cartilage between bone
     no movement
     e.g. found in skull.
  2. Slightly moveable joints:
     have cartilage between bones
     flexibility with little movement
     found between vertebrae.
  3. Moveable joints (synovial):
     have cartilage, synovial fluid and synovial membranes between bones
     four types of synovial joint: ball and socket (hip), hinge (knee), gliding (ankle) and pivot (top of spine).
- Muscles contract and relax so they need to be pulled to their original shape.
  - Muscles are found in antagonistic pairs, e.g. triceps (extensor) and biceps (flexor) in arm.
- Osteoarthritis arises where the joints wear out. Rheumatoid arthritis is where the body attacks its own joints. Can be prevented by weight-free exercise. A surgeon can replace damaged joints.
- Osteoporosis is the loss of bone density. It is more common in women, and can be prevented by taking calcium and vitamin D, and weight-bearing exercise.

HL
- The skeleton is originally cartilage and is gradually replaced by bone tissue (ossification). This is done by osteoblasts at the growth plates. When the growth plates are ossified then increased growth is impossible.
  - In adults bone is continuously broken down and replaced.
  - This is controlled by the parathyroid hormone.
  - Osteoblasts make new bone: some osteoblasts are trapped (osteocytes); osteoclasts break down bone and the process repeats.

The Musculoskeletal System

Review questions

01 (a) What is the purpose of the musculoskeletal system?
(b) What are the functions of the skeleton?

02 (a) Distinguish between the axial and appendicular skeleton.
(b) Name the parts of the axial skeleton and state their functions.
(c) Name the parts of the appendicular skeleton.

03 (a) Label the regions labelled A to E on the diagram of a backbone.
(b) To which region are the ribs attached?
(c) What are the functions of the ribs?

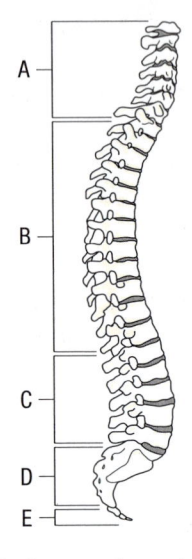

04 (a) Draw a simple diagram of a pentadactyl limb.
(b) Why is this structure used as evidence for evolution?

05 (a) Draw a labelled diagram of a L.S. through a long bone.
(b) Give the functions of the parts you have labelled.

06 (a) List the three main types of joint.
(b) Give a named example of each of these.
(c) Give one location for each example in (b).

07 (a) Draw a diagram of a synovial joint.
(b) Give the function of each part labelled.

08 (a) What is meant by the term 'antagonistic pair'?
(b) Why are muscles found as antagonistic pairs?
(c) Give an example of an antagonistic pair in humans.
(d) What are the differences between tendons and ligaments?
(e) What is the function of cartilage?
(f) Name two places in the body where cartilage is found.
(g) Name two places, other than the skeleton, where cartilage is found.

09 (a) What is osteoporosis?
(b) What causes osteoporosis and what is a possible preventative measure?

10 (a) What is ossification?
(b) Why does ossification take place?

11 (a) Describe the process of bone formation.
(b) What hormone controls the process of bone manufacture?
(c) Why does there have to be a good blood supply to bones?

Examination style questions

Section A

01 (a) The diagram shows an example of antagonistic muscles and part of the appendicular skeleton. Identify the parts labelled A, B, C and D.

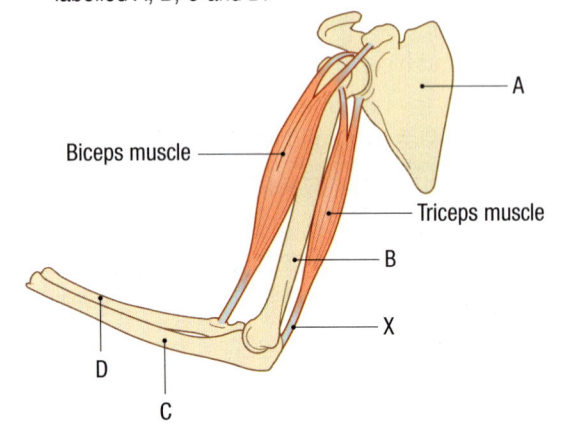

(b) Explain the term antagonistic muscles.
(c) State which muscle, the biceps or triceps, contracts to raise the lower arm.
(d) Identify the structure labelled X, which connects muscle to bone.
(e) State the function of X.

02 (a) What are the two parts to the skeleton?
(b) Give the four functions of the skeleton.
(c) Name two types of synovial joints.
(d) Give a precise location in the body where each can be found.
(e) What is the function of cartilage at the joint?

Section C

03 (a) There are three major types of joint in the human skeleton. Distinguish between slightly moveable and synovial joints.
(b) List three synovial joints and give their location.

Examination style questions

(c) State the function of a named joint.
(d) Outline the role of osteoblasts and cartilage in the formation of bone.
(e) Give two factors that affect the continued renewal of bone throughout our life.

04 The diagram shows a longitudinal section of a long bone and a freely moveable joint.

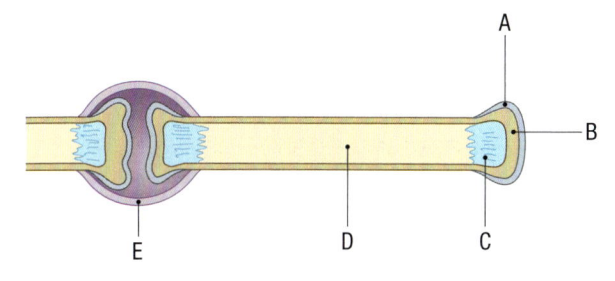

(a) Give an example of a freely moveable joint.
(b) Identify the parts labelled A, B, C and D of the long bone.
(c) Name the fluid in the joint cavity. What is its function?
(d) Explain the function of the part labelled A.
(e) Explain the function of the part labelled E.
(f) Movement is one function of the skeleton. State two other functions of the skeleton.

05 (a) (i) What do you think would be the problems caused if the bones were:
   1. Completely solid?
   2. Totally hollow?
   (ii) Describe the appendicular skeleton.
(b) (i) Describe the structure of a synovial joint with the aid of a labelled diagram.
   (ii) Give a function of each labelled part.
   (iii) Muscles are found as antagonistic pairs. Explain this statement.
   (iv) Describe how such a pair of muscles can move the arm.
(c) (i) What is the difference between an osteoblast and an osteoclast?
   (ii) Describe how these work together to produce new bone tissue.
   (iii) Give one cause, treatment and preventative measure for any bone disorder.

Leaving Certificate examination questions

Section A

01 Study the diagram of a synovial joint and then answer the following questions.

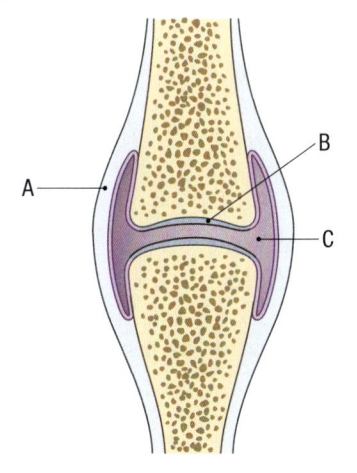

(a) Name tissue A.
(b) Give a function of A.
(c) Name tissue B.
(d) Name the fluid in C.
(e) Give a function of the fluid in C.

2007 OL Q. 6

02 (a) The diagram shows the macroscopic structure of part of a long bone.

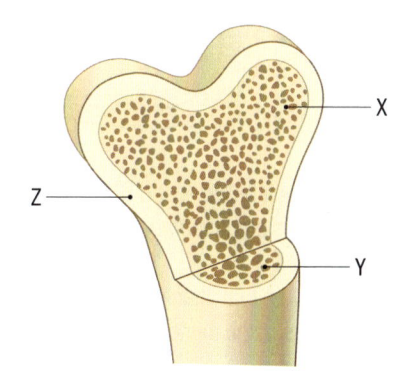

(i) Name a long bone in the human body.
(ii) Name parts X, Y and Z in the diagram.
(iii) State a function of X.
(iv) State a function of Y.
(b) (i) Show clearly on the diagram where you would expect to find cartilage.
(ii) State **one** role of **this** cartilage.

2012 HL Q. 3

32 The Musculoskeletal System

Leaving Certificate examination questions

03 (a) The diagram shows a longitudinal section of a long bone.

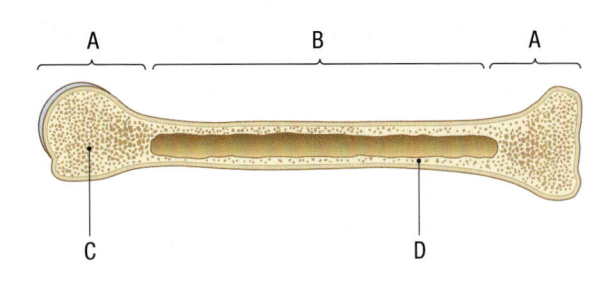

(i) Name the parts of the diagram labelled A, B, C, D.
(ii) Where are the discs in the human backbone?
(iii) What is the function of the discs in the human backbone?

(b) Give a role for **each** of the following in the human body:
(i) yellow bone marrow, (ii) red bone marrow.

2009 HL Q. 4

Section C

04 The diagram shows muscles and bones in a human arm.

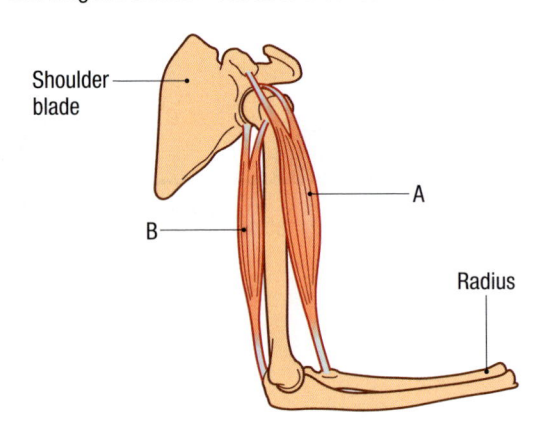

(i) Name the muscles labelled A and B.
(ii) These two muscles are an *antagonistic pair*. What does this mean?
(iii) Name the structures that attach muscles to bones.
(iv) Describe the roles of the muscles A **and** B in raising the forearm.
(v) What general name is given to places in the body where two or more bones meet?
(vi) 1. Name **one** disorder of the human musculoskeletal system.
2. Suggest **one** cause and **one** treatment for the disorder referred to in (vi) 1. above.

2014 OL Q. 4 (a)

05 The diagram shows a synovial joint.

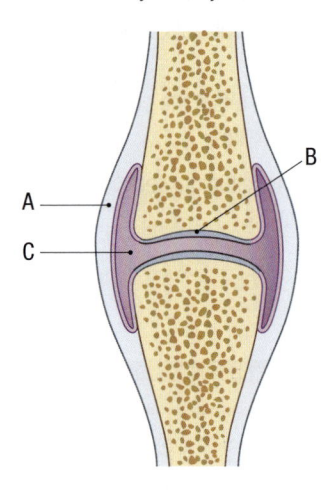

(i) Name the parts labelled A, B and C.
(ii) Give two functions of the human skeleton.
(iii) Vertebrae in the neck are called cervical vertebrae. Name and give the exact location of two other types of vertebrae.
(iv) Name one disorder of the musculoskeletal system.

2013 OL Q. 14 (b)

06 The diagram shows the bones of the human arm.

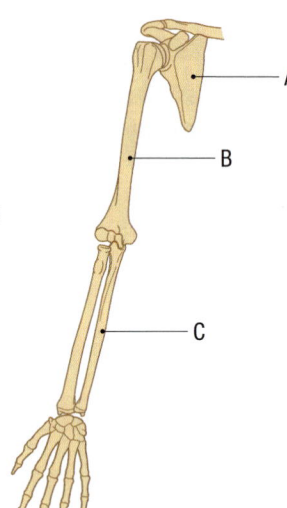

(i) Name the parts labelled A, B and C.
(ii) What structures attach a muscle to a bone?
(iii) Which upper arm muscle contracts to raise the lower arm?
(iv) What is meant by the term *antagonistic pair* in reference to muscles?
(v) Name the type of joint at the elbow.
(vi) Apart from movement, give **one** other function of the skeleton.
(vii) Suggest **one** reason why the bones of birds are almost hollow.

2010 OL Q. 15 (b)

Leaving Certificate examination questions

07 (i) Name the **type** of joint shown in the diagram.

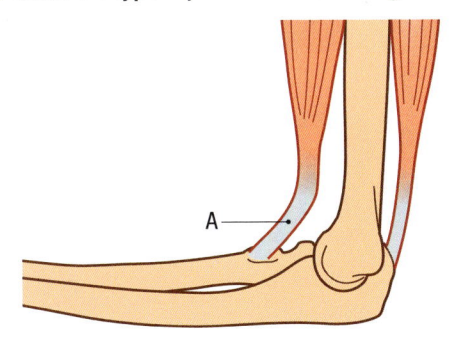

(ii) Name the structure labelled A, which attaches muscle to bone.
(iii) Explain what is meant by an *antagonistic muscle pair*.

2014 HL Q. 11 (a)

08 Answer the following questions in relation to the human musculoskeletal system.
(i) Give **three** roles of the skeleton.
(ii) Explain what is meant by the axial skeleton.
(iii) Give a function for each of the following:
1. Red marrow, 2. Cartilage, 3. Tendon.
(iv) Explain what is meant by an antagonistic muscle pair and give an example in the human body.
(v) Suggest a treatment for a named disorder of the musculoskeletal system.

2008 HL Q. 15 (a)

09 (i) Draw a diagram to show the structure of a synovial joint. Label **three** parts of the joint that you have drawn, other than bones.
(ii) Explain the functions of the three parts that you have labelled.
(iii) Name a disorder of the musculoskeletal system.
(iv) Give a possible cause of the disorder that you have named in (iii) and suggest a treatment for it.

2006 HL Q. 15 (a)

Past examination questions

OL	2014 Q. 14 (a)	2013 Q. 14 (a)	2010 Q. 15 (b)	2007 Q. 6	2006 Q. 15 (c)	2004 Q. 1 (b), Q 4
HL	2014 Q. 11 (a)	2012 Q. 3	2009 Q. 4	2008 Q. 15 (a)	2006 Q. 15 (a)	
	2005 Q. 3 (d), Q 14 (c) (iii)					

3 The Human Defence System

After studying this chapter you should be able to:

1. Describe the general defence system including the skin, the mucous membranes and the phagocytic white blood cells.
2. Describe the specific defence system.
3. Describe the antibody–antigen response.
4. Define induced immunity.
5. Explain immunisation and vaccination.
6. **HL** Describe the types of lymphocytes found in the body.
7. **HL** Explain the role of B and T cells in the specific defence system.

Defence against disease

Humans live in a world in which their bodies are awash with microbes. Many of these attack our bodies and try to enter them in an attempt to live within. Humans have a defence system that continuously defends the body from these microbes. The microbes attempt to enter the body through one of its openings such as the nose, the mouth or the opening of the reproductive system. They may also enter through a cut in the skin. These **pathogens** – as such disease-causing microbes are called – will live on the tissue of the human or produce poisons (**toxins**) which are released into the body. The body defends itself in a number of ways. These methods can be divided into two main types:

1. The **general defence system** that prevents the introduction of microbes into the body and acts against all microbes if they do get in.
2. The **specific defence system** that kills particular microbes as they enter the body.

> A **pathogen** is a disease-causing organism.

The general defence system

The general defence system prevents the entry of microbes by acting as a barrier and by destroying microbes once they are within the body.

1. The skin is an effective barrier to most microbes. Cells dividing at the bottom of the epidermis produce the skin. These cells become flattened as they are pushed up to the uppermost layer. These flattened skin cells are shed when they reach the top of the skin and they carry microbes away with them (Fig 27.5). The skin only covers the exposed surface of the body, and the tubes in the body leading from the various openings cannot be protected in this manner.
2. The **oil (sebaceous) glands** in the skin release sebum that kills bacteria.
3. The respiratory system is protected by **mucus-producing cells**. This mucus traps the microbes. Cells containing **cilia** line the tubes, and these little hairs sweep the mucus to the throat where the mucus and microbes are swallowed and killed in the stomach by the acid produced there. Coughing and sneezing will also help to remove some foreign bodies.

4. Body fluids produced in exposed areas, i.e. tears, urine or saliva, all contain an enzyme, **lysozyme**, which bursts bacteria by putting holes in the walls of bacteria, thus letting water enter.
5. The walls of the vagina produce carbohydrates that beneficial (**symbiotic**) bacteria convert into **lactic acid**. This acid inhibits the growth of pathogens.
6. The blood will **clot** preventing pathogens entering the body and loss of blood.

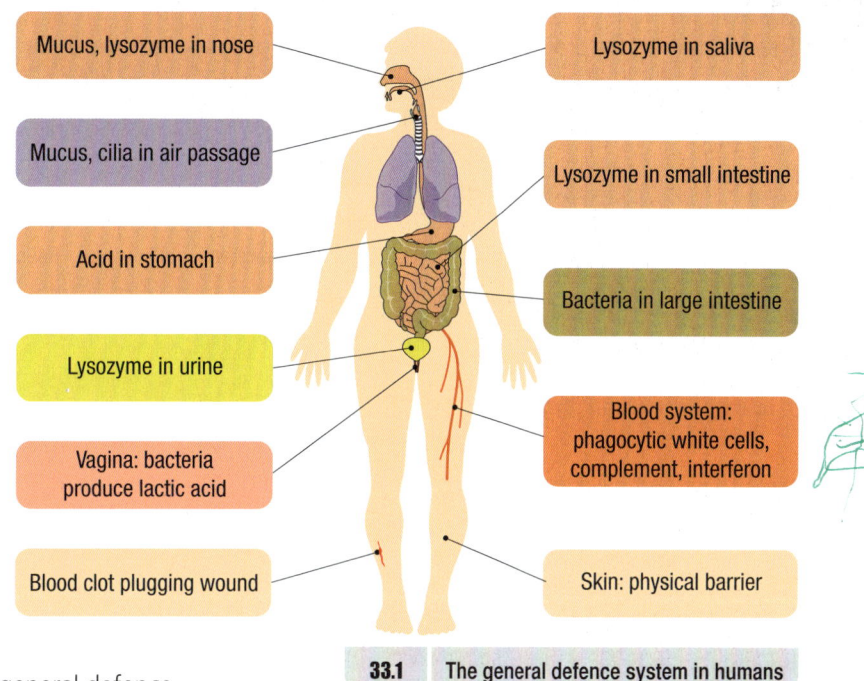

Should the microbes get beyond these barriers to entry, then the body has a number of methods to defend itself. The general defence system (Fig 33.1) uses a number of non-specific responses to rid the body of microbes.

7. The most obvious is the **inflammatory reaction**. This causes swelling and redness at the site of infection, as the temperature rises and the number of white blood cells in the area increases.
8. Many of these white blood cells destroy the microbes by engulfing and destroying them. These cells are called **phagocytic white blood cells**, and are largely responsible for the production of pus at the site of an infection (Fig 33.2).
9. There are also proteins produced in the blood system which protect cells from bacteria. These proteins, called **complement**, produce holes in bacterial walls causing bacteria to fill with fluid and burst. Cells infected by viruses release a protein, **interferon**, which makes the surrounding cells resistant to the virus and helps limit the spread of the virus.

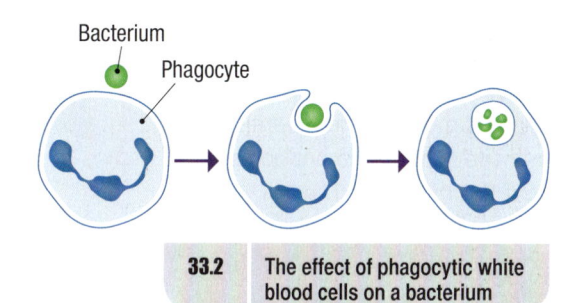

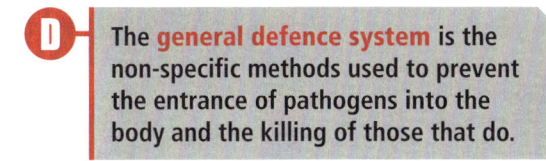

> The **general defence system** is the non-specific methods used to prevent the entrance of pathogens into the body and the killing of those that do.

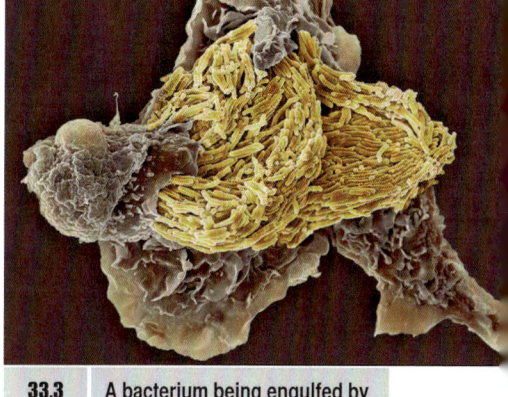

33.1 The general defence system in humans

33.2 The effect of phagocytic white blood cells on a bacterium

33.3 A bacterium being engulfed by a white blood cell

The specific defence system

The body has a specific defence system, also called the **immune response**. This system produces an individual response to each foreign body (**antigen**). Certain white blood cells called **lymphocytes** are produced in the **red bone marrow** and found in the **spleen**, the **thymus**, the **lymph system** and the **blood**. The spleen is a small organ found beside the stomach behind the lower ribs and the thymus is a gland found behind the top of the breast bone.

> The **specific defence system** or immune response is the defence against pathogens using antibodies or particular white blood cells.

> **Immunity** is the ability to defend against a disease.

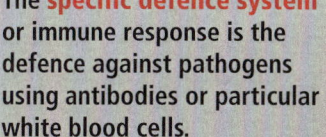

33 The Human Defence System

These lymphocytes produce proteins called **antibodies** to **antigens**. Each antigen causes a specific antibody to be produced that binds to the wall of the invading microbe and helps to destroy it. A person is born with millions of lymphocytes each capable of producing a different antibody.

> **D** An **antigen** is a substance that causes lymphocytes to produce antibodies.

> **D** **Antibodies** are proteins produced by a lymphocyte in response to an antigen.

3 When a microbe enters the body, lymphocytes attempt to attach their antibodies to the surface of the microbe (Fig 33.4). The structure it attempts to attach to is called an antigen. Eventually the correct match is found and that white blood cell reproduces quickly to produce thousands of copies of itself. As each white blood cell releases more and more antibodies into the system, the antibodies coat the microbes. The cell wall of the microbe becomes permeable and the cell either bursts or the phagocytes identify the antibody-coated microbes and digest them, and so the microbes are destroyed.

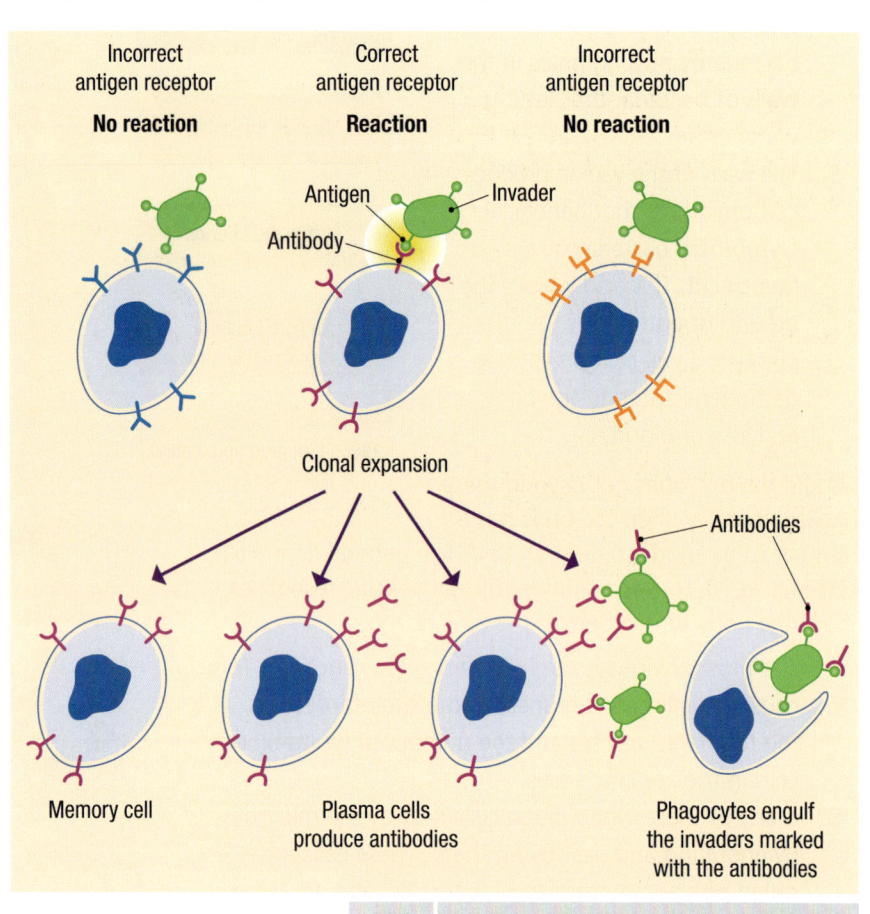

33.4 The production of antibodies by lymphocytes

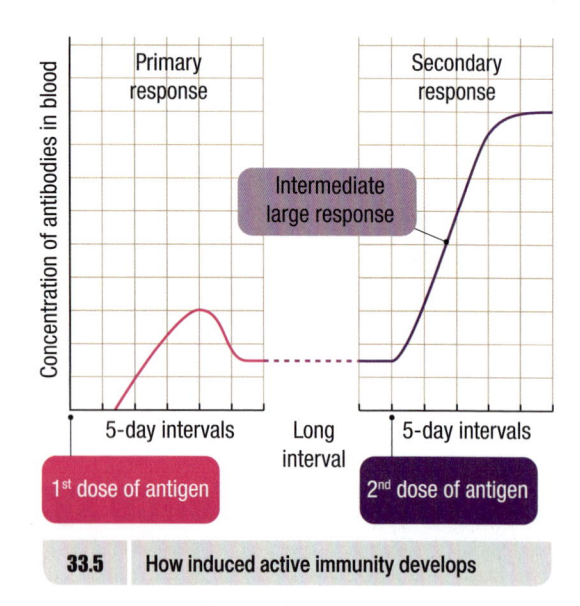

Once the body has learnt to produce the correct antibody the body remembers them. Should the same microbe try to reinfect the body, an immediate response occurs that produces large numbers of the antibody. This process ensures that humans do not normally get the same **4** infectious disease twice. This results in a process known as **induced active immunity** (Fig 33.5).

> **D** **Induced immunity** is when the body contains (or has the ability to produce) specific antibodies against particular antigens.

- **Active immunity** gives long term-immunity.
- This occurs naturally when a person gets a disease and the body produces the correct antibody and retains the ability to prevent future infection.
- **5** This same effect can be generated artificially using a form of **immunisation** often called **vaccination**. In this process, a non-disease causing form of the microbe, or part of the microbe is injected (or given orally) into a person. This is called a **vaccine**. The person's immune response is started and the correct antibodies against the disease are produced. Should this person at a later date be exposed to the same disease, the correct antibodies are present in their blood to prevent infection, e.g. the MMR injection which protects against measles, mumps and rubella.

33.5 How induced active immunity develops

The Human Defence System | 33

> **Active immunity** is when a person has the ability to produce their own antibodies against a disease.

> A **vaccine** is a substance introduced into a person to induce an antibody response leading to immunity to that disease.

> **Vaccination** is the introduction of a non-disease causing dose of a microbe so as to generate an active immune response.

> **Passive immunity** is when a person receives the antibodies that have been made by another organism, against a disease, without the ability to produce their own antibodies.

- In **passive immunity**, the body gets antibodies from someone else, and this generates a short-term defence against the disease.

- In newborn babies, passive immunity occurs naturally as they receive antibodies from their mother in breast milk. Breast-feeding reduces the incidence of diarrhoea in babies due to this effect.

- Passive immunity can be artificially induced in a person by **immunisation**. In this process, an injection of antibodies against a specific disease is given to the person, e.g. the anti-tetanus injection. In passive immunity, the immunity to the disease is short-lived as the donated antibodies are eventually destroyed.

- Passive immunity can be used if a response is required faster than the person could manufacture their own antibodies, i.e. a tetanus injection following a puncture wound. Or it could be administered if the vaccination is too expensive.

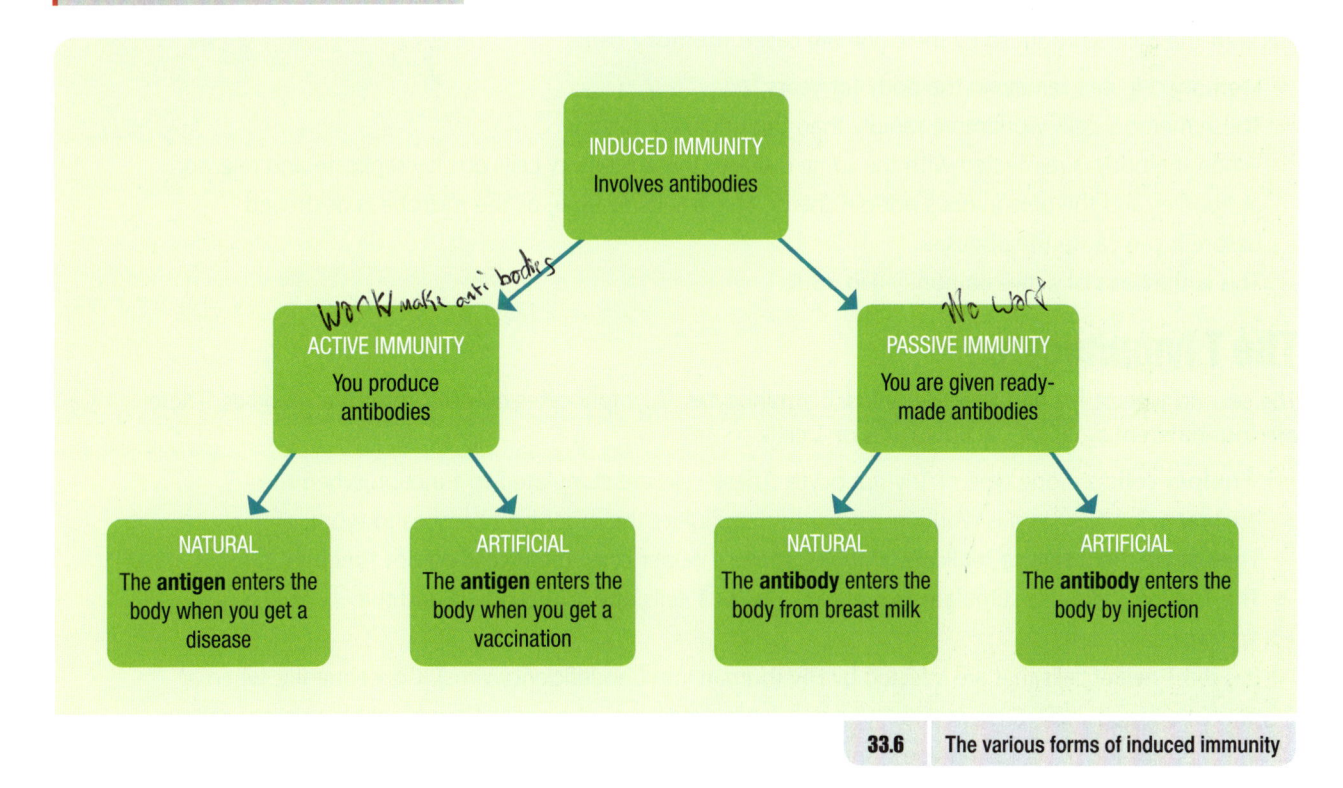

33.6 The various forms of induced immunity

HL Lymphocytes

There are two types of lymphocytes produced in the body (Fig 33.7). **B lymphocytes**, which mature in the red bone marrow and produce antibodies, and **T lymphocytes** that mature in the thymus gland and are largely active in controlling the immune response, as we will see later.

The B lymphocytes

The B lymphocytes are the lymphocytes that produce antibodies. As has already been seen, these antibodies are produced in response to antigens. At birth, humans have some 10 million different **clones** of B lymphocytes (a clone is a group of identical cells).

- Each B lymphocyte clone has its own specific antibody that it can produce in response to an antigen.
- This antibody is attached to the surface of the B cell.
- When this antibody comes in contact with an antigen it can attach to, it stimulates the B cell to replicate and to release lots of antibodies into the blood.
- As a result, the body is full of specific B cells that are all capable of releasing a specific antibody that binds to the antigen. These are called plasma cells.
- Microbes that have antibodies attached to them are then attacked by other cells in the immune system and are destroyed.

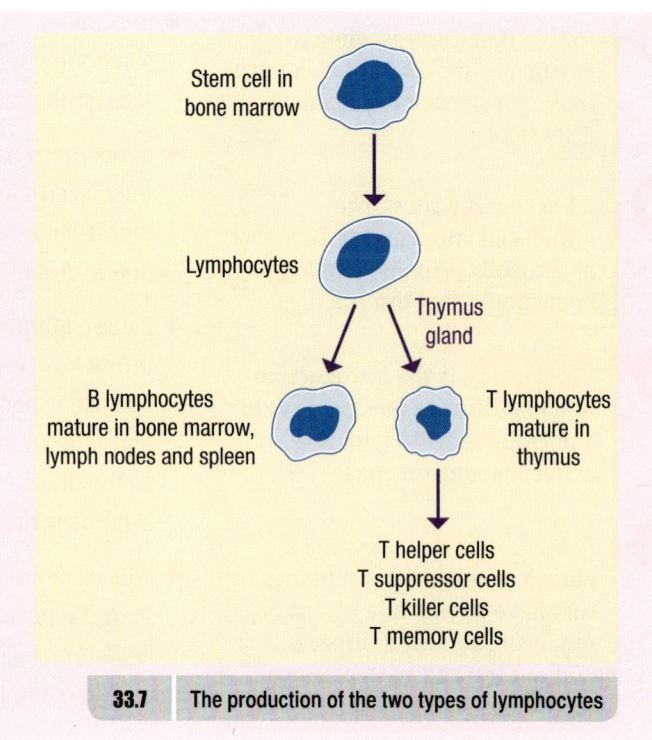

33.7 The production of the two types of lymphocytes

Some of the B cells produced by the clone are called **memory cells**.

- Memory cells can remain in the body for years.
- These memory cells work more rapidly than the original B cells.
- When the body is reinfected with the same disease, these memory cells quickly replicate and release antibodies and the person does not get the disease a second time, as the microbe is destroyed before it can cause the disease.
- This is the basis of active immunity (Fig 33.5).

The T lymphocytes

The second type of lymphocytes are called T lymphocytes. T lymphocytes do not produce antibodies. There are four different types of T lymphocytes or T cells:

- **T helper cells** are one type of T lymphocyte. These cells are stimulated to function when the general defence system is working, and in turn stimulate the other lymphocytes to work.
- They cause the B cells to replicate. Without these T helper cells, the B cells do not function.
- The T helper cells also stimulate two other types of T cells, the **T killer cells** and the **T suppressor cells**.
- It is the T helper cells that are infected by HIV (human immunodeficiency virus). Consequently, when a patient develops AIDS (acquired immune deficiency syndrome), the patient is susceptible to many other infections as the patient's immune system is compromised.
- T killer cells destroy cells infected by viruses, and they also attack any foreign cells in the body. This can cause organ rejection in organ transplant patients.
- T suppressor cells will reduce the immune response of other cells. This prevents the immune system from over-reacting to an infection (Fig 33.8).

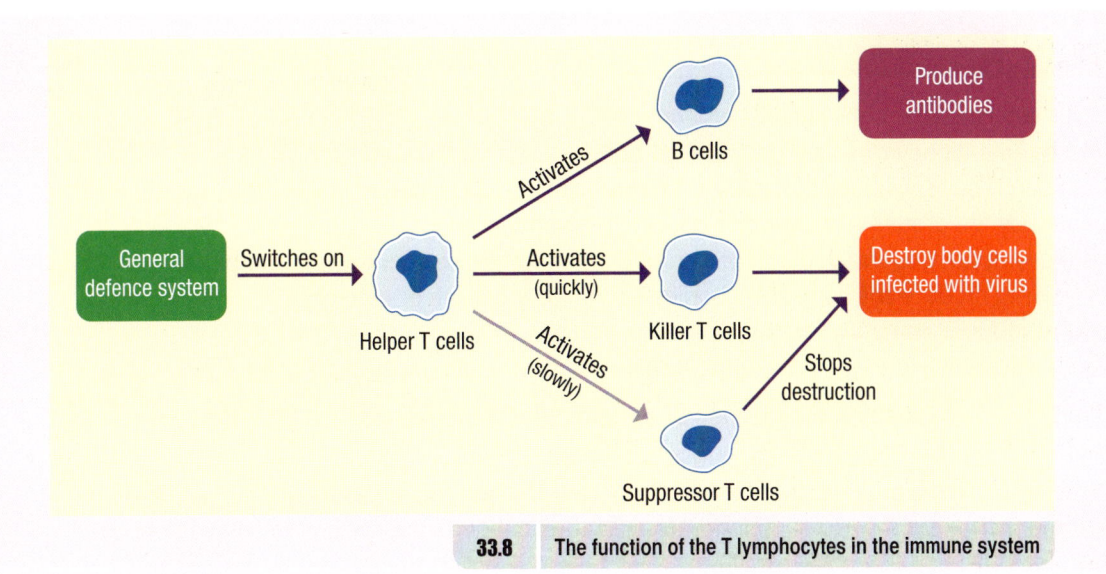

HL

33.8 The function of the T lymphocytes in the immune system

- **T memory cells** are long-lived and are produced when the T lymphocytes are stimulated into action. The T memory cells survive in the circulatory system for a long time and help the immune system to react more quickly if it is attacked by a disease a second time.

Summary

- Immunity is the ability to resist infection.
- The general defence system is the non-specific methods used to prevent entry of pathogens and it can destroy all microbes.

Structure or process	Role
Skin	Is an effective barrier, and sheds microbes along with epidermis
Sebum (oil) in skin	Kills microbes
Respiratory system: cilia and mucus	Traps microbes and sweeps them into the stomach.
Tears	Contain lysozyme to kill microbes
Vaginal bacteria	Produce lactic acid to kill microbes
Clotting mechanism	Clot blood to prevent loss
Inflammation	Causes temperature to rise and an increase of white blood cells to kill microbes
Phagocytic white blood cells	'Eat' microbes
Complement	Makes holes in bacterial cells
Interferon	Makes cells virus-resistant

- The specific defence system or immune response is the defence against pathogens using antibodies.

33 The Human Defence System

Summary

- The specific defence system (the immune system):
  - Produces an antibody to an antigen (foreign body).
  - An antigen is any substance that causes the production of an antibody.
  - An antibody is a protein produced in response to an antigen.
  - Uses the lymphocytes (white blood cells) found in the lymph, spleen, thymus and blood.
  - Can learn to produce the correct antibodies, so you only get the disease once.
  - Produces induced immunity (active or passive).
- Active immunity is when a person has the ability to produce their own antibodies against a disease.
- Active immunity develops after an infection or a vaccination. It provides long-lasting protection.
- Passive immunity means that antibodies are acquired, for instance in mother's milk. Disease will not be contracted while the antibodies are present (passive). The antibodies can be given in an injection (immunisation). This is a short-lived defence because the antibodies are not produced by the body's cells (see Fig 33.6).
- A vaccine is a substance introduced into a person to induce an antibody response leading to immunity to that disease.

HL
- There are two types of lymphocytes: B cells and T cells.
- B cells are made and mature in the bone marrow.
  - Each B lymphocyte clone produces its own specific antibodies.
  - The antibody is attached to the surface of the cell, and will switch on the cell if it meets its antigen. This will cause production of large amounts of the antibody. The antibody will then destroy the disease.
  - After infection, memory B cells are left, which give long-term immunity to disease.
- T cells are made in the bone marrow and mature in the thymus gland.
- T lymphocytes are subdivided into four types:
  - T helper cells. Turn on other lymphocytes. These are affected by HIV.
  - T killer cells kill damaged cells and foreign cells.
  - T suppressor cells reduce immune response.
  - T memory cells speed up any subsequent action of the T cells.
  - A way to remember these types is the phrase '**K**ill the **H**elper, **S**uppress the **M**emory'.

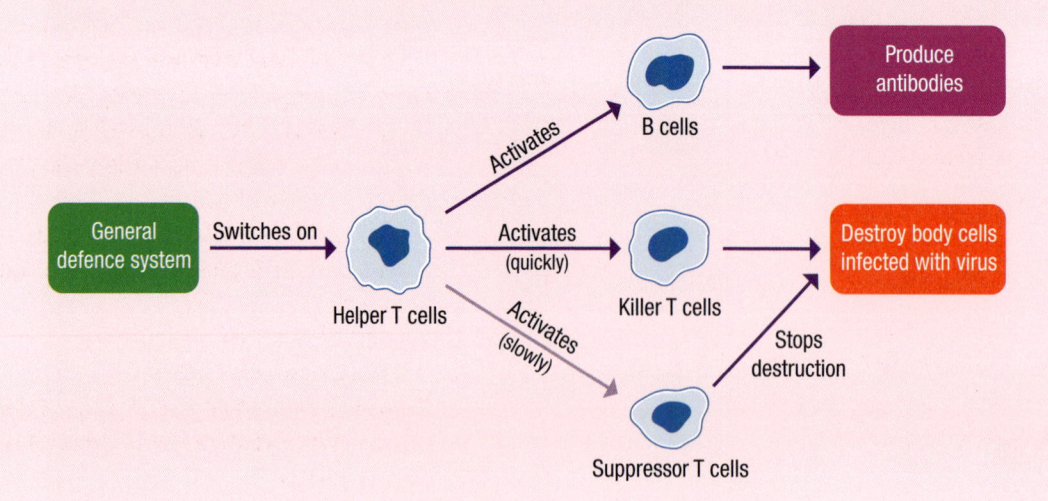

The Human Defence System

Review questions

01
(a) Why is it necessary to have a defence system?
(b) What are pathogens?
(c) What is immunity?

02
(a) What is the general defence system?
(b) Describe six ways in which the body defends itself using the general defence system.
(c) Explain the major difference between the general and the specific defence systems.

03
(a) What is the specific immune response?
(b) What role do white blood cells play in this system?
(c) What is the name given to these white blood cells?

04
(a) What is an antibody?
(b) What is an antigen?
(c) How are antigens and antibodies related?

05
(a) How is it that people usually get chickenpox only once?
(b) Is this an example of induced active immunity?
(c) Explain your answer in (b).

06
(a) What is a vaccination?
(b) How does a vaccination work?
(c) Name two vaccinations that you have had and the diseases they protect against.

07
(a) Distinguish between active and passive immunity.
(b) Give one example of each type of immunity.
(c) Is not catching the cold that your friend has an example of active or passive immunity?

08
(a) What are lymphocytes?
(b) Where are B lymphocytes produced?
(c) Where do they mature?
(d) What is the function of B lymphocytes?

09
(a) Describe the role B lymphocytes play in the specific defence system.
(b) What is the importance of B memory cells?

10
(a) List the types of T lymphocytes found in the immune response.
(b) Describe the role of each of the cells you named in (a).
(c) Describe how all the lymphocyte cells interact with each other.
(d) How does the HIV virus have its effect?

Examination style questions

Section A

01
(a) What is the general defence system?
(b) What is its function?
(c) What is a lymphocyte?
(d) Which defence system is it part of?
(e) Explain your answer in (d).

02
(a) What is an antibody?
(b) How is an antibody related to an antigen?
(c) What produces an antibody?
(d) What is passive immunity?
(e) Describe two ways in which a person might get passive immunity.

Section C

03
(a) (i) What is a pathogen?
 (ii) What type of chemical is present on the surface of a pathogen that is targeted by the immune system?
(b) (i) The skin is part of the general defence system of the body. State two ways that the skin protects us against pathogens.
 (ii) Some of our defensive white cells are <u>phagocytic</u>. Explain the meaning of the underlined term.
 (iii) Distinguish between antigen and antibody.
 (iv) Vaccination is used to immunise us against specific pathogens. Explain how vaccination gives us the ability to protect ourselves successfully should that pathogen penetrate our general defence system and gain entry into the body.
 (v) Suggest why it is important that a vaccination contains a diluted (harmless) form of the disease or its toxin.
(c) (i) What are lymphocytes?
 (ii) Where are these cells produced?
 (iii) Lymphocytes are further divided into T cells and B cells. Distinguish between those two different types of lymphocytes.
 (iv) Explain the role of each of the following in destroying a bacterial infection such as TB.
 Phagocyte
 B-lymphocyte
 Any two types of T-lymphocytes

33 The Human Defence System

Examination style questions

04 (a) (i) Distinguish between the general defence system and the specific defence system.
(ii) Describe three ways in which the general defence system carries out its function.
(iii) What is induced immunity?
(iv) Induced immunity can be generated when a person is vaccinated. Outline how vaccination works to protect against a particular pathogen.
(b) (i) What is the difference between active and passive immunity?
(ii) Describe two ways a person might get passive immunity.
(iii) Why is active immunity more useful for a person?
(iv) When might a doctor use passive immunity in treating a disease?

05 In the final years of the 19th century, Dublin was hit by a major outbreak of typhoid fever. A resident of Dublin, Mary Mallon, lost her entire family and emigrated to the USA. Mary became an excellent cook and was much in demand. However, she was dogged by bad luck and after working for a few months in any one household, typhoid would break out. Mary would move on to other employment (with very good references). In 1906 when typhoid broke out in General Warren's house, the cases were investigated as it was unusual for typhoid to be found in wealthy people's households since good sanitation was available.

The only common link in all the cases was Mary Mallon and she was discovered to be a 'healthy carrier'. This was the first time this condition was identified. Mary was originally kept at a hospital but later released on condition that she did not return to cooking. This, however, she did and another outbreak was discovered in a hospital where she was working. This time the public got to hear of the effect of Mary, who was called 'Typhoid Mary' in the press. She was nearly lynched by an angry mob. As it was impossible to get rid of the typhoid microbes from Mary, she spent the rest of her life living in a house attached to the hospital.

(a) What is a healthy carrier?
(b) How do you think Mary passed on the disease?
(c) Describe the mechanism by which most people recover from a case of typhoid.
(d) What measures could Mary have taken to reduce the likelihood of passing on the disease?
(e) How would doctors solve the problem of a typhoid carrier today?
(f) If you were trying to trace the source of the outbreak in 1906 in a scientific manner, what would you have done?

Leaving Certificate examination questions

Section A

01 During 2009 swine flu spread through the population of many countries. Younger people were more at risk of becoming ill with swine flu than older people. Using your knowledge of the immune system, suggest a reason for this.

2010 HL Q. 6 (c)

Section C

02 (i) What term is used to describe organisms that cause disease?
(ii) The general defence system tries to prevent disease-causing organisms entering the body. List **two** parts of the general defence system in the body.
(iii) 1. Distinguish between active immunity and passive immunity by defining each.
2. Which of these produces the longest-lasting immunity?
(v) Some people receive vaccinations to protect them from disease. What is meant by the term *vaccination*?

2014 OL Q. 14 (b)

03 (i) Distinguish clearly between antibodies and antibiotics by writing a note about each.
(ii) In relation to antibodies, distinguish between active and passive immunity.
(iii) Using your knowledge of antibiotics and bacteria, suggest why a person is more likely to pick up an infection in hospital than at home.

2013 HL Q. 12 (c)

04 (i) Name a group of white blood cells, other than lymphocytes.
(ii) Lymphocytes may be divided into B cells and T cells. B cells produce antibodies.
1. What is the role of antibodies in the body?
2. Name any **three** types of T cell.
3. State a role of **each** of the T cell types that you named in part 2.

2012 HL Q. 15 (b)

The Human Defence System

Leaving Certificate examination questions

05
(i) What is meant by the term immunity?
(ii) Outline briefly the role of B lymphocytes in the human immune system.
(iii) Distinguish between active and passive immunity.
(iv) "Vaccination gives rise to active immunity". Explain this statement.
(v) In certain situations a person is given a specific antibody rather than being vaccinated.
  1. Is this an example of active or passive immunity?
  2. Under what circumstances might an antibody, rather than a vaccination, be given?
  3. Comment on the duration of immunity that follows the administration of an antibody.

2007 HL Q. 14 (c)

06
(i) What is meant by the term immunity? Distinguish between active and passive immunity.
(ii) Describe two ways in which the skin helps to defend the body against pathogenic micro-organisms.
(iii) Lymphocytes play a vital role in the body's immune system. To which group of blood cells do lymphocytes belong? Name two types of lymphocyte and state a role of each.
(iv) What is the purpose of vaccination?

SEC Sample HL Q. 15 (b)

Past examination questions

OL	2014 Q. 14 (b) (i)–(iii) and (v)	2011 Q. 15 (c) (iii)–(v)		

HL	2013 Q. 12 (c)	2012 Q. 15 (b) (ii) and (iii)	2010 Q. 6 (c)	2009 Q. 15 (c) (i)	2007 Q. 14 (c)
	2006 Q. 6 (e)	2005 Q. 15 (a)	SEC Sample Q. 15 (b)		

34 Sexual Reproduction in Flowering Plants

After studying this chapter you should be able to:

1. Explain the terms reproduction and distinguish between asexual and sexual reproduction.
2. Appreciate the great variety of types of flower.
3. Draw a labelled diagram of a named flower and state the function of each part.
4. State what produces the male and female gamete.
5. (HL) Describe, in detail, pollen grain development and embryo sac development.
6. Define the term pollination and the methods of pollination – self-pollination and cross-pollination.
7. Describe the differences between and adaptations of wind and animal pollinated flowers.
8. Define fertilisation and describe 'double' fertilisation.
9. Describe seed structure.
10. Distinguish between (a) named endospermic and non-endospermic seeds and (b) named monocot and dicot seeds.
11. Outline the role of plant growth regulators in fruit development.
12. Explain how seedless fruits may be produced.
13. Describe the various methods of fruit and seed dispersal and explain the need for dispersal.
14. Define and state the advantages of dormancy.
15. Define germination and describe the stages of seedling growth.
16. Outline the factors necessary for germination and the role of respiration and digestion in germination.
17. Describe an investigation to show the effect of water, oxygen and correct temperature on germination.
18. Describe an investigation to show digestive activity during germination.

Reproduction

Reproduction is the ability of **organisms** to produce new individuals. If a type of organism is unable to reproduce, it becomes extinct. The continuity of life is therefore dependent on reproduction.

There are two types of reproduction: **asexual reproduction** and **sexual reproduction**.

Asexual reproduction

- Does not involve the fusion of **gametes** (involves only one parent).
- The offspring are produced as a result of **mitosis**.
- The new individuals (offspring) are identical to the parent.
- This type of reproduction is common in bacteria, fungi, *Amoeba* and plants.

Sexual reproduction

- Usually involves the fusion of male and female gametes (involves two parents).
- Gametes are **haploid** and their production usually involves **meiosis**.
- Because the **zygote** results from the joining of **chromosomes** in the nuclei of the two gametes, the offspring will not be identical to the parents.
- Sexual reproduction is common in animals and many plants.

34.1 A variety of plant life

Sexual reproduction in the flowering plant

2 Flowering plants are the most successful group of plants. They have adapted to live in almost every habitat on Earth except Antarctica. This is in part due to their ability to reproduce sexually without the need for water to be present. You have only to look around you to see the huge variety of flowering plants that exist (Fig 34.1).

Flower structure

3 The **flower** is the reproductive organ of a flowering plant. Flowers are formed from buds. A typical flower consists of a group of modified leaves arranged in rings or whorls. There are four main whorls in a flower. Starting from the outside there are the sepals, followed by the petals, stamens and carpels (Table 34.1 and Fig 34.2). The flower sits on the swollen stem tip, known as the receptacle.

Flowers differ in the number and arrangement of their flower parts.

Part	Description	Function(s)
Receptacle	Tip of stem	Forms the base of the flower
Sepals	Leaf-like, usually green	Protect flower before it blooms
Petals	Usually coloured	Attract animal pollinators, e.g. insects
Stamens	Made up of anther and filament	Male part of the flower
Anther	Sac-like structure at top of filament	Produces pollen grains that produce the male gametes
Filament	Stalk-like structure	Supports the anther and supplies food and water to the anther
Carpel	Made up of stigma, style and ovary	Female part of the flower
Stigma	Top of the carpel	To trap and hold pollen
Style	Neck of the carpel	Connects stigma to ovary
Ovary	Female reproductive organ	Contains ovules
Ovule	Bears an embryo sac	Produces the egg
Nectary	Sugar sac, usually at the base of the petals	Provides energy-rich food for pollinators

Table 34.1 Flower parts and functions

34 Sexual Reproduction in Flowering Plants

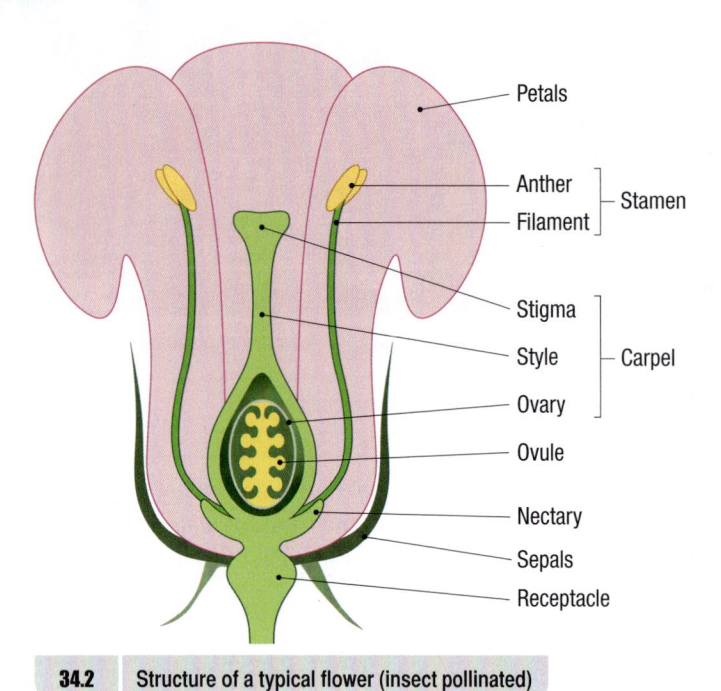

34.2 Structure of a typical flower (insect pollinated)

The life cycle of a typical flowering plant (Fig 34.3) involves a number of steps:

1. Gamete formation
2. **Pollination**
3. **Fertilisation**
4. **Seed** and **fruit** formation
5. Seed and fruit dispersal
6. **Dormancy**
7. **Germination**

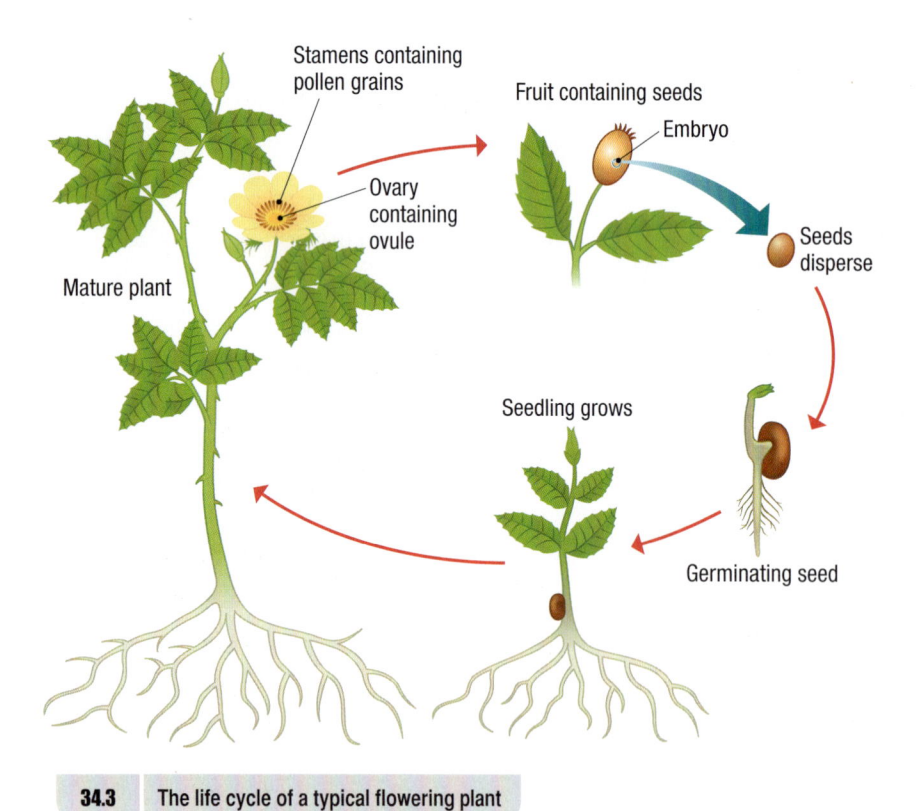

34.3 The life cycle of a typical flowering plant

1. Gamete formation

Pollen grains are formed in the **anther**. The pollen grain produces the male gamete.

The female gamete is produced in the **embryo sac** in the ovule (Fig 34.4). The embryo sac produces the egg cell and polar nuclei which both have a role in fertilisation in the flowering plant.

Sexual Reproduction in Flowering Plants | 34

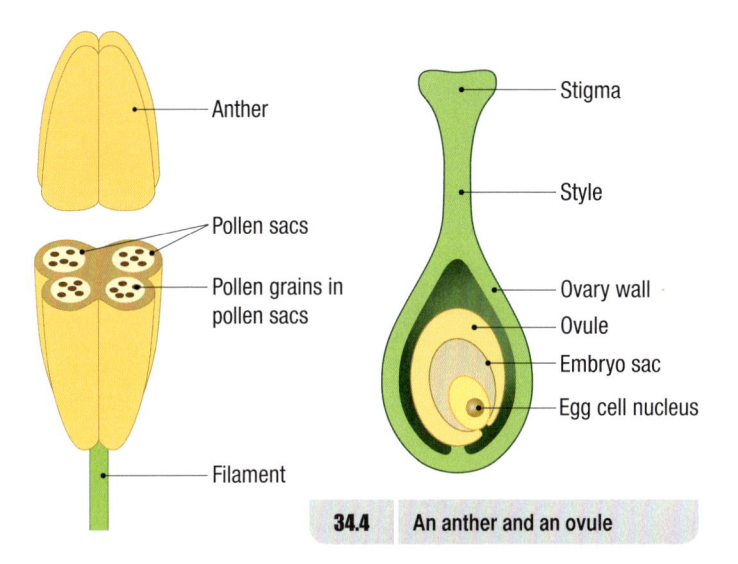

34.4 An anther and an ovule

HL Development of the pollen grain

- The stamens consist of a filament and an anther.
- Pollen grains form in the anther.
- Each anther contains four pollen sacs which contain many microspore (pollen) mother cells.
- Each pollen sac is lined by a special layer of cells known as the tapetum, which provides nutrients for the developing pollen grains.
- All the cells of the flowering plant are **diploid**. Each microspore mother cell (2n) divides by **meiosis** to produce four haploid microspores.
- The microspores become the pollen grains. The pollen grain is not a gamete, it produces the male gametes.
- The nucleus of each pollen grain divides by **mitosis** to produce two nuclei enclosed by a thick wall. One of these nuclei is known as the tube nucleus (which will form the pollen tube), the other is the generative nucleus. Each of these nuclei is haploid, because they have been produced by mitosis of the haploid nucleus of the pollen grain.
- Following pollination, the generative nucleus divides by mitosis to produce two male gametes.

In summary, pollen grains (Fig 34.5) form from microspores. The mature pollen grain consists of a tube cell nucleus and two haploid male gamete nuclei. As we shall see, each of these gamete nuclei has a role to play during fertilisation.

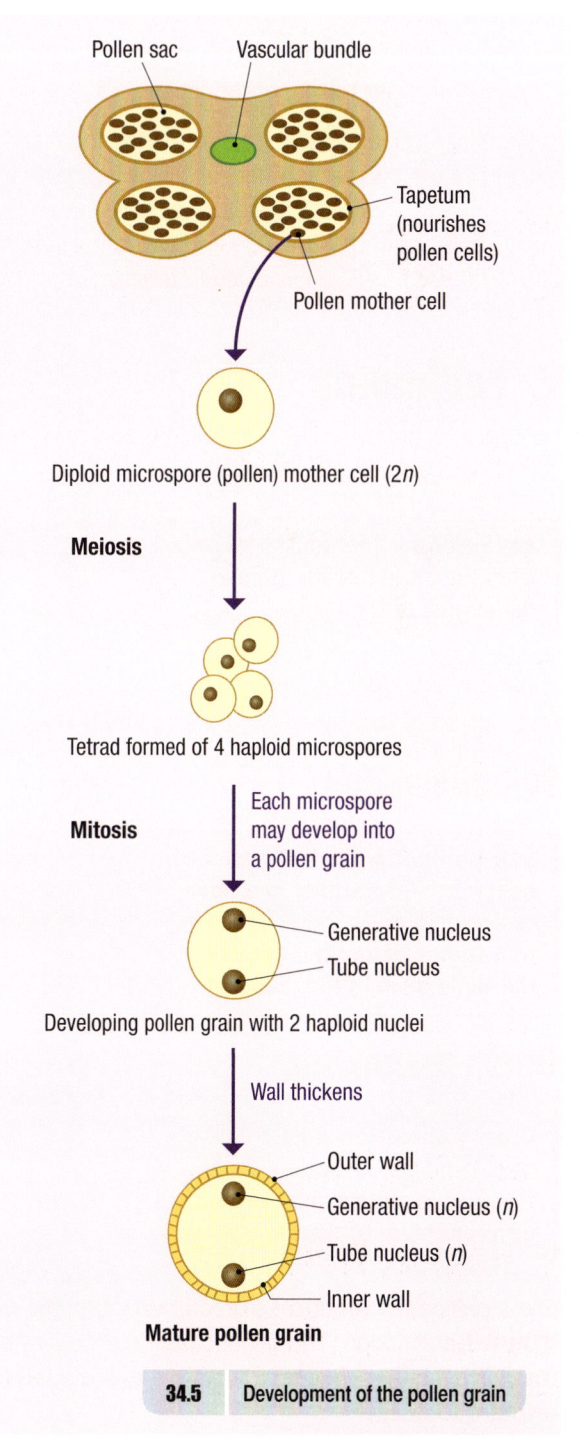

34.5 Development of the pollen grain

UNIT 3 THE ORGANISM 445

HL Embryo sac development

- The carpel of the flower houses one or more ovules (2n).
- Each ovule consists of a nutritious tissue called the nucellus, inside which lies a special cell – the embryo sac mother cell (also known as the megaspore mother cell).
- The embryo sac mother cell divides by meiosis to produce four haploid cells.
- Three of these cells disintegrate and the remaining cell is called the embryo sac or megaspore (n).
- The nucleus of the embryo sac now divides three times by mitosis to form eight haploid nuclei.
- These nuclei arrange themselves in the embryo sac as shown in Fig 34.6. The egg cell is to one end and the two polar nuclei are towards the middle of the embryo sac. The remaining five nuclei play no further role in reproduction.

In summary, the egg cell forms from an embryo sac mother cell in the ovule. The embryo sac mother cell divides once by meiosis and then three times by mitosis. The mature embryo sac consists of eight haploid nuclei, one of which is the egg and two others are the polar nuclei. Each of these nuclei are involved in fertilisation.

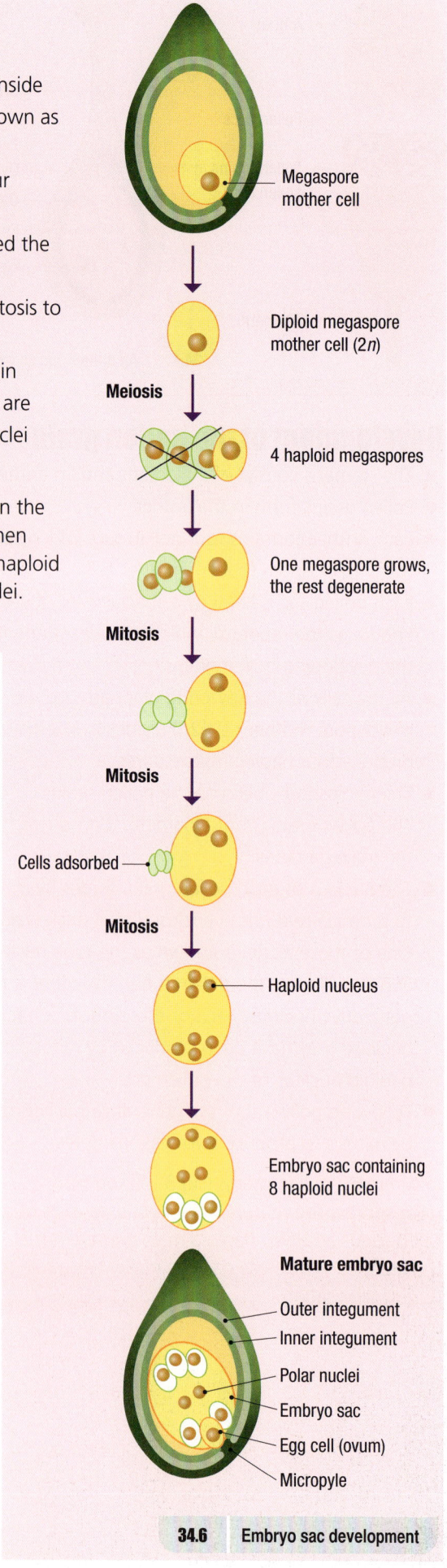

2. Pollination

For reproduction to occur, the pollen grains must reach the carpel. This event is called **pollination**.

> **Pollination** is the transfer of pollen from the anther of the stamen to the stigma of the carpel.

There are two types of pollination: **self-pollination** and **cross-pollination** (Fig 34.7).

Self-pollination

> **Self-pollination** is the transfer of pollen from the anther of a flower to a stigma of the same flower or to a stigma of another flower on the same plant in the ground.

Cross-pollination

> **Cross-pollination** is the transfer of pollen from an anther of one flower to a stigma of a flower of a different plant of the same species.

Cross-pollination produces a greater variety in the offspring than self-pollination. This genetic mixing produces plants that have a better chance of survival and are often more resistant to disease.

34.6 Embryo sac development

(Diagram labels: Megaspore mother cell; Diploid megaspore mother cell (2n); Meiosis; 4 haploid megaspores; One megaspore grows, the rest degenerate; Mitosis; Mitosis; Cells adsorbed; Mitosis; Haploid nucleus; Embryo sac containing 8 haploid nuclei; Mature embryo sac — Outer integument, Inner integument, Polar nuclei, Embryo sac, Egg cell (ovum), Micropyle)

34.7(a) Self-pollination

34.7(b) Cross-pollination

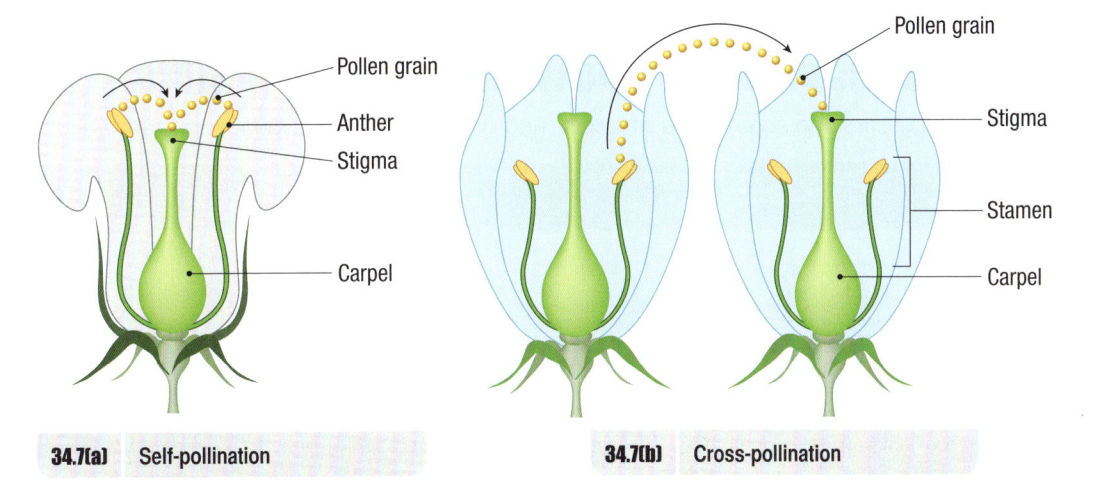

Agents of pollination

Cross-pollination is commonly carried out by the action of wind, or of animals, usually insects. In Ireland, insects such as bees (Fig 34.8), moths and butterflies are the most common agents of pollination, but in the tropics, fruit bats and birds such as the hummingbird are effective pollinators. Animals that pollinate flowers carry pollen on their body as they move from flower to flower searching for nectar.

Animal-pollinated flowers

Animal-pollinated flowers have various features to attract the pollinators. These include:

- brightly coloured petals;
- scent;
- nectar (an energy-rich food) and pollen (protein-rich food), which act as a reward to the pollinator.

The flower parts are adapted to encourage pollinators to visit (see Table 34.2).

34.8 Bees are good pollinators

Wind-pollinated flowers

Flowers that use the wind to transfer pollen do not need brightly coloured petals, nectar or scent. Wind pollination is a chancy affair: there is only a slim chance that pollen will land on the stigma of a flower of the same species. To overcome this, wind-pollinated flowers produce huge numbers of pollen grains and their flower parts are adapted to releasing and trapping large amounts of pollen.

Typical wind-pollinated plants include the grasses and many trees, e.g. the oak, sycamore, birch and hazel (Fig 34.9).

34.9 Wind-pollinated flowers of hazel

34 Sexual Reproduction in Flowering Plants

Features and adaptations of insect- and wind-pollinated flowers

Table 34.2 summarises the characteristics and adaptations of insect- and wind-pollinated flowers.

	Characteristic	Adaptation
1. Insect-pollinated flowers, e.g. buttercup, rose	Flowers usually conspicuous	Readily available to insects
	Petals may be brightly coloured	To attract insects
	Nectary may be present	To reward the insect
	Flowers may have scent	To attract insects
	Pollen grains tend to be sticky	To attach to insect's body
	Flower parts (stigmas/stamens) held within the flower	To force insect to forage
2. Wind-pollinated flowers, e.g. rye grass, oak	Flowers not conspicuous	Attraction of wind not necessary
	Dull/green coloured bracts, no nectaries	Attraction of wind not necessary
	Flowers not scented	Attraction of pollinators not necessary
	Pollen grains light and small	Easily carried by the wind
	Anthers and stigma hang outside the flower	For easy release and entrapment of pollen
	Large volume of pollen produced	Allows for wastage

Table 34.2 Adaptations of insect- and wind-pollinated flowers

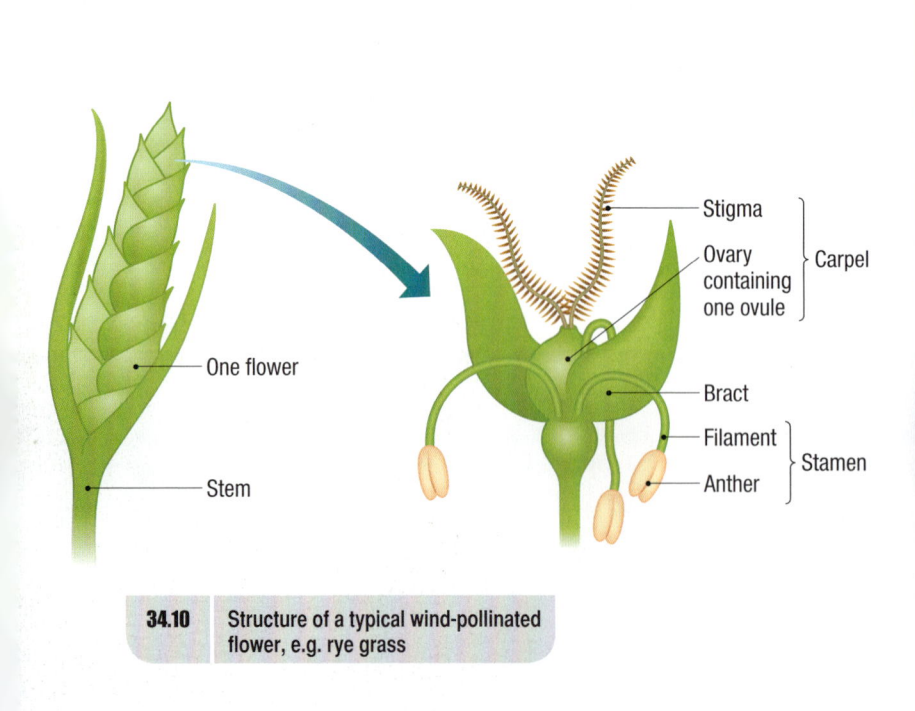

34.10 Structure of a typical wind-pollinated flower, e.g. rye grass

34.11 A mixture of pollen grains, can you identify the wind pollinating pollen?

Sexual Reproduction in Flowering Plants | 34

3. Fertilisation
Events leading up to fertilisation

- When the pollen grain attaches to the stigma and it starts to grow (germinates), it forms a pollen tube that grows down through the style to the micropyle of the embryo sac.
- The generative nucleus divides by mitosis (if it has not already done so) to form two male gametes.
- The growth of the pollen tube is stimulated by sugars produced by the style.
- The nucleus of the pollen tube controls the growth of the tube and it is attracted to the ovule by chemicals secreted by the tissues of the ovary and ovule. This is an example of **chemotropism**.
- Finally the pollen tube arrives at the micropyle.

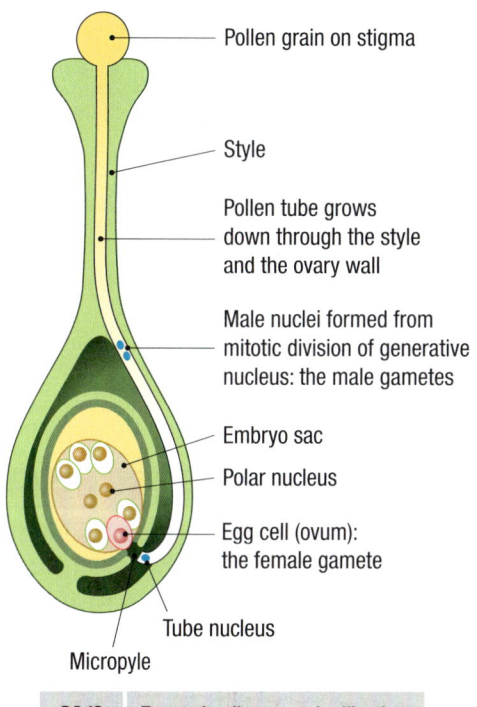

Double Fertilisation in the flowering plant

Fertilisation occurs when one of the male gametes moves into the embryo sac and fuses with the egg cell to form a diploid zygote (1 in Fig 34.13). The second male gamete fuses with the two polar nuclei to form the triploid endosperm (2 in Fig 34.13). Because of these two 'fusings', **fertilisation** in flowering plants is sometimes referred to as '**double fertilisation**' (Fig 34.13). The zygote develops into an **embryo** plant and the endosperm forms a food supply for the developing embryo. Finally, the whole contents of the ovule become the seed.

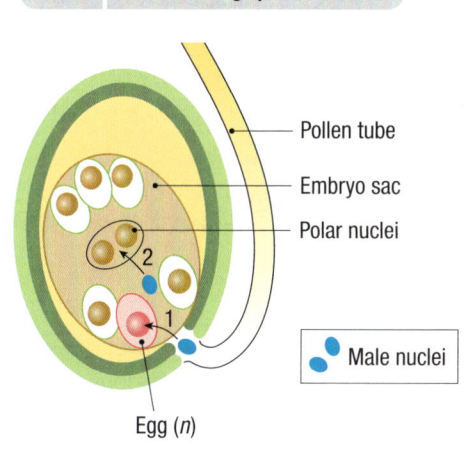

> **Fertilisation** is the fusion of the egg nucleus with one of the male gamete nuclei, to form a diploid zygote.

4. Seed and fruit formation

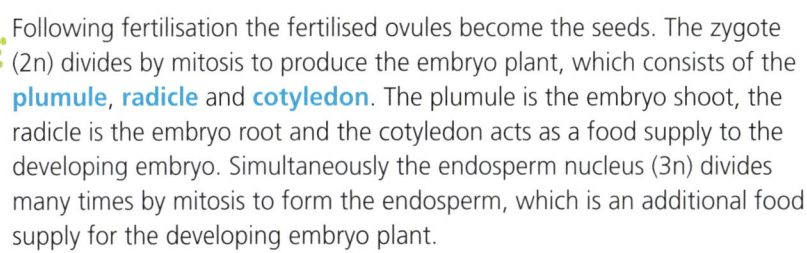

Following fertilisation the fertilised ovules become the seeds. The zygote (2n) divides by mitosis to produce the embryo plant, which consists of the **plumule**, **radicle** and **cotyledon**. The plumule is the embryo shoot, the radicle is the embryo root and the cotyledon acts as a food supply to the developing embryo. Simultaneously the endosperm nucleus (3n) divides many times by mitosis to form the endosperm, which is an additional food supply for the developing embryo plant.

The wall of the ovule becomes the coat of the seed, the **testa**. The seeds release **auxins** (growth regulators) that cause the fruit to form and the ovary develops into the fruit.

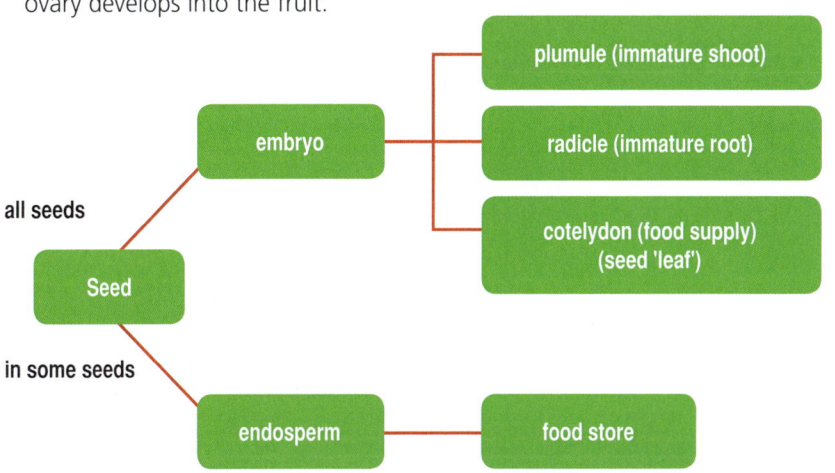

34.12 Events leading up to fertilisation

34.13 Double fertilisation in the flowering plant

34.14 Broad bean seeds in a pod

Structure	Fate
Zygote (2n)	Becomes the embryo plant
Fertilised ovule	Becomes the seed
Wall of the ovule	Becomes the testa (seed coat)
Ovary	Becomes the fruit
Endosperm nucleus (3n)	Becomes the endosperm, a food store for the developing embryo

Table 34.3 The fate of flower structures, following fertilisation

Seed types and structure

When they are mature, seeds lose water and become hard and dry. In this form they can withstand adverse conditions such as cold or drought and can be dispersed away from the parent plant. Dispersal is necessary to prevent the new plants (seedlings) from competing with the parent plant for water, light and minerals (see page 452).

Classification of seeds

Mature seeds are classified on the basis of two features:
- The number of cotyledons – embryonic 'seed leaves'.
- The presence or absence of endosperm (a food store) in the mature seed.

Seeds with one 'seed leaf' or cotyledon are classed as **monocotyledons** (monocots), e.g. maize, grass, oats. Monocots rarely store food in the cotyledon, rather they store it in the endosperm and are classed as **endospermic seeds** (Fig 34.15).

The endosperm of wheat seeds is full of starch, and this is the part of the wheat seed that is ground up to make white flour. The white material that forms when popcorn is made is the endosperm.

Seeds with two 'seed leaves' are classed as **dicotyledons** (dicots), e.g. broad bean, snapdragon, buttercup. In general, most dicotyledons use up their endosperm before the seed is mature and are known as **non-endospermic seeds** (Fig 34.16).

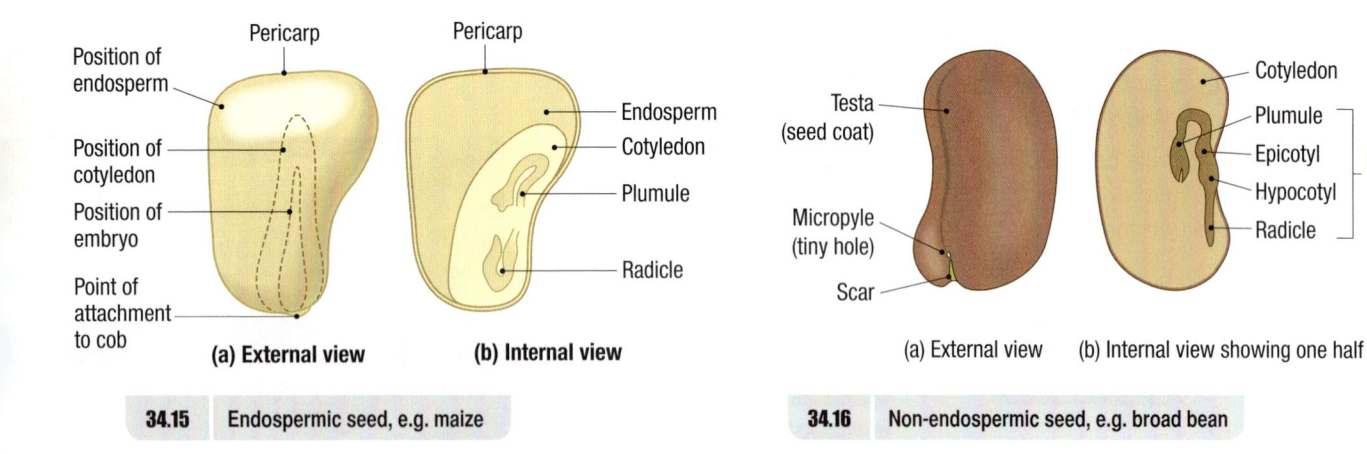

34.15 Endospermic seed, e.g. maize

34.16 Non-endospermic seed, e.g. broad bean

Sexual Reproduction in Flowering Plants | 34

34.17 A variety of fruits

Fruits

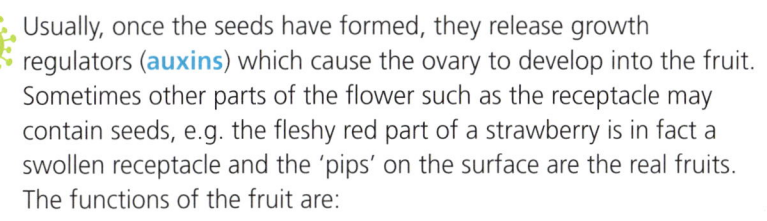

11 Usually, once the seeds have formed, they release growth regulators (**auxins**) which cause the ovary to develop into the fruit. Sometimes other parts of the flower such as the receptacle may contain seeds, e.g. the fleshy red part of a strawberry is in fact a swollen receptacle and the 'pips' on the surface are the real fruits. The functions of the fruit are:
1. To protect the seeds.
2. To enable the seeds to be dispersed.

How seedless fruits form

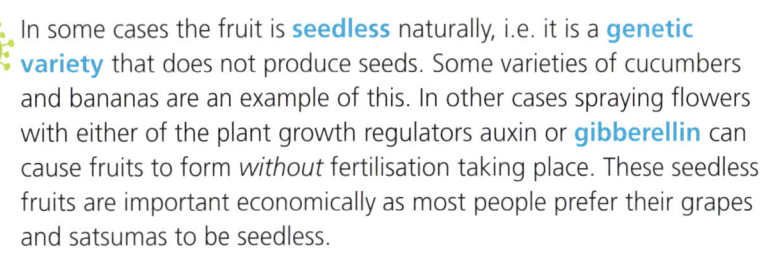

12 In some cases the fruit is **seedless** naturally, i.e. it is a **genetic variety** that does not produce seeds. Some varieties of cucumbers and bananas are an example of this. In other cases spraying flowers with either of the plant growth regulators auxin or **gibberellin** can cause fruits to form *without* fertilisation taking place. These seedless fruits are important economically as most people prefer their grapes and satsumas to be seedless.

Gibberellin can also cause bigger and larger fruits to form. To achieve more marketable products, the plant growth regulator **ethene** is used to ripen fruits like bananas and tomatoes.

Ethene can also de-green the skins of oranges and lemons. These fruits normally remain green due to the high level of chlorophyll in the rind.

5. Fruit and seed dispersal

13 The dispersal of seeds and fruits is necessary to:
- Prevent overcrowding and competition for resources, such as water and light.
- It also allows the plant species to colonise new areas.

34.18 Seedless fruits

34 Sexual Reproduction in Flowering Plants

There are a variety of different dispersal methods such as wind, water, animals and self-dispersal.

Method of dispersal	Feature of seed/fruit to aid dispersal	Example	
Wind	Usually light and may be winged or have hairy tufts	Sycamore 'helicopters', dandelion 'parachutes'	34.19 Wind dispersal
Water	Have air spaces which increase buoyancy and are light	Plants that live in water, e.g. water lilies. Plants that live along rivers and streams, e.g. willow	34.20 Water dispersal
Animal	Hooked and sticky to catch onto an animal's body. Juicy and/or tasty, seeds are indigestible and pass out in faeces/droppings	Stick-weed, raspberries, acorns of oak, beech nuts	34.21 Animal dispersal
Self	In a pod or container that can burst open to release the seeds	Beans and peas	34.22 Self-dispersal

Table 34.4 Methods of seed dispersal

6. Dormancy

The majority of seeds do not begin to grow as soon as they have been dispersed even if all the conditions of growth are present. Instead, they go through a resting or dormant period when their metabolic rate is very low. It is only following this period of **dormancy** that the seeds will germinate (grow into a new plant).

> **Dormancy** is a period when a seed does not germinate, despite favourable conditions being present.

During dormancy, the embryo plant remains alive and capable of further growth. Seeds which retain their ability to germinate are said to be **viable**. Some seeds remain viable for only a few days, e.g. willow, whereas others have been found to remain viable for months and even years. The majority of garden and agricultural seeds will remain viable for at least a year and maybe even longer, as long as they are stored dry.

Seed banks store many varieties of crop seeds in a dried out (dormant) state. This ensures the preservation of large numbers of different varieties of crops for agricultural and horticultural uses.

Advantages of dormancy

As most of our seeds are dispersed in late summer and autumn:

- Dormancy ensures the new plant will not be affected by the harsh winter conditions of frost and low temperatures.
- Another advantage of dormancy is that it allows time for the immature embryo of many seeds to ripen.
- It also allows more time for seeds to be dispersed and to colonise new areas.

Dormancy in agriculture and horticulture

Knowing how long the dormant period is for a particular seed type allows the grower to provide optimum storage conditions for the seeds and choose when to sow the seeds.

In some seeds dormancy can be artificially broken by:

- Soaking the seeds in water for a period of time before sowing.
- Scratching the seeds with a knife to break the testa (scarifying).
- Exposing the seeds to a cold temperature.

7. Germination

> **Germination** is the re-growth of the embryo plant, following a period of dormancy.

Germination is the start of the growth of the embryo in a seed. For a seed to germinate, certain environmental conditions must be present. These are **water**, **oxygen** and a **suitable temperature**. As you will see in Investigation 34.1, unless all three factors are present, germination will not occur.

Germination of a typical seed, e.g. the broad bean

- The seed absorbs water through the micropyle and swells. The testa splits.
- The food store (in the cotyledons and/or endosperm) is **digested** to a soluble form.
- The products diffuse to the embryo plant and are used to produce **ATP** and new cells.
- The radicle bursts through the testa and grows down into the soil.
- The hooked plumule emerges later and grows up out of the soil. Above the soil the plumule straightens out and the young leaves develop, which begin to **photosynthesise**.
- Meanwhile, underground, the radicle has developed into a main (primary) root, with branching lateral roots.

34.23 Germination of a broad bean seed

- The cotyledons remain below the ground, where they act as a food supply for the embryo plant. As the food store is used up, the cotyledons gradually wither and shrivel up.

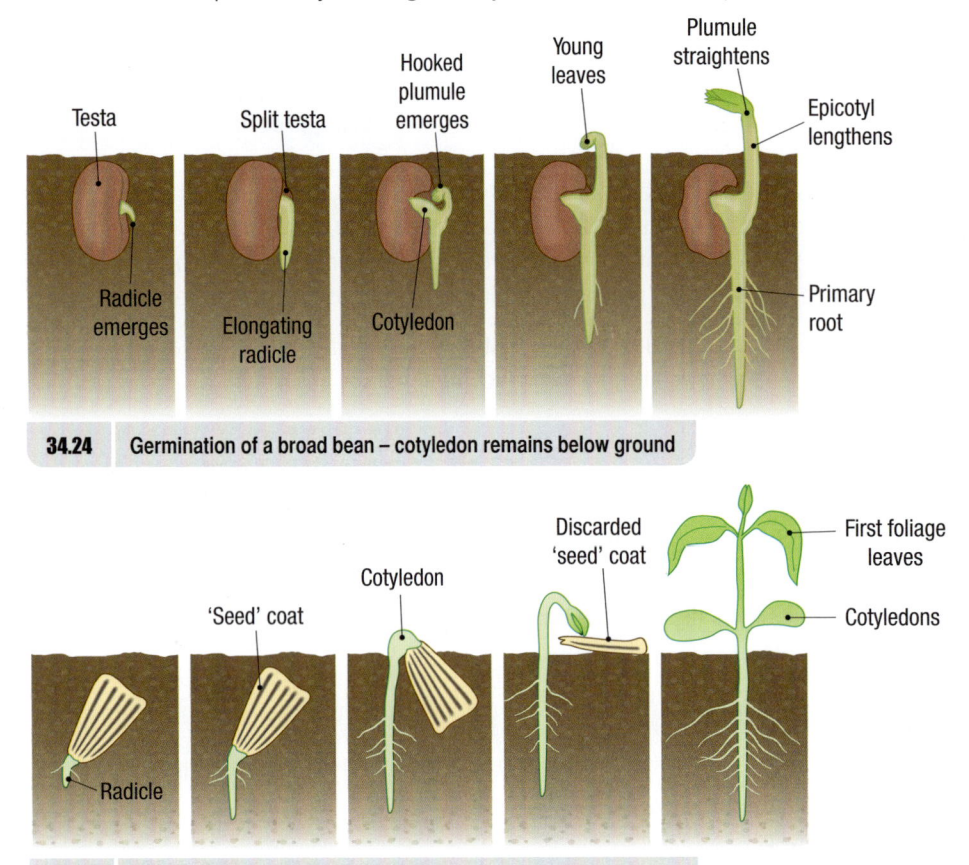

34.24 Germination of a broad bean – cotyledon remains below ground

34.25 Germination of a sunflower – cotyledon comes above ground

Factors necessary for germination

Seeds need water, oxygen and a suitable temperature in order to germinate.

1. Water is necessary to activate the **cytoplasm** of the cells and to provide a medium in which the chemical reactions can occur. Enzymes in the cells of the cotyledon become active and begin the breakdown of the food store. The products formed provide the raw materials (glucose and amino acids) for growth of the embryo plant. In Investigation 34.2, you can find out about the role of digestive **enzymes** in germination.
2. A suitable temperature is required for the chemical reactions to occur. The temperature may vary from plant to plant, but, generally speaking, temperatures above 5°C and below 40°C allow germination to occur.
3. Oxygen is essential to allow the seeds to respire aerobically and so produce enough energy for the process of germination.

Two main events that occur during germination

1. Digestion of the food stores.
2. **Respiration** and cell division.

Enzyme	Food store digested	Product(s) formed	Use of products
Amylase Maltase	Starch Maltose	Maltose Glucose	Respired to make energy Used to form cellulose for cell walls
Proteinase	Proteins	Amino acids	To make cell proteins, e.g. enzymes To form cell membranes
Lipase	Lipids	Fatty acids and glycerol	Respired to make energy To form cell membranes

Table 34.5 The digestion and use of the food store in a seed

Sexual Reproduction in Flowering Plants | 34

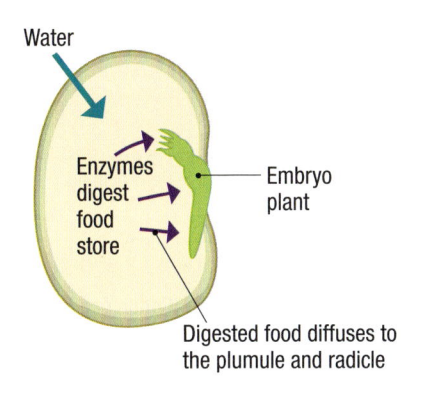

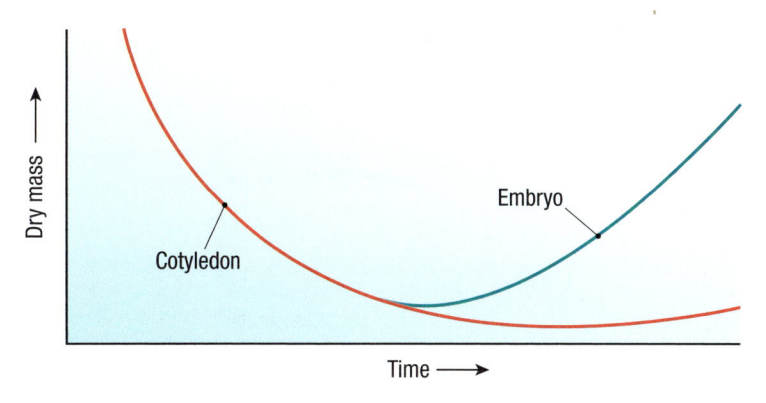

34.26 Digestion during germination

34.27 Changes in mass with time during germination

Investigation 34.1

To investigate the effect of water, oxygen and correct temperature on germination

Procedure

1. Label four Petri dishes A, B, C, D.

2. Place a circle of cotton wool into each Petri dish.

3. Treat each dish as follows:

   Dish A – add 10 cm³ distilled water, scatter on 8–10 cress or mustard seeds, place in anaerobic jar in an incubator at 20°C for 2–3 days (this dish has no oxygen).

   Dish B – add 10 cm³ distilled water, scatter on 8–10 cress or mustard seeds, place in an incubator at 20°C for 2–3 days (this dish has moisture, oxygen and a suitable temperature, it acts as the control).

   Dish C – add 10 cm³ distilled water, scatter on 8–10 cress or mustard seeds, place in a refrigerator for 2–3 days (this dish does not have the correct temperature).

   Dish D – scatter on 8–10 cress or mustard seeds, place dish in an incubator at 20°C for 2–3 days (this dish has no moisture).

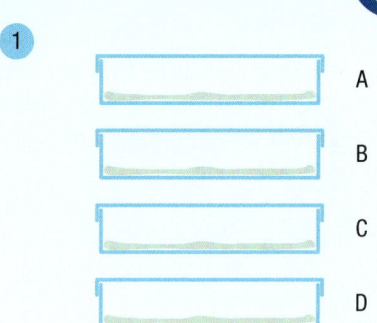

1. Label four Petri dishes A, B, C and D. Place cotton wool in the base of each dish.

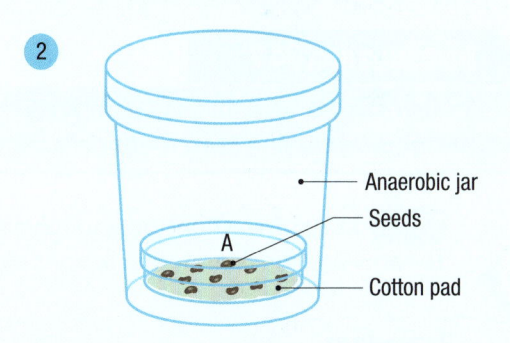

2. In dish A place 10 seeds and wet the cotton wool. Put in an anaerobic jar – this lacks oxygen.

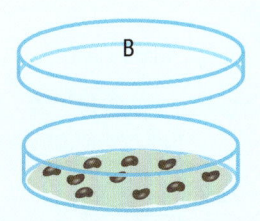

3. Place 10 seeds in dish B and wet the cotton wool. This dish has all of the ideal conditions and acts as the control.

LIFE LEAVING CERTIFICATE BIOLOGY | UNIT 3 THE ORGANISM | 455

34 | Sexual Reproduction in Flowering Plants

4

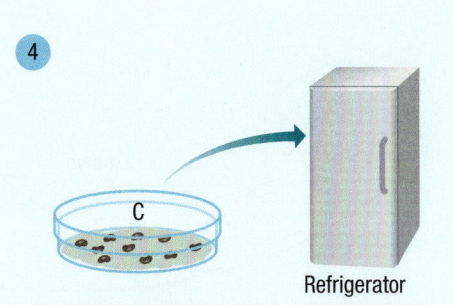

Wet the cotton wool in dish C.
Place 10 seeds on the cotton wool.
Put the dish in the refrigerator –
this dish lacks a suitable temperature.

5 — Petri dish lid, Seeds, Cotton pad

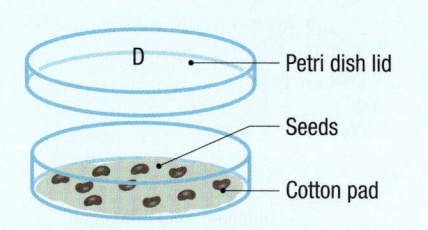

In dish D place 10 seeds. Leave the
cotton wool dry – this dish lacks water.

4. After 2–3 days check each dish for signs of germination.
5. Record your results in a table and form a conclusion.
6. Seedlings will grow from the seeds in dish B, which shows that all three factors must be present for germination to occur.

6 — Incubator at 25°C

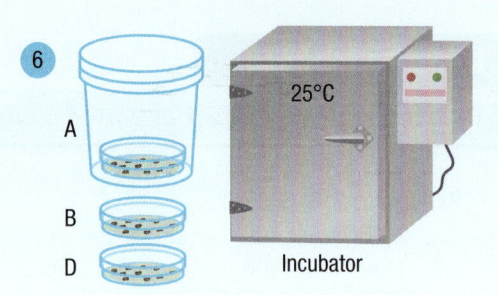

Place dishes A (in anaerobic jar), B and D into an incubator at 25°C. Check the dishes after 2–3 days and record results.

34.2B To investigate the conditions for germination

Investigation 34.2

To investigate the digestive activity in seeds during germination using starch agar plates

Note: In this investigation you have the choice of using starch agar plates to check for amylases or skimmed milk agar plates to check for proteinases.

Procedure

1. Boil two pre-soaked broad bean seeds in a beaker of water for 10 minutes (to denature the enzymes).
2. Label two prepared starch agar plates A and B.

1 Swab the bench with disinfectant. (Disinfectant, Cloth, Table)

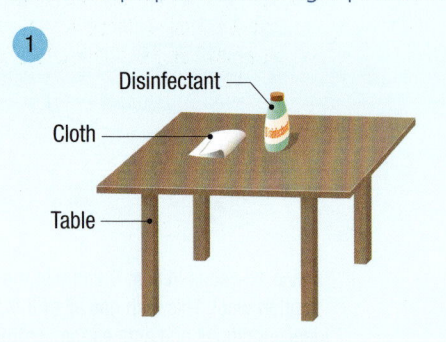

2 Label the agar plates 'boiled (control)' and 'unboiled'. (Boiled / Unboiled — Starch or skimmed milk sterile agar plates.)

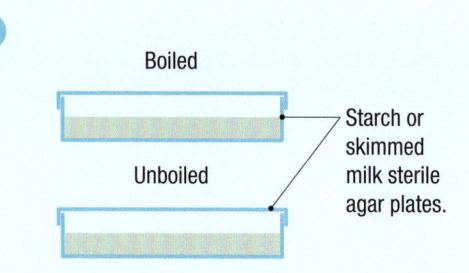

3. Label two small beakers A and B and half fill each with disinfectant solution (to kill any fungi that might be on the seed surface and could digest the starch in the agar).

4. Remove the boiled seeds to beaker A and leave for 10 minutes.

5. Place a second set of two un-boiled broad bean seeds in beaker B for 10 minutes.

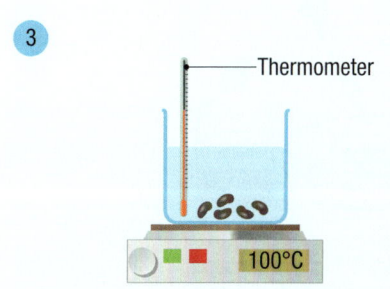

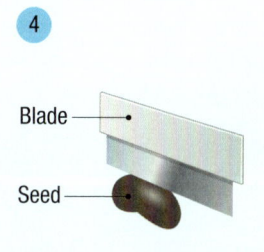

3 Boil half the seeds for 10 minutes.

4 Split all of the seeds in half.

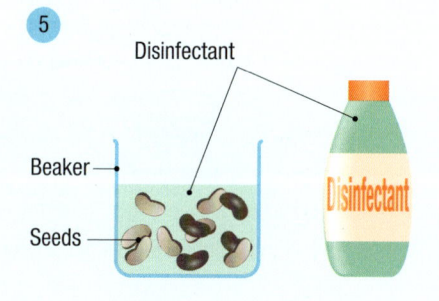

5 Soak the seed halves in disinfectant for 10 minutes.

6. Using a sterile forceps remove the boiled seeds from beaker A and rinse in distilled water (to remove the disinfectant).

7. Using a sterile forceps remove the un-boiled seeds from beaker B and rinse in distilled water.

8. On a sterile board carefully remove the testa from each seed.

6 Rinse the seed halves twice in water.

7 Flame the forceps to sterilise it.

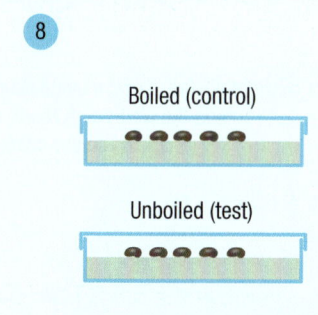

8 Place the boiled seeds face down on the plate labelled 'boiled'. Place the unboiled seeds face down on the plate labelled 'un-boiled'.

9. Use a sterile backed blade to cut each seed in half lengthwise. Remember to keep the boiled and un-boiled seeds separate.

10. Open the lid of dish A by a small amount. Using a sterile forceps, place each boiled seed half, face downwards, onto the surface of the starch agar. (Placing the seed face down ensures the enzymes in the seed are in contact with the agar.) Replace the lid.

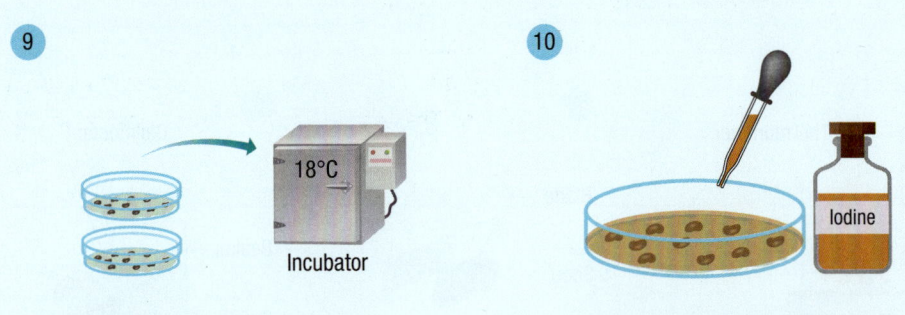

Incubate at 18°C – 20°C for 48 hours.

Remove the seeds: if using starch agar, flood the plates with iodine and record colour changes.

11. Open the lid of dish B by a small amount. Using a sterile forceps, place each un-boiled seed half, face downwards onto the surface of the starch agar. Replace the lid.

12. Place the two agar plates in an incubator for 2–3 days at 20°C.

Remove the seeds: if using skimmed milk agar, flood the plates with Biuret reagent and record colour changes.

Expected result.

34.29 To investigate digestive activity in seeds

13. Remove the seeds from the surface of each dish.

14. To test for digestive activity, flood each dish with a solution of iodine. Leave for 2–3 minutes.

15. Pour off excess iodine solution.

16. Examine the surface of the dishes and note any colour changes.

17. Record your results and form a conclusion.

18. Clear/brown zones should appear on the agar surface under the un-boiled seed halves. This shows that the substrate starch has been broken down. A blue-black colour should be present under the boiled seed halves, indicating that no digestion has occurred.

Summary

- Flowering plants can reproduce sexually and asexually.
- Sexual reproduction produces genetic variation in the offspring.
- The flower is the reproductive organ of a flowering plant.
- The flower parts consist of four layers:
  - Sepals, usually green, protect the flower before it blooms.
  - Petals, usually coloured, that attract animal pollinators.
  - Stamens, consisting of a stalk called the filament and an anther which produces the pollen grains.
  - Carpel(s) consisting of the stigma, style and ovary. The ovary contains ovules (see Table 34.1).
- Sexual reproduction involves the following stages:
  1. Gamete formation.
  2. Pollination.
  3. Fertilisation.
  4. Seed and fruit formation.
  5. Seed and fruit dispersal.
  6. Dormancy.
  7. Germination.
- 1. Gamete formation
  - Pollen grains produce the male gametes.
  - The embryo sac in the ovule produces an egg cell.

HL
- Pollen grain (microspore) development occurs in the anthers.
  - Microspore mother cells (2n) in pollen sacs divide by meiosis to produce microspores (n).
  - Each microspore nucleus divides by mitosis to produce a generative and a tube nucleus.
  - Generative nucleus later divides by mitosis to produce two male gamete nuclei.
  - Embryo sac (megaspore) development occurs in the ovule.
  - Megaspore mother cells (2n) divide by meiosis to produce four haploid cells.
  - Three of these disintegrate and one survives as the embryo sac (megaspore).
  - The embryo sac nucleus divides by mitosis three times to produce eight haploid nuclei, one of which is the egg and two others the polar nuclei.

- 2. Pollination
  - Pollination is the transfer of pollen from the anther to the stigmas.
  - Self-pollination is the transfer of pollen within a flower or to another flower on the same plant.
  - Cross-pollination is the transfer of pollen from one plant to another plant of the same species.
  - Cross-pollination ensures a greater mixing of plant genes than self-pollination.
  - The agents (methods) of cross-pollination are (a) wind or (b) animals, such as insects.
  - Animal-pollinated flowers differ from wind-pollinated flowers (see Table 34.2).
  - After pollination, a pollen tube grows down to the ovary to the micropyle, carrying with it the male gametes.

- 3. Fertilisation
  - Fertilisation occurs when one of the male gamete nuclei fuses with the egg nucleus to form a diploid zygote. This is the first fertilisation.
  - The second fertilisation occurs when the second male nucleus fuses with the two polar nuclei to form a triploid endosperm nucleus.
  - Both fertilisations occur in the embryo sac.

34 Sexual Reproduction in Flowering Plants

Summary

4. **Seed and fruit formation**
   - Following the second fertilisation, the endosperm nucleus forms the endosperm, a food store.
   - The zygote divides by mitosis to become the embryo plant and the cotyledon.
   - The ovule becomes the seed.
   - The ovary becomes the fruit.
   - Seeds consist of an embryo plant and a food store (cotyledon and/or endosperm).
   - In some seeds, the only food store is the cotyledon (seed leaf); in others a cotyledon and the endosperm form the food tissue.
   - Seeds that contain one cotyledon are described as monocotyledons, e.g. maize; seeds with two cotyledons are described as dicotyledons, e.g. broad bean.
   - Mature seeds that also contain endosperm are described as endospermic seeds, e.g. maize.
   - Seeds without an endosperm at maturity are described as non-endospermic seeds, e.g. broad bean.
   - In general monocots store food in the endosperm.
   - A fruit is a mature ovary usually containing seeds. The functions of the fruit are protection and dispersal.
   - Seedless fruits can be produced naturally due to genetic variety in some plants and artificially by spraying flowers with plant growth regulators, such as auxin.
   - Plant growth regulators can also be used to ripen fruits such as melons and lemons.

5. **Fruit and seed dispersal**
   - Seeds and fruits are dispersed by a number of agents, namely wind, animal, self and water. Fruits have special features that enable them to be so dispersed (see Table 34.4).
   - Dispersal is necessary to prevent overcrowding and competition for water, minerals and light and to allow plants to survive and colonise new areas.

6. **Dormancy**
   - Dormancy is a resting period for seeds during which the embryo plant remains alive and capable of growth, i.e. it remains viable but does not grow. Dormancy allows:
     time for seeds to be dispersed;
     embryo plants to mature;
     survival in adverse conditions.

7. **Germination**
   - Germination occurs when the embryo in a seed begins to regrow.
   - The factors necessary for germination are water, oxygen and a suitable temperature.
   - Water is needed to provide a medium for chemical reactions. Oxygen is needed for the production of energy in respiration, and the chemical reactions in the cells will only occur if the temperature is suitable.
   - During germination, the embryo plant grows as a result of receiving food from the breakdown of carbohydrate and protein in the cotyledons and endosperm, if present, using enzymes (see Table 34.5).

Review questions

01 (a) Copy the diagram below.
(b) Give the name of each of the parts labelled A to G.
(c) State the function of each of parts A, B, D and E.

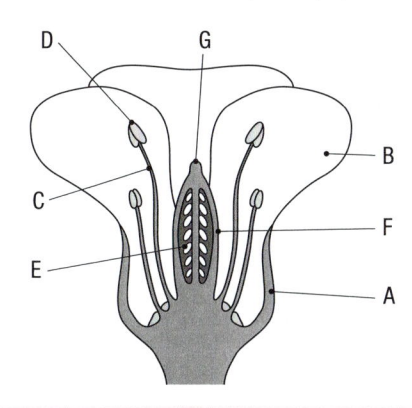

02 (a) Describe the development of pollen grains from microspore mother cells.
(b) Outline the role of meiosis and mitosis in the formation of the mature embryo sac.
(c) Draw a labelled diagram to show the detailed structure of a mature embryo sac.

03 (a) Explain the term pollination.
(b) State two common agents of pollination.
(c) Name an animal-pollinated flower and a wind-pollinated flower.
(d) Suggest two ways in which pollen from wind-pollinated flowers is different from animal-pollinated flowers.
(e) List three other features that distinguish animal-pollinated and wind-pollinated flowers.

04 (a) Distinguish between cross-pollination and self-pollination.
(b) Give one advantage of cross-pollination.

05 (a) Draw a diagram to illustrate the main features of a wind-pollinated flower.
(b) Name two wind-pollinated flowers.
(c) Do you think wind pollination is better for plants than insect pollination?

06 Distinguish between: (a) petals and sepals, (b) anther and ovule, (c) pollination and fertilisation, (d) a gamete and a zygote.

07 (a) Draw a labelled diagram of a mature ovule of a flowering plant. Include the following labels: ovule, integuments, micropyle, polar nuclei, egg cell and embryo sac.
(b) Are the polar nuclei haploid, diploid or triploid?
(c) With what do the polar nuclei fuse at fertilisation?
(d) What is the name of the product of (c) and what is its role in the seed?

08 (a) Define the term fertilisation.
(b) Describe the two 'fertilisations' in the flowering plant.
(c) Where do these two 'fertilisations' occur?

09 (a) Following fertilisation, describe what happens to the following parts of the flower: the petals, the ovule, the endosperm, the stamens, the zygote.
(b) What is a seed?
(c) Draw a labelled diagram of: (i) the external structure and (ii) the internal structure of a seed such as the broad bean.

10 (a) Seeds are classified on the basis of the number of cotyledons they have and on the presence or absence of an endosperm. Explain the underlined terms.
(b) Distinguish between monocotyledenous seeds and dicotyledenous seeds. Give a named example in each case.
(c) Which of the following is/are an example of a non-endospermic dicotyledenous seed: grass, pea, wheat, corn?

11 (a) What is a fruit?
(b) List the functions of the fruit to a plant.
(c) Name two fruits.
(d) Name two seedless fruits and explain how they are formed.
(e) What advantage are seedless fruits to humans?
(f) Can seedless fruits produce new plants? Explain your answer.

12 (a) What is seed and fruit dispersal?
(b) What are some of the problems for plants if their seeds are not dispersed?
(c) List four methods of fruit and seed dispersal. In each case, mention a feature of the seed or fruit that is an adaptation to the method of dispersal.
(d) Which of the following plant seeds/fruits are not wind-dispersed: sycamore, strawberry, grass, dandelion, plum.

13 Before growth can begin, a seed may go through a period of inactivity.
(a) What term is used to describe this period of inactivity?
(b) Give two reasons for this period of inactivity.
(c) What term is used to describe the process by which a seed begins to grow?

14 (a) What is germination?
(b) List the environmental factors necessary for seeds to germinate.
(c) Outline the reason each of the factors you list in (b) are required for germination.
(d) Give an account of the process of germination in a named seed.

34 Sexual Reproduction in Flowering Plants

Review questions

15 (a) Describe an experiment to show the effect of varying temperature on the germination of seeds.
(b) Explain how you would recognise that germination had taken place.

16 If a plant has a diploid number of chromosomes of 28, state the number of chromosomes present in the following:
(a) An egg nucleus.
(b) A pollen nucleus.
(c) The zygote.
(d) The embryo.
(e) The cotyledon.
(f) The endosperm.

17 Distinguish between each the following:
(a) Haploid and diploid.
(b) Pollination and fertilisation.
(c) Monocotyledens and dicotyledens.
(d) Endospermic and non-endospermic seeds.
(e) Dormancy and germination.

18 During germination, enzymes break down stored food in the cotyledons and endosperm. Describe an experiment you could carry out to verify this statement.

Dry weight can be described as the weight of a tissue which remains after all water has been removed from it. How do you think dry weight can be determined in a laboratory?

Examination style questions

Section A

01 The diagram shows the internal structure of a broad bean seed.

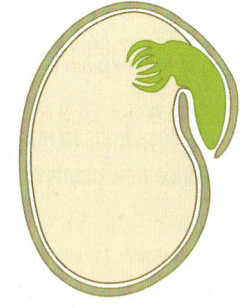

(a) Copy the diagram of the broad bean seed and label the following parts, using clear lines and the appropriate letter.

Part	Letter
Plumule	A
Cotyledon	B
Radicle	C
Testa	D

(b) Which labelled part becomes the shoot of the plant?
(c) Describe the result you would expect to get if iodine solution is poured over the part labelled B.
(d) What does this result tell you about the function of B?
(e) Match the word in the left-hand column with the correct description in the right-hand column. Write your answer in sentences, e.g. The testa ....

Testa — stores food
Radicle — protects the seed
Embryo — the young root
Cotyledon — contains the plumule and radicle

02 Distinguish between the following pairs of terms:
(a) Anther and stamen.
(b) Ovary and ovule.
(c) Petal and sepal.
(d) Cotyledon and endosperm.
(e) Monocots and dicots.

03 (a) Copy the diagram shown into your copy.
(b) Use the following letters to label the diagram you have drawn using clear lines and the appropriate letter.
Ovary – P, Anther – R, Stigma – S, Stamen – T
(c) Is the flower insect-pollinated or wind-pollinated?
(d) State two ways in which the flower shows adaptation to the method of pollination used.
(e) Name a plant that has a flower of this type.

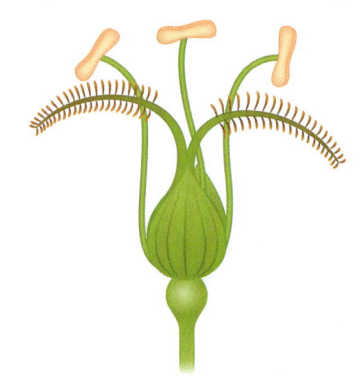

Section B

04 (a) (i) Name the stage most seeds go through immediately before they germinate.
(ii) What advantage is this stage to the plant?

Examination style questions

05 (b) The apparatus shown has been set up to show that a particular factor is needed for seeds to germinate.

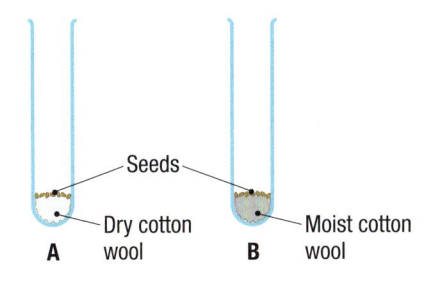

(i) What factor, needed for germination, is being tested for using the apparatus shown?
(ii) Describe the result you would expect in tube A after 2–3 days.
(iii) Test tube B acts as the control. Explain the purpose of setting up a control in this experiment.
(iv) Why were 5–6 seeds used in each test tube rather than just one seed in each?
(v) How would you keep the test tubes at constant temperature during the experiment?

05 (a) (i) Name a large food storage molecule that might be present in seeds.
(ii) Name the enzyme that breaks down the food molecule you have named.

(b) If conditions are suitable seeds will germinate into seedlings. During the process of germination enzymes break down (digest) the large food storage molecules in the seed. The seedlings use the products of the breakdown for growth. The diagram shows the set-up you might use to show digestive activity during germination.

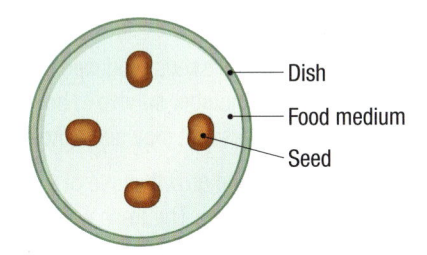

(i) Describe how you transferred the seed halves to the agar.
(ii) Why are the seed halves placed face downwards on the agar?
(iii) For how long must the dishes be left before being tested for digestive activity?
(iv) Why must the seeds be left for this time?
(v) Describe how you tested the dishes for digestive activity.
(vi) Describe the results you would expect.
(vii) What conclusions can you draw from these results?

06 (a) A seed contains a non-growing plant embryo at a very low rate of metabolism.

(i) Explain what is meant by seed germination.
(ii) Explain the term embryo plant.

(b) You carried out an investigation into the effect of water, oxygen and temperature on seed germination. Answer the following questions in relation to that investigation.
(i) At what temperature did you run the water and oxygen procedure?
(ii) Describe the control set-up for the water investigation.
(iii) Describe the experiment set-up for the water investigation.
(iv) How did you remove the oxygen from the air surrounding the seeds in the control for the oxygen investigation?
(v) How did you maintain one set of seeds at low temperature (4°C) for the temperature investigation?
(vi) What was the result of all the controls?
(vii) Give one way in which you ensured this was a fair test.
(viii) Explain the need for oxygen during seed germination.

07 (a) (i) What is meant by seed dormancy?
(ii) Why is a period of dormancy necessary for plants?

(b) The following questions refer to the investigation of digestive activity in seeds during germination.
(i) Why is it necessary to first soak the seeds in water overnight?
(ii) What food medium would be used in the plate?
(iii) Why is it necessary to ensure all dishes, food medium, materials and seeds are sterile?
(iv) Describe the control used in this investigation.
(v) Name the reagent used to test for digestive activity.
(vi) What will be observed in a plate that would indicate that digestion of the food medium took place?
(vii) Name the species of seeds used in the above germination experiment.
(viii) Some of the food reserve in seeds is used for increase in cell number and mass but most of the food is used up in what process?

Section C

08 (a) (i) Define fertilisation.
(ii) Where does fertilisation occur in a flowering plant?

(b) The diagram shows a section through a typical flower.

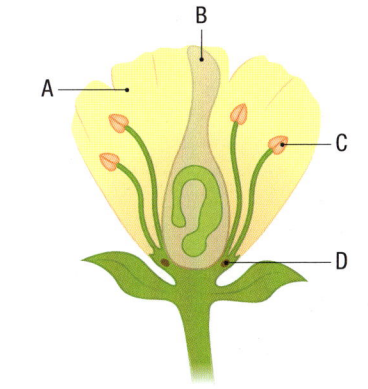

Examination style questions

  (i) Identify the structures labelled A to D.
  (ii) Give two ways in which this flower is adapted for insect pollination.
  (iii) Give two ways in which the structure of a wind-pollinated flower, such as that of grass, would differ from the flower shown.
(c) (i) After fertilisation, what does the ovary become?
  (ii) Give two reasons why seed dispersal is important for plants.
  (iii) Name two methods of seed dispersal and describe in each case how the seed is adapted for the method named.

09 (a) Give the function of each of the following parts of a flower: receptacle, anther, stigma, ovule.
(b) Distinguish between pollination and fertilisation.
(c) Outline the events leading up to fertilisation in the flowering plant.
(d) Name the two products of fertilisation in the flowering plant and state whether they are haploid, diploid or triploid.
(e) Name a flowering plant.

10 The diagram shows the structure of a non-endospermic and an endospermic seed.
  (i) Name the parts labelled A, B, C, D in seed X.
  (ii) Seed X is non-endospermic. What is the evidence for this in the diagram?
  (iii) Name the part labelled F in seed Y.
  (iv) Name two parts in a seed where food may be stored.
  (v) Seeds are the dispersal agents of flowering plants. Give two advantages of dispersal.
  (vi) In relation to seeds what is meant by the term dormancy? Give one advantage of dormancy.

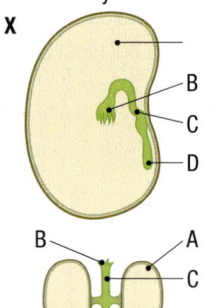

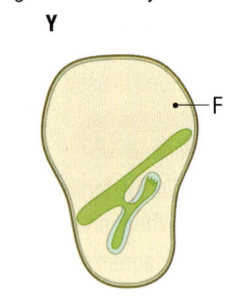

11 The diagram shows a mature embryo sac in the ovule of a flowering plant.
  (i) Outline the stages of development of the embryo sac from the diploid megaspore mother cell in the ovule.
  (ii) Name the parts labelled A, B and C. 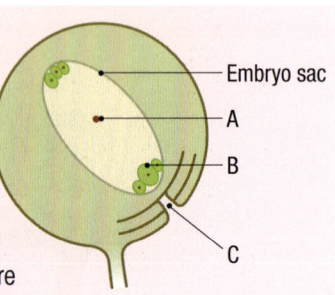
  (iii) Which of the labelled parts fuse(s) to form the endosperm?
  (iv) In this plant the diploid number of chromosomes is 16. How many chromosomes would you expect to find in the nucleus labelled B?
  (v) Why is the pollen grain not the male gamete?

12 Two hundred French bean seeds were planted in trays in a greenhouse. Each week 20 seedlings were picked, their water removed and weighed. The results are shown below.

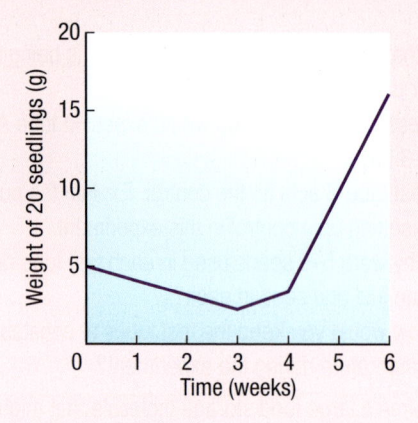

(a) Suggest why the water was removed from the seedlings before weighing them.
(b) Why were 20 seedlings weighed each week, rather than just a single seed?
(c) Describe the changes in the weight of the seedlings over the 6 weeks.
(d) What process occurring in the seedlings in the first 3 weeks would account for the loss in weight?
(e) Can you explain why there was an increase in weight after the first 4 weeks?
(f) Of the large number of seeds produced each year by a plant, only a limited number survive to become mature plants. List five factors that may affect the survival rate.

13 The graph below shows the growth curve of a plant from the time it germinates until it dies. The fresh weight (weight of tissues with water) indicated at A is that of a seed from the plant some time after the seed was dispersed. Examine the graph and answer the questions that follow.

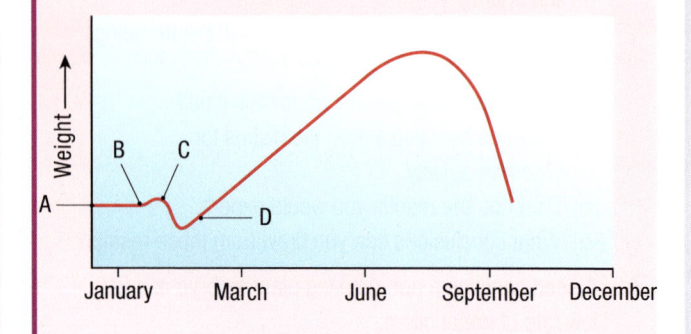

34 Sexual Reproduction in Flowering Plants

Examination style questions

(a) What term is given to the period of time in the plant's life cycle between stage A and B on the graph? State the importance of this period.

(b) Give the name for the stage in the plant's life cycle that begins at B. Give one reason for (i) the increase in fresh weight between B and C, and (ii) the decrease in fresh weight between C and D.

(c) Fresh weight increases rapidly from D. Explain what is happening to account for this rise.

(d) Copy the graph and mark F on it where you think flowering of this plant is likely to begin and G where seed dispersal is likely to occur.

(e) Suggest what benefits can be gained from keeping certain seeds in a 'seed bank'.

Leaving Certificate examination questions

Section A

01 The diagram shows the external structure of a stamen.

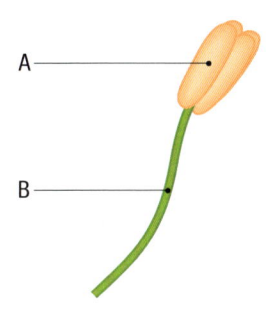

(a) Name A and B.
(b) Where is pollen produced, in A or in B?
(c) To which part of a flower is pollen carried?
(d) What is meant by cross-pollination?
(e) Name two methods of cross-pollination.

2005 OL Q. 3

02 The diagram shows a young plant growing in a tilted seed box.

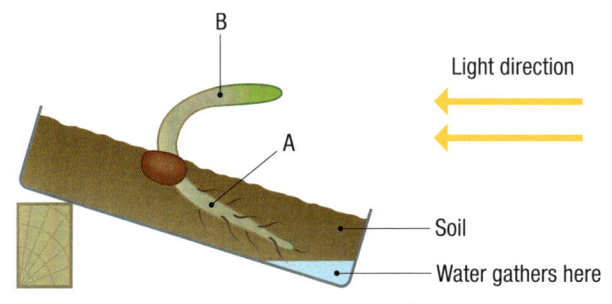

(a) From which structure in the seed did A develop?

2009 HL Q. 2

03 (a) Light is essential for the germination of seeds. T F
(b) Endosperm is a food reserve in some seeds. T F

2005 HL Q. 3

Section B

04 (a) (i) What is meant by the term digestion?
(ii) Name a carbohydrate you would expect to find **stored** in a seed.

(b) Answer the following questions in relation to practical work you carried out to investigate digestive activity in germinating seeds.
(i) What type of agar did you use in this investigation?
(ii) The seeds were divided into two batches. One batch was used untreated.
How did you treat the other batch of seeds before using them in the investigation?
Why was such treatment necessary?
(iv) Describe how you carried out the investigation **and** indicate clearly how you showed whether or not digestion had occurred.
(v) Give the results of your investigation.
 1. Untreated seeds.
 2. Treated seeds.

2014 OL Q. 8

05 (a) (i) What is meant by the term *digestion*?
(ii) Why does digestion occur in seeds during germination?

(b) Answer the following questions in relation to practical work you carried out to investigate digestive activity in germinating seeds.
(i) Name a plant that provides suitable seeds for this investigation.
(ii) The seeds were divided into two batches. One batch was used untreated.
How did you treat the other batch of seeds before using them in the investigation?
(iii) Explain why you treated the second batch of seeds in the way described in (ii).
(iv) Describe how you carried out the investigation. In your description outline how you demonstrated that digestion had occurred.
(v) Give the results of your investigation.

2009 OL Q. 9

Leaving Certificate examination questions

06 (a) (i) What is meant by the germination of seeds?
(ii) Seeds may remain inactive for a period before germination. What term is used to describe this period of inactivity?
(b) Answer the following questions about an investigation that you carried out on the effect of water, oxygen and temperature on germination.
   (i) What seeds did you use?
   (ii) Explain how you set up a control for the investigation.
   (iii) How did you deprive some of the seeds of oxygen?
   (iv) How did you ensure that some of the seeds were deprived of a suitable temperature for germination?
   (v) State the results of the investigation, including those of the control.

2008 OL Q. 9

07 (a) (i) Name a part of a seed in which food for germination is stored.
(ii) Name the **three** factors necessary for seeds to germinate.
(b) Answer the following questions on seed germination.
   (i) At the start of the investigation to show digestive activity during germination the seeds were sterilised.
      1. Why is this necessary?
      2. How did you sterilise the seeds?
   (ii) Name the substance that is used as a medium on which to germinate the seeds.
   (iii) What substance, to be digested by the seeds, was added to the above medium?
   (iv) What control did you use in this demonstration?
   (v) How did you demonstrate that digestive activity had taken place?

2014 HL Q. 7

08 Answer the following in relation to investigations that you carried out in the course of your practical studies.
When investigating digestive activity during seed germination:
1. How did you supply a substrate suitable for the digestive enzymes?
2. How did you ensure that no digestive enzymes were available on the control plate?

2013 HL Q. 9 (b) (iv)

09 Answer the following in relation to investigations that you carried out in the course of your practical studies.
(i) What type of agar plates did you use when investigating the digestive activity of seeds?
(ii) How did you demonstrate that digestive activity had taken place in the investigation referred to in part (i)?

2012 HL Q. 7 (b) (iii), (iv)

10 In the case of starch or skimmed-milk agar plates, state:
1. An investigation in which you used it.
2. The precise purpose for its use in the investigation that you have indicated.

2006 HL Q. 7 (b) (ii)

Section C

11 The diagram shows the structure of a flower.

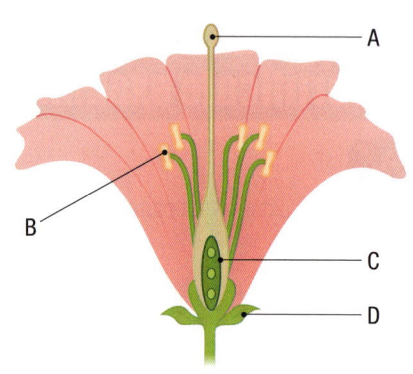

(i) Name the parts labelled A, B, C and D.
(ii) What is meant by the term **pollination**?
(iii) Give **two** methods of pollination in plants.
(iv) What is the next step after pollination in the lifecycle of the plant?
(v) Suggest a substance that flowers produce that may cause hay fever in some people.

2013 OL Q. 15 (a)

12 (a) (i) Name the **two** main types of reproduction.
(ii) Explain the term *fertilisation*.
(b) The flower is the organ of reproduction in many plants.
   (i) What part of the flower produces pollen?
   (ii) After fertilisation, what part of the flower becomes the fruit?
   (iii) Give **two** methods of seed dispersal in plants.
   (iv) Why is it necessary for plants to disperse their seeds?
   (v) What is the advantage of dormancy to seeds?
   (vi) Give **three** conditions necessary for seeds to germinate.

2012 OL Q. 12 (a), (b)

13 (a) (i) Draw a large labelled diagram to show the internal structure of a flower.
(ii) Give **two** ways by which pollen is transferred from one flower to another.
(iii) After fertilisation, what part of the flower becomes the fruit?

Leaving Certificate examination questions

(iv) Many seedless fruits, e.g. grapes, are available in shops today. State **one** way of forming seedless fruits.

(v) Sometimes artificial methods are used to propagate (reproduce) plants. Name any **two** methods of artificially propagating plants.

2011 OL Q. 15 (a)

14
(i) What is meant by *fertilisation*?
(ii) Name the part of the flower in each case:
   1. Where fertilisation occurs.
   2. That becomes the fruit.
(iii) Each seed is made up of an <u>embryo</u>, a food store and a seed coat (testa). One function of fruit is to aid <u>dispersal</u>. Explain **each** of the underlined terms.

Blackberries   **Sycamore fruit**

(iv) By which method are the seeds of **each** of the fruits shown above dispersed?
(v) What term is given to the growth of an embryo into a plant?
(vi) In order for this growth to be successful, certain environmental conditions must be present. Name any **two** of these conditions.

2010 OL Q. 14 (c)

15
(i) Name a part of the flower from which fruit forms.
(ii) Give three examples of the ways in which fruits are involved in seed dispersal.
(iii) Suggest why it is necessary for a plant to disperse its seeds.
(iv) Following dispersal most seeds enter a period of *dormancy*. What is *dormancy*?
(v) Give an advantage of dormancy.
(vi) Name the stage in the plant's life cycle that follows dormancy.
(vii) State one way in which it is possible to produce seedless fruits in horticulture.

2009 OL Q. 14 (c)

16
(i) In the table below, which letter gives the correct order of events in the life cycle of a flowering plant – A, B, C, D or E?

A	germination seed and fruit formation growth pollination fertilisation dispersal
B	germination fertilisation seed and fruit formation growth dispersal pollination
C	germination fertilisation growth seed and fruit formation pollination dispersal
D	germination growth pollination fertilisation seed and fruit formation dispersal
E	germination seed and fruit formation growth fertilisation dispersal pollination

(ii) Distinguish clearly between pollination and fertilisation.
(iii) State a location in the seed where food is stored.
(iv) What is germination?
(v) State **three** factors necessary for the germination of a seed.

2007 OL Q. 14 (c)

17
(i) Name:
   1. The site of production of a pollen grain.
   2. The structure on which it must land to complete pollination.
(ii) Name two methods of cross-pollination.
(iii) Many species of plant have mechanisms that prevent self-pollination. Suggest how such plants could benefit from this.
(iv) Describe in detail the events that follow the arrival of a pollen grain at the destination referred to in (i), up to and including fertilisation.
(v) Which part of a flower usually develops into a fruit?

2014 HL Q. 14 (a)

18
(i) Give a brief account of the role of **each** of the following in flowering plant reproduction.
   1. Petal.
   2. Anther.
   3. Stigma.
(ii) Name **one** structure through which the pollen tube grows in order to reach the embryo sac.
(iii) Within the pollen tube the generative nucleus divides to form two male gametes.
   1. What type of division takes place?
   2. With what does **each** male gamete fuse in the embryo sac?
   3. Name the product of **each** fusion.

Sexual Reproduction in Flowering Plants

Leaving Certificate examination questions

(iv) As the seed forms following fertilisation, a food store develops in one of two structures. Name any **one** of these structures.

2012 HL Q. 14 (a)

19 (a) Give a role for each of the following parts of a flower: sepals, anther, stigma.

(b) (i) Describe the development of pollen grains from microspore mother cells.
(ii) What is meant by the term *fertilisation*?
(iii) Give a brief account of the process of fertilisation in flowering plants.

(c) (i) What is meant by the **dormancy** of seeds?
(ii) Give **one** way in which the dormancy of seeds is of benefit to plants.
(iii) Suggest **one** way in which a knowledge of dormancy is useful to farmers and gardeners.
(iv) Water, oxygen and a suitable temperature are all required for the germination of seeds. In the case of **each** of these factors describe its effect on the process of germination.
(v) Which part of the embryo in a germinating seed gives rise to each of the following parts of the seedling?
1. The root.
2. The shoot.

2010 HL Q. 13

20 (i) From what structure in the carpel does the seed develop?
(ii) State two locations in the seed where food may be stored.
(iii) The embryo plant within the seed has a number of parts. List two of these parts, apart from food stores, and give a role for each of them.
(iv) Following dispersal, the seed undergoes a period of dormancy. What is dormancy?
(v) Suggest two advantages of dormancy.

2007 HL Q. 14 (a)

21 Answer the following in relation to sexual reproduction in flowering plants.
(i) State a role for each of the following: sepal, anther, stigma, ovary.
(ii) Distinguish between pollination and fertilisation.
(iii) The two male gametes in the pollen tube are derived from the generative nucleus. Do these gametes form as a result of mitosis or meiosis? Explain your answer.
(iv) Describe the fate of each of the male gametes.
(v) State **one** method that is used to produce seedless fruits.

2006 HL Q. 14 (a)

22 The diagram shows a vertical section through a carpel.

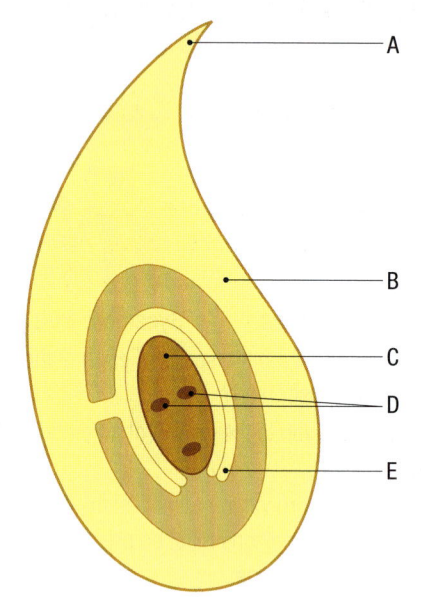

(i) Name A, B, C, D, E.
(ii) What happens to the two nuclei labelled D?
(iii) In the case of B and E state what may happen to each of them after fertilisation.
(iv) Copy the diagram into your answer book and add a pollen tube that has completed its growth. Label the nuclei in the pollen tube.

2004 HL Q. 14 (a)

Past examination questions

OL	2014 Q. 8	2013 Q. 15 (a)	2012 Q. 12 (a), (b)	2011 Q. 8 (b) (ii), Q. 15 (a)	2010 Q. 14 (c)
	2009 Q. 9, 14 (c)	2008 Q. 9, Q. 14 (a)	2007 Q. 14 (c)	2006 Q. 14 (c)	2005 Q. 3, Q. 9	2004 Q. 14

HL	2014 Q. 7, Q. 14 (a)	2013 Q. 9 (b) (iv)	2012 Q. 7 (b) (iii)–(v), Q. 14 (a)	2010 Q. 13
	2009 Q. 8, Q. 15 (c)	2007 Q. 14 (a)	2006 Q. 7 (b) (ii), (iv), Q. 14 (a)	2004 Q. 14 (a)

Asexual Reproduction in Flowering Plants

35

After studying this chapter you should be able to:

1. Explain the term vegetative propagation.
2. Describe one example of vegetative propagation from a stem, root, leaf and bud.
3. Explain what is meant by artificial propagation in flowering plants.
4. Describe any four methods used to artificially propagate plants.
5. Compare vegetative propagation with reproduction by seed.

Asexual reproduction

Asexual reproduction is another name for **vegetative propagation** or **vegetative reproduction** in plants. It is reproduction without the fusion of **gametes**, and many plants reproduce by this means. During vegetative reproduction, part of a plant becomes separated from the parent plant and then grows, by **mitosis** (see Chapter 11) into a new plant. As a result of this type of reproduction, the parent plant and its offspring are genetically identical, i.e. they have the same **genes**.

> **Vegetative propagation** is asexual reproduction in plants. It involves the production of new plants without the fusion of gametes.

In vegetative propagation, each new plant usually develops from an axillary bud on the stem of the parent plant. Parts of the parent plant, for example a stem or root, are specially modified for the purpose.

Clones

Cloning is the production of genetically identical organisms by means of asexual reproduction. **Clones** are produced by mitosis.

All of the methods of vegetative reproduction mentioned in this chapter, both natural and artificial are examples of cloning.

Natural vegetative propagation

SYLLABUS REQUIREMENT:
You need one example from stem, root, leaf and bud.

Modified stems
Runners

A **runner** is a branch of the main stem of a plant which 'runs' or grows across the surface of the ground. Runners develop from axillary buds at the base of the stem of the parent plant. The terminal bud of the runner sends up a daughter shoot and new roots form down into the soil. Eventually the part of the stem between the parent and the daughter plant dies away. In this way one plant can give rise to several plants. The strawberry plant reproduces asexually by means of runners (Fig 35.1).

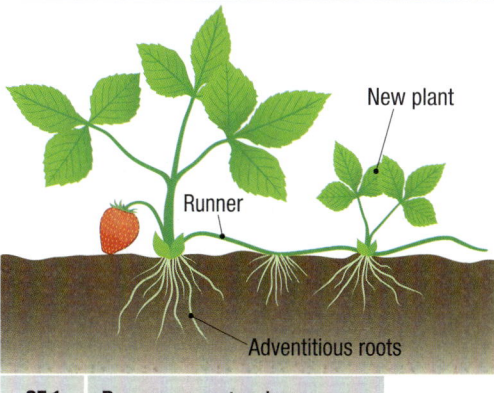

35.1 Runners, e.g. strawberry

Stem tubers

A **stem tuber** is an underground stem swollen with stored food and capable of vegetative propagation. The potato is a good example of a stem tuber. The 'eyes' on the potato are lateral buds. These produce new shoots and roots using the store of food in the tuber. The old (parent) tuber eventually dies away. Potatoes that we eat are all grown from what we call 'seed potatoes', i.e. potato tubers which produce the new potato plants. This is the method by which potatoes are grown both commercially and in a garden or allotment (Fig 35.2).

Modified roots

Root tuber

Root tubers (Fig 35.3) form when the fibrous roots of plants, such as the dahlia (Fig 35.4), become swollen with food reserves. An axillary bud lies at the top of each tuber near the base of the stem. It is from this bud that the new shoot grows. At the end of the growing season (autumn), the parent plant dies down and each root tuber, together with its bud, remains in the ground.

The next summer each bud can give rise to a new plant. As time goes on a number of root tubers form and these can be split by hand, each one being a potential new plant.

35.2 Stem tubers, e.g. potatoes

35.3 Root tuber

35.4 Dahlia plants

Modified leaves

Plantlets

Some plants, e.g. *Bryophyllum*, have leaves that give rise to **plantlets** along the margins of the leaves. When the plantlets (Fig 35.5) reach a certain size they fall off, take root and grow into new plants.

Modified buds

Bulbs

A **bulb** is a modified bud. It consists of a very small stem bearing a main terminal flower bud and one or more lateral buds, surrounded by thick fleshy leaves. These leaves are swollen with stored food.

In spring, the terminal bud produces new leaves and the flower. After flowering, the leaves continue to make food which passes back into the bulb for storage. New bulbs may develop from the lateral buds. In this way the bulbs act as a means of asexual reproduction. Daffodils, onion and garlic are all examples of bulbs (Fig 35.6).

35.5 *Bryophyllum* with plantlets

Asexual Reproduction in Flowering Plants | 35

35.6 An onion bulb is a modified bud.

In addition to reproduction, many of these modified structures store food (see Chapter 22). The food store enables the plant to survive through dormant periods of their life cycle.

Artificial vegetative propagation

Being able to produce new plants by means of artificial vegetative propagation is very important in agriculture and horticulture. Once a plant with desirable characteristics, such a large flowers or sweet fruits, has been bred, growers can use artificial propagation to produce more, identical plants. Artificial methods are much faster and more reliable than reproduction by seed and the offspring will all have the same genetic make-up. Many houseplants, trees and shrubs are propagated in this way.

SYLLABUS REQUIREMENT:
You need to know four methods of artificial propagation.

Methods of artificial propagation

Cuttings

One method of artificial propagation is to take a **cutting**. A young shoot is cut, at an angle, just below a node (Fig 35.7). The cutting is placed in water or well-watered compost until roots appear. **Auxins** (see Chapter 28) produced in the growing tip pass down to the base of the cutting where they stimulate roots to develop. Many house and garden plants can be propagated by taking cuttings, e.g. geraniums.

35.7 Taking a cutting

Grafting

Another commonly used method of artificial vegetative propagation is **grafting**. This involves attaching together cut surfaces of two separate plants (usually of the same genus) to combine some of the benefits of each. The plant to be propagated is known as the **scion** and the plant onto which it is grafted is called the **rootstock**. Grafting provides faster propagation than cuttings or seeds and is commonly used in the production of fruit trees, vines and roses (Fig 35.8).

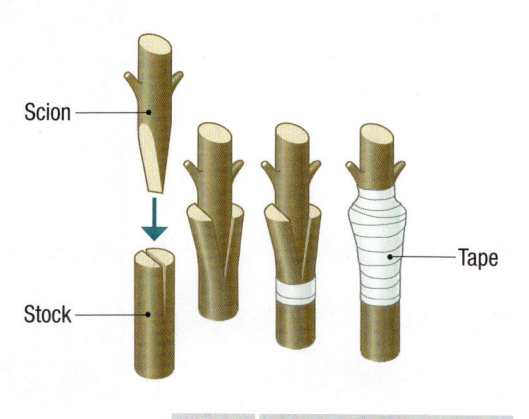

35.8 Grafting

Layering

In this method of artificial propagation, a strong healthy stem of a plant is cut across at an internode. The stem is then pegged down just under the soil (Fig 35.9). Adventitious roots are stimulated to form at the point of the cut and eventually a new shoot will grow up from the cut. **Layering** is particularly useful in propagating woody plants that have a flexible stem such as the blackberry.

Micropropagation (tissue culture)

Individual **cells** can be removed from a plant, and then grown in the laboratory in a procedure known as **tissue culture**. In tissue culture, a whole plant can be grown from a small piece of stem, root or leaf tissue. The procedure involves removing cells from the parent plant and placing them in a **sterile** culture medium in the laboratory. If suitable conditions such as pH, temperature, growth factors and oxygen concentration are present the cells divide by mitosis. Once the **tissue** develops into a tiny plantlet, it can be divided up again to produce many identical plants (see also Chapter 13).

Micropropagation (Fig 35.10) has enormous economic potential for the mass production of houseplants and in the commercial growth of crops such as bananas and strawberries. Tissue culture produces very large numbers of plants much more quickly than cuttings. It can greatly assist plant breeders to check cells for a particular feature, such as resistance to chemicals or to a particular disease organism.

35.9 Simple layering

35.10 Micropropagation

Advantages of artificial vegetative propagation

1. It allows the horticulturalist to **control the desirable features** of the plant to be grown.
2. It is **faster** than natural vegetative propagation.
3. It is **more reliable**.

Comparison between vegetative propagation and reproduction by seed

Vegetative propagation	Reproduction by seed
Produces offspring genetically identical to the parents. Useful when you want to cultivate a plant variety with particular characteristics.	Produces greater variety of offspring. Genes from different parents are mixed.
New individuals tend to grow close to the parent thus increasing competition.	Seed dispersal ensures offspring do not compete with parents.
It is a very reliable method of obtaining new plants as it does not depend on pollination, fertilisation and seed dispersal.	Pollination and dispersal rely on external agents (wind and animals), which is wasteful of both pollen and seeds.
Any weakness or susceptibility to disease is passed on quickly.	Variations in offspring allow for resistance to disease and for evolution.
New plants are produced in a short space of time.	The new plants take a long time to reach maturity.

Table 35.1 Comparison between vegetative propagation and seed reproduction

Summary

- Vegetative propagation is asexual reproduction in plants.
- Asexual reproduction produces offspring that are genetically identical to the parent plant.
- Such offspring are produced by mitosis and are known as clones.

Vegetative propagation	
Natural methods	Artificial methods
1. Modified stem, e.g. tuber (potato)	1. Taking cuttings (geraniums)
2. Modified root, e.g. tuber (dahlia)	2. Grafting (vines, apple trees)
3. Modified leaf, e.g. plantlets (*Bryophyllum*)	3. Layering (carnations)
4. Modified bud, e.g. bulbs (onion)	4. Micropropagation (bananas)

- A comparison between vegetative propagation and reproduction by seed can be found in Table 35.1.

35 Asexual Reproduction in Flowering Plants

Review questions

01 Vegetative propagation occurs in many plants.
 (a) What is vegetative propagation?
 (b) Name any two methods of vegetative propagation.
 (c) Describe the genetic make-up of the offspring of vegetative propagation.
 (d) Name the type of cell division that is used in vegetative propagation.

02 (a) Name a modified stem.
 (b) Draw a diagram of the modified stem you have named.
 (c) Explain how the modified stem carries out vegetative propagation.

03 Distinguish between each of the following:
 (a) sexual and asexual reproduction
 (b) a potato and a bulb
 (c) cuttings and grafting.

04 The diagram shows a vertical section through a bulb.
 (a) Name the parts labelled A to E.
 (b) State the functions of parts B and C.

 (c) Daffodils are plants that form bulbs. Name two other plants which form bulbs.

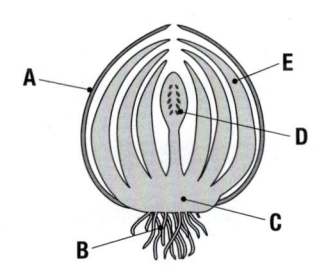

05 Use Table 35.1 to:
 (a) list two advantages of vegetative propagation
 (b) list two advantages of sexual reproduction in flowering plants
 (c) list two disadvantages of vegetative propagation
 (d) list two disadvantages of sexual reproduction in flowering plants.

06 Cloning is widely used in horticulture. By reference to a named example of an artificial clone, suggest one possible advantage and one possible disadvantage of cloning.

Examination style questions

Section A

01 Many flowering plants can reproduce by means of <u>vegetative propagation</u>.
 (a) Explain the underlined term.
 (b) Select from the following list, one example in each case, of a modification for vegetative propagation of the plant parts named.
    bulb   cutting   tuber   plantlet
   (i) Stem.
   (ii) Leaf.
   (iii) Bud.
 (c) (i) Give two advantages of vegetative propagation.
   (ii) Give one disadvantage of vegetative propagation.

02 The diagrams show a bulb in vertical section and a potato tuber.
 (i) Name the parts of the bulb labelled A, B, C.
 (ii) Name a plant that produces a bulb.
 (iii) Is the plant you name in (ii) a monocot or a dicot?
 (iv) What evidence is there in the diagram of the tuber that it is a modified stem?
 (v) Give an example of another type of modified stem other than a tuber.

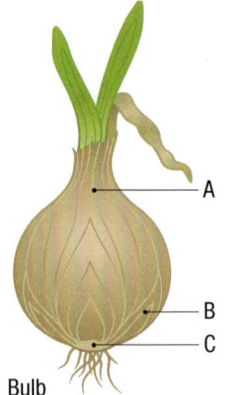

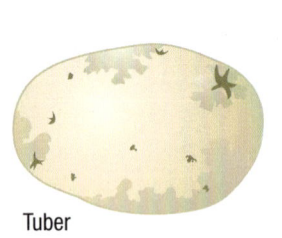

Section C

03 (a) Suggest a biological reason for each of the following:
   (i) Taking cuttings from a hedge.
   (ii) Not removing the leaves of daffodil plants until 6 weeks after flowering.
   (iii) Grafting apple trees rather than growing apples from seed.

Examination style questions

(b) (i) What is vegetative propagation?
(ii) Give an example of a modified stem and a modified root involved in vegetative propagation.
(iii) Artificial vegetative propagation is a common horticultural method of producing new plants of a particular variety. Name two types of artificial vegetative propagation and describe the method involved in one of them.
(iv) State two advantages of vegetative propagation.

04 Vegetative propagation occurs in many plants.
(a) Give another name for vegetative propagation.
(b) Name two natural methods of vegetative propagation.
(c) Describe how a named plant carries out one of the methods named in (b).
(d) Give one disadvantage of vegetative propagation.

Leaving Certificate examination questions

Section A

01 The diagram shows a strawberry plant from which a runner has given rise to a daughter plant.

(a) The runner is a modified stem. How could you tell this from (i) external observation, (ii) viewing a thin section of it under the microscope?
(b) What term is used for the type of asexual reproduction that produced the daughter plant?
(c) Would you expect the daughter plant to be haploid or diploid? Explain your answer.
(d) What evidence is there in the diagram that sexual reproduction has also taken place?
(e) Give one method, other than runners, and not involving seeds, that is used by horticulturalists to produce new plants.

2013 HL Q. 4

Section C

02 (i) What is meant by the term vegetative propagation?
(ii) Give one example of vegetative propagation in plants and state whether it involves a stem, a root, a bud or a leaf.
(iii) State two ways that vegetative propagation differs from reproduction by seed.
(iv) Artificial propagation is widely used in horticulture. Give two examples of artificial propagation carried out by gardeners or horticulturalists.
(v) Give one advantage and one disadvantage of artificial propagation.

2013 OL Q. 15 (b)

03 (i) What is meant by *vegetative propagation*?
(ii) Horticulturists use a number of methods to artificially propagate plants. Suggest **one** advantage of artificial propagation.
(iii) Describe **two** methods used by horticulturists to artificially propagate plants.
(iv) Give **two** differences between vegetative propagation and propagation involving seeds.

2009 HL Q. 15 (a)

Past examination questions

OL	2013 Q. 15 (b)	2005 Q. 15 (b)	
HL	2013 Q. 4	2009 Q. 15 (a)	SEC Sample Q. 14 (b)

Human Reproduction 1: The Reproductive Systems and the Menstrual Cycle

36

After studying this chapter you should be able to:

1. Identify and draw the main parts of the human male reproductive system, the associated glands and a sperm cell.
2. Describe the function of each labelled part including the role of meiosis in sperm production.
3. Describe the role of testosterone in the development and maintenance of the adult male.
4. Define secondary sexual characteristics and give examples in males and females.
5. Identify and draw the main parts of the human female reproductive system, the associated glands and an egg cell.
6. Describe the function of each labelled part, including the role of meiosis in egg production.
7. Describe the role of oestrogen and progesterone in the development and maintenance of the adult female.
8. Explain the term menstrual cycle and describe the events of the menstrual cycle, including the role of oestrogen and progesterone.
9. **HL** Describe the menstrual cycle and its hormonal control in detail.
10. **HL** Define menstrual disorder and describe one possible cause, prevention and treatment of one menstrual disorder (endometriosis or fibroids).

Human reproduction

1. **Sexual reproduction** in humans involves the male and female reproductive organs. These structures produce the **gametes**, the sperm and the egg, and special chemicals called **hormones** which control the process. The reproductive organs are specially designed to allow **fertilisation** to take place and for the fertilised egg, the **zygote**, to develop into a new human being within the body of the woman.

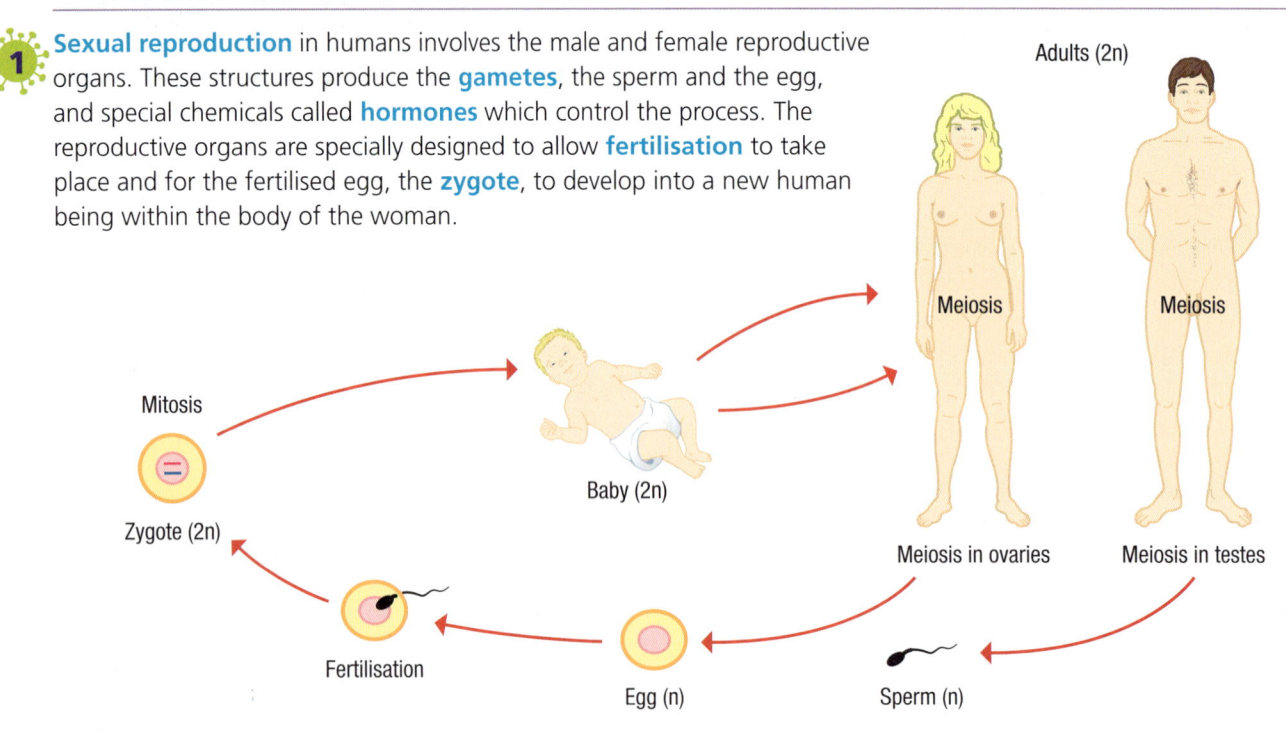

36.1 The life cycle of humans

36
Human Reproduction 1: The Reproductive Systems and the Menstrual Cycle

The male reproductive system

Sperm are produced in the **testes**, which are small organs enclosed by a fold of tissue called the scrotal sac (**scrotum**). Because viable sperm can only be produced at a temperature 2°C lower than the normal body temperature, the scrotal sac lies outside the abdomen. (Viable sperm are those that are capable of fertilising an egg.) When a baby boy is developing in the womb, his testes lie in the abdomen, but before or soon after birth, the testes move down into the scrotal sac.

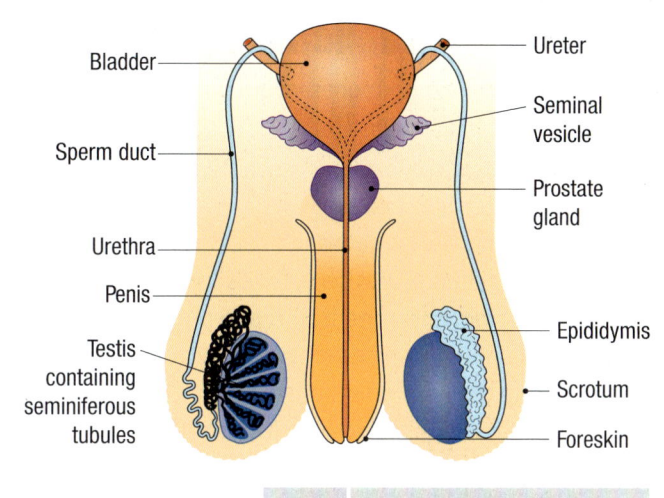

Each testis consists of a series of coiled tubules in which the sperm are made. Sperm cells are produced when **diploid** (2n) cells in the testes divide by **meiosis** and produce **haploid** (n) sperm cells. Sperm cells consist of three parts:

- A head, containing a haploid nucleus and an **acrosome** containing **enzymes**.
- A mid-piece, containing many **mitochondria** that produce energy.
- A tail that allows the sperm to swim.

Once produced, the sperm move into a larger tube called the **epididymis** where they mature and are stored.

The epididymis leads into a narrow muscular tube, the **sperm duct** (vas deferens). Each sperm duct runs up into the abdomen where it joins the urethra as it leaves the bladder. As sperm pass through the sperm ducts, they collect fluid from the **seminal vesicles** and the **prostate gland** which lies near the base of the bladder. The prostate gland produces a fluid which, together with the sperm, forms **semen**. The fluid from the seminal vesicles has a high fructose content, which provides nourishment and enables the sperm to swim. The fluid from the prostate gland increases the volume of the semen. Finally, as the sperm passes down the urethra, it receives fluid from the **Cowper's gland**.

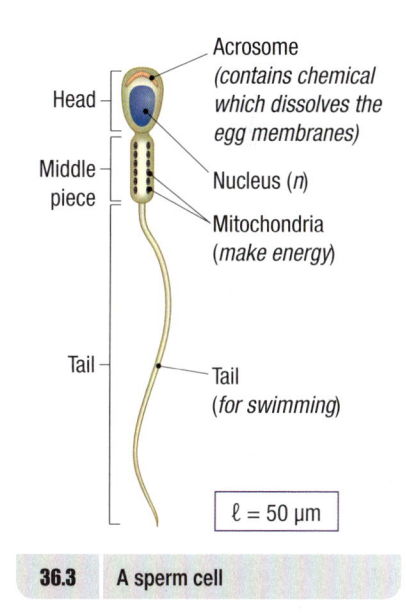

Sperm leave the body from the top of the penis. The top or head of the penis is extremely sensitive to touch and is protected by a fold of skin called the foreskin.

36.2 The male reproductive organs

36.3 A sperm cell

Part	Function
Testis	Produces sperm and hormones.
Scrotum	Holds testis at a temperature cool enough for sperm production.
Epididymus	Allows sperm to be stored and become mature.
Sperm duct (vas Deferens)	Transports sperm from testis to urethra.
Urethra	Transports sperm.
Seminal vesicle	Produces seminal fluid which allows sperm to swim and provides nutrients.
Prostate gland	Produces seminal fluid, which allows sperm to swim and provides nutrients.
Cowper's gland	Produces seminal fluid, which allows sperm to swim and provides nutrients.
Penis	Organ of sperm release.

Table 36.1 The parts and functions of the male reproductive organs and associated glands

The male reproductive hormones

There are three main hormones involved in male reproduction (see Chapter 31).

1. **Follicle stimulating hormone (FSH)**. FSH is produced in the **pituitary gland** which lies just below the brain. It travels in the bloodstream to the testes where it causes certain cells to produce sperm.
2. **Luteinising hormone (LH)** is also produced by the pituitary. LH causes other cells in the testes to produce the hormone testosterone.
3. **Testosterone** is important in the growth and development of boys. At puberty testosterone causes the sex organs to mature, the penis to enlarge, the shoulders to broaden, the voice to deepen, and body and facial hair (beard) to grow. These features are known as **secondary sexual characteristics**. The hormone testosterone continues to be produced and maintains these features throughout the adult life of a male. In addition, testosterone works with FSH in the production of sperm.

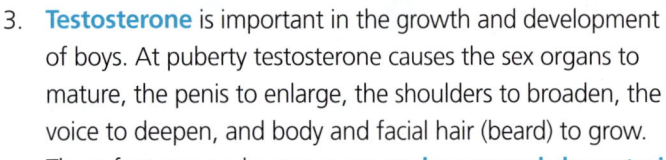

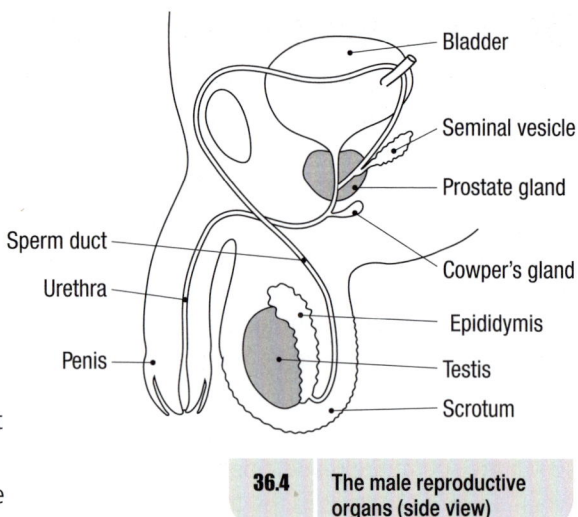

36.4 The male reproductive organs (side view)

> **D** **Secondary sexual characteristics** are features that develop during puberty, but are not essential for reproduction.

The female reproductive organs

The female reproductive organs lie in the pelvic cavity and consist of the **ovaries**, **oviducts** (fallopian tubes), **uterus** (womb) and **vagina**.

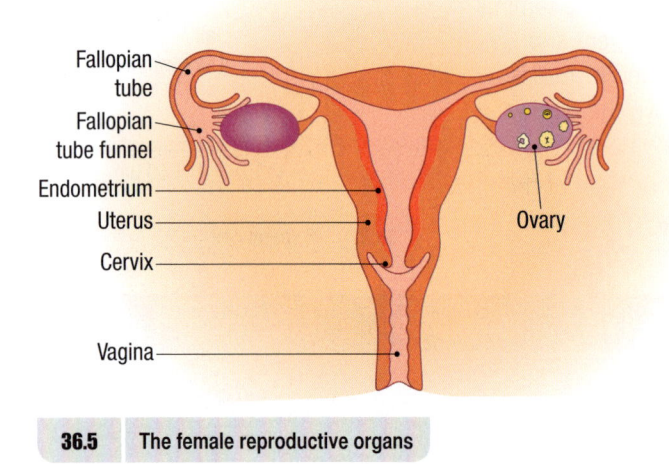

36.5 The female reproductive organs

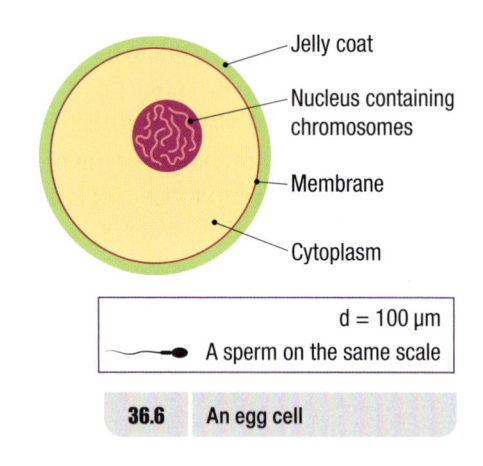

36.6 An egg cell

d = 100 μm
A sperm on the same scale

The ovaries

The ovaries produce eggs and the hormones **oestrogen** and **progesterone**. When a girl is born, she already has thousands of immature egg cells in her ovaries. Each month from puberty onwards (10–12 years), until the menopause (45–50 years), a number of these cells begin to grow. As they mature, a fluid-filled sac called a **Graafian follicle** forms around each one. Usually one follicle matures faster than the others, and the rest degenerate or break down. Inside this follicle an egg cell (ovum) forms as a result of **meiosis** (Fig 36.6). Egg cells are larger than sperm. They have a thin wall, a **haploid** nucleus and thousands of mitochondria to produce energy. The mature follicle, with its egg cell, now moves to the surface of the ovary and releases the egg into the oviduct (**ovulation**). An egg can live for 24–48 hours.

> **D** **Ovulation** is the release of an egg from the ovary.

Human Reproduction 1: The Reproductive Systems and the Menstrual Cycle 36

What happens after ovulation?

After ovulation, the egg that is released from the ovary is wafted into the Fallopian tube (oviduct) by the Fallopian funnel. The egg passes down the narrow tube of the oviduct by means of **cilia** and **peristalsis**, and on into the uterus. Unless the egg meets a sperm cell and they fuse, the egg cell will die within 2 days and pass out of the body through the vagina.

If the egg meets a sperm and they fuse, fertilisation is said to have occurred. The fertilised egg, now called the zygote, begins to divide by mitosis to form an embryo, and at the same time it travels down the oviduct into the uterus. Here, if the embryo attaches to the lining of the uterus, **pregnancy** begins. The wall of the uterus is lined with a special layer of cells and blood vessels called the **endometrium** (see Chapter 37), which provide a nutritious layer for the embryo to embed into. **Implantation** is the name given to the embedding of the embryo into the endometrium.

> **D** — **Implantation** is when the embryo embeds in the endometrium.

The cervix and vagina

The base or neck of the uterus is called the **cervix**, and this leads into the vagina, a muscular tube about 10 cm long. The function of the vagina is to hold the penis during sexual intercourse, and it is the birth canal through which the baby passes at birth. The vaginal opening is surrounded and protected by an area called the vulva. Above the vaginal opening lies the opening to the urethra.

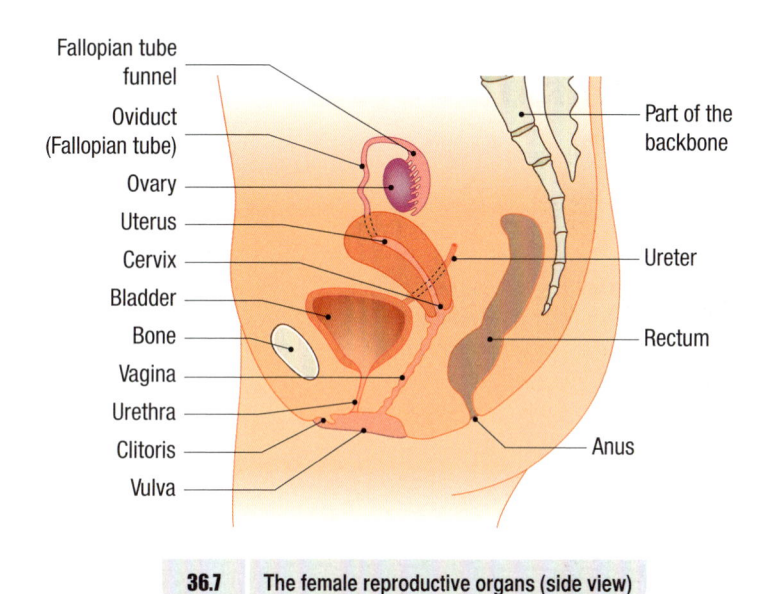

36.7 The female reproductive organs (side view)

Part	Function
Ovaries	Produce eggs and the hormones oestrogen and progesterone.
Fallopian tube (oviduct)	Transports egg to the uterus. Site of fertilisation.
Uterus	Holds the developing baby during pregnancy.
Endometrium	Allows attachment of the embryo during pregnancy.
Cervix	Closes during pregnancy.
Vagina	To hold the penis during intercourse and acts as the birth canal.

Table 36.2 The parts and functions of the female reproductive organs

The female reproductive hormones

As already mentioned the ovaries produce the hormones oestrogen and progesterone.

1. Oestrogen has two main roles:
   - To cause the lining of the uterus (the endometrium) to thicken in preparation for implantation.
   - The development of the secondary sexual characteristics. These include the enlargement and growth of the breasts, widening of the hips and the development of body hair, in particular in the underarm and pubic regions.
2. Progesterone keeps the endometrium built up in preparation for pregnancy.
3. Follicle stimulating hormone (FSH) is produced in the pituitary gland. It travels in the bloodstream to the ovaries where it causes the Graafian follicles and egg to form.
4. Luteinising hormone (LH) is also produced by the pituitary. LH causes ovulation.

SYLLABUS REQUIREMENT:

See page 481 for HL detail of these hormones.

The menstrual cycle

The **menstrual cycle** is a series of events during which the body prepares for pregnancy. The cycle usually lasts for 28 days, but this can vary from one girl or woman to another. Some cycles are shorter and others longer than the typical 28-day cycle.

> The **menstrual cycle** is the female monthly cycle in which an egg is released and the endometrium is shed.

> **Menstruation** is the shedding of the endometrium.

When an egg is released from an ovary the lining of the uterus prepares to receive the egg in case it is fertilised. If the egg is not fertilised, the endometrium is no longer needed, and it is shed from the body. The shedding of the endometrium is called **menstruation**, or having a period. Menstruation involves a small amount of blood and lining cells passing out through the vagina over a period of about 5 days.

In a typical menstrual cycle the following sequence of events occurs (Fig 36.8).

- Day 1: Menstruation occurs, i.e. the cells and endometrium are shed. At the same time, a Graafian follicle begins to develop and produce an egg in one of the ovaries.
- Day 5–13: As the follicle ripens, it releases oestrogen. Oestrogen travels in the bloodstream from the ovary to the uterus where it causes the repair of the endometrium.
- Day 14: The mature egg is released from the ovary into the oviduct. Ovulation has occurred.
- Days 15–21: The empty follicle becomes a new structure called the corpus luteum or 'yellow body' because of its colour. The corpus luteum begins to secrete progesterone as well as oestrogen. Progesterone travels to the uterus where it makes the lining of the uterus soft and spongy so that if the egg is fertilised, it will embed into the endometrium easily.
- Days 21–28: If the egg is not fertilised, it degenerates and passes out of the body. The corpus luteum breaks down. Over the next week, the progesterone and oestrogen levels drop, the endometrium begins to break down, and finally it is shed. Menstruation has begun again.

36.8 The menstrual cycle

> The **fertile period** is the time during a menstrual cycle when an egg may be fertilised.

The time during the cycle when fertilisation can occur is known as the **fertile period**. This is 2–3 days either side of ovulation. You will learn more about **fertilisation** in the next chapter.

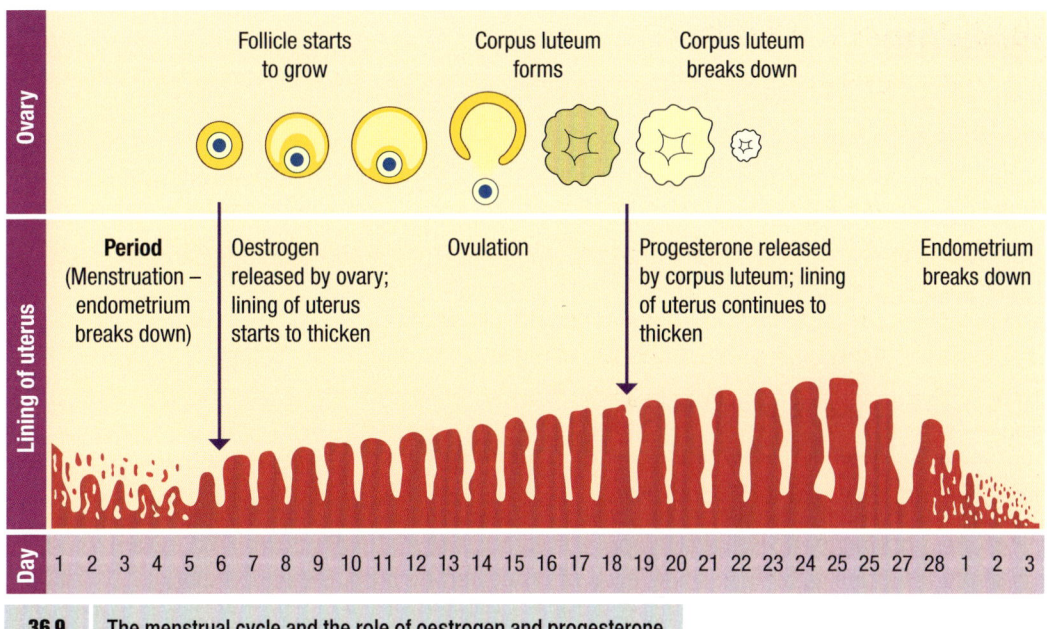

36.9 The menstrual cycle and the role of oestrogen and progesterone

HL The menstrual cycle and its hormonal control in more detail

The menstrual cycle is controlled by four hormones: follicle stimulating hormone (FSH), luteinising hormone (LH), oestrogen and progesterone. The hormones are produced so that the events of the cycle happen in the correct sequence. The roles of these hormones are given below.

Follicle stimulating hormone (FSH)

On day 1 of the menstrual cycle, the endometrium is shed. This stimulates the release of FSH from the pituitary gland. FSH travels in the bloodstream to an ovary where it:

- causes a number of Graafian follicles in the ovary to develop;
- stimulates cells in the follicles to secrete oestrogen.

Oestrogen

Oestrogen is produced by the follicles in the ovary and it travels to the uterus where it:

- causes the endometrium to be repaired so it will be ready to receive an **embryo** if fertilisation occurs;
- high levels of oestrogen cause production of FSH from the pituitary to be inhibited – this prevents further follicles becoming active if this month's egg happens to be fertilised; this is an example of **negative feedback** (see Chapter 31 for more details);
- the level of oestrogen peaks just before ovulation is due to take place, and this causes a surge of luteinising hormone (LH) to be released from the pituitary.

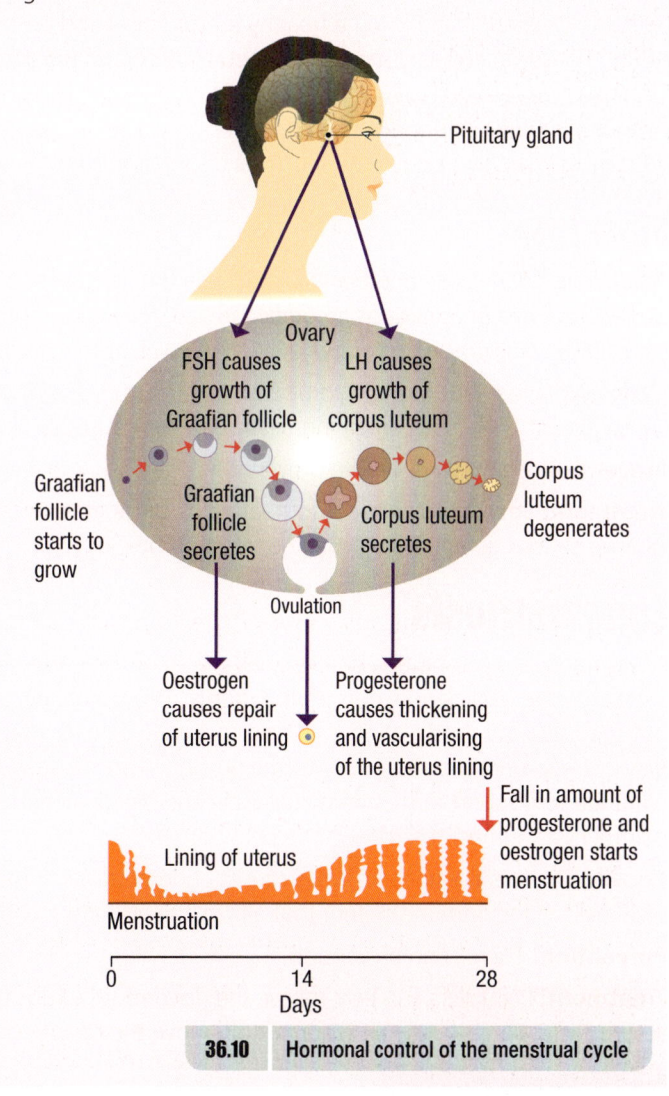

36.10 Hormonal control of the menstrual cycle

HL Luteinising hormone (LH)

Luteinising hormone is produced by the pituitary gland and travels to the ovary:

- LH causes ovulation to occur on day 14.
- Once ovulation occurs, a woman can conceive a baby if she has sexual intercourse or if there are sperm already present in her fallopian tubes.
- LH causes the empty follicle to seal up and become the corpus luteum. The corpus luteum secretes the hormones progesterone and oestrogen.

Progesterone

Progesterone is produced by the corpus luteum in the ovary:

- It causes the further repair of the endometrium in preparation for implantation.
- As levels of progesterone rise, they inhibit FSH and LH.

However, as the levels of these hormones (FSH and LH) drop, the corpus luteum breaks down. This in turn causes the production of progesterone to decline. If the levels of progesterone drop, the endometrium cannot be maintained and it is shed – menstruation begins again.

Also, as a result of low progesterone, the production of FSH and LH by the pituitary is no longer inhibited and the next cycle can begin.

Menstrual disorders

Menstruation is a normal healthy process, and most women have no problems with their periods. However, because it depends on having a healthy uterus lining and on the interaction of hormones, the delicate balance of the menstrual cycle can be easily upset. Disorders of menstruation include **fibroids** and **endometriosis**.

> **SYLLABUS REQUIREMENT:**
> You need to know about one menstrual disorder, fibroids or endometriosis.

Fibroids

A fibroid is a non-cancerous (benign) growth in the uterus. Fibroids may be as small as a pea or as large as an orange in size. They consist of muscle and connective tissue which grow slowly within the wall of the uterus (Fig 36.11).

Cause: Not clear, but thought to be associated with levels of oestrogen, e.g. oral contraceptives containing oestrogen can cause fibroids to enlarge.

Prevention: There is no known prevention.

Treatment: Small fibroids need no treatment. Large fibroids that are causing serious complications may be removed by surgery.

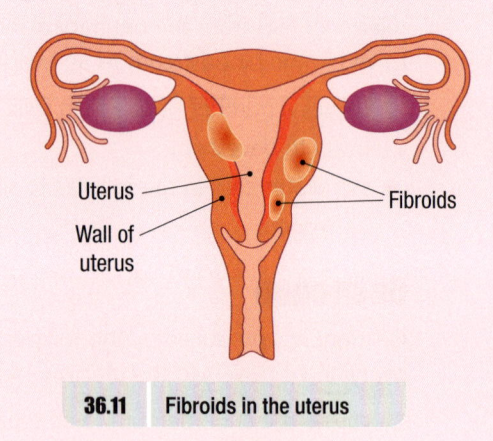

36.11 Fibroids in the uterus

Endometriosis

Endometriosis is a condition where small pieces of the endometrium are found in other parts of the body, such as in the pelvic cavity outside the uterus. This occurs when some fragments of the endometrium are not shed during menstruation in the normal way. Instead, they pass up into the oviducts and out into the pelvic cavity. Here they may stick to the outside of the ovaries, bladder, uterus and vagina. The fragments continue to respond to the menstrual cycle and bleed each month. The blood cannot escape and it causes painful cysts (lumps) to grow on the pelvic organs.

Causes: Doctors are not sure what causes endometriosis. It may be due to a hormone imbalance or a weakness in the immune system that allows the endometrial fragments to become attached.

Prevention: There is no prevention.

Treatment: Painkillers can help relieve the discomfort. Drugs may be given to prevent menstruation, and in severe cases, surgery may be required to remove the cysts.

Human Reproduction 1: The Reproductive Systems and the Menstrual Cycle

Summary

- The male gametes are the sperm, produced in the testes by meiosis and released from the body via the penis.
- For the parts and functions of the male reproductive organs, see Table 36.1.
- The production of sperm is under the control of the hormones follicle stimulating hormone (FSH) and testosterone.
- Testosterone is also responsible for the development of the secondary sexual characteristics in the male.
- Luteinising hormone (LH) causes the production of testosterone.
- Secondary sexual characteristics are the features that develop during puberty, e.g. body hair and broader shoulders in the male; breast development and wider hips in females.
- The female gametes are the eggs, produced in the ovaries by meiosis. Usually only one egg is produced each month during a woman's fertile years (approximately 12–55).
- For the parts and functions of the female reproductive system, see Table 36.2.
- The production of eggs is under the control of the hormones FSH and oestrogen.
- Oestrogen is also responsible for the development of the secondary sexual characteristics in the female.
- Ovulation is the release of an egg from the ovary. If fertilisation does not occur, the egg dies after approximately 48 hours and passes out of the body.
- The menstrual cycle is the female monthly cycle in which an egg is released and the endometrium is shed.
- The menstrual cycle is controlled by the female sex hormones.
- Events of a typical menstrual cycle:
  - Days 1–5: Menstruation occurs, an egg is produced in the ovary by meiosis.
  - Days 6–14: The endometrium repairs in preparation for pregnancy.
  - Day 14: Ovulation occurs.
  - Days 14–28: The endometrium thickens, the egg travels to the uterus and passes out of the body if fertilisation does not occur.

Male/female	Hormone	Site of production	Site of action	Function(s)
Male	FSH	Pituitary	Testes	1. Stimulates production of sperm.
	LH	Pituitary	Testes	2. Stimulates production of testosterone.
	Testosterone	Testes	All around the body	3. Responsible for secondary sexual characteristics and sperm production.
Female	FSH	Pituitary	Ovary	1. Stimulates Graafian follicle and egg to form. 2. Stimulates ovary to produce oestrogen.
	LH	Pituitary	Ovary	1. Causes ovulation. 2. Causes the Graafian follicle to become the corpus luteum.
	Oestrogen	Ovary	Uterus	1. Causes the endometrium to repair. 2. High levels inhibit FSH and stimulate LH.
	Progesterone	Ovary	Uterus	1. Maintains the endometrium (and pregnancy if it occurs). 2. Inhibits FSH and LH.
	Oxytocin	Pituitary	Uterus and breasts	1. Stimulates labour and 2. breasts to release milk.
	Prolactin	Pituitary	Breasts	1. Stimulates milk production.

Table 36.3 Summary of reproductive hormones

Summary

- Hormone control of the menstrual cycle

Hormone	Site of production	Site of action	Role in the menstrual cycle
FSH	Pituitary	Ovary	1. Stimulates Graafian follicle and egg to form. 2. Stimulates ovary to produce oestrogen.
Oestrogen	Ovary	Uterus	1. Causes the endometrium to repair. 2. High levels inhibit FSH and stimulate LH.
LH	Pituitary	Ovary	1. Causes ovulation. 2. Causes the Graafian follicle to become the corpus luteum. 3. Corpus luteum produces progesterone.
Progesterone	Ovary	Uterus	1. Maintains the endometrium in case implantation occurs. 2. Inhibits FSH and LH. 3. Which then inhibit progesterone and the endometrium is shed. 4. The cycle begins again.

Table 36.4 Hormonal control of the menstrual cycle

- Disorders of the menstrual cycle include fibroids and endometriosis.

> **SYLLABUS REQUIREMENT:**
> You need to know about one menstrual disorder, fibroids or endometriosis.

	Fibroids	Endometriosis
Cause	Unknown, may be due to oestrogen	May be due to a hormone imbalance
Prevention	None	None
Treatment	Surgery if fibroid is very large	Painkillers

Table 36.5 Menstrual disorders

Human Reproduction 1: The Reproductive Systems and the Menstrual Cycle — 36

Review questions

01 Explain each of the following terms: sexual reproduction, asexual reproduction, gamete and zygote.

02 (a) Copy the diagram below of the human male reproductive organs.
(b) Label the following parts: testis, scrotum, epididymis, vas deferens (sperm duct), penis, urethra, Cowper's gland, seminal vesicle, prostate gland.
(c) Give the main function of each of the parts you have labelled.

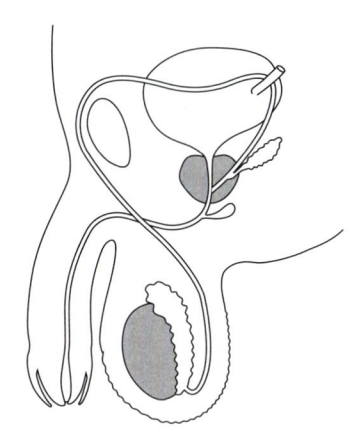

03 (a) Identify the parts labelled A, B, C, D, E, F of the female reproductive system.
(b) Give one function for each of the parts labelled. 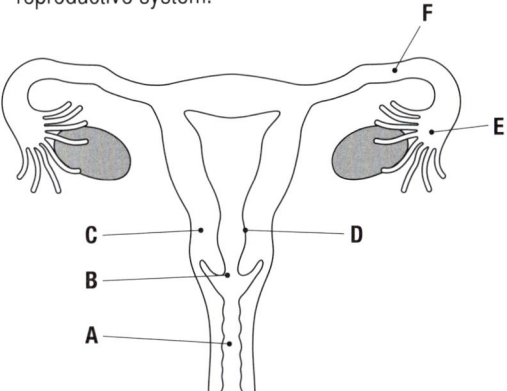

04 (a) Compare a sperm cell and an egg cell under the following headings: (i) shape, (ii) structure, (iii) size, (iv) number of chromosomes in the nucleus, (v) presence of mitochondria.
(b) Many more sperm cells are produced than eggs. Suggest why you think this is so.

05 (a) What is a hormone?
(b) Name the three male reproductive hormones.
(c) State which of the hormones is responsible for (i) sperm production, (ii) testosterone production.
(d) Suggest what might happen if there was a deficiency of FSH in a man.

06 (a) Explain what you understand by the term puberty.
(b) Define secondary sexual characteristics.
(c) List three secondary sexual characteristics in males and three in females.
(d) What controls the development of these characteristics?

07 (a) What is the menstrual cycle?
(b) What is the function of the menstrual cycle?
(c) On which day in a normal 28 day cycle do the following occur: (i) ovulation, (ii) menstruation?
(d) A woman has a regular 28-day cycle. An egg is released on 6 June.
  (i) Over which dates in the cycle would fertilisation be most likely to occur?
  (ii) If the egg is not fertilised how soon after 6 June will the woman's next period start?
  (iii) How long does a period normally last?
(e) Sometimes disorders of the menstrual cycle may occur.
  (i) Name a menstrual disorder, state what causes it, and indicate a suitable treatment.

08 (a) Name the four hormones that regulate the menstrual cycle.
(b) State where each of the four hormones is produced.
(c) Indicate where each of the hormones is active.
(d) Give two functions for each hormone in the cycle.

Examination style questions

Section A

01 The diagram shows the male reproductive system.
(a) Name the parts labelled A, B, C, D and E.
(b) Name the structure where sperm are formed.
(c) Name a hormone secreted by the structure labelled D and state its functions.
(d) Which of the labelled parts contribute to the composition of semen?
(e) State one function of the seminal vesicle.

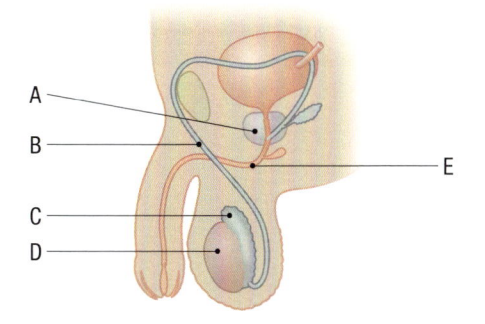

Human Reproduction 1: The Reproductive Systems and the Menstrual Cycle

Examination style questions

02 Copy the table below into your copy book. From the list below select the part of the reproductive organs that best matches the function listed.

epididymis   prostate gland   ovary   scrotum   fallopian tube

Part	Function
	Site of fertilisation
	Holds the testes
	Secretes hormones
	Stores sperm

03 The following information refers to the human menstrual cycle. The diagram illustrates how the thickness of the endometrium changes during the human menstrual cycle. The different phases of the menstrual cycle are numbered 1, 2, 3, etc.

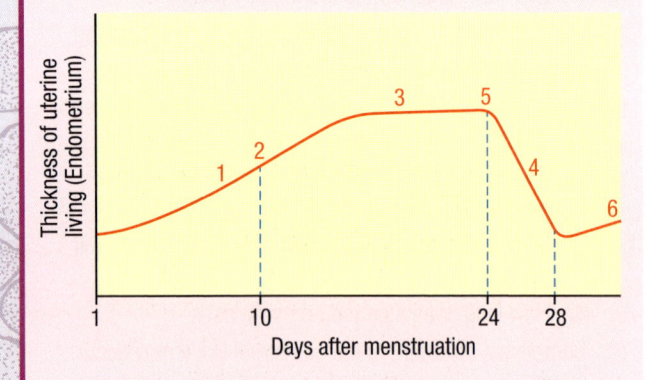

(a) Name the hormone that stimulates the repair of the endometrium following menstruation.
(b) Copy and draw a line graph in the space above the diagram to illustrate the changes in the level of this hormone over the time period shown.
(c) In what phase of the cycle would ovulation most likely occur?
(d) What structure gives rise to the corpus luteum?
(e) In what numbered phase of the cycle would the corpus luteum begin to degenerate?
(f) What event in the endometrium follows degeneration of the corpus luteum?

04 State whether the following statements are true or false. If a statement is false, give the correct answer.

(a) Sperm cells are a type of gamete.
(b) The time in a woman's life when she starts to produce eggs is known as the menopause.
(c) Ovulation is the release of an egg from the ovary.
(d) Testosterone is a male sex hormone.
(e) Progesterone is responsible for the secondary sexual characteristics in the female.
(f) On average menstruation lasts for 28 days.
(g) The urethra connects the testis to the penis.

05 Answer the following questions in connection with the menstrual cycle of human females.

(a) Name the hormone whose decline causes menstruation.
(b) Which hormone is then secreted by the pituitary and stimulates the formation of a new Graafian follicle?
(c) Name the hormone, secreted by the developing Graafian follicle, that brings about the formation of a new uterine lining.
(d) Where are Graafian follicles located in the female reproductive system?
(e) What type of nuclear division is responsible for the formation of the female gamete?
(f) Name the hormone that causes ovulation.
(g) On what day is ovulation likely to occur in a normal 28-day menstrual cycle?
(h) What structure is produced from the Graafian follicle after ovulation?
(i) What happens to this structure if implantation does not occur?
(j) Endometriosis and fibroids are classed as menstrual disorders. State how one of these disorders may be treated.

Section C

06 (a) (i) Define the term secondary sexual characteristics.
(ii) The testes, in addition to producing sperm, produce a male hormone. Name this hormone and describe the changes this hormone makes in a boy's body during puberty.
(b) (i) Draw a large labelled diagram of the male reproductive system of the human.

Examination style questions

(ii) Name which part(s) of the system is/are responsible for each of the following: storage of sperm, release of sperm, formation of semen.
(iii) Suggest a reason why the testes are found in the scrotal sacs and not inside the body cavity.
(iv) Draw a labelled diagram of a human sperm cell and a human egg cell.
(v) How many chromosomes are present in normal human gametes?
(vi) Name the type of cell division that is used to produce sperm. Explain why this type of cell division is used to produce gametes.

07 (a) (i) Distinguish between the menstrual cycle and menstruation.
(ii) What is the function of the menstrual cycle?
(b) Examine the diagram below of a typical 28-day menstrual cycle and answer the following questions.

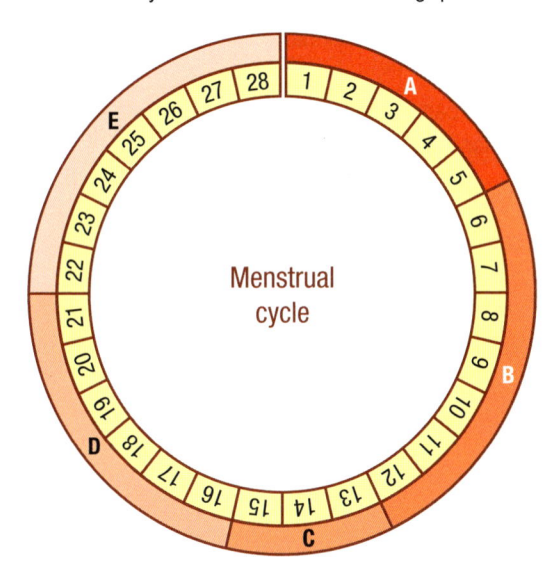

(i) Name the events marked A, B and C.
(ii) Between which days of the cycle can the following occur: (a) ovulation, (b) menstruation, (c) formation of the Graafian follicle, (d) breakdown of the corpus luteum.
(iii) If, instead of this being a 28-day cycle, the cycle lasted for 36 days. On which day in this cycle is ovulation likely to occur?
(iv) What event will stop the menstrual cycle from occurring?

(c) Write notes on each of the following: (i) Male reproductive hormones. (ii) Secondary sexual characteristics. (iii) Ovulation.

08 (a) (i) Distinguish between ovulation and implantation.
(ii) Which of the above requires luteinising hormone to occur?
(b) The diagram summarises changes in the ovary and in the uterus during a 28-day menstrual cycle in a woman, assuming that fertilisation does not take place. (Relate each event to time.)

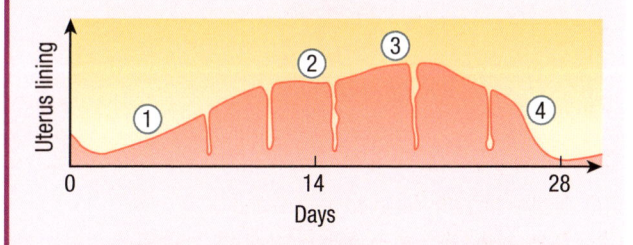

(i) Where is the Graafian follicle located?
(ii) Briefly describe what happens to the Graafian follicle at ovulation.
(iii) What changes take place in the endometrium at the start of the 28-day cycle?
(iv) Outline the connection between oestrogen and progesterone levels to the changes in the Graafian follicle and the endometrium.
(c) (i) What do the letters FSH stand for?
(ii) Name the gland that secretes FSH.
(iii) Suggest what would happen if, for some reason, a woman was unable to produce any FSH.
(iv) Name a menstrual disorder and describe a possible cause, prevention and treatment for the named disorder.

36 Human Reproduction 1: The Reproductive Systems and the Menstrual Cycle

Leaving Certificate examination questions

Section A

01 The diagram shows the human female reproductive system.

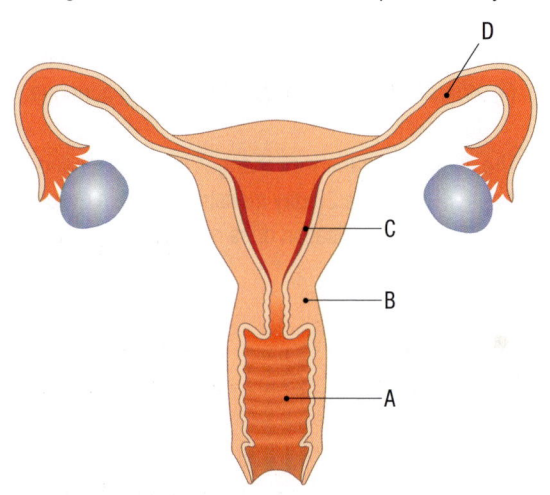

(a) Name the parts labelled A, B, C and D.
(b) State **one** function of the part labelled C in the diagram.

2014 OL Q. 3

02 The diagram shows the reproductive system of a human female.

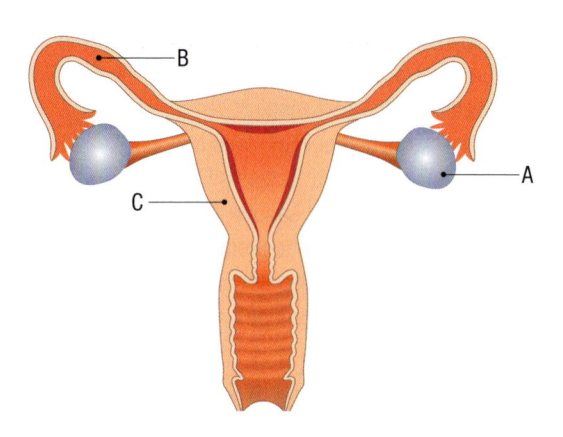

(a) Name A, B and C.
(b) In which of the parts A, B or C is the ovum (egg) formed?
(c) What is meant by fertilisation?
(d) In which of the parts A, B or C does fertilisation occur?
(e) Give one cause of female infertility.

2006 OL Q. 5

03 The diagram shows the female reproductive system.

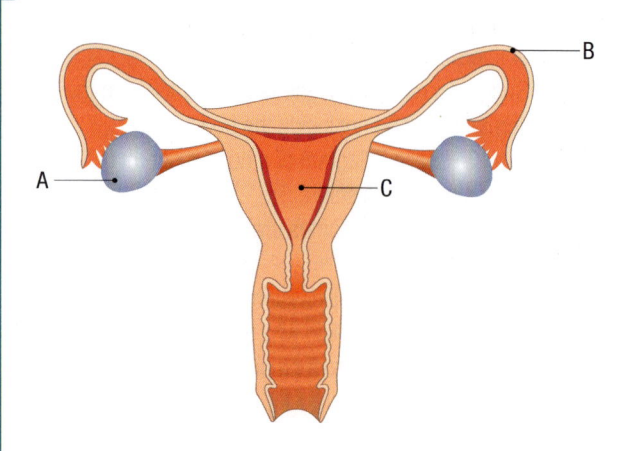

(a) Identify parts A, B and C.
(b) Using the letters X, Y and Z and arrows, identify each of the following on the diagram: endometrium (X), where fertilisation normally occurs (Y), where meiosis occurs (Z).
(c) Which part of the female reproductive system is influenced by both FSH and LH?

2008 HL Q. 6

04 The graphs illustrate changes in the levels of two hormones, A and B, which are involved in the development of the endometrium, during the human female menstrual cycle.

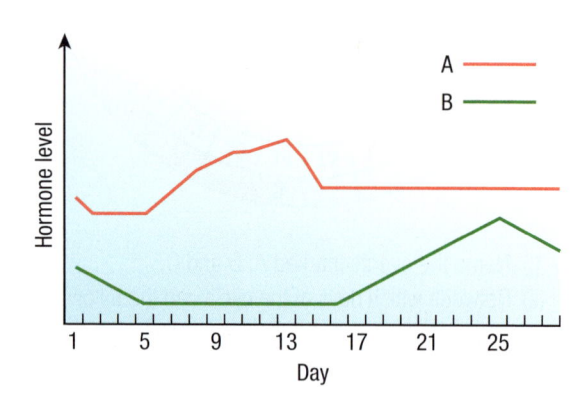

(a) Name one of these hormones.
(b) What happens in the ovary around day 14 of the cycle?
(c) Apart from the two hormones illustrated, another hormone called FSH has a role in the cycle.
   (i) Where is FSH produced?
   (ii) Give one function of FSH.
(d) Which graph, A or B, represents the hormone secreted by the *corpus luteum* (yellow body)?
(e) Draw a line graph in the space above A and B to illustrate the changes that take place in the thickness of the endometrium over the course of the cycle.

2007 HL Q. 4

Leaving Certificate examination questions

Section C

05 The diagram shows the human male reproductive system.
  (i) Name the parts A, B, C.
  (ii) Name **one** male sex hormone.
  (iii) What is the function of the prostate gland?
  (iv) Suggest a reason why the structure containing part D must be kept below body temperature.
  (v) In which labelled part does meiosis occur?

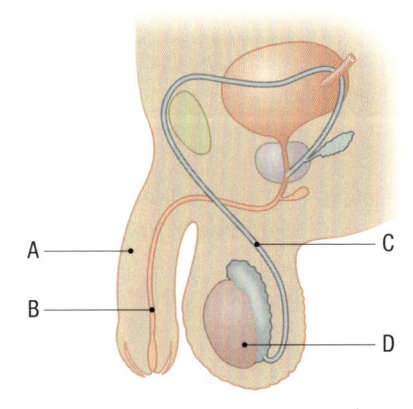

2014 OL Q. 14 (c)

06 (a) (i) Explain the term secondary sexual characteristics.
  (ii) Give **two** examples of secondary sexual characteristics in males.
  (b) The diagram shows a regular female menstrual cycle.

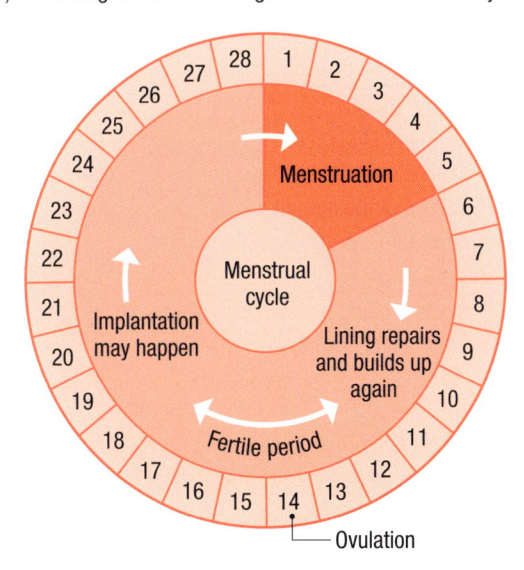

  (i) What happens in the womb during menstruation (days 1–5)?
  (ii) Explain the term *ovulation*.
  (iii) What is meant by the *fertile period*?
  (iv) Where does fertilisation occur in the female body?
  (v) Explain the term *implantation*.
  (vi) Name **two** female hormones that have a role in the menstrual cycle.
  (vii) What happens to the menstrual cycle when a woman reaches the menopause?

2013 OL Q. 12

07 The diagram shows a human sperm cell.

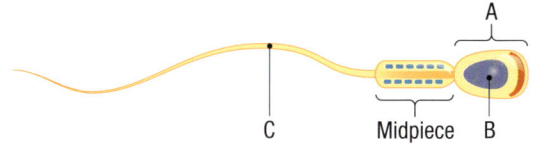

  (i) Name the parts labelled A, B and C.
  (ii) What is the function of the mid-piece of the sperm?
  (iii) Name the hormone responsible for sperm production.

2012 OL Q. 12 (c)

08 (i) Draw a large labelled diagram of the human female reproductive system.
  (ii) Indicate clearly on your diagram where each of the following events takes place:
    1. Ovulation
    2. Fertilisation

2011 OL Q. 14 (a)

09 The diagram shows the human male reproductive system.

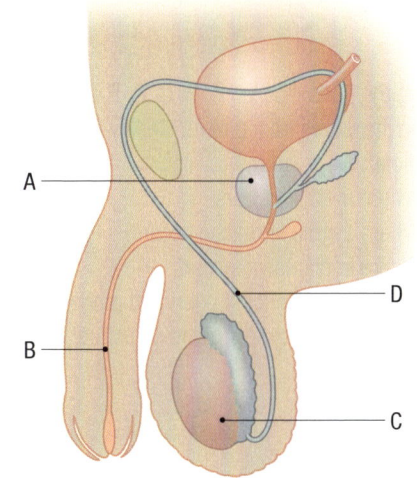

  (i) Name the parts A, B, C and D.
  (ii) What is the function of part D?
  (iii) Name the principal male sex hormone.
  (iv) Name **two** male secondary sexual characteristics.
  (v) Draw a labelled diagram of a human sperm cell.

2010 OL Q. 14 (a)

10 (i) Draw a large labelled diagram of the reproductive system of the human female.
  (ii) Indicate on your diagram where each of the following events takes place: fertilisation, implantation.

36 | Human Reproduction 1: The Reproductive Systems and the Menstrual Cycle

Leaving Certificate examination questions

(iii) What is the menstrual cycle? Outline the main events of the menstrual cycle.

2005 OL Q. 14 (b)

11 (a) (i) In humans, widening of the female hips is one example of *physical changes that distinguish the sexes but are not essential for reproduction*. To what term does the definition in italics refer?

(ii) What term is used for the time in a young person's life when such changes take place?

(iii) Name the hormone that maintains such changes throughout the life of a male.

(b) The diagram shows the reproductive system of the human female.

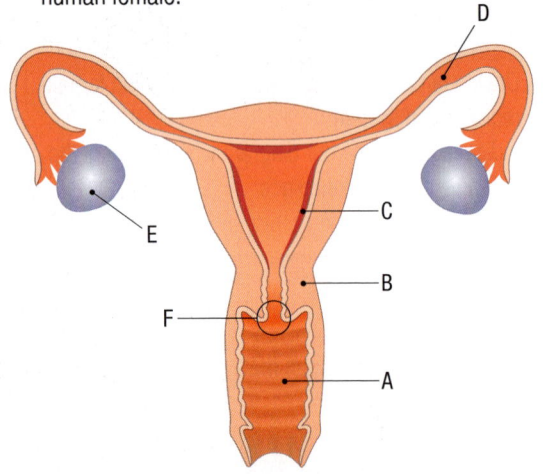

(i) Name the parts labelled A, B, C, D, E and F.
(ii) Using the letters from part (i), identify the following locations:
   1. Where meiosis occurs.
   2. Where zygote formation occurs.
   3. Where implantation occurs.
(iii) Describe the role of oestrogen **and** progesterone in the control of the events of the menstrual cycle.

2013 HL Q. 13

12 (i) What is semen?

(ii) Draw a labelled diagram of the reproductive system of the human male.
On your diagram, indicate clearly **and** name the part at which **each** of the following occurs:
   1. Production of sperm cells.
   2. Maturing of sperm cells.
   3. Mixing of fluid with sperm cells.
   4. Transport of semen.
(iii) State **two** secondary sexual characteristics of the human male.
(iv) What maintains the secondary sexual characteristics in the adult human male?

2010 HL Q. 15 (a)

13 (i) Draw a diagram of the reproductive system of the human female. On your diagram indicate where the following occur:
   1. Meiosis.
   2. Fertilisation.
   3. Implantation.
(ii) Give an account of the role of either oestrogen **or** progesterone in the menstrual cycle.
(iii) Name a human female menstrual disorder. In the case of this disorder give:
   1. A possible cause.
   2. A method of treatment.

2009 HL Q. 14 (a)

14 (a) (i) Where is testosterone secreted in the body of the human male?
(ii) Give a brief account of the role of testosterone.
(b) (i) Draw a large labelled diagram of the reproductive system of the human male.
(ii) Where are sperm produced?
(iii) State **two** ways in which sperm differ from ova (eggs).
(iv) Name a gland that secretes seminal fluid.
(v) State a function of seminal fluid.

2005 HL Q. 13

Past examination questions

OL	2014 Q. 3, Q. 14 (c) (i)–(v)	2013 Q. 12 (a), (c)	2012 Q. 12 (c) (i)–(iii)	2010 Q. 14 (a)
	2006 Q. 5	2005 Q. 14 (b)	2004 Q. 11 (a), (b)	

HL	2013 Q. 13 (a), (b)	2010 Q. 15 (a)	2009 Q. 14 (a)	2008 Q. 6
	2007 Q. 4, Q. 15 (a) (i)–(iv)	2006 Q. 15 (c) (i)	2005 Q. 13 (a), (b)	2004 Q. 14 (b) (i)

Human Reproduction 2: From Fertilisation to Birth

37

After studying this chapter you should be able to:

1. Outline the stages of copulation in both male and female.
2. Define fertilisation.
3. Compare the survival time of an egg and sperm cell.
4. Explain the term fertile period.
5. Explain infertility.
6. State one cause of male and female infertility and corrective measures.
7. Define and explain the process of *in vitro* fertilisation.
8. Define and state the location of fertilisation, implantation and placenta formation.
9. Describe the functions of the placenta.
10. **HL** Describe in more detail the sequence of development from the fertilised egg, morula, blastocyst, implanted blastocyst up to the end of the third month.
11. **HL** Define the term germ layer and state two structures that develop from each of the ectoderm, mesoderm and endoderm layers.
12. Explain the amnion and state its function.
13. Describe the process of birth.
14. Describe the role of hormones in the process of birth.
15. Describe lactation including the role of hormones and the benefits of breastfeeding.
16. Explain birth control (contraception) and outline natural, mechanical, chemical and surgical methods of contraception.

Copulation and fertilisation

Fertilisation is the fusion of a sperm and egg to form a **zygote**. Normally fertilisation occurs in the female fallopian tube (oviduct). So in order for fertilisation to occur, an egg and sperm **cell** must meet in an oviduct. This is usually achieved by **copulation**. Copulation literally means to join or unite, and it is more commonly known as sexual intercourse or making love.

D — **Copulation** means sexual intercourse.

During intercourse, **sexual arousal** causes the penis to become stiff and erect. This event is called having an erection. It is caused by blood being pumped into the many blood spaces in the wall of the penis faster than it can drain away. In the female, sexual arousal leads to the erection of the clitoris and the secretion of mucus by the wall of the vagina.

The erect penis enters the vagina, which has become lubricated by the mucus lining. The rhythmic movements of the penis in the vagina cause semen to be ejaculated (released) into the vagina near the cervix. During ejaculation the man experiences a pleasurable feeling called an **orgasm**. Stimulation of the clitoris may also produce an orgasm in the female.

37 Human Reproduction 2: From Fertilisation to Birth

The fluids secreted by the seminal vesicles and prostate glands, together with the mucus secreted by the cervix, and muscular contraction of the cervix and uterus enable the sperm to swim through the cervix, into the uterus and up into the **oviducts**. The sperm are very small, many are not the correct shape and most swim in the wrong direction. So millions of sperm are ejaculated at a time to ensure that some sperm reach an oviduct where there might be an egg.

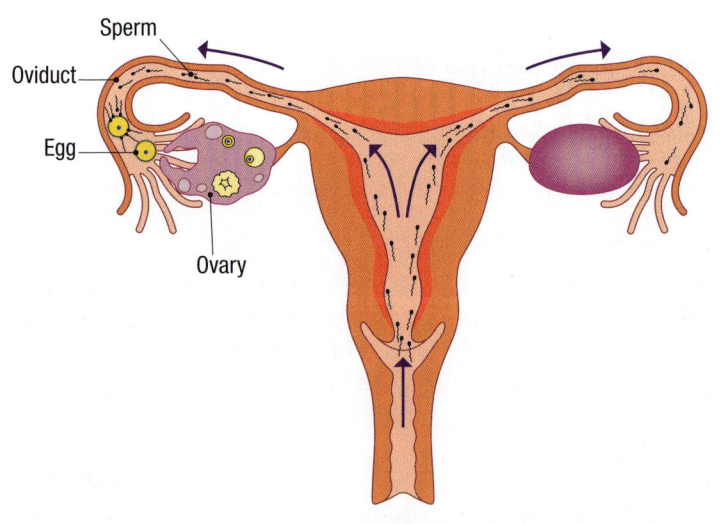

37.1 The pathway of sperm

Fertilisation

Of the millions of sperm cells ejaculated, only a few hundred reach the oviducts and only one will fertilise an egg. This happens as follows:

The acrosome at the head of the sperm cell releases digestive **enzymes** which break down the outer membrane of the egg. As soon as one sperm enters the egg cell, the membrane changes and prevents the entry of other sperm. Any other sperm cells die away. Only the head of the sperm cell, which contains the nucleus, passes into the egg. The mid-piece (with all the **mitochondria**) and the tail remain outside.

Fertilisation occurs when the sperm nucleus and the egg nucleus fuse to form the **diploid** zygote. In other words, the **chromosomes** of the sperm join with the chromosomes of the egg.

> **Fertilisation** is the fusion of a sperm cell nucleus with an egg cell nucleus to produce a diploid zygote.

Survival time of the egg and sperm

Sperm cells can live and be capable of fertilising an egg for up to 5 days after being released into the female body. The egg itself remains fertile for 12–24 hours. In a menstrual cycle that happens to be strictly 28 days, the period in the cycle when intercourse could result in fertilisation is between days 12 and 16 of that cycle. The period of time in the cycle when an egg can be fertilised is known as the **fertile period**.

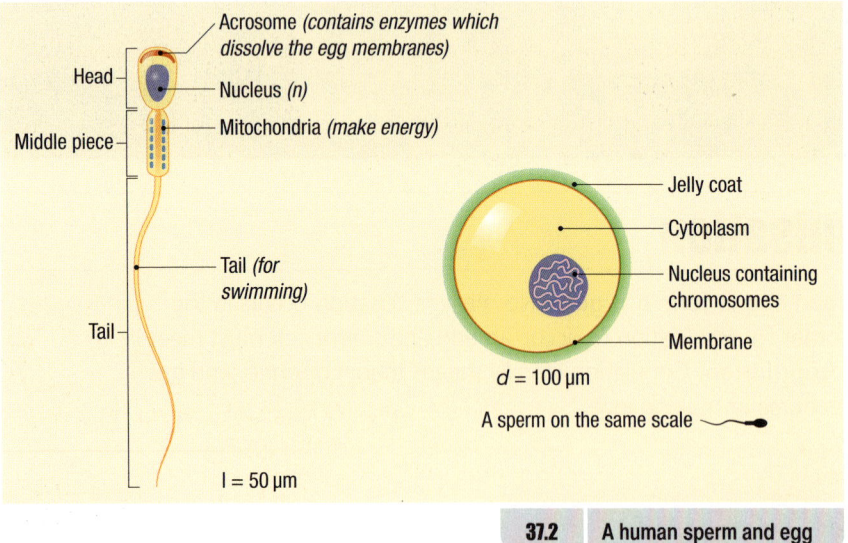

> The **fertile period** is the time during a menstrual cycle when an egg can be fertilised.

37.2 A human sperm and egg

Infertility

Some couples are unable to conceive. The inability to conceive is called **infertility**. **Conception** (fertilisation, followed by **pregnancy**) depends on many things: healthy and plentiful sperm, healthy eggs and endometrium, a clear passage between the ovary and the uterus, and sufficient **hormone** production in both male and female. A problem with any one of the above factors can lead to infertility.

In general, about 40% of infertility cases are due to factors which affect men, another 40% are due to factors affecting women and the remaining 20% are due to a combination of both.

> **Infertility** is the inability to produce gametes or to conceive.

Human Reproduction 2: From Fertilisation to Birth | **37**

Male infertility

SYLLABUS REQUIREMENT:

You need to know about one cause of male infertility.

Causes

The main cause of male infertility is the inability to produce enough healthy sperm. Men with a low sperm count, less than 20 million sperm per cubic centimetre of semen, are considered sterile. Chronic alcohol abuse, cigarette and cannabis smoking have been linked with low sperm count. Sperm that cannot swim properly and insufficient testosterone production are also causes of male infertility.

Corrective measures

Treatment of male infertility is limited. Changes in diet and lifestyle may prove helpful, e.g. reducing alcohol intake. If the cause is due to lack of testosterone, drug therapy may be useful. *In vitro* fertilisation (IVF), as described below, can be used as a treatment for male infertility.

Female infertility

SYLLABUS REQUIREMENT:

You need to know about one cause of female infertility.

Causes

One cause of female infertility is blockage of the oviducts which prevents the egg from being fertilised and passing into the uterus. Another cause of female infertility is the inability to produce and or release eggs.

Corrective measures

If the oviduct blockage is small, surgery can be performed to clear the blockage. In cases of severely damaged oviducts, *in vitro* fertilisation is the only way that conception may be achieved (see below). Inability to produce eggs is normally due to a hormone imbalance and it may be treated with drugs.

In vitro fertilisation

IVF is a method of treating some types of infertility. The technique involves removing an egg from an ovary and fertilising it outside the body. In vitro means 'in glass' and it refers to the dish in which the fertilisation occurs.

Babies born as a result of IVF are sometimes referred to as test-tube babies. But this is a misnomer because although fertilisation occurs in a dish (glass), pregnancy and development of the embryo occurs in the mother's uterus.

> **D**
> *In vitro* fertilisation is the fusion of an egg and sperm outside the body.

The technique

- Early in the **menstrual cycle**, the woman is given hormones to cause the production of several eggs instead of the normal one egg.
- The developing **follicles** are monitored by ultrasound scanning.
- Immediately before **ovulation**, the eggs are removed through a narrow needle and transferred to a nutrient fluid in a Petri dish.
- The man's sperm are mixed with the eggs and the dish is placed in an incubator.
- After a few days the eggs are examined to see if fertilisation has occurred and **embryos** have begun to grow.
- If they have, one or two embryos are placed in the woman's uterus, and hopefully one may become **implanted**.

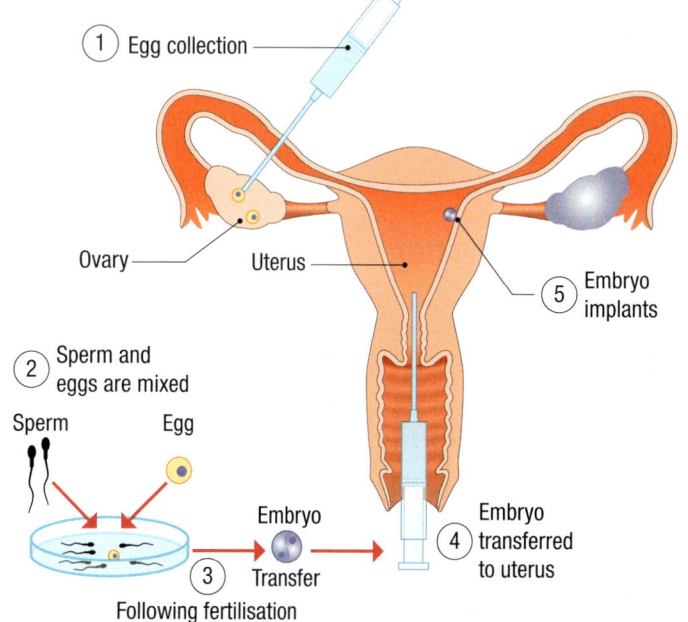

37.3 The process of IVF

37 Human Reproduction 2: From Fertilisation to Birth

- Usually, following an implantation, a normal pregnancy and birth will follow, although the percentage of implantations that occur is quite low.

Sometimes any 'extra' embryos are frozen for later use or they may be destroyed. The first successful birth as a result of *in vitro* fertilisation took place in England in 1978.

Implantation and human pregnancy

Following fertilisation, the zygote begins to divide to form the embryo. It travels down the oviduct to the uterus where, approximately 7 days after fertilisation, it embeds (implants) into the **endometrium** and pregnancy begins. Fertilisation, followed by pregnancy, are together referred to as conception.

> **Implantation** is when the embryo embeds into the endometrium.

Human pregnancy

Implantation of the embryo is complete 14 days after fertilisation, and once it has occurred, pregnancy is said to be established. In humans, pregnancy lasts for 38 weeks. This figure means that 38 weeks after fertilisation, the baby will be due to be born. The time between conception and birth is called the gestation period. Menstruation does not occur during pregnancy.

Once implanted, the embryo cells continue to divide and become specialised, forming all the tissues and organs of a new human being. After 8 weeks, the embryo looks like a tiny human being and becomes known as the **foetus** (fetus, Latin = offspring). During the following weeks and months, the foetus grows rapidly and the uterus swells to allow for the increase in size.

The placenta

The **placenta** is a disc-shaped structure formed from tissues of both the embryo and the mother (endometrium). In the placenta, the blood of the mother and the foetus lie close together, but they never mix. The placenta is attached to the embryo by the **umbilical cord**. The placenta is fully formed by the end of the 12th week of pregnancy.

Functions of the placenta

1. Exchange of materials

Digested food (amino acids and glucose), oxygen, minerals and **antibodies** pass from the mother's blood to the foetus by **diffusion** and **active transport**. Drugs, alcohol, **viruses** and chemicals in cigarette smoke can also pass into the foetus (see section on health in pregnancy below). Wastes made in the foetus, such as carbon dioxide, urea and excess water pass from the foetus into the mother's blood.

37.4 The placenta and foetus

2. Acts as a barrier

The placenta acts as a barrier against the blood pressure of the mother, which might at times be too great for the foetus. It also protects the foetus from the mother's immune system, which might otherwise reject the foetus as foreign.

3. Endocrine gland

The placenta acts as an **endocrine gland** (temporary). It takes over the role of the corpus luteum in the ovary and secretes **progesterone** and **oestrogen**. These hormones maintain the endometrium, prevent ovulation and prepare the breasts to produce milk once the baby is born.

Human Reproduction 2: From Fertilisation to Birth | 37

Health in pregnancy

Cigarette smoking in pregnancy increases the risk of babies being born underweight. This is due to reduced oxygen reaching the cells of the embryo.

Taking drugs and heavy drinking can damage the growth of the baby's cells, particularly those of the brain and spinal cord.

Eating a healthy diet before and during pregnancy greatly improves the chances of conception and the healthy development of the foetus. It is now well known that folic acid (one of the B vitamins) is essential for the correct development of the spinal cord.

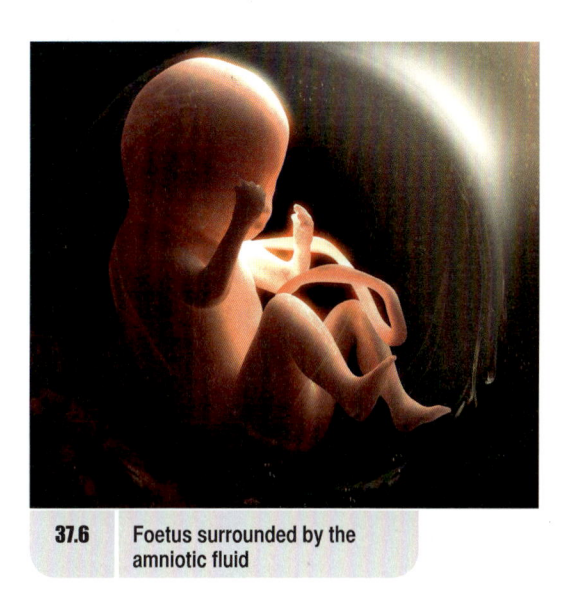

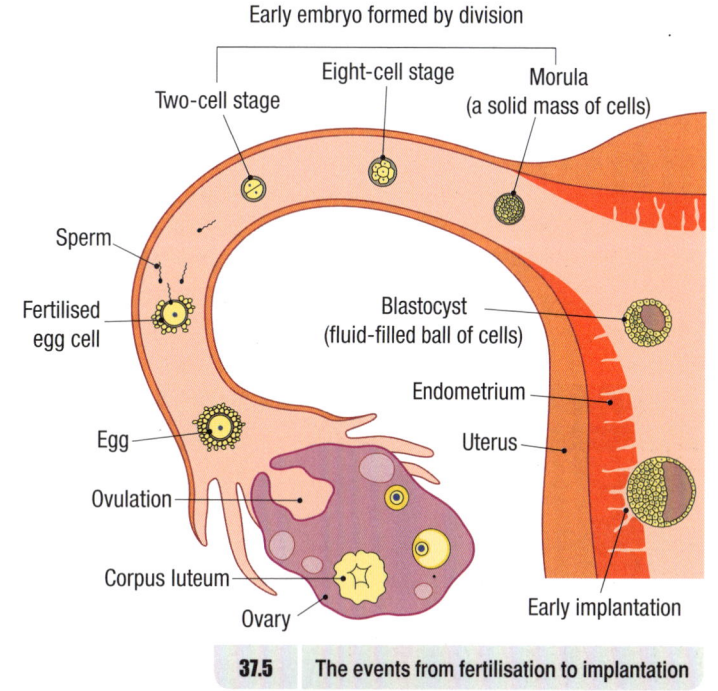

37.6 Foetus surrounded by the amniotic fluid

37.5 The events from fertilisation to implantation

HL Development of the embryo up to the third month

Shortly after fertilisation, the zygote begins to divide many times by mitosis. This results in a solid ball of unspecialised (undifferentiated) cells called the **morula** (32 cells). The morula is wafted down the fallopian tube to the uterus by **cilia** and **peristalsis**. The cells of the morula continue to divide and form a fluid-filled ball of cells called the **blastocyst**. The blastocyst consists of an outer layer of cells called the trophoblast, which forms the placenta and a small inner mass of cells which becomes the embryo. Details of the placenta, its formation and functions can be found on page 494.

D The **morula** is a solid ball of cells.

D The **blastocyst** is a fluid-filled ball of cells.

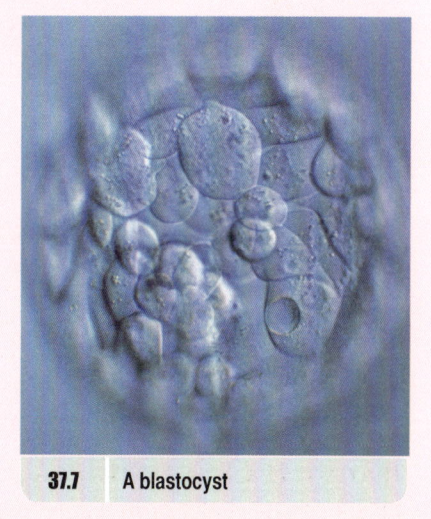

37.7 A blastocyst

Implantation

Some 7 days after fertilisation, the blastocyst moves into the uterus and embeds into the endometrium. This is implantation. Initially, the **trophoblast** layer forms finger-like projections called **villi** (see Fig 25.9), which absorb nutrients from the endometrium and pass them to the embryo cells. Later, this nutritive role is taken on by the placenta itself. The trophoblast also forms the series of membranes, the chorion and **amnion**, which surround and protect the embryo as it grows (see Fig 37.9).

Implantation is when the embryo embeds into the endometrium. **D**

37 Human Reproduction 2: From Fertilisation to Birth

HL Development of the embryo

The embryo develops from the small mass of cells in the blastocyst. These cells organise themselves into three layers, called **germ layers**. These layers are very important because each one forms certain parts of the body. The outside layer is the **ectoderm**, the middle layer is the **mesoderm** and the innermost layer is the **endoderm**. Table 37.1 lists the main organ systems that develop from the three germ layers.

> A **germ layer** is a group of cells in the embryo that give rise to the body organs.

Ecotoderm	Mesoderm	Endoderm

Becomes the
  Brain
  Spinal cord
  Skin, hair and nails
	Becomes the
	  Muscles
	  Heart
	  Skeleton
	  Blood and blood vessels
	  Kidneys
	  Reproductive organs
		Becomes the linings of the
		  Gut
		  Lungs
		  Pancreas
		  Liver
		  Blood vessels
		  Urethra

Table 37.1 The organs and structures that develop from the germ layers

Time after fertilisation	Events
24 hours	Zygote divides to form two cells.
3 days	Morula reaches the uterus.
7 days	Implantation of blastocyst begins.
14 days	Implantation complete.
1.5 weeks	Blood cells are forming.
3.5 weeks	CNS begins to develop; heart forms and starts to beat; blood vessels form.
4 weeks	Arm and leg buds begin to appear, umbilical cord forms, a tail is visible (length = 5.6 mm).
5 weeks	All the internal organs, i.e. liver, kidney, lungs and sex organs, have begun to form.
6 weeks	The eyes are visible and the nose and ears are forming; the arms and legs grow rapidly (l = 10 mm).
8 weeks	The face becomes more human, the tail has gone; muscles and bones develop; most of the internal organs are formed. The embryo now becomes known as the foetus (l = 25 mm).
12 weeks (end of third month)	Cells in the foetus are still actively growing and becoming specialised. Finger and toe nails form, hair, eyebrows and eyelashes can be seen. The placenta is fully formed. It is now possible to tell if the foetus is male or female. The foetus weighs 14 g (l = 85 mm).

Table 37.2 Development of the embryo up to the end of the third month

Human Reproduction 2: From Fertilisation to Birth | 37

Once the first three months are over, the foetus continues to grow and develop until finally it is ready to be born. The average weight of a newborn baby is 3.4 kg and the average length of a baby is 51 cm. What began as a single cell following fertilisation is now a fully formed human baby, made up of millions and millions of different cells. A wondrous growth!

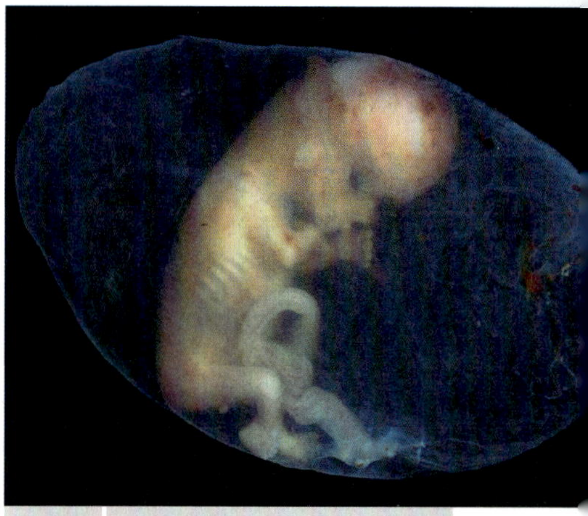

The amnion

12 The foetus is surrounded by a thin membrane called the **amnion**. The amnion encloses a cavity called the amniotic cavity, which contains **amniotic fluid** (Fig 37.9). The foetus floats in this fluid and is protected and cushioned by it. The amniotic fluid protects the foetus from drying out and from changes in temperature.

37.8 The embryo at 6 weeks

D The **amnion** is a membrane which surrounds the embryo and secretes amniotic fluid.

Birth

13 In humans, pregnancy lasts 280 days from the last period (or 266 days (38 weeks) after conception). After this time, the baby is born. The process of birth is known as **labour**, and it occurs in three stages.

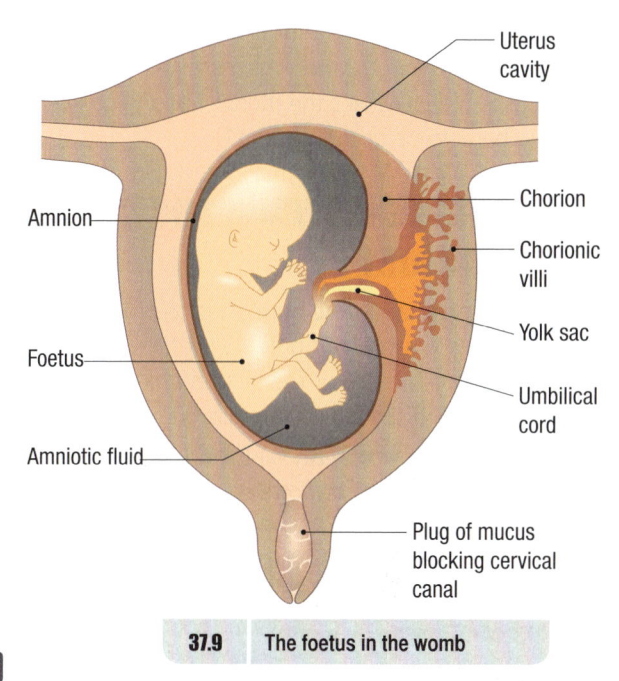

The first stage of labour (6–18 hours)

Labour begins when the muscle wall of the uterus begins to contract. At first the mother feels gentle contractions which do not occur very often. The contractions gradually get stronger and more frequent causing the cervix to open (dilate) to allow the baby's head to pass through.

Around this time, the amniotic membrane surrounding the baby bursts releasing the amniotic fluid through the vagina. This event is known as the 'breaking of the waters', and it is usually a sure sign that the baby is ready to be born.

37.9 The foetus in the womb

The second stage of labour (20–60 minutes)

In the second stage of labour, strong contractions of the uterus cause the baby's head to be pushed down through the vagina. Once the head is 'born', the shoulders emerge, one following the other, and then the rest of the baby slides out. The baby is still attached to the mother by the umbilical cord and placenta. Once the umbilical cord stops pulsating, it is tied (clamped) and cut. This causes no pain to the baby and the scar that remains on the abdomen becomes your navel or 'belly button'.

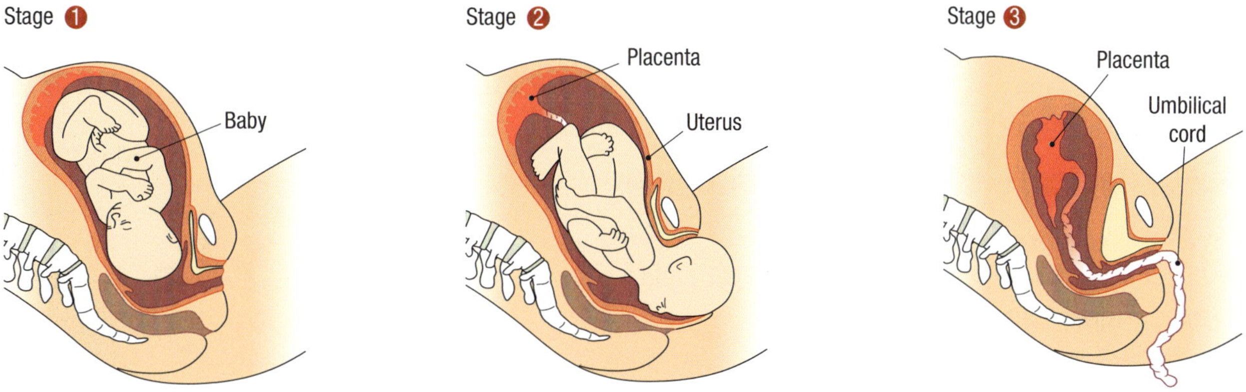

Stage 1 — Baby

Stage 2 — Placenta, Uterus
The actual birth

Stage 3 — Placenta, Umbilical cord
The placenta (afterbirth) is expelled

37.10 The three stages of labour

The third stage of labour (5–15 minutes)

In the final stage of labour, further contractions loosen and expel the placenta, the other membranes that surrounded the foetus and the remains of the umbilical cord. Collectively, these structures are known as the afterbirth.

Following childbirth, the endometrium repairs and the uterus returns to its normal size. If the mother is not breastfeeding her baby (see below), the menstrual cycle can start again in about 6–8 weeks.

The role of hormones in the birth process

Just before labour begins, the levels of progesterone and oestrogen drop. This removes the effect of progesterone on the uterus, and the wall now begins to contract. In addition, it allows the hormone **oxytocin** to be released by the **pituitary gland** which lies just under the brain. Oxytocin also causes the uterus wall to contract to allow the baby to be born (Fig 37.11).

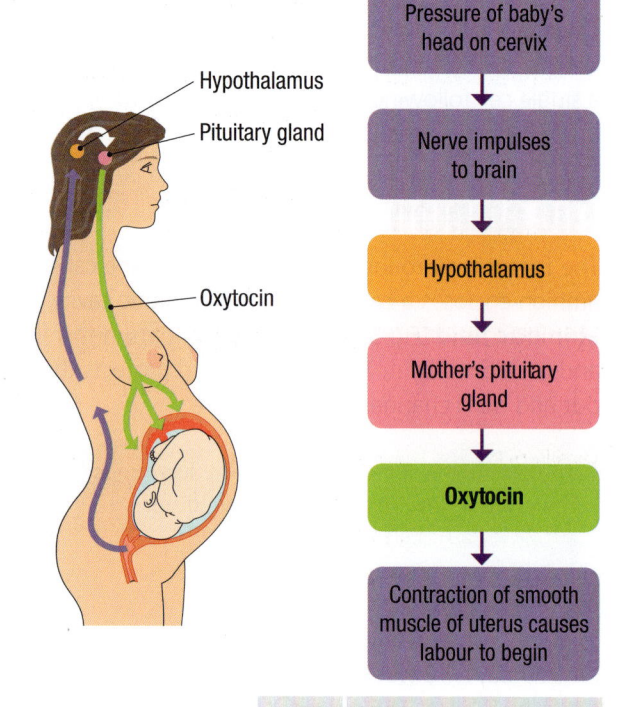

Production of milk and breastfeeding (lactation)

During pregnancy, the hormones oestrogen and progesterone cause the breasts to enlarge and prepare for the production of milk. Milk is the only food a baby needs for the first few months of its life. A young baby has no teeth, and its digestive system is not capable of digesting solid food.

The hormone **prolactin** is needed for the production of milk and oxytocin stimulates the nipples to release the milk. During pregnancy, the secretion of prolactin is inhibited by progesterone and oestrogen. At birth, the levels of the latter hormones decline, and this stimulates the pituitary gland to secrete prolactin. It takes two or three days after the baby is born for milk to be produced.

During this time, the breasts produce **colostrum**. Colostrum contains food in the form of protein and important antibodies, which help protect the newborn infant from certain diseases and allergies. After about 3–4 days, the breasts produce milk containing all the protein, fat, sugars, vitamins and minerals the baby needs for the first few months of its life.

When a healthy newborn baby is put to the breast, it sucks on the nipple. This stimulates the release of milk and causes more milk to be made. The more the baby suckles the greater the secretion of prolactin and of milk. As long as the mother has a healthy diet and rest, there should be a plentiful supply of milk for the baby. If a mother chooses not to breast feed, the breasts stop making milk and return to their normal size within a few days.

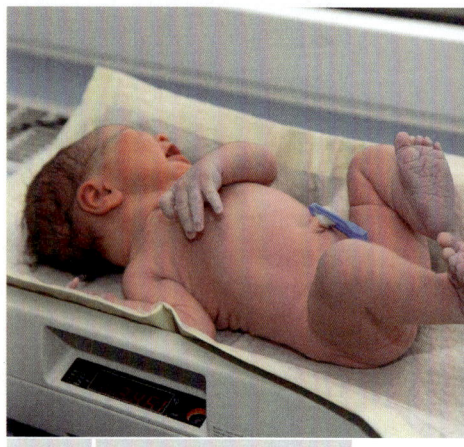

The biological benefits of breastfeeding

Breastfeeding is good for the baby and good for the mother:

- Breast milk is the perfect food for a human baby and it is always at the correct temperature.

37.11 The role of oxytocin in the process of birth

37.12 A newborn baby

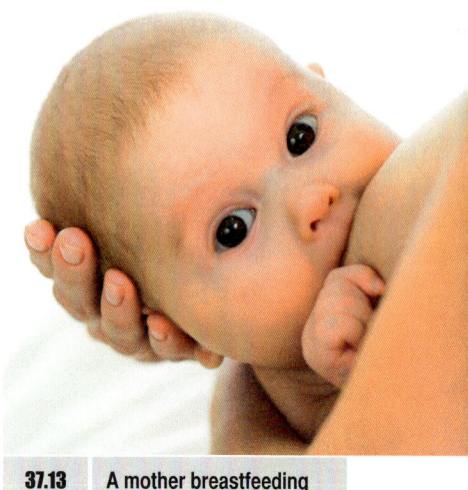

37.13 A mother breastfeeding her baby

- Breast milk contains antibodies, which protect against allergies and illnesses.
- Breast milk can help the mother to lose weight after the birth of her baby, and it helps the uterus contract back to its normal size more quickly.
- Breastfeeding allows the mother and baby to 'bond', because of the close physical relationship it involves.
- Breastfeeding can help delay the return of the menstrual cycle and ovulation, a fact used in many cultures to allow natural spacing of the birth of children. This is because suckling inhibits FSH and LH production.

Birth control (contraception)

It is possible, at least in theory, for a woman to have a baby every year from the time she starts to ovulate until the menopause. Most couples want to limit the number of children that they have. Birth control or family planning is when a couple want to prevent pregnancy. There are many methods of birth control, and most of them involve some form of contraception.

Contraception can be achieved in four different ways: natural, chemical, mechanical and surgical.

D — **Contraception** means to prevent fertilisation and pregnancy.

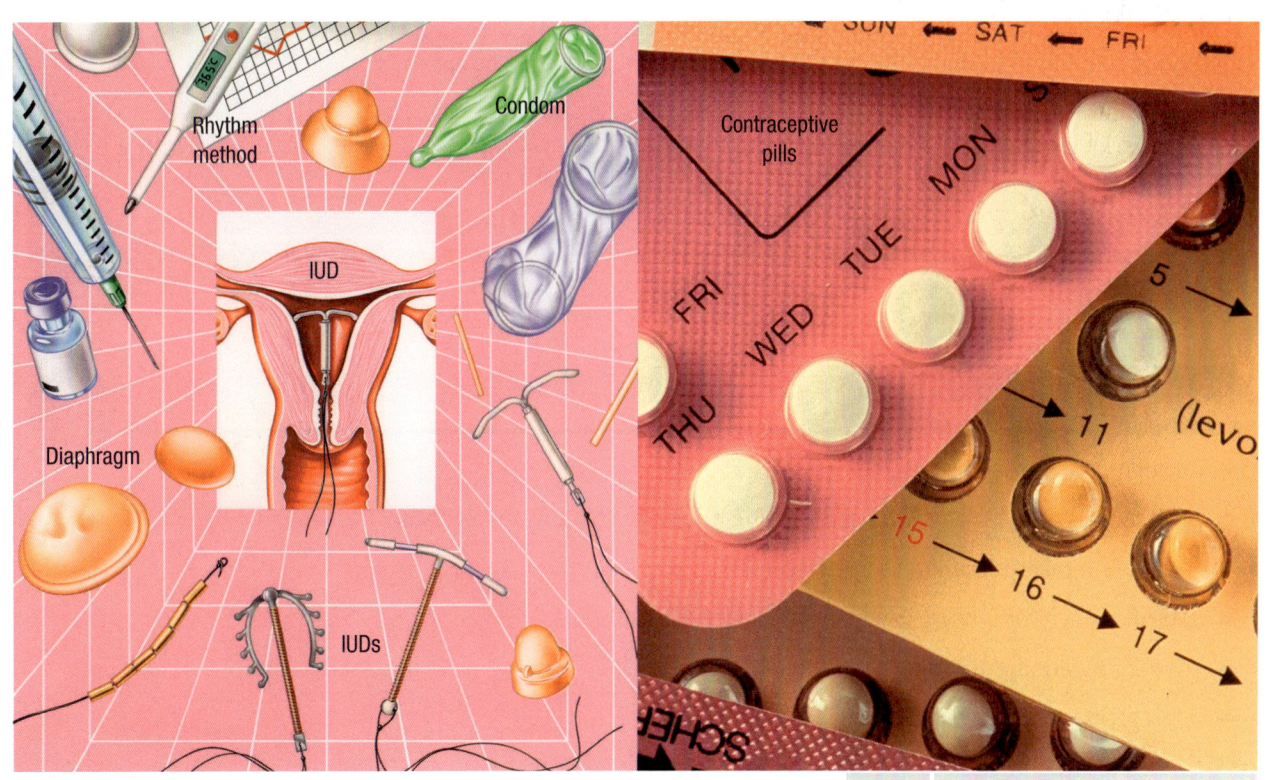

37.14 Various methods of contraception

Type	Method	Procedure	Mode of action	Effectiveness
Natural	Rhythm	Work out the fertile period	Avoid intercourse for 5 days before and 5 days after ovulation	70%
Mechanical	IUD (intra-uterine device)	Strip of plastic bent into a loop or coil and placed in uterus	Prevents implantation	90%
Chemical	The pill	Tablet containing oestrogen and/or progesterone taken daily	Prevents ovulation	99.9%
	Morning after pill	Tablet containing high levels of oestrogen	Prevents ovulation and implantatation	
	Contraceptive implant	Small plastic rod inserted into the inner part of upper arm. Releases progesterone over a period of years.	Prevents ovulation	
Barrier	Diaphragm	Dome-shaped device placed at cervix	Prevents sperm entering uterus	90%
	Condom	Sheath that fits over erect penis	Prevents sperm entering vagina	85%
Surgical sterilisation – female	Tubal ligation	Oviducts are cut and tied	Prevents eggs meeting sperm	100%
Surgical sterilisation – male	Vasectomy	Sperm ducts are cut and tied	Prevents sperm leaving the penis	100%

Table 37.3 Methods of contraception

Summary

- Copulation is sexual intercourse.
- Fertilisation is the fusion of the sperm and egg cell nuclei to form a zygote.
- Fertilisation takes place in the fallopian tube.
- Sperm can live for 5 days. The egg can live for 12–24 hours.
- The fertile period is the time in the menstrual cycle when fertilisation is possible.
- Infertility is an inability to conceive.
- Causes of male infertility: low sperm count, hormone imbalance.
- Causes of female infertility include inability to produce eggs and blocked fallopian tubes.
- Corrective measures for infertility include hormone treatment, surgery to clear blocked fallopian tubes and IVF.

Human Reproduction 2: From Fertilisation to Birth

Summary

- IVF involves the fusion of an egg and sperm outside the body.
  - The woman is given hormones to increase egg production.
  - Eggs are removed to a Petri dish with a nutrient medium.
  - Sperm are added.
  - If fertilisation and embryo formation occur, one or two embryos are implanted into the mother.
  - Pregnancy follows.

- Human pregnancy lasts for 38 weeks (from fertilisation).

- Following fertilisation, the zygote divides many times by mitosis to form the embryo. Once the embryo reaches the uterus, it embeds into the lining, the endometrium. Implantation is the embedding of the embryo into the endometrium.

- After about 12 weeks, a structure called the placenta forms, which acts as a link between the mother and the foetus.

- The placenta is formed from the tissue of the mother and of the embryo.

- The functions of the placenta are:
  - to exchange materials between the mother and the foetus, e.g. gases and nutrients;
  - to attach the foetus to the wall of the uterus;
  - to protect the foetus against changes in the mother's blood pressure;
  - to act as an endocrine gland by secreting hormones, oestrogen and progesterone – progesterone maintains the pregnancy by preventing the uterus contracting.

HL • Following fertilisation, the zygote divides by mitosis to produce the morula and then the hollow blastocyst. The blastocyst implants in the endometrium and continues to develop. The inner mass of cells becomes the embryo and the outer layer, the trophoblast, forms the chorion and amnion membranes. The chorion, together with the endometrium of the mother, forms the placenta. The embryo cells form three germ layers, the ectoderm, mesoderm and endoderm. These layers form the organs of the body (see Table 37.3).

- By week 4, the heart, brain and blood vessels have formed. By week 5, all the internal organs are forming. By week 6, the sense organs and limbs are growing. By week 8, most of the internal organs are formed. The embryo now becomes known as the foetus.

- By the end of the third month (12 weeks), the foetus is complete, but is still tiny and it will be another 6 months before it is fully mature. The placenta is fully formed.

- Birth involves the three stages of labour:
  - Stage 1, lasts the longest. During this stage, contractions of the uterus wall cause the cervix to widen.
  - Stage 2, in which contractions of the uterus wall strengthen and the baby is pushed out through the vagina.
  - Stage 3, in which the placenta and its membranes are expelled from the body as the afterbirth.

- The hormone oxytocin causes the uterine wall to contract during labour and it stimulates the breasts to secrete milk. Prolactin causes milk to be produced once the baby is born.

- Breast milk is the perfect food for human babies: it is produced at the correct temperature, it provides a balanced diet for the baby in the first months of life, and it contains protective antibodies.

- Contraception means preventing fertilisation and pregnancy. There are natural, mechanical, chemical and surgical methods of contraception (see Table 37.3).

Human Reproduction 2: From Fertilisation to Birth

Review questions

01 (a) Explain the terms fertilisation and zygote.
(b) Draw a diagram of the human female reproductive organs and mark on the diagram the location of each of the following:
  (i) Where an egg is produced.
  (ii) Where fertilisation usually occurs.
  (iii) Where implantation occurs.
  (iv) Where ejaculation occurs.

02 (a) Outline the pathway taken by a sperm cell from the time it is made in the testis until it meets an egg cell.
(b) Describe the events that then take place leading up to fertilisation.
(c) Sperm can live inside the female for up to 5 days, and the egg can live for 24 hours after being released. If ovulation occurs on the 13th day of the menstrual cycle of a woman, on which days of the cycle could sexual intercourse result in pregnancy? What is the name given to this period of time?

03 Distinguish between the following:
(a) ovary and oviduct,
(b) ovulation and fertilisation,
(c) implantation and copulation.

04 Some couples may be infertile.
(a) What does being infertile mean?
(b) Describe one cause of male infertility and one cause of female infertility.
(c) How can the causes of infertility you mention be treated?

05 (a) Why is the term 'test-tube' baby a misnomer?
(b) What is *in vitro* fertilisation (IVF)?
(c) Outline one situation in which IVF is used.
(d) Describe the main steps involved in IVF.
(e) Suggest one ethical issue associated with the process of IVF.

06 (a) How long does a human pregnancy last from conception (give your answer in days or weeks)?
(b) Distinguish between the embryo and the foetus.
(c) At what stage does the embryo become known as the foetus?

07 (a) What is the placenta?
(b) From what two tissues is the placenta formed?
(c) One function of the placenta is the exchange of materials between the foetus and the mother. (i) Name the process by which materials are exchanged. (ii) Give examples of materials that pass into and out of the foetus.
(d) Describe two other functions of the placenta.
(e) Name a hormone that maintains the placenta.

08 Distinguish between:
(a) fertilisation and implantation,
(b) morula and blastocyst,
(c) ectoderm and endoderm.

09 (a) Describe the events from the time the zygote is formed until implantation is complete.
(b) What type of cell division brings about these events?
(c) Name the three primary germ layers and for each layer name two tissues or organs produced from it.

10 (a) What is the amnion?
(b) What does the amnion produce?
(c) State the function of the amnion.

11 The diagram shows a foetus in the uterus during the first stage of birth.
(a) Name the parts A, B, C, D.
(b) State two functions of C.
(c) What is the function of B? And from what is B formed?
(d) Identify two features from the diagram that tells you that the diagram is showing the first stage of labour.
(e) Describe what happens during the third stage of labour.
(f) Suggest why a pregnant woman must be careful not to smoke or drink alcohol and be careful what she eats, particularly during the first 8 weeks of the pregnancy.

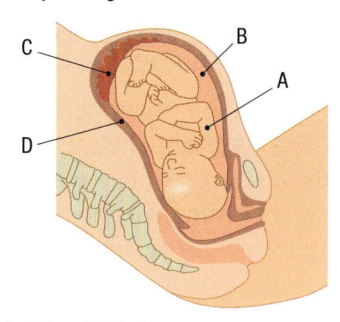

Milk is the first food of babies.

12 (a) Where is the milk produced?
(b) Name the hormone involved in milk (i) production, (ii) secretion.
(c) What triggers milk to be secreted?
(d) Outline three biological advantages of breastfeeding.
(e) In spite of the advantages, many women choose not to breastfeed their babies. Suggest a reason why you think this is the case.

13 (a) What is meant by the term contraception?
(b) Distinguish between natural and chemical methods of contraception.
(c) Give one example of a barrier method of contraception.
(d) (i) Classify the following as chemical, mechanical or surgical methods of contraception: condom; the pill; the diaphragm; vasectomy.
  (ii) Identify the contraceptives used by males from the following list: condom; the pill; the diaphragm; vasectomy.
(e) Outline one advantage and one disadvantage of contraception to humans.

Examination style questions

01 Answer the following by selecting the correct answer from the list in each case.
  (i) In humans fertilisation normally occurs in:
      (a) uterus   (b) oviduct   (c) vagina   (d) ovary
  (ii) A fertilised egg divides to form a ball of cells called a/an:
      (a) embryo   (b) amnion   (c) zygote   (d) foetus
  (iii) Which of the following describes the fertilised egg sinking into the endometrium?
      (a) ovulation   (b) implantation   (c) gestation   (d) menstruation
  (iv) Which of the following is not involved in pregnancy:
      (a) conception   (b) copulation   (c) contraception   (d) gestation
  (v) In humans pregnancy lasts approximately:
      (a) 28 days   (b) 40 days   (c) 28 weeks   (d) 40 weeks

02 The diagram shows a foetus in the uterus just before birth.

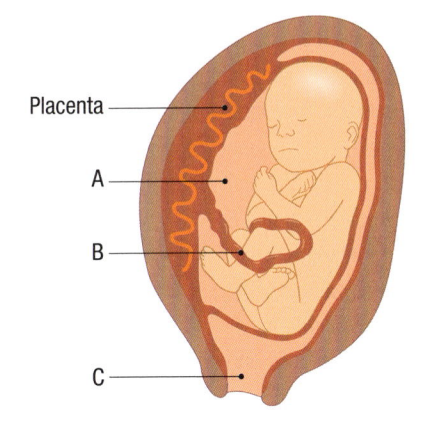

  (i) Name the parts labelled A, B, C.
  (ii) Give the function of A.
  (iii) One function of the placenta is to produce hormones. Name a hormone produced by the placenta.
  (iv) Name a substance that, if passed across the placenta, could be harmful to the baby.

03 The diagrams show the events from <u>fertilisation</u> at A to <u>implantation</u> at D.
  (a) Define the underlined terms as they apply to the human.
  (b) Name the structures at B and C.
  (c) State the type of cell division at X.
  (d) Name the part of the uterus in which C implants.
  (e) Roughly how many days after fertilisation is implantation complete?

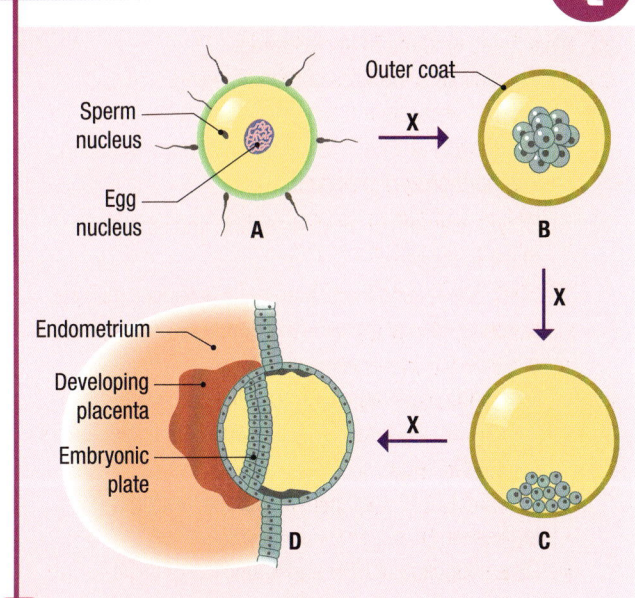

04 (a) Explain the term germ layer.
  (b) From what in the blastocyst are germ layers formed?
  (c) Copy and complete the table below.

Germ layer	Tissue/organ formed
	Endothelial lining of the arteries
Mesoderm	
	Brain and nails

  (d) Suggest why it is important that the menstrual cycle should stop during pregnancy.

Section C

05 (a) (i) What is meant by infertility?
      (ii) State one cause of infertility in the human female.
      (iii) Outline one corrective measure (treatment) for the cause you have named in (ii).
  (b) Sexual reproduction in humans involves the fusion of the male and female gametes.
      (i) Where does the fusion of gametes, i.e. fertilisation, normally take place?
      (ii) Name the type of cell division that produces gametes in humans.
      (iii) Name the human male gamete.
      (iv) Draw a labelled diagram of the male gamete.
      (v) At what age do boys start to produce gametes?
      (vi) Name the hormone responsible for the production of the male gamete and give one other function of this hormone.

37 Human Reproduction 2: From Fertilisation to Birth

Examination style questions

(c) Write notes on three of the following:
  (i) The biological benefits of breastfeeding.
  (ii) *In vitro* fertilisation.
  (iii) Mechanical and chemical methods of contraception.
  (iv) The hormones of pregnancy.

06 (a) (i) Draw a diagram of a human sperm and label three major features.
  (ii) State one reason the human male produces millions of sperm cells at a time unlike the single egg that is produced by the female.

(b) (i) By means of a diagram, outline the path taken by a sperm from the time of ejaculation in the vagina until it meets the egg.
  (ii) Give the events that then take place leading to fertilisation.
  (iii) Give a function of FSH and a function of LH in relation to the male reproductive system.

(c) (i) What is the placenta?
  (ii) From what is the placenta formed?
  (iii) Why is the placenta necessary?
  (iv) How are materials exchanged across the placenta?
  (v) Name three substances that are exchanged.
  (vi) Describe what happens to the placenta in the third stage of labour.

07 Human chorionic gonadotrophin (HCG) is a <u>hormone</u> produced in early pregnancy by the <u>trophoblast</u> in the blastocyst. HCG is essential to establish and maintain early pregnancy. Its role is to maintain progesterone production from the <u>corpus luteum</u> in the ovary, until the placenta is fully formed. Once this happens levels of HCG decline and production of progesterone is carried out by the placenta.

The graph below shows the changes in hormones during pregnancy. Using information in the passage above and the graph, answer the following questions:

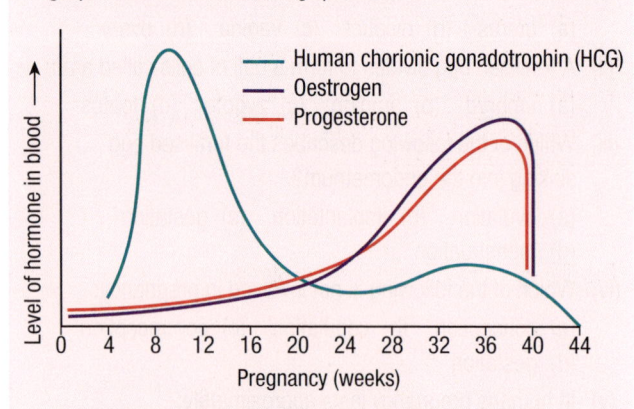

(a) What structure produces HCG?
(b) Outline the changes that take place in the levels of HCG during the time shown in the graph.
(c) At what time in the pregnancy does the level of HCG decline? What is the reason for this decline?
(d) Progesterone levels remain high during pregnancy. State two sources of progesterone.
(e) In which week(s) of pregnancy do the levels of progesterone begin to drop? What effect does this drop in level have on the uterus?
(f) During pregnancy the breasts are stimulated to develop milk ducts. Following the birth of the baby these milk ducts begin to secrete milk. Name the hormone involved in the production of milk and outline the benefits of breast milk to the baby.

Leaving Certificate examination questions

Section C

01 The diagram shows the foetus in the womb.

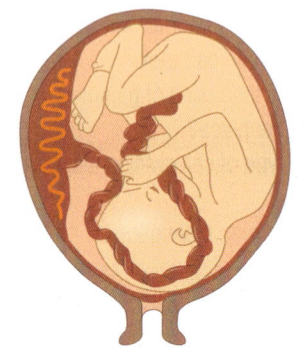

(i) Give **two** functions of the placenta.
(ii) Give the **three** stages of childbirth.
(iii) Many babies are breast fed after birth. Give **two** biological benefits of breastfeeding.
(iv) What is meant by the term *infertility*?
(v) *In vitro* fertilisation is a method used to treat infertility. What is meant by *in vitro fertilisation*?

2013 OL Q. 12 (b)

02 (i) Give **one** cause of infertility in men.
(ii) Explain the term *contraception*.
(iii) Name **two** methods of contraception.

2012 OL Q. 12 (c)

Human Reproduction 2: From Fertilisation to Birth 37

Leaving Certificate examination questions

03 (i) What does the term *infertility* mean?
(ii) *In vitro* fertilisation is a method used to treat infertility. What is meant by the term *in vitro* in relation to fertilisation?
(iii) Give **one** cause of infertility in women.
(iv) As a result of fertility treatment, an embryo develops successfully from an *in vitro* fertilisation. What is the next step for the embryo?

2011 OL Q. 14 (a)

04 The diagram shows a foetus in the uterus.

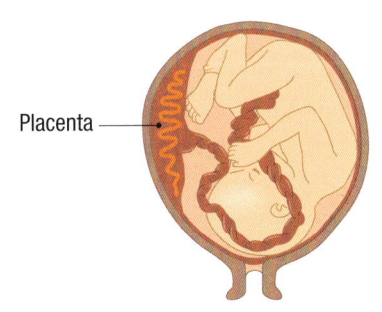

Placenta

(i) From what tissues is the placenta formed?
(ii) Give **two** functions of the placenta.
(iii) Describe the process of birth.
(iv) Give any **one** biological benefit of breastfeeding.
(v) List **two** methods of contraception.

2010 OL Q. 14 (b)

05 Answer the following questions in relation to the development of a human zygote.
(i) By which type of cell division does the zygote divide?
(ii) Further divisions result in the formation of a morula. What is the next developmental stage after the morula?
(iii) The placenta forms from tissues of the mother and the foetus. Give **two** roles of the placenta.
(iv) Give **one** change experienced by the mother that indicates to her that the birth process is starting.
(v) Give a short account of the birth process.

2013 HL Q. 13 (c)

06 Answer the following questions from your knowledge of early human development in the womb.
(i) 1. Name the **three** germ layers in the early human embryo.
 2. For **each** germ layer name a structure in the adult body that develops from it.
(ii) From which tissues does the placenta develop?
(iii) 1. What is the amnion?
 2. Explain the importance of the amnion for the foetus.

2012 HL Q. 14 (b)

07 Suggest a biological explanation for the following observation:
(i) As long as a baby feeds regularly from its mother's breast (or if a breast pump is regularly used) the milk will continue to flow.

2010 HL Q. 15 (c)

08 Write notes on **three** of the following.
(i) Menstruation and a disorder of menstruation.
(ii) Biological benefits of breastfeeding.
(iii) Survival times for sperm and ova.
(iv) Formation and functions of the placenta.

2006 HL Q. 15 (c)

09 (i) What is meant by contraception?
(ii) Give an example of a surgical method of male contraception. Suggest an advantage and a disadvantage of the method that you have named.
(iii) List **three** methods of contraception other than surgical. In your answer you may refer to either or both sexes.
(iv) Suggest a possible effect on a human population that may result from an increased availability of contraception.

2005 HL Q. 13 (c)

Past examination questions

OL	2014 Q. 3 (c), (d), Q. 14 (c) (vi), (vii)	2013 Q. 12 (b)	2012 Q. 12 (c) (iv)–(vi)	2011 Q. 14 (a)
	2010 Q. 14 (b)	2006 Q. 5		

HL	2013 Q. 13 (c)	2012 Q. 14 (b)	2010 Q. 15 (c) (i)	2009 Q. 14 (b)	2007 Q. 15 (a) (v)
	2006 Q. 15 (c) (ii)–(iv)	2005 Q. 13 (c)	2004 Q. 14 (b) (iii), (iv), (c)	2004 Q. 11 (c)	

38 The Examination

The aim of this chapter is to give you advice and guidelines for preparing for the exam and answering the examination paper.

Preparation

Studying Biology

As with all of your subjects in the Leaving Certificate, it is important that you study in the most effective way possible for **you**. There is a large amount of material to cover in Biology and there are a large number of facts, terms and definitions that you will need to learn. To do this you must develop a **good study technique**. It is vital that this is developed early in your study of the subject so that you do not find yourself with too much work to cover in the last year of your course. You should develop a **regular study habit**. You should try to study at the same time, in the same place, every day. This will mean that you will settle down to productive study quickly and efficiently. If study is to be most effective it should be a regular and relatively brief activity without cramming for exams. It should be done in blocks of about two or two-and-a-half hours. Within this you should study in blocks of 20 to 40 minutes, with the last 5 or 10 minutes used to review what you have done in the previous 15 or 30 minutes. Remember, study is most productive when you undertake it during periods of maximum concentration. It is important that you realise that **time spent on study does not necessarily equal work done!**

When you are studying you should always have a pen (or pencil) in your hand and you should summarise your work as you go along. This summarising can take many forms:

- You could write short notes on cards (to minimise what you write). (See the section *Write notes on* below.)
- You could in some instances draw labelled diagrams, such as when studying the human body systems, for learning parts and functions.
- You could make up rhymes and phrases/mnemonics to remember material, for example:
  - **P**eas **M**ake **A**wful **T**arts (for the four stages of mitosis).
  - In DNA the p**y**rimidines (with a '**y**') bases are the ones with a 'y' in their name – th**y**mine and c**y**tosine. Purines have no 'y' – adenine and guanine.
  - The DNA purines are double-ringed –they have two 'n's in their name – ade**nin**e and gua**nin**e.
  - The tricuspid valve in the heart is the one on the right-hand side. **T**ricuspid has an 'r' and so does '**r**ight'.
- You could construct mind maps (this requires you to draw a diagram showing the connections between the different parts of the topic (see Fig 38.1).
- You could produce placemats and use graphic organisers to make comparisons.
- You could use flow charts to describe biochemical pathways such as photosynthesis and respiration.

Mind map example

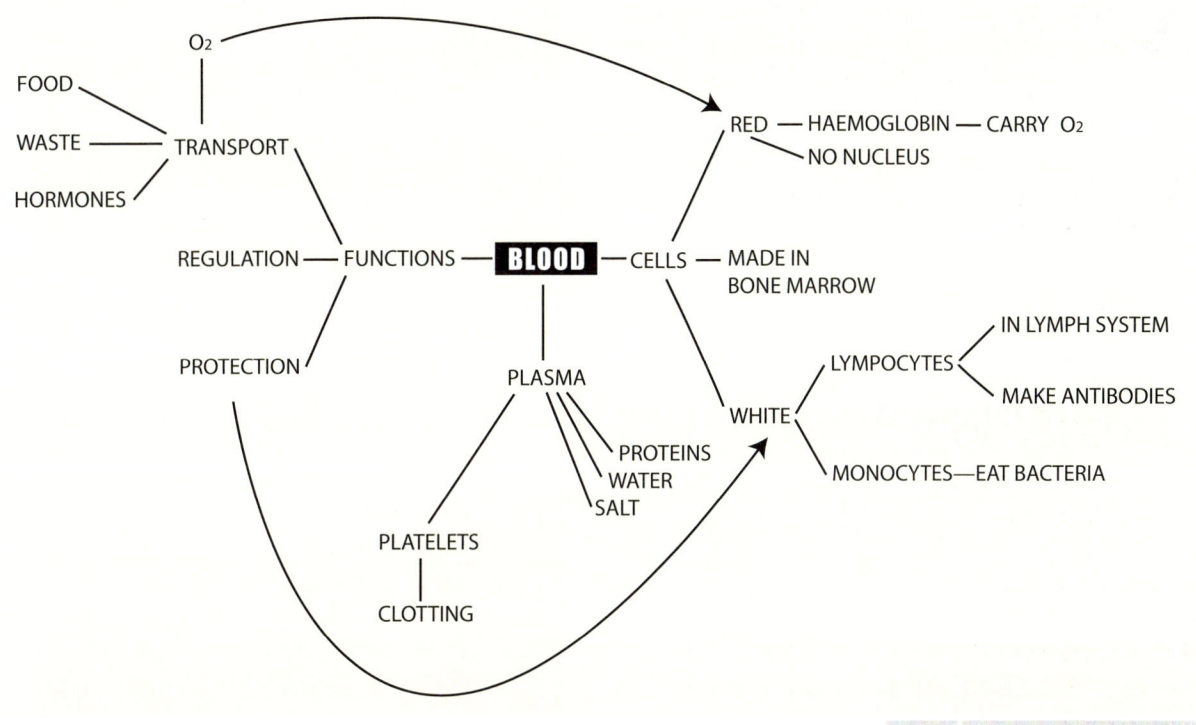

```
        O₂
FOOD              RED — HAEMOGLOBIN — CARRY O₂
WASE — TRANSPORT       NO NUCLEUS
HORMONES

REGULATION — FUNCTIONS — BLOOD — CELLS — MADE IN
                                          BONE MARROW
                                                    IN LYMPH SYSTEM
                                          LYMPOCYTES
PROTECTION       PLASMA                             MAKE ANTIBODIES
                                          WHITE
                  PROTEINS
                  WATER                   MONOCYTES — EAT BACTERIA
                  SALT
        PLATELETS
           |
        CLOTTING
```

38.1 Partial mind map of blood

Setting goals

Before you start studying a topic you should set yourself a goal, e.g. I will be able to do the first four learning outcomes of this topic or I will produce a mind map or a question to answer, e.g. 'What affects the rate of photosynthesis?' This will focus your study and make it more productive. The summaries you produce will be your first port of call when you come to revise the topic. This will make your revision easier and shorter as you will not have to read through the text again (unless you find in a particular topic that your notes are not good enough).

You will also find that the very act of producing summaries will increase your understanding of the topic as you pick out the important concepts from the material being studied. It is important to remember that this process should be an active one, where you are thinking about the material and deciding what is important, not just transcribing sections of the text. Keep referring back to the learning outcomes.

Remember to reward yourself when you have **achieved** the goals you set yourself at the beginning of your study period – watch that programme on the TV, catch up on social media, go training, or for a walk, play a match at the end of the week, etc.

It is a good idea to get up and move around/stretch when you have finished a topic during your two hours of study.

Check your progress regularly as you study to make sure you are learning the material:

- Look at the learning outcome. Have you covered it? Can you do what it describes?
- Try to answer the review and exam style questions at the end of the chapter.
- Attempt to answer exam questions (in the same time as allowed in the exam).
- See if you can reproduce your mind maps or summary/placemat sheets.
- Draw a labelled diagram of the item.

38 | The Examination

Revision

It is important for your success in exams that you learn to revise effectively. Much research has been undertaken on this subject and these studies have led to a number of key recommendations that you need to consider when revising.

1. How to organise your revision.
2. Length of time spent revising.
3. How often revision should be undertaken.

1. Organising your revision

- You should make a revision timetable well in advance of your exams and you should stick to this timetable to the best of your ability.
- Pay particular attention to the areas you have difficulty understanding (it is easy revising what you already know). Check your notes – which parts of your notes do you not understand? Study these areas.
- It can be useful to work with someone else. They can teach you the topics they understand better and you do the same for them. You will remember much more of any topic that you have to teach someone else!

2. Length of time

- You should divide your time between learning material and practising exam questions.
- Research has shown that if you study for a fixed period of time you remember more from the beginning and end of that period. This means that if you divide up your two-hour study period into shorter periods with short 'stretch' breaks every 30 minutes or so then your productivity will be much greater, as shown in Fig 38.2.

3. Frequency of revision

- The frequency of your revision is very important. It has been demonstrated that you will quickly forget most of the material you read if you study it only once. This is shown in Fig 38.3. However studies also show that planned revision can greatly improve recall. If you revise after 10 minutes, your recall will improve and it will develop even further if you review the material after one day and one week (see Fig 38.4). Best practice suggests that reviewing material five times is required to move the material from your short-term memory to your long-term memory.

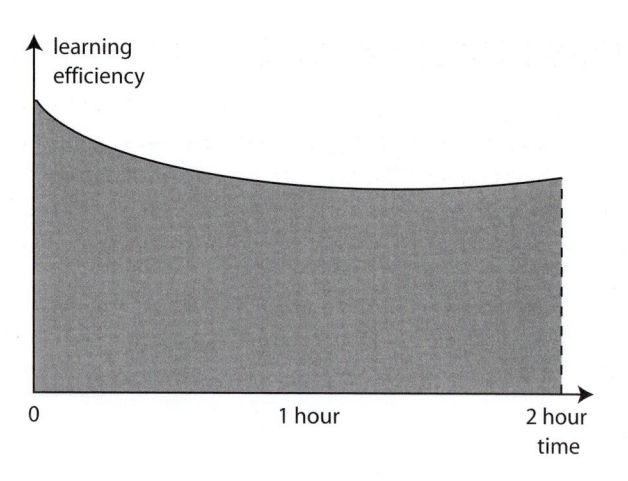

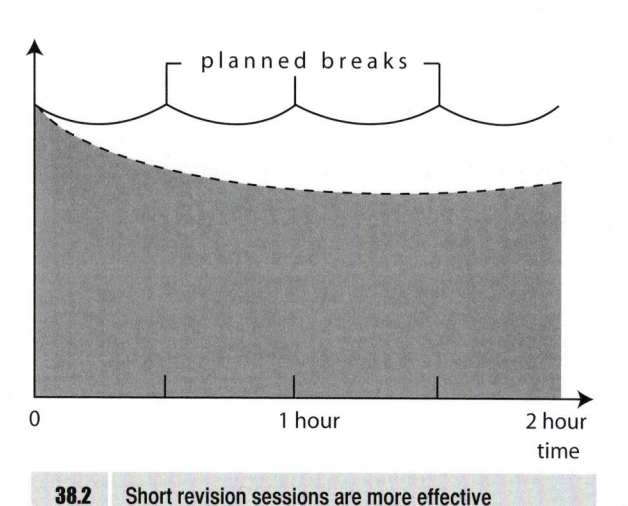

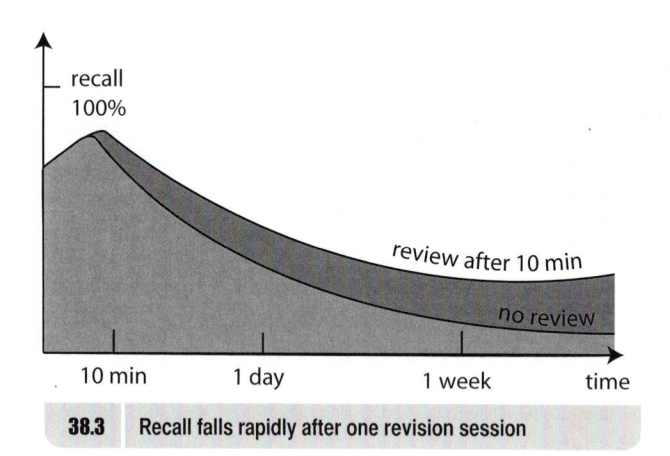

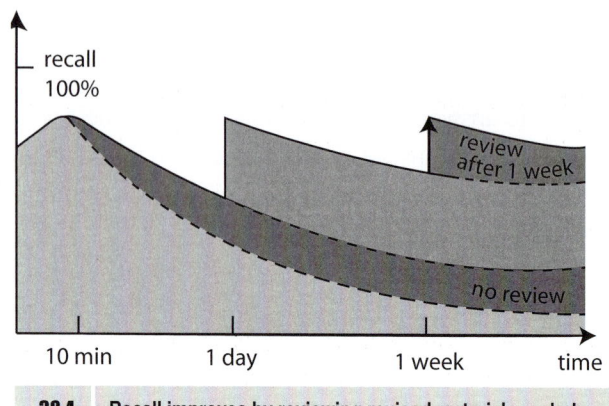

38.2 Short revision sessions are more effective

38.3 Recall falls rapidly after one revision session

38.4 Recall improves by reviewing revised material regularly

The structure and rubric of the exam paper

It is very important that you know and understand the layout of the Biology exam paper before the exam. Some subject exams have more than one paper, e.g. English, Maths and Irish each have two papers. This means that many students sit ten or more exam papers during the Leaving Certificate and each one has a different structure and rubric. The rubric is the detail of what you have been asked to do during the examination, e.g. how many questions to answer, where to answer them, etc. It is essential that you know which sections and questions you have to answer and the choice you have within each section or question.

The front page of the Leaving Certificate Biology paper, both Higher and Ordinary Level, has the same structure and rubric:

Some guidance with answering the paper

The Biology exam paper consists of 15 questions. The total number of marks for the exam is 400.

In general the unit mark is 3 marks per correct answer but this may vary. This will help you decide how many points to give in your answer, particularly in Section C.

Section B

- Section B consists of three questions, of which **two** are to be attempted. The answers to these questions are to be filled in on the exam paper itself.
- Each question is worth 30 marks, so Section B carries 60 marks, or 15% of the total mark.
- In Section B the questions relate to the Mandatory Student Activities and can be taken from any Unit. It is worth noting that 11 out of the 22 mandatory activities are found in Unit 2.

Recommended time: 30 minutes (15 minutes per question including reading time).

Section A   Answer any **five** questions from this section.
Each question carries 20 marks.
Write your answers in the spaces provided on **this examination paper**.

Section B   Answer **two** questions from this section.
Each question carries 30 marks.
Write your answers in the spaces provided on **this examination paper**.

Section C   Answer **four** questions from this section.
Each question carries 60 marks.
Write your answers in the spaces provided in the **answer book**.

You must return this examination paper with your answer book at the end of the examination.

Section A

- Section A consists of six questions, **five** of which must be attempted. The answers to these questions are to be filled in on the exam paper itself.
- Answers should be short, note style.
- Each question is worth 20 marks, so Section A carries 100 marks, or 25% of the marks of the total paper.
- In Section A there will be 2 questions from Unit 1, 2 questions from Unit 2 and 2 questions from Unit 3.
- The golden rule is to 'leave no blank space' – attempt every part of each question and attempt all six.

Recommended time: 30 minutes, including reading time.

Section C

- Section C consists of six questions, of which **four** are to be answered. The answers to these questions are to be written into a separate answer book.
- Each question is worth 60 marks, so Section C is worth 60% of the total marks for the exam.
- In Section C, there is **one** question from Unit 1, **two** questions from Unit 2 and three questions from Unit 3.
- In questions 10, 11, 12 and 13 there are three parts: (a) 9 marks, (b) 27 marks, (c) 24 marks.
- There is a degree of internal choice in questions 14 and 15, where you are required to answer two out of three parts, and each is worth 30 marks.

Recommended time: 120 minutes (30 minutes per question including reading time).

Knowing the number of marks per question and the fact that the unit mark is 3 marks, you can calculate how many points to give in your answer. For example, if the question carries 24 marks, then you should have 8 points (8 × 3 marks) in your answer.

It is not necessary for you to remember the rubric off by heart but you should keep checking at the start of each section how many questions you are required to attempt.

Understanding the rubric and knowing how to allocate time are essential for success. Class tests, house exams and mock exams all help prepare you for the final Leaving Certificate papers.

Practising past exam questions and using the marking schemes intelligently will improve performance (see State Examinations Commission website for marking schemes). The learning outcomes in each chapter are there to guide you through the syllabus, which is also available on the NCCA website. Use these to prepare in advance of studying a topic, to catch up if you have been absent, to assess your learning and to prepare for tests and exams.

Tips for answering the exam paper

- When you get the exam paper, don't panic. Read carefully through each question on the whole paper. There will be questions that you know the answers to and you can mark these – but do not start doing them at this stage. Reading through the paper allows you find questions that you know the answers to and this will give you confidence.
- In Section A, fill in your answers on the exam paper, in pen. Remember, if you give more answers than you are asked for in a section of the exam, then any extra wrong answer will cancel out a correct answer, i.e. if you are asked for two benefits of bacteria to man and you give three but one is not a benefit, you will only get marked for **one** correct answer.

(The points above also apply to Sections A and B.)

- Always attempt the required number of questions. *Marks are lost each year because candidates do not attempt the required number of questions.* In Section C you have to attempt **four** questions. If you only answer three then you can only get a maximum of 180 marks (3 × 60 marks). Answering four questions gives you the chance of getting 240 marks (4 × 60 marks). Again, a comment from the Chief Examiner's 2013 report states that "there is plenty of time to complete the required number of questions". It is better to use that time to answer the required number of questions as fully as possible and not to try and complete every question on the paper'. **Quality**, i.e. fully answering the question asked, is better than **quantity**, i.e. trying to answer every question on the exam paper.
- Read each question carefully and underline the key words which indicate what you are expected to do. (See separate section on *Keywords used in questions*.)
- Keep referring back to the question to (a) ensure you attempt all of it and (b) prevent yourself going off the point. According to the Chief Examiner's report 2013 the more successful candidates were those who took care to answer exactly what a particular question or part of a question actually asked.
- Watch your timing. If you go over the recommended time for a question, STOP, leave a full page (so you can return and complete later if you have time) and go on to your next question.
- Time per sub-section: 9 marks = 5 minutes, 24 marks = 12 minutes, 27 marks = 13 minutes.
- You may answer the questions in any order you wish, e.g. 12, 15, 11, 10, etc., but you should answer sub-section questions in order (a), (b), (c).
- Remember to put the question number and the sub-section letters in the left-hand margin. It is very important that the examiner can find his/her way around your script.
- Make sure to read the whole question through before deciding to choose it. Later parts of a question may be more or less difficult for you.
- Do not spend too long on any one question or part of a question. If you are stuck leave a space and come back later.
- Remember it is more difficult to get 100% on half of the question than to get 50% on all of the required questions.
- Be as precise as you can and do not write too much.
- Where appropriate, use well labelled diagrams. These should be neatly drawn with a pencil (do not colour). The diagrams should be of a reasonable size and in proportion, with a title and labels.
- Use the correct scientific terms. Candidates, particularly at Higher Level, are expected to recognise and use correct biological terms.
- **Make sure your writing is legible.**

Key words used in exam questions

The wording of questions is all-important. You need to understand the terms used in questions so that you can answer them correctly.

Below is a list of some of the terms that appear frequently in biology questions.

Briefly/Concisely	Give the main points in short sentences.
Comment on	For example, 'Comment on the validity of…'. Say whether the statement is true or false (if appropriate) giving your reasons.
Compare	Mention similarities and differences.
Contrast	Mention differences only.
Define	Give the exact meaning of the term or word. (Note: If the term is a compound term such as dicotyledon, then both the 'di' and 'cotyledon' need to be explained.)
Describe	Give a detailed account using diagrams where appropriate.
Discuss	Explain and give both sides of the issue.
Distinguish	Give a definition or explain of both terms by writing a sentence about each.
Draw	Draw a diagram that is at least half A4 page size, in proportion and labelled (unless directed otherwise).
Explain	Give reasons why something is the case or how something happens.
Identify	Recognise and name.
Illustrate	Use labelled diagrams.
List	Give as a list of words one after the other.
Outline	State the main points (similar to Briefly/Concisely).
State	Give the main features in brief form.
Summarise	Give a concise account.
Suggest	Put forward ideas or thoughts either from your learned knowledge or from information in the question. This type of question is asking you to 'think outside the box'.
What is the fate of	State what will happen to something, where it goes, what it does.

Write notes on

If asked to write notes on a topic, you should give a number of points, usually three or four, describing the item in terms of what it is, what is its structure, what is its location, what is its function, an example, etc. Diagrams are not accepted in this type of answer.

Diagrams

- Use a good quality HB pencil. Colour is not required (unless specified).
- Brilliant sketches are not expected, but make sure all the parts you want to show are clearly visible.
- Diagrams should be of reasonable size, in proportion and have a title.
- ALWAYS label your diagrams. You get zero marks if there are no labels on your diagram.
- Make sure that your label line touches the item you are naming. Do this by touching the part(s) to be named with your pencil and bring the label line out, off the diagram, and then write the name of the part.
- Don't be frightened of drawing diagrams – if it is big and all the important parts are present, in the correct places and labelled then the drawing will score full marks.

Graphs and graphing

When you carry out most experiments you are looking at the relationships between two variables. Graphs are frequently used to look at these relationships. If you are given graphs in your exam there are only three things you will be asked to do:

Draw it, describe it or **explain it**

1. **If asked to draw a graph from a set of data or to copy a graph from the exam paper.**
   When you draw a graph remember the following:
   (a) Use a good quality HB pencil.
   (b) Ask for and **use** graph paper if you have been given figures (numbers) to plot. Graph paper is **not** required if you are giving a trend graph, e.g. draw a graph to show how pH affects enzyme action.
   (c) Label each axis giving the appropriate units. The *x*-axis is the horizontal one. The letter '*x*' is a 'cross' and the *x*-axis goes 'across' the page.
   (d) Use a scale that best fills the graph paper.
   (e) Plot each point accurately and join with a pencil line to show the shape of the graph.
   (f) If drawing a predator–prey graph, remember the predator line will be lower and slightly to the right of the prey line.

2. **Reading/describing graphs**
   If you are describing the graph imagine you are talking to a person who cannot see the graph so describe it exactly, giving beginning and ending points.
   - Block off the graph (from its start) as the graph line changes.
   - Make a comment at each change, e.g. 1. At pH 4 the rate of reaction is low. 2. As pH changes from 4 to 6 the rate of reaction increases rapidly. 3. At pH 6 the rate is at its maximum (optimum pH for this reaction). 4. From pH 6 to 8 the rate of reaction declines quickly.
   - Don't forget to comment on the starting and finishing points.

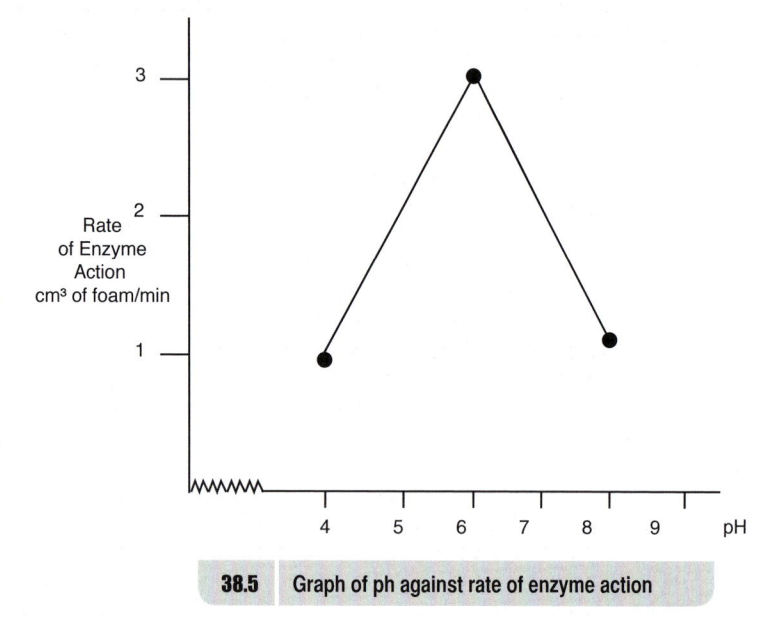

   38.5 Graph of ph against rate of enzyme action

3. **Explaining graphs**
   When you are explaining a graph use your biology knowledge to explain the relationship (connection) that the graph demonstrates, for example:
   As the pH changes, the shape of the enzyme changes. At a pH of 6 the enzyme shape allows it to work most effectively. This is known as the optimum pH for the enzyme. As the pH changes from 6 the shape of the enzyme changes so it loses its function. The further the pH is from 6 the greater the change in shape and hence the greater the loss of function.

In conclusion

Have a look at the Chief Examiner's 'Recommendations to Teachers and Students' from the 2013 report on the Biology exam (see the SEC website archive for the Chief Examiner's Report), in which the following key points are made:

- Practice past exam questions.
- Use biological terminology.
- Read questions carefully.
- Practice drawings – they should be large, tidy, accurate and labelled.
- Explain compound terms in full.
- Follow the instructions in the questions.
- Work on accurate explanation of terms

Good luck with your exam. If you have prepared well and keep calm before and during the exam, you will be successful.

Glossary

HL = Higher Level only

2,4-D, a synthetic auxin used as a selective weedkiller in lawns. It kills dicot plants.
Abiotic, the influence of a non-living part of the environment on an organism.
Abscisic acid, growth inhibitor found in plants.
Absorption, movement of digested food molecules into the bloodstream.
Acetylcholine, a common neurotransmitter.
Acquired variations, differences within a species that develop over the life of the organism.
Activation energy, the amount of free energy needed to start a chemical reaction.
Active immunity, when a person has the ability to produce their own antibodies against a disease.
Active site, the place on the enzyme where the substrate attaches and the reaction takes place. **(HL)**
Active transport, the absorption of molecules into cells against the concentration gradient, using energy.
ADH (anti-diuretic hormone), a hormone, produced by the hypothalamus, which causes water retention in the kidney. **(HL)**
Adrenal gland, gland situated on top of the kidneys.
Adrenaline, hormone produced by the adrenal gland (sometimes called the 'fight or flight' hormone).
Aerobic respiration, the breakdown of food (carbohydrate) to release energy.
Afterbirth, the common name for the placenta; remains of the umbilical cord and the other membranes that surrounded the foetus and which are expelled from the uterus after the baby has been delivered.
Alleles, alternative forms of the same genes.
Alveolus (plural, alveoli), tiny air sac found at the end of the bronchioles in the lung. Site of gaseous exchange.
Amino acid, building block of all proteins.
Amnion, a membrane which surrounds the embryo and secretes amniotic fluid.
Anabolic, reactions in which smaller molecules are combined to form larger molecules.
Anaerobic respiration, the breakdown of food (carbohydrate) in the absence of oxygen releasing energy.
Angiosperm, flowering plant, bearing seeds in a protective covering (fruit).
Antagonistic muscles, pairs of muscles that pull against each other.
Antibiotics, chemicals produced by micro-organisms that are toxic to bacteria.
Antibodies, proteins produced by a lymphocyte in response to an antigen.
Antigen, a substance that causes lymphocytes to produce antibodies.
Apical dominance, the suppression of the growth of lateral buds by the terminal bud. **(HL)**
Appendicular skeleton, comprises the girdles and the limbs.
Aquatic factors, those that affect organisms that live in water.
Aqueous humour, fluid found between the lens and cornea.
Artery, thick-walled blood vessel, carries blood away from the heart.
Asepsis, excluding microbes from as much of the environment as possible.
Asexual reproduction, reproduction that does not involve the manufacture or fusion of gametes. Produces offspring genetically identical to the parent.
Asthma, breathing disorder caused by narrowing of the bronchioles.
ATP (adenosine triphosphate), traps and transfers energy for cell reactions. **(HL)**
Atrium, upper chamber of the heart (receives blood).
Autoclave, a piece of equipment, which heats steam under pressure to raise the temperature to 120°C, that sterilises everything contained within it.
Autoimmune disease, a disease where the person's own immune system attacks their own body.
Autosome, a chromosome that does not have a role in determining the sex of the individual.
Autotrophic bacteria, bacteria capable of making their own food using energy.
Auxin, growth promoters produced by plants that regulate cell elongation and division.
A-V node, group of muscle cells lying in the septum between the right atrium and right ventricle, involved in the heartbeat. **(HL)**
Axial skeleton, comprises the skull, vertebral column, ribs and sternum.
Axon, a cytoplasmic fibre in a neurone that carries messages away from a cell body and releases a neurotransmitter.
Batch flow method, production in which a fixed amount of nutrients are added to a bioreactor which is emptied of its contents at the end of production.
Behaviour, the response of an organism to changes in its environment (internal and external).
Bile, fluid produced by the liver containing bile salts, bile pigments and cholesterol.
Binary fission, a form of asexual reproduction where a cell divides into two evenly sized new cells.
Biodiversity (or biological diversity), a term used to describe the variety of living things on Earth.
Biology, the study of living things.
Biomass, the amount of living matter present at any level in a food chain. Biomass may be measured as either living mass or dry mass.
Biomolecules, the chemicals found in living things.
Bioprocessing, the use of organisms, cells or enzymes to make specific products.
Bioreactor, a vessel (usually large) in which cells, organisms or enzymes are placed to manufacture specific products.
Biosphere, the parts of the Earth and its atmosphere in which life can exist.
Biotechnology, the use of organisms, cells or enzymes to make specific products.
Biotic, an organism's influence on another organism.
Birth control, limiting the number of children born to a couple.
Bladder, a sac filled with fluid or air. In the urinary system this holds the urine produced by the kidneys.
Blastocyst, a fluid-filled ball of cells. **(HL)**
Blind spot, the part of the retina where the nerves leave the eye and there are no receptors and no vision.
Blood grouping, classification of blood on the basis of the particular antigen present on a person's red blood cells.

Glossary

Blood pressure, the force of blood as it passes through an artery.
Blood vessel, tube for transporting blood, e.g. arteries, veins and capillaries.
Bone, hard connective tissue making up the skeleton.
Bowman's capsule, a double-walled, cup-shaped chamber at the start of the nephron. **(HL)**
Brain, an enlargement at the top of the spinal cord where most decisions of the nervous system are taken, and where information from the senses is interpreted.
Breast milk, the most natural food for a human baby containing the correct balance of nutrients and important antibodies.
Bronchitis, breathing disorder caused by build-up of mucus in the bronchi.
Budding, a form of asexual reproduction where a cell divides into two unevenly sized cells.
Bulb, a group of modified leaves, swollen with food reserves.
Cancer, the abnormal and uncontrolled growth of cells by mitosis.
Capillary, very narrow blood vessel with a wall only one cell thick, forms link between arterioles and venules.
Carcinogen, any factor that can transform a normal cell into a cancer cell.
Cardiac cycle, the sequence of events in a single heartbeat.
Carnivore, an animal which feeds on other animals only, e.g. fox, ladybird.
Carrier, a person who is heterozygous for a gene is said to be a carrier of the recessive gene.
Cartilage, elastic connective tissue found mainly at joints.
Catabolic, reactions in which larger molecules are broken down to form smaller molecules.
Catalysts, have the ability to speed up (or indeed slow down) chemical reactions without being used up in the reaction.
Cell body, the part of the neuron containing the nucleus.
Cell continuity, means that all cells develop from pre-existing cells.
Cell plate, a structure found in plant cells at telophase. Believed to be the origin of the middle lamella between the two new cells. **(HL)**
Cells, the basic unit of life.
Cellular energy, the energy stored in the chemicals found in cells.
Central nervous system (CNS), a group of nerves which control the nervous system, i.e. the brain and spinal cord.
Centriole, a cell organelle found in pairs in certain cells. They produce the spindle fibres that are used in cell division. **(HL)**
Centromere, a region of the chromosome that holds sister chromatids together and where the spindle fibre attaches to the chromosome. **(HL)**
Cerebellum, part of the hindbrain which is situated beneath the back of the cerebrum and controls coordination and balance.
Cerebrum, the front section of the brain where consciousness resides.
Characteristic, a feature which is identified with an organism or an object.
Chemoreceptor, a sensory receptor that responds to changes in the chemical environment.
Chemical digestion, the breakdown of food into smaller molecules by enzymes, stomach acid or bile.
Chemosynthetic bacteria, bacteria that are capable of making their own food using energy from a chemical reaction.
Chloroplast, a membrane-bound organelle found in plant cells.
Cholesterol, fatty substance made in the liver from certain animal fats in the diet. Involved in the hardening of the arteries.
Chorion, one of a number of membranes surrounding the embryo; involved in placenta formation.
Choroid, a pigmented layer inside the sclera of the eye. Prevents internal reflection.
Chromatid pair, a chromosome and its replicated copy held together at the centromere. This is found during cell division. **(HL)**
Chromatin, long strands of DNA and protein that form chromosomes.
Chromosome, a structure made of DNA and protein which can be inherited.
Ciliary body, swollen front section of choroid in the eye containing the ciliary muscle.
Ciliary muscle, circular muscle used for focusing of the lens in the eye.
Cleavage, the division of the cell cytoplasm into two at the end of cell division. **(HL)**
Climatic factors, the weather conditions that affect organisms in an ecosystem.
Clone, a genetically identical offspring.
Closed circulatory system, blood contained within blood vessels, e.g. in humans.
Cocci, spherical bacteria.
Cochlea, coiled structure in the inner ear sensitive to sound.
Coenzyme, non-protein chemical essential for the functioning of certain enzymes. Often these are made from water-soluble vitamins in heterotrophs. **(HL)**
Coleoptile, a sheath that originally surrounds the top of a seedling of the grass family. **(HL)**
Colostrum, a thick yellowish fluid produced by the breasts after a baby is born. It contains protein and valuable antibodies and is replaced by breast milk.
Commensalism, when two organisms live together where one benefits but does not harm its host.
Community, made up of groups of different species living together.
Competition, the struggle between organisms for resources that are in short supply, such as food or light.
Complement, a blood protein that makes holes in the surface of bacteria.
Compound, a substance made up of two or more different elements combined together chemically, e.g. carbon dioxide (CO_2).
Concentration gradient, a difference of concentration of molecules between two different areas. The greater this difference, the greater the rate of diffusion.
Conception, when a fertilised egg becomes implanted in the uterus wall and pregnancy begins.
Cones, light-sensitive receptors in the eye giving colour vision.
Connective tissue, cells found in a matrix used for attaching organs together or for protection.
Conservation, the wise management of our environment.
Consumer, an organism that feeds off another organism, e.g. herbivores, carnivores, omnivores.
Contest competition, an active physical confrontation between two organisms in which only one wins the resource. **(HL)**
Continuous flow method, production that involves maintaining the microbes in the log phase of growth by the addition of fresh medium.

Glossary

Continuity, the ability of organisms to exist from one generation to the next.
Contraception, the prevention of fertilisation and pregnancy.
Contractile vacuole, a vacuole found in simple, aquatic organisms. This vacuole uses energy to expel excess water out of the cell.
Control, a standard against which the experiment is compared.
Copulation, sexual intercourse.
Cornea, transparent section of sclera at the front of the eye which helps in the focus of light.
Coronary (cardiac) blood vessels, artery and vein which surround and supply the heart muscle with blood.
Corpus callosum, a section of nerve fibres found in the brain connecting the two halves of the cerebrum together.
Cotyledon, an embryonic seed leaf.
Cross-pollination, the transfer of pollen from an anther of one flower to a stigma of a flower of a different plant of the same species.
Cuticle, non-cellular waxy layer secreted by the dermal layers of a plant. It prevents excess water loss.
Cytokinins, group of growth promoters found in plants.
Cytoplasm, the contents of a cell excluding the nucleus.
Cytosol, the contents of a cell excluding the cell organelles.
Data, the measurements, observations or information gathered from an experiment.
Deamination, the breakdown of excess amino acids in the liver.
Decomposer, micro-organism which brings about the decay of plant and animal tissues.
Denatured, when an enzyme has permanently lost its function due to loss of shape. **(HL)**
Dendrite, a cytoplasmic fibre that collects and carries messages towards a cell body of a nerve cell.
Dental formula, a formula indicating the number of each type of tooth in a mammal.
Desiccation, drying out.
Detritus, decaying plant and animal material.
Diastole, relaxation of heart muscle. **(HL)**
Dicotyledons, plants that have two seed leaves.
Diffusion, the movement of molecules from areas of high concentration to areas of lower concentration.
Digestion, the breakdown of large food molecules into smaller soluble ones.
Dihybrid cross, a genetic cross in which two traits are being examined together. **(HL)**
Diploid cell (2n), contains two copies of each chromosome.
Disaccharide, carbohydrate consisting of two sugar molecules.
DNA (deoxyribonucleic acid), the nucleic acid that forms the genetic material found in most organisms.
DNA profiling, the process of making a pattern of bands from a person's DNA to compare with other DNA patterns.
Dominant allele, the allele that is expressed in the heterozygous condition.
Dopamine, a neurotransmitter.
Dormancy, a period when a seed does not germinate, despite favourable conditions being present.
Double-blind testing, a method of preventing bias where neither the tester nor the person being tested knows who is getting the placebo or who is getting the test chemical.
Dry mass, the mass of a substance or organism with the water removed.
Eardrum, a membrane dividing the outer ear from the middle ear.
Ear ossicles, the three smallest bones in the body found in the middle ear.
Ecological pyramid, a model for comparing different communities in the ecosystem in order of different feeding (trophic) levels.
Ecology, the study of the interaction between groups of organisms and their environment.
Ecosystem, organisms and their interactions with the environment.
Ectotherm, an animal whose body temperature varies with the external temperature.
Edaphic factors, soil factors that affect organisms.
Effector, a structure used by an organism to respond to a stimulus, i.e. a muscle or gland.
Egestion, the removal of undigested material from the body.
Element, a substance consisting of only one type of atom, e.g. carbon (C), oxygen (O), hydrogen (H).
Embryo (human), term given to the unborn baby from the time of conception until it is eight weeks old.
Embryo sac, produces the female gamete in flowering plants.
Endocrine glands, ductless glands that produce hormones.
Endocrine system, a set of endocrine glands found in an animal coordinating a slower and more widespread response than the nervous system.
Endometrium, the lining of the inside wall of the uterus.
Endosperm, food store present in some seeds, e.g. in maize. Produced from fusion of polar nuclei and a sperm nucleus.
Endotherm, an animal who maintains its body temperature independent of the external environment.
Environment, the surroundings of an organism.
Enzymes, protein catalysts found in living organisms.
Ethene (ethylene), plant growth regulator which has a number of different effects, i.e. it inhibits longitudinal growth, causes leaf fall and affects fruit ripening.
Ethics, refers to whether something is right or wrong.
Eukaryotic cell, a cell that has a nucleus and other membrane-bound organelles. **(HL)**
Eustachian canal, a tube connecting the middle ear to the throat used to equalise pressure on each side of the eardrum.
Evolution, the changes between members of a species and the emergence of new species from older species over time, in response to change in the environment, due to natural selection.
Exons, parts of the DNA molecule that code for proteins.
Excretion, the removal of the wastes of metabolism (the wastes made in the cells of an organism).
Exhaling, breathing out.
Exocrine glands, glands that have ducts (tubes) leaving them which carry their products.

Glossary

Experiment, a series of steps carried out to test a hypothesis.
Exponential phase, the stage of rapid growth of microbes as they double in number in a set time. (HL)
Extensor, muscle that straightens out a joint.
Exteroceptors, sensory receptors which monitor external changes, e.g. taste receptors.
Fair test, when carrying out an experiment you make sure that you change only one factor while keeping all other conditions the same.
Fallopian tube, the oviduct which links the ovary and the uterus. Fertilisation usually occurs in the fallopian tube.
Fat, a lipid that is solid at room temperature.
Feedback, occurs when the level of hormone in the blood controls the production of another hormone or the production of itself. (HL)
Fermentation, see anaerobic respiration.
Fertile period, the time during a menstrual cycle when an egg may be fertilised.
Fertilisation, fusion of a sperm cell nucleus with an egg cell nucleus to produce a diploid zygote.
Fetus, alternative spelling for foetus.
Flagellum, a hair-like filament found in cells used for locomotion.
Flexor, muscle that bends a joint.
Flower, a modified bud. Reproductive structure of the plant.
Foetus, name given to the unborn baby from the end of the eighth week of pregnancy until birth.
Follicle, fluid-filled sac in which the egg develops.
Follicle stimulating hormone (FSH), sex hormone produced by the pituitary. Causes egg production in the female and sperm production in the male.
Food chain, the feeding relationship between organisms in which energy is transferred
Food web, two or more intersecting food chains.
Fovea, the part of the retina that has the most cones and it has the most accurate vision.
Freely movable (synovial) joints, where bones are held together by ligaments and are separated by fluid and cartilage.
Fruit, plant structure formed from a mature ovary, usually containing seeds.
Gametangium, structure that produces gametes in *Rhizopus*.
Gamete, haploid sex cell capable of fusion.
Ganglion, a swelling on a nerve containing the cell bodies of the neurons.
Gaseous exchange, term used to describe the exchange of the gases oxygen and carbon dioxide between an organism and its environment.
Gastric, term describing anything related to the stomach, e.g. gastric juice.
Gene expression, the process of converting the information in a gene into a protein.
Gene, a section of DNA that codes for a particular protein.
Genetic disorder, conditions that result from the inheritance of mutations in specific genes or chromosomes or a change in chromosome number.
General defence system, the non-specific methods used to prevent the entrance of pathogens into the body and the killing of those that do.
Genetic engineering, the alteration and manipulation of genes.
Genetics, the study of the effect of genes and the inheritance of genes.
Genetic screening, the testing of people to see whether they have a specific gene.
Genotype, the genetic make-up of the organism.
Germination, the re-growth of the embryo plant, following a period of dormancy.
Germ layer, a group of cells in the embryo that give rise to the body organs. (HL)
Gibberellins, group of plant growth regulators.
Glomerulus, a knot of blood capillaries found in the Bowman's capsule. (HL)
Glomerular filtrate, plasma that passes from the blood into the Bowman's capsule.
Glycolysis, the first stage of respiration that converts glucose into pyruvic acid. This occurs in the cytosol of the cell. (HL)
Grey matter, the part of the CNS that contains cell bodies and has a darker colour.
Guard cells, specialised epidermal cells surrounding a stoma in plants.
Habitat, the place where an organism lives.
Haemoglobin, iron-containing pigment found in red blood cells.
Haploid cell (n), contains one copy of each chromosome.
Herbaceous, plant which does not produce a woody stem, e.g. grasses, buttercups.
Herbivore, an organism that eats plant material only, e.g. rabbit, greenfly.
Heredity, the passing of traits, using genes, from one generation to the next.
Heterotrophs, organisms which are not capable of making their own food.
Heterozygous, an individual that has different alleles for a trait.
Homeostasis, the maintenance of a constant internal environment.
Homologous chromosomes, pairs of chromosomes that have genes at the same position on them which control the same traits.
Homologous structure, a structure found on two different organisms that originates from a common ancestral structure, e.g. pentadactyl limb.
Homozygous, an individual that has identical alleles.
Hormone, chemical messengers produced in ductless glands, carried in the blood, for use in another part of the body.
Host, the cell or organism a parasite is living in.
Human chorionic gonadotrophin (HCG), a hormone secreted by the blastocyst (and later the placenta) which maintains the corpus luteum in the ovary. High levels of HCG in the urine are an indication that pregnancy has occurred.
Hydrogen bonds, weak bonds between areas of a molecule or molecules that are slightly charged. These hold the two sides of the DNA molecule together. (HL)
Hypermetropia (long-sightedness), the inability to focus on objects close to the eye.
Hyphae, thread-like filament that makes up a fungus.
Hypothalamus, part of the midbrain, above the pituitary gland that controls homeostasis in the body and the pituitary gland.
Hypothesis, an educated guess based on observation.

Glossary

IAA (indoleacetic acid), a plant growth regulator (auxin) which causes elongation of plant cells.
Immobilised enzymes, biological catalysts attached to an inert material chemically or physically.
Immobilised cells, cells attached to an inert material by chemical or physical means.
Immovable (fibrous) joints, where two bones are held tightly together by connective tissue.
Immune response, the specific defence system or immune response is the defence against pathogens using antibodies or particular white blood cells.
Immunity, the ability to defend against a disease.
Immunisation, either the injection of antibodies into a person to produce a passive immune response or the injection of antigens into a person to produce an active immune response.
Implantation, when the embryo embeds into the endometrium.
Incomplete dominance, neither allele masks the expression of the other.
Induced fit theory, the theory that the shape of the active site of an enzyme changes to give a perfect fit between the enzyme and its substrate.
Induced immunity, when the body contains (or has the ability to produce) specific antibodies against particular antigens.
Infertility, the inability to produce gametes or to conceive.
Inflammatory reaction, redness, swelling and rise in temperature that surrounds the site of infection.
Ingestion, taking food into the mouth.
Inhaling, breathing in.
Inherited variations, differences within a species that are controlled by genes.
Inorganic molecule, molecules that do not contain both carbon and hydrogen, e.g. CO_2, NaCl.
Insulin, the hormone produced by the pancreas that helps to control blood sugar level. Lack of insulin causes diabetes mellitus.
Interferon, a cellular protein that produces a reaction in surrounding cells to protect them against viral infection.
Interneuron, a nerve cell that carries messages between nerve cells.
Internode, space on stem between nodes.
Interoceptors, sensory receptors which monitor internal changes i.e. stretch receptors in the muscles.
Introns, pieces of DNA that do not code for proteins, also known as junk genes.
Interphase, the interval between successive nuclear divisions, when no activity of the chromosomes is visible. It is the period when much cell activity takes place.
***In vitro* fertilisation (IVF),** the fusion of an egg and sperm outside the body.
Ion, a charged particle or atom, e.g. Na^+, NH_4
Iris, a pigmented diaphragm of muscle in front of the lens controlling the amount of light entering the eye.
Islets of Langerhans, the hormone-secreting cells of the pancreas.
Joints, the junction between two bones.
Junk genes, see non-coding DNA.
Karyogram, a diagram or photograph of the chromosomes in a cell arranged in pairs and in order of size.
Kidney, the main organ of excretion of nitrogenous waste.
Krebs cycle, a cyclical pathway, which is the second stage in respiration during which CO_2 is released and many electrons. These electrons, when passed down the electron carrying chain, generate ATP. (HL)
Labour, another name for the process of giving birth.
Lag phase, Number of bacteria do not increase. Bacteria adjusting to the environment and learning to produce the correct enzymes for the food source. (HL)
Law of Segregation, states that organisms contain two factors for every trait. These factors separate in gamete formation, producing gametes with only one copy of each factor. (HL)
Law of Independent Assortment, states that either member of a member of a pair of alleles can pass into a gamete with either member of another pair of alleles. (HL)
Lens, transparent structure used to focus light. Also part of a microscope used to focus objects.
Lenticels, specialised pores in woody stems used for gaseous exchange.
Life, something that possesses the characteristics of both metabolism and continuity.
Ligament, elastic connective tissue, connects bone to bone.
Light-dependent stage, the first stage in photosynthesis when light energy is used to produce ATP and NADPH. (HL)
Light-independent stage, the second stage of photosynthesis where ATP and NADPH are used to make carbohydrate from CO_2. (HL)
Linked genes, where genes for different traits are contained on the same chromosome and tend to be inherited together. (HL)
Locus, the position of the gene on a chromosome.
Luteinising hormone (LH), sex hormone produced by the pituitary. Causes ovulation in the female and testosterone production in the male.
Lymph, a pale yellow-coloured fluid containing water, white blood cells, proteins and lipids (but no red blood cells or platelets).
Lymph nodes, small swellings along the length of many lymph vessels. Lymph nodes filter bacteria and produce and store white blood cells.
Lymph vessels, blind-ending tubes that carry lymph. Many lymph vessels have valves.
Lymphocyte, a type of white blood cell, made originally in the bone marrow, matures in the lymph nodes. Protects against disease by producing antibodies. (HL)
Lysis, destruction of the cell.
Lysogenic cells, cells that have viral DNA incorporated in their DNA with no apparent ill effects.
Lysozyme, a protein-digesting enzyme that breaks open cell membranes.
Malt, grain that has been allowed to germinate. Used in brewing.
Mechanoreceptors, receptors that respond to physical changes.
Mechanical digestion, the breakdown of food into smaller pieces by physical means such as teeth, chewing, churning.
Medulla oblongata, the part of the brain immediately above the spinal cord. Controls involuntary muscles including heartbeat and breathing.
Meiosis, a form of cell division in which the cell nucleus divides into four producing four haploid nuclei all genetically different.
Menstrual cycle, the female monthly cycle in which an egg is released and the endometrium is shed.

Glossary

Menstruation, the shedding of the endometrium.
Meristem, a region of active cell division (mitosis) in plants.
Metabolism, the sum of all the chemical reactions that occur in an organism.
Micropropagation, the growth of a new plant from a piece of stem, root or leaf tissue.
Milk (deciduous) teeth, the first set of teeth in the mammal.
Mitochondrion, a membrane bound structure found in a cell. The site of aerobic respiration.
Mitosis, a form of cell division that produces two genetically identical daughter cells which are also identical with the original cell.
Molecule, the smallest unit of a chemical substance, e.g. O_2 consists of one molecule of oxygen, CO_2 is one molecule of carbon dioxide, $C_6H_{12}O_6$ is one molecule of glucose.
Monocotyledons, plants that have one seed leaf.
Monocyte, a type of white blood cell which engulfs bacteria. **(HL)**
Monohybrid cross, a genetic cross in which one trait is being examined.
Monosaccharide, carbohydrate consisting of one sugar molecule.
Morula, a solid ball of cells. **(HL)**.
Motor neuron, a nerve cell that carries messages from the CNS to an effector.
mRNA, a nucleic acid used to carry messages from the nucleus to the ribosomes for transcription into protein.
Mucus, a slippery fluid, secreted by mucus membranes and glands in the body e.g. mucus lines and protects the respiratory system.
Musculoskeletal system, the combined muscle and skeleton systems used together for movement.
Mutualism, when two organisms of different species live together and both benefit.
Mutagens, agents that change the DNA in a cell.
Mutation, a change in the structure or amount of DNA in an organism.
Mycelium, a group of hyphae forming a single fungus.
Myelin sheath, a fatty-like layer formed by the membrane of the Schwann cells which is found on many dendrites or axons in the nervous system. This increases the speed of the nervous message.
Myopia (short-sightedness), the inability to focus on objects at a distance from the eye.
NAD (nicotinamide adenine dinucleotide), traps and transfers hydrogen ions and electrons in cell reactions. **(HL)**
NADP (nicotinamide adenine dinucleotide phosphate), traps and transfers hydrogen ions and electrons in cell reactions. **(HL)**
Natural selection, the mechanism by which members of a species, with genetic traits that allow them to survive in their environment, reproduce and pass these traits to the next generation.
Negative feedback, occurs when the increasing level of a hormone in the blood stops the production of itself. **(HL)**
Nephron, the functional unit of the kidney. **(HL)**
Nervous system, a set of nervous tissue used by the animal to detect and carry information about the environment and to co-ordinate a response to that environment. In general giving a rapid response.
Neuron, a nerve cell.
Neurotransmitter, a chemical that carries a nerve message across a synapse.
Niche, the role of an organism in the ecosystem.
Node of Ranvier, small gaps on the axon or dendrite between each Schwann cell of some nerve cells. These speed up the nerve messages.
Node, place on a stem to which leaves attach.
Notochord, rod-like piece of tissue found between the nerve cord and the gut. Present at some stage in all vertebrates.
Non-coding DNA (junk gene), an area of a chromosome that does not produce a protein.
Non-nuclear DNA, DNA not contained in the nucleus that is passed from one generation to the next.
Nucleoid, the area of the prokaryotic cell where the DNA is found. **(HL)**
Nucleotide, a molecule comprising a sugar with phosphate and one of four bases attached. It is a building block of DNA.
Nutrient recycling, the way nutrients are exchanged between the biotic and abiotic parts of the ecosystem.
Nutrition, the getting/producing and use of food.
Obligate aerobe, an organism that can only live in the presence of oxygen.
Obligate anaerobe, an organism that can only live in the absence of oxygen.
Obligate parasites, can only replicate within another living cell.
Oestrogen, female sex hormone produced by the ovary.
Offspring, the new individuals produced in reproduction, i.e. the young.
Oil, a lipid that is liquid at room temperature.
Omnivore, animals which eat both plants and animals, e.g. humans, badgers.
Oncogene, a cancer-causing gene.
Open circulatory system, blood not contained within blood vessels, e.g. in insects.
Organ, a group of tissues that work together to carry out a function.
Organelle, a structure found within a cell that carries out a specific function. A membrane surrounds most organelles.
Organic molecule, molecules that contain both carbon and hydrogen, e.g. $C_6H_{12}O_6$ (glucose).
Organisation, organisms are made up of cells (which are themselves highly organised), tissues, organs and systems.
Organism, a living thing.
Organ systems, groups of organs working together to undertake specific functions.
Osmoregulation, the control of the water and salt levels in the cell or the organism.
Osmosis, the movement of water from an area of high concentration of water to an area of lower concentration of water, across a semi-permeable membrane.
Ossification, the process by which cartilage is replaced by bone in the skeleton. **(HL)**
Osteoarthritis, a form of bone disease where the synovial joints wear away.
Osteoblasts, bone-producing cells. **(HL)**
Osteoclasts, bone-digesting cells. **(HL)**

Glossary

Osteoporosis, a skeletal disease in which bone density is lost.
Oval window, a membrane covered opening into the inner ear.
Ovary, reproductive organ and endocrine gland in females.
Oviduct, another name for the fallopian tube.
Ovulation, the release of an egg from the ovary.
Oxytocin, a hormone secreted by the pituitary gland which causes the wall of the uterus to contract during labour.
Pacemaker, group of muscle cells in the heart which control the heartbeat.
Pancreas, gland situated below the stomach. Has both an exocrine and endocrine function (dual function gland).
Parasitism, a relationship between two organisms of different species living together where one benefits and does harm to the other. (HL)
Parathyroids, glands situated behind the thyroid gland.
Passive immunity, when a person receives the antibodies that have been made by another organism, against a disease, without the ability to produce their own antibodies.
Pasteurised, the heating of substances, i.e. milk, to 72°C for 15 seconds followed by rapid cooling. This process kills all the bacterial cells (but not spores) present in the milk and prolongs its shelf-life.
Pathogens, disease-causing organisms.
Pectoral girdle, the bones that attach the arms to the axial skeleton.
Peer review, the checking of a person's work by others who work in the same field or profession.
Pelvic girdle (pelvis), the fused bones that attach the legs to the skeleton.
Pentadactyl limb, the five-fingered (digit) limb found in some form in nearly all terrestrial vertebrates.
Peptidoglycan, a chemical unique to bacterial cell walls. (HL)
Percentage cover, the area of the ground covered by a species of plant in a quadrat.
Percentage frequency, the chance of finding a particular plant (or sedentary animal) in a quadrat.
Peripheral nervous system (PNS), the nerves that carry messages to and from the CNS.
Peristalsis, the waves of muscular contraction of the gut wall that moves the food along.
Permanent teeth, the second set of teeth in the mammal.
Phagocytic white blood cells, blood cells of the immune system that engulf and digest foreign material in the body.
Phenotype, the physical appearance of the organism and is produced by the interaction of the genotype and the environment.
Phospholipid, lipid containing one phosphate and two fatty acids.
Photoreceptors, receptors that respond to light.
Photosynthesis, the process in which plants make carbohydrate and oxygen using (sun)light energy, water, carbon dioxide and chlorophyll.
Photosynthetic bacteria, bacteria that use sunlight to make their own food.
Pinna, the external part of the outer ear.
Pituitary gland (master gland), a gland attached to the base of the midbrain which produces hormones.
Placenta, structure formed from tissues of the embryo (chorion) and the mother (endometrium) and through which food and waste are exchanged. The placenta also secretes hormones.
Plant growth regulator, a chemical that at very low concentrations affects the development of plants.
Plasma, liquid part of the blood composed of water and dissolved solutes.
Plasmid, small, circular, extra-chromosomal DNA found in micro-organisms, including bacteria and yeast. Often carries genes conferring drug resistance.
Plasmolysis, the loss of turgor pressure in plant cell due to loss of water from the cytoplasm.
PNS, see peripheral nervous system.
Polysaccharide, carbohydrate consisting of many sugar molecules.
Pollen grain, produces male gametes.
Pollination, the transfer of pollen from the anther of the stamen to the stigma of the carpel.
Pollutant, any harmful addition to the environment.
Pollution, the addition of harmful substances to the environment.
Population, the number of a particular species living in a particular ecosystem.
Predation, the act of hunting, killing and eating prey. (HL)
Predator, the organism that hunts, kills and eats its prey. (HL)
Pregnancy, the period from conception to birth – 266 days in humans.
Prey, the organism that is eaten by the predator. (HL)
Principle, a proven theory.
Producer, organisms which make their own food, e.g. green plants.
Product, the chemical or chemicals made in the reaction.
Progesterone, female sex hormone produced by the ovary.
Prokaryotic cell, a cell that does not possess a nucleus or other membrane-bound organelles. (HL)
Prolactin, a hormone secreted by the pituitary gland that controls the production of breast milk.
Proprioceptors, receptors that give information about the position and movement of the body.
Protoplasm, the contents of a cell excluding the vacuoles and cell wall.
Pseudopodia, a temporary extension of the cell cytoplasm.
Pulse, the expansion and contraction of the arteries due to the pumping action of the heart.
Punnett square, a mathematical device used to show all the possible genotypes of a genetic cross.
Pupil, hole in the centre of the iris of the eye.
Pure-breeding, organisms that always produce offspring identical to themselves and are homozygous for a trait. (HL)
Pyramid of numbers, used to show the numbers of individuals at each trophic level of a food chain.
Qualitative survey, records if a species is present or not.
Quantitative survey, records the numbers of a species present.

Glossary

Receptor, a structure used to receive a stimulus, i.e. a pain receptor in the skin.
Recessive allele, the allele that is only expressed in the homozygous condition.
Red bone marrow, tissue found in spongy bone that produces blood cells.
Reflex action, the unthinking response to a nerve stimulus.
Reflex arc, the nerve pathway of a reflex action.
Replicate, (a) A repeat of an experiment or procedure. (b) The production of an identical copy of a cell or DNA.
Replication, the production of an identical copy of the DNA in a cell.
Reproduction, the ability of an organism to produce new individuals of its own kind.
Respiration, the breakdown of food (carbohydrate) to release energy.
Respiratory surface, specialised region for gas exchange, e.g. gills of fish, lungs (alveoli) of humans.
Response, the ability of organisms to react to both internal and external changes.
Retina, light-sensitive layer at back of eye.
Reverse transcriptase, an enzyme, which transcribes RNA into DNA.
Rhesus factor, a blood group system based on the presence or absence of factor D antigen in the blood.
Rheumatoid arthritis, an inflammatory disease of the joints.
Rhizoid, short fungal hypha that grows down into the substrate. Used for anchorage and absorption of digested food.
Rhizome, an underground stem swollen with food reserves.
Ribosome, a cell organelle without an enveloping membrane that is found attached to membranes or free in the cytoplasm. It is made of RNA and is the site of protein synthesis.
Ribs, the bones attached to the vertebrae in the chest region.
RNA (ribonucleic acid), a type of nucleic acid which differs from the structure of DNA in that it is usually single-stranded and it contains the sugar ribose (not deoxyribose), and it replaces the base thymine with the base uracil.
Rods, light-sensitive receptors giving black and white vision.
Root pressure, the force that pushes water up the stem from the root.
Round window, a membrane covered exit from the inner ear.
rRNA, structural RNA that makes the ribosomes. Used in the manufacture of proteins. **(HL)**
Salt, a compound of a metal and a non-metal, e.g. NaCl, $MgSO_4$. When a salt dissolves in water, it breaks up into ions. $NaCl = Na^+ + Cl^-$.
S-A node (pacemaker), controls heartbeat. **(HL)**
Saprophytes, organisms which get their food from dead organisms commonly called decomposers.
Schwann cell, the specialised cell that wraps itself around neurones to form the myelin sheath.
Scientific method, a step-by-step process which leads to knowledge.
Sclera, white outer coat of eye.
Scramble competition, a struggle between organisms for a scarce resource in which each organisms gets some of the resource. **(HL)**
Secondary sexual characteristics, features that develop during puberty, but are not essential for reproduction.
Seed, embryo plant with a food store.
Selectively permeable or semi-permeable membrane, a membrane that does not allow free passage of all molecules across it, i.e. the cell membrane.
Self-pollination, the transfer of pollen from the anther of a flower to a stigma of the same flower or to a stigma of another flower on the same plant in the ground.
Semen, fluid containing sperm and fluid from the seminal vesicles, prostate gland and Cowper's gland.
Semicircular canals, apparatus in inner ear used to detect movement.
Sensory neuron, a nerve cell that carries messages to the CNS from a sense organ.
Sensory system, a set of sense organs in animals used to detect information about the environment.
Sex chromosome, a chromosome having a role in determining the sex of an individual. (also known as heterosomes).
Sex-linked genes, genes found on the X chromosome or on the Y chromosome.
Sexual reproduction, reproduction involving fusion of gametes that produces offspring, which contain characteristics of both parents.
Single-celled protein (SCP), microbes used as foodstuff in an animal or human diet. **(HL)**
Skeleton, a framework of bones and cartilage used for support and movement and protection.
Slightly movable (cartilaginous) joints, where two bones are separated by cartilage only, e.g. between the vertebrae.
Solar energy, the energy that come from the sun.
Species, a group of organisms that can interbreed and produce fertile offspring.
Specific defence system (immune response), the defence against pathogens using antibodies or particular white blood cells.
Sperm duct (vas deferens), tube in male which carries sperm from the testis to the urethra.
Sphincter muscle, a ring of muscle surrounding an opening which controls the movement of substances through it.
Spindle, a structure which develops during cell division in some cells. The spindle both pulls the sister chromatids to either pole of the cell and pushes the poles apart during mitosis. **(HL)**
Sporangiophore, aerial hyphae that support the sporangium.
Sporangium, structure at end of sporangiophore that produces and stores spores.
Spore, a reproductive structure, often single-celled, which produce new offspring. It may have a protective coat to withstand adverse conditions. Does not store food.
Sterile, (a) being infertile, (b) free from all microbes.
Sternum, the breastbone.
Steroids, a set of lipid molecules based on a series of ring-like carbon structures.
Stomata (singular, stoma), a small pore in the epidermis (dermal tissue) of a plant leaf. Functions in gaseous exchange.
Substrate, the chemical or chemicals with which the enzyme reacts.
Symbiosis, a relationship between two organisms of different species in which at least one of them benefits.
Symbiotic organisms, organisms of one species that live in close relationship with another species where at least one organism benefits.

Glossary

Synapse, the region where two neurons meet.
Synaptic knob, a swelling at the end of an axon.
Synaptic cleft, the gap between two neurons.
Synovial joint, a freely movable joint comprised of synovial membrane and fluid and cartilage.
Systole, contraction of heart muscle. (HL)
Tendon, non-elastic connective tissue used to attach muscle to bone.
Testis, reproductive organ (gonad) and endocrine gland in the male.
Testosterone, male sex hormone, produced by the testes.
Thalamus, part of the midbrain, under the cerebrum, that processes most sensory information.
Theory, a hypothesis that is supported by experiment.
Thermoreceptors, receptors that respond to changes in temperature.
Theory, a hypothesis that is supported by experiment.
Threshold, the minimum stimulation required to send a message along a neuron.
Thyroid gland, a gland situated in the front of the neck.
Thyroxine, the hormone produced by the thyroid gland.
Tissue culture, the growth of cells in a medium outside an organism.
Tissues, groups of similar cells that have the same structure and function.
Toxins, poisonous chemicals produced by organisms.
Transformed, an organism in which the DNA has been changed by the addition of extra DNA.
Transgenic organism, an organism whose genetic make-up has been altered by the addition of a gene by genetic engineering.
Transcription, the copying of a section of DNA, a gene, into mRNA.
Translation, the manufacture of protein based on the sequence of bases on the mRNA. (HL)
Transpiration, the loss of water vapour from the surface of a plant.
tRNA (transfer RNA), a form of RNA which has a specific amino acid attached to one end to correspond with three unpaired bases exposed at one section of the molecule. Used in the manufacture of proteins. (HL)
Trophic level, a feeding level in a food chain.
Trophoblast, the outer cells of the blastocyst.
Tropism, a growth response of a plant to a directional stimulus.
Turgid cell, a plant cell in which the contents of the cell are pushing against the cell wall due to turgor pressure.
Turgor pressure, the force of the cell contents against the cell wall in plant cells.
Ultrasound scanning, technique in which very high frequency sound waves (too high for us to hear) are passed into the body. The echoes which reflect back are detected and analysed, giving a picture of the internal organs.
Ureter, tube carrying urine (urea and water) away from the kidney to the bladder.
Urethra, tube carrying urine out of the bladder.
Urination, the release of urine from the bladder along the urethra.
Vaccination, the introduction of a non-disease causing dose of a microbe so as to generate an active immune response.
Vaccine, a substance introduced into a person to induce an antibody response leading to immunity to that disease.
Valve, flap of tissue which prevents a back-flow of fluid, e.g. blood. Found in veins, lymph vessels and the heart.
Variable, a factor which may change during an experiment, e.g. temperature.
Variation, the difference between individuals of the same species.
Vascular system, system concerned with the transport of substances.
Vascular tissue, cells concerned with transport, e.g. xylem and phloem in plants, and blood in animals.
Vas deferens, or sperm duct transports sperm from the testis to the urethra.
Vegetative propagation, asexual reproduction in plants. It involves the production of new plants without the fusion of gametes.
Vein, thin-walled blood vessel with valves, carries blood towards the heart.
Ventricle, lower chamber of heart (releases blood).
Vertebrae, the 26 individual bones in the vertebral column.
Vertebrate, animal possessing a backbone.
Vertebral column, the bones comprising the backbone.
Vestigial structure, a tissue or organ whose size has been reduced over evolutionary time due to loss of function.
Villi, finger-like projections from the lining of the small intestine wall. Function in the absorption of digested food.
Virus, a group of sub-cellular infectious agents.
Vitreous humour, jelly-like material found behind the lens.
Warfarin, a rat poison which functions by preventing blood clotting (is also used to prevent heart attacks).
Waste management, the way we deal with our waste.
White matter, the part of the CNS that contains the axons and has a lighter colour.
Xylem tracheid, water- and mineral-transporting cell which has tapered end walls but lacks spiral thickening on side walls.
Xylem vessel, water- and mineral-transporting cell lacking end walls, and with spiral thickening of lignin, on side walls.
Yellow bone marrow, tissue found in the centre of large bones that is used for fat storage.
Zygospore, a zygote with a resistant coating to survive adverse conditions.
Zygote, a diploid cell produced by the fusion of two gametes.

Index

A

abiotic factors, ecosystems 35, 42, 72, 79, 88
absorption
    digestive system 333
    nutrition 337–39, 340
acceptor molecule 157
ADH (anti-diuretic hormone) 370–71, 413, 414
ADP (adenosine diphosphate) 146
adrenal glands, endocrine system 413, 414
adrenaline, endocrine system 413
algal bloom 50
allele 178, 197, 198
amino acid 21, 137
anabolism 12, 136, 138, 148
anaemia 326
animal kingdom 235, 236, 239
animal tissue 107–8, 112
    connective tissue 107, 108
    epithelial tissue 107
    muscular tissue 107, 108
    nervous tissue 107
antagonistic muscles, musculoskeletal system 424
anther, flowering plant 444, 445
antibiotics 7, 8, 246–47
    resistance 246
antibodies 434, 438
    white blood cells 326, 327
apical dominance, plants 383
aquatic factors, ecosystems 35, 36, 42
asepsis 264
    bacteria 247–48, 260
ATP (adenosine triphosphate) 145–46, 148, 156–57, 166, 171
autoclave 247, 260–61
autosomes, chromosomes 202
autotrophic nutrition 14, 235, 244, 289, 295, 332, 340
axon, neuron 389, 395

B

bacteria 242–52
    disease and antibiotics 246–47, 252
    factors affecting growth 245
    growth curves 249
    industrial microbiology 249–51
    nutrition 244, 252
        chemosynthetic 244, 252
        photosynthetic 244, 252
        saprophytes 244, 252
        symbiotes
            commensalism 244, 252
            mutualism 244, 252
            parasitism 244, 252
    reproduction 243
    sterility and asepsis 247–48, 252
    structure 243, 252
    types 242
bases
    complementary base pairs 181
    purine 181
    pyramidine 181
belt transect 84
binomial system 234
biodiversity 12
biology 2
biomolecules 18
bioprocessing 144
bioreactor 109, 144, 168, 249
biosphere 35, 42, 136–37
biotechnology 168
biotic factors, ecosystems 35, 42
bladder 367
blood 325–29
    blood cells 325–27, 329
        platelets 325, 327, 329
        red blood cells 325, 329
        white blood cells 325, 329
            lymphocytes 326
            monocytes 326, 327
    blood clotting 327, 329
    blood groups 327–28, 329
    functions 327, 329
    plasma 325, 329
blood clotting 433, 437
brain
    medulla oblongata 355
    see also sense organs
breathing system 350–53, 358
    disorders 356, 359
    mechanism 353
    structure 351, 358
        alveoli 351, 352, 358, 359
    transport of oxygen and carbon dioxide 355
bronchiole 351
bronchus 351

C

carbohydrates 19–20, 27
    elements 19
    functions 19
        metabolic 20
        structural 20
    structure 19
    test for presence of carbohydrates 25, 28
carbon cycle 40–43
cardiac cycle 310
cardiac muscle 305
carnivores 36, 43, 332, 340
cartilage 108, 351
catabolism 12, 136, 138, 148
catalysts 137
cell continuity, cells 125–26, 130, 131, 221, 442
cells 13
    active transport 118, 120
    cell continuity 124–31
        cell cycle 125, 182
        cell division 124, 131
            cancer 129–30, 131
        chromosomes 124–25
        meiosis 125–26, 130, 131, 221
        mitosis 125–29, 130, 131
    cell diversity 107–12
        organs 110–11
        tissues 107–8, 112
            cultures 109, 112
    see also animal tissue; plants, plant tissue
cell metabolism 136–37, 145–46, 148
    see also photosynthesis; respiration
cell structure 95–103
    animal cell 96–97, 98
    cell membrane 96–97, 103, 120
    cell wall 98, 103
    chloroplasts 98–99, 103, 108, 211
    cytoplasm 96, 97
    eukaryotic cells 102, 103, 248
    mitochondria 98–99, 103, 165–66, 170, 211, 248
    nucleolus 97, 103
    nucleus 97, 99, 103
    organelles 13, 96
    plant cell 97–98
    prokaryotic cells 102, 103, 127, 248
    protoplasm 96
    ribosomes 99–100, 103, 188
    vacuole 97–98, 103
cell theory 4, 95
diffusion 115–16, 120
energy *see* photosynthesis
enzymes 136–48
    action 137
    activation energy 138, 143
    active site 138
    denaturation 139–43
    effect of pH 139–41, 148
    effect of temperature 141–43, 148
    immobilisation 144, 148, 168, 172
    induced fit theory 138, 148
    industrial uses 144
    metabolism 136–37
    specificity 138
    structure 137
    membrane 115–18, 120
    osmosis 116–18, 120, 290
    see also nutrition; photosynthesis; respiration
cellulose 20
central nervous system (CNS) 389, 391–93, 395
cerebellum, brain 392, 393, 396
cerebrum, brain 392, 396, 401
chemical elements 17–28
    dissolved salts 18
    main elements 18
    trace elements 18
chemosynthetic, nutrition 244, 252
chlorophyll 154, 157
chloroplast 98–99, 103, 108, 154, 211, 248, 349
choroid, eye 404, 405, 407
chromatin 124–25, 131
chromosomes 179, 198, 442
    autosomes 202
    cells 124–25
    DNA (deoxyribonucleic acid) 179, 190
    genetic mutation 222–23
    genetic variation 221–22
    heterosomes 202
cilia 351, 352

Index

circulatory system 301–17
   blood flow 308
   blood vessels 303
      arteries 303, 305
      capillaries 303, 304, 305
      valves 303, 304
      veins 303, 305
   closed 302
   heart 305–8
      atrium 306–7
      valves 306
      ventricle 306–7
   heartbeat 310–11
   portal system 308
   pulmonary circulation 303, 308
   systemic circulation 303, 308
class, classification 234
classification 234–37
   binomial system 234
   five-kingdom system 235–37, 239
climatic factors, ecosystems 35, 36, 42
cochlea, ear 403
codon, DNA 187, 188
coleoptile 382–83, 384
commensalism, nutrition 244
competition
   adaptive techniques 60, 61, 67
   contest competition 60, 61, 67
   ecosystems 35, 43
   population control 60–62, 65, 67
   scramble competition 60, 61, 67
complementary base pairs, bases 181
concentration gradient 116
conjunctiva, eye 404, 407
connective tissue, animal tissue 107, 108
consumers, ecosystems 35, 36, 43
continuity 12–13, 15
contractile vacuole 117, 120, 263
cornea, eye 404, 407
coronary blood vessels 305
corrosive 5
cortex 367
   kidney 370
cotyledon 278, 282
cuticle 291
cytoplasm 96, 170, 189
   cell structure 96, 97
cytosol 165

D

Darwin, Charles 223–24, 228
decomposers, ecosystems 35, 43
defence system 432–38
   general defences
      beneficial bacteria 433
      blood clotting 433, 437
      body fluids 433, 437
      inflammatory reaction 433, 437
      mucous membranes 432, 437
      phagocytic white blood cells 433, 437
      sebaceous (oil) glands 432, 437
      skin 432, 437
   specific defences 433–38
      antibodies 434, 438
      antigen 434
      immunity 433
         induced immunity 434, 438
         lymphocytes 435–37, 438
dendrites, neurons 389, 395
detritovores 43
detritus food chain 37
diastole 310
dicotyledon 278–79, 282
diffusion 115–16, 120, 301, 366
digestion, nutrition 333–34, 340, 341
digestive enzymes 139, 334, 337
dihybrid crosses, genetics 205–6, 208
diploid 124–25, 131, 179, 199, 221
disaccharides 19
DNA (deoxyribonucleic acid) 97, 99, 107, 124–25, 131, 178–91
   chromosomes 179, 190
   coding and non-coding data 180, 183
   genes 178–79, 190
   genetic screening 184, 190
   profiling 183–84, 190
   protein synthesis 187–88, 190–91
   replication 182, 190
   reproduction 179
   structure 180–81
   see also genetics
dominant allele 198
dormancy, flowering plants 453, 459, 460
double helix, DNA 181

E

ear 403, 406–7
   cochlea 403
   Eustachian tube 403
   ossicles 403
      anvil 403
      hammer 403
      stirrup 403
   pinna 403, 406
ecology 34–43
   conservation 51–52, 55
   energy flow 36–37, 39, 42
   environmental factors 35–36, 42
      abiotic factors 35, 42
      biotic factors 35, 42
   environmental impact of humans 49–55
   food chains 37
   habitat 40, 42
   niche 40
   nutrient recycling 40–42
   pyramid of numbers 38–39, 43, 86
      limitations 39, 43
   trophic levels 38–39, 43
   waste management 53–55
      micro-organisms 55
   see also ecosystem; populations
ecosystem 34–35, 72–88
   abiotic factors 35, 42, 72, 79, 86
   adaptations of plants and animals to habitat 74–75, 86
   biotic factors 35, 42, 72
   community 73
   edaphic factors 35, 36, 42
   fieldwork steps 75–87
   habitats 73–75, 76
   identification key 78–79
   see also investigations; surveys
ectotherm 357, 359
edaphic factors, ecosystem 35, 36, 42
egestion
   digestive system 333
   nutrition 333, 339, 340
embryo sac, flowering plant 444, 445
endocrine system 388, 412–17
   endocrine glands 412, 416
      adrenal glands 413, 414
      hypothalamus 413, 414
      ovaries 414
      pancreas 413, 414
      parathyroid glands 413, 414
      pituitary gland 413, 414
      testes 414
      thyroid gland 413, 414
   hormones 412, 414, 416–17, 421, 478, 480
      feedback mechanism 415–16, 417
      over- or underproduction 414–15, 416–17
endotherm 357, 359
enzymes 22
epiglottis 351
epithelial tissue, animal tissue 107
eukaryotic cells, cells 102, 103, 248
Eustachian tube, ear 403
eutrophication 42, 50
excretion 13, 14, 15, 365–69
   humans 366–71
   plants 365–66, 372
exocrine glands 412, 416
exons (coding DNA) 180
experiment 3
   bias (prejudice) 4, 5–6, 8
   control 4, 5, 8
   double-blind testing 5, 6, 7
   replicate 3, 5, 6, 8
eye 404–6, 407
   choroid 404, 405, 407
   conjunctiva 404, 407
   cornea 404, 407
   fovea 404, 405
   iris 404, 405, 407
   pupil 404, 405
   retina 404, 407
   rods and cones 405, 407
   sclera 404, 407

F

family, classification 234
fats *see* lipids
fatty acids 20
fertilisation
   flowering plants 449, 459
   reproductive system 491, 492, 500
fertilisers, agricultural 50–51
flammable 5
Fleming, Sir Alexander 8
flowering plants 271–82
   asexual reproduction 442, 459, 469–73
      clones 469
      vegetative propagation 469–73
         artificial 471–73
         natural 469–71
   classification 278–79
   root system 272, 295

Index

sexual reproduction 442, 443, 459
    flower structure 443, 444
    life cycle 443, 459–60
        dormancy 453, 459, 460
        fertilisation 449, 459
        fruit and seed dispersal
            451–52, 459, 460
        gamete formation 444–46, 459
        germination 453–55, 459, 460
        pollination 446–48, 459
        seed and fruit formation
            449–51, 459, 460
    shoot system 272–74, 295
        buds 272
        flowers 273
        leaves 273
    storage 293–94, 295
    transport 289–92
        carbon dioxide 293, 295
        minerals 293, 295
        water 290–92, 295
            cohesion-tension model 292, 295
            root pressure 290, 295
            transpiration 291, 295
food *see* carbohydrates; chemical elements; lipids; proteins; vitamins
food chains 14, 37, 43, 86
    pollution 51
    trophic levels 38–39
food preservation 120
food test investigations 24–26, 28
    test for presence of carbohydrates 25
    test for presence of fats 26
    test for presence of protein 26
food web 38, 43, 86
fovea, eye 404, 405
freedom from bias 4, 5–6, 8
    double-blind testing 5, 6
    large sample size 5, 6
    random selection 5, 6
    replicates 5, 6
FSH (follicle stimulating hormone) 413, 478, 480, 483
fungus kingdom 235, 236, 239, 256–64
    classification 256, 264
    nutrition 257, 264
    see also Rhizopus; yeast

G

gamete formation, flowering plants 444–46, 459
gametes 125, 179, 199, 221
gaseous exchange, homeostasis 349–59
genes, DNA (deoxyribonucleic acid) 178–79, 190
genetic screening, DNA (deoxyribonucleic acid) 184, 190
genetics
    evolution 223–25, 227
    gene expression 178
    genes 125, 178–79, 197–202, 211
    genetic engineering 109, 225–27, 228
    genetic inheritance 197–212

genetic variation 221–23, 227
incomplete dominance 201–2, 208, 212
linked genes 209–10
sex determination 202, 212
sex-linked genes 210–11
sexual reproduction 199–202, 221, 227
see also Darwin, Charles; Mendel, Gregor; Wallace, Alfred
genotype 198, 212
genus, classification 234
germination, flowering plants 453–55, 459, 460
glottis 351
glucose 158
glycerol 20
glycolysis 166
grazing food chain 37
grey matter, brain 392, 396
growth curves
    bacteria 249
    population 65–66, 67
growth hormone, endocrine system 414

H

haemoglobin 326, 355
haploid 125, 179, 199, 442
hearing *see* sense organs, hearing
herbivores 36, 43, 332, 340
heredity 197, 211
heterosomes, chromosomes 202
heterotrophic nutrition 14, 235, 244, 332, 340
    types 332
heterozygous 198, 199
homeostasis 348–59, 365
    gaseous exchange 349–59
    human 350–53
    plant 349–50
    skin 357–58, 359
    see also breathing system; excretion
homozygous 198, 199
hormones *see* endocrine system
human *see* blood; breathing system; circulatory system; defence system; endocrine system; excretion; musculoskeletal system; nervous system; nutrition; reproductive system; sense organs
Huntington's disease 8
hypermetropia, vision defect 405
hypothalamus
    brain 392, 396
    endocrine system 413, 414
hypothesis 3, 4, 8

I

IAA (indoleacetic acid), auxin 379
immunisation 437, 438
    active immunity 434, 435, 438
    passive immunity 434, 435, 438
incinerators 53
inflorescence 273
ingestion, nutrition 333, 340

introns (non-coding DNA) 180
investigations
    demonstration of osmosis 119
    digestive activity in seeds during germination 456–58
    dissect and display a sheep heart 309–10
    effect of growth regulator on plant tissue 380–82
    effect of pH on catalase activity rate 139–41
    effect of temperature on catalase activity rate 141–43
    effect of water, oxygen and temp on germination 455–56
    estimate percentage cover 82
    estimate population of animal species using capture/recapture method 85
    growth of yeast 261–62
    investigate effect of exercise on breathing rate 353–54
    isolating DNA from onion cells 185–86
    measure the influence of carbon dioxide on rate of photosynthesis 156
    measure the influence of light on rate of photosynthesis 155
    measure the light intensity in habitat 80
    measure percentage frequency 83
    measure the pH of soil in habitat 80
    measure the temperature of soil in habitat 80
    observing animal cells using light microscope 100–101
    observing plant cells using light microscope 101
    prepare an enzyme immobilisation 144–45
    prepare T.S. of dicotyledonous stem 280–81
    production of ethanol by yeast 169
    test for presence of carbohydrates 25, 28
    test for presence of fats 26, 28
    test for presence of protein 26, 28
    testing for polysaccharides 25
iodoform test 169, 172
iris, eye 404, 405, 407
irritant 5

K

kidney
    excretion 367–71, 372
    nephron structure 368–71, 372
        afferent arteriole 368
        Bowman's capsule 368–69, 370, 372
        collecting duct 368, 369, 372
        distal convoluted tubule 368, 369, 372
        efferent arteriole 368
        glomerulus 368–69
        loop of Henlé 368, 369, 372

Index

osmoregulation 370–71
  proximal convoluted tubule 368, 369, 372
kingdom, classification 234
Krebs cycle 167

L

lamina 273
landfill 53
larynx (voice box) 351
lenticels 366
  plant 349
LH (luteinising hormone) 413, 478, 480, 483
life 12–15
  characteristics 13–15
  see also chemical elements; organism
lignin 277
line transect 84
lipids 20–21, 27
  elements 20
  metabolic 21
  phospholipids 20–21
  sources 21
  structure 20, 21
  test for presence of fats 26, 28
lipoproteins 21
liver 336–37, 341, 368
locus, genes 198
lungs 351, 358, 366, 372
lymphocytes 435–37, 438
  white blood cells 326
lysogenic cells 238
lysozyme, enzyme 433

M

medulla, kidney 367, 368
medulla oblongata 396
  brain 355, 392, 393
meiosis 125–26, 130, 131, 221, 442
Mendel, Gregor 203–10, 212
  Law of Independent Assortment 207–8
  Law of Segregation 204
  modern explanation of results 204–5
meninges, brain 391, 396
meristem 274, 281, 379
metabolism 12, 14, 15, 19, 24, 39, 153
  anabolic reactions 24
  catabolic reactions 24
microscope
  electron 95
  light 95
minerals 23, 28, 43
mitochondria 98–99, 103, 165–66, 170, 211, 248
mitosis 125–29, 130, 131, 442
  prophase 127
  metaphase 127
  anaphase 127–28
  telophase 128
Monera (Prokaryotae) kingdom 235, 239, 242–52
  see also bacteria
monocotyledon 278–79, 282
monocytes, white blood cells 326, 327
monosaccharides 19

mRNA (messenger RNA) 187
multicellular, organism 13
muscular tissue, animal tissue 107, 108
musculoskeletal system 421–27
  bone structure 421, 423–24, 426–27
    growth 426
  disorders 425, 427
  human skeleton 421–24, 426–27
    appendicular 421, 422–23, 426–27
    axial 421, 422, 426–27
    functions 421, 426
  joints 423, 427
  movement
    cartilage 421, 425, 427
    ligaments 421, 425, 427
    muscles 424, 425, 427
    tendons 421, 424–25, 427
mutation
  chromosome 222–23, 227
  gene 222, 227
mutualism 339
  nutrition 244
  population control 63–64
myelin sheath, neuron 390, 396
myopia, vision defect 405–6

N

NAD (nicotinamide adenine dinucleotide) 146–47, 148
NADH 146–47, 148
NADP (nicotinamide adenine dinucleotide phosphate) 147, 148
NADPH 147, 148, 156–57
nephron, kidney 367–71, 372
nervous system 388–96
  central nervous system (CNS) 389, 391–93, 395
    brain 389, 391–93
    drugs 391
    spinal cord 389, 393, 396
  disorders 395, 396
  peripheral nervous system (PNS) 389, 394, 395
    neurons 389–91, 395–96
      interneurons 390, 396
      message transfer 390, 396
      motor neurons 390, 396
      neurotransmitters 391, 396
      sensory neurons 36, 390–91
      synapse 390–91, 396
      synaptic cleft 390–91
    reflex actions 394, 396
  see also endocrine system
nervous tissue, animal tissue 107
nitrates 50
nitrogen cycle 40–43, 50
non-nuclear inheritance, genetics 211, 212
non-reducing sugar 25
nucleolus, cell structure 97, 103
nucleotide 188
  DNA 181
nutrition 332–41
  absorption 337–39, 340
    colon 339, 341
    small intestine, ileum 335–36, 337–39, 340, 341

balanced diet 339–40, 341
digestion 333–34, 340, 341
  chemical 334, 340, 341
  digestive enzymes 139, 334, 337, 340
  liver 336–37, 341
  mechanical 333–34, 340
  pancreas 336, 340, 341
  peristalsis 334–35, 340
  small intestine 335–36
    duodenum 335–36, 340, 341
  stomach 335, 340, 341
egestion 333, 339, 340
  large intestine 339
heterotrophs 332, 340
ingestion 333, 340
symbiotic bacteria 339, 341

O

obligate parasites 237
omnivores 43, 332, 340
order, classification 234
organelles 13, 96, 116
organism 12, 111, 112
  organisation 13, 15
  reproduction 13, 15
  response 13, 14, 15
  see also blood; cells; classification; excretion; homeostasis; nutrition; viruses
osmoregulation 117, 263, 367, 370–72
osmosis, cells 116–18, 120, 290
ossicles, ear 403
ossification, bone development 426, 427
osteoblasts, bone development 426, 427
osteocytes, bone development 426, 427
ovaries
  endocrine system 414
  reproductive system 478
oxidising 5
oxyhaemoglobin 326, 355

P

pancreas
  endocrine system 413, 414
    islets of Langerhans 413
parasitism 257
  nutrition 244
  population control 60, 63–64
parathyroid gland, endocrine system 413, 414
pathogen 243, 246, 432
peer review 3
pepsin 139
peptide bond 21–22
  enzymes 137
peptidoglycan 248
pericardium 305
peripheral nervous system (PNS) 389, 394, 395
pesticides
  agricultural 50–51
  biological pest control 51
petiole 273
phagocytic white blood cells 433, 437
pharynx (throat) 351
phenotype 198, 212

Index

phloem 277, 278, 282, 289
phosphates 50
phospholipids 116
photophosphorylation 157
photosynthesis 14, 20, 22, 136–37, 147, 153–59, 166, 244, 252, 289, 349
    chlorophyll 157, 159
    horticulture 156, 159
    light-dependent stage 156–58
    light-independent stage 157, 158
    process 153–54, 159
phylum, classification 234
pinna, ear 403, 406
pituitary gland 396, 413
    endocrine system 413, 414
    kidney 370
placebo 6
plants
    excretion 365–66
    plant cells, osmosis 118
    plant kingdom 235, 236, 239
    plant tissue 107–8, 112, 274–78, 281, 349
        dermal tissue 107, 108, 275–76, 281, 349
        ground tissue 107, 275–76, 281, 349
        growth and tissues in plants 274–75
        meristematic tissue 107, 108
        vascular tissue 107, 275–78, 281
    response to stimuli 377–84
        plant growth regulators (PGRs) 379–80
            abscisic acid 379
            auxins 377, 379, 382–83, 384, 451
                IAA (indoleacetic acid) 379, 384
            commercial use 380, 384
            cytokinins 379
            ethene (ethylene) 379, 384, 451
            gibberellin 379, 451
        protection 383–84
        tropisms 377–79, 384
            chemotropism 378, 379, 384, 449
            geotropism 378, 379, 384
            hydrotropism 378, 379, 384
            phototropism 378, 379, 383, 384
            thigmotropism 378, 379, 384
    see also flowering plants
plasma, blood 325, 329
plasmolysis 118
pleural membranes 351
pollen, flowering plants 445
pollination, flowering plants 446–48, 459
pollution 49–55
    agricultural 49, 50–51, 55
    domestic 49, 55
    industrial 49, 55
polysaccharides 19, 20
    testing for 25
populations 60–67
    general population curves 65–66, 67
    human 65–66, 67
    population dynamics 65–66
    population size 60–61, 67
predation
    adaptations 62–63
    population control 60, 62–63, 65, 67
    predator/prey relationships 63
principle 4, 8
probability, genetics 205
producers, ecosystems 35, 36, 43
product, enzymes 137
Prokaryotae (Monera) kingdom 235, 239, 242–52
prokaryotic cells 102, 103, 127, 248
proteins 21–22, 27
    cell structure 96
    elements 21
    metabolic 22
    sources 22
    structure 21, 22
    test for presence of protein 26, 28
Protist (Protoctista) kingdom 235, 236, 239, 262–63, 264
protoplasm, cell structure 96
Punnett square 200
pupil, eye 404, 405
purine, bases 181
pyrimidine, bases 181
pyruvic acid (pyruvate) 166, 171

Q

quadrat 81, 88

R

receptors, sense organs 401, 402, 406
recessive allele 198
recycling 53
reducing sugar 25
renal system 367–71
replication, DNA (deoxyribonucleic acid) 182, 190
reproduction, bacteria 243
reproductive system 476–84
    birth 497–98, 500
    birth control 499–500
    copulation 491–92, 500
    female 478–79
    fertilisation 491, 492, 500
    human pregnancy 494–97, 500
    implantation 494
    infertility 493–94, 500
    lactation and breastfeeding 498–99, 500
    male 477–78
    menstrual system 480–82, 483
respiration 20, 153, 165–72, 355
    aerobic 165–66, 170, 171
    anaerobic 165, 166, 170, 172
    industrial fermentation 168
    Krebs cycle 167, 171
    plants 365
    stages
        first stage 166–67, 170
        second stage 167, 170
retina, eye 404, 407
rhesus factors, blood grouping 328, 329
Rhizopus 258–59, 264
ribosomes, cell structure 99–100, 103, 188
RNA (ribonucleic acid) 97, 187
root pressure 290
root system, flowering plants 272, 295

S

safety symbols 5
saprophytes 244, 252, 257
scientific journals 3
scientific method 2–8
    ethics 8
    limitations 7, 8
    steps 4, 8
sclera, eye 404, 407
sebaceous (oil) glands 432, 437
sense organs 401–7
    hearing 402–3, 406–7
        balance 403
        defects 403–4
    receptors 401, 402, 406
        chemoreceptors 401, 406
        mechanoreceptors 401, 406
        photoreceptors 401, 404, 405, 406
        proprioceptors 401
        thermoreceptors 401, 406
    taste and smell 402
    touch 402
    vision 404–6
        defects 405–6, 407
sessile 273
shoot system, flowering plants 272–74, 295
skeleton see musculoskeletal system
skin 372, 432, 437
    excretion 367
    homeostasis 357–58, 359
soil factors, ecosystems see edaphic factors
species 197, 211, 221
    speciation 224
    see also classification
sphincter muscle 367
sterility 264
    bacteria 247–48, 260–61
stomata 153, 154, 273, 291, 349, 358, 365
substrate
    bioprocessing 168
    enzymes 137, 148
surveys 81–86, 88
    abundance estimates 81
    capture/recapture method 85, 88
    percentage cover 81–82, 83, 88
    percentage frequency 83, 88
    qualitative 81–84, 88
    quantitative 81, 85, 88
    random sampling 81
    source of errors 86, 88
    transects 84, 85, 88
symbiosis 41–42
    population control 60, 63–64, 65, 67
    see also mutualism; parasitism
symbiotes, nutrition 244, 252
symbiotic relationship 41–42, 244, 339
systole 310

T

testes
    endocrine system 414
    reproductive system 477
thalamus, brain 392, 393, 396
theory 4, 8
thymus, endocrine system 414
thyroid gland, endocrine system 413, 414
toxic 5
trachea (windpipe) 351
transcription, DNA 187, 188
transgenic organisms 226–27
translation 189
    DNA 187
transpiration 273
    flowering plants 291, 295
transport in humans see circulatory system
TRH (thyroid releasing hormone) 413, 414
triglyceride 20
tRNA (transfer RNA) 188–89
tropism, plant 377–79
trypsin 139
TSH (thyroid stimulating hormone) 413, 414

U

unicellular, organism 13
ureter 367
urethra 367
    reproductive system 477
urinary system, excretion 367

V

vaccination 238, 434, 435
vacuole, cell structure 97–98, 103
variation, genetic 221
vegetative propagation, flowering plants 469–73
vestigial structures 224–25
viruses 237–39, 239
    replication 237–38
    structure 237
vision see sense organs, vision
vitamins 23, 27
fat-soluble 23
water-soluble 23

W

Wallace, Alfred 223–24, 228
water 24, 28
white matter, brain 392, 396

X

xylem 154, 277, 278, 282, 289

Y

yeast 260, 264

Z

zygote 179, 199, 442

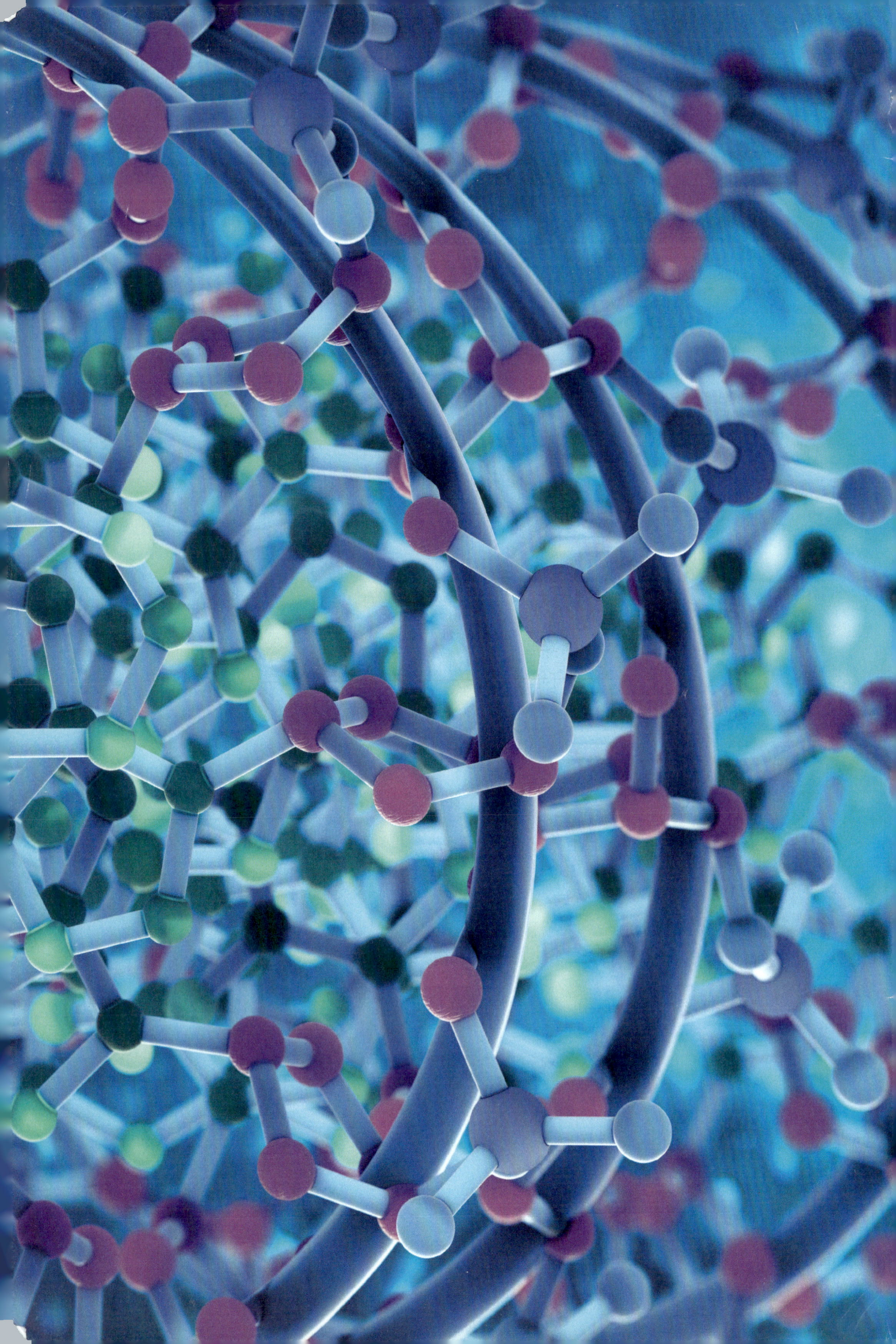